THE ANNUAL OBITUARY 1990

THE ANNUAL OBITUARY 1990

Editor
DEBORAH ANDREWS

St J

St James Press

Chicago and London

For further information, write:
ST. JAMES PRESS
233 East Ontario Street
Chicago 60611, U.S.A

or

2-6 Boundary Row
London SE1 8HP, England

British Library Cataloguing in Publication Data

The Annual Obituary 1990.
1. Biography—Periodicals
920′.02′05 CT100

ISBN 1-55862-092-3

First published in the U.S.A. and U.K. 1991.

CONTENTS

EDITOR'S NOTE

Many of the people in this book have, in their own fields, made history, or at least been etched in its shadow. The obvious link between them is that they all died in 1990. This would seem perhaps a loose bond. Behind Chinese horoscopes is the belief that those born in the same year have characteristics in common; but there is not a similar unifying scheme for a shared time of death. It is however fascinating to see the cross-referencing that occurs between the 342 distinguished individuals in **The Annual Obituary 1990**.

Most obviously, a private friendship, and one that had also been hugely influential in the establishment of American music, ended when *Aaron Copland*'s death followed *Leonard Bernstein*'s by just two months. In the world of business, *Armand Hammer* issued a valedictory tribute to fellow multi-millionaire, *Malcolm Forbes*, only months before he also was to die. *Lord Rothschild* and Lord Swann, who worked together as young research biologists, are linked here by the year of their death. As chairman of the BBC, *Lord Swann* worked with the then director-general, *Sir Ian Trethowan*, who also died in this year.

The musical version, **Leave It To Me**, of a *Bella Spewack* play, shot *Mary Martin* to stardom. *Jack Gilford*'s career was launched by *Jay Gorney*'s **Meet the People**. *Joel McCrea* danced in a film with *Greta Garbo* and was in **The Silver Cord** with *Irene Dunne* (who was in **Anna and the King of Siam** with *Sir Rex Harrison*), and in **Union Pacific** with *Barbara Stanwyck* (who played with *Joan Bennett* in **There's Always Tomorrow**). *Delphine Seyrig* was memorable in *Jacques Demy*'s film **Peau d'âne**. *Jill Ireland*'s first screen role was in *Michael Powell*'s **Oh Rosalinda**! *Pearl Bailey* was in the film of **Porgy and Bess**, choreographed by *Hermes Pan*. *Anne Revere* was in the film of *Anya Seton*'s **Dragonwyck** and *Athene Seyler* in that of *Dodie Smith*'s **Dear Octopus**. *Jim Henson* worked on the film of *Roald Dahl*'s **The Witches**. *Ava Gardner* was photographed by *Norman Parkinson*.

Jimmy Van Heusen composed for *Sammy Davis Jr*. *Walter Davis Jr* played with *Art Blakey*'s Jazz Messengers. *Blakey, Dexter Gordon* and *Sarah Vaughan* have all played in the Billy Eckstine band. *Margaret Craske* taught *Dame Peggy van Praagh*. *Peggy Glanville-Hicks* based her opera, **Sappho**, on a *Lawrence Durrell* play. *Elizabeth Harwood* sang in the Glyndebourne production of **Der Rosenkavalier** designed by *Erté*. *Leonard Bernstein* was one of *William S. Paley*'s top recording artists at CBS.

Away from entertainment, we see that *Max Gordon* worked as associate architect to *Gordon Bunshaft* in New York. *Victor Lasky* wrote a book on *Arthur J. Goldberg*. *Malcolm Muggeridge* took part in *Joseph McCulloch*'s "Dialogues". Two people in this book were credited with inventing the phrase "the Establishment" — *A.J.P. Taylor* actually did.

For ease of reference, the entrants in **The Annual Obituary** are both indexed alphabetically and categorized by profession. In each case, a descriptive essay is followed by a listings-style section giving biographical details, works and achievements.

Special acknowledgement is due to researcher Paul Stevens, to listings compilers Kelly King Boyd and Mary Jean Evers and to Miren Lopategui, J. R. Colliss Harvey and Juliette Bright, for proof-reading. Last but certainly not least, thanks are also extended to this year's writers.

Deborah Andrews
London

Alphabetical Index of Entrants

Index of Entrants by Profession

The index is divided into the following categories:

Actors, Actresses and Entertainers

Anthropologists and Archaeologists

Architects, Planners and Preservationists

Art Historians, Collectors and Critics

Artists

Astronomers and Astrophysicists

Aviators, Aviation Experts and Aerodynamicists

Biographers and Memoirists

Biologists, Botanists and Naturalists

Business Executives and Industrialists

Chefs, Food Writers and Restaurateurs

Chemists, Biochemists and Nutritionists

Children's Writers

Clergy and Religious Scholars and Theorists

Composers, Arrangers and Songwriters

Dancers and Choreographers

Designers, Design Writers and Fashion Writers

Diplomats

Directors

Earth Scientists (including Geologists)

Economists, Financial Specialists and Bankers

Educators, Educationists and Educational and Foundation/Association Administrators

Engineers and Technologists

Essayists

Farmers, Horticulturists and Agriculturists

Heads of State, Presidents, Premiers and Governors General

Historians and Classicists

Illustrators, Cartoonists and Animators

Intelligence Agents and Officers

Inventors

Journalists and Editors (including Travel Writers)

Judges and Lawyers

Labour Leaders

Librarians, Museum Curators and Antiquarians

Literary Scholars and Critics

Medical Practitioners and Researchers

Military Officers and Strategists

Musical Performers and Conductors

Novelists and Short Story Writers (including Humorists)

Philanthropists

Philosophers

Photographers

Physicists

Playwrights and Scriptwriters

Poets

Politicians

Producers and Administrators (Film, Stage and Television)

Psychiatrists, Psychologists and Psychotherapists

Public and Government Officials

Publishers and Newspaper Proprietors

Radio and Television Personalities

Social, Political and Human Rights Activists

Sociologists

Sports and Games Figures

Theatrical/Music Impresarios

Translators

Contributors

Jamie Ambrose
Harry Andrews
Ian Armour
Ian A. Bell
Terence Boughton
Edmund Bradley
David Brady
Juliette Bright
Molly Brown
Patricia Burgess
Mary Cadogan
Alison Classe
Francis Coleman
Scott Coombs
Margaret Cornell
Tom Cullen
Christopher Downing
Emma Dyer
Jane Ehrlich
John Gill
Stella Goodwin
Elizabeth Gordon
Anastasia N. Hackett
Dilys Hartog
Caroline Heslop
Rodney Hoare
Christie Horn
Peter Hutchings
Linda Jennings
Caryl Joyce
Richard Kisch
Maria Lauret
Greg Ledger
Jehanne Le Quesne
Miren Lopategui
Lucinda Lubbock
Linden Nicoll
Paula Nuttall
Margaret Osborne
Julian Petley
Eddie Playfair
Joanna Price
Mary Scott
Alyn Shipton
Denise Silvester-Carr
Caroline B.D. Smith
Jackie Smith
Robert Snell
Philip de Souza
Timothy D. Spry
Christopher Stevens
Paul Stevens
Paul Tappenden
Nicholas Thomas
Paul Tweddle
Steve Voce
Jane Walker
Ian Weightman
Sara Wheeler
Sue Wilson
Claudia Woolgar

THE ANNUAL OBITUARY 1990

JANUARY

EVANGELOS AVEROFF-TOSSITSAS

Greek Politician and Writer
***Born* Trikkala, Greece, 17 April 1910**
***Died* Athens, Greece, 2 January 1990**

One of the best-known of post-World War II Greek politicians of the "old school", firmly conservative, pro-royalist, pro-West, staunchly anti-Communist, Evangelos Averoff was the scion of a wealthy middle-class family from the mountain area of central Greece. His paternal grandfather, George Averoff, had been a substantial benefactor to charitable causes in the region and beyond, most notably in repairs to the Olympic Stadium, and his grandson was to continue in that tradition of service, both in active politics and as a notable author of historical works, both fact and fiction.

Evangelos Averoff used to describe himself as "a farmer, politician and playwright", and it was perhaps in that order that the priorities of his long service to his country lay. He was the first Greek to develop the cultivation of hard wheat on his family estates. The Averoffs are Vlahs, members of the Hellenophile Latin-speaking Aromân people of the Pindus mountains, and with the help of his nephew Janis Averoff, the mayor of Metsovo, Evangelos Averoff devoted much attention to reviving the prosperity and traditional culture of the local mountain communities. The family mansion houses an Aromân museum and library, and from there Averoff continued the tradition of generous hospitality including, it is rumoured, oustanding breakfasts. He added the name of Tossitsas to his own in deference to Baron Michael Tossitsas, the last descendant of the wealthy Epirus family, who made Averoff sole executor of his will and dispenser of vast sums to charitable agricultural projects in his native region, two of the most notable being the cultivation of vineyards on French lines on the Metsovo slopes and the setting up of a museum of regional arts and crafts.

Trained as a lawyer and economist at the University of Lausanne, Averoff was destined to take up a career in the wider sphere of national rather than regional life. His first public appointment as governor of Corfu in 1941 led to his imprisonment after the German invasion. Elected deputy for Epirus in 1946 in the first free elections to be held in Greece for ten years, Averoff was a strong supporter of the royalist cause, first in the national referendum which brought back King George and then in the three years of civil war against the Communists, later vividly described in his book *The Fire and the Axe.* Averoff was immediately brought into the post-war government as minister of provisions and then of national economy in the process of rebuilding the war-torn economy under the Truman Plan. But his main contribution was to be in the field of foreign affairs. Known later as "the bridge-maker", his achievements as foreign minister in the first government of

Constantine Karamanlis (1956–63) included the 1960 agreement with Britain and Turkey for the independence of Cyprus, an agreement which was to come unstuck with the disastrous events of the early 1970s and the Turkish annexation of the north-eastern part of the island. Later Averoff was to write a magisterial history of the Cyprus problem, *Lost Opportunities: a History of the Cyprus Problem.*

The colonels' *coup d'état* of 1967 found Averoff — at that time minister of agriculture — again trying to bridge the gap between military dictatorship, which he detested, and his fellow right-wing politicians who were loyal to the young King Constantine. In this he inevitably failed and was put under house arrest for his allegedly subversive activities. His support for the monarchy remained unshakeable, however, even to the point of supporting an attempt on the part of the Greek Navy to persuade the King to proclaim a government in exile — again a failure which this time landed Averoff in prison.

The overthrow of the junta in 1974 restored democratic government under Averoff's respected political mentor, Karamanlis, at the head of the New Democracy Party, of which Averoff himself was later to become leader in opposition to the Papandreou Socialist government. But during the remainder of the 1970s he was to achieve the peak of his political career as minister of defence in Karamanlis's government, with his rebuilding of the armed forces both in equipment and morale. The defeat of the New Democracy Party by the Socialists in the 1981 election marked the end of conservative rule. After three years as its leader, Averoff gave way in 1984 to the party's support for its current head, becoming its honorary president — a position he retained until his death.

A man of wide culture and considerable international standing as a writer — he was fluent in several languages and his history of the civil war was originally written in French — Averoff was awarded literary prizes by the Academy of Athens and the City of Paris, and several of his works have been translated into English, French and Italian. Averoff's long political career — from his election as the youngest deputy in 1946 to his deputy premiership in 1981 — spanned times of pride and shame in his country's modern history. Throughout, his wise statesmanship was to retain the trust of a large proportion — the best of the traditionalists — of his fellow countrymen, and the respect of the world at large.

Born Evangelos Averoff. **Parents** Anastasious and Efthymia Averoff. **Marriage** Diamantina Lykiardopoulou. **Children** Natalie and Tatiana. **Education** Public school, Athens; School of Political, Legal and Economic Sciences, University of Lausanne, Switzerland, graduated summa cum laude, 1930. **Military service** Resistance worker, Epirus and Thessaly, interned for two years, northern Italy, World War II. **Career** Governor, Corfu, 1941; Liberal member of parliament, 1946–56; minister of supply, 1948; minister of provisions, 1949–50; minister of national economy, 1950–51; under-secretary of foreign affairs, 1951–52; National Radical Union member of parliament, 1956; minister of agriculture, February-May, 1956, 1967; minister of foreign affairs, 1956–63; minister of national defence, 1974–81; deputy prime minister, June-October 1981; leader New Democracy Party, 1981–84, honorary president, 1984 onwards; member-at-large of parliament, 1984 onwards. **Related activities** Director of repatriation of hostages, Greek Embassy, Rome, 1945; delegate, United Nations, 1956, 1957; imprisoned, later under house arrest, 1967–74; political adviser, mutiny of the Navy, 1973, imprisoned, July 1973. **Other activities** Journalist, *Gazette de Lausanne;* first publication, *Union Douanière Balkanique,* 1933; creator, numerous philanthropic institutions; pioneer, agricultural projects; endowed museum of regional arts and crafts. **Offices and memberships** Member, Athens Club. **Awards and honours** Honorary doctorate, University of Lausanne, 1939; prize for *Contributions to the Investigation of Greece's Population Problems,* Academy of Athens, 1939; Grand Cross, Order of the Phoenix; Commander, Royal Hellenic Navy, 1945; Prix littéraire de la cité de Paris, 1976. **Publications** (non-fiction, unless stated) *Union Douanière Balkanique,* 1933; *Contributions to the Investigation* *of Greece's Population Problems,* 1939; *Freedom or Death,* 1945; *The Foreign Policy of Greece,* 1960; *The Cry of the Land* (fiction), 1964; *The Land of Sorrow* (fiction), 1966; *The Delphic Land* (fiction), 1968; *When the Gods Used to Forget* (fiction), 1969; *When the Gods Used to Bless* (fiction), 1971; *Return to Mycenae* (play), 1973; *The Fire and the Axe,* 1973; *Lost Opportunities: a History of the Cyprus Problem,* 1981. **Cause of death** Heart attack, at age 79.

LADY EVE BALFOUR

British Pioneer of Organic Farming

Born **London, England, 16 July 1898**

Died **14 January 1990**

Lady Eve Balfour, farmer, saxophonist, pilot, sailor and detective writer, had many achievements to her name, but she will be best remembered for her unique role in the formation of the organic farming movement in Britain and for founding the Soil Association, a respected organization with a growing membership, devoted to educating the farming establishment and the general public alike on the merits of organic farming. An imposing woman, gifted at communicating her central message of the intimate and interdependent relationship of people, soil, food and health, she was delighted that her philosophy, for many years regarded as the height of crankiness, found acceptance and even respectability by the end of her life. Its simple but profound message is expressed in the stated aims of the Soil Association: "It encourages an ecological approach to agriculture and offers organic husbandry as the real long-term option rather than chemical farming which is causing havoc to the land and the environment." In recognition of her achievement in founding the Soil Association, Lady Eve, as she was usually known, was awarded an OBE in the 1990 New Year's Honours List, shortly before her death. The day after she died, Mrs Thatcher's government announced the first ever British grant to help farmers convert to organic methods.

Lady Eve's aristocratic family produced its fair share of prime ministers, namely the Marquess of Salisbury and Lady Eve's uncle A. J. Balfour, affectionately known to her as "Nunkie". The first two years of her life were spent mainly in Dublin where her father, Gerald Balfour, MP, was chief secretary for Ireland. Her mother, Lady Betty, was the eldest daughter of the 1st Earl of Lytton, poet and viceroy of India. Educated privately, her later childhood was divided between Fisher's Hill, near the southern English town of Woking, in a house designed for her parents by another distinguished uncle, architect Edwin Lutyens, and Whittingehame in East Lothian, the parliamentary Scottish seat of bachelor uncle, "A. J.". Lady Eve claimed that the interesting guests at "Nunkie's" house parties and the influence of her older cousins formed the basis of her education.

Always of an independent mind, she had already decided at the age of 12 to become a farmer and, in 1915, went to Reading University to read for a diploma in agriculture. In the last year of World War I, she had her first job, training Land Army girls on a farm on behalf of the Women's War Agricultural Committee. In 1918 she was barely 20, so became "officially" 25 in order to qualify for the job, recounting later: "They were all older than me and they were *tough*!" In 1919 she and her sister bought New Bells Farm in the Suffolk village of Haughley near Stowmarket and Lady Eve began farming in earnest.

The 1930s were a formative time for Eve Balfour. She gained useful campaigning experience when championing the cause of local farmers fighting against the unpopular tithe tax. This had been introduced some hundred years before and stipulated that one-tenth of the value of certain crops should be paid in tax — a punitive system for Depression-struck farmers. Her pamphlet and the evidence she submitted to the Royal Commission helped to change the law. During these years, too, she was formulating her farming philosophy, becoming critical of the intensification of orthodox farming. She was much influenced by a book called *Famine in England,* written by Lord Lymington in 1938, which questioned whether intensive farming could be sustained, and introduced her to the relationship between different agricultural methods, healthy soil and the "wholeness" of food. It inspired Lady Eve to undertake her own research and, in 1939, she set up the Haughley Experiment on her own farm and on the neighbouring farm of her friend Alice Debenham, to compare scientifically organic and inorganic methods of farming.

An important marker in Lady Eve's life was the writing of her book, *The Living Soil,* written during World War II and published in 1943. The book was written primarily to gain support for the research on her own farm, although its influence extended much further. Reprinted nine times, it became a classic for the organic movement which it helped to create. In it she brought together pioneering work in different fields of health. As she explained in her Introduction: "My subject is food, which concerns everyone; it is health, which concerns everyone; it is the soil, which concerns everyone — though they may not realize it — and it is the history of certain recent researches linking these three vital subjects." In a tribute to Lady Eve, another founder member of the Soil Association, Mary Langman, shed light on her colleague's determined and indefatigable character, recounting that at the time of writing her book, Lady Eve was working full-time on the farm and, hard hit by the inter-war Depression in English corn-growing counties, was living very simply and cheaply in a caravan, surrounded by relevant books from the public library. She went on: "I have heard her describe writing chapters in her head — polishing sentences as she sat on the tractor, for she was a fastidious writer — and then in the evenings getting these down on paper before she dropped off to sleep."

The success of *The Living Soil* led to the beginnings of what came to be known as "the organic movement" and, in 1946, to the foundation of the Soil Association by Lady Eve Balfour and other like-minded people, including doctors from the Pioneer Health Centre in Peckham, south London, whose research, from a more medical standpoint, had been moving in the same direction. The Association's aims were to bring together those working in similar directions, to help bring about research and to collect and distribute the knowledge gained. Its early educational aims were furthered by its journal *Mother Earth* and by the zeal of Lady Eve, the Association's first president, in undertaking lecturing trips abroad, especially in the late 1940s and early 1950s. In 1951, on a trip to the United States, she told *The New Yorker* of the benefits of her organic vegetarian diet, which she claimed had cured her of rheumatism, tooth decay and colds, saying, "I was able to sweep a whole armory of medicines and patent remedies into the dustbin." She enjoyed these trips hugely and also visited Australia, many European countries and Israel.

Despite growing support, with 3000 members by 1952, the Soil Association was often in financial crisis because of the heavy cost of research for the Haughley Experiment. Despite Lady Eve's own unwavering commitment to the project, not all members felt that this burden was worthwhile, believing that the Association should be demonstrating rather than testing the benefits of organic farming. Indeed, the debts incurred by research proved too much for a voluntary charitable institution and caused the loss of the farms in 1970, a personal blow for Lady Eve. However, the results of her research were published in 1975 in an addendum to a reprint of *The Living Soil,* and remain an invaluable document.

Since its infancy, the Soil Association has evolved, retaining its educational role but becoming more involved in campaigning and in establishing standards for organically grown produce, and British farmers and gardeners entitled to use the Soil Association symbol enjoy high respect. In 1990, the Soil Association is campaigning for "20% organic by the year 2000". The controversy has continued over the years between those who wished the Soil Association to concentrate on its campaigning role and those who, like Lady Eve, wished it to retain its early emphasis on research. It is interesting that the Soil Association re-committed itself in 1989 to an emphasis on diet, health and education and to a more international outlook. This wider perspective had been in evidence in the early days, with concern for Third World agriculture expressed on the pages of *Mother Earth.*

Eve Balfour was a woman of action and loved best the practical work on the farm or tasks such as working with local groups to set up trial plots for agricultural shows. When she retired in 1984, she found the time at last to grow all her own vegetables. At various times, she was general secretary of the Soil Association and manager of the research farm but was said to be more at ease in the second role, never really enjoying administration nor the internal politics of the organic movement. Although at times autocratic, she respected the democratic decisions of the Soil Association Council and enjoyed working with others, especially those whose creative genius she recognized. One such was E.F. Schumacher, author of the influential *Small is Beautiful,* with whom she worked closely when he was president of the Association. Her many activities included corresponding widely with scientists and farmers both at home and abroad, lecturing, contributing to annual residential Soil Association courses, and setting up college courses for those new to organic agriculture. During the post-war years when organic agriculture was so out of step with mainstream views and derided by many so-called experts, Lady Eve played a crucial inspirational role in keeping alternative ideas alive. She was fiercely loyal to those who supported her, though perhaps over-wary towards those within the movement who opposed her.

As years went by, public consciousness was raised on both sides of the Atlantic of the need to safeguard the environment. In the US in the 1960s, Rachel Carson's book *Silent Spring,* alerted the world to the toxic effects on the environment of chemical pesticides. In Britain the influence was increasingly felt of enthusiastic organic gardeners such as Lawrence D. Hills, (q.v.)who set up his own Henry Doubleday Research Association and popularized the vital role of the plant comfrey in organic gardening. Organic farming is now also firmly supported by such influential figures as Prince Charles, the heir to the British throne. Even during those harder early years, Eve Balfour, though regarded by many as an eccentric mystic, managed, through her faith in proper scientific research, to forge some valuable links across the agricultural divide with some of the more open-minded academic soil scientists. More importantly, she helped to create a new synthesis of ideas which have had a profound influence in the last part of the twentieth century, pushing farming experts and the public alike to "think green".

Despite her great commitment to organic farming, Lady Eve was never a one-track person, and her other activities included forming a dance band, locally very popular, in which she played saxophone. She gained her pilot's licence in the 1930s, but regretted that she was too old to deliver aircraft from factories to airfields in World War II. She took great pleasure in crewing for her brother when he went on annual summer sailing trips to Scandinavia. As E.B. Balfour, she wrote three detective novels with Beryl Hearnden, the most successful of which, *Paper Moon,* was translated into several languages. She had a sense of humour too and reportedly replied to a group interested in nutrition when asked about her diet: "Oh, don't model yourself on me. I drink gin and tonic and smoke cigarettes. As long as you're good 75 per cent of the time, the remaining 25 per cent will look after itself." In 1963, she moved to Theberton near the Suffolk coast but still made frequent visits to Haughley. In 1985, the year following her retirement, the Soil Association moved to Bristol in south-west England.

Mary Langman sums up what she sees Eve Balfour's greatest achievement: "Historically, I do not think that she herself will come to be seen as one of the great originators, a role she never herself claimed, but rather as one who worked continuously and with the most acute perception to bring together insights derived from different fields of scientific research and practical experience: all related to her central themes of nutrition and health, and their relation to the soil." Lady Eve knew that this was an on-going process, still in its early stages, and it is worth remembering that in the year of her death, BBC Radio 4's *Food Programme* reported that the British government was spending 9.5 million pounds a day on subsidizing conventional agriculture compared with just 726 pounds a day on research and development of organic agriculture. Without a doubt, Lady Eve Balfour helped to bring about this first small step by government toward organic farming methods.

Born Evelyn Barbara Balfour. **Pseudonym** E.B. Balfour. **Parents** Gerald, member of parliament and chief secretary for Ireland, and Lady Betty (Lytton) Balfour. **Education** Reading University, 1915, diploma in agriculture, 1917. **Career** Farmer, 1918 onwards; trained Land Army girls, Women's War Agricultural Committee, 1918; owner, with sister, New Bells Farm, Haughley, Suffolk, 1919–84, Walnut Tree Farm, 1930s–1984. **Related activities** Haughley Experiment, initiator, with Alice Debenham, 1939, director, 1939–84; publication of *The Living Soil,* 1943; founder, Soil Association, 1946, organizing secretary, 1946, lecturer, America, Australia, Europe, 1940s and 1950s; guest, Israeli Ministry of Agriculture. **Other activities** Founder, dance band, saxophonist, 1920s; campaigner against tithe tax, 1930s; pilot, 1930–39; sailor; author, detective stories, under pseudonym. **Offices and memberships** Soil Association, 1946 onwards. **Awards and honours** Officer of the Order of the British Empire, 1990. **Radio** *Prophets Returned,* BBC Radio 4, 1989. **Publications** (include) *The Living Soil,* 1943; (with Beryl Hearnden) *Paper Moon* (novel). **Cause of death** Undisclosed, at age 91. **Further reading** *The Living Earth,* quarterly journal of the Soil Association.

JOHN BLACKING

British Social Anthropologist

***Born* Guildford, Surrey, 22 October 1928**

***Died* Belfast, Northern Ireland, 24 January 1990**

John Blacking was a man in love with the whole process of human life. He had, he said, no hobbies in the true sense of that word. What he did have was an unlimited interest in, and love of, the underlying structures of human culture and social interaction and a seemingly unlimited supply of energy with which to pursue this interest and similarly to enthuse those around him.

He was the eldest child, and only son, of a strict Anglo-Catholic ecclesiastical architect and grew up in the cathedral city of Salisbury in the west country. He was educated at the independent school of Sherborne after which he was commissioned into the prestigious regiment of Coldstream Guards for military service, having excelled in the Officer Cadet Training Unit and been awarded the Belt of Honour. He was also a talented musician.

During his time on active duty in Malaya he led a platoon of irregulars drawn from the Aboriginal population. Many young men from a similar upper-middle-class background of that time would have regarded them as "merely natives" and not part of the "real" world. But Blacking developed a respect for the differences between their two cultures and a desire to discover more. Thus he chose subsequently to study social anthropology at Cambridge University where the renowned Meyer Fortes had recently taken the Chair.

After Cambridge he returned briefly to Malaya but found his respect for the rights of other people at variance with his advisory duties and subsequently ended up in Paris where he pursued his alternative interest of music. In fact this was to prove one of the pivotal periods of his life. He began working on the anthropology of music at the Musée de L'Homme with André Schaeffner and, on his advice, gave up his aim for a career as a concert pianist and accepted a job in South Africa at the International Library of African Music, founded by another musician with an interest in folklore, Hugh Tracey. (Blacking did not, however, abandon music. He continued to play — to a very high standard throughout his life — and took a great interest in choral music. He was also a choirmaster.)

It was now that Blacking really served the apprenticeship for his future work in the field of ethnomusicology. He learned recording methods, transcription and analysis, and worked on his first field studies — in Mozambique and Zululand. He subsequently spent nearly two years in intensive fieldwork amongst the Venda people of the northern Transvaal. Although an anthropologist, of course, examines all aspects of a particular culture and, in particular, the culture of ritual, Blacking concentrated on music as the key idiom in which cultural norms, values and expectations are expressed and can be perceived. His basic ethnography of Venda music was published in 1965, followed two years later by *Venda Children's Songs: A Study in Ethnomusicological Analysis*. These were trail-blazers in the anthropological study of music. Unlike his contemporary in the USA, Alan Merriam, Blacking did not wish to marry the findings of musical analysis with those of anthropology. He saw music *and* its cultural context as interrelated parts of the total system. This he called "cultural analysis" which may, in part, account for his greater popularity in the USA. In North America the discipline is seen in terms of cultural wholes and specificity. The British–French tradition is far more concerned with the search for universal theory.

Following his fieldwork Blacking became a lecturer at the University of Witwatersrand in South Africa. There he moved gradually up the hierarchy, being appointed professor in 1965 and becoming a source of inspiration, often subversive, to all who chose to listen to him. He was never afraid of personal action or involvement where apartheid was concerned. He consistently ignored its barriers in his personal life and, when his relationship with Zureena Desai, the medical student who eventually became his second wife, was discovered, he was prosecuted under the notorious Immorality Act. This forbade sexual relations between Black and White. He managed to turn the tables on the authorities during the ensuing trial by making fun of the whole proceedings, not least the surveillance methods employed by the police. They had spent a not inconsiderable period of time hanging from tree branches in an attempt to peer into his bedroom. Happily, this Act was later repealed.

In the early 1970s Blacking was appointed professor to the first Chair of Social Anthropology at Queen's University, Belfast. Here he proceeded to make the department a centre of excellence by international standards. The fact that, from his earliest days in Belfast, the Irish "troubles" were in loud and visible evidence (bombs and the devastation of terrorist action could be heard and seen from the windows of the department) never hindered him in the development of an institutional base from which to spread the gospel of ethnomusicology. He had not allowed the fall-out from discrimination and injustice to deter him from his beliefs when in South Africa: he was certainly not going to permit it to inhibit him back home in the United Kingdom.

Blacking's department rapidly attracted high-calibre post-graduate students from throughout the world. They were drawn by his reputation, by the university's willingness to recognize qualifications from little-known institutions, and by the British Council who provided many with scholarships. Most overseas students based their research on fieldwork in their own areas. Blacking himself gained immensely from the richness of the data they brought to study. His colleagues, however, did not allow him to slip too far into the American tradition of cultural relativity. Ladislav Holy and his fellow Czechoslovakian, Melan Stuchlik, contributed a strong theoretical focus to the work at Queen's. Blacking took this on board and used it in developing the freshness of approach employed in his later writing.

Blacking was always incredibly busy, lecturing throughout the world, spending several semesters at American universities and, from 1981 to 1983, was chairman of the Society for Ethnomusicology. He was the first non-American resident to hold the position. He also founded the European

Seminar in Ethnomusicology. His interests were not confined solely to the level of high academia, however. He scripted and introduced a television series on dance and was particularly influential in bringing about the introduction of all relevant forms of ethnic music into British state schools. This was not simply to reflect the different musical heritages of children in a multi-cultural society but to offer young people of all intellectual abilities access to what he regarded as the greatest human universal.

Although he died with still so much planned work yet to be done, Blacking's achievements were nonetheless both large and recognized. He left a substantial body of published work and was made a member of the Royal Irish Academy in 1984, awarded the Rivers Memorial Medal of the British Royal Anthropological Institute in 1986, and made professor emeritus at Queen's six months before his death. His greatest memorial however lies in the continuation of his work through his former students at Queen's. They carry his message forward throughout the world.

Born John Anthony Randall Blacking. **Parents** William, ecclesiastical architect, and Margaret (Waymouth) Blacking. **Marriages** 1) Brenda Eleonora Gebers (dissolved); 2) Zureena Rukshana Desai. **Children** Caroline (deceased), Jessica, Fiona (deceased), Laura and Valentine, by first marriage; four daughters by second. **Education** Sherborne School, Dorset; King's College, Cambridge, BA in social anthropology, 1953, MA, 1957; studied piano and anthropology of music under André Schaeffner, Musée de L'Homme, 1954; University of Witwatersrand, Johannesburg, PhD, 1965, DLitt, 1972. **Military service** British Army, commissioned in Coldstream Guards, 1948–49, served in Malaya. **Career** Assistant adviser on Aborigines, Malaya, 1953; musicologist, International Library of African Music, South Africa, 1954–57; fieldworker, anthropological scholarship, northern Transvaal, 1956–58; lecturer in social anthropology and African administration, University of Witwatersrand, Johannesburg, South Africa, honorary lecturer in music, 1959–65, professor of social anthropology, chairman of African Studies Programme, 1966–69; professor of social anthropology, Queen's University, Belfast, Northern Ireland, 1970, professor emeritus, 1989 onwards; visiting professor: Western Michigan University, 1969–72, Makerere University, University of Pittsburgh. **Related activities** General editor, Cambridge University Press series in Ethnomusicology; member, Council for National Academic Awards; founder, director, European Seminar in Ethnomusicology, 1981 onwards; honorary director of research, international cultural performing arts project, Goldsmiths' College, London. **Offices and memberships** Fellow, Royal Anthropological Institute; member: Association of Social Anthropologists of the British Commonwealth, International Folk Music Council, Musicological Society of Australia, Society for Ethnomusicology, United States of America, chairman, 1981–83. **Awards and honours** (include) Elected member,Royal Irish Academy, 1984; Rivers Memorial Medal, Royal Anthropological Institute, 1986; Fumio prize, Tokyo, 1989. **Recordings** *Music from Petauke,* Album I, 1962, Album II, 1965. **Publications** (include) *Black Background: the Childhood of a South African Girl,* 1964; *Venda Children's Songs: A Study in Ethnomusicological Analysis,* 1967; *Process and Product in Human Society,* 1969; *How Musical Is Man?,* 1973; *Man and Fellowman,* 1974; (with Joann W. Kealiinohomoku) *The Performing Arts: Music and Dance,* 1979; (editor, with Philip V. Tobias) Antonio de Almeida, *Bushmen and Other Non-Bantu Peoples of Angola: Three Lectures,* 1965; (editor) *The Anthropology of the Body,* 1977. **Cause of death** Cancer, at age 61.

IAN CHARLESON

British Actor

***Born* Edinburgh, Scotland, 11 August 1949**

***Died* London, England, 6 January 1990**

In the final act of Shakespeare's masterpiece, Hamlet observes, "If it be now, 'tis not to come; if it be not to come, it will be now; if it be not now, yet it will come: the readiness is all. Since no man of aught he leaves knows aught, what is't to leave betimes? Let be." It is the comment of a man matured to the point where he can accept the inevitability of his own death. There is a peculiar and poignant irony in the fact that Ian Charleson's final public performance was in this role, a show which brought the audience to its feet, at some level no doubt aware — as he knew all too well — that he was dying. Two months later, his agent announced his death from septicaemia after a brave, dignified struggle against the onset of Aids.

Charleson was that very rare thing, an actor universally liked, both within and without the profession. His bravery in the final months of his life and the integrity with which he fought the ravages of his condition won him much admiration, particularly in view of his constant pain as a result of both the disease and the various therapies used to combat it. To the outside world, he had an acute sinus condition, a euphemism used to explain his bloated face and swollen eyes. Close friends however knew, and many others guessed the true explanation, in spite of Charleson's jokes in rehearsal about his distorted appearance: "When I come on, all you'll hear is the rustle of programmes as people flick through, saying, 'Who's he? Who's he?' " At times, he was almost too weak to fight the final duel; he was forced to miss a number of performances altogether, in his own eyes, a serious lapse in professionalism — "If they're paying you, you should turn up," he commented. *Hamlet* is, of all Shakespeare's plays, the most concerned with mortality, charting the path of a man in his prime on an inevitable journey to his own death. For at least one critic, his was the quintessential Hamlet of his generation, a performance of extraordinary intensity that had much to do with the dignity and courage with which he faced his own end.

The son of a working-class Edinburgh family, Charleson won a bursary to the fee-paying Royal High School. From there, he went to Edinburgh University to read architecture, though much of his time was given over to student theatre. He decided to give up a career as an architect to go onto the professional stage, although his father looked on the entertainment profession as a haven for "a lot of strange people", whom he defined when pressed as "nancy boys". Stout reassurances, together with a bursary to the London Academy of Music and Dramatic Art (LAMDA), confirmed parental and family support for his decision to train for the theatre.

Charleson's early career was filled with apparently effortless success. He was plucked straight from LAMDA by Frank Dunlop to join his company at the Young Vic, where, after an initiation at the Edinburgh Festival as one of the many brothers in the musical *Joseph and the Amazing Technicolour Dreamcoat,* he went on to make a strong impression in roles such as the fiery Jimmy Porter in John Osborne's *Look Back in Anger.* He subsequently gave his first Hamlet with the Cambridge Theatre Company in 1975, of which he later said, "Nobody saw it, but I learnt a lot." Various jobs followed, but it was not until he was invited to dinner by film producer David Puttnam to discuss the part of Scottish preacher and athlete, Eric Liddell, that his career really took off. "There were not too many Scots actors who could run very fast," he recalled with typically ironic detachment. *Chariots of Fire* was what Hollywood calls a "low-concept movie" — one whose plot cannot be summed up in two sentences — and its enormous appeal and consequent commercial success came as something of a surprise to both makers and backers. When the film went on to win an Oscar, Charleson looked set to become a major movie star.

In common with many in his profession, however, he was torn between his desire to make it in the international arena and his ambition to become a great classical actor. Curiously equivocal about the trappings of success, he had little patience with the routine milk-round of press conferences and chat shows — sick of the inanity of it all, he flew home in the middle of a publicity tour for *Chariots*. He later refused to do the expected thing and go to Hollywood to wait for offers. None was forthcoming, and it was the stage that claimed the vast bulk of his time for the rest of his career.

Several seasons' work at the National Theatre saw him first as Sky Masterson, the Broadway gambler, in a much-praised and hugely popular revival of the musical *Guys and Dolls,* allowing him an opportunity to display his very fine tenor voice; this was followed by the lead in Sam Shepherd's *Fool for Love.* His performance as Brick in Tennessee Williams's *Cat on a Hot Tin Roof* also drew many plaudits, being a gutsy and credible portrayal of the alcoholic repressed homosexual.

Charleson was, in many ways, an actor's actor, highly sensitive to those on stage and displaying a precision and grace that made him highly watchable. While never an overpowering, sexually magnetic stage presence in the mould of, say, Olivier or Burton, he commanded attention apparently without trying. On a personal level, he inspired loyal friendships and intense admiration. Fellow actor, Hilton McRae, said of his time at Stratford with the Royal Shakespeare Company, "Almost everyone — man or woman — was in love with him." His final courageous decision, with the admirable support of his family, not to disguise the cause of his death, was entirely in keeping with an honesty and independence that informed his whole life.

Born Ian Charleson. **Parents** John, printer, and Jane Charleson. **Education** Royal High School, Edinburgh; scholar, Edinburgh University, MA in architecture, 1970; London Academy of Music and Dramatic Art. **Career** Professional début, as Gad in *Joseph and the Amazing Technicolour Dreamcoat,* with Young Vic company, 1972; New York début with Young Vic company as Lucentio in *The Taming of the Shrew,* Ottavio in *Scapino,* Brian Curtis in *French Without Tears,* Brooklyn Academy of Music, 1974; film début in *Jubilee,* 1978; starred as Eric Liddell in *Chariots of Fire,* 1981. **Stage** (in London, unless otherwise indicated) *Joseph and the Amazing Technicolour Dreamcoat,* Edinburgh, 1972; with Young Vic company: *Look Back in Anger, Rosencrantz and Guildenstern Are Dead,* 1972–74; *The Taming of the Shrew,* New York, 1974; *Scapino,* New York, 1974; *French Without Tears,* New York, 1974; *Hamlet,* Cambridge, England, 1975; *Otherwise Engaged,* 1975; *Julius Caesar,* 1977; *Volpone,* 1977; *Hunchback of Notre Dame,* 1977; *The Tempest,* Stratford-upon-Avon, 1978; *The Taming of the Shrew,* Stratford-upon-Avon, 1978; *Love's Labour's Lost,* Stratford-upon-Avon, 1978; *Piaf,* Stratford-upon-Avon (Other Place), 1978; *Love's Labour's Lost,* 1979; *Once in a Lifetime,* 1979; *The Innocent Man,* 1979; *Piaf,* 1979; *Guys and Dolls,* 1983; *Fool for Love,* 1985; *After Aida,* 1986; show for Queen's birthday, Windsor Castle, 1986; *Cat on a Hot Tin Roof,* 1989; *Hamlet,* 1989. **Films** (include) *Jubilee*, 1978; *Chariots of Fire,* 1981; *Gandhi,* 1982; *Greystoke: The Legend of Tarzan, Lord of the Apes*,1984; *Car Trouble*, 1986. **Television** (includes) *Rock Follies; Churchill's People; The Paradise Run; All's Well that Ends Well; Julius Caesar; Antony and Cleopatra; Month in the Country; Oxbridge Blues; Troubles; Codename Kyril; The Sun Also Rises; Master of the Game; Louisiana.* **Cause of death** Aids-related septicaemia, at age 40.

JOSEPH S. CLARK

American Politician

***Born* Philadelphia, Pennsylvania, 21 October 1901**

***Died* Philadelphia, Pennsylvania, 12 January 1990**

"There is nothing wrong with the Declaration of Independence. These truths are self-evident. All men are created equal. What is wrong is the way the Declaration is soft-pedaled by those who wish to limit its application... And those who wish to do so, who venerate what they call constitutional government, are in control of Congress."

Joseph Clark wrote this in 1964, after seven years as senator and after having seen first-hand the rigor mortis that was setting in on Capitol Hill. Clark had entered the Senate with the naïve assumption that its purpose was to make laws. Instead, he discovered that it was bound by a series of archaic practices that undermined party responsibility, divorced it from the electorate, and consistently thwarted any meaningful government. Moreover,this trend was being encouraged by what he saw as "a self-perpetuating oligarchy" of congressmen. Clark had entered local politics to pursue political reform, and upon reaching the Senate it became his main focus. In the course of his 12 years in Congress, he became an intelligent supporter of civil rights, an early critic of the Vietnam war and Congress's leading maverick.

A friend once described Clark as "a rebel by nature", but in the beginning he did not look much like one. He was born into a wealthy, patrician family who lived in Chestnut Hill, one of Philadelphia's well-to-do suburbs. His father was a former tennis champion and then a prominent lawyer. His family ran an investment firm and had substantial coal and oil interests. Young Clark was an athlete and a prize-winning student in school and in college. He graduated Phi Beta Kappa and *magna cum laude* from Harvard in 1923. After receiving his law degrees and being admitted to the Pennsylvania Bar in 1926, Clark pursued a traditional upper-class career as a lawyer and civic leader. He dabbled in city politics in the 1930s, adopting a Right-leaning liberal philosophy. Then, on a tip from a friend in Washington, Clark entered the Army Air Force in August 1941. He entered as a captain, and after serving deputy chief of staff in the India-China-Burma theatre, left as a colonel.

His impressive list of credentials would certainly have been enough to secure Clark's position in Philadelphia society if he had chosen it. But he had other ideas. He was one of a new generation of politicians whose activism and idealism would culminate in John F. Kennedy's "New Frontier" policies. He became part of a reforming group, dissatisfied with the notorious practices of the Republican party-machine, which had controlled Philadelphia politics since 1884, and determined to put an end to corruption.

By 1951, the call for reform was growing. The Republicans were embroiled in several scandals involving embezzlement, fraud and extortion. Clark was also at odds with the Democratic leadership, who offered mayoral candidates "who had no real stake in the city". Although the Party bosses did not regard him as a serious candidate, he ran for mayor in 1952. Using a broom to symbolize his designs on corruption, Clark turned a 200,000-vote Republican majority into a landslide victory for the Democrats.

Under Clark, Philadelphia city government was streamlined and professionalized. A new city charter was adopted, departments merged, and the investigative powers of the mayor increased. Clark shunned patronage, reformed the civil service, cleared slums, and sponsored extensive urban redevelopment. In 1956, a grateful city gave him the Philadelphia Award for "instituting good government", making Clark the first politician to win it. Riding the wave of appreciation, and despite the indifference of leading Democrats, Clark was easily elected to the Senate, where he fully expected to pursue the policies of the Democratic platforms of 1952 and 1956.

He was wrong. In his view, the eighty-fifth Congress was applying itself to the business of accomplishing as little work as possible in 1957. Over the budget, civil rights and procedural rules, the leadership thwarted action at every turn. Clark saw the main force behind the inertia as the senator from Texas, Lyndon B. Johnson. Clark and Johnson had a poor relationship from the beginning. Clark did not like the "Johnson Treatment" of hard-sell tactics, and Johnson considered Clark a nuisance. Several northern liberals had gained seats in the 1956 election and formed a small coalition against the Johnson camp, but they still were not strong enough to force any issues.

In one of his first speeches as senator, Clark attacked the procedures that "penalize those who seek action in the national interest". By 1959, the liberal opposition had begun to bite; and with Kennedy's election to the presidency in 1960 (and Johnson's removal to the vice-presidency), Clark enjoyed new status and influence. He wrote and sponsored two major pieces of legislation: the Area Redevelopment Act in 1961, which encouraged industrial development in depressed areas, and the Manpower Development and Training Act in 1962, which offered extensive federal aid for training and retraining workers. Kennedy asked Clark to prepare the agenda for civil rights legislation in 1961, and in 1962 he was appointed to the Democratic steering committee, which determines all committee assignments in the Senate. Under Kennedy, Clark and his liberal Democratic colleagues gained ground.

But it did not last long. Southern conservatives were still powerful, and when Kennedy's assassination put Johnson in the Oval Office, the reform movement was stymied. The aid mandated by the Manpower Development and Training Act was gutted and the system replaced by the Economic Development Administration in 1965. Clark's proposals to continue liberal reform were repeatedly voted down. Civil rights continued to make painfully slow progress. In 1964, Clark supported Johnson's pivotal Gulf of Tonkin resolution, but soon withdrew his support as Congress became bitterly divided over Vietnam.

Back in Pennsylvania, too, his reform movement was lagging. Clark's rhetoric, characterizing candidates in the 1963 primaries as "sleazy", for example, actually rallied the opposition. Clark was then blamed for the poor showing the Democrats made that year, and the Democratic leadership finally regarded him as a liability. His third senatorial campaign was handicapped by this opposition, as well as by the appearance of a young and progressive Republican candidate. He lost his seat by over 200,000 votes.

Clark's efforts in the Senate never quite got the results he sought. The scathing criticisms he made in 1964, in a book called *Congress: The Sapless Branch,* are today still valid. Congress, he claimed, had lost its vigour and effectiveness because it was still living in the "horse-and-buggy era". The consequence has been ineffective leadership and, more importantly, a loss of faith. This breeds apathy and cynicism in the electorate and the budget battles of 1957 and 1990 show that the situation has not changed. Clark thought that it would; and when it did, he said that "this maverick will consent to be branded".

Born Joseph Sill Clark. **Parents** Joseph Sill, lawyer, and Kate Richardson (Avery) Clark. **Marriages** 1) Noel Hall, 1935; 2) Iris Richey. **Children** Joseph and Noel, by first marriage. **Education** Chestnut Hill Academy, Philadelphia; Middlesex School, Massachusetts, 1919; Harvard University, Cambridge, Massachusetts, BS, magna cum laude, 1923; University of Pennsylvania, Philadelphia, LLB, 1926. **Military service** United States Army Air Force, 1941–45, served in China, Burma, India, retired as colonel. **Career** Admitted to Pennsylvania Bar, 1926; associate: Clark, Clark, McCarthy and Wagner, 1926–33, Dechert, Bok, Smith and Clark, Philadelphia, from 1934; deputy attorney general of Pennsylvania, 1934–35; city controller,

Philadelphia, 1949–51; mayor of Philadelphia, 1952–56; United States senator from Pennsylvania, 1957–68. **Related activities** Chairman: citizens' committee for Truman and Barkley, 1948, Philadelphia chapter, Americans for Democratic Action, 1948–49; founder, president, Members of Congress for Peace through Law; president World Federalists of the United States of America, 1969–71; chairman, Coalition on National Priorities and Military Policy, 1969–73. **Offices and memberships** Member: Pennsylvania Merit League, Public Charities Association of Pennsylvania, Bureau of Municipal Research, Pennsylvania, Committee of Seventy, Philadelphia, Citizen's Council on City Planning, Philadelphia, Juristic Society, Sharswood Law Club, Junior Legal Club, Americans for Democratic Action, American Legion and Veterans of Foreign Wars, American Philosophical Society, Phi Beta Kappa; on board of overseers, Harvard, 1953–59; trustee, Fund for Peace; fellow, American Academy of Arts and Sciences; vice-president, American Academy of Political and Social Sciences; on board of directors, Arms Control Association. **Awards and honours** Bronze Star, Legion of Merit, United States; Military Order of the British Empire; Honorary Wings of the Chinese Air Force; LLD: Temple University, Harvard, 1952, Drexel Institute, 1957, University of Pennsylvania, 1963, Haverford College, 1966, Franklin and Marshall College, 1967; Doctor of Civil Law, Susquehanna University, 1961; Doctor of Literature, Lincoln University, 1961; Philadelphia Award for instituting good government in the city, 1956. **Publications** *The Senate Establishment,* 1963; *Congress: The Sapless Branch,* 1964; *Readings in Congressional Reform,* 1966. **Cause of death** Undisclosed, at age 88.

ARNAUD d'USSEAU

American Playwright and Screenwriter

Born **Los Angeles, California, 18 April 1916**

Died **Manhattan, New York, 29 January 1990**

The name does not roll easily off the tongue, nor does it bring to the mind of the general public any immediate associations, yet it is safe to say that Arnaud d'Usseau will be remembered in dramatic circles for two things: his best-known plays *(Tomorrow the World* and *Deep Are the Roots,* both written in conjunction with James Gow) and his blacklisting by Senator Joseph McCarthy during the Communist witch-hunts of 1950s America.

D'Usseau came by his interest in the stage and screen naturally enough: his father was a movie producer and scenarist, his mother was an actress. No one was surprised when, after graduation, the young man chose an "expressive" type of career, beginning with journalism. At first he worked for the United Press service in Arizona, but soon left when a Hollywood studio offered him a job as a set dresser.

The jump from journalism to set co-ordination might seem a strange one, but for d'Usseau, the dresser job was a means to an end; soon afterwards he landed an assignment to write a treatment of a mystery story for RKO movie studios with a view to production. The thriller, *One Crowded Night,* was successfully shot by the company and appeared in 1940 — quite a coup for d'Usseau, who admitted that he "had never read a mystery story" in his life. Despite that fact, the young writer was immediately cast by the Hollywood scene as "a mystery writer", a label which he found somewhat difficult to shake off.

He was not the only one. On the RKO lot, d'Usseau's path crossed with that of James Gow, another young screenwriter whose success with the adaptation of opera for the movies had resulted in the same type-casting problem. Soon the two writers were collaborating on a comedy in a bid to escape from mysteries and opera. The result was *Repent at Leisure* which was produced in 1941 — but neither author was allowed to write the screen version because, they were told, "it's not your kind of picture".

If the screen world proved too caught up in types, the young men reasoned, then they would try their luck on the stage, and so the pair began collaborating on various plays. In the meantime, d'Usseau left RKO to join Twentieth Century-Fox. There he worked on the screenplays of several motion pictures including *Who Is Hope Shuyler?, The Man Who Wouldn't Die, Twelve Men in a Box,* and *Just Off Broadway;* most have since been consigned to the late-night realms of television's B-movies. Eventually, however, Gow and d'Usseau came up with a winner, a story about a Nazi-trained teenager adopted by an American couple. They began writing the play in July 1942 — one sat at the typewriter while the other paced the floor — and by November the first draft of what was to become *Tomorrow the World* was complete. By 1943, the play was running on Broadway.

Tomorrow the World did not just make it to Broadway; it ran for 499 performances there and then transferred to London for 398 performances in 1944. The critics and the public at large loved it, even though parts of the work were generally thought to be uneven. Lewis Nichols of *The New York Times,* for example, wrote that the play contained flaws, but stated that "it gives an audience an evening that is sometimes moving, sometimes exciting and, in general, all on the credit side of the ledger" — not a bad review for a supposed mystery writer and opera adapter. "Vastly effective, at times rather luridly ridiculous" was how Howard Barnes of the *Herald Tribune* thought of it; nonetheless, a movie version of the play came out in 1944, produced by Ring Lardner Jr, one of the future "Hollywood Ten" who would later be jailed for standing their ground during the Congressional Investigation led by Joseph McCarthy into alleged Communist influences within the film industry.

That, however, was yet to come. In the meantime, the duo of Gow and d'Usseau did not rest on their laurels, but embarked on their third joint writing effort, this time a story of racial injustice. *Deep Are the Roots* appeared on Broadway in 1945 and achieved 477 performances, as well as a decent run in London's West End two years later. The play tells the story of a black soldier who returns to his home town in the South after the war and is subsequently forced to re-learn his role in society. *Roots* is considered to be d'Usseau's best work and it was one of the ten "Best Plays" chosen by Burns Mantle in the 1945–46 edition of the annual publication of the same name.

D'Usseau's reputation seemed to be climbing at that time, but when his name hit the headlines again, it was in conjunction with a very different subject. In 1953 the playwright refused on principle to answer questions concerning proposed connections with the Communist Party (in fact, he had none) and nearly came to blows with the leader of the inquisition, Senator McCarthy, during the House Un-American Committee's hearings. He would gladly debate communism and capitalism, d'Usseau told the fanatical McCarthy, but "not where you have everything stacked". D'Usseau, like so many other film-makers and writers of the time, was blacklisted by Hollywood and forced to flee to Europe for work. Ironically, he continued to write for the Hollywood scene under a variety of pseudonyms.

Before his departure, d'Usseau had collaborated on his fifth and final effort with Gow, a comedy called *The Story of Sarah* which opened in 1950. He had also teamed up with the legendarily witty Dorothy Parker to produce a psychological drama, *The Ladies of the Corridor,* about a group of lonely women in a residential hotel. While his exile lasted, d'Usseau lived mostly in France and Spain, but he eventually returned to the United States and settled in New York City, where he taught writing at New York University — the same university at which he had studied journalism as a young man.

At the time of his death, the playwright was awaiting the Broadway opening of his final work, *Bledsoe,* which had been postponed from spring, 1989. It may give us more insight into d'Usseau's own experiences, for *Bledsoe* follows the life of an exiled American writer in Rome.

Born Arnaud d'Usseau. **Parents** Leon, screenplay writer and film producer, and Ottola (Nesmith), actress, d'Usseau. **Marriages** 1) Susan Wells, 1938; 2) Marie-Christine. **Children** One son and one daughter, Emmanuel and Guadalupe. **Education** Beverly Hills High School, Los Angeles; studied journalism, New York University. **Military service** United States Army Signal Corps, 1943–45. **Career** Book clerk, 1932; writer, United Press, Arizona; set dresser, Hollywood; first movie treatment, *One Crowded Night,* 1940; first collaboration with James Gow, *Repent at Leisure,* 1941; blacklisted by Hollywood during McCarthy era, moved to Europe, 1953; lecturer in writing: New York University, School of Visual Art, New York City. **Writings** (plays, unless otherwise indicated) *One Crowded Night* (screenplay), 1940; (with James Gow) *Repent at Leisure,* 1941; (with James Gow) *How Like an Angel,* 1941; with Twentieth Century-Fox, from 1942: *Who Is Hope Schuyler?* (screenplay), *The Man Who Wouldn't Die* (screenplay), *Twelve Men in a Box* (screenplay), *Just Off Broadway* (screenplay), 1942; (with James Gow) *Tomorrow the World,* 1943; (with James Gow) *Deep Are the Roots,* 1945; (with James Gow) *Legend of Sarah,* 1950; (with Dorothy Parker) *The Ladies of the Corridor,* 1953; *Bledsoe,* production originally scheduled 1989. **Cause of death** Stomach cancer, at age 73.

HAROLD EDGERTON

American Engineer and Photographer

***Born* Freemont, Nebraska, 6 April 1903**

***Died* Cambridge, Massachusetts, 4 January 1990**

Lovers of the flashing lights and pounding beat of today's disco's have cause to be grateful to Professor Harold "Doc" Edgerton, inventor of the modern stroboscope — although *his* musical taste ran mainly to quieter country-and-western music. The pulsing strobe light which illuminates the dance floor, causing every movement to seem strangely jerky — almost robotic — is essentially the same device that Edgerton pioneered in 1931 and spent the rest of his life perfecting.

Putting aside such frivolous application, it is also true that every camera-user who relies on an electronic flash to illuminate his or her subject is applying an Edgerton invention. The scientific uses of Edgerton's high-speed stroboscopes are wide-ranging. However, he was no mere inventor, letting others apply his technology. He worked with naturalists studying bird, bat and insect flight; oceanographers studying the sea floor; archaeologists studying lost civilizations and aerodynamicists studying aeroplane shock waves.

His taste for adventure and his passion for taking pictures with his own equipment took him to the bottom of the sea with Jacques Cousteau, the French marine biologist, and involved him in the planning of the Allies' "D-Day" invasion of France during World War II, as well as drawing him into Scotland's Loch Ness, Lake Titicaca in the Andes and a number of important shipwrecks in Europe and America.

Although Edgerton regarded all his photographs as scientific documents, some of his most striking pictures have crossed over into the realm of art. His famous splashing milkdrop, for instance, hangs in the Museum of Modern Art in New York.

So how did Edgerton's stroboscope revolutionize photography? To take a still photograph or a frame in a moving film, the light-sensitive film must be exposed to light for a certain period of time (the exposure). The earliest surviving photograph, taken in 1827 by Joseph Nicephore Niepce, required an eight-hour exposure. The view from Niepce's study appeared rather blurry because the sun and shadows had moved somewhat during the exposure. Since then, exposure times have been progressively shortened by shutter, film and lighting technology. Edgerton's achievement represents the pinnacle of this process.

If the light is strong enough and the film sufficiently sensitive, the exposure can be made shorter and shorter allowing us to "freeze" briefer and briefer instants of time. To get these very short exposures mechanically the camera's shutter has to be opened and shut extremely fast. Unfortunately there is a limit to how fast the shutter can "click" — giving a minimum exposure of 1/1500th of a second. Using Edgerton's stroboscopic flashlight, however, it has been possible to reduce the length of exposure beyond the limits of what is possible with a shutter.

A stroboscope is simply a very powerful light which is able to flash on and off very fast. Stroboscopes existed, as curiosities, before Edgerton. His contribution was to increase massively the intensity of the light, reduce the length of the flash and increase the flash speed electronically.

By using a tube of Xenon gas, which provides light more intense than the sun (equivalent in fact to 40,000 50-watt bulbs) and ensuring that each flash lasts less than 1/10,000th of a second, Edgerton was able to break new ground in short exposure photography. If such lights flash on and off up to 100 times every second, multiple exposure photographs can be obtained which combine several instants in one picture. Separate frozen views of a moving subject can be seen together, allowing the viewer to "dissect" a rapid movement, such as a golfer's swing or a footballer's kick.

If this technique is combined with ultra-high-speed moving film (2000 frames per second for example) each separate flash can coincide with a new frame of the film which is rushing past an open shutter at over 80 miles an hour. A rapid event such as an explosion or the flapping of a hummingbird's wings can be "slowed" down by playing back the resulting film at normal speed. This has given scientists a powerful tool in the study of very rapid events. In Edgerton's own words, it allows "time itself to be chopped up into small bits and frozen so that it suits our needs".

Surely if a light is being switched on and off, however fast, the viewer will be aware of a flickering on the film? Luckily, the human eye cannot cope with more than about ten new images per second. If a light is flashed on an object any faster than this, the object will seem to us to be constantly illuminated, the human viewer being unaware of the darkness between each flash — although it is there.

When we look at an object which is vibrating or spinning at a constant speed, such as a tuning fork, a wheel or a dragonfly's wings, the flashes of a stroboscope can be synchronized to the speed of the moving object. At this speed the object will appear to be absolutely motionless. Near this speed it will appear to be moving very slowly. This is because the very short regular flashes "catch" the object in the same, or nearly the same, position each time around. Our eyes only perceive what is illuminated — cutting out every movement in between. The result is the isolation of the instant. What seemed like an impossibly rapid event can be made to stand still or run as slowly or as fast as necessary.

As a boy, Edgerton learned about photography from an uncle and he bought his first camera at the age of 15. His first roll of indoor pictures was underexposed, leading him to consider the need for a carefully controlled source of light — a flash. Later, as an undergraduate student at the University of Nebraska, he had a summer job at the Nebraska Power and Light Company where the vibrating and rotating parts may have initiated his interest in capturing rapid events on film.

In 1930, while he was a graduate student at the Massachusetts Insitute of Technology (MIT) studying the movement of generator rotors, he was suddenly aware that a moving rotor he was examining appeared to be stationary. This was because of the stroboscopic effect of a mercury arc rectifier which happened to be producing rapid bolts of light nearby. Edgerton decided to reproduce this effect and produced his first high-speed stroboscope in 1931.

Edgerton's famous picture of the crown-shaped splash of a drop of milk was taken in 1938 while he was trying to popularize the use of his stroboscope. By 1940, his striking photographs had made

Edgerton's work famous and, following the film, *Quicker than a Wink,* on which he collaborated, it seemed a career as MGM's special effects king beckoned. However, Edgerton recounts that his relatively unreliable cameras simply couldn't run to Hollywood schedules: "They got tired of me... once in a while the camera would quit and they'd all get disgusted because time was being lost."

The military, however, were not slow to see the possibilities of strobe technology to aerial reconnaissance during World War II. Edgerton's equipment was used to illuminate and photograph the French coast through cloud and at night in order to study German troop movements just before the Allied invasion of Normandy known as D-Day. This successful operation was the first stage in the eventual liberation of Europe.

In 1947, Edgerton and two former students, Kenneth Germeshausen and Herbert Grier, capitalized on this military link-up by setting up E.G. & G., now a multi-million-dollar operation. The company produces the electronic systems that detonate, trigger and measure nuclear tests and have operated an exclusive franchise for this work with the Atomic Energy Commission.

By 1953 Edgerton had teamed up with Jacques Cousteau to apply stroboscopic photography to underwater exploration. He set about designing an electronic flash tube and camera which could survive the extremely high pressures (eight-and-a-half tonnes per square inch) at the bottom of the ocean.

In 1958, ever at the forefront of technology, Edgerton developed a system for photographing the shockwaves around aircraft in flight, using a strobe and a Scotchlite screen which reflects light back to the camera. The shockwaves deflect the light, creating a characteristic pattern of light and shade.

Edgerton contributed much to developments in the field of sonar — the use of reflected pulses of sound to analyse the sea floor and locate objects which may be buried under it — notably the "pinger" and "boomer" which apply this effect in different ways. Combined with his underwater experience and sense of adventure, this led him to help locate and photograph a number of important shipwrecks including the American Civil War ship *Monitor* — an early iron-clad gunboat which sank in a gale off the North Carolina coast in 1862. From 1976, he was also involved in the, so far fruitless, search for the legendary Loch Ness monster. Despite several visits, the resident of that deep and murky Scottish trench did not exhibit the same interest in Edgerton's bright lights that the sharks and turtles had shown when the equipment was tested beforehand at the New England Aquarium. His dives in search of treasure at the bottom of the high-altitude lake Titicaca in the Bolivian Andes also proved fruitless though fascinating.

In 1969, defying cold war suspicion, Edgerton joined a team of Soviet oceanographers aboard the prestigious *Akademik Kurchatov* survey ship. Together they took the first pictures of the rift valley in the mid-Atlantic, where two continental plates are in collision.

Edgerton's equipment also assisted in locating the *Titanic* in 1986 as well as lost cities such as the Mediterranean coastal city of Caesarea, destroyed by earthquakes and tidal waves in the thirteenth century and now buried off the coast of Israel.

Harold Edgerton, like earlier pioneers of photography, developed a technology which extended our awareness of the world. Like the radio telescope or the electron microscope, his inventions allowed our senses to make a great leap forward. He was not consciously an artist, but his arresting photographs inspire wonder and fascination in every fresh observer. The bullets shooting through apples, playing cards and light bulbs, as well as the multi-exposure shots of the golfer's swing or the insect's wings; all give us new insights into the commonplace. As such they qualify as works of art. It is hardly surprising that when Britain's National Museum of Photography, Film and Television gave Edgerton its second international award in 1989, it was for "a lifetime's contribution to the art and science of photography".

Born Harold Eugene Edgerton. **Parents** Frank Eugene, lawyer, and Mary Nettie (Coe) Edgerton. **Marriage** Esther May Garrett, teacher, 1928. **Children** Mary, Robert and William (died 1957). **Education** University of Nebraska, Lincoln, BS, 1925; Massachusetts Institute of Technology, Cambridge, MA, 1927, DSc, 1931. **Military service** Consultant, United States Army, in Italy, France, England, 1942–43. **Career** Electrical engineer: Nebraska Power and Light Company, 1921–25 (university vacations), General Electric Company, Schenectady, New York, 1925–26; instructor, Massachusetts Institute of Technology, Cambridge, 1928–32, assistant professor, 1932–38, associate professor, 1938–48, professor of electrical measurement, 1948–66, Institute Professor Emeritus, 1966 onwards. **Related activities** Founding partner, E.G. & G. Incorporated, 1933, vice-president, 1947–66, chairman, board of directors, 1954–66, honorary chairman until 1972; collaborated on MGM film *Quicker than a Wink,* 1940; member: Woods Hole Oceanographic Institution, Boston Museum of Science. **Offices and memberships** Fellow: Institute of Electrical and Electronic Engineers, Photographic Society of America, Society of Motion Picture and Television Engineers, Royal Photographic Society of Great Britain; Academy of Applied Science; Academy of Underwater Arts and Sciences; American Academy of Arts and Sciences; American Philosophical Society; Marine Technology Society; National Academy of Sciences, 1964; National Academy of Engineering, 1966; Society of Photographic Engineers; Explorers Club; New England Aquarium; Photographers Association of New England; Sigma Xi; Sigma Tau. **Awards and honours** (include) Royal Photographic Society of London Medal, 1936; Potts Medal, Franklin Institute, 1941; Medal of Freedom, United States government, 1946; Doctor of Engineering, University of Nebraska, 1948; Master of Photography, Photographers Association of America, 1949; Joseph A. Sprague Memorial Award, National Press Photographic Association, 1949; Franklin L. Burr Prize, National Geographic Society, 1953; Progress Medal Award, Photographic Society of America, 1955; Progress Award, Society of Motion Picture and Television Engineers, 1959; George W. Harris Achievement Award, Photographers Association of America, 1959; Boston Sea Rovers Award, 1961; Gordon Y. Billard Award, Massachusetts Institute of Technology, 1962; E.I. DuPont Gold Medal, Society of Motion Picture and Television Engineers, 1962; Industrial Photographers Association National Award, 1963; Silver Progress Medal, Royal Photographic Society of Great Britain, 1964; Morris E. Leeds Award, Institute of Electrical and Electronic Engineers, 1965; Richardson Medal, Optical Society of America, 1968; John Oliver LaGorce Gold Medal, National Geographic Society, 1968; LLD: Doane College, 1969, University of South Carolina, 1969; Alan Gordon Memorial Award, Society of Photo-Optical Instrumentation Engineers, 1969; Albert A. Michelson Medal, Franklin Institute, 1969; NOGI Award, Underwater Society of America, 1973; Holley Medal, American Society of Mechanical Engineers, 1973; National Medal of Science from President of the United States, 1973; Lockheed Award, Marine Technology Society, 1978; DSc, Washington University, 1979; Culture Award, Deutsche Gesellschaft für Photographie, West Germany, 1981; International Award, (British) National Museum of Photography, Film and Television, 1989; honorary member: Boston Camera Club, Boston Sea Rovers, Fairhaven Whalers Club; eminent member, Eta Kappa Nu; numerous other awards for photography and engineering. **Inventions** Stroboscopic high-speed motion and still photography apparatus; designer: underwater camera, high-resolution sonar equipment. **Individual exhibitions** *Seeing the Unseen,* Ikon Gallery, Birmingham, 1976; Margaret Compton Gallery, Massachussetts Institute of Technology, Cambridge, 1977; Vision Gallery, Boston, 1977; Stephen Wirtz Gallery, San Francisco, 1977; G. Ray Hawkins Gallery, Los Angeles, 1977; Galerie Agathe Gaillard, Paris, 1978; Museum of Science, Boston, 1980; Gallery of Photographs, New Haven, Connecticut, 1981; Haverford College, Pennsylvania, 1981; Daniel Wolf Inc, New York, 1981; University of Nebraska, Lincoln, 1982; *The Split Second,* Silver Image Gallery, Columbus, Ohio, 1986. **Group exhibitions** (include) *Hundert Jahre Photographie 1839–1939,* Museum Folkwang, Essen, 1959; *The Sense of Abstraction,* Museum of Modern Art, New York, 1960; *The Painter and the Photograph: From Delacroix to Warhol,* University of New Mexico, Albuquerque, 1964; *Photos from the Sam Wagstaff Collection,* Corcoran Gallery,

Washington, DC, 1978; *Fleeting Gestures: Dance Photographs,* International Center of Photography, New York, 1979; *Life: The First Decade 1936–45,* Grey Art Gallery, New York University, 1979; *Floods of Light,* The Photographers' Gallery, London, 1982; *Invention and Allegory,* Daniel Wolf Inc, New York, 1983; *Sammlung Gruber,* Museum Ludwig, Cologne, 1984. **Collections** Massachusetts Institute of Technology, Cambridge; International Museum of Photography, George Eastman House, Rochester, New York; Plainsman Museum, Aurora, Nebraska; Gernsheim Collection, University of Texas at Austin; Science Museum, London; Bibliothèque Nationale, Paris; Centre Georges Pompidou, Paris; Moderna Museet, Stockholm; Museum Ludwig, Cologne. **Publications** (With J.R. Killian) *Flash: Seeing the Unseen,* 1939; (contributor) Arthur A. Allen, *Stalking Birds with Color Camera,* 1951; *Electronic Flash: Strobe,* 1970; (with J.R. Killian) *Moments of Vision: The Stroboscopic Revolution in Photography,* 1979; contributor to technical and photographic journals; *Sonar Images,* 1986. **Cause of death** Heart attack, at age 86. **Further reading** Lucia Moholy, *A Hundred Years of Photography 1839–1939,* 1939; Raymond Lecuyer, *Histoire de la Photographie,* 1945; Helmut and Alison Gernsheim, *Hundert Jahre Photographie 1839–1930 aus der Sammlung Gernsheim* (exhibition catalogue), 1959; John Wolbarst (editor), *Polaroid Portfolio No.1,* 1959; Van Deren Coke, *The Painter and the Photograph: From Delacroix to Warhol,* 1964; John Szarkowski, *Looking at Photographs: 100 Pictures from the Collection of the Museum of Modern Art,* 1973; Cecil Beaton and Gail Buckland, *The Magic Image,* 1975; Peter Tausk, *Geschichte der Fotografie im 20. Jahrhundert,* 1977, also published as *Photography in the 20th Century,* 1980; Ake Sidwall, Sune Jonsson, Ulf Hard af Segerstad, *Tusen och en Bild* (exhibition catalogue), 1978; Arne Lewis (designer) *A Book of Photographs from the Collection of Sam Wagstaff,* 1978; Erika Billeter, *Amerika Fotografie 1920–1940,* 1979; Robert Littman, Ralph Graves, Doris C. O'Neill, *Life: The First Decade 1936–1945,* 1979; Lee D. Witkin, Barbara London, *The Photograph Collector's Guide,* 1979; Roland Barthes, *La Chambre claire,* 1980; Rupert Martin, *Floods of Light: Flash Photography 1951–1981* (exhibition catalogue), 1982; Siegfried Gohr (foreword), *Sammlung Gruber; Photographie des 20. Jahrhunderts,* 1984; Harry N. Abrahams, *Stopping Time* (collection of Edgerton's photographs), 1987; *Contemporary Photographers,* 1988.

INDIA EDWARDS

American Political Activist and Journalist

***Born* Chicago, Illinois, 1895**

***Died* Sebastopol, California, 14 January 1990**

"Sometimes I feel like a ghoul", commented India Edwards when explaining how she got women into federal jobs. "I'd read the obits, and as soon as a man had died, I'd rush over over to the White House and suggest a woman to replace him." Such was the character of this formidable woman who dedicated her political life to getting women into positions of power in a male-dominated American political scene.

Coming into adulthood at a time when women were very much in the background of public life, Edwards managed to get a job on the staff of the *Chicago Tribune,* eventually working as society editor and women's editor. She spent 22 years in that position, sharpening her confidence and burnishing her ideal of seeing women in politics. In 1942, at the time of her third marriage which took her away from the *Chicago Tribune* and into Washington, DC, she began to make the acquaintance of some of the most powerful men in the Democratic Party.

Her most important friendship was with President Harry S. Truman. During his re-election campaign tour in 1948, where pollsters were predicting Truman's loss to Republican hopeful Thomas Dewey, Truman remarked, "India, sometimes I think there are only two people who believe I will win. You and me." She replied, "That's enough." (The rest is history as Truman won a surprise victory.) Most importantly, because of India Edwards's loyalty and support, Truman appointed more women to top jobs than any preceding president. Among those appointed under Edwards's influence were the first woman US ambassador, Eugenia Anderson (as ambassador to Denmark), Perle Mesta (as minister to Luxembourg), Ruth Bryan Rhode (as alternate delegate to the United Nations) and Georgia Neese Clark (as treasurer of the United States).

In 1950 Edwards was unanimously elected to the Democratic Party's National Committee and became vice-chairwoman, in which position she continued to campaign for other presidential hopefuls. She remained active in politics for the next 30 years, most recently backing the campaign of Democratic nominee for president, Gary Hart.

Politics was not her only cause. She also devoted herself to other organizations such as the Health and Welfare Council, Girls Clubs of America and the Women's Medical College (now Medical College of Pennsylvania).

Because the equality of women was the biggest single issue of her life, and progress so hard won, she was remarkably surprised by the nomination of Geraldine Ferraro as vice-presidential candidate in 1984. It was an event she did not expect to see in her own lifetime.

India Edwards's life and work are explained in detail in her 1977 memoirs, *Pulling No Punches,* a title suggested by President Truman. However, her personality and unbounded energy were best described by her husband Herbert, "She is a rushing mountain torrent. She's so intense that when she has to rest, she wears herself out with the intensity of resting."

Born India. **Marriages** 1) Mr Moffett, 1924; 2) Name unknown; 3) Herbert T. Edwards, state department official, 1942 (died 1970s). **Children** India (died 1979) and John Holbrook (died 1944), from first marriage. **Education** Schools in St Louis. **Career** Reporter *Chicago Tribune,* society editor, women's editor until 1942; Democratic Party campaigner, 1944 onwards; scriptwriter, Democratic party headquarters, speechwriter, 1944; executive secretary of the women's division, Democratic National Committee, 1945–1947, associate director, 1947–48, executive director, 1948–50, vice-chairwoman, 1950; delegate for presidential candidate, Gary Hart, 1984. **Related activities** Active on behalf of Washington, DC, Health and Welfare Council, Girls Clubs of America, Women's Medical College (now Medical College of Pennsylvania). **Offices and memberships** Member, Washington Press Club. **Publication** *Pulling No Punches* (memoirs), 1977. **Cause of death** Undisclosed, at age 94.

LADY ELWYN-JONES

British Writer and Artist

***Born* Manchester, England, 1904**

***Died* Brighton, East Sussex, 26 January 1990**

Polly Elwyn-Jones, who was also known by her own name of Pearl Binder, has been described as a Bohemian in the heart of the British establishment.

The daughter of a Jewish tailor, she left home at the age of 21 with a total of three pounds in her pocket (then enough to survive for a couple of weeks) and settled in London's East End where she became entranced by the mixture of indigenous people and, both as artist and writer, began to chronicle their lives, in particular those of the street traders (the costermongers) and the history of their own "royalty" — the Pearly Kings and Queens.

"Lady Polly", as she came to be known affectionately — especially in the United States — quickly established herself and became a hostess noted for her beer and liver-sausage parties at which there was always plenty of everything for the guests except sufficient space! Over the next ten years she worked in both London and Paris as an illustrator on various journals, including *Vogue,* and later took up radio broadcasting and some television work. She rapidly became well known.

In the mid-1930s she met a Welshman, Frederick Elwyn Jones who was five years her junior. He came from a working-class background but had just left the prestigious university of Cambridge and was reading for the Bar. "He had just left Cambridge", his future wife recalled, "and, though he was the son of a tin-plate worker, he didn't look at all like a working-class boy to me. I was full of thoughts about Russian peasants and life in the East End." But, perhaps because of their common interest in socialist and anti-Fascist causes, their relationship flourished. They married in 1937.

Her husband rose to prominence early in his career. He was a member of the British team at the Nuremberg trials in 1945 and, later that year, became a MP for an East End constituency in the Labour landslide which ousted the British wartime leader, Winston Churchill. Their marriage was, however, strengthened by their independence of each other and Elwyn-Jones encouraged his wife to pursue her own career. There were frequent separations deriving from his legal and political journeys overseas but Lady Elwyn-Jones had long had her own agenda. She travelled, especially in Russia and China, looking at art forms as they emerged in the everyday life of ordinary people. She was not just a visitor of galleries but also concerned to discover what people painted for their own walls, how they fashioned and decorated their tools, and how their social position and striving contributed to their art. In this vein were her books on the history of costume and manners such as *The Peacock's Tale* and *Muffs and Morals* and also, in later years, her books on trade union banners and the Pearlies, both of which located a "native" art form in its specific history and social context.

Her husband's knighthood came in 1964 when he became Attorney General and a Privy Councillor. His elevation to the House of Lords came with his life peerage in 1974 when he became Lord High Chancellor of Great Britain and took the title Baron Elwyn-Jones.

One of her first parties as the Lord Chancellor's Lady was for the Pearly Kings and Queens in the State Apartments at Westminster — a party also attended by Queen Elizabeth, the Queen Mother, whose strong relationship with, and respect for, East Londoners dated from the days of the bombing during World War II. A rousing good time was had by all.

Lady Elwyn-Jones loved the atmosphere of Westminster. Her painterly eye saw the beauty of the Thames river at night when it was empty of daytime bustle. "It was like Venice," she later recalled, "with all the buildings reflected. I would wander around at two in the morning, drawing". She also left her own mark there. In the House of Lords are now 22 stained glass windows by her commemorating former Lord Chancellors.

Lady Elwyn-Jones did not, however, eschew family life. Along with her many interests and activities, she also found time for her beloved children and, later, grandchildren. One of the greatest joys of *not* being the Lord Chancellor's Lady, which came about in 1979, lay in having more time for the latter.

Lady Elwyn-Jones was able to find joy in almost everything she undertook. And one of the ways in which she expressed this was her clothes. She wore enormous and elaborate hats and was quite likely to be seen in her beloved East End in a costume more suited to a Buckingham Palace Garden Party. But possibly her greatest joy lay in her marriage. It lasted 52 years until Lord Elwyn-Jones's death in December 1989. She survived him by only a few weeks.

Born Pearl Binder. **Father** A tailor. **Marriage** Frederick Elwyn Jones, barrister, member of parliament and one-time Labour Lord Chancellor, 1937. **Children** Josephine, Daniel and

Elizabeth. **Education** Attended evening classes, Manchester School of Art; Academie Colarossi, Paris; Central School of Art and Design, London. **Career** Illustrator, *Le Rire,* Paris, 1926; first publication as illustrator, *Bed and Breakfast* by Coralie Hobson, 1926; illustrator for *Vogue, The Sketch, Harper's Bazaar,* London, 1927; first publication as author, *Odd Jobs,* 1935; illustrator for British Broadcasting Corporation, from 1939; radio broadcaster and television presenter. **Related activities** Sculptor, lithographer: exhibited in London, Moscow, Sydney, Paris, Hong Kong and other major cities; artist in stained glass, responsible for 22 memorial windows, House of Lords. **Offices and memberships** Fellow, Royal Anthropological Institute. **Collections** British Museum; Victoria and Albert Museum. **Publications** (under name Pearl Binder, all self-illustrated) *Odd Jobs,* 1935; *Misha and Masha,* 1936; *Misha Learns English,* 1942; *Russian Families,* 1942; *Muffs and Morals,* 1953; *The Peacock's Tail,* 1958; *Look at Clothes,* 1959; *The English Inside Out: An Up-to-Date Report on Morals and Manners in England,* 1961; *Pigeons and People,* 1967; *Ladies Only,* 1972; *Magic Symbols of the World,* 1972; *Treacle Terrace: A Story of Children and Their Parents With Pictures and a Moral,* 1974; *The Pearlies: A Social Record,* 1975; *Treasure Islands: The Trials of the Ocean Islanders,* 1977; **Publications as illustrator** Coralie Hobson, *Bed and Breakfast,* 1926; Lancelot de Giberne Sieveking, *All Children Must Be Paid For,* 1927; Jane Austen, *Persuasion,* 1928; John Skelton, *The Tunning of Elynour Rumming,* 1928; Jack H. Driberg, *People of the Small Arrow,* 1930; Thomas Burke, *The Real East End,* 1932; Gerard Labrunie de Nerval, *Aurelia,* translated by Richard Aldington, 1932; Philip Godfrey, *Back-stage: A Survey of the Contemporary English Theatre From Behind the Scenes,* 1933; Louis Golding, *The Dance Goes On,* 1937; Bertha Malnick (compiler), *Life in Russia,* 1938; Alan Lomax, *Harriet and Her Harmonium: An American Adventure With Thirteen Folk Songs From the Lomax Collection,* 1955; Kermit Goell, *Pocahontas,* 1963; Josephine Marquand, *Chi Ming and the Tiger Kitten,* 1965; Josephine Marquand, *Chi Ming and the Lion Dance,* 1969; Josephine Marquand, *Chi Ming and the Jade Earring,* 1970; Josephine Marquand, *Chi Ming and the Writing Lesson,* 1970; Josephine Gladstone, *Zadig,* 1976. **Other works** *When the Summer Comes Again* (musical). **Cause of death** Undisclosed, at age 85.

LORD GARDINER

British Lawyer

Born **England, 30 May 1900**

Died **London, England, 7 January 1990**

The "rebel advocate" was Muriel Box's title of the biography she wrote of her husband, Lord Gardiner. Yet few rebels achieve such high office — that of the Lord High Chancellor of Great Britain and eighth in order of precedence after the Queen.

The Lord Chancellor is a member of the government, a minister of the Crown; and he is responsible for the administration of British Justice. But Lord Gardiner's political experience was limited to fighting one seat as a Labour candidate. And his experience as a judge was non-existent. Yet even the Conservative prime minister seems to have shared in the general assumption that only Gardiner could be the Labour Lord Chancellor. For Lord Gardiner was not a politician in spirit — he was a reformer who set out to humanize the law and who made real progress in the service of many causes.

Gerald Gardiner was born the son of a successful businessman who married into the Prussian nobility. In appearance and manner he was a typical product of the English upper classes and he received a very English education at Harrow and Magdalen College, Oxford. But even as an undergraduate he showed distinct signs of having interests which for a man of his background were decidedly unconventional. He was greatly attracted to the stage and remained so all his life. While at Oxford he was remarkable for the extreme elegance of his appearance which was sufficiently marked to provoke the formation of a "Society for Ruffling Gerald Gardiner's Hair". He is also unique among Lord Chancellors for having been sent down from Oxford. His "sin" was not of the frivolous, hell-raising sort, beloved of the young aristocrat. Far from it. As editor of the student publication *Isis* he had been guilty of advocating women's rights.

After a short period in the Army at the end of World War I he studied for the Bar to which he was called in 1925 — to become, thereafter, a practising barrister. He also — another unusual move for a man of his class — joined the Peace Pledge Union within months of his demobilization.

By the time World War II broke out in 1939 he had built up a flourishing junior practice. He had found time to develop an interest in many worthy causes — the abolition of capital punishment, the rehabilitation of offenders, the reform of the law relating to marriage and sexual offences. And he had become a member of the Labour Party.

In World War I he had been a commissioned officer in the Coldstream Guards. In World War II his deep feelings against the taking of human life led him to become a member of a team of conscientious objectors in the Friends Ambulance Unit. Writes John Saunders, who headed the team, "Gerald worked as hard as anyone... He was evidently a good deal older than the rest of us. Always impeccably turned out, he once asked me if his trousers had a sufficiently sharp crease." But Saunders also attributes good relations with the military personnel at the camp to "the friendly, modest and quite evidently unthreatening person of Gerald Gardiner."

Hostilities over, Gardiner returned to his legal practice, took Silk (became a King's Counsel) and achieved a commanding position at the Bar. This is hardly surprising, given the causes which he chose to champion. In the Electrical Trades Union trial he appeared for union leader Frank Chapple, whose accusation against the Communist officials for rigging the ballot was upheld. But by far the most celebrated of his appearances was as defence counsel in the first case to be brought under the 1959 Obscene Publications Act against Penguin Books for their publication of D.H. Lawrence's *Lady Chatterley's Lover*. It was one of Gardiner's greatest triumphs to secure Penguin's acquittal.

In 1951 Gardiner contested the parliamentary seat of West Croydon in outer London. He achieved a creditable near miss — which excursion was the sum total of his "experience" as a politician.

Having served on the General Council of the Bar for some years, Gardiner was appointed its chairman for 1958 and 1959. He also sat on the Lord Chancellor's Law Reform Committee. And his passion for law reform found expression in his book, *Capital Punishment as a Deterrent.*

In December 1963, on the nomination of Harold Wilson, Gardiner was created a life peer. When, following his narrow victory at the polls, Wilson became prime minister, it was inevitable that he should choose Lord Gardiner for Lord Chancellor: though Gardiner was the first man in modern history to fill the position without having been either an MP or a judge.

He could have been a judge. He was once offered a judgeship, but briskly refused it. The reason he gave — "Wouldn't feel I had done a real day's work" — was perhaps not the whole truth. Commentators suggest that he declined appointment to the High Court because — until the abolition of capital punishment in 1965 — that would have required him to pronounce the death sentence, against the very concept of which his conscience revolted.

As Lord Chancellor he could influence changes in the law and the legal system. He did so. After 35 years of personal involvement in the campaign against capital punishment he spoke, as Lord Chancellor, in the House of Lords debate which led to its abolition. His appearance was always impressive and his bearing made him a formidable figure. He told the House,

When my grandfather was 21, a boy of nine who had set fire to a house was hanged at Chelmsford. In a previous year a little way back, a boy of seven and his sister of eleven were hanged at Lyne... In 1930 the Select Committee of the House of Commons reported: "Our prolonged examination of the situation in foreign countries has increasingly confirmed us in the assurance that capital punishment may now be abolished in this country without endangering life or property, or impairing the security of society..."

The House agreed by 220 votes to 174 to end hanging.

Gardiner continued to devote his attention to penal reform and to the rehabilitation of offenders. Writes Louis Blom-Cooper, chairman of the Howard League for Penal Reform, "Quite apart from his notable contribution in the movement which led to the abolition of the death penalty, he was a proponent of studied progress towards the humanising of our prisons and the rehabilitation of prisoners." He broke with precedent in appointing a businessman (Lord Beeching) as chairman of the Royal Commission charged with overhauling the whole machinery of the criminal courts. He warmly welcomed the commission's far-reaching recommendations which, after his retirement, were embodied in the 1971 Courts Act.

Gardiner took the issue of so-called sexual offences to heart. During his term as Lord Chancellor the laws on homosexuality were humanized. He also reformed the law on abortion and he paid great attention to judicial appointments; he was pleased to be able to add to the number of women holding office and he appointed the first woman High Court Judge.

He took a special interest in the working of the law. He instituted the first comprehensive and compulsory training scheme for Justices of the Peace. Though they continued to serve unpaid they would at least be no longer unlearned. It is to Gardiner that Britain owes the present system of selection of magistrates by advisory committees which sift out the unsuitable and interview the promising — as well as the rule by which all new justices must undertake training and experienced justices undergo refresher courses.

The law commissions, set up under his aegis, were created to organize the process of law reform and were derived from the co-operative work of Labour Party lawyers under his direction. And the ombudsman, or parliamentary commissioner for administration — the citizen's guard against governmental maladministration — proved a boon in itself as well as a forerunner of similar protection in the Health Service and in local government.

In addition to all this activity, Lord Gardiner also had to study government papers and political dispatches. He took little part in general politics; but he was responsible for the administration of justice throughout the country, had to select judges, to give an eye to the appointment of magistrates and to the work of over a thousand administrative tribunals.

But these were only a fraction of his duties. The Lord Chancellor is automatically a member of the British cabinet and must be on hand to advise his colleagues on policy decisions. He had, for instance, to justify the increased costs of Legal Aid — the assistance granted to people who cannot afford to defend themselves in court. As a member of the cabinet Lord Gardiner had the potential for political power. But he made little impact upon the political scene and remained to the end almost unknown to the general public. Perhaps his natural shyness, combined with his distaste for the trivia of party warfare, brought this about. He was always approachable and receptive; but he gave little impression of warmth.

The reforms which he desired were not merely changes, however important, in the law and the legal system. Far more deeply, he wanted changes in society — swifter movement towards equality, the elimination of poverty, a better understanding of crime and the treatment of offenders, a freer, less inhibited society. He was impatient of the delays imposed by the democratic machine to which he strongly adhered.

He always said he would retire at the age of 70. A few days after his seventieth birthday Labour went into opposition. So it was forced upon him. But it is pretty certain that he was glad to retire when he did. He sat, for a time, on the Opposition Front Bench in the Lords. In 1971 he retired to the back benches, saying he hoped to introduce some Bills of his own and "even have some fun".

As a backbencher he continued to make his voice heard in the service of a range of causes. A number of organizations sought — and were given — the benefit of his advice. He was the chairman of the Justice committee whose recommendations were to lead to the Rehabilitation of Offenders Act in 1974 which allowed minor offenders to live their lives unburdened by their criminal record. He was also president of the Howard League for Penal Reform.

In 1972 he served on a government-appointed committee inquiring into the questioning of suspected terrorists. His — minority — opinion was that the methods of interrogation being used by the security forces were unacceptable. This did not save him from a narrow encounter with an IRA bomb. In 1975 his conclusion, as the chair of another government committee, that detention without trial for terrorists was justified, came as a surprise to some of his supporters.

In his retirement — at long last — he decided to embark on a course of further study. He was appointed chancellor of the Open University in 1973. He immediately registered as a student in the social sciences course. He found economics "extremely tough" but writing essays for tutors young enough to be his children was easier than writing judgments. He graduated in 1977 and took great pleasure in lining up in the Strand with a window cleaner, a traffic warden and a cook to receive his degree.

In his eighties Gardiner was a firm supporter of the various causes with which he had so far been associated. In 1980 he was the chairman of the World Disarmament Campaign; in 1984 he supported arguments in favour of an independent prosecuting authority for England. In other words, he was a reformer to the last. Said his second wife, Muriel Box, who wrote *The Rebel Advocate* and whom he married after passing his seventieth birthday, "He is kind, gentle, very courteous and completely dedicated to his work." History, says one commentator, could provide him with no better epitaph.

Born Gerald Austin Gardiner. **Parents** Sir Robert, shipping director, and Lady Gardiner, German baroness. **Marriages** 1) Lesly Trounson, 1925 (died 1966); 2) Muriel Box, film producer, 1970. **Children** One daughter, Carol, by first marriage. **Education** Harrow School, London; Magdalen College, Oxford, MA; Open University, BA in social sciences, 1977. **Military service** Second lieutenant, Coldstream Guards, 1918; Friends Ambulance Unit, 1943–35. **Career** Called to the Bar, 1925; Kings Counsel, 1948; Master of the Bench of the Inner Temple, 1955; alderman, London County Council, 1961–63; privy councillor, 1964; Lord High Chancellor of Great Britain, 1964–70; chancellor of the Open University, 1973–78. **Related activities** Member, Committee on Supreme Court Practice and Procedure, 1947–53; member, Lord Chancellor's Law Reform Committee, 1952–63; chairman, General Council of the Bar, 1958, 1959; member, Longford Committee, 1963; co-editor, with Andrew Martin, *Law Reform Now,* 1963; chairman, Council of Justice; member, International Committee of Jurists, 1971 onwards; joint chairman, National Campaign for Abolition of Capital Punishment; chairman, World Disarmament Campaign, 1980. **Other activities** President: Oxford Union, Oxford University Dramatic Society, 1924. **Offices and memberships** (include) Member: Peace Pledge Union, Labour party; founder, Society of Labour Lawyers, president until 1980; president, Howard League for Penal Reform. **Awards and honours** Created Baron Gardiner of Kittisford 1963; Honorary LLD: Southampton, 1965, London, 1969, Manitoba, 1969, Law Society of Upper Canada, 1969, Birmingham, 1971, Melbourne, 1973; Doctor of the University of York, 1966; Companion of Honour, 1975. **Publications** (include) *Capital Punishment as a Deterrent,* 1965; (joint-editor) *Law Reform Now,* 1963. **Cause of death** Undisclosed, at age 89. **Further reading** Muriel Box, *Rebel Advocate,* 1983.

AVA GARDNER

American Actress

***Born* Grabton, North Carolina, 24 December 1922**

***Died* London, England, 25 January 1990**

Ava Gardner *was* different. She was, in her own words, one Hollywood star "who hadn't tried to slash her wrists, taken sleeping pills or kick a cop in the shins". Her appetite was for life and everything basic in it: love, drink, good food, honest and open behaviour (although paradoxically she was always presented as the enigmatic female). On occasion, her straight talking won admiration — or trouble. (On the set of *On the Beach* in Australia, in 1958, she commented, "I'm here to make a film about the end of the world, and this sure is the place for it." Local residents were not amused.)

Gardner is often recalled as (and perhaps reduced to) the siren who filled the sexual stop-gap between Rita Hayworth and Marilyn Monroe. In the 60-odd films which spanned her career, most of her roles were of the torchy, temptress type which is hardly surprising, given her stunning good looks. She was statuesque, shapely and sensual. Her acting range, however, was artificially constricted by the studios, particularly MGM, but her performances earned her respect from directors and audiences alike. Unfortunately, her talent for comedy was never explored. Gardner herself had no illusions about her stardom. "I've always done my best to be professional in movies because I'm such a rotten actress. I'm embarrassed to look at myself on the screen. I've never been able to figure out what it is, but there is something terribly lacking." Many would dispute her opinion, as the love affair between the actress and her public lasted more than 40 years — a testimony to her appeal and professionalism.

Born in Grabton, a small town in North Carolina, Ava Lavinia Gardner was the youngest of seven children. For once, the studios allowed her real name to be used as her "stage" name, inventing Lucy Ann Johnson as her "real" one! Her father was a tobacco and cotton farmer, as well as a store-owner. Even after losing land to the Depression, the Gardners were never quite as poor as the publicity machine later implied. Gardner did, however, consider herself a country girl at heart, with "ordinary values".

At 17 she was spotted by MGM, after her photographer brother-in-law sent them her picture, and was given a variety of lessons (including elocution and a tinker in the make-up room). "They told me to take the gum out of my mouth", she remembered. "I was never so embarrassed in my life." From 1940 until 1960, she had starring roles in romantic films, with her male co-stars reading like a *Who's Who* list of desirable young men of the time: Clark Gable, Humphrey Bogart, James Mason, Burt Lancaster, Gregory Peck and Richard Burton. The publicity machine invented stories linking her with every one of them. Despite the fact that she heartily disliked the gossip, finding it foolish, and directly opposed to her own unpretentious and honest attitudes, she was unable to avoid the overwhelming press circus, later blaming it for ruining much of her life.

Gardner's film début came in 1942 with Robert Siodmak's *We Were Dancing*. This was followed by 20 unimportant potboilers, as MGM did not seem to know what to do with her. Her first real break was in *The Killers* in 1946, Ernest Hemingway's story of an ex-fighter found murdered. In this she played what was to become her *femme fatale* role, opposite a young Burt Lancaster. The Hemingway film was a great success; Gardner later appeared in two other films by the writer, *The Snows of Kilimanjaro,* with Gregory Peck and Susan Hayward, and *The Sun Also Rises*. Hemingway was profoundly impressed with her, referring to her as "Daughter".

Throughout her career, she portrayed strong, sultry women who had a spirited attitude to the world and its morals. She was a torch singer in *The Hucksters,* an outspoken, wise-cracking playgirl in *Mogambo* (trapped in the jungle with Clark Gable, with whom she became fast friends), and a tormented soul in *Bhowani Junction,* with Stewart Granger. *Mogambo* earned her an Oscar nomination in 1953. This was a lusty remake of *Red Dust,* with Gable repeating his role from the 1932 film, and Gardner replacing Jean Harlow. Her performance was considered one of her best.

The public and press were given no reason (and sought none) for assuming Gardner was anything more than her publicity-machine portrayal. Her complexity of character (which included great warmth and generosity) was ignored. "I was a victim of image", she later said. "Because...I played all those sexy broads, people made the mistake of thinking I was like that off the screen. They couldn't have been more wrong. Although no-one believes it, I am pathologically shy."

At the age of 19, Gardner married Mickey Rooney, a studio stablemate (who is said to have arranged for a publicity department minion to accompany them on their honeymoon). Sixteen months later, they were divorced. In 1945 she married bandleader Artie Shaw. Blaming his attempts to make her more of an intellectual than she wished to be, she divorced him a year later. Two failed marriages fuelled her reputation as a difficult tempest of a woman. She, for her part, often indicated that she would be delighted to give up acting "for one good man I could love and marry and cook and make a home for, who would stick around for the rest of my life." Her friendship, stormy as it was, with billionaire Howard Hughes, was fanned by the press into a headline-grabbing affair, although the reality is likely to have been very different.

In 1950 Gardner met Frank Sinatra, and they were married one year later, becoming one of the most photographed couples in Hollywood. Six years later, they divorced. Her career was still blossoming, while his had hit a low point. When the singer co-wrote the classic song, "I'm A Fool To Want You", it was reportedly a heart-broken tribute to his ex-wife.

Gardner's films in these 1950s years were now box-office successes, including *Show Boat* (her final-frame blown kiss, as she stands on the deck of the departing *Cotton Blossom* is one of the more affecting scenes), *Pandora and the Flying Dutchman, Mogambo,* and the semi-autobiographical *Barefoot Contessa,* in which she wildly flamencoed her way through the Hollywood jet-set. She was billed as "The Most Beautiful Animal in the World", and the world believed it. In 1958, Gardner left the MGM studios and headed for Europe and a career as an independent actress. There is no doubt that her acting took on a greater depth and sensitivity as a result. Although she had recently been a smash in *Bhowani Junction* with Stewart Granger, and in *The Sun Also Rises* (where the chemistry with Tyrone Power and Errol Flynn was palpable), Gardner continued to be more interested in living her life than she was her legend. She divided her time between Madrid and London.

Throughout the 1960s, Gardner continued to remain visible, with a new and flattering tint of world-weariness, in films such as *55 Days at Peking* in 1963, with Charlton Heston and David Niven, and *Seven Days in May,* a military-scheme picture by John Frankenheimer, with Burt Lancaster and Frederic March, in 1964. That same year she turned in one of her finest performances in Tennessee Williams's (and John Huston's) *The Night of the Iguana,* with Richard Burton and Deborah Kerr. Her dignified Sarah in Huston's epic *The Bible,* in 1966, helped lift the heavy-handedness of the film. Huston cast her again, in his *The Life and Times of Judge Roy Bean* in 1972, in which she portrayed actress Lillie Langtry. Huston praised her for her directness and no-nonsense approach to her work. It was a consistent compliment, as Gardner was the true professional.

Gardner developed a warm friendship with the British poet, Robert Graves, and they corresponded for several years, a fact known by few of her fans. When Graves died, she donated her letters to St John's College, Oxford, where an archive of his material is being established. She described her letters as "illiterate scribbles", and explained that she was "often drunk in those days, which made 'em worse".

After making the disaster film *Earthquake,* in 1974, Gardner appeared in a number of unremarkable films, although her performance in the disastrous American–Russian collaboration,

The Blue Bird, in 1976, outshone everyone else's including Elizabeth Taylor's. (The two were not great friends on the set, it was rumoured.) Gardner's name continued to be a draw. Now in her early fifties, she continued to be a bewitching presence on the big screen. But when she turned to television, she felt uncomfortable, and her performances were not complimented. Roles in a mini-series, *A.D.,* and in the mediocre *Dallas* spin-off, *Knots Landing,* were strictly, she told a critic, "For the loot, honey, for the loot. I needed the money."

Gardner settled in London, a city she loved, remarking that it was perfect for her, as the English "mind their own goddamn business". She took advantage of her position to ignore the press. Never a recluse, more a European exile (self-imposed exile, although she had illnesses to battle against), Gardner lived in her flat with her long-term companion/housekeeper and Welsh corgi. Until the end, Frank Sinatra, with whom she remained in warm contact, paid her medical bills. At 67 she died of pneumonia.

Director Joseph Mankiewicz (*Barefoot Contessa*) said of her, "I don't think Ava ever put body and soul into her performances. She put body and soul into living a life." Gardner always showed the woman behind the face, which made her beauty more real; as film critic Pauline Kael put it, she looked "slightly used, and therefore more beautiful". Ava Gardner also proved that there is no such thing as "too much" woman — only that there is often "too little" world.

Born Ava Lavinia Gardner. **Parents** Jonas B. tenant farmer and store-owner, and Mary Elizabeth Gardner. **Marriages** 1) Mickey Rooney, film actor, 1942 (divorced 1943); 2) Artie Shaw, bandleader, 1945 (divorced 1946); 3) Frank Sinatra, singer and actor, 1951 (divorced 1957). **Education** High school, Smithfield, North Carolina; Atlantic Christian College, Wilson, North Carolina. **Career** Film actress, 1941 onwards; film début, *We Were Dancing,* 1942. **Films** *We Were Dancing,* 1942; *Joe Smith American,* 1942; *Sunday Punch,* 1942; *This Time for Keeps,* 1942; *Calling Dr. Gillespie,* 1942; *Kid Glove Killer,* 1942; *Pilot No. 5,* 1943; *Hitler's Madman,* 1943; *Ghosts on the Loose,* 1943; *Reunion in France,* 1943; *Du Barry Was a Lady,* 1943; *Young Ideas,* 1943; *Lost Angel,* 1943; *Swing Fever,* 1944; *Music for Millions,* 1944; *Three Men in White,* 1944; *Blonde Fever,* 1944; *Maisie Goes To Reno,* 1944; *Two Girls and a Sailor,* 1944; *She Went to the Races,* 1945; *Whistle Stop,* 1946; *The Killers,* 1946; *The Hucksters,* 1947; *Singapore,* 1947; *One Touch of Venus,* 1948; *The Bribe,* 1949; *The Great Sinner,* 1949; *East Side, West Side,* 1949; *My Forbidden Past,* 1951; *Show Boat,* 1951; *Pandora and the Flying Dutchman,* 1951; *Lone Star,* 1952; *The Snows of Kilimanjaro,* 1952; *Ride Vaquero!,* 1953; *The Band Wagon,* 1953; *Mogambo,* 1953; *Knights of the Round Table,* 1954; *The Barefoot Contessa,* 1954; *Bhowani Junction,* 1956; *The Little Hut,* 1957; *The Sun Also Rises,* 1957; *The Naked Maja,* 1959; *On the Beach,* 1959; *The Angel Wore Red,* 1960; *55 Days at Peking,* 1963; *Seven Days in May,* 1964; *The Night of the Iguana,* 1964; *The Bible,* 1966; *Mayerling,* 1968; *The Devil's Widow,* 1971; *The Life and Times of Judge Roy Bean,* 1972; *Earthquake,* 1974; *Permission to Kill,* 1975; *The Blue Bird,* 1976; *The Cassandra Crossing,* 1977; *The Sentinel,* 1977; *City on Fire,* 1979; *The Kidnapping of the President,* 1980; *Priest of Love,* 1980; *Regina,* 1982. **Television** *A.D.,* 1984; *Knots Landing,* 1985; *The Long Hot Summer,* 1985; *Harem,* 1986. **Publication** *Ava: My Story,* 1990. **Cause of death** Pneumonia, at age 67. **Further reading** David Hanna, *Ava,* 1960; *International Dictionary of Films and Filmmakers,* volume three, 1986; Jane Ellen Wayne, *Ava's Men: The Private Life of Ava Gardner,* 1991.

ARTHUR GOLDBERG

American Statesman and Lawyer

Born **Chicago, Illinois, 8 August 1908**

Died **Washington, DC, 19 January 1990**

Mention Arthur Goldberg's name, and the question inevitably will arise: How could he have traded a lifetime appointment on the United States Supreme Court — the highest honour the American legal profession has to offer — for the thankless task of representing President Lyndon Johnson's administration at the United Nations during the build-up of American forces in Vietnam? On the day he was appointed as United States ambassador to the United Nations, Goldberg admitted, "In all candour, I would rather the President had not asked me to undertake this duty."

Arthur Goldberg had come a long way before reaching these dizzy heights of American public office. He was born in Chicago, one of eight children of Joseph and Rebecca Goldberg, Jewish immigrants from Russia. Like many children of immigrants of his generation, Goldberg seized the opportunities offered by the American public school and higher education system. He completed his undergraduate work at DePaul University in Chicago and then moved across town to Northwestern University Law School where he graduated in 1929 at the top of his class. For a while he worked for a law firm in which — the Depression just having started — he was asked to specialize in mortgage foreclosures. This had no appeal for Goldberg who finally opened his own law office and soon began to concentrate on labour law, an area that was attracting idealistic young lawyers who were able to take advantage of the Depression era legislation to further the trades union movement. In 1931 he married Dorothy Kurgans who, in addition to her own career as an artist, tirelessly supported her husband in his work throughout their long life together.

During the 1930s and 1940s, Goldberg represented several major unions in strike negotiations and litigation, interrupting this work from 1942 to 1944 for war service at the Office of Strategic Services. In 1948 he began a 13-year role as general counsel, first for the Congress of Industrial Organizations (CIO) and the United Steelworkers of America, and then from 1955 for the combined AFL-CIO, after the CIO joined with the American Federation of Labor, a merger he planned and negotiated. By the end of this period of his life, he was generally recognized as one of the nation's leading labour lawyers with extraordinary arbitration skills. In 1960 he was an active supporter of John F. Kennedy's presidential campaign. It was his reputation in labour law coupled with a warm relationship with Kennedy that brought him into Kennedy's cabinet as secretary of labor in 1961.

As secretary of labor Goldberg argued that the government should actively try to settle labour-management conflicts that were detrimental to national interests. In his first 24 hours on the job he negotiated an end to a strike that had shut down New York harbour. He also intervened in a dispute between the Metropolitan Opera and its orchestra members. In 1962, he made an important contribution to Kennedy's famous confrontation with the steel industry, working successfully behind the scenes to convince the industry to back down on a price rise.

Kennedy's high esteem for Arthur Goldberg led him to appoint Goldberg in August 1962 to the United States Supreme Court, to replace Felix Frankfurter, who was retiring. This was the unofficially recognized "Jewish seat" of the nine seats on the Supreme Court (a tradition which ended in 1969 with the resignation of Abe Fortas, Goldberg's successor). In the early 1960s, when conservatives in Congress hindered Kennedy's attempts to enact civil rights legislation, the United States Supreme Court was the most dynamic and "activist" force in national life. This suited

Goldberg with his zest for innovation in the law. When Goldberg was appointed, he provided, in many cases, the necessary fifth vote to transform the previous dissents of Justices Warren, Black, Douglas and Brennan into a liberal majority. The Court, headed by Chief Justice Earl Warren and thus known as the Warren Court, was now able to apply the American Constitution to protect, more than any Court before or since, the rights of the poor and underprivileged. Although Goldberg was only on the Court for three years, he played a crucial role in this mission. Goldberg wrote the majority opinion in *Escobedo v. Illinois* which established a constitutional right to counsel immediately upon arrest. Later, in *Griswold v. Connecticut,* he wrote an influential concurring opinion in which he argued that the United States Constitution, in addition to its enumerated rights, provides the basis for the creation of unwritten fundamental rights such as the right to privacy. This was a precursor to the *Roe v. Wade* decision in 1973 which established a woman's constitutional right to an abortion.

Mr Justice Goldberg's brief tenure on the United States Supreme Court will, unfortunately, be best remembered for the way he ended it. After Adlai Stevenson's death in July 1965, President Johnson wanted to appoint someone of similar stature as United States ambassador to the United Nations. He called Goldberg and said that he needed "an outstanding American to deal with the crisis at the UN" (this was the Article 19 deadlock in which several countries were refusing to pay their dues), and to guide him to an early settlement of the Vietnam war. Goldberg was reluctant to leave his position on the Supreme Court which he regarded as the fulfilment of his life's ambition. But Johnson applied considerable pressure to persuade him to resign, stating that he wanted to get the benefit of "America's greatest negotiator in reaching a peaceful solution — and soon" to the war in Vietnam. As Goldberg told one of his Supreme Court law clerks, "My President has told me I can save American soldiers' lives" by working on the Vietnam peace agreement. Goldberg had a great horror of the Vietnam war and probably also had an exaggerated respect for the potential of the United Nations as peacemaker. He also had a strong sense of public service and patriotism.

Goldberg said: "Although I would love nothing more than to live out my years on the Supreme Court, America has been too good to me for me to turn down its President." He saw, in the end, no alternative: "I have accepted, as one simply must." It seems very likely that there was an implicit understanding with President Johnson that he would be reappointed to the Supreme Court, although that opportunity never, in fact, materialized. There has even been speculation that Johnson offered Goldberg the vice-presidency in his next administration, which Johnson may have viewed with some confidence in 1965, though by 1968 he had decided to step down. Johnson later wrote in his book, *The Vantage Point,* that he had asked Goldberg to leave the Supreme Court because he had heard that Goldberg was "bored" with his work on the Court. When he read this, Goldberg was so outraged that he telephoned and demanded back the painting Dorothy Goldberg had given him during his presidency, saying "You don't deserve it."

In the final analysis, Goldberg was duped by Johnson who did not give him his promised role in the Vietnam peace negotiations. Though he had, as it turned out, little influence on Vietnam, Goldberg was effective in dealing with some key United Nations issues. As United States ambassador, he lost no time in diffusing the Article 19 crisis at the UN and in helping to resolve the Indo-Pakistan war by stressing the importance of private negotiations, a technique he had learnt from his days in settling labour disputes. Many feel that Goldberg's finest hour at the UN was his role in drafting Security Council Resolution 242, which was passed in November 1967 after the Six Day War and which has provided a basis for peace negotiations in the Middle East ever since. The Arabs generally recognized Goldberg's fairness in these negotiations, notwithstanding his sympathy with Israel. In January 1968, when North Korea seized the USS *Pueblo,* Goldberg persuaded the President to use diplomacy rather than force to secure the release of the crew. Despite this achievement, by February 1968, Goldberg's relations with President Johnson took a markedly downward turn. The American defeat and huge loss of lives during the North

Vietnamese Tet offensive made Goldberg realize the uselessness of his efforts to bring about peace. Johnson had consistently left Goldberg out of the loop in many crucial policy discussions on Vietnam and when arrangements were finally concluded for four-party negotiations (the United States, South Vietnam, North Vietnam, and the Viet Cong), in Paris, Johnson failed to pick Goldberg as one of the US representatives. Goldberg would have resigned in early 1968 but, at Johnson's request, postponed his resignation long enough to ensure the ratification of the Nuclear Non-Proliferation Treaty.

After leaving the UN in 1968, Goldberg never again had the opportunity for such high-powered public service. All but four of his remaining years were those of a Republican presidency, so Goldberg, an ardent liberal, returned to private life. He served for a while as president of the American Jewish Committee and became a member of a large Manhattan law firm. In 1970, he ran as liberal Democratic candidate for the office of governor of New York but, public speaking never being his strong point, he did not prove to be an effective campaigner and was soundly defeated. In 1971 he moved his law practice from New York to Washington, DC, also teaching at Washington's American University. In his legal work, he was involved in various international arbitration cases and in 1977 briefly resumed public service under President Jimmy Carter as a United States ambassador-at-large, focusing on human rights issues.

When given the opportunity, Goldberg applied his prodigious drive and creativity to what he believed were crucial areas of public life — trades unionism, political and legal activism and international diplomacy. The final irony is that Goldberg gave up his position on the United States Supreme Court to serve his country when, in fact, he could have best served it by staying on.

Born Arthur Joseph Goldberg. **Parents** Joseph and Rebecca Goldberg. **Marriage** Dorothy Kurgans, 1931 (died 1988). **Children** Barbara and Robert. **Education** Day student, Crane Junior College, attended evening classes, DePaul University, Chicago, Illinois; Northwestern University Law School, Evanston, Illinois, DJur, 1929, PhD, summa cum laude, 1930. **Military Service** Major, United States Army, Office of Strategic Services, 1942–44. **Career** Called to Illinois Bar, 1929; lawyer, Chicago, 1929–48; lecturer, John Marshall Law School and Chicago School of Industrial Relations, 1944; general counsel: United Steelworkers of America, Congress of Industrial Organizations, 1948–61; special counsel, merged American Federation of Labor, Congress of Industrial Organizations, 1955–61; secretary of labor, 1961; associate justice of the Supreme Court, 1962–65; United States representative, United Nations, 1965–68; lawyer: New York, 1968, Washington, DC, 1971 onwards; lecturer, American University, Washington, DC, 1971 onwards; ambassador-at-large, United States delegation, first review conference of 1977 Helsinki European Security and Co-operation accords, 1977. **Related activities** Campaign manager for Hubert Humphrey, New York, 1968; Democratic candidate for governorship of New York, 1970. **Other activities** President, American Jewish Committee, 1968–69. **Cause of death** Coronary artery disease, at age 81. **Further reading** Victor Lasky (q.v.) *Arthur J Goldberg: The Old and the New,* 1970; Robert Shogan, *A Question of Judgment: The Fortas Case and the Struggle for the Supreme Court,* 1972; Dorothy Goldberg, *A Private View of a Public Life,* 1975; Seymour Maxwell Finger, *Your Man at the U.N.,* 1980; H.J. Abraham, *Freedom and the Court: Civil Rights and Liberties in the United States,* 1982; Bernard Schwartz and Stephan Lisher, *Inside the Warren Court, 1953–69,* 1983; H.J. Abraham, *Justices and Presidents: A Political History of Appointments to the Supreme Court,* 1985.

ALDO GUCCI

Italian Luxury Goods Retailer

***Born* Florence, Italy, 26 May 1905**

***Died* Rome, Italy, 20 January 1990**

The Gucci publicity machine has sometimes attempted to trace the history of the luxury goods dynasty back to saddlers who served the Medici, princes of Renaissance Florence. In fact it seems more likely that the business which Aldo Gucci made great was founded by his father Guccio in the 1920s. Spiritually, though not genetically, the Guccis with their perpetual internecine power struggles seem to have a lot in common with that other Italian family of the Renaissance, the Borgias.

It is sad that in old age Aldo Gucci never had the peace to relax and enjoy the considerable fruits of his labours. But then again, peace is not something that the Guccis have gone in for.

Of Guccio's four sons (one of them illegitimate), Aldo was the only one who gave the leather shop in the Via Condotti, Florence, his undivided attention. It was Aldo who spotted the business's growth potential, and who imparted to the Gucci products their characteristic look, including, apparently, the GG logo and horsey themes that are so recognizable today.

Aldo Gucci was more of an entrepreneur than the highly conservative Guccio had ever been. As soon as he began working in the shop he began to find all sorts of possibilities for expansion. A pattern quickly began to emerge. Aldo would propose a scheme, perhaps the creation of a new product line; Guccio would oppose it with threats and imprecations, and tell Aldo that he could do what he liked as long as he, Guccio, was not involved, and that he would have to get his finance from the bank. Apparently Guccio would then covertly tell the bank that he would underwrite the scheme. This way he could claim credit when the schemes succeeded, or continue to disown them if they failed.

It was with this limited degree of paternal blessing that Aldo Gucci opened the first Gucci branch in Rome just before the war. His adventurousness was vindicated by subsequent events. For much of the war Rome was treated as an "open city" by the Allies and the shop was able to continue trading. After the war the branch proved to be an ideal jumping-off point for expanding the business. Aldo introduced a number of cheaper product lines which had such a success as souvenirs for the Allied troops and other visitors that he was encouraged to think about opening more branches, abroad. Even Guccio began to like this idea, particularly when Princess Elizabeth visited the shop in Florence and remarked that "We have nothing like this in England" — though he was less impressed by the fact that the royal visitor spent no money.

Aldo's brother Rodolfo had been a film actor before the war. After 1945 he began to take more of an interest in the family business, and enthusiastically supported the idea of overseas branches. Paris's rue de Rivoli and London's Bond Street, both of them prestigious shopping areas for the well-off, were the agreed sites for the new ventures. It was left to Aldo to secure the shop sites, staff them and launch the new stores. Such was their success, that by 1952 Aldo was determined to open in New York. Guccio again tried to put the brakes on, so Aldo went ahead and made the arrangements anyway.

That was the last time Guccio performed his trick of approving one of Aldo's schemes after the event. Guccio died in 1953, leaving the business to his three legitimate sons in equal shares, even though almost all the other members of the family regarded Aldo as the author of the company's success.

Guccio's daughter Grimalda, who with her husband had given Guccio and Aldo considerable support, were overlooked in the will. Having expected a share of the empire, Grimalda took her brothers to court. The brothers convinced the court that they'd reached a settlement with her, leaving her feeling cheated. Giovanni, Grimalda's husband, told Aldo that she had been treated disgracefully, and from that day onwards, Aldo never darkened her door again. This episode was just a pale shadow of the litigation and family feuding that was to come.

Although Aldo owned only a third of the shares in the business, his dynamism and authority made him the effective head of the enterprise. He spent a lot of time in the US, where the Gucci style and workmanship made the New York shop an overnight hit. More shops opened, strung across the country from Philadelphia to San Francisco. With all this going on, to say nothing of his life as a New York socialite, Aldo failed to see the trouble that was fermenting in his own family.

Aldo's personal relations had never been anything like as successful as his business ones. Before the war, he had married a British woman, Olwen Price, who was visiting Florence as maid to a Romanian princess. Olwen and Aldo seem to have had a hasty wedding and to have become estranged shortly afterwards, though Aldo continued to visit Olwen from time to time and Olwen bore him three sons and a daughter.

Meanwhile Aldo, who had a reputation for being extremely attractive to women, had various mistresses. For many years he wanted to marry one of them, the beautiful Bruna, by whom he had a daughter (and with whom he is said to have lived out much of his old age), but Olwen Gucci steadfastly refused to divorce him. The relationship between their parents had understandably upset the young sons as they were growing up. Paolo, in particular, regularly stood up to Aldo, who on one occasion beat the boy with a (Gucci) belt, admittedly after Paolo had thrown a cup of coffee at him.

Now Aldo's three sons had grown up to join the family business, and, in an echo of Aldo's earlier relationship with Guccio, were beginning to show dissatisfaction with the distribution of power. Aldo paid little attention to their complaints. Paolo, in particular, was highly critical of the company's lack of direction, and wanted to do something about the inefficient way in which he considered the products were designed, made and marketed. He was keen to license merchandisers to distribute Gucci products more widely than could be achieved through their own retail outlets.

Paolo was given the position of head of design, but soon found that this was little more than a sop: his uncles would put new products into production without any consultation. The lack of any financial control in the company made his position meaningless, he felt.

Meanwhile the Gucci empire continued to widen. A branch opened in Japan in 1965, and in 1967 Aldo realized his life-long dream of relocating the Florence shop in the city's ultra-luxurious Via Tornabuoni. In 1971 Aldo tried unsuccessfully to get his brothers to agree to go public in order to make it easier to finance still further expansion.

After the death of their brother Vasco, Aldo and Rodolfo bought his shares from his widow. These shares were split 50–50 but Aldo distributed ten per cent of his 50 per cent among his sons, a move which paved the way for his later downfall. Rodolfo kept all his shares because he was at this time estranged from his only son, Maurizio, who had married against his will.

When, in 1978, Paolo fell out irreparably with Rodolfo after the latter had overruled him once too often, Aldo invited Paolo to come to New York and work with him. Paolo soon found he couldn't work with Aldo either. According to one story, Aldo was in the habit of making a fool of the by now middle-aged Paolo, officially a vice-president and managing director of the American Gucci corporation, in front of the shop staff.

Things came to a head when Rodolfo wrote to fire Paolo from his Italian position and Paolo took Rodolfo to court for unfair dismissal. When Aldo got wind of this lawsuit, and of the fact that Paolo was considering launching his own product range, he too fired Paolo and began litigation to stop him trading under his own name. Unbeknown to Aldo, Paolo had been gathering evidence of massive tax "irregularities" in Gucci's US operation. Paolo now tried to use these papers to force Aldo to let him carry out his plan of launching his own range under the trademark Paolo Gucci.

Aldo would not yield and, although Paolo seems to have tried to get the tax papers back before the matter came to court, he was unable to put the brakes on the wheels which he had set in motion.

In the midst of the tax case came an unexpected blow. On Rodolfo's death in 1983, his son, Maurizio, had taken over his half-share in the company. Getting hold of the proxy vote for some shares of Paolo's (so that he temporarily controlled more than his own 50 per cent of the voting rights) he ousted Aldo from the presidency. Aldo was said to be heartbroken by this loss.

On top of this, the tax case in the US culminated in the octogenarian Aldo Gucci being sentenced in 1986 to a year and a day in prison plus a large fine. Although the prison was more like a hotel and Aldo served a mere four months of his sentence, the ignominy must have hurt, try though Aldo might to put the blame for the tax irregularities on an accountant. Most of his family were unsympathetic to his plight.

In the meantime, Maurizio's own affairs also came under scrutiny. There were allegations of forgery relating to a document by which Rodolfo had apparently made his shares in the firm over to Maurizio before his death (removing the liability for estate duties). These allegations led to Maurizio being temporarily suspended as president, though he was later restored to power.

At present half of the business is owned by Maurizio Gucci, who is making the distribution policies more exclusive and the products even more up-market than they were under his uncle Aldo. The other half was sold by Aldo and his sons to a Middle-Eastern bank. Litigation over Paolo's plan to trade under his own name continues: Paolo lost the most recent round in the London High Court. A further row arose on Aldo's death: he had left his 20 million pounds to his mistress Bruna and her child, and nothing to Olwen, Paolo or his brothers, who are now taking legal action to invalidate the will. According to one estimate, Gucci lawsuits have cost two million pounds in lawsuits over the past five years — good news for lawyers.

Aldo Gucci's energy, determination and sense of style made the family name a byword for fine Italian design and workmanship, epitomized by the famous Gucci moccasin which film stars and other jet-setters rushed to buy. The less elegant conduct of his family, in which his obstinacy played its part, seem to have done little to tarnish the reputation of the products. In 1989 the company turned over 125 million pounds.

The architect of the turbulent empire died an extremely rich man. It seems impossible that he died a happy one. On the other hand, an employee who saw him a couple of weeks before he died said that he seemed cheerful. Perhaps the vendetta had become a way of life.

Born Aldo Gucci. **Father** Guccio Gucci, leather goods manufacturer. **Marriage** Olwen Price. **Children** Giorgio, Paolo, Roberto and Patricia from the marriage; one daughter from outside the marriage. **Career** Leather goods executive and designer, 1938 onwards; chairman, Guccio Gucci Soc. r.l., Italy, director, Gucci Limited, London, Gucci Soc. Resp. Limited, Paris, until 1984, Gucci America, 1953–84. **Other activities** Imprisoned for tax evasion, 1986. **Collection** Gucci moccasin, Museum of Modern Art, New York. **Cause of death** Cerebral haemorrhage, at age 84. **Further reading** Gerald McKnight, *Gucci: A House Divided,* 1987.

ALAN HALE JR

American Actor

Born **Los Angeles, California, 1918 or 1921**

Died **Los Angeles, California, 2 January 1990**

"Wasn't he Errol Flynn's sidekick in all those films?"

"No, that was his father."

Because Alan Hale Jr, best-known as the stocky, soft-hearted Skipper in the 1960s television sitcom, *Gilligan's Island,* eventually became the spitting image of his famous father, the mistake by his fans was understandable. The fact that Hale Sr's old films were shown on late-night television was a source of bemusement as well.

However, unlike his father, who starred in hundreds of films, Hale Jr found his acting niche in television. His films, such as his first, *To the Shores of Tripoli,* in 1942, with John Payne and Maureen O'Hara, were rather routine. Not even small roles in *One Sunday Afternoon,* Raoul Walsh's tepid musical remake of *Strawberry Blonde,* or *Young At Heart* with Frank Sinatra and Doris Day, or *The True Story of Jesse James,* with Robert Wagner and Jeffrey Hunt, could propel the well-liked, easy-going actor to stardom. Most sources claim that Hale participated in 65 films. Leslie Halliwell's *Filmgoer's Companion* lists eight — "and many others".

Hale's first television series, in the early 1950s, was the adventure show *Biff Baker USA*. He went on to appear in the popular but short-lived *Casey Jones* situation comedy and, eventually, in *The Good Guys.* None of these ever fully showcased Hale's cheerful professionalism and excellent sense of comedic timing. However, his name became a household one with *Gilligan's Island* in the 1960s, a primetime sitcom that was often deplored by TV critics for its unchallenging humour and weak plotlines — and which was one of the more successful shows of decade.

A motley group of castaways, shipwrecked on an island after what was supposed to be a three-hour cruise, included Bob Denver (formerly the popular beatnik Maynard G. Krebs in an earlier sitcom, *The Loves of Dobie Gillis*) as the inept first-mate. Also starring were Jim Backus as the blowhard millionaire Thurston Howell III, and Tina Louise (in her first and last "flowering" upon the screen) as a sexy actress. Hale's jovial skipper proved to be the most likeable of the stable, and reinforced the show's increasing popularity when it went into syndication, particularly with the younger audience. A "reunion" in 1978 followed, along with two specials in 1979 and 1981. Some people felt that Hale's refusal to take his character (and perhaps himself) too seriously added to the fun of the series; his style, along with his physical gesturing, smacked of vaudeville in its broadness.

Hale kept his image of his most successful role alive, even wearing the Skipper's hat as he welcomed the public into his popular restaurant in West Hollywood, Alan Hale's Lobster Barrel. With the exception of an early stint in the Coast Guard, Hale remained in the Los Angeles area throughout his life, and was named Los Angeles Senior Citizen of the Year in 1972.

Born Alan Hale Junior. **Parents** Alan, actor, and Gretchen (Hartman), actress, Hale. **Marriage** Naomi. **Children** Three sons and one daughter. **Military service** Coast Guard, World War II. **Career** Film and television actor, 1930s onwards. **Other activities** Restaurateur, Alan Hale's Lobster Barrel, West Hollywood, Los Angeles, 1980s. **Awards and honours** Named Senior Citizen of the Year, Los Angeles, 1972. **Films** (include) *Wild Boys of the Road,* 1933; *To the Shores of Tripoli,* 1942; *One Sunday Afternoon,* 1948; *Four Days' Leave,* 1950; *The Gunfighter,* 1950; *West Point Story,* 1950; *The Big Trees,* 1952; *Rogue Cop,* 1954; *Young at Heart,* 1954; *The Indian Fighter,* 1955; *The Killer Is Loose,* 1956; *The True Story of Jesse James,* 1957. **Television** (includes) *Biff Baker USA,* 1952–53; *Casey Jones,* 1957; *Gilligan's Island,* 1964–67; *The Good Guys,* 1968–70, *Gilligan's Island* sequel specials, 1978, 1979, 1981. **Cause of death** Cancer, at age 68 or 71.

CHARLES HERNU

French Politician

***Born* Quimper, France, 3 July 1923**

***Died* Villeurbanne, France, 17 January 1990**

Did Charles Hernu cold-bloodedly order the bombing by French agents of the Greenpeace ship *Rainbow Warrior* in July 1985 — an attack which killed one man on board and sunk the ship — or was the initiative taken by senior officers within the French armed forces?

Whatever the truth, Charles Hernu — France's bullish defence minister at the time — paid for the *Rainbow Warrior* scandal with his resignation. A harsh punishment if he was indeed blameless, as he claimed; but if as the senior elected politician in the Defence Ministry he was responsible for ordering the attack, a mere resignation seems a small price to have paid.

We may never know the whole story. As one French newspaper commented: "He takes the full story of that episode to the grave." The nearest Hernu came to admitting any kind of guilt was two years after the incident, when he told the newspaper *Le Monde:* "Yes, there were such orders. They were bungled. I covered up and I paid the price." His choice of newspaper for his confession was ironic, as *Le Monde* had been principally responsible for hounding him out of office in the first place.

This much we do know: In 1985 the international environmental pressure group Greenpeace sent a group to the Pacific in their vessel, *Rainbow Warrior* — a former trawler which had been fitted with sails in order to save fuel and stay out of port for longer. The Greenpeace crew were planning to disrupt French nuclear tests which were once again taking place near the Mururoa atoll in French Polynesia, 2500 miles from mainland New Zealand and roughly the same distance from the US's fiftieth state. The Greenpeace mission was intended to keep the issue of the dangers of nuclear testing in the public eye and step up pressure on the French government to halt such tests. Local Polynesians were themselves planning to work with Greenpeace by attempting a spectacular landing on the islands with their longboats.

One night, while the *Rainbow Warrior* was moored in Auckland, New Zealand, two underwater bombs were attached magnetically to the ship's hull by divers. The bombs blew a massive hole in the hull — sinking the *Rainbow Warrior* and killing a photographer who was on board. New Zealand is a difficult place to escape from if you're in a hurry, and those responsible were soon caught. It quickly emerged that the bombing team were members of the French State Security Service, the DGSE. There was an international outcry and, at home, growing demands for the prosecution of all senior officials who had been aware of the secret DGSE mission to New Zealand.

By September 1985, the affair was threatening the very survival of France's Socialist government. Something had to be done. Both Hernu and the admiral who headed the DGSE resigned. The French prime minister, Laurent Fabius, told his people on national television that the decision to sabotage the Greenpeace mission had been a bad one. Hernu continued to claim he was not implicated and that senior officers had "hidden the truth" from him. The scandal simmered down but irreparable damage had been done to relations between France and the South Pacific states. The *Rainbow Warrior* affair was also held responsible for the defeat of the French Socialists in the 1986 general election.

Did Hernu consciously order such an unprovoked act of aggression against an unarmed vessel in another state's waters? After he and his officials discussed intelligence reports about Greenpeace's activities in the Pacific, it is clear that he did sign a document authorizing the DGSE to "forecast and anticipate the actions of Greenpeace". Were the DGSE over-zealous in their interpretation of "anticipate" or was it intended as a blank cheque authorizing state-sponsored sabotage?

In the nature of these operations, there is very little background paperwork detailing the operation. The full story could only emerge if the participants could be persuaded to be entirely truthful about what was said and how it was interpreted.

Charles Hernu was the son of a police officer. During World War II he joined the Resistance in the French city of Lyon and served briefly in the French Army at the end of the war. After a brief career as a journalist he was elected to the French National Assembly (lower house of parliament) in 1956. He collaborated with another ambitious young Socialist MP. This was François Mitterrand who was many years later to become president of France.

Hernu worked closely with Mitterrand during his first challenge for the presidency in 1965. He became a close personal friend of the Socialist leader as they brought together the disparate groups on the non-Communist left to create a major national party capable of winning power and getting a president elected.

One of Hernu's contributions to the revival of the Centre-left in French politics was to found the Jacobin Club in 1954 which became one of the most influential of the *clubs Républicains*. This is the name given in France to political think-tanks/debating societies which enable like-minded people to come together and develop new political ideas which can then be popularized by the political parties which adopt them.

In the late 1950s and early 1960s the French Left was divided about its attitude to the new constitution (the 5th Republic) promoted by President de Gaulle. This created a more powerful presidency — something of which many on the left were highly suspicious. Hernu was able to combine 54 of the *clubs Républicains* into the *Convention des Institutions Républicaines* which argued that the Left should not attempt to change the constitution of the 5th Republic when it gained power.

Hernu's other major achievement was to persuade a somewhat sceptical Socialist Party to support another Gaullist policy; that of maintaining France's independent nuclear deterrent or strike force (*force de frappe*). In a party of schoolteachers and office-workers Hernu, with his love of military regalia, was one of the very few who took a serious interest in defence policy. Combined with his close association with Mitterrand, his expertise helped him to establish himself as the party's principal defence spokesperson. He used this position to argue that there should be no tension between an incoming Socialist government and the military — the party would have enough problems without disgruntled generals to cope with.

When the Left finally did come to power in the elections that followed Mitterrand's presidential victory in 1981, it was inevitable that Hernu should become defence minister. At first, he suspended the French nuclear test programme. However, after pressure from service chiefs, he reversed this policy within days. France was once again committed to a full programme of testing and Charles Hernu, as defence minister, was the programme's staunchest defender. This was despite the growing tide of protest from environmental groups and foreign governments — notably the Lange administration in New Zealand — which had the country designated a nuclear weapon-free zone.

Hernu was also a good friend of the military in other ways; increasing their spending overall and allocating a significant 30 per cent of total defence expenditure to nuclear weapons. His close association with the services he was supposed to control made him deeply unpopular with many of his party colleagues — both for economic and environment reasons. However, France is a country which is proud of its independence and continuing military strength. Tanks and missile launchers are cheered by thousands as they roll down the Champs Elysées in Paris every year on 14 July. Hernu's "macho" stance clearly endeared him to many French people. Even the *Rainbow Warrior* affair did not apparently do his popular reputation much harm. He was re-elected to the Assembly with an increased majority in 1986 and remained mayor of the Lyon suburb of Villeurbanne until his death.

Many believe that in the *Rainbow Warrior* affair, an otherwise respected international power perpetrated nothing less than a terrorist act in foreign waters. But there is still a strong body of opinion in France which believes that the sinking of the *Rainbow Warrior* was perfectly justified in the national interest. Those holding this view would argue that Charles Hernu's only problem was that he was found out. Hernu benefited from that strand of nationalism which he did so much to bolster during his life.

Born Charles Hernu. **Parents** Eugène, policeman, and Laurence (Prost) Hernu. **Marriages** Five; 5) Martine Borg, 1988. **Children** Four children. **Education** Collège des Minimes, Lyon. **Military service** French Resistance and French Army, World War II. **Career** Journalist, *Le Jacobin,* 1954; deputy for Seine, National Assembly, 1956–58; mayor of Villeurbanne, 1977 onwards; deputy for Rhône, National Assembly, 1978 onwards; minister of defence, 1981–85. **Related activities** Secretary, Foreign Affairs Committee, 1956–58; secretary-general, Colloques juridiques, 1960; general delegate, Fédération de la gauche démocrate et socialiste, 1965–67, one-time vice-president; general delegate, chairman, Presidium, Conventions des institutions républicaines until 1970; technical adviser, Centre nationale du commerce extérieur; one-time secretary general, Fédération Nationale des Elus Socialistes et Républicains; one-time president, Conventions pour l'Armée Nouvelle; editor, periodical, *Armée Nouvelle.* **Offices and memberships** Founder member with Pierre Mendès, Parti Socialiste Unifie, 1963; founder, Jacobin Club; president, Villeurbanne basketball team. **Publications** *La Colère usurpée,* 1959; *Priorité à gauche,* 1969; *Soldat citoyen,* 1975; *Chroniques d'attente,* 1976; *Nous les grands,* 1980. **Cause of death** Heart attack, at age 66.

GORDON JACKSON

British Actor

Born **Glasgow, Scotland, 19 December 1923**

Died **London, England, 14 January 1990**

Imagine the populations of each of the United States standing together with the population of the United Kingdom; the resulting mass represents approximately the number of people worldwide who would instantly recognize the precise, straitlaced Scottish butler from *Upstairs, Downstairs,* the hugely successful British television series that ran for five years in the early 1970s. Gordon Jackson's portrayal of Hudson made him a familiar figure in homes all over the world, yet he remained an unassuming figure, never playing the star, in spite of an extremely impressive list of credits spanning some 100 feature films, together with numerous stage and television appearances.

He was born in Glasgow and, in common with fellow countrymen the world over, he never lost his mellifluous Scottish brogue, a feature that was to become his trade mark. Although he had some experience of acting as a child, appearing in BBC radio plays, he went straight from Hillhead High School into Rolls Royce as an engineering draughtsman at the age of 17. World War II, as with so many other performers, gave him a start in uplifting war films such as *The Foreman Went to France, San Demetrio, London* and *Millions Like Us.* His fresh-faced innocence and callow good looks read well on the big screen and, following pressure from Rolls Royce to make up his mind, he chose acting as his career.

Jackson's lack of training proved no handicap; rather, a persistent nervousness about the business of performing stayed with him for the rest of his career, and fostered a painstaking, committed approach that proved highly successful. "People think of me as a very dedicated actor," he once commented, "but in fact it is sheer fear and wanting to get it right." He slipped easily into character roles, almost invariably Scottish and frequently in uniform, and appeared totally at his ease in a number of Ealing comedies such as *Whisky Galore.* His screen career prospered, leading to substantial roles in *Tunes of Glory* with Alec Guinness and John Mills, *Mutiny on the Bounty,* where he relished the opportunity of observing Marlon Brando and Trevor Howard at work, and *The Great Escape,* where his ability to portray genuine openness and honesty was put to good use as the German-speaking prisoner in disguise making a fatal lapse into English in response to a wily Nazi Officer's "Good luck".

His appearance in the classic *The Prime of Miss Jean Brodie* with Maggie Smith in 1968 won him much acclaim, but it was the casting of *Upstairs, Downstairs* two years later that set the seal on his fame. "It just sounded like another part. I don't think any of us thought it would become all those episodes and be such a big success." True to type, Jackson never watched a single one of the series' 75 episodes, although he was eternally grateful for the financial security it provided. His performance as Hudson won him the 1975 award for Best Actor from the Royal Television Society. With sales throughout the world, and such a seemingly real-life portrayal, it would not have been surprising had Hudson suffocated many future working opportunities. However, in spite of being in his own words "underconfident and too tentative — never a go-getter", Jackson was lucky enough to secure a contrasting role in another highly successful television series, this time as the granite-jawed Special Branch policeman Cowley in *The Professionals.* A further five years in that series kept him almost constantly on screens throughout the world, as both proved major successes on the lucrative US market.

His stage appearances, though relatively infrequent, were enthusiastically tackled, and he attracted good notices for his performances in Orson Welles's production of *Moby Dick* in 1955, Banquo to Alec Guinness's *Macbeth* at the Royal Court Theatre and Horatio in Tony Richardson's 1969 production of *Hamlet* at London's Round House, this last transferring to New York.

He worked very regularly, appearing in television dramas such as Nevil Shute's *A Town Like Alice,* shot in Australia, and the BBC's *The Winslow Boy.* The fame and recognition left him curiously unspoiled. A genuinely modest man, he once dismissed his achievements with the characteristically self-effacing comment, "I'm just a well-known face." This amiable lack of conceit won him many friends in the business, complementing perfectly his innate and thorough professionalism.

Born Gordon Cameron Jackson. **Parents** Thomas, teacher of printing, and Margaret (Fletcher) Jackson. **Marriage** Rona Anderson, actress, 1951. **Children** Graham and Roderick. **Education** Hillhead High School, Glasgow. **Career** BBC Radio actor as a child; engineering draughtsman, Rolls-Royce, until becoming a full-time actor; film début, *The Foreman Went to France,* 1942; stage début, as Dudley in *George and Margaret,* MSU Theatre, Rutherglen, Scotland, 1943; London début, as Able Seaman McIntosh in *Seagulls Over Sorrento,* Apollo, 1951; New York début, as Horatio in *Hamlet,* Lunt-Fontanne, 1969. **Awards and honours** Clarence Derwent Award for role of Horatio, 1969; Royal Television Society Award for Best Actor, 1975; Emmy, 1976; Officer of the Order of the British Empire, 1979. **Stage** (in London, unless otherwise indicated) *George and Margaret,* Rutherglen, Scotland, 1943; in repertory, Glasgow, Worthing, Perth; *Master of Men,* Glasgow, 1944; *Seagulls Over Sorrento,* 1951; *Moby Dick,* 1955; *The Soldier's Tale,* 1958; *Macbeth,* 1966; *The Soldier's Tale,* Edinburgh Festival, 1967; *Wise Child,* 1967; *This Story of Yours,* 1968; *Hamlet,* 1969; *The Signalman's Apprentice,* Oxford, 1969; *Hedda Gabler,* Stratford, Ontario, 1970; *Oedipus,* 1970; *The Soldier's Tale,* 1970; *The Lovers of Viorne,* 1971; *Veterans,* 1972; *What Every Woman Knows,* 1973; *Macbeth,* 1975; *Noah,* Chichester Festival, 1976; *Twelfth Night,* Chichester Festival, 1976. **Films** (include) *The Foreman Went to*

France, 1942; *Millions Like Us,* 1943; *Nine Men,* 1943; *San Demetrio,* 1944; *London,* 1944; *Pink String and Sealing Wax,* 1945; *The Captive Heart,* 1946; *Against the Wind,* 1947; *Eureka Stockade,* 1948; *Whisky Galore,* 1948; *The Lady with a Lamp,* 1951; *Meet Mr Lucifer,* 1954; *Pacific Destiny,* 1956; *Tunes of Glory,* 1960; *The Great Escape,* 1962; *Those Magnificent Men in their Flying Machines,* 1964; *The Ipcress File,* 1965; *Cast a Giant Shadow,* 1966; *The Fighting Prince of Donegal,* 1966; *The Prime of Miss Jean Brodie,* 1968; *Run Wild Run Free,* 1969; *Kidnapped,* 1972; *Russian Roulette,* 1975; *Spectre* (television), 1977; *The Medusa Touch,* 1977; *The Last Giraffe* (television), 1977; *A Town Like Alice* (television), 1980; *The Shooting Party,* 1984. **Television** (includes) *Upstairs, Downstairs,* 1970–75; *The Professionals,* 1977–81; *My Brother Tom,* 1987; *The Winslow Boy,* 1988. **Cause of death** Undisclosed, at age 66.

PATRICK KELLY

American Fashion Designer

Born **Vicksburg, Mississippi, 24 September 1949 or 1954**

Died **Paris, France, 1 January 1990**

"People have to make happy clothes; there's just too much sadness in the world", Patrick Kelly once told an interviewer. The designer's whimsical women's fashions, adorned with quirky buttons, feathers, bows, and piccaninny pins, were as cheerful and optimistic as they were outrageous. The first black American to become a member of the powerful *Chambre Syndicale de la Couture,* the Parisian Fashion Designers' Guild, Kelly rose from the fleamarket stalls at Clignancourt to the rarefied air of the *Cour Carée du Louvre* exhibition in only three years. His slinky, stretchy styles earned him the title "King of Cling" and the patronage of countless celebrities, from rock stars Madonna and Grace Jones and actresses Jane Seymour and Bette Davis, to the Princess of Wales.

Though Kelly grew up on a Mississippi corn, pecan and squash farm and spent much of his youth working in the fields with his brothers and grandfather, he developed an early interest in women's fashion. His mother was a home economics teacher, and his aunt, an accomplished seamstress. But it was his grandmother, Ethel Rainey, who introduced him to the world of fashion. From a young age he was entranced by her copies of *Vogue* and *Harper's Bazaar,* and perplexed by the total absence of black models in the magazines. He resolved then to redress the balance. Around the same time he taught himself to sew with the help of his aunt, picked up the basics of sketching from his mother, and began designing prom dresses for neighbourhood girls.

Most influential of all, however, were the Sunday fashion displays among the congregation at the Vicksburg Baptist Church. There, Kelly remembered, "the ladies [were] just as fierce as the ladies at Yves Saint Laurent haute-couture shows." This, together with his grandmother's habit of replacing his missing buttons with new ones in myriad colours and configurations, inspired his choice of bright, unexpected fabrics and fanciful button adornments for his later designs.

Despite Kelly's obvious talent in art and design, his early interest in fashion was discouraged. It was not considered an appropriate career for a man. After graduating from Vicksburg Senior High School in 1972, he won a scholarship to study history at Jackson State University. He dropped out after only 18 months, resolving to "educate himself" instead.

Kelly spent the next few years of his life on the fringes of the fashion world, eking out a Bohemian existence in Atlanta and then in New York. To earn money, he collected clothes for an Atlanta veterans' organization, decorated windows at an Yves Saint Laurent boutique, and sold stained glass retrieved from derelict buildings. Eventually he opened his own antique-clothing business. Among the secondhand garments he peddled were some of his own prototype designs. He also staged several fashion shows, and through this made the acquaintance of successful model Pat Cleveland, who eventually persuaded him to leave Atlanta for New York.

New York, however, did not welcome the young, black designer with open arms. After 18 months at Parsons School of Design, during which he earned his tuition by creating clothes for black models, students and disco dancers, Kelly attempted to establish himself on Seventh Avenue. Everywhere he went, the doors were closed. At his friend Pat Cleveland's suggestion — and with the help of a complimentary ticket — he boarded a plane for Paris. "It's difficult getting discovered in America", he remembered. "I was one of thousands trying to make it in an enormous, impersonal industry." Once he arrived in Paris, he never looked back.

While he was not an instant success, Kelly's humour, ingenuity, and determination kept him going. Upon his arrival in Paris he was offered a job as costume designer for a popular night-club and discothèque. Having borrowed an ancient Singer sewing machine, he established a small costume workshop in his hotel room. Between assignments he designed his own coats and sold them, first on the Boulevard Saint-Germain, then in a market stall at Porte de Clignancourt. But it was not until 1985, several years after Kelly's arrival in Paris, that his avant-garde designs first came to the attention of the French fashion élite.

Some time earlier, Kelly had devised a series of curious dresses — simple, unseamed, skin-tight cylinders made from black cotton tube cloth and adorned with colourful buttons — and offered them for sale in Clignancourt. They proved popular among market shoppers, but remained largely invisible until Françoise Chassagnac, a former Dior model and owner of the trendy Victoire boutiques, happened to notice one among the racks. She was immediately captivated by the design and offered Kelly showroom space and the capital to prepare his ready-to-wear collection. In February 1985, the French edition of *Elle* magazine devoted six full-colour pages to Kelly's spring–summer collection. Immediately afterwards, the Victoire boutiques were deluged with orders.

Before long, Kelly was mounting his own exhibitions and exporting his designs to important American retailers, such as Bergdorf Goodman and Bloomingdales. By 1986 he had established his own business, Patrick Kelly Paris, in collaboration with his close companion, Björn Amelan, and the following year accepted the backing of American clothing giant Warnaco. The affiliation provided him with the security he needed to open his own Paris boutique. By 1988, his designs had made such an impact that he was unanimously elected a member of the exclusive *Chambre Syndicale*. Of its 44 members, Kelly was the only American.

While brightly coloured buttons, sequins, feathers, and gimmicks of all descriptions were Kelly's trademarks, his garments were as versatile as they were extravagant. Creations ranged from sparkly, strapless sheaths for disco-dancers to casual pantsuits and streamlined denim and black knit skirts. His designs, he claimed, were for women of all ages, sizes and proportions. "Other designers try to improve on what's there or cover everything up, but with my clothes I'm saying [that] whether you're fat or skinny, have big hips or no hips at all, you're beautiful just the way you are." The upbeat, inspirational tone was typical of him. For 1990 he had planned a less costly — but equally fun — fashion line, followed by a selection of fragrances, jewellery, and accessories.

When it came to his own attire, Patrick Kelly favoured the "rural chic" or "hillbilly" effect. Invariably clad in oversized overalls, a tee shirt, day-glo running shoes, and a baseball cap with a jauntily upturned rim, he was an unlikely representative of Parisian haute-couture. But his clownish, gregarious nature won him the affection of public and press alike. Kelly, wrote Betty Goodwin of the *Los Angeles Times,* was "as approachable as your next-door neighbor". Whatever his actual age — never divulged by Kelly to interviewers — he was at the height of his creative talents when he died.

Born Patrick Kelly. **Parents** Danie, variously fishmonger, insurance agent, and Letha Kelly, teacher. **Education** Vicksburg Senior High School, Mississippi, 1972; studied art history and black history, Jackson State University, Mississippi; Parsons School of Design, New York. **Career** Employed variously: collected, sorted clothes for AMVET, window decorator, Yves Saint Laurent's Rive Gauche boutique, seller, stained glass, owner, antique-clothing business, staged fashion shows, Atlanta, Georgia, 1974; worked in New York; costume designer, Le Palace, Paris, 1979 or 1980–1982; first ready-to-wear collection, 1985; founder, with Björn Amelan, Patrick Kelly Paris, 1986; opened Patrick Kelly boutique, Paris, 1987; first collection, Louvre, 1988. **Offices and memberships** Chambre Syndicale, 1988. **Cause of death** Bone marrow disease and brain tumour, at age 35 to 40.

ARTHUR KENNEDY

American Actor

***Born* Worcester, Massachusetts, 17 February 1914**

***Died* Branford, Connecticut, 5 January 1990**

There are actors, and then there are stars; and the actors who are not stars often have a difficult time. They may add a great deal to a performance, but they rarely enjoy proper recognition. They are known as *character* and *supporting* actors, and never quite achieve the individual prestige that stardom brings. Arthur Kennedy was one of America's most successful character actors, on stage and on film. His work in the original productions of several plays by Arthur Miller established his reputation in the theatre, and his versatility on the screen made him a top actor in Hollywood. The movie critic David Thompson once described him as "one of the subtlest American supporting actors", and many commentators have remarked on Kennedy's sensitivity and insight as an actor. He appeared in scores of productions on and off Broadway and in over 20 films. He won a Tony Award in 1949 and was a five-time Oscar nominee. His performances, often considered equal to those of Bogart and Brando, were praised by colleagues as diverse as James Cagney and Laurence Olivier.

Kennedy was best at revealing the human side of villainous characters and the dark streaks in admirable ones. This "dimension" made him ideal for roles which highlighted or questioned the motives of the leading characters. The pinnacle of his stage career was his portrayal of Biff Loman in Miller's *Death of a Salesman,* which earned him his Tony Award, and his performance alongside Olivier in Jean Anouilh's *Becket.* In the movies, he played everything from a drunken school janitor in *Peyton Place* to a newspaper reporter in *Lawrence of Arabia,* not to mention his ubiquitous presence in Westerns. Even so, Kennedy was nagged by personal doubt throughout his career, especially when preparing for a role. A friend of Kennedy's once described him as being "always...in a turmoil", though it generally ended in success rather than failure.

When he was a boy, Kennedy wanted to be a jockey but he went on to study drama at the Carnegie Institute of Technology. He began his acting career in New York City at the height of the Depression, but was able to join a touring repertory company at the Globe Theatre in 1936. Here, he gained experience in classical and Shakespearian drama. In 1940, a turning point came from a different direction. James Cagney had seen Kennedy's work and convinced him to take a part in the Warner Brothers film *City for Conquest.* At the time, most of Warner Brothers' major male stars — Humphrey Bogart, Edward G. Robinson and Cagney — were ageing, and the studio was looking for fresh talent. The performance led to a contract and a rapid succession of film roles, leading up to his enlistment in 1943.

Following the war, Kennedy returned to the stage and began the most seminal period in his career. In film, his efforts culminated in 1951's *Bright Victory,* in which he played a soldier coming to grips with his blindness. It was the same year Bogart starred in *The African Queen* and Brando starred in *A Streetcar Named Desire,* but it was to Kennedy that the New York critics gave their Best Actor award.

Kennedy made numerous films in the 1940s and 1950s, but his most important performances at this time were in the theatre. He returned to Broadway in 1947 to play in Miller's *All My Sons.* As David Shipman wrote in London's *The Independent,* "Kennedy was exactly the sort of young man America believed had fought for them — gentle, idealistic, courteous"; but in *All My Sons,* his character returns from the war to find his father exposed as a war profiteer. Two years later Kennedy appeared in *Death of a Salesman* as the disappointed, and disappointing, eldest son. Kennedy was applauded for the "strength and dignity" with which he sustained such a turbulent and complicated role. After taking the lead role in *The Crucible,* also by Miller, in which a Salem farmer must defend himself and his wife against charges of witchcraft, Kennedy emerged as a significant figure in American drama.

These praises never quite convinced Kennedy of his own worth, however. He did not pursue stardom, but he was deeply concerned about the economic status of actors and especially about the quality of his own performances. One commentator noted that he became so worried about his preparation for a play that he frequently isolated himself during rehearsals "in order to spare his family torture". Every role seemed to represent his downfall to him, but it was precisely that deeply personal involvement which produced the sincerity and naturalness in his acting.

In 1952, he moved back east from Hollywood, partly because he feared that the screen acting might undermine his ability to sustain a stage performance. He remained a prolific screen actor, beginning his long string of gun-slinging Westerns. He played every sort of goodie and baddie, though he once said he had greater satisfaction with the bad-guy roles. The film role with which he is most widely associated came in 1962, when he played the crusty, sceptical reporter, Jackson Bentley, in David Lean's *Lawrence of Arabia;* a role which has received renewed acclaim after the film's 1989 restoration.

Perhaps his crowning achievement in the theatre came at this time. The 1960 production of Anouilh's *Becket,* which dramatizes the relationship between King Henry II of England and his friend Thomas à Becket, had already been highly popular. The title role had been successfully rendered by Olivier, but when Anthony Quinn abandoned the role of King Henry, Olivier took over and Kennedy took Olivier's place. The cast then played to record houses in Boston, Washington and New York City. Kennedy was praised for offering a restrained, memorable performance, adding "conscience" to the role of the reluctant archbishop.

The 1970s were devoted mainly to Spanish and Italian Westerns, and in the 1980s thyroid cancer and an eye disease forced him into retirement. He returned to the screen shortly before his death, completing *Grandpa* just four months before he died. Kennedy's career is significant because he created several important characters, but the best epitaph comes from a description Olivier once gave of him. To Olivier, Kennedy was "that lovely actor".

Born John Arthur Kennedy. **Parents** J.T. Kennedy, dentist, and Helen (Thompson) Kennedy. **Marriage** Mary Cheffey, actress, 1938 (died 1975). **Children** Terence and Laurie. **Education** South High School and Worcester Academy, Massachusetts; studied drama, Carnegie Institute of Technology, Pittsburgh, Pennsylvania. **Military service** United States Air Force, 1943–45. **Career** Actor, 1934 onwards; with Globe Theatre's touring repertory company, 1936; New York début, as Bushy in *King Richard II,* St James, 1937; film début, *City for Conquest,*

1940. **Awards and honours** Antoinette Perry (Tony) Award for role in *Death of a Salesman,* 1949; Academy Award nominations for *Champion,* 1949, *Bright Victory,* 1951, *Trial,* 1955, *Peyton Place,* 1957, *Some Came Running,* 1959; New York Film Critics Award for Best Actor, 1951. **Stage** *King Richard II,* 1937; *Henry IV (Part I),* 1939; *Madam, Will You Walk,* 1939; *Life and Death of an American,* 1939; *International Incident,* 1940; *All My Sons,* 1947; *Death of a Salesman,* 1949–50; *See the Jaguar,* 1952; *The Crucible,* 1953; *Time Limit,* 1956; *The Loud Red Patrick,* 1956; *Becket,* 1961; *The Price,* 1968; *Veronica's Room, 1973.* **Films** (include) *City for Conquest,* 1940; *High Sierra,* 1941; *Strange Alibi,* 1941; *Knockout,* 1941; *Highway West,* 1941; *Bad Men of Missouri,* 1941; *They Died with Their Boots On,* 1941; *Desperate Journey,* 1942; *Air Force,* 1943; *Devotion,* 1946; *Cheyenne,* 1947; *Boomerang,* 1947; *Too Late for Tears,* 1949; *Champion,* 1949; *The Window,* 1949; *The Walking Hills,* 1949; *Chicago Deadline,* 1949; *The Glass Menagerie,* 1950; *Bright Victory,* 1951; *Red Mountain,* 1952; *Rancho Notorious,* 1952; *The Girl in White,* 1952; *The Lusty Men,* 1952; *Impulse,* 1954; *The Man from Laramie,* 1955; *The Naked Dawn,* 1955; *Trial,* 1955; *The Desperate Hours,* 1955; *Crashout,* 1955; *The Rawhide Years,* 1956; *Peyton Place,* 1957; *Twilight for the Gods,* 1958; *Some Came Running,* 1958; *A Summer Place,* 1959; *Elmer Gantry,* 1960; *Home Is the Hero,* 1961; *Claudelle Inglish,* 1961; *Murder She Said,* 1962; *Hemingway's Adventures of a Young Man,* 1962; *Barabbas,* 1962; *Lawrence of Arabia,* 1962; *Cheyenne Autumn,* 1964; *Joy in the Morning,* 1965; *Murieta,* 1965; *Italiano Brava Gente,* 1965; *Fantastic Voyage,* 1966; *Nevada Smith,* 1966; *Monday's Child,* 1967; *The Prodigal Gun,* 1968; *The Day of the Evil Gun,* 1968; *Dead or Alive,* 1968; *Hail Hero,* 1969; *The Movie Murderer* (television), 1970; *Glory Boy,* 1971; *A Death of Innocence* (television), 1971; *The President's Plane is Missing* (television), 1971; *Crawlspace* (television), 1972; *Nakia* (television), 1974; *The Sentinel,* 1977; *Brutal Justice,* 1978; *The Tempter,* 1978; *Grandpa,* 1989. **Television** (includes) *Divided We Stand,* 1959; *The Third Commandment,* 1959; *Not Without Honor,* 1960. **Cause of death** Cancer, at age 75.

PETER KNEEBONE

British Graphic Designer and Illustrator

Born **Middlesbrough, Yorkshire, 4 April 1923**

Died **Paris, France, 30 January 1990**

The name Peter Jack George Kneebone, sounds like the stuff of folk tale or nursery rhyme — maybe the sort of gentleman who'd eat only pumpkin, or no fat or, shown a pudding, put his thumb in it. In fact, there was very little of the homespun about this Peter Kneebone. As his obituarist in the London *Times* put it, "His style was a reflection of his own personality — witty, perceptive, economical and always memorable." What is more, he came to favour bespoke shirts inspired by wallpaper designs.

He was born of an English father and a French mother in the town of Middlesbrough, in the north-east of England, in 1923. In 1942 he went south to University College, Oxford, to study politics and philosophy. This was in the middle of World War II, and so after only a year in the City of Dreaming Spires, he joined the Royal Navy to become a liaison officer in Italy. The war's end in 1945 found Kneebone in Cairo. Here he served as naval broadcasting representative, which was a nice job for the right man as it covered the roles of announcer, producer, scriptwriter and newsreader, and carried with it the rank of lieutenant. By 1948 he had returned to Oxford, completed his studies, and gained a Master of Arts degree. There was now in the offing the ambitious Festival of Britain. Finally mounted in 1951, it was conceived as a celebration and a tonic, with events up and down the islands, and a splendid exhibition of technology — and a funfair — in London. (The only remaining evidence, the Festival Hall on the Thames's South Bank, remains a popular concert venue today.) Kneebone became assistant to the director of exhibitions, with reponsibility for the logistics of planning the care and display of some 100,000 artefacts. As *The Times* said, "he co-ordinated what was probably the most significant galaxy of British design talent in this century."

Little as yet had been seen of Kneebone's own design talent. He was to spend the new decade developing it diversely. In 1952 he directed and illustrated a BBC television adaptation of T.S. Eliot's *Old Possum's Book of Practical Cats.* Two books designed and illustrated by Kneebone then appeared — *Look Before You Elope* and *Sexes and Sevenths.* As a freelance, he produced illustrations for many leading British magazines — notably *The Observer* magazine. His style at the time was calculated to amuse and full of detail, but a shift of emphasis in his work led to the pared-down drawing which became characteristic. The transition was informed partly by his interest in the now familiar area of corporate identity — the image of the large corporation in all its visual aspects. He was becoming a graphic designer more than an illustrator, and addressing his abilities to a variety of projects and commissions, from the Shell Oil company, to the National Fund for Research into Crippling Diseases.

Kneebone wrote: "Not having a conventional professional training has kept me open-minded about my work and open-minded about its direction... It has also meant that I have been preoccupied with style and techniques as means rather than as ends." The last sentence is significant, because it indicates his approach to the craft of design, which was that of the problem-solver. His intellectual training inclined him to a certain rigour, so that he would make long and painstaking inquiry into exactly what communication was required to be expressed in any project which he undertook. His genius, though, lay in distillation. In his own words, "The aim of simplicity is to make clear something that is not simple." And Kneebone's visual solutions are evidence of just that. Moreover, he was blessed with humour, which again he used as a tool. Brevity is the soul of wit,and wit the soul of brevity; an illustration can be remembered better than a block of text. To all these ends, he evolved in his drawing a Kneebone "family", "half-human, half not", described with a steely line and an absolute minimum of decoration. Kneebone had a friend who, as director of a voluntary organization, grumbled that his workmates seemed too dense to read a balance sheet. Kneebone soon presented him with a drawing headed "The Bare Facts". Here were Teddy Bear derivatives labelled Income from Donations, Research Expenditure etc, trying to balance a seesaw. Later in *How to Interview* and *How to be Interviewed,* commissioned by the British Institute of Management, Kneebone achieved a series of similar crystalline sophistications.

He was also bilingual (thanks to his parentage), cosmopolitan, and an educator. From 1963 onwards he became increasingly involved in the teaching of design. He was co-ordinator of post-graduate studies at London's Central School of Art and Design, and went on to similar positions in France. After his second marriage, in 1976, he lived in Paris, but kept a flat in Kew, west London, and continued to spend much time in that city. He was chairman and eventually vice-president of the Society of Industrial Artists, and active in similar French organizations. The International Council of Graphic Design Associations, founded in 1963, was dedicated to increasing the understanding and use of visual and graphic communications world-wide. It was Kneebone who fertilized the idea, nurtured the result and became its president in 1979.

As already suggested, it's a fine thing to play with and speculate about the power of names. Might they not influence the fate, personality, or the business of their owners? What does Kneebone suggest? A hinge, a connection, something which joins and makes separate parts work, something essential, functional, something without fleshy distraction — and so on. If he had any taste himself for this sort of *jeu d'esprit,* Kneebone would have kept it firmly in its place, for he had a discipline, and an unerring sense of purpose, to teach and explain. "We design", he said, "for others."

Born Peter Jack George Kneebone. **Marriages** 1) Catherine Shanks, 1958 (divorced 1976); 2) Françoise Jollant, 1976. **Children** Anna, Jonathan, Sophie and Lucy from the first marriage. **Education** University College, Oxford, studied philosophy, politics and languages, 1942–43, 1946–48, MA, 1948. **Military service** Royal Naval Volunteer Reserve, liaison officer, Italy, naval broadcasting representative, lieutenant, 1943–46. **Career** Assistant to the director of exhibitions, Festival of Britain, London, 1951; television producer, British Broadcasting Corporation, London, 1952–53; freelance designer, Paris, London, 1952–90; head of complementary studies, Kingston School of Art, Surrey, 1963–66; co-ordinator of post-graduate studies, Central School of Art and Design, London, 1967–74; visual communications co-ordinator, École Nationale des Beaux-Arts, Nancy, 1980–89; visiting tutor: University of Paris VII, 1978–81, Parsons School of Design, Paris, 1981–88. **Related activities** Editor, journal of the Society of Industrial Artists, 1955; signage consultant: Philips Corporation, Netherlands, 1969–76, Ministry of Industry, Paris, 1974–77; design consultant: National Fund for Research into Crippling Diseases, London, 1969–74, Salle Pleyel concert halls, Paris, 1980–81, Ministry of Research, Paris, 1981–88, Centre National d'Art Contemporain, Villa Arson, Nice, 1983, Europrospective conference, Paris, 1986–87. **Offices and memberships** Secretary, International Council of Graphic Design Associations (IOCGRADA), 1963, secretary-general, 1977–79, president, 1979–81; fellow, Chartered Society of Designers, chairman, vice-president; member, Society of Typographic Designers. **Awards and honours** President's Trophy, International Council of Graphic Design Associations, 1970; IBM fellowship, Aspen Design Conference, Colorado, 1980. **Works** (as book designer and illustrator, unless otherwise indicated) *Old Possum's Book of Practical Cats* (television programme director, illustrator), BBC, 1952; *Look Before You Elope,* 1952; *Oiling the Wheels,* for Shell, 1955–58; corporate identity and graphics, for the National Fund for Research into Crippling Diseases, 1955–75; *Happy Families* (typeface calendar) for Monotype Corporation, 1963; *English Pronunciation Illustrated,* 1965; *Baby's Book,* 1971; *Look Behind You,* 1973; *How to Interview* and *How to Be Interviewed* (illustrator), British Institute of Management, 1975–80; *How to Recruit,* British Institute of Management, 1970s; Sign systems, Third Architectural Psychology Conference, Strasbourg, 1976; corporate identity and graphics, Salle Pleyel concert halls, Paris, 1980–81; CPE Centre, visual identity and publications design, ministry of research, Paris, 1981–89; visual identity and graphics, Europrospective conference, Paris, 1987; also, illustrator for Central Office of Information, National Economic Development Office, Institute of Directors, Imperial Chemical Industries, National Council of Voluntary Organisations. **Exhibitions** *Funny Peculiar: Illustrations by Peter Kneebone,* Kilkenny, 1984; *Design Français 1960–1980: Trois Decennies,* Centre Georges Pompidou, Paris, 1988. **Publications** *Look Before You Elope,* 1952; *Sexes and Sevenths,* 1953; *Oiling the Wheels,* 1957; (translator) *The Art of Afghanistan,* 1967; (co-author) *How to Interview,* 1975; *A Signature for Singapore,* 1979; (co-author) *How to Be Interviewed,* 1980; *Signaletique,* 1980; also contributor, illustrator, *The Observer, News Chronicle, The Sunday Times, Radio Times, New Scientist.* **Cause of death** Undisclosed, at age 66. **Further reading** *Designers in Britain,* 1951–71; R.D. Usherwood, *Drawing for the Radio Times,* 1961; James Holland, *Minerva at Fifty,* 1980; *Trademarks and Symbols of the World,* 1987; *Trademarks Collection: Europe I,* 1988; Margo Rouard and Françoise Jollant Kneebone, *Design Français 1960–1980: Trois Decennies,* 1988; *Contemporary Designers,* 1990.

ROSE KUSHNER

American Author and Public Health Advocate

***Born* Baltimore, Maryland, 22 June 1929**

***Died* Washington, DC, 7 January 1990**

Rose Kushner's career as an advocate for better breast cancer treatment for women began one Saturday night in June 1974 while she was having a bath. In a moment she never forgot, she found a lump (which turned out to be malignant) on one of her breasts. This discovery catapulted her into fighting first for improved breast cancer care for herself, and then into leading a national crusade to change the way the disease is treated. Many of the steps she advocated were at first rejected by American breast cancer experts but are now common practice in the United States.

In her own breast cancer treatment, Rose Kushner's first clash with American medical convention was in her refusal to submit to the "one-step" procedure. In the mid-1970s in the United States, a woman would have to undergo what Kushner regarded as the "barbaric custom" of doing a diagnostic biopsy and a mastectomy (if necessary) in a single procedure. Kushner believed that a woman needed time, after a cancer diagnosis, to assess her options and to find the best surgeon available to remove the breast.

Determined not to undergo the "one-step" procedure, Kushner finally, after making 18 telephone calls, found a surgeon who would remove only the lump. After the biopsy, when the lump in her breast did prove to be malignant, she angered the physicians she consulted in Washington, DC, and New York still further by insisting on modified radical surgery rather than the Halsted mastectomy, the standard procedure. She felt that the modified surgery would be preferable because the surgeon, while still removing her breast, would not remove the muscles in the chest wall beneath the breast. She discovered that at Roswell Park, in Buffalo, New York, the oldest cancer hospital in the world, Halsted mastectomies were never done, and that there she could have a modified radical mastectomy. Her surgery and convalescence went smoothly and the experience left her with a zeal to change the way patients with breast cancer are treated.

Rose Kushner was, by chance, in the best place in the United States to promote her cause. She lived with her husband, Harvey Kushner, in an affluent Maryland suburb of Washington, DC, which gave her the benefit of being not only a ten-minute drive from two of the finest medical libraries in the country — the National Library of Medicine and the Library of the National Institute of Health — but also within easy reach of Congress for her later lobbying efforts. The National Institute of Health is a major medical research facility and Kushner did not hesitate both to use its library and to interview its doctors to get first-hand information on the latest medical advances.

By 1974, Rose Kushner had been a freelance writer for many years. Her journalistic experience, which in the late 1960s had taken her to Vietnam to cover the war, stood her in good stead as a public health advocate. She claimed she started to take notes from the day she found the lump in her breast, to use in anticipated published writing. This was her way of dealing with her condition, and she described the approach as "cathartic". Kushner regarded her own mission of demystifying the medical profession as a cause in the spirit of the Watergate era: "I, like most writers — especially those living in and around Washington — abhor secrets. To us, a secret is something to dig out and tell to the public." She also drew on the American consumer activist movement: "changing the way medicine is practiced is up to us consumers". Her campaign was launched at a time of increasing feminist awareness in the United States. She decried the notion that mastectomies were a part of a vicious male plot to defile women but did continually encourage women to stand up to the predominantly male medical profession to be sure that they got the best care possible.

Untiring in her persistent efforts to bring about major change in breast surgery, Kushner completed in 1975 her pioneering book *Breast Cancer,* which was revised in 1977 and appeared as *Why Me?* (subtitled *What Every Woman Should Know About Breast Cancer to Save Her Life).* What had begun as Kushner's personal "crusade" to do away with the "one-step" procedure, for which there was no valid medical justification, was quickly picked up by women's groups, many surgeons, health insurance companies and by the federal government. In Massachusetts and in California, in 1979 and 1980 respectively, the legislature passed a law requiring all women to be told every treatment option, if they should have breast cancer. In 1979, Rose Kushner was the only lay member of a National Institute of Health panel that not only put an end to the Halsted mastectomy, but also recommended the "two-step" procedure for most cases.

Rose Kushner did not stop at these victories. In 1978, she won a landmark suit against the US Department of Health and Human Services and the Food and Drug Administration to require labels on birth control pills warning women who had had breast cancer to avoid the pill. She founded a counselling service and telephone hotline which until 1981 was run from her home. She became so well known that letters addressed simply to "Mrs Breast Cancer, Kensington, Maryland" would reach her mailbox. Through extensive travels to international conferences and foreign hospitals she found out about alternative methods of treating breast cancer by speaking to specialists from western and eastern Europe and Japan. In 1982, she wrote a new version of her previous two books, called *Alternatives,* in which she discussed benign breast disease, chemotherapy, early signs of recurrence or metastasis and breast reconstruction. From 1980 to 1986, she was a member of the Breast Cancer Advisory Board and in 1989 was appointed to the American Cancer Society's Breast Cancer Task Force. In 1988, she founded a political action committee to press for more federal funding for breast cancer. She became an advocate for increased use of lumpectomy in which the malignant lump is removed but the rest of the breast is left. At the time of her death, she was lobbying to require health insurance companies to cover mammograms.

In 1990, Rose Kushner was awarded posthumously the Society of Surgical Oncology's award for outstanding contributions by a lay person to fight cancer. This was "poetic justice" said her husband because the society's members had "booed her off the stage in 1975" after she had challenged their standard treatments. Rose Kushner died on 7 January 1990 of breast cancer. In the previous 15 years she had done much to improve breast cancer treatment in the US and to educate American women about alternative treatments. Her efforts had been the result of her vigorous and tenacious attitude. As she said herself, "It does no harm to have a streak of stubbornness, and a loud voice as well."

Born Rose Rehert. **Parents** Israel, tailor, and Fannie (Gravitz) Rehert. **Marriage** Harvey David Kushner, systems analyst, 1951. **Children** Two boys and a girl, Gantt, Todd and Lesley. **Education** Johns Hopkins University, Baltimore, Maryland, 1946–47; Baltimore Junior College, 1950–51; Montgomery Community College, Rockville, Maryland, 1963–65; University of Maryland, College Park, BS, summa cum laude, 1972. **Career** Research assistant, Pavlovian laboratory, Johns Hopkins University School of Medicine, Baltimore, 1947–51; medical-surgical secretary, local community hospitals, 1952–56; technical writer, Operations Research Incorporated, Silver Spring, Maryland, 1960–68; correspondent, *Baltimore Sun,* South Vietnam, 1967; freelance science writer, 1960s onwards. **Related activities** Founder, Breast Cancer Advisory Center, Kensington, Maryland, 1975, executive vice-president, 1975 onwards; patient adviser, consultant, breast cancer working group, Office of Cancer Communications, National Cancer Institute and Bureau of Radiology Health; member, National Breast Cancer Advisory Board, 1980–86; member, American Cancer Society's Breast Cancer Task Force, department of epidemiology, National Cancer Institute, 1989; consultant, women and health roundtable, National Women's Health Network. **Offices and memberships** Member: Pavlovian Society of North America, American Medical Writers Association, American Nursing Association, American Society of Journalists and Authors, Congressional Periodicals Press Gallery, White House Correspondents Association, Washington Independent Writers Association, Federation of American Scientists, Association of Community Cancer Centers, National Academy of Scientists, Sigma Delta Chi, Kappa Tau Alpha, Phi Kappa Phi. **Awards and honours** First Prize for feature writing, Sigma Delta Chi, 1971; National Media Award for newspaper publications, American Psychological Association, 1974; Distinguished Medical Writing Award, American Medical Writers Association, Mid-Atlantic chapter: 1975, 1979, 1980; Top Ten Books Award, American Library Association, 1975; James Ewing Award for oustanding contributions by a lay person in fight against cancer, Society of Surgical Oncology, 1990. **Publications** *Breast Cancer: A Personal History and an Investigative Report,* 1975; *Why Me? What Every Woman Should Know About Breast Cancer to Save Her Life,* 1975; *Alternatives: New Developments in the War on Breast Cancer,* 1984. **Cause of death** Breast cancer, at age 60.

ALBERTO LLERAS CAMARGO

Colombian Journalist and Former President

***Born* Bogotá, Colombia, 3 July 1906**

***Died* Bogotá, Colombia, 4 January 1990**

Small of stature, quietly spoken, unflamboyant to the point of being almost retiring, Alberto Lleras Camargo was yet one of the most influential politicians in his country's post-World War II history and a leading statesman in the South American region.

Something of a rebel in his youth, he left university without taking his degree, to become prominent as a writer in the leading Bogotá papers befor he was 20 and also in the Argentine press in the late 1920s. He was appointed editor-in-chief of the leading liberal Colombian newspaper, *El Tiempo,* at the tender age of 24. The son of a respected Liberal family — his paternal grandfather had once served as foreign minister and his mother's side boasted a former president, General Sergio Camargo — he grew up in modest circumstances but with a tradition of public service. It was through journalism that Lleras Camargo was first to come into politics, and his influence as a political writer was to provide a major strand throughout his career.

In the early 1930s the long dominance of the Conservative Party came to an end in Colombia, and Lleras Camargo was enlisted into the first reforming Liberal government of the new era, holding posts including minister of education and minister of foreign affairs, in which capacity he led the Colombian delegation to the San Francisco Conference which set up the United Nations. It was during his service to this government that he was to take up the presidency of his country for the first time when the then president, Alfonso López Pumarejo, resigned in 1945 after only three years of his four-year term of office. This was only a brief tenure of power. Conflicts within his party led to their putting up two candidates in the 1946 elections, and thus to the return of a Conservative government.

Lleras withdrew to his old love — journalism. But his stint as foreign minister, preceded by a few months as his country's ambassador to Washington in 1943, had introduced him to the wider politics of the American continent, and in March 1947 he was elected director-general of the Pan

American Union, the first South American to hold the post. Within a year this had been reorganized as the Organization of American States (OAS), with Lleras as its secretary-general — a post he held until August 1954. This was in many ways the happiest period of his public career. Vigorously anti-Communist — he was bitterly opposed later on to Castro's policies — and strongly supportive of the United States' role in the American hemisphere, he was largely responsible for shaping the OAS into the powerful instrument for peaceful settlement of border disputes which it has since remained. This same hemispheric interest was to lead him later to help establish greater regional co-operation with the setting up of the Latin American Free Trade Association, and to suppport the Alliance for Progress.

But he was inevitably to be drawn back into his own country's politics, if only because of his continued journalistic activities, now extended to broadcasting. Moreover, the increasing civil unrest following General Rojas Pinilla's seizure of power in mid-1953 led him to take steps to try to restore constitutional government, particularly after his election as leader of the Liberal Party. In the summer of 1956 he went to Spain to confer with the exiled Conservative Party leader, Dr Laureano Gómez. The two men agreed on a bi-partisan policy which was to edge Pinilla out of office and institute the 16-year truce which arranged for the equal sharing of all offices and the alternation of the presidency between the two parties. Lleras was the prime architect of what has since been seen as this somewhat controversial National Front, but, whatever its democratic shortcomings, it restored civilian rule and brought an end to sectarian fighting.

Lleras was to be its first president from 1958 to 1962 — the only man on whom the two parties could agree. He instituted some much-needed reforms. First and foremost, and reflecting his major interest, he restored freedom of speech, of the press and of public assembly. He embarked on a programme of austerity, with higher taxes and cuts in public expenditure, to put the economy on a sounder financial footing — again an indication of his support in the country. He also initiated the first agrarian reform legislation and drew up a ten-year social and economic development plan, with particular emphasis on one of Colombia's greatest needs, cheap housing schemes. Who knows how the country might have developed had he been able to continue in power, but after his four-year stint his own National Front arrangements ensured his succession by a Conservative. He himself retired from active politics but continued his influence behind the scenes through his new venture — a current affairs magazine *Visión* which enjoys wide circulation throughout Latin America.

Born Alberto Lleras Camargo. **Parents** Felipe Lleras Triano and Sofía Camargo. **Marriage** Berta Puga, 1931. **Children** Consuelo, Ximena, Marcela and Alberto. **Education** Military academy, Bogotá; Colegio Mayor de Nuestra Señora del Rosario; School of Law and Political Science, National University of Bogotá. **Career** Journalist, *La República, El Espectador,* Bogotá; reporter, *El Tiempo,* Bogotá; journalist, *La Nación,* and other newspapers and magazines, Buenos Aires, Argentina, 1926–29; staff correspondent, *El Mundo,* 1929; editor-in-chief, *El Tiempo,* chief editor, *La Tarde,* 1930; deputy, Chamber of Deputies, 1930, 1941, also speaker, 1931,1933, 1941; minister of the interior, 1935–38; minister of education, 1938; founder *El Liberal,* 1938, director and editor, 1938–42; senator, 1943; ambassador to the United States, 1943; minister of foreign affairs, 1944; president of Colombia, 1945–46, 1958–62; founder, *Semana,* 1946, editor briefly; editor, *El Independiente,* 1956; chairman, editorial staff, *Visión,* 1962 onwards. **Related activities** Secretary-general, Liberal Party; secretary, Colombian delegation, Seventh International Conference of American States, 1934; general secretary, Colombian president, Dr Alfonso López Pumarejo, 1934; Colombian delegate, Inter-American Conference for the Maintenance of Peace, Buenos Aires, 1936; member, executive committee, Liberal Party, 1941; leader: Colombian delegation, Chapultepec Conference, Mexico, 1944, United Nations Conference on International Organizations, San Francisco, 1945; director-general, Pan American

Union, 1947–48; secretary-general, Organization of American States (formerly Pan American Union), 1948–54; president: University of Los Andes, 1954–56, National Association of Radio Broadcasters, 1954; member, United Nations committee into Hungarian revolt, 1956; director, Liberal Party, 1956; founder, Latin American Free Trade Association, 1961. **Awards and honours** Honorary doctorates: Harvard, Yale, Colombia, Princeton and other universities of Latin America and United States; Maria Moors Cabot Gold Medal, Colombia University, for significant contributions to international friendship, 1947; honorary colonel, Colombian Army. **Publication** *Mi gente* (memoirs). **Cause of death** Undisclosed, at age 83.

LORD McALPINE OF MOFFAT

British Industrialist

***Born* 23 April 1907**

***Died* 7 January 1990**

For centuries, visitors to St Paul's Cathedral in London have read and obeyed the epitaph to its architect, Christopher Wren: *Si monumentum requiris, circumspice* — If you seek a monument, look around you. Anyone who looks around them in late-twentieth-century London can hardly help seeing the monuments of Robert Edwin McAlpine, Lord McAlpine of Moffat. Some of London's most conspicuous post-war buildings, including the National Theatre and the Shell Centre, both on the South Bank of the Thames, went up when he was director of London projects for his family firm of Sir Robert McAlpine.

The firm had its roots in the Victorian construction industry. Though it was founded by his grandfather, the eponymous Sir Robert, a Scottish bricklayer, the young Edwin believed that it was his father William Hepburn McAlpine who had "made" the business, and he was determined to sustain his father's work. On leaving his public school, Oundle, at the age of 18, he went straight into the family business, becoming a partner three years later. He spent some time familiarizing himself with the basics of construction and civil engineering, but it soon became clear that his greatest strengths had little to do with buildings and everything to do with people.

He was one of nature's salesmen, instinctively sniffing out an opportunity, speedily turning the opportunity into a deal, but then, as the deal became a project, becoming impatient to move on to the next prospect. Other members of the family, notably McAlpine's cousin Sir Robin McAlpine, had complementary abilities and interests: they managed the execution of the orders while Edwin McAlpine went off to win more business. He would, however, continue to keep a critical eye on the progress of construction projects, realizing that tight project control and customer satisfaction were essential to future sales.

One of the opportunities McAlpine identified for his company was as builders for the nuclear power industry, then in its infancy. Britain's Atomic Energy Authority had decided that each power station would be built as a "turn-key" project, with a single contractor taking responsibility for the whole station. This meant that, to be in the running for a contract, a builder needed to ally with a generator manufacturer. In 1955, McAlpine became deputy chairman of the Nuclear Power Plant Company (NPPC), one of four such consortia formed to tender for nuclear power station business. McAlpine's was subcontracted by NPPC to build plants at Bradwell in England and Latina in Italy.

McAlpine became chairman of NPPC in 1959. About the same time, a fifth consortium appeared on the scene to compete for the business of constructing nuclear power stations. The Central

Electricity Generating Board called a meeting to advise the five chairmen that some rationalization was needed if all were to survive. With a characteristic piece of fast footwork and use of his contacts, McAlpine negotiated a merger with another consortium on the way home from the meeting. He offered a lift, in his company's private black cab, to his friend Lord Chandos, head of the AEI-John Thompson Nuclear Energy Company. By the end of the short trip, it had been agreed that the consortia would merge, and that Chandos would be chairman.

At first deputy chairman of the resultant company, The Nuclear Power Group (TNPG), McAlpine took over as chairman on Chandos's retirement in 1966. In 1975, TNPG became part of the National Nuclear Corporation, with which McAlpine had no direct involvement. In the meantime, he had been instrumental in the construction of a total of seven nuclear reactors.

Among these, TNPG had built two Advanced Gas-Cooled Reactors (AGRs) at the Hinkley "B" and Hunterson "B" stations. Although all the AGRs suffered from problems, especially vibration, the Hinkley and Hunterson reactors were considered comparatively successful examples of the genre, and were used as models for other stations at Heysham and Torness. In the 1980s, McAlpine was to be an enthusiastic proponent of the AGR at the enquiry into the proposed Sizewell "B" project. He argued that the AGR's relative safety justified the price differential over the American Pressurized Water Reactor (PWR) (as implicted in the Three Mile Island incident). Nonetheless, the PWR was chosen for Sizewell "B".

At the time of his death, Britain had called a halt to the construction of further nuclear power stations, but McAlpine, convinced that more would be needed in future, was in the process of submitting a discussion document on the subject to the secretary of state for energy.

McAlpine's interest in the power industry was not confined to nuclear energy. The Nuclear Power Group had undertaken the construction of an oil-fired power station at Inverkip in Scotland. He involved the family firm in the investigation of "alternative" energy sources; they are currently engaged in the construction of wind-powered generators and tidal barrages.

McAlpine became chairman of British Nuclear Associates in 1973. This was just one of a long list of formal and informal networks through which he gathered information from and wielded influence over the construction and energy industries and the world at large. For instance, there was the Dorchester Group of building contractors, who originally met to discuss their interests at the Dorchester, one of the most elegant of the hotels in London's Park Lane, for over 20 years owned by the McAlpine family. And then there were the parties.

He was always holding parties. For many years he held a Christmas lunch for 1000 guests in the Dorchester. In 1970, the trade journal *Construction News* listed some of the celebrities at the lunch and mischievously pointed out that while the party was in progress it would be "virtually impossible to get a Cabinet quorum". In later years, the annual McAlpine beano was a cocktail party of mammoth proportions — 1400 invitees in 1989 — at the McAlpine-built and owned Hotel Inter-Continental, every November. These were only the most visible of a seemingly endless succession of social events.

McAlpine would give monthly lunches, the prize exhibit at which wold be a cabinet minister to whom the other 20 or so guests were encouraged to put questions and opinions. Sir Peter Hall, then of the National Theatre, a guest at one of the Dorchester lunches, reported: "I must have heard people offering to 'have a word with' someone at least eight times as a solution to some problem or other". Clearly, the guests at the parties were expected both to enjoy themselves and to make themselves useful.

This systematic hob-nobbing with the powerful, and with the "Great and Good" of the British establishment, can be seen either as sensible use of one's contacts or as taking unfair advantage of the "old boy" network, depending on your point of view. Construction-industry rivals of the McAlpines were sometimes heard to allege that their planning applications went through unnaturally smoothly, for instance. But even if this were so, it would be unrealistic to expect industrialists to abstain from trying to use their influence out of a sense of fairness to their competitors. Favouritism in public life reflects not so much on the favoured but on those who abuse their positions of responsibility.

Newarthill, the holding company which owns Sir Robert McAlpine, went public in 1978. McAlpine became a director and the family retained control: it was recently reported that the majority shareholding was divided among 18 family members and 13 family trusts.

For recreation — it was not one of his more successful investments — McAlpine bred race-horses. A member of the Jockey Club, and a well-known figure on the racing field, he owned and bred horses under both sets of rules: that is, for flat racing and steeplechasing. He had his own stud in Oxfordshire, near his home in Henley-on-Thames, and employed four trainers. But despite some high points, such as winning the Erroll Stakes at Ascot in 1962, he never in all his 40 years of racing won any of the classic events for three-year-olds (the Derby, Oaks, One Thousand Guineas, Two Thousand Guineas or St Leger).

He was made a life peer in 1980 and subsequently inherited his ancestral title on the death of his older brother. He and his family were and are staunch supporters of the Conservative Party. In his work and leisure pursuits McAlpine cannot be described otherwise than as a pillar of the Establishment. But even those acquaintances who did not particularly admire what he stood for remember him as a charming, generous man of great personal integrity.

Born Robert Edwin McAlpine. **Parents** William Hepburn, chairman, Sir Robert McAlpine and Sons, and Margaret (Donnison) McAlpine. **Marriages** 1) Ella Mary Gardner Garnett, 1930 (died 1987); 2) Nancy Hooper, 1988. **Children** Three sons and one daughter, oldest son, William. **Education** Oundle School, Peterborough, 1925. **Career** Sir Robert McAlpine and Sons, 1925, partner, 1928 onwards, later director and chairman; chairman, Development Securities; director, Newarthill, 1978 onwards; chairman, Greycoat London Estates, Limited, 1978 onwards. **Related activities** Deputy chairman, Nuclear Power Plant Company, 1955, chairman, 1959; deputy chairman, Nuclear Power Group, 1959, chairman, 1966–75; deputy chairman, British Nuclear Associates, 1973 onwards. **Other activities** Racehorse breeder and owner; farmer. **Offices and memberships** Chairman of the trustees, Apprentice School Charitable Trust, 1980 onwards; member, Jockey Club; vice-president, National Children's Home, 1986 onwards. **Awards and honours** Knighted, 1963; created life peer, Baron McAlpine of Moffat, 1980; inherited family baronetcy, 1983. **Constructions** (include) Shell Centre, London; National Theatre, London; nuclear power stations: Bardwell, Dungeness, Oldbury-on-Severn, Hinckley "B", Hunterson "B", Inverkip, Scotland, Latina, Italy. **Cause of death** Undisclosed, at age 82. **Further reading** Tony Hall, *Nuclear Politics,* 1986; David Morrell, *Indictment: Power and Politics in the Construction Industry,* 1987.

DREW MIDDLETON

American Journalist

***Born* New York, 14 October 1913**

***Died* Manhattan, New York, 10 January 1990**

In nearly half a century of reporting, mostly for *The New York Times,* Drew Middleton observed the comings and goings of "presidents and prime ministers, monarchs and mountebanks, heroes and rogues", as he wrote in his memoirs. "In all stages of sobriety and sanity", he added. Lumped together, they formed part of what he called "the huge, changing kaleidoscopic world of international affairs."

It is as a war correspondent during World War II, however, that Middleton is best remembered. From the beginning of the conflict until its end he covered the ebb and flow of battle in North Africa and in western Europe, sometimes with the Allied Forces on foot, sometimes from the nose of a bomber, or again from a landing craft under shell-fire off the Normandy coast. His reports earned him the respect of colleagues and the confidence of such wartime leaders as Dwight D. Eisenhower and Winston Churchill.

In his memoirs he describes hearing Churchill being "brutally frank about the situation in the Far East and the Middle East" at a bleak moment in the war. But then, Middleton recalled, "As I rose to go, he said: 'Do not be downcast. My experience is that the spirit of free men can overcome all.'"

Drew Middleton was born in New York of a family which, on his mother's side, had links with a famous American theatrical clan. John Drew Barrymore, the stage and screen actor, was its most notable member. Educated in Manhattan and in South Orange, New Jersey, Middleton graduated from Syracuse University, where he distinguished himself as a sports writer on the campus newspaper. After graduating, he took up reporting and sports writing professionally, and soon came to the notice of the Associated Press, which hired him and sent to London in 1939. He had no opportunity to cover sporting events abroad, for in September that year Hitler invaded Poland.

Meanwhile, on his first night in London, Middleton had wandered into a pub off Oxford Street. "Like most Americans," he wrote, "I had been brought up on the myth that all Englishmen are aloof, monosyllabic, cold to strangers." This chance pub encounter was to change all of his preconceived notions. Far from being cold and aloof his fellow convives drew him into a furious argument over the relative merits of rival soccer teams. It was the beginning of what was to be a lifetime love affair with Britain.

Press colleagues at first didn't know what to make of the chubby pipe-smoker who had joined their ranks, though some were inclined to disapprove of his prankishness. For example, his penchant for pretending to light cigars with five-pound notes in front of awe-stricken RAF pilots was held to be a menace to Anglo-American relations. In time he settled down, and proved his worth as a reporter.

Middleton never lost his fear of the bombing raids over London, as he confessed. On the night of 25 September 1940, he was bedded down in the basement of the Associated Press building when the whiz-z-z of a falling bomb followed by the wham of its explosion bounced him off his cot. "Fire flared in the street", he wrote, "...lighting up a crater eighteen feet by thirty...I stumbled through streets littered with broken glass." Although it became a familiar experience the Blitz never lost its terror.

Middleton was not lacking in pluck, however, when in August 1942 he accompanied the ill-fated commando raid on Dieppe. The motor launch he was aboard had its quota of reserves as well as pressmen, and was continually bombed and strafed. Middleton's comment: "It's no fun shooting back with a pencil when you look like any other commando to the Germans." His coverage of the Dieppe raid earned him an invitation to join *The New York Times,* which he promptly accepted.

October 1942 found Middleton aboard a US Navy transport bound for Africa, where the Allies were about to open a second front. In Algiers Middleton noted General de Gaulle's popularity and picked him as the likely winner of the Free French stakes as opposed to General Giraud, whom the US State Department was backing. This perspicacity earned Middleton kudos as a sharp political observer.

Occasionally his reportage took on a poetic quality as when harking back to the American Civil War, he described a Tunisian battlefield thus: "You can follow the path of those soldiers through the wheat as you could follow the path of Pickett's charge through the summer wheat at

Gettysburg." But mostly his was the hard-hitting prose of a generation inspired by Ernest Hemingway. "Machine-gun fire swept the streets", he wrote of the Allied capture of Aachen in 1944. "Bullets hit the walls of our house and whispered as they ricocheted."

Middleton's posting, in 1946, to the *Times*'s bureau in Moscow lasted a year, the Russians having refused him permission to return at the end of that time. "He must have done a good job there", a colleague commented. He then spent seven years in Bonn, where he was never happy, being out of sympathy with Konrad Adenauer's Germany.

In 1953 his lifetime's ambition was fulfilled when he was made chief of *The New York Times*'s London bureau. Middleton arrived in Britain during what he called "the Soft Twilight of Empire", meaning the period when Britain, having lost an empire, had yet to find a post-war role.

The London to which he returned was totally unlike the one he had known during the Blitz. As he noted sadly, "the British proletarian has developed tastes in food, amusement, clothing and living conditions that...are not far apart from those of his American counter-part."

If Brits now wore American-style jeans Middleton still had his suits tailored in Savile Row. A lover of British-style club life, he joined the Beefsteak and Garrick. The decade ending in 1963 marked the happiest days of his life abroad, he later claimed.

After the London assignment Middleton served as European correspondent covering everything from the North Atlantic Treaty Organization to the European Economic Community in Brussels. Returning to the United States in 1970 he became the *New York Times*'s military correspondent until his retirement in 1984.

Middleton remained thoroughly American, although his British ties were deep-rooted. In March 1942 he had taken time out from the Tunisian battlefront to come to London and to marry Winifred Estelle Mansel-Edwards (known to her friends as "Stevie"), the daughter of the chief of the Welsh Home Guard, thus adding to those ties. He prized the Order of the British Empire, of which he was made an honorary Commander in 1985, as much as he did the United States Medal of Freedom, which was likewise conferred on him.

Middleton was never happier than when he dropped in at the Garrick to drink with a crony, unless it was when he was invited to take tea at Buckingham Palace, an occasion which caused his colleagues to refer to him with a smile as "Sir Drew". In both his native and his adopted country Drew Middleton was acknowledged by those who knew him to be a gentleman in a profession where gentlemen do not often succeed.

Born Drew Middleton. **Parents** Elmer Thomas, businessman, and Jean (Drew) Middleton. **Marriage** Winifred Estelle Mansel-Edwards, 1942. **Children** One daughter, Judith. **Education** Columbia High School, South Orange, New Jersey, 1931; Syracuse University, New York, BS in journalism, 1935. **Career** Sports editor, *Eagle News,* Poughkeepsie, New York, 1936; reporter, *Poughkeepsie Evening Star,* 1936–37; sports writer, Associated Press, New York Office, 1939; war correspondent: attached to British Expeditionary Force, France, Belgium, 1939–40, to Royal Air Force, British Home Army, 1940–41, to United States Army as correspondent in Iceland, 1941–42, to Allied Forces, London, 1942; staff member, *The New York Times,* London, 1942; correspondent in Tunisia, Algeria, Mediterranean area and Allied Headquarters, Algiers, 1942–43; with United States 8th Air Force and Royal Air Force Bomber Command, 1943–44; accredited, United States First Army and Supreme Headquarters, Allied Expeditionary Force, 1944–45; at Frankfurt, Berlin and International Military Tribunal trials, Nürenberg, Germany, 1945–46; chief correspondent, *The New York Times,* 1946–84: to Union of Soviet Socialist Republics, 1946–47, Germany, 1947–53, London, 1953–63, Paris, 1963–65, United Nations, 1965–68, European affairs correspondent, 1968–70, military correspondent, 1970–84; twice-weekly columnist, special feature writer, *The New York Times,* 1984 onwards. **Offices and memberships** Member: Delta Upsilon, Phi Kappa Alpha. **Awards and honours** International

News Service Medal for Dieppe coverage, 1942; Headliners Club Award for best foreign correspondent, North African campaign, 1943; United States Navy Certificate of Merit, 1945; United States Medal of Freedom, 1948; Order of the British Empire, military division, 1947; honorary life member, Garrick Club, 1981; honorary Commander of the Order of the British Empire, 1985. **Publications** *Our Share of Night,* 1946; *The Struggle for Germany,* 1949; *The Defense of Western Europe,* 1952; *These Are the British,* 1957; *The Sky Suspended,* 1960; *The Supreme Choice,* 1963; *The Atlantic Community,* 1965; *Retreat from Victory,* 1973; *Where Has Last July Gone?,* 1974; *Can America Win the Next War,* 1975; *Submarine,* 1976; *The Duel of the Giants: China and Russia in Asia,* 1978; *Crossroads of Moden Warfare,* 1983; (with Gene Brown) *Southeast Asia,* 1985. **Cause of death** Undisclosed, at age 76.

LEWIS MUMFORD

American Architectural, Social and Literary Critic and Writer

Born **Long Island, New York, 19 October 1895**

Died **Amenia, New York, 26 January 1990**

> The curse of all great cities is the quantity of everything they have to contain, from people to cars. Cars should be cleared away from city centers and the space they devour should be restored to public transport...We desperately need those trains and buses. We also need cheap small taxis. Because it is now a simple matter to build 35-storey buildings, we have to have them, although they are wholly without justification, are really there for prestige or capital gain — for anything, in fact, but a practical purpose.

A timely critique indeed on the congested cities of the 1990s, the world over; but it wasn't voiced in 1990, nor even in the 1980s. These words were written 30 years ago by Lewis Mumford, visionary of the city of the future and town planner *extraordinaire.*

Mumford was fascinated by cities. According to one of his disciples, Brendan Gill, "If one were obliged to reduce his books to a single sentence, it might be 'The city is civilization.'" Yet Mumford was also a vociferous critic of modern cities during a period of uncontrolled urban expansion all over the globe.

He was born in that most metropolitan of cities — New York — the illegitimate son of a lawyer, and grew up in modest circumstances on the West Side. By the time he reached high school, he was showing signs of an independent mind — "my interest widened and my marks worsened", he recalled in later years. He attended New York City College, then Columbia University and the New School for Social Research. He thought of becoming an engineer; he wrote a few unproduced plays, and he began his literary career at the age of 19 with a contribution to *Forum* magazine.

During World War I he was a Navy radio operator. He became associate editor of the *Fortnightly Dial,* then acting editor of the *Sociological Review* in London, and co-editor of *American Caravan,* an annual publication which attempted to give a broad perspective of contemporary American writing. In 1925 he lectured on American literature and in 1929 on sociology at the Geneva School in International Studies and from 1930 to 1939 was visiting lecturer at Dartmouth College.

But the event which was to be the major influence on all his subsequent thinking took place in 1915; he came across the writings of Patrick Geddes. Geddes was a Scottish town planner, geographer, scientist, sociologist and educationist. He was idealistic to the point of Utopianism, he was determined to break the bounds of individual disciplines and he promoted the concept of regional planning — of viewing the city within its wider context. Mumford resembled his hero in more than his ideas about planning. As Mumford's obituarist in the London *Times* remarked, "He had the same darting imagination, with flashes of humour, and the same capacity for seeing relationships in facts of history that are not obviously connected." Even the title of his first book, *The Story of Utopias,* published in 1922, reflects his debt to Geddes.

Mumford also wrote for the *Journal of the American Institute of Architects,* then a focus for concern about the housing crisis in America. His reading on this subject led him to the British concept of the garden city. This seemed to him, and to other similar thinkers, an answer to New York's problems. If the city was to flourish it could not be allowed to get any bigger; future growth should be diverted to satellite towns with low-rise housing, instead of "clinging to the sardonic funeral towers of metropolitan finance" — producing what he called "subtopia" around dying central districts.

In 1923 he and his colleagues formed the Regional Planning Association of America. Their efforts led to the development of Sunnyside Gardens, an experimental housing project in Queens, just across the East River from Manhattan. In line with Mumford's theories, this was a mixed-income, high density garden suburb. He and his wife lived there for ten years.

Mumford's early books included perceptive literary and art criticism such as *The Brown Decades* which encouraged Americans to re-evaluate their painting and architecture of the post-Civil-War period. He also — again looking to the past — wrote a book about Herman Melville.

In 1932 Mumford moved further into the public eye when he took over the "Sky Line" column on architecture in *The New Yorker.* For the next 30 years he produced some of the world's most distinguished architectural journalism. *Technics and Civilization,* published in 1934, was the first of his books to attract world-wide interest. In it he focused on one of his enduring themes — the role of the machine. In his appreciation of the dehumanizing and tyrannical consequences of machine worship, Mumford was very much a product of his time, of the industrial economy into which he was born and which was so powerful and persuasive. He was also a product of his past: American Utopian thinkers from Emerson on have been drawn to the idea of the city and mechanization and its impact on the nation, with a fascinated ambivalence. In this book Mumford argues, as Emerson did a century before, for acceptance of the machine, for humanistic instead of profit-making reasons. "Its ultimate aim", he declared, "is leisure — that is, the release of other organic capacities."

In 1938 he published *The Culture of Cities,* an encyclopaedic work surveying the history of civilization as represented by the development of the city. Following Geddes, he advocated planning policies based on the region rather than the metropolis. These included the creation of a permanent green belt, together with new towns within the larger urban region.

Mumford's approach to planning and architecture was, above all, a humanist's approach. For him, buildings, like cities themselves, were of interest as expressions of human societies and ideals; and he saw how science and technology were creating "a uniform, all-enveloping super planetary super structure, designed for automatic operation." So he loathed architect Le Corbusier for his "technological fetishism", preferring designs which — in two of his favourite terms — had "biological vitality" and were on a "human scale". His own description of his visit to the ancient Italian town of Pompeii, brings vividly to life his Utopian vision of a metropolis constructed not for the creation of wealth but for the benefit of its inhabitants:

> When one considers the amount of space and fine building given to Pompeii's temples, its markets, its law courts, its stadium, its handsome theater, all conceived and built on the human scale, with great nobility of form, one realizes that American towns far more wealthy

and populous than Pompeii do not, except in very rare cases, have anything like this kind of civic equipment, even in makeshift form...

Profoundly American as he was, Mumford was European in his concern with urban life and historical continuity. He was a frequent visitor to Britain and took a beneficial interest in town planning there. In 1965 he was consulted over the long-running saga over the proposal for a ring road which would run through Christ Church Meadow, Oxford. His advice was categorical: the road might be "a final solution for Oxford in the sense that Hitler's extermination policy was called a final solution for the Jews."

For although at first Mumford was interested in the landscaping of new roads and bridges, he soon became an early critic of remorseless motorway building. In 1943 he complained, prophetically, that "express highways would be admirable if they were related to anything except the desire, on the part of the more prosperous, to get out of New York as fast as possible; actually, their function is to increase the planless decentralization of the metropolis and thereby pile up such a load of decaying properties in the centre as to hasten the final exodus."

In 1961, when he was awarded the Royal Gold Medal for Architecture at the Royal Institute of British Architects, the message in his acceptance speech was much the same. He spoke of how subservience to the private car had destroyed American cities and warned, "One must render to the machine only what belongs to the machine and render to Man all that belongs to Man."

During all these years he continued to write prolifically. Although *Technics and Civilization* and *The Culture of Cities* remain the books for which he is likely to be most widely remembered, he produced, in all, more than 30 volumes, including *The City in History* for which he received the National Book Award in 1961 and which one critic has described as a masterly fusion of "historical narrative with propaganda for the great movement for socialized planning in which he played so articulate a part."

His attack on the dominance of the machine continued unabated. As he put it in *Art and Technics* in 1952: "If you fall in love with a machine there is something wrong with your love life. If you worship a machine there is something wrong with your religion."

Mumford also widened his attack to include new technological threats to humanity. His critique of the motor car ("this piece of defective rolling stock"), extended to supersonic aeroplanes. He had always deplored what he saw as the tendency of people in the West to separate themselves from nature and from their primitive instincts; now he saw the ultimate development of these destructive tendencies in the centralized, post-war, nuclear superpower. Of nuclear weapons he wrote, "until we have controlled these weapons nothing else will matter".

But he was, at the last, a Utopian and an optimist (in true Emersonian mould) about the resourcefulness of the human spirit. "For those of us who have thrown off the myth of the machine, the next move is ours: for the gates of the technocratic prison will open automatically, despite their ancient rusty hinges, as soon as we choose to walk out."

He did not underestimate the profound changes which would have to take place. In one of his last books, *The Pentagon of Power,* he warned that "reformers who would treat the campaign against environmental and human degradation solely in terms of improved technological facilities, like the reduction of gasoline in motor cars, see only a small part of the problem. Nothing less than a profound reorientation of our vaunted technological 'way of life' will save this planet from becoming a lifeless desert."

Mumford's criticisms of uncontrolled urban growth and unco-ordinated traffic planning are as pertinent today as when he wrote them and contain as valid a message for the future as they ever did. But, while he warned of the dangers of dependence on technology, he also envisaged man becoming master of the machine. Or as Brendan Gill puts it: "Robert Frost wrote, 'I had a lover's quarrel with the world,' and so, indefatigably, did Mumford." Perhaps that statement, too, contains a — more hopeful — message for our future.

Born Lewis Mumford. **Parents** Lewis, lawyer, and Elvina Conradina (Baron), housekeeper, Mumford. **Marriage** Sophia Wittenberg, 1921. **Children** Geddes (killed in action 1944) and Alison. **Education** Stuyvesant Technical High School, New York, 1909–12; City College of New York, 1912–17; Columbia University, New York, 1915–16; New School for Social Research, New York, 1919. **Military service** United States Navy, radio electrician, second class, 1918–19. **Career** Investigator, dress and waist industry, 1916; laboratory assistant, United States Bureau of Standards, New York, 1917; special investigator, New York Housing and Planning Commission, 1924; lecturer: New School for Social Research, 1925, Geneva School of International Studies, 1925, 1929; visiting professor, Dartmouth College, Hanover, New Hampshire, 1929–35; lecturer, Columbia University, 1931–35; professor, Stanford University, California, 1942–44; Earle Lecturer, Pacific Institute of Religion, 1947; visiting professor, North Carolina State University, Raleigh, 1948–52; Bampton Lecturer, Columbia University, 1951; professor of city planning, University of Pennsylvania, Philadelphia, 1951–56, Ford Professor, 1959–61; visiting professor: Massachusetts Institute of Technology, Cambridge, 1957–61, University of California, Berkeley, 1961–62; Saposnekow Lecturer, City College of New York, 1962; senior fellow, Wesleyan University Center for Advance Studies, Middletown, Connecticut, 1962–64; visiting lecturer, Massachusetts Institute of Technology, 1973–74, Charles Abrams Professor, 1975. **Related activities** Associate editor, *Fortnightly Dial,* 1919; acting editor, *Sociological Review,* London, 1920; contributing editor, *New Republic,* 1927–40; columnist, "The Sky Line", *The New Yorker,* 1932; member, Board of Higher Education, New York, 1935–37; member, American Council on Education Commission on Teacher Education, 1938–44. **Offices and memberships** Founder member, Regional Planning Association of America, 1923; vice-president, Société Européenne de Culture; member, American Academy of Arts and Sciences; member, American Academy of Arts and Letters, president, 1963–65. **Awards and honours** Guggenheim fellowship: 1932, 1938, 1956; Townsend Harris Medal, 1939; honorary fellow, Stanford University, 1941; honorary associate, Royal Institute of British Architects, 1942, fellow; Ebenezer Howard Memorial Medal, 1946; honorary member: Town Planning Institute, 1946, American Institute of Planners, 1955, Town Planning Institute of Canada, 1960, American Institute of Architects, Colegio del Arquitectas del Peru; Fairmount Park Art Association Medal of Honour, 1953; Town Planning Institute Gold Medal, 1957; honorary member, Phi Beta Kappa, 1957; Royal Gold Medal, Royal Institute of British Architects 1961; Award of Merit, American Institute of Architects, 1962; National Book Award, 1962; Medal of Freedom, 1964; Silver Medal, American Society of Planning Officials, 1965; Emerson-Thoreau Medal, 1965; LLD, University of Edinburgh, 1965; Kaufman International Design Award, 1965; Doctor of Architecture, University of Rome, 1967; Leonardo da Vinci Medal, Society for the History of Technology, 1969; Gold Medal, American Academy, 1970; Hodgkins Medal, Smithsonian Institution, 1971; Thomas Jefferson Memorial Foundation Medal, 1972; National Medal for Literature, 1972; honorary Knight Commander of the Order of the British Empire, 1975; Prix Mondial del Duca, 1976. **Publications — Planning and social and literary criticism** *The Story of Utopias,* 1922, *Sticks and Stones: A Study of American Architecture and Civilisation,* 1924; *Aesthetics: A Dialogue,* 1925; *The Golden Day: A Study in American Experience and Culture,* 1926, also published as *The Golden Day: A Study in American Literature and Culture,* 1933; *Architecture,* 1926; *American Taste,* 1929; *Herman Melville,* 1929, revised edition published as *Herman Melville: A Study of His Life,* 1963; *The Brown Decades: A Study of the Arts in America 1865–1895,* 1931; *Technics and Civilization,* 1934; *Whither Honolulu?,* 1938; *The Culture of Cities,* 1938; *Men Must Act,* 1939; *Regional Planning in the Pacific Northwest: A Memorandum,* 1939; *Faith for Living,* 1941; *The South in Architecture,* 1941; (with Herbert Agar and Frank Kingdon) *World-Wide Civil War,* 1942; *The School of Humanities: A Description,* 1942; *New World Theme,* 1943; *The Social Foundations of Post-War Building,* 1943; *The Condition of Man,* 1944; *The Plan of London County,* 1945; *City*

Development: Studies in Disintegration and Renewal, 1945; *Values for Survival: Essays, Addresses, and Letters on Politics and Education,* 1946, also published as *Programme for Survival,* 1946; *Atomic War — The Way Out,* 1948; *Man as Interpreter,* 1950; *The Conduct of Life,* 1951; *Art and Technics,* 1952; *Towards a Free World: Long-Range Planning under Democratic Control,* 1952; *In the Name of Sanity,* 1954; *The Human Prospect,* edited by Harry T. Moore and Karl W. Deutsch, 1955; *From the Ground Up: Observations on Contemporary Architecture, Housing, Highway Building, and Civic Design,* 1956; *The Transformation of Man,* 1956; *The Human Way Out,* 1958; *The Role of the Creative Arts in Contemporary Society,* 1958; *The City in History: Its Origins, Its Transformations, and Its Prospects,* 1961; *Social Responsibility in the Business Community,* 1961; *The Highway and the City,* 1964; *Myth of the Machine:* 1. *Technics and Human Development,* 1967, 2. *The Pentagon of Power,* 1971; *The Urban Prospect,* 1968; *Interpretations and Forecasts 1922–1972: Studies in Literature, History, Biography, Technics, and Contemporary Society,* 1973; *Architecture as a Home for Man: Essays for "Architectural Record",* edited by Jeanne M. Davern, 1975; *The Lewis Mumford Reader,* 1986. **Other publications** *Thomas Beer, Aristocrat of Letters,* 1944; *Green Memories: The Story of Geddes Mumford,* 1947; *The Van Wyck Brooks-Lewis Mumford Letters: The Record of a Literary Friendship,* 1970; *The Letters of Lewis Mumford and Frederic J. Osborn: A Transatlantic Dialogue,* edited by Michael R. Hughes, 1971, also published as *Lewis Mumford and Frederic J. Osborn: A Transatlantic Dialogue,* 1972; *Findings and Keepings 1914–1936 (Analects for an Autobiography),* 1975; *My Works and Days: A Personal Chronicle 1895–1975,* 1979; *Sketches of Life: The Autobiography of Lewis Mumford: The Early Years,* 1982; freelance contributor to many magazines and journals. **Publications as editor** (With others) *The American Caravan: A Yearbook of American Literature* and *The Second* and *The New American Caravan, American Caravan IV,* and *The New Caravan,* five volumes, 1927–36; *America and Alfred Stieglitz: A Collective Portrait,* 1934; *Roots of Contemporary American Architecture,* 1952; *Essays and Journals* by Ralph Waldo Emerson, 1968; *The Ecological Basis of Planning,* by Artur Glikson, 1971. **Cause of death** Undisclosed, at age 94. **Further reading** Elmer S. Newman, *Lewis Mumford: A Bibliography 1914–1970,* 1971; David R. Conran, *Education for Transformation: Implications of Lewis Mumford's Ecohumanism,* 1976; *Thinkers of the Twentieth Century,* 1987; Donald Miller, *Lewis Mumford: A Life,* 1989.

BRONKO NAGURSKI

Canadian Football Player

***Born* Rainy River, Canada, 3 November 1908**

***Died* International Falls, Minnesota,7 January 1990**

One of the first genuine stars of the gridiron game, Bronko Nagurski played with a fearful combination of power and aggression. At 6 feet, 2 inches, the 225-pounder might not appear to be an imposing athlete by today's standards, but in the mid 1930s, his bullish appetite for the game introduced a whole new meaning to the phrase "power play". "I was a straight downfield runner. I wouldn't, or couldn't dodge anybody", admitted this charter member of the Pro Football Hall of Fame. "If somebody got in my way, I ran through them."

The crowds and the commentators of that time loved him for his bullishness; and tales about his legendary size and bone-crunching power entered the archives of the game. Folklore has it, for instance, that he was "discovered" in 1925 by Minnesota coach Clarence "Doc" Spears, who drove past a farm and noticed a muscular young man ploughing a field...without a horse. When Spears stopped on the pretence of asking for directions, he was amazed to see Nagurski use the plough to point him in the right direction.

Another favourite tale about Nagurski centres on a day when he was playing for the Chicago Bears. The crowd had spilled onto the field, near to the goal line, and were being controlled by mounted police, when Nagurski crashed into and through the end zone with such force, it is said, that he knocked over one of the horses and its rider.

Born to Ukrainian parents in Rainy River, Ontario, Nagurski grew up in International Falls, where his very first schoolteacher presented him with the nickname of "Bronko" after being unable to understand his mother's pronunciation of his first name.

Football came naturally to Nagurski. He not only became a three-time all-American during his three-year spell at the University of Minnesota, but was also the only player to be honoured as an all-American at two positions in one season: defensive tackle and full back.

Rumours of his outstanding prowess travelled quickly into the professional leagues — helped, no doubt, by the stories which spread about him breaking three ribs in one match, only to return the next day to play tackle. He was duly signed by George Halas in 1930, to join the famous Red Grange in the Chicago Bears' backfield.

Together, they helped the team to win the championships of 1932 and 1933. The following season, Nagurski took on the role of blocking back for Beatle Feathers who, in turn, was able to rush for 1004 yards to become the first NFL back to surpass 1000 yards. In his nine seasons in the NFL, Nagurski was voted All Pro three times, and gained 2778 yards rushing. There were few things he could not do — and did not do — on the football field; and as if to emphasize that fact, in his first game for the Bears, he even threw two touchdown passes against the New York Giants.

He retired from football in 1937, supposedly because Bears' George Halas did not offer him enough money. In a 1972 interview, Nagurski reflected, "We used to say Coach Halas tossed nickels around like they were manhole covers. People told me I could get into wrestling and make millions. I did it for about 12-14 years. It was tough work, and I didn't make millions."

Despite being rejected for military service because of damage to his knees and ankles, Nagurski did spend many years as a professional wrestler. Eventually, he returned for one more season, in 1943, as a defensive tackle with the Bears, helping them to win the championship again.

He wrestled until 1960 when, losing interest altogether in football, and finding movement increasingly painful, he became a virtual recluse, spending his time fishing, gardening or watching television. "I want people to remember the way I was, and not the way I am", he said. And in many respects, he got his wish. For it is tales of his powerhouse play in the NFL which are remembeed and still told to this day.

There's the tale about a scoring run he made for the Bears at Wrigley Field when, on a touchdown gallop, he sent two linebackers flying in opposite directions, stomped over a defending halfback, crashed into an interfering safety man, rebounded off the goalposts and finally smacked into the stadium's brick wall. On returning to the huddle, he simply reported: "That last guy hit me awfully hard."

Born Bronislau Nagurski. **Children** Four sons and two daughters. **Education** University of Minnesota, Minneapolis, 1927–29. **Career** All American, University of Minnesota, 1927–29; full back, Chicago Bears, 1930–37, defensive tackle, 1943; professional wrestler, 1937–1960; also, petrol station operator, 1937 onwards. **Awards and honours** Charter member, Pro Football Hall of Fame, 1963. **Cause of death** Undisclosed, at age 81.

LAURENCE PETER

Canadian Educationist

***Born* Vancouver, Canada, 16 September 1919**

***Died* Palos Verdes, California, 12 January 1990**

Laurence Peter achieved eponymity in his own lifetime, when the Peter Principle moved into the English language alongside Parkinson's and Murphy's laws. He formulated what the London *Times* described as "The melancholy doctrine of the inevitability of incompetence in human affairs". And his determined anti-meliorism ensured him financial security.

He was born in 1919, to a poor family in Vancouver. "We cut wood out of the bush to give us fuel and grew most of our food in the garden", he once told an interviewer. Peter sought an academic career, and worked his way through college before becoming a teacher in the Canadian public school system. Having earned a doctorate in education from Washington State College, he taught at the universities of British Columbia and Southern California. It was while teaching at the latter that he produced his notable bit of mischief, *The Peter Principle,* subtitled *Why Things Always Go Wrong.* (The book was co-written with Raymond Hull, a British-born freelance writer.) At first it lived up to its name. McGraw Hill, who had previously published a textbook by Peter, declined to take on this one: "I can foresee no commercial possibilities for such a book and can consequently offer no encouragement", wrote the editor. Thirty publishers and 30 more rejection slips later, William Morrow paid 2500 dollars for the manuscript and ordered a 10,000-copy run.

The central contention of the Peter Principle is that "In a hierarchy every employee tends to rise to his level of incompetence." The average employee's reward for a job well done is routine promotion. This is fine until eventually, inevitably, that employee reaches a level beyond his or her competence. Here, in a job he or she cannot cope with, the employee becomes defensive, obstructive and a menace to the organization. So, logically, every bureaucracy is made up almost entirely of people inadequate for their posts. To use another Peter apophthegm, "the cream rises until it sours", or again, "In every thriving organization there is a considerable accumulation of dead wood at executive level." He went on to catalogue the symptoms — ulcers, allergies, alcoholism and Tabulatory Gigantism (who's got the larger desk?). In his analysis, the big corporations were by no means alone in their susceptibility to the Peter Principle. The author's beady eye found it operating in school systems, government agencies, churches and political parties. It was in short "the key to the whole structure of civilization". Something less than complete conviction might have been detected when its comprehensive application was extended to that oddly resonant twentieth-century phenomenon, the lost sock in the laundrette. And Peter did say, eventually, that he was only kidding.

The world he satirized could not get enough. One print run followed another, as, 15 weeks after its first publication, the book appeared in the *New York Times* non-fiction best-seller list. It stayed there for 33 consecutive weeks, 20 of them at the top. Success in many other countries followed, and at the last count, the book has been translated into 38 languages. It is estimated that world-wide sales exceed ten million copies. The corporations came forward with many job offers, but Peter refused them. He didn't want to test his theory that closely.

He had other, idiosyncratic, fish to fry. These included the No Bull Peace Prize ("Because the Nobel Peace Prize keeps being awarded to people who have really nothing to do with peace"), and the Peter University. Established in his garage, the "university" dispensed the degree Doctor of Competence. On receiving his, Buckminster Fuller said it was the academic award he'd been awaiting all his life; a City of London gardener who was similarly honoured for his one-man campaign against dog-dirt on the streets has apparently recorded no comment.

Though troubled by illness, Peter produced eleven more books, including the four-volume study *Competencies for Teaching: Systems of Accountability for Teacher Education,* and several other Peter plans and prescriptions. These dwell further on how things go wrong, and offer to put them right. He also co-wrote *The Laughter Prescription* with the humorist Bill Dana. By this time, he was living in a suburb of Palos Verdes where, he thought, many of his neighbours regarded Ronald Reagan as a Communist agent.

Britain excited Peter's gloomy prognoses — he discovered a public transport system which refused to stop in case it fell behind schedule — as did his native Canada. ("The chief national characteristic is dullness", he declared of his homeland.) Towards the end of his life, he was receiving enquiries about his work from China and the USSR. The Peter Principle, we may infer, is ideology-proof.

Born Laurence Johnston Peter. **Marriage** Irene Howe, 1967. **Children** John, Edward, Margaret and Alice. **Education** Western Washington State College, BA, 1957, MA in education, 1958; Washington State College, PhD, 1963. **Career** Teacher, Vancouver; psychologist; assistant professor, University of British Columbia; professor of education, University of Southern California, 1966–70; first publication, *Prescriptive Teaching.* **Related activities** Founder, Peter University. **Publications** *Prescriptive Teaching;* (with Raymond Hull) *The Peter Principle: Why Things Always Go Wrong,* 1969; *The Peter Prescription,* 1972; *The Peter Plan,* 1975; *Peter's Quotations,* 1977; *Peter's People,* 1980; *Peter's Almanac,* 1982; (with Bill Dana) *The Laughter Prescription,* 1982; *Why Things Go Wrong,* 1985; *The Peter Pyramid: Or Will We Ever Get The Point?,* 1986; *Competencies for Teaching: Systems of Accountability for Teacher Education.* **Cause of death** Complications after a stroke suffered in 1988, at age 70.

LIEUTENANT-GENERAL SAMUEL PHILLIPS

American Aviator and Space Flight Administrator

***Born* Springerville, Arizona, 19 February 1921**

***Died* Los Angeles, California, 31 January 1990**

No technical achievement this century has so excited and astonished the world as landing man on the moon in July 1969. There had been previous marvels in space flights: the launching of satellites, men orbiting the earth, space vehicles docking and a flight round the moon and back, but this culminating achievement was visible as well as extraordinary. Around the world people could look up at the bright, full moon, and accept the incredible fact that men in strange, inflated space suits were moving in slow, bouncy motion on its fine powdery surface. They could accept it because they were also able to see it on television.

The technical achievement was stupendous, but although the astronauts themselves became household names, the ranks of designers, scientists, engineers and technicians who formed the team which accomplished the remarkable feat were mainly anonymous. And few could have given the name of, or had even heard of, the team leader who controlled the whole enterprise, the director of NASA's Apollo Space Program. In fact it was Lieutenant-General Sam Phillips.

Although born in Arizona, Phillips grew up in Cheyenne, Wyoming. While still at high school, he spent much of his spare time at the CAA (Civil Aeronautics Authority) radio station, based at Cheyenne Airport. As he later recalled in conversation, "I got to know the people, and they educated and trained me I guess in radio. And I wound up learning a lot and becoming progressively more interested and through that became interested in airplanes." He obtained his commercial radio licence at this time, and never let it lapse. He continued to spend time at Cheyenne Airport during his vacation breaks from studying for his BSc in electrical engineering at the University of Wyoming. During one summer, he enrolled in a flying course which was part of the Civilian Pilot Training Program, and obtained his private flying licence.

By the time he graduated, in 1943, World War II was well underway, and Phillips promptly entered the regular army as a second lieutenant, shortly transferring to the Air Corps. He joined the US 8th Air Force in England, and was involved, with the 364th Fighter Group, in combat over Europe. During that time and later, he flew almost every type of plane in the Air Force, ranging from the P-38 to the most modern jet fighters.

When the war was over he moved to European Headquarters in Frankfurt, becoming director of operations at the armament laboratory working on the B-52 bomber project. For a while he returned to his studies, this time at the University of Michigan, and after taking his Master's degree in engineering, he spent several years at Wright Patterson Air Force base in Ohio on research and development.

In 1956 he returned to England, this time as chief of logistics for the 7th Air Division of Strategic Air Command. From now on Phillips's professional interest was concentrated on missiles. Nato's missile defences were being formed, as part of the cold war, and he played an important part in its planning, as well as helping form the Anglo-American agreement by which Britain was able to use the American Thor missile.

In 1959 he was appointed director of the Minuteman Intercontinental Ballistic Missile Program, and his success in that task during the next four years marked him as suitable for a high position in the National Aeronautics and Space Administration. NASA had been set up by the US government in 1958.

He was recruited into NASA in February 1964, by which time he was a major general, by Dr George Mueller, a specialist in ballistic missiles and space probes. At the time Dr Mueller stated, "General Phillips's experience in managing the Minuteman Program for the Air Force, where he met or exceeded all program objectives including schedules and costs, brings to NASA the high qualifications necessary for carrying out the large and complex Apollo program." Wernher von Braun, the rocket designer, was to say later that it was these two men who "successfully shaped the three NASA centres involved in the lunar landing program into a team."

Phillips's task was immense. He described it as having "to oversee the design, construction and testing of flight and ground equipment, and the training of thousands of technicians; and to see that the millions of parts of Apollo come together at the right time and place." A six-footer, he wore civilian clothes and worked in his shirt-sleeves, but his bearing was always military. His was the central role, holding daily meetings, making telephone calls, or visiting plants or the contractors.

The programme was not a steady success story, for in January 1967, when the three pilots were in their Apollo 1 spacecraft simulating the launch that was to put them in orbit the following month, fire broke out, probably caused by faulty electrical equipment. Boosted by the pure oxygen atmosphere, it spread rapidly through the capsule, and the groundcrew were unable to open the hatch which could not be freed from inside. The three men died, and the whole program was set back. Phillips had to issue the report of the investigations, which was very critical of one of the contractors, and get the programme forging ahead again. His efforts were supported "from the top", as it was feared the Russians were planning their own spectacular moon landing.

By Christmas 1968 came the first circumlunar journey with Apollo 8. In May 1969 Apollo 10 was launched, and at that time Werhner von Braun publicly singled out General Phillips as the man to whom the greatest credit belonged for the achievements of the programme. The Apollo 10 lunar module, with three astronauts on board, orbited the moon, coming within ten miles of its surface.

A landing was not attempted because the radar system had not been tested in flight. After that success Phillips said to his wife, "I hope I have enough strength for Number 11."

July that year saw the culmination, the achievement that enthralled the world. The three astronauts landed the lunar module of Apollo 11 on the Sea of Tranquility, and the first man emerged, watched by television cameras, to stand on the surface. Rarely has there been such a spectacular triumph. And when the module lifted off successfully, Phillips was able to announce to the enthralled news conference, "The men and equipment that are Apollo 11 have performed to perfection." However he was honest enough to say, "In my opinion we damn near didn't make it. I think we came awfully close to having to abort."

Soon after this triumph he left the space programme to return to the Air Force, and he commanded the Space and Missile System Organization until 1972, when he became director of the National Security Agency. In 1973 he became commander of the Air Force Strategic Air Command, and he retired, a four-star general, two years later.

His retirement was not idle. The aerospace company TRW employed him as an adviser until 1986. In January 1986 came the Challenger disaster, when the American space shuttle blew up seconds after the lift-off, killing its crew of seven. NASA called Phillips back to conduct a management review and to recommend changes in the organization of the space agency. The radical overhaul that followed owed much to his expertise and experience.

When he died, NASA issued a statement which is unequivocal in its praise: "Sam Phillips was in the first rank of those who led the United States on our epic journey to the moon in the 1960s. He was also among the first to come back to NASA after the Challenger accident to lend his efforts toward renewing NASA and returning America to preeminence in space flight."

Born Samuel Cochran Phillips. **Marriage** Betty Ann. **Children** Dana, Janie and Kathleen. **Education** University of Wyoming, BSc, electrical engineering, 1942; University of Michigan, Ann Arbor, MS, electrical engineering, 1950. **Career** United States Army, lieutenant of infantry, 1942; Army Air Corps, 8th Air Force, in England, 1944–45; director of operations, European headquarters, armament laboratory, Frankfurt, 1947; staff member, Wright Patterson Air Force base, Ohio, 1950–56; chief of logistics, 7th Air Division, Strategic Air Command, 1956; director, Minuteman Intercontinental Ballistic Missile Programme, 1959–63; director, Apollo Program, National Aeronautics and Space Administration, 1964–69; commander, Space and Missile System Organization, United States Air Force, 1969–72; director, National Security Agency, defense department, 1972–73; commander, Air Force Strategic Air Command, 1973; retired as general, 1975; general manager, Energy Systems Management Division, TRW, vice-president, Defense Systems Group, 1984–86, adviser, to 1986. **Related activities** Participant, Anglo-American agreement on use of Thor ICMB; member, Committee for the Human Exploration of Space, National Research Council; chairman, management review into Challenger disaster, National Aeronautics and Space Administration, 1986, led study group to up-date report, 1988. **Offices and memberhips** Member, National Academy of Engineers. **Awards and honours** Distinguished Flying Cross; Croix de Guerre; Legion of Merit; Distinguished Service Medal, National Aeronautics and Space Administration; LLD, University of Wyoming. **Cause of death** Cancer, at age 68.

BHAGWAN SHREE RAJNEESH

Indian Guru

***Born* Kutchwara, India, 11 December 1931**

***Died* Poona, India, 19 January 1990**

"Osho — never born never died", reads the inscription carved in gold on the memorial stone in Poona of the man known to most of the world as Bhagwan Shree Rajneesh. "Sex Guru" of the 1970s, prophet of ecstasy, author of over 600 books, founder of the "orange people" and of the ill-famed Rashneeshpuram communes in Poona and Oregon, Rajneesh was also a multi-millionaire whose personal fleet of over 90 Rolls Royce cars scandalized the world almost as much as did his teachings on free love and sexual bliss.

Born the oldest son of a large family, in a small town in central India, Rajneesh began adult life as a teacher of philosophy at Jabalpur University. In 1966 he took to the road as a travelling orator and religious teacher, and in 1970 settled in Poona with seven disciples. It was at this point that he took for himself the name of Bhagwan, the Hindi word for "god".

Almost from the beginning the Bhagwan seems to have aimed the message of his "first and only religion" primarily at the West and at the affluent. His discourses in English and in Hindi became popular with western travellers and the ashram in Poona an essential stopover for seekers on the eastern trail. By the time the Indian tax authorities caught up with him in 1981, his followers claimed for the Bhagwan 10,000 disciples back home in Poona and another 20,000 around the world.

Rajneesh arrived in the United States later that year with his mother, a Rolls Royce and some 4000 energetic disciples. They bought and renovated a 164,000-acre ranch in Oregon, near the small town of Antelope, turning it, in four years, into a flourishing commune with orchards, vineyard, vegetable and fish farms, a 160-bed hotel, shopping mall, meditation centre, airport and landing strip. Visiting journalists wrote in wonder of the place, describing with some kind of awe the largely middle-class and affluent pink-robed, chanting and saintly "sannyasin" (as the disciplines called themselves), wondering what kind of New Age Utopia this really was.

The fact that the Master protected himself on his daily drives around the commune with armed guards and helicopters, that he spent much of his time watching children's television while leaving the running of the place to his secretary, Ma Anand Sheela, and that disillusioned disciples, like Hugh Milne (seven years personal secretary and bodyguard of the Bhagwan) suffered his "considerable wrath" on leaving Rashneeshpuram, seem to have escaped the notice of most of the sannyasin. The end came in 1985 when, after a series of scandals, both the Bhagwan and his secretary were arrested on a series of charges which included attempted murder, the mass poisoning of the inhabitants of Antelope, drug-smuggling and embezzlement. Ma Anand Sheela went to prison for four years. The Bhagwan, who confessed guilt to the charge of immigration fraud, was expelled from the United States with a fine and a ten-year suspended prison sentence.

Refused entry by 21 countries, the Bhagwan and his entourage finally returned to Poona where, in a rare moment of modesty, he dropped the honorific Bhagwan (or "god") for the name of Osho ("teacher" — "he on whom the heavens shower flowers"). It says something for the vitality of his movement that, within a few years, the ashram in Poona was once again a flourishing concern with some 15,000 members, all of whom believed their Master the innocent victim of an American-government-inspired campaign of lies and slander, one of the most vicious being the persistent story that Osho's continual ill-health was due to infection with Aids.

The spread of the Aids epidemic inevitably had its effect on the message of free love and eroticism preached by Rajneesh. Delighted critics wrote with glee of the new rubber-gloved and condomed approach advocated by the Master who apparently now told the disciples to wash with pure alcohol before embarking on sex. Compulsory blood tests were demanded of all visitors to the commune. Sceptics who dismissed the Bhagwan's teachings as nothing but eastern mysticism, minus the discipline, and western pop psychology with a lot of hedonism thrown in, welcomed a turn of events which seemed to confirm everything they had always said. Puritans saw it as some kind of divine retribution on the person who once boasted that he had made love to more women than any other man on earth.

Corrupt and criminal the Bhagwan may have been, and his behaviour an outrage to civilized opinion both in India and the West. It seems hard, however, to dismiss a movement which at one time or another attracted some half a million people, simply as claptrap. Like any other successful religious leader, Rajneesh evidently had a compelling and charismatic presence. The English writer Bernard Levin was moved to describe him as "the conduit along which the vital force of the universe flows". Others spoke of his hypnotic gaze which seemed to fix each of his listeners individually. Hugh Milne judged that his gift was not just that of oratory or insight but also, "an ability to convey a sense of unconditional love that was nothing short of life-changing for those who experienced it."

"I am here" Rajneesh said, "to create a million mystics in the world — that's my purpose and that's my joy and celebration." "Surrender to me and I will transform you, that is my promise" read a banner floating above his public lectures. It was a promise that touched off a chord in many who felt dissatisfied with the arid spirituality of traditional religion and with the empty materialism of western society.

"Osho believed that society's obsession with sexuality was a product of repression and a product in particular of Christianity. He taught that we were split by religious conditioning — that the body was bad and the soul was good. He wanted to get sex out of the brain and back to the genitals where it belonged", wrote one follower. Another affirmed that, "what we were looking for was not sexual licence but love, joy, freedom and an opportunity to find our own authentic being." Even the religious affairs correspondent of the *Guardian* newspaper, who stressed his distrust of all gurus, confessed that he had always found the followers of the Bhagwan "more joyful people than most" — "and none of them were fools".

In cocking a snook at established religion, Rajneesh seems to have highlighted one of its more important gaps. Healing the psycho-sexual split, bringing together the soul and the body, has now become one of the central messages of New Age theology. It is preached by Green Christianity and is central to the idea of "creation spirituality" developed by the Dominician friar Matthew Fox. Osho who never lived and never died, stirred up a fair amount of dust and scandal and left behind more than his share of shattered lives. Could it be that he also shamed us into putting back a bit of joy and love and celebration into our own beliefs? If this is so then the sannyasin, prostrate in Poona before a larger-than-life-size video image of the Master, jumping up and down and shouting "Hoo" or laughing their way through the Mystic Rose Meditation, become not so much a threat or a shock, more just dated and old-fashioned.

Born (Sources differ) Acharya Rajneesh, Chandra Mohan Jain or Madhya Pradesh II. **Pseudonyms** Bhagwan Shree Rajneesh; Osho. **Parents** Swami Dev Teertha, businessman, and Saraswati (Devi) Bharati. **Education** Jabalpur University, BA, 1955; University of Saugar, MA, 1957. **Career** Philosophy teacher; Zen, Taoist, Tantric master, 1966 onwards; took name Bhagwan, settled in Poona, India, 1970s, settled in commune, Oregon, United States, 1981–85; returned to Poona, India, 1986. **Other activities** Collector, Rolls Royces; deported from United States for violations of immigration law, 1985. **Publications** (include, under pseudonym, unless otherwise indicated) *I Am the Gate,* 1972; *The Book of Secrets: Vigyana Bhairava Tantra,* vol I, 1974, vol II, 1975, vol III, 1976, vols IV–V, 1976; *The Way of the White Clouds,* 1975, revised edition published as *My Way: The Way of the White Clouds,* 1978; *No Water, No Moon,* 1975; *The Mustard Seed: The Gospel According to Thomas,* 1975; *Roots and Wings,* 1975; *...And the Flowers Showered,* 1975; *Tantra the Supreme Understanding: Tilopa's "Song of Mahamudra",* 1975, also published as *Only One Sky,* 1976; *Neither This Nor That: Sosan,* 1975; *Yoga, the Alpha and Omega: Patanjali,* vols I–III, 1976, vols IV–VIII, 1977, vols IX–X, 1978; *Just Like That,* 1976; *Hammer on the Rock,* 1976; *The Hidden Harmony: The Fragments of Heraclitus,* 1976; *When the Shoe Fits: The Sayings of Chuang Tzu,* 1976; *Returning to the Source,* 1976; *Tao, the Three Treasures: The Tao Te Ching of Lao Tzu,* vols I–III, 1976, vol IV, 1977; *The Ultimate Alchemy: Atma Pooja Upanishad,* vol II, 1976, vol I, 1977; *Until You Die,* 1976, also published as *Straight to Freedom; The Grass Grows by Itself,* 1976; *Come Follow Me: The Four Gospels,* vol I, 1976, vols II–IV, 1977; *Vedanta, Seven Steps to Samadhi: Akshya Upanishad,* 1976; *The True Sage,* 1976; *Nirvana: The Last Nightmare,* 1976; *The Empty Boat: The Stories of Chuang Tzu,* 1976; *Meditation: The Art of Ecstasy,* 1976, also published as *Meditation: The Art of Inner Ecstasy,* 1977; *Above All, Don't Wobble,* 1977; *The Supreme Doctrine: Kenopanishad,* 1977; *Nothing to Lose But Your Head,* 1977; *The Search: The Ten Zen Bulls,* 1977; *Dang Dang Doko Dang,* 1977; *Ancient Music in the Pines,* 1977; *The Beloved: The Baul Mystics,* vol I, 1977, vol II, 1978; *Be Realistic: Plan for a Miracle,* 1977; *A Sudden Clash of Thunder,* 1977; *The Psychology of the Esoteric,* 1977; (under name Acharya Rajneesh) *The Mysteries of Life and Death,* translated from Hindi by Malini Bisen, 1978; *The Cypress in the Courtyard,* 1978; *Get Out of Your Own Way,* 1978; *The New Alchemy to Turn You On — Mabel Collins' "Light on the Path",* 1978; *The Discipline of Transcendence: The Sutra of Forty-Two Chapters,* four vols, 1978; *Ecstasy, the Forgotten Language: Kabir,* 1978; *The Art of Dying,* 1978; *Beloved of My Heart,* 1978; *A Rose Is a Rose Is a Rose,* 1978; *Dance Your Way to God,* 1978; *The Great Nothing,* 1978; *God is Not for Sale,* 1978; *The Divine Melody: Kabir,* 1978; *The Path of Love: Kabir,* 1978; *The Heart Sutra: The Prajnaparamita Hridayam Sutra,* 1978; *The Passion for the Impossible,* 1978; *Tao, the Pathless Path: The Sayings of Lieh Tzu,* vol II, 1978, vol I, 1979; *Zen: The Path of Paradox,* vol I, 1978, vols II–III, 1979; *The Shadow of the Whip,* 1978; *This Very Body the Buddha: Hakuin's "Song of Meditation",* 1978; *The Supreme Understanding,* 1978; *Dimensions Beyond the Known,* 1978; *The Tantra Vision: The Royal Song of Saraha,* vols I–II, 1979; *The Diamond Sutra: The Vajrachchedika Prajnaparamita Sutra,* 1979; *The Rajneesh Nothing Book* (blank pages), 1979; *Blessed Are the Ignorant,* 1979; *Walk Without Feet, Fly Without Wings, and Think Without Mind,* 1979; *The Buddha Disease,* 1979; *This Is It,* 1979; *The Revolution: Kabir,* 1979; *Take It Easy: Ikkyu,* 2 vols, 1979; *From Sex to Superconsciousness,* 1979; *Sufis: The People of the Path,* 2 vols, I, 1979; *The Zero Experience,* 1979; *For Madmen Only — Price of Admission: Your Mind,* 1979; *The First Principle: Talks on Zen,* 1979; *The Mind of Bhagwan Shree Rajneesh,* 1980; *The Guest: Talks on Kabir,* 1981; *Books I have Loved,* 1985; *Glimpses of a Golden Childhood,* 1985; *The Rajneesh Bible,* 1985; *Notes of a Madman,* 1985; *The Last Testament: Interviews with the World Press,* 1986; also author of over 100 books in Hindi, 1975 onwards. **Cause of death** Heart failure, at age 58. **Further reading** R.C. Prasad, *The Mystic of Feeling,* 1970; Ma Prem Divya, *Lord of the Full Moon: Life With Bhagwan Shree Rajneesh,* 1979; Bernard Gunther, *Dying for Enlightenment,* 1979; Ma Satya Bharti, *The Ultimate Risk,* 1979; Frances Fitzgerald, *Cities on a Hill,* 1986; *Yes Osho* (newsletter issued in Poona), 1990.

SEMPRINI

Italian/British Concert Pianist and Popular Entertainer

***Born* Bath, Somerset, 27 March 1908**

***Died* Brixham, Devon, 19 January 1990**

Alberto Semprini, more often billed simply as "Semprini", had a remarkable flair for popularizing classical music with vastly assorted audiences. His enthusiasm was always infectious, and it was enhanced rather than abated during his long-running BBC radio series *Semprini Serenade.* Introduced by what soon became his catch-phrase ("Old ones, new ones — loved ones, neglected ones") this programme commanded a large and devoted audience from the beginning of the 1950s for a quarter of a century.

Purists occasionally complained of his "treacly touch", even erroneously suggesting similarities between his style and the over-the-top flamboyance of the American pianist Liberace, but Semprini's presentation of both light and classical music suffered no gross distortions; both his piano-playing and his personality came across without the need for gimickry or glamorous trappings.

His ability to keep his finger on the pulse of the British BBC Light Programme public might well have sprung from English aspects of his background. Despite his wholly Italian name his mother was an English opera singer, who met his father — an Italian horn player — while both were working for a British touring opera company. Semprini spent the first ten years of his life in England, and was educated at the Bath Forum School. His musical skills quickly became apparent and he was sent to the Conservatorio Verdi in Milan when the family moved there in 1918.

He studied piano, composition and conducting and was such a talented pupil that he was soon playing at La Scala for the great Toscanini, who is supposed to have then remarked "So, we have a member of the musical staff in knee-pants." Semprini pursued a highly successful career in Italy between the two world wars as a pianist, and a conductor in many leading opera houses. In 1933 he joined another pianist, Bormioli, with whom he played duets throughout Europe, before forming his own Symphonic Rhythm Orchestra for the Italian broadcasting service.

The outbreak of World War II, which Italy entered in 1940, caused Semprini an acute conflict of loyalties. Britain and Italy were on opposing sides and, although he had dual nationality, Semprini was eligible for conscription under Italian military law. He went into hiding in and around San Remo until 1943, and, with the Allied advance into southern Italy, reported to Field Security and started to take part in troop concerts. He became the chief attraction at many of these, touring forward units with his piano mounted on the back of a 15-hundredweight truck. Amongst his audience was Michael Brennan, a young actor, who suggested that he should become Semprini's agent and arrange a career in England for him after the war.

Britain was then to become his base and his home. Despite a shaky start with the BBC, when he was expected to imitate the piano-playing style of Charlie Kunz which was very different from his own, Semprini soon became a household name. With his appreciation of classical and popular music, as well as certain schools of jazz, he claimed that his concerts and broadcasts widened people's musical horizons. Schubert and Chopin became the icing on the cake of current hit music, and he claimed that he appealed to the heart rather than the head of his audiences.

Semprini retained his Italianate, handsome appearance throughout his long career. His performances were often in cabaret where, in impeccable evening dress and with soft-spoken charm, he kept alive the "light cocktail" style of entertaining which had been popular during the pre-war years.

Despite his attractive appearance, he performed surprisingly infrequently on television, apart from Eric Robinson's BBC series *Music For You*. He was a prolific composer as well as a performer. Fellow musicians praised his dedication and lack of pretension. A typical comment (from singer Ian Wallace) appeared in the British newspaper *The Independent;* "Though he was the star turn, he always smilingly insisted that we finish the concert with a joint performance of the *Hippopotamus Song,* a typically generous gesture".

Semprini was a keen worker for charities, and in 1972 was made an Officer of the Order of St John of Jerusalem. Officially retiring from performances in 1982 his services to music and to Britain were recognized in the following year when he was appointed OBE.

Sadly, Semprini was to suffer from Alzheimer's disease for some time before he died.

Born Fernando Riccardo Alberto Semprini. **Parents** Father, horn player; mother, an opera singer. **Marriages** Two marriages; 2) Consuelo. **Children** Five sons; two from first marriage, three from second marriage. **Education** Bath Forum School, Avon; Conservatorio Verdi, Milan. **Military service** In hiding, Italy, 1939–43; entertainer for Entertainments National Service Association, 1943–45. **Career** Repetiteur, La Scala, Milan; pianist, conductor, entertainer, 1939–82; also toured Europe with pianist Bormioli, 1930s; founder and pianist, orchestra, Symphonic Rhythm, 1930s; toured Spain, 1945–48; on BBC radio, from 1949. **Awards and honours** Officer of the Order of St John of Jerusalem, 1972; Officer of the Order of the British Empire, 1983. **Television** *Music for You; This Is Your Life.* **Radio** (includes) *Semprini Serenade.* **Cause of death** Alzheimer's disease, at age 81.

HARRY SHAPIRO

American Anthropologist

Born **Boston, Massachusetts, 19 March 1902**

Died **Manhattan, New York, 7 January 1990**

Professor Harry Shapiro was one of America's most respected physical anthropologists whose work in the forensic field also made him one of the best known to a much wider public. In addition he devoted a large portion of his life and work towards promoting a clearer understanding of the way in which the human species has evolved and developed — primarily as the result of the combining of environmental factors with cultural ones. He was one of the first to realize, as a result of his own research and fieldwork, that race, in itself, cracked no direct evolutionary whip over mankind. Rather environmental pressures were responsible for the selection and fostering of beneficial genetic traits in any given population.

Shapiro was educated at Harvard, where he also gained his doctorate in 1926, the same year he began his lifelong association with the American Museum of Natural History, New York. He joined as an assistant curator in the Department of Anthropology. Five years later he became an associate curator and, in 1942, was appointed chairman of the department and curator of physical anthropology. He held both posts until his official retirement in 1970 but continued lecturing both at the museum and at Columbia University, where he had been appointed professor in 1938.

Throughout his early working years Shapiro was regularly involved in researching in the field. As early as 1927 he was in the West Indies and within another two years had spent many months on the Polynesian Islands of the Central Pacific where he conducted population studies. He found natives of partly Caucasian origin and subsequently published on the distribution of blood grouping in Polynesia.

His next expedition followed swiftly. He went to Quebec to work on issues relating to the French population of Canada. He subsequently became a research professor at the University of Hawaii where he had been invited to study both the Chinese-Hawaiian population and the Japanese. Realizing the importance of balancing his findings, he also investigated relations of immigrants still living in China and Japan. He found a number of physical variations which gave clear indications that immigrants differed demonstrably from relatives who remained in their native countries. He also found further variation in immigrants' children. This was the study that led him to understand that race was no base on which to evaluate or assess physical quality. This should be measured solely by efficiency.

Shapiro's next research task was one of the most interesting to a wider public. Over a period of years he studied the inhabitants of Pitcairn Island in the South Pacific where six British sailors from the naval ship HMS *Bounty* had settled with nine Polynesian women from Tahiti following the historic mutiny. He was able to document what was later described as "the most extensive record of human experiment in cross-matching between two races and their consequent close inbreeding through six generations". Because the islanders had kept complete and accurate records of all births, marriages and deaths from well before 1800, Shapiro was able to follow all the ramifications of frequent and close inbreeding. It is now widely known, of course, that cross-cousin marriage is often the preferred, if not required, form of marriage amongst people of many differing cultures, but at the time it was popularly believed to endanger both the physical health and mental vigour of the children of such marriages. Shapiro's findings were quite the contrary. He was later able to assert that the current population of the island had a good medical record and that the people were robust and healthy despite the frequent cousin, nephew–aunt and niece–uncle marriages.

One further piece of fieldwork prior to his becoming chairman of the museum's Anthropology Department related to the investigation of a prehistoric town at Point Hope in Alaska which added weight to the emerging theory that the first American settlers had migrated across the Bering Strait from Asia. The remains indicated a sizeable settlement with 800 buildings and a population estimated at 3000. They had become extinct about 2000 years ago but clearly had not been Eskimo because of basic differences in tool construction and their greater concentration on the hunting of land animals.

It was World War II which took Shapiro's work into the forensic field. He became a civilian consultant to the American Graves Registration and, when Congress ruled that all war dead had to be returned to the US, Shapiro went to Europe where he introduced the present system of anatomical identification, primarily on the evidence from bones, teeth and hair for those sad cases where no other evidence was available. So successful were his methods that they have been widely used by others and, in addition, applied to the identification of murder victims. He was often consulted by the New York City police.

Shapiro's most controversial moment came in early 1952 when the Chinese Communist regime charged him with having custody of the ancient remains of Peking Man. It was said that the Americans had stolen and smuggled the bones to the Museum of Natural History back in 1941. Shapiro defended vehemently his own and the museum's innocence in the matter. However there had been just such an attempt by US marines and, unfortunately for the history of the whole of mankind, the bones disappeared. The truth of the matter is unlikely ever to emerge.

Intellectually Shapiro was a generous man. Recognizing that anthropology had diversified so rapidly that no one writer could handle all aspects of the discipline, he chose not to sacrifice the authority that comes from an expert writing on his own speciality. Readers, he felt, deserved better than secondhand material, no matter how brilliantly presented. Thus, when editing *Man, Culture, and Society* for the Oxford University Press, Shapiro's choice of contributors ranged widely and came from many universities throughout the USA. However his selection did not stop there. He also invited contributions from staff of British universities and from the renowned French social anthropologist, Claude Lévi-Strauss.

Shapiro was widely respected within his discipline, at various times being president of the American Anthropological Association, the American Ethnological Society and the American Eugenics Society. He was also a member of the National Research Council, the American Academy of Arts and Sciences and the Association of American Indian Affairs. In addition he was awarded, in 1964, the Theodore Roosevelt Distinguished Service Medal.

His lasting memorial will be the Hall of the Biology of Man at the museum. First opened in 1961 it attracted wide critical and public acclaim. Currently under renovation, the hall will re-open in 1992, once more giving testimony to Shapiro's vision and service.

Born Harry Lionel Shapiro. **Parents** Jacob and Rose (Clemens) Shapiro. **Marriage** Janice Sandler, artist, 1938 (died 1962). **Children** Thomas, Harriet and James. **Education** Boston Latin School, Massachusetts, 1919; Harvard University, Cambridge, Massachusetts, Detur Prize winner, John Harvard scholar, AB, magna cum laude, 1923, AM, 1925, on Thaw fellowship, PhD, 1926. **Career** Anthropological researcher, Norfolk Island, South Pacific, on Bishop Museum Fellowship, Yale University, 1923–24; tutor, Harvard University, 1925–26; assistant curator, American Museum of Natural History, New York, 1926–31, associate curator of anthropology, 1931–41, curator of physical anthropology and chairman, Department of Anthropology, 1942–70, curator and chairman emeritus, 1970 onwards; also, research professor, University of Hawaii, 1930–35; professor, Columbia University, 1938–74; visiting professor, University of Pittsburgh, 1970; scientific resident, Lehman College, New York City, 1979 onwards. **Related activities** Member Association of American Indian Affairs, board of directors, 1947–55; board member, Field Foundation, 1966–71; consultant, Louise Wise Services for Children, New York City, on board of directors, 1985 onwards. **Other activities** Civilian consultant to quartermaster general's office, American Graves Registration Command, 1945 onwards. **Offices and memberships** President, American Anthropological Association, 1948; member, American Ethnological Society, president, 1942–43; member, American Eugenics Society, president, 1955–62; member, American Association of Physical Anthropology, secretary 1935–39, vice-president, 1941–42; member, National Academy of Sciences, council member, 1957–60; member, National Research Council, chairman, anthropology and psychology division, 1953–57; member, American Academy of Arts and Sciences; member, New York Academy of Sciences, anthropology chairman. **Awards and honours** Theodore Roosevelt Distinguished Service Medal, 1964; Contribution to Science Award, New York Academy of Sciences, 1977; Research in Forensic Anthropology Award, American Academy of Forensic Sciences, 1983; honorary associate, Bernice P. Bishop Museum, Honolulu; Die Anthropologische Wien, honorary fellow. **Publications** *Heritage of the Bounty,* 1936, revised edition published as *The Pitcairn Islanders,* 1968; *Migration and Environment,* 1939; (editor) *Man, Culture, and Society,* 1956; *Aspects of Culture,* 1957; *The Jewish People: A Biological History,* 1960; (contributor) *The Race Question in Modern Science: Race and Science,* 1961; *Peking Man,* 1974. **Cause of death** Undisclosed, at age 87.

RUSKIN SPEAR

British Painter

***Born* London, England, 30 June 1911**

***Died* London, England, 17 January 1990**

Contrary to what one might expect, the full Christian names of Augustus John Ruskin Spear were not chosen for their artistic associations. His mother named him Augustus after his father, John after her father and Ruskin after the son of the — artistically minded — family with whom she was in service as a cook. It was nevertheless fortuitous and appropriate, given Spear's position as one of the foremost British painters of his generation and a leading figure in the British art world, that he bore the names of another British painter, Augustus John, and Britain's most renowned art critic, John Ruskin.

Spear was born in the riverside west-London district of Hammersmith, where he spent most of his life and which was the inspiration for much of his work. His father was a coach-painter and Spear grew up in an atmosphere of fine craftsmanship, nurtured further at the Brook Green School, for crippled children, which he attended as a result of contracting polio, where the stress was on painting, lettering and music. His artistic talent was recognized early on, when he won a scholarship aged 15 to the Hammersmith School of Art. This was followed by a more prestigious scholarship at 20 to the Royal College of Art under Sir William Rothenstein, whose emphasis on drawing reinforced Spear's own talent as a draughtsman.

After this lengthy and thorough training Spear went on to his first teaching post at Croydon Art Schools, south London, in 1935. He gained it in an unconventional manner when the Principal, who was interested in palmistry, read his hand during the interview and decided he was promising. Exempt from military service during World War II on account of his polio-induced lameness, Spear continued to teach at a number of London art schools as well as drawing for *Vogue,* working as a picture restorer and playing jazz piano in clubs, bars and dance-halls.

The Royal Academy of Arts, where Spear had first exhibited in 1932, appointed him an Associate in 1944. His election was strongly opposed by the then president, Sir Alfred Munnings, who, Spear assumed, was ill-disposed to his working-class background as well as to the unromantic subject-matter of his work. A painting of a mother potting her baby submitted by Spear for that year's exhibition so outraged Munnings that it had to be withdrawn. Principally, though, Munnings feared that Spear would introduce an unwelcome modern element into the Academy, and was in due course justified as Spear, although ever a loyal Academician, did much to revitalize the institution by encouraging the participation of the "modern chaps" Munnings abhorred.

Another pillar of the British art establishment, the Royal College of Art, also felt the refreshing force of Spear's influence. He was a teacher there from 1948 to 1975, during which time some of the most outstanding names in modern British painting — Bratby, Greaves, Blake, Hockney, Kitaj, Auerbach — passed under his tutelage. His teaching was demanding and ironic, but always sympathetic and tolerant of new approaches. One former student, Anthony Green, now himself an RA, sums up his generation's debt to Spear and his then colleagues at the RCA — Carel Weight, Robert Buhler and Roger de Grey — thus: "People used to say they didn't teach enough, they were always in the pub drinking pink gins. But they allowed young artists to flower, they were very talented growers of talent. Their own work and teaching was a wedge of British art which is the cornerstone of what has developed since."

Spear's own work was essentially traditionalist. A critic once denigrated him as belonging to a line of British painters descended from his namesake Augustus John, who "flirted with modernism but could never bring themselves to take it to heart". His paintings combine masterly draughtsmanship and formal composition with great feeling for the handling of paint, tonal values and richness of colour. He was a true metropolitan artist, charting London life in the tradition of Hogarth and Rowlandson, Sickert and the Camden Town group, whose artistic heir he was. His evocations of glistening wet Hammersmith streets, deserted District Line railway stations and the misty Thames are as redolent of their locality as his studies of its inhabitants in pubs and barbers' shops. The unaffected directness of his character studies also caused Spear to be favourably compared with such painters of everyday life as Brouwer and Rembrandt, Manet and Degas.

The penetrating vision tempered with sympathy, and occasionally irony, which informs Spear's paintings of anonymous Londoners, together with his ability to capture likeness and personality, qualified him to be a first-rate portraitist. His sitters included some of the most distinguished public figures of the day, notably Sir Laurence Olivier, and the Archbishop of Canterbury, Lord Ramsay. Spear was, however, best known for his satirical portraits of the famous which, during the 1960s and 1970s, achieved him a degree of notoriety. Often taken from photographs and swiftly executed, these quasi-caricatures bear titles such as *Harold Wilson with Pipe Smoke* (the former prime minister wreathed in smoke as if in a Brouwer inn-scene), *Poet Laureate Afloat* (John Betjeman looking ill at ease in a rowing boat against a lyrical background) and *True Blue* (Margaret Thatcher when leader of the opposition). These unsolicited portraits were not always well received by their subjects. Winston Churchill exploded: "Go away, you horrible man", while Mrs Thatcher proclaimed: "It's terrible. Let's get away from it as fast as we can."

By the late 1950s Spear's financial success was assured. He was patronized by the Arts and British councils, exhibited at home and abroad, notably in the important *Looking at People* exhibition which travelled to Moscow in 1957, and is represented in many permanent collections. His eminence in the British art world was acknowledged with the award of the CBE in 1979 and a retrospective exhibition at the Royal Academy in 1980. One commentator noted, though, that "His life has changed little since he was an uproarious and strikingly handsome student with barely a shilling to his name." Spear himself once defined his pursuits as "Painting, breathing, drinking". Gregarious, fun-loving and generous of spirit, he was a man large in both physical presence and personality, who assumed a sardonic gruffness to conceal diffidence and modesty, and whose sharp wit was often aimed against himself. He despised the ever-increasing pretentiousness and commercialism of the art world. "What he liked", recalls Anthony Green, "was people turning up at the RA and buying a ticket and having a laugh with him at a bit of mackerel wrapped in newspaper or a jolly barmaid. He was a people's artist."

Born Augustus John Ruskin Spear. **Parents** Augustus, coach-painter, and Jane, cook, Spear. **Marriage** Mary Hill, 1935. **Children** Roger and Rachel. **Education** Brook Green School, Hammersmith, London; Hammersmith School of Art; studied under Sir William Rothenstein, Royal College of Art, Kensington, London, diploma, 1934. **Career** First exhibited at the Royal Academy, 1932; teacher, Croydon Art Schools, 1935, also at Sidcup College of Art, St Martin's and Hammersmith School of Art, 1939–45; illustrator, *Vogue* magazine, 1942–44; teacher, Royal College of Art, 1948–75. **Other activities** Member, jazz band, Symphonic Syncopators. **Offices and memberships** Elected London Group, 1942, president, 1949–50; Associate of the Royal Academy, 1944; Royal Academician, 1954. **Awards and honours** Commander of the Order of the British Empire. **Exhibitions** (include) *Looking at People* (joint), Pushkin Museum, Moscow, 1957; Retrospective, Royal Academy, 1980; has also exhibited in Paris, United States, Belgium, South Africa, Australia, New Zealand. **Commissions** (include) Altar Piece, RAF Memorial Church, St Clement Danes, 1959; four mural panels, P&O liner, *Canberra;* Sir Ralph Richardson as Falstaff, National Theatre; also, works purchased by Chantrey Bequest, Contemporary Art Society, Arts Council of Great Britain, British Council. **Portraits**

The Queen; Princess Margaret; Lord Adrian; Herbert Butterfield; Sir Stewart Duke-Elder; Sir Laurence Olivier as Macbeth (Stratford Memorial Theatre); Lord Chandos; Sir Ian Jacob; Sir Robin Darwin; Miss Ruth Cohen; Sir Eric Ashby; S.S. Eriks, KBE; Lord Ramsey, Archbishop of Canterbury; Sir Aubrey Lewis; Arthur Armitage; 5th Duke of Westminster; Sir Hugh Greene; Lord Goodman; Dr Charles Bosanquet; Sir James Tait; Sir John Mellor; Sir Geoffrey Taylor; Sir Peter Allen; Sir Maurice Bridgemen; Lord Butler of Saffron Walden; Sir Geoffrey Howe; Sir David Willcocks, CBE, MC; Professor Dame Sheila Sherlock; Sir Cyril Clarke; Edward Ardizonne; Lucien Ercolani; Sir Ralph Richardson as Falstaff; Sir John Kendrew; Cliff Richard; Francis Bacon (National Portrait Gallery); Lord Wilson of Rievaulx (National Portrait Gallery); Lord Redcliffe-Maud (National Portrait Gallery); Sir Alan Herbert (National Portrait Gallery); Lord Hailsham (National Portrait Gallery); self-portrait (National Portrait Gallery), 1982. **Other works** (include) *Man Selling Postcards,* 1946; *Man with a Cap,* 1948; *Ravenscourt Park,* 1950; *Hammersmith Broadway,* 1950; *Friday Night,* 1958; also: *Brown Ale/The Hampshire Hog, Success Story, Harold Wilson with Pipe Smoke, Mrs Barbara Castle at the RA Banquet, Poet Laureate Afloat,* Sir John Betjeman, *True Blue,* Mrs Thatcher, *The Blue Hat,* Mrs Thatcher, *The White Hat,* Princess Anne, *Homage to Barnett Newman, Trouble in Paradise Row, Still-life with Fish, Conversation about Vacuum Cleaners, Harry's Cafe.* **Cause of death** Undisclosed, at age 78.

BARBARA STANWYCK

American Actress

Born **Brooklyn, New York, 16 July 1907**

Died **Santa Monica, California, 20 January 1990**

In a show-business career spanning 60 years and a dazzling range of stage, film and television roles, Barbara Stanwyck is best remembered for her portrayal of Phyllis Dietrickson, the treacherous, two-timing wife in the 1944 classic *Double Indemnity.* Her searing performance brought her her third Oscar nomination and helped to establish her as one of Hollywood's finest melodramatic actresses. But the *femme fatale* was only part of Stanwyck's vast and varied repertoire. Praised throughout her life for a "natural" style which emphasized strength and sincerity over glamour and artifice, she was one of the industry's best-liked, hardest working, and most professional stars. In 1982 the Motion Picture Academy awarded her an honorary Oscar, citing her as an "artist of impeccable grace and beauty, a dedicated actress and one of the great ladies of Hollywood." Over the years she appeared in more than 84 theatrical films and three long-running television series.

The youngest of five children, Barbara Stanwyck was born Ruby Stevens in Brooklyn, New York. Her mother died when she was four, and her father, a bricklayer, deserted the family shortly afterwards. Left to board in a series of foster homes, Stanwyck learned survival at an early age. At 13 she dropped out of school to earn a living, first as a department store package wrapper, then as a telephone operator, receptionist, and filing clerk. She saved her pennies for the cinema, and in her spare time studied dancing with a vaudevillian friend. By the age of 15 she had landed her first job in show business — as a chorus girl at several local speakeasies and cabarets. She soon advanced to the Ziegfeld Follies, and at 18 was talent-spotted by Broadway producer Willard Mack, who cast her in the part of a cabaret dancer in his new Broadway melodrama, *The Noose.* It was he who changed her name from Ruby Stevens to the more elegant and theatrical-sounding "Barbara Stanwyck", inspired by a billboard notice.

Though her original part was small and insignificant, Stanwyck was soon promoted to a leading role, and *Theatre* magazine singled her out as a "real discovery". When *The Noose* finished its nine-month run, producer Arthur Hopkins, entranced by what he described as Stanwyck's "rough poignancy", cast her in the leading role of Bonny in *Burlesque,* a part she played on Broadway for the next two years.

While her career was thriving, Stanwyck's personal life was in turmoil. Distraught over the tragic death of her lover, Rex Cherryman, in 1928, she turned for solace to vaudeville actor Frank Fay. They were married later that year. Though the relationship ended in 1935, Fay proved an invaluable ally in her drive for professional recognition. In 1929 he took her with him to Hollywood, where, through his influence, she came to the attention of the industry's top producers. Before long, her talent and success had outshone his.

Stanwyck spent her first few years in Hollywood under contract to both Warner Brothers and Columbia Pictures. Here, leading directors, such as William Wellman and Frank Capra, offered her ample opportunities to develop her large and wide-ranging abilities. They found her as affable and level-headed as she was talented. She "gave her all the first time she tried a scene", Capra remembered. Cecil B. De Mille later wrote that he had never worked with an actress who was "more cooperative, less temperamental, and a better workman". Her modesty, generosity, and conscientiousness won her the affectionate nickname "Missy".

Stanwyck's association with Capra was to prove a long and fruitful one. In 1930 he cast her in her first important movie role, that of an adventuress redeemed by love in the melodrama *Ladies of Leisure.* Over the next three years she appeared in a string of other Capra vehicles, including *The Miracle Woman*, *Forbidden,* and perhaps most memorable of all, *The Bitter Tea of General Yen.* She also starred in the Western, *Annie Oakley,* and in 1937 played the title role in *Stella Dallas,* a performance which earned her her first Academy Award nomination. Two years later she married actor Robert Taylor, one of Hollywood's leading men. The marriage ended in 1951.

Stanwyck's career reached its pinnacle in the early 1940s, with such memorable films as *Ball of Fire*, *Meet John Doe* and *The Lady Eve.* Then, in 1944, came Raymond Chandler's suspense thriller *Double Indemnity.* Otis L. Gernsey of the *New York Herald Tribune* described her cool, insolent portrayal of the murderous wife as one of the five outstanding performances of the year. Around the same time, the Internal Revenue Service revealed that Barbara Stanwyck, now as prodigious a star as Joan Crawford and Bette Davis, was the highest paid woman in the United States.

Yet, despite her enormous appeal, Stanwyck lacked the glitz and glamour of the matinée idol. Though she was nominated for an Academy Award on four separate occasions, the only Oscar she ever received was an honorary statuette for dramatic excellence, issued some 30 years after her movie career had ended.

Following her sterling performance in *Double Indemnity,* Stanwyck went on to play leading roles in a host of powerful melodramas, including *The Strange Love of Martha Ivers*, *Sorry, Wrong Number* and *The File on Thelma Jordan.* When, in the late 1950s and early 1960s, her film career began to fade, she turned to television, gaining a whole new following as Victoria Barkley, charismatic matriarch of the Barkley clan in the award-winning Western series *The Big Valley.* She also starred in a popular anthology programme, *The Barbara Stanwyck Show,* and in the early 1980s emerged from semi-retirement to deliver a memorable performance as Mary Carson in the mini-series, *The Thorn Birds.* Though some critics were less than impressed, her work in television won her many new admirers and three Emmy Awards.

As gutsy and determined as the characters she portrayed, Stanwyck steadfastly refused to use a double when filming dangerous scenes, and was seriously injured on more than one occasion. She was equally adamant in her refusal to dye her silvering hair. "You have to know when you've had your hour in the sun", she told an interviewer in 1981. "To be old is death here [in Hollywood]. I think it's kind of silly. Be glad you're healthy. Be glad you can get out of bed on your own." In 1987 she became the eighth person — and the second woman — to receive the American Film Institute's prestigious Life Achievement Award.

Born Ruby Stevens. **Father** A bricklayer. **Marriages** 1) Frank Fay, vaudeville actor, 1928 (divorced 1935); 2) Robert Taylor, film actor, 1939 (divorced 1951). **Children** One adopted son, Dion Anthony Fay. **Education** Schools in Brooklyn, New York. **Career** Employed variously from age of 13: parcel wrapper, telephone operator, pattern cutter, receptionist, clerk; night-club dancer; first appeared in musical comedy; on tour with *Ziegfeld Follies,* 1923, 1925; acting début, *The Noose,* 1926; film début, *Broadway Nights,* 1927; on contract with Warner Brothers and Columbia, 1931; freelance actress, 1935 onwards; radio début, *Lux Radio Theatre,* 1936; on television, 1960 onwards. **Related activities** Founder, Barwyck Corporation production company, 1956. **Awards and honours** Best Actress Academy nominations: for *Stella Dallas,* 1937, for *Ball of Fire,* 1941, for *Double Indemnity,* 1944, for *Sorry, Wrong Number,* 1948; co-recipient, Special Jury Prize for Ensemble Acting, Venice Festival, for *Executive Suite,* 1954; Emmy, for *The Barbara Stanwyck Show,* 1961; Emmy, for *The Big Valley,* 1966; Emmy, for *The Thorn Birds,* 1982; Special Academy Award, 1982; Life Achievement Award, American Film Institute, 1987. **Stage** *Ziegfeld Follies of 1923* (dancer); *Keep Kool* (dancer); *A Night in Spain* (dancer); *A Night in Venice* (dancer); *Scandals* (dancer); *The Noose,* 1926, *Burlesque,* 1927. **Films** *Broadway Nights,* 1927; *The Locked Door,* 1929; *Mexicali Rose,* 1929; *Ladies of Leisure,* 1930; *Illicit,* 1931; *Ten Cents a Dance,* 1931; *Night Nurse,* 1931; *The Miracle Woman,* 1931; *Forbidden,* 1932; *Shopworn,* 1932; *So Big,* 1932; *The Purchase Price,* 1932; *The Bitter Tea of General Yen,* 1933; *Ladies They Talk About,* 1933; *Baby Face,* 1933; *Even in My Heart,* 1933; *Gambling Lady,* 1934; *A Lost Lady,* 1934; *The Secret Bride,* 1935; *The Woman in Red,* 1935; *Red Salute,* 1935; *Annie Oakley,* 1935; *A Message to Garcia,* 1936; *The Bride Walks Out,* 1936; *His Brother's Wife,* 1936; *Banjo on My Knee,* 1936; *The Plough and the Stars,* 1936; *Interns Can't Take Money,* 1937; *This Is My Affair,* 1937; *Stella Dallas,* 1937; *Breakfast for Two,* 1937; *Always Goodbye,* 1938; *The Mad Miss Manton,* 1938; *Union Pacific,* 1939; *Golden Boy,* 1939; *Remember the Night,* 1940; *The Lady Eve,* 1940; *Meet John Doe,* 1941; *You Belong to Me,* 1941; *Ball of Fire,* 1941; *The Great Man's Lady,* 1942; *The Gay Sisters,* 1942; *Lady of Burlesque,* 1943; *Flesh and Fantasy,* 1943; *Double Indemnity,* 1944; *Hollywood Canteen,* 1944; *Christmas in Connecticut,* 1945; *My Reputation,* 1946; *The Bride Wore Boots,* 1946; *The Strange Love of Martha Ivers,* 1946; *California,* 1946; *The Two Mrs. Carrolls,* 1947; *The Other Half,* 1947; *Cry Wolf,* 1947; *Variety Girl,* 1947; *B.R.'s Daughter,* 1948; *Sorry, Wrong Number,* 1948; *The Lady Gambles,* 1949; *East Side, West Side,* 1950; *The File on Thelma Jordan,* 1950; *No Man of Her Own,* 1950; *The Furies,* 1950; *The Man with a Cloak,* 1951; *Clash by Night,* 1952; *Jeopardy,* 1953; *Titanic,* 1953; *All I Desire,* 1953; *The Moonlighter,* 1953; *Blowing Wild,* 1953; *Executive Suite,* 1954; *Witness to Murder,* 1954; *Cattle Queen of Montana,* 1954; *The Violent Men,* 1955; *Escape to Burma,* 1955; *There's Always Tomorrow,* 1956; *The Maverick Queen,* 1956; *These Wilder Years,* 1956; *Crime of Passion,* 1957; *Trooper Hook,* 1957; *Forty Guns,* 1957; *Walk on the Wild Side,* 1962; *Roustabout,* 1964; *The Night Walker,* 1965; *The House That Wouldn't Die* (television), 1970; *A Taste of Evil* (television), 1971; *The Letters* (television), 1973. **Television** (includes) *The Barbara Stanwyck Show,* 1960–61; *The Big Valley* (series), 1965–69; *The Thorn Birds* (mini-series), 1983; *The Colbys* (series), 1985 onwards. **Cause of death** Congestive heart failure, at age 82. **Further reading** Ella Smith, *Starring Miss Barbara Stanwyck,* 1974; Jerry Vermilye, *Barbara Stanwyck,* 1975; Al DiOrio, *Barbara Stanwyck: A Biography,* 1983; Jane Ellen Wayne, *Stanwyck: The Untold Biography,* 1986; *International Dictionary of Films and Filmmakers,* volume three, 1986.

HORACE STONEHAM

American Baseball Club Owner

Born **Jersey City, New Jersey, 10 July 1903**

Died **Scottsdale, Arizona, 8 January 1990**

Few people can claim to have changed, historically, the character of a sport during their lifetime. But among those who could was Horace Stoneham.

One of a dying breed of baseball entrepreneurs with no other outside business or corporate interests, Stoneham, it might be argued, did not possess the character of a visionary or a pioneer. Quiet, shy and retiring to the point of being reclusive, he was nevertheless stubbornly independent and, more to the point, perfectly capable of carrying through his decision to move his major league franchise from one side of America to the other. His controversial decisions could make people from coast to coast in America either love or loathe him. And no decision epitomized this better than his determination to move the Giants to San Francisco.

Born in Jersey City in 1903, he took control of the Giants in 1936, after the death of his father, Charles A. Stoneham, who had bought the club in 1919 in partnership with John McGraw and Judge Francis McQuade.

At the age of 32, Horace Stoneham might have been the sport's youngest executive, but he knew the Giants inside-out, having worked at the club since high school days: selling tickets, helping the ground crew, and learning everything about the way in which a major league ball club was run. Before the historic move, his teams won the National League penants in 1936, 1937, 1951 — and 1954, when the Giants also presented him with his only World Series triumph.

A dedicated executive, he was passionate about the fortunes of the Giants. When attendances started falling off at the antiquated Polo Grounds in New York, he began to look for solutions. Fortunes were particularly bleak in 1957 and, at about the same time, former San Francisco mayor George Christopher was eager to attract a major league franchise to the city, and sent Judge Francis McCarty on a mission to New York to bring the first major league team to the West Coast.

Confirmation of the move was made in August 1957 — just two months before Walter O'Malley announced his decision to move the Brooklyn Dodgers to Los Angeles. Thus a special two-team rivalry from the East Coast was transplanted to the West Coast of America. Whether Stoneham was totally aware of the heartache (East Coast) and ecstasy (West Coast) he caused is difficult to say. But in California, both he and O'Malley were treated as heroes for bringing two of the most famous teams to the state.

Stoneham had been promised a new stadium, but had to play the 1958 and 1959 seasons at the 21,000-seat Seals Stadium. Every game was a sell-out, as San Francisco baseball fans flocked to see a combination of great stars and exciting young rookies in action.

Candlestick Park eventually opened in 1960, and the Giants prospered there for ten years, winning the National League title in 1962 (but losing to the Yankees in the seventh game of the World Series 1–0), and attracting 1.5 million fans despite the cold weather and windy conditions experienced in the stadium.

The 1970s, however, brought more torrid times for Stoneham and his Giants. The team finished second five times, but as the fans grew tired of waiting for the ultimate success, and the more established players passed their prime, interest waned. The arrival of Charles O'Finley's A's at Oakland from Kansas City did not help Stoneham's cause. And by 1974, the Giants were attracting just 519,991 fans — the lowest figure in the whole of the major league.

Stoneham, a baseball man through and through, did not believe in sideshows and match-night promotions to entertain the crowds; and he kept the club solvent by selling his star players. He knew all about victory and profit, as well as defeat and failure. He made one final baseball decision, and in 1976 sold the Giants' franchise (after considering moves to Toronto and Denver) to Bob Lurie and Bud Herseth for eight million dollars. It was a sad ending to Stoneham's lifelong involvement in the sport.

Lurie paid tribute to the man, and also recognized how badly the sale had affected him. "He was a wonderful gentleman and a heck of a guy", began Lurie. "It was a real disappointment when he had to sell the club. We invited him to our special events, but he never came."

Instead, the shy Stoneham spent his 13 years of retirement well away from the major league, and only occasionally showed up at the Giants' spring training camps in Arizona — where he had made his home with his wife, Valleda, many years earlier. Sitting there quietly, in his regular seat high in the stands down the left field line, he troubled no one, and remained as reclusive as ever.

Born Horace Charles Stoneham. **Father** Charles A. Stoneham, owner, chief executive, Giants baseball team. **Marriage** Valleda. **Children** Charles and Mary. **Education** Hun, Loyola and Pawling Schools. **Career** Copper miner, California, briefly; president, principal owner, Giants, 1936–76. **Cause of death** Undisclosed, at age 86.

JOHNNY SYLVESTER

American Baseball Fan and Businessman

***Born* 1915**

***Died* Mineola, New York, 12 January 1990**

"Who the hell is Johnny Sylvester?" The question is said to have been asked by Babe Ruth, the finest baseball player ever to wield a bat. Yet legend has it that it was actually a gesture of kindness on his behalf which led to the name of Johnny Sylvester entering baseball's folklore in the first place.

The story goes that at the age of eleven, Sylvester was thought to be dying from an infection caused by a kick to the head from a horse on his father's estate in Essex Falls, New Jersey. His father, Horace C. Sylvester, a vice-president of National City Bank in New York, cabled the New York Yankees asking for an autographed ball for his dying son.

Two balls duly arrived by airmail. One came from the Yankees' opponents in the World Series, the St Louis Cardinals. The other was accompanied with the special message: "I'll knock a homer for you on Wednesday." Wednesday was Game 4 of the 1926 World Series; Babe Ruth hit three home runs for "my little sick pal"; and Johnny made a miraculous recovery.

How much of that story is based on the truth, and how much of it was blown out of all proportion by a sentimental press, will probably never be known. But one thing that *is* known for sure is that it resulted in widespread fame for little Johnny, whose story was portrayed in the 1948 movie *The Babe Ruth Story*. Sylvester, however, refused to be star-struck. Having recovered from his illness, he went on to live a full life, playing for Princeton's hockey team, serving as a naval officer in World War II, and eventually becoming the president of the Long Island packaging machinery company, Amscomatic Inc.

He seldom entered the debate over how much of the Babe Ruth story was true, and refused to discuss its colourful interpretation on the big screen. "He didn't have an opinion on the movie", explained a lifelong friend, Joseph Hazen. "Johnny didn't care about publicity." A college roommate, Anthony Rytina, threw a little more light on Sylvester's coyness on the matter when he noted: "Johnny never said it helped him get better. But we always kidded him about being the famous Johnny Sylvester."

At one time described as "the best known boy in America", Sylvester's brief brush with the great Babe Ruth has been the subject of much debate for almost three-quarters of a century. Greg Schwalenberg, of Baltimore's Babe Ruth Birthplace Museum, claims it was an extension of the truth, and that the slugger's message was simply, "I'll knock a homer for Wednesday's game." For his part, Ruth always showed a genuine affection to ailing children, making countless visits to orphanages and hospitals, and in later life admitting, "Fear of disappointing kids always causes me more worry than anything else."

Having been so vividly reported by the press in 1926, the story of Ruth's gesture — and Sylvester's incredible recovery — was fiercely defended by the optimists, and the subject of much scorn from the doubters. The latter group, for instance, point to another part of the tale, when Sylvester's uncle was said to have approached Babe Ruth some months after the event. He began by saying, "Mr Ruth, I just want to thank you again for what you did for Johnny."

"Glad to do it", responded Ruth. "How is Johnny?"

"He's fine. He's home and everything looks OK."

"That's good. Give him my regards", concluded Ruth, who waited until the man had left before turning to a group of journalists and saying, "Now who the hell is Johnny Sylvester?"

A photograph of the two of them together casts some doubt on the accuracy of the reporting of the conversation. There certainly seems no doubt that Johnny Sylvester was seriously ill in 1926 and was given only 30 minutes to live before his father tried to fulfill his dying wish; that the baseball and message probably did reach him; and that Ruth did hit three homers in that game. But from that moment, it was probably coincidence and vivid imagination which took over.

Such is the stuff legends are made of. It is typical that the postscript to the story failed to attract anything like the same level of attention. For Ruth is said to have written to Sylvester again before Game 6, promising, "I will try to knock you another homer, maybe two today." But he failed to hit one. The Yankees lost — as they did the next day, when an unpromised homer by Ruth proved insufficient to save the Yankees, or the World Series.

Born John Dale Sylvester. **Father** Horace C. Sylvester, banker. **Children** One son, John Jr. **Education** Princeton University, New Jersey, 1937. **Military service** Lieutenant, United States Navy, World War II. **Career** President, Amscomatic Incorporated, packaging machinery company, Long Island City, New York. **Film** (about) *The Babe Ruth Story,* 1948. **Cause of death** Undisclosed, at age 74. **Further reading** Robert Cramer, *Babe,* 1974.

TERRY-THOMAS

British Actor

***Born* London, England, 14 July 1911**

***Died* Godalming, Surrey, 8 January 1990**

Terry-Thomas began his 1990 autobiography with some of the descriptions offered by critics through his career: "Terry-Thomas with his permanent air of caddish disdain... bounder... aristocratic rogue... upper-class English twit... genuine English eccentric... one of the last real gentlemen... wet, genteel Englishman... high-bred idiot... cheeky blighter... camel-haired cad... amiable buffoon... pompous Englishman... twentieth-century dandy... stinker... king of the cads...." Such phrases instantly conjure up one of the most easily recognizable of film stars, whose gap-toothed smile, military moustache, florid accent and dapper dress sense cropped up in (and too often propped up) so many films in the 1950s and 1960s.

Yet Terry-Thomas, while invariably playing himself, managed to create a persona whose appeal to film audiences in the 1950s was based on more than just his well-polished comic ability. In those dour days, with its rationing and its collapsing empire, Britain welcomed the fruity humour of Terry-Thomas, with his loud waistcoats, exaggerated vowels, and over-familiar manner. His manner of dress, to a British audience of the time, connoted either a homosexual or a "spiv". Resolutely heterosexual (as his autobiography frequently and rather charmlessly confirms), Terry-Thomas indeed had the flashy air of a spiv. He was the comic incarnation of the sort of ex-minor-public-schoolboys whose shady dealings were such a feature of post-war British culture.

Though sometimes seen as aristocratic, Terry-Thomas, as British audiences (rather than American ones) may have suspected, was not quite the genuine article. To his own disgust, he was born and raised in Finchley, a suburb of London which was, at most, respectable. As he himself said, "I've cashed in on playing the lower-middle-class pretending to be upper-class." Though educated privately, he was unable subsequently to join the British Army, despite being his school's star cadet officer, since an officer at that time needed an independent income. Instead he took a rather less glamorous job as a transport clerk at Smithfield Meat Market. Though he remained there six years, he made a mark less with his abilities as a clerk than with his regular attire of a buttonhole, a silver-topped Malacca cane and slip-on suede shoes, and his star turns in the company's amateur dramatic society.

He developed his show-business career in the early 1930s through organizing and playing the ukelele with a band called the Rhythm Maniacs, through dancing as a professional at the Cricklewood Palais, and by impersonating well-known singers on the cabaret circuit. In World War II he served in the Army, rising to the rank of sergeant. His success in ENSA, the Forces Entertainment wing, ensured that, like many of his colleagues, he went on to the London stage on his release, with a part in Sid Field's *Piccadilly Hayride.* His popularity with British audiences was consolidated by radio work and by his own TV show, *How Do You View,* in 1951, so that by the time of his first feature film appearance in 1956, his was a familiar face.

It is for his film appearances that Terry-Thomas will be remembered, as new generations, seeing his work reshown on TV, relish his improbably plummy drawl, and his inevitable catch-phrases. As Major Hitchcock in the Boulting Brothers' *Private's Progress,* he described his troops, memorably, as "a shower! An absolute *shower*!" Similarly, the lecherous charm underlying the apparently innocent enquiry, "How do you do?" delighted audiences then and now. Yet his film work in the late 1950s, from his pseudo-intellectual in *Lucky Jim* to his crooked personnel manager in *I'm All Right, Jack,* and from his bumbling diplomat in *Carleton-Browne of the FO* to the hilariously bumptious cad in *School for Scoundrels*, showed Terry Thomas carrying off subtly different, yet similarly priceless studies of fraudulent Englishmen, with a talent whose depth was perhaps never fully tapped.

By 1960, he was a genuine star, if only as a cameo performer, and inevitably Hollywood beckoned. By happy coincidence, a shift in English culture was occurring which threatened to make his brand of humour an anachronism. Some excellent work (opposite Jack Lemmon in *How to Murder Your Wife,* for example), was almost overshadowed by a series of cameo roles in less-than-challenging, though financially rewarding, projects. Struck by the amount of money available merely for reproducing what Americans saw as an archetypal Britisher on film, Terry-Thomas was able to finance an extravagant life-style without ever extending or developing his considerable comic talents. Although he was never less than watchable, the projects became more obscure and his career waned.

His unusual name was the result of several experiments. Disliking his given name, Tom Stevens, he decided to spell it backwards. But Mot Snevets gave way to Thomas Terry, until confusion with the Terry acting family prompted the adoption of Terry Thomas. The subsequent hyphen, he would often point out, matched the trademark gap between his front teeth. Later, he was delighted when his name was adopted by the field of orthopaedic surgery, to describe the gap produced by a disruption of the ligaments in the carpal bones of the wrist.

In the mid-1970s he was diagnosed as having Parkinson's disease, and spent the later years of his life struggling to pay for medical treatment. Despite having earned huge sums of money, by the mid-1980s Terry-Thomas had been forced to sell the home he had built in Ibiza, and was reduced to living in a cramped flat in south London, nursed by his second wife, Belinda. A picture in the British press, showing this once immaculately turned out *bon vivant* huddled in a blanket, almost unrecognizable and all too clearly stricken by his illness, prompted a charity show from fellow British entertainers. It is to be hoped that he was, at the last, aware of the tremendous affection in which he was held.

Born Thomas Terry Hoar Stevens. **Parents** Ernest Frank, businessman, and Ellen Elizabeth (Hoar) Stevens. **Marriages** 1) Ida Patlanskey, dancer, 1938 (divorced 1962); 2) Belinda Cunningham, 1963. **Children** Two sons, Tiger and Cushan, by second marriage. **Education** Ardingly College, Sussex. **Military service** Royal Corps of Signals, 1941–46, sergeant; also Entertainments National Service Association. **Career** Employed variously: transport clerk, Union Cold Storage Company, dancer, dancing teacher, played in band, Rhythm Maniacs, film, radio extra, in cabaret; on radio from 1938; West End début, *Piccadilly Hayride,* Prince of Wales Theatre, 1946–47; first Royal Variety Performance, 1946; film début, *Helter Skelter,* 1949; on television, from 1951. **Awards and honours** Four military service medals, World War II. **Stage** *Rhythm in the Air* (dancer), 1930s; *Stars in Battledress,* 1945–46; *Piccadilly Hayride,* 1946–47; *Dick Whittington,* 1953; *Humpty Dumpty,* 1954; *Room for Two,* 1955; *Large as Life,* 1958. **Films** *Helter Skelter,* 1949; *Private's Progress,* 1956; *Green Man,* 1956; *Brothers-in-Law,* 1957; *Lucky Jim,* 1957; *Murder at St Trinian's,* 1957; *The Naked Truth/Your Past is Showing,* 1958; *Tom Thumb,* 1958; *Happy is the Bride,* 1958; *Carleton-Browne of the FO,* 1958; *I'm All Right, Jack,* 1959; *Too Many Crooks,* 1959; *Make Mine Mink,* 1960; *Man in a Cocked Hat,* 1960; *School for Scoundrels,* 1960; *His and Hers,* 1960; *A Matter of Who,* 1961; *Operation Snatch,* 1961; *Bachelor Flat,* 1961; *The Wonderful World of the Brothers Grimm,* 1961; *Kill or Cure,* 1962; *It's a Mad Mad Mad Mad World,* 1962; *Wild Affair,* 1963; *The Mouse on the Moon,* 1963; *How to Murder Your Wife,* 1964; *You Must be Joking,* 1965; *Those Magnificent Men in Their Flying Machines,* 1965; *Munster Go Home,* 1966; *Kiss the Girls and Make Them Die,* 1966; *Rocket to the Moon,* 1967; *The Perils of Pauline,* 1967; *Don't Look Now,* 1968; *Where Were You When the Lights Went Out?,* 1968; *2000 Years Later,* 1969; *Monte Carlo or Bust,* 1969; *Thirteen,* 1970; *Seven Times Seven,* 1970; *Arthur, Arthur,* 1970; *Atlantic Wall,* 1970; *The Abominable Dr Phibes,* 1970; *Lei, Lui, Loro, la Legge,* 1971; *Dr Phibes Rises Again,* 1972; *The Heroes,* 1972; *Vault of Horror,* 1973; *Side by Side,* 1975; *Spanish Fly,* 1975; *The Bawdy Adventures of Tom Jones,* 1976; *The Last Remake of Beau Geste,* 1977; *The Hound of the Baskervilles,* 1978. **Television** (includes) *How Do You View,* 1951–52; *Bird in Hand,* 1955; *Strictly T-T,* 1956; *What's My Line?; My Wildest Dream; Ed Sullivan Show; The Old Campaigner,* 1968. **Radio** *Friends to Tea,* 1938; *To Town With Terry,* 1948–49; *Top of the Town,* 1951–52. **Publications** *Filling the Gap,* 1959; *Terry-Thomas Tells Tales: An Autobiography,* 1990. **Cause of death** Parkinson's disease, at age 78.

DAME PEGGY van PRAAGH

British Ballet Dancer and Founder of the Australian Ballet

***Born* London, England, 1 September 1910**

***Died* Melbourne, Australia, 15 January 1990**

Peggy van Praagh was one of a remarkable corps of dancers who developed ballet in Britain where no indigenous classical dance had previously existed. In the wake of interest generated by Pavlova and expatriate Russian impresarios in the 1920s, she and a number of other dancers built fledgling troupes into national and international ballet companies over a period of 40 years. At the time of her death, she was one of eight former ballerinas whose artistic and administrative contribution to the balletic art had been recognized with the title "Dame".

Her career in England spanned more than a quarter of a century but, possibly, because in the second half of her life she was the missionary who fostered and consolidated the growing interest in classical dance in Australia, she was not as well known in her country of birth as the other dance "dames" — Genée, de Valois, Rambert, Markova, Fonteyn, Grey and Park. In Australia, she was held in affectionate esteem and her importance in the cultural life of that country may be judged by the fact that her death was a leading item on Australian television and radio news bulletins.

Peggy van Praagh went to Australia shortly after the death in 1959 of the Czech dancer, Edouard Borovansky. For years, Borovansky, who had danced with Pavlova and been a *premier danseur* with Colonel de Basil's Ballet Russe, had struggled, often on the verge of bankruptcy, to keep a company and school afloat in Melbourne. Van Praagh's acceptance of the invitation to take temporary charge of the ailing company proved one of the most decisive steps of her life. The former principal dancer and ballet mistress from Sadler's Wells Theatre Ballet urged the Australian government to consider setting up a national company. No one was more surprised than she when they agreed, on condition that she ran it. The Borovansky Ballet was absorbed into the New Australian Ballet and Peggy van Praagh became artistic director in 1963, a post she held until 1974, sharing it for some years with Sir Robert Helpmann. She returned in 1978 to lead the company through a management crisis.

Experience gained as a guest producer with national companies in Toronto, Munich and Stockholm in the late 1950s stood her in good stead but the strongest influences she brought to Australia were those learned in earlier years as a dancer and teacher in London.

The daughter of a family doctor, Peggy van Praagh was born in London and educated at King Alfred School in Hampstead. Her enthusiasm for dance had been fired at the age of three when she was taken to a pantomime, and her youthful Terpsichorean party-pieces for relatives and friends pointed the way to her future. At a time when there were few opportunities for English dancers on stage, she became a teacher. She studied with Tamara Karsavina, was trained in the Cecchetti method of classical dance by its greatest exponent, Margaret Craske (q.v.), and Agnes de Mille schooled her in modern dance. She became a fellow and examiner of the Cecchetti Society and taught in dance companies and schools.

Her stage début, dancing with Anton Dolin, was at the London Coliseum in 1929. She later danced in Anthony Tudor's *Adam and Eve* with the Camargo Society and throughout most of the 1930s was with Ballet Rambert, her big break occurring when she took the role of the formidable ex-mistress of the bridegroom in Tudor's *Jardin aux Lilas.* Her long and fruitful association with Tudor led to her creating roles in his *Dark Elegies, Gala Performance* and *Soirée Musicale,* all ballets which have become standard repertoire works. When Tudor formed the London Ballet in 1938 she was one of its two principal ballerinas and on his departure for America a year later, she and Maud Lloyd took over the direction of the company. One of their innovative entertainments was a revolutionary idea for which they are still remembered; lunch-time ballet with members of the company at the Arts Theatre during the Blitz.

In 1941, van Praagh joined Sadler's Wells Ballet, the company founded over a decade earlier by Ninette de Valois. Her main task was to teach but she was soon dancing leading roles, her most notable performances being the Blue Girl in Ashton's *Les Patineurs* and a Swanilda in *Coppelia* that remained a benchmark for future generations. Her strong technique and expressive dramatic range were particularly suited to demi-character roles.

Her abilities as a teacher and organizer were recognized when the main company moved to the Royal Opera House, Covent Garden, in 1946. While de Valois was engaged in laying the foundations of what became the Royal Ballet, van Praagh, first as ballet mistress and then as assistant director, stayed with the Sadler's Wells Theatre Ballet and this ten years saw a great flowering of the balletic art in England. Her theatrical flair and musicality, combined with her administrative and tutorial skills, produced a rich repertoire. Under her guidance a generation of fine dancers emerged, among them David Blair, Elaine Fifield and Maryon Lane. She nurtured and encouraged young choreographers, two of whom, John Cranko and Kenneth MacMillan, achieved international fame.

In spite of her successful tenure with Sadler's Wells, van Praagh never felt she was a "child" of the company. She was the adoptive daughter, the newcomer from Ballet Rambert, and in a reorganization in 1956 she was disappointed when the directorship of the Royal Ballet's touring company (as Sadler's Wells Theatre Ballet became) went to someone else. Determined to succeed elsewhere, she freelanced as a guest producer overseas, directed Norsk Ballet from 1957 to 1958, taught in the USA and was with the Ballet du Marquis de Cuevas when she gave Rudolf Nureyev his first classes after his defection to the West.

But it is for the next period of her life that Peggy van Praagh will always be remembered. Not only did she export British classical dance techniques to Australia but she developed an indigenous style, establishing not only a ballet company which reached international standards of performance but a school and a choreographic expression, though she regretted that she never discovered a choreographic talent to match those she had nurtured in London. She was, of course, greatly assisted by the flamboyant Robert Helpmann: she was the backbone of the company, raising money, speaking to councils, boards and politicians, teaching, moulding the dancers, and generating audience interest: Helpmann was the big star with the clout to make the headlines. She invited international guest artists to Melbourne and she produced many classical ballets, winning a coveted prize at the International Festival of Dance in Paris in 1965 for her version of *Giselle.* She took Australian Ballet on overseas tours, to London in 1967, to Canada, South Africa and to the Far East and China.

Dame Peggy's last years were marred by ill-health. She was arthritic and, despite two hip operations, she never recovered her former vitality, yet she rarely allowed her afflictions to suppress her natural zest for life.

Her contribution to dance and the cultural life of Australia was recognized by the Australian people and government and, in the last 25 years of her life, Peggy van Praagh was given many awards and honours for a life dedicated to ballet, and to Australian Ballet in particular.

Born Peggy van Praagh. **Father** A doctor. **Education** King Alfred School, Hampstead, London; trained in classical ballet by Aimée Phipps, Margaret Craske, Tamara Karsavina, Vera Volkova, in modern dance by Agnes de Mille; awarded diploma, advanced examination, Cecchetti Society, 1932. **Emigration** Left United Kingdom for Australia, 1960. **Career** Ballet teacher; stage début, *Revolution,* with Anton Dolin's company, London Coliseum, 1929; dancer, Ballet Rambert, 1933–38; director, London Ballet (with Maud Lloyd), 1939–40; dancer, Sadler's Wells

Theatre Ballet, 1941–46, producer and ballet master, 1946, associate director, 1952–55; freelance ballet producer, television director, Europe and United States, 1955–62; guest producer, National Ballet of Canada, Bavarian Opera House, Munich Opera House, Royal Theatre Stockholm, 1956–57; director, Norsk Ballet, 1957–58; director, Edinburgh International Ballet, Edinburgh Festival, 1958; teacher, Royal Ballet School, 1959, 1974–78; guest teacher, Jacob's Pillow, United States of America, 1959, Ballet du Marquis de Cuevas, 1961; Borovansky Ballet, director, 1960; artistic director, Australian Ballet (with Sir Robert Helpmann from 1965), 1963–74, 1978–79; guest teacher, Australian Ballet School, 1975–82. **Related activities** Fellow and examiner, Cecchetti Society; council member, Australian Ballet School; competition juror, Moscow. **Awards and honours** Queen Elizabeth II Coronation Award, Royal Academy of Dancing, 1965; Officer of the Order of the British Empire, 1966; Dame Commander of the Order of the British Empire, 1970; honorary degrees: University of New England, 1974, Melbourne University, 1981; Distinguished Artist Award, Australia Council, 1975. **Ballets** *Revolution,* 1929; *Adam and Eve,* 1932; *Mephisto Valse,* 1934; *Valentine's Eve,* 1935; *Circus Wives,* 1935; *The Planets,* 1937; *Dark Elegies,* 1937; *Jardin aux Lilas,* 1938; *Gala Performance; Soirée Musicale; Coppelia; Les Patineurs; Les Rendezvous* (producer); *Coppelia* (producer); *Les Sylphides* (producer); *Giselle* (producer). **Publications** (include) *How I Became a Dancer* (for children), 1954; (with Peter Brinson), *The Choreographic Art,* 1963. **Cause of death** Undisclosed, at age 79.

ROMAN VISHNIAC

Russian/American Microbiologist and Photographer

Born **Pavlovsk, Russia, 19 August 1897**

Died **Manhattan, New York, 22 January 1990**

Many of the images we have formed of eastern European Jewry before it was wiped out by the Nazis are based on Roman Vishniac's photographs. It is through his lens that we who have not been there, know the ghettos and *shtetls* of Poland, Czechoslovakia, Hungary, Lithuania, Latvia and Romania. It is through Vishniac's eyes that we have seen the suffering of the hungry children, of the peddlers and street vendors, of the homeless and unemployed; through his eyes also we have witnessed the joys of religious rituals and family celebrations, of studying the Bible and the Talmud.

Roman Vishniac, who was born into a Jewish family near St Petersburg (now Leningrad) in 1897, was actually trained as a zoologist at university in Moscow and pursued an eminent career in the field of microbiology. After obtaining his doctorate, he taught biology until a shortage of doctors at the Front during World War I motivated him to take part in a government-sponsored course in medicine. He then, however, followed his family, who had left Russia in the aftermath of the Russian Revolution, via the newly established state of Latvia to Germany.

They settled in Berlin where Vishniac continued his research in microbiology, studied oriental art and began to investigate optics. The latter prompted him to take up photography and to embark on his project of chronicling Jewish life in eastern Europe.

Living in Berlin in the pre-war years, Vishniac experienced the rising anti-Semitism and the support for Hitler who had made it "his mission to exterminate all Jews". Vishniac knew that he could not save his people, but he made it *his* mission to save their memory. "I felt that the world was about to be cast into the mad shadow of Nazism and that the outcome would be the annihilation of a people who had no spokesman to record their plight."

Without anyone wanting to join him, and having been warned by everyone of the dangers involved, Vishniac set out on his four-year voyage through Poland, Lithuania, Latvia, Hungary, Romania and Czechoslovakia in 1935. In order not to be suspected of being a spy and not to offend religious Jews who adhered to the "prohibition against making graven images", Vishniac was often forced to use a hidden camera. He nevertheless took more than 16,000 photographs of which only 2000 were spared from confiscation. Some of those photographs were published in 1942 in a book entitled *Polish Jews: A Pictorial Record,* but many were only published 30 years later in the volume *A Vanished World.*

The photographs are a record of the poverty in the Jewish ghettos of eastern Europe. They tell of those suffering from the economic boycott of Poland's three-and-a-half million Jews fostered by the government and the Church in the late 1930s. They chronicle the lives of people who have lost their jobs from one day to the other, who were forced out of business and could not pay their rent anymore. They show over-crowded flats, beggars and hungry children on the streets, peddlers and people transporting freight by handcarts or on their back — the only occupation permitted to the Jews of Warsaw after the boycott. There are photographs of a market in Lask where a guard made sure that Jews and non-Jews were separated and did not buy each other's goods. There is a record of the open sewers in the Jewish quarter of Lublin, images of anti-Semitic demonstrations by Poland's National Democratic Party, and many photographs of unknown sad faces, of lives which were later brought to an end in the Nazi concentration camps.

Then again there are images of singing Hasidim, groups of devout Jews who sought to serve and unite with God through enthusiasm and ecstasy. There are photographs of old sages and scholars, of students of Kabbalism (Jewish mysticism) and of children studying the Talmud, the compendium of Jewish law. We see children waiting in line for the ritual bath, the *mikva,* men surrounding a stand with newspapers in Yiddish, families celebrating a Jewish holiday and children playing outside. Yet, both the happy and the sad faces were doomed to the same fate; only very few of Vishniac's subjects survived the Holocaust.

Vishniac himself escaped death by fleeing from Germany to France in 1939. After the establishment of the Vichy government, however, he was put in a concentration camp. Permission to emigrate to America saved his and his family's lives and they arrived in New York in December 1940.

In New York Vishniac at first earned a living with portrait photography, but gradually achieved some success in microphotography. He won the top award at the annual exhibition of the New York chapter of the Biological Photographic Association for three successive years. After several years of freelance work, during which he developed a technique involving the use of polarized light, Vishniac was appointed research associate at the Albert Einstein College of Medicine in 1957. He later taught biology at Yeshiva University and helped to plan an educational film series which employed Vishniac's own cinematographic techniques covering his research into the physiology of protozoa. Vishniac was also appointed professor of humanities at the Pratt Institute and became visiting professor at Rhode Island School of Design in Providence. In 1971 the International Center for Photography mounted an exhibition of both his scientific and historical works.

During all those years Roman Vishniac was engaged in publicizing the catastrophic events of the Holocaust. He gave lectures and exhibited his photographs throughout the United States and Europe. Until the end he fulfilled the essential task of his life: not to, as Elie Wiesel put it, allow oblivion to defeat memory.

Born Roman Vishniac. **Father** Solomon Vishniac, umbrella manufacturer. **Marriages** Two marriages; 2) Edith, 1947. **Children** Wolf and Mara, from first marriage. **Education** Private academy, St Petersburg (now Leningrad), gold medal for scholarship; Shanyavsky University, Moscow, 1914–20; PhD in zoology, 1920; studied medicine, 1917–20; studied oriental art,

University of Berlin, 1920s. **Emigration** Left Russia for Germany, 1920; left Germany for France, 1939; left France for United States, 1940; naturalized, 1946. **Military service** Tsarist, Kerensky and Soviet Armies, Russia, 1914–17. **Career** Assistant professor of biology, Shanyavsky University, Moscow; medical, scientific researcher, Berlin, 1920–35; freelance photographer, Germany and eastern Europe, 1935–39; freelance portrait and medical microphotographer, New York, 1940 onwards; also, research associate, Albert Einstein College of Medicine, 1957; biology lecturer, Yeshiva University, 1961–62; Chevron Professor of Creativity, Pratt Institute, New York; visiting professor of art, Rhode Island School of Design, Providence. **Related activities** Project director, *Living Biology* series, Yeshiva University. **Other activities** Imprisoned as stateless person, Du Richard, Annot, France, 1940. **Offices and memberships** One-time president, New York Entomological Society; fellow: New York Academy of Sciences, Royal Microscopical Society (United Kingdom), Biological Association; member: American Society of Protozoologists, National Association of Biology Teachers. **Awards and honours** Best-of-the-show Award, New York chapter of the Biological Photographic Association, 1952, 1953, 1954; Memorial Award, American Society of Magazine Photographers, 1956; Grand Prize in Art in Photography, "Art in the USA: 1959", 1959: Honor Award, American Society of Magazine Photographers, 1965. **Individual exhibitions** Musée du Louvre, Paris, 1939; Teachers College, New York, 1941; *Through the Looking-Glass,* IBM Gallery, New York, 1962; *The Concerns of Roman Vishniac,* Jewish Museum, New York, 1971; The Photographers' Gallery, London, 1973; *Jewish Ghettos of Eastern Europe 1936–39,* Witkin Gallery, New York, 1977; Photopia Gallery, Philadelphia, 1979; Chrysler Museum, Norfolk, Virginia, 1985. **Group exhibitions** (include) *The Sense of Abstraction,* Museum of Modern Art, New York, 1960; *3 Photographers in Colour,* with Helen Levitt and William Garnett, Museum of Modern Art, New York, 1963; *The Concerned Photographer II,* Israel Museum, Jerusalem, 1973; *10th Anniversary Show,* Witkin Gallery, New York, 1979; *Life: The First Decade 1936–45,* Grey Art Gallery, New York University, 1979; *The Imaginary Photo Museum,* Kuntshalle, Cologne, 1980; *International Photography. 1920–80,* Australian National Gallery, Canberra, 1982; *Lichtbildnisse: Das Portrat in der Fotografie,* Rheinisches Landesmuseum, Bonn, 1982. **Collections** Museum of Modern Art, New York; Jewish Museum, New York; Library of Congress, Washington, DC; Smithsonian Institution, Washington, DC; International Center of Photography, New York. **Publications** *Polish Jews: A Pictorial Record,* with text by Abraham Joshua Heschel, New York, 1942, also published as *Les Juifs de Passe,* 1979; *A Day of Pleasure,* with text by Isaac Bashevis Singer, 1969; *Building Blocks of Life,* 1971; *Roman Vishniac,* with text by Eugene Kinkead, 1974; *Roman Vishniac: The Vanished World of the Shtetl,* 1978, also published as *The Life That Disappeared,* 1980; *Roman Vishniac: Einstein,* 1980; *A Vanished World,* with foreword by Elie Wiesel, 1983. **Cause of death** Cancer of the colon, at age 92. **Further reading** Stanley Rayfield, editor, *How Life Gets the Story: Behind the Scenes in Photo-Journalism,* 1955; John Walbarst, editor, *Polaroid Portfolio No 1,* 1959; Cornell Capa, editor, *The Concerned Photographer II,* 1972; Cecil Beaton and Gail Buckland, *The Magic Image,* 1975; Lee D. Witkin with foreword by Carol Brown, *A Ten Year Salute,* 1979; Robert Littman, Ralph Graves and Doris C. O'Neill, *Life: The First Decade 1936–1945,* 1979; Lee D. Witkin and Barbara London, *The Photograph Collector's Guide,* 1979; Helmut Gernsheim, Renate and L. Fritz Gruber and others, *The Imaginary Photo Museum,* 1981; Klaus Honnef, editor, *Lichtbildnise: Das Portrat in der Fotografie,* 1982; *Contemporary Photographers,* 1988.

HERBERT WEHNER

German Politician

***Born* Dresden, East Germany, 11 July 1906**

***Died* Bad Godesberg, West Germany, 19 January 1990**

It is somewhat ironic that Herbert Wehner will go down in history as being one of the most influential political figures of his time. According to Anthony Glees, writing in the London *Independent* newspaper, Wehner was "virtually unknown outside his own country...he looked engagingly ordinary, a bit like an old-fashioned country GP [family physician]". Intensely private, quite unapproachable even to his most intimate colleagues, this grim-faced, irascible, pipe-smoking man was largely responsible for the transformation of German politics, in particular, the intercourse between East and West. It is a sad twist of fate that, even as Wehner lay dying in Bad Godesberg on the outskirts of Bonn, the great goal of his lifetime — the unification of the two Germanies — was already in sight. It was no mere chance that the one ministerial post he accepted was that for All-German Affairs. He will always — in his native country, at least — be remembered as "a boulder in the desert of German politics".

Like that of many modern leading political figures, Wehner's background was a humble one. Born in 1906 in Dresden, he was the son of a cobbler and a seamstress. After attending the *Realschule* there, he initially studied to become a salesman. In the meantime, however, the unstable Weimar Republic was unfolding all around him, and it wasn't long before the future political leader had turned his career interests to journalism — and subsequently Communism. It was no coincidence that his first jobs consisted of editing several left-wing publications.

Even in his youth, Wehner was a man of conviction. By 1927, at the age of 21, he had become a member of the KPD, the German Communist Party. This Stalinist organization took its orders directly from the Kremlin and, as such, was a sworn enemy of the first German Social Democratic movement (the SPD) — even going so far as to co-operate with the Hitler regime in order to combat it. Not surprisingly, a good deal of Wehner's own work was specifically directed against the SPD, and soon he had been called by the KPD to Berlin, where he built a reputation as an organizer and public speaker. By 1931, he had become assistant to the KPD leader Ernst Thaelmann, but his initial service was short-lived: the Nazis seized control of power in 1933, forcing Stalin — and subsequently the German Communists — to quickly revise their political policies.

The focus of the KPD's action shifted from the destruction of the SPD to the protection of the Soviet Union, at that time, the only Communist state in the world. Since Hitler threatened all forms of power, the KPD ceased co-operation with the Nazi regime and its activities were forced underground. Wehner, one of the KPD's prize agents, was sent by Comintern (*Com*munist *Intern*ational, the co-ordinating body of Socialist organizations established in 1929) to Prague, where he was soon arrested. After his release, he travelled to Moscow where he devoted himself to co-ordinating the Communist resistance movement against the Nazis and served as an official on Comintern's executive committee. Fortunately for Wehner, he was favoured by Stalin, who actually killed more of the KPD leaders than Hitler did; after being interrogated by Stalin's secret police on charges of alleged Trotsky sympathizing, he was then sent to Sweden and instructed to establish a network of agents to patrol the northern borders of the Third Reich. In 1942, however, Wehner was arrested again — this time by the Swedish security police. He was sentenced to prison for espionage and violation of Sweden's neutral status.

Wehner was released in 1944, returning to Germany in 1945. Whether due to the prison sentence or other factors prior to that, the Herbert Wehner who crossed the border into his fatherland that year was no longer a Communist. Although his faith in the mission of the working classes was not shaken, he said that he could no longer accept that East European Communism was concerned with the preservation of genuine Socialist values; he had also allegedly become a Christian. Thus, when Wehner resumed his career as a journalist, this time his sympathies were with his old opponent, the SPD. The second phase of his political life had begun.

Despite the suspicion which lingered due to his former Communist connections, Wehner quickly rose to power within the SPD. In 1949 he won a seat in the first Bundestag and took up his position as minister of the influential All-German Committee; in 1952 he was elected to the party executive. After forming an alliance with Willy Brandt and Fritz Erler, he began to work relentlessly towards putting the SPD into the seat of German power over the rival right-wing CDU. During the mid-1960s, his rivals within the SPD — for Wehner was not one to pull punches even where his own colleagues were concerned — anonymously accused him of still being a closet Stalinist and stated that he was unfit for government. Wehner's response was quick and biting: if people like himself were not allowed to serve West German democracy, he declared, it was surely more of a comment on democracy than on him. The threats held little sway in the end, for, in 1966, the SPD and the CDU had come together to form a coalition government.

It was during this time that Wehner took his position as minister for all-German affairs, and devoted himself to forging a link between East German Communism and West German Democracy. "The two parts of Germany must speak to each other as equals", he stated, "though neither need accept the other as equal." Even so, Wehner was not blind to East Germany's failings (he pointed continually at the political prisoners — some of them SPD members — who were held there, for example); it was simply his dream, he said, to see the creation of a Germany peacefully reunified through dialogue.

In 1969, Willy Brandt, more or less Wehner's protégé, became chancellor of West Germany, but Wehner still held the reins of power. When it was discovered in 1974 that Brandt's chief aide was in fact a top secret agent for East Germany, Wehner forced a furious Brandt to resign in order to save the SPD's credibility. It was also he who steered Helmut Schmidt into the chancellorship in Brandt's stead. In 1983, Helmut Kohl and the CDU came to power, and Wehner, along with Schimdt, bowed gracefully out of the political limelight. It was time, he decided, to retire.

His work for the reunification of Germany, however, had not gone unnoticed by either party, nor indeed, by the European political world. The Warsaw government awarded Wehner Poland's highest decoration for a foreigner in recognition of his successes in helping to reconcile Poles and West Germans. The German Trade Union Federation as well presented him with its highest award for "contributing to conditions that have made working people into economic citizens instead of economic vassals." His ever-present dialogue between East and West had forged the way for the eventual reunification of Germany, a day that, sadly, he did not quite live to see.

Upon his death, Hans-Jochen Vogel, chairman of the SPD, declared that his party had "lost one of its extraordinary fighters, who served his people and his party as only a few in his generation did." Chancellor Helmut Kohl of the rival CDU agreed: "Herbert Wehner never avoided political conflict. He wounded and suffered wounds, but he won respect and recognition beyond party boundaries."

Herbert Wehner's obsession with privacy means that very little is known of his personal life. He was married three times; when his second wife Charlotte died in 1979, he married Greta, her daughter by a previous marriage.

Born Herbert Wehner. **Parents** Father, cobbler; mother, seamstress. **Marriages** Three marriages; 2) Charlotte (died 1979); 3) Greta, 1983. **Emigration** Left Germany for Czechoslovakia, France, Soviet Union and Sweden, 1935–46; left Germany for Sweden, 1983. **Education** Realschule, Dresden. **Career** Member, Saxony Provincial Parliament, 1930–32; scientific assistant, Sweden; editor, party newspaper, Hamburg; member, Bundestag, 1949–83; minister of all-German affairs, 1966–69. **Related activities** Member, central committee, Communist Party, 1930s; official, Cominform Executive Committee, Moscow; chairman, All-German Committee, Bundestag, 1949; chairman, Hamburg Union Sozialdemokratische Partei Deutschlands and deputy chairman, federal Sozialdemokratische Partei Deutschlands, 1958–73; member of executive, parliamentary party, 1952, chairman, 1969–83. **Offices and memberships** Member, Communist Party, 1927–42. **Awards and honours** Highest decoration for a foreigner for work to reconcile Poles and West Germans, Poland, 1983; highest award, German Trade Union Federation, 1983. **Cause of death** Diabetes, Alzeimer's disease and sclerosis, at age 83.

SIR MARTIN WILKINSON

British Financier and Administrator

***Born* 4 June 1911**

***Died* 22 January 1990**

In 1971 a senior stockbroker wrote to the London *Times* to protest that the Stock Exchange did not exist to perform a public service but was, rather, a private gentleman's club. This was not the sort of remark which Sir Martin Wilkinson, then chairman of the Stock Exchange, would have welcomed. He was struggling to convince the government of the day that it was not so, and to convince the Exchange's members that it should not be.

As a member of a family well known in the City of London for two centuries, Wilkinson was not, perhaps, an obvious candidate for the role of reformer. He had considerable respect and affection for City and family tradition, to the extent of requesting a memorial service in the same church and with exactly the same content as that of his father. And yet his background, and the respect in which his family was held, doubtless worked in his favour as he laboured to change the Stock Exchange from a gentleman's club to a professional organization fit to face the late twentieth century and beyond. His own intelligence and open-mindedness enabled him to consider and debate each proposed reform on its own merits.

Wilkinson was following a family tradition when he joined the stockbroking firm of de Zoete and Gorton in 1930, on leaving Repton school. De Zoetes was an old-established firm — described by some as "a bit Victorian" in fact — with a special interest in Far Eastern business. Following two earlier generations of his family who had been partners in de Zoetes, Wilkinson got his partnership in 1936. (He would become a senior partner of the merged firm of de Zoete and Bevan in 1970.) He resumed his City career after a wartime spell in the Royal Air Force from 1940 to 1945.

His father, Sir Robert Wilkinson, had served with distinction as deputy chairman of the Stock Exchange for the ten years from 1936. Martin Wilkinson was elected to the Council of the Stock Exchange in 1959, and became deputy to the chairman, Lord Ritchie of Dundee, in 1963. The following year Ritchie was too ill to discharge his duties, so Wilkinson had effectively been acting as chairman for a year when he officially assumed the chair in 1965.

During the eight years of his chairmanship, Wilkinson fought to modernize the Stock Exchange while retaining the more valuable of its traditions. In doing so, he had to cope with difficulties both inside and outside the Exchange (as well as with his own serious health problems). Some of his reforms had to be carried through in the face of vigorous opposition from the more conservative members. And, in the outside world, he had to defend the Exchange and its practices against the

Labour government of the day, which attacked the City and its institutions, by both verbal and fiscal means, for being out of touch with the real worlds of industry and commerce.

In 1970, rules were changed to allow the brokers and jobbers of the Stock Exchange to raise finance by becoming limited partnerships or companies; members of bodies which chose to do so remained personally liable for their debts, however. This move was designed to facilitate competition between participants without undermining their sense of responsibility. Wilkinson felt strongly about the need for complete probity, condemning insider dealing as "no better than theft" (but predicting accurately that if and when it became a criminal offence, few prosecutions would be brought to successful conclusions).

In the other reforms which he supported, there was a similar balance between the lifting of restrictions on competition on the one hand, and the tightening up of professional supervision on the other. Reforms in the latter category included the introduction of a qualifying examination for new members, and, outside the Exchange itself, support for the introduction of a panel to enforce the pre-existing but often-flouted Code on Takeovers and Mergers.

Liberalizing reforms included the removal of restrictions against advertising, and against foreigners becoming members of the Exchange, or members trading overseas. Wilkinson was a strong advocate of the admission of women to the Exchange; though his attempts to get this reform passed by the council in 1967 and 1968 failed, he had the gratification in 1973 of seeing the first woman member admitted. Her admission was an inevitable corollary of the amalgamation of the various stock exchanges of the United Kingdom and Republic of Ireland, some of which already admitted women, into the Stock Exchange.

Wilkinson, as founder chairman of the Federation of Stock Exchanges of Great Britain and Ireland from 1965, played a central role in this amalgamation. He also oversaw the demolition and reconstruction of the Stock Exchange's premises to allow it to accommodate the requirements of modern telecommunications and information processing; this was an organizational feat, involving, as it did, a shift of the Exchange's operations and personnel into temporary accommodation, and back. At the opening ceremony for the new building, which took place in 1972 when Britain was entering the European Economic Community, Wilkinson predicted that London would become "the leading financial centre in an enlarged domestic market of the expanded EEC", a prophecy which is now coming true.

He was a persuasive speaker who used both logic and trenchant humour to dissolve opposition. A retiring man, he set little store by his knighthood, and, when he was in hospital, told a nurse that he "did not remember" what he had got it for. He did not particularly enjoy the City dinners mandatory to one of his standing, and was occasionally to be seen eating baked beans on toast at London Bridge station as an antidote.

He maintained that excessive drinking and excessive smoking would counteract one another, since one dilated the arteries and the other constricted them. His other interests, in gardening and cricket, were undoubtedly healthier pastimes.

Wilkinson retired as chairman of the Stock Exchange in 1973, and from de Zoetes in 1976. He lived to see the Stock Exchange transformed beyond recognition by a series of shocks culminating in the deregulatory "Big Bang". Not all of the changes met with his approval; for instance, he lamented the end of the trading floor, made redundant by the advent of electronic dealing systems. But it is certain that his reforms left a Stock Exchange better equipped to face the hi-tech and competitive future than the gentleman's club he had found.

Born Robert Francis Martin Wilkinson. **Parents** Sir Robert Pelham, deputy chairman, Stock Exchange, 1936–46, and Phyllis Marion Wilkinson. **Marriage** Dora Esmé Arendt, 1936. **Children** Three daughters. **Education** Repton School, Derbyshire. **Military service** Royal Air Force, 1940–45. **Career** On staff, de Zoete and Gorton (de Zoete and Bevan, 1970 onwards), 1930, partner, 1936, senior partner, 1970–76, consultant, 1976 onwards; member, Stock Exchange, 1933, member of council, 1959, deputy chairman, 1963–65, chairman, 1965–73. **Related activities** Founder chairman, Federation of Stock Exchanges of Great Britain and Ireland, 1965–73; member, Panel on Takeovers and Mergers, 1968; chairman, Altifund, 1976–81. **Offices and memberships** Director, City of London Brewery Trust, chairman, 1977–78; past Master, Worshipful Company of Needlemakers. **Awards and honours** Knighted, 1969; Her Majesty's Lieutenant, City of London, 1973. **Cause of death** Undisclosed, at age 78.

GROUP CAPTAIN F.W. WINTERBOTHAM

British Intelligence Officer, Writer and Farmer

Born **Gloucestershire, England, 16 April 1897**

Died **28 January 1990**

Accepted for pilot training in the British Royal Flying Corps on the grounds of being a good horseman, Fred Winterbotham found himself in a borrowed Nieport fighter over Passchendaele, behind enemy lines, on 13 July 1917. Alas, he was without his talisman, a blue silk garter, trophy of a wartime night out in Amiens, France, and was duly shot down and captured. It was as a prisoner of war that he picked up the German which was to be so important in his subsequent remarkable career and which was to enable him some years later to chat with Hitler about the chivalry of aerial dog-fights during World War I.

That career was to bring Winterbotham into the close confidence of Allied commanders during World War II when he came to oversee the dissemination of intelligence won from the breaking of the German Enigma code, a story which only became public in 1974 with the publication of his book, *The Ultra Secret.* Ultra, as the project was called, was the greatest secret of the war and was of incalculable value, from giving an early indication of Hitler's postponement of plans to invade Britain to aiding the organization of the Allied invasion of mainland Europe. And Ultra decrypts were known to many simply as "Fred".

A group of academics was formed early in the war to work on cracking the Germans' supposedly unbreakable code. That work involved the first development of electronic computers and the building of a wooden mock-up of the German cypher machine from information provided by a Polish mechanic who had been employed in its construction. Later, an original machine was stolen. In April 1940, Winterbotham was brought in to organize the translation, distribution and security of the intelligence gleaned by the code-breakers.

His association with intelligence work had begun in the late 1920s when he sought to break out of his, by then, settled life as a pedigree-stock breeder deep in the countryside of southern England. In 1929 the Deputy Chief of the Air Staff appointed him to take over a new Air Intelligence Section of the British secret service organization, MI6. Subsequently, Winterbotham spent much time in Germany befriending leading Nazis in an effort to learn details of the military buildup there. His efforts led him to valuable information about the rearmament of the *Luftwaffe,* being made an honorary member of the Luftwaffe Club when it was founded in Berlin in 1935. There he chatted with young pilots and got to know about the characteristics of the new Stuka dive-bombers and the techniques of *Blitzkrieg.*

He won the confidence of Alfred Rosenberg, editor of the Nazi newspaper and philosopher of Naziism, who introduced Winterbotham to the Führer himself. After some initial banter about

World War I "dog-fights", Hitler talked at length about the *Luftwaffe* and enabled Winterbotham to go on to meet military leaders such as generals von Reicheneau, Lörzer and Kesselring. Over lunch von Reicheneau spoke about German plans to invade Russia.

But Winterbotham was frustrated to discover that back in Britain the government and civil service were not receptive to this information. Prime Minister Baldwin in particular was concerned that any moves towards British rearmament would not go down well with voters. In his first book of war reminiscences, *Secret and Personal,* which was published in 1969 and makes no mention of Ultra, Winterbotham recalls with some acrimony that Baldwin disingenuously referred in Parliament to having been misled about Germany's true air strength when the facts finally became clear.

Undeterred however Winterbotham sought to supplement his work in Germany by developing a new technique of high-altitude aerial photography. He had two Lockheed executive aircraft brought over from the United States, painted pale blue and equipped with cameras heated by a stream of warm air to prevent frosting in the cold airstream. He also hired an extrovert Australian pilot, Sydney Cotton, who posed as a rich film-maker searching for locations, and thereby managed to photograph German bases and Italian military installations in North Africa. It was in the wake of this coup that Winterbotham had hoped to take command of the first Royal Air Force Photographic Reconnaissance Unit but he was put in charge of the Ultra project instead.

Fred Winterbotham's books have something of an air of an old-fashioned boys' adventure comic. And his background fitted him as a hero of that style. He was born the son of a solicitor of Stroud, an old country town in the south-west of England. As a boy he flew box-kites, then a new invention, with his grandfather on the local common. His mother hired a French nanny so that he could learn the language early and later he was educated at the famous English public school, Charterhouse. As a youth he was sent on a world tour to round off his education. He described that tour as "a brilliant preparation for what lay ahead". Early in World War I, in 1915, he became an officer in the Royal Gloucestershire Hussars Yeomanry, but when the regiment's horses were withdrawn the following year he applied to the Royal Flying Corps, later to become the Royal Air Force.

After release from wartime captivity in Germany, Winterbotham went to Christ Church, Oxford, to read for a law degree. There he bought some riding equipment from the Prince of Serbia, a fellow undergraduate, so that he could play polo and join the foxhunts. After graduating and by then in his early thirties, he turned to the life of a country gentleman, farming until the beginnings of his career in intelligence.

When this career led to his assignment to the Ultra project he took on the job with gusto and a high degree of expertise. He set up his own intelligence hut, named "Station X", at Bletchley Park, in the country west of London, which then housed the war section of the Government Code and Cypher School. There he assembled top mathematicians and German-speaking Royal Air Force officers to work on the code-breaking and translation.

It was imperative that the maximum secrecy should be maintained and Winterbotham was ruthlessly strict in limiting the dissemination of Ultra intelligence and making sure that it was only used in a way which would give no clue to the Germans that their code had been broken. He was secretly amused to hear a submarine commander describe his astonishing luck at always surfacing at the rear of a German supply convoy. To carry the information to the relevant commanders, Winterbotham set up special liaison units at strategic points to receive encoded information and make it available when appropriate.

Churchill referred to Ultra intelligence as his "golden eggs" and held Winterbotham in considerable esteem. The two were often in touch by telephone and Churchill authorized Winterbotham's visits to operational theatres to ensure that the information was being ultilized properly. The Group Captain also came to be known and respected by top American commanders including Eisenhower and Spaatz. He briefed American officers before they were authorized to receive Ultra, and towards the end of the war an agreement was signed between British and Americans unifying the handling of Ultra intelligence world-wide. This agreement established common practice very much along the lines of that laid down by Winterbotham.

Despite his important work during the war, or rather because of its highly secret nature, he was not offered a high-ranking position in peace-time and chose instead to work as an executive for the civilian British Overseas Airways Corporation. He then moved on to work in colonial development, and finally returned to farming in 1952. The only recognition for his work remained the relatively modest honour of Commander of the British Empire and it was to be more than 20 years before Witherbotham received government approval for *The Ultra Secret.* It became an international best-seller, though it was the object of strong disapproval from some of his former colleagues who thought that their original oath of secrecy ought still to be respected.

Born Frederick William Winterbotham. **Father** F. Winterbotham, solicitor. **Marriages** 1) 1921; 2) 1947. **Children** One son and two daughters from first marriage, one daughter from second marriage. **Education** Charterhouse, Godalming, Surrey; studied law, Christ Church, Oxford, 1919. **Military service** Officer, Royal Gloucestershire Hussars Yeomanry, 1915; officer, Royal Flying Corps, No 29 Squadron, 1916–19; prisoner-of-war, 1917. **Career** Pedigree stock breeder, 1920–29; commander, air intelligence section, MI6, 1929–40; deviser and commander, special liaison units, Ultra, Bletchley Park, 1940–45, retired as group captain; executive, British Overseas Airways Corporation, 1945–48; on staff, Colonial Development Corporation, 1948–52; farmer, 1952 onwards. **Awards and honours** Honorary member, Luftwaffe Club, Berlin, 1935; Commander of the Order of the British Empire, 1943. **Publications** *Secret and Personal,* 1969; *The Ultra Secret,* 1974; *The Nazi Connection,* 1978; *The Ultra Spy,* 1989. **Cause of death** Undisclosed, at age 92.

FEBRUARY

RHYS ADRIAN

British Radio and Television Dramatist
***Born* London, England, 28 February 1928**
***Died* London, England, 8 February 1990**

Although more prolific than many of his BBC contemporaries, Adrian was less well known. He had cultivated an anonymity that traditionally radio presenters and writers have struggled to avoid. This obscurity allowed him to pursue his three major preoccupations — watching, writing and drinking — in peace. Happily for Adrian, these activities were mutually conducive. His office was more often than not a table in the corner of his local pub, from which he was able to observe, record — and participate in — the unfolding of the drama of real life which characterized his work. As a dramatist Adrian was concerned with sub-text; with what underlies the trivia of everyday life. As a patron of public houses, his concern was for the quality of the beer.

Rhys Adrian Griffiths's father was a Welsh coal miner, and his mother an English artists' model. His father had been awarded a painting scholarship to London and although talented, failed as an artist. Adrian's mother was 17 when she married and not much older when she divorced. The product of this union spent very little of his early education attending school, preferring even as a child to learn by observation rather than by rote. His only formal education was provided by a sergeant whom Adrian befriended during his National Service in the Royal Air Force towards the end of World War II. The officer encouraged him to "read good books" and thus educated, Adrian began to write.

In the early 1950s, after demobilization, Adrian took a variety of freelance jobs in London. He worked as an assistant stage manager on a number of West End theatre shows, where he developed a passion for both dramatic art and a particular dancer in the chorus of the musical *Gay's the Word*. He married Mavis Trail, a former member of the Ballet Rambert and later a painter, while they were both working on the show. For some time Adrian worked as a cinema projectionist, perhaps enjoying observing the audiences as much as he enjoyed the films.

Throughout this period Adrian continued to write, mostly short stories. He also began to adopt a series of pseudonyms, using permutations of his real name, such as L.A. Reece and L.R. Adrian. He later claimed that the disguises were to avoid being thought of as "just another Welsh playwright". With the pre-eminence of Dylan Thomas and Alun Owen in the 1950s, pretenders to their literary thrones would almost certainly have fallen. However, those who knew Adrian suspected genuine self-effacement and the desire on his part for something else to hide behind, the better to watch others.

In 1955, Adrian entered and won a short story competition run by a national Sunday newspaper, *The Observer*. His story caught the attention of Martin Esslin, then the head of the BBC Drama Department, who convinced him that his style was most suited to radio. His first play, *The Man on the Gate*, was broadcast the following year. As Adrian's career began his search for the right *nom de plume* ended; he settled for an amalgamation of his two first names: Rhys Adrian.

The development of television in the late 1950s threatened the future of radio as a medium for drama. However its survival was ensured by the calibre of the writers who were working for the BBC at the time. Adrian was fortunate to have the footsteps of Samuel Beckett, Harold Pinter and John Mortimer to follow in. Despite the daunting shadows of these colleagues, Adrian wrote prolifically and successfully. Throughout the 1960s he was producing at least one play, and as many as three, every year. He also began to write screenplays for television but the static nature of his work, and the concentration on the minutiae of speech and behaviour, lent itself more naturally to radio.

Adrian chose titles for his work which were either one word, or long and idiosyncratic. They were always intriguing, and occasionally gave rise to concern about what might lie beneath them. His play *Too Old for Donkeys* was banned by the BBC in 1963, presumably for the suggestion of bestiality in the title, although no inference of such activities was contained in the play. Adrian was never sure why the play was banned and it was perhaps his unswerving sense of the ridiculous which led him to call his next play *A Nice Clean Sheet of Paper.*

His work was often mistakenly compared with Harold Pinter's; stylistically they were similar, but Adrian was never controversial in the way that Pinter was. The nearest Adrian got to controversy was in 1972 when his play *Memories of a Sly Pornographer* gave rise to debate in the House of Lords. The noble guardians of morality of the day considered the play "too rude" to be broadcast, although the Member who instigated the debate had not actually read or heard the play.

Nearly all Adrian's plays were comic, and nearly all were infused with a sense of sadness. He had a rare gift for capturing in dialogue the social rituals and hierarchies that exist in ordinary exchanges; his characters sounded like people, and not merely actors. Where Pinter found menace in human attempts at communication, Adrian found genuine pathos and humour. His work always produced an atmosphere of warmly mocked desperation, and a sense of the grave difficulties people have in articulating deeply held beliefs. It was quintessentially "English". It is ironic then that he should have been better known — and better paid — elsewhere. He was particularly popular in Germany and Scandinavia, and he won literary prizes in Italy in 1970 and 1979. It was not until the 1980s that he was rewarded (twice) with the Giles Cooper prize for radio drama in England.

Adrian's plays were ostensibly variations on a single theme: the place of the individual in a world of complex and often conflicting moral values. They were also variations on a single setting: the pub. John Tydeman, a producer and director at the BBC, who directed 27 of Adrian's plays, would sigh on receipt of the latest: "Oh not another play with scenes set in a pub!" Invariably, Adrian would reply: "But this one will be different." Miraculously it was.

Born Rhys Adrian Griffiths. **Parents** Father, former miner and painter; mother, artists' model. **Marriage** Mavis Trail, ballet dancer and painter, 1952. **Children** Two sons. **Military service** Clerk, national service, Royal Air Force. **Career** Employed variously in entertainment business, as assistant stage manager, cinema projectionist; author of radio and television plays; first radio play, *The Man on the Gate,* 1956. **Awards and honours** Prix Italia for *Evelyn*, 1970; Prix Futura for *The Clerks*, 1979; Giles Cooper Award: for *Watching the Plays Together*, 1982, for *Outpatient*, 1985. **Radio plays** (include) *The Man on the Gate,* 1956; *The Passionate Thinker*, 1957; *The Prizewinner*,1960; *Betsie*, 1960; *The Bridge*, 1961; *No Licence for Singing*, 1961; *Too Old for Donkeys*, 1963; *A Nice Clean Sheet of Paper*,1963, published in *New Radio Drama*, 1966; *A*

Room to Let, 1963; *Sunday, The First of May*, 1964; *Between the Two of Us*, 1967; *Ella*, 1968; *Echoes*, 1969; *Evelyn*, 1969; *I'll Love You Always, Always*, 1970; *The Gardeners of My Youth*, 1970, staged, 1976; *Mr and Mrs Squirrel*, 1971; *A Chance Encounter*, 1972; *Memoirs of a Sly Pornographer*, 1972; *Angle*, 1975; *The Night Nurse Slept in the Day Room*, 1976; *Buffet*, 1976; *The Clerks*, 1978, published in *BBC Radio Playscripts*, 1979; *Passing Through*, 1981; *Watching the Plays Together*, 1982, published in *Best Radio Plays of 1982*, 1983; *Passing Time*, 1983; *Outpatient*, 1985, published in *Best Radio Plays of 1985*, 1986; *Crossroads*, 1985; *Toytown*, 1987; *Upended*, 1988; *Why Leo?*, 1988. **Television plays** *Protest*, 1960, published in *New Granada Plays*, 1961; *Helen and Edward and Henry*, 1965; *Stan's Day Out*, 1967; *The Drummer and the Bloke*, 1968; *The Foxtrot*; 1971, *No Charge for Extra Service*, 1971; *Thrills Galore*, 1972; *The Withered Arm*, 1973; *The Joke*, 1974; *The Cafeteria*, 1974; *Tea at Four*, 1975; *Mr and Mrs Bureaucrat*, 1978; *Getting It on Concorde*, 1979. **Cause of death** Undisclosed, at age 61. **Further reading** *Contemporary Dramatists*, 1988.

LESLIE AMES

British Cricketer

***Born* Elham, Kent, 3 December 1905**

***Died* Canterbury, Kent, 26 February 1990**

The venerable and most perceptive cricket writer John Arlott assessed Les Ames as "the finest wicketkeeper-batsman in the history of the game and one of its most courteous and effective administrators." Another of the game's luminaries, R.C. Robertson-Glasgow, wrote: "That Ames should do two things superbly seems to aggravate many who cannot do either of them at all." There was indeed much to envy in his fortune — a long and happy life spent playing and watching cricket.

He was born in 1905 to a family of enthusiastic cricketers in the village of Elham, in the fertile county of Kent. Curiously, one of his earliest mentors was a cricketing Scot — which is approaching oxymoron. This was F.A. Mackinnon, the Chief of his Clan. (Why he was living in Kent, we do not know.) The Mackinnon, as protocol would have him called, gave Ames his first bat at the age of four, and thereafter kept a pawky eye on his career. At Harvey Grammar School, Folkestone, Ames attracted the attention of the Kent county cricket coach. He duly joined the club in 1923; already a strong batsman, he was ordered to train as wicketkeeper. Three seasons later he had made the position his own, and was starting to get runs. (This time the Mackinnon sent him a silver claymore.)

Wicketkeeping is an exhausting task, demanding physical labour, mental alertness and complete concentration for long periods of time. Ames was ideally equipped; a natural athlete who also played professional soccer for several seasons, and who was always immensely fit. By 1931 he was regular wicketkeeper for England, and giving a series of superlative displays which lasted until the outbreak of World War II. To slow bowling, particularly that of his Kent team-mate "Tich" Freeman, he worked low and very close to the stumps; to the fiery fast bowling of Larwood, Voce and Allen he made ground to take wide catches. On the so-called "Bodyline", series, the tour of Australia in 1932–33, these three wreaked havoc, and they credited Ames with not missing one chance off them, or any other. At London's Oval ground, against the West Indies in 1933, he conceded but a single bye in two innings. His Test total was 97 dismissals, 23 stumped and 74 caught.

Ames owed his first international caps to his superiority as a batsman, and the strength of the England side in the 1930s owed much to his orthodox, though free-scoring, presence at the crease. He played in 47 test matches and made 2434 runs (including eight centuries) at an average of 40.56, which no wicketkeeper-batsman has yet bettered. Against New Zealand in 1931, Ames was partner in a record eighth-wicket stand of 246, and his highest personal international score was 149 against the West Indies in Kingston, Jamaica. For Kent, too, he was a prolific and rapid run-maker, usually coming in at number three. He scored 102 centuries for his county, and in 1933, against Gloucestershire, hit his personal highest total of 295.

During World War II Ames served in the Royal Air Force and attained the rank of squadron leader. Returning in peace-time to Kent cricket, he handed the wicketkeeping gloves to the brilliant extrovert young Godfrey Evans, who was to succeed him behind the stumps for England, too. (The same young G. Evans made his final appearance, keeping wicket for a charity side at the age of 70, in the summer of 1990.) Despite attacks of fibrositis, Ames batted on as a senior professional until 1951; afterwards he became the county coach and later manager. From 1950 to 1958 he was an England selector as well as a member of the Cricket Council and of the committee of the Marylebone Cricket Club. For the latter, he took three sides on tour.

Under Ames's stewardship, Kent cricket prospered after a long period in the doldrums. Captained by Colin Cowdrey (who captained England as well), the team were three times runners-up in the county championship, and outright winners — for the first time since 1913 — in 1974. Ames was well liked as a manager, being without prejudice, and a sound judge of men, though forthright when he had a point to make. He held firmly to traditional values and scorned foul play or rule-bending. Even as a player, he was described as "a quiet, smiling executioner; as near to being sorry for his victim as his lethal profession permits". E.W. Swanton attributed Ames's philosophy and disposition to a happy boyhood and to his formative years being spent "in a Kent side rich in character, and with an approach to the game which at this distance seems impossibly idealistic ... what a model for a naturally enterprising young batsman!"

Ames leaves one record apparently secure against time. Since records have been kept, only four wicketkeepers have made 1000 runs and secured 100 victims in a season. One is John Murray of Middlesex; the other three are Les Ames.

Born Leslie Ethelbert George Ames. Marriages Two marriages; 2) Bunty. **Children** One son and one daughter from first marriage. **Education** Harvey Grammar School, Folkestone, Kent. **Military service** Royal Air Force, 1940–46, retired as squadron leader. **Career** Apprentice, Kent County Cricket Club, 1923, county wicketkeeper, 1927–44, and batsman, 1927–51, coach, 1951–57, manager and secretary, 1957, president, 1975; team member, Players v Gentlemen, 1928–47; wicketkeeper and batsman, England, 1929–39, selector, 1950–58. **Related activities** Member, Cricket Council; committee member, Marylebone Cricket Club. **Other activities** Professional, Football League (played for Clapton, now Leyton, Orient and Gillingham). **Awards and honours** Lawrence Trophy for fastest century of the season, twice; Commander of the Order of the British Empire; honorary member, Marylebone Cricket Club. **Test matches** (Home): Australia, 1934, 1938, South Africa, 1929, 1935, West Indies, 1933, New Zealand, 1931, 1937, India, 1932; (away): Australia, 1932–34, 1936–37, South Africa, 1938–39, West Indies, 1929–30, 1934–35, New Zealand, 1932–33. **Other tours** (include) Marylebone Cricket Club tour of Australia, 1928–29; captain, Commonwealth XI to India and Ceylon, 1950–51. **Highest scores** Test match: England v West Indies, 149, 1929–30; for Kent, Kent v Gloucestershire, 295, Folkestone, 1933; best scoring season, 3058 runs, 1933; best bowling, 2–23, Kent v Surrey, Oval, 1946; most wicketkeeping dismissals, 127, 1929; 100 dismissals or more in season, with 1000 runs, 1928, 1929, 1932; 64 stumpings, 1932; world Test record and record for all cricket at Lords, added 246 for eighth wicket, England v New Zealand, 1931; county record, added 277 for fifth wicket, Kent v New Zealanders, Canterbury, 1931. **Cause of death** Undisclosed, at age 84.

TONY CONIGLIARO

American Baseball Player

***Born* Revere, Massachusetts, 7 January 1945**

***Died* Boston, Massachusetts, 24 February 1990**

Tragedy, sadness and sheer bad luck dogged Tony Conigliaro's private and professional life. But perhaps the greatest tragedy of all is that his career is not recalled in baseball history in terms of record-breaking or match-winning statistics, pennants or rings, or his achievements at the plate, so much as by one horrific — and, sadly, famous — incident at Boston's Fenway Park on the evening of 18 August 1967.

It was a moment that characterized the entire existence of the man known as "Tony C". The Red Sox — in the year they called "The Impossible Dream" — were on the rise under new manager Dick Williams. The pennant would be won thanks to Carl Yastrzemski, Jim Lonborg, John Wyatt ... and Tony Conigliaro who, up to 18 August, had slammed 20 homers and 67 RBI's.

He came to the plate that evening as a 22-year-old with a glittering career stretching out in front of him. Earlier that season, he had become the youngest major league player to hit 100 home runs. The previous season he had been voted Boston's "Most Valuable Player". And the Red Sox great, Johnny Pesky, summed up his potential with the words: "Some say he was the best-looking young hitter they've ever seen. I never saw Ruth or Gehrig, but I saw Ted Williams, and Williams said he [Conigliaro] was another Joe DiMaggio."

The pitch that effectively ended his rise to greatness was delivered by the Angels' Jack Hamilton. As the ball crunched into Conigliaro's face, fracturing his cheekbone and dislocating his jaw, the crowd at Fenway Park fell silent. Dick Dew, a sportswriter covering the game, said later: "It stopped everybody in the place because of the sound of it ... You knew the injury was serious the moment you heard it."

Conigliaro himself provided a vivid, almost slow-motion, account of the incident in his autobiography, *Seeing It Through*. "The ball came sailing right toward my chin", he wrote.

> Normally a hitter can jerk his head back a fraction and the ball will buzz by. But this pitch seemed to follow me in. I know I didn't freeze. I definitely made a move to get out of the way of the ball. In fact, I jerked my head back so hard that my helmet flipped off just before impact ... When the ball was about four feet from my head I knew it would get me. And I knew it would hurt because Hamilton was such a hard thrower. I was frightened. I threw my hands up in front of my face and saw the ball follow me back and hit me square on the left side of the head. As soon as it crunched into me, it felt as if the ball would go in on one side of my head and come out the other; my legs gave up and I went down like a sack of potatoes. Just before everything went dark, I saw the ball bounce straight down on home plate. It was the last thing I saw for several days.

When he finally recovered consciousness and looked at his reflection in the mirror for the first time, Conigliaro could see the imprint of stitches on his face where the ball had hit him. Doctors told him that if it had been an inch or two higher, it would have killed him. They also advised him that the vision in his left eye was so badly impaired that it was unlikely he would ever play baseball again. To someone who once observed, "I love being on a baseball field; it's my life", that news came as a shattering blow. His depression was not helped by the fact that his apartment in Boston overlooked Fenway Park's right field.

An attempted comeback that season failed. Unable to knock even the bat boy's pitches very far, he was forced to sit out the remainder of the season. And on the night the Red Sox players celebrated their pennant win, Conigliaro reportedly sat in front of his locker, crying.

It all added up to one of the saddest stories in the history of baseball. The son of a Boston factory worker, Conigliaro had excelled in all sports at school, especially ice hockey, which — ironically — his father had persuaded him to give up for fear of injury. He was called up to the Red Sox as a center fielder in 1964, switched to right field, and in 1965 led the American Baseball League in home runs.

Never married, he explained in his autobiography: "I made up my mind not to get married until I got my complete fling out of life". But Boston sports writers inflated his reputation as a "playboy", causing the slugging outfielder to respond angrily at the time: "I'm no angel, but I'm all business when it comes to baseball."

After Hamilton's pitch, however, Conigliaro seemed to be out of that business for good. He went into the Instructional League as a pitcher, and considered retirement; but minor league manager Billy Gardner kept insisting that he should take batting practice and, suddenly, Tony C. started hitting again. It was, in his own words, "a miracle".

On the opening day of the 1969 season, Conigliaro was back in the Red Sox line-up; and in a story-book return, he hit Pete Richert's fastball over the left field fence to win the game in the tenth inning. "The guy's were all reaching for me at one time", he recalled. "Reggie [Smith] and Rico [Petrocelli], Yaz and everybody. They were pounding my back and I was being hugged to death. Then Dick Williams came over and kissed me on the cheek. At that moment, I could have bit him in the neck."

Conigliaro's dislike of the Boston manager had grown from the time when he was recovering in hospital. All the Red Sox players — and Angels pitcher Jack Hamilton — visited him regularly. Williams, however, failed to appear at all; and the following year he summarized his team's chances of a second pennant without Conigliaro with the words: "We did it without his butt last year, and we'll do it without his butt this year."

Conigliaro won the Major League's Comeback Player of the Year Award in 1969, and had his best season the following year with 36 homers and 116 RBI's. But just when everything seemed to be going so well again for Conigliaro, everything changed. In October 1970, the simmering resentment between player and manager led to Conigliaro being traded, controversially, to the Angels, where his career hit a slump. After the first half of the 1971 season, he retired — citing his recurring vision difficulties as the reason. He tried making a second comeback with Boston in 1975, but played in just 21 games, before leaving the sport for good.

Life away from baseball was a little kinder to Conigliaro. He spent time as a sportscaster, and — with varying degrees of success — pursued business interests.

But in 1982, just two days after an audition to broadcast Red Sox games, he suffered a heart attack which left him clinically dead for minutes, in a coma for four months, brain damaged, and in need of constant medical care and attention for the rest of his life. His mother, Theresa, summed up Tony's ill-luck: "Every time he was the happiest, he got knocked down. He got beaned in Boston when he was doing great. When he was excited, he got knocked down." And she added, "For eight years I cried for Tony. He suffered so much ... now he's at peace."

Born Anthony Richard Conigliaro. **Parents** Salvatore, factory manager, and Theresa Conigliaro. **Education** St Mary's High School, Lynn, Massachusetts. **Career** Signed by Boston Red Sox, 1962; assigned to Wellsville, New York, A League team, 1963; transferred to Boston Red Sox, 1964–67; injured 1967, sight believed permanently impaired; discovered return of near-perfect vision, 1968; player, Winter Instructional League, Sarasota, Florida, 1968; returned to Boston Red Sox, 1969–70; traded to California Angels, 1970–71; retired from baseball due to impaired vision, 1971; staged comeback, Boston Red Sox, 1975; retired, 1975. **Related activities** Sports commentator. **Other activities** Formed rock group, Tony C. and the All Night Workers, 1968; owner, Tony C.'s Girls, Incorporated, employment agency; owner, health food store. **Awards and honours** Most Valuable Player, New York-Pennsylvania League, 1963; Most Valuable Player, Boston Red Sox, 1965; Comeback Player of the Year Award, 1969. **Recording** "Playing The Field", RCA. **Publication** (With Jack Zanger) *Seeing It Through* (autobiography), 1970. **Cause of death** Kidney failure, at age 45.

MARGARET CRASKE

British Ballet Dancer and Teacher

Born **Norfolk, England, 26 November 1892**

Died **Myrtle Beach, South Carolina, 18 February 1990**

Classical ballet, more than any other art form, relies on a living tradition which is handed down from generation to generation. Attending a ballet today at the Royal Opera House, Covent Garden, or the New York Met, it is surprising to reflect that a dancer's performance has been directly influenced by an unbroken line of teachers who can be tracked back from the present day right through to the origins of the art in seventeenth-century France. Margaret Craske, who was one of the greatest teachers of classical ballet this century, has her own special place in this vital process.

Rural England at the end of the nineteenth century was an unlikely place to find expert ballet tuition, and it was not until Craske came to London in 1918, to study with the great Italian dancer and teacher, Enrico Cecchetti, that her serious training began. By this time she was in her mid-twenties and it was late to contemplate a significant career as a performer. However she danced as a soloist with the Royal Italian Ballet and she was also chosen by Dame Ninette de Valois, one of the most influential founders of English ballet, to form part of a dance troupe which toured the music-hall circuit. Craske recalled this time fondly saying, "It was divine. That was absolutely the most wonderful audience in the world. If they didn't like you they threw things." Most of the time the bemused audience didn't appreciate the classical dance which was a new medium to them, and the enterprise was short lived.

Following a brief period dancing with Diaghilev's legendary Ballets Russes, Craske decided the time had come to give up performing and she set up her own dancing school. By this time she had studied with Cecchetti for four years and had thoroughly absorbed his methods. Cecchetti, who had been ballet master to the Imperial Russian Ballet before coming to the West with the Diaghilev Company, was a teacher of genius. He had brought the virtuosity for which Italian ballet was renowned to the Russian Company, and he had been largely responsible for helping them to create the technical prowess and bravura performances which became known as the Russian style.

Cecchetti was so impressed with Craske's teaching that he awarded her a certificate which qualified her to give classes in his method. She also assisted on the production of *A Manual of Classical Theatrical Dancing (Cecchetti Method),* which was the definitive work on the maestro's theories. Later Craske wrote *The Theory and Practice of Allegro in Classical Ballet*, with Cyril Beaumont, and *The Theory and Practice of Advanced Allegro in Classical Ballet*, with Derra de Moroda, both of which were based on Cecchetti's techniques.

Craske set up her studio in West Street near Cambridge Circus, the heart of London's theatreland. As well as classes in classical dance Craske included lessons in anatomy, history of dance and Spanish dance in her syllabus — innovative at that time. She soon established a considerable reputation as a teacher and, during the 1930s, many luminaries of the dance world passed through her doors. Among her pupils were Mary Skeaping of the Royal Swedish Ballet, Peggy van Praagh (q.v.), who went on to found the Australian Ballet, and Frederick Ashton, who was to become the most influential choreographer and director to the British Royal Ballet. Later Ashton wrote of the Cecchetti style which he learnt from Craske: "It inculcates a wonderful feeling for line and correct positioning of the use of head movement and *épaulement* which, if properly absorbed, will be of incalculable use through a dancer's career." Ashton was to draw on this knowledge in many of his ballets, notably *A Month In the Country* which he created 50 years after he had attended Craske's classes.

Craske's career changed direction at the end of the decade. She became a disciple of the spiritual teacher Meher Baba and she spent seven years in India learning and practising his philosophy. By 1946 she was ready for a new challenge and Meher Baba suggested she should try teaching dance in America. American Ballet Theater invited her to become the Company's teacher and ballet mistress. Four years later she was appointed director of the newly formed Metropolitan Opera Ballet School, beginning an association which was to last 20 years. Craske also taught at Robert Ossario's Manhattan School of Dance. Among her many students during this long period were Nora Kaye, Melissa Hayden, Paul Taylor and Sallie Wilson.

Craske was much loved by generations of students. A former student, Nancy Reed, described her as "a little ball of energy. She was a tiny woman — maybe all of five feet tall — with little feet in pink ballet slippers. She'd wear bell-bottomed trousers to teach in, and her feet would dart out of these trousers like humming birds, the pants flapping." Craske had forceful ideas which she expressed with clarity, and although she was always excited by new forms of dance, she was not to be fooled by the lack of intellectual rigour which characterized some of the more abstract companies of recent years. As she put it in an interview in 1983, "There is no room in the world for dancers running around and around the stage and then kicking their right ear. That doesn't mean a thing."

Craske remained a disciple of Meher Baba and from time to time she would return to India for a period of philosophical reflection. She continued to teach until well into her nineties but towards the end of her life she retired to Myrtle Beach, a centre of Meher Baba's teaching. However her visitors were quite likely to be given an impromptu ballet class when they came to see her there.

Margaret Craske's influence is still clearly to be seen in many of the great ballet companies of the world, where her former students are dancers, choreographers, directors and teachers. Through her extended influence, she has become a part of the tradition of classical dance.

Born Margaret Craske. **Emigration** Left England for US, 1946. **Career** Trained with Enrico Cecchetti, 1918–23; dancer, Diaghilev's Ballets Russes, 1920; dancer, Ninette de Valois troupe, London music-hall circuit, 1921; dancer, Carl Rosa Opera Ballet Company, London; illustration model, texts on Cecchetti method, from 1922; founded own ballet school; ballet mistress, Sadler's Wells (now Royal Ballet); studied with Meher Baba, India, 1931, 1939–46; ballet master, Ballet Theater, New York, 1947; assistant director, Metropolitan Opera Ballet, faculty, Ballet School, 1950–66; faculty, Dance Department, Juilliard School, 1950–66; faculty, Jacob's Pillow; ballet mistress, Manhattan Festival Ballet, 1968; studio, Manhattan School of Dance, 1961–86; retired 1986. **Related activities** Examiner, Imperial Society of Teachers of Dancing, London. **Other activities** Director, Meher Spiritual Center, Myrtle Beach, North Carolina. **Publications** (Contributor) *A Manual of Classical Theatrical Dancing (Cecchetti Method)*; (with C.W. Beaumont) *The Theory and Practice of Allegro in Classical Ballet*, 1930; (with Derra de Moroda) *The Theory and Practice of Advanced Allegro in Classical Ballet*, 1956; *The Dance of Love*, 1980; *Still Dancing with Love*, 1990. **Cause of death** Undisclosed, at age 97.

FABIA DRAKE

British Actress

***Born* Herne Bay, Kent, 20 January 1904**

***Died* London, England, 28 February 1990**

Fabia Drake played almost every major female role on the British stage, but she will be remembered mostly for her television portrayals of elderly yet imperious women. She fought debilitating stage fright throughout her career and despite performances with such notables as Laurence Olivier and Peggy Ashcroft, Drake's importance in the history of British stage and screen acting has often been overlooked.

She was born Ethel McGlinchy in Herne Bay on the south coast of England. Her father was an unsuccessful Irish actor and her mother, Annie, was Scottish. Drake remained relentlessly English, the product of the Royal Academy of Dramatic Art more than of her Celtic heritage. Her desire to act began almost before she could talk and Drake feigned an illness, managing to convince her parents to have her removed from her primary school. In 1914 Drake, aged nine, became the youngest pupil ever to attend the Academy of Dramatic Art — now RADA — under the tutelage of Kenneth Barnes. She managed to convince Barnes of her promising, if idiosyncratic, style of acting by insisting at her audition that in order to perform her speech as Katherine in *The Taming of the Shrew*, she "*must* make an entrance".

Drake quickly established herself as something of a child prodigy at the Academy. After her tenth birthday she had her professional stage début, playing a hermit land crab in *The Cockyolly Bird* at a London theatre. This inauspicious beginning inspired the formidable child to greater things. Two years later, Drake was cast in *The Happy Family* alongside a 16-year-old Noël Coward, whom she re-christened "Cowardy Custard". At 12 Drake played her first Shakespearian role, in *Twelfth Night*, this time with Laurence Olivier, two years her junior, who was to become a lifelong friend. In 1916, the same year as her performance with Olivier, Drake played Falstaff's page in a professional production of *The Merry Wives of Windsor*. The lead was played by the legendary Ellen Terry.

Drake left the Academy in 1917 to resume her education in Paris, but returned as a part-time student five years later. The early 1920s proved to be a difficult period for Drake, both personally and professionally. After the ease of her early success she began to suffer from the stage fright which eventually forced her to retire from the theatre. This pre-performance panic was attributed to guilt over the event in her childhood which had freed her to act in the first instance. Drake consulted psychiatrists and Indian gurus in an attempt to rid herself of this affliction, but fear continued to follow her.

On her return to London, Drake embarked on a series of small parts in West End theatres. Despite the growing voice of the suffragette movement, Drake was attempting to earn a living in a world where female intelligence was still often considered surplus to requirements. One (male) critic wrote of her 1926 performance in *The Scarlet Lady*: "Miss Fabia Drake is probably the best *ingénue* on the present-day stage, and provided she is able to conceal her brains, will one day make a popular success." He added, ironically, in the light of her paralysing stage fright, "She suggests health, physical, mental and moral."

In 1929 the director, W. Bridges-Adams asked Drake to join the Stratford Festival Company for a tour of North America. It was an enormous risk on his part; Drake had played Shakespeare only once professionally, and was required to learn six major parts in the three weeks before the tour was due to begin. This she managed to do, and having survived the physical and emotional strain of the tour, she returned to Britain to enjoy a run of some celebrity as a Shakespearian actress. Drake appeared in some ground-breaking productions. In 1933 she was Lady Macbeth in the director Komisarjevsky's so-called "aluminium revival". The actors were required to oil their skins so that they would shine against the scrolled aluminium of the sets. That autumn she played Rosalind in the London revival of *As You Like It*. It was Drake's favourite role, but her last in any Shakespearian production.

After her marriage to Maxwell Turner, a barrister — and later an Old Bailey judge — whom she met through his playwright brother, John Hastings Turner, Drake retired from the theatre. She said that retirement was a release from the horrors of stage fright. She didn't appear on stage at all during World War II, but in 1946 directed her first play, Robert Donat's revival of *Much Ado About Nothing*. At this time Drake also began to teach at the Academy of Dramatic Art. In the classroom she was formidable and demanded a great deal from her students. An actor who studied under her at the Academy commented: "Any inflection, emotion, gesture or intonation that appeared to her other than utterly genuine was ruthlessly exposed."

Drake's acting career resumed around the early 1950s when she began to be cast in film roles. It is these performances that gave rise to her being identified as a "crusty, domineering character". Drake received good reviews for her performance in the 1948 film *All Over the Town*, albeit for a cameo role. In 1954 she appeared in *Fast and Loose*, another minor role in a minor British film. The performances were always carefully honed and well-received, despite her usually fleeting presence on the screen. Although stage acting was her first love, the medium of film — and later, of television — relieved her of the anxieties of live performance, and she did discover on celluloid a niche of sorts.

Drake's husband died in 1960 and for a while she retired from acting altogether. What she called her *amitié amoureuse* with the distinguished archaeologist, Sir Mortimer Wheeler, began some years later and lasted for ten years. Drake continued to pursue her film and television career. In 1978 her autobiography *Blind Fortune* was published, with a preface written by her friend Laurence Olivier. It was not until she was in her eighties that Drake really found public recognition. In 1982 she appeared as Mabel in the major British television film, *The Jewel in the Crown*, with Peggy Ashcroft. Three years later she played Miss Catherine Allen in the film, *A Room With a View*. A serious accident after filming again forced Drake to retire from acting. She returned, aged 86, to record a BBC radio production of *The Forsyte Chronicles* (based on Galsworthy's *The Forsyte Saga*). Hours after completing a scene in which she enacted the death of her character, Fabia Drake died.

Born Ethel McGlinchy. **Parents** Francis Drake, actor, and Annie (Dalton) McGlinchy. **Marriage** Maxwell Turner, barrister, 1938 (died 1960). **Children** One daughter, Deirdre. **Education** Royal Academy of Dramatic Art, London, 1914–17, and later on Vedrenne scholarship, 1922; schools in Paris and London. **Career** Professional, début, a crab in *The Cockyolly Bird*, Court (now Royal Court) Theatre, London, 1913; with Stratford-upon-Avon Festival Company, 1929–30, 1932, 1933; début as director, *Much Ado About Nothing*, Aldwych theatre, London, 1946. **Related activities** Teacher, Royal College of Dramatic Art, World War II. **Stage** (in London unless otherwise indicated) *The Fairy Doll*, 1913 (stage début); *The Cockyolly Bird*, 1914; *Brer Rabbit and Mr Fox*, 1914; *The Happy Family*, 1916; *The Merry Wives of Windsor*, Brighton, 1916; *Twelfth Night*, 1917; *The Happy Family*, 1917; *Major Barbara*, 1921; *Quarantine*, 1922; *Secrets*, 1922; *Hassan*, 1923; *The Creaking Chair*, 1924; *Possessions*, 1925; *Easy Money*, 1925; *Twelfth Night*, 1925; *The Scarlet Lady*, 1926; *Escape*, 1927; *The Spot on the Sun*, 1927; *The Wrecker*, 1927; *The Silver Cord*, 1928; *Loyalties*, 1928; *The Love-Lorn Lady*, 1928; *Young Love*, 1929; *Macbeth* (on tour, United States and Canada), 1929; *Much Ado About Nothing* (on tour, United States and Canada), 1929; *No. 17*, 1930; *The World of Light*, 1931; *King Henry IV Part I*,

1932; *The Merchant of Venice*, 1932; *Cecilia*, 1933; *As You Like It*, 1933; *Poison Flower*, Croydon, 1934; *The Rose Without a Thorn*, 1934; *Sixteen*, 1934; *Our Mutual Father*, 1934; *Lady Precious Stream*, 1934; Frolic Wind, 1935; *Anthony and Anna*, 1935; *Indian Summer*, 1936; *Comedienne*, 1938; *Much Ado About Nothing* (director), 1946; *The Nightingale*, 1947. **Films** (include) *Meet Mr Penny*, 1938; *All Over the Town*, 1948; *Young Wives' Tale*, 1951; *Fast and Loose*, 1954; *The Good Companions*, 1957; *A Room With a View*, 1985; *Valmont*, 1989. **Television** (includes) *The Pallisers; The Jewel in the Crown; The World of Wooster; The Rainbow*. **Radio** (includes) *The Forsyte Chronicles*, 1990. **Publication** *Blind Fortune* (autobiography), 1978. **Cause of death** Undisclosed, at age 86.

JOSÉ NAPOLEÓN DUARTE

El Salvadoran Former President

Born **San Salvador, 23 November 1925**

Died **San Salvador, 24 February 1990**

Seldom can a man have come to power with higher hopes than José Napoleón Duarte, when in 1984 he became his country's first freely elected president in half a century. And the hopes of the free world — and especially of the United States — rode with him. Confident in his self-inspired mission to bring peace and democracy to a land torn by civil war and ravaged by long years of corruption and military rule, and with that confidence in no way shaken by his experience as head of the military junta in the early 1980s, Duarte took office determined to negotiate with the Farabundo Martí National Liberation Front (FMLN) guerrillas and to crush the death squads of the extremist right-wing elements entrenched in the Salvadoran Army. Once, in an interview, he had compared himself to Moses and described his life's ambition as to lead his people out of their slavery, poverty and brutality. Perhaps, like all endowed with a Messianic streak, his great mistake was to believe that his was a God-given mission. Certainly, by the end of his career, he was to feel — as he confessed to a close friend — that God had forsaken him.

And yet, his career began so well. The son of a tailor and confectioner who struck it lucky, he was active in politics while still a high-school student, taking part in the general strike of 1944. He then managed to get himself to Notre Dame University in the United States, from where he returned home with an engineering degree, to marry the daughter of a wealthy building contractor. His fellow students at Notre Dame had already noted his self-confidence; he is said to have tried for the college football team without ever having played the game. His now comfortable circumstances enabled him to embark almost at once on his favoured career in politics. His reputation gained a solid base from his three reforming terms as elected mayor of San Salvador in the 1960s, and he rapidly became the leader of the Christian Democratic Party, which he had helped to found in 1960.

In 1972 he ran for president at the head of a strategic coalition of Christian Democrats and Communists — a foolhardy venture in a country long dominated by military rule, and for which Duarte was to pay the penalty of a brutal beating up by the army followed by a seven-year exile in Venezuela. This experience at the hands of the army was to scar him for life, but in no way did it shake his belief in his political destiny. If he could not beat the military junta, then he would join it — anything so long as he had the chance to save his country. Following a fresh coup, he returned home and in March 1980 joined a military-civilian junta formed in an attempt to restore order as El Salvador sank into the anarchy of civil war. That same month saw the murder of Archbishop

Romero, followed later in the year by the murder of four American nuns — only the most publicized among more than an estimated 10,000 murders in that year alone. But Duarte, by this time the president of the junta, refused to acknowledge that his military colleagues were themselves the masters of the notorious death squads. He justified his continuing membership of the junta as unavoidable if he was to fulfil his mission.

Duarte's belief seemed vindicated when he won the presidential election in 1984 against his notorious right-wing opponent Major Roberto D'Aubuisson. Duarte promised peace and the end of what he called his country's "culture of violence", but his attempts to negotiate with the left-wing guerrillas were soon still-born. As was, indeed, his own hold on the situation. In reality, the army was still in control and inevitably the death squads increased their activities as his administration crumbled. Admittedly, the fates were against him. The country suffered a devastating earthquake and ever deepening poverty, his own daughter was kidnapped and held to ransom, and his son was involved in a corruption scandal; at the same time, his political support fell away, disillusioned not least by his "tainted" record of collusion with the military. Only the flow of US aid remained staunchly behind him, but in the eyes of his fellow countrymen he, and they, paid heavily for this support — and in some cases exaggeratedly, as on his visit to Washington in 1988 when he ostentatiously bowed to kiss the American flag.

This close identification with the United States brought opposition not only from the left-wing guerrillas but also from the ultra right-wing nationalists. In the 1989 presidential election the Christian Democrats suffered a devastating defeat at the hands of the right-wing National Republican Alliance (ARENA) Party. But by then Duarte was in any case out of the battle; he was struck down with terminal cancer. His one positive achievement might be said to have been his struggle to hang on to office until he could hand over to a constitutionally elected civilian successor, albeit of an extremist type which immediately stimulated the guerrillas to launch a major new offensive in the civil war he had tried so ineffectually to bring to an end.

One of the many jokes about Duarte during his seven years of exile was that he was physically too big to be called Napoleón and that El Salvador was too small for him to be Bonaparte. Perhaps it was a cruel fate that baptised him with the name of a man of destiny. Fundamentally an honest man — he was never accused of any personal corruption — and assuredly a staunch patriot, his tragedy was that he was faced with a situation bigger than he was or than perhaps any man could tackle single-handed.

Born José Napoleón Duarte Fuentes. **Parents** José Jesus Duarte, tailor and confectioner, and Amelia Fuentes de Duarte, former domestic servant and seamstress. **Marriage** María Ines Durán, 1925. **Children** Inés and three other daughters; Alejandro and one other son. **Education** Liceo Salvadoreno, San Salvador; Notre Dame University, South Bend, Indiana, BS in civil engineering, 1948. **Career** Partner, construction firm, also teacher, National University and military academy; mayor, San Salvador, 1964–70; Christian Democrat and Communist coalition presidential candidate, 1972; imprisoned, then exiled to Venezuela, 1972–77, engineer, Caracas; member, five-man ruling junta, 1980; president, 1980–82, 1984–89. **Related activities** Co-founder Christian Democrat Party, member, organizing committee, 1960, head, organization branch, secretary-general from 1961. **Cause of death** Cancer, at age 64.

HENRY FAIRLIE

British Journalist

***Born* London, England, 13 January 1924**

***Died* Washington, DC, 25 February 1990**

Henry Fairlie is often, among other things, credited with creating the term "the Establishment" by using it in one of his columns which examined the British political scene. As usual, the general public has misconstrued the truth of the matter. Fairlie did not actually coin the term (it was originally used by A.J.P. Taylor (q.v.)); he merely defined it — the whole matrix of official and social relations within which power is exercised — thereby granting it colloquial status. It was the method — the pure journalistic skill — by which he defined the term, however, that caused the public to credit him with its origin, for Fairlie's genius was such that it caused his bad debts, missed deadlines and erratic nature to be forgotten into the bargain. Dependable he was not, but Henry Fairlie was a highly talented journalist when he chose to deploy his powers and thus the world has forgiven him for his not-so-little foibles.

If one believes in the influence of heredity, then Fairlie came by his talent for writing *and* his unreliable nature quite naturally enough. His father James had moved from Scotland to London to become the news editor for the *Evening Standard* newspaper, and the young Fairlie claimed to relish the story of his death: one evening James Fairlie, inebriated after a dinner for Lord Beaverbrook, was placed into the hands of a taxi-driver in Fleet Street who was given instructions to drive him home. "When he got there, he was dead!" Fairlie would howl with laughter when repeating the story. "That's how I'd like to go!"

In addition to a weakness for drink and the ladies, Henry Fairlie also inherited his father's coal-black hair, his constantly red face, and intense eyes — and, according to his obituarist in *The Daily Telegraph* newspaper, "that deep melancholia which sometimes strikes the Scots."

One of six children, Henry Fairlie attended Highgate School in north London and from there went on to attend the University of Oxford where, at Corpus Christi College, he took a degree in modern history in 1945. Even as a young man, Fairlie was diagnosed as having heart trouble and so missed out on military service during World War II. Instead, he went straight from university life into the world of newspapers, first writing parliamentary reports for the *Manchester Evening News* and contributing to the *Glasgow Herald*, before proceeding to *The Observer* (a major Sunday newspaper). He remained with *The Observer* for two years, working as a general feature writer, before he left to join *The Times* in 1950. His first position here was as an obituarist, but soon it became clear that Fairlie had a natural talent for interpreting correctly political issues, and before long he had become the *Times*'s leader writer and a respected political editorial writer.

In 1955, the young journalist left *The Times* to join the staff of the *Spectator*, the UK's established weekly political and literary magazine. Although he spent a relatively short period as its political columnist, it was at the *Spectator* that Fairlie's real reputation as a political writer was confirmed. Initially, he wrote a commentary under the *nom de guerre* of "The Trimmer"; soon he was putting his own name to it. As Paul Johnson rightly stated in the London *Independent* newspaper, "The big men of all parties read and, more important, reflected on, what he wrote, and when he came out into the open ... his column was regarded as the shrewdest and best informed. It was also highly entertaining".

The column at the *Spectator* was the same in which Fairlie used the term "the Establishment", which, as stated above, will always be associated with him. More importantly, however, was the consistent accuracy which pervaded every column he wrote. "He had a remarkable instinct for sensing the direction in which political breezes were blowing," wrote Brian Inglis in the *Guardian*, and *The Daily Telegraph* shared that opinion: "He established himself as a gifted writer with an instinctive feeling for politics ... As a political columnist he followed in a tradition begun by his predecessor Hugh Massingham, of the inquisitive, intuitive essay. He took a serious, even grave view of political life, as an honourable calling whose practitioners were engaged in work of high importance."

No one can or would wish to deny that Henry Fairlie took politics seriously, yet on other matters — just as serious to most of us — he could be infuriatingly irresponsible. As Brian Inglis lamented (and he was not the only one) Fairlie "left many a newspaper a poorer place". After his stint at the *Spectator*, Fairlie went freelance, writing for journals and newspapers such as *Punch*, the *Daily Mail*, *Time and Tide* and the *Daily Express*. They loved him, but only for a short time: due to his neglect to open any sort of letter that "looked official", Fairlie was forever behind in rent payments and debts of various kinds; he often took to living in whatever publication's offices he happened to be working for at the time, and his arrival usually coincided with the mysterious disappearnce of books (he pawned them to raise cash) and other items of office equipment.

Nonetheless, Fairlie was much sought after as a journalist as well as a broadcaster — but here, like everywhere else, he characteristically "put his foot in it". During one such programme he made some scandalous remarks about the author Lady Antonia Fraser — at the time, a friend of his — who quite understandably sued both him and the BBC for libel. Because Fairlie never opened his mail, however, he ignored his summons, behaviour which, on a previons occasion, had led him to be arrested for contempt of court, prompting his long-suffering wife Lisette to say, "Well, at least tonight I shall know where Henry is." Shortly after the libel case, convinced he was in danger of going to prison, Fairlie abandoned his wife and family and fled to the United States in 1966.

Here, he began his love–hate relationship with America liking, so he said, the country's freedom and informality but not "the connection between power, wealth and glamour that now exists in Washington." Nonetheless, Fairlie remained in the US for the rest of his life, writing for numerous publications there: *The New York Times, Harper's, The Atlantic,* and *The New Republic*, where he more or less maintained a permanent relationship. The *Republic*'s editor, Hendril Hertzberg, explained,

> He was independent-minded, which made it hard for him to maintain a relationship with any publication. He claimed to be a true conservative, but it always looked a lot to me like liberalism. He was known as a curmudgeon, but that does not do him justice, because he had a big heart. He was an American patriot and a British patriot and a Scottish patriot — all these patriotisms co-existed quite comfortably in his bosom.

In between writing his columns, Fairlie had also found the time and discipline required to produce several books (although there were many more he had promised, received advances for, and never written). The first of these was *The Life of Politics*, published in 1969, which, according to the London *Times*, "set forth what amounted to his political credo. It took issue with what was regarded as critical orthodoxy in the late 1960s — namely that Parliament had become a cypher, power was concentrated in the hands of the bureaucracy, and that all a Prime Minister had to do was to placate the bureaucrats, as being the source of his own power." But that was not all: "Fairlie", *The Times* went on, "defended the British political system from these generally accepted charges and reiterated his faith in Parliament and its members." This book is considered by most to have been his finest work.

Among the other titles to his credit are the 1973 *The Kennedy Promise*, in which he analysed the presidential campaign and administration of John F. Kennedy (although he "badly exaggerated Kennedy's neglect of domestic affairs", wrote R.D. Novak in the *National Review*, his "overriding insight of what was wrong with Kennedy is worth considering"). *The Spoiled Child of the Western World* followed in 1976; this work was concerned with the need for the United States to "recover its morale and equilibrium". Other titles include *The Parties* and *The Seven Deadly Sins Today*. Just as in his native Britain, Fairlie's genius kept him out of severe scrapes in the United States, where he was forgiven more often than not for his habitual misconduct.

Perhaps Brian Inglis, who worked with Fairlie at the *Spectator*, best sums him up in his book, *Downstart*:

> As a colleague, Henry was maddening. He had a remarkable attraction for girls, coupled with devilry in arranging his schedule so that they were forever ringing up to find where he was, and why he wasn't where he said he would be to meet them. His copy tended to arrive long after it was promised; he boasted that he had never missed a deadline, but our Wednesday evenings were plagued by his near-misses. He was infuriatingly elusive, his telephone either remaining unanswered or, more commonly, off the hook. Yet he had that charm which made it impossible to be angry with him when he eventually showed up at the office — often needing to borrow a pound or two to finance his evening out.

Not surprisingly, the last Inglis, among others, heard of Fairlie, was that he was working on his autobiography. The provisional title? *Bite the Hand that Feeds You.*

Born Henry Jones Fairlie. **Parents** James, journalist, and Rita (Vernon) Fairlie. **Marriage** Elizabeth (Lisette) Todd Phillips, 1949. **Children** Simon, Charlotte and Emma. **Education** Highgate School, London; Corpus Christi College, Oxford, BA, modern history, 1945. **Emigration** Left England for the United States, 1966. **Career** Parliamentary correspondent, *Manchester Evening News*, columnist, *Glasgow Herald*, 1945–48; feature writer, *The Observer*, 1948–50; political editorial writer, *The Times*, London, 1950–54; political columnist under name, "The Trimmer", *Spectator*, 1955; freelance writer, late 1950s onwards, for *Punch*, the *Daily Mail, The Times, Encounter, The Observer, Time and Tide, Daily Express, The Sunday Telegraph,* London and *The New Republic, Washington Post, Baltimore Sun, The New York Times,* United States. **Publications** *The Life of Politics*, 1969; *The Kennedy Promise*, 1973; *The Spoiled Child of the Western World: The Miscarriage of the American Idea in Our Time*, 1976; *The Parties: Republicans and Democrats in This Century*, 1973; *The Seven Deadly Sins Today*, 1978; *Bite the Hand that Feeds You* (unfinished autobiography). **Cause of death** Undisclosed, at age 66.

MALCOLM FORBES

American Publisher

***Born* Brooklyn, New York, 19 August 1919**

***Died* Far Hills, New Jersey, 24 February 1990**

Malcolm Forbes, multi-millionaire publisher and art collector, was sometimes confused in the American mind with Superman, of comic-strip fame. His habit of arriving at charity balls astride a motorbike, for example, put Americans in mind of that other hero. Forbes would dismount, remove his goggles and his Hell's Angel leather gear to reveal a man-about-town in impeccable evening wear. Did not Clark Kent of the comic-strip do the same in reverse, changing before one's eyes from a wimp into the soaring man in the cape?

When Superman Forbes took time out from air-ballooning over China to squire actress Elizabeth Taylor around town it was as though the American Dream "had been made flesh and dwelt among us", as one commentator explained. It was also good for business, as Forbes himself might have put it. He excelled at marketing himself as part of a product, in his case *Forbes* magazine, a semi-monthly journal of business and finance.

This publication, which was founded by his father, was the basis of Forbes's holdings, variously estimated as worth between 400 million and one billion dollars. During his stewardship Forbes built up the magazine to 735,000 readers. In the 1980s it pulled ahead of *Fortune* in advertising space and gained ground on *Business Week*, these being its two main rivals. It was all due to "sheer ability, spelled I-N-H-E-R-I-T-A-N-C-E", Forbes quipped.

Forbes's holdings included a private plane, a yacht and an island in the South Pacific named Lauthala, over which he requested that his ashes be scattered. They also included such exotic real estate as a château in Normandy, a mansion overlooking the River Thames in London, a palace in Morocco and a 260-square-mile ranch in Colorado.

Born in Brooklyn, Forbes was the third son of a Scottish emigrant, "Bertie" Forbes, who founded *Forbes* magazine in 1917. During school holidays young Forbes worked in the mail room in order to learn the family business from the ground up. Upon his graduation from Princeton University in 1941 he was cited as the undergraduate "who has contributed most to Princeton".

During World War II Forbes served as a machine gunner with the 84th Infantry Division in Europe, where he was severely wounded in combat. He was discharged from the Army with the Bronze Star, the Purple Heart, and a slight limp, which remained with him for the rest of his days.

In 1946 he married Roberta Laidlaw, whose father was an investment broker; and the couple went to live in Far Hills, New Jersey on an estate they named Timberfield. They were divorced in 1985.

Forbes's first choice of a career was politics, with publishing as a sideline. In 1951 he was elected to a six-year term as a New Jersey state senator, and became one of the first Republicans to back Dwight D. Eisenhower for president. In 1957 Forbes was defeated as the Republican candidate for governor of New Jersey. Thereafter his active interest in politics waned.

Forbes's climb up the ladder of the family enterprise was a gradual one until the death of his elder brother in 1968, when he gained complete control as publisher, president, editor-in-chief and sole owner of *Forbes* magazine. In a lively column he wrote himself, Forbes filled the magazine with his likes and dislikes, ranging from a puff piece for a favourite restaurant to a sharp dig at a peddler of junk bonds.

Not until he was in his fifties did Forbes make an impact upon the public as an eccentric and big-time spender. By then Forbes on his Harley-Davidson motorcycle had roared from Warsaw to Moscow — this at a time when many of his peers, on the advice of their doctors, had taken up croquet as being less strenuous than squash.

By then, too, Forbes had become a familiar figure in the art salerooms. When he bid two million dollars for a bejewelled Easter egg that Carl Fabergé had designed for a Russian tsar the auctioneer brought his hammer down and announced: "The score now stands at Kremlin 10, Forbes 11." Before the year was out the publishing magnate had increased his score to a round dozen.

Forbes's overriding passion, however, was hot-air ballooning. In November 1973, he became the first person ever to cross the United States in a balloon when he flew from Coos Bay, Oregon, to the Chesapeake Bay. In the process he broke six world records. The following year he nearly lost his life when the tiny aluminium gondola, in which he was hoping to cross the Atlantic, was dragged across a concrete runway as the balloon supporting it broke free from its moorings.

To the argument that balloons were dangerous, foolish and a waste of money, Forbes countered that they were a good promotional gimmick for the magazine. The same was true of the Fabergé eggs, which were placed on display at the firm's Fifth Avenue headquarters. As sole owner of Forbes, Inc., the publisher was not accountable to shareholders.

Some were puzzled by the magazine's motto, "Capitalist Tool", which was also the name of the firm's private jet. In addition to its usual meanings, "tool" could designate a flunky, one who allowed himself to be manipulated. By his extravagance was Forbes holding the social system of which he was so much a part up to ridicule and contempt, or was it simply a childish delight in the things that money could buy?

In particular his profligacy came under criticism when shortly before his death he flew 800 guests, including Elizabeth Taylor and former secretary of state Henry Kissinger, to Tangier to celebrate his seventieth birthday. The cost: nearly two million dollars. On the other hand, Forbes gave lavishly to charity, one of his last donations being a million dollars for Aids research.

Forbes gave capitalism a human face, according to industrialist Armand Hammer (q.v.) a verdict in which David Dinkins, the mayor of New York City agreed, adding that the publisher was a "creative and vibrant character". "He was the quintessential American — optimistic, buoyant, and lots of fun", Henry Kissinger declared.

Forbes left four sons, one daughter, 12 Fabergé eggs, six hot-air balloon records, 68 Harley-Davidson motorcycles, 75,000 toy soldiers, and a business said to be worth ten million dollars a year.

Born Malcolm Forbes. **Parents** Albert Charles Forbes, founder *Forbes* magazine, and Adelaide (Stevenson) Forbes. **Marriage** Roberta Laidlaw, 1946 (divorced 1985). **Children** Malcolm, Robert, Christopher, Timothy and Moira. **Education** Lawrenceville School, New Jersey, 1937; Woodrow Wilson School of Public and International Affairs, Princeton University, New Jersey, AB, political science, 1941. **Military service** Staff sergeant, 334th Infantry, 84th Infantry Division, in France, Belgium, Holland, Germany, 1943–45. **Career** Founder, undergraduate magazine, the *Nassau Sovereign*, while at college; owner and publisher: *Fairfield Times*, Lancaster, Ohio, 1941, *Lancaster Tribune*, 1943; assistant to the publisher, *Forbes* magazine, 1945, associate publisher, 1947, publisher and editor, 1954, editor-in-chief, sole owner, 1957, onwards; vice-president, Forbes Incorporated, 1947, president, 1964 onwards; founder, *Nation's Heritage*, president and publisher, 1948–49; owner, publisher, *Egg* magazine, 1989. **Related activities** Vice-president, Investors Advisory Institute, 1948, president, 1954–64. **Other activities** Borough councillor, Bernardsville, New Jersey, 1949; senator, New Jersey state, 1951–57; founder, chairman, New Jersey Ike-Nixon clubs, 1951; Republican candidate for governorship of New Jersey, 1957; New Jersey delegate-at-large, Republican National Convention, 1960; owner, Slegers-Forbes Inc., 1960 onwards; collector, motorcycles, property, paintings, Fabergé eggs and jewels; balloonist, 1972 onwards, first person to cross the United States in a hot-air balloon, 1973; holder, six official world ballooning records; member, corporate America bridge team. **Offices and memberships** Member: St Andrew's Society, Association of the United States Army, New Jersey Historical Society, Confrérie des Chevaliers du Tastevin, National Aeronautic Association, International Balloonists' Association, Balloon Federation of America, Aircraft Owners and Pitts Association, Lighter Than Air Society, British Balloon and Airship Club. **Awards and honours** Class of 1901 Medal, Princeton, 1941; Bronze Star, 1945; Purple Heart, 1945; Freedom Foundation Medal, for *Nation's Heritage*, 1949; named New Jersey Young Man of the Year, New Jersey Junior Chamber of Commerce, 1951; Doctor of Humane Letters, Nasson College, Springvale, 1966; Doctor of Law, Oklahoma Christian College, 1973; Doctor of Literature, Millikin University, Decatur, Illinois, 1974; Harmon Aeronauts' Trophy, 1974. **Publications** (include) *Fact and Comment*, 1974. **Cause of death** Heart attack, at age 70. **Further reading** Christopher Winans, *Malcolm Forbes*, 1991.

LIEUTENANT-GENERAL JAMES GAVIN

American Military Commander and Diplomat

Born **Brooklyn, New York, 22 March 1907**

Died **Baltimore, Maryland, 23 February 1990**

In World War II, dropping troops on the field of battle by parachute was one of the most successful, if controversial, tactical innovations. James Gavin emerged as one of the stars of airborne warfare, and at the age of 37 became the youngest officer ever to hold divisional command in the war.

He was also an outspoken critic of American military strategy in the cold war era, and it was for this independence of mind that he was chosen by President Kennedy to represent the United States in France in the early 1960s. Later it was American involvement in Vietnam which incurred his withering disapproval.

Gavin was orphaned while still a baby, and his adoptive parents, Martin and Mary Gavin, brought him up in the coal-mining Mount Carmel region of Pennsylvania. The Gavins were not well-off, and before young James left school at the age of 14 he had already worked part-time as a newspaper boy, coal picker and barber's assistant. For three years he was employed first as a shoe-shop clerk, then running service stations.

It was to complete his education that Gavin finally decided to join the Army in 1924 at the age of 17, a move which provided the key to a meteoric career. Enlisted in the coastal artillery and posted to Panama, he attended evening classes for the equivalent of high-school graduation standard. In 1925 he was accepted, against all the odds, for cadet training at West Point Military Academy.

At West Point he displayed the same determination to apply himself: many of his most profitable study hours were won by rising at 4.30 am, and spending the interval before reveille quietly reading in the basement latrines.

Commissioned in 1929, Gavin had early experience with aircraft at the Air Corps Primary Flying School at Brooks Field in Texas. Most of his postings in the inter-war period, however, were to infantry regiments in Arizona, Oklahoma, the Philippines and Washington State.

In August 1940 Captain Gavin was appointed as an instructor in tactics at West Point. It was in this period that his study of the German campaigns then being conducted in Europe convinced him of the tactical importance of airborne warfare. Such was his enthusiasm for this new form of troop deployment that, in September 1941, he secured a transfer to the Parachute School. Within a few months he was training paratroops himself at Fort Benning in Georgia. By April 1942 he was head of military operations for Airborne Command at Fort Bragg, North Carolina, and attended staff college later that year with the temporary rank of lieutenant-colonel.

Gavin's aptitude for paratroop command was obvious. So was his personal success as a field commander. He was a believer in close contact with the men he led, often stopping for genuine conversation. No one under his command could ever feel that Gavin was remote from their interests, or did not share their dangers.

Appointed to command the 505th Parachute Infantry Regiment in August 1942, Gavin devoted the next year to training his men in parachute drops. Roughly half this time was spent in North Africa, in preparation for the crucial Allied landings in Sicily. With the Axis powers on the retreat in Russia, and chased out of North Africa, Allied strategy in 1943 hinged on a successful, two-stage invasion of Italy through Sicily and the Straits of Messina. Paratroops dropped behind the enemy's coastal defences were to play a vital role in the operation.

On the night of 9–10 July 1943 Gavin's regiment headed the drop into Sicily. They did not have everything their own way; some two dozen American aircraft were shot down by their own artillery support, and one in ten of the paratroop force was killed. "Jumping Jim" Gavin proved his inspirational qualities in the Sicily landings. As on later drops he was always "first out of the door". In the words of one of his men, "He could jump higher, shout louder, spit farther and fight harder than any man I ever saw." He was also remarkably calm in combat, and successfully directed his men in a counter-attack against the German forces opposing them.

The 505th next saw action on 14 September, in support of the landings at Salerno on the Italian mainland. Shortly after the Salerno drop Gavin was singled out for temporary promotion to brigadier-general, and appointed assistant commander of the 82nd Airborne Division, of which the 505th was a part. He was seconded to the London headquarters of General Eisenhower, supreme allied commander in Europe, during the winter of 1943 to 1944, to advise on the airborne tactics for the forthcoming Normandy landings.

Before returning to the 82nd Airborne to prepare for D-Day, Gavin thus had an opportunity to help shape the Allied use of paratroops in Normandy. He made it clear how essential it was to avoid dropping units too far in the enemy's rear, where they would be at the mercy of more heavily armed units. Equally important, paratroops would not make much difference on the landing beaches themselves; their value was in dislocating enemy defences in the immediate rear of the front line.

Parachute landings in Operation Overlord were on a hitherto unprecedented scale involving three separate airborne divisions. Gavin dropped on 6 June with the 82nd Division in support of the American VII Corps on Utah Beach. By mid-August the Allied forces had broken out of the Normandy beachhead, and the advance across northern Europe began. Gavin was in an even more important position by now, for on 15 August he was given the command of the 82nd Airborne itself.

In the north European campaigns of 1944 to 1945, the 82nd Airborne Division became something of a legend. It covered the most ground, spent the highest number of continuous days in combat, and accounted for the most enemy losses. Much of this was due to Gavin's driving energy and qualities of leadership.

The Division's highest profile was as part of Operation Market Garden, the drive to secure bridgeheads on the right bank of the Rhine in the Netherlands. Gavin's troops were successfully dropped in the region of Nijmegen; but the parallel drop at Arnhem was a disaster, with the paratroops overwhelmed before Allied armoured units could come to their support.

After Nijmegen Gavin was promoted to major-general, the youngest in the Army. He again achieved prominence during the Ardennes counter-offensive by the Germans, or Battle of the Bulge, when General Montgomery ordered the 82nd to withdraw in conformity with the rest of the hard-pressed Allied forces. Gavin's protest that the 82nd had never yet yielded an inch of ground was overruled by Montgomery, probably wisely.

Gavin's progress after the war reflected the golden opinion that had been formed of him during it. After briefly sharing the occupation of Berlin with his division, he returned to the United States in December 1945, and remained in command of the 82nd at Fort Bragg until 1948. In 1947 he published a model account of his experiences and reflections as a paratrooper, *Airborne Warfare*.

He served for a year as chief of staff to the Chicago-based Fifth Army, and in April 1949 was appointed to the office of the secretary of defence, as the Army representative on the Weapons Systems Evaluation Group. From 1951 to 1954 he was based with American forces in Europe, returning to Washington in the latter year as assistant chief of the research and development department in the Pentagon. Between 1955 and 1958, as a lieutenant-general, he headed Research and Development. It was here, however, that Gavin's serious disagreement with American defence policy began to surface. In both these posts, it should be noted, Gavin made an important contribution to the development of the long-range missile, and to the tactical use of helicopters as troop carriers. Both innovations have shaped tactics to this day.

Early in the Eisenhower administration, defence policy showed an increasing tendency to rely on the strategic potential of nuclear weapons as an alternative to conventional forces. This was in part motivated by cost: by investing heavily in strategic nuclear weapons, the government could, and did, cut back its conventional strength. An overwhelming preponderance of nuclear weaponry, however, also implied the possible use of nuclear weapons for non-military as well as military purposes. This was opposed by a number of influential voices in the academic world, including Henry Kissinger. Such critics argued that a sizeable conventional force was essential if the United States were to remain capable of acting decisively in world politics, without the constant threat of nuclear weapons.

Gavin also objected strongly to this "New Look" policy of Defence Secretary Charles E. Wilson. His objections were tactical: an army without the development of tactical conventional weapons and training would be useless for any limited, ie non-nuclear, warfare; and despite the existence of nuclear weapons it was limited warfare, he argued, which was more likely to occur. Realizing that his arguments were having little effect on Wilson, Gavin announced his resignation from the Army days before his promotion to full general. As he put it, "I won't compromise my principles, and I won't go along with the Pentagon system."

That same year (1958), he published a detailed critique of the "New Look" policy, *War and Peace in the Space Age*. The basic thesis was that the United States must possess the conventional forces and flexibility to cope with limited as well as nuclear war.

Gavin's ideas began to sink in in the early 1960s, when the concept of massive nuclear retaliation by either superpower appeared increasingly self-defeating. In the meantime Gavin had accepted a job as vice-president of a management and industrial research consultancy, Arthur D. Little Inc. in Cambridge, Massachusetts, and became its chairman in 1960.

His book and his record as a plain-spoken fighting man, however, had attracted the serious attention of the then Senator John F. Kennedy, who reviewed favourably *War and Peace in the Space Age*. The result was an invitation to act as the Kennedy administration's ambassador to France in 1961.

Gavin spoke virtually no French and had no ambition as a diplomat, and Kennedy's initiative has usually been explained as a desire to "match one obstreperous general (de Gaulle) with another". It was improbable, though, that the presence of even so engaging a personality as Gavin in Paris could have papered over the differences between France and the United States in this period. Instead, Gavin was soon under attack from within the Kennedy administration for having "gone native", and actually arguing that the US should assist France in building up its independent nuclear deterrent. His appointment lasted only 18 months.

Gavin went back to his consultancy chairmanship, but resurfaced in the mid-1960s as an unexpected critic of the Vietnam war. For Gavin the whole American involvement in Vietnam lacked any clear or justifiable purpose. The policy of attrition was self-defeating, and was diverting US resources from what Gavin considered the real trouble spot, the Middle East, where Soviet influence appeared to be real and growing. After a ten-day trip to Vietnam in 1967 he returned to announce, in a public lecture, that "We are in a tragedy".

During the 1968 primaries Gavin actually spent some time trying to induce the Republican Party to field a peace candidate. According to some accounts, he himself was briefly promoted by influential Republicans as a candidate, but dissociated himself from the attempt immediately.

Gavin retired from business in 1977. His memoirs, *On to Berlin*, appeared the following year.

Born James Maurice (last name unknown). **Parents** (by adoption) Martin and Mary (Tearle) Gavin. **Marriages** Two marriages;2) Jean Emert Duncan. **Children** Barbara, from first marriage, Caroline, Patricia, Aileen and Chloë, from second marriage. **Education** Local schools, Mount Carmel, Pennsylvania; cadet, United States Military Academy, West Point, 1925–29; Air Corps Primary Flying School, Brooks Field, Texas; Infantry School, Fort Benning, Georgia; Parachute School, 1941; Command and General Staff School, Fort Leavenworth, Kansas, 1942.

Career Clerk, shoe shop; manager, petrol stations; private, coast artillery, 1924; corporal, United States Army; commissioned, second lieutenant, infantry, 1929; with 25th Infantry, Arizona; with 38th and 29th infantries, Fort Sill, Oklahoma; with 57th Infantry (Philippine Scouts); captain, 7th Infantry, Vancouver Barracks, Washington; instructor in tactics, West Point, 1940–41; plans and training officer, Provisional Parachute Group, Fort Benning, Georgia, 1941; chief of military operations, Airborne Command, Fort Bragg, North Carolina, became lieutenant-colonel, 1942; commander, 505th Parachute Infantry Regiment, 1942–43; brigadier-general, 1943; assistant commander, 82nd Airborne Division, 1943, commander, 1944–48; became major-general (temporary), 1944; chief of staff, Fifth Army, Chicago, 1948; Army member, Weapons System Evaluation Group, Washington; chief of staff, Allied forces, southern Europe, 1951; commander, United States Seventh Corps, Germany, 1952–54; assistant chief of staff, Plans and Operations, Pentagon, 1954; deputy chief of staff, Plans and Research, Pentagon, 1955; lieutenant-general (permanent), 1955; chief of research and development, 1955–57; retired from Army, 1958; vice-president, Arthur D. Little, Inc., 1958, president, chairman, 1960–77; ambassador to France, 1961–63. **Related activities** Airborne adviser, Supreme Commander, London, 1943; American representative, City Kommandantura, 1945; member, Council on Foreign Relations; delegate, Atlantic Congress; member, New Frontiers of Technology Committee, United States Chamber of Commerce; member, Republican campaign, 1968 presidential elections. **Offices and memberships** Fellow, Harvard Center of International Affairs; life trustee, Tufts University; member: American Academy of Arts and Sciences, National Council of the Atlantic Union Committee. **Awards and honours** Distinguished Service Cross with oak leaf cluster; Distinguished Service Medal; Silver Star with oak leaf cluster; Bronze Star Medal; Purple Heart; Distinguished Service Order, Great Britain; Croix de Guerre, France; Legion of Honour, France; Order of Alexander Nevsky, Russia; Order of Orange-Nassau, Netherlands; Order Courenne, Belgium. **Publications** *Airborne Warfare*, 1947; *War and Peace in the Space Age*, 1958; *Crisis Now*, 1968; *On to Berlin* (memoirs), 1978. **Cause of death** Parkinson's disease, at age 82.

KEITH HARING

American Artist

Born **Kutztown, Pennsylvania, 4 May 1958**

Died **Manhattan, New York, 16 February 1990**

He used a near-naked Grace Jones, "the ultimate body", for his canvas. He dressed Madonna in squiggly hand-painted jackets. He had one-man shows in all the major art galleries, in all the big metropolitan centres, all over the world. He was an Aids activist, and a champion of street culture. Most of all Keith Haring was an artist who appealed to all kinds of people, designer of the most striking visual language to hit the United States and Europe at any time in the post-war period. His work crossed geographical and cultural boundaries with ease and made a nonsense of distinctions between high and mass art in the age of technology.

The "meteoric rise" of certain contemporary artists of the New York scene has become somewhat of a cliché in art criticism-speak. Yet in the case of Haring, it is very much a live and apt metaphor. Because indeed Keith Haring "arrived" in the early to mid-1980s as if from outer space, dotting the urban landscape of downtown (and underground) New York with his characteristic cookie-cutter outlined radiant babies, barking dogs and dancing figures. At first, these distinctive shapes signified little more than a more imaginative way of saying "Keith Haring was here", but they gradually evolved into a unique vocabulary when he added crosses and light bulbs, television sets, mythical-looking creatures and a host of semi-abstract forms. From graffiti-kid to multi-millionaire international artist: such is the story of Keith Haring.

Like a meteor, his life and art were a bright flash, brief but incredibly intense, and leaving a lasting impression. Haring's light never reached the stage of burnout however. In the full flow of his creative powers and while enjoying huge popular success, he died at the age of 31 — an Aids victim like so many of his contemporaries in the arts and entertainment world.

Explaining the rationale behind his work and acknowledging one of the major influences on it, Keith Haring told the magazine *Flash Art* in 1984: "The role of the artist has to be different from what it was 50, or even 20 years ago. I am continually amazed at the number of artists who continue working as if the camera were never invented, as if Andy Warhol never existed, as if airplanes and computers and videotape were never heard of." This was his artistic credo: taking art out of the studios and the art galleries into the streets, abandoning realism (though not representation) and making full use of the new democratic materials of everyday life: advertising hoardings, walls, the marking pen and industrial paints. In his statement Haring singled out Andy Warhol, whose popular visual style, derived from advertising, was clearly a precedent for Haring's own brand of street-culture. Warhol's images, together with Roy Lichtenstein's blown-up strip cartoons, must be credited with doing the groundwork that prepared the art world for Keith Haring. Still, it has to be remembered that Haring was radically different as well, and in many ways more innovative than either of these luminaries of American Pop Art; he did not confine himself to the mainstream and commercial visual language of American popular culture. Instead, Haring fused it in a unique and revolutionary way with Afro-American and Latino forms. This lent his art its wholly individual and instantly recognizable air of what used to be called "primitivism": simple, highly efficient and evocative colours and shapes reminiscent of Aztec and African art. In addition, Haring's keen interest in popular cultural forms, especially as practised on the streets of the Bronx and in Harlem, danced into his art in the shape of contorted figures doing the hip-hop and electric boogie — with sparks flying everywhere.

But Haring fused more than cultural differences and the palpable tensions of New York's multi-ethnic life. In 1982 he used the Spectacolor billboard over Times Square to flash one of his drawings for an entire month, displacing the crass images of advertising. In this way Haring managed to merge street culture with high art, and the new technological media with the ancient crafts of mural and body-painting. An artist of the 1980s in every possible sense, he nevertheless sought to restore art to what he saw as its traditional and rightful place: art should be playful and exploratory without shunning social critique — he wanted his work to "make people think".

Keith Haring was born in a small town in Pennsylvania in 1958. From an early age he invented and illustrated wild and funny stories (inspired by television strip cartoons) in collaboration with his father, a foreman in a Western Electric plant. In search of further training and excitement, Haring went to New York at the age of 20 to attend the School of Visual Arts. Here he soon reached the conclusion that "high" art, abstract expressionist painting such as he was encouraged to pursue at the school, had had its day. What he saw on the subway was much more interesting: street-kids who used advertising boards and spraycans as their easel and oils. This was a movable art, "paintings that travelled to you instead of vice versa", as he later explained. Haring soon joined the graffiti kids, taking care to paint (rather than spray) on black paper which he stuck on unused advertising space. This gave his work a distinctive "framed" look, as if of "real" paintings which had gone astray *en route* to a "real" art gallery. Just like his spraying companions, however, Haring was arrested numerous times for defiling public property, and even on occasion thrown into an overnight cell. But a funny thing happened: increasingly the policemen whose job it was forcibly to remove him from his "studio", confessed to liking his work. By the time he had become a celebrity, they even started asking for his signature.

Taking his art out onto the streets did not mean that education at the School of Visual Arts had been entirely wasted on Keith Haring. The course in semiotics (the study of signs) which he had taken there proved particularly formative as he progressed from subway "paintings" to above-ground murals and gallery pieces. Soon his symbolic and evocative drawings were everywhere, evolving as he went on from the playful and joyful babies and dancers to the more sinister and critical visual symbols of Christian crosses, figures with television sets for heads seemingly in the process of electrifying themselves, and mythical creatures with grotesque genitals. If it was to be expected that these wry and graphic comments on the force of religion, on the destructive effects of consumer and media culture and more especially on the demonization of Aids would win him no friends in the art establishment, such was not the case. The more enlightened critics and dealers, always on the lookout for something new, immediately recognized the importance of his work. That famous Maecenas of contemporary art, the appropriately named Henry Geldzahler, for example, engaged Haring in a project to re-decorate the Palladium, a ritzy disco-cum-night-club. Major exhibitions of Haring's work were staged in Los Angeles, London, Amsterdam and Sydney, as well as in his own backyard, New York. He could call Andy Warhol, Boy George, Yoko Ono and Madonna his friends, and he threw lavish parties for them and the numerous people he worked with from SoHo and the Bronx. As an admirer told the press years later, he became "an artist nobody doesn't love". Haring's golden years were the mid and late 1980s, when he made himself a not-too-moderate fortune, lots of famous and infamous friends, and a reputation as champion of the marginalized and oppressed. Although international exhibitions and his private clients made increasing demands on his time, Haring also continued to paint in the style to which he was accustomed: outdoors, on the walls of hospitals, in schoolyards, and in his own Pop Shop, which he opened on Lafayette Street in 1986. Going commercial, selling posters and tee-shirts, mugs, diaries and socks imprinted with his designs, attracted much criticism from those who preferred to see Haring as a big-time gallery artist. But his defence was cogent, emphasizing his anti-elitism as well as the snobbery of his critics. First of all he said "art is nothing if you don't reach every segment of the people", and secondly he pointed out that if he just wanted to make a lot of money quickly he'd be better off selling all his work, down to the most casual doodle, as an "original artwork" through his dealer Tony Shafrazi. The tumult died down, and Haring concentrated again on his many projects: sets for ballets, murals for Mount Sinai Hospital in New York, a "Subway Show" at Lehman College in the Bronx, sculptures exhibited by Leo Castelli, and a mural of the Ten Commandments (which Haring had to look up in the Bible the night before starting) for the Musée d'Art Contemporain de Bordeaux. Proving that he was not in it for the money, he also initiated projects with neighbourhood kids, contributed to *Live Aid* in 1985 and the Campaign for Nuclear Disarmament, and made a series of images on the plight of Blacks in South Africa and the United States. One of his last works was a mural entitled *Once Upon a Time* which he contributed to the ACT UP Stop the Church campaign held in New York at the end of 1989, in protest against the anti-gay religious fever sweeping the country at that time in the wake of the Aids scare.

Keith Haring's art was committed to the breaking down of barriers of all kinds. He spoke across the divides of class, race, gender, sexuality and ethnicity. When in 1986 he painted 100 yards of the Berlin Wall in the colours of the German flags with a chain of interlinked human figures superimposed upon it, the breaking down of barriers became an almost literal thing. Haring commented at the time: "It is a humanistic gesture, a political and subversive act — an attempt to psychologically destroy the wall by painting it." In the 1960s young people had believed in "living the revolution" before it had happened; Haring's decision to paint the Berlin Wall was in this sense a prefigurative act worthy of that icon of 1960s culture, the poet Allen Ginsberg (whom Haring greatly admired). Three years after he painted it the Berlin Wall came down, only a few months before Aids put up a final barrier between Keith Haring and the many people whose world is darkened by his untimely death.

Born Keith Haring. **Parents** Allen, electricity plant foreman, and Joan Haring. **Education** Kutztown High School, Pennsylvania; School of Visual Arts, New York, 1979–80. **Career** Artist, 1980 onwards; first exhibition, Westbeth Painters Space, West Village, 1981; artist-in-residence, Montreux Jazz Festival, Switzerland, 1983; first published collection, *Art in Transit*, 1984. **Related activities** Clothes and stage set designer; founder/owner, the Pop Shop, New York, 1986. **Individual exhibitions** Westbeth Painters Space, 1981; Club 57, New York, 1981; Rotterdam Arts Council, 1982; Tony Shafrazi Gallery, New York, 1983; Leo Castelli Gallery, 1985; Shafrazi Gallery, 1985; Leo Castelli Gallery, 1986; Alexander Roussos Gallery, London; also exhibited in Tokyo, Milan, Basel, Munich, Amsterdam. **Group exhibitions** Club 57; *1982 Documenta*, Kassel, Germany, 1982; *Urban Kisses*, Institute of Contemporary Art, London, 1982; *Beast: Animal Imagery in Recent Painting*, P.S. Gallery, Long Island City, New York, 1982; *New York Today*, Carnegie–Mellon University, Pittsburgh, 1983; Whitney Museum of American Art Biennial, New York, 1983; São Paulo Bienal, 1983; San Francisco Museum of Modern Art, 1984; Hirshhorn Museum, Washington, DC, 1984; *Disarming Images: Art for Nuclear Disarmament*, 1984; Venice Biennale, 1984; *Subway Show*, Lehman College, New York, 1985; Biennale de Paris, 1985; *Life in the Big City: Contemporary Artistic Responses to the Urban Experience*, Rhode Island School of Design, Providence, 1986. **Works** (include) *Painted Man*, 1983; Videotape commercial, Zürich, Switzerland, 1984; set and prop designs, *Secret Pastures*, 1984; curtain design for *The Marriage of Heaven and Hell*, Ballet National de Marseille, 1985; *Michael Stewart: USA*, *Portrait of Macho Camacho*, 1985; mural, Musée d'Art Contemporain de Bordeaux, France, 1985; set decoration for rock group Duran Duran, 1985; murals, Mount Sinai Hospital, New York, 1986; first-day cover commemorating United Nations International Youth Year, 1985; mural, Berlin Wall, 1986; murals for Necker Children's Hospital, Paris; *A Pile of Crowns for Jean-Michel Basquiat*, 1988; posters for "Act Up" campaign, 1989. **Collections** Dag Hammarskjöld Plaza Sculpture Garden, United Nations headquarters, New York; Museum of Modern Art, Rio de Janeiro. **Publication** *Art in Transit, Subway Drawings by Keith Haring*, 1984. **Cause of death** Aids, at age 31.

SIR WILLIAM KESWICK

British Businessman and Art Collector

***Born* Yokohama, Japan, 6 December 1903**

***Died* London, England, 16 February 1990**

The history of British trade in the Far East is very much that of the Scots merchant house of Jardine Matheson. Equally, the story of Jardine's has been inextricably intertwined with that of the Keswick family.

Sir William Keswick, who was called "Tony" by his friends, was the great-great-grand-nephew of William Jardine, who co-founded the firm in 1832. His paternal grandfather, William, and father, Henry, both became head or "taipan" of Jardine's, and there was never serious doubt that William would follow in their footsteps.

He was born in Yokohama, Japan (where Jardine's had had an office since 1859). He came to England for his formal education, at Winchester, the public school, and Trinity College, Cambridge, but immediately afterwards returned to the Far East to begin his business training and induction into the ways of Jardine's. He took up his duties in Harbin, Manchuria, in 1925. After a nine-year tour of Jardine's offices, he was ready to assume charge. As taipan, he based himself in the company's official head office in Hong Kong between 1934 and 1935, and in Shanghai, then the most commercially important of the offices, from 1935 to 1940.

He became a prominent figure in Shanghai society (literally as well as figuratively, as he was conspicuously tall and well-built). Shanghai was a major international business centre with special areas or "concessions" set aside for foreign traders. Keswick became chairman of the Shanghai Municipal Council in 1938, a position which made him "mayor" of the expatriate business community. His influence encouraged the formation of friendly links between Chinese and European business interests.

At the onset of World War II, Keswick returned to Britain, and visited Washington as part of a British shipping mission, but soon he was back, assisting Churchill's minister of state for the Far East, Duff Cooper, who was based in Singapore but travelling the area to monitor the political situation. Cooper's brief was chiefly to keep an eye on the Japanese who, it was correctly suspected, were about to enter the war. Keswick was especially qualified to advise Cooper by his dealings with the Japanese in Manchuria.

Perhaps it was this activity which made Keswick the target of an assassination attempt in January 1941. So many had fled Shanghai that the city could not raise sufficient finance at current rates of taxation. A ratepayers' meeting was convened at Shanghai racecourse to discuss increasing the rates. As Keswick, still the chairman of the Municipal Council, addressed the meeting, a Japanese by the name of Haiyashi took a pot-shot at him, from point-blank range. Keswick escaped with a grazed rib, which good fortune some attributed to the thick overcoat which he was wearing at the time. Shortly afterwards, Keswick left the Far East to take a more active part in the war. He served with HQ 21 Army Group under Montgomery in Egypt, becoming a brigadier.

He was never to live in China again. It was traditional in the Keswick family for the men to devote their youth to the family firm in the East and then, having discharged that duty, to return to Britain and live out their years in the comfort of the family estate at Glenkiln, in Dumfriesshire, Scotland

Although this Keswick followed the custom to the extent of returning to Britain for good after the war, he certainly cannot be said to have retired. The family's investments in Jardine's meant that he retained a large measure of control over the company, and on the strength of this power continued to be regarded by his associates as unofficial "king" of Hong Kong. And one important post after another came his way. He was director, and, from 1949, chairman of Jardine's London arm, Matheson & Co. Beyond Jardine's, he became a director of British Petroleum, and governor of the Hudson Bay Company, another venerable British trading company predating Jardine's by a couple of hundred years.

As a director of the Bank of England, Keswick underwent the traumatic experience of giving evidence to a tribunal set up in 1957 to investigate an alleged leak of an imminent increase in the Bank Rate from five to seven per cent. It appeared that certain companies, including Matheson's, had begun to sell off their sterling government securities, or gilts, prior to the announcement of the rate increase, indicating that they were trading on insider knowledge.

Attaching more importance to the concept of honour than many a twentieth-century financier, Keswick felt the implied accusations keenly, even after the tribunal completely exonerated him. One piece of the evidence adduced in his favour was a message from Keswick to Jardine's in Hong Kong, which had been clamouring to get out of gilts. Keswick had finally conceded agreement with the words "this is anti-British and derogatory to sterling, but on balance it makes sense".

Two other offices which Keswick held reveal a patronage of the arts of which he was inclined to make light before his City associates. He became a trustee of the National Theatre, and, partly through his old school-fellow and friend, Kenneth Clark, a trustee of the National Gallery.

Another of Keswick's friends was the world-famous sculptor Henry Moore. Keswick would visit Moore's studio, and bought or commissioned important works including *Standing Figure* and *King and Queen*. The wild landscape of his grouse moor at Glenkiln was used to display monumental sculptures by Moore and Epstein, to great advantage, perhaps in an echo of the sculpture gardens which he had experienced in the East.

The sculpture "park" attracted world-wide attention, so much so that Keswick began to complain that visiting art critics were upsetting his grouse. For he was a traditional Scots laird to the extent of listing shooting and fishing as recreations in his *Who's Who* entry. (He and a friend are said to have shot 2000 snipe in a weekend, back in China in the 1930s.)

Most of his interests, though, were less conventional. He grew plants, particularly exotic trees and lilies, some of them collected in the East. Hot-air ballooning was a favourite, though infrequent, pastime. He loved harp music and enjoyed regular command performances by a harpist in the garden of his house on the outskirts of London. According to one anecdote, he summoned a French horn-player to play with her, but insisted that he play from the top of a tree so as not to overpower the sound of the harp.

Keswick retired as chairman of Matheson's in 1966, but the family involvement with Jardine Matheson continues. His oldest son Henry has been chairman of Matheson's since 1975, and his youngest, Simon, is a director. Both have held and hold other major positions within the Jardine empire.

Sir William Keswick saw a major restructuring of Jardine Matheson after World War II, when, of necessity, its interests became concentrated on Hong Kong. His heirs will have to grapple with equally momentous changes in the run-up to 1997 when Hong Kong will be taken over by the People's Republic of China. No doubt Sir William, always keen to meet an adventure or an opportunity head-on, would have liked to be there too.

Born William Johnston Keswick. **Father** Major Henry Keswick, businessman. **Marriage** Mary Lindley, 1937. **Children** Three sons, oldest Henry and youngest Simon, and one daughter. **Education** Winchester College, Hampshire; Trinity College, Cambridge, 1925. **Military service** Brigadier, staff duties 21 Army Group, Egypt, Washington, World War II. **Career** Executive, Jardine, Matheson & Company Limited, Shanghai, 1925–26, Beijing, Manchuria and Tientsin, 1926–34; taipan, Jardine, Matheson & Company Limited, Hong Kong, 1934–35, Shanghai, 1935–40; director, Matheson & Company Limited, 1943–75, chairman, 1949–66, non-executive director, 1966–75; director, the Hudson Bay Company, 1943–72, governor, 1952–65; director: Bank of England, 1955–73, British Petroleum Company Limited, 1950–73; chairman, various public companies in Far East. **Related activities** Chairman, Shanghai Municipal Council of late International Settlement, 1938–41; member, Royal Commission on Taxation of Profits and Income. **Other activities** Seconded to staff of Duff Cooper, minister of state for the Far East, 1941; collector of sculptures and rare plants; balloonist. **Offices and memberships** Member, Royal Company of Archers; trustee: National Gallery, 1964–71, National Theatre. **Awards and honours** Knighted, 1972. **Cause of death** Undisclosed, at age 86.

VICTOR LASKY

American Journalist and Author

***Born* Liberty, New York, 7 January 1918**

***Died* Washington, DC, 22 February 1990**

Whatever else one might say about Victor Lasky, best-selling author and newspaper columnist, he was not thin-skinned. "I dish it out, I can take it", he once explained. He might well have made it his motto.

During four decades, in books, in newspaper columns, and in lectures, he "dished it out" in a personal crusade against subversives in high places. In Lasky's usage "subversive" was an omnibus term which included Communists and those whom he called "woolly-minded liberals", notably President John F. Kennedy.

Accused of being a hatchet-man for the far right in politics and of showing unfair bias in his writing, Lasky answered that he never paid attention to political criticism. "I let my readers decide." That his readers found for Lasky more often than not is attested by the frequency with which his books made best-seller lists despite being lambasted by his critics.

Victor Lasky was born in Liberty, New York, graduated from Brooklyn College, and began his career in journalism as a copy boy on *The New York Journal-American*. He was soon hired as a reporter by *The Chicago Sun*. During World War II he was on the staff of the Army newspaper, *Stars and Stripes*.

Lasky's post-war career took off when he co-wrote for *The New York World-Telegram* a series of articles on Communist infiltration of American institutions. The series won the Pulitzer Prize for 1947, and established Lasky as an expert on subversion.

His coverage of the trial of Alger Hiss, former State Department official convicted of perjury for denying that he had been a Soviet agent, yielded a best-seller, *Seeds of Treason*, written in collaboration with Ralph de Toledano. Lasky next turned his attention to political biography of the debunking variety, choosing as his first subject President Kennedy. The resultant *J.F.K., The Man and the Myth* was a scissors-and-paste job, and as such panned by *Time* magazine as a collation of "every bit of anti-Kennedy rumour, gossip, innuendo, and fact."

Lasky was dogged by bad luck in the case of both Kennedy brothers. The *JFK* biography appeared shortly before the President was assassinated. *Robert F. Kennedy: The Myth and the Man* was published soon after its eponymous subject had been gunned down in a Los Angeles hotel ballroom, thus necessitating extensive rejigging and leaving Lasky open to the charge of making "tasteless ... comments on a man who could not defend himself" *(The New York Times Book Review)*. When this was followed in due course by *Jimmy Carter: The Man and the Myth* the dominant reaction was, "Oh, no, not again." Lasky appeared to be scraping the bottom of the barrel, mythologically speaking.

In contrast, *It Didn't Start with Watergate*, which was published in 1977, was an attempt on Lasky's part to vindicate ex-president Richard M. Nixon by pointing to the misdeeds of his Democratic predecessors in office. Presidents from Franklin D. Roosevelt to Lyndon B. Johnson had resorted to "dirty tricks", including wiretaps and illegal break-ins, according to Lasky.

For 18 years Lasky wrote a syndicated column, "Say It Straight", for the North American Newspaper Alliance. He also wrote and lectured for Accuracy in Media, a conservative watchdog group whose mission was to keep an eye on newspapers suspected of showing a liberal bias.

Lasky lived to see the cold war give way to co-existence, a process started by a president whom he could not have labelled a "woolly-minded liberal", Ronald Reagan. The old crusader never lowered his guard, however. As the glacier that had covered East–West relations began to melt Lasky gave one last warning. "I do hope we're not falling for Communist tricks again", he said.

Born Victor Lasky. **Parents** Max and Bella (Polen) Lasky. **Marriage** Patricia Pratt, 1952. **Education** Brooklyn College (now Brooklyn College of the City University of New York), BA, 1940. **Military service** Correspondent, *Stars and Stripes*, United States Army, Europe, 1942–46. **Career** Reporter, *The Chicago Sun*, Chicago, Illinois, 1941; copywriter, *The New York Journal-American,* 1941; reporter, *The New York World-Telegram*, New York City, 1946–50; screenwriter, Metro-Goldwyn-Mayer, Culver City, California, 1951–52; writer, RKO General Teleradio, New York City, 1955–56; press officer, Radio Liberty, New York, 1956–61; author of column, "Say It Straight", syndicated by North American Newspaper Alliance, 1962–80. **Related activities** Lecturer and writer, Accuracy in Media. **Other activities** Publicity adviser, Richard Nixon's presidential campaign, 1960. **Offices and memberships** Member: National Press Club, Overseas Press Club, Authors League of America. **Awards and honours** Pulitzer Prize, for series on Communist infiltration, 1947; Academy Award nomination, for documentary film *The Hoaxters,* 1952; *It Didn't Start with Watergate*, Conservative Book Club selection, 1977; Doctor of Letters, Ashland College, 1983. **Publications** (include) (with Ralph de Toledano) *Seeds of Treason*, 1950; (with Allen Rivken) *The Hoaxters* (documentary), 1952; *The American Legion Reader*, 1954; *John F. Kennedy: What's Behind the Image?*, 1960; *J.F.K., The Man and the Myth*, 1963; *The Ugly Russian*, 1965; *Robert F. Kennedy: the Myth and the Man*, 1968; (with George Murphy) *Say, Didn't You Used to be George Murphy?*, 1970; *Arthur J. Goldberg* [q.v.]: *The Old and the New*, 1970; *It Didn't Start with Watergate,* 1977; *Jimmy Carter: The Man and the Myth,* 1979; *Never Complain, Never Explain: The Story of Henry Ford II*, 1981. **Cause of death** Abdominal cancer, at age 72.

MEL LEWIS

American Jazz Drummer and Bandleader

***Born* Buffalo, New York, 10 May 1929**

***Died* Manhattan, New York, 3 February 1990**

Paradoxically for so modest and low-profiled a man, Mel Lewis held two of the flashiest jobs in jazz. He was a drummer and he was a bandleader. So too was Buddy Rich and yet the two men, although their skills were similar, could not have been more different. The wise-cracking Rich had an electric rapport with his audiences. The self-effacing Lewis even went so far as to have someone else make his stage announcements for him.

On the other hand, when Lewis felt strongly about something, he could be as forthright as Rich. He was a realist and hated pretence of any kind. He recognized the need to play "commercial" music to make a living. "If you don't want to play it, get your own band", he said.

Born Melvin Sokoloff, he was the thinking man's drummer, displaying musical taste superior to that of any other drummer one could think of. His genius was to improve the performance of everyone he played with, whether it was that of an instrumental soloist, a singer or an entire orchestra. Consequently he appeared on few, if any, bad recordings and worked across the widest spectrum of jazz, accompanying such basic blues singers as Jimmy Witherspoon on the one hand, and helping to produce the vintage wine of jazz that was the Thad Jones–Mel Lewis Jazz Orchestra on the other.

"I'm thankful", he said, "for having gotten to play with almost every good jazzman around during my career, from Dixieland to avant-garde. I feel sorry for the guy who's in one bag all his life. He's missing out on the fun. Ben Webster, Dizzy Gillespie, Coleman Hawkins, Louis Armstrong, Eric Dolphy, Muggsy Spanier, Richard Davis, Eddie Sauter, Gunther Schuller — I've worked with all of them."

He was instrumental in forcing the Stan Kenton band to swing for the first time. When he joined he found a ponderous and inflexible band style which stifled the possibility of a loose, rhythmic jazz sound. When the Kenton band was due to visit Britain in 1956 Lewis refused to travel unless the bass player in the band, whom he thought to be inadequate, was fired. Kenton took Lewis's advice and replaced the man with Curtis Counce, and the Kenton band achieved an exciting jazz sound on that tour that had a colossal impact on its listeners. One could have been forgiven for having thought that Kenton's previous bands operated only on the principle of "louder, louder". The sound was loud still, but with Lewis on board there was more variation in the dynamics, and most important of all the rhythm section took on a pithy swing previously unknown in the context.

Mel Lewis's father was a professional drummer in the Buffalo area of New York where the family lived, but young Mel never studied drumming, learning music by playing the baritone horn and tuba. When he was 16 he changed to drums and began his professional career with clarinettist Lenny Lewis's band. Subsequently he worked for the bands of Boyd Raeburn, Alvino Rey, Ray Anthony and Tex Beneke in the years between 1948 and 1954, when he joined Stan Kenton (the ever-courteous Kenton telephoned Beneke and apologized for taking his drummer).

"Not only did Stan inspire you to play, when he found a talent he featured it. Now that I'm a leader, I think that one of the most important things is that the audience always knows who is in the band, and I learned that from Stan. That's how I got known. Stan made sure that everybody knew that Mel Lewis was playing drums. That's how Stan created names. I learned from him how to treat a young player to help him develop. A lot of my ideas came from Stan." Lewis stayed with Kenton, working at the same time in small groups led by Frank Rosolino and Hampton Hawes, until 1957. Eventually he left the band because "Stan was changing back to the more experimental kind of music. I'm a swinger, a jazz player." He moved to Los Angeles where he worked in television and radio and led a quintet with the tenor saxophonist Bill Holman. He played also with the bands of Gerald Wilson and Terry Gibbs. The latter gave him his permanent nickname "the Tailor" ("because he walks like my tailor").

By now Lewis was so much in demand that he began to commute between Los Angeles and New York for a multitude of different jobs. In 1960 at the instigation of his friend Bob Brookmeyer, valve trombone player in the group, he joined Gerry Mulligan's Concert Jazz Band, one of the most inventive, traditional and yet free-thinking jazz groups of the day. Although it was world famous, Mulligan's band didn't work on a regular basis, coming together only when Mulligan had found enough work to make it viable and Lewis was able to take the time to tour Europe with Dizzy Gillespie's quintet in 1961 and to make the infamous Russian trip with the Benny Goodman Orchestra the following year. Goodman's eccentric behaviour on this historic visit alienated just about all the musicians in his group.

Lewis remained in the Mulligan band for three years and then in 1963, with trumpeter Thad Jones, whom he had befriended while with Mulligan, formed a rehearsal band (a group that played for fun and not money). Many of the top musicians in the city, some from the Kenton, Ellington and Basie bands, joined, and eventually the new band began meeting regularly at the Village Vanguard on Monday evenings, a night when the club was normally closed.

The quality of the musicians and the high standard of music written for the band, mostly by Thad Jones and Bob Brookmeyer, soon turned this into one of the best and most inventive bands in the world. Life at the Vanguard was too parochial for such a potent force and, as the Thad Jones–Mel Lewis Jazz Orchestra, the group began a series of world-wide tours. This writer remembers a wonderful night at Manchester's Free Trade Hall when the plane carrying the band's sheet music and uniforms had gone astray. Famous for its easy-going good nature, there was much laughing among the musicians as the shirt-sleeved orchestra improvised the evening's music on the spot.

The band reeled from the blow when Thad Jones left in 1978 and moved to Scandinavia where he took over the Danish Radio Big Band. Mel Lewis stayed in New York and picked up the reins of the Jazz Orchestra. By now many of the big-name musicians in the band had moved on and had been replaced by younger men. Lewis called on Bob Brookmeyer to take on the creation of a new library. Brookmeyer, then recovering from a period away from jazz, responded with huge enthusiasm and took over the role of composer, arranger and music director that had previously been Jones's. Although it remained an excellent and tasteful band it never achieved the quality of the star-drenched band of Thad Jones's day.

"Fifteen musicians and a drummer" was one of the old definitions of a big band. Not with Lewis in it, for he was invariably the arbiter of good taste and his mere presence was a hallmark of excellence in any context. He had an enviable musical sensitivity in any musical setting, and probably made more jazz recordings than any other drummer.

Born Melvin Sokoloff. **Father** A professional drummer. **Marriage** Doris. **Children** Lori and Donna. **Career** Dance-band drummer, Buffalo, New York: with Lenny Lewis, with Boyd Raeburn, 1948, Alvino Rey, 1948–49, Ray Anthony, 1949–50, 1953–54, Tex Beneke, 1950–54; with Stan Kenton, 1954–57; with Frank Rosolino's quintet and Hampton Hawe's trio, briefly; leader, with Bill Holman, quintet, Los Angeles, 1958; with Terry Gibbs and Gerald Wilson, 1959–62; with Gerry Mulligan Concert Jazz Band, New York, 1960; toured Europe with Dizzy Gillespie, 1961; toured Union of Soviet Socialist Republics with Benny Goodman, 1962; formed Thad Jones–Mel Lewis Orchestra with Jones, New York, 1965, became sole leader, 1978. **Recordings** (include) as leader: *Mel Lewis and Friends*, A&M Hor. 716, 1976, *Live at the Village Vanguard*, with Thad Jones, SolS 18, 1967, *Central Park North*, with Thad Jones, SolS 18058, 1969, *Consummation*, with Thad Jones, BN 84, 1970, *Suite for Pops*, with Thad Jones, A&M Hor. 701, 1972, 1975, *The Thad Jones/Mel Lewis Quartet*, AH 3, 1977, *Mean What You Say*, with Thad Jones and Pepper Adams, Mile, *Body and Soul* with Al Cohn and Zoot Sims, Muse, *The You and Me That Used to Be*, with Jimmy Rushing, RCA; as sideman: S. Kenton, *Contemporary Concepts*, Cap T666, 1955, S. Kenton, *On Fire!*, Cap T731, 1956, B. Holman, *The Fabulous Bill Holman*, 57188, 1957, W. Herman, *Woody Herman's New Big Band at the Monterey Festival*, Atl. 1328, 1959, G. Mulligan, *A Concert in Jazz*, 68415, 1961, D Gillespie, *New Continent*, Lml. 86022, 1962. **Cause of death** Melanoma, at age 60.

DOUGLAS LONG

British Journalist, Editor and Newspaper Executive

***Born* London, England, 9 February 1925**

***Died* London, England, 7 February 1990**

Douglas Long was a hard news man turned hard-nosed newspaper manager. And a man whose career began after it ended. Twice.

The archetypal British journalist of the 1940s was an aggressive foot-in-the-door, notepad-toting reporter. In the 1960s he sat in a noisy, smoky newsroom on Fleet Street, bashed out his copy on a manual typewriter and spent his lunch-times in "watering holes" such as The Cheshire Cheese. In the 1970s new communications technology changed those newsrooms beyond recognition. The 1980s was the decade of new ventures and of a massive exodus from Fleet Street. Douglas Long was in on all these developments: as one of the foremost of its practitioners and — after his "retirement" — as an instigator of new ventures in the world of British newspapers.

He was born where he latterly lived — in London. After education at Wandsworth School, south London he had little time to consider a career before becoming, of necessity given the outbreak of war, a soldier. He served in the Indian cavalry regiments where he eventually became a captain in Probyn's Horse. Thereafter he always retained a touch of the officer-class presentation about him with his well-cut suits and his crisp speech.

Soon after demobilization Long joined the now long defunct *Daily Graphic* as a reporter, and found the vocation which was to last the rest of his life. He became a feature writer, gaining the experience on which he later built his reputation as a hard newsman and thruster. In 1948 at the age of 23 he headed north to the *Daily Record* in Glasgow. For the next six years he remained there — and his progress was steady rather than dramatic.

In 1955 he landed the job which really launched him, Scottish editor to the *Daily Herald*, and three years later returned to London as the *Herald's* chief news and features editor. These were tricky times at the *Herald*. The newspaper was owned by Odhams in rather queasy partnership with the Trades Union Congress. Ian Waller, while political correspondent on *The Sunday Telegraph*, recalled "the tragic history of the *Daily Herald*, with the intolerable conditions imposed on its editor and staff and the insistence that it should be the uncritical mouthpiece of the unions and Labour leadership ..." But the difficult, shoe-string conditions brought out the best in Douglas Long; admittedly he was irritable and irascible — he was also intuitive and effective. Although the paper was inexorably fading, he still managed to produce what the readers wanted. Unfortunately, the readers became fewer and fewer as they were claimed either by death or by richer newspapers.

At that time the International Publishing Company, headed by Cecil King, was the most successful newspaper and magazine organization in Britain: IPC bought Odhams lock, stock and barrel. Some publications continued to appear under the old company name; but the *Herald* was transformed into the IPC *Sun* with the slogan "Born of the age we live in." Douglas Long stayed on as its chief news editor/features editor.

"There were two alternative policies open to the IPC management when they decided to replace the Herald", wrote Ian Waller. "Either to produce a quality left-wing paper ... seeking to 'fill the gap' between the popular and the heavies: bright, with good news coverage of a serious quality, but radical in flavour. Or it could attempt to beat the *Daily Express* at its own game, becoming sensational and vigorous. But unfortunately the *Sun* has fallen between the two." And — a problem which still dogs left-wing publications in Britain — the paper failed to attract sufficient advertising. So the *Sun* also died in the age it in which it lived; it was taken over by Rupert Murdoch.

But Long had already been spotted by Don Ryder, chairman of Reed International. This was the era of newspaper takeovers and counter-takeovers; Reed bought IPC, once again retaining the old name on many of its products. And Long, in 1969, was appointed general manager of what was left of what had been Odhams.

Much later, in the late 1970s, Cedric Pulford, attending an address which Douglas Long gave to the Mirror Group's editorial trainees, asked Long why he had crossed over into management. His reply was notably straightforward: "Because I thought no one was going to make me an editor [of an entire paper]." He didn't amplify; perhaps, according to Pulford, he was not brash enough for the "pop" end of the business. Or perhaps he was ideally suited to his new role. He knew the business inside out from his years as a reporter; he was also, right from the early days, that rare bird among journalists — neat and tidy in his administration. So it was not really surprising that he accepted the move to management.

Long progressed quickly in this sphere. The newspaper part of Odhams became the Mirror Group and in 1972 he became its deputy chief executive; on the strength, it was said, of scoring a million or so points in one of those management training games so beloved of costly consultants. In 1980 he succeeded Percy Roberts as managing director and chief executive of the Mirror Group. By 1984 he was Group chief executive and vice-chairman. He was one of only two who knew of Reed's plans to float the Mirror Group. It was a tremendous disappointment to him when a series of problems made Reed abort the flotation and sell to yet another tycoon, Robert Maxwell.

It was midnight, one night in July 1984 in the Holborn Circus headquarters of the *Mirror*. At that hour the editorial offices of a "daily" are still awake and buzzing. And at that hour Maxwell arrived to announce that he was the new owner. Maxwell moved in; Long moved out.

He was then almost 60 and – well compensated and pensioned — had no financial worries. Everyone expected that would be the end of his long and already considerable career. Instead he walked out of one era of newspaper history — a famously frustrating one for managers — and into another. "Remember," said one of the men he left behind him, "he was as fit as a flea then." Certainly he and his wife Barbara played tennis and swam regularly.

So it wasn't really so unpredictable that he was approached to help launch *The Independent*. Writes Matthew Symonds,

> Andreas Whittam Smith and I first discussed starting a newspaper on All Fools Day 1985 ... In our conceit, we were very clear about the kind of paper we wanted to see launched, who would write for it and even who the readers would be.
>
> However, it did not take us long to realise that, although we had a fair idea about how the journalistic product might be created, we knew almost nothing about the practical details of paper-buying, printing, distribution and all the myriad other things essential to the making of the "daily miracle" which do not take place on the editorial floor. We badly needed to talk to someone who did.

He remembered Long.

Symonds and Long knew each other only slightly. But the ex-Mirror Group man agreed to meet and his response to the idea of *The Independent* was immediately one of encouragement and enthusiasm. "It must have been bliss to him", writes a contemporary. Says Symonds, "He explained that he was enjoying his retirement, but would be happy to allow Andreas and me to pick his brains".

Inevitably, Douglas Long became increasingly involved and contributed much with much zest. He was a professional; his management expertise helped to avoid the errors which led to the initial failure of *Today*, launched by comparative amateur Eddie Shah. Long was also widely known and respected; he was able to obtain the all-important backing from the City.

In 1986 he became the managing director of Newspaper Publishing plc (*The Independent*). "He laboured heroically," according to Symonds, "appearing at over 60 presentations, negotiating contracts, sometimes banging heads together; always he was firmly practical and wise. When he left *The Independent*, his job was essentially done. A new national newspaper had been established. It could not have happened without Douglas Long."

He retired once more. The share situation on *The Independent* would have made him a very rich man. However, having tasted that very particular excitement and satisfaction of a new start in a new newspaper world, he did it again. He took his experience and his enthusiasm over to the Clerkenwell premises of *The Sunday Correspondent* as founding chairman. For a second time he presided over a successful launch (although the paper was to be short-lived).

In these late ventures, he was able to introduce new ideas and to change the working methods from those which had frustrated him and his colleagues in the decade before. He had been a hard news man; he knew the score. Many journalists will remember him now as never forgetting who creates newspapers and doing his best to see they were rewarded. His most frequent phrase when the pay battle raged was: "OK. Give it to them. It's only money."

Douglas Long survived the takeovers and counter-takeovers of Fleet Street in the 1960s and 1970s. He played a crucial role in establishing two quality newspapers floated by new communications technology and the advertising boom of the 1980s. But he did not survive to tackle a third "retirement" venture. He was attacked by cancer and after only a brief illness died just short of his sixty-fifth birthday.

Born Adrian Douglas Long. **Parents** Harold Edgar and Kate Long. **Marriage** Vera Barbara Wellstead, 1949. **Children** One son, Mark. **Education** Wandsworth School, London. **Military**

service Royal Deccan Horse, 43rd Cavalry, Probyn's Horse, captain, Indian Army, 1943–47. **Career** Reporter, feature writer: *Daily Graphic*, 1947, *Daily Record*, Glasgow, 1948–54; Scottish editor, *Daily Herald*, 1955–57, chief news and features editor, *Daily Herald* and the *Sun*, 1958–68; general manager, Odhams, 1969–71; deputy manager, Mirror Group Newspapers Limited, director, deputy chief executive, 1972–79, chief executive, 1980–84, group chief executive, 1984, vice-chairman, 1984; chairman: Syndication International, 1975–84, Mirrorair Limited, 1981–84; director: Odhams Newspapers Limited, 1976–84, Mirror M&G Management Limited, 1976–84, *Scottish Daily Record and Sunday Mail*, 1977–84, Reed Publishing Pension Trustees Limited, 1980–84, Reed Publishing Holdings Limited, 1981–85, Mirror Group Pension Trustees Limited, 1981-84; co-founder, managing director, Newspaper Publishing plc, *The Independent*, 1986-88, *The Sunday Correspondent*, 1988–90. **Related activities** Consultant, Surrey Business Enterprise Limited, 1985 onwards; member, Press Council, 1986 onwards. **Offices and memberships** Member: President's Association, American Management Association, Institute of Directors, British Institute of Management; fellow, Royal Society of Arts, 1987. **Cause of death** Cancer of the liver, at age 64. **Further reading** Ian Waller, "The Left-Wing Press", in *The Left,* editor, Gerald Kaufman, 1966.

LORD MACLEAN

British Courtier and Scout

Born **Isle of Mull, Scotland, 5 May 1916**

Died **Hampton Court Palace, London, 8 February 1990**

It was 1981. Romantics and Royal-watchers the world over sat glued to their television screens with bated breath and damp handkerchieves as young Diana Spencer arrived at St Paul's Cathedral to wed her prince. A decade earlier: the old guard of the Boy Scout movement sat around their campfires appalled at plans to abolish the traditional shorts and wide straw hats which had made the scout instantly recognizable the world over. One man was behind these two very different landmarks in modern history — Charles Hector Fitzroy Maclean.

He was born into a romantic historical tradition of his own. He was the second son of Hector Fitzroy Maclean of the Clan Maclean of Duart whose lineage is traced to "Gillean of the Battleaxe", founder of the clan Gillean in the thirteenth century and thence — through a Celtic abbot of Lismore and the Royal House of Lorn — to the ancient kings of Dalriada. The family home, which had been rebuilt by Maclean's grandfather, was perched on a windswept promontory on the Isle of Mull off the west coast of Scotland.

But Maclean was sent south for his education — far south to Dorset. Hardly had he finished his education there when, in 1936, his grandfather died, at the age of 101, and the young Maclean succeeded him as 11th Baronet and 27th Chief of the Clan.

When war broke out he served as an officer in the Scots Guards. He fought in France, Belgium, Holland and Germany. He landed on the beaches of Normandy. He crossed the Rhine with William Whitelaw and Robert Runcie (later to become a leading politician and Archbishop of Canterbury respectively) as fellow officers. He was mentioned in despatches and retired with the rank of major.

In 1947, back on the farm, Maclean bred Highland cattle and Blackface sheep. He was also unstinting in public service. In 1954 he was appointed lord-lieutenant (the Queen's representative) of the county of Argyll and in 1955 became a JP. Indeed, throughout his life he found time for numerous organizations from military service bodies to the Outward Bound Trust: from the Camping Club to the Scottish National Fatstock Club. He was also a director of Distillers.

As an eight-year-old Charles had joined the Wolf Cubs. His interest in the Boy Scout movement persisted into adulthood and in 1954 he became chief commissioner for Scotland for the Boy Scouts Association. Five years later he became chief scout of the UK and Overseas Branches. By his own account he had found "the form of service I was looking for".

He had an instinctive rapport with the young and was never stuffy. It was jocularly said that "Chips" — his nickname — Maclean was best known for his knees, which were regularly exposed in his capacity as chief scout, and of course, by his kilt in his role as chief of the clan Maclean.

But the short trousers of the Boy Scouts were soon swept away by Chips in a whirlwind of reform. Under his aegis a 24-man working party set out to revolutionize the scouting image. "Little Johnny of the Peewits" with badges down to the elbow was out. Scouts were henceforth to be Scouts, not Boy Scouts. New adventure pursuits, such as gliding and caving, were added to the traditional activities of camping, tying endless varieties of knots and lighting fires without matches. He even enlisted a pop group in his campaign. "We must do more to show that scouting is really swinging and 'with it'", declared Maclean.

Maclean was much criticized by traditionalists; but his package of reforms ensured that the Scout Movement in the 1970s was respected and admired as a modern educational force. Said Sir William Gladstone, who succeeded him as chief scout, "he had boldly grasped the nettle and, against some strong conservative opposition, had given the Scout Movement its new look ... His courage made my task an easy one."

In 1975 Lord Maclean stood down as chief scout. He had in the meantime become Lord Chamberlain of the Queen's Household and a life peer. The Lord Chamberlain's job — in a nutshell — is to organize State visits by foreign heads of state, court ceremonies and garden parties. His other duties range from the maintenance of the royal palaces and residences to matters of precedence: from the flying of flags to the care of the Queen's swans. He also issues warrants to tradespeople who enjoy the royal patronage.

Lord Maclean's first ceremonial assignment, the funeral of the Duke of Windsor in 1972, was a difficult one, given the relationship of the Crown to the Windsors. But he presided over the melancholy occasion with superb tact — and with the most meticulous attention to protocol. The Royal-watchers who assembled at Heathrow, ready to pounce on the slightest error, noted with approval that his farewell to the Duchess of Windsor did not include a bow. He was also responsible for the state funerals of the Duke of Gloucester and Lord Mountbatten. At the latter his eye for detail was apparent when he discreetly rearranged a wreath on the coffin and straightened a banner.

Maclean's owlish figure, carrying his white wand of office and often walking backwards, became a familiar sight on television during the state occasions he organized so superbly. Happy occasions as well as sad ones. He master-minded the Silver Wedding and Silver Jubilee celebrations of the Queen and the marriage of Princess Anne and Captain Mark Phillips in Westminster Abbey. And the job had its lighter side. On one occasion he had to advise the Queen on whether she ought to retain her right to every whale and sturgeon washed up on the British coastline. After due consideration it was decided against, as the right was of no benefit to the Crown and might well prove a nuisance.

But the highlight of this perfectionist's term as Lord Chamberlain of Her Majesty's Household was without doubt the wedding of the Prince and Princess of Wales in 1981. He and his staff spent months making careful preparations for the service, the great procession to and from the Palace and Clarence House and the reception that followed. He even vetted all commemorative items — and upset the British textile industry by his ruling that "Charles and Di" tee-shirts should not be permitted to adorn the chests of the kingdom. The reward for all his work was a grateful kiss from the bride at Waterloo Station — which took Maclean by surprise, but set the seal of royal approval on his efforts.

"Chips" Maclean retired as Lord Chamberlain in 1984 and received the rare honour of the Royal Victorian Chain. The next year he was appointed chief steward of Hampton Court Palace. Here, as in the Household, he was much loved by his staff. For his attention to detail extended to the welfare of those who worked for him; every year he arranged for members of the domestic staffs of the royal houses to have a day trip on the royal yacht. Not that he broadcast this fact; a taste for public acclaim played no part in the character of this meticulous, hard-working man behind the scenes of the uniquely British pageant of so many royal ceremonies.

Born Charles Hector Fitzroy Maclean. **Parents** Hector F. and Winifred Joan (Wilding) Maclean. **Marriage** Elizabeth Mann, 1941. **Children** The honorable Lachlan Hector Charles Maclean and the honourable Janet Maclean. **Education** Canford School, Wimborne, Dorset. **Military service** Scots Guards, Armoured Division, World War II, mentioned in despatches, retired as major, 1947. **Career** Chief of the Clan of Maclean, 1936–90; Lord Chamberlain of Her Majesty's Household, 1971–84; Permanent Lord in Waiting, 1984 onwards; lieutenant, Royal Company of Archers, Queen's Body Guard for Scotland; chancellor, Royal Victorian Order, 1971–84; chief steward of Hampton Court Palace, 1985–90. **Related activities** Lord Lieutenant of Argyll, 1954 onwards; justice of the peace, Argyll, 1955; Lord High Commissioner, General Assembly of the Church of Scotland, 1984, 1985. **Other activities** Chief commissioner for Scotland, Boy Scouts Association, 1954–59, chief scout of the United Kingdom and Overseas branches, 1959–71, chief scout of the Commonwealth, 1959–75; breeder, Highland cattle, Blackface sheep. **Offices and memberships** Patron: Coombe Trust Fund, Roland House, British Red Cross Society, Scottish branch, Argyll Division; vice-patron, Argyll and Sutherland Highlanders Regimental Association; president: Territorial Auxiliary and Volunteer Reserve Association, Argyll British Forces Help Society, Lord Robert's Workshops; convenor, Standing Council of Scottish Chiefs; vice-president: Highland Cattle Society, National Playing Fields Association, Scottish branch, National Small-bore Rifle Association (ex officio), Camping Club of Great Britain, Trefoil Residential School for Physically Handicapped Children, Casualties Union; council member: Earl Haig Officers Memorial Fund, Scottish Naval, Military and Air Forces Veteran Residences, Royal Zoological Society, Outward Bound Trust; life member: Highland and Agricultural Society of Scotland, Highland Cattle Society, Scottish National Fatstock Club, Royal Agricultural Society of England. **Awards and honours** Knight Commander, Order of the British Empire, 1967; knighted, 1969; Knight Grand Cross of the Royal Victorian Order, 1971; created life peer, Baron Maclean of Duart and Morvern in the County of Argyll, 1971; privy councillor, 1971; Royal Victorian Chain, 1984; Bronze Wolf, Scout Association; honorary patron, Friends of World Scouting; honorary president: Argyll County Scout Council, Toc H, Scouts Friendly Society. **Publication** *Only* (juvenile), 1979. **Cause of death** Undisclosed, at age 73.

JOHN MERIVALE

British/Canadian Actor

***Born* Toronto, Canada, 1 December 1917**

***Died* London, England, 6 February 1990**

"The last call I ever got from him", wrote John Merivale's friend and colleague, playwright William Douglas-Home, "came through a week or two ago [after his death] when he rang up from hospital to ask how we had fared during the storm. That illustrates his kindness and concern for others: bestowing kindness on his friends and those he loved was his life's work apart from acting." This is a fitting epitaph for the man the dramatic profession knew as the "gentleman actor". For John Merivale was chosen time and again to lend his special type of *gentillesse* to stage and screen, perhaps because the qualities of kindness, modesty, concern and sympathy were an intrinsic part of his make-up in real life. He may well have been "more of a sound supporting actor than a star himself", as Peter Cotes has written in the London and Manchester *Guardian*, but his reputation as a human being has placed him in the highest echelon the acting profession has to offer.

Merivale was born into a dramatic family; his father, Philip Merivale, was a one-time matinée idol, while his mother, Viva Birkett, was an actress in her own right. When his father remarried, it was to the actress-manager Gladys Cooper. Thus the young John or "Jack" Merivale, as he was known to his friends, was surrounded by the world of stage and screen even before he had decided to embark on that course as his own career.

Although born in Canada, Merivale's education took place in England, first at Rugby School, then at New College, Oxford. His university years were cut short, however, due in part to lack of funds: his father had invested heavily in a disastrous production of a Shakespeare play, so the family was forced to tighten its belt. Nonetheless, Merivale was able to train with the renowned Old Vic theatre company during the early 1930s, and in 1933 he made his film début with a minuscule role as a newsboy — in what, exactly, not many of his friends remember. His roles quickly became more substantial, and he followed his inauspicious beginning with parts in such pictures as *If Winter Comes*, *A Night to Remember* (in which he won admiration for his portrayal of the husband who goes down with the *Titanic*), and *Circus of Horrors*. During 1938, however, he returned to the stage as an understudy in a production of *A Midsummer Night's Dream*, held in London's open-air theatre in Regent's Park. There was more to this appearance than meets the eye: also in the cast at that time was actress Vivien Leigh, who wished Merivale luck when he took over the role. Merivale would eventually conduct a discreet and romantic affair with Leigh — but more of that later.

In the meantime, he decided to develop his early career in the United States, where, in 1940, he appeared on Broadway in the Laurence Olivier-Vivien Leigh production of *Romeo and Juliet*. Then, World War II intervened, and Merivale, ever one for noble causes, served throughout the conflict as a pilot in both the British Royal Air Force and the Royal Canadian Air Force. He had married the actress Jan Sterling in 1941, but it was a marriage which barely survived the war (they were divorced in 1948).

Directly after World War II, Merivale became involved in more successful acting projects, such as the New York staging of the Cecil Beaton production of Wilde's *Lady Windermere's Fan*. Both Beaton himself and Merivale's step-brother, the brilliant but highly unstable John Buckmaster, were in the cast; the latter caused Merivale no end of concern due to his never-ending conflicts with the police and other authorities. One of the "legends" of Merivale's life concerns a visit by himself and a horribly hung-over Noël Coward to the unfortunate Buckmaster, who at that time was an inmate of a Long Island sanitorium. It was largely due to Merivale's efforts that his step-brother was allowed to return to England.

Merivale returned to England himself in 1948, after appearing with Rex Harrison (q.v.) in *Anne of a Thousand Days* – and, of course, divorcing Jan Sterling. In the early 1950s, he began a new career in the then-new medium of television. He hadn't given up the stage, however, and in London he began to make a greater name for himself by taking roles in comedies, such as William Douglas-Home's *The Reluctant Débutante* in 1955, in which he starred with Anna Massey. The show later transferred to New York, a move which took the young actor back across the Atlantic where he afterwards took the part of Armand in the Broadway production of Giraudoux's *Duel of Angels* in 1960. It was during this year that his affair with Vivien Leigh began; she had recently separated from Olivier, whom she would continue to love, but not be able to live with, for the rest of her life.

Professionally, the move was a bad one for Merivale, who ended up sacrificing much of his own career in order to cope with the ups and downs of the screen star's turbulent last years. "Jack's role was to pick up the pieces", said Leigh's biographer Hugo Vickers. "This he did with great sensitivity. Jack shared Vivien's wider interests. They loved to explore, and they were both alarmingly adept at *The Times* crossword. Jack was also very good at handling Vivien when in the worst clutches of her manic depression." Merivale's love for Vivien Leigh was, by all accounts, complete, and when she died in 1967 (it was Merivale who found her body), he was left utterly bereft. Nearly two years later, however, Merivale met the "third actress in his life", Dinah Sheridan, who ended up playing the same role for him that he had played for Vivien Leigh: that of a supportive and completely devoted partner. They met while performing a play called *Robert's Wife* at the Yvonne Arnaud Theatre in Guildford, England, and subsequently shared their lives from that time until Merivale's death. It is largely due to Sheridan's devotion and careful nursing — the actor suffered from a hereditary disease which required him to undergo dialysis three times a week — that John Merivale was able to live the complete life he did. It came as no surprise to anyone to hear him say, just a few days before he died, that he was indeed "a very lucky man".

"Good looking and tall with courtesy and charm, he appeared the perfect English gentleman", stated the London *Daily Telegraph* newspaper. This was true both on-stage and off. As William Douglas-Home knew Merivale for over 30 years, it seems fitting to let him have the last word.

> One is lost in admiration for the way in which he gave up his career to comfort and care for her [Vivien Leigh] during her last years, bringing her comparative tranquility and a belated happiness. But what of his own happiness? ... I find it an inspiring story, a romantic one as well and with a very happy ending. A good-looking, humorous and kindly man, who devoted many years to looking after an unhappy lady, and who then became ill himself, just when he had met a beautiful, unselfish actress in the shape of Dinah Sheridan: with whom he lived happily ever after, as will Dinah, with the memories she has of him.

Born John Merivale. **Parents** Philip, actor, and Viva Birkett, actress, Merivale. **Marriages** 1) Jan Sterling, actress, 1941 (divorced 1948); 2) Dinah Sheridan, actress, 1986. **Education** Rugby School, Warwickshire; New College, Oxford; Old Vic School, London. **Military service** Pilot, Royal Air Force and Royal Canadian Air Force, 86th squadron, World War II. **Career** Actor, 1930s onwards; film début, 1933. **Stage** (in London unless otherwise indicated) *A Midsummer Night's Dream*, 1938; *Romeo and Juliet*, New York, 1940; *Lady Windermere's Fan*, New York, 1946; *Anne of a Thousand Days*, New York, 1948; *Venus Observed*, New York, 1952; *The Reluctant Débutante*, 1955; *Duel of Angels*, 1958; *Ivanov*, New York, 1965; *Robert's Wife*, Guildford, 1968; also: *The Sacred Flame, The Last of Mrs Cheyney, Time Out of Mind*. **Films** (include) *A Night to Remember*, 1941; *If Winter Comes*, 1948; *The Battle of the River Plate*, 1956; *Circus of Horrors*, 1960; *80,000 Suspects*, 1963; *The List of Adrian Messenger*, 1963; *King Rat*, 1965; *Arabesque*, 1966. **Television** (includes) *The Gentle Goddess; No Time for Comedy; The Third Man, The Verdict is Yours; The Judge's Story*. **Cause of death** Pneumonia, at age 72.

GEORGES de MESTRAL

Swiss Inventor

***Born* St-Saphorin-Sur-Morges, Switzerland, 19 June 1907**

***Died* Commugny, Switzerland, 8 February 1990**

Enough of it is produced each year to circle the globe twice. It can be found in almost every nation on Earth. It's even been to the moon. A group of international inventors voted it one of the most important inventions of the twentieth century. It has many uses: keeping an astronaut in zero gravity from floating off the floor, holding an artificial heart in place, and fastening everything from shoes, handbags and spectacle cases to almost any type of clothing you can think of, from children's wear to spacesuits. So what is this stuff and who do we have to thank for it? It's Velcro, of course, and the man to thank is Georges de Mestral.

It's often the case that the greatest ideas are the simplest. Velcro is a perfect example; it's based on the humble burr. Like many other great ideas, it came about almost by accident.

One day in 1941, Georges de Mestral came home from a walk in the woods with his dog and noticed that both his trousers and the dog's ears were covered with burrs. Another man would have brushed them off and forgotten about it. Even de Mestral might have ignored them if it had happened at another time. But a recent evening out had been ruined by a stubbornly stuck zip on his wife's dress, and fastenings had been on his mind ever since. He knew there had to be a better way: one which didn't require chains, slides or metal parts.

The tenacity of the burrs intrigued him. He studied them under a microscope and observed that their outer skins bristled with tiny hooks. This was obviously the secret of their adhesive properties, and became the basis of de Mestral's new system: two compatible nylon strips, one covered with tiny hooks, just like those on a burr, the other covered in loops. Pressed together, they hold firm yet can be quickly peeled apart and re-adjusted. It has been estimated that Velcro (the name is a combination of "velvet" and "crochet", the French word for hook) can be opened and closed up to 50,000 times without loss of power.

Did Velcro make Georges de Mestral an instant millionaire? Hardly. More than 15 years passed between the incident with the burrs and the opening of the first Velcro factory, in 1957 at Aubonne, Switzerland. Then, in the 1960s, Velcro passed into the public domain and de Mestral found himself competing against manufacturers who could produce and sell his invention cheaper than he could. This experience turned him into a strong advocate of more effective patent protection.

Velcro was not his only invention, just his most well-known. He began actively designing and building at a very early age, obtaining his first patent before he was 15 years old, and continued producing new ideas and taking an interest in all things scientific throughout his life. He was the first person to propose the idea of fibre optics, and his many inventions included various toys, gear wheels, turbines, plastic cartridges, compartmented boxes for dispensing medicine and most recently, something which his wife described as "one stupid little thing that sold very well": an asparagus peeler.

Born Georges de Mestral. **Marriages** 1) Jeanette Schnyder, 1931; 2) Monique Panchaud, 1950; 3) Helen Dale, 1958. **Children** Two sons by first marriage, one son by second marriage. **Education** Polytechnicum, Lausanne. **Career** Engineer; inventor of Velcro, 1941; founder, Velcro factory, Aubonne, 1957. **Awards and honours** Member of honour, Swiss Society of Engineers and Architects, 1978. **Inventions** (include) Velcro; asparagus peeler; medicines container; hair curler. **Cause of death** Undisclosed, at age 82.

COLIN MILBURN

British Cricketer

***Born* Burnopfield, County Durham, 23 October 1941**

***Died* Darlington, North Yorkshire, 28 February 1990**

In the last 30 years of English cricket, only Ian Botham has stirred the native public in the way that Colin Milburn did. When the rotund "Ollie" came out to bat, a demonstration of style and power could palpably be anticipated. It was often provided; alas, not nearly as often as it might have been, for Milburn's career was cut short by bitter misfortune.

He came from Burnopfield, County Durham, in the north-east of England. His father was a successful cricketer in the local leagues, and young Colin received thorough instruction in the sport. Educated at Stanley Grammar School, he was playing for his county by the age of 18, and in 1959 he scored 100 notable runs against the Indian touring team. Like other Durham men before and after him, Milburn joined Northamptonshire County Cricket Club. By 1962 he had secured a regular place in the first team, and four years after that he was chosen for the English national side.

English cricket was going through a very drab phase at the time, with defensive tactics and poor crowds. It needed a Milburn. He was a shortish young man, and already upwards of 18 stone in weight, much of which one commentator unerringly described as "Honest-to-goodness fat". Bulk is not an important factor in the make-up of a good batsman, but allied to timing and technique, as in Milburn's case, the results were spectacular. Moreover, he had an attractive and extremely affable personality which projected strongly from the cricket field. England's opponent in 1966 was the formidable West Indies team, captained by Sir Garfield Sobers. In the first Test, Milburn scored 0 and 94. In the second, he saved the match for his side by scoring 126 not out, while his injured partner defended one-handed at the other end. As the light failed, Milburn waxed, and struck the aggressive West Indies bowlers for 6 after six. At the close of play, he was carried shoulder high (it took a few of them) from the pitch.

Cricketing greatness seemed to beckon, but Milburn could not find consistent favour with the Test selectors, and made only seven further appearances over the next three years, before he left to play for the Western Australia state team. With them he made his personal best score of 243 runs — 181 of them in a two-hour afternoon stint. He was quickly summoned to reinforce an England team on tour in what was then East Pakistan, now Bangladesh. As a player and as a comrade, he had been badly missed by his fellows: "His arrival was greeted with such unconfined delight by the rest of the team that a troubled tour took on a new light", wrote his obituarist in the London *Times*. Within a week, Milburn had scored a "sparkling" 139 at Karachi. (The adjective is courtesy of *Wisden*, the cricketers' Bible). Again he was talked of as England's opening bat for the coming decade.

In May 1969, he was involved in a car crash. His head went through the windscreen, his left eye damaged beyond repair, and his right one injured too. Milburn responded with astonishing fortitude: "His infectious good humour and indomitable spirit raised morale throughout the hospital", wrote the hospital management committee in its annual report. But here, at the age of 27, his career was effectively over. In 1973 he played again for Northamptonshire, but with his sight so drastically impaired, the odds were stacked against him. He did some coaching and some cricket commentaries for the radio, still the fat man with a liberal fund of joviality, which made him friends everywhere. He kept his depressions private, but sadly, he never found the steady alternative employment that he needed.

In his nine-year first class career, Milburn scored 23 centuries. He was a useful medium-pace bowler, and despite his girth, an agile fielder close to the bat, breaking the Northants record by taking 43 catches in a season. Any opening batsman must confront fresh bowlers and a new ball, and Milburn faced the world's fastest. His technique was both immaculate and savage; he hit the ball formidably hard and with metronomic perfection. He was very brave, loving to hook the fast, rising ball off his nose and into the crowd, who loved him. The England selectors complained that Milburn was "unreliable" — which he was, because he played his attacking shots more frequently than others, and so increased his chances of getting out. These same selectors might have paid more heed to the unique quality which Milburn brought to the game as an entertainer. The journalist Mathew Engel articulated many people's thoughts in an eloquent tribute to Ollie, saying that cricket should be played, "as Milburn played it, with a twinkle. It is a spectacle which demands skill and decency, and a sense of fun. If English cricket rediscovers that, it would be the man's best possible memorial."

Born Colin Milburn. **Father** Jack Milburn, Tyneside Senior League cricket professional. **Education** Stanley Grammar School, County Durham. **Career** Batsman, Durham Cricket Club, 1959, 1975–76; batsman, Northamptonshire County Cricket Club, 1960–74, county cap, 1963, testimonial, 1971; Test début, at Old Trafford, England v West Indies, 1966; batsman, Western Australia, 1966–67, 1968–69; test commentator, British Broadcasting Corporation, also, England tour courier. **Awards and honours** Lawrence Trophy for fastest 100 of season, 1967; honorary member, Marylebone Cricket Club. **Test matches** Nine, 1966–69: West Indies, four times, 1966, India, 1967, Australia, twice, 1968; Pakistan, 1968–69; Test match average, 46.71. **Tours** East Africa, for Marylebone Cricket Club, 1963–64; West Indies, for Marylebone Cricket Club, 1967–68; Pakistan, 1968–69. **Highest scores** Batting: in Test match, 139, England v Pakistan, Karachi, 1968–69; 243, Western Australia v Queensland, Brisbane, 1968–69; scored 100 before lunch three times, 1966; scored 1000 runs in year, five times, 1963–67; bowling: 6–59, Northamptonshire v Glamorgan, Swansea, 1962. **First-class matches** Played in 225; batting innings, 435; outs, 34; runs, 13,262; average score, 33.07; 100s, 23; bowling — runs, 3171; wickets, 99; average 32.03; caught, 226; most catches, 43, 1964. **Publication** *Largely Cricket* (autobiography), 1968. **Cause of death** Heart attack, at age 48.

NORMAN PARKINSON

British Photographer

***Born* London, England, 21 April 1913**

***Died* Singapore, 15 February 1990**

There were great photographers before Parks and there are some succeeding him but it is questionable whether any ever has had or will have a lens as loving of women as his. It also seems unlikely that any other "snapper", as he liked to describe himself, will do quite as much for so very many sitters.

Norman Parkinson (born Ronald William Parkinson Smith) was the product of a professional middle-class family of sufficient, but modest, means who appeared to have little academic ability at school but did show a modicum of artistic talent. His parents, as concerned as he about his future in the post-Depression world, apprenticed him to a fashionable Bond Street photographer in London's West End, Speaight and Sons, whose clients included the then Duke and Duchess of York who, within six years, were to become the King and Queen of England. Thus, as he later said, "The whole thing has come full circle. When old man Speaight was photographing the Queen Mother and George VI with Princess Margaret and Princess Elizabeth, I was putting the film in the camera."

In 1934, together with Norman Kibblewhite, he opened his own studio in nearby Dover Street under their amalgamated names of Norman and Parkinson. When the partnership ended he kept the name. It was quickly becoming well known. Most of his work at this time lay in society portraits, at which he excelled, becoming also a deb's delight. His height — he was a commanding figure of six-and-a-half feet — and his dandyish dress endeared him to women. They also realized, even in those early days, that he had a genuine love of women and their beauty. He revelled in the erotic and tended to play the eccentric. He was unable to risk using a camera without wearing his trademark — a Kashmiri bridal cap. Replacements had to be worn in on top to assimilate the magic. He did not believe in taking unnecessary chances!

When he moved into fashion he introduced a new dimension. Not for him the artificial stuffy and scented interiors of salons. He took his models into the reality of outdoors — to beaches, golf courses, farmyards and the streets. Against breakwaters on the Isle of Wight he asked model Pamela Minchin to jump off a post with her arms flung wide. The resulting print confirmed everything he had hoped for and he remembered that moment for the rest of his life. Recalling it in what was to prove his last interview, with Brian Appleyard and published in London's *The Sunday Times*, he said, "When I pulled that picture out of the soup, it confirmed to me for the rest of my life that I had to be a photographer. I was absolutely amazed by the magic of it."

This pursuit of naturalism could override consideration of the model. He once sat Wenda Rogerson, the model who became his third and lasting wife, on an ostrich in Africa. It promptly shot off into the distance pursued by shouts from Parks of, "More profile, Wenda! More profile!"

During the 1930s Parkinson's fashion and portraiture work appeared regularly in the British edition of *Harper's Bazaar* and the (now long defunct) weekly *The Bystander*, for which he did a great deal of photojournalism. Many of his most notable early portraits were taken at this period. There were memorable shots of the Sitwells, couturier Charles James, and of Rose Kennedy, then the elegant and admired wife of the American ambassador to Britain.

From 1937 to 1940 he did a series of photographic recruitment essays for the British armed services and then, during World War II, he combined fashion and society work with reconnaissance photography over France, and with propaganda. After the war he moved back to freelance work and began his long association with Condé Nast publications, his work appearing in all editions of *Vogue* and *House and Garden*. This lasted until the 1970s with only a four-year break when he became an associate contributing editor of *Queen*, a glossy British monthly which, under the editorship of Jocelyn Stevens, broke new ground and enjoyed a high reputation in the early 1960s.

To follow his earlier work, Parkinson now began to build up a most impressive collection of portraits which also included a larger than usual number of men. Painter Augustus John, composer Ralph Vaughan Williams, writer C.S. Lewis, singer Kathleen Ferrier — who died tragically young from cancer in 1953 — and Lord David Cecil, all provided memorable sittings. He also moved into advertising. But Parks didn't just photograph the people he was sent. He was also always on the look out for new beauties whom he would seek out, circumspectly, on the street and, on occasion, from parades of models.

"One day in 1959," he later wrote in his book *Lifework*,

> I rang Lucie Clayton [of the model agency] and asked her to put on a "cattle market" as we would unglamorously call them. Upstairs 30 nervous young girls were sitting around like wallflowers. An hour later I was downstairs drinking tea in the office.
>
> "There you are, Parks, not much there as we told you."
>
> "What do you mean? You have a star up there. Celia Hammond."
>
> "But Parks, you can't be serious, she looks like a Burmese or something."
>
> "That's the whole point and I'll book her all day on Wednesday for *Queen* magazine."

He did so and Celia Hammond appeared in swimsuits on a fur rug — shot from above with a thumb in her mouth; as a panama-hatted schoolgirl on a railway station; and in luxurious evening dresses in stately homes. After a year's contract with *Queen* she became an international star. Commented Marit Allen, a colleague at the time, "Parks understood the dynamics of the Sixties. He used his sense of reportage, and his sophistication, experience and wit to put together the ingredients for a great fashion sitting, with never a backward glance at the young Turks snapping at his professional heels."

The wit of Parks was recalled by Douglas Lowndes, who was involved in the UK launch of Camay soap. "I persuaded Norman to take the colour photographs for use in elected women's magazines. He delivered dozens of gorgeous pictures of the girl in the pink bath, including one in which he indulged in one of his impish jokes: the soap was being offered to the girl by a huge masculine hand in the foreground: owner invisible. At the time (1957), extremely risqúe."

Parkinson was, by the 1970s, moving back into royal circles and the portraits which received his widest public circulation. The arrival in the 1960s of a new breed of "snappers", the Trinity of Bailey, Donovan and Duffy, took him into the Establishment hierarchy, a position sealed when he was called to Buckingham Palace to photograph Prince Charles and the younger Royals. They were feeling the need of something a little more modern than Cecil Beaton who was, after all, "Granny's photographer"! In the event he became one of the Queen Mother's most noted photographers too. He took extended portfolios for her seventy-fifth, eightieth and eighty-fifth Birthdays. One of the portraits for the eightieth was used on postage stamps to commemorate the occasion.

Over his last two decades he photographed all members of the royal family on many occasions although, towards the end, he too found himself in the role of "Granny's photographer" and a preference for younger people creeping in, particularly with the Princess of Wales. His favourite royal subject was Princess Anne, now the Princess Royal. He recognized her as a supremely beautiful woman: her image usually being ignored because of her interest in horses — another of Parkinson's passions. For her twenty-first Birthday portraits he saw she had the full treatment with extensive professional make-up and advice and continued this through her engagement to Mark Phillips. Without playing down any of her own personality and interests he produced photographs showing her glamour, especially on the back of a horse.

This was typical of Parks. He knew the image was an illusion but saw no point in using the camera to attack or to expose. He was utterly against the modern trend of catching "victims" in states of disarray guaranteed to cause unhappiness. He wanted to make his subjects happy. This he could do by helping them relax and capturing the good things of the present which he knew was, inevitably, fleeting. He appreciated that being photographed felt unnatural and immodest and set out to overcome this. "If I have time," he once said, "I always like to watch them in a mirror. With Elizabeth Taylor I try to come in after she's been at her make-up for about half an hour ... and talk to her in the mirror. You shouldn't see them raw or too early. About 2 pm is the best time for a session, when the face has had time to settle. The mirror, you see, is woman's greatest enemy. They spend a lot of time in front of the mirror, trying."

But, of course, the psychology of approaching a woman through her looking-glass is a stroke of genius because that is the one place where it *is* permissible to be narcissistic — where she rehearses her daily image. By becoming part of her beauty process Parks was the better able to capture and to immortalize the illusion.

But his love for, and understanding of, women was by no means confined to his professional life. He was not by nature monogamous — a fact he freely admitted — and his first two marriages failed. His marriage to Wenda Rogerson (formerly an actress who had been discovered by Cecil Beaton and was introduced to him as a new model when he was working for *Vogue*) came in 1945, and she understood that he genuinely saw her sex as the more important gender. He found women more courageous, more industrious and more honest than men. Their life together, in London and the English countryside and, later, their home on Tobago where Parkinson took up pig farming and horse breeding, was extremely happy. When Wenda died, very suddenly in London in 1987, Parks was devastated. And then their beautiful Tobago home was equally devastated by fire. To escape his sorrow he threw himself into an ever more hectic schedule of work. He was in Malaysia, working on an assignment, when he collapsed with a cerebral haemorrhage.

Most of Parkinson's work was done outside the studio. In another interview published in the British weekly *The Independent on Sunday* he recalled that, by the end, "I shall have recorded the pendulum arc of over 70 years. When I've gone to that darkroom in the sky, I hope people will realise … that I recorded a large proportion of the twentieth century. That is not unimportant."

Nor is the fact that the record is beautiful in itself.

Born Ronald William Parkinson Smith. **Parents** William Parkinson, barrister, and Louie (Cobley) Smith. **Marriages** Three marriages; 3) Wenda Rogerson, actress and model, 1945 (died 1987). **Children** One son, Simon. **Education** Westminster School, London, 1927–31; apprentice, court photographers, Speaight and Sons Limited, Bond Street, London, 1931–33. **Career** Opened own studio with Norman Kibblewhite, Dover Street, London, 1934; photographer for British edition, *Harper's Bazaar* and *The Bystander*, 1935–40; photographic essayist, British Armed Services recruitment drive, 1937–39; reconnaissance photographer, Royal Air Force, 1940–45; portrait and fashion photographer, *Vogue*, 1945–60; advertising début, 1952; associate contributing editor, *Queen*, 1960–64; freelance photographer for *Vogue, Life, Elle, Town and Country*, 1964 onwards. **Other activities** Farmer, Gloucestershire, Worcestershire and Oxfordshire, 1937–60, Tobago, 1964 onwards; founder, Porkinson Banger Company. **Offices and memberships** Fellow, International Institute of Photography, 1975. **Awards and honours** Honorary fellow, Royal Photographic Society, 1968; Commander of the Order of the British Empire, 1975; Lifetime Achievement Award, American Society of Magazine Photographers, 1983; Gold Award, Design and Art Directors Association, London, 1984, Silver Award, 1985; Hasselblad Gold Award, Göteborg, Sweden, 1985; Doctor of Fine Arts, University of Miami, Florida, 1986. **Individual exhibitions** (in London unless otherwise indicated) Parkinson Studio, 1935; Jaeger Showrooms, 1960; The Photographers' Gallery, 1978; *50 Years of Fashion and Portraits* (retrospective), National Portrait Gallery, 1981; Sotheby's, New York, 1983; International Center of Photography, New York (retrospective), 1983; *Notable Diamonds*, Arts Institute of Chicago, 1985, on tour, 1985–86. **Group exhibitions** (include, in London unless otherwise indicated) *Exposition Internationale*, Paris, 1937; *Biennale di Fotografia*, Venice, 1957; *The Mask of Beauty*, National Portrait Gallery, 1972; *Fashion 1900–1939*, Victoria and Albert Museum, 1975; *Happy and Glorious: 6 Reigns of Royal Photography*, National Portrait Gallery, 1977; *The Queen Mother: A Celebration*, National Portrait Gallery, 1980; *Modern British Photography* 1919–39, Museum of Modern Art, Oxford, 1980; *British Photography 1955–65*, The Photographers' Gallery, 1983; *Sammlung Gruber*, Museum Ludwig, Cologne, 1984; *Shots of Style*, Victoria and Albert Museum, 1985. **Collections** National Portrait Gallery, London; Victoria and Albert Museum, London; Museum Ludwig, Cologne; Sotheby's, London and New York; Hamilton Gallery, London; National Museum of Photography, Bradford, Yorkshire. **Portraits** (include) Princess Anne, 21st birthday and engagement pictures; Queen Elizabeth, the Queen Mother, official 80th and 85th birthday photographs. **Publications** *Sisters under the Skin*, 1978; *Fifty Years of Style and Fashion*, 1983, also published as *Lifework*, 1984; *Would You Let Your Daughter …?*, 1985, **Cause of death** Brain haemorrhage, at age 76. **Further reading** Alexander Liberman with an introduction by A.B. Louchheim, *The Art and Technique of Color Photography: A Treasury of Color Photographs by the Staff Photographers of Vogue, House and Garden, and Glamour*, 1951; L. Fritz Gruber, editor, *Beauty: Variations on the Theme Woman by Masters of the Camera — Past and Present*, 1965; Valerie Lloyd and others, *Fashion 1900–1939* (exhibition catalogue), 1975; Cecil Beaton and Gail Buckland, *The Magic Image*, 1975; Nancy Hall-Duncan, *The History of Fashion Photography*, 1979; David Mellor, *Modern British Photography 1919–39* (exhibition catalogue), 1980; *50 Years of Portraits and Fashion: Photographs by Norman Parkinson* (exhibition catalogue), 1981; Sue Davies, Michael Rand, Mark Boxer and others, *British Photography 1955–65: The Master Craftsmen in Print* (exhibition catalogue), 1983; Siegfried Gohr, foreword, *Sammlung Gruber: Photographie des 20. Jahrhunderts* (exhibition catalogue), 1984; Martin Harrison, *Shots of Style: Great Fashion Photographs Chosen by David Bailey*, 1985; *Contemporary Photographers*, 1988.

SANDRO PERTINI

Italian Former President

***Born* Stella San Giovanni, near Savona, Italy, 25 September 1896**

***Died* Rome, Italy, 24 February 1990**

It was not for nothing that former president Alessandro Pertini of Italy was known throughout his public career as "Sandro". A man of outstanding honesty and rigid principle, he stood for the very best in the Italian people at a time when *la classe politica* had become besmirched even at its very pinnacle, with his predecessor as president being forced to resign over allegations of involvement in the Lockheed bribery scandal, and in return he was beloved by them in a way seldom accorded to twentieth-century Italian politicians. But then, Sandro Pertini was no ordinary vote-catching politician; he simply had the common touch. As their president, he shared his fellow countrymen's joys and sorrows; none more excited than he as he watched the Italian football team win the World Cup in 1982, none more distressed at the unsuccessful attempt to rescue a five-year-old boy trapped down a well outside Rome, none more angered by the bureaucratic delays in getting aid to the Naples earthquake victims in 1980.

He refused to move into the Quirinale palace on his assumption of the presidency, but chose to remain in his flat overlooking the Trevi fountain, instead opening his official residence to visits from schoolchildren, all 600,000 of whom he received personally and painstakingly answered their questions. It was said that he insisted on paying his own air fares — a habit without precedent in an age of political "perks". His political trademark was his utter probity. The embodiment of the Resistance — he was imprisoned by both Fascists and Nazis — he reached the peak of his career at a time when his country's political life had plumbed the depths, with the terrorism of the Red Brigades culminating in the assassination of the prime minister, Aldo Moro. Pertini was elected president by the largest number of votes ever gained by an Italian presidential candidate and his tenure of office brought a breath of fresh air to the political scene. As one correspondent put it, "He was a sport, capable of giving politicians a good name".

Born into a landowning family and a lawyer by training, Pertini moved into politics immediately after his service in World War I, as a founder member of the Italian Socialist Party. Inevitably he came up against the Fascists after their seizure of power in 1922. In all, he spent nearly ten years in prison for his anti-Fascist activities, punctuated by his escape to France with his fellow Socialist Filippo Turati. In the last years of World War II he led the Resistance against the Nazis.

With such impeccable credentials, he was inevitably elected a member of the constituent assembly which drew up the constitution of the new post-war Italian republic. He remained a parliamentarian — first as deputy speaker of the Chamber of Deputies for two consecutive terms from 1968, and then as the Chamber's president. He had hoped to win the Italian presidency in 1971, but lost to the continued ascendancy of the Christian Democrats. "I'm too old", he decided.

But seven years later, at the age of 81, he was to emerge as the compromise candidate with unprecedented all-party support. This time he declared "I'm not old. I'm ancient, but I'm not blind, deaf or dumb." And he proved it. He was to do more than any other Italian politician of this century to restore credibility to his country's political institutions. Though a lifelong Socialist, he stood above the political fray. Without fear or favour, he hit out at the abuses he saw around him, publicly condemning the terrorism of the Red Brigades, the Mafia, the P2 masonic conspiracy. He was the first president to appoint a non-Christian Democratic prime minister. When he heard that the then Communist Party leader Berlinguer was dying, he had him brought to Rome in the presidential plane. Though a lifelong non-believer and anti-clericalist, he struck up an extraordinarily cordial friendship with Pope John Paul II and kept a vigil outside his hospital room when the latter was shot in 1981. The story goes that he was sure he would get into heaven (if there was such a place) "because Pope Wojtyla will give me a push".

And his fellow countrymen would endorse this sentiment about the most popular president they have ever had. The sincerity of his belief in the innate goodness and honesty of the ordinary men (and women) in the street revived their belief in themselves at a time of despair and restored their pride in their country's institutions.

Born Alessandro Pertini. **Father** A farmer. **Marriage** Carla Voltolina, Resistance worker and psychiatrist. **Education** Degrees in political science and law. **Military service** Lieutenant, artillery, decorated, World War I; in force against German troops, Porta San Paolo, Rome, arrested, escaped, 1944. **Career** Elected to Constituent Assembly for Genoa-Florence-Naples, 1946; life senator, 1948, 1953, 1958, 1963, 1968; elected representative for Genoa, Chamber of Deputies, deputy speaker, 1963–68, president, 1968–76; president of Italy, 1978–85. **Related activities** Member, Socialist Party, 1918; arrested for anti-Fascist publications, Italy, 1925, France, 1927; imprisoned, 1926, 1928–35, in political detention camp, 1935–43; member, executive council, Italian Socialist Party, 1943; secretary, Socialist Party in Italy, 1944; organizer, insurrections, northern Italy, 1945; member, Socialist Party administration, 1945–48; chairman, Socialist Parliamentary Group. **Other activities** Journalist; variously employed, France, Italy, 1925–29; general manager, *Il lavoro nuovo*, 1945–46, 1950–53; editor, *Avanti*, 1945–48. **Awards and honours** Gold Medal of Valour, Resistance movement, World War II. **Publication** *Six Convictions, Two Prison Escapes* (autobiography). **Cause of death** Undisclosed, at age 93.

MICHAEL POWELL

British Film Director, Producer and Writer

***Born* Bekesbourne, Kent, 30 September 1905**

***Died* Avening, Gloucestershire, 19 February 1990**

"Of his generation, he was unquestionably the most innovative and most creatively brilliant film maker this country ever boasted." Thus Sir Richard Attenborough on the occasion of Michael Powell's death, in a judgement with which few now would probably disagree. However, it was not always so, and for many — too many — years, one of the British cinema's few real stylists and genuine *auteurs* was virtually unable to work in his own country, while his extraordinary *oeuvre* remained the victim of critical neglect or, worse still, disdain. This was particularly the case after the "scandal" of *Peeping Tom* (the real scandal, of course, being its critical and commercial reception and not, as was thought at the time, its subject-matter), although this was by no means the first time that Powell and his films had been the subject of controversy and the victim of half-baked critical maulings; furthermore, his career had been in decline during the 1950s — along with the rest of the British film industry. In the 1960s, in Britain at least, Powell's remarkable achievements were celebrated only sporadically, oppositionally and at the margins, in small magazines such as *Motion* and *Movie*. With the next decade, however, his reputation widened.

In 1970 the National Film Theatre in London screens a season of 14 of Powell's films, and the season's organizer, Kevin Gough-Yates, edits a booklet on the director and his long-term collaborator, Emeric Pressburger. The same year also sees the publication of the book *A Mirror For England* by Raymond Durgnat, one of Powell's most steadfast and perceptive champions, which includes a sustained discussion of his *oeuvre*. As the decade progresses, critical attitudes towards cinema in general at last begin to change, and Powell benefits in particular from the growth of "auteurism" and an increased interest in non-realist forms. In 1978 Powell is honoured with a complete-as-possible retrospective at the National Film Theatre; *The Life and Death of Colonel Blimp* is reconstructed by the National Film Archive, and the British Film Institute (BFI) publishes *Powell, Pressburger and Others*, edited by Ian Christie, a valuable collection of essays and documents putting Powell's work in its proper perspective and also analysing the reasons for his critical neglect and denigration in his native land. New and restored prints of Powell's masterpieces are shown to new, young audiences both in Britain and the US, audiences unaffected by the critical prejudices that had hitherto blighted Powell's reputation; directors such as Scorsese and Coppola publicly credit much of their inspiration to Powell's films; *Peeping Tom* is finally recognized for the masterpiece that it is; retrospectives are held at the Museum of Modern Art in New York, the Art Institute of Chicago and elsewhere; Powell is made a fellow of the BFI in 1983; in 1986 Ian Christie publishes the seminal study of the director, *Arrows of Desire*; and Powell is also made senior director-in-residence at Coppola's Zoetrope Studios, thus becoming an honorary "movie brat" at 75. In 1984 he marries Scorsese's long-time editor, Thelma Schoonmaker.

Powell's "problem" lay in the fact that his cinema was a far cry indeed from the realism, restraint and "good taste" so highly regarded by British film-makers and critics alike. Think of the pantheon of directors of British cinema and names like Carol Reed and Anthony Asquith come to mind; whereas Powell has been variously compared with Minnelli, Godard, Welles, Gance and Vidor — not necessarily a compliment in narrow British critical terms! Thus while Powell himself dismissed Reed as "a watchmaker, passionless", the influential critic Richard Winnington was dismissing Powell and Pressburger's *A Matter of Life and Death* as "even further away from the essential realism and true business of the British movie than their two recent films *I Know Where I'm Going* and *A Canterbury Tale*." Powell's flamboyance, virtuosity and, in particular, his ravishing use of Technicolor, were sometimes criticized as being too "American", and indeed he himself admitted that "I suppose it is this strong predilection and admiration for everything American in the lively arts that makes the English critics and literary ladies and gents suspicious of me". But he added, using an apple metaphor, "I never wanted to go to America and make their pictures for them. I wanted to make English ones. I was English to the core, as English as a Cox's Orange Pippin, as English as a Worcester Pearmain."

The point about Powell is that he explored and personified a quite different kind of "Englishness" to the realism of a Grierson, the restraint and "good taste" of an Asquith, or the literariness of so many others: Powell's England is that of the Romantic and the Gothic. As Raymond Durgnat so aptly sums it up in *A Mirror For England*:

> Powell has been dismissed as a "mere" technician, but if so, he's an eccentric one, in the sense of that proverbially English phenomenon, an eccentric Colonel. When stiff upper lip Colonels retire from matter-of-fact activities like strategy and gunnery, they notoriously embrace soft-centred systems of mystical belief. Similarly, where Powell the brilliant technician leaves off, there appears a man with a disciplined foible for romantic mysticisms of every kind: for militarism (his Prussian officers and his Queen's Guards), for the English countryside *(A Canterbury Tale)*, for the fate-time warp (*A Matter of Life and Death*), for sex-maniacs (*Peeping Tom*), for a sex-maddened nun on Tibetan peaks (*Black Narcissus*), for the wild Celtic fringe (*The Edge of the World*, *I Know Where I'm Going*), for the spiritual hothouse of opera-ballet (*The Red Shoes*, *Tales of Hoffman*). He opens up the romantic veins of his sober subjects: even *The Small Back Room*, most of which is the best filmization of Nigel Balchin, blossoms into expressionist DTs with David Farrar vainly striving to scramble up the sheer smooth sides of a gigantic Scotch-bottle ... Had Powell and the cinema, and Technicolor,

flourished in the first half of the nineteenth century instead of the twentieth, the period, in fact, of Romanticism encountering Victorian realism, Powell might have been working with the cultural grain instead of against it. His cravings are audacious, constant, uncertain, he turns this way and that, restlessly seeking out different genres, styles, symbols. In a sense, he's Britain's Abel Gance.

Powell's best known early work, *The Edge of the World*, made after an apprenticeship of over 20 "quota quickies", was well received precisely *because* it was perceived as a film in the much-vaunted realist vein, being praised by no less a figure than Grierson himself and compared by C.A. Lejeune to Flaherty's *Man of Aran*. However, both the subject-matter and the elaborate style of his films soon began to cause consternation, and he, like Hitchcock (soon to leave British shores for a more congenial cinematic climate), began to acquire the reputation of being merely a clever-clever, and somewhat tasteless, technician. According to Durgnat the dominant view was that Powell was a "stylist and a rhetorician, camouflaging the absence of idea by a weakness for grandiose, out-of-context effect". But it was not just the supposed formal "excesses" that proved too much for the British critics and other arbiters of taste and acceptability; more disturbing still were Powell's excavations of the underside of English stiff-upper-lippery. Thus, for example, *The Life and Death of Colonel Blimp* offended Churchill and the Ministry of Information on account of its satirical representation of Britain's military élite; the heady mixture of convent life and eroticism in *Black Narcissus* outraged certain religious sensibilities (indeed, in the US the Legion of Decency managed to get the film severely cut); the figure of the local magistrate and big-wig who pours glue into the hair of local girls who fraternize with American soldiers was thought by some to be quite out of place in the wartime *A Canterbury Tale*. (Seen from a different perspective, of course, this extraordinary evocation of English landscape and tradition can be regarded, as Gavin Millar put it, as "conceivably the most profoundly and self-consciously patriotic film ever made ... unmistakably British but deeply unjingoistic".) The crowning controversy came, of course, with *Peeping Tom*, described by Powell himself as "a very tender film, a very nice one" but greeted on opening with a torrent of abuse in the press, which put the wind up distributors and exhibitors alike and virtually finished Powell's British career. According to Derek Hill in *Tribune*, "the only really satisfactory way to dispose of *Peeping Tom* would be to shovel it up and flush it swiftly down the nearest sewer", whilst the *New Statesman* argued that it "stinks more than anything else in British films since *The Stranglers of Bombay*" and the *Daily Worker* dismissed it as "perverted nonsense" and "wholly evil". Such extreme reactions were the rule, not the exception, and mirrored the treatment handed out to *Psycho* the same year.

The real irony of all this, of course, is that had Powell been anything other than English he would not have made the films that he did: like English horror films and Gainsborough melodramas (equally despised and reviled by the mainstream British critics at the time) they are simply the recto to the verso of the dominant realist aesthetic and its attendant notions of "restraint" and "style-less" style. But perhaps the last word here should go to Durgnat, one of Powell's oldest and most loyal champions, who, as long ago as 1965, in an article in *Motion*, recognized that

> he remains an upholder, through its lean years, of the Méliès tradition. His films shed not a little light on English thought and the English soul, in its restraints, its pusillanimity, its nostalgia for a German expressionism, its coy amorality. But their authenticity, in terms of some conventionalised realism, isn't the only criterion; at their flimsiest, they still engross and reward one's attention, they give pleasure by half-belonging to *our* world and half to their own", relating to a "spectacular cinema which asks the audience to relish the spectacle *as such*, to a school of "Cinema" which is always exquisitely conscious of not only its cinematic effects but its cinematic *nature*.

Born Michael Latham Powell. **Parents** Thomas William, hop farmer and hotelier, and Mabel (Corbett) Powell. **Marriages** 1) Name unknown, 1927 (dissolved); 2) Frances Reidy, 1943 (died 1983); 3) Thelma Schoonmaker, film editor, 1984. **Children** Two sons, Kevin and Columba. **Education** King's School, Canterbury, Kent, 1916–18; Dulwich College, London, 1918–21. **Career** Joined National Provincial Bank, 1922; with Metro-Goldwyn-Mayer film company, 1925–28, assistant to Rex Ingram, south of France, 1925, still photographer, Hitchcock; film directing début, *Two Crowded Hours*, 1931; on contract with Alexander Korda, 1938; first collaboration with Pressburger, *The Spy in Black*, 1939; stage directing début, *The Fifth Column*, 1945. **Related activities** Co-founder and managing director with Pressburger, The Archers, 1943–57; senior director-in-residence, Francis Ford Coppola's Zeotrope Studios; film lecturer, Dartmouth College, New Hampshire, 1981; supervisor, *Pavlova*, Anglo-Union of Soviet Socialist Republics productions, 1983–85. **Offices and memberships** Fellow: British Academy of Film and Television Arts, 1981, British Film Institute, 1983, Royal Geographical Society. **Awards and honours** Academy Award for *49th Parallel*, 1940; honorary DLitt: East Anglia University, 1978, Kent University, 1984; Special Award, with Emeric Pressburger, British Film Institute, 1978; Golden Lion of Venice Award, 1982; honorary doctorate, Royal College of Art, 1987. **Stage** (as producer and director) *The Fifth Column*, 1945; *The Skipper Next to God*, 1947; *Heloise*, 1951; *Hanging Judge*, 1955. **Films** (as director) *Two Crowded Hours*, 1931; *My Friend the King*, 1931; *Rynox*, 1931; *The Rasp*, 1931; *The Star Reporter*, 1932; *Hotel Splendide*, 1932; *C.O.D.*, 1932; *His Lordship*, 1932; *Born Lucky*, 1932; *The Fire Raisers* (also, co-screenplay), 1933; *Red Ensign* (also co-screenplay), 1934; *The Night of the Party*, 1934; *Something Always Happens*, 1934; *The Girl in the Crowd*, 1934; *Lazybones*, 1935; *The Love Test*, 1935; *The Phantom Light*, 1935; *The Price of a Song*, 1935; *Someday*, 1935; *The Man Behind the Mask*, 1936; *Crown Versus Stevens*, 1936; *Her Last Affair*, 1936; *The Brown Wallet*, 1936; *The Edge of the World* (also screenplay), 1937; *The Spy in Black* (*U-Boat*), 1939; *The Lion Has Wings* (co-director), 1939; *Contraband* (*Blackout*), 1940; *The Thief of Bagdad* (co-director), 1940; *49th Parallel* (*The Original Story of the Invaders*), 1941; *One of Our Aircraft Is Missing*, 1942; (produced, directed, scripted by The Archers company): *The Life and Death of Colonel Blimp*, 1943; *The Volunteer*, 1943; *A Canterbury Tale*, 1944; *I Know Where I'm Going*, 1945; *A Matter of Life and Death* (*Stairway to Heaven*), 1946; *Black Narcissus*, 1947; *The Red Shoes*, 1948; *The Small Back Room* (*Hour of Glory*), 1949; *Gone to Earth* (*The Wild Heart*), 1950; *The Elusive Pimpernel* (*The Fighting Pimpernel*), 1950; *The Tales of Hoffman*, 1951; *Oh Rosalinda!*, 1955; *The Battle of the River Plate* (*Pursuit of the Graf Spee*), 1956; *Ill Met By Moonlight* (*Intelligence Service, Night Ambush*), 1956; (as producer and director): *Luna de miel* (*Honeymoon*), 1956; *Peeping Tom*, 1960; *Queen's Guards*, 1961; *Bluebeard's Castle* (director only), 1964; *They're a Weird Mob*, 1966; *Sebastian* (co-producer only), 1968; *Age of Consent*, 1969; *The Boy Who Turned Yellow*, 1972; *Trikimia* (*The Tempest*) (also screenplay), 1974; *Return to the Edge of the World*, 1978. **Television** *Espionage; The Defenders*. **Publications** *2000,000 Feet on Foula*, 1938; *The Edge of the World, A Waiting Game*, 1975; (with Emeric Pressburger) *The Red Shoes*, 1978; *A Life in Movies* (autobiography), 1986. **Cause of death** Prostate cancer, at age 84. **Further reading** Raymond Durgnat, *A Mirror for England*, 1970; I. Christie, editor, *Powell, Pressburger, and Others*, 1978; Ian Christie, *Arrows of Desire*, 1986; *International Dictionary of Films and Filmmakers*, volume two, 1991.

JOHNNIE RAY

American Popular Singer

***Born* Dallas, Oregon, 14 January 1927**

***Died* Los Angeles, California, 25 February 1990**

Johnnie Ray was the first controversial pop superstar, a precursor to Elvis Presley and comparable in stature to The Beatles in their heyday. His records sold in the millions and his stage performances inspired hysteria in countless thousands of young women. For the era — he had his first major hit, "Cry", in 1951 — his overwrought stage performance was an extraordinary sight; a skinny young man appearing to go to pieces on stage in front of an audience of sobbing and screaming teenage girls. Little wonder that conservative observers at the time saw Ray as a symbol of the moral decline thought to be creeping through America in those cold war years.

Before Ray, there had only been polite (and resolutely white) big-band croon, sung by stars such as Frank Sinatra, Rosemary Clooney and Bing Crosby, or songs by hack writers paid by the bar. If the big-band swing songs were not gentrified black jazz compositions, they tended to be popular show tunes re-sprung with a little jive rhythm.

Ray was, if not the catalyst, then the rupture between this anodyne fare and the alarums of the rock'n'roll music that Elvis Presley would soon popularize — to further parental dismay. A contemporary photograph of Ray shows him distraught onstage, in tears, hand holding his head in grief, his face that of a relative arriving at the scene of a fatal car crash. The voice the girls in the audience were screaming at was a strange distillation of the despairing tones of jazz singer Billie Holiday, but they were not to know this.

What appears to have produced this voice was an accident at the age of eleven. Ray was being playfully thrown around in a blanket by some friends. The blanket slipped, he fell, hit his head badly, and was totally deaf for the next four years. His recovery was aided only by an obtrusive hearing aid, something he would have to wear for life. He was bullied at school and traumatized for life by this impairment, but it produced the voice, an extraordinary sound driven by his own personal unhappiness (it has been said that Ray was a repressed homosexual), that led Ray to be lionized, in one of the first great examples of pop hyperbole, as the Nabob of Sob, also known as the Prince of Wails. Many have argued — and still argue — that he could not really sing, merely bellow through a hearing impediment. But his style was also inspired by the blues, and Ray was unique for his time — the first white soul singer.

He came from a working-class background, and was of part American Indian and part white American parentage. He was musically precocious, mastering the rudiments of the piano at the age of three. He began singing in clubs in Detroit, accompanying himself on piano, in the late 1940s. It was a chance meeting with legendary black singer LaVern Baker and her manager that helped him along with his music, introducing him to the black blues and rhythm and blues culture, and he soon won a deal with the Okeh Records label in Detroit. His first single, "Whiskey and Gin", self-penned, was a minor hit. It was his second single, "Cry", that made him a star, while its B-side "The Little White Cloud That Cried" went on to become the best-selling record of 1952. Soon, Ray needed a regular police escort to keep the droves of fans who flocked to his concerts from tearing at his clothes and attempting to snip locks of hair from his head with scissors. He might be said single-handedly to have invented the screaming pop fan.

More hits began to climb into the upper reaches of the American and foreign charts: "Please, Mr Sun", "Walkin' My Baby Back Home", "Somebody Stole My Gal", "Such a Night", "Just Walking in the Rain" and others. His 1957 album, *The Big Beat*, reached the American top 20, and his last hit, "I'll Never Fall in Love Again", reached the top 30 in 1958. It is estimated that the original release of "Cry", its re-releases and cover versions may have sold in excess of 25 million copies world-wide.

Having effectively prepared the ground for the wilder excesses of Elvis Presley and the new rock'n'roll, Ray enjoyed massive fame but pop was not kind to him. He drew huge audiences in England and Australia, although continental audiences, perhaps resistant to American cultural influences, were cool. At home in America, newer, younger and even more shocking performers were appearing. Rebellious youth culture was burgeoning; it was the era of teen icons like Dean and Brando. While the pop-star machine did not make Ray its first victim, he was its first casualty. He made money, and is said to have invested it shrewdly for the future, but by 1958 his career at the front line of pop was over.

Several attempted comebacks, and an unhappy foray into acting in the 1954 film, *There's No Business Like Show Business*, followed his early success, but Ray's private life went into decline. He was married briefly in the early 1950s, but soon divorced, and by the beginning of the 1960s Ray was a self-confessed alcoholic. He retired from touring in 1965, although he made a comeback tour in 1974. While for the audiences this was pure nostalgia, for Ray it was disappointing. He continued to play the cabaret circuit until recently. His last public appearance was in October 1989 in Salem, Oregon.

It is probably difficult for younger people and those with an aversion to popular music to appreciate Ray's standing in the history of pop. He was no musical genius but his appearance in 1951 was crucial in the development of the music, perhaps as revolutionary as later performers who changed the course of popular music. One classic image of Ray on stage, dressed in black, eyes closed, body thrashing and face contorted, has eerie echoes of the personal terrors suffered on stage by the late Ian Curtis, singer with the seminal Manchester, England, new-wave group, Joy Division. There is no stylistic similarity, but time may prove that both men had a comparable influence.

Born John Ray. **Father** A sawmill worker. **Marriage** Marilyn Morrison, 1952 (divorced 1954). **Career** Singer, pianist, night-clubs and bars, Los Angeles and mid-West, 1940s; first hit, "Cry", 1951; on contract with Okeh Records, 1951, with Columbia, 1952; London Palladium début, 1953; British "comeback" tour, 1974; performed sporadically up to 1989. **Films** *There's No Business Like Show Business*, 1954. **Songs** (include) "Whiskey and Gin", 1951; "Cry"/"The Little White Cloud That Cried", 1951; "Tell The Lady I Said Goodbye"; "Please, Mr Sun"/"Here I Am — Broken-Hearted", 1952; "What's The Use"; "All Of Me", 1952; "Walkin' My Baby Back Home", 1952; "Somebody Stole My Gal", 1953; "Candy Lips", 1953; "Such a Night", 1954; "If You Believe", 1954; "Alexander's Ragtime Band", 1954; "Just Walking in the Rain", 1956; "You Don't Owe Me a Thing", 1956–57; *The Big Beat*, 1957; "Good Evening Friends"/"Up Above My Head", 1957; "I'll Never Fall in Love Again", 1958. **Cause of death** Liver failure, at age 63. **Further reading** I. Whitcomb, *After the Ball: Pop Music from Rag to Rock*, 1973; *Whole Lotta Shakin': A Rock and Roll Scrapbook*, 1982.

DEL SHANNON

American Popular Musician and Composer

***Born* Coopersville, Michigan, 30 December 1939**

***Died* Santa Clarita, California, 8 February 1990**

His contribution to popular music was small and his career brief, but Del Shannon is assured a place in rock legend by one song alone, "Runaway". His canon stretches to little more than a dozen singles and a sextet of albums, only a handful of those memorable, but musicians and critics alike revere him as a master.

He only began to play the guitar at the age of 14, but by his late teens was already writing and performing his own material. Drafted into the armed forces and sent to Europe, he became a regular performer on the forces radio programme, *Get Up and Go*. He began playing in bands on his return from Germany, particularly in the house band of the Hi-Lo Club in Battle Creek, Michigan, where a DJ heard Shannon and passed a live tape to a local entrepreneur. Signed to New York record label Big Top, Shannon and co-writer Max Crook wrote and recorded "Runaway", with its locomotive guitar riff and primitive electronic sound effects, in only two studio sessions.

Released early in 1961, "Runaway" became America's number one song for four weeks in April, and dominated the British charts for the same amount of time only two months later. Shannon and Crook also gave the world the sound of the Musitron, a precursor to the keyboard-operated synthesizer — it was much copied on releases by lesser performers hoping to emulate its unique sound and apparent success.

Shannon swiftly followed this release with his other famous tune, "Hats Off to Larry", which made the American top five, the British top ten, and inadvertently started an obscure cult of "Hats Off to ..." tribute songs — Led Zeppelin's later "Hats Off to [Roy] Harper" being among the most notable.

Shannon's output in this period was furious: two more singles, "So Long Baby" and "Hey! Little Girl", were released before the end of the year, followed by "Cry Myself to Sleep" and "The Swiss Maid", the next summer, but none repeated the top five success of those first two singles. Some gained respectable chart placings, but only "Little Town Flirt" came near, reaching the American top 20 and British charts. Some later releases barely got into the top 100.

While his hold on the American charts, indeed the American teen consciousness, was slipping, his reputation was buoyant enough in Britain for Shannon to appear on the same bill as The Beatles at the Royal Albert Hall in London. An admirer of The Beatles, and wanting to help them gain an American audience, he offered to, and in fact did, record the Lennon–McCartney tune, "From Me to You", for release as a single in the United States. It made the seventies in the American charts, and was the first Beatles song to chart in America. While the subsequent *Little Town Flirt* album reached the American top 20, Shannon's career was in decline — overshadowed, paradoxically, by the very music he wanted to showcase. A latecomer to the rock'n'roll revolution, he peaked at a time when popular music was diversifying into the almost tribal styles that would emerge on both sides of the Atlantic in the mid-1960s.

It was also about this time that Shannon became embroiled in complex and costly contract battles, first in 1963 with his original managers and then with successive record labels. He returned to the American top ten in 1965, after a three-year absence, with "Keep Searchin" ("We'll Follow the Sun"), and repeated that success in Britain, but subsequent releases faltered and Shannon became involved in further contractual battles with record companies. In 1967 he recorded an album with Rolling Stones manager Andrew Loog-Oldham which would sit in the label vaults for more than a decade, and in 1969 became a producer himself, most famously with friend Brian Hyland, who had a hit with their cover version of The Impressions' "Gypsy Woman", which became a million-seller.

Afterwards, Shannon's output became more erratic, although he more than survived on royalties from the original "Runaway" and the estimated 200-plus covers of the song — the number itself is a measure of the song's status. A variety of admirers helped produce comeback recordings for Shannon — Dave Edmunds in 1974, Jeff Lynne of the Electric Light Orchestra in 1975, and Tom Petty in 1982 — but while the critics applauded, the public was not interested. He continued to record, and played a number of what were, in essence, nostalgia rock'n'roll package tours. But he was clearly disillusioned and perhaps even depressed at his lack of success in later years. When police found him shot dead in his home with his own rifle by his side, they recorded death by apparent suicide — a fairly rock'n'roll way to go.

The fact that he took his first name from the name of a stylish Cadillac car and his surname from a wrestler he met in a night-club gives an idea of the ethos or milieu that produced Shannon: mythical young small-town America as celebrated in films, books and songs of the last 40 years. Compared to some his output was slight, but his most famous song and its abiding status gives a glimpse of what to the consensus makes great rock'n'roll: the ability to transcend mere entertainment and connect with popular taste and imagination with such force as to stamp an individual's personality on a time.

Born Charles Weeden Westover. **Father** A roadworker. **Marriage** Bonnie. **Military service** National serviceman, American Army, West Germany, 1958. **Career** Clerk, bowling ball manufacturers; début, *Get Up and Go* forces radio show, West Germany, 1958; resident guitarist and singer, Hi-Lo Club and carpet salesman, Battle Creek, Michigan; on contract with Harry Balk and Irving Micahnik, 1960; on contract with Embee Productions, and Big Top Records; composed with Max Crook, first hit, "Runaway", 1961; forms own record label, Berlee Records, 1963; recorded with Amy Records, New York, 1964; on contract with Liberty Records, Los Angeles, 1966; début as record producer with Brian Hyland, "Gypsy Woman", 1970; on contract with US Island Records, 1975; on contract with Warner Brothers, 1984. **Film** *It's Trad, Dad,* 1962. **Recordings** "Runaway", Big Top 3067, 1961; "Hats Off to Larry", Big Top 3075, 1961; "So Long Baby", 1961; "Hey! Little Girl", 1961; "You Never Talked About Me", 1962; "Cry Myself to Sleep", 1962; "The Swiss Maid", 1962; "Little Town Flirt", 1963; "Two Kinds of Teardrops", 1963; *Hats Off to Del Shannon*, 1963; "From Me to You", 1963; *Little Town Flirt*, 1963; "Two Silhouettes", 1963; "Sue's Gotta Be Mine", 1963; "Mary Jane", 1963; "Do You Want to Dance", 1964; "Handy Man", Amy, 1964; "Sings Hank Williams", 1965; "1,660 Seconds", 1965; "Keep Searchin'"/"We'll Follow the Sun", Amy 915, 1965; "I Go to Pieces", 1965; "Stranger in Town", 1965; "Break Up", 1965; "The Big Hurt", 1966; "This Is My Bag", Liberty, 1966; "Total Commitment", 1966; *Home and Away*, Liberty, recorded but not released 1967; "Baby It's You" (as arranger), 1969; "Gypsy Woman" (as producer), 1970; "Del Shannon Sings", Post, 1970; *Live in England*, UA S29474, 1973; *Best of Del Shannon*, Polydor, 1973; "And the Music Plays On", 1974; "Tell Her No", 1975; "Cry Baby Cry", 1975; *Del Shannon: The Vintage Years*, Sire 37082, 1975; *Drop Down And Get Me*, Elektra, 1982; "Sea of Love", 1982; "In My Arms Again", 1984. **Cause of death** Suicide by shooting, at age 50.

KATE SIMON

Polish/American Travel Writer

Born **Warsaw, Poland, 5 December 1912**

Died **Manhattan, New York, 4 February 1990**

When Kate Simon's first and best-known travel guide, *New York Places and Pleasures: An Uncommon Guidebook*, appeared in 1959, she proved beyond all doubt that it does not take an out-of-towner to appreciate the Big Apple. Though she travelled widely, producing memorable studies of Mexico City, Paris, Rome and London, together with two vivid autobiographies, it is for her unusual, affectionate portrait of her teeming hometown on the Hudson — a city she claimed to know "as well as [her] own body — that she is best remembered. *New York Places and Pleasures*, which sold more than 100,000 copies in its first three years and underwent four revisions, is still regarded as one of the most popular, most readable guides to New York City.

The daughter of a Polish shoemaker, Kate Simon was born Kaila Grobsmith in a Warsaw ghetto. When she was four, her father left for New York, and shortly afterwards she and her mother and brother secured steerage tickets to follow him. From the Lower East Side, the family moved briefly to Harlem, then to the Tremont section of the Bronx, where Simon spent her formative years. Later, she recalled the period in *Bronx Primitive: Portraits in a Childhood*, the first volume in her three-part autobiography. In the second, *A Wider World: Portraits in an Adolescence*, she chronicles her rebellious teenage years. Her realistic, unsentimental account earned her the praise of *New York Times* critic Robert Pinskey, who hailed her "clean and unpretentious prose style", her "aristocratic disdain for cant", and her "frank worldliness".

Despite the protests of her tyrannical father, Simon went on to study at competitive James Monroe High School and then at Hunter College, where she earned a Bachelor's degree. After graduating she held a succession of editorial posts, first with the Book-of-the-Month Club, then with *Publishers' Weekly*, and finally with the *The New Republic* and *The Nation*, where she reviewed the work of contemporary writers.

Although she did not publish her first book until 1959, Simon had spent her adolescence and early adulthood gathering enough experiences and observations to fill a library. "I really started to work on it [*New York Places and Pleasures*], without knowing I was doing so, at fourteen, during summer vacation from high school in the Bronx", she remembered. "I wandered around the city with fascinated curiosity ... I'd spend a day walking and a day writing." The guidebook that evolved reflected her highly personal, unconventional approach, and her *penchant* for forgotten corners and unlikely or exotic characters.

Following the publication of *New York Places and Pleasures*, Simon went on to write a similar guide to Mexico, a country she had first explored in the 1940s. True to form, she shunned the traditional tourist traps and concentrated on less obvious, more evocative areas. "I give only a couple of paragraphs to Acapulco, which to me is not what's endearing about Mexico, but a great many pages to Guanajuato, which is", she explained in a *New Yorker* interview. "It's [Guanajuato] one of those angry-cat cities. It doesn't wag its tail at you, the way a dog does." Her own advice to travellers mirrored her own techniques: "Walk slowly, look, listen, smell." Eavesdropping was never out of order.

Over the years, she produced ten travel books and received awards from the National Book Critics Circle and the English Speaking Union. According to Sybil S. Steinberg of *Publishers' Weekly*, Simon's guides were "in a class by themselves, distinctly personal guides of rare good taste and discernment". J.H. Plumb of *The New York Times Book Review* called her work "incomparable" in making "one of the dullest forms of literature a brilliant work of art." Shortly before her death she completed a third volume of her memoirs, tentatively titled *Etchings on an Hour Glass*, in which she recalled her student life, her marriages and her career.

Born Kaila Grobsmith. **Father** A shoemaker. **Marriages** 1) Stanley Goldman, doctor (died 1942), 2) Robert Simon, publisher (divorced 1960). **Children** One daughter, Alexandra, by first marriage. **Education** James Monroe High School, New York; AB, Hunter College, New York. **Emigration** Left Poland for the United States, 1916. **Career** Editor, various organizations, including Book-of-the-Month Club, *Publishers' Weekly*; book reviewer, *The New Republic*, *The Nation*; first travel book, *New York Places and Pleasures: An Uncommon Guidebook*, 1959. **Awards and honours** Awards from the National Book Critics Circle and English Speaking Union, both for travel writing. **Publications** *New York Places and Pleasures: An Uncommon Guidebook*, 1959; *Italy: The Places in Between,* 1970; *England's Green and Pleasant Lane*, 1974; *Fifth Avenue: A Very Social History*, 1978; *Bronx Primitive: Portraits in a Childhood* (autobiography), 1982; *A Wider World: Portraits in an Adolescence* (autobiography), 1986; *A Renaissance*

Tapestry: The Gonzaga of Mantua, 1988; *Etchings on an Hour Glass* (autobiography), to be published; also a travel book on Mexico City. **Cause of death** Cancer, at age 77.

IPHIGENE OCHS SULZBERGER

American Newspaper Heiress and Philanthropist

***Born* Cincinnati, Ohio, 19 September 1892**

***Died* Stamford, Connecticut, 26 February 1990**

As daughter, wife, mother-in-law, and mother to three generations of *New York Times* publishers, Iphigene Ochs Sulzberger played a quiet yet essential role in helping to shape the history of one of the most important newspapers in the United States. "Through her, the continuity of family control from father to husband to son-in-law to son has been maintained for over 60 years", wrote Barbara Tuchman in the foreword to Sulzberger's memoirs, "and, through her, it will be passed on to the next generation — her grandchildren."

A member of the *Times*'s governing board for 56 years, Iphigene Ochs Sulzberger was once described in an editorial as "something like its conscience". She also embraced a wide variety of philanthropic causes, including the environment, education and civil rights, and was a frequent and favoured guest of prominent politicians. Her maternal grandfather, Isaac M. Wise, was the founder of American Reform Judaism.

Iphigene Bertha Ochs Sulzberger, known to family and friends as "If" or "Iffy", once observed that her life "revolved around newspapers". Few could disagree. The night she was born, her father, Adolph S. Ochs, then publisher of the *Chattanooga Times*, was in New York lobbying to get smaller papers, such as his own, accepted in the Associated Press. Four years later he bought the faltering *New York Times*, and the family moved east from Tennessee to New York.

The only child of an indulgent yet perfectionist father, Iphigene Ochs enjoyed a privileged upbringing. She was educated at home until the age of eight, gaining a thorough grounding in history and literature by delving into what she described as "one-syllable history books on Rome and Greece and France and the United States" supplied by her parents. She also visited the Metropolitan, the Natural History Museum, and the New York theatre, and, from age eight on, accompanied her parents on annual excursions to Europe. Her love of travel was to last throughout her life. Still, the highest point of her week, she remembered, was her Sunday perambulation through Central Park in the company of her father. He also took her with him to luncheons with important business and political figures, and, occasionally, to the composing room at *The New York Times*.

Iphigene Ochs continued her education at two Manhattan day schools, and in 1910 went on to Barnard College. Here, she recalled, "I discovered that learning could be a joy." Yet, despite her studies, she refused to languish in an academic cocoon. During her college years she also worked at the Henry Street Settlement, at the Cedar Knolls School for disturbed children, and in the Jewish Big Sister Program, developing a strong and unwavering commitment to social service. In her senior year at Barnard she enrolled in a course at the Columbia School of Journalism, but later denied that she harboured any real ambition to follow her father into the profession. Instead, she was content to spend the rest of her life on the sidelines, informed but — except in a few rare and memorable cases — unobtrusive. Besides, her father had often maintained that a newspaper office was no place for a woman.

While studying at Barnard she also met, and later married, Arthur Hayes Sulzberger, the son of a southern cotton merchant. At the end of World War I they settled in New York, where Sulzberger joined *The New York Times* and his wife occupied herself with making a home and rearing the couple's four children. When they had grown, she turned her boundless energy and enthusiasm to education and philanthropy.

When her father died in 1935, Iphigene Sulzberger and her husband both became trustees of the *Times*; thanks to her intervention, Arthur Sulzberger was also elected president and publisher. When he retired in 1961, he was succeeded by her son-in-law, Orvil E. Dryfoos, and in 1963, by her son, Arthur Ochs Sulzberger.

During World War II, Iphigene Sulzberger moved briefly from the newspaper's sidelines and onto its staff, accepting a position as director of special events in the *Times*'s promotion department. Here, she helped to assist the war effort, civilian defence and conservation, and encouraged the use of the *Times* as an educational tool in schools and colleges. She also initiated educational forums on world affairs, and, during this period, inspired a series of Pulitzer Prize-winning articles that revealed the public's astonishing lack of interest and competence in history.

Throughout her life, she was a diligent and regular reader of *The New York Times*, occasionally disagreeing with its views and writing droll — and usually anonymous — letters to the editor. Her greatest quarrel with the paper concerned the presidential elections of 1952 and 1956, when she supported Democrat Adlai Stevenson over the paper's choice, Republican Dwight D. Eisenhower. But, more often than not, she preferred to express her opinions quietly, within the confines of the family. "I know, as every wife and mother does, how best to influence the men of the family into doing the right thing", she once remarked.

Outside the family and the newspaper, Sulzberger focused her energies on education and conservation. For 16 years she served as president of the Park Association, a volunteer group dedicated to improving New York City's parks, and in 1976 received the annual Parks Council Award for her continuing work on environmental issues. She also sat on the board of Barnard College from 1937 to 1968, and in 1951 received an honorary Doctor of Laws degree from Columbia University. Then, in January 1978, Bishop College of Dallas, then the largest predominantly black institution of higher learning in the American south-west awarded her an honorary Doctorate of Humanities. At that time, she was commended for having been the largest single private donor in the history of the United Negro College Fund. Her interests also ranged as far afield as Antarctica, where explorer Admiral Richard Byrd was moved to name a glacier and an Arctic waterway for her.

At the age of 87, Iphigene Ochs Sulzberger recited her personal memoirs to one of her 13 grandchildren. These were subsequently printed for private perusal, and in 1979 they were published in book form under the title *Iphigene*. In them she reveals the lively, adventurous spirit and boundless optimism that made her the pillar of one of America's most powerful and influential families. "The more one has seen in life, the more questions one raises, the more one realizes that ... nothing is impossible", she writes. Nearly ten years later, at 97, she was as curious and enthusiastic as ever.

Born Iphigene Bertha Ochs. **Parents** Adolph S., newspaper proprietor, and Iphigenia (Wise) Ochs. **Marriage** Arthur Hays Sulzberger, newspaper publisher, 1917. **Children** Marian, Ruth, Judith and Arthur. **Education** Dr Sachs School for Girls, Manhattan, New York: Benjamin-Dean School, Manhattan, New York; Barnard College, New York, 1910; Columbia School of Journalism, New York, 1912. **Career** Director, *The New York Times*, 1917–73, director emeritus, 1973 onwards, trustee, 1935 onwards, director, special events, World War II, trustee stock trust. **Related activities** Committee member, *Dictionary of American Biography*; advisory committee member, works of Thomas Jefferson. **Other activities** Worked in Henry Street

Settlement, Jewish Big Sister Program and Cedar Knolls School for disturbed children, as a student; member, Park Association, 1928 onwards, president, 1934–50, chairman, 1950–57; member, Musical Talent in Our Schools, World War II; active in Metropolitan Museum of Art; active in State Communities Aid Assocation, the National Urban League, the Association on American Indian Affairs, the New York Girl Scout Council. **Offices and memberships** Board member, Barnard College, 1937–68, trustee emeritus, 1968 onwards; trustee, Hebrew Union College-Jewish Institute of Religion; board member: Cedar Knolls School, Federation of Jewish Philanthropists; on board of managers, Inwood House; director, Yaddo, Saratoga Springs, New York. **Awards and honours** Doctor of Laws, Columbia University, 1951; Distinguished Service Award, New York Botanical Garden, 1965; honorary DLitt, Jewish Theological Seminary, 1968; Doctorate of Humane Letters: Hebrew Union College-Jewish Institute of Religion, 1973, University of Chattanooga; Parks Council Award, 1976; Doctorate of Humanities, Bishop College of Dallas, 1978; award, New York City Board of Education, 1978; honorary chairman, Central Park Conservancy, 1980; Distinguished Alumna Award, Barnard College; Gold Medal for distinguished service to humanity, National Institute of Social Sciences. **Publication** *Iphigene*, 1979. **Cause of death** Respiratory failure, at age 97.

SIR ERNEST TITTERTON

British Nuclear Physicist

***Born* Tamworth, Staffordshire, 4 March 1916**

***Died* Canberra, Australia, 8 February 1990**

The dropping of two atomic bombs on Japan in 1945 was to affect the lives of all who had helped develop them. Some, like Mark Oliphant, were to feel so guilty they regarded themselves as a form of war criminal. Few were to feel entirely happy at their participation, but Sir Ernest Titterton was one of them. "These two weapons", he was to say later, "caused enormous damage. Everybody was very sad that it was so. Nevertheless it had to be done. We had to swap 200,000 Japanese lives for literally millions of lives of our people. It's a curious way of looking at it, but it was a humanitarian act."

His views, and those of Oliphant, were poles apart on this subject, but Titterton's whole career had been bound up with Oliphant's from a very early stage. In the late 1930s, when at university at Birmingham, England, not far from his home town, he became Professor Mark Oliphant's first research student. When war broke out in 1939 Titterton worked for the Admiralty on radar, Asdic and the detection of magnetic mines, but Oliphant then introduced him into Tube Alloys, the team working on the feasibility of making an atomic bomb. It was headed by Peierls and Frisch, two *émigrés* excluded from the Admiralty research. It was their famous memorandum, in 1940, which showed for the first time that a "super bomb" could be created based on a nuclear chain reaction.

In 1943, when the development became a joint one with the Americans, Oliphant and Titterton were among the group of British scientists, 19 in all, who joined the Manhattan Project. Titterton was still in his twenties, but had earned himself a reputation as an outstanding experimentalist. He led the group working on the instrumentation and timing involved in actually firing the first bomb, which exploded at Alamogordo. The explosion was to last for considerably less than a millionth of a second, and the task of setting up the arming and firing sequence, and operating the instruments remotely to give ultra-fast time references of the processes taking place during the explosion, was extraordinarily complex technically. The whole success of the experiment depended on it.

The bombs were dropped, the war ended, and Titterton stayed on at Los Alamos until 1947, after the McMahon Act terminated Anglo-American co-operation, as head of the Electronics Division. In 1946, during the atomic weapon trials on Bikini Atoll, he gave the countdown and detonation order for the tests. As his identity was kept secret, the radio operator at Bikini dubbed him "The Voice of Abraham".

From Los Alamos Titterton returned to England, working at the Atomic Energy Research Establishment at Harwell, but in 1950 Mark Oliphant, who was in charge of physics research at the new Australian University at Canberra, invited him to be head of the department of nuclear physics there, and Titterton was to remain at that university for the rest of his working life.

But relations between Titterton and Oliphant were not to be easy in the new country they adopted. Titterton was a small, squat, somewhat pugnacious man, with complete conviction in the future of nuclear energy and nuclear weapons. Oliphant, who had the greatest respect for Titterton's professional brilliance, was much more sensitive and caring.

Titterton's strong advocacy in the benefits of science and nuclear energy in particular led him to play a distinctly controversial role in the British nuclear weapon tests in central Australia during the 1950s and early 1960s. He chaired a small group of Australian scientists, the Atomic Weapons Tests Safety Committee, which liaised with the British. Titterton was probably chosen for that role, rather than Oliphant who was Australia's pre-eminent nuclear physicist, because the latter's "soft" politics might have offended the Americans; for these were the McCarthy years.

Titterton's actions at that time were not to be publicly aired for many years, not until the Australian Royal Commission into the safety aspects of the tests in the 1980s. It was said that at those tests he showed more allegiance to his old country than his new one, and that he allowed unsafe testing and concealed information from the Australian government when he felt "to do so would suit the interests of the United Kingdom Government and the testing programme." But it may have been simply that he was valuing the interests of science too highly against the interests of humanity.

His firm advocacy of nuclear energy and nuclear weapons made many enemies, for as a subject it is a fence which divides, and few can sit on. It is interesting that in spite of an abundant supply of uranium, Australia has never developed nuclear power in either form.

But his work at the Australian National University was remarkable. At Los Alamos and in Britain he had mixed with the foremost nuclear physicists of the world, and these contacts were invaluable in establishing a thriving nuclear physics department with a world-class laboratory. Several accelerators were installed, including, in 1975, the 14UD Pelletron, at that time the world's highest voltage electrostatic accelerator.

His main studies concerned rare modes of fission and the photo disintegration and spectroscopy of light nuclei. In directing the research he had great drive and enthusiasm and he expected the same from his staff. Fools were not suffered gladly. Small and brusque, those meeting him felt he would either accept or ignore them, depending on his appraisal of their work and worth.

At the Royal Commission he was asked by the lawyers if he had any scepticism of his fellow scientists. "I do not have very much scepticism of scientists as a group", he replied. "I have considerable scepticism of some of them. And I have huge scepticism of pseudo-scientists who learn a little and think they know a lot."

After a very energetic life his last three years were tragic. A freak car accident left him quadriplegic, able to use only the muscles of his head and neck. His brain was still agile, and whereas other men would have lost their courage with their other faculties, Titterton found a new cause to advocate with passion; that of euthanasia. And for the first time in 40 years he found himself on the same side as his former mentor, Mark Oliphant.

Born Ernest William Titterton. **Parents** William Alfred, paper manufacturer, and Elizabeth (Smith) Titterton. **Marriage** Peggy Eileen Johnson, chemist 1942 (divorced 1986).

Children Two daughters and one son, Elizabeth, Andrew and Ashley. **Education** Queen Elizabeth's Grammar School, Tamworth, Staffordshire; University of Birmingham, BSc, 1937, BSc with honours, 1938, Diploma in Education, 1939, MSc, 1940, PhD, 1942. **Career** Research officer, Admiralty, 1939–43; member, British Scientific Mission on atomic bomb development (Manhattan Project), United States of America, 1943–47; senior member, Timing Group, 1st atomic bomb test, Alamogordo, new Mexico, 1945; head, Electronics Division, Los Alamos Laboratory, United States of America, 1946–47; group leader, research team, Atomic Energy Research Establishment, Harwell, England, 1947–50; professor of nuclear physics, Australian National University, 1950–81, professor emeritus, 1981 onwards, dean, Research School of Physical Sciences, 1966–68, director, 1968–73; also, lecturer, United Nations, writer for television and broadcaster. **Related activities** Adviser on instrumentation, Bikini Atomic Weapons Test, 1946; member, Australian Atomic Energy Commission Scientific Advisory Committee, 1955–64; deputy chairman, Australian Atomic Weapons Safety Committee, 1954–56; chairman, Atomic Weapons Tests Safety Committee, 1957–73; member, Defence Research and Development Policy Committee, 1958–75; member, National Radiation Advisory Committee, 1957–73. **Offices and memberships** Vice-president, Australian Institute of Nuclear Science and Engineering, 1968–72, president, 1973–75; fellow: Royal Society of Arts, Australian Academy of Science; member: Australian Academy of Forensic Sciences, Royal Society of Arts and Sciences. **Awards and honours** Elizabeth Cadbury Prize; Companion of the Order of St Michael and St George, 1957; knighted, 1970. **Publications** *Facing the Atomic Future*, 1954; *Progress in Nuclear Physics Four*, 1955; *Selected Lectures in Modern Physics*, 1958; (with F.P. Robotham) *Inside the Atom*, 1966; *Uranium: Energy Source of the Future?*, 1979. **Cause of death** Undisclosed, at age 73.

JIMMY VAN HEUSEN

American Composer

Born **Syracuse, New York, 26 January 1913**

Died **Rancho Mirage, California, 6 February 1990**

Expelled from high school for singing "My Canary Has Rings Under His Eyes" (a mildly salacious song he'd heard on the radio) during a school assembly, then expelled from another school a year later for being what school officials described as "a little bum hanging around poolrooms", he grew up to be a notorious hellraiser who once told an interviewer, "I dig chicks, booze, music and Sinatra — in that order." He was certainly telling the truth about his likes, but he wasn't truthful about the order. Luckily for us, music was definitely his first, and most important, love. There can't be many people in the English-speaking world who can't hum at least one or two of his songs, which include such Oscar winners as "Swinging' on a Star" (from *Going My Way*), "All the Way" (*The Joker Is Wild*), "High Hopes" (*A Hole in the Head*), and "Call Me Irresponsible" (*Papa's Delicate Condition*).

Born Edward Chester Babcock, he was still in high school when he took a job at a local radio station and the manager insisted that he change his name. He looked out of the window and saw a billboard advertising Van Heusen shirts, so that was the name he took. He added "James" just because he liked the sound of it. Years later, Van Heusen recalled that the station manager was delighted with the new name and that he was happy with it himself because "my parents did not know I was skipping school".

In the early 1930s he formed a songwriting partnership with Jerry Arlen, the younger brother of his next-door neighbour, Harold Arlen. When Harold was unable to fulfil a songwriting commitment for Harlem's Cotton Club, Van Heusen and Jerry took the job over. The revue was a flop, and Van Heusen later described the song he wrote for it as "terrible". Some hard times followed, during which he supported himself by means of various jobs, from waiting on tables to operating a freight elevator to playing piano in a bordello.

By 1939, teamed up with a new lyricist, Eddie de Lange, he had written the music for a Broadway show, *Swingin' the Dream*, a swing version of Shakespeare's *A Midsummer Night's Dream*. Despite music played by Benny Goodman and a cast that included Louis Armstrong as Bottom, the show was a disaster, playing only 13 performances. The show may have flopped, but it provided Van Heusen's career with a much-needed boost: his first hit. "Darn That Dream", one of the songs from the show, was recorded by several different artists, including Dinah Shore, and sold more than 200,000 copies in sheet music by the end of 1940.

As one of Tin Pan Alley's most successful composers, with 60 songs published in just one season, Van Heusen's next stop was Hollywood. With his new lyricist, Johnny Burke, he began a long and profitable association with Bing Crosby. Altogether, Van Heusen wrote the music for 23 Bing Crosby films, including six of the famous "Road" pictures, in which co-star Bob Hope played a character with a name rather familiar to Van Heusen: Chester Babcock.

Such was the string of hits produced by Burke and Van Heusen that Bing Crosby referred to them as the "Gold Dust Twins". At one time they were under contract to Twentieth Century-Fox, MGM, Columbia and International Studios, all at the same time.

During World War II, Van Heusen, who had earned a pilot's licence in 1937 and owned his own plane, became a test pilot for Lockheed. As he said in an interview years later, "Having two names now stood me in good stead. I was able to continue writing songs under the name of James Van Heusen and the 120 test pilots in the pilot house at Lockheed did not know for at least a year and a half that the Edward Babcock in their midst was the ... James Van Heusen whose song 'Sunday, Monday or Always' was currently on *Your Hit Parade*, and I was just 'one of the guys'." He didn't tell the studio about it, either, "because, as Johnny Burke warned me at the time, if they knew I was test-flying airplanes at Lockheed they would not assign me to a picture in the middle of which I might be killed flying a sick airplane."

The Burke–Van Heusen partnership began to falter in the 1950s. Burke's health was failing, and their Broadway show, *Carnival in Flanders*, closed after only six performances. Frank Sinatra, whose own career was in a slump, suggested that Van Heusen should work with Sammy Cahn. After Van Heusen's death, Cahn wrote, "one day the phone rang and it was Sinatra saying, 'I'd like you to do a song with Van Heusen.' ... I said, 'No, no. He's a team with Burke.' They were joined at the hip." Finally, Cahn agreed to meet with Van Heusen. He went over to his house, and suddenly the doorbell rang and Johnny Burke came in. For a lyric-writer, that's like being caught with somebody else's wife."

Their first song together was "The Tender Trap", a major hit for Frank Sinatra, and the beginning of Van Heusen's associate membership of the "Rat Pack". Bing Crosby, while trying to cut down on his drinking, used to avoid Van Heusen after dark. Not Sinatra. Van Heusen used to joke that he ought to get more than 50 per cent from a song because he spent "so much time with Sinatra", while Sammy Cahn has written of Sinatra, "Sinatra thinks he's Van Heusen ... but he can't pass the physical."

Sinatra recorded 76 songs by Van Heusen, more than any other composer. Like Van Heusen's mother, Sinatra always called him "Chester", and in concerts often used to dedicate songs to him with the words, "This one's for Chester."

The hits written by Van Heusen and Cahn did more than revive Sinatra's career, they gave him a chance to branch out into a variety of personae, from the swinging 1950s hipster of "Come Fly with

Me" to the wide-eyed optimist of "High Hopes" to the brooding nostalgic of "September of My Years". Of course, a great deal of this was due to the lyrics of Sammy Cahn, who wrote of his collaboration with Van Heusen, "When he wrote with Burke, the Irish poet, as we called him, the songs were lacier, more fragile ... I wrote down-to-earth, more abrasive lyrics for him."

The lyrics often came first. Some composers find this too restricting; they find themselves trapped by a regular metrical pattern. Van Heusen, however, was able to create a totally free-wheeling melody while remaining true to every nuance of the lyrics. If Sammy Cahn asked for an extra grace note so he could add an "and" or "but", Van Heusen would just tell him he'd write him another tune. Van Heusen would occasionally suggest some alteration to the lyrics, such as when he and Cahn were writing a song for Bing Crosby to sing in the 1960 film, *High Time*. They had to write a love song for a widower to sing to a widow. They had quite a bit of trouble with that one, and then Cahn came up with the title and the first two lines of "The Second Time Around":

> Love is wonderful the second time around
> Just as beautiful with both feet on the ground.

Van Heusen stopped him and said, "No. What you want to say is,

> Love is *lovelier* the second time around
> Just as *wonderful* with both feet on the ground."

Cahn said that after that, the song just wrote itself. According to Cahn, "A good composer is the editor of the lyric, the one who has to decide if it's a print."

With Sammy Cahn as his partner, Van Heusen made a few more attempts at writing for Broadway, but they never achieved the level of success they had in films. Their longest running show was *Skyscraper*, an adaptation of Elmer Rice's *Dream Girl*, which ran for 248 performances. The two also wrote for television, winning two Emmys before their partnership was dissolved in the early 1970s and Van Heusen finally retired.

He once said, "I was lucky to go to Hollywood in the days when it was still making original musicals or Jimmy Van Heusen might have gone the way of Edward Chester Babcock. I was also lucky to have Frank and Bing to sing my songs. They brought out the best in them — and me."

It would seem that Hollywood, and Frank, and Bing, were the lucky ones.

Born Edward Chester Babcock. **Parents** Arthur Edward, building contractor, and Ida Mae (Williams) Babcock. **Marriage** Bobbie Perlberg, 1970. **Education** Central High School, Syracuse, New York; Czenovia Seminary, New York; Syracuse University, New York, 1930–32. **Career** Radio announcer, WSYR, Syracuse, while still at school; own programme, WFBL, Syracuse; formed songwriting partnership with Jerry Arlen, first collaboration, "Harlem Hospitality", Cotton Club Revue, New York, 1933; moved to New York City, employed variously as waiter, elevator operator, staff pianist; formed partnership with lyricist, bandleader, Eddie de Lange, 1938; first Broadway musical score, *Swingin' the Dream*, 1939; collaborated with lyricist Johnny Burke, 1940–53; first film score, *Love Thy Neighbor*, with Burke, 1940; with Burke, formed publishing company, Burke & Van Heusen Incorporated, 1944; founded Van Heusen Incorporated, 1950; collaborated with Sammy Cahn, 1955 to early 1970s; with Cahn also composed for night-clubs, theatrical appearances by Paul Anka, Lena Horne, Nat King Cole, Sammy Davis Jr (q.v.) and others. **Related activities** Toured army camps, 1942. **Other activities** Test pilot, Lockheed aircraft company, 1942–44. **Awards and honours** Oscar for "Swinging on a Star", 1944; United States Treasury Department, citation, plaque, silver medal, for helping promote sale of war and victory bonds, 1946; Emmys for "Love and Marriage", 1956, for *Jack and the Beanstalk*, 1966; Oscars for "All the Way", 1957, for "High Hopes", 1959, for "Call Me Irresponsible", 1963; honorary citizen of Texas, 1958; Distinguished Alumnus Award, Czenovia Seminary, 1961;

elected to Songwriters Hall of Fame, 1971. **Compositions** "Harlem Hospitality", 1933; "It's the Dreamer in Me", 1938; "So Help Me", 1938; "Deep in a Dream", 1938; "Good for Nothin'", 1938; "Heaven Can Wait", 1939; "All I Remember Is You", 1939; "Can I Help It", 1939; "Darn That Dream", 1939; "Speaking of Heaven", 1939; "Oh You Crazy Moon", 1939; "You Think of Everything", 1939; "All This and Heaven Too", 1939; "Looking Is Yesterday", 1939; "Imagination", 1939; "Isn't That Just Like Love?", 1940; "Dearest, Darest I?", 1940; "Do You Know Why?", 1940; "Polka Dots and Moonbeams", 1940; "Humpty Dumpty Heart", 1940; "It's Always You", 1941; "Ain't Got a Dime in My Pocket", 1941; "Birds of a Feather", 1941; "Moonlight Becomes You", 1942; "Sunday, Monday or Always", 1943; "If You Please", 1943; "Swinging on a Star", 1944; "The Day After Forever", 1944; "Suddenly It's Spring", 1944; "It Could Happen to You", 1944; "Like Someone in Love", 1944; "Sleigh Ride in July", 1944; "Friend of Yours", 1945; "Aren't You Glad You're You", 1946; "Welcome to My Dreams", 1946; "It's Anybody's Spring", 1946; "Put It There, Pal", 1946"; "Personality", 1946; "Just My Luck", 1946; "Harmony", 1946; "As Long As I'm Dreaming", 1947; "My Heart Is a Hobo", 1947; "Smile Right Back at the Sun", 1947; "But Beautiful", 1948; "Country Style", 1948; "You Don't Have to Know the Language", 1948; "You're in Love with Someone", 1949; "Once and for Always", 1949; "When Is Sometime?", 1949; "And You'll Be Home", 1950; "Sunshine Cake", 1950; "Here's That Rainy Day", 1953; "That Very Necessary You", 1953; "Call Me Irresponsible", 1955; "The Man with the Golden Arm", 1955; "Love and Marriage", 1956; "All the Way", 1957; "To Love and Be Loved", 1958; "Indiscreet", 1958; "Only the Lonely", 1958; "Come Dance with Me", 1959; "High Hopes", 1959; "Come Fly with Me", 1959; "No One Cares", 1959; "The Second Time Around", 1960; "A Pocketful of Miracles", 1961; "Ring-A-Ding-Ding", 1961; "The Boys' Night Out", 1962; "Warmer Than a Whisper", 1962; "My Kind of Town", 1964; "Love Is a Bore", 1964; "Where Love Has Gone", 1964; "September of My Years", 1965; "Everybody has a Right to Be Wrong", 1965; "I'll Only Miss Her When I Think of Her", 1965; "Walking Happy", 1966; "Thoroughly Modern Millie", 1967. **Scores** *Swingin' the Dream*, 1939; *Love Thy Neighbor*, 1940; *Playmates*, 1941; *Road to Singapore*, 1941; *Road to Zanzibar*, 1941; *Road to Morocco*, 1942; *Dixie*, 1943; *Going My Way*, 1944; *And the Angels Sing*, 1944; *Bell of the Yukon*, 1944; *Lady in the Dark*, 1944; *The Great John L*, 1945; *Nellie Bly*, 1946; *The Bells of St Mary's*, 1946; *The Road to Utopia*, 1946; *Welcome Stranger*, 1947; *Road to Rio*, 1948; *Top o' the Morning*, 1949; *A Connecticut Yankee*, 1949; *Mr Music*, 1950; *Sunshine Cake*, 1950; *Carnival in Flanders*, 1953; *Not as a Stranger*, 1955; *The Tender Trap*, 1955; *The Man with the Golden Arm*, 1955; *Our Town*, 1956; *Anything Goes*, 1956: *The Joker Is Wild*, 1957; *Some Came Running*, 1958; *Indiscreet*, 1958; *A Hole in the Head*, 1959; *High Time*, 1960; *A Pocketful of Miracles*, 1961; *The Boys' Night Out*, 1962; *The Road to Hong Kong*, 1962; *Papa's Delicate Condition*, 1963; *Robin and the 7 Hoods*, 1964; *Where Love Has Gone*, 1964; *Skyscraper*, 1965; *Walking Happy*, 1966; *Thoroughly Modern Millie*, 1967. **Television** (includes) *Our Town*, 1955; *Frank Sinatra Show*, 1959–60; *Potomac Madness*, 1960; *Jack and the Beanstalk*, 1966; *The Legend of Robin Hood*, 1968; *Journey Back to Oz*, 1971. **Cause of death** Undisclosed, at age 77. **Further reading** D. Ewen, *Great Men of American Popular Song*, 1970; A. Wilder, *American Popular Song: The Great Innovators 1900–1950*, 1975.

GREVILLE WYNNE

British Intelligence Agent

***Born* Shropshire, England, 1919**

***Died* London, England, 27 February 1990**

Greville Wynne saw himself as a cold war warrier and lived his life at the interface between fact and fiction. He almost admitted a few years before his death that he could not always distinguish one from the other and even his ghost writer, John Gilbert, acknowledged a tendency to "enlarge and romanticise" as being part of his personality.

Greville Maynard Wynne came from a modest background. His early childhood was spent in South Wales where his father was an engineering worker and from whom Wynne gained his own interest in the field. He later studied engineering as an extra-mural student at Nottingham University prior to World War II.

Just how he was really recruited into British Intelligence is not known. His own version was that in the year before the war, when he was 19, he reported a man in a Nottingham factory for transmitting messages to Germany. This, he claimed, led to his serving in low-level intelligence in the UK for the duration, monitoring the activities of suspected Nazi sympathizers for MI5. He claimed that he ended the war with the rank of major and subsequently elevated himself to lieutenant-colonel. In fact the record shows that Wynne had been rejected by an officers' training course and was assigned to an anti-aircraft battery as an ordinary soldier. He never received a commission.

After the war he started his own electrical engineering firm and proved himself a successful businessman. In 1955, according to his own version once more, he was contacted by a former MI5 boss who hinted that trade in eastern Europe might be a fruitful area to pursue. Wynne seized the challenge and began what he obviously saw as a glamorous career as a British agent.

The record shows that he travelled in eastern Europe as a businessman and, in November 1962 and within days of the Cuban missile crisis, was picked up by the KGB while giving a party for Hungarian clients in Budapest. He was flown to Moscow for interrogation and a month later Colonel Oleg Penkovsky of the Soviet Military Intelligence Agency (the GRU) was arrested and charged with supplying political, military and scientific secrets to western agents over a period of 16 months.

The two men were arraigned together. At their four-day show trial Penkovsky was sentenced to death for treason. It was claimed he had supplied over 5000 items of sensitive information to the West at a crucial stage in the relationship between the two blocs. Wynne was sentenced to eight years for acting as his go-between with both American and British intelligence agencies. They had met several times in London and Paris as well as the Soviet Union itself.

Wynne was sentenced to three years' imprisonment and five years in a labour camp. In the event he served only 17 months — in the Lubyanka prior to the trial and thereafter in the punishment prison of Vladimir. He was freed in a spy swap at a Berlin border checkpoint in April 1964. In return the British gave up Gordon Lonsdale, a KGB man who had, while wearing the guise of a Canadian businessman, been caught by Scotland Yard's Special Branch together with a number of others in January 1961.

Wynne did, in fact, play a pivotal part in the transmission of vital information which enabled President Kennedy to call Khrushchev's bluff over the deployment of Soviet missiles in Cuba and to force a withdrawal. He also clearly suffered severely in prison. Photographs taken following his return to the UK show a gaunt and haggard face which contrasts strongly with the full and assured look he had previously.

But when he came to tell his own story, first in his book *The Man from Moscow* which came out in 1967, the embroidery began. In the introduction to his book, *The Man from Odessa*, he included a remark made by the secretary of the D-Notice Committee (which has power to suppress sensitive information) to the effect that "certain passages ... would almost certainly have been objectionable on security grounds, had they been true"! When one recalls, in more recent years, the efforts to prevent the memoirs of a "spy catcher" being published in the UK, it becomes clear that Wynne's recollections must have been more fantasy than fact. His tales of holding out against KGB interrogation (having taken far greater punishment in "practice" from his masters), of trying to rescue a Soviet military intelligence officer from Odessa and even of meeting, with Penkovsky, President Kennedy back in 1961 have all been proved false.

The truth is that he was a clearly unhappy man after his return to the West. He drifted around the Mediterranean, dabbling in property development and horticulture — with some success — but failed to find his true *métier*. He was said to have developed a drinking problem and his first marriage ended in 1970. His second marriage also ended acrimoniously, Wynne admitting, "The moment it really gets down to family life, things go wrong."

Born Greville Maynard Wynne. **Father** An engineer. **Marriages** 1) Sheila (divorced 1970); 2) Herma van Burean, 1970 (separated). **Children** One son from first marriage. **Education** Extra-mural student of engineering, Nottingham University. **Military service** Private, anti-aircraft battery. **Career** Electrical engineer, Nottingham; exporter of industrial electrical equipment, 1950; variously employed as property developer, Malta and the Canaries, rose cultivator, Majorca; in property business on retirement, Majorca. **Other activities** In British intelligence, from 1938; unofficial intelligence agent, MI6, 1960; arrested, Budapest, 1962; tried, Moscow, 1963; sentenced to eight years' hard labour, imprisoned, Lubyanka and Vladimir prisons; exchanged for Conon Molody (also known as Gordon Lonsdale), 1964. **Publications** *The Man from Moscow*, 1967; *Contact on Gorky Street*, 1968; *The Man from Odessa*, 1981. **Cause of death** Cancer of the throat, at age 71. **Further reading** Oleg Penkovsky, *The Penkovsky Papers*, 1965.

MARCH

BRUNO BETTELHEIM

Austrian/American Psychoanalyst
***Born* Vienna, Austria, 28 August 1903**
***Died* Silver Spring, Maryland, 13 March 1990**

It was on the anniversary of the German invasion of Austria, 52 years earlier, that Bruno Bettelheim ended his life in the way that he had lived it: wilfully and after careful consideration. Like his contemporary and fellow-survivor of the Nazi camps Primo Levi, suicide was not a final desperate act annihilating a life devoted to the exploration of what it is to be human, warts and all. Neither Levi nor Bettelheim were in the end defeated by survivor's guilt; instead, the fact that they chose their own death must — perhaps paradoxically — be seen as a decision to take into their own hands what had been taken from so many other Jews by force. Some wars never end, and as Bettelheim once said, the memory of the camps left him with "a lifelong battle to invest life with meaning". Both men were deeply marked by the horrors of the concentration camps, and although through their work they used the experience for the moral advancement of humanity, no amount of public recognition and respect could ever undo the enormity of that psychological burden.

After the war, Bettelheim's was a battle not only for the meaning of his own life, but primarily for that of autistic and otherwise disadvantaged children whom he saw as equally the victims of loss of self. The many books Bettelheim wrote both on his work with problem-children and on the art of parenting earned him a reputation as the "grand old man of psychoanalysis" in the post-war period. With his 1976 book on fairy-tales, *The Uses of Enchantment,* and his "Dialogues with Mothers" in *Ladies' Home Journal,* written during the 1960s, he reached a wide popular audience as well as an academic one for his ideas on pedagogy. He became known chiefly as an advocate of permissiveness in the bringing up of children, but if this marked him out as a liberal — people called him "Dr Yes" — Bettelheim was never an uncontroversial figure. Casting himself in the role of a maverick and enjoying the confrontation with received ideas, he managed to arouse controversy within the psychoanalytic profession, in the Jewish community and among the people with whom he had worked as a child psychiatrist. After his death there was renewed scandal when former pupils of the school where he worked for nearly 30 years questioned publicly his integrity and alleged that he never practised the care and respect that he preached. Contrary to his public image of a gentle man, he could be gruff in personal contact, cultivating a combative and provocative debating style. Asked once by a journalist why he seemed to thrive on confrontation, Bettelheim characteristically responded with a counter-question: "What good is it having a friend who always agrees with you?" Of course, he supplied his own answer: "Completely worthless."

Bruno Bettelheim was born into a family of non-religious Austrian Jews in 1903. As was expected in his milieu, he did well at the Reform *Realgymnasium* and went on to study philosophy and psychology at the University of Vienna where he obtained his PhD in 1938. Earlier young Bruno had become interested in psychoanalysis, but for an ulterior purpose, as later he was fondly to recall. During his schooldays he had been in love with a girl who was reading the work of Sigmund Freud, so he thought he had better gain some knowledge of it too. The effort did not pay off however: Otto Fenichel (who later also became a famous analyst) got the girl and Bettelheim was left with psychoanalysis. He went into therapy with Richard Senda soon after, not — as he was keen to point out — to be cured of the trauma of unrequited love, but "in order to gain clarity". In keeping with this intellectual stance he said he saw it as "very much a joint undertaking".

Bettelheim began his work on autism in 1932, when he took a child into his home in order to provide it with the round-the-clock attention that he believed such children (who do not respond to the normal range of social and emotional stimulus) needed. This work was cut short when in 1938 the Nazis invaded Austria. Bettelheim was arrested and interned first in Buchenwald and then in Dachau, but on the intercession of Eleanor Roosevelt, the President's wife, and of Herbert Lehman, then governor of New York, he was released 18 months later. Deeply traumatized by what he had observed in the camps, Bettelheim arrived in the United States in 1939. Two years later he married Gertrude Weinfeld, with whom he was to have three children: Naomi, Ruth and Eric. No doubt having a family helped the Bettelheims to re-establish themselves and to put down roots; in 1944 Bettelheim was naturalized as an American citizen.

Although his interest in children and the development of the self pre-dated his experience of the Nazi camps, Bettelheim could not just take up work where he had left off. In America, he started with straight academic jobs, first as a research associate at the University of Chicago, then as associate professor at Rockford College, Illinois. He moved back to the University of Chicago in 1944, as assistant professor concerned with educational psychology and psychiatry. From 1952 until 1973 he was a full professor there, but it was not this side of his career that gained him his international reputation. The Sonia Shankman Orthogenic School, also in Chicago, was the place where Bettelheim put most of his considerable energies in the years between the end of World War II and his retirement in the early 1970s. It was here that he developed his theories of child-rearing, claiming like Freud that the treatment of "abnormal" children can teach us important lessons about what normal children need and want as well. Bettelheim established a new regime at the school, which did *not* focus on intensive psychoanalytic work so much as on the provision of a stable, loving and playful environment in which the children, however difficult and disturbed in their behaviour, were always treated with respect. Believing that the 24-hour engagement with children's needs might reverse a process of destruction of the self, Bettelheim sought to prove that an environment which was the antithesis of Dachau and Buchenwald (a regime of systematic humiliation and torture) might redeem the most difficult of hard cases: children imprisoned in their own fears and in their inability to make contact with the outside world. *Love Is Not Enough: The Treatment of Emotionally Disturbed Children,* published in 1950, eloquently argued the case for treating children with due attention for the validity of their experience so that they may grow up with respect for others too: "I believe people do the right thing not because they are scared to death but because their self-respect requires it." In *Truants from Life: The Rehabilitation of Emotionally Disturbed Children,* Bettelheim illustrated this thesis with four case-studies of children he had treated successfully. One of these, the story of Joey "the electric boy", became world famous when Bettelheim used it in a 1959 article for *Scientific American* entitled "Individual and Mass Behavior in Extreme Situations". This article became required reading for US Army personnel stationed in Europe and had a strong impact on the treatment of psychological withdrawal due to shock.

Bettelheim's achievements at the Sonia Shankman School established his reputation in child psychology and provided the groundwork for many of his later books. Both the 1967 *The Empty*

Fortress: Infantile Autism and the Birth of the Self and *The Children of the Dream,* published in 1969, became classics in the field. The latter, a study of children reared in the kibbutzim of Israel, attracted particular attention for its relevance to 1960s experiments with communal living inspired by the counter-culture and the New Left. Bettelheim's conclusions, although based on too small a sample to have empirical validity, were interesting: he saw the kibbutz children as emotionally stable, secure and responsible, though also somewhat lacking in imagination and independent thinking.

Unexpectedly, and in contrast with Dr Spock, his rival in the child psychology field, Bettelheim had no sympathy with the adults of the 1960s who protested against the Vietnam war and called for the liberation of imagination. These rebels he said were "stuck at the stage of the temper tantrum" — a provocation which contradicted his fame as the advocate of permissiveness and landed him with the new nickname, "Dr No". In later years, especially after his retirement when Bettelheim became even more productive as a writer and thinker, other controversies surfaced. One of the most painful was that over his statements on the "Jewish ghetto mentality", expressed most fully in the posthumously published *Recollections and Reflections* but also aired during his life in various publications and interviews.

By "ghetto thinking" Bettelheim meant a mode of Jewish behaviour before and during World War II which was characterized by the tendency to ingratiate oneself with the powers that be rather than to resist, and to accommodate and adapt to repression rather than to challenge it. He therefore saw the Jews not as archetypal victims, but as people who unconsciously colluded with the Nazis in their own destruction: "It was inertia that led millions of Jews into the ghettos that the SS created for them. It was inertia that made hundreds of thousands sit home, waiting for their executioners." These words, coming from a Jew and a survivor at that, were very hard to swallow for many people. They did, however, leave out an important part of Bettelheim's argument which it was more convenient for his detractors to forget. For, as perceptive critics have pointed out, Bettelheim was not engaging in a crass psychoanalytical reversal of blaming the victim. Instead, he argued that anti-Semitism had not been invented by the Nazis, and that the long tradition of pogroms and persecution of Jews in Europe had forced them *historically* into adaptation and non-resistance as a mode of survival which then became ingrained in the Jewish character. "Freedom from ghetto thinking" was Bettelheim's answer to this phenomenon; the battle over not only the Jewish but the general problem of the victim-mentality has continued to rage ever since.

All of Bettelheim's work then was informed, in some way or other, by his experience of the concentration camps, including the searing critiques of psychoanalysis itself which he delivered from time to time in his writings. Psychoanalysis as it developed in theory and as a therapeutic practice after Freud had become too clinical, Bettelheim felt. It was good at taking people's psyche apart and helping them to understand how it worked, but not at putting people *as human beings* back together again. In his 1982 re-evaluation of Freud, *Freud and Man's Soul,* Bettelheim charged that psychoanalysis had become too enmeshed in clinical dogma and that the subtleties and the human concerns that Freud expressed in his writings about not just the minds of people but their souls (in German, *Seele*) had all too often got lost in (mis)translation.

Towards the end of his life Bettelheim published two works which will surely continue to be widely read for a long time to come. One, *The Uses of Enchantment: The Meaning and Importance of Fairy Tales* re-emphasized the importance of fantasy in a child's life, fairy tales being an occasion for children to live through fear in the imagination and thereby purging themselves of it in real life. The other, *A Good Enough Parent: A Book on Child-Rearing,* was described by Bettelheim himself as "the summation of my life's work" in which he argued once more that "the most important thing is for a child to be respected, to be taken care of, and to be made welcome in the world...There are no perfect parents and no perfect children, but every parent can be good enough". With this as his credo, it was all the more disturbing that after his death some shadow was cast over Bettelheim's own credentials as a "good enough" substitute parent for his charges at the Sonia Shankman School. If one were to be true to Bettelheim's beliefs, then the experience some of his pupils alleged they had had of cruelty and abuse suffered at his own hands could not just be dismissed. The saddest thing is, perhaps, that these accusations were not aired during his lifetime when he was still able to defend himself.

Born Bruno Bettelheim. **Parents** Anton and Paula (Seidler) Bettelheim. **Marriage** Gertrud Weinfeld, social worker, teacher and researcher, 1941 (died 1984). **Children** Ruth, Naomi and Eric. **Education** Reform Realgymnasium, Vienna, 1921; studied philosophy and psychology, University of Vienna, PhD in psychology, 1938. **Emigration** Left Austria for United States, 1939; naturalized 1944. **Career** Studied autistic children, 1932–38; prisoner, Dachau and Buchenwald concentration camps, 1938–39, released after intervention of Eleanor Roosevelt and Herbert Lehman, governor of New York; research associate, Progressive Education Association, University of Chicago, 1939–41; associate professor of psychology, Rockford College, Illinois, 1942–44; published "Individual and Mass Behavior in Extreme Situations", 1943; assistant professor, University of Chicago, 1944–47, head, Sonia Shankman Orthogenic School, University of Chicago, 1944–73, associate professor, 1947–52, professor of educational psychology, 1952–73, Stella M. Rowley Distinguished Service Professor of Education, 1963–73, professor of psychology and psychiatry, 1963–73. **Related activities** Fellow, Center for Advanced Study in the Behavioral Sciences, Stanford, California, 1971–72. **Other activites** Columnist, *Ladies' Home Journal;* contributor, *Commentary.* **Offices and memberships** Founding member, American Academy of Education; fellow, American Psychological Association, American Orthopsychiatric Association; member, American Academy of Arts and Sciences, American Philosophical Association, American Association of University Professors, American Sociological Association, Chicago Psychoanalytical Society. **Awards and honours** Honorary doctorate: Cornell University; diplomate, American Psychological Association; *The Uses of Enchantment,* National Book Award, National Book Critics' Circle Award. **Publications** (include) "Individual and Mass Behavior in Extreme Situations", *Scientific American,* 1943; *Love Is Not Enough: The Treatment of Emotionally Disturbed Children,* 1950; (with Morris Janowitz) *Dynamics of Prejudice: A Psychological and Sociological Study of Veterans,* 1950, expanded edition as *Social Change and Prejudice, Including Dynamics of Prejudice,* 1964; *Overcoming Prejudice,* 1953; *Symbolic Wounds: Puberty Rites and the Envious Male,* 1954; *Truants from Life: The Rehabilitation of Emotionally Disturbed Children,* 1955; *The Informed Heart: Autonomy in a Mass Age,* 1960; *Paul and Mary: Two Cases from "Truants from Life",* 1961; (with others) *Youth: Challenge and Change,* 1961; *Child Guidance — A Community Responsibility: An Address, with a Summary of Public Provisions for Child Guidance Services to Michigan Communities,* 1962; *Dialogues with Mothers,* 1962; *The Empty Fortress: Infantile Autism and the Birth of the Self,* 1967; *Mental Health in the Slums: Preliminary Draft,* 1968; *The Children of the Dream,* 1969, published in England as *The Children of the Dream: Communal Child-Rearing and Its Implications for Society,* 1971; *Food to Nurture the Mind,* 1970; *Obsolete Youth: Toward a Psychograph of Adolescent Rebellion,* 1970; (with others) *Moral Education: Five Lectures,* 1970; *A Home for the Heart,* 1974; *The Uses of Enchantment: The Meaning and Importance of Fairy Tales,* 1976; *Surviving, and Other Essays,* 1979; (with Karen Zelan) *On Learning to Read: The Child's Fascination with Meaning,* 1982; *Freud and Man's Soul,* 1982; *A Good Enough Parent: A Book on Child-Rearing,* 1987; *Freud's Vienna and Other Essays,* 1990; *Recollections and Reflections* (autobiography), 1990. **Cause of death** Suicide by asphyxiation, at age 86. **Further reading** Geneviève Bersihand, *Bettelheim,* 1971; *Thinkers of the Twentieth Century,* 1987.

HARRY BRIDGES

Australian/American Labour Leader

***Born* Melbourne, Australia, 28 July 1901**

***Died* San Francisco, California, 30 March 1990**

Harry Bridges, one of the best known American labour leaders of his day, was, literally, the ugly duckling who turned into a swan. This was a wiry man with a hatchet face, a sharp tongue and a permanently twisted fist that seemed to prove his familiarity with the sign of his trade, the docker's hook. For some 50 years, he was the bugbear of "big business" and anti-Communist trade union bosses. He was hounded by Senator Joseph McCarthy's inquisition, libelled, slandered, abused and jailed as an alleged Communist card-holder, and saw off two deportation orders. Yet he ultimately died in the odour of sanctity in San Francisco as a revered elder statesmen of American labour.

Bridges defied every attempt by opponents to prove he was a card-carrying Communist. Hedley Stone, a renegade Communist, former official of the National Maritime Union, was practically reduced to hysterics when challenged in court to prove his allegations. He shouted, "I couldn't prove a duck was a duck and the whole world says 'That is a duck' and it quacks like a duck, and that is what I was taught, that it was a duck, and I was raised that way, so until my dying day, until they change a duck to another name, I am going to answer when people point at it, that that is a duck."

Born in a comfortable suburb of Melbourne, then capital of Australia, in 1901, Bridges was the son of a prosperous real-estate agent and a mother who was a staunch supporter of Irish independence. Bridges attended a Catholic school, but left at 16, and soon rejected prospects of life as a clerk. Influenced by his taste for Jack London's vivid writing, he ran off to sea and survived several shipwrecks, once being saved by staying afloat on his father's mandolin.

Jack London's intensely individualistic brand of socialism was absorbed by the young Bridges, and in 1921 he joined the International Workers of the World movement, the "Wobblies", having jumped ship on arrival at New Orleans to join a picket line of wharfees on strike. The strike was eventually sold out, or so Bridges believed, by American Federation of Labor officials.

Three years later, Bridges quit the Wobblies. In 1933 he started a dynamic campaign, seeking to transform West Coast waterfront trade union organization and break the stranglehold of corrupt union bosses and employers, with their notorious "shape-up" system. This was the system under which union officials compelled dockers to "kickback" wages to officials, who weeded out suspected militants and "trouble-makers". The racket also existed on the US East Coast and was brought to world-wide attention in the outstanding film, *On the Waterfront* (1954) and also featured in the novel, *No Exit from Brooklyn.* A series of violent and bloody waterside strikes between 1934 and 1937 brought huge picket lines and demonstrations. Two men were killed and hundreds injured on "Bloody Thursday" when city-wide strikes stopped San Francisco in its tracks. These eventually led to the formation of the new International Longshoremen's and Warehousemen's Union, affiliated to the new Committee for Industrial Organization, which was led by the miners' leader, John L. Lewis. Bridges, the longshoremen's president, became CIO regional director for the Pacific Coast and a member of the CIO's executive board.

Attempts to force the government to deport Bridges as a dangerous Communist began in 1938, when the secretary for labor, Frances Perkins, issued a deportation warrent. Bridges was still an Australian citizen and could only be deported if allegations of membership of the Communist Party could be proved. James M. Landis, dean of the Harvard Law School, ruled after a nine-week hearing that Bridges was "energetically radical" but that there was no evidence that he "tried to realize these aims by undemocratic or unconstitutional methods." In 1940, the House of Representatives voted by 380 to 42 for Bridges's deportation. This was pronounced unconstitutional. Another attempt, led by the FBI under Edgar Hoover, failed in May 1942.

In 1950, Bridges was convicted of perjury for swearing he had not been a Communist when he took out citizienship papers some years earlier. He spent three weeks in jail, but the Supreme Court cleared him in 1953. Bridges said, "Ninety per cent of the evidence against me was true, but the one thing I did not do was to affiliate with the Communist Party." All charges against him were dropped and the Supreme Court declared, "The record in this case will stand for ever as a monument to man's intolerance of man. Seldom, if ever, in the history of this nation has there been such a concentrated and relentless crusade to deport an individual because he dared to exercise the freedom that belongs to him as a human being, and is guaranteed to him under the Constitution."

In 1970, Bridges was made a member of the San Francisco Port Commission. The ugly duckling was well on the way to becoming a swan. He retired in 1977, saying, "I've noticed that when the bastard's retiring, people say he's not so bad after all." As leader of the longshoremen he had earned only 27,000 dollars a year — far less than many of his members. He insisted that it was the rank and file that had built his union. "I just got the credit", he said in 1985, "I just happened to be around at the right time."

Born Alfred Bryant Renton Bridges. **Parents** Alfred Ernest, real-estate agent, and Julia (Dorgan) Bridges. **Marriages** 1) Agnes Brown, 1921 (dissolved); 2) Nancy Fenton Berdecio, dancer, 1946; 3) Noriko. **Children** Julie, Robert, Jackie and Katherine. **Education** St Brendan's parochial school, 1913–17. **Emigration** Left Australia for United States, 1920; incomplete applications for citizenship, 1921, 1928; ordered deported by Secretary of Labor Frances Perkins as Communist, 1938, reversed 1939; House of Representatives failed to pass bill for deportation, 1940; investigated by Federal Bureau of Investigation, 1941–42; ordered deported by courts, 1941, overruled, 1942; Supreme Court invalidated deportation order, 1945; awarded citizenship, 1945; indicted for perjury for denying Communist Party membership at naturalization hearings, 1949, found guilty and sentenced to five years' imprisonment, 1950, appealed, judgment overturned by Supreme Court, 1953. **Career** Clerk, retail stationery store, 1917; seaman, 1918–23, shipwrecked twice; arrived United States, 1920; oil rigger, 1921; supported maritime strike, New Orleans, 1921; member, Industrial Workers of the World, 1921–24, organizer; quartermaster, *Lydonia*; longshoreman, San Francisco, 1922, forced to join company union, 1923; unsuccessfully tried to establish rival union, International Longshoremen's Association, 1924; writer, *The Waterfront Worker,* 1932, editor, 1933–36; organized San Francisco local, International Longshoremen's Association, 1933; chairman, Joint Maritime Strike Committee, 1934; organized Maritime Federation of the Pacific, 1935; led Maritime Federation strike, 1937; led International Longshoremen's Association's Pacific locals into Congress of Industrial Organizations, 1937; founder, International Longshoremen's and Warehousemen's Union, president, 1937–77. **Related activities** Pacific Coast regional director, Congress of Industrial Organizations, executive board member, 1937–50; chairman, on labor-management panel, *San Francisco Chronicle* Forum, 1945; member, Port Commission, San Francisco, 1970–82. **Cause of death** Emphysema, at age 88.

CAPUCINE

French Model and Actress

***Born* Toulon, France, 6 January 1923 or 1933**

***Died* Lausanne, Switzerland, 17 March 1990**

Capucine, whose actual date of birth as Germaine Lefebvre remains something of a mystery, was a classic French beauty whose career inevitably moved on into the films of the 1960s but in which, like most other models, she failed to excel. Her two best roles came with Peter Sellers whose sexual advances she managed to evade in both *The Pink Panther* and *What's New Pussycat?*.

Difficult as it is to separate fact from studio fiction, it seems certain that she was discovered by a commercial photographer while sightseeing in Paris. He persuaded her to sit for him and, despite original plans for a teaching career, she was lured into fashion modelling, at which she did excel. By the end of the 1950s she had reached the top of her profession in France.

She then caught the eye of American film producer Charles Feldman. He took her to Hollywood to test for *Song Without End* in which she made her début opposite Dirk Bogarde. The film was a heavily romanticized biography of Franz Liszt, and Capucine, although much praised for her face and figure, failed to deliver the goods as an actress. She freely admitted that she had learned no acting whatsoever until the film began and was also, at the time, hurriedly trying to master the English language. This she did rather charmingly as those who saw her in the Sellers's comedies will recall. It has to be admitted, however, that she never did master the art of acting although Feldman continued to promote her in his own films until he died in 1968 and, in her two films with William Holden (*The Lion* and *The Seventh Dawn*) she was actually playing opposite a man with whom she was romantically involved off-screen. Like many another model, she was simply not able to project feeling onto film.

By the end of the 1960s she had virtually finished with English-speaking cinema except for a few minor roles. The 1970s found her working in European productions in France, Italy and Spain but even here she had parts of little importance and, as time went by, she proved unable to make a successful move into character parts. Sadly, she did not age well and when she returned to the Panther series in the 1980s both *Trail of the Pink Panther* and *Curse of the Pink Panther* were poor endings to the very funny original movies. With Sellers himself already dead and his original co-star David Niven very seriously ill, the latter proved a sorry epitaph.

Despite her lack of talent Capucine has to be admired for her determination to continue in the cinema and her acceptance of her fall from international status. She did seriously try to become an actress and although she had already an early failed marriage her fairly long relationship with Holden did not end in total acrimony. Although it was over by the end of the 1960s he obviously remembered her with some affection. When Holden, also a Swiss resident, died in 1981 he bequeathed her a legacy of 50,000 dollars — a small sum by Hollywood standards, but enough to acknowledge her importance in his life.

Her last years were marred by depression. She withdrew into herself and lived an isolated life in her eighth-floor apartment with only three cats for company. Her death came with her suicide as she threw herself to the ground.

Born Germaine Lefebvre. **Father** Industrialist. **Career** Film début, *Rendezvous de Juillet,* 1949; haute couture model, Dior, Givenchy; moved to Hollywood; studied drama with Gregory Ratoff; contracted to producer Charles K. Feldman; English-language film début, *Song Without End,* 1960; returned to Europe, 1968, final film appearance, *The Curse of the Pink Panther,* 1983.

Films *Song Without End,* 1960; *North to Alaska,* 1960; *A Walk on the Wild Side,* 1962; *The Pink Panther,* 1963; *The Seventh Dawn,* 1964; *What's New Pussycat?,* 1965; *The Honey Pot,* 1967; *The Queens,* 1967; *Fraulein Doktor,* 1968; *Satyricon,* 1969; *Las Crueles,* 1971; *Red Sun,* 1972; *Jaguar Lives,* 1978; *Ritratto di Borghese in Nero,* 1978; *Arabian Adventure,* 1979; *Martin Eden* (television), 1979; *Trail of the Pink Panther,* 1982; *Curse of the Pink Panther,* 1983. **Cause of death** Suicide, at age 57 or 67.

GEORGE COSTAKIS

Greek Art Collector

Born **Moscow, Russia, 1912**

Died **Athens, Greece, 9 March 1990**

Historians and enthusiasts of twentieth-century art owe an inestimable debt to George Costakis, who alone was responsible for resurrecting and saving from oblivion the abstract art of revolutionary Russia. Costakis amassed the single greatest private collection of Russian avant-garde paintings and drawings at a time when such works were banned by the Soviet authorities and almost completely unknown in the West.

The son of a wealthy Greek tobacco merchant resident in Moscow, who lost his money in the 1917 Revolution, George Costakis was forced to leave off his education and earn a living at a very young age. Starting out as a car mechanic, he became a driver at Moscow's Greek legation in 1929. On the closure of the legation after the Hitler–Stalin pact of 1939 he was offered the opportunity of emigrating to the United States, but declined since his wife and children, Soviet citizens, were denied exit visas. He house-sat the Finnish embassy until 1943 when he was taken on as a driver by the Canadian embassy. His organizational talents soon asserted themselves; he was seconded to the British embassy to superintend entertainments for Winston Churchill's visit to Moscow in 1943, and eventually became the Canadian embassy's chief administrative officer, remaining there for 34 years, until his departure from the Soviet Union.

As early as the 1930s Costakis had begun collecting, although he as yet knew nothing of Russian avant-garde art, which had already fallen into disrepute and was completely neglected. Antiques were then readily available in Moscow and Leningrad from the dispossessed middle and upper classes, especially to those who, like Costakis, earned salaries in hard currencies. He bought Old Master paintings, silver, porcelain and rugs, some of which he in turn sold during the lean war years to keep his wife and family.

When in 1946 he saw his first Russian abstract painting, a green stripe on a white canvas of 1917 by Olga Rozanova, it was a revelation. "I brought it home to my flat, with the silver, the carpets and so forth, and I realized that I had lived until then with closed windows", he recalled. Seized with enthusiasm he began what he described as his "private archaeological excavation of avant-garde art", seeking out paintings from the Abstract, Constructivist, Cubist and Supremacist movements that had flourished in Russia until about 1925. Many were bought from the artists, who, having suffered under the Stalinist purges, their work banned and discredited by a regime which promoted Socialist Realism, were in some cases incredulous of Costakis's interest, but in others regarded him as restoring their self-esteem.

The privileged position afforded by the diplomatic world enabled Costakis to build up a formidable collection of paintings and drawings by artists whose names were virtually unheard-of in the West, such as Kasimir Malevich, Wassily Kandinsky, Alexander Rodchenko and Vladimir Tatlin. His Moscow apartment, crammed with pictures, became a haven for devotees of the avant-garde, native and foreign; visitors included artist, Marc Chagall, the composer Igor Stravinsky, President Kennedy, and the directors of several European and American museums. Costakis himself undertook a lecture tour of the US in 1973. Numerous contemporary Soviet artists who were not admitted to the Union of Artists were helped by his patronage. By the mid-1970s the attention he was attracting resulted in a number of "warnings" from the KGB: there was a suspicious burglary at his apartment and a fire at his country dacha, and Costakis realized that he was "sitting on a barrel of dynamite".

Assisted by friends in high places, in 1977 he began negotiating with the authorities for permission to emigrate. The outcome was that in 1978 he and his family left the Soviet Union for Athens, taking with them some 1200 paintings and drawings, one-fifth of the Costakis collection. The remainder stayed in the Soviet Union, the property of Moscow's Tretyakov Gallery. In Greece he himself took up painting, in a vivid, expressive style, and began lending works for international exhibitions, notably at the Guggenheim Museum, New York and the Royal Academy, London. His contribution to preserving an important part of the national heritage was eventually acknowledged by the Soviet authorities in an exhibition of donors to state galleries at the New Tretyakov in 1986, which included 16 works from his collection. This was the occasion of a triumphant return visit by Costakis to Moscow which, notwithstanding his Greek nationality, he always regarded as his native city.

Born George Dionysevich Costakis. **Father** Tobacco merchant. **Marriage** Zinaida Panfiova, 1931. **Children** Aleki, Natasha and Alexander. **Emigration** Left Soviet Union for Greece, 1977. **Career** Motor mechanic; chauffeur, Greek legation, Moscow, 1929–35, 1938–39; collected icons, Russian silver, porcelain and sixteenth- and seventeenth-century Dutch paintings from 1930; motor mechanic, 1935–38; caretaker, Finnish embassy, 1939–43; administrator, Canadian embassy, 1943–77; began collecting Soviet avant-garde paintings, 1946; built collection of 10,000 drawings and paintings; negotiated permission to emigrate with 1200 paintings, rest to Tretyakov Gallery, Moscow, 1977; collection exhibited and cataglogued, Guggenheim Museum, New York, 1981. **Related activities** Lecture tour, United States, 1973. **Exhibitions** *Art of the Avant-Garde in Russia: Selections from the George Costakis Collection,* Guggenheim Museum, New York, 1981; Royal Academy, London, 1983; also: University of Newcastle on Tyne, Dusseldorf, Munich, Hanover, Montreal. **Cause of death** Heart failure, at age 77. **Further reading** Margit Rowell and Angelica Zander Rudenstine, *Art of the Avant-Garde in Russia: Selections from the George Costakis Collection* (exhibition catalogue), 1981; Angelica Zander Rudenstine, *Russian Avant-Garde Art: The George Costakis Collection,* 1981.

JOHN DEXTER

British Theatre and Opera Director

***Born* Derby, England, 2 August 1925**

***Died* London, England, 23 March 1990**

"Don't tell me: show me!" was a favourite rallying cry from John Dexter as he worked on a production. True to his own philosophy, Dexter once encouraged playwright, Peter Shaffer, to complete *Black Comedy* — his play which takes place during a power cut — by going to his cottage, removing all the fuses, and then making his escape, leaving Shaffer to experience what it was really like staggering around in the dark. He was a director with great energy and an imagination which translated itself into some exceptional theatrical moments, and he was also a man who could be hard to work with, and who appears to have had more success on the theatre, than on the opera, stage.

The son of a plumber, Dexter left school at 14 and went to work in a factory. It was probably from these early days that he developed his fixation with class. He confessed once, in a rare interview (for *The New York Times*), "I was never quite sure whether we were lower-middle class or working class. I'm still more class-ridden than practically anybody I know. It bothers me no end." Despite his paranoia about his Midlands accent Dexter had a successful career in the Army, attaining the rank of sergeant and serving in North Africa and the Middle East. But he wanted to act, and when he was seconded to the Army's entertainment division Dexter discovered his talent for the stage.

But life was no easier then than it is now for would-be actors, and after three years at six pounds a week as an assistant stage manager in the Clevedon provincial repertory company, Dexter got a job making pies and packing ice-cream on the night-shift at Wall's Ice Cream Company. Determined not to desert the theatre altogether, days were spent directing amateur productions and doing the rounds of casting offices. As for the acting...Dexter landed the part of Police Constable Bryden in the BBC radio soap opera *The Archers*. It was a role he later tried hard to forget.

The hard work of daytime rehearsals and night-time ice-cream packing paid off in 1957. The playwright John Osborne, who had seen and admired one of Dexter's amateur productions, introduced him to George Devine, the director of the English Stage Company. At that stage the company had only just acquired the lease for the Royal Court Theatre in London — indeed it had only opened the year before. Nevertheless Devine was impressed by Dexter's obvious enthusiasm and took him on as a directorial assistant. It was a step into the unknown for Dexter as much as for Devine — but it was a risk which paid off in style.

Recalling his early days at the Royal Court Theatre, Dexter remembered wading through all the unsolicited manuscripts which the theatre's interest in new writing provoked. "The most interesting were the 'mad plays' — page after page of the same four-letter words in big capital letters. You were afraid to dismiss them too quickly and maybe miss another Beckett or Ionesco." Dexter spent several years at the Royal Court; he was a rarity as he was non-Oxbridge (indeed non-university) educated, but he held his own and soon established a considerable reputation as a director.

Dexter's two chief "finds" while at the Royal Court were Arnold Wesker and Peter Shaffer, and he is closely associated with their early work. During these years Dexter became known as a "playwright's director" because he had such a keen eye for what was wrong with a script, and had the ability to put it right. He is supposed to have told Arnold Wesker once, "If you don't shut up, Arnold, I'll direct this play as you've written it."

Spotted by Laurence Olivier, Dexter was invited to join the National Theatre company in 1963. Together with William Gaskill, Dexter became Olivier's assistant director and over the next few years (1963–1966, and then again 1971–1975) he directed productions which have gone down in the memories and history books of the theatre. Dexter raised *Hobson's Choice* into a comedic version of *King Lear*, for example, and directed Olivier in a controversial new production of *Othello*. Still talked about is Dexter's production of Peter Shaffer's *Equus* in 1973 which is remembered by those who were there as one of the most exciting first nights seen during the National company's tenure of the Old Vic theatre.

Equus transferred with great success to the Plymouth Theater on Broadway the following year and public enthusiasm kept it running until well into 1976. Anthony Hopkins, Tony Perkins and Richard Burton all played in the key role of the psychiatrist, Dysart, and Dexter brilliantly created horses on stage with wire equine masks and hoof-like shoes for the actors. New York drama critics proclaimed it "breath-taking" and "unfailingly excellent".

In 1974 Dexter was made director of productions at New York's Metropolitan Opera House (the Met). Earlier experience of opera work had been mainly in Hamburg where Dexter's production of Verdi's *Vespri Siciliani* ensured that he was noticed as an opera director. He had also directed Berlioz's *Benvenuto Cellini* at Covent Garden, but after his appointment at the Met it was *Vespri* which he introduced into the repertory.

Critical feelings remain mixed about the success of Dexter's tenure at the Met. His appointment was on the basis of a triumvirate with the conductor James Levine and the administrator Anthony Bliss. The idea was that they were to have equal authority, but relationships did not run smoothly and power struggles ensued. The result was that Dexter stepped down to be production adviser in 1981, and it is said that he was "sacked" in 1984.

Putting aside the "boardroom" wrangles, it appears that all was not perfect on the stage either. Dexter undoubtedly had several triumphs (best remembered is his production of Berg's *Lulu*), but, conservative at the best of times, the Met audience wanted superb productions of *Aida, La Traviata, Don Pasquale.* The energy with which Dexter approached the challenge of relatively unfamiliar works was not, it seems, matched in his handling of the Met's basic repertory. One New York critic, Dale Harris, recalls "[Dexter] could think of nothing better than to distract the audience with gimmickry. His *Bartered Bride,* in Tony Harrison's clumsy, uncomic translation, was miscalculated in tone, speed and scope." In 1981 Dexter redeemed his reputation with a triple bill of *Parade, Les Mamelles de Tiresias* and *L'Enfant et les sortilèges.* David Hockney was commissioned to design the sets, and amid high praise — "miraculously beautiful" — Dexter and Hockney enjoyed perhaps their finest hour in New York.

During the late 1980s Dexter's health began to deteriorate. He was diagnosed as suffering from diabetes and he began to have trouble walking. Undeterred Dexter continued to work on a freelance basis, his last big production being the long-running play, *M. Butterfly.* Even when he was in hospital, Dexter was working with great enthusiasm with Howard Brenton and Tariq Ali on the ideas for *Moscow Gold.* His bed was strewn with notes, books on Russia and Shostakovich CDs...but Dexter never survived to see the production open. As Brenton and Ali wrote in the *Guardian* newspaper after his death, "We were privileged to have seen John Dexter working on our play in full blaze. It was an unforgettable and joyous six weeks with a director who was touched with genius, a lion of a man whose voice continues to resound in our heads."

John Dexter was a great director who showed all the energy and drive he had learnt under apprenticeship with George Devine. He was a director not afraid of facing a challenge or doing things differently. All his work may not have been entirely successful, but the triumphs will be remembered as significant productions. Michael Billington, a friend for eight years, paid fine tribute to Dexter the director and Dexter the man, "His death has robbed the British theatre and his many friends of one of nature's life-enhancers."

Born John Dexter. **Parents** Harry James, plumber and waterworks inspector, and Rose Dexter. **Military service** Sergeant, British Army, World War II, served North Africa and Middle East, seconded to entertainment division as actor. **Career** Lathe operator, plumbing equipment shop, 1939; contracted polio, 1946; assistant stage manager, Clevedon repertory company, 1948–51; night shift, Wall's Ice Cream Company, 1951; directed amateur productions, 1951–55; actor, *The Archers,* BBC radio; assistant director, English Stage Company, 1957, first professional production staged; associate director, National Theatre, 1963–66, 1971–75; first opera directed, *Benvenuto Cellini,* Covent Garden, 1966; director of productions, Metropolitan Opera, New York, 1974–81, production adviser, 1981–84; appointed artistic director, Stratford Shakespeare Festival, Canada, 1980, invitation rescinded due to protests. **Awards and honours** Best Director,

Antoinette Perry (Tony) Award, *Equus,* 1975, *M. Butterfly,* 1988. **Stage — theatre** (includes) *Yes — and After,* 1957; *Each in His Own Wilderness,* 1958; *Chicken Soup With Barley,* 1958; *Roots,* 1959; *The Kitchen,* 1959; *Last Day in Dreamland,* 1959; *A Glimpse of the Sea,* 1959; *Chicken Soup With Barley,* 1960; *This Year, Next Year,* 1960; *I'm Talking About Jerusalem,* 1960; *Toys in the Attic,* 1960; *The Kitchen,* 1961; *South,* 1961; *The Keep,* 1961, 1962; *My Place,* 1962; *England, Our England,* 1962; (co-directed) *Chips With Everything,* 1962; *The Blood of the Bambergs,* 1962; *The Sponge Room,* 1962; (co-directed) *Squat Betty,* 1962; *Jackie the Jumper,* 1963; *Half-a-Sixpence,* 1963; *Saint Joan,* 1963; *Chips With Everything,* 1963; *Hobson's Choice,* 1964; *Othello,* 1964; (co-directed) *Royal Hunt of the Sun,* 1964; (co-directed) *Armstrong's Last Goodnight,* 1965; *Black Comedy,* 1965; *A Bond Honoured,* 1966; *The Storm,* 1966; *A Woman Killed with Kindness,* 1971; (co-directed) *Tyger,* 1971; *The Good-Natur'd Man,* 1971; *The Misanthrope,* 1973, 1975; *Equus,* 1973, 1974; *The Party,* 1973; *Phaedra Britannica,* 1975; *Do I Hear a Waltz?,* 1965; *Royal Hunt of the Sun,* 1965; *Black Comedy and White Lies,* 1967; *The Unknown Soldier and His Wife,* 1967; *Wise Child,* 1967; *The Old Ones,* 1972; *In Praise of Love,* 1973; *Pygmalion,* 1974; *Galileo,* 1980; *The Glass Menagerie,* 1983; *The Cocktail Party,* 1986; *M. Butterfly,* 1988; *Threepenny Opera,* 1989. **Stage — opera** *Benvenuto Cellini,* 1966; *Devils of Loudun,* 1974; *Lulu,* 1977; *The Rise and Fall of the City of Mahagonny,* 1979; *Parade,* 1981; *Les Mamelles de Tiresias,* 1981; *L'Enfant et les sortilièges,* 1983; *Nightingale,* 1981; *The Rite of Spring,* 1982; *The Nightingale,* 1982; *Oedipus Rex,* 1982; *La forza del destino; Das Entführung aus dem Serail,* 1984; *La buona figliuola,* 1985; also: *Vespri Siciliana, From the House of the Dead, Boris Godunov, Un ballo in maschera, Aida, Le Prophète, Dialogues des Carmélites, Billy Budd, Bartered Bride.* **Films** *The Virgin Soldiers,* 1967; *The Sidelong Glances of a Pigeon Kicker,* 1970; *I Want What I Want,* 1972. **Cause of death** Heart failure, at age 64. **Further reading** Jim Hiley, *Theatre at Work: The Story of the National Theatre's Production of "Galileo",* 1981.

RUTH GLASS

German/British Sociologist

Born **Berlin, Germany, 30 June 1912**

Died **London, England, 7 March 1990**

Among their colleagues at London University, Ruth Glass and her husband were known as the Heloise and Abelard of sociological research. Ruth Glass was a Marxist who abhorred the pretensions of the Left and their "dusty dogmas and Utopian dreams". Her political affiliations were inseparable from her academic interests and she saw it as the responsibility of sociologists to bring about social change by influencing changes in government policy. Glass refused to confine her deeply held beliefs to the classroom; she wrote prolifically to newspapers and academic journals, always challenging perceptions of the prevailing social order and always attempting to demolish the structures of oppression.

The passionate, often furious, nature of her fight against systematic class and racial discrimination perhaps had its roots in Glass's early experiences in Germany. She was born Ruth Lazarus into a distinguished Jewish family. As a teenager, she deferred university entrance to work on a radical left-wing newspaper in Berlin. Her early style of incisive journalism and her commitment to political action made her popular with the leading figures of the Left, who would meet at the Romanische Café in the city. She claimed to have lost her virginity, by her own design, to one of her role models from the Café. Glass's political education was not dissimilar to that of another of her role models, Rosa Luxemburg.

As a student in 1932 at Berlin University, she published a study of youth unemployment in the city, bringing to her academic studies the same wit and articulateness that characterized her journalism. However her education was interrupted by the Nazi threat, and Glass escaped to Geneva, and briefly to Prague, before arriving in London in the mid-1930s. She resumed her degree in social studies, at the London School of Economics, where she met and married her first husband, Henry Durant, a pioneer of public opinion surveys. The marriage was dissolved in 1941, after six years, by which time Glass was working as a research officer at Columbia University in New York. Glass returned to London in 1942 and married the demographer, David Glass.

During World War II her study of the London "Watling" housing estate was published. The book established Glass's reputation as a social scientist in Britain. More importantly, *Watling* offered important insights into, and sensitivity towards, the human aspects of housing. Perhaps more than any other research social scientist, Glass influenced the government rebuilding programme which followed the war. Hers was one of the few voices tempering this dramatic period of construction with a cry for acknowledgement of the emotional needs of those whose homes had been destroyed. Where academic input into town-planning had previously focused on architectural values, and the proximity of amenities for newly created communities, Glass was pressing for an understanding of relationships between people, as well as of their relationship to their environment. It remained a source of sadness to her that the ideas she was expressing so urgently in the 1940s were still having to be touted 40 years later.

Glass joined the Government Ministry for Town and Country Planning in 1948, where she was able to help implement some of her ideas. The often obstructive attitude of her colleagues at the Ministry led Glass to return to the academic life after two years. Her critique of "social engineering" and her disdain for "simple recipes taken from short order cook books" caused some consternation amongst members of the Planning Department; Glass had an abrasive manner, and the combined effect of her drive and her gender made her a formidable opponent. In the male-orientated world of government planning departments, Glass was something of a blot of the new London landscape being created.

In 1951 Glass founded the Centre for Urban Studies, initially as a new research department at University College, London. While she continued to take an active interest in housing development, Glass became increasingly interested in questions of immigration and race relations in Britain. With the arrival of great numbers of immigrants in the 1950s, Glass was provided with another instance of injustice in which to channel her unfaltering energy. Drawing parallels between the Indian caste system and the treatment of West Indians arriving in Britain, Glass wrote *Newcomers,* a powerful denouncement of xenophobia and a reflection on the opportunity that immigrants give to a society to "recognise its own blind spots".

An inability to forgive injustice and oppression informed all of Glass's work. She was against the idea of research for its own sake and her career was characterized by a willingness to involve herself in political debate. She campaigned against the Immigration Laws in the 1960s, not only for their part in perpetuating poverty in the developing world, but also for the fear and racial stereotyping they encouraged in Britain. Above all else Glass was struggling towards "a widening horizon of human integrity". She was not encouraged by the neo-Marxism of the late 1960s, disclaiming it as mere abstraction. For Glass the value of social research combined with political debate was its potential to resist on behalf of others.

Glass was further disappointed by the social policies of Thatcherism. She perceived that with the new divisions of poverty created in the 1980s, the will and ability to resist them was being eroded. She continued to lecture after her retirement from the Centre for Urban Studies, but colleagues wrote that after the death of her husband in 1978, Glass began to retreat into sadness and despair.

As one put it: "She was an all-purpose ball of fire even though what she increasing reduced to ashes was herself."

Born Ruth Lazarus. **Parents** Eli and Lilly Lazarus. **Marriages** 1) Henry Durant, statistician, 1935 (divorced 1941); 2) David V. Glass, demographer, 1942 (died 1978). **Children** Helen and Robert, from second marriage. **Education** Geneva University; Berlin University; London School of Economics; Columbia University, New York. **Emigration** Left Berlin for London. **Career** Reporter Berlin; senior research officer, Bureau of Applied Social Research, Columbia University, 1940–42; research officer, Ministry of Town and Country Planning, 1948–50; director, Society Research Unit, Department of Town Planning, University College, London, 1951–58, honorary research associate, 1951–71, visiting professor, 1972–85, honorary research fellow, 1986, founding director, Centre for Urban Studies, 1958–90. **Related activities** Visiting professor: Essex University, 1980–86, Institute of Education, University of London, 1984–87; editorial adviser: *London Journal, International Journal of Urban and Regional Research, Sage Urban Studies Abstracts.* **Other activities** Contributor: *Town Planning Review, Architectural Review, Population Studies, International Social Science Journal, Monthly Review, Transactions of the World Congresses of Sociology, New Society.* **Offices and memberships** Member, International Sociological Association; chair, Urban Sociological Research Committee. **Awards and honours** Honorary fellow, Royal Institute of British Architects, 1972; honorary LittD, Sheffield University, 1982. **Publications** *Watling: A Social Survey,* 1939; (editor) *The Social Background of a Plan,* 1948; *Urban Sociology in Great Britain,* 1955; (with H. Pollins) *Newcomers: The West Indians in London,* 1960; (editor) *London: Aspects of Change,* 1964; *London's Housing Needs,* 1965; *Housing in Camden,* 1969; *Clichés of Urban Doom, 1988.* **Cause of death** Undisclosed, at age 77.

RAY GOULDING

American Comedian

***Born* Lowell,** Massachusetts, 20 March 1922

***Died* Long Island, New York, 26 March 1990**

Bob and Ray were a team best known for their gentle satire which, though hilariously funny, was often so on target and presented in such a realistic way that it got taken seriously. They told their radio listeners that they could receive a "home-dismantling kit" by writing to the Smithsonian Institution in Washington, DC, and hundreds of people wrote in for one. Another time they announced that transcripts of their radio scripts were available from the Library of Congress, to the puzzlement of government staff who found themselves inundated with requests. In the early days of the Kennedy administration, a book was published called *Who's in Charge Here?* The book was a collection of photographs of world leaders and politicians with humorous cartoon-style bubble captions. Bob and Ray wrote the introduction to the book, explaining that in order to see the *real* captions, you had to hold the book up to an ultra-violet light. Across America, people switched on the ultra-violet and searched in vain.

This genial ribbing of the American public began shortly after the end of World War II, when Ray Goulding left the Army to take a job as a weekday morning newscaster on WHDH Radio in Boston. He and the disc jockey Bob Elliott began to banter back and forth throughout the show, and as Bob Elliott recalls, "it got longer and longer. We never said 'Let's be a comedy team.' But the chemistry was there, and nobody told us to stop, so we just kept on."

Given their own show by WHDH, *Matinée with Bob and Ray,* they won a legion of devoted followers throughout New England. When asked how they decided who would get top billing, Ray's standard reply was always that if the word had been "matinob" instead of "matinée", the show would have been called "Matinob with Ray and Bob".

National recognition led to a punishing schedule. When asked about their early days in radio, Ray told *The New Yorker* magazine,

> We did *Matinée with Bob and Ray* for five years, until the summer of 1951. Then we got a contract with NBC to do a fifteen-minute network show every evening, from five-forty-five to six, plus one hour on Saturday nights, from nine to ten, most of it ad lib. We moved to New York and also did a daily two-and-a-half-hour show on WNBC, from six to eight-thirty, and an NBC television show for fifteen minutes in the evening. At one point, we were doing the WINS early-morning show every morning, a WOR show in the evening during the week, and the *Monitor* show on NBC for eight hours on Saturday and eight hours on Sunday. We did *Monitor* live. It was before they started using tape. If a line broke down somewhere, they'd cut to us, and we had to be there, ready to go on.

They finally quit their early morning shows because of sheer exhaustion, but with the advent of taping, they returned to the morning airwaves.

They were in the middle of taping a morning show when they heard the news of President Kennedy's assassination. Ray immediately stopped the taping, but "There was some idiot around there who tried to tell me I *had* to do it. I said to him, 'You're not going to have *my* voice on the air tomorrow morning!'" Bob and Ray did very little political humour after that because as Ray said, "Politics became a very unfunny subject after 1963. The assassination of Kennedy really sapped me."

They found plenty of material in other areas, though. With a cast of characters such as the bumbling interviewer Wally Ballou, the all-purpose know-it-all Mary McGoon, and the Piel brothers (featured in a series of television commercials for Piel's Beer), there was always something to poke fun at, and they were so busy doing radio and television throughout the 1960s that when they were offered a Broadway run in 1964, they had to turn it down for lack of time. They found the time eventually, in 1970, and their show, *The Two and Only,* was a real crowd-pleaser, with a writer for *The New Yorker* noting that it was the first time in years he'd heard so much "genuinely relaxed" laughter from an audience.

"Relaxed" is the key word. That was what made Bob and Ray so darn funny; they were perfectly relaxed, just a couple of guys talking. Their timing was exquisite, voices cutting over each other, sentences sometimes left unfinished, just like a real conversation. It didn't matter that Ray Goulding was a large man who spoke with a booming baritone, when he played a soap-opera heroine with a coloratura falsetto it seemed the most natural thing in the world, because he made it seem that way. Another thing about Bob and Ray: no matter how laid-back and deadpan the delivery, it was obvious they were having a great time. They liked each other, and it showed. As Bob said after the death of his long-time partner, "We had no rivalry, just great mutual respect."

Humour has changed a lot in recent years. A modern comedian's persona is often aggressive and strident, even cruel, the exact opposite of Bob and Ray's gentle kidding. But how much of the modern comic's material (once you take away the shouting) will still be funny 30 years from now? Perhaps Bob and Ray's *style* of humour seems dated now, but their simple little sketches, like the one in which they offered "at laughably low prices, sweaters in two styles: turtle or V-neck. State what kind of neck you have", will always raise at least a smile, no matter how jaded future generations may turn out to be.

Born Raymond Walter Goulding. **Parents** Thomas M., mill overseer, and Mary (Philbin) Goulding. **Marriage** Elizabeth Leader, 1945. **Children** Raymond, Thomas, Barbara, Bryant,

Mark and Melissa. **Education** Lowell High School, Massachusetts, 1935–39. **Military service** First lieutenant, United States Army, 1942–46. **Career** Radio announcer, Lowell, Massachusetts, 1939–40; announcer, WEEI, Boston, 1940–42; newscaster, WHDH, Boston, 1946, formed partnership with Bob Elliott, 1946; *Matinée with Bob and Ray* programme, WHDH, 1947–1951, transferred to New York, initially for NBC, late 1951; first television series, NBC, 1951; president, Goulding, Elliott, Greybar Productions, Incorporated, New York, 1954–88; first film appearance, *Cold Turkey,* 1969; first Broadway appearance, *The Two and Only* (with Bob Elliott), 1970–71. **Offices and memberships** Member: American Federation of Television and Radio Artists, American Guild of Variety Artists, Screen Actors Guild. **Awards and honours** Two Peabody Broadcasting Awards, Academy of Television Arts and Sciences; several Clio Awards for performances in television commercials. **Radio** *Matinée with Bob and Ray,* WHDH, 1947–51; *The Bob and Ray Show,* NBC, CBS, ABC, National Public Radio, WINS, WHN, WOR; *Monitor,* NBC; numerous other appearances. **Radio characters created by Bob and Ray** (include) Wally Ballou, radio interviewer; Mary McGoon, cookery expert; the Piel Brothers (Harry and Bert); O. Leo Leahy, author; Mary Backstayge, Backstage Wife. **Publications** (all with Bob Elliott) *Bob and Ray's Story of Linda Lovely and the Fleebus,* 1960; *Bob and Ray: The Two and Only,* 1970; *Write If You Get Work: The Best of Bob and Ray,* 1975. **Cause of death** Kidney failure, at age 68.

JANE GRIGSON

British Cookery Writer

Born **Gloucester, England, 13 March 1928**

Died **Broad Town, Wiltshire, 12 March 1990**

One of Jane Grigson's best-loved books, *Good Things,* begins with the words: "This is not a manual of cookery, but a book about enjoying food". This epitomizes Grigson's commitment to food as one of the great pleasures of life as well as one of its necessities. Well educated and intelligent, Grigson took food writing seriously but she was never grand or pretentious and she made cooking fun.

Grigson was born in the west country but grew up in the north of England when her father's work as a town clerk took the family to Sunderland when she was four years old. After the outbreak of World War II, the Sunderland shipyards became a tempting target for German bombing raids so Grigson and her sister were sent to boarding school in Westmorland. After leaving school Grigson read English at Newnham College, Cambridge, and then spent a short time studying and travelling in Italy.

Returning to England Grigson worked for a time as an assistant in art galleries in Cambridge and London, before landing a job in publishing. She was appointed as a picture researcher for a series of books called "People, Places, Things and Ideas" which was being brought out by Thames and Hudson. The editor of the series was the eminent poet and critic, Geoffrey Grigson, and as Joy Law, one of their colleagues of that time, has written, "Jane and Geoffrey fell in love with each other and I am happy to think that they never fell out of it."

For the next 30 years Jane and Geoffrey Grigson managed that rare feat of living life on their own terms despite the fact that they often had to get by on comparatively little money. They set up home in London, moving to a farmhouse in Wiltshire when their daughter, Sophie, arrived on the scene in 1959. A few years later they bought a small house in the French village of Troo and from then on they divided their year between these two homes. After her marriage Grigson continued to work in publishing, specializing in translations from Italian. She won the John Florio prize for her translation of the eighteenth-century jurist, Beccaria's, treatise, *Of Crimes and Punishments.*

Grigson had developed a keen interest in food preparation from an early age and she had become an accomplished cook. Cooking cannot have been an easy task in her French home, which was an enlarged and extended cave dwelling where the kitchen consisted of a couple of gas rings and a grill. However it was here that her professional career as a cookery writer began.

Grigson's first cookery publication was *Charcuterie and French Pork Cooking* which appeared in 1967. With this book she established a standard for excellence which was to be maintained throughout all her subsequent works. Grigson's books were all meticulously researched. They are written in a clear and lucid prose and enriched by the depth of her scholarship, vast knowledge of literature and sheer love of life. What other cookery writer would introduce her recipes for cherries with a description of a painting by Memling in the Uffizi gallery, in which "Jesus sits on Mary's knee, ivory pale against her rust-coloured robe, with a cherry clutched in one hand, symbol of the Heaven he had left behind", and then follow this up with an apt quotation from the seventeenth-century English poet and cherry-lover, Robert Herrick?

For all her formidable intellect Grigson never talked down to her readers. Her recipes were easy to understand and, what is more, they always worked. Following the success of her first cookery book, Grigson was invited to write for the colour magazine of the Sunday newspaper, *The Observer.* From 1968 until the time of her death, she was that newspaper's cookery correspondent. The articles she researched and wrote often formed the basis for her subsequent books, most notably *Good Things* and *Food with the Famous.* Two of her most successful books were *Jane Grigson's Vegetable Book* and *Jane Grigson's Fruit Book.* She received the Glenfiddich Writer of the Year award and also the Andrée Simon Memorial Prize for both of these classic works.

Grigson's range was extremely wide. She moved happily between foreign cuisine and traditional English regional cooking, writing knowledgeably on such subjects as the almost lost art of tripe preparation, and devoting a whole book (*The Mushroom Feast*) to fungi. In what was to be her last series for *The Observer,* she took great delight in giving authentic recipes for hamburgers, pizzas, ice-cream and a whole range of foods which have been reduced to synthetic tastelessness by the fast-food industry.

Grigson was passionate about the importance of using really fresh food and good quality produce. In her last years, scandalized by inept government policies on intensive farming, she became a strong campaigner, supporting small independent producers and lambasting the Ministry of Agriculture.

Grigson's husband, Geoffrey, died in 1985 after a protracted illness and she was devastated by the loss. She was beginning to recover from this bleak period when she discovered that she had the cancer which was to kill her. With typical openness she wrote about her illness, and the diet she was using in her fight against it, in order to help other sufferers. She received a tremendous response from her readers who sent hundreds of letters of support.

As well as being one of the best-known cookery writers of her generation, Grigson was also one of the best loved. She was unselfish in her encouragement of younger cookery writers and she was particularly delighted with the success of her daughter, Sophie, who is ably following in her footsteps. After her death numerous tributes to Grigson appeared from readers, fellow cookery writers and long-time friends, all of which spoke of the warmth of her personality and generosity of spirit. This was perhaps best summed up by that doyenne of cookery writers, Elizabeth David, who wrote "as a writer Jane leaves an unfillable gap. As a friend she is irreplaceable." Grigson was renowned for her great sense of humour and she would surely have been pleased that at her well-attended memorial service, the proceedings began with a rendition of "Sheep May Safely Graze".

Born Jane McIntire. **Parents** George Shipley, town clerk, and Doris (Berkley) McIntire. **Marriage** Geoffrey Grigson, poet and critic (died 1985). **Children** One daughter,

Sophie. **Education** Casterton School, Westmorland; Newnham College, Cambridge, BA, 1949. **Career** Assistant, Heffers Art Gallery, Cambridge, 1950–51; assistant, Walker's Art Gallery, London, 1952–53; editorial assistant, George Rainbird Limited, London, 1953–54; editorial assistant, Thames and Hudson Limited, London, 1954–55; freelance writer, editor and translator since 1955; first translation published, 1963; first book published (with Geoffrey Grigson), 1965; first cookery book published, 1967. **Related activities** Cookery correspondent, *The Observer* magazine, 1968–90. **Offices and memberships** Member, Wine and Food Society. **Awards and honours** John Florio translation prize for Cesare Beccaria's *Of Crimes and Punishments,* 1966; Cookery Writer of the Year for *English Food,* 1974; Glenfiddich Writer of the Year Award for *Jane Grigson's Vegetable Book,* 1978, for *Jane Grigson's Fruit Book,* 1982; André Simon Memorial Prize for *Jane Grigson's Vegetable Book,* 1978, for *Jane Grigson's Fruit Book,* 1982. **Publications — cookery** *Charcuterie and French Pork Cookery,* 1967; *Good Things,* 1971; *Fish Cookery,* 1973; *English Food,* 1974; *The Mushroom Feast,* 1975; *Jane Grigson's Vegetable Book,* 1978; *Food with the Famous,* 1979; *Jane Grigson's Fruit Book,* 1982; *The Observer Guide to European Cookery,* 1983; *The Observer Guide to British Cookery,* 1983; *Jane Grigson's British Cookery,* 1984; (with Charlotte Knox) *Exotic Fruit and Vegetables,* 1986. **Publications — translations** *Scano Boa* by Giovanni A. Cibotto, 1963; (with Father Kenelm Foster) *Of Crimes and Punishments* by Cesare Beccaria, 1964. **Other publications** (With Geoffrey Grigson) *Shapes and Stories,* 1965; (with Geoffrey Grigson) *More Shapes and Stories,* 1967. **Cause of death** Cancer, at age 61.

HALSTON

American Fashion Designer

Born **Des Moines, Iowa, 23 April 1932**

Died **San Francisco, California, 26 March 1990**

He didn't just dress the beautiful people; he was one of them himself. His clients were the rich and famous of America, and they didn't just tolerate this boy from Iowa, they made him a friend, a confidant, a man to be seen with. Charming, handsome and cultivated, he was the first American designer-celebrity, his face gracing the society pages almost as frequently as his designs dominated the fashion spread of the late 1960s and early 1970s.

In December 1971, Eugenia Sheppard announced in the *New York Post* that Halston's "special brand of casual but sexy has become one of the most recognizable and individual looks in American fashion". In 1972, *Newsweek* magazine hailed him as "the premier fashion designer in America".

It was simplicity that set the Halston style apart. The look up to then had been the tie-dyed hippie peasant, complete with jangling earrings and sometimes even bells. He stripped away all the fussy details and introduced a sort of fashion minimalism: easy, unstructured clothing that was (like Halston himself) equally at home sipping cocktails in an uptown duplex or dancing in a downtown dive.

Born Roy Halston Frowick, he was only 12 or 13 when he surprised his family by presenting his mother with a hat he'd made himself. "We all wondered how the hell and why he did it", his brother Robert recalled in 1972 for *Newsweek.* "But it was a smash and really flattered my mother." He was 21 when he opened his own millinery salon in Chicago's Ambassador Hotel. His first client was Fran Allison of the children's television puppet show, *Kukla, Fran and Ollie.* Soon his clients included Gloria Swanson, Kim Novak and Deborah Kerr.

In 1958, he moved to New York and got a job with Lily Daché, then a prominent milliner. Within a year he moved to the exclusive department store, Bergdorf Goodman, where his "incredible clientele" included Marilyn Monroe and Jacqueline Kennedy, who catapulted Halston into national stardom when she wore one of his pillbox hats for her husband's presidential inauguration.

By the early 1960s, hats had fallen out of favour and were rapidly disappearing from the fashion scene, so Halston moved into the field of women's clothing. His first collection was launched by Bergdorf Goodman in 1966. Two years later, with backing from Mrs Paley, wife of the founder of CBS TV, William S. Paley (q.v.), he went into business for himself.

Before long, Halston proved that as well as an eye for beauty, he had a head for commerce. His business rapidly grew from a one-floor custom shop to a national chain of boutiques. As he explained in 1976, "Most designers come out of school and get a job as a sketcher in a big fashion house. Then they get an assistant, and then they get a chance to go onto a bigger house, but they're never involved in the business community. I've always been involved. Even when I was designing at Bergdorf Goodman, I was also running a department."

In 1973, he sold his five-year-old business to the Norton Simon conglomerate for 16 million dollars. Basically, what he sold was his name. The deal gave Norton Simon the right to use Halston's name on things he did not design, and required him to obtain permission before he could use his name on anything. The arrangement worked well for a decade, but when the corporation changed management, Halston made several attempts to retain the right to design under his own name, none of them successful.

A 1982 deal to produce a Halston line for J.C. Penney, an inexpensive American chain store, caused the up-market Bergdorf Goodman to drop everything by their former employee. To Halston's credit, he was unperturbed by this snub. "I love J.C. Penney", he said, "and I've always wanted to entertain a larger public. J.C. Penney sells to half the American people." Despite this bravado, it was the beginning of the end. Within two years, Halston Enterprises had been spun off by its latest owner, a food conglomerate. Unable to buy back his business and the rights to his name, Halston himself was dropped by the company.

But it is not for his adventures and misadventures in the world of corporate finance that Halston will be remembered. It will be for his lasting impact on fashion around the world and his famous penchant for the flashy night-life of New York City. His life-style was always as newsworthy as his fashion design. He often invited his favourite clients to informal luncheons at his salon or his apartment. A regular member of Andy Warhol's "Factory" crowd, his wilder side is documented in Warhol's diaries. He was so devoted to the trendy and exclusive Manhattan night-club, Studio 54, that he altered his office hours to accommodate his time spent there, which was usually until 4 or 5 am. In a recent interview, he defended his time spent night-clubbing as necessary, "A lot of the socializing I did...was related to business. I had to do it then."

In January 1990, he sold the Manhattan townhouse which had been his home for 15 years, and moved to California to be near his sister and two brothers. In March, he died from Aids.

Fashion is a business that depends on change; trends come and go, often lasting months rather than years. But 20 years have passed since Halston became a household name, and many of his designs are every bit as inviting and refreshing today as they were then. As Sal Ruggiero, fashion director of the major department store Marshall Field & Co., said upon hearing of Halston's death, "If any time was the best for his clothes, it's now — lean, clean, with beautiful fabrics wonderfully cut, which is always what he stood for."

Born Roy Halston Frowick. **Father** An accountant. **Education** Bosse High School, Evansville, Indiana; University of Indiana; Chicago Art Institute. **Career** Designed first hat (for mother), 1945; designed window displays, Carson Pirie Scott & Company, Chicago, to 1957; freelance milliner; opened first millinery salon, Chicago, 1952–56; designed hats for Lily Daché, New York,

1958–59; assistant milliner, Bergdorf Goodman, New York, 1959, chief milliner, Bergdorf Goodman, New York, 1959, chief milliner, designed first ready-to-wear collection, 1966; created pillbox hat for Jacqueline Kennedy to wear to presidential inauguration, 1961; founded Halston-USA collection (millinery), 1968; designed couture collection, 1968; first solo collection, 1968; founded Halston International (for knitwear), 1970; founded Halston Originals (ready-to-wear), 1972, acquired by Norton Simon and renamed Halston Enterprises, 1973, unsuccessfully tried to repurchase, 1984; opened New York boutique, 1972; launched Halston perfume, 1975; initiated Halston III line for J.C. Penney, 1982–83. **Awards and honours** Coty Special Award for millinery innovations, 1962, for first solo collection, 1969; "Winnie" award, Coty American Fashion Critics Award, 1971, 1972; Coty Hall of Fame, 1974. **Productions designed** *Clytemnestra* (ballet) for Martha Graham; *The Act* (Broadway) For Liza Minnelli. **Cause of death** Aids, at age 57. **Further reading** *Contemporary Designers,* 1990.

TOM HARMON

American Football Player and Broadcaster

***Born* Gary, Indiana, 1920**

***Died* Westwood, California, 15 March 1990**

To the public, Tom Harmon's greatest day of pride and glory came in 1940 when, on his final appearance as an all-American tailback for the University of Michigan, he led his team to a 40–0 romp against Ohio State, running in three touchdowns, passing for two more, kicking four extra points, and averaging 50 yards with three punts.

More privately, Harmon himself might have highlighted his wedding day, when his bride, former actress Elyse Knox, wore a dress made from the white silk parachute which saved his life the second time he was shot down over Asia during World War II.

In a full and varied life, Harmon succeeded in making his mark on almost everything he touched. But it is perhaps as an elusive six-foot, 195-pound single-wing tailback football player that "Greater than Grange" will be remembered. His playing career reached its peak in 1940 when he won the Heisman Trophy, the Maxwell Award, the Walter Camp Trophy and Associated Press Athlete of the Year honours.

In three seasons with the Michigan Wolverines, Harmon scored 237 points in 24 appearances, and ran for 2134 yards. Better still, he earned his nickname for scoring 33 touchdowns — two more than the outstanding Red Grange had scored in the mid-1920s for Illinois. Will Perry, Michigan's associate athletic director, would later note: "Tom Harmon was probably the greatest football player we've ever had at Michigan. He was truly a legendary sports hero who was on the cover of *Time* and *Life* magazines. At a time in this country when there was no television, everybody knew who Tommy Harmon was."

All of this prompted the biggest professional football club of the day, the Chicago Bears, to make him the first pick of the 1940 National Football League draft. But Harmon — who had already surprised football commentators when he collected the Heisman Trophy by stating he had no intention of playing professionally — signed instead with the New York Americans, and made his professional début at the Yankee Stadium.

As with so many other sportsmen of his generation, a glittering professional career was cut short by the onset of war, during which he served with the US Army Air Corps as a fighter pilot, and earned a Purple Heart and Silver Star. He was twice reported missing in action: the first time in April 1943, when he crashed in the jungles of Dutch Guiana and had to march through swamps and rain forests for four days before being rescued and guided to safety; and later in the same year when he baled out over China.

Back in the United States after the war, he spent the 1946 and 1947 seasons with the Los Angeles Rams. But combat injuries to his legs had left him without his famous speed and power; and after a largely disappointing and unimpressive return, he turned to his first love — sports broadcasting.

"Sports casting was the only job I ever wanted. It was the thing I loved because it put me among people I knew and wanted to be with", a very contented Harmon was to note in later life. Having majored in speech at college, he earned as much national recognition for his work with the microphone as he ever did for his efforts on the grid.

He remained active for all his life, and died of a heart attack after completing a round of golf at the Bel Air Country Club.

Born Thomas Harmon. **Marriage** Elyse Knox, actress, 1944. **Children** Mark, Kristin and Kelly. **Education** University of Michigan, BA in speech, 1941. **Military service** Fighter pilot, United States Army Air Corps, 1941–45, twice reported missing. **Career** Single-wing tailback, University of Michigan, 1939–40, scored 237 points in 24 games, ran for 2134 yards in 398 attempts, completed 101 of 233 passes for 1399 yards, amassed 3533 yards on offense, scored 33 touchdowns in three seasons (breaking record); starred in *Harmon of Michigan* (based on his life), 1941; first choice, Chicago Bears in National Football League selection draft, but joined New York Americans, 1941; played for Los Angeles Rams, 1946–48; sports broadcaster based in Los Angeles, from 1948; sports director, Hughes Television Network, 1974. **Awards and honours** All-American, 1939, 1940; Heisman Trophy, 1940; Maxwell Award, 1940; Walter Camp Trophy, 1940; Associated Press Athlete of the Year, 1940; World War II medals: Silver Star, Purple Heart. **Film** *Harmon of Michigan,* 1941. **Cause of death** Heart attack, at age 70.

ROSAMOND LEHMANN

British Novelist

Born **Bourne End, Buckinghamshire, 3 February 1901**

Died **London, England, 12 March 1990**

"No English writer has told of the pain of women in love more truly or movingly...of what it felt like to be a woman", Marghanita Laski wrote of Rosamond Lehmann. This was no mean praise coming from a fellow novelist well versed in English literature's treatment of women's emotional lives. Laski's admiring statement was elicited by *The Echoing Grove,* published in 1953 and as representative a sample of Lehmann's concerns and style as any of her seven novels. Illicit love affairs, sexual mores in a changing world, social and political upheavals in the middle years of the century — this is the stuff that Rosamond Lehmann's fiction is made of, and *The Echoing Grove* is no exception. The novel takes for its basic plot the relationship between two sisters and one man, who is husband to the one and lover to the other of the two women. In a technically innovative way — even within the terms of her own *oeuvre* — Lehmann explored this knot of emotional bonds by telling the same events from different perspectives, thus exposing the complexities of each character's psychological reality. Yet despite the positive reception of this, her sixth novel, what resounded from *The Echoing Grove* was silence: between 1953 and 1967 Rosamond Lehmann ceased to write. She only returned to the literary scene briefly, with a volume of autobiography and a last — disappointing — novel in 1977. It is not clear whether this lengthy silence was caused by a series of crises in her personal life, or by the fact that her characteristic themes ceased to inspire her in old age, but critics agreed that she never found the form of her previous works again.

As the poet Stephen Spender once said, Rosamond Lehmann was "one of the most beautiful women of her generation", an epithet which stayed with her throughout life. She was, in a sense, born beautiful, the daughter of Alice Davis, a woman renowned for her looks and for her charm as hostess to a wide circle of intellectuals and artists. More or less from babyhood, Rosamond was endowed by her mother with a sensitive nature, a lively interest in the arts and a craving for the admiration of her peers. Her father, the Liberal MP and contributor to the satirical magazine *Punch,* Rudolph Lehmann, provided her with the intellectual and political environment typical of a free-thinking upper-middle-class English household.

Sheltered from the ravages of World War I, Lehmann received a private education at home from various governesses and tutors until she went to Girton College, Cambridge, on a scholarship in 1920. There she met — as well as many of her lifelong friends — the Hon Walter Runciman, who became her first husband in 1923. The couple divorced five years later.

In the meantime *Dusty Answer* had been published to universal critical acclaim. Although Lehmann later regretted the large share this first novel had in building her literary reputation, the story about a young girl's trials and tribulations in growing up already showed some of its author's trademarks: lyrical writing, sensitive characters, and a plot which revolves more around emotional than external events. *Dusty Answer* was an especially great success in France, probably because of its subject-matter which in retrospect invites comparison with that other, later, best-seller about a young girl's precocious development, *Bonjour Tristesse.* But unlike Françoise Sagan, who never equalled her first literary achievement, Rosamond Lehmann quickly recovered her cool after the initial flush of success. Deliberately changing tack, she set to work on another novel, *A Note in Music,* which was partly based on her own unhappy experiences of living in Newcastle, no longer an idealistic young girl but now a married woman feeling isolated in an alien social environment. As different from *Dusty Answer* as could be, *A Note in Music* was perhaps too different from what the reviewers expected of Lehmann, and they panned it unanimously. With *Invitation to the Waltz* in 1932 however Lehmann returned to the more familiar, nostalgic terrain of a young girl's existence filled with dances and tea parties at country houses. This story, and the sequel *The Weather in the Streets,* again found favour with a large readership, and a film version which merged the two novels into one script appeared later.

Legend has it that Rosamond Lehmann was born in the middle of a thunderstorm on the day of Queen Victoria's funeral. If there is a symbolic significance to this — the fact that her life began at the end of the sexually restrictive Victorian era — then it must surely be found in *The Weather in the Streets.* The book aroused controversy: American publishers were disconcerted by the frank description of abortion, a theme whose time obviously had not yet quite come. Nevertheless, *The Weather in the Streets* became one of Lehmann's best-loved works, not only because of its ground-breaking discussion of a young woman's affair with a married man, but also because of its atmospheric description of the late 1930s as a time of restlessness and uncertainty. The novel seemed to anticipate the upheaval on the world political stage which was soon to come.

In contrast with the tortured subject matter of her books however, the 1930s were not an unhappy time for Lehmann. She was part of an extended group of artistic and intellectual friends, whose ramifications reached to the famous Bloomsbury group of which Virginia Woolf was a key member. Nor was Rosamond Lehmann the only one of the family to move in these Bohemian circles. Her brother John shared publishing ventures with the Woolfs, and sister Beatrix starred on the London stage as an actress. Shortly before the outbreak of World War II Beatrix Lehmann played the lead in her sister's only play, *No More Music.* For a time there was personal happiness too. In 1928 Rosamond Lehmann had married for the second time and with the birth of a daughter and a son she settled down to family life with the painter, and future Lord Milford, Wogan Philipps. Like many artists and intellectuals of the time (including Beatrix Lehmann and the aforementioned Stephen Spender), Philipps was a Communist. The frequent discussions of the contemporary political scene which he and his wife had over the dinner-table filtered into Lehmann's later novels, which portray their characters with an acute consciousness of the formative role of class and background. In *The Ballad and the Source,* for example, published in the year of her divorce from Wogan Philipps (1944), there is a strong theme of disintegration of the old order, a sense of "a defeat somewhere, a failure of the vital impulse". Clearly, this sense of failure was applicable to both her personal situation and the anticipated devastation of World War II, but Lehmann's work remains ambiguous on the question whether — politically speaking — the defeat of the old order was to be mourned or celebrated. Nostalgia for youth and the stable world of a comfortable middle-class existence remained a feature. Never herself a card-carrying Communist, nor a feminist for that matter — despite her persistent interest in the sexual and emotional conditions of women's lives — she always held herself aloof from ideological affiliations. Even when later in life she converted to Christianity, Lehmann could not commit her faith to any of the established churches and turned to spiritualism instead — an unconventional choice.

In her work this change of focus from the life of the emotions to that of the soul became evident only with the publication of the 1967 *The Swan in the Evening: Fragments of an Inner Life.* This was an autobiographical account of her experience of psychic encounters in dreams and visions with her deceased daughter, Sally. Sally's death of polio at the age of 21, on the threshold of adulthood, had a devastating impact on Rosamond Lehmann's life and was probably the cause of her long literary silence after *The Echoing Grove.* Alongside a disastrous love-affair with the poet Cecil Day Lewis, which left her emotionally depleted, the loss of her daughter was the final straw which motivated Lehmann to look elsewhere for spiritual sustenance and comfort.

Earlier in her career, Rosamond Lehmann had written to her brother John: "You suffer, as I always did, from a fatal facility. It is so easy for us to write. I personally am only just beginning to find it terribly difficult, and feel a little more hopeful". After 1958, the year of Sally's death, all hope was temporarily lost, only to re-surface in Christian faith and a belief in life after death, which for Lehmann became the condition of sanity. She gained no converts among her intellectual friends. Because of what they saw as an embarrassing loss of rationality, Lehmann's intellectual social circle was faintly embarrassed by *The Swan in the Evening* as well as by *A Sea Grape Tree,* her final novel.

Yet there can be little doubt that spiritualism sustained the author in her mature years and old age, when blindness and general ill-health prevented her from what she loved doing most — reading and writing. For as long as she could, Rosamond Lehmann remained active in the literary sphere as a reviewer, president of the British PEN, and council member of the Society of Authors. In 1982 the Queen recognized her services to English literary life by including her on the Honours List: she became a CBE. What pleased her at least as much, however, was the re-publication of some of her novels during the 1980s, at a time when she could no longer write or take part in public life and when the memory of her previous novelistic successes seemed to have been swept away on the tides of literary fashion. Virago, the all-women publishing house, re-issued Lehmann's work which once more brought her sackfuls of letters from grateful readers. This literary resurrection was a fitting tribute to a woman who by all accounts remained as beautiful in her blue-rinse days as she had been in Cambridge in the 1920s, who resisted old age as much as she could and who did not believe in the finality of death anyway.

Born Rosamond Nina Lehmann. **Parents** Rudolph, newspaper editor, founder of *Granta, Punch* contributor and Liberal member of parliament, and Alice (Davis) Lehmann. **Marriages** 1) The

Honourable Walter Runciman, later Viscount Runciman, 1923 (divorced 1928); 2) the Honourable Wogan Philipps, later Lord Milford, painter, 1928 (divorced 1944). **Children** Sally (died 1958) and Hugo, from second marriage. **Education** Educated at home; scholarship in English Literature, Girton College, Cambridge, BA, 1922. **Career** First novel published, 1927; first play produced, London, 1939; co-director, John Lehmann Limited, publishers, London, 1946–53; "rediscovered" by Virago Press, 1982. **Offices and memberships** President, Poets, Playwrights, Editors, Essayists, Novelists English Centre, international vice-president; council member, Society of Authors; vice-president, College of Psychic Studies. **Awards and honours** Denyse Clairouin Prize, for translation, 1948; commandant, Order of Arts and Letters, France, 1968; Commander of the Order of the British Empire, 1982. **Novels** *Dusty Answer,* 1927; *A Note in Music,* 1930; *Invitation to the Waltz,* 1932; *The Weather in the Streets,* 1936; *The Ballad and the Source,* 1944; *The Echoing Grove,* 1953; *The Sea-Grape Tree,* 1976. **Other publications** *A Letter to a Sister,* 1931; *No More Music* (play), 1939; (editor with others) *Orion: A Miscellany 1–3* (three volumes), 1945–46; *The Gipsy's Baby and Other Stories* (short stories), 1947; (translator) *Geneviève* by Jacques Lemarchand, 1947; (translator) *Children of the Game* by Jean Cocteau, 1955, published in US as *The Holy Terrors,* 1957, published as *Les Enfants terribles,* 1976; (with W. Tudor Pole) *A Man Seen Afar,* 1965; *The Swan in the Evening: Fragments of an Inner Life* (autobiography), 1967; (with Cynthia Sandys) *Letters from Our Daughters* (two volumes), 1972; (editor with Cynthia Sandys) *The Awakening Letters,* 1978; *Rosamond Lehmann's Album,* 1985. **Manuscript collections** King's College, Cambridge; University of Texas, Austin. **Cause of death** Undisclosed, at age 89. **Further reading** M. T. Gustafson, "Rosamond Lehmann: A Bibliography", *Twentieth Century Literature 4,* 1959; Diana E. Le Stourgeon, *Rosamond Lehmann,* 1965; Gillian Tindall, *Rosamond Lehmann: An Appreciation,* 1985; *Contemporary Novelists,* 1986; *Reference Guide to English Literature,* 1988.

JACK LINDSAY

Australian Writer, Poet and Scholar

Born **Melbourne, Australia, 20 October 1900**

Died **Cambridge, England, 8 March 1990**

The systematic exorcism of this original and fascinating figure from English cultural history is hardly surprising. Despite his presence as one of the shaping intellects of British cultural life in this century, Lindsay's Marxist viewpoint and Communist affiliation have made him wholly intolerable to some post-war chroniclers and readers. Despite titanic productivity in the areas of prose, classical scholarship, theatre and criticism, less than half a dozen of his books were still in print at the time of his death. "He was the last Communist writer of that heroic generation matured in the 1930s", wrote Stanley Mitchell. "In a culturally insular Communist Party, Lindsay was a door into world literature." His books have sold millions of copies in the Soviet Union and eastern Europe, and up until the 1950s, Lindsay was hugely popular in the West. But his unswerving Marxism and unorthodox humanism could not be digested by the cold war mentality. He was almost expelled by the Communist Party in 1949, over his association with Jean-Paul Sartre, and in the West you will struggle to find him mentioned in literary histories of the 1930s and 1940s. First, he was applauded for being one of the few writers who could combine political commitment with literary excellence; later, he was condemned for his "crude propaganda". This proves our myopia, rather than Lindsay's.

The first period in Lindsay's life stretched from his birth to the 1930s, during which he conceived of himself "as a poet and nothing else". His father was the graphic artist Norman Lindsay — now an Australian national institution, but then reviled as obscene. When he was nine years old, Jack Lindsay's parents separated, and Jack and his brothers (including Philip, also a well-known historical novelist) followed their mother to Brisbane. Later, young Jack won a scholarship to Queensland University to study classics and achieved a first at the age of 20. He began criticizing the university, published a poem based on one of his father's etchings, and was subsequently expelled. Undaunted, Lindsay tried to ignite a literary movement in Sydney with a quarterly magazine called *Vision*. From his flat in north Sydney, he tried to promote an aesthetic based largely on the ideas of his father and incorporating the traditions of Keats, Blake, Nietzsche, Aristophanes and Theocritus, among others. The project misfired, but Lindsay was encouraged by a friend, John Kirtley, and by the letterpress movement of the 1920s, to emigrate to England.

In 1926, he and Kirtley came to England and set up the Fanfrolico Press. Acting as editor, typographer and writer, Lindsay spent four years publishing contemporary poetry (much of it his own), reprints of risqué sixteenth- and seventeenth-century texts, and classical light erotica, translated by Lindsay. He continued to reprint his father's work, accompanied by illustrations by Lionel Ellis and Edward Bawden. He was "attempting to invade the English scene with what we called the Australian Renaissance" and to develop a dialectical aesthetic. Linday's intellectualism, however radical, was out of step with Britain in the aftermath of the General Strike, which nearly brought down the government. The *London Aphrodite* sought energetically to stir its readers by attacking pedantry on the one hand and anti-intellectualism on the other. It was the closest thing Britain had to the French Dadaist movement, but it was forced to shut down after six issues in 1929. In fact, the foray into magazines had so weakened the press's finances that it too was forced to close by the end of the year.

Vigorous, experimental and daring it may have been, but the business of the Fanfrolico Press was essentially academic. Still, it had been an ambitious project, and not the only one to fall on hard times in the 1930s. More importantly, there were two consequences that flowed from the press's demise. It had left Lindsay completely broke, bringing the bailiffs down on him and forcing him out of London. It had shown him, too, that he needed "to find a new basis" for his work. Poetry, and his quest into its nature, had led him into a box canyon. The first consequence led him into Devon and Cornwall and "extreme hardship", where he eked out a living as a reviewer. The second led him in 1936 to the writings of Karl Marx.

Here is where the transformation occurred. The key Lindsay needed to make his synthesis work lay in the historical dialectic; not as Utopian, but as material. Lindsay once wrote that in Marx, "I had reached bedrock"; and for the first time he was able "to grasp the real historical forces...to grasp the ancient world as a place in history, moving to the present." For the first time, seeing the material effects of unemployment, Lindsay felt "the role of the people in history". This link between the historic and the contemporary became Lindsay's major preoccupation, and inaugurated his most prolific period.

Although he continued to write poetry, Lindsay's ideas now found their expression in a more appropriate form — the historical novel. Two years before his conversion to Marxism, about the same time Robert Graves published *I, Claudius,* Lindsay began his trilogy of novels dealing with the Cataline rebellion in 63 BC. Instead of focusing on the excesses of the imperial family, these books brought the *entire society* to life. By choosing moments of fundamental crisis, and by using the fictional mode, Lindsay was able to make history immediate. Periods of revolutionary struggle always involve the great human forces — growth and decay, integrity and corruption, "alienation...and the struggle against alienation" — and through the historical novel Lindsay successfully wove his scholarship, philosophy, and political alignment.

His method was still essentially poetic, but by "seeking a basis in social existence" he had turned the process "inside out". His devotion to poetry led him to translate the ancient poets, then led him into criticism, then history, philosophy, anthropology and psychoanalysis, in an ever-broadening circle. His new formulae brought together "the sensuous immediacy of experience...the tragic pattern of conflict...[and] the related pattern of death–rebirth." Before, revealing these elements in a purely poetic structure had left them hollow and unresounding. As Andy Croft pointed out in a useful radio evaluation of Lindsay's work, using history as a contact point (and then crystallized by Marx) had given them vitality and relevance. Linday's Roman trilogy was met with critical acclaim and popularity. He went on to write a full 16 historical novels before 1941, in addition to other prose works, verse translations and a large number of stories and works of criticism.

Lindsay had launched himself into the forefront of political and literary activity in the 1930s. After he had turned to Marxism and the Communist Party, he discovered he was not alone. During this period of crisis in capitalism, many of Lindsay's old colleagues were looking for other solutions. He wrote for the *Daily Worker* and *Left Review,* and participated in the cultural activities of the Popular Front, fighting for social reform and against Fascism. The struggle to defeat Fascism required a "re-definition of Englishness" and a reclaiming of Britain for the common people:

> Come, you Anabaptists and you Levellers. Come, you muddletonians and bedlamites. Fall in behind us, comrades! Come, Luddites. Come, you men of the Charter, singing your songs of defiance on the blackened hills. Come from the mines and the looms. Come from the ploughlands. Come and tramp the streets of Birmingham and London, you angry millions. You workers. Your voice snarls in the clang of the flaring foundries. Your voice rips louder than ravens claws in the morning. You are speaking and you were not meant to speak. You are waking, comrades!

It was with this background that Lindsay produced his greatest work of historical fiction, *1649,* part of another trilogy. It looks back to another turbulent period in British history, following the execution of Charles I, and traces the suppression of Republican Levellers and their offshoot, the Diggers, by Oliver Cromwell. It is a rich evocation of seventeenth-century life, epic in scope, a story of the defeat of the popular aspirations unleashed by the Civil War, and the rising commercialism of the middle class. In this passage, Lindsay is at his best:

> This is how the effort to bring liberty to England had ended. When the...troopers, with refreshed horses, had ridden into Burford as the clock chimed midnight, they had surrounded the town. Will Thompson and a dozen others had escaped from the farther end and somehow gained horses before daybreak, but the rest of the regiment and volunteer detachments were cornered. After a brief consultation, they raised at dawn the white flag of surrender — and a parley at which an assurance of safety was promised. But Captain Thompson, he was not a man to think one check meant the end of England's struggle for liberty...He'd sworn to free England, and he meant it. He fled on horseback. They harried him for days. He fled through the springtime. He heard the danger call of the redshank, and he slept under the sweet blossoms. He saw the plants pushing up through the dead leaves, the blackbirds scratching with little sideways jumps in the forest of beeches, the moorhen hiding under the sycamore roots in the stream bank. He saw it all, he smelt the spring, harried across England. They cornered him in Northamptonshire, behind the barn where the pigs were rooting in the mud. A corporal with seven bullets in his carbine caught him at last.

In the words of Andy Croft, "the English landscape here is a winter's elegy for broken social relations, a love song for the place these men were fighting over, and a springtime promise of change." Lindsay the novelist always portrayed history as an indelible force which motivates people in ways and with consequences they don't understand, and as largely irrational, i.e.

unreflected consciousness. Even unsympathetic critics like David Smith thought *1649* "gave to Marxist ideology a life and conviction that few British novelists had so far been able to do."

During the 1930s and 1940s, Lindsay was doing much more than writing fiction. He pursued the ideal of mass culture, experimental theatre, and began work in social and cultural history. This work laid the foundations for "a native, popular, Marxist historical tradition." Major contributions to the field by E.P. Thompson and Raymond Williams are indebted to him. World War II saw Lindsay at the height of his powers and reputation. In 1939, one of his poems, an anti-Fascist "declamator poem", was performed in Trafalgar Square. In 1941 he enlisted, and eventually he wound up at the Army Bureau of Current Affairs, Theatre Unit, where he produced plays for the troops. He also found time to write several books and edit the Communist Party's cultural journal *Our Time*. Taking advantage of the anti-Fascist feeling, Lindsay helped develop a form of agit-prop in the form of street theatre, tracts and pamphlets, and radio drama — the likes of which would not been seen again until the 1960s.

The abundance of his energies was staggering, and his output enormous. He wrote and translated over 160 books in all, including 39 novels, eleven plays, eleven volumes of verse, and 60 non-fiction titles. He edited another 18. Highlights among these are his biographies of Blake, Mark Antony, Dickens, Cézanne, John Bunyan, and his personal encounters with Edith Sitwell, Louis Aragon, Tristan Tzara and others. Once, in his late sixties, he wrote "I am hard at work on Cézanne and I have just signed up for a big book on the Origins of Alchemy. At the moment [I am] correcting the galley proofs of my huge book on the Roman Nile. The Graeco-Roman book is on the way. Bernard [Miles] is trying to lure me into a modern *Pilgrim's Progress*...and so on."

The end of the war, the break-up of the anti-Fascist alliance, and the election of a Labour government mark the beginning of the third and final stage in Lindsay's life. The cultural upsurge in the populace waned, many writers abandoned their political stance, and the government of Clement Attlee pursued policies on the arts and housing that represented to Lindsay a betrayal. Lindsay registered his disappointment in a long series of novels, generally entitled "The British Way". His powers of characterization, description and plotting had not diminished. However, the disaffection between Lindsay and the fashionable intelligence was mutual. He could not find a publisher for his poems on the French Resistance. Eleven of his "British Way" Novels were not even noticed in the press. When they deigned to review his books, he was labelled "a mouthpiece of the Moscow Foreign Office", and his work was slighted for its "pedestrian Marxism". Although he continued to write fiction and verse, the bulk of his output from this period shifted to straightforward scholarship, history and criticism.

Sectarians on the other side of the political world were also annoyed by Lindsay's individuality. Where in the West he was accused of a dogmatic adherence to Marxism, in the Soviet Union he was attacked for abandoning it. Lindsay was already familiar with the leading figures of the Resistance, but after the war he took an active interest in Sartre, who was anti-Marx. Lindsay had continually applied himself to "the problem of developing Marxism", and in 1949 questioned the sacrosanct "Base-Superstructure" model in *Marx and Contemporary Science*. The paper was ostensibly a reply to Karl Popper's *The Open Society and Its Enemies*, but it was also a rejection of Stalinism. This nearly resulted in Lindsay's expulsion from the party. It did not happen, but Stalin's crimes and the invasion of Hungary sorely tried his allegiance. After his eightieth birthday, Lindsay foreshadowed, in theoretical terms, the revolutions of 1989 in his *The Crisis of Marxism* (1981), proving that he was always ahead of those around him.

Jack Lindsay is still gagged, although the changes he predicted may prepare the way for a reassessment of his life and work. To those who knew him, he was "magic", and many people visited him in East Anglia. Poet Roy Fuller called him "translator, polymath, biographer, poet — man!"; to another poet, Edith Sitwell, he was "a saint". He was always ready to listen to others and help them with their work; of his own, he once said, "I always feel my work lies ahead". Or, "Just past the straining finger tips it lies."

Born Jack Lindsay. **Pseudonyms** Richard Preston, Peter Meadows. **Parents** Norman Alfred William, writer and artist, and Kathleen (Parkinson) Lindsay. **Marriages** 1) Janet Beaton; 2) Ann Davies (died 1954); 3) Meta Waterdrinker, art potter, 1958. **Children** Philip and Helen, from third marriage. **Education** Brisbane Grammar School; University of Queensland, Brisbane, 1918–21, BA (first-class honours) in classics, 1921. **Emigration** Left Australia for England, 1926. **Military service** Royal Corps of Signals, British Army, 1941–45, seconded to War Office as scriptwriter, 1943–45. **Career** Co-editor, *Vision,* Sydney, 1923–24; first poetry published, 1923; first play published, 1927; proprietor and director, Fanfrolico Press, London, 1927–30; co-editor, *London Aphrodite,* 1928–29; moved to west country, 1930; first novel published, 1931; editor, *Poetry and the People,* London, 1938–39; editor, *Anvil,* London, 1947; co-editor, *Arena,* London, 1949–51. **Offices and memberships** Fellow: Royal Society of Literature, 1945, Ancient Monuments Society, 1961, Australian Academy of Humanities; member: Egyptian Exploration Society, Roman Society, Hellenic Society, Essex Archaeological Society, Suffolk Archaeological Society. **Awards and honours** Australian Literature Society Couch Gold Medal, 1960; Order of Merit (USSR), 1968; honorary DLitt, University of Queensland, 1973; member, Order of Australia, 1981. **Novels** *Cressida's First Lover,* 1931; *Rome for Sale,* 1934; *Caesar Is Dead,* 1934; *Last Days with Cleopatra,* 1935; *Despoiling Venus,* 1935; *Storm at Sea,* 1935; *The Wanderings of Wenamen: 1115–1114 B.C.,* 1936; (as Richard Preston) *Shadow and Flame,* 1936; *Adam of a New World,* 1936; *Sue Verney,* 1937; (as Richard Preston) *End of Cornwall,* 1937; *1649: A Novel of a Year,* 1938; *Brief Light: A Novel of Catullus,* 1939; *Lost Birthright,* 1939; *Giuliano the Magnificent* (adapted from a work by Dorothy Johnson), 1940; *Light in Italy,* 1941; *Hannibal Takes a Hand,* 1941; *The Stormy Violence,* 1941; *We Shall Return: A Novel of Dunkirk and the French Campaign,* 1942; *Beyond Terror: A Novel of the Battle of Crete,* 1943; *The Barriers Are Down: A Tale of the Collapse of a Civilisation,* 1945; *Hullo Stranger,* 1945; *Time to Live,* 1946; *The Subtle Knot,* 1947; *Men of Forty-Eight,* 1948; *Fires in Smithfield,* 1950; *The Passionate Pastoral,* 1951; *Betrayed Spring: A Novel of the British Way,* 1953; *Rising Tide,* 1953; *The Moment of Choice,* 1955; *A Local Habitation: A Novel of the British Way,* 1957; *The Great Oak: A Story of 1549,* 1957; *The Revolt of the Sons,* 1960; *All on the Never-Never: A Novel of the British Way of Life,* 1961; *The Way the Ball Bounces,* 1962; *Masks and Faces,* 1963; *Choice of Times,* 1964; *Thunder Underground: A Story of Nero's Rome,* 1965; *The Blood-Vote,* 1985. **Short stories** *Come Home at Last and Other Stories,* 1936; *Death of a Spartan King and Two Other Stories of the Ancient World,* 1974. **Plays** *Marino Faliero: A Verse Play,* 1927; *Helen Comes of Age: Three Original Plays in Verse* (includes *Ragnild* and *Bussy d'Amboise*), 1927; *Hereward: A Verse Drama,* 1930; *The Whole Armour of God,* 1944; *Robin of England,* 1945; (with B. Coombes) *The Face of Coal,* 1946; (adapter) *Iphigenia in Aulis* by Euripides, 1967; (adapter) *Hecuba* by Euripides, 1967; (adapter) *Electra* by Euripides, 1967; (adapter) *Orestes* by Euripides, 1967; (adapter) *Nathan the Wise* by Lessing, 1967. **Verse** *Fauns and Ladies,* 1923; *The Pleasante Conceited Narrative of Panurge's Fantastic Ally Brocaded Codpiece,* 1924; *The Spanish Main and Tavern,* 1924; *The Passionate Neatherd,* 1926; *Into Action: The Battle of Dieppe,* 1942; *Second Front,* 1944, *Clue of Darkness,* 1949; *Peace Is Our Answer,* 1950; *Three Letters to Nikolai Tikhonov,* 1951; *Three Elegies,* 1957; *Faces and Places,* 1974; *Collected Poems,* 1981. **Non-fiction works** *William Blake: Creative Will and the Poetic Image,* 1927; *Dionysos: or, Nietzsche contra Nietzsche: An Essay in Lyrical Philosophy,* 1928; *The Romans,* 1935; *Runaway* (juvenile), 1935; *Rebels of the Goldfields* (juvenile), 1936; *Marc Antony: His World and His Contemporaries,* 1936; *John Bunyan: Maker of Myths,* 1937; *The Anatomy of Spirit: An Enquiry into the Origins of Religious Emotions,* 1937; *To Arms! A Story of Ancient Gaul* (juvenile), 1938; *England, My England,* 1930; *A Short History of Culture,* 1939; *The Dons Sight Devon: A Story of the Defeat of the Invincible Armada* (juvenile), 1942; *Perspective for Poetry,* 1944; *British Achievement in Art and Music,* 1945; *Mulk Raj Anand: A Critical Essay,* 1948; *Song of a Falling World: Culture During the Break-up of the Roman Empire (A.D. 350–600),* 1948; *Marxism* *and Contemporary Science; or, The Fulness of Life,* 1949; *A World Ahead: Journal of a Soviet Journey,* 1950; *Charles Dickens: A Biographical and Critical Study,* 1950; *Byzantium into Europe: The Story of Byzantium as the first Europe (362–1204* A.D.*) and Its Further Contributions till 1453* A.D., 1952; (with M. Cornforth) *Rumanian Summer,* 1953; *Civil War in England: The Cromwellian Revolution,* 1954; *George Meredith: His Life and Work,* 1956; *The Romans Were Here: The Roman Period in Britain and Its Place in Our History,* 1956; *After the Thirties: The Novel in Britain and Its Future,* 1956; *Arthur and His Times: Britain in the Dark Ages,* 1958; *The Discovery of Britain: A Guide to Archaeology,* 1958; *1764: The Hurly-Burly of Daily Life Exemplified in One Year of the 18th Century,* 1959; *The Writing on the Wall: An Account of Pompeii in Its Last Days,* 1960; *Death of the Hero: French Painting from David to Delacroix,* 1960; *William Morris: Writer,* 1961; *Daily Life in Roman Egypt,* 1963; *Nine Days' Hero: Wat Tyler,* 1964; *The Clashing Rocks: A Study of Early Greek Religion and Culture, and the Origins of Drama,* 1965; *Leisure and Pleasure in Roman Egypt,* 1965; *Our Anglo-Saxon Heritage,* 1965; *J.M.W. Turner: His Life and Work: A Critical Biography,* 1966; *Our Roman Heritage,* 1967; *Meetings with Poets: Memories of Dylan Thomas, Edith Sitwell, Louis Aragon, Paul Eluard, Tristan Tzara,* 1968; *Men and Gods on the Roman Nile,* 1968; *The Ancient World: Manners and Morals,* 1968; *Cézanne: His Life and Art,* 1969; *The Origins of Alchemy in Graeco-Roman Egypt,* 1970; *Cleopatra,* 1971; *Origins of Astrology,* 1971; *Gustave Courbet: His Life and Work,* 1974; *Helen of Troy: Woman and Goddess,* 1974; *Blast-Power and Ballistics: Concepts of Force and Energy in the Ancient World,* 1974; *The Normans and Their World,* 1975; *William Morris: His Life and Work,* 1975; *Decay and Renewal: Critical Essays on Twentieth Century Writing,* 1976; *The Troubadours and Their World of the Twelfth and Thirteenth Centuries,* 1976; *Hogarth: His Art and World,* 1979; *William Blake: His Life and Work,* 1978; *The Monster City: Defoe's London 1688–1730,* 1978; *Thomas Gainsborough: His Life and Art,* 1981; *The Crisis in Marxism,* 1981; *Turner: The Man and His Art,* 1985. **Works edited** (With Kenneth Slessor) *Poetry in Australia,* 1923; (with P. Warlock) *Loveing Mad Tom: Bedlamite Verses of the XVI and XVII Centuries,* 1927; *The Metamorphosis of Aiax* by Sir John Harington, 1928; *The Parlement of Pratlers,* 1928; (as Peter Meadows) *Delighted Earth* by Robert Herrick, 1928; *Inspiration, 1928; Letters of Philip Stanhope, Second Earl of Chesterfield,* 1930; (with Edgell Rickword) *A Handbook of Freedom: A Record of English Democracy Through Twelve Centuries,* 1939; (with Maurice Carpenter and Honor Arundel) *New Lyrical Ballads,* 1945; *Anvil: Life and the Arts: A Miscellany,* 1947; *New Development Series,* 1947–48; *Herrick: A Selection,* 1948; *William Morris: A Selection,* 1948; (with Randall Swingler) *Key Poets,* 1950; *Barefoot* by Z. Stancu, 1950; *Paintings and Drawings of Leslie Hurry,* 1952; *The Sunset Ship: Poems of J.M.W. Turner,* 1966; *The Autobiography of Joseph Priestly,* 1970. **Works translated** *Lysistrata* by Aristophanes, 1926; *Propertius in Love,* 1927; *Satyricon and Poems* by Petronius, 1927; *Homage to Sappho,* 1928; *Complete Poems of Theocritus,* 1929; *Hymns to Aphrodite* by Homer, 1929; *Women in Parliament* by Aristophanes, 1929; *The Mimiambs of Herondas, 1929; The Complete Poetry of Gaius Catullus,* 1930; *Sulpicia's Garland: Roman Poems,* 1930; *Patchwork Quilt: Poems by Ausonius,* 1930; *The Golden Ass,* by Apuleius, 1931; *I Am a Roman,* 1934; *Medieval Latin Poets,* 1934; *Daphnis and Chloe* by Longus, 1948; (with S. Jolly) *Song of Peace* by V. Nezval, 1951; *Poems of Adam Mickiewicz,* 1957; *Russian Poetry 1917–1955,* 1957; *Asklepiades in Love,* 1960; *Modern Russian Poetry,* 1960; *Cause, Principle, and Unity: 5 Dialogues* by Giordano Bruno, 1962; *Ribaldry of Ancient Greece,* 1965; *Ribaldry of Ancient Rome,* 1965; *The Elegy of Haido* by Tefcros Anthias, 1966; *The Age of Akhenaten* by Eleonore Bille-de-Mot, 1967; *Greece, I Keep My Vigil for You* by Tefcros Anthias, 1968; *The Twelve, and The Scythians* by Alexander Blok, 1982. **Autobiographical works** *Life Rarely Tells: An Autobiographical Account Ending in the Year 1921 and Situated Mostly in Brisbane, Queensland,* 1958; *The Roaring Twenties: Literary Life in Sydney, New South Wales, in the Years 1921–26,* 1960; *Fanfrolico and After,* 1962. **Manuscript**

collection University of Queensland, St Lucia. **Cause of death** Undisclosed, at age 89. **Further reading** Alick West, *Mountain in the Sunlight,* 1958; Edgell Rickword (editor) *A Garland for Jack Lindsay,* 1980; Bernard Smith (editor), *Culture and History: Essays Presented to Jack Lindsay,* 1984; Robert Mackie (editor) *Jack Lindsay: The Thirties and Forties,* 1984; *Contemporary Novelists,* 1986; *Twentieth-Century Romance and Historical Writers,* 1990; *Reference Guide to English Literature,* 1991. **Further resources** Andy Croft, "Red Letter Days" 2: *Jack Lindsay,* BBC Radio 4, September 1990.

JAY LOVESTONE

American Political Activist

Born **Lithuania, Russia, 24 December 1898**

Died **Manhattan, New York, 7 March 1990**

Probably one of the hardest positions to sustain in the United States is that of the dedicated Communist. In a land where the word "Communism" is shrouded with suspicion and anyone remotely connected with it immediately branded a renegade or traitor, Communists are a breed that tend to work, for the most part, underground. There are exceptions to that rule and one of them was Jay Lovestone.

Russian by birth, Lovestone was brought to America by his parents at the age of nine. Because he was of Jewish extraction his hatred for tsarist Russia was well ingrained and he was deeply stirred by the 1917 Bolshevik Revolution. He turned his political interests towards this new order. In 1918 when he graduated from the City College of New York he was deeply involved in the Socialist and Communist movements and he helped to establish the American Communist Party. His first post was as editor of their newspaper *The Communist.*

His star began to rise in the Communist scene until, in 1923, he opposed Stalin in his defence of Nicolai Bukharin, the powerful head of the Comintern, the Communist International. It was an event that would not only change the course of his life, but also turn his political ideas around.

In 1929, Lovestone was called to a meeting with Stalin in Moscow where, it is said, Stalin not only expelled Lovestone from the party, but was intent that he should not leave the Soviet Union alive. Lovestone, however, managed to escape through Danzig with the help of false identity papers. He was to say in later years about his interview with Stalin, "He wasn't used to being told the truth."

When Lovestone returned to the United States he continued his work with the labour movement, becoming the head of the Communist Party of the United States, which would later change its name to the Independent Labor League of America. The group was disbanded in 1940, by which time Lovestone had concluded that Communism, rather than being a saviour of the working classes, was in reality a totalitarian conspiracy directed from the Kremlin.

He now put his political weight behind the Committee to Defend America which sought support for Britain and the other Allies in the early days of World War II. In addition, in 1943, he was named international affairs director for the International Ladies Garment Workers Union, a prestigious post in a large organization.

Following the war Lovestone became executive secretary to the International Confederation of Free Trade Unions whose purpose it was to oppose the Communist-dominated organization, World Federation of Trade Unions. He had now come full circle from being a staunch supporter of the Communist movement to being "married to the idea of preventing the Kremlin from dominating the world".

Backed by the CIA and the State Department of the United States, Lovestone helped build anti-Communist unions in other countries. His work also continued with the AFL-CIO (the newly merged American Federation of Labor and the Congress of Industrial Organizations). Principally, he directed programmes in Latin America through the Institute for Free Labor Development, and with the International Labor Organization, an arm of the United Nations. He had by this time collected a valuable network of informers, enabling him to predict developments in the Communist world way ahead of any other source. Even after retirement he continued to work as a consultant to the AFL-CIO and to the Ladies Garment Workers Union.

Born Jacob Liebstein. **Father** A cantor. **Education** City College, New York, BA, 1918. **Emigration** Left Russia for US, 1907. **Career** Editor, *The Communist,* official underground organ, American Communist Party, 1921, national secretary, 1922–27, secretary-general, 1927–29; argued for separate American Communist plan for change; called to Moscow by Stalin, 1929, forcibly detained but escaped, 1929, ordered expelled from American Communist Party, 1929; founder, Communist Party of the United States, later Independent Labor League of America, disbanded 1940; rejected Communism; international affairs director, International Ladies Garment Workers Union, 1943; headed drive to rid organized labour of communist influence, 1944; executive secretary, International Confederation of Free Trade Unions; international affairs director, American Federation of Labor-Congress of Industrial Organizations, to 1974, consultant, 1974–85. **Related activities** Leader, Committee to Defend America, 1939–43; on board of directors: Atlantic Council, Council on Foreign Relations, Committee on the Present Danger; member, Labor Advisory Committee, president; member, international committee, National Planning Association. **Awards and honours** Grand Cross of Merit, Republic of Germany; commander, Order of Merit, Republic of Italy. **Cause of death** Undisclosed, at age 91.

JOSEPH McCULLOCH

British Priest

***Born* Liverpool, England, 31 August 1908**

***Died* London, England, 4 March 1990**

"I'm sure I don't know, says the Great Bell of Bow" in the children's jingle about the churches of the City of London. True Cockneys, it is said, are born within the sound of Bow Bells. The church of St-Mary-le-Bow, Cheapside, was built by the Normans, destroyed in the Great Fire, rebuilt by Sir Christopher Wren, destroyed again by the Blitz and finally restored by the Reverend Joseph McCulloch, rector of Bow from 1959 to 1979.

The Bow Bells jingle suited Joseph McCulloch well. A doubting prelate, author of books like *A Parson in Revolt,* and *The Faith that must Offend,* he was never one of those on whom the priest's mantle sits lightly. His was one of those challenging, questioning minds with which the Church of England is sometimes blessed, even if it rarely offers them the distinction they deserve. This seems to have been the case with McCulloch, who would have made a brilliant Dean of Westminster, who was once considered for the post of head of religious affairs broadcasting at the BBC, but whose greatest distinction remains the work he put into the rectorship at Bow.

McCulloch made Bow into one of the most exciting churches in London. The famous lunch-time "Dialogues" which he introduced, and which ran for more than ten years, filled the church to bursting point each Tuesday. McCulloch and some well-known public figures debated the burning issues of the day from two giant pulpits set either side of the central aisle. Yehudi Menuhin, Bernard Levin, Enoch Powell, Germaine Greer and Malcolm Muggeridge (q.v.) were among his chosen interlocutors. Some of the dialogues were published, others televised. At the time it seemed that McCulloch had achieved a break-through for the Church. As Robert Stepford, then Bishop of London, commented wryly, "it's our one link with the outside world".

Joseph McCulloch had a past that would have delighted the pen of Trollope. A working-class lad from Anglo-Catholic Liverpool he won a scholarship to study theology at Oxford. After ordination he had to escape from his first parish in a hurry. A novel, *Charming Manners,* published under a pseudonym, roused the ire of certain parishioners whose characters McCulloch had not taken the trouble to disguise. Rescued by the cricketing Canon, H.F. Gillingham (whose daughter, Betty, McCulloch married), McCulloch again came to grief as a curate in a Westminster parish whose rector did not appreciate the changes initiated in his absence. Even the career as a religious affairs broadcaster that he cultivated assiduously through the 1930s and 1940s, went through its awkward patches. For a year during the war McCulloch was banned from the air, presumably because of his controversial views — views that also lost him his job as army chaplain when he made them known in a letter of complaint to the chaplain general.

Bow was not the only almost defunct church into which McCulloch was able to breathe new life and energy. When he and his wife arrived at St Mary's, Chatham, in 1943, they formed a congregation of two. Within a few years the church was full and the Rector a well-known figure propping up the bar of the Red Lion Inn where he conducted a one-man "brains trust" each Sunday evening. McCulloch's book about Chatham, *The Medway Adventure,* attracted the praise of the lay thinker Joseph Oldham who compared it favourably with his own Bishop's report, *Towards the Conversion of the Church of England,* published in 1946. McCulloch's comment that he had become so unused to praise in Church circles that Oldham's words were worth more to him "than a chorus of praise from the whole bench of bishops", reflects his permanent uneasiness with the ecclesiastical hierarchy.

Like many rebels and non-conformists within the Establishment, McCulloch seems to have been an essentially lonely man, and after his retirement from Bow and the death of his wife, became something of a recluse. His friends found him always a witty conversationalist and an inspiring preacher, saying that in his last years he became concerned, like Jung (whom he read thoroughly), with a search for the true self. Discontent with the parochial system of the Church and the life-style imposed on priests was another issue. McCulloch stated that in another life he would only take Holy Orders if he could work and earn money in the outside community. "My experience as a clergyman has been the process of discovering", he wrote, "the extent and nature of the intolerable imprisonment of Christian priesthood". It is interesting that, to the outside observer, Joseph McCulloch would seem to have been more adept at escaping that imprisonment than the great majority of Anglican priests among whom he worked.

Born Joseph McCulloch. **Marriage** Betty Gillingham, 1935 (deceased). **Children** Christopher, Gabriel and Jane. **Education** Scholar, Exeter College, Oxford, BA in theology. **Career** Took orders in the Anglican church, 1931; appointed curate, Blundellsands, Liverpool, 1931, forced to leave after pseudonymously published *Charmed Lives* revealed as his, 1932; curate, Lee, London; curate, St John's Smith Square, London, forced to leave after Rector discovered certain initiatives had been begun without permission, 1935; rector, Turweston, Buckinghamshire, 1935–38; rector, Great Warley, Essex, 1938–43; chaplain, anti-aircraft brigade, 1939–41; rector, St Mary's Chatham, Kent, 1943–49; rector, St Mary's Warwick, 1949–59; rector, St Mary-le-Bow, London, 1959–79, instituted "Dialogues" between himself and other communicators; retired, 1979. **Related activities** BBC broadcaster. **Other activities** Labour councillor, Chatham.

Publications *Charmed Lives*; *Limping Sway*; *A Parson in Revolt*; *The Divine Drama*; *The Faith that must Offend*; *We Have Our Orders*; *The Trumpet Shall Sound*; *The Medway Adventure*; *Door of the Cave*; *My Affair with the Church* (autobiography). **Cause of death** Undisclosed, at age 81.

WALTER S. MACK

American Businessman

***Born* Manhattan, New York, 19 October 1895**

***Died* Manhattan, New York, 18 March 1990**

With the death of Walter S. Mack, members of the "Pepsi Generation" can salute the man who not only gave them their all-time second favourite soft drink, but also put the can in their hands. For Mack was the marketing genius who stole the limelight from the Coca-Cola company with his incredible talent for marketing and advertising.

A Harvard graduate, Mack had by the early 1930s already earned himself a reputation as a financial wizard, with a special ability for recognizing ailing companies with potential and turning them into success stories. In 1938 he became president of a cola company which was selling its formula in syrup form distributed to candy store soda fountains. The name of the company was Pepsi.

Within a year profits soared. Shares in Pepsi rose from 70 to 190 dollars. In order to continue the rising success, Mack turned his sights on Coca-Cola, the number-one cola on the market. He knew he would have to cut into the rival drink's market share and directed all his abilities towards selling techniques.

His first move was to win a court battle enabling him to add the word "Cola" to the end of his product name. Then he turned to advertising. Indelibly etched into the subconscious of every American growing up in the 1950s and early 1960s is Mack's Pepsi jingle:

Pepsi-Cola hits the spot
Twelve full ounces, that's a lot,
Twice as much for a nickel, too
Pepsi-Cola is the drink for you.

The creation of this jingle was not the only innovation of this shrewd salesman. For it was Mack who put Pepsi-Cola in cans to rival the curvaceous green bottles of the Coca-Cola company.

Walter Mack's uniqueness does not end with financial success, for here was a rare animal indeed. Not only was he a classic capitalist, but his business acumen was always softened by benevolence. He saw to it that his company funded college scholarships as well as art exhibitions, inner-city youth projects and day centres for members of the military. These Pepsi-Cola-sponsored projects, along with its advertising campaign, helped to establish the company name.

In 1956, Mack resigned his presidency and board chairmanship over battles with the board over some of his innovative ideas. While his career with Pepsi was at an end, Mack's working life continued. He became involved as an officer with a wide range of manufacturing, investment and mining companies. In 1978, at the age of 82, he re-emerged from retirement and along with other retired cola company executives set up King Cola World Corporation. This new company failed, but those who worked with Mack claimed it was a worthwhile experience. He also found time to write an autobiography entitled *No Time Lost* — an appropriate title indeed.

Born Walter Staunton Mack Junior. **Parents** Walter Staunton, cloth trader, and Alice (Ranger) Mack. **Marriages** 1) Marion Reckford, 1922 (divorced 1944); 2) Ruth Juergensen, 1945 (died 1986). **Children** Anthony and Florence, from first marriage; Alice and Walter, from second marriage. **Education** De Witt Clinton High School, New York; Harvard University, Cambridge, Massachusetts, 1913–17, BA, 1917. **Military service** Ensign, United States Navy, 1917–18. **Career** Salesman, Bedford Mills, Incorporated, textile house, 1918, president, 1926–31; vice-president, William B. Nichols and Company, investment bankers, 1931; vice-president, Equity Corporation, 1931; president, Phoenix Securities Corporation, 1931; unsuccessful Republican state senator candidate, 1932; president, Pepsi-Cola Company, 1938–51, masterminded challenge to Coca-Cola, from 1939–51, board chairman, 1951–56; credited with invention of soft drink in cans, 1953; founded King Cola World Corporation, 1978. **Related activities** Board chairman, United Cigar-Whelan Stores, Aminex Resources, Aminex Petroleum, Nedick's, C & C Cola. **Other activities** Republican National Convention delegate, 1940; chairman, New York Police Athletic League benefit, 1942–43; vice-chairman, Industrial Salvage Committee for Greater New York; honorary and active chairman, Red Cross, United Service Organization, Beverage Division of the National Safety Council, Incorporated, War Production Fund to Conserve Manpower; chairman, War Fund Drive, 1943; member, Fire Protection Committee of the New York City War Council; committee member, New York mayor's Local Defense Council and Business Advisory Committee; incorporator, New York City Center of Music and Drama; advisory committee member, New York's World Fair; director: Mexican Chamber of Commerce, Cuban Chamber of Commerce, Queens County Chamber of Commerce, China-American Council for Commerce and Industry; treasurer, Republican County Committee of New York. **Offices and memberships** Trustee and treasurer, Temple Emanu-El, New York; trustee, Mount Sinai Hospital. **Publication** *No Time Lost* (autobiography), 1982. **Cause of death** Heart disease, at age 94.

HAROLD MEDINA

American Federal Judge

***Born* Brooklyn, New York, 16 February 1888**

***Died* Westwood, New Jersey, 14 March 1990**

"I always wanted to be a judge; I am having a wonderful time as a judge, and I haven't the slightest idea of ever doing anything else." In his own words, Harold Medina summed up his brilliant career and service to his country as a United States federal judge. It was a career that began on a promising basis and never once faltered through more than 70 years service.

Medina began his career as a graduate from the prestigious Columbia Law School. He graduated with honours and with the Ordronneaux Prize for the highest standing in the school. Like most young lawyers he started as a law clerk, at eight dollars a week. In order to supplement this income, he began to coach law students for the Bar examinations in a special cram course that he originated. He began with four students and at the end of his career as tutor he had coached 39,788 pupils. A contemporary remarked, "Medina has turned out more lawyers than most law schools."

At the same time Medina had begun his own law firm in partnership with Eugene A. Sherpick. He established a reputation for winning the most difficult cases, utilizing his vast knowledge and brilliant interpretation of the law. Then on 1 July 1947, at the age of 59, a time when most attorneys are looking towards retirement, he was nominated by President Truman to become a federal judge in the Southern District of New York. The appointment meant giving up a 100,000-dollar law practice for a salary of 15,000 dollars as a judge. For Medina there was no contest, "I've made plenty of money", he remarked. "Now I'd like to do something for my country. I guess the best thing I have to contribute is law."

His most famous trial was soon to follow as he presided over the case of eleven Communist leaders charged under the Smith Act for conspiracy to teach and advocate the overthrow of the federal government by force. Not only was it a landmark case, but it came at the starting shot of the American anti-Communist witch-hunts. For nine months the case dragged on and Medina was constantly barraged with abuse from the defending attorneys. The case became famous for its disruption, confusion and unendurable delays. Yet Medina was able to maintain his calmness, dignity and professional detachment throughout. At one point he was to remark to the defending lawyers, "you will not goad me into making any statements which will create errors in this courtroom."

It was an overwhelmingly long and complicated case involving over five million words of testimony. The eleven defendants were convicted and the five defence attorneys handed sentences of up to six months for contempt of court. It was a decision upheld by the United States Supreme Court by a six to two decision.

Following the trial Medina found, to his embarrassment, that he had become something of a hero among the conservative anti-Communists who were championing him. It was not a role he believed he fitted or, indeed, one he wanted to play. "I wasn't anti-Communist or anti-anything else", he was later to say. He tried to explain that his only motive was to be fair in the face of continued provocation.

In the years that followed Medina continued his career in the United States Court of Appeals, taking over from Learned Hand. In that job he handled one of the most famous anti-trust cases involving investment banking, and his 420-page opinion dismissing the case became a textbook on investment banking.

In 1958 at the age of 70, Medina retired from the bench, but remained as a "senior" judge in which capacity he handed down various influential opinions. He continued in this role until the age of 92 by which time he was recognized as a champion of free speech and a free press. He enjoyed ten years of retirement. At his death at the age of 102 he was the oldest federal judge and the oldest Princeton alumnus.

Born Harold Raymond Medina. **Parents** Joaquin A., import and export businessman, and Elizabeth (Fash) Medina. **Marriage** Ethel Forde Hillyer, 1911 (died 1971). **Children** Harold and Standish. **Education** Public School 44, New York City; Princeton University, New Jersey, highest honours in French, BA, 1909; Columbia University, New York, LLB, 1912. **Career** Admitted to New York Bar, 1912; offered cram course in law, 1912–40; practised law, Davies, Auerbach and Cornell, New York City, 1915–18; lecturer, Columbia University, 1915–17, associate in law, 1917–25, associate professor of law, 1925–47; formed law firm with Eugene A. Sherpick, 1918–47; appointed judge, US District Court, Southern District, New York, 1947–51, US circuit judge, Court of Appeals for Second Circuit, 1951–58, senior circuit judge, 1958–80, retired 1980; presided over trial of eleven American Communist Party members, 1949. **Other activities** Vice-president and director, family import-export business; life trustee emeritus, Teachers College, Columbia University; alumni federation president, Columbia University; president, Columbia Law School alumni association, 1935–1938; chairman, advisory council of the modern language department (Romance division), Princeton University; charter trustee emeritus, Princeton University; trustee, Good Samaritan Hospital and Dispensary. **Offices and memberships** Fellow, American Academy of Arts and Sciences; member, American Bar Association, subcommittee of the special committee on the improvement of judicial procedure; member, New York Bar Association, committee on uniform laws, 1920–34, committee on the civil practice act, 1929–35, special committee in connection with the Law Revision Commission, 1935–47, committee on improvement in judicial administration and the committee on jurisdiction of the Court of Appeals, 1941; member, City of New York Bar Association, executive committee chairman, 1945; member: New York County Lawyers Association, American Judicature Society, New York Law Society. **Awards and honours** Ordronneaux Prize, Columbia Law School, 1912; medal for conspicuous service, Columbia University alumni association, 1933; various awards: Freedom Foundation, Holland Society, New York Board of Trade, National Institute of Social Science, Brooklyn College, National Society of New England Women, Sons of the American Revolution, Texas Bill of Rights Foundation; Eleanor Van Rensselaer Medal, National Society of Colonial Women; Justice award, American Judicature Society, 1971; Harold R. Medina Professorship established, Columbia Law School, 1973; Harold R. Medina Courtroom dedicated, Columbia Law School, 1981; James Madison award, National Broadcast Editorial Association, 1976; distinguished Public Service award, Ohio Newspaper Association, 1976. **Publications** (include) *Pleading and Practice under New Civil Practice Act,* 1922; *Cases on Federal Jurisdiction and Procedure,* 1925; *Cases on New York Pleading and Practice,* 1928; *Cases and Materials on Jurisdiction of Courts,* 1931; *Medina's New York Civil Practice Manual,* 1932; (editor) Bostwick's *Lawyers' Manual* (fourth edition), 1934; *Digest of New York Statute Law,* 1941; *Summary of New York Pleading Practice and Evidence,* 1941; *Judge Medina Speaks,* 1954; *The Anatomy of Freedom,* 1959. **Cause of death** Undisclosed, at age 102.

GARY MERRILL

American Actor

***Born* Hartford, Connecticut, 2 August 1915**

***Died* Falmouth, Maine, 5 March 1990**

It is tempting to conjecture what Gary Merrill's future might have been, had he known that the pinnacle of his career was reached when he was only 35 years old. The film was *All About Eve,* when he portrayed the young stage director who was in love with the ageing, tempestuous star (Bette Davis) being undermined by an ambitious protégée (Anne Baxter). Written and directed by Joseph L. Mankiewicz and co-starring the stalwart cast of George Sanders, Celeste Holm, Thelma Ritter and a few minutes of a young and breathy Marilyn Monroe, the film won an Oscar for Best Picture — and, in no time, the status of a classic.

In what is considered another of those Tinseltown tales, both Merrill and Davis identified with their characters so completely that they carried on playing the duo for the next ten years, officially. (Merrill divorced his wife, Barbara Leeds, first, although with indecent haste, according to the censorious press.) Two more films with the Davis/Merrill (as opposed to the Merrill/Davis) team followed: an unintentionally amusing English thriller, *Another Man's Poison,* a title which critics felt summed up the female lead star. Gossip columnists referred to Davis as "a middle-aged matron" and to Merrill as "Mr Bette Davis". *Phone Call from a Stranger,* in 1952, left Merrill the lion's share of the action, as a survivor of a plane crash visiting the families of the dead. Neither film proved healthy for the couple's careers. Later that year, however, Merrill gained more praise for his deft portrayal of a man who believes he has committed a murder, in *Night Without Sleep.* More conjecture is possible: without this success, Merrill's career could have sunk without further ripple.

The son of an insurance salesman, Merrill's stage career began, not quite as the spear-carrier, but as a crowd member in *The Eternal Road* in 1937. Later that year he toured in a production of *Brother Rat,* worked in radio, the Helen Hayes Theater, then the Theater Guild. As a result of his first screen performance, in the 1944 *Winged Victory*, directed by George Cukor, he was offered the plum role of the reporter in the stage version of *Born Yesterday* with Paul Douglas, two years later.

Darryl Zanuck was also impressed with his performance in the small role of an air force commander in the 1948 film, *Slattery's Hurricane,* and signed him to a contract with Twentieth Century-Fox. Although he played well in several films within the next few years, notably as the demoralized CO replaced by Gregory Peck in *Twelve O'Clock High,* and as the villain in *Where the Sidewalk Ends,* his craggy good-looks and bushy eyebrows stereotyped him, in true Hollywood-Machine fashion, as the dour, determined — and limited — character. *All About Eve* was a departure, and gave a glimmer, to the perceptive, of what else Merrill could handle. What he could not handle was Davis.

Merrill was the last of Davis's four husbands, but it appeared that his was the only photograph still hanging on her wall by the 1980s. In 1989 he said, "Subconsciously we just went on after the movie was finished. As the demands of real life set in, we realized the premise was wrong." The marriage had also not done much for Merrill's career, an unexpected result. Roles for the two of them became fewer, and Fox was growing disenchanted. Both settled for a life of domesticity in Connecticut. Davis was quoted as agreeing with her ex-husband's analysis of their marriage: "He wanted to believe that I was Margo Channing. I thought he was Bill Sampson, this strong, protective, secure man...most of all I resented the waste of his talent. I could tolerate everything else, if he had shown some discipline." "I had no drive, really" Merrill agreed. And the difficulty of living in his wife's shadow caused him to seek solace elsewhere, primarily in the bottle. After a disastrous tour of 67 cities, where the two of them read Carl Sandburg's works, they divorced in 1960.

Merrill then embarked on a long, well-publicized relationship with Rita Hayworth. His autobiography, *Bette, Rita and the Rest of My Life,* details his weakness for older screen goddesses.

Merrill's films after his marriage ended were primarily "B" ones, including *The Wonderful Country,* a brooding Western with Robert Mitchum as a gun-runner; *The Savage Eye,* a contrived drama about a divorcée beginning her life again; *Around the World Under the Sea,* an undistinguished under-water tour with Lloyd Bridges (who else?), and *Huckleberry Finn.* He also made appearances in television dramas, and did voice-overs for documentaries. His attempts to rekindle a stage career usually met with good reviews: *Step on a Crack* and *The Hemingway Hero,* both in the 1960s, and *Morning's at Seven,* in 1980, all produced notable performances.

From 1971 Merrill sought solace in a nineteenth-century lighthouse by the sea at Cape Elizabeth, Maine. Politically a liberal, he actively supported Edmund Muskie's successful campaign for Maine's governorship in 1953, and participated in the Selma to Montgomery, Alabama, civil-rights march in 1965. However, his disapproval of President Johnson's handling of the Vietnam war caused him to switch political parties; in 1968 he ran an unsuccessful primary campaign as a pacifist candidate for a congressional seat.

Born Gary Merrill. **Father** Insurance salesman. **Marriages** 1) Barbara Leeds (divorced 1950); 2) Bette Davis, 1950 (divorced 1960). **Children** Michael and Margot, adopted during second marriage. **Education** Bowdoin College, Maine; Trinity College, Hartford, Connecticut. **Military service** US Army, 1941–45. **Career** Regional theatre; first stage appearance, *The Eternal Road,* 1937; first major role, *Brother Rat,* 1937; worked in radio; joined Helen Hayes Theater, joined Theater Guild; first major Broadway role, *See My Lawyer,* 1939; first film appearance, *Winged Victory,* 1944; contract player, Twentieth Century-Fox, from 1949; toured with Bette Davis in *An Evening with Carl Sandburg,* 1959. **Other activities** Supported Edmund Muskie for governor of Maine, 1953; participated Selma to Montgomery civil-rights march, 1965; ran unsuccessfully for Congress, Maine, 1968. **Awards and honours** Monte Carlo television festival award, *Summer Is Forever,* 1970. **Stage** (includes) *Brother Rat,* 1937; *See My Lawyer,* 1939; *This Is the Army,* 1943; *Born Yesterday,* 1945; *At War with the Army; An Evening with Carl Sandburg,* 1959; *Step on a Crack,* 1962; *The Hemingway Hero,* 1967; *Rosebloom,* 1971; *Morning's at Seven,* 1980. **Films** (include) *Winged Victory,* 1944; *Slattery's Hurricane,* 1948; *Twelve O'Clock High,* 1949; *Where the Sidewalk Ends,* 1950; *All About Eve,* 1950; *Decision Before Dawn,* 1951; *Another Man's Poison,* 1951; *Phone Call from a Stranger,* 1953; *Night Without Sleep,* 1952; *Blueprint for Murder,* 1953; *The Human Jungle,* 1954; *The Black Dakotas,* 1954; *Bermuda Affair,* 1956; *The Wonderful Country,* 1959; *The Pleasure of His Company,* 1961; *The Woman Who Wouldn't Die,* 1965; *Around the World Under the Sea,* 1966; *Destination Inner Space,* 1966; *Catacombs,* 1966; *The Power,* 1968; *Huckleberry Finn,* 1974; *Thieves,* 1977. **Television** (includes) *The Mash,* 1954; *Young Dr Kildare,* 1973; *Summer Is Forever,* 1970; *Reporter,* 1974; *The Making of Liberty* (narrator), 1986. **Publication** *Bette, Rita and the Rest of My Life* (autobiography), 1989. **Cause of death** Lung cancer, at age 74.

VICE-ADMIRAL WILLIAM RABORN

American Naval Officer and Intelligence Chief

Born **Decatur, Texas, 6 June 1905**

Died **McLean, Virginia, 7 March 1990**

William Francis "Red" Raborn was a good example of the sort of technocratic naval officer who has come to prominence in the age of air power and the guided missile. He was responsible, in the late 1950s, for the development of the Polaris underwater missile, a weapons system which has had a profound effect on the balance of nuclear terror ever since.

Latterly Raborn achieved an unhappy notoriety as one of the more controversial directors of the Central Intelligence Agency in recent times. It would not be too much of an exaggeration to say that he was laughed out of the job as a political innocent.

Raborn was born the son of a Baptist preacher in Texas, but his secondary education was in Oklahoma. At an early age he decided on a career in the Navy, and attended the US Naval Academy at Annapolis, Maryland. He was commissioned as an ensign in 1928 and also completed a degree in sciences. For the next eleven years he served on a succession of ships as a junior gunnery officer, but in 1933 applied for a place on the Naval Air Station's flying course at Pensacola, Florida. He qualified as a pilot the next year.

A series of appointments with carrier fighter squadrons followed, including an experimental cold weather cruise off Alaska on board USS *Ranger* in 1936. Until 1940 Raborn alternated sea service with a term as flying instructor at Pensacola. In 1940 he helped set up an Aviation Gunnery School at Barbers Point in the Hawaiian Islands, and was at this post when the Japanese attacked Pearl Harbor in December 1941. Later he ran the Free Gunnery School at Kaneohe Bay.

Raborn in fact spent most of the war in aviation training rather than on combat duty; the final such appointment was in the office of the deputy chief of naval operations for air in 1943. In 1944 he at last got a chance to see active service, as the executive officer on board the aircraft carrier USS *Hancock.* On 7 April 1945 *Hancock* was struck in the flight deck by a Japanese bomb, and Raborn was directly responsible for controlling the raging fires in what has always been the highest risk area of an aircraft carrier.

While he was still serving on *Hancock* Raborn was promoted to captain, in March 1945. In the immediate post-war period he served as chief of staff to a task force and carrier group in the Pacific, then as operations officer for Fleet Air Command on the American West Coast. In 1949 came the first of a number of appointments which were to involve him totally in a new breed of weaponry, guided missiles. For a year he worked at the Bureau of Ordnance in Washington, DC, on this subject.

His first sea command, between July 1950 and August 1951, was USS *Bairoko,* stationed off Japan. There followed a spell at Naval War College in Rhode Island, then a job at Naval Operations as assistant director of the guided missile division. Raborn's last sea-going command was USS *Bennington,* but a few weeks after he took over, in April 1954, the ship was devastated by a chain reaction of explosions while on manoeuvres off Newport, Rhode Island. Ninety-one of the crew were killed, and although Raborn was commended for his handling of the disaster, he never took *Bennington* to sea again.

In December 1955, after a period on the operations staff of the Atlantic Fleet, he was chosen to head a project to which not many in the Navy attached much urgency, that of developing a submarine-launched missile system.

The Fleet Ballistic Missile Program or, as it came to be known, the Polaris project, turned out to be one of the big success stories in post-war weapons development, and to a large extent this was due to Raborn's administrative ability. Always the man for achieving practical results by dint of organization and hard work, he managed to deliver a workable underwater missile system a full three years ahead of schedule.

Two decisions have been seen as crucial to the success of the Polaris project. One was Raborn's decision to concentrate on producing a missile of a much shorter range than originally envisaged, of no more than 1500 miles. This lessened fuel and other physical requirements and made the goal that much more feasible. The other was the choice of rocket. Initial planning had involved the Jupiter rocket, whose liquid fuel was known to be highly volatile. Raborn was persuaded by the hydrogen bomb expert, Edward Teller, that a solid fuel rocket, which would in addition be much smaller, was essential.

The first successful launch of a Polaris missile, in July 1960, was not only well ahead of schedule but dead on target as well. By 1961 the United States had its first missile-equipped submarine, the *George Washington,* in commission. The impact of introducing Polaris was immediate. Strategically, it gave the West a whole new edge in the nuclear arms race, since a force of submarines, which could fire intercontinental missiles from anywhere in the world's oceans, presented the Soviet Union with a formidable challenge. Politically, Polaris has had the advantage of being a weapons system which other Nato governments, such as the UK and France, could take on board, without incurring the odium of having nuclear missiles stationed on their soil.

Raborn's next assignment for government was of a completely different nature. After retiring from the Navy in 1963, he spent the next two years as vice-president of the Aerojet General Corporation in California. But in April 1965, President Johnson asked him to take over the Central Intelligence Agency. Johnson, by his own account, had searched the country for the right man, and could find none better than Raborn. The President was thoroughly dissatisfied with the CIA's contribution to the Vietnam war, and thought that a proven administrator like Raborn would provide better intelligence and show a greater flair for clandestine operations.

It proved a considerable misjudgement. Raborn was undoubtedly a good organizer, but as director of the CIA he showed little political awareness and, if even some of the stories told are true, a remarkable ignorance of world affairs. The story goes that at a meeting with the political analyst Ray Cline and others, Raborn was being briefed on the continuing dispute between China and the Soviet Union. His first response was to ask, "Do we have positive proof of it?"

The CIA had a reputation for being full of unorthodox intellectuals with an alarming tendency to concoct their own remedies for the world's ills. Raborn clearly needed to exert some control, but his inability to get along with his academic advisers soon had the entire Agency at sixes and sevens. Cline, for instance, who had led the immoderate laughter at Raborn's ignorance, was soon transferred to a post in Germany. Raborn relied increasingly on non-academic personnel, and trawled the ranks of retired agents to bring in people more congenial to him. Morale went into a tailspin.

Some changes were welcome, and showed Raborn at his innovative best. The introduction of computers to cope with the Agency's daily torrent of information was essential. A more selective type of recruiting was begun at the universities in an effort to get the right mix of intelligence and practicality in personnel. But there was no denying Raborn's failure to get the CIA behind him, or to overcome its institutional quirks. He resigned in June 1966 after hardly a year in office, and retired to the world of business.

Born William Francis Raborn Junior. **Parents** William Francis, Baptist preacher, and Cornelia (Moore) Raborn. **Marriage** Mildred T. Terrill, 1955. **Children** Priscilla and William. **Education** US Naval Academy, Annapolis, Maryland, BS, 1928. **Naval career** Ensign, 1928; sea duty, 1928–40; USS *Texas,* USS *Twiggs,* USS *Dickerson,* USS *Ranger,* USS *Portland;* naval aviator, 1934; co-founder, Aviation Gunnery School, Barbers Point, Hawaii, also officer-in-charge, Free Gunnery School, Kaneohe Bay, Hawaii, 1940–42; in office of deputy chief of naval operations for air, 1943; executive officer, USS *Hancock,* 1943–45; made captain, 1945; chief of staff, Task Force 77, Western Pacific, 1945–47; operations officer, Fleet Air Command, West Coast, 1947–49; guided missile research and development, Bureau of Ordnance, Washington, DC, 1949–50; commander, USS *Bairoko,* 1950–51; Naval War College, Newport, Rhode Island, 1951–52; assistant director, Guided Missile Division, Office of Naval Operations, 1952–54; commanding officer, USS *Bennington,* 1954–55; assistant chief of staff to commander-in-chief, Atlantic Fleet, 1955; director, Office of Special Projects, Polaris project, 1955; deputy chief, Naval Operations (Develt), 1962; retired as admiral, 1963. **Civilian career** Vice-president, program management, Aerojet General Corporation, Azusa, California, 1963–65, industrial consultant; director, Central Intelligence Agency, 1965–66; president, W.F. Raborn Company Incorporated, McLean, Virginia, 1966–86. **Related activities** Director: Curtiss Wright Corporation, Avemco, E-Sys Incorporated, S.A.I. Corporation, Wackenhut Corporation. **Awards and honours** Silver Star, 1945; Bronze Star Medal, 1951; Commendation Medal, 1954; Distinguished Service Medal, 1960; National Security Medal, 1966. **Cause of death** Cardiac arrest, at age 84.

WALTER ROBERTS

American Climatologist

***Born* West Bridgewater, Massachusetts, 20 August 1915**

***Died* Boulder, Colorado, 12 March 1990**

Global warming, the greenhouse effect and man's damage to the atmosphere are common topics of conversation these days. Destruction of the ozone layer causes widespread concern. Climatology is a recognized science, and learned conferences on possible changes in climate occur frequently. Yet the concentration on these topics is very recent, and people like Walter Roberts, who studied climate and the factors that affected it over many decades, are very rare. Indeed he played a crucial role in defining the science of climatology, and from the 1940s onwards not only did he carry out pioneering work in his studies of the sun and climate, but he established centres where bands of scientists could pursue such studies, including the High Altitude Observatory and the National Center for Atmospheric Research in Boulder, Colorado.

Son of a Massachusetts farmer, Walter Orr Roberts would be expected to have more awareness of the atmospheric conditions than a town-dweller. After obtaining his Bachelor's degree in physics and mathematics at Amherst College, Massachusetts, he went for a summer job with the Eastman Kodak Company, and they helped him to go to graduate school at Harvard for which he always felt grateful. When he left Harvard to join the Harvard College Laboratory he told the director of Kodak research, "You know, you've done all this for me, for us, and I took the graduate fellowship with the expectation of coming back to Kodak, and now I'm not coming back to Kodak." The reply came, "If you do well in science, Kodak will be well repaid." And they were.

At Harvard Roberts studied for his Master's degree in solar astrophysics, and it was in February 1939, after his first year there, that he was asked by Donald Menzel to take on the completion of a coronagraph.

In 1930 a French astronomer, Bernard Lyot, had succeeded in building an instrument which, using simple optical principles, had managed to block out the photosphere of the sun in the way the moon does in a total eclipse, and view the corona round the edge. Menzel had seen the two coronagraphs Lyot was operating and had obtained a grant from the Weather Bureau to build one in the USA, in the hope that daily observations of the corona might help predict the weather. He had subcontracted the work to a Cambridge instrument company, and the money had run out before it was completed.

While pursuing his MA degree, Walter Roberts completed the instrument, and in March 1940 managed to secure pictures of solar prominences at a time of moderate solar activity. It was worth going ahead and finding a suitable high altitude station for it.

Menzel had been born in Denver, and he went to Colorado to select a site. A mining company provided one on Fremont Pass at 11,520 feet high. They also put up a small house next to a building which could be used for the observations.

Roberts persuaded his fiancée to marry him in June 1940; they put parts of the dismantled coronagraph in the back of their old car, and headed west. The coronagraph was installed and, by the time of Pearl Harbor, Roberts and his wife, Janet, were taking daily readings of the red and green lines of the corona. They had established a connection between increases in brightness in the corona and later radio storms. This worked sufficiently well for the military to provide support for the research. As the details formed part of Roberts's PhD thesis, it was classified.

Almost every day for seven years, Walt and Janet Roberts carried out the readings in the mountaintop observatory by themselves, but in 1946 the team expanded. Shortly afterwards photographs were obtained of the giant H-alpha prominence, or stream of hot gases from the surface of the sun, later known as "Grandpa". These were studied widely by scientists for the next 20 years.

The observation post was now promoted. "If you are going to incorporate into an observatory," Menzel said to Roberts over the phone one day, "you will need a name." "A name? How about High Altitude Laboratory?" came the instant reply. So the HAO was born.

The observatory expanded, and, in 1952, sent an expedition to Khartoum for the total eclipse of the sun which occurred there. Photographs of the chromospheric flash taken were so good they made all previous ones obsolete, and no new ones are necessary.

Expansion cost money but, Walter Roberts, apart from being a builder, was an enthusiast and a warm friend. Many firms were persuaded by him to contribute funds, and his standing with even the humblest employees was such that they were even willing to forgo a month's salary when times were hard.

By 1955 Roberts and a colleague suggested that sudden changes in the upper atmosphere, caused by "invisible but potent barrages of solar radiation that did not quite reach the earth", were responsible for big weather shifts, though they could not explain how the lower atmosphere was influenced by these bursts. However, in March 1958, when there was an extraordinary number of solar flares, no radical changes in the weather followed.

In 1960 the US government created the National Center for Atmospheric Research, and Boulder, with Dr Roberts as director, was the obvious choice. He described the aim of the centre as attracting some of the most intelligent researchers from almost every branch of natural science, "sparking germinal research at the many institutions with which it is to work, and weaving the results into the grand pattern of furthering all human knowledge about the atmosphere." His interests were becoming wider and were embracing everything from global warming and the nuclear winter to famine and the world's rising population. "I have a very strong feeling", he said, "that science exists to serve human betterment and improve human welfare. It is wonderful to have the opportunity given us by society to do basic research, but in return, we have a very important moral responsibility to apply that research to benefitting humanity."

His fame was growing as his horizons became wider. It was largely as a result of his work and his reputation that Boulder became a centre for space studies and rocket science and research. From 1974 to 1981 he directed the Program on Food, Climate and the World's Future for the Aspen Institute for Humanistic Studies, while he served on dozens of committees and boards including Earthwatch, the World Wildlife Fund, American Academy of Arts and Sciences (of which he was president) and Space Biospheres Ventures.

It was certainly fitting that Walter Roberts was the first scientist to receive the United Nations Environment Leadership Medal.

Born Walter Orr Roberts. **Parents** Ernest Marion, farmer, and Alice Eliott (Orr) Roberts. **Marriage** Janet Naomi Smock, 1940. **Children** David, Alan, Jennifer and Jonathan. **Education** Amherst College, Massachusetts, BA, 1938; Harvard University, Cambridge, Massachusetts, MA, 1940, PhD, 1943. **Career** Operator, High Altitude Observatory, Climax, Colorado, 1940–47, director, Boulder/Climax, 1940–60, director in charge of solar research program, 1947–50; instructor, Harvard University, 1947–48; instructor, Radcliffe College, 1947–48; research associate, Harvard College Observatory, 1948–73; professor-at-large, University of Colorado 1952–56; professor of astro-geophysics 1956–88, professor emeritus, 1988; director, National Center for Atmospheric Research, 1960–70, research associate, 1975–90; director, Program on Food, Climate and the World's Future, Aspen Institute for Humanistic Studies, 1974–81, trustee, 1970–90; (with Russell Schweickart) established national computer dialogue on global warming with USSR (Greenhouse-Glassnost Conference), 1988. **Related activities** Trustee, University Corporation on Atmospheric Research, 1959, president, 1960–73, president emeritus, 1980–90; associate editor: *Journal of Geophysical Research,* 1960–64; advisory committee member, World Meteorological Organization, 1963–68; member, US National Commission for Unesco, 1964–67; editorial board, *Science,* 1970–72, *Journal of Planetary and Space Science, National Science Foundation Journal of History,* 1972; trustee, International Federation of Institutes of Advanced Study, 1971–81, chairman, program committee; member, committee on international environmental programs, 1971–77, National Academy of Science, 1972–73, chairman, committee on arctic science and technology; consultant/committee member, Report on State of Human Environment, UN Stockholm Conference, 1972; member, defense science board, Department of Defense, 1972–75; member, bureau committee on the effects of solar terrestrial disturbances in lower atmosphere, Special Committee on Solar Terrestrial Physics, from 1972; member, subcommittee US-USSR cooperative program on man's impact on the environment, Department of State, 1973–80; secretary, Marconi International Fellowship

Council, from 1974; visiting committee member, Smithsonian Astrophysics Observatory, 1975–78; founding board member, task force on science and technology, Civilian/Military Institute, Air Force Academy, 1975–83; member, Council on Science and Technology for Development, from 1977; board of directors, International Institute of Environment and Development, 1971–76, Worldwatch Institute, 1975–85. **Other activities** Trustee: Mitre Corporation, 1960–90, Amherst College, 1964–70, Max C. Fleischmann Foundation, 1967–80, Charles F. Kettering foundation, 1964–70, Upper Atmosphere Research Corporation, 1971–74. **Offices and memberships** Fellow, American Association for the Advancement of Science, director, 1963–70, president, 1967, member, committee on arid lands, 1973–83; member: American Academy of Arts and Sciences, Royal Astronomical Society, Academy of Independent Scholars, Aspen Society of Fellows, American Rocket Society, American Astronomical Society, Academy of Science, American Geophysical Union, American Philosophical Society, Federation of American Scientists, American Institute of Aeronautics and Astronautics, International Academy of Astronautics, International Society of Ecological Modelling, World Future Society, Council on Foreign Relations, Royal Society of Arts, International Institute of Communications, International Mountain Society, American Council of UN University. **Awards and honours** (include) Bancroft Prize in astronomy, Amherst College, 1938, John Woodruff Simpson Fellowship for advanced study, 1938; honorary DSc: Ripon College, 1958, Harvard University, 1959, Colorado College, 1962, C.W. Post College of Long Island University, 1964, Carleton College, 1966, Southwestern at Memphis, 1968, University of Colorado, 1968, University of Denver, 1969, University of Alaska, 1975; recipient, Hodgkins medal, Smithsonian Institution, 1973; Mitchell Prize, 1979; United Nations Environmental Leadership Medal, 1989. **Publications** (Contributor) *The Sun,* 1953; (contributor) *Vistas in Astronautics,* 1958; (with Paul R. Ehrlich, Carl Sagan and Donald Kennedy) *The Cold and the Dark,* 1984. **Cause of death** Cancer, at age 74.

LORD ROTHSCHILD

British Scientist, Government Adviser and Intelligence Agent

***Born* 31 October 1910**

***Died* London, England, 20 March 1990**

Polymaths must be stimulating company for those lucky enough to move in such circles, but they are not always easy companions. Such a man was the third Baron Rothschild — scientist, businessman, civil servant, counter-spy, writer, bibliophile, cricketer, musician — there seemed no end to his interests and he excelled in all of them. He was also a hospitable host in London and in his beautiful house on the Backs at Cambridge, and a generous friend and patron. At the same time, his temper was on a short fuse — his grandfather had the reputation of being "one of the two rudest men in England" — and Victor Rothschild was never one to suffer fools gladly. Why should he, when he had so many other things to do with his time? Lord Zuckerman, a fellow scientist and a close friend, tells how at the beginning of World War II Victor Rothschild asked him, with a certain bitterness, how he could expect to be taken seriously when he was a Rothschild, a Lord, a millionaire and a Jew, to which Zuckerman laughingly replied that most people would give a lot if they could enjoy even two if his disabilities.

Certainly Nathaniel Mayer Victor Rothschild was born into a charmed circle. One of the seventh generation of the international Jewish banking family, with influential connections in all the capitals of Europe, the world was his oyster from the start. But Victor was never one to take the easy way. Not for him the social whirl of the eligible bachelor or a comfortable place in the family firm. He was always unorthodox, of independent — some would say arrogant — turn of mind. After a conventional education at Harrow, he followed on almost automatically to that next bastion of privilege — Trinity College, Cambridge. But there he broke away and opted for an ordinary pass degree in French, physiology and English rather than the regular grind of Parts One and Two of the Natural Science Tripos. The natural sciences were always a major interest — had not his uncle, the second Baron, been a distinguished international zoologist? — and after graduation he plunged into research at the Cambridge Zoology Laboratory on the fertilization of frogs' eggs, a piece of work which earned him a Fellowship at Trinity in 1935.

At the same time he was keenly interested in motor racing, water skiing, music (he was a gifted pianist, both classical and jazz), and collecting eighteenth-century books and Impressionist paintings. He was also a talented cricketer. He always regretted not getting his Blue at Cambridge, especially since he had played for Harrow and, while still a schoolboy, for his county team when he achieved the feat of scoring 37 against the redoubtable body-line bowling of the mighty Larwood. Typically, he got himself invited to play for his county against the University and knocked up a century! But cricket took up too much time and Rothschild was seriously into his biology. His research on fertilization and parthenogenesis was ultimately to win him the much-coveted honour of a Fellowship of the Royal Society and kept him in touch with the Department of Zoology at Cambridge where he was assistant director of research from 1950 to 1970.

On the outbreak of World War II Rothschild was immediately recruited into the anti-sabotage section of Military Intelligence. This was highly dangerous work, and in 1944 he was awarded the George Medal for a particularly courageous defusing of a bomb. He continued his experiments after the liberation of France, and terrified the servants of his French cousin by testing out high explosives among the treasures of the latter's Paris flat. His more clandestine activities earned him a tribute from President Truman as "one of the world's greatest experts on counter-espionage". It was this period of his life which was to have repercussions later on when rumours began to circulate about his connections with the notorious spies, Burgess, Maclean, Philby and Blunt. Certainly Rothschild knew them well, he was a fellow member of the Apostles (a semi-secret society) at Cambridge; and he never made any secret of his left-wing views — he ultimately took his seat in the House of Lords after the war as a Labour peer. His later connection with Peter Wright, of *Spycatcher* notoriety, brought up speculation that he might be the "Fifth Man", and there were calls in the House of Commons for his prosecution under the Official Secrets Act. (In fact, there is more evidence to suggest that, far from protecting his old friend, Rothschild actually had a hand in exposing Philby.) He publicly called on the Director-General of MI5 to clear his name, and was totally exonerated — though at first somewhat grudgingly — by the Prime Minister and ultimately by the Attorney General. The strain of the long investigations told, however, on a man as proud, and as devoted to the public service, as Rothschild.

Lord Rothschild was always his own man. Rothschilds, he used to say, are quick to take and quick to give offence. And the third Baron was prepared to speak his mind without fear or favour. Never more so than during his three years (1971 to 1974) as the head of Mr Heath's new Central Policy Research Staff in the Cabinet Office (the "think-tank"). It was a surprising appointment for a Conservative prime minister to make, and yet it was an inspired one. Rothschild had already served for ten years from 1948 as chairman of the Agricultural Research Council and then throughout the 1960s as head of the research programme of the Royal Dutch Shell Group. Heath caught him just as he had reached the compulsory retiring age at Shell and was looking around for new fields to conquer. "His time as the founding head of the think-tank was the perfect crown for his career of service to his country in war and peace", writes one of his young recruits, William Waldegrave. His unique blend of scientific and managerial talents could now be put to good use on the country's many problems: the coal industry, shipbuilding, nuclear power, race relations, the computer industry were some of the subjects reported on, and warnings were given of the impending oil crisis. Characteristically, one of the first reports was his own on Research and Development, which put the cat among the pigeons with its revolutionary proposal for the reorganization of all government-funded scientific research and development on the "customer-contractor" principle — an idea based on his commercial experience, and anathema to the worlds of scientists and civil servants. But the think-tank had been set up to be, in the words of another of its members, "the grit in the smooth-running Whitehall machine". Rothschild understood this well, and only a man of his intellectual and physical stature — and, let's face it, sheer wealth and influence — could have faced up to government ministers and the civil service mandarins to highlight the nation's problems. As Waldegrave says, "Rothschild bent his will and intellect, his patriotism and his aristocratic sense of duty to the task of trying to make a reality of a belief he held until his dying day: namely, that there must be rational solutions to our problems."

It was not till he left the think-tank that Rothschild had time to take part in the affairs of his family bank, and then only to sort out family wrangles. One of his last acts of public service was to chair the Royal Commission on Gambling, whose report did much to expose the myriad opportunities for fraud in the industry. But like so many of his exposures, its recommendations came to nothing. This was all of a piece with his general technocratic approach. He was impatient with the amateurishness and inefficiency of much of the British way of life, as reflected in two of his books — *Meditations of a Broomstick* and *Random Variables.* As his sister Miriam used to say, "Every country gets the Rothschilds it deserves", but perhaps Victor Rothschild deserved better than the rather grudging treatment meted out to him by his country. But then, "Renaissance men" such as he are not born for a time of, at best, national stagnation.

Born Nathaniel Mayer Victor Rothschild. **Father** Honourable Nathaniel Charles Rothschild. **Marriages** 1) Barbara Hutchinson, 1933 (divorced 1945); 2) Teresa Mayor, 1946. **Children** Jacob, Sarah and Miranda, from first marriage; Emma, Victoria, Amschel and one son (deceased), from second marriage. **Education** Harrow School, London; Trinity College, Cambridge. **Military service** Anti-sabotage section, Military Intelligence 5. **Career** Fertilization research, Cambridge, 1935–39; succeeded uncle as third Baron Rothschild, 1937; chairman, Agricultural Research Council, 1948–58; assistant director of research, Department of Zoology, Cambridge University, 1950–70; vice-chairman, Shell Research Limited, 1961–63, chairman, 1963–70; chairman, Shell Research NV, 1967–70; director: Shell Chemicals UK Limited, 1963–70; Shell Internationale Research Mij, 1965–70; Shell International Gas, 1969–70; research co-ordinator, Royal Dutch Shell Group, 1965–70; director general and first permanent under-secretary, Central Policy Review Staff, Cabinet Office, 1971–74; director, N. M. Rothschild and Sons, chairman, 1975–76; director, Rothschild Incorporated, 1976–85; chairman, Rothschilds Continuation, 1976–88; chairman, Rothschilds Continuation Holdings AG, 1983–88; chairman, Biotechnology Investments Limited, 1981–90. **Related activities** Director, British Overseas Airways Corporation, 1946–58. **Other activities** Member: BBC General Advisory Council, 1952–56, Council for Scientific Policy, 1965–67, Central Advisory Council for Science and Technology, 1969; Fourth Royal Society Technology Lecture, 1970; Trueman Wood Lecturer, Royal Society of Arts, 1972; Dimbleby Lecturer, 1978; chairman: Royal Commission on Gambling, 1976–78, Enquiry into the Social Science Research Council, 1982. **Awards and honours** Prize-Fellow, Trinity College, Cambridge, 1935–39, honorary fellow, 1961; George Medal 1944; American Legion of Merit; American Bronze Star; Knight of the Most Venerable Order of the Hospital of St John of Jerusalem, 1948; Fellow of the Royal Society, 1953; honorary fellow: Bellairs Research Institute of McGill University, Barbados, 1960, Weizmann Institute of Science, Rehovoth, 1962, Wolfson College, Cambridge University, 1966, Institute of Biology, 1971, Imperial College, 1975,

Royal Society of Edinburgh, 1986; honorary DSc: Newcastle University, 1964, Manchester University, 1966, Technion University, Haifa, 1968, City University, 1972, Bath University, 1978; Melchett Medal, 1971; honorary PhD: Tel Aviv University, 1971, Hebrew University, Jerusalem, 1975, Bar-Ilan University, Israel, 1980; Royal Society of Arts medal, 1972; Knight Grand Cross of the Order of the British Empire, 1975; honorary LLD, University of London, 1977; honorary DUniv, University of York, 1980; Fellow, Royal Statistical Society, 1984. **Publications** *The History of Tom Jones, A Changeling,* 1951; *The Rothschild Library,* 1954; *Fertilization,* 1956; *A Classification of Living Animals,* 1961; *A Framework for Government Research and Development,* 1971; *The Rothschild Family Tree,* 1973; *Meditations of a Broomstick,* 1977; *You Have It, Madam,* 1980; *The Shadow of a Great Man,* 1982; *Random Variables,* 1984; (with N. Logothetis) *Probability Distributions,* 1986; and many scientific papers. **Cause of death** Undisclosed, at age 79.

CHARLOTTE SITTERLY

American Astrophysicist

Born **Ercildoun, Pennsylvania, 24 September 1898**

Died **Washington, DC, 3 March 1990**

The extremely hot, luminous centres of stars emit light in a continuous spectrum, covering the whole range of colours from red to violet smoothly. But as this light comes through the star's atmosphere of cooler gases, particular frequencies of light are absorbed by them, so that when the light is examined on earth, lines on the spectra show the missing frequencies. In this way scientists can tell a great deal about the constitution of the atmospheres of the stars, as well as other qualities such as their speed of rotation and the rate at which they are moving away from the earth. For a considerable time one of the foremost authorities on solar and stellar spectra was Charlotte Sitterly.

She was born Charlotte Emma Moore deep in Quaker country in Pennsylvania. Her father was a superintendent of schools and her mother a schoolteacher and they gave the young Charlotte, and her three brothers and two sisters, a deep love of learning. From the local public schools she moved to Swarthmore College where she graduated in mathematics in 1920, picking up not only her BA degree but the inspiration, from a physics professor, that she should go for a career in astronomy.

She went to Princeton, to work in the University Observatory as a mathematical computer, and her research on atomic spectra and astrophysical problems was with Professor Henry Norris Russell, an eminent astronomer, who had developed a theory of stellar evolution from spectroscopic studies. Five years later she moved to a similar job at Mount Wilson Observatory in Pasadena, California, and it was at the University of California that she obtained her PhD in 1931, with a thesis on the atomic lines in the sun-spot spectrum.

She returned to Princeton University Observatory, where she remained for 14 years, during which time she married Dr Bancroft Walter Sitterly, an astronomer and physicist also working at Princeton.

In 1945 she joined the National Bureau of Standards, and here her remarkable analytical and organizing powers came into play. She was involved in compiling tables of the atomic energy levels obtained from the analysis of optical spectra. These tables became standard works, keeping astrophysicists supplied with the essential laboratory data required for their research into stellar phenomena. She also had many other publications to her credit.

This invaluable work received considerable recognition from professional societies and the US government. She was awarded honorary degrees at home and abroad, and received the Federal Women's Award, which recognizes women who have made outstanding contributions to federal service, the year it was inaugurated. She was also the first woman foreign associate of the Royal Astronomical Society of London.

The careful, systematic analysis of atomic spectra and their publication for use world-wide was only part of her achievement, for she did considerable original research, and her own interpretation of the data gained her wide renown. One achievement was the recognition of technitium in the solar spectrum. This element is produced as a result of atom-splitting in nuclear reactors, but it decays radio-actively and is not found naturally on earth. However Charlotte Sitterly discovered it in the spectrum of sunlight, the first indication that it can exist naturally anywhere, although how it can is not yet understood.

Short — she was less than five feet tall — she nevertheless had a commanding manner. Her concern for international co-operation between scientists was one reason for her keenness to travel. She was also worried about the future provision of scientists, and stressed the importance of basic subjects in education. "I would urge the secondary schools to limit the duties of the teacher to teaching fundamentals if we are to survive as a nation", she said. "Many students today lack the ability to write concisely, clearly and correctly. They need the discipline afforded by language teaching, and they need basic training in thinking such as is developed in scientific studies." These are sentiments that many would echo.

Born Charlotte Emma Moore. **Parents** George Winfield, superintendent of schools, and Elizabeth Palmer (Walton), schoolteacher, Moore. **Marriage** Bancroft Walker Sitterly, astronomer and physicist, 1937 (deceased). **Education** Coatesville High School, Pennsylvania, 1916; Swarthmore College, Pennsylvania, BA in mathematics, 1920; University of California at Berkeley, PhD in astronomy, 1931. **Career** Computer, Princeton Observatory, 1920–25, 1928–29, research assistant, 1931–36, research associate, 1936–45; researcher, Mount Wilson Observatory, 1925–28; physicist, Atomic Physics Division, National Bureau of Standards, 1945–68, Office of Standard Reference Data, 1968–70, US Naval Research Laboratory, 1971–78; retired 1978. **Related activities** Member, committee on line spectra of elements, National Research Council; member, commission on standard wavelengths and spectral tables, International Astronautical Union, 1950–64, commission on fundamental spectroscopic data, president, 1961–67; member, joint commission on spectroscopy, International Council of Scientific Unions, 1950–58, committee on data science and technology, 1966–70; member, triple union commission on spectroscopy, International Union of Pure and Applied Physics, 1960–65; contributor: *Astrophysical Journal, Journal of the Optical Society of America, Journal of Research of the National Bureau of Standards.* **Offices and memberships** Member, American Association for the Advancement of Science, Astronomical Section, vice-president, 1952; fellow, American Physical Society; fellow, Optical Society of America; member, American Astronomical Society, vice-president, 1958–60; honorary member, Society of Applied Spectroscopy; member, Astronomical Society of the Pacific; member, Academy of Sciences; member, Philosophical Society; elected member, Royal Astronomical Society, London, 1949. **Awards and honours** Elected to Phi Beta Kappa, Swarthmore College, 1920; Lick Fellowship, University of California at Berkeley, 1931; Cannon Prize, American Astronomical Society, 1937; Silver Medal, US Department of Commerce, 1951, Gold Medal, 1960; Federal Women's Award, 1961; honorary DSc: Swarthmore College, 1962, University of Kiel, 1968, University of Michigan, 1971; Cannon Centennial Medal, Wesley College, 1963; National Civil Service League Career Service Award, 1966; William F. Meggers Award, Optical Society of America, 1972. **Publications** (include) (With Henry Norris Russell) *Presence of Predicted Iron Lines in the Solar Spectrum of Iron,* 1928; *Some Results from the Study of* *the Atomic Lines in the Sun-Spot Spectrum,* 1932; *A Multiplet Table of Astrophysical Interest,* 1933; *New Identifications of Solar Lines,* 1937; (with Henry Norris Russell) *The Masses of the Stars,* 1940; *Atomic Energy Levels as Derived from the Analyses of Optical Spectra* (three volumes), 1945, 1952, 1958; (with Harold D. Babcock) *The Solar Spectrum,* 1947; *An Ultraviolet Multiplet Table,* 1950. **Cause of death** Heart failure, at age 91.

REAR-ADMIRAL SIR MATTHEW SLATTERY

British Naval Airman and Aviation Administrator

***Born* 12 May 1902**

***Died* England, 16 March 1990**

In 1918, at the end of World War I, the Royal Air Force was formed, and one of its functions was to take over control of naval aviation from the Royal Navy. The Fleet Air Arm remained part of the RAF until 1937, when it was returned to the Navy. During its years under RAF command, a small band of regular naval officers transferred to the Fleet Air Arm and were responsible for the development of deck landings on aircraft carriers and the general tactical principles of using naval aircraft in wartime. One of these officers was a young lieutenant, Matthew Slattery.

Slattery had entered the Navy as a midshipman in 1916, after attending the Royal Naval Colleges at Osborne and Dartmouth. He qualified as a pilot in 1924 and achieved rapid promotion, becoming a captain — the youngest in the Service — in 1938. In these years Britain's naval aircraft and carrier forces were being rapidly built up in preparation for the coming war, and as director of Air Material at the Admiralty Slattery had responsibility for the large-scale production of such aircraft as the Swordfish torpedo-spotter-reconnaissance biplane and the "navalized" versions of the Hawker Hurricane and Supermarine Spitfire fighters. Later he supervised procurement of American carrier-borne aircraft for the Royal Navy.

In 1941 he went to sea again in command of the light cruiser *Cleopatra,* a brand-new ship with an inexperienced crew which was promptly attacked by German dive-bombers as it entered harbour in Malta. Slattery was — perhaps unfairly — accused of "inefficiency" by his superiors and deprived of his command, returning shortly thereafter to the Admiralty as director-general of Naval Aircraft Development and Production, and from 1942 until the end of the war he continued to carry heavy responsibility in this field.

In 1948, aged 46, he retired from the Royal Navy with the rank of rear-admiral. His long experience of administration, an ability to handle detail and deal with committees, coupled with a refreshingly direct manner of speech, fitted him ideally for high office in the aircraft industry, and he became first the managing director and later the chairman of Short Brothers and Harland in Belfast. This company was then working closely with the Bristol Aeroplane Company on the Britannia airliner, and so he became a Bristol director in 1957, as well as special adviser to the prime minister, Harold Macmillan, on the problems of transporting oil from the Middle East after the closing of the Suez Canal. He also became a non-executive director of the National Bank, of which his father H.F. Slattery had been chairman.

Slattery's aviation experience had not extended to the airline business, but in June 1960 he was appointed by Duncan Sandys to be chairman of the British Overseas Airways Corporation (BOAC), a nationalized concern at that time. His appointment upset some of the senior BOAC staff, but he was soon to show himself as an able and forthright leader. The position of chairman of a nationalized corporation is never an easy one, being open to political criticism in addition to the usual commercial disciplines, but Slattery managed to halve the airline's ton-per-mile costs and considerably reduce costs in other areas. He was distinctly sceptical about the commercial viability of the new supersonic airliner Concorde, which was then in the early study phase.

By 1962, in spite of Slattery's economies, BOAC was showing a heavy loss of 64 million pounds. He defended himself forthrightly on the grounds that the government had expected the airline to do much that was not wholly commercial, such as the development of advanced technology, and then to pay interest on the money which it had lost, a policy which he described as "bloody crazy". However, in the following year a new minister, Julian Amory, carried out a further investigation of BOAC's finances and declared that there had been "very serious weaknesses in management", which led to Slattery's resignation in somewhat acrimonious circumstances.

He served for the remainder of his active life in a number of appointments, notably as chairman of R. and W. Hawthorn, Leslie, the company which had built the light cruiser *Cleopatra* which he had briefly commanded in wartime. His delight in the English countryside and its pursuits took him in retirement to Warninglid in Sussex where he was able to spend the rest of his life.

Born Matthew Sausse Slattery. **Parents** H.F. Slattery, banker. **Marriage** Mica Mary Swain, 1925. **Children** Two sons and one daughter. **Education** Stoneyhurst College, Lancashire; Royal Navy Colleges, Osborne and Dartmouth. **Military career** Joined Royal Navy, 1916; midshipman, HMS *Dublin,* 1919; joined Fleet Air Arm, 1924; first sea command, HMS *Winchelsea,* 1935; executive officer, HMS *Sussex,* 1937–38; promoted captain, 1938; director, Air Material, Admiralty, 1939–41; commanded HMS *Cleopatra,* 1941–42; appointed director-general of Naval Aircraft Development and Production, Ministry of Aircraft Production, 1941, chief naval representative, 1943; vice-controller (air) and chief of naval air equipment at Admiralty; chief naval representative, 1943 on Supply Council, Ministry of Supply, 1945–48; retired list, 1948. **Civilian career** Managing director, Short Brothers and Harland Limited, Belfast, Northern Ireland, 1948–52, chairman and managing director, 1952–60; chairman, Bristol Aircraft Limited, 1957–60; director, Bristol Aeroplane Company Limited, 1957–60; Special Adviser to Prime Minister on Transport of Middle East Oil, 1957–59; chairman: British Overseas Airways Corporation-Cunard Limited, 1962–63; chairman, R. and W. Hawthorn, Leslie and Company, 1966–73. **Related activities** Chairman, (SB Realisations) Limited, 1952–60; director, National Bank Limited, 1959–60, 1963–69; vice-chairman, Air Requirements Board, 1960–74; board member: Williams and Glyn's Bank, Swan Hunter Shipbuilders Limited. **Awards and honours** Commander, US Legion of Merit; fellow, Royal Aeronautical Society, 1946; Companion of the Order of the Bath, 1946; honorary doctorate, Queen's University, Belfast, 1954; knighted 1955; Knight Commander of the Order of the British Empire, 1960. **Cause of death** Undisclosed, at age 87.

PHILIPPE SOUPAULT

French Poet, Novelist and Journalist

Born **Chaville, France, 2 August 1897**

Died **Paris, France, 11 March 1990**

"The Surrealist atmosphere created by automatic writing is especially conducive to the production of the most beautiful images... everything is valid when it comes to obtaining the desired suddenness from certain associations". These words by André Breton, co-founder of the Surrealist movement with Louis Aragon and Philippe Soupault, describe both the method and effect of the latter's poetry. William Carlos Williams, the North American poet who became Soupault's friend, wrote, when translating Soupault's novel *Les Dernières Nuits de Paris,* that "there is a simplicity of phrase emphasising the elusive reality of words". This description complements the critic Matthew Josephson's evocation of Soupault's work as "deceptively simple, often gossamer light, like the smoke of his perpetual cigarettes, yet composed of sharp images and dashes of strong colour."

Less than a decade after the inception of the Surrealist movement, Soupault was "excommunicated" from it by his autocratic friend and colleague, André Breton, nicknamed the "Pope". Consequently, Soupault wrote prolifically and variously without quite the recognition he deserved. Breton's "differences" with Soupault seemed to stem from the latter's need to experiment with different forms, including the unacceptably "literary" novel. Although he was accused of betrayal, Soupault's work remained faithful to the inspiration of the Surrealist movement, which was, unarguably, to a large extent his own inspiration. Like Breton and Aragon, he concluded that it had become necessary to resolve the tensions between man's daily life and his inner world, fusing them together at the point where, as Breton put it in one of his most succinct and frequently quoted pronouncements, "life and death, the real and the imagined, past and future, the communicable and the incommunicable cease to be perceived as contradictions". The disparate images which ordinarily flood into the mind unchecked were brought together in the Surrealist poems through the process of automatic writing, or "spoken thought".

Soupault was born rich, related to the Renault family whom he subsequently pilloried in his novel *Le Grand Homme.* His father was a doctor who wrote a standard text on stomach cancer, and young Philippe was educated at the Sorbonne. Breton and Aragon, incidentally, were both medical students. Philippe Soupault's seventeenth birthday was perhaps not the happiest of occasions, as it coincided with the declaration of war in Europe. Improving his English in Folkestone, on England's south coast, he was recalled home and joined the artillery in 1915. A year later he was poisoned by a typhoid injection and spent six months in hospital where he began to write poetry.

The collective experience of the younger generation in World War I was probably the most significant factor in the creation of a Surrealist movement. Soupault described it as causing him "terrible suffering", and felt, as had many Engish contemporary poets, that no one was using art or literature to express this feeling. He labelled the "luminaries" of French thought "imposters" and continued to rail against them in the strongest of terms. "After this four-year war", he wrote, "which conjured up for all those who lived through it tragedy full of blood and fury and also of mud, those who were ironically called *littérateurs du territoire* expected to continue to impose their dictates and exercise their evil influence."

Soupault did not reject absolutely the poetry of his countrymen and spoke of Apollinaire, whom he met and to whom he sent his first volume of poetry, *Aquarium,* in reverential terms: "Guillaume Apollinaire seemed to me to be the only poet who refused to conform and wished to explore a new world; he became my friend and exercised a great influence." Apollinaire introduced him to Breton.

After work at the Oil and Petrol Commissariat, Soupault would meet Breton and walk to the Hotel des Grands Hommes in the Place Panthéon where they would read their poems to each other. Their first composition, and the one which is generally acknowledged to have germinated the seeds of Surrealism as a movement, is *Les Champs Magnétiques.* Soupault described its composition:

> In the course of our research we established that the mind, liberated from all critical pressures and academic habits offered not logical repositions but images, and that if we accepted what the psychiatrist Pierre Janet had called "automatic writing" we could obtain texts which

> would describe a hitherto unexplored universe. Breton and I therefore decided to spend a fortnight in collaboration which we would publish without correcting or erasing anything, and with growing faith we read the texts obtained by this method and decided to publish them under the title *Les Champs Magnétiques*. From this was born what we at first prudently called a method and which we then baptised Surrealism in memory of Guillaume Apollinaire who had used the term to describe his poem, "Onirocritique".

Meanwhile, Tristan Tzara was spreading disorder in Zürich with Dadaism, his mocking, anti-bourgeois art movement. His artistically anarchic influence reached Soupault and his circle and in 1920, the Paris Dadaists arranged a hoax announcement that Charlie Chaplin was about to appear and declare himself a Dadaist. William Carlos Williams, writing of his first impressions of Soupault, expressed bafflement: "He [Soupault] was a very amusing person, really amusing, all wound up in Dadaism. I didn't really understand what Dadaism was, but I liked Soupault."

In 1919 the pointedly anti-literary magazine *Littérature* was founded, with Louis Aragon, Soupault and Breton as its editors. The first Surrealist manifesto in 1924 signalled Breton's intention of establishing a doctrine that demanded absolute fidelity to its stated aims. A year earlier many of the eighteen who signed the manifesto had also taken part in a sustained, published attack on Anatole France. But by this time Soupault had already begun writing novels, like the authors he had once rejected. Breton considered that this was shoring up the barriers of the old guard. Soupault had also opened his own bookshop, Librairie Six. Stirring up a good deal of malicious gossip about Breton in his wake, Soupault was ejected from the movement along with Antonin Artaud, playwright and former director of the "Central Bureau of Surrealist Research". Soupault commented, "I never accepted being excluded. Excluded from what? By whom? Surrealism wasn't a church, a Masonic lodge,...a police regiment."

Perhaps Soupault's interests were too wide-ranging to be contained in Breton's increasingly finely honed theories and strictures. Perhaps Soupault could not accept that a movement of the absurd should have formulated "rules", although the original impetus for the movement came from the notion of creating a new order and energy from the waste of the everyday rather than merely the desire to detonate anarchic tensions.

While North American writers flocked to Paris, Soupault became fascinated by the corresponding trends in their literature and art. In 1930 he wrote *Charlot* (about Chaplin) and *The American Influence in France*. He also taught a course in French literature in the United States.

The second world war had scarcely less influence on Soupault than did the first. In 1938 he founded Radio Tunis at the suggestion of Léon Blum, the Socialist leader, and after a period in the Free French Station in Algiers was consequently imprisoned by the Vichy government for propagandist activities. His 1940 novel, *Les Moissonneurs,* was confiscated by the authorities and has never come to light again. One poem that survived his period in prison was his *Ode à Londres bombardé,* written as a tribute to fellow broadcasters at the BBC World Service. Soupault's career as a broadcaster resumed after his release and following a period of world travel and teaching. He became Director of Foreign Programmes for Radio Télévision Française.

In 1974 Soupault was honoured by the Académie Française, but perhaps a more significant token of recognition was the retrospective exhibition at the cultural centre in Montreuil in 1989. For this, a commemorative album was issued, tracing Soupault's links with other key modernist figures from Marcel Proust, whom he had met as a young man, to William Faulkner and James Joyce.

Born Philippe Soupault. **Parents** Maurice, hospital doctor, and Cécile (Dancongnée) Soupault. **Marriages** Two marriages; 2) Meta-Erna Niemeyer, 1936. **Children** Nicole, from first marriage; Christine, from second marriage. **Education** Lycée Condorcet, Paris; Sorbonne, Paris. **Military service** French Army, 1914–18. **Career** First volume of poetry published, 1917;

joined Oil and Petrol Commissariat, Paris, 1919; founded (with André Breton and Louis Aragon) *Littérature,* 1919; founder, Surrealist movement, 1922, expelled 1926; opened Librairie Six bookshop, 1923; first novel appeared, 1923; journalist; travelled: Europe, 1925–28, United States, 1929 and USSR, 1930; founded Radio-Tunis, 1938, director, 1938–40, ousted by Vichy government, 1940; arrested and imprisoned, around 1941; faculty, Swarthmore College, 1944; American emissary, provisional government of de Gaulle; director of foreign broadcasts, Radio Télévision Française, programme producer; editor, *Europe Revue.* **Awards and honours** Poetry grand prize, Académie Française, 1974; grand prize, Society of Men of Letters, 1977; Saint-Simon prize, for *Mémoires de l'oubli, 1981.* **Exhibitions** *Philippe Soupault le voyageur magnétique,* Montreuil cultural centre, 1989. **Novels** *Le Bon Apôtre,* 1923; *Les Frères Durandeau,* 1924; *Le Nègre,* 1927; *Les Dernières Nuits de Paris,* 1928, published in English as *The Last Nights of Paris,* 1929; *Le Grand Homme,* 1929; *Les Moribonds,* 1934; *Les Moissonneurs,* confiscated by Vichy police, 1940, never published. **Plays** (With André Breton) *S'il vous plaît,* published in English as *If You Please,* 1964; also: *Vous m'oubliez, La Fille qui fait des miracles, Rendez-vous I.* **Essays and critical works** (include) *Guillaume Apollinaire,* 1927; *Henri Rousseau, le douanier,* 1927; *Lautrémont,* 1927; *William Blake,* 1928, also published in English, 1928; *Baudelaire,* 1931; *Profils perdus, Eugène Labiche, Lautréamont, Collection fantôme,* 1974; *Ecrits de cinéma, 1918–1931,* 1979; *Vingt mille et un jours* 1980; *Ecrits sur la peinture,* 1980; *Mémoires de l'oubli,* 1981. **Poems** *Aquarium,* 1917; (with André Breton) *Les Champs Magnétiques,* 1919; *Ode à Londres bombardé,* 1944, published in English as *Ode to Bombed London,* 1944; *Poésies complètes: Chansons, Poèmes et Poésies, 1917–73,* 1973. **Other publications** (include) *Histoire d'un blanc* (autobiography), 1927; *Charlot,* 1930; *The American Influence in France,* 1930; *Le Temps des assassins,* 1945, published in English as *Age of Assassins,* 1946. **Cause of death** Undisclosed at age 92. **Further reading** H.-J. Dupuy, *Philippe Soupault,* 1957; Michael Benedikt, *The Poetry of Surrealism,* 1974.

LORD STEWART OF FULHAM

British Politician

Born **London, England, 6 November 1906**

Died **London, England, 10 March 1990**

A noose hung from the gallery. There were shouts of: "Hang him!" There was a continuous chant of "Ho, Ho, Ho Chi Minh". It was 1970; the 1960s — the decade of student protest, of demonstrations against the proliferation of nucelar weapons and against the Vietnam war — had barely drawn to a close. Before the year was out Michael Stewart, foreign and commonwealth secretary in Harold Wilson's Labour government, would find himself out of office for ever. Now, as he stood on a platform before the undergraduates of Oxford University, he faced more immediate evidence of the public hostility his policies inspired.

Stewart is described by contemporaries as a man who "gave the impression of a colourless personality", "a small, neat man with an unimpressive figure and an unattractive voice" and a man with a "greyness of impact". Yet though he eschewed the theatrical in his speeches, he met, time and again, with theatrical gestures in response. Though his views were reasonable and reasoned, they split his party and forced passions to run high — in the House of Commons as well as on the platform where he now confronted a barrage of abuse.

It was his second term as foreign secretary. He was tipped to become prime minister; but he didn't. His high ability and wide knowledge made him one of Wilson's most trusted aides; but he never achieved greatness in the eyes of the world. He was, according to his private secretary, Sir Nicholas Henderson, "an unsung foreign secretary".

Wherein lay his failure to reach the pinnacle of British politics? Many commentators liken him to Clement Attlee; and there are parallels. Like the former Labour prime minister he came from middle-class origins — he was the son of a schoolmaster. Like Attlee, he joined the Labour Party in revolt against poverty and unemployment in the Britain of the 1920s. But Attlee became prime minister in 1945; Stewart, with similar ideals, similar abilities was a fish out of water 15 years later. He was a "grey man" in one of the most colourful eras of the century, the era of Swinging London, The Beatles and the mini skirt.

Even in his undergraduate days at St John's College, Oxford, Stewart was logical, rational and a stickler for detail. Professor Roger Wilson remembers him as the secretary of the University Labour Club.

> On one occasion...a visiting left-wing woman journalist reported in some detail on a visit to the Soviet Union. Among her details was that one of the few important industries free from government regulation was the manufacture of men's braces. Stewart included this in the minutes which he read out at the next meeting. A fussy little man...rose from the back to question the importance of the point. Stewart brought the house down with his, "It's what the lady said."

After Oxford, Stewart taught in schools in London and, after World War II, in Working Men's Colleges, before becoming, in 1945, MP for the London constituency of Fulham East. His first position in the government — after only three years — was as under-secretary of state for war. When the Labour Party moved into Opposition he became housing spokesman and came, for a while, into his own.

For when Stewart spoke in the House he was transformed. Wrote Henderson, "To have any idea of his high quality, you had to hear him address an audience. He came to life on his feet. It was as if he suffered stage fright in reverse. The bigger the audience, the more confident and fluent he became." So he made an outstanding impression in the Commons, particularly for his exposure of the evils of Rachmanism — the exploitation of tenants by unscrupulous landlords. And in 1963 he topped the polls in the elections for the shadow cabinet.

In 1964 when Wilson formed his government he made Stewart minister of education. Stewart was a strong believer in comprehensive education and a critic of exclusive public schools. But, characteristically, he advocated reform of these institutions rather than the abolition many socialists of that generation favoured. He constantly practised moderation and restraint, virtues not always well regarded in the party when political passions were running high.

It was by accident that Stewart, in 1965, first went to the Foreign Office. Patrick Gordon-Walker, the appointed foreign secretary, lost his seat and Stewart was drafted in to replace him. The civil servants who welcomed him were impressed by his good manners, his regard for duty, his intellect, and his commitment to high ideals. When a proposal about disarmament was being discussed, he said to a startled senior official: "You have told me well the interests of Her Majesty's Government. What are the interests of mankind?"

He offered the same blunt humanitarian approach to President Johnson. When the US ambassador in Saigon said that no limit existed to the potential escalation of the Vietnam war, Stewart responded that the US should not just consider what was militarily appropriate but should display, in the words of the Declaration of Independence, "a decent respect for the opinions of mankind."

But high intellect and high ideals were not enough to bring him accolades — or even public respect — over the difficult issue of Vietnam. Labour foreign policy was to maintain a close relationship with the US: to keep President Johnson sweet without yielding to his pleas to send in British troops. But left-wingers thought Stewart too sympathetic to America. When Johnson authorized bombing attacks on the North, they demanded he should condemn the American action. This, Stewart told them, would not be right. The North had attacked America's ally, South Vietnam, and the attacker's territory could not be treated as inviolate.

The alternative to uttering useless condemnations was, in his view, to try to bring both sides to the conference table. He was as good as his word. According to Harold Wilson he helped to steer American thinking towards a negotiated settlement. In December 1965 he appeared on Russian television and appealed to Russia to join Britain in calling a conference of all governments involved in the Vietnam crisis. And, urged to give more emphasis to Britain's positive views about the settlement, he accepted an invitation to take part in a three-day teach-in at the Oxford Union.

Henry Cabot Lodge, the US ambassador, had already spoken for America at the event and had gone down badly. Civil servants uttered dire warnings of humiliation at the hands of a Communist-controlled meeting. But Stewart spoke fluently and powerfully from a few notes, arguing that the Americans were ready for talks without conditions and the Communists were not. And for once, on this occasion, he was heartily applauded.

In 1966 Stewart switched departments to become secretary of state for economic affairs, a role in which he was effectively deputy to Harold Wilson. He did not conceal from his closest friends his hope of becoming prime minister. But at the Department of Economic Affairs (DEA), as at the Foreign Office, Stewart allowed himself to be thrown on the defensive: partly perhaps because of his impatience with what appeared to him to be erroneous criticisms of his policy. The DEA he turned almost wholly into an organ for enforcing a statutory prices and incomes policy. It was a controversial policy, but, as always, Stewart did his duty, even in the face of what he himself called a "harsh, unfriendly atmosphere".

In March 1968 he returned to the Foreign Office where he remained as secretary of state until the defeat of the Wilson government in 1970. This time he confronted not only continuing problems over Vietnam but also the dilemma posed in Nigeria by the secession of the Ibos from the Federation. Nigeria reminded the British government of its promise some years earlier to supply arms in case of need. Now that need had come.

The Labour Party was as divided over this Biafran crisis as it was over Vietnam. Everyone, Stewart included, hated the idea of selling arms and prolonging a war. Yet, he said, "If we refused we were siding with the secessionists and breaking the promise at independence." He won the day; but Harold Wilson used to say that if Stewart had not threatened to resign it would have been difficult to carry the policy through cabinet.

Stewart did have tangible successes. He was gratified by the signing in London in 1968 of the Astronauts Rescue Treaty and later of the Non-Proliferation Treaty. One of the achievements which gave him particular satisfaction was his face-to-face persuasion of President Tito of Yugoslavia to free a British student who had been jailed for six years after a road accident. But over the largest issues of the day his reason and impeccable logic did not prevail. According to his private secretary they had no hope of doing so. Given Britain's economic weakness, the shadow of Vietnam and many residual problems of Empire, he could not, Henderson believes, have stamped British foreign policy with any enduring mark. But by strength of reason and by his integrity, he prevented many possible disasters — serious deterioration in British relations with the US or setting a dangerous precedent for Africa if he had equivocated over Biafra.

Wrote Harold Wilson of these years, "Recalling now the villification and the violence of the demonstrations that marked so much of Michael Stewart's two periods at the FO I have every reason for saying that his critics were as wrong in their misrepresentation of what he was seeking to achieve as in their persistent undervaluation of his untiring efforts, his influence and his achievements." But this could have been no consolation to Stewart in 1970 as he faced that angry audience of Oxford students screaming for his resignation. Nor, after Labour lost power, for his failure to be elected to the shadow cabinet.

In the 1970s he filled other important positions as a backbencher and in 1975 he became leader of the first Labour members of the European Parliament. "But", writes fellow MEP John Ardwick, "he did not enjoy the job. I would find him sitting alone at night in his hotel room with a teetotal drink before him, happy to receive a bit of company but without the will to ask people in."

Yet, ironically, it was at this late stage of a disappointing career that some of his real abilities were recognized by at least one staunch left-winger. Tam Dalyell was Stewart's deputy during his first 18 months in the European Parliament. He writes,

> The obvious quality of his mind and his dignity at all times greatly impressed European politicians of every political hue, and gave a weight to the Parliament that was not so easily attained in the 1970s. As one who had been horrified by his vehement defence at the Oxford Union and elsewhere of the US position in Vietnam and had believed that he was too rigid on prices and incomes policy, I can only pay tribute to his charm and leadership in Strasbourg, Luxembourg and Brussels.

Stewart became Lord Stewart of Fulham in 1979 and he and his wife Mary (also a peer) always stayed on conscientiously to vote in the House of Lords, no matter how late the hour. After Mary's death in 1984 he carried on as before, saying, "To have useful and interesting work to do and enough money and leisure to do it properly, is as much happiness as is good for the sons of Adam." It was a modest, unassuming statement by a man who, in other circumstances, could have achieved real greatness and real public acclaim. Michael Stewart was a man of high integrity and high intellect in an age when passion and personality counted for more in the world of politics than these very solid strengths.

Robert Born Michael Maitland Stewart. **Parents** Robert Wallace, schoolmaster and textbook writer, and Eva Stewart. **Marriage** Mary Elizabeth Henderson Birkinshaw, later Baroness Stewart of Alvechurch, magistrate and hospital governor, 1941 (died 1984). **Education** Christ's Hospital, Sussex; classical scholarship, St John's College, Oxford, first-class honours in classical moderations, first-class honours in philosophy, politics and economics, BA 1929. **Military service** Army Intelligence Corps, 1942; Army Educational Corps, 1943; commissioned and promoted to captain, 1944; served Egypt, Lebanon and Palestine. **Career** Combined studies with work, League of Nations Secretariat, Geneva, 1929–30; assistant master, Merchant Taylors' School, 1930–31; assistant master, Coopers' Company's School, 1931–42; unsuccessful Labour candidate for member of parliament, West Lewisham, 1931, 1935; elected Labour member of parliament, Fulham East, 1945–55, Fulham, 1955–74, Hammersmith and Fulham, 1974–79; member, European parliament, 1975–76; entered House of Lords as life peer, 1979. **Related activities** Lecturer, Workers' Educational Association; vice-chamberlain of Her Majesty's household, 1947–51, comptroller, 1946–47; under-secretary of state for war, 1947–51; parliamentary secretary, ministry of supply, 1951; secretary of state for education and science, 1964–65; secretary of state for foreign affairs, 1965–66; first secretary of state, 1966–68; secretary of state for economic affairs, 1966–67; secretary of state for foreign and commonwealth affairs, 1968–70. **Other activities** President, Trade Union Committee for Transatlantic Understanding, from 1979. **Offices and memberships** President, Oxford Union, 1929; president, H.G. Wells Society, from 1982. **Awards and honours** Privy Councillor, 1964; Honorary fellow, St John's College, Oxford, 1965; honorary LLD, University of Leeds, 1966; freeman of Hammersmith, 1967; Companion of Honour, 1969; honorary DSc, University of Benin, 1972; created life peer, Baron Stewart of Fulham, of Fulham in Greater London, 1979. **Publications** *The Forty Hour Week*, 1936; *Bias and Education for*

Democracy, 1937; *The British Approach to Politics,* 1938; *Modern Forms of Government,* 1959; *Life and Labour* (autobiography), 1980; *European Security: The Case Against Unilateral Nuclear Disarmament,* 1981. **Cause of death** Undisclosed, at age 83.

LOLA SZLADITS

Hungarian/American Librarian
Born **Budapest, Hungary, 11 March 1923**
Died **Manhattan, New York, 30 March 1990**

To Lola Szladits T.S. Eliot was "Tom", W.H. Auden was "Wystan" and Virginia Woolf was simply "Virginia". Not that she knew these famous writers in person; her familiarity — both intimate and scholarly — was with their precious manuscripts.

For 20 years Lola Szladits was curator of the Berg Collection at the New York Public Library, one of the world's most important repositories of English and American literature. She was an expert in these fields with a refined appreciation of the subtleties of English language; yet she was Hungarian by birth and retained the accent which revealed her origins throughout her life. She retained also the exuberance, the sense of humour and the passion which she brought to the post when she first accepted it in 1955. "Whatever Lola wants", she was apt to joke, "Lola gets."

In the auction room she commanded the generous purchase funds with which the Berg Collection was endowed. For petty cash she had to rely on the New York Library's budget and therefore suffered like the rest of the establishment in times of financial stringency. She rose to the challenge; only hours away from the opening of one important exhibition she bought Windolene from her own purse to polish the glass cases before the public were admitted. She remarked at the time — with characteristic frankness — that she thought the library's supply of toilet paper would just about last till the end of the month.

In short, Lola Szladits was a living contradiction of the popular picture of an academic librarian — of a grey, dry, serious, cerebral, prim person. "In an age of drab conformity", writes one commentator, "where librarians seem to care more about user statistics than books, Lola Szladits was a colourful and larger than life figure."

She was born Lola Abel in Budapest in 1923 and obtained her doctorate in Hungary in 1946 before doing post-graduate work in Paris, at the Sorbonne; in London, at University College, and in New York at Columbia University. In 1950 she immigrated to the United States where she worked as an indexer, as a librarian of rare books for the New York Academy of Medicine and then for the New York Public Library. In 1956 she became an American citizen, and in 1969 she became the Berg's curator.

The Henry W. and Albert A. Berg Collection of English and American literature was begun by the two doctors whose name it bears. Its treasures include the manuscripts of Joseph Conrad's novel *Chance,* T.S. Eliot's poem *The Waste Land* and 33 volumes of Virginia Woolf's diaries. Under Lola's direction — everyone from the president of the library to her assistants called Dr Szladits by her first name — its cultural assets were immeasurably increased.

She scoured England to bargain for diaries and first editions to add to the Berg's shelves. In the auction room she was a bold player, turning her face against "crazy" prices but homing in on lots which would suit the Berg — and then heaven help the opposition! In the United States she persuaded authors to think of the collection first when parting with their papers.

By these means she acquired manuscripts by W.B. Yeats, Robert Graves and Saul Bellow. She turned the Berg into the leading centre for Auden studies. She maintained a constant flow of good things into her reading and exhibition rooms on the third floor of the library on Fifth Avenue. And she enjoyed them. She liked to reach for the exact quotation from one of the tens of thousands of documents in the collection. She did not wrap what she had found in the librarian's equivalent of cotton wool.

Of course she was — understandably — protective of the treasures in her care. She was said to defend the Berg and its reputation as a mother tiger defends its cubs, and to those who were impatient of the collection's bureaucratic access procedures she gave short shrift; but to the serious scholar she was a good friend. She did not see the Berg as a musty repository of the past but as a working collection to be used by biographers from all over the world.

"It has to be used." These were her words to Whitney Balliett, who wrote a profile on her in *The New Yorker* in 1984 — the first such article about a librarian in the prestigious magazine's history. "It is alive", she went on. "My role at the Berg is to stand still and allow the collection to grow."

Stand still, she did not. She was a workaholic who lived, breathed and slept the Berg collection. But grow, it did. So, in addition to Auden's notes, she established or expanded files on Conrad Aiken, H.G. Wells, Muriel Rukeyser, Evelyn Waugh, Samuel Beckett, William Faulkner, May Sarton, Washington Irving, Walt Whitman and Oliver Wendell Holmes. "I am buying for eternity", she pronounced.

In 1989, when she organized a show on diarists, it included 50 of her famous authors, among them Elizabeth Barrett Browning, Herman Melville and, of course, Virginia Woolf. Lola liked especially to quote "Virginia" who said, "Fortunately intellect has no gender."

Reflected Paul Fasana of New York Public Library after Dr Szladits's death: "Lola was an original. Her standards, for herself and for others, were high and at times unattainable. Her dedication to the ideal of literary scholarship was fierce. But she was also loving and human." She was no repressive, silent figure, flitting, finger to lip, between the shelves. She was real and alive and passionate — about literature. She should, according to another commentator, "be counted one of the greatest collection-builders of the twentieth century."

Born Lola Leontin Abel. **Parents** Bodog and Margit (Stern) Abel. **Marriage** Charles Szladits, law professor, 1950 (died 1986). **Education** Peter Pazmany University, Budapest, Hungary, PhD, 1946; Columbia University, New York, 1946–47; Sorbonne, Paris, 1948; University College, London, Diploma of Librarianship, 1950. **Emigration** Left Europe for the United States, 1950, naturalized, 1956. **Career** Oriental librarian, Courtauld Institute of Art, London, 1948–50; indexer, National Health Council, New York City, 1950–51; first assistant, rare book room, New York Academy of Medicine, New York City, 1951–55; library assistant, art division, New York Public Library, New York City, 1955; first assistant, Berg Collection, 1955–69; curator, Berg Collection of English and American Literature, 1969–90; council member: Princeton Library, New York, 1979 onwards, Rosenbach Foundation Library, 1980 onwards, *Dictionary of Literary Biography,* 1981–84. **Other activities** Medical secretary, Allied Control Commission, United States Forces in Hungary, 1945–46. **Offices and memberships** Fellow, Morgan Library, Library Association of England; member, Bibliography Society of America, on council, 1976–82; member: English-Speaking Union, New York Historical Society, Keats-Shelley Association of America, director, 1974 onwards. **Publications** (include) *Independence* (exhibition catalogue), 1975; *Book Collecting: A Modern Guide,* 1977; *The Thirties in England* (exhibition catalogue), 1979. **Cause of death** Undisclosed, at age 67.

COMMANDER BRADWELL TURNER

British Naval Officer

***Born* England, 7 April 1907**

***Died* England, 21 March 1990**

Throughout its almost 900 years of service, the history of the Royal Navy is punctuated by famous sayings attributed to many senior officers and admirals. On a night in February 1940, yet another was added to the list by a not-so-very-senior officer. "The Navy's here!" was the cry with which Bradwell Turner led the boarding party from HMS *Cossack* to capture the German supply vessel *Altmark.*

Educated at Christ's Hospital school, Turner joined the Royal Navy as a cadet at the RN College Osborne on the Isle of Wight in 1921, and from there he transferred to Britannia College, Dartmouth. After Dartmouth his career followed the usual route of a "between the wars" naval officer. This was: the training squadron, appointment to a capital ship as a midshipman and, after being promoted to sub-lieutenant, transfer to HMS *Excellent* and HMS *Vernon* for gunnery and torpedo courses. He then went on to the RN College, Greenwich, and his examination for lieutenant.

The outbreak of war in 1939 found Turner as a lieutenant-commander serving as first lieutenant in the Tribal class destroyer HMS *Cossack,* then the leader of the fourth destroyer flotilla (captain, Phillip Vian) of the Home Fleet.

On 13 December 1939 the German heavy cruiser (pocket battleship) *Graf Spee,* had been brought to action and defeated by three light cruisers — *Ajax, Exeter* and *Achilles* — off the River Plate. From the outbreak of war until she was sunk, *Graf Spee* had been doing duty as a commerce raider, and during this time she had sunk nine British merchant ships and had taken almost 300 seamen prisoners. But where were they held? Certainly not aboard *Graf Spee* — all of the ship's company had been landed before she was scuttled — so the whereabouts of these men remained a mystery. There were few friendly ports in the South Atlantic where the raider could replenish with stores and oil fuel to remain at sea for any length of time, therefore she must have an auxiliary vessel in company to carry out these very important and necessary tasks. A chance remark by a British merchant navy officer who had been in Montevideo at the time of the action, suggested that the *Graf Spee*'s supply ship might be the *Altmark* and perhaps the prisoners were aboard her.

For two months *Altmark* hid in the South Atlantic before attempting to make her way back to Germany. Bad weather helped her to pass undetected between Iceland and the Faeroes, but on 14 February she was sighted by an RAF reconnaissance aircraft making toward Norwegian waters. Ships of the fourth destroyer flotilla were ordered to intercept and search, but by the time *Cossack* had made contact, *Altmark* had taken refuge in Jösing Fjord. As the British ship entered the fjord, she was met by two Norwegian torpedo boats whose commander claimed that she had been boarded, inspected, carried no arms and had no prisoners aboard. She was therefore given permission to proceed to Germany using Norwegian waters. When this reply was shown to the First Lord of the Admiralty (Winston Churchill) he was convinced that the prisoners were on board, and he immediately sent a signal ordering Captain Vian to board and search *Altmark* with or without Norwegian co-operation.

During the hours of darkness of 16 February *Cossack* entered the fjord and with a boarding party under Lieutenant-Commander Turner standing by on the fo'c's'le, steered for the enemy. The two Norwegian patrol boats stood passively by, but the German captain altered course and made for *Cossack,* intending to ram. Instead the German ship ran herself aground and by skilful use of helm and engines Captain Vian got his ship close alongside the enemy. As the two ships came together, Turner jumped on to *Altmark's* deck, and it was then that he shouted his famous cry, "The Navy's here". While the boarding party made their way, covering all ladders and hatchways, Turner made for the bridge to demand the ship's surrender. After a spirited action, in which the Germans lost four men killed and five wounded, the prize was secured and the White Ensign hoisted. When the hatches were opened 299 men poured onto the upper deck. Some had been taken prisoner almost from the day that hostilities had commenced. Transferred to the British destroyers, they were quickly given passage home to Leith, Scotland, where a joyous welcome awaited them.

For his part in the action, Lieutenant Commander Turner received the Distinguished Service Order. He saw further service during the war and was later promoted to the rank of commander. Soon after the end of hostilities he contracted polio and this curtailed his very promising career. Although removed from the active list he remained in the Royal Navy until 1957, his last appointment being naval attaché to Norway. After retirement from the Service he worked for many years as an executive for the electronics firm, Marconi. During this period of his life, he undertook a further challenge: he read for the Bar — by correspondence, and although he passed all of the required examinations, he never practised law. However, his knowledge was put to good use as a JP for Chelmsford, where he was the chairman of the bench for many years.

As well as making a niche for himself in the history of the Royal Navy by his exploits in February 1940, Commander Bradwell Turner made a further contribution to Britain's war effort. In the spring of 1940 a popular song was written called "The Navy's Here" telling the story of the capture of *Altmark*. It was sung with great gusto and feeling by merchant seamen at the Merchant Navy Club in London throughout the war.

Born Bradwell Talbot Turner. **Parents** A.F. and A.I. Turner. **Marriage** Mary G.B. Nixon, 1937. **Children** Three daughters. **Education** Christ's Hospital, Sussex; Royal Naval Colleges Osborne and Dartmouth. **Military service** Joined Royal Navy, 1921; led boarding party from HMS *Cossack* to rescue prisoners on German prison ship *Altmark,* 1940; naval attaché, Oslo, Norway, 1954–57; retired, 1957. **Career** Barrister-at-Law, 1956 (never practised); Marconi Company, 1957–72. **Related activities** Justice of the Peace, Chelmsford, Essex, 1962, chairman of the bench, 1974–77. **Offices and memberships** Member, Institute of Electrical Engineers, 1946. **Awards and honours** Companion of the Distinguished Service Order, 1940; Officer, Legion of Merit, USA, 1945; Officer of the Order of the British Empire, 1951; Commander of the Royal Victorian Order, 1955. **Cause of death** Undisclosed, at age 82.

AN WANG

Chinese/American Inventor and Computer Manufacturer

***Born* Shanghai, China, 7 February 1920**

***Died* Boston, Massachusetts, 24 March 1990**

In the brief history of computing, individuals who are both inventors and successful entrepreneurs are hard to find. Dr An Wang was such an individual, and anyone who has experienced the amazement and delight of switching from a typewriter to a screen-based word-processor can attest the importance of at least one of his inventions.

Wang held 40 patents altogether. Although the word-processor is perhaps his most enduring and familiar contribution to Information Technology, and is certainly the one which made him a multi-millionaire, his first invention arguably played a more important part in computer history. This was "core memory" which Wang invented in 1948, only weeks after joining the Harvard Computation Laboratory and encountering computers for the first time. By allowing the computer to store information in a reasonably compact way, and to retrieve it at high speed, core memory made high-speed computer processing possible in the two decades before the microchip.

Wang had arrived at Harvard via a circuitous and often arduous route from his native Shanghai. Despite the fact that he had been born into a loving family, first the civil war between Communists and Kuomintang, and then the Japanese invasion of China, had separated him from his family and made his youth lonely and sad. He lost both his parents and his elder sister during World War II. Accentuating the positive, he said in his autobiography that his early isolation had given him confidence and self-sufficiency.

It was convenient for him to attend the school where his father taught, in the small town of Kun San 30 miles from Shanghai. This school had no classes below the third grade, however, so Wang started his education alongside children two years older than he was. He was well able to keep up, and soon showed a notable flair for mathematics — though he was so much smaller than his classmates that he afterwards joked that in their football games, he was not so much a goal-keeper as a target. At home his family taught him English and instilled the traditional values of Confucian philosophy. In his early teens he became a boarder at Shanghai Provincial High School, and at 16 he was ready to begin his higher education in electrical engineering at Chiao-Tung University in Shanghai, having come top in the entrance examination.

Shanghai's strategic importance made it a target for the Japanese. They occupied the city in 1937, at the end of Wang's freshman year. The university moved for safety into the French Concession. This area, set aside for French traders to carry on their business, was secure from the Japanese, at least until Europe entered the war. From then on, Wang and his fellow-students pursued their undergraduate studies in what was in effect a nine-square-mile island in the middle of the war zone.

On graduation Wang spent a year as a teaching assistant at the university. Wanting to contribute to the war effort and realizing that the Japanese would soon penetrate the concessions, Wang and eight of his fellows went to work in Kweilin, in the Chinese interior, at a centre producing radio equipment for Chinese government troops. Still only 21, Wang found himself in charge of his own design group. He enjoyed the challenge of improvising substitutes for components which were unavailable, and said afterwards that he had learned a lot from the entrepreneurial atmosphere which prevailed in Kweilin.

The Japanese advance continued through China. Towards the end of 1944 the Kweilin group had to bale out. Wang had already applied to join a programme whereby Chinese engineers would spend a period as apprentices in the United States. This scheme was designed to ensure that China had the knowhow it would need in the post-war reconstruction period. Wang was accepted.

After a long journey, the latter part by sea from Calcutta, Wang arrived in the US in June 1945. The looked-for apprenticeship was not immediately forthcoming, but in the meantime Wang and some colleagues were accepted by Harvard as post-graduate students. Wang took a Master's degree in applied physics after a mere two semesters. As no more funding for Chinese students was forthcoming from China, Wang's friends at Harvard arranged teaching work and scholarships to allow him to do a PhD. His speciality was nonlinear mechanics; he had no involvement at that time with the top-secret, defence-orientated computer development which was going on at Harvard under Howard Aiken, designer of the pioneering Mark I computer.

After 16 months' work, Wang had completed his PhD studies. By 1947 the outcome of the civil war in China was a foregone conclusion. Wang did not want to return to China under the Communist regime, which he felt would not allow him the freedom he had experienced in the US. Accordingly he began to look for a job.

He regarded the fact that he went into computing at all, like much else in his life, as a matter of luck. Apart from courses he had taken in digital electronic circuitry while doing his PhD, he knew little about it. He had in fact applied for a job with an aeronautic engineering firm, and it was only disheartenment with the bureaucracy of the application forms that made him wander into the computation laboratory to see if there was any chance of a job with Howard Aiken.

In May 1948 Wang began work as a research fellow under the redoubtable Aiken. By now computer research had refocused away from defence applications and towards the development of a general-purpose computing machine, the Mark IV. Work was being hampered by the fact that all the information storage devices available, such as the rotating magnetic drum, involved mechanical movement before the information could be written or read. Not only did this make them subject to breakdown, but it also restricted the speed of computation.

As his first task in the lab, Aiken asked Wang to solve this critical problem of writing and reading magnetic information without mechanical motion. Aiken can hardly have anticipated how quickly Wang would come up with the solution — he had the germ of an idea immediately and in a few weeks had a fully-worked-out method.

Wang decided to represent each binary digit or "bit" of information by the magnetic direction or flux of a small doughnut-shaped piece of magnetic material, called a core. (The doughnut shape was chosen because it required only a small electric current to create the required magnetic field.) A positive flux could represent a binary one and a negative flux a binary zero. The information could be read by trying to remagnetize the core, which would generate an electric pulse if the flux was successfully changed. The realization that this method of reading would destroy the information at first posed a problem for Wang, but he soon realized that the information could immediately be written back again.

Wang's invention of cores was fundamental to computing until the emergence of viable semiconductor technology in the late 1960s, when silicon chips took over as the primary method of storing information. Even after that, cores continued in occasional use, having the advantage that they retain their information even if the power source is lost.

Despite his obvious pride in his invention, Wang afterwards reproached himself for not having gone on to invent the best method of linking the cores together. He had wired them together in a series, but this made it cumbersome to get to a specific bit of data; it was Jay Forrester, from the Massachusetts Institute of Technology, who saw that they could be linked in a matrix structure to allow immediate access to any bit (with half the current required to read or write the bit coming along the horizontal wire and half along the vertical).

However, the basic idea of the core was Wang's and he filed patent applications, fully intending to exploit his discovery. Harvard's interest in computers would soon end, he foresaw, as they were becoming less of an experimental area and more part of mainstream technology. Eager to provide for his family (he had now married and had a son) he set up his own business, Wang Laboratories, opening for business in modest Boston premises on 30 June 1951.

Thanks to diligent attendance at trade shows, Wang made a profit in his first year. Some of his revenue came from wiring up and selling the cores, but an increasing amount came from consultancy, and from contracts to design and build special purpose digital equipment, for instance for counting red and white blood corpuscles. Though none of the devices was of lasting importance to Wang, the facility for digital electronics design which he developed was to become the mainstay of his business.

IBM were becoming interested in his patent for core, which Wang offered to sell to them for 2.5 million dollars. Tactics which IBM used in their negotiations were alleged by Wang to have involved playing him off against another inventor with a supposedly conflicting patent claim. With or without foul play, IBM succeeded in buying the patent for 400,000 dollars.

Wang refused to be embittered by what he regarded as IBM's unfair dealings with him. In the late 1950s, he used the money to develop new products for his company to sell, including the Weditrol, a digital control device for machine tools such as lathes, and a precursor of the industrial robots which are so prevalent today. He became involved with a firm called Compugraphics, which specified a phototypesetting machine to be designed and manufactured by Wang's firm. Sales of this successful machine, the Linasec, took Wang turnover past the million-dollar mark for the first time in 1964. When, the following year, Compugraphics decided to take over the manufacture of the machine, Wang needed a new product, quickly.

Fortunately the Laboratories were on the point of launching LOCI, the "logarithmic calculating instrument" machine for scientific use, which was shortly followed by the more user-friendly, business-orientated Model 300. Though described as desk-top calculators, the machines were large (the Model 300 had its processor separate from the keyboard so that the former could be put on the floor under the desk). They were also incredibly expensive by the standards of today's calculators (6500 dollars for the LOCI and 1695 dollars for the Model 300).

However, the calculators were a completely new idea and filled an unmet need "somewhere between the slide rule and the minicomputer" as Wang afterwards said. They were very popular and took sales to 6.9 million dollars in 1967. By this time the company had 400 employees and an international sales network with offices in the UK, Belgium and Taiwan. The company went public to great acclaim — the shares were offered at 12.50 dollars and at the end of the first day's trading were selling at 40.50 dollars. Wang was convinced that the success of the float was partly due to the popularity of his calculators with Wall Street traders. The Wang family retained a controlling interest in the company.

By 1970, however, the price of calculators was dropping rapidly. Wang had another important hunch: with the advent of microchips, he foresaw that calculators would soon become even cheaper. It would be no market for a firm like his, which was not in the business of manufacturing chips. Despite the fact that calculators represented 70 per cent of his sales, and in the teeth of vociferous opposition from his colleagues, he decided to get out of calculators.

Wang had begun to dabble in general purpose computers, having bought a data processing company, Philip Hankins Inc., to gain programming expertise. He had developed two computers and was soon to launch another, the 2200, precursor of the VS range. Wang Laboratories had been experimenting with one of IBM's early editing typewriters, and now Wang had the idea of applying computer technology to the editing of office text. The 1200, their first offering in the word-processing market, was launched in 1971 and was not all that dissimilar to the IBM editing typewriter, in that it did not have a display screen.

In the mid-1970s came the breakthrough: a brand-new, screen-based word-processor. The prototype was unveiled at a trade show in New York and aroused unprecedented interest, with prospective customers queueing ten-deep to see the machine demonstrated. And they liked what they saw. Menu-based programs made the machine outstandingly easy to use.

Sales rocketed, boosted by television publicity campaigns pitting Wang as David against the Goliath of IBM. The analogy worked: the word-processors were a unique product which enabled Wang to gain a foot-hold in blue-chip companies previously locked into buying from IBM. Often Wang could sell mini-computers on the back of the word-processors. Sales topped 2 billion dollars in 1984.

The company was able to dominate the office automation market for a decade, but sadly, by the time An Wang died, his luck seemed to have changed. Competitive word-processing systems had proliferated. The trend in Information Technology was towards standardization of desk-top equipment based around the IBM Personal Computer range and Unix networks. Wang Laboratories ignored this trend for too long, providing compatibility between its own products but not attempting to comply with the industry standard. The company lost 424 million dollars in fiscal 1989, and, at the time of An Wang's death, was embarking on a radical restructuring programme involving extensive redundancies and asset sales in an attempt to avoid the threat of a take-over.

Though Wang came in for personal criticism over his company's problems, he had in fact retired in 1986 and had been replaced as president by his son Frederick. When the company ran into serious problems in 1989, An Wang intervened to bring in a new president, Richard Miller, from outside the company. The family continue to be represented on the board of the company and to have a controlling interest in it.

Wang always put his successes down to common sense and adaptability combined with luck, rather than to genius. His leadership style tended towards the democratic except when a firmly-held conviction led him to overrule his colleagues, for instance when he decided to get out of calculators. He did his best to foster the abilities of his staff, to the extent that he was sometimes taken to task for his reluctance to recruit management externally.

Much of the personal wealth that he accrued was used to make generous academic, civic and medical endowments. He was proud of having buildings and institutes named after him, not from personal vanity but from pride in his origins. When he started his company, and later, when it went public, he had firmly rejected suggestions that it would succeed better under a less exotic name than his own. An Wang fulfilled spectacularly his ambition of proving to the West that the Chinese were capable of more things than running laundries and restaurants.

Born An Wang. **Parents** Yin Lu, English teacher and traditional Chinese medicine practitioner, and Zen Wan (Chien) Wang. **Marriage** Lorraine Chiu, 1949. **Children** Frederick, Courtney and Juliette. **Education** At school in Kun San; Shanghai Provincial High School; Chiao-Tung University, BS in electrical engineering, 1940; Harvard University, Cambridge, Massachusetts, MSc, 1946, PhD in applied physics and engineering, 1948. **Emigration** Left China for US, 1945; naturalized US citizen, 1955. **Career** Teaching assistant, Chiao-Tung University, 1940–41; engineer, Central Radio Works, Kweilin, China, 1941–45; research fellow, Computation Laboratory, Harvard University, 1948–51; invented and patented magnetic core memory, 1948; owner, Wang Laboratories, 1951–55; president, Wang Laboratories Incorporated, 1955–83, 1985–86, chairman, 1955–90; designed: first electronic typesetter, LINASEC, 1962, first electronic scientific desk calculator, LOCI, 1964, first successful word-processing system, 1972; received 40 patents; founded Wang Institute of Graduate Studies, 1979. **Offices and memberships** Fellow, Institute of Electrical and Electronics Engineers; fellow, American Academy of Arts and Sciences. **Awards and honours** Honorary DSc, Lowell Technological Institute, 1971, South-eastern Massachusetts University, 1981; honorary doctor of commercial science, Suffolk University, 1980; Medal of Achievement, American Electronics Association, 1984; US Medal of Liberty, 1986; US National Inventors Hall of Fame. **Publications** (With Eugene Linden) *Lessons: An Autobiography,* 1986. **Cause of death** Cancer of the oesophagus, at age 70.

WILLIAM APPLEMAN WILLIAMS

American Historian

***Born* Atlantic, Iowa, 12 June 1921**

***Died* Newport, Oregon, 5 March 1990**

In the historiography of the cold war much has changed since the mid-1960s. Before then, because of the prevailing climate of unquestioning anti-Communism, critical accounts of the western powers' relations with the Soviet Union after 1945 were thin on the ground.

The so-called New Left, or revisionist, school of historians which emerged after about 1965 stood the existing orthodoxy on its head. To historians like David Horowitz and Gar Alperovitz it was the

United States, not the Soviet Union, which started the cold war, by ignoring the legitimate security concerns of Stalin's Russia in pursuit of its own imperialist goals. Much of the revisionists' work was quickly shown to be as one-sided as anything produced at the height of the cold war, and their use of evidence in particular was often selective and always polemical. Nevertheless the New Left introduced a breath of fresh air into the cold war debate, and at least encouraged Americans to think more critically of their role in the world.

The man who more than any other can be said to have sparked off this controversy was William Appleman Williams. His *The Tragedy of American Diplomacy,* though published in 1959, only started to make an impact on the historical profession some years later. In its basic premises, as well as its weaknesses, however, Williams's work contained all the ingredients of the New Left revisionism. It attributed the breakdown in superpower relations to American policy, and was frankly apologetic for the Soviet Union. It also expressed something unusual in American historiography, a distaste for power politics as such, which imbued all of Williams's work.

Williams was born on a farm in Iowa, and received his higher education as a cadet at the Naval Academy in Annapolis, Maryland. He did a degree in engineering, and upon graduating was almost immediately swept into the war in the Pacific. He was wounded and spent more than a year recovering.

With the war over, Williams's career took a totally new direction. He enrolled as a graduate student in history at the University of Wisconsin, completing his MA and PhD there. His doctoral thesis was on the United States' reaction to the Bolshevik Revolution of 1917 and showed, for the times, a remarkable readiness to criticize American policy. As a young man, Williams made no secret of his interest in Marxism, and his choice of subject may well have been a principled protest against the current McCarthyite witch-hunts. Out of this subject came the material for his first published work, *American-Russian Relations, 1781–1947,* in 1952. This, and the subsequent *The Shaping of American Diplomacy, 1750–1955,* were typical of all Williams's books in that they covered a very large time-span.

In 1957 he secured a teaching appointment at Wisconsin, where he remained until 1968. In the latter year he transferred to the history faculty at Oregon State University.

His early research encouraged him to see a connection between the American frontier mentality, made famous by the historian Frederick Jackson Turner, and American foreign policy. United States governments from a very early point in the country's history, he suggested, reflected an innate urge to expand which did not stop at the physical frontiers of the United States but, in the twentieth century, had continued outwards.

The Tragedy of American Diplomacy was the logical fruit of these reflections. At its core was the contention that American policy since the turn of the century had been determined by the drive to establish an "Open Door World". This meant the free movement of goods and capital, which the consolidation of Soviet control over eastern Europe in 1945 naturally threatened.

In his explanation of this policy, Williams identified two strands, but never specified which one he considered dominant. Was America's "Open Door" policy (as a Marxist would argue) the consequence of an economic need to export surplus goods and profits? And if so, where did the fact that the United States, in this period, was largely self-sufficient in both raw materials and markets, fit in? Or was American expansion primarily ideological, a doctrinaire fixation with the virtues of free trade and the need to impose American values on the outside world? Certainly there was more to the ideological argument than met the eye; and recently, in the aftermath of the cold war, some scholars have taken up the idea that American policy-makers inevitably evolved an ideology of democracy and free enterprise to counteract the Soviet ideology of communism.

Whether either of these interpretations adequately explained US policy in 1945, however, is another matter. David Horowitz might describe Williams's book as "perhaps the finest interpretive essay on American foreign policy ever written", but other historians pointed out grave inconsistencies in Williams's supporting evidence.

Robert James Maddox, for instance, in a critique of the New Left in 1973, discovered that Williams had frequently conflated different documents to make them appear as if they were a single source; had elided passages in documents which did not support, and in fact often contradicted his thesis; and for some of the most central arguments in his book relied on what could be described as a "proof by lack of evidence" technique. If no evidence had been unearthed to disprove what Williams wanted to prove, then that seemed to make it true in his eyes. "The mortal weakness of Williams' interpretation," wrote Maddox, "lay in his inability to produce even the scantiest evidence that American policymakers actually regarded an Open Door in Eastern Europe as the critical factor, rather than as one of many subsidiary goals, in relations with Russia."

It is hard to avoid concluding that Williams's preference for the broad sweep of historical events, rather than the minutiae of narrower periods, seriously weakened his analysis. As a writer he was inspiring; as an historian his methods left something to be desired. His subsequent publications confirmed this tendency, even down to their titles. *The Contours of American History* appeared in 1962, followed in 1969 by the more ambitious *The Roots of the Modern American Empire.*

By the time the latter book was published not only had Williams's earlier work been seized upon by revisionist historians, but the Vietnam war had altered radically the public mood towards American power. Williams's words therefore fell on a much more congenial soil. His continuing thesis that American history had been expansionist since the eighteenth century now struck many people as essentially true. In a sense Williams was now going beyond his own audience, however, in that he concluded that international trade and overseas commitments, of themselves, produced imperialism and war.

Williams's alternative verged on the Utopian, but has since become the mainstay of radical politics in the industrialized world. According to this, a small state which would be truly responsive to its citizens' needs, and which would have greater regard for the environment, was preferable to the mega-state the US had made of itself.

His last major work, *America Confronts a Revolutionary World: 1776–1976,* published in the bicentenary of the American Revolution, carried these ideas to their logical conclusion. The stress was all on the right of mankind to self-determination, whether as a people or as a community or, ultimately, as individuals.

"The act of imposing one people's morality upon another people", he wrote, "is an imperial denial of self-determination." "Once begun, there is no end of empire except war and more war."

Despite the rough reception of his works by other professional historians, there is no denying that much of Williams's basic message about the United States as an imperial power has sunk in with many Americans. There is less hubristic talk, these days, about America as the "champion of the free world", and a greater readiness to question the economic and ideological roots of American involvement overseas.

Where Williams perhaps went wrong was in neglecting to prove the link between his brilliant *aperçus* and the factual record of American policy. He and his followers have also tended to ignore the extent to which America's involvement in the outside world has been forced upon it, and the element of genuine, if misguided and often self-deluding, idealism which accompanied this process.

Williams retired from Oregon State University in 1986, but continued to teach as an emeritus professor. He spent the last four years of his life in the sort of small community he had come to idealize, at Waldport, Oregon.

Born William Appleman Williams. **Marriage** Wendy. **Children** One son and two daughters: Ward, Kyenne and Savoy. **Education** US Naval Academy, Annapolis, Maryland, BS in engineering; University of Wisconsin, Madison, MA, PhD in American history. **Military service** US Navy, 1941–45. **Career** Associate professor, University of Wisconsin, 1957–1960, professor,

1960–68; professor, Oregon State University, 1968–86, emeritus professor, 1986–90. **Related activities** Fulbright professor, University of Melbourne, 1977; lecturer, Oregon Coast Community College, 1989. **Offices and memberships** President, Organization of American Historians, 1980. **Publications** *American-Russian Relations, 1781–1947,* 1952; *The Shaping of American Diplomacy, 1750–1955,* 1956; *The Tragedy of American Diplomacy,* 1959; *The Contours of American History,* 1962; *The Roots of the Modern American Empire,* 1969; *America Confronts a Revolutionary World: 1776–1976,* 1976; *Empire as a Way of Life,* 1980. **Cause of death** Cancer, at age 68. **Further reading** Robert James Maddox, *The New Left and the Origins of the Cold War,* 1973.

LEV YASHIN

Russian Football Player

Born **Moscow, USSR, 22 October 1929**

Died **21 March 1990**

There is a consensus of opinion among soccer experts that Lev Yashin stands among the greatest — possibly he *was* the greatest — that the goal-keeping fraternity has produced. Certainly, he was one of the first Soviet sportsmen to become a household name outside of his own country, and by the end of his career, his reputation and his popularity transcended all national boundaries.

He was born in Moscow in 1929. As a boy he played ice hockey and basketball, boxed and ran, but in general showed little distinction at sport. At 14 he left school to become a fitter in the Red October aircraft factory, and began to play soccer in the forward line of the works team. Only after doing his national service did he show obvious ability as a goalkeeper; and this was for the Moscow Dynamo ice hockey team. His talent attracted the football side of the same name. They poached him to be groomed as successor to their famous "Tiger" Khomich. When Khomich was tamed by injury, Yashin succeeded him. He came to international attention four years later, when a Soviet team won the Olympic tournament in Melbourne, Australia, and rose to full prominence during the 1958 World Cup in Sweden.

During the first half of the 1960s, the international soccer community saw Yashin at his very best. His inspirational performances brought the Soviets success in two European Nations' Cup Finals (now called the European championships), in 1960 and 1964; once as outright winners and once as runners-up. In between times he was European Footballer of the Year in 1963 and, that same year, delighted the crowd at London's Wembley Stadium on the occasion of the English Football Association's Centenary. Yashin appeared in goal for an all-star side chosen from the cream of international talent, against an English eleven. He produced what was now his stock in trade — the impossible save — stopping a point-blank header from the raucous Bobby Smith of Tottenham Hotspur, and drew storms of applause from the 100,000 capacity crowd. For the 1966 World Cup he was back in England, though, at the age of 36, no longer the automatic choice in the Soviet goal. However, his talismanic qualities were widely looked to when a steadily improving Soviet team met West Germany in the semi-finals. It seemed that the right choice had been made when a sprightly Yashin flung himself to hold a 30-yard free-kick with both hands; but even he could not save the game when a sending-off reduced his team to ten men.

At the age of 40, Yashin broke his wrist in a training session. "My age is beginning to tell", he admitted laconically, and in the next season announced his plan to retire. An invitation match was organized for his swansong: Bobby Charlton of England, Jacinto Fachetti of Italy, and Gerd Mueller of Germany were among those who turned out to pay tribute at Moscow's huge Lenin Central Stadium. After making saves from all of them, Yashin left the pitch to a standing ovation, for the last time.

His career in first-class soccer had lasted 21 years, during which time he'd won the Russian league five times with Moscow Dynamo, and appeared 78 times for the USSR. On retirement, he went into management with Dynamo, and became deputy chairman of the Soviet Football Association. He continued to live modestly in his two-bedroom flat, but did not enjoy continual good health. Always a heavy smoker, he suffered a thrombosis, and had a leg amputated later in his life.

Yashin was tall, lean and long-limbed, which is a good shape for a goalkeeper to be, as it aids aerial ability and reach. Like the other great goalkeepers, he had lightning reactions and acrobatic agility, and like them, too, he possessed the art which hides the art: he could anticipate, see the ball early, pick up its flight, pace and weight in order to position himself and make his job look easy. He kept his most spectacular resources for use in emergencies, and it took the world's best attacking players to push him to that exertion. His fans called him the "Octopus" for obvious reasons, and the "Black Panther" because of the black strip which he always wore on the field. Yashin's love of the game shone through his play, and he was a chivalrous opponent; it was his sportsmanship as well as his ability which made him such an international favourite, and set him alongside the likes of Bobby Charlton and Pele in the popular imagination. An old comrade was Billy Wright, who captained Wolverhampton Wanderers and England. On hearing of Yashin's death he said, "He was a marvellous goalkeeper...we became good friends even though he couldn't speak English and I couldn't speak Russian. His sense of fun came through the black he always wore."

Born Lev Ivanovich Yashin. **Career** Fitter, Red October aircraft factory, Moscow, 1943; goalkeeper, Moscow Dynamo ice hockey team; goalkeeper, Moscow Dynamo soccer team, 1951–72, management from 1972; Olympic gold medallist, Melbourne, 1956; member, Rest of World team, Football Association Centenary match, Wembley, 1963; played in 813 matches; capped 78 times; played in four World Cups, 1954, 1958, 1962, 1966. **Related activities** Deputy chairman, Presidium of the Soccer Federation of the USSR. **Awards and honours** European Footballer of the Year, 1963. **Cause of death** Stomach cancer, at age 60.

APRIL

RALPH ABERNATHY

American Civil Rights Leader and Clergyman
***Born* Linden, Alabama, 11 March 1926**
***Died* Atlanta, Georgia, 17 April 1990**

To live in the shadow of a great and respected man is a difficult and frustrating thing to do. Such was the life of Ralph Abernathy who will for ever be remembered as Martin Luther King's right-hand man. Although he sacrificed and fought as hard as the renowned leader, he would never gain the prominence or respect that was associated with King.

Grandson of a slave, Abernathy was born in Linden, Alabama. His father owned a 500-acre farm in Marengo County, was a great supporter of the local black high school and was said to be the first Black ever to serve on a grand jury in the United States. Abernathy was well educated, taking degrees in mathematics and sociology. However, the turning point of his life came when, as a student at Atlanta, he heard Martin Luther King preach at the Ebenezer Baptist Church. He was later to comment that upon hearing King, "I knew he was a wonderful man."

The two both became pastors in Montgomery, Alabama, in 1951 and quickly became close friends. Four years later when a Montgomery black seamstress, Rosa Parks, refused to give up her seat on a bus to a white person, and was arrested, Abernathy sprang into action. He called a meeting at which he proposed the boycotting of buses by Blacks and, together with King, organized the Montgomery Improvement Association. Their aim was to do away with segregation on buses.

King was elected to the presidency of that organization and Abernathy ungrudgingly took a back-seat position. It was to be the pattern of his career. Years later in an interview he would claim that he never resented King's leadership. "We started out together and I knew someone had to be the leader...We were never rivals."

The boycott lasted one year with the Blacks of Montgomery walking to work or using the 300-car transportation pool that was arranged by Abernathy's organization. On 21 December 1956 they won their fight as buses became desegregated. Fired by their success, King and Abernathy called a meeting in January 1957 at the Ebenezer Baptist Church in Atlanta, of all black leaders from ten southern states, and organized the now famous Southern Christian Leadership Conference (SCLC). It was the beginning of the civil rights movement in the United States.

Again, King was elected president while Abernathy became secretary-treasurer. Both men were now targets for extremists and their lives were constantly in danger. During this conference, Abernathy's home and church in Montgomery were bombed. His wife and baby daughter, who were inside the house at the time, escaped unharmed but the church was destroyed and had to be rebuilt.

What marked the uniqueness of this organization was its firm commitment to non-violence. They subscribed to a programme of civil disobedience as practised by the Indian leader Mahatma Gandhi, but first described by the great American author Henry David Thoreau. Abernathy once stated, "Violence is the weapon of the weak and non-violence is the weapon of the strong. It's the job of the state troopers to use mace on us. It's our job to keep marching. It's their job to put us in jail. It's our job to be in jail." Step by step the movement gained momentum, desegregating restaurants, universities and institutions across the country. King and Abernathy not only shared the work of the organization but, more often than not, a jail cell during their many arrests. Abernathy would later say, "Whenever Dr King and I would go to jail together we would spend the first 24 hours fasting to purify our souls in order that we would have no hatred in our hearts toward the jailer and a stronger determination to tear down the system responsible."

In the early 1960s when the civil rights movement was at its height, King named Abernathy as his successor. It was becoming increasingly clear to King that at any moment he might lose his life and he wanted to be assured of the leadership of the SCLC. In the meantime, both King and Abernathy were concerned that the movement seemed only to be benefiting the black middle class. With the introduction of technology, thousands of unskilled workers, both black and white, were slipping further and further into despair. The SCLC began to focus on getting the United States government to deal with the problems of the poor in the technological age. They launched the Poor People's Campaign in December 1967.

In April 1968 King's prediction of his own death was to come to pass. While standing on a balcony of a motel room in Memphis, Tennessee, King was mortally wounded by a sniper's bullet. Abernathy was standing beside him when the bullet struck and at the risk of his own life stayed on the balcony, cradling Martin Luther King's head.

Now as leader, Abernathy took hold of the reins of the SCLC, vowing to wage "the most militant and aggressive non-violent war ever waged by the civil rights movement." In May 1968, he organized and led a demonstration in Washington, DC, which brought in caravans of unemployed from departure points in the North-east, the South, the Mid-west, the West and the Rocky Mountains. Three thousand plywood huts were erected in Potomac Park and two thousand others erected around the Washington area. Abernathy named the newly erected village Resurrection City, USA.

On 15 May 1968, Abernathy met with senators and representatives, presenting them with the demands of the Poor People's Campaign, which asked for assurances of jobs or guaranteed incomes for the unemployed. A decision was made to create an informal congressional committee of eight senators and eight representatives to meet regularly with the campaign leaders. On 19 June, 50,000 sympathetic Americans of all classes joined the residents of Resurrection City in a rally at the Lincoln Memorial. Five days later, when the Poor People refused to disband at the expiration of their permit, police moved in, closed down the campsite and arrested Abernathy. He spent 20 days in jail. But the protest was to leave an indelible mark on the politics of the United States.

As the years passed, the SCLC began to lose its influence. When Abernathy resigned he claimed that King's widow, Coretta Scott King, was diverting attention away from the SCLC and towards the King Center for Non-Violent Social Change.

In 1977 he made an unsuccessful bid for Congress and returned to his post as pastor at the West Hunter Street Baptist Church in Atlanta. He was beginning to lose support as the young accused him of being too conservative. Then in 1980, when he threw his support behind Ronald Reagan's bid for the presidency, other leaders of the civil rights movement began to distance themselves from him. The biggest blow of all to his colleagues was the publication of his 1989 book, *And the Walls Came Tumbling Down,* which alleged that King had adulterous relationships. Many in the movement felt that he had betrayed the memory of his friend.

Nonetheless, Abernathy had dedicated his life to the civil rights movement in America, suffered the indignities of those who instigate great social change, and sacrificed much of his personal life for the cause. He should be remembered not so much for being Martin Luther King's shadow, as for being King's inspiration.

Born Ralph David Abernathy. **Parents** William L., farmer, and Louivery (Bell) Abernathy. **Marriage** Juanita Odessa Jones, teacher, 1952. **Children** Juandalynn, Donzaleigh, Ralph and Kwame. **Education** Linden Academy, Alabama; Alabama State College, Montgomery, BA in mathematics, 1950; Atlanta University, Georgia, MA in sociology, 1951; Allen University, LLD, 1960. **Military service** US Army, World War II. **Career** Ordained minister, Baptist Church, 1948; pastor: Demopolis Baptist Church, 1948–51, First Baptist Church, Montgomery, Alabama, 1951–61, West Hunter Street Baptist Church, Atlanta, 1961–90; personnel counsellor, Alabama State College, 1951, instructor of social sciences, 1951; organizer, Montgomery Improvement Association, 1955; initiator, bus boycott, Montgomery, 1955, organizer, 1957; home and church bombed, 1957; founder (with Martin Luther King), Southern Christian Leadership Conference, 1957, financial secretary-treasurer, 1957–68, vice-president-at-arge, 1961–68, president, 1968–77; launched (with Martin Luther King) Poor People's Campaign, Resurrection City, Washington, 1967, leader, 1968; present, Martin Luther King's assassination, Memphis, Tennessee, 1968; addressed United Nations, 1971; unsuccessfully ran for Congress, 1977. **Related activities** Chairman, Commission on Racism and Apartheid; organizer/chairman, Operation Breadbasket, Atlanta; advisory council member, Congress of Racial Equality; participant, World Peace Council Presidential Committee Meeting, Santiago, Chile, 1972; on board of directors, Industrial Areas Foundation, Chicago. **Offices and memberships** Member: Atlanta Ministers Union, American Red Cross, American Cancer Society, Young Men's Christian Association, National Association for the Advancement of Colored People. **Awards and honours** Honorary LLD: Southampton College, 1969, Long Island University, 1969, Alabama State University, Montgomery, 1974; honorary DD: Morehouse College, 1971, Kalamazoo College, 1978; recipient, German Democratic Republic Peace medal, 1971. **Publication** *And the Walls Came Tumbling Down* (autobiography), 1989. **Cause of death** Heart attack, at age 64. **Further reading** Martin Luther King, *Stride Toward Freedom,* 1958.

HAROLD BALLARD

Canadian Hockey Executive

***Born* 30 July 1903**

***Died* Toronto, Canada, 11 April 1990**

Compromise was not a word in Harold Ballard's vocabulary. While his final listing in the Toronto Maple Leafs' press guide described him as someone "basically just doing whatever he pleases, regardless of what anyone thinks", the organization's promotional brochure simply called him "one of the most loved and hated men in Canada".

Never afraid to speak his mind on any subject, Ballard was the darling of the Toronto press — providing them with quotes which not only attracted attention and controversy, but also brought him more coverage than anyone else in the public eye. Soon after becoming the president of the Maple Leafs in 1972, for instance, he removed a picture of Queen Elizabeth II from the stadium, saying, "I just booted her out. She never gave me anything. Never paid any taxes for me."

He once described the Russians as "parasites and barnacles who steal our money", and took great pride in having put a Maple Leaf sticker on Lenin's tomb. In 1983, he cancelled a scheduled performance of the Moscow State Circus at the Maple Leaf Gardens, in what he described as a gesture of retaliation for the shooting down of the South Korean airliner. Two years later he went one better, when, in the final minutes of a match at the stadium between the Canadian Olympic team and a touring Moscow Dynamo outfit, fans watched in surprise as the following message was flashed up on the electronic scoreboard: "Korean Airlines Flight 007 Shot Down By The Russians. Don't Cheer. Just Boo — Harold."

The son of a machinery company foreman credited with having invented the tube skates used by hockey players, Harold Ballard was an investor in the Maple Leaf Gardens during its construction in 1931. He worked his way to the top — eventually owning the Canada's best-known ice hockey team, and the less-well-known Hamilton Tiger-Cats football team.

The man who, as an aide to the Canadian ice hockey team in 1928, had carried the country's flag during the Olympic Games' opening ceremony, was seldom out of the spotlight; and his private affairs were at times as well documented by the media as his professional career. He spent a year in prison for fraud after it was discovered that money had been diverted from the club into his own account. He delighted in calling his own daughter "a reptile". And though he never remarried after the death of his first wife, Dorothy, in 1969, he did become the close companion of Yolanda MacMillan, who changed her name to Ballard in 1987.

Despite his high profile, the Maple Leafs experienced a lean decade under his ownership. The president of the National Hockey League, John Ziegler, called him "an original, colourful and challenging individual". But for his part, Ballard was less cryptic in his response, and described Ziegler as "a know-nothing shrimp".

Big, burly, and sporting a mop of bright orange hair, Ballard was never afraid to resort to more direct action if words were not enough — as hockey legend "King" Clancy was to discover one night. The two men were in a bar when Clancy accidentally knocked over a fan's glass of beer. As the fan protested long and loudly, Ballard — then in his mid-seventies — grounded him with one mighty blow. "I was afraid. I though we were both going to get arrested", admitted Clancy. "Harold never gave it another thought. He said it served the guy right. That it would do him some good."

His team's fortunes may have shown signs of slow improvement, but Ballard himself could never be said to have turned over a new leaf. In early 1990, he and Yolanda MacMillan finally took out a marriage licence while visiting the Cayman Islands. But just two hours before the ceremony, the would-be bridegroom backed out and was subsequently declared mentally incompetent. His final days, meanwhile, were spent in courtroom battles with his own children.

Born Edwin Harold Ballard. **Parents** Sidney Eustace, machinery company foreman, and Mary (Garner), boarding-house keeper, Ballard. **Marriage** Dorothy Higgs (died 1969). **Children** William, Harold and Mary. **Career** Flag carrier, Canadian Olympic team, 1928; investor, Maple Leaf Gardens, 1931, director, 1972–90; manager: Sea Fleas amateur hockey team, West Toronto National Juniors Team; manager, Toronto Marlboros, president; imprisoned for fraud for diverting Maple Leafs funds to own account, 1971; owner, Toronto Maple Leafs, president, 1972–90; owner, Hamilton Tiger-Cats football team. **Cause of death** Diabetes-related heart problems, at age 86. **Further reading** Dick Beddoes, *Pal Hal*.

JOHN BEATTIE

British Anthropologist

Born **Liverpool, Lancashire, 8 May 1915**

Died **Letchworth, Hertfordshire, 13 April 1990**

John Beattie was a rare specimen among anthropologists. He managed to comply with the ritual demands of the academic life — chairing committees and attending meetings — without losing either the exotic appeal of the subject or the interest of his students. His practical approach to anthropology and his lucid, humorous style of presentation earned Beattie a reputation as one of the key figures in the evolution of the discipline in Britain. Whilst other anthropologists in the 1950s and 1960s were attempting to make names for themselves, Beattie was making a name for anthropology.

Beattie grew up in County Wicklow, Ireland, and after graduating from Trinity College, Dublin, in 1937 with a degree in philosophy, he took the Civil Service examination at Oxford. He spent 12 years in the Colonial Civil Service, working in southern Tanganyika (now Tanzania), and later in Dar es Salaam, on the coast. He took rather a scholarly approach to administration, learning the local languages fluently in order to gain a better understanding of the problems facing the Tanzanians at that time in their history. His humanitarian and liberal attitude towards development, and his genuine affection for the country and its people, made him an effective administrator and later, a respected cultural historian.

Beattie's empathy and understanding of the enormous difficulties experienced by the Tanzanians in their struggle towards political independence in the 1950s was perhaps rare during the era of often counter-progressive colonial rule. When he left the Service in 1949 to continue his anthropological studies at Oxford, he took with him a belief in the potential for the discipline to facilitate change. His basic approach, to both administration and anthropology, was pragmatic and thorough, based on rigorous thought. Beattie returned to Africa in 1951 to carry out field work in the Kingdom of Bunyoro, Uganda. He arrived at a time when the Bunyoro were fighting to restore the status of their kingdom, which had been reduced by war over boundary rights with neighbouring territories. Beattie's ethnographic work was not disinterested, and he negotiated with administrators on behalf of the Bunyoro, who bestowed on him an honorary indigenous name.

Returning to Oxford in 1953, Beattie was appointed lecturer in social anthropology, a post he held for 20 years. In the 1960s when anthropological theory was tending towards Lévi-Strauss's abstract, structuralist approach, Beattie was espousing a view which gave weight to observation and the oral traditions of the societies being studied. It was an unpopular theoretical approach at the time, but one which gained validity in the 1970s and made anthropology more accessible to a wider audience.

His book *Other Cultures*, based on lectures he had given at Oxford, rapidly became a seminal text after its publication in 1964 and is still widely used as an introduction to the subject. Where many anthropological texts offered insights largely into the cultural values of the author, Beattie's writing provided a valuable record of the Ugandan experience of post-colonial development. He would elaborate on concepts of meaning, ritual and spiritual experience, while always keeping the ethnographic evidence in view. It is fitting that the importance of his written work has been recognized by universities in the developing world and is not merely filling shelves in British schools.

Beattie left Oxford in 1971 to take up a professorship at the University of Leiden in the Netherlands. As an authority on East African societies he was much in demand as a visiting lecturer, and travelled widely until his retirement in 1975. Relieved of the demands of teaching, Beattie continued to write and to play host to passing anthropologists returning from their own field work. Although recent unrest in Uganda made it difficult for Beattie to keep in touch with his friends there, he continued to provide financial assistance to promising Ugandan students. Retirement also provided Beattie with a chance to develop on a larger canvas the doodling he had turned to an art form to avert his boredom at university meetings.

Born John Hugh Marshall Beattie. **Parents** John Crawford, civil servant, and Jean M. (Jones) Beattie. **Marriage** Honor M. Davy, 1946 (died 1978). **Children** Hugh and Frances. **Education** Trinity College, Dublin, BA, 1937; Oxford University, BLitt, 1951, DPhil, 1956. **Career** Administrative service, Tanganyika Territory (now Tanzania), 1940–49; field study, Bunyoro, Uganda, 1950–55; director, East African Institute of Social Research, Kampala; lecturer in social anthropology, Oxford University, 1953–71; professor of African studies (cultural anthropology and sociology), University of Leiden, Netherlands, 1971–75; supernumerary fellow, Linacre College, Oxford, 1976–90. **Related activities** Fellow, Center for Advanced Study in the Behavioral Sciences, Stanford, California, 1959–60; Malinowski Lecturer, London School of Economics and Political Science, University of London, 1965. **Offices and memberships** Member: Royal Anthropological Institute of Great Britain and Ireland, African Studies Association, Association of Social Anthropologists of the Commonwealth. **Publications** *Nyoro Kinship, Marriage and Affinity*, 1958; *Bunyoro: An African Kingdom*, 1960; *Other Cultures: Aims, Methods and Achievements in Social Anthropology*, 1964; *Understanding an African Kingdom: Bunyoro*, 1965; (editor with John Middleton) *Spirit Mediumship and Society in Africa*, 1969; *The Nyoro State*, 1971; (editor with R. G. Lienhardt) *Studies in Social Anthropology: Essays in Memory of E. E. Evans-Pritchard by His Former Oxford Colleagues*, 1975; "Representations of the Self in Traditional Africa", *Africa*, 1980. **Cause of death** Undisclosed, at age 74.

LORD BRUCE-GARDYNE

British Politician and Journalist

***Born* Angus, Scotland, 12 April 1930**

***Died* London, England, 15 April 1990**

He rode an old bicycle. On wet days he would arrive at the office of *The Daily Telegraph* in yellow oilskins and scatter raindrops over all. According to the then editor of the paper, William Deedes, he "gracefully camouflaged abundant talent and a first class mind with some endearing idiosyncracies." As minister of state at the Treasury he took the almost unprecedented step of refusing to use his ministerial car. He was known to his enormous circle of friends simply as "Jock". Wrote Nicholas Ridley who was secretary of state for trade and industry when "Jock" died: "He enriched any gathering or activity with his eccentricity and his wit and his combative views." The then prime minister, Mrs Thatcher, characterized him as "never afraid to challenge orthodoxy although it was always done with good humour."

Eccentrics — especially in England — are much loved and much revered. More than 500 people filled Parliament's church, St Margaret's Westminster, for a memorial service after Lord Bruce-Gardyne's death. The list of those attending reads like a page, or several, from *Who's Who*. Yet Bruce-Gardyne's independence of mind was also his political downfall.

He distinguished himself both as a journalist and a politician, but he was, according to leading British political writer Ian Aitkin, "a man who never quite made up his mind whether he was a journalist or a politician." "Judged purely by the record..." Aitken continues, "there can be no doubt that he was better at journalism than he was at politics." Certainly it was his contacts in journalism which brought about the debacle which sounded the death knell of his political career.

Lord Bruce-Gardyne was born into an old Scottish land-owning family. He was educated at Winchester College, from where he gained a scholarship to Magdalen College, Oxford. In 1953 he joined the Foreign Service. But he was not cut out to be a diplomat. After this eminently conventional start to life and after three gloomy years at the British embassy in Sofia he called it a day. He opted to become a journalist.

In 1956 he became the Paris correspondent for the *Financial Times*. He proved to be an outstandingly good foreign correspondent: bold, resourceful and with a wide range of contacts in every sphere. In 1950 he moved back to England to become foreign editor of the *Statist*. And in 1962 he caught the bug of politics. He was selected for the safe Conservative seat of South Angus, near his family home, and won it at the 1964 general election, just as his party was going out of office for 13 years.

Bruce-Gardyne was — before his time — an instinctive monetarist. "The only way to suspend the law of supply and demand in an advanced industrial society for very long," he once wrote, "is with the tanks." Says Mrs Thatcher of him: "He was among the first in the Conservative Party to rediscover the importance of monetary policy and of encouraging market forces and competition." He soon found himself under the influence of Enoch Powell, along with two other young Tory MPs, Nicholas Ridley and John Biffen. His political creed was set for his life; he was a Thatcherite before Thatcher. Perhaps because of this, he remained on the backbenches under Edward Heath's leadership of the party. At the same time he held the post of foreign editor of *The Spectator* journal — appointed by Nigel Lawson, the then editor.

In 1970 when the Conservatives moved into government, Bruce-Gardyne became parliamentary private secretary to the secretary of state for Scotland. But two years later he was sufficiently out of step with Heath's brand of managerial capitalism to threaten to resign when the government caved in to a sit-in in the Glasgow dockyards. It was characteristic of his loyalty to the party that he did not make his reasons for resigning public.

It was at this time that Nicholas Ridley worked most closely with him. He writes: "He hammered home the message that the money supply must be kept under control and demolished the conventional wisdom that demand management was all that mattered...It was then that he made his reputation, and then that he laid the foundations for Mrs Thatcher's victory in 1979."

But meanwhile, Bruce-Gardyne, like the government itself, was defeated at the polls in 1974. Once again he turned to writing and established a name as a versatile freelance journalist and produced, in this period, three books; one, *The Power Game*, in collaboration with Nigel Lawson. In 1977 he was invited to join *The Daily Telegraph* as a leader writer. William Deedes paints an endearing picture of the eccentric Jock at work: "He wrote his copy at great speed, faster than any serious writer I have known. Given the subject, usually an awkward economic one, he would approach a typewriter, beg the loan of one's plastic card to draw coffee from the office vending machine, light a cigarette, and immediately start striking the keys. For reasons of his own, he spurned the modern word-processor."

In 1979 with the election of Margaret Thatcher as prime minister he returned to Parliament and was tipped as a candidate for office. But his customary independence of mind intervened; some articles he wrote around the time of the election that suggested the difficulty the Tories would have in implementing their programme, temporarily set back his chances.

For another two years he continued his work on the *Telegraph*. It was not until the reshuffle in autumn 1981 that he was rewarded for his hostility to all things Heathite with a ministerial job at the

Treasury. In the same year he was moved to the post of financial secretary, traditionally one of the stepping stones to the highest offices.

He was well liked by both colleagues and civil servants. And he always retained his sense of fun, never became pompous. Nicholas Ridley recalls that while making a difficult speech in the Commons, he felt his feet being swept to one side and looked down to find "Jock" crawling on all fours. "Having finally recovered from this disturbance and finished my speech I sat down. I asked him what the hell he was doing. 'I lost my spectacles', he said. 'I was only looking for them.'" He had other eccentric adventures, as when he got into trouble answering a parliamentary question on VAT on sanitary towels and when he had an accident on his bicycle when his red box of ministerial papers fell onto the road and burst open, scattering secret Budget documents all over the street.

All was well in Westminster, but trouble was brewing in his constituency. There were complaints that he spent too much time in London; and, true enough, he found the rituals of being a constituency MP tedious. The leaking by an unscrupulous third party of a private letter he wrote to financial journalist Samuel Brittan proved the last straw.

In this letter he shared his views over the Falklands campaign, which was then in progress. His views were distinctly heretical. "The Falklanders", he wrote, "could quite easily be re-settled elsewhere on the globe at a far higher standard of living." The left-wing journal, the *New Statesman* printed the letter in full. The Prime Minister's reaction was said to have been "explosive". After a 20-minute interview with her — in which he offered to resign — he issued a statement of "deep regret" for what had happened. In return, she allowed him to retain his office. But his constituents were not so forgiving. After boundary changes in 1983 he was not re-adopted and his career in the Commons came to an end.

Mrs Thatcher showed remarkable personal kindness in bringing him back into Parliament — this time the House of Lords — by giving him a life peerage. But he never held office again; he returned to his typewriter.

It was while he was battering at the keys that Bruce-Gardyne felt the first intimations of the disease of which he was to die. Finding he could not hit the right keys, he went to his doctor, then to hospital for tests. The verdict was a brain tumour too far gone for successful surgery.

Politicians and editors all pay tribute to the courage and humour with which he faced his inevitable death. Despite the immense pain of his treatment and the discomfort and weakness the illness inflicted on him, he never showed self-pity; indeed his determination and strength extended his life well beyond what his doctors expected. He continued to attend and to speak in the Lords; and he wrote movingly about his illness in *The Spectator* and the *Telegraph*. He continued writing almost up until he died.

Said Margaret Thatcher in a statement afterwards: "He was a marvellous colleague, loyal but always retaining an independence of mind." The *Daily Telegraph* leader column expressed a similar depth of regret in rather different terms: "His apparent flippancy and cynicism did not forward his political career, but masked the shrewdest instincts about the realities of government. He added immeasurably to the gaiety of nations, and we shall miss him greatly."

Born John Bruce-Gardyne. **Parents** Captain Evan, naval captain and tenth Laird of Middleton, Angus, and Joan (McLaren) Bruce-Gardyne. **Marriage** Sarah Louisa Mary Maitland, 1959. **Children** Adam, Thomas, and one daughter. **Education** Winchester College, Hampshire; scholar, Magdalen College, Oxford. **Military service** National service, 1951–53. **Career** Served London and Sofia, foreign service, 1953–56; Paris correspondent, *Financial Times*, 1956–60; foreign editor, *Statist*, 1961–64; Conservative member of parliament for South Angus, Scotland, 1964–74, for Knutsford, Cheshire, 1979–83; foreign editor, *The Spectator*, 1964–70, columnist, 1983–90; parliamentary private secretary to secretary of state for Scotland, 1970–72; editorial writer, *The Daily Telegraph*, 1977–81, 1984–90; columnist, *The Sunday Telegraph*, 1979–81, 1984–

90; minister of state, Treasury, 1981, economic secretary, 1981–83; entered House of Lords as life peer, 1983. **Related activities** Vice-chairman, Conservative Parliamentary Finance Committee, 1972–74, 1979–80; consultant, Northern Engineering Industries, 1979–81, 1985–90; director: Central Trustee Savings Bank, 1983–85, Trustee Savings Bank plc, 1985–90, Trustee Savings Bank England and Wales plc, 1985–90, London and Northern Group plc, 1985–87. **Awards and honours** Created life peer, Baron Bruce-Gardyne of Kirkden in the District of Angus, 1983. **Publications** *Whatever Happened to the Quiet Revolution?*, 1974; *Scotland in 1980*, 1975; (with Nigel Lawson) *The Power Game*, 1976; *Mrs Thatcher's First Administration: The Prophets Confounded*, 1984; *Minsters and Mandarins: Inside the Whitehall Village* (autobiography), 1986. **Cause of death** Brain tumour, at age 60.

JIMMY CHIPPERFIELD

British Circus Owner and Safari Park Pioneer

***Born* Corsham, Wiltshire, 17 July 1912**

***Died* Middle Wallop, Hampshire, 20 April 1990**

If the literary genre, magical realism, is still fashionable by the time you read this, you might think you've stumbled into a bit of it. But no: what follows is exotically true.

James Seaton Methuen Chipperfield was born in 1912, in the top bunk of a mahogany wagon which happened to be parked near the village of Corsham in Wiltshire. The family had owned a travelling circus for six generations — he later liked to say that a Chipperfield had organized entertainment for King Charles II. The itinerant life denied Chipperfield any conventional education; instead he learned wire-walking, business on the trapeze and wrestling with bears — the latter skill took him as far as the famous London Palladium Theatre. At the age of 16 he fell in love with Rosie Purchase, the beautiful daughter of another circus family, who danced in the lions' cage. After six years of parental opposition, they eloped.

With the outbreak of World War II in 1939, Chipperfield determined to become a fighter pilot with the Royal Air Force. As they saw it, he was less than A1 material, being deficient to the tune of any maths at all, and one kidney (a bear-hug had accounted for the other; he was also embroidered with leonine lacerations). Not one whit abashed, he ignored the medical reports, found a village school that would accept him, and sat down with the children to learn trigonometry. Eventually he got his wish, and flew Mosquito aircraft.

When peace returned, he rejoined the circus with his brother Dick and travelled Europe with a troupe which grew to outrival that of Bertram Mills, a similarly ambitious dynast in the circus business. By 1955, however, questions about the condition of animals in captivity were turning public taste against the circus, and Chipperfield decided to diversify. He began to farm, and to train animals for Walt Disney films. Also, he founded a zoo, in Southampton. The search for stock took him to the game reserves of East Africa, where he captured animals and exported them back to England. This involved him in a number of controversies, and a rancorous relationship with the London Zoo, but the whole experience stimulated the atavistic showbusinessman in him to adapt his service to current requirements.

What he had seen on the great African plains was the reverse of his previous operation: the beautiful, dangerous animals ran wild, and the people stayed in cages, though mobile ones — motor cars. Thus was born the concept of the safari park. What Chipperfield now needed was a backer with plenty of land. Well, there were members of the British aristocracy with just that, and plenty of them looking for ways to help with the upkeep of their expensive stately homes. The first to bite was the Marquis of Bath. At Easter 1966 he invested his ancient parkland at Longleat with some live heraldry — Chipperfield's imported bestiary. *The Times* called it "dangerous folly", and the British Parliament called it stupid, but Chipperfield had cracked it. The British public could now pay to drive, or be driven, through crowds of lions, antelopes and the like, apparently at large in the spacious backyards of the nobility. Other such enterprises, usually in partnership with the landowner, opened at Woburn, Knowsley, Blair Drummond, Lambton and Bewdley.

He managed his new empire shrewdly, and became a millionaire. While delighting in the Rolls-Royce, the private aircraft and the indoor swimming pool, he did not neglect his animal benefactors, like Congo the zebra or James the chimpanzee, who would take tea (or coffee) with guests. Fiercely proud of his own family and their achievements, Chipperfield had to suffer the death of two sons. The first died of tetanus at the age of six, the second, who inherited all his father's dash and his empathy with animals, was killed in a car crash in Uganda. It was left to his daughter, Mary, to carry on the family circus tradition.

Born James Seaton Methuen Chipperfield. **Parents** Circus performers. **Marriage** Rose Purchase, circus performer, 1934. **Children** James (deceased), Richard (died 1975), Mary, Margaret and John. **Military service** Pilot, Royal Air Force, World War II. **Career** Circus performer, tightrope walker, trapeze artist; partner (with brother), travelling circus, 1945–55; animal trainer; founded zoo, Southampton, invented the safari park, Longleat, 1965, Woburn, Knowsley, Blair Drummond, Lambton, Bewdley. **Publication** *My Wild Life* (autobiography), 1975. **Cause of death** Undisclosed, at age 77. **Further reading** Ted Seago, *High Endeavour: The story of Jimmy, a lion tamer now Pilot Officer in the Royal Air Force*, 1944.

PETER DOHERTY

British Football Player and Manager

***Born* Magherafelt, Londonderry, 5 June 1913**

***Died* Blackpool, Lancashire, 6 April 1990**

Arguably the greatest Irish inside forward of all time, Peter Doherty was a complete footballer, admired by his colleagues and feared by opposing defenders. Quick, versatile, industrious and volatile, he enjoyed a fine career, and after hanging up his boots, was manager of the national team at the time of its finest hour, in 1958, when Northern Ireland strode into the World Cup finals for the first time, and shocked the footballing world by daring to reach the quarter finals.

The captain of that particular team — the great Danny Blanchflower — later paid a glowing tribute to Doherty. "He was", said Blanchflower, "the great North Star that twinkled brightly in the heavens, promising untold glory, beckoning me to follow, and always showing the way."

It was all such a long way from the start of Doherty's football career. This had eventually taken root with Glentoran of the Irish League after a false start at Coleraine, and a brief reliance on income supplied from his work as a brickie, then a bus conductor. Then, at the age of 19, the doors to the English Football League were opened up to him, when Blackpool signed him for what proved to be the bargain price of 2000 pounds.

Doherty's talents were quickly recognized, and after three seasons with Blackpool, he was already a member of the Irish squad, as well as the focus of many First Division clubs' attention. It was Manchester City who eventually won the race for his signature, and he quickly repaid the 10,000-pounds transfer fee, as he proved to be the final link in the 1937 Championship-winning team.

A classic inside forward, Doherty was more than just a goal scorer — although he did score 30 of City's 107 goals in that first season. Displaying a Trojan appetite for work, he linked the defence and attack; and such was the industry he displayed, that many commentators of the day expressed a fear that he might burn himself out prematurely. Happily they were wrong, and it was not the player, but the club, who ran out of steam. For Manchester City was relegated from the First Division just one season after winning the title.

World War II interrupted the playing career of Peter Doherty, who spent five years as a PTI (physical training instructor) sergeant. There were, however, occasions when he was able to pull on a pair of football boots, and to do what he knew best. One particularly famous occasion was later recalled by Maurice Edelston, who described Doherty's part in Ireland's 7–4 loss to a Combined Services team at Windsor Park. "Peter almost played us off the park by himself", said Edelston, noting that Doherty scored all four Irish goals. "He might have got another four...he was almost a one-man team — and if Ireland had had two Doherty's that day, I shudder to think what might have happened."

After the war, Doherty featured in a Derby County team noted for its fine football. Forming a famous partnership with the great Raich Carter, he helped the Rams to victory in the first post-war FA Cup Final, in 1946. But ticket allocation for that match proved a source of conflict between the player and club, and Doherty put in a transfer request, moving to Huddersfield Town, and saving them from almost certain relegation. In 1950, aged 36, he joined Third Division Doncaster Rovers as player-manager and scored 36 goals in a promotion-winning season.

Flame-haired, and with a temperament to match, Doherty's fiery nature made him an uncomfortable employee. Doncaster Rovers' board of directors, for instance, could simply not handle him, and Doherty resigned to become manager of Bristol City and Northern Ireland. Able to call on the likes of Danny Blanchflower and Jimmy McIlroy, he led Ireland to its first win against England at Wembley in 1957, and then directed the campaign which saw Ireland, the giant-killers, reach the quarter finals of the 1958 World Cup Finals.

People who knew him well remember not only his volatility, but also his friendly good humour. Proud and independent, he stood up for what he believed in, and fought especially hard against the exploitation of the professional footballer. It is interesting, for example, to hear one of the greatest footballers of his time say of his own transfer from Blackpool to Manchester City: "I might as well have been a bale of merchandise."

Doherty, having scored 197 goals in 403 league matches, eventually drifted out of the game. But his contribution was never forgotten.

Born Peter Doherty. **Marriage** Jessie. **Children** One son, Paul. **Military service** PTI sergeant, Royal Air Force, World War II. **Career** Brickie; bus conductor; inside forward for Coleraine, Glentoran, Blackpool, 1933–36, Manchester City, 1936–39, Derby (guested), 1939–45, Derby, 1946, Huddersfield, 1946–48; player-manager, Doncaster Rovers, 1949–52; retired 1953; manager, Bristol City, 1958; manager, Northern Ireland, 1958; played 403 league games, scored 197 goals; 16 caps for Ireland. **Cause of death** Undisclosed, at age 76.

ERTÉ

Russian/French Designer

Born **St Petersburg, Russia, 23 November 1892**

Died **Paris, France, 21 April 1990**

In 1912 a young man arrived in Paris from St Petersburg (now Leningrad). Like so many others of artistic inclination at that time he came in search of fame and fortune without knowing quite what he would do to woo that elusive Dame. His first venture into the world of art was inauspicious. Employment as a designer in "an obscure, second-rate fashion house" was hardly a promising start for the young hopeful and, what is more, it did not last long. Yet some errors of judgement can make history: when the proprietor of Maison Caroline sacked Romain de Tirtoff (Erté's given name) because he "had no talent for fashion design", the man unwittingly launched one of this century's greatest costume designers on a glittering career. For this young Russian was no ordinary fashion designer; in fact, he abhorred the very idea of fashion which he saw as merely another kind of — seasonally adjusted — uniformity. Even at the start of his career, Romain de Tirtoff had a different idea of dress: "I firmly believe that every human being has a duty to make himself as attractive as possible. Clothes are a kind of alchemy: they can transform human beings into things of beauty or ugliness."

Having changed his name to Erté — the French pronunciation of his initials — the aspiring alchemist/clothes designer was soon taken on by Paul Poiret, and began to get interested in the theatre. Dressed in outrageously extravagant costume, Erté attended the first nights of such major cultural events as Stravinsky's *Le Sacre du printemps* (1913) causing a stir amongst the spectators and nearly upstaging the performance they had come to see. Here the ancient adage "if you can't beat them, join them" held true, and it was not long before the theatre directors asked Erté to work for them as a designer. He started by designing costumes for the young dancer, Mata Hari (later to be shot by the Germans as a spy), in the 1913 show *Le Minaret*. This was an exotic Arabian Nights-type production in which he could give his imagination full rein. But Etré was never content to operate merely behind the scenes. It was by now expected of him to turn up on first nights dressed in grand style — on one occasion that meant a coat of red velvet and ermine, long red gloves and glittering earrings, the whole ensemble topped by a scarlet turban.

In his designs for Mata Hari and in his later work the influence of the East was evident, something which has been traced back to the Persian and Indian miniatures which Erté as a child had often seen in St Petersburg's world-famous Hermitage museum. There were other childhood factors as well which can help account for Erté's later very distinctive style of design. He was born the son of Russian aristocrats and grew up amidst the material and cultural wealth of late-nineteenth-century St Petersburg. Although his father, a military man, was dismayed by Erté's interest in dance and painting and preferred him to engage in the boisterous boys' games which would prepare him for a naval career, his mother from the beginning encouraged the pursuit of art and beauty. Reputedly Erté designed his first dress for her at the age of six; together they explored the shops on Nevsky Prospekt, the theatre (where they saw Diaghilev's first productions) and, of course, the Hermitage. By the time Erté finished school, having won distinctions and commendations from his art and dance teachers, even the father had come round: the passport and ticket to Paris were a present from him.

Following hot on the heels of his theatrical success with *Le Minaret* and *L'Orient merveilleux* Erté was commissioned to design covers for the chic fashion magazine *Harper's Bazaar*. This became a long-standing connection which lasted until the mid-1930s and lent Erté the distinction of becoming known in the popular imagination as "the Father of Art Deco". Instantly recognizable as small works of art, his cover designs defined the magazine's house-style and identified the magazine with the main decorative trend of the period. Bent over his drawing table scattered with magazine photographs, sketches and plans, Erté did not let the life of the Roaring Twenties pass him by however. Involvement with the quintessential Parisian revue, the Folies-Bergère, and its American equivalent, the Ziegfeld Follies, on Broadway, drew him into metropolitan high life and provided him with ample opportunity to make spectacular public appearances, dressed like a film star in gold lamé, diamond-studded velvet, and even a hoop skirt. Hollywood was, indeed, not far off but a sojourn in the world of film at the invitation of William Randolph Hearst proved a disappointment. This was the age of big-budget musicals and revues and although Erté did work on lavish productions such as Irving Berlin's *Music Box* and George White's *Scandals* there were too many problems with funding for Hollywood to hold his attention for long. Back in Paris there was plenty of work waiting and plenty of fun to be had.

It was all the more of a shock, then, when with the economic crash in 1929 Erté lost virtually all his money and much of his confidence in the economic security he had never been without. Gone were the days of conspicuous consumption and dazzling displays — as it seemed, overnight. Erté did not lose his touch however. Soon he manifested himself again as a reincarnation of the mythical Midas: everything he touched changed into gold. This was true both of the elaborate stage-sets he designed for numerous theatrical and ballet productions in the 1930s and 1940s, which glittered and gleamed with gilt-draped props and costumes, and of his personal fortune which he amassed through demanding to be paid only in gold. In the company of such divas as Victoria de Los Angeles and the legendary Anna Pavlova this was hardly seen as a pathological obsession; in a world where eccentricity was the norm Erté's flamboyant idiosyncrasies were heartily indulged. Even the sobering experience of working with British theatre companies in the 1940s, when money was short, did not dull his appetite for glamour and display — predictably, given the need for escape during those hard times and given Erté's personal charm, the British loved him for it.

"The Father of Art Deco" would never have earned that title however if he had merely been a canny eccentric whose ideas were right for the time. Perhaps Erté's greatest achievement was the merging of art and craft, that ancient and troublesome twosome which has dogged so much of twentieth-century aesthetic judgement. For Erté, art and design were one and Art Deco was the movement in which he could best express his multiple talents, without regard for the world's prejudice against practical and applied work as "not really art" but merely a matter of technique or skill. As Erté himself said, Art Deco "for the first time fused pure with applied art, which had previously been considered fairly contemptible."

It is certainly true that in his work in the theatre, Erté was as concerned with finding technical solutions to practical problems encountered in the execution of his vision, as he was with the pure aesthetics of it. A master of invention, his "human curtains", collective costumes and *tableaux vivants* were never short of sensational and they shifted significantly the standards of technical ingenuity in the theatre. At the same time, it has to be said that much of what is remembered of Erté's work today would traditionally come into the fine art category: drawings, lithographs, and sculptures, even if these overlap considerably with his design work: costumes, illustrations, furniture and jewellery. That he was also capable of good abstract work was demonstrated in 1964 with an exhibition of painted wood and metal sculptures, which he called *formes picturales*.

It was around that time, when his fame as a designer had begun to fade, that Erté was re-discovered by Jacques Damase, the French writer, and Eric Estorick, owner of the Grosvenor Gallery in London. They encouraged him to do more graphic work in order to reach a wider audience than his other designs had hitherto found. A series of related lithographs with titles such as *The Precious Stones*, *Signs of the Zodiac* and *The Seven Deadly Sins* was particularly successful. With the revival of interest in Erté came also commercialization. To the dismay of the serious art world, all of a sudden the shops were flooded with cheap Erté reproductions (especially a series of drawings called *Alphabet*) as well as jewellery, not to mention the mugs, dolls and diaries. And of course, the royalties kept rolling in. Meanwhile, the man himself continued to work as he had always done; in 1980 Erté's spectacular sets and costumes for a production of *Der Rosenkavalier* at the Glyndebourne Festival Opera in England attracted the highest critical praise.

Apart from the sheer range and quality of his work and the fertility of his imagination, Erté was remarkable also for his enormous productivity. Totalling the fruits of his labours in the 1975 autobiography *Things I Remember*, Erté estimated his output as some 16,000 designs, not including the things he did *not* remember nor all the work he was yet to do right up until the time of his death. Quantity was clearly important, and it is very characteristic of Erté that the title of the autobiography puts the emphasis on *things*. For despite the wonderful and dreamlike nature of his dressed-up figures and sets, Erté's was a profoundly material world in which the inanimate could come to life just as easily as the reverse could happen: the human figure reduced to thing-ness. It has often been remarked that this was especially the case with Erté's female figures and his clothes for women, which typically constrict and constrain the body with skirts tightly wrapped around the legs, sashes, belts and chain-like jewellery. Woman in bondage was a persistent theme and there are good reasons to believe that when the French cultural critic Roland Barthes, writing in the 1980s, pointed out that "Erté's mythological purgatory is Woman" he was hinting at something that went rather deeper that merely style.

Erté's public life was littered with "things" which together make up a glittering career, but they shed little light on the private person. It seems strange that he never returned to Russia in all of his 95 years for example, and that despite his extrovert image his was really, for long stretches of time, a solitary existence. For most of his life a flat near the Bois de Boulogne which he shared with cats and a parrot was his habitat. He also spent a lot of his time in the Bahamas and in Majorca, where he was rebuilding a recently acquired *finca*. As with clothes, he looked upon interior design also as a magical process of transformation which would tailor his physical environment to the needs of fantasy and the desire to act out different roles, to be different people. In old age he came to look — in the words of an admirer — "like a retired duchess", but for someone who made and wore unisex clothing well before the 1960s "invented" it and who took great pleasure in cross-dressing no matter what outrage it caused, this look seemed entirely appropriate. Certainly, like a duchess, Erté grew old gracefully and with dignity, keeping himself in trim on a diet of exercise and work. Amusement came from travel, the company of friends... and work. Work, he once explained "has been my mother and father, my wife, my friend, my mistress and my children. It has been my life."

Born Romain de Tirtoff. **Parents** Admiral Piotr Ivanovich, naval officer, and Natalia Mikhailovna (Nikolenko) de Tirtoff. **Education** Kronstadt College, St Petersburg (now Leningrad), 1904–11; studied painting and drawing under Repine and Lossewsky, Academy of Fine Arts, St Petersburg, 1906–11; studied painting, Académie Julian, Paris, 1912. **Emigration** Left Russia for France, 1912, later naturalized. **Career** First drawings published, *Damsky Mir* (Woman's World) magazine, 1912; fashion artist, for couturier Paul Poiret, Paris, 1912–13; designed costumes for Mata Hari, 1913; stage costume designer: Théâtre de la Renaissance, Le Bataclan, Théâtre Femina, Folies Bergère, Théâtre Sarah Bernhardt, Bal Tabarin, Théâtre du Vieux Columbier, Paris, Saville Theatre, London, from 1913, *George White's Scandals*, Winter Garden, New York, World's Fair, New York City, 1939; designed collections for: B. Altman, Henri Bendel, New York, 1915–17; freelance illustrator for: *Harper's Bazaar*, 1915–37, *Vogue*, *Cosmopolitan*, *Delineator*, New York, *Femina*, *L'Illustration*, *Le Gaulois artistique*, *La Gazette du bon ton*, *Art et industrie*, *Plaisir de France*, Paris, *The Sketch*, *Illustrated London News*, London, from 1915; freelance film costume designer, Cosmopolitan Films, 1919; contract costume designer, Metro-Goldwyn-Mayer film company, 1925; began publishing series of lithographs: *Les Chiffres*,

1968, *Les Pierres Précieuses*, 1969, *Les Quatre Saisons*, 1970, *The Four Aces*, 1974, *Alphabet*, 1977. **Awards and honours** Honorary member: Motion Picture and Television Costume Designers Guild, New York; L'Ordre de Mérite Culturel, France, 1972; Officier de l'Ordre des Arts et des Lettres, France, 1976; honorary degree, Royal College of Art, 1989. **Stage designs** (include) *Le Minaret*, 1913; *La Fête de St Cyr*; *Panachot the Dictator*; *Gobette of Paris*; *L'Orient Merveilleux*; *George White's Scandals*; Irving Berlin's *Music Box*; *Ziegfeld Follies*; *Greenwich Village Follies*; *Manhattan Mary*; *Chant du Tzigane*; *Phi-Phi*; *Sappho*; *Phèdre*; *It's in the Bag*; *Stardust*; Radio City's *Easter Parade*. **Operas designed** (include) *Don Pasquale*, 1944; *Les Mamelles de Tirésias*, 1947; *La Traviata*, 1951; *Castor et Pollux*, 1961; *Der Rosenkavalier*, 1980; *Anatol*, 1985. **Ballets designed** (include) *Mother Goose*; *Self-Portrait*; *The Enchanted Mill*; *Le Coiffeur Miracle* (filmed); *Edition Spéciale* (filmed). **Films designed** (include) *Restless Sex*, 1920; *The Mystic*, 1925; *Bright Lights*, 1925; *Time, the Comedian*, 1925; *Dance Madness*, 1925; *La Bohème*, 1925; *Paris* (never filmed), 1925; *Ben Hur*, 1925. **Exhibitions** Madison Hotel, New York, 1925; Galerie Charpentier, Paris, 1926, 1929; Galerie du Studio, Brussels, 1927; Warren and Cox, New York, 1929; Waldorf Astoria Hotel, New York, 1935; Galerie Ror Volmar, Paris, 1964; Galerie la Motte, Paris, 1965; *Les Années 25*, Musée des Arts Décoratifs, Paris, 1966; Galerie Jacques Perrin, Paris, 1966; Galleria Milano, Milan, 1966; Grosvenor Gallery, London, 1967; Galleria Lambert-Monet-Geneva, 1972; *Romantic and Glamorous Hollywood Design*, Metropolitan Museum of Art, New York, 1974; Electrum Gallery, London, 1975. **Collections** Metropolitan Museum of Art, New York; Museum of Modern Art, New York; Victoria and Albert Museum, London. **Publications** (Illustrator) *Ermyntrude and Esmeralda* by Lytton Strachey, 1969; (illustrator) *The Beatles Illustrated* by Alan Aldridge, 1969; *Erté Fashions*, 1972; *Things I Remember: An Autobiography*, 1975; *Designs by Erté: Fashion Drawings and Illustrations from "Harper's Bazaar"*, 1976; *Erté Graphics: Five Complete Suites*, 1978; *Erté*, 1978; *Erté's Theatrical Costumes in Full Color* (edited by Salome Estorick), 1979; *Erté's Costumes and Sets for Der Rosenkavalier*, 1980; *Erté's Fashion Designs: 218 Illustrations from "Harper's Bazaar" 1918–1932*, 1981; *Erté at Ninety: The Complete Graphics*, 1982; *Erté at Ninety-Five*, 1987. **Cause of death** Undisclosed, at age 97. **Further reading** Giuliana Veronesi, *Romain de Tirtoff—Erté* (exhibition catalogue), 1966; *Erté* (exhibition catalogue), 1967; Charles Spencer, *Erté*, 1970; Roland Barthes, *Erté*, 1972; Stella Carter, *Designs by Erté*, 1977; *Contemporary Designers*, 1990.

ALDO FABRIZI

Italian Actor, Director and Screenwriter

Born **Rome, Italy, 1 November 1905**

Died **Rome, Italy, 2 April 1990**

Aldo Fabrizi was an actor whose reputation, at least outside his own country, was built around one particular film—despite the fact that he acted in several films before, and over 60 afterwards (some of which he co-scripted). But *Roma, città aperta*, or *Rome, Open City*, Roberto Rossellini's painfully loving 1946 classic of a town in the grip of the German Occupation, was the film. Fabrizi portrayed Don Pietro, the defiant priest who was executed by the Nazis for protecting his own people. The impassioned nature of his character as well as his "of the common people" loyalty, was shared by Fabrizi himself. The part fitted him as perfectly as possible. And the audiences, as well as the critics, took notice.

Born in the slums of Rome, Fabrizi would recount later his memories of going to bed hungry. But he was proud of his background, and of his earthy Roman dialect, which he used to great effect (as he did his mastery of other local accents) in his early days on the vaudeville and radio circuits. He, fortunately, had grown disillusioned with his earlier career, as a horse-carriage and tram-driver.

In his films from 1942 onwards Fabrizi frequently portrayed an ordinary, unsophisticated Roman, wise in the ways of street life. But his first role, in the 1942 *Avanti c'è posto*, and indeed his next three, caused no great stir. When he was cast, and forever remembered, as a priest, many were surprised to learn of his music-hall background. In fact, it was a member of his troupe, a young Federico Fellini (who later used one of Fabrizi's old routines in his first film, *Lights of Variety* in 1950), who, as co-collaborator on *Rome, Open City*, recommended him. The film itself started out as a documentary about Don Morosini, a real priest whose fate was similar to that of Don Pietro. Fellini later recounted the difficulty in convincing Fabrizi to play the role. "But what if the Germans return?" he was asked by the anxious actor.

Fabrizi cemented his growing reputation as an actor in Luigi Zampere's 1943 film, *Vivere in pace*, with his role of Uncle Tigna, the head of a family who gives protection to two American soldiers, one black, in his home. His finely-honed — at times *roughly* so, in other films! — sense of comedy, sharpened the inevitable tragic ending.

Although Fabrizi made many films afterwards, they proved to be unnoteworthy in either script or direction. Rossellini, who brought out the best in him, according to many critics, directed him to good effect in *Flowers of St Francis* in 1950. But few of his films were seen internationally. Nevertheless, his talents as a character actor brought a spark of life and of joy in all but the dullest script. In 1951's *Guardie e ladri*, Fabrizi's portrayal of a policeman given three months to find a thief, only to end up befriending the man's family, was one of his finer performances.

Fabrizi also tried his hand at directing; of his four films, *Emigrantes*, about a family leaving for the Argentine, was the best. However, like the rest, it never made a real impact on the international market — a strong criterion, especially for Italy's post-war films, for success. He had better luck in the theatre, particularly as the papal executioner in the musical comedy, *Rugantino*, which reached New York in 1964 to acclaim.

In 1967 Fabrizi worked briefly in Hollywood, joining Sylvia Koscina, Tammy Grimes and others in *Three Bites of the Apple*, a flimsy comedy meant to promote then-rising star David McCallum. By now Fabrizi seemed to parody himself, with his bulky body and enthusiastic gesticulation. More and more, food played an important role in his life and he wrote several cookery books, sometimes with recipes in verse. Soon his appreciation for fine culinary fare extended not only his girth but his desire for public appreciation of it. He sometimes recited his recipes and could talk on almost any topic, à la Peter Ustinov — often with outrageous humour.

Although it can be concluded that Fabrizi's strength came from his personification of national characters, with precision, style and affection, the last word must go to James Agee: "I don't agree with those who talk of Fabrizi as a great actor. As an actor he seems thoroughly experienced, astute, uninhibited and no more. His grandeur is as a man. His good luck is his solid equipment as an artist and his magnificent equipment in face, and lowering head and burly body, to make visible certain kinds of greatness."

Born Aldo Fabrizi. **Marriage** Beatrice Rocchi (deceased). **Children** Massimo and one other. **Career** Horse-carriage and tram driver; variety theatre comedian, 1931; dialect comedian, radio and music-hall; film début, 1942; first script filmed, 1942; directional début, 1949; appeared on Broadway, *Rugantino*, 1964; published several cookery books. **Films as actor** (include) *Avanti c'è posto* (also co-scripted), 1942; *Campo dei Fiori (The Peddler and the Lady)*, 1943; *L'ultima carrozzella*, 1943; *Circo equestre Za-Bum*, 1944; *Roma, città aperta* (*Rome, Open City/Open City*), 1945; *Mio figlio professore (Professor My Son)*, 1946; *Vivere in pace (To Live in Peace)* (also co-scripted), 1946; *Il delitto di Giovani Episcopo* (*Flesh Will Surrender*) (also co-scripted), 1947; *Tombola, paradiso nero*, 1947; *Natale al campo 119* (*Escape into Dreams*) (also co-scripted), 1948; *Antonio di Padova* (*Anthony of Padua*), 1949; *Prima comunione* (*Father's Dilemma*), 1950; *Francesco — giullare di Dio* (*Flowers of St Francis*), 1950; *Vita di cani* (*It's a Dog's Life*), 1950; *Guardie e ladri* (*Cops and Robbers*) (also co-scripted), 1951; *Parigi è sempre Parigi*, 1951; *Signori in carrozo* (also co-scripted), 1951; Tre passi anord (*Three Steps North*), 1951; *Cameriera bella presenza offresi,* 1951; "Il carrettino dei libri vecchi", episode of *Altri tempi* (*Times Gone By/In Olden Days/Infidelity*), 1952; *Cinque poveri in automobile* (*The Lucky Five*), 1952; *La voce del silenzio*, 1952; *L'età dell'amore*, 1953; *Siamo tutti inquilini*, 1953; *Cose da pazzi*, 1953; "Garibaldina", episode of *Cento anni d'amore*, 1954; *Accadde al penitenziario*, 1955; *Carosello di varietà*, 1955; *I due compari*, 1955; *Io piaccio*, 1955; *Donatella*, 1956; *Guardia, guardia scelta, brigadiere e maresciallo*, 1956; *Mi permette, babbo?*, 1956; *I pappagalli*, 1956; *Un po' di cielo*, 1956; *Festa di maggio* (*Premier May*), 1957; *I prepontenti*, 1958; *Fernando I, re di Napoli*, 1959; *Prepotenti più di prima*, 1959; *I tartassati (*The Overtaxed), 1959; *La sposa bella* (*The Angel Wore Red*), 1959; *Un militare e mezzo*, 1960; *Totó, Fabrizi e i giovani d'oggi*, 1950; *Gerarchi si muore*, 1962; *Le meraviglie di Aladino* (*The Wonders of Aladdin*), 1962; *Orazi e Curiazi* (*Duel of Champions*), 1962; *I quattro monaci*, 1962; *Twist, ninfette e vitelloni*, 1962; *I quattro moschettieri*, 1963; *Totò contro i quattro*, 1963; *Fra Manisco cerca quai* 1965; *I quattro tassisti* 1964; *La donna è una cosa meravigliosa*, 1964; *Made in Italy*, 1965; *Sette monici d'oro*, 1966; *Three Bites of the Apple*, 1967; *Cose di cosa Nostra* (*The Godson*), 1971; *La Tosca*, 1973; *Non toccate la donna bianca*, 1973; *Permettete che ami vostre figlia?* (*Madam, Permit Me to Love Your Daughter/Claretta and Ben*), 1974; *C'eravamo tanti amati* (*We All Loved Each Other So Much/Those Were the Years*), 1974; *I baroni*, 1974; *Il ginecologo della mutua* (*Ladies Doctor*), 1977. **Films directed and scripted** (include) *Emigrantes*, 1949; *Benvenuto reverrendo!*, 1950; *La famiglia Passaguai*, 1951; *La Famiglia Passaguai fa fortuna*, 1952; *Papa diventa Mamma*, 1952; *Una di quelle*, 1953; "Marsini stretta", episode of *Questa è la vita* (*Of Life and Love*), 1954; *Hanno rubato un tram*, 1955; *Il maestro* (*The Teacher and the Miracle*), 1958. **Cause of death** Heart attack, at age 84. **Further reading** *International Dictionary of Films and Filmmakers*, volume three, 1986.

JOHN HENRY FAULK

American Humorist

***Born* Austin, Texas, 21 August 1913**

***Died* Austin, Texas, 9 April 1990**

John Henry Faulk, humorist and radio personality, had many of the qualities which he attributed to the mockingbird. Not only was the mockingbird a songster without peers, according to Faulk, but it was "one of the most independent and cantankerous fellows in the feathered world." Admirers would quarrel with the use of "cantankerous" to describe Faulk, though many of the hillbilly characters he wove tales around on his radio programmes would qualify as such. He was, however, an independent spirit, all would agree.

It was this spirit which prompted Faulk to take up arms against the McCarthyite witch-hunters who, in the 1950s, were busy black-listing entertainers suspected of having Communist leanings. Faulk won his battle, but at great cost to himself and to his family. For six years, while the libel suit against his detractors was pending, no radio or television network would hire him.

As a humorist, Faulk was hailed as the "new Will Rogers", a misleading comparison. Rogers's humour was topical; he took delight in taking sly digs at congressmen and other fat cats. Besides, he was a showman, relying upon a ten-gallon Stetson, cowboy chaps and a twirling rope to give him the proper homespun image (Rogers starred in Ziegfeld *Follies* as well as in films). In contrast, Faulk (whose true medium was radio) was brilliant in imitating the characters he had encountered in his travels in the Texas Panhandle. He did for Texas folklore what Woody Guthrie had done for the Oklahoma variety.

Faulk, who smoked a pipe and favoured cloth caps, was born in Austin, Texas, the son of a judge. He took a Master's degree in folklore at the University of Texas and went on to teach the subject there. During World War II he was rejected in the call-up because of poor eyesight and served with the American Red Cross in the Middle East, before being allowed to join the US Army in a limited-service capacity.

Faulk was hosting a radio show in Paterson, New Jersey, when he came to the notice of a Columbia Broadcasting System executive, who, having heard Faulk's tall tales at a party, invited him to create a network programme. The result was the long-running *Johnny's Front Porch*. Faulk worked on many CBS television and radio shows but, in 1957, he was suddenly fired without explanation, though his ratings were high.

The answer was not long in forthcoming. Faulk had been named as a Communist suspect by Aware, Inc, a self-appointed watchdog group formed to "combat the Communist conspiracy in entertainment communications". Aware's proof? Faulk had run for office in the American Federation of Television and Radio Artists on an anti-blacklisting slate. Also he had attended a United Nations dinner for Andrei Gromyko, the Soviet foreign minister.

Faulk sued Aware, Inc, and two of its founders for libel. He hired a shrewd criminal lawyer, Louis Nizer, to plead his suit. To tide him over financially while the case dragged on in the courts, Faulk opened a small advertising agency in Austin.

In June 1962 a jury awarded Faulk a record 3.5 million dollars, later reduced on appeal to 725,000 dollars. He collected only a fraction of this latter sum, however, as Aware had become insolvent. But he had broken the black-listers' stranglehold on the entertainment industry. Belated recognition of his contribution came in October 1975 when CBS broadcast *Fear on Trial*, based on Faulk's own account of his libel action.

In recent years Faulk was a popular figure on the university lecture circuit, where he gave fresh insights on such unhumorous topics as civil rights. He also wrote and performed a one-man show, *Pear Orchard*, detailing the further adventures of the cracker-barrel characters who had appeared in *Johnny's Front Porch*.

Faulk was prized by such broadcasting colleagues as Edgar R. Murrow and Walter Cronkite as a doughty fighter against injustice, to which the Texan might have replied that he had done no more than any other independent and cantankerous fellow would have done.

Born John Henry Faulk. **Parents** John Henry, judge, and Martha Cynthia (Miner) Faulk. **Marriages** Two marriages; 2) Elizabeth Peake, 1965. **Children** Tannehill, Johanna, Evelyn and Frank, from first marriage; John Henry, from second marriage. **Education** University of Texas, BA in English, 1936, MA in folklore, 1940. **Military service** US Army, 1944–46. **Career** Lecturer, English Department, University of Texas, Austin, 1942; field director, American Red Cross, Cairo, Egypt, 1942–44; radio programme host, 1946–48; created *Johnny's Front Porch*, 1949; *John Henry Faulk Show*, 1951–57; television programmes, CBS television, 1951–57; elected to office on anti-blacklist platform, American Federation of Television and Radio Artists, 1955; accused of Communist ties by Aware Incorporated, 1956; contract terminated by CBS, 1957; owner, advertising firm, Austin, Texas, 1957–62; sued Aware Incorporated, 1957–62, awarded damages; first film appearance, 1963; regular contributor, *Hee-Haw* television programme; wrote and performed, *Pear Orchard* one-man show; consultant, TV-film adaptation of

Fear on Trial, 1975. **Other activities** Served with American Red Cross, World War II, Precinct chairman, Austin Democratic Committee; member, Travis County Democratic Executive Committee. **Offices and memberships** Member, International Platform Association, board of governors, 1967; member, American Federation of Television and Radio Artists, vice-president; member, Screen Actors Guild. **Awards and honours** Fellow, Julius Rosenwald Foundation, 1941–42. **Films** *All the Way Home*, 1963; *The Best Man*, 1964. **Television** *John Henry Faulk Show*, 1951–57; *It's News to Me*, *Leave It to the Girls*, *Walk a Mile for a Camel*, 1953–55. **Radio** *Johnny's Front Porch*, 1949. **Publication** *Fear on Trial*, 1964. **Cause of death** Cancer, at age 76.

PETER FULLER

British Art Critic

***Born* Damascus, Syria, August 1947**

***Died* Near Oxford, England, 28 April 1990**

Within the British art world Peter Fuller's was one of the most "Establishment" of all dissident voices. Once christened "the red Tory" by artist and writer Victor Burgin, Fuller had constructed a niche for himself as guardian of the good sense and timeless values of English art, under threat from a transatlantic Modernist conspiracy to erase standards, good taste and draughtsmanship from the aesthetic agenda.

He did more than any other contemporary critic to formulate and maintain an English figurative romantic tradition which he firmly believed in upholding, constructed as it was upon fairly recent precedent. The tradition evolved into his only preoccupation, spawning a criticism that could be seen as regressive and reactionary but which was perfect for its time.

A graduate of Peterhouse College, Cambridge, in the late 1960s, Fuller achieved his final stance only after he had flirted with and rejected the Marxist philosophy fashionable at that time. His career began, like that of his then mentor, the critic John Berger, as a writer for the left-wing journal *New Society*. Here, in the 1970s, he produced a series of articles broadly expounding the "true faith". His Marxism was however short-lived and by the 1980s he had repudiated Berger and all that he stands for and taken up the mantle of the foremost art critic for Prime Minister Thatcher's New Victorian Britain.

At *New Society* and concurrently at *Art Monthly*, Fuller had written volubly in support of his then unshakeable Marxism, indulging in skirmishes with the art world from the perspective of the Left. His belligerent style never really changed, he simply underwent a transformation which concentrated his skills as a apologist for the Right. His aplomb as a self-publicist, together with his oratorical style of journalism, made certain that his new position of antagonism toward the art world caused as much if not more furore than had his old one. He continued to write for a variety of newspapers and journals, founding his own quarterly art magazine, *Modern Painters*, in 1988.

Fuller was often accused of inconsistency, having altered his opinions radically over the years. More charitably, he could been seen to have been engaged upon a search for a guiding philosophical precept. His initial enthusiasm for Freud, elaborated in two books, *The Champions* and *Art and Psychoanalysis*, was superseded by his preoccupation with Marx. This in turn was jettisoned to be displaced by the English spirituality of that most eminent of Victorians, the art critic John Ruskin. All three assumed in their turn an enormous importance for Fuller, who defended and enlarged upon their views with characteristic intransigence.

As the critic all others loved to hate, Fuller stirred up debate around issues which assumed some importance through his own tenacity and rhetorical skills. Latterly, through the medium of *Modern Painters*, he addressed himself to an audience convinced of the degeneracy of modern art and offered salvation through a neo-Ruskinite revival. Like many critics who are perhaps more inclined toward journalism than academia, Peter Fuller had a touching faith in the quality of his own taste as a benchmark of artistic excellence. His writing often displayed a combination of erudition, prejudice and anecdote but never ceased to be challenging. Bellicose in the extreme, Fuller characterized his position as one of "belligerent entrenchment". Always provocative, often outrageous, Fuller's pronouncements were the judgements of one who believed in the importance and rectitude of his own position.

By encouraging an unholy alliance with the Thatcherites, as an art critical proponent of "Victorian values", Fuller established himself as the point from which all others could map out their positions. Fellow critic Waldemar Januszczak said upon his death "Without Peter Fuller to disagree with, the British art world has lost most of its immediate geography."

Born Peter Michael Fuller. **Parents** Harold William Charles, doctor, and Marjorie (Noyes) Fuller. **Marriages** 1) Colette Mejean, teacher, 1972 (dissolved); 2) Stephanie Burns, 1985. **Children** Sylvia, from first marriage; Laurence, from second marriage. **Education** Epsom College, Surrey; Peterhouse College, Cambridge, BA in English, MA, 1968. **Career** Staff writer, *City Press*, London, 1968–69; contributor: *Black Dwarf*, *Seven Days*, *New Society*, *Art Monthly*, *Village Voice*, *Art Forum*, *New Left Review*; founder/editor, *Modern Painters* magazine, 1988; art critic, *The Sunday Telegraph*, 1989–90. **Publications** (With John Halliday) *The Psychology of Gambling*, 1974; (contributor) *New Stories I*, 1976; *The Champions*, 1977; (contributor) *New Stories II*, 1977; *Robert Natkin*, 1980; *Art and Psychoanalysis*, 1980; *The Crisis of the Fine Arts*, 1980; *Seeing Berger*, 1980, republished as *Seeing Through Berger*, 1989; *Images of God: Consolations of Lost Illusions*, 1985; *The Australian Scapegoat*, 1986; *Marches Past* (autobiography), 1986; *Theoria: art and the absence of grace*, 1988. **Cause of death** Automobile accident, at age 42.

GRETA GARBO

Swedish/American Actress

Born **Stockholm, Sweden, 18 September 1905**

Died **Manhattan, New York, 15 April 1990**

Of all the art forms, film is the most personal: the viewer becomes trapped in the star's persona, so closely that their identities almost merge. Of the gods and goddesses raised above common humanity, none has surpassed Greta Garbo, the most exalted and the most exclusive. The star's seeming remoteness is the core of her appeal. Garbo's aloofness and mystery in over 25 movies in only 19 years made her probably the best known woman in the world, and her legend did not stop with her retirement, at the age of 36. She was dubbed "the incomparable one"; "the flaming icicle"; "the supreme symbol of inscrutable tragedy"; the Scandinavian sphinx"; "the woman of mystery"; "the woman who wants to be alone". Garbo was spoken of, even by more sober critics, as unequalled and unparalleled, so far superior to any other woman on the screen that she had to be classed apart.

But in 1918 in a backstreet barber's shop in Stockholm's shipyards, Garbo was a large, lively teenager, the lather-girl, chatting up the clientele. Fully grown and over-large at 12, her father's early death a year later left her the family bread-winner. Her first break came in trade films for the department store where she'd become a milliner's assistant. In these comic shorts, Greta Gustafsson showed "How Not to Dress" and "How Not to Behave in a Restaurant". She looked like a mature woman at 15 but was hardly less gauche than the comic character she portrayed. But she always had a reputation for being ambitious and the Royal Dramatic Theatre School saw in her dramatic potential, awarding her a scholarship for two years from the month of her eighteenth birthday.

The plump mature-looking young woman was little changed when famous Scandinavian director, Mauritz Stiller, picked her out of the drama school ranks with the famous remark "You get a face like that in front of the camera only once in the century." As her Svengali, he set about creating her, rather as Von Sternberg was to do later with Marlene Dietrich. She was almost named Gabor after an obscure Hungarian prince but a variation was selected to replace the too-common Gustafsson. Stiller cast her in the Swedish classic *The Atonement of Gösta Berling*, a European success for both director and star. The two were in Berlin, living lavishly on film development money, hoping for a stroke of luck, when Louis B. Mayer of Metro-Goldwyn-Mayer encountered Stiller in the hotel lobby. He offered Stiller an MGM contract, which Stiller only accepted when the studio agreed to take on Greta Garbo. Mayer showed his reluctance, remarking disparagingly, "American men like their women to be slimmer".

Having told her mother, "I will be back in a year", Garbo arrived with Stiller in New York to almost no reception, though a proper one followed in Hollywood, complete with little girls in Scandinavian dress singing folk tunes on the train platform. No one thought this large mature woman could be under 21, with a contract invalid until signed by her mother. She was not what they'd expected and was for some time a laughing stock. The MGM star machine however set about grooming her. She shed 26 pounds; her eyebrows were plucked, her hairline changed and her teeth capped. She was transformed into a film immortal.

Stiller was the true star-maker. When Garbo was cast in her first MGM film, *The Torrent*, he secretly rehearsed her at night. He advised, in fact insisted, on how she should be shot. He himself was one of the first masters of the close-up and in all her career, Garbo was rarely photographed in long shot, where her awkwardness, or at least lankiness, would have been exposed. Stiller even insisted that she be shot only on the most expensive film stock to maximize the quality of the close-ups. She herself modelled her acting on her favourite Swedish star, now forgotten, whom she described as "So much soul and so tired, always". This, too, Stiller exaggerated by arranging it so that she was bored and overtired before they eventually got to her takes.

The Nordic sphinx as a Spanish peasant in *The Torrent* was enough of a success to lead to a pairing with Stiller in *The Temptress*. Stiller was not the "company man" that Hollywood expected and was removed from the film. He suffered a similar fate on pictures for other studios before returning to Sweden only to die soon afterwards — clutching a photograph of Garbo.

Garbo was devastated by Stiller's removal from the picture. He still coached her but her confidence was shattered. Without Stiller on the set, she developed a nervous twitch: uncontrollable blinking that threatened the completion of the film and her entire career. By chance, the director discovered that by playing Garbo in slow motion the blinking problem wasn't noticeable. Garbo in slow motion was even more languorous and was that much more effective. It was literally still-life acting. So it was almost by accident that the strained look became her style, dramatically counterpointing the desperation of the characters she played.

Garbo made her first and only personal appearance at a Hollywood *première*. When asked if she spoke English yet, she replied "Not von vord", to howls of laughter. She felt they were laughing at, not with, her and never attended another *première* in her entire career.

Actually she was hardly mentioned in the reviews of her first films. But the MGM contract was generous enough for her already to be able to afford a house, a car and servants. The studio notables and producer, Irving Thalberg, had noticed her and she was cast in *Flesh and the Devil*, with John Gilbert, Hollywood's idol and highest paid star. A compulsive romantic, Gilbert contrived to live the role he was playing off-screen as well as on. A raging love affair began, curing Garbo of her melancholia over Stiller, igniting their film scenes and giving the press office something to write about.

The public's insatiable appetite for Garbo stories had begun, leaving the MGM press office with a particular problem. Garbo's limited English did not extend to the slang of Hollywood's press. She was always badly misunderstood and genuinely could not see why the public had any interest in her opinions on any topic from politics to the desirability of men with moustaches.

Character actor Lon Chaney (of *The Hunchback of Notre Dame*) sympathized with her increasing agony. He advised her "Mystery has served me well — it could do as much for you." The MGM publicity department took over, building her up as a "woman of mystery". In the hands of her new manager, Henry Edington, she became the most exclusive female star in Hollywood. He negotiated a record salary approaching 5000 dollars a week, and built an image of enigmatic aloneness that she played up to in her films. By playing up her secretiveness, she got her privacy and she got people talking about her.

Garbo was now a full-blown star, not just another leading lady. Three films a year followed for several years. In all of them she played a deeply sensual woman whose love for the hero led to the abandonment of old loyalties and ultimate tragedy. Sin punished satisfied the censors, while allowing for the horizontal love scenes that had become her trademark. These are not *Hollywood's* great movie stories, it was Garbo who transformed them into classics.

Contemporary columnist Malcolm Oettinger, on the set of *Love*, was mesmerized by the sight of Garbo in the arms of John Gilbert. "The air was surcharged, the atmosphere glowed. As they embraced unaware of anyone else, the heat curled the walls, blistered the chairs, all but stifled in its intensity... she sits back and looks at you through heavy-lidded, half-closed eyes, her lips parted in a tempting smile. She represents 'Sex Incarnate'." In *Love* she played Tolstoy's Anna Karenina. She was now a megastar, acting the role of a mother of a ten-year-old son — but Garbo herself was only 22 years old.

Off-screen, after countless film costumes, she preferred simply to wear trousers and shirts and flat shoes (although Hollywood would not admit to stocking anything as gauche as flat shoes). She preferred not to socialize but had her own close friends whom she saw often. Her real-estate investments made her one of the richest women in the world, yet she still sent money home to her family in Sweden. She finally got back to visit them before risking all with her first talking picture.

Anna Christie was the vehicle, sold quite simply with the promise, "Garbo Talks". Talkies ruined countless careers including John Gilbert's. But Garbo cultivated deep tones which were an international sensation. One "supreme romantic tragedy" followed the next: *Camille*, *Queen Christina*, *Anna Karenina* (again), mostly with director Clarence Brown. But with the war, her European audiences dried up and Americans were tired of period pieces. Garbo proved herself the comedienne in director Ernst Lubitsch's *Ninotchka*, sold as "Garbo Laughs". *Two-Faced Woman*, a screwball comedy, was not such a success and Garbo retired "temporarily" during the war. She was 36. She never returned to the screen.

For almost the next 50 years, she was instantly recognizable — incognito — in her camouflage uniform of dark glasses, tea-cosy hat, raincoat and trousers, grocery shopping near her New York apartment. She lived a spartan life, seemingly alone and unhappy in only two rooms of the larger apartment. But alone meant tea in London with Mrs Anthony Eden, wife of the then prime minister, or at the Sporting Club in Monte Carlo with Aristotle Onassis. She was tenuously engaged to English photographer and designer Cecil Beaton, and was romantically linked (often with fabrication) to 100 famous men. We don't know the details, for although she is said to have read every article ever written about her, she would allow no official biography.

As for her screen presence, her magnetic charm has never been truly defined; the mysterious ingredients of her beauty are elusive. She was a professional and let her work stand for her. As MGM "hyped" prophetically, "Once seen, never forgotten". Truly a case of "what more could be said about a picture — see it". Never a dramatic, narrative actress, with her unique still-life acting, always shot in the close-ups and angles Stiller had advised, she made every drab vehicle memorable.

For years after he directed her, the famous George Cukor would still point out the chair in which Garbo sat by his pool. Idolized even at the pinnacle of Hollywood, she truly merits the exalted status that has been attached to her.

Born Greta Lovisa Gustafsson. **Parents** Karl, unskilled labourer, and Anna Gustafsson. **Education** Catherine Elementary School, Stockholm, 1912–19; Royal Dramatic Theatre School, Stockholm, 1922–24. **Emigration** Left Sweden for US, 1925, naturalized 1951. **Career** Barber's shop latherer, 1920; in millinery department, Bergstrom's department store, model, 1921–22; advertising films for PUB and the Co-operative Society of Stockholm; film début, 1921; met Mauritz Stiller and cast in leading role in his *The Atonement of Gösta Berling*, 1923; contract player, Metro-Goldwyn-Mayer, Hollywood, 1925–41; first Hollywood film, *The Torrent*, 1926; first sound film, *Anna Christie*, 1930; retired, 1941; agreed to appear in but later withdrew from *La Duchesse de Langeais*, 1949. **Awards and honours** Received Academy Award nomination for best actress: *Anna Christie*, 1929/30, *Romance*, 1929/30, *Camille*, 1937, *Ninotchka*, 1939; received New York Film Critics' Society Best Actress Award: for *Anna Karenina*, 1935, for *Camille*, 1936; Special Academy Award, 1954. **Films** *En lyckoriddare* (*A Fortune Hunter*), 1921; *Herr och fru Stockholm* (*Mr and Mrs Stockholm, How Not to Dress*), 1921; *Our Daily Bread*, 1921; *Luffar-Petter* (*Peter the Tramp*), 1922; *Gösta Berlings Saga* (*The Atonement of Gösta Berling*), 1924; *Die Freudlose Gasse* (*The Joyless Street*), 1925; *The Torrent*, 1926; *The Temptress*, 1926; *Flesh and the Devil*, 1926; *Love*, 1927; *The Divine Woman*, 1928; *The Mysterious Lady*, 1928; *A Woman of Affairs*, 1928; *Wild Orchids*, 1929; *A Man's Man*, 1929; *The Single Standard*, 1929; *The Kiss*, 1929; *Anna Christie*, 1930; *Romance*, 1930; *Inspiration*, 1931; *Susan Lenox: Her Fall and Rise*, 1931; *Mata Hari*, 1932; *Grand Hotel*, 1932; *As You Desire Me*, 1932; *Queen Christina*, 1933; *The Painted Veil*, 1934; *Anna Karenina*, 1935; *Camille*, 1936; *Conquest*, 1937; *Ninotchka*, 1939; *Two-Faced Woman*, 1941. **Cause of death** Kidney disease, at age 84. **Further reading** Cesar Arconada, *Leben der Greta Garbo,* 1930; Franz Blei, *Die Göttliche Garbo*, 1930; Cesar Arconada, *Vita di Greta Garbo*, 1930; Rilla Page Palmborg, *The Private Life of Greta Garbo*, 1931; Roland Wild, *Greta Garbo*, 1933; Richard Kühn, *Greta Garbo: Der Weg einer Frau und Künstlerin*, 1935; Alexander Lernet Holenia, *Greta Garbo: Ein Wunder in Bildern*, 1937; E. E. Laing, *Greta Garbo: The Story of a Specialist*, 1946; John Bainbridge, *Garbo*, 1955; John Wallin, *Garbo en stjärnas väg*, 1955; Fritiof Billquist, *Garbo: A Biography*, 1960; Mercedes de Acosta, *Here Lies the Heart*; Michael Conway, Dion McGregor and Marc Ricci, *The Films of Greta Garbo*, 1963; Fausto Montesanti, *Greta Garbo*, 1963; Raymond Durgnat and John Kobal, *Greta Garbo*, 1964; Fernando Darte, *Greta Garbo*, 1965; Norman Zierold, *Garbo*, 1969; Sjolander Ture, *Garbo*, 1971; Marjorie Rosen, *Popcorn Venus*, 1973; Richard Corliss, *Greta Garbo*, 1974; Charles Affron, *Star Acting: Gish, Garbo, Davis*, 1977; Frederick Sands and Sven Broman, *The Divine Garbo*, 1979; Alexander Walker, *Greta Garbo: A Portrait*, 1980; George Linton, *Greta Garbo*, 1981; *International Dictionary of Films and Filmmakers*, volume three, 1986; Antoni Gronowicz, *Garbo: Her Story*, 1990.

NORMAN GIBBS

British Historian

***Born* 17 April 1910**

***Died* 20 April 1990**

In his early thirties Norman Gibbs was to be found on the tank gunnery ranges at Lulworth Cove on the south coast of England, where he worked as an instructor in the 1st King's Dragoon Guards during the opening years of World War II. It was from there that he was transferred to the historical section of the British government cabinet office as one of the first officers to begin work on the official history of the war. And it was those studies which were to lead, just ten years later, to Gibbs's election as Chichele Professor of the History of War at Oxford University, a post he was to retain for 24 years, until 1977. In that year, he was made an emeritus fellow of All Souls College.

At the cabinet office he began by studying the role of British troops in Egypt prior to the war and how their training and preparation fitted them for facing Rommel's army in the Western Desert. He then assisted Professor W. K. Hancock and wrote a study of the changing relations between government and military in Britain during the previous hundred years.

His Oxford career had begun in 1928 when he gained an open exhibition to Magdalen College from his London grammar school. He read history and became a "senior demy", a graduate student of the college, under the historian K. B. McFarlane, going on to complete a doctorate in 1935 entitled, "The History of Reading in the Later Middle Ages". After working for a short period as an assistant lecturer at University College, London, Gibbs returned to Oxford as tutor in modern history at Merton College. After three years, war interrupted, and then changed, the direction of his studies and when he resumed his fellowship after the war he taught both modern history and the Oxford "PPE" course: philosophy, politics and economics.

The Chichele Chair had been set up in 1909 but, later, the issue of whether offering war studies at university was morally suspect had come under question. At the time when Gibbs took over the post (from Cyril Falls) the very survival of the Chair was in doubt. Gibbs's tenure, however, began with a notable address on the origins of the British Committee of Imperial Defence (published in 1955), and ended with war studies being held in much higher esteem because of his efforts. His long and painstaking research culminated in the publication in 1976 of the first volume of his *History of the Second World War* and he became well known in the United States, holding visiting posts at US universities and, finally, at the US Military Academy, West Point, where a very successful year led to his being awarded the Outstanding Civilian Service Medal.

One of Gibbs's concerns was to make academic opportunities available to military personnel. To that end he arranged undergraduate courses for senior officers at Oxford and helped to establish Ministry of Defence fellowships and lectureships in other universities. He also lectured widely at military institutions in Britain and overseas. He became chairman of the Naval Education Advisory Council, a member of the International Council of the Institute for Strategic Studies and sponsored a series of NATO conferences at St John's College, Oxford, which attracted annually both academics and senior NATO officials, including the supreme allied commander, Europe. All of these activities contributed a great deal to cementing closer ties between governments, universities and armed forces.

Gibbs also took an interest in education at a level prior to university studies. For ten years, he was chairman of the Oxford "O" and "A" level schools examinations (the nationally attested exams for 16 and 18 year-olds at that time) world-wide. What helped make Norman Gibbs's tenure of the Chichele Chair so successful was that he brought to it a combination of familiarity with both the academic and military spheres. At the same time as he was forging links between these, he was also pursuing his own research and encouraging a growing band of post-graduates, so that he was able to hand on a very active tradition of research when he retired from the post. That familiarity with academia also extended to the arcane details of the organization of Oxford University so that, as a fellow of All Souls College during his professorship, he was able to see through college reforms. Tall and good-looking, with a reputation for applying himself kindly and cheerfully to diverse problems, he sat on numerous committees and took responsibility for a new scheme of visiting fellowships at All Souls, a radical change which needed delicate handling. His efforts even extended to overseeing the restocking of the All Souls cellars after the austerity of the post-war years, perhaps not the most onerous of the many duties he undertook.

On Norman Gibbs's eightieth birthday, three days before his death, a dinner was held in his honour at All Souls which was attended by colleagues, friends and former students from around the world. There he was presented with the proofs of a collection of essays dedicated to him and to be published under the title, *The Limitations of Military Power*.

Born Norman Henry Gibbs. **Marriage** 1) Joan Frances Leslie-Melville, 1941 (divorced 1954); 2) Kathleen Phebe Emmett, 1955 (died 1989). **Children** Two daughters, from first marriage. **Education** At (grammar) school in London; open exhibitioner, Magdalen College, Oxford, 1928, senior demy, 1931, first-class honours in history, BA, 1931, MA, DPhil in medieval history, 1935. **Military service** First King's Dragoon Guards, 1939–45, tank gunnery instructor, 1939–43, seconded to historical section, War Cabinet Office, 1943–45. **Career** Assistant lecturer, University College, London, 1934–35; fellow and tutor in modern history, Merton College, Oxford, 1936–39, in modern history and philosophy, politics and economics, 1945–53; Chichele Professor of the History of War, Oxford University, 1953–77; emeritus fellow, All Souls, Oxford, 1977–90. **Related activities** Chairman, Oxford ordinary and advanced level examinations, 1967–77, research associate, Center for International Studies, Princeton University, 1965–66; visiting professor: University of New Brunswick, 1975–76, United States Military Academy, West Point, 1978–79, National University of Singapore, 1982–84. **Other activities** Chairman, Naval Education Advisory Committee; international council member, Institute for Strategic Studies; council member, Royal United Service Institution. **Awards and honours** US Outstanding Civilian Service Medal, 1979. **Publications** (Editor of second edition) *British Cabinet System* by A. B. Keith, 1952; *The Origins of the Committee of Imperial Defence*, 1955; *Rearmament Policy*; (contributor) *Cambridge Modern History*; (contributor) *L'Europe du XIXme et du XXme siècles*, 1966; (editor) *The Soviet System and Democratic Society*, 1967; *History of the Second World War: The Grand Strategy*, 1976. **Cause of death** Undisclosed, at age 80. **Further reading** *The Limitations of Military Power (festschrift)*, 1990.

PAULETTE GODDARD

American Actress

Born **Whitestone, New York, 3 June 1905 or 1911**

Died **Porto Ronco, Switzerland, 23 April 1990**

Paulette Goddard was the woman of whom Anita Loos once said: "I always thought gentlemen preferred blondes until I met Paulette." Beautiful, naturally bright, and above all, versatile, she could be described as a "glamour girl" only in the sense that she knew instinctively how to attract people to the glamour that they wanted to see, without losing her integrity or warmth. As a young, bottle-blonde Ziegfeld girl she once organized a protest, and plenty of publicity for herself, against her employer for allegedly preferring brunettes, while Chaplin, her second husband, persuaded her to return to her natural chestnut hair colour to play the waif in *Modern Times*.

Paulette Goddard was born Pauline Marion Levy in Whitestone, New York. When she worked for Hal Roach in Hollywood, she contributed to her publicity file with the comment: "Paulette Goddard and Oscar Wilde say that any woman who tells her age tells anything." The most likely date of her birth is 3 June 1905, although the second, more commonly quoted one, is six years later. Goddard's Uncle Charlie was a successful businessman who gave, by all accounts, "the best parties on Long Island". Well-known people flocked to his house and the young Paulette, weary of moving from town to town after her parents' divorce, sensed that she could find a secure future for herself in a life of celebrity.

Leaving school at the age of 14 and nicely aware of her good looks, she began work as a fashion model and dancer. Her first Ziegfeld show was *No Foolin'* in 1926, followed by *Rio Rita*. Perhaps the most significant consequence for Goddard of her brief marriage to a wealthy lumber-merchant, Edgar W. James, was the substantial divorce settlement she received from him and with which she launched herself upon Hollywood. Certainly financial independence as much as looks and talent set her apart from the other shapely, blonde hopefuls at this stage in her career. It is possible that this first failed marriage also gave her a determination to succeed, wisely.

Goddard was a bit-part actress when she met Chaplin. He was 43, twice married and searching for a beautiful girl to play a destitute orphan in his new feature, *Modern Times*, which was to be the last major silent picture made in Hollywood. He described the story as one of "two non-descripts trying to get along in modern times". In fact, what he required from his prospective co-star was far removed from this: not only did she have to be a remarkable beauty and actress, she also had to communicate with him, both as the little tramp, and as the charismatic film star, while revealing personal qualities able to satisfy the demands of the audience. Playwright William Saroyan's 1941 description of Paulette Goddard comes closest to showing why she was perfect for the part. "What she has is an inner twinkle, and it goes around in a strictly non-sorrowing frame, all of it is attractively tough, challenging mischievous, coquettish, wicked and absolutely innocent".

Goddard often told the story of her first day on the set.

> When I turned up to make *Modern Times* I was wearing the full rig. Charlie took one look at me, shook his head and said "That's not it. That's definitely not it". He told me to take off my shoes, change my suit and remove my make-up. Then he threw a bucket of water all over me... He saw an "animal quality" in me that people have found so useful; the "gamine, barefoot actress".

During the film, Goddard studied literature, Spanish, French and psychology. Then the couple left to sail to China, Indonesia and Bali, where they were married, secretly, at sea. After *Modern Times* Goddard stood out as the leading contender for the part of Scarlett O'Hara in David O. Selznick's *Gone with the Wind*. She certainly believed that she had been chosen after the screen tests, but without rancour, told the bitter story of being "runner-up". "Selznick had as good as decided on me. I gave a tennis party to celebrate and Laurence Olivier turned up with his girlfriend, Vivien Leigh. Selznick took one look and that was that."

Jean Renoir, the French director, for whom she starred in *Diary of a Chambermaid*, once said of her: "She keeps company only with remarkable men, but she changes them often." During the break-up of her marriage with Chaplin, she began to fulfil this pattern, which continued for the remainder of her life. She had a minor flirtation with the 80-year-old H. G. Wells and the composer

George Gershwin was a passionate admirer. In 1938, her father, who had been libelled by *Collier's* magazine, allegedly losing his job because of this, sued Goddard for 600 dollars per month support payment, doubling the amount she already paid to him. Escaping from a good deal of unfavourable publicity, she flew to Mexico to meet a friend of Gershwin's, the muralist and artist Diego Rivera. Finding him under house arrest, she charmed her way past the police guards and flew with him to Texas to headlines of "Screen star rescues artist". Rivera, living in California, painted her face on the women figures in his murals. In *The Tree of Life*, dressed all in white, she and Rivera embrace a tree.

Goddard's film career progressed at a leisurely rate; she had the sophistication necessary for comedy and could be sultry or gutsy as the role required in melodrama. In 1939 she played opposite Bob Hope in *The Cat and the Canary* and was then cast in three grandiose epics for De Mille. Her natural vivacity served her well in the 1946 picture *Kitty* in which she plays a guttersnipe who snatches Thomas Gainsborough's shoe-buckle. Rather than prosecute her, he paints her portrait. The *New York World Telegraph's* critic wrote: "Paulette Goddard has worked up a blazing temperament to go with her ravishing beauty in the title role." Her co-stars certainly recognized her ability to infuse a scene with warmth and confidence. Ray Milland, with whom she starred in *The Lady Has Plans*, *Reap the Wild Wind* and *The Crystal Ball*, called her "the most honest actress that he had ever worked with", while Robert Benchley said simply, "She could charm a rock".

Joking that she now kept her engagement rings on a necklace, Paulette Goddard married Burgess Meredith, who co-wrote *Diary of a Chambermaid* for her. The newly married couple starred together in the play *Winterset* in Dublin and then she left for England, where she played Mrs Chevely in *An Ideal Husband* for Alexander Korda. Of her final marriage, in 1958 to Erich Maria Remarque, author of *All Quiet on the Western Front*, she commented: "I'm gregarious and he's sedentary. It works out fine." They lived together in a town overlooking Lake Maggiore in Switzerland, the move marking her semi-retirement from films. After his death, she sold her collection of Impressionist paintings for nearly three million dollars, giving a large proportion of the proceeds in scholarships to drama students. Her procession of remarkable men continued, to include a fascination with Andy Warhol who, naming her as one of his "Twelve Favourite Women", photographed her in white fox fur and announced his intention of writing her biography. After 80 hours of interviews, Paulette Goddard proudly announced that she had "told him nothing". In one of the last interviews that she gave, however, she spoke emphatically about her earlier career, refusing to accept that she had been a "glamour girl" and linking the term with its original, derogatory meaning. She said: "Glamour means a spell of charm — as one who deceives the sight. I don't want to be phony. I want to be real."

Born Pauline Marion Levy. **Marriages** 1) Edgar W. James, lumber-merchant, 1927 (divorced 1929); 2) Charlie Chaplin, actor, 1936 (divorced 1942); 3) Burgess Meredith, actor, 1944 (divorced 1949); 4) Erich Maria Remarque, writer, 1958 (died 1970). **Education** Mount St Dominic's Academy, Caldwell, New Jersey. **Career** Model, from 1925; stage début in Ziegfeld's *No Foolin'*, 1926; moved to North Carolina on marriage, 1927–29; contract player: Roach, Goldwyn, 1929–32; tutored by Chaplin, 1933–36; contracted to David O. Selznick under special arrangement with Chaplin, 1938; contract player, Paramount Studios, 1939–52; United Services Organization Far East tour, 1944; appeared in *Winterset*, Dublin, 1947; first television appearances, 1950; lived mainly in Europe, from 1954. **Stage** *No Foolin'*, 1927; *Winterset*, 1947; *Waltz of the Toreadors*, 1957; *Caesar and Cleopatra*. **Films** *Rio Rita*, 1929; *The Locked Door*, 1929; *Berth Marks*, 1931; *City Streets*, 1931; *The Girl Habit*, 1931; *The Mouthpiece*, 1932; *Show Business*, 1932; *Young Ironsides*, 1932; *Pack Up Your Troubles*, 1932; *Girl Grief*, 1932; *The Kid from Spain*, 1932; *Roman Scandals*, 1933; *Kid Millions*, 1934; *Modern Times*, 1936; *The Young in Heart*, 1938; *Dramatic School*, 1938; *The Women*, 1939; *The Cat and the Canary*, 1939; *The Ghost Breakers*, 1940; *The*

Great Dictator, 1940; *North West Mounted Police*, 1940; *Second Chorus*, 1940; *Pot o' Gold*, 1941; *Hold Back the Dawn*, 1941; *Nothing But the Truth*, 1941; *The Lady Has Plans*, 1941; *Reap the Wild Wind*, 1941; *The Forest Rangers*, 1942; *The Crystal Ball*, 1942; *Star Spangled Rhythm*, 1942; *So Proudly We Hail*, 1943; *Standing Room Only*, 1944; *I Love a Soldier*, 1944; *Duffy's Tavern*, 1945; *Kitty*, 1945; *Diary of a Chambermaid*, 1946; *Suddenly It's Spring*, 1947; *Variety Girl*, 1947; *Unconquered*, 1947; *A Miracle Can Happen*, 1947; *An Ideal Husband*, 1947; *Hazard*, 1948; *Bride of Vengeance*, 1949; *Anna Lucasta*, 1948; *The Torch*, 1949; *Babes in Baghdad*, 1952; *Vice Squad*, 1953; *Paris Model*, 1953; *Charge of the Lancers*, 1953; *Sins of Jezebel*, 1953; *The Stranger Came Home*, 1954; *Gli indifferenti* (*A Time of Indifference*), 1963; *The Snoop Sisters* (television), 1972. **Cause of death** Heart failure, at age 78 or 84. **Further reading** J. R. Parish, *The Paramount Pretties*, 1972; J. Morella and E. Z. Epstein, *Paulette*, 1985; *International Dictionary of Films and Filmmakers*, volume three, 1986.

DEXTER GORDON

American Jazz Saxophonist and Actor

Born **Log Angeles, California, 27 February 1923**

Died **Philadelphia, Pennsylvania, 25 April 1990**

Dexter Gordon exerted his greatest influence on jazz during the 1940s, but due fame didn't catch up with him until decades later when his charismatic personality caused him to be singled out not just as a great jazz inventor, but also as a film star and actor.

Although he also played the soprano saxophone in his later years, it was on tenor that he was one of the prime movers in the modern jazz of the 1940s that came to be known as bebop. He set the role for his instrument in the way that Charlie Parker had done for the alto, Dizzy Gillespie for the trumpet and Bud Powell for the piano.

His 6 feet, 5 inches and good looks marked him out even before you noticed the unusually relaxed amble with which he carried his frame from place to place. He was, if you will, ultimately hip.

Gordon did his re-thinking of the role of the tenor sax at a time when the florid style of Coleman Hawkins and the ascetic, lean playing of Lester Young had provided two very clear paths for young players to follow. Gordon slipped between the two, although his terse, unembroidered solos owed much more to Young than to Hawkins. He learned much from Charlie Parker, too, although Parker's incandescent playing was suited only to the alto. When reinterpreted by Gordon it became smoother and less angular.

He was a master of "quotes" — fitting bits of other songs into whatever he happened to be playing with great skill and humour. He was also very receptive to new ideas, even when he became older. He inspired the young John Coltrane and was aware enough to take the influence back when he heard the giant strides that Coltrane had taken. No one will ever know just how many great saxophone players he influenced, but among the better known were Jimmy Heath, Coltrane, Allen Eager, Jackie McLean, Sonny Rollins and Clifford Jordan.

Gordon first took up the clarinet, studying harmony and musical theory from the age of 13. He was soon playing with contemporary Los Angelenos Charlie Mingus and Buddy Collette. When he was 15 he took on the alto saxophone and made the final change to the tenor two years later. He left school in 1940 and joined a local band called the Harlem Collegians. In December of that year he joined the Lionel Hampton band and stayed there for three years. The extrovert Hampton provided a platform which allowed Dexter to make a name for himself amongst saxophonists from coast to coast. One of his disciples was Sonny Stitt. "I rode 35 miles on my bicycle", Stitt remembered, "from my home to Flint, Michigan, to hear Dexter with Hampton. But he was good, what he had to play. Later on, of course, I really heard him when I joined Billy Eckstine in '45. Boy! He was out front of that band, shouting like a trumpet man. He was doing it right even then!"

Gordon claimed that he wasn't really aware of the more voluptuous tenor styles of Coleman Hawkins and Ben Webster until he was well past his formative years. During these he had listened to Dick Wilson and Herschel Evans as well as Lester Young. He also drew inspiration from a non-tenor saxophonist, trumpeter Roy Eldridge.

When he left Hampton, Gordon played first with a sextet led by Lester Young's brother, the drummer Lee Young. Joining the Fletcher Henderson Orchestra in 1943, he thus completed a remarkable line for Henderson who had had in turn over the years, Coleman Hawkins, Lester Young, Ben Webster and Chu Berry in his solo tenor chair. Dexter led his own quintet in Los Angeles that same year, using Harry Edison on trumpet and Nat "King" Cole on piano. In 1944 he joined Louis Armstrong's big band for six months and then joined the turbulent new big band led by Billy Eckstine.

Billy's band held the cream of the young beboppers, including from time to time, Charlie Parker, Dizzy Gillespie, Fats Navarro, Sarah Vaughan (q.v.), Art Blakey (q.v.), Gene Ammons and Sonny Stitt. Dexter travelled with the band to New York, where it made records for the DeLuxe and National labels, and finally settled in the city. Said Gordon, "Sonny Stitt was on the band and sounding like a whirlwind then. Part of the sax section was called the Unholy Four — Stitt, myself, John Jackson and Leo Parker. We liked to rehearse so we'd get our parts first from Jerry Valentine, the trombonist-arranger with the band. We'd room together, hang out together. We were so full of tempestuous youth that things didn't always go too smoothly." It was while with Eckstine's band that he came under the influence of Dizzy Gillespie and, as he put it, "dug other things besides Lester".

While with Lionel Hampton Gordon had been required to take part in crowd-pleasing tenor saxophone battles with the frenetic Illinois Jacquet, a man who specialized in screaming high notes. Gordon slipped easily into this form of playing and loved the way in which he and Jacquet were able to strike ideas off each other. He developed the method with more sophistication but amidst no less excitement when he and Gene Ammons played tenor duets in the Eckstine band. The two were featured on the band's recording of "Blowin' The Blues Away", the first really successful saxophone tandem in jazz. Gordon identified himself further with the style when he recorded a series of battles with Wardell Gray, another long, tall tenor. Gray's style was more closely based on Lester Young's than Gordon's and the two men showed an affinity in duet which has perhaps not been matched by any tenor players since. The two constantly inspired each other and the success of "The Chase" brought real fame to both of them. "The Chase" took up two sides of a record featuring the two horns in chase choruses (following each other) reducing evenly from 32 bars a piece to 16, eight and then four bars. Recorded in 1947, the record became the Dial label's biggest seller, out-selling even Charlie Parker's classic work for the same label.

Gordon's solos on his 1945 recordings with Dizzy Gillespie's Sextet ("Groovin' High" and "Blue 'n' Boogie") showed an astute harmonic awareness, and yet his clarity of line meant that his work could reach out easily to non-musician listeners. In 1945, too, he played at the Spotlite Club on New York's Fifty-second Street in a group that included Charlie Parker, Miles Davis, Bud Powell and Max Roach. "Bird would leave Miles and me with our mouths open every night", Gordon said.

Gordon returned to Los Angeles in 1946 and developed his partnership with Wardell Gray at a club called Jack's Basket. "There'd be a lot of cats on the stand, but by the end of the session it would wind up with Wardell and myself. "The Chase" grew out of this." Both men were addicted to heroin and Gray died in 1955 in disputed circumstances but certainly suffering from an overdose. Drugs and drink remained a problem for Gordon during most of his career and his addiction was to keep him away from the jazz scene for long periods, by way of both prison sentences and periods of ill health.

The quantity of his recordings dwindled from the time of his first incarceration in 1952, although in 1955 he played in at least three fine recording sessions. After one of his convictions he was sent to Chino, an open prison, and here his interest in acting began. He had a part in the film *Unchained*. "I had a few lines, but when I was seen playing the tenor, the soundtrack wasn't me."

Playwright Carl Thaler hired Gordon in 1960 for the Los Angeles production of Jack Gelber's play about drug addicts, *The Connection*. Gordon wrote the music for the play, led the band, which appeared on stage, and also took one of the main speaking roles. "One supposes the fact that the musicians on stage are all Negro is also symbolic", wrote John Tynan in a highly critical review. "Not so", said Gordon. "I simply looked for the best musicians I could find."

Because of his drug convictions Gordon was restricted by parole conditions and, like Billie Holiday, was unable to obtain a cabaret card, a permit to work, from the New York city authorities. Despite the resurgence of his career in a superb series of recordings for the Blue Note label in the early 1960s, this meant that he was unable to play in the city that was the most important source of employment for a jazz musician. He decided to move to Europe and, in autumn 1962, began a stay of 14 years in Copenhagen, broken only by brief visits to the USA in 1965, 1969 and 1970.

Gordon gave new impetus to the jazz scene in Europe as his still-potent influence took hold of the younger players. He made many broadcasts on Danish radio — these have subsequently been released on compact discs and show that the high standards achieved with his Blue Note recordings were no flash in the pan. He also recorded with a wide range of American peers including Stan Getz, Ben Webster, Jackie McLean, Charlie Mingus and Johnny Griffin.

He didn't return to the US until 1976, when he intended simply to visit his homeland and then return to Denmark. But the visit demonstrated to him that he had become fashionable again there. Each of the jazz clubs at which he played was sold out and such was the demand for return visits that he came back home permanently in 1977. Especially notable was his appearance with the ill-starred Woody Shaw's band at the Village Vanguard. He made another series of good recordings, this time for CBS, which, while they were not up to the standards of the Blue Note sessions or the broadcasts in Denmark, showed a man still in possession of great musical powers.

Gordon was more or less in retirement from 1983 until 1986 when he was asked to take the leading role in Bertrand Tavernier's film *Round Midnight*. Tavernier recalled,

> As soon as I started to think about this project, I decided it would be much more interesting to try a musician as an actor, rather than the reverse. There were precise gestures, movements, some relationship between the musician and the reed that I'd seen in documentaries, but that I'd never found in any feature film. I saw a film of Dexter Gordon in concert that I found absolutely stunning! The way he was moving his hands, the way he was walking, the movement of his feet — everything! Dexter was unique.

Gordon was nominated for an Academy Award as best actor for his work. Shortly before his death he completed work in the film *Awakenings* with Robin Williams and Robert De Niro, where Dexter was cast as a patient in a psychiatric ward.

Having set the style of bebop tenor in the 1940s Gordon saw no need to do much but fine tune his style in the decades that followed. He slipped easily into the modern harmony of the 1960s and 1970s and remained a viable soloist until the end, a man gifted with an eloquent and beautiful style of ballad playing and a fierce and unflagging inventiveness on his faster outpourings.

Born Dexter Keith Gordon. **Father** Doctor. **Marriage** Maxine. **Children** Robin, Deirdre, Mikael, Benjamin and Woody. **Education** Jefferson High School. **Career** Studied clarinet from

1936; studied saxophone with Lloyd Reese, played with other Reese pupils including Charlie Mingus and Buddy Collette; played with The Harlem Collegians; joined Lionel Hampton's touring band, 1940–43; appeared in Louis Armstrong "Soundies" (three-minute films); first solo recordings as leader of quintet with Nat "King" Cole as sideman, 1943; played with Lee Young, Jesse Price and the Fletcher Henderson Orchestra, 1944; joined Louis Armstrong band, 1944; played with Billy Eckstine's band, 1944–45; recorded "bebop" with Eckstine, Dizzy Gillespie, Fats Navarro, 1944; formed own group, Three Deuces; alternated between East and West Coast engagements, 1945–50; fought "saxophone duels" with Wardell Gray, 1947–52; playing curtailed by drug problems, 1952–60; imprisoned for heroin possession, 1952–54, 1956–60; composer/musician/actor, *The Connection* (play by Jack Gelber), 1960; recording contract, Blue Note records, 1961–65; toured US, 1960–62; based in Copenhagen, 1962–77, appeared in *Just Jazz*, PBS, 1971; toured Europe; toured Japan, 1975; returned to US, 1977; retired, 1983–86; concentrated on film acting, 1986–90. **Related activities** Taught for Worker's Cultural Foundation, Malmo, Sweden; taught for Jazz and Youth Society, Vallkilde, Denmark, 1968. **Awards and honours** Won *Down Beat* reader's poll, 1971; Academy Award nomination for best actor, for *Round Midnight*, 1986. **Compositions** (include) "Antabus"; "Candlelight Lady"; "The Apartment"; "Ernie's Tune"; "Tivoli"; "The Girl With The Purple Eyes"; "The Rainbow People"; "Montmartre"; "Boston Bernie"; "Fried Banana"; "Mrs Miniver"; "Valse Robin"; "The Panther"; "Stanley the Steamer". **Stage** *The Connection* (actor, composer, bandleader), 1960. **Films** *Unchained* (actor), 1955; *Round Midnight* (actor and musician), 1986; *Awakenings* (actor), 1990. **Albums** (include) *Master Takes: The Savoy Recordings with Bud Powell, Fats Navarro and Tadd Dameron/Long Tall Dexter*, Savoy, 1945–47; *Dexter: The Dial Sessions*, Storyville, 1947; (with Wardell Gray) *The Chase*, Savoy, 1947; *The Bethlehem Years*, Bethlehem, 1955; *Doin' Allright*, Blue Note, 1961; *Dexter Calling*, Blue Note, 1961; *Go*, Blue Note, 1962; *Our Man in Paris*, Blue Note, 1963; *More than You Know*, 1975; *Homecoming*, Columbia, 1976; *Biting the Apple*, Steeplechase, 1976; *Round Midnight*, Columbia, 1986; also: *Jazz Concert — West Coast*, Savoy, *The Foremost*, Onyx/Polydor, (sideman) Billy Eckstine's *Together*, *Dexter Blows Hot and Cool*, (sideman) Wardell Gray's *Central Avenue*, Prestige, *A Swing' Affair*, Blue Note, *One Flight Up*, Blue Note, *Dexter Gordon*, Blue Note, *The Apartment, The Meeting*, (with J. McLean) *The Source*, Steeple, *Tower of Power*, *More Power*, *The Panther*, *The Jumpin' Blues*, *Generation*, *Blues A La Suisse*, *Tangerine*, *Ca' Purange*, Prestige, *Montmartre Collection*, Blue Lion, *A Day in Copenhangen*, BASF, *Charlie Parker Memorial*, Chess, *Newport in New York: The Jam Sessions* Volume 3 and 4, Cobble, *The Foremost*; *Gettin' Around*, *Blues Walk*, Black Lion. **Singles** (include) "I Found a New Baby"/"Rosetta", Mercury/Clef 8900, 1943; (with Billy Eckstine) "Blowin' The Blues Away", Deluxe 2001, 1944; "Groovin' High"; (with Dizzy Gillespie) "Blue 'N' Boogie", Guild 1001, 1945; "Long Tall Dexter", Savoy 603, 1946; (with Wardell Gray) "The Chase", Dial 1017, 1947; also: "The Steeplechase", "Rocks 'N' Shoals", "The Duel", "Move", "I Guess I'll Hang My Tears Out To Dry"; "Dexter's Minor Mad"; "Blow Mr Dexter"; "Dexter Rides Again". **Cause of death** Kidney failure and throat cancer, at age 67. **Further reading** R. Nieus, *A Discography of Dexter Gordon*, 1986; T. Sjogren, *Long Tall Dexter: The Discography of Dexter Gordon*, 1986.

ARTHUR HOUGHTON JR

American Industrialist and Arts Patron

Born **Corning, New York, 12 December 1906**

Died **Venice, Florida, 3 April 1990**

Arthur Amory Houghton Jr may well have been born to privilege but he nonetheless was a man of very wide interests who gave generously both of his time and money because he believed things should be done and because he cared enough to see them through to completion.

He was the great-grandson of Amory Houghton, a founder of Corning Glass Works in 1851. After St Paul's School, Concord, New Hampshire, he went to Harvard and, under the influence of the great librarian, George Parker Winship, became entranced by books. It was a lifelong passion. After Harvard he returned to Corning for a year to join the family firm and work his way through its various departments but when he moved to New York he was able to pursue his love with intelligence and diligence.

He made the acquaintance of the great A. S. R. Rosenbach, the celebrated "Doctor" of the book world and whose excursions into the great libraries of Britain furnished him with many gems for serious collectors with serious bank accounts. Houghton spent happy evenings at Rosenbach's and usually left with something, such as a Restoration play that took his eye, tucked under his arm. This was his discreet manner of saying thank-you. But he was also a deeply committed collector, in particular of English literature. With Rosenbach's assistance he built up one of the world's richest collections of poetry and prose from the Elizabethan and Jacobean eras. He was also interested in the Romantic period and was able to create the finest collection of Keats's manuscripts in private hands. Houghton also had a good eye for rare books outside his chosen field and acquired, among other items, a 42-line Gutenberg Bible which he later sold when insurance would only cover it while in a bank vault.

His interest in rare books became widely known — the circle is a comparatively small one — and it was felt that William (Bill) Jackson, whom Houghton had met through Rosenbach, was the librarian needed for Harvard's rare book collections. Houghton built the library, which still bears his name, and endowed the post. This led to a happy relationship continuing until Bill Jackson's death in 1959. He bestowed his Keats collection on it but, although Harvard had confidently expected the rest of his library, it was eventually sold, the bulk being auctioned by the London house of Christie's in 1979 and 1980. It realised more than 2.5 million pounds and that was after the private sale of such items as the Gutenberg Bible.

In his business life Houghton showed an equal dedication to achieving perfection. When he took over the presidency of the Corning subsidiary, Steuben Glass, in 1933 he felt its products to be below standard. It is rumoured that within a month of taking control he and a vice-president spent a Sunday destroying every item in a company warehouse. He had decided to create a new business that would combine excellence in design with superb crystal. He dedicated himself to producing, as he said, "glass which would rank in history among man's greatest achievements". He brought in highly regarded design experts and, in little more than a year, had a whole new range of tableware, cocktail sets and some ornamental items, selling well from the firm's own new store on New York's Fifth Avenue. The reputation of Steuben Glass was set to go from strength to strength.

Although retaining the presidency of Steuben, Houghton became curator of rare books at Washington's Library of Congress for two years from 1940 and subsequently spent three years of war service with the Army Air Corps.

It was after World War II that his interest in the arts generally broadened to include education and, over time, he became involved with more than 100 different organizations, joining not for the usual reasons of sociability or status but simply because something needed to be done and he felt able to facilitate that.

One of his longer involvements was with the Metropolitan Museum of Art. He served on the board for over 20 years and during his presidency, from 1964 to 1969, was involved with the redrawing of the museum's charter to modernize its administrative and curatorial systems. He subsequently became the museum's chairman. He also took on much of the responsibility for its centennial celebrations in 1970 and was instrumental in the development of its ethnic (or so-called "primitive") art collection. He was also closely involved with the New York Philharmonic Symphony Orchestra and its relocation from Carnegie Hall to Lincoln Center.

Houghton's public commitments were huge and included chairmanships of the American Trust for the British Library (part of London's British Museum), Cooper-Union University and the Parsons School of Design. He also set up the Corning Glass Center for the company's own centennial and from which evolved the Corning Museum of Glass. This he believed to be one of his most significant achievements.

Houghton however was generous in every respect. His giving was thoughtful and always appropriate: in 1960, for example, he donated 273 acres of land on the outskirts of Corning for building the Community College; his Maryland estate he transferred to the Aspen Institute, an international public policy study organization; and his breeding herd of Black Angus cattle went to the University of Maryland. The heritage of the United States has much to thank him for.

Born Arthur Amory Houghton Junior. **Marriages** Four; 4) Nina Rodale. **Children** One son and two daughters by previous marriages, Arthur, Sylvia and Hollister. **Education** St Paul's School, Concord, New Hampshire; Harvard University, Cambridge, Massachusetts, 1925–29. **Military service** Officer, Army Air Corps, 1942–45. **Career** Vice-president Corning Glass Works, Upper New York State, 1935–42; president Steuben Glass, 1933–72, chairman, 1972–78; director: USX Corporation and New York Life Insurance Company. **Related activities** Creator, Corning Glass Center, 1951. **Other activities** Bibliophile, book collector, 1929 onwards; curator of rare books, Library of Congress, Washington, 1940–42; endower, Houghton Library, Harvard, 1942; vice-chairman, committee for creation of the Lincoln Center for the Performing Arts; donator: site for Corning Community College, 1960 and Wye Plantation to Aspen Institute. **Offices and memberships** Board member, Metropolitan Museum, New York, 1952–74, president, 1964–69, chairman, 1969–72; board member, New York Philharmonic, 1952–65, chairman, 1958–63; chairman: the American Trust for the British Library, Cooper-Union University, Parsons School of Design, Institute of International Education; vice-president: Corning Glass Museum, Pierpont Morgan Library, English-Speaking Union of the United States; overseer, Harvard University; vice-chairman, Fund for the Advancement of Education. **Awards and honours** Honorary trustee: Parsons School of Design, United States Trust Company of New York. **Cause of death** Undisclosed, at age 83.

IVAR LO-JOHANSSON

Swedish Novelist, Essayist and Autobiographer

***Born* Ösmo, Sweden, 23 February 1901**

***Died* Stockholm, Sweden, 11 April 1990**

They said he could easily have won the Nobel Prize for literature. They said his writings were largely responsible for the abolition of a near-feudal system of farming which held many people —

including his own father — effectively in thrall. They said he was the "grand old man" of Swedish literature. They said lots of praiseworthy things, but in fact the literary world at large knows very little about Ivar Lo-Johansson. Of his 50 books, numerous short stories, innumerable articles and several pamphlets, one work and one work only — *Lyckan* (*Bodies of Love*) — has been translated into English, and only a few others into German, French and Russian. Only the Swedes, and those fortunate few who read the language, can truly know the reasons why Ivar Lo-Johansson, or Ivar Lo as he was sometimes called, is considered to be a "prolific and first-class writer", as his countryman Alvar Alsterdal describes him.

It is nothing new to say that a writer came from poor beginnings, but in the case of Lo-Johansson, the truth of such a statement was pitifully real. His father, Gottfrid, was an illiterate labourer, a member of the impoverished *statare* class of farmers who received no salaries, but earned their only payment in kind. His mother, Lovisa, was also engaged in manual labour. Lo-Johansson stood such conditions just so long: while still a youth, he "broke violently away" from his parents, as Björn Kumm put in the London *Independent*. We know that, thereafter, he lived the next few years on the road, in, literally, a hand-to-mouth existence, supporting himself by a series of odd-jobs which included stone-cutting and, of course, farming. Although he had experienced no formal schooling to speak of, the young Lo-Johansson managed to educate himself, first by reading widely in public libraries, and later by travelling to other countries such as Britain and France to learn their languages and study their cultures. Because of this, he has been likened to George Orwell and Jack London, both of whom did their time as "down-and-outs". For Lo-Johansson, however, there was not a lot of choice in the matter: he, like the ordinary poverty-stricken people he worked and lived with, effectively had nothing to lose.

Thus it is not surprising to learn that, years later, he defined his task as an author as follows: "Roughly speaking, I consider a writer's tasks to be principally two. One is taking care of the language. The other is to rebel against oppression." He began to achieve these aims in the early 1920s, when his books turned the spotlight on poverty and the harsh conditions of the working class in France and Britain and, of course, in his native Sweden. His series of novels about Swedish farm-workers which began in 1933 with *Godnatt, jord* (Goodnight, Earth), exposed the truth about the near-feudal conditions in which they lived. Yet Lo-Johansson did much more than expose oppression; he somehow managed to convey its message with the utmost artistry — something, Alvar Alsterdal rightly declares, that is "rare in social realism", and a characteristic that has resulted in his work begin compared to that of John Steinbeck and Erskine Caldwell. His literary portraits of the *statare* women are regarded as his most masterful, perhaps because they were taken in part from his mother, whose inbred passive acceptance of a brutal social order he had witnessed from childhood. Many regard his *Bara on mor* (Only a Mother), to be his greatest work.

Novels were not his only weapons. Lo-Johansson wrote countless articles concerned with social criticism, taking as his subjects the Swedish gypsy culture on one hand, and the plight of the aged on the other. He also made inroads into a hitherto forbidden literary zone in Sweden, sexuality, by writing pamphlets in which he advocated a drastic relaxation of sexual division among the young; the separation of the sexes, he claimed, resulted in the transformation of Swedish boys into a generation of "miserable loners". In his 1946 novel, *Geniet* (The Genius), Lo-Johansson shocked the nation by portraying a highly sexed adolescent who actually dies because his sexual drives are forbidden their natural release.

His capacity to shock was nothing new. In 1935, Lo-Johansson had already given his readers cause to ponder by writing *Kungsgaten* (King's Street), which depicted the Stockholm *demi-monde* as seen through the eyes of two naïve farm boys. In typical Lo-Johansson style, the novel pulled no punches in its forthright depiction of prostitution.

Although his other works were perhaps not so blatantly disturbing, they were nonetheless movingly true to life. In *Analfabeten* (The Illiterate), the first of his autobiographical series of eight novels, Lo-Johansson created a vivid portrait of his father, a man who remained illiterate all his life, yet somehow managed to retain his dignity and independence. The subject matter promises little in the way of comedy, yet in a departure from the stereotyped Swedish nature, Lo-Johansson endowed the autobiographical cycle with a great deal of humour and, occasionally, gentle irony, as well.

One subject the writer did not view humorously, however, was the world of what he described as "haughty academics". To this sector belonged the clique of Swedish writers who formed the Swedish academy, and Lo-Johansson roasted them soundly in *Författaren* (The Writer), in 1956, as well as in his later works of the 1970s and 1980s. This fact, no doubt, had something to do with his not winning the Nobel Prize for literature in what has come to be known as the "Swedish year" of 1974. It is doubtful that Lo-Johansson himself minded very much, for he was always a man used to living modestly. From 1934 until shortly before his death, he lived in a small apartment in the southern section of Stockholm. Here he did all of his writing, and here he avoided one of the most time-consuming activities of the literati: speaking to writers' groups. When he did agree to make speeches, the author preferred to do so at trade union gatherings. This fitted in with his personal philosophy for, although he had attained fame and a comfortable living from his writing, thus raising himself far above the poverty line of the working class, Lo-Johansson always felt it his duty to keep language and literature from being the exclusive property of the rich.

"In his long life of struggle for justice, he produced many pamphlets of a philosophical nature, demonstrating that he was no naïve protester but a profound man capable of producing, at his best, great imaginative art." Thus did his obituarist in the London *Times* sum up the life of one of the great figures of modern Scandinavian literature. Unfortunately, his final sentence is all too true: "His international reputation is yet to come." This writer, like many other lovers of literature, is still waiting for it.

Born Karl Ivar Lo-Johansson. **Parents** Gottfrid, farm labourer, and Lovisa (Ersson), labourer, Lo-Johansson. **Career** Stone-cutter; farm-hand; journalist; workman in France, England and Hungary, 1925–29; first book published, 1927; first novel published, 1932; first poetry published, 1958. **Awards and honours** Dobloug Prize, 1953, 1973; honorary PhD, University of Uppsala, 1964; Nordic Council Prize, 1979. **Publications** *Måana är död* (Mana is Dead), 1932; *Godnatt, jord* (Goodnight, Earth), 1933; *Kungsgatan* (King's Street), 1935; *Statarna* (The Farm Labourers), two volumes, 1936–37; *Bara en mor* (Only a Mother), 1939; *Jordproletärerna* (Proletarians of the Soil), 1941; *Traktorn* (The Tractor), 1943; *Geniet: En roman om pubertet* (The Genius: A Novel of Puberty), 1947; *Ungdomsnoveller* (Stories of Youth), 1948; Autobiographical series: *Analfabeten* (The Illiterate), *Gåardfarihandlaren* (The Peddler), *Stockholmaren* (The Stockholmer), *Journalisten* (The Journalist), *Författaren* (The Writer), *Socialisten* (The Socialist), *Soldaten* (The Soldier), *Proletärförtfattaren* (The Proletarian Writer), eight volumes, 1951–60; *Lyckan (Bodies of Love)*, 1962; *Astronomens hus* (Astronomer's House), 1966; *Elektra, kvinna âr 2070* (Woman of the Year 2070), 1967; *Passionerna: Älskog*, 1968; *Martyrerna* (The Martyrs), 1968; *Girigbukarna* (The Misers), 1969; *Karriäristerna* (The Careerists), 1969; *Vällustingarna* (The Libertines), 1970; *Lögnhalsarna* (The Liars), 1971; *Vishetslärarna* (The Teachers of Wisdom), 1972; *Ordets makt: Historien om spraket* (The Power of Words), 1973; *Nunnan i Vadstena: Sedeskildringar* (The Nun of Vadstena), 1973; *Folket och herrarna* (The People and the Masters), 1973; *Furstarna: en krönika från Gustav Vasa till Karl XII* (The Rulers), 1974; *Lastbara berättelser* (Stories of Vice), 1974; *Passionsnoveller I-II* (Stories of Passion) (selection), two volumes, 1974; *En arbetares liv: Proletärnoveller* (A Worker's Life: Proletarian Stories), 1977. **Verse** *Ur klyvnadens tid* (The Splitting Time), 1958. **Other publications** *Vagabondliv i Frankrike* (Vagabondage in France), 1927; *Kolet i våld* (The Coal's Power), 1928; *Statarliv* (Farm Labourers' Lives), 1941; *Stridsskrifter*, 1946; *Statarna i bild* (Farm Labourers in Pictures), 1948; *Monism*, 1948; *Ålderdom* (Old Age),

1949; *Vagabondliv* (Vagabondage), 1949; *Ålderdoms-Sverige* (Sweden for the Aged), 1952; *Okänt Paris* (Unknown Paris), 1954; *Zigenarväg* (Gypsy Ways), 1955; *Att skriva en roman* (Writing a Novel), 1957; *Zigenare* (Gypsies), 1963; *Statarnas liv och död* (Farm Labourers Alive and Dead) (selection), 1963; *Statarskolan i litteraturen* (Farm Labourers Literary School), 1972; *Dagbok fron 20-talet I-II* (Diary from the Twenties), 1974; *Stridsskrifter I-II* (Polemical Pamphlets), 1974; *Dagar och dagsverken: Debatter och memoarer* (Days and Days' Work), 1975; *Under de gröna ekarna i Sörmland* (Under the Green Oaks in Sörmland), 1976; *Passioner i urval* (selection), 1976; *Den sociala fotobildboken* (The Social Photograph Book), 1977; *Pubertet* (Puberty) (autobiography), 1978; *Asfalt* (Asphalt) (autobiography), 1979; *Tröskeln* (The Threshold) (autobiography), 1982. **Cause of death** Undisclosed, at age 89. **Further reading** Mauritz Edström, *Lo-Johansson*, 1954, revised as *Avan, kärleken, klassen: En bok om Lo-Johanssons författarskap*, 1976; Ragnar Oldberg, *Lo-Johansson*, 1957; Ragnar Oldberg and Lars Furuland, *Lo-Johansson i tryscksvärtans ljus*, 1961; Bertil Palmqvist, *Om Lo-Johansson*, 1974; Ola Holmgren, *Kärlek och ära*, 1978; *Contemporary Foreign Language Writers*, 1984.

LOUIS NELSON

American Jazz Trombonist

Born **New Orleans, Louisiana, 17 September 1902**

Died **New Orleans, Louisiana, 5 April 1990**

To thousands of jazz enthusiasts in all parts of the world, Louis Nelson was the embodiment of New Orleans jazz. Whether playing at the former art gallery turned music venue, Preservation Hall; touring with his own band or the Legends of Jazz; or appearing at the top of the bill on festivals from Switzerland to Japan, the silver-haired, gentlemanly figure of Louis Nelson represented to his listeners a personal link to the very origins of jazz.

"Mister Nelson" as he was known, was the son of a well-to-do professional Creole family in turn-of-the-century New Orleans. His father was a doctor and his mother (who played the piano) a graduate of the Boston Conservatory of Music. When young Louis was two, the family moved from Touro Street in New Orleans to Napoleonville (about 80 miles to the west). The family was musical — his father and sister played piano and organ, and his brother George played saxophone. Despite the relative isolation of Napoleonville, Nelson was able to take lessons on alto horn from Claiborne Williams (a well-known brass and concert bandleader from Donaldsonville who later led bands in Baton Rouge). This early training stood him in good stead when he changed to trombone at around the age of 16, and he found work with Joe Gabriel's band from Thibodeaux.

Coming to New Orleans in 1926, Nelson played with Kid Harris's band, but soon afterwards joined Sidney Desvigne who led the orchestra aboard the Streckfus line steamer *Capitol*. Nelson stayed with Desvigne for some years, performing as far afield as St Paul, Minnesota, the northern limit of their boat's itinerary, and where the band sometimes stayed for a short summer season. In the group were pianist and composer Steve Lewis, banjoist Manuel Sayles and bassist Ransom Knowling (all of whom were pioneers of jazz recording) as well as Louis Barbarin on drums, whose brother Paul was already famous as Louis Armstrong's percussionist.

After leaving Desvigne in 1935, Nelson worked with other New Orleans bandleaders, including Buddy Petit, Kid Rena, Chris Kelly, Bebe Ridgely and Fats Pichon. During the Depression he played in the WPA band as first trombonist, and during World War II played in various naval bands. In the 1950s, Nelson was a part-time musician, working also for the Post Office. In 1954, he joined the band of Kid Thomas Valentine, remaining in the group for almost 20 years. Kid Thomas played a raw energetic style of jazz, and the polished, urbane trombone style which Nelson favoured for ballads was a perfect foil for the stabbing staccato phrasing of Thomas. On up-tempo numbers, Nelson was capable of blistering power and played with a huge tone. At its best, Kid Thomas and his Algiers Stompers (as the band was known) was the finest of the New Orleans bands of the 1950s and 1960s. For them the term "revivalism" was a misnomer: they were playing the music they had grown up with. No current pop song was off-limits (Nelson and saxophonist Emanuel Paul would painstakingly teach new songs to their fellow non-reading bandsmen) and these were mixed with traditional blues, marches and rags from the very origins of New Orleans's musical heritage.

The band played at many venues in New Orleans, including Speck's Moulin Rouge, The Tip Top and Fireman's Hall. In 1959, the band was recorded at the WDSO radio station, and the result issued as *Kid Thomas Valentine and his Creole Jazz Band* on Arhoolie and Seventy-Seven records. Captured on tape two years before Preservation Hall began, the Kid Thomas band provides the perfect backdrop to Nelson's trombone. Although Nelson was to record dozens of sessions later in his career, nothing that he did better captures the essence of New Orleans jazz, and his contribution to it, than this 1959 recording.

Once art dealer, Larry Borenstein, and enthusiast Ken Mills and Barbara Reid had begun to hold sessions at 726 St Peter Street in the Vieux Carré of New Orleans, a new era opened up for the elder generation of local musicians. Preservation Hall, as the place was called, became a mecca for enthusiasts from all parts of the world, hoping to hear "authentic" jazz. Most of the players of Nelson's generation were to work there regularly, although few of those who participated in the early 1960s were still as vital a part of the Hall's music in 1990 as Nelson. As the hard and impoverished lives many of his contemporaries had led saw them dying only a year or two into the new-found success of regular musical employment, Nelson, in the company of a handful of other pioneers, seemed somehow immortal. Despite heart murmurs and the toll of constant travelling, Nelson's playing did not diminish as he neared his ninetieth year. Had he not been the victim of a hit-and-run car accident some ten days before his death, Nelson seemed fair set to continue playing for many years to come. It is characteristic of his great strength and personal resolve that even after the accident he was preparing himself to appear at the French Quarter Festival, before the effects of his injuries overcame him.

Nelson recorded for Bill Russell's American Music label in the 1940s, going on to play and record with many musicians, including George Lewis, Percy Humphrey, the Legends of Jazz and the New Orleans Joymakers. In the Legends, a band of New Orleans veterans led by the expatriate English drummer Barry Martyn, Nelson toured the US and Europe many times, introducing traditional jazz to thousands of people, and he continued to fulfil this role as the leader of his own All-Stars from 1984, which, in addition to playing weekly in New Orleans's Palm Court Cafe, were top of the bill at many international festivals. Nelson surrounded himself with pioneers of jazz, including guitarist Danny Barker, bassist Chester Zardis and clarinettist Pud Brown, but he also included younger players in his group, including pianist Butch Thompson, trumpeter John Brunious and drummer Stanley Stephens. Preservation Hall and its musicians continues, but with the death of Louis Nelson it lost the last first-generation pioneer of New Orleans jazz trombone.

Born Louis Nelson. **Parents** Father, doctor; mother, pianist. **Children** One daughter, Anna. **Military service** Played in bands; US Navy, World War II, discharged as Musician First Class. **Career** Played alto horn; switched to trombone; played with Joe Gabriel; played with Kid Harris Dixieland band, from c. 1926; played with Sidney Desvigne, c. 1927–35; played with (among others) buddy Petit, Kid Rena, Chris Kelly, Bebe Ridgeley, Fats Pinchon; played in Works

Progress Administration's WPA big band; played with William Ridgeley's Original Tuxedo Orchestra, 1936; rejoined Desvigne; from 1945, played with Kid Howard, Kid Sheik, DeDe Pierce, played with (brass bands) John Casimir, Kid Howard, George Williams, also worked part-time for Post Office; played and recorded with Kid Thomas Valentine, from 1954; toured Japan and Europe with George Lewis, from 1960; played at Preservation Hall, New Orleans, from 1961; first overseas tour (Britain and Belgium), 1966; played at New Orleans Jazz and Heritage Festival, from 1969; toured with Percy Humphrey and the New Orleans Joymakers, from 1970; toured as soloist with the Legends of Jazz, from 1970; toured with Kid Thomas and Sammy Rimington, from 1970 also played with George Lewis, Kid Howard and Billie and DeDe Pierce; led All-Stars, from 1984. **Recordings** (include) *Kid Thomas at Moulin Rouge*, Center 14, 1955; *Kid Thomas Valentine and his Creole Jazz Band*, Arhoolie/Seventy-Seven, 1959; *Louis Nelson Big Four*, GHB 25–6, 1963. **Cause of death** Injuries suffered from car accident, at age 87.

HENRY PALMER

British Radio Astronomer

***Born* Monmouth, Wales, 16 September 1926**

***Died* 28 April 1990**

At the very fringes of space, at the furthest distances of which man has obtained any evidence, are objects called quasars. They are so far away that the light emitted by some may have taken 15,000,000,000 years to reach the earth. To be seen at all, quasars, which look like faint stars, must have been shining hundreds of times more brightly than a big galaxy like the Milky Way in which we live, when they emitted their light.

But quasars were not discovered simply by being seen. "Quasar" is short for 3C 273 quasi-stellar sources, and the first one was classified when a Dutch-born US observer found that the source of radio waves classified as 3C 273 was not a galaxy, as had been expected, but appeared to be a star. And the quasar's spectrum had such a large red-shift that it had to be at a far greater distance than anything discovered up to then. Hundreds of other quasars have been found subsequently.

How had the radio source been identified? By radio interferometry. And one of the pioneering scientists who developed the techniques involved was Henry Palmer.

Palmer's interest in radio astronomy did not begin until after he had completed his education at Oxford, where the thesis submitted for his DPhil was on ice particle nuclei in the atmosphere. Joining the University of Manchester as an assistant lecturer in physics, he became interested in the research being carried out at Jodrell Bank, the Nuffield Radio Astronomy Laboratories connected with the university. Under the supervision of Sir Bernard Lovell, a series of radio telescopes had been built on this site, including a steerable telescope with a 250-foot parabolic dish which was for a long time the largest in the world.

Lacking the clear skies and the clean air of isolated and higher locations, Manchester was not the place for research with optical telescopes, but radio waves, which penetrate cloud and haze, could be detected as well there as elsewhere.

Radio astronomy was still in its infancy. Radio waves had been detected from outer space in 1931, and in 1942 some British radar operatives detected for the first time bursts of radio energy from the sun. By 1950 six or seven discrete, celestial sources of radio energy had been detected. With the new, immense, steerable radio dish a whole range of exciting research had been undertaken.

Radio, however, has a severe limitation compared with light. Its wavelength is about a million times longer than those of visible light, so to obtain equivalent resolution to an optical telescope, a radio receiver would have to be correspondingly immense. Fortunately the reflector does not have to be solid — wire netting reflects radio waves very well — nor does it have to be particularly smooth unless required for wavelengths of less than about four inches.

To locate, and measure the diameter of, sources of radio waves, straightforward observation is impossible. Some other method is required to resolve the directions and widths of sources to any accuracy, and interferometry is used. In this, two or more widely separated sources are required, each dish being pointed at the source. There is a phase difference between the waves reaching each source. With the earth spinning on its axis, computer analysis of the signals obtained over many days mimics the effect of a huge optical telescope.

When Palmer arrived at Jodrell Bank, the nature of localized radio sources was a major problem, and he was to study it for the next 27 years. To begin with he used the 218-foot transit telescope with a mobile broadside array of 35 square miles as a cable connected phase correlation interferometer. Using the maximum baseline of the interferometer, 1000-metre or 500 wavelengths, he could not resolve 15 of the 23 radio sources being examined. The baseline had to be increased, and this was done by using a radio connection between the two aerials to replace the cable, a substitution which raised many difficulties requiring solution.

To improve resolution, relying on the rotation of the earth to provide the interferometer fringe frequency was found inadequate, and Palmer, with Hanbury Brown and A. R. Thompson, incorporated a rotating mag-slip phase-shifter. In conjunction with a radio link, the baseline between the two aerials could be increased to several miles, the resolution improving to less than 12 arcseconds.

When Palmer was able to use the 250-foot steerable telescope as the home station of the interferometer, and three cylindrical paraboloids with a collecting area of 100 square miles, instead of the small broadside array, he measured the angular diameters of 384 sources. Accompanied by an enthusiastic band of young research workers, he would transport a 25-foot radio telescope round sites in northern England, eventually using a baseline of 115 kilometres or 61,000 wavelengths. He achieved resolutions down to two arcseconds, equivalent to the apparant diameter of a small coin at a distance of two kilometres. At the penultimate site he showed that seven of the sources examined had angular diameters of less than three arcseconds, and it was during the optical search for these sources that one was identified by Sandage as a relatively bright "stellar" object, as opposed to a galaxy. This was the first optical identification of a "quasar", although it was not until three years later, when Schmidt discovered their high red-shift, that they were properly classified.

To begin with Palmer was working under Hanbury Brown, but when Hanbury Brown left for Australia in 1962 Palmer became senior member of the group at Jodrell Bank. The telescopes improved, and baselines of multi-million wavelengths were developed in Britain and overseas, particularly in Canada. The work done at Jodrell Bank led astronomers to the furthest reaches of the universe, studying galaxy-formation almost at the beginning of time.

As he developed his ideas, Palmer realized the limitations of the two-element interferometer, and suggested an array of several linked radio telescopes providing simultaneous baselines across Britain. It was a proposal of his that led to the Merlin radio mapping array, the main research tool at Jodrell Bank today.

In 1979 he was given a year's leave to work with the advanced project group of a division of Philips Electronic and Associated Companies. He was always a devoted husband and father, and family reasons, together with his enthusiasm for sailing, decided him to retire from Jodrell Bank and remain in the south of England. For his final work he joined the Independent Broadcasting Authority as engineering information officer, and was involved in frequency planning.

Born Henry Proctor Palmer. **Marriage** Esmé Kemp, 1951. **Children** One son and two daughters. **Education** Giggleswick School, North Yorkshire; University of Oxford, BA, 1947;

DPhil in meteorology, 1952. **Career** Assistant lecturer, Manchester University, with research work at Nuffield Radio Astronomy Laboratories Jodrell Bank, 1952–67, reader, 1967–80; measured angular diameters of radio emission sources which led to the discovery of quasars; designed the Merlin radio mapping array for mapping quasars, Jodrell Bank, 1974; with advanced projects group, MEL, a division of Philips Electronic and Associated Industries, 1979–80; engineering information officer, Technical Information Facilities section, Independent Broadcasting Authority, 1981–86. **Awards and honours** Honorary DSc, University of Manchester, 1980. **Cause of death** Undisclosed, at age 63.

SABICAS

Spanish Flamenco Guitarist

Born **Pamplona, Spain, 1917**

Died **Manhattan, New York, 14 April 1990**

One of the finest solo guitarists of his time, Sabicas took the art of flamenco, or gypsy music, into new realms by establishing the flamenco guitar as an instrument in its own right rather than a mere accompaniment to a musical troupe. The achievement was a remarkable one, and all the more so because his birthplace and background were geographically, culturally and musically far removed from the natural home of flamenco.

Sabicas was born into a gypsy family in Pamplona, northern Spain — a far cry from the southern province of Andalucia, the natural home of the gypsy. His real name was Agustin Castellon, but his craving for a particular type of broad bean, or *habica*, led to his being call *El nino de las habicas* (Little broadbeans kid). *Las habicas* soon became "Sabicas", and the nickname stuck for life.

Sabicas was always very proud of his gypsy heritage. "I'm a gypsy, and for the gypsies, this is our music" he once said. His extraordinary skill with the guitar was recognized at a very early age — it was said that he played flamenco brilliantly by the time he was seven or eight years old. He later recalled these years: "My father played a little, and when I was five years old, I picked up a guitar, just to make noise. By the time I was eight, I had an audience." His brilliance was almost frightening. In an interview, a friend, the well-known Spanish guitarist Paco Peña, told of how Sabicas was, as a child, taken by his mother to a guitar teacher to get proper tuition. The teacher asked him to play something. Peña recalled Sabicas's description of the incident: "I played a run and the teacher practically threw us out of the house, saying we were making fun of him."

His runs (*picadas*) were to become legendary, as was his overall mastery of the guitar. There was an effortless quality to his playing which was belied by his supreme dedication. Before each concert he would practise for up to six hours a day on one of his seven guitars. When his recording *Flamenco Puro* first appeared in Spain, it took the world of flamenco by storm. Up till then, the flamenco guitar had merely been considered as an adjunct to a troupe of singers and dancers — never had such exquisite playing been heard by the flamenco guitar as a solo instrument. As Peña later remarked, "life changed, guitarists began to see a new world of music unfolding in front of them. Sabicas played pure flamenco with a level of technical perfection nobody suspected existed until then."

Despite his success in Spain, however, it was not until Sabicas went to Buenos Aires in the late 1930s that he developed into a concert artist with a world-wide reputation. It was then that he toured North and South American countries with Carmen Amaya, a celebrated flamenco dancer with whom he was often romantically linked. In the 1940s, he went on to appear in a few Hollywood films with her — times he clearly always cherished, for in later life he still carried pictures of himself with stars such as Marlon Brando, Gary Cooper and Charlie Chaplin. Although he became a resident of the USA, making his permanent home in Manhattan, Sabicas continued with several European and American tours until, in 1959, he made his first solo appearance in New York at Town Hall, in the first solo flamenco concert to have been given in the United States.

Despite his own undoubted success, Sabicas was always willing to provide help and encouragement when it was needed. Paco Peña recalled how when he first heard Sabicas play, in London, he was so overwhelmed by the complex detail of Sabicas's playing that he felt incapable of ever fully appreciating, learning and playing his music. "Don't worry," Sabicas told him, "you just listen now, you won't know it yet but maybe in a year, maybe later, you will remember. It will come back to you in one way or another." Years later, when Peña made his own professional début in New York, he rang Sabicas, expressing his nervousness, not only about the concert, but about the fact that Sabicas himself would be there to listen to him. Yet again, Sabicas was able to offer reassuring words: "The guitar is a beautiful instrument. Try to make it sound beautiful and play that which *you* want to play. Don't worry if it is your own music or mine. You relax and be honest about what you can do." Peña found his comments enormously helpful, and was able to relax into the concert.

Sabicas's last New York performance was at Carnegie Hall on 3 June 1989, where he was honoured by the Spanish government, though on this occasion he shared the bill with, amongst others, the flamenco guitarist Paco de Lucia, whom he described as "my true disciple". Even so late in his career, the master had clearly not lost his touch. Stephen Holdern, reviewing the concert in *The New York Times* wrote: "Sabicas's style is characterized by a soft, ringing tone; clear simply sculpted arrangements, and an unusually relaxed sense of rhythm that at moments almost cuts loose and swings gently."

Perhaps fittingly, his last public performance was in his own native country, Spain, when, in August, he played as part of a memorial tribute to his old friend, Carmen Amaya in a concert near Barcelona. After this, his health began to decline, and he died eight months later, leaving a generous legacy of artistry and commitment to the emotion, fire and spirit of flamenco that has, for many, been unequalled in our time.

Born Agustin Castellon. **Children** One son and one daughter, Agustin and Margarita. **Career** Guitarist, 1930s onwards; toured North and South America with Carmen Amaya, 1930s; played in films with Carmen Amaya, 1940s; New York début as soloist, Town Hall, 1959. **Awards and honours** Honoured by Spanish government, Carnegie Hall, 1989. **Recordings** (include) *Flamenco Puro*; *The Fabulous Guitars of Sabicas and Escudero*. **Cause of death** Multiple strokes and pneumonia, at age 73.

C. R. SMITH

American Airline Executive

***Born* Minerva, Texas, 9 September 1899**

***Died* Annapolis, Maryland, 4 April 1990**

In his own fashion C. R. Smith was a tribute to the American way of life. Rising above the poverty he was born to, he managed to help support his own family (his mother and six siblings), finish his education and help establish one of the most important airline companies in America.

Born in Texas, Cyrus Rowlett Smith spent his childhood with a family that wandered over a wide area of Texas and Louisiana, stopping wherever his father was able to find work. When Smith was nine years old, his father abandoned the family leaving Smith's mother with seven children of whom Smith was the eldest son. But they were an enterprising group and, through co-operative effort and the expert management of his mother, they were able to support themselves. They accomplished this amazing feat with Mrs Smith teaching and taking in boarders, and each child going to work as soon as he or she came of age. All the money earned was put into a common fund which not only provided them with the necessities of life, but also enabled all seven children to attend college.

Between the ages of nine and 16, Smith held various low-paying jobs, but in 1915 he was able to obtain a position as a bookkeeper and teller for the First National Bank of Whitney. With that experience behind him he was able to move on to a better paying position as bookkeeper in a cotton mill in Hillsboro. He remained there until 1919 when he took a job with the franchise-tax department of the Secretary of State in Austin. Although he was earning a very good salary, he was not satisfied. He felt that now he had practical experience, what he needed was a formal education. At the age of 21 he entered the University of Texas, specializing in business administration and law. Being a full-time student did not stop this industrious personality from carrying on a part-time job with the Federal Reserve Bank, running a one-man advertising agency and belonging to two fraternities. He also found time to serve as president of his junior class and the public-speaking club.

After graduating, in 1924, he took a regular position as a junior clerk in a Dallas accounting firm, soon becoming known as an expert in business management. It was at this time that he became acquainted with A. P. Barrett, a Texas utilities magnate who offered him the job of assistant treasurer in the Texas-Louisiana Power Company.

He had been in this position for three years when the power company acquired Texas Air Transport, an air-mail firm which served Dallas-Fort Worth and Brownsville to Houston. Barrett chose Smith to manage the new acquisition. It was the beginning of the creation of one of the biggest airline companies in America.

In a short time Smith consolidated the company with other lines, forming the Southern Air Transport, which carried not only mail, but some passengers as well. He also earned his transport pilot's licence.

Between 1929 and 1934 the company kept on growing, constantly acquiring other companies and expanding its routes. But its administration was faulty and it began to lose money. In 1934 the Post Office cancelled its mail contracts. In order to survive, the company had to reorganize. In February 1934 American Airlines was created, and by October C. R. Smith had become its president. By 1945 American Airlines was the leading domestic airline in the United States.

During the war years Smith resigned as president and director of the airline in order to enter the Army as a colonel with the Air Corps Ferrying Command, where he was involved in flying Lend-Lease planes bound for Britain to take-off points in America. By 1942 it was necessary to rush supplies as well as planes to American troops. Smith's command was soon reorganized into the Air Transport Command and he became chief-of-staff.

Smith retired from the service after VE Day in 1945, having been awarded the Distinguished Service Medal, the Legion of Merit and the Air Medal. He returned to American Airlines as chairman of the Board and he remained in charge until 1968, when he became secretary of commerce in the last year of President Lyndon B. Johnson's administration.

After retiring, he became a partner in the investment banking firm of Lazard Frères and Company. However, in 1975 he went back to the chairmanship of American Airlines to help it through a management crisis.

When asked in 1950 what made him go into the aviation business, C. R. Smith replied, "The people in aviation made me want to get into it. Vigorous people with a sense of humour, their minds big enough to think of the whole world all at once! People whose vision doesn't stop at the horizon." It is also an apt description of his own energetic life.

Born Cyril Rowlett Smith. **Parents** Roy Edgerton and Marion (Burck) Smith, schoolteacher. **Marriage** Elizabeth Lewis Manget, 1934 (dissolved). **Children** One son, Douglas. **Education** University of Texas, 1920–24. **Military service** Colonel, US Army Air Force, 1942–45, chief-of-staff, 1942, brigadier general, 1942, deputy commander, Air Transport Command, 1942–45, major general, 1945. **Career** Bookkeeper and teller, First National Bank of Whitney, Texas, 1915–16; bookkeeper, cotton mill, Hillsboro, Texas, 1916–19; bookkeeper, Texas Secretary of State franchise-tax department, 1919–20; part-time bank examiner, 1920–24; founded advertising agency; public accountant, Peat Marwick Mitchell and Company, Dallas, 1924–26; assistant treasurer, Texas-Louisiana Power Company, Fort Worth, 1926–28; vice-president, Texas Air Transport, Incorporated, 1929–30; Texas vice-president of operations, American Airways (American Airlines from 1934), 1930–33, vice-president, 1934, president, 1934–42, board chairman, 1946–68, chairman, 1973–74, chief executive officer, 1973–74; US Secretary of Commerce, 1968–70; partner, Lazard Frères and Company, 1970–73. **Awards and honours** Distinguished Service Medal; Legion of Merit; US Air Medal; Commander of the Order of the British Empire; Wright Brothers Award; Billy Mitchell Award; Aviation Hall of Fame, 1974; Business Hall of Fame, 1975. **Cause of death** Undisclosed, at age 90.

BELLA SPEWACK

American Dramatist and Screenwriter

Born **Hungary, 25 March 1899**

Died **Manhattan, New York, 27 April 1990**

Bella Spewack achieved the unusual distinction of having written an adaptation of a Shakespeare play that was arguably more popular than the original. *Kiss me Kate* — her adaptation of *The Taming of the Shrew* — was a remarkable achievement in many ways: its first run on Broadway lasted for over 1000 performances; it rescued the career of its composer, Cole Porter; and although a very loose reworking, it was argued that *Kiss Me Kate* introduced an entirely new audience to the work of the Bard. It was, as one critic put it, "A dazzling example of how to build a plot all around and in between the lines of the Shakespearian original without doing the structure any fundamental harm."

Spewack was born the the Transylvanian region of what is now Romania. Shortly after her birth, she and her mother moved to New York. Her father, Adolph Cohen, was not much in evidence after the move and Spewack later enigmatically told journalists that "there was no father". She grew up in the Lower East Side of Manhattan and graduated from Washington Irving High School in 1917. Finding her first job proved to be problematic during World War I but Spewack was eventually hired by the editor of a socialist newspaper, *The New York Call*. He was evidently impressed by Spewack's youthful outspokenness and her radical political views. Other editors were equally impressed and Spewack eventually moved on to the *Evening Mail* before turning to freelance feature-writing for *The New York Times* and the *New York Herald Tribune*. She also became a freelance publicist, working for, amongst others, the Girl Scouts Association. Her big publicity coup here was made with the invention of the Girl Scout Cookie, a recipe that remains an integral part of contemporary Girl Scout ethics.

Spewack's journalism caught the attention of another young immigrant writer, Sam Spewack, then a reporter on the New York newspaper, *The World*. Bella said after her marriage to Sam in 1922 that he had fallen in love not with her but with her writing. Immediately after their marriage the Spewacks were posted to Moscow as foreign correspondents for *The World*. In Moscow and other eastern European postings, the Spewacks perfected the art of finding humour in adversity. As one of the very few women foreign correspondents, and aged only 27, Bella Spewack achieved considerable journalistic acclaim for the stories she filed back to *The World*. The period between the two world wars was one of dramatic change in American foreign policy in Europe and the Spewacks were already turning the events of the time to fiction.

They returned to New York in 1926. Sam Spewack continued to write for *The World* while Bella became a theatrical press-agent. Around this time the Spewacks began their partnership as scriptwriters. Their first Broadway success, *Clear All Wires*, was based on their experiences in Moscow and was an immediate success in New York in 1932. The play was ostensibly a cruel commentary on eastern European politics and American Foreign Office stupidity. Spewack had no such pretensions about it: it was a farce and it made audiences laugh. The play was later turned into a musical — *Leave It To Me* — notable not only for its long run on Broadway, but also for such Cole Porter classics as "My Heart Belongs To Daddy". The original Broadway run shot to stardom the sparkling Mary Martin (q.v.), and also featured a young and obscure dancer, Gene Kelly, in the chorus. The Spewacks discovered early in their careers how to keep audiences amused in the face of even the most banal action. If Bella Spewack was a pragmatist, she was a pragmatist with a sense of humour.

Spewack and her husband wrote consistently together throughout the 1930s and 1940s. Almost every year one of their plays or musicals was performed on Broadway and many of them were taken up by producers in Hollywood wanting to emulate their success on celluloid. Their play *Boy Meets Girl* — which was later filmed with James Cagney — is perhaps typical of their formulaic approach to writing. The main character, a screenwriter, explains on their behalf: "Listen. I've been writing stories for eleven years: boy meets girl, boy loses girl, boy gets girl, girl meets boy, girl loses boy, girl gets boy, love will find a way, love never loses, put your money on love." It was a formula that served the Spewacks well and in the post-Depression years they were just what Broadway and Hollywood needed.

The Spewacks were part of a rich seam of American light dramatists. Their contemporaries included Kaufman and Hart and Hecht and MacArthur, none of whom pleaded artistic licence; they were all basically technicians offering grateful audiences "dances, scenery, girls and boys". The Spewacks were, like the others, clever and prolific writers although they had the advantage of Bella's experience in public relations and her considerable business acumen. And, like the others, they had one brilliant idea.

The original idea for *Kiss Me Kate* came from a producer, Saint Subber, who had been working on the film version of *The Taming of the Shrew*. He thought the off-set arguments of its leading actors, Alfred Lunt and Lynn Fontanne, could be turned into a musical comedy. Bella Spewack was not initially keen on the idea since she considered *The Shrew* to be one of Shakespeare's "flops". She was finally convinced to pursue the project when Cole Porter agreed to write the music. Porter had been reluctant to work again with the Spewacks after the ten-year lull in his career following their first collaboration. The final product was a triumph for all three; Porter for the first time wrote songs based on a script, which gave the play a dramatic and musical coherence that other musicals lacked; and the Spewacks had a new laurel to rest upon. When asked by a brave reporter to explain the "message" of *Kiss Me Kate* Bella Spewack said, "Same as Shakespeare's.

Slap your wife around; she'll thank you for it." (She had already redeemed herself for this anti-feminist statement 30 years earlier when she refused to edit the women's page of a newspaper on the grounds that "women can read the whole paper".)

The success of *Kiss Me Kate* in 1948 was never matched by any of the Spewacks' subsequent plays or films. Indeed by the mid-1950s the Spewacks were out of favour with both producers and critics. Their play *Festival* in 1955 received terrible reviews and was threatened with early closure. Bella Spewack launched a publicity campaign to save it by appearing on stage after each performance and imploring the audience to get their friends to see it. Remarkably, *Festival* survived. Few producers have survived the blow of a bad review in New York, but the Spewacks' career went on. And on.

Born Bella Cohen. **Parents** Adolph and Fanny (Lang) Cohen. **Marriage** Samuel Spewack, 1921 (died 1971). **Education** Washington Irving High School, New York, 1917. **Emigration** Left Transylvania for US, 1900, naturalized. **Career** New York newspaper reporter, *Yorkville Home News*, *The New York Call*, *Evening Mail*, and *The Morning World*; feature writer, New York *Herald Tribune* and *The New York Times*; national publicity director, Camp Fire Girls and Girl Scouts, invented Girl Scout Cookies; (with Sam Spewack) foreign correspondent in Russia and Europe, 1922–26; theatrical press-agent, Morris Gest; began writing plays in collaboration with Sam Spewack, 1926; first play presented, *The Solitaire Man*, 1926; first screenplay filmed, *The Secret Witness*, 1931; first Broadway success, *Clear All Wires*, 1932. **Awards and honours** Antoinette Perry (Tony) award for *Kiss Me Kate*, 1949. **Stage** (includes) *The Solitaire Man*, 1926; *Poppa*, 1928; *The War Song*, 1928; *Clear All Wires*, 1932; *Spring Song*, 1934; *Boy Meets Girl*, 1935; *Leave It To Me*, 1938; *Miss Swan Expects*, 1939; *Woman Bites Dog*, 1946; *Kiss Me Kate*, 1948; *Two Blind Mice*, 1949; *The Golden State* (produced only), 1950; *My Three Angels* (adapted from the French play of Albert Husson), 1953; *Festival*, 1955. **Films** (include) *The Nuisance*; *The Secret Witness*, 1932; *The Gay Bride*, 1934; *The Cat and the Fiddle*, 1934; *Rendezvous*, 1935; *Boy Meets Girl*, 1938; *Vogues of 1938*, 1938; *Three Loves has Nancy*, 1938; *My Favourite Wife*, 1940; *Weekend at the Waldorf*, 1945; *Kiss Me Kate*, 1953; *Move Over Darling*, 1963. **Cause of death** Undisclosed, at age 91.

SARAH VAUGHAN

American Jazz Singer

***Born* Newark, New Jersey, 27 March 1924**

***Died* Los Angeles, California, 3 April 1990**

Together with Billie Holiday and Ella Fitzgerald, Sarah Vaughan was one of the most accomplished female singers in jazz. The youngest of the three, Vaughan was also to make her initial reputation by singing bebop, the style of modern jazz pioneered by Dizzy Gillespie and Charlie Parker in the early 1940s. Although Vaughan made a large number of purely commercial recordings of popular songs with minimal jazz content, and her delivery, flair and style in this context marked her out as remarkable, it is her substantial contribution to the development of jazz singing, and her legacy of jazz records that make her the most significant post-World War II jazz singer.

The origins of her musical career lie in the Mount Zion Baptist Church, Newark, where she sang in the choir, and became organist at an early age. Equipped with a sound keyboard technique, she was to join the big band of Earl Hines as second pianist in 1943. Hines first heard her at the Apollo Theater in New York on a night when Ella Fitzgerald was to appear: "Before Ella came on, they brought out this girl who had got a week's engagement...for winning the talent contest the past Wednesday. Sarah was standing there, flat-footed, no personality at all..."But if Hines was unimpressed with her appearance, he was sufficiently taken with her voice to ask her immediately to join his band. As a pianist, she could be a member of the American Federation of Musicians (the musicians' union) and Hines found that this avoided problems with the Variety Artists' union and reckless managers trying to get her to sign exclusive representation contracts. Singer Billy Eckstine was also with Hines's band as a trumpeter *manqué*, and also joined the AFM. Vaughan was to become pianist in Eckstine's band, and after working with this pioneering group (which contained most of the men who were to develop bebop) she came to make her great recording of "Lover Man" in 1945, with Dizzy Gillespie and Charlie Parker (both of whom had played in Eckstine's band). Two years later, with Billy Eckstine's band, Vaughan recorded "It's Magic" which proved to be one of her greatest and most enduring commercial hits.

Also in 1947, Sarah Vaughan married George Treadwell, who undertook her management, and radically altered her style of stage appearance and her repertory. She began to command substantial earnings, and between 1949 and 1954 was under exclusive contract to Columbia, who focused on her commercial (rather than her jazz) talents. A subsequent agreement with Mercury records broadened her artistic scope, and she was to record numerous jazz performances for their EmArcy subsidiary. In the same way that Vaughan's 1940s jazz performances were linked to the modern jazz movement through Parker and Gillespie, she remained in the forefront of artistic development in the 1950s by recording with such players as Clifford Brown and Cannonball Adderley. Quincy Jones composed and arranged for many of Vaughan's records during this period. After leaving the Mercury label, Vaughan did not record for some time, eventually opting to work for Norman Granz's Pablo label.

Remarriage and changes of management affected the emphasis in her career, but she remained successful throughout the 1960s, and the next two decades, touring indefatigably, recording prodigiously, and working in a variety of musical environments, from the minimal accompaniment of guitar and bass to big bands and symphony orchestras. From time to time, captured on recordings such as her 1973 Tokyo concert, she would sing alone to her own piano accompaniment. Her version of Hoagy Carmichael's "The Nearness of You" from that recording demonstrates the flexibility of her range and timbre as well as her control over dynamics (in this case heightened by the sensitivity of her piano playing).

In many of her recordings, and stage appearances, Vaughan's supporting group was a piano-bass-drums trio. Her accompanists were always at the highest artistic level, and included Bob James, Carl Schroeder, Roland Hanna and (on record) Oscar Peterson. As recently as 1982, Vaughan won a Grammy Award for best female jazz vocalist for her album *Gershwin Live!* It is testimony to her range and skill that four years later she appeared with Kiri Te Kanawa and José Carreras on a full scale re-recording of the musical *South Pacific*, and in such daunting vocal company, she more than held her own. Films of the making of that recording show her complete professionalism in the studio, her remarkable control of pitch and timing, even when overdubbing to pre-recorded accompaniment, as well as hinting at the shades of prima donna behaviour that occasionally came to the fore in her last years (many jazz critics recalling her temperamental displays at the Nice Jazz Festival).

Although Vaughan was survived by Ella Fitzgerald, the latter never became fully at home with the nuances of modern jazz singing. Of the three great female vocalists in jazz history, Sarah Vaughan — for all her forays into other musical genres — remains the one to have created and developed a totally convincing approach to using the voice as a modern jazz improvising instrument.

Born Sarah Lois Vaughan. **Parents** Asbury, carpenter and amateur guitarist and pianist, and Ada (Baylor), laundress and choir singer, Vaughan. **Marriages** 1) George Treadwell, manager and trumpeter, 1947 (divorced 1956); 2) Clyde B. Atkins, professional football player, 1959 (divorced 1968); 3) Marshall Fisher, restaurant owner, 1971 (divorced 1977); 4) Waymon Reed, musician, 1978 (dissolved). **Children** One daughter, Deborah. **Education** Studied piano and organ; Arts High School, Newark, New Jersey. **Career** Won first prize, amateur contest, Apollo Theatre, Harlem, 1942, played one-week engagement; vocalist and second pianist, Earl "Fatha" Hines group, 1943–44; vocalist, Billy Eckstine's band, 1944–45; first recording (with Billy Eckstine), "I'll Wait And Pray", 1944; first solo recording, Continental Records, 1945; joined John Kirby's group, Copacabana, New York, 1945–46; joined J. C. Heard sextet, Café Society Downtown, 1946; took on George Treadwell as manager, 1947; recording contract, Columbia Records, 1949–53; first television appearances around 1951; recording contract, Mercury Records, 1953; first European tour, 1953; US tour with Birdland Stars of '57, 1957; appeared in television variety shows with Jackie Gleason, Ed Sullivan, Perry Como, from 1950; appeared briefly in films, from 1951; international tour with Count Basie and his orchestra, 1964; command performance, White House, 1965; reduced touring from 1967; vocal for sound track, *Cactus Flower*, 1969; recording contract, Mainstream Records, 1972; Newport Jazz Festival, 1974; filmed concert, PBS, 1974; performed for President Gerald Ford and President Valéry Giscard d'Estaing, Martinique, 1975; recording contract, Mainstream Records; recording contract, Pablo Records. **Awards and honours** Best new star, *Esquire* magazine, 1947; best female singer, *Downbeat* magazine, 1947–52, 1973, 1975–79; best female singer, *Metronome* magazine, 1948–53; best female singer, *Jazz Journal International*, 1978; Grammy Award for best jazz vocal performance, *Gershwin Live!*, 1982. **Films** *Murder Inc.*, 1950; *Disc Jockey*, 1951; *Harlem Follies*, 1955. **Albums** (include) *Great Songs from Hit Shows*, Mercury, 1953; *In Hi-Fi*, EmArcy 36058, 1955; *Sassy*, EmArcy 36089, 1956; *No 'Count Sarah* Mercury 20441, 1958; *After Hours*, Roulette 793721, 1961; *Sassy Swings the Tivoli*, EmArcy 832788, 1963; *Sarah Plus Two*, Roulette 52118, 1964; *Sarah Vaughan — Michel Legrand*, Mstr. 361, 1972; *Live in Japan*, Mstr. 401, 1973; *How Long Has This Been Going On?*, Pablo 2310–821, 1978; *Sarah Vaughan/Duke Ellington Songbook I and II*, Pablo 2312–111 and 2312–116, 1980; *Crazy and Mixed Up*, Pablo 2312 137, 1982; *South Pacific*, CBS, 1987; *Brazilian Romance*, Columbia, FM42519, 1987; *Dizzy Gillespie — Sarah Vaughan — Charlie Parker*, Jazzline JL20286; *Compact Jazz: Sarah Vaughan*, Vogue 830699–2; *After Hours at London House*, Mercury 20383; *Sarah Vaughan Sings the George Gershwin Songbook*, EmArcy 814 1871; *At Mr Kelly's*, Mercury 20326; *At the Blue Note*, Mercury 200094; *Favorites*, Harmony 7208; *Great*, Harmony 7158; *Sarah Vaughan with Her Trio*, EmArcy 36109; *In a Pensive Mood*, Rond. 102; *In a Romantic Mood*, Mercury 20223; *Linger Awhile*, Columbia CL 914; *Sarah*, EmArcy 36004; *Sarah Vaughan*, Lion 70052; *Sings*, Rond. 853; *Songs of Broadway*, Rond. 35; *Vaughan and Violins*, Mercury 20370; *Wonderful Sarah*, Mercury 20219; *Sarah Vaughan Sings*, Masterseal MS–55; *The Divine Sarah Vaughan: The Columbia Years, 1949–53*, Columbia 44165; *The Complete Sarah Vaughan on Mercury, Volume I: Great Jazz Years, 1954–56*, Mercury 826320; (with Billy Eckstine) *Irving Berlin Songbook*, Verve 822526. **Singles** (include) (With Billy Eckstine) "I'll Wait And Pray", 1944; (with Dizzy Gillespie) "Lover Man", 1945; "All Too Soon", 1945; "Body and Soul", 1946; (with John Kirby) "It Might As Well Be Spring", 1946; "Tenderly", 1947; "It's Magic", 1947; "I Cover the Waterfront", 1947; "Mean To Me", 1949; "Make Yourself Comfortable", 1953; "Lullaby of Birdland", 1954; "Whatever Lola Wants", 1955; "Mr Wonderful", 1956; "Misty", 1957; "Broken-Hearted Melody", 1958; "A Lover's Concerto", 1966. **Cause of death** Lung cancer, at age 66. **Further reading** R. Leydi, *Sarah Vaughan*, 1961.

ANTOINE VITEZ

French Theatre Director

***Born* Paris, France, 20 December 1930**

***Died* Paris, France, 30 April 1990**

That one of France's great theatre intellectuals should describe himself as "a simple peasant", reveals the paradox at the heart of Antoine Vitez's work. A member of the Communist Party for much of his life, Vitez wanted the theatre to be accessible to all, and yet it was the intellectual community which appreciated his productions and made him director of the Comédie Française — the pillar of French classical theatre. Vitez spoke of creating "elitist theatre for everyone" and this paradox remained with him throughout his life.

The son of a Hungarian photographer and his Normandy wife, Vitez grew up in an active anarchist environment, and quickly adopted the left-wing convictions of his parents. He worked as a secretary for the Communist writer Louis Aragon and, at the age of 27, joined the French Communist Party. Despite this dedication to Communism (a dedication which lasted until 1980 and Russia's invasion of Afghanistan), Vitez's first passion was his desire to act and to work in the theatre.

When he failed to enter the Conservatoire National Supérieur d'Art Dramatique Vitez turned instead to the study of eastern languages — enabling him to declare later that to understand Stanislavski one should read him in the original Russian. Determined to break into the world of the theatre, Vitez applied his knowledge of languages to the translation of German, Greek and Russian plays and novels, and also worked in several regional theatres. Vitez's ambition, however, stretched beyond a string of small roles and the life of a strolling player.

Any training as such that Vitez acquired was in non-conformist schools and it appears that he was battling against the well-established view that the arts were for the Parisian élite. It was not until 1966 that Vitez got his first big opportunity as the tide of opinion began to change, and he was given the chance to direct Sophocles' *Electra* and Mayakovsky's *Bath-house* at Caen. But Vitez was not going to stop there. His conviction that theatre should be taken to the masses directed his work throughout the 1960s, and led to his becoming a founder member of a people's theatre movement in the Parisian red belt and nearby suburbs. The movement soon became known as 'the Red Belt' and performed in the most unlikely of venues — gymnasiums, school playgrounds and town halls — all in defiance of placing "theatre" in an established, formal performance space, and instead reaching out with greater accessibility to a wider, more "popular" audience.

Though some of Vitez's work was successful in this respect, it nevertheless showed an intellectual quality which thwarted his own ideals. So eager was he to do something different, that his productions often seemed too self-consciously experimental or artificial in some way, and he cared little whether he baffled or bored his audience. A fine example of this would be his 1987 production of Claudel's *Le Soulier de satin* at the Avignon Festival. On seeing the first performance Sacha Guitry had exclaimed, "Fortunately we were not presented with the pair." Vitez, undeterred, presented "the pair" by doubling the usual performance time to 12 hours. Exhausted, critics and audiences were baffled *and* bored, and it is only time which has shown this production to be an important step in theatrical history.

In remembering Vitez the director, one must not forget Vitez the teacher. Following the political upheaval which swept across France in 1968, Vitez was appointed to teach a course at the Paris Conservatoire. It was not respectful adherence to the traditions of the Comédie Française which became Vitez's hallmark. Rather he is quoted as saying that he liked to teach his actors and students "irrespect toward what Brecht called the terrorism of the classics". Vitez encouraged inventiveness and set about developing new definitions of acting. He refused to see the actor as one piece in the huge jigsaw of the stage. Instead the actor, for him, was the *raison d'être* of the theatre; the theatre was his or her milieu. In this one can see the influence of Stanislavski working on Vitez, and though he did not adhere to the extremes of social realism demanded by the great Russian, he urged his students and actors to search within when preparing for a role.

In addition to 13 years at the Conservatoire, Vitez was director of studies of the Theatre of Nations University in 1965, and a teacher at the Jacques Lacoq Mime School from 1966 to 1970. He gained a considerable reputation as a teacher and a set of films was made of his classes entitled *Cinq leçons de théâtre*.

As a director Vitez secured his name through the work he did at the Théâtre National de Chaillot. From 1972 to 1974 he was co-artistic director under Jack Lang — later the French minister of culture — and in 1981, he returned as artistic director. During this time his work retained an unpredictable edge as he refused to establish a recognizable Vitez style. What remained unchanged, however, was his belief in the role of the actor. This was reflected in the work he did with the designer, Yannis Kokkos, whose simple sets pitched the emphasis on the actors.

Two years before his death, this man who sought to stretch theatre beyond its normal performance bounds — both in terms of production and audience — and who sought to give space to contemporary playwrights, side-by-side with the classical masters, was appointed head of the Comédie Française. This bastion of classical French theatre suddenly had a man at its helm for whom, to quote Douglas Johnson, "no modern play was too obscure".

This did not mean that Vitez showed a lack of interest in the classics — his productions of Molière and Racine were famous. But he is credited with modernizing the repertory of the Comédie Française. He put on Jean-Paul Sartre's *Huis clos*, and his final production was Brecht's *Galileo* — only the second time that Brecht had been performed at the Comédie Française. Antoine Vitez was a man of ideals, but he was also a man of imagination, intelligence and guts. All four qualities are talents of great value in the theatre, and one can only wonder what further steps on to new ground the Comédie Française might have taken had Antoine Vitez not died so soon.

Born Antoine Vitez. **Father** Photographer. **Marriage** Agnès van Molder. **Children** Jeanne and Marie. **Career** Actor, 1949; studied with Tania Balachova; personal secretary to Louis Aragon, translator of German, Greek and Russian plays and novels; worked with marionettes, 1962; presented a lecture/production of Mayakovsky's work, 1964; theatre director, 1966–90; director of studies, Theatre of Nations University, 1965; instructor, Jacques Lacoq Mime School, 1966–70; professor, Conservatoire National d'Art Dramatique, 1968–81; opera director; director, Théâtre National de Chaillot, 1972–74, artistic director, 1981–88, classes filmed as *Cinq leçons de théâtre*; founder, Théâtre des Quartiers d'Ivry, Paris, 1972; director, Comédie Française, Paris, 1988–90. **Offices and memberships** Member, French Communist Party, 1950–80. **Stage** (includes) *Electra*, 1966; *Le Procès d'Emile Henry*, 1966; *Bath-house*, 1966; *Le Dragon*, 1968, *La Grande Enquête de François-Félix Kulpa*, 1968; *La Parade*, 1969; *Le Précepteur*, 1970; *La Mouette*, 1970; *Electra*, 1971; *Faust*, 1972; *Mother Courage*, 1973; *m = M, 1973; Gospel According to St John*, 1974; *Les Miracles*, 1974; *Le Pique-nique de Claretta*, 1974; *Phèdre*, 1975; *Catherine*, 1975; *Partage de midi*, 1976; *La Ballade de Mr Punch*, 1976; *Iphigénie-Hôtel*, 1977; *Grisélidis*, 1977; *Les Burgraves*, 1977; *L'École des femmes*, 1978; *Don Juan*, 1978; *Le Misanthrope*, 1978; *Tartuffe*, 1978; *The Inspector General*, 1980; *Faust*, 1981; *Britannicus*, 1981; *Hamlet*, 1983; *Hernani*, 1985; *Le Soulier de satin*, 1987; *Apprentice Sorcerers*, 1988; *Huis-clos*, 1989; *La Célestine*, 1989; *Un transport amoureux*, 1989; *Galileo*, 1990; also *Triumph of Love*; *Tombeau pour 500,000 soldats*; *Entretiens avec M. Said Hammadi, ouvrier algérien*. **Opera** (includes) *Le nozze de Figaro*, 1979; *Macbeth*, 1984. **Cause of death** Brain haemorrhage, at age 59.

CLIFTON R. WHARTON

American Diplomat

***Born* Baltimore, Maryland, 11 May 1899**

***Died* Phoenix, Arizona, 25 April 1990**

In 1958 it was widely reported that the country of Romania was sharply critical of the United States for supressing black people. One can only imagine the Romanians' surprise when, in the same year, President Eisenhower appointed African-American Clifton R. Wharton to the post of US minister to Romania.

With Bachelor's and Master's degrees in law from Boston University, Wharton joined the State Department as a law clerk in 1925. In the previous year the US government had formed a career Foreign Service department and Wharton, after almost a year of clerking, passed both the written and oral examinations. Like most black people in the service he was immediately assigned to a small tropical country: he served as third secretary at the US embassy in Monrovia, Liberia. Then from 1930 until 1941 he was consul in Las Palmas in the Canary Islands. At the end of this period he was transferred to Tananarive, Madagascar where he was to serve for three years as consul.

Wharton became an expert on West African affairs. He had a seemingly inborn talent for working with both his colleagues and local officials. As a result, for years after leaving the area, people in West Africa with whom he had dealt often asked after him.

In 1945 he was moved on to Ponta Degada in the Azores Islands as the American delegate, and three months after his posting became consul there. Much of the time he was concerned with the American air base, Lages, situated on the Island of Terceira. As he represented the civilian side of the government, he concentrated his duties on protecting the rights of civilians working on the base and with maintaining good relations with the Portuguese authorities.

Wharton's distinguished service there led to his biggest career break — a posting as consul and first secretary in Lisbon in October 1949. It was the first important diplomatic posting of a black man. The next year he was promoted to the office of consul general.

In 1953 Wharton was again reassigned. This time he was appointed as consul general in Marseilles in southern France. While he reported generally on political and economic conditions in the area, he was particularly concerned with the regulation of American shipping in this large seaport.

In 1958 another career breakthrough came to him as he became the first black American career diplomat to be named chief of a diplomatic mission. He was assigned the post of minister to Romania and the next year was promoted to the Foreign Service rank of career minister.

He remained in Bucharest until March 1961 when he was appointed as ambassador to Norway. When he retired three years later, Secretary of State Dean Rusk said, "Yours has been an outstanding career, and I am sure you take pride in the fine reputation you have earned."

Clifton R. Wharton not only distinguished himself in his career, but in doing so paved the way for other black Americans in the diplomatic service.

Born Clifton Reginald Wharton. **Parents** William B. and Rosalind (Griffin) Wharton. **Marriages** 1) Harriette Banks, 1924 (dissolved); 2) Evangeline L. Spears, 1949. **Children** Clifton, William, Mary, and Richard, from first marriage. **Education** English High School, Boston; Boston University LLB (cum laude), 1920, LLM, 1923. **Career** Called to Massachusetts Bar, 1920; began practising law, Boston, 1920; examiner, Veterans Bureau, Washington, DC, 1924; law clerk, US Department of State, 1925; entered US Foreign Service, 1925; third secretary,

Liberian embassy, 1925–27, vice-consul, 1927–29, occasional chargé d'affaires, 1930–41; consul, Las Palmas, Canary Islands, 1930–41; consul, Tananarive, Madagascar, 1942–45; American delegate, Ponta Delgada, Azores Islands, 1945, consul, 1945–49; consul, Lisbon, Portugal, 1949–50, first secretary, 1949–50, consul general, 1950–53; consul general, Marseilles, France, 1953–57; US minister to Romania, 1958–61; appointed career minister, 1959; ambassador, Norway, 1961–64; retired, 1964. **Cause of death** Undisclosed, at age 90.

AUBREY WILLIAMS

Guyanese Painter

Born **Georgetown, British Guiana, 8 May 1926**

Died **London, England, 27 April 1990**

A major exponent in Britain of abstract expressionism and a prominent figure on London's Afro-Caribbean art scene, Aubrey Williams, although a contemporary painter of great energy and seriousness of purpose, never achieved adequate recognition from the British art establishment. This is probably attributable — at least in part — to his Guyanese origins, themselves crucial to his painting. Born and brought up in the then colony of British Guiana, now Guyana, Williams initially worked as an agricultural officer in the civil service. Guyana then, as Williams later commented, "was coming out of colonial bondage. It was a boiling cauldron". Williams's support of economically repressed local farmers caused the authorities to post him to the remote north-west corner of the country, where he spent two years working amongst the Warrau, a native Indian tribe in the rain forest. This experience, anticipated with dismay by Williams at the outset, proved to be of inestimable value to his thought and work; it was there, as he later recalled, "that I discovered myself as an artist".

Williams had in fact shown an early aptitude for drawing and had been involved with the Working People's Art Group run by the Guyanese artist and teacher E. R. Burrowes. In 1952 he arrived in London as an agriculture student, but soon changed course and enrolled for a year at St Martin's School of Art. Thereafter he made London his home. Like so many of his contemporaries, he was profoundly influenced by the New York School of abstract expressionism, particularly Jackson Pollock and Arshile Gorky. To this he brought a unique combination of cultural elements culled from his knowledge of early South American civilizations, and his widely contrasting Guyanese experiences of political upheaval and primitive tribal life. Denis Bowen, former director of the New Vision Centre Gallery in London, where Williams was to exhibit, describes his work as having "its own mysterious atmosphere, possessed by surging forms imbued with a hypnotic depth of feeling for the past and present seen as one totality."

Initially, with his first one-man show at London's Archer Gallery in 1955, Williams met with critical approbation, but was subsequently cold-shouldered by British critics. Although he continued to exhibit in Britain, notably in the show entitled *Commonwealth Art Today* at the Commonwealth Institute, London, and received the Commonwealth Prize for painting in 1965, it was in continental Europe and the Americas that his reputation was established. He participated in a number of shows, including the Saō Paolo Biennale of 1967, culminating in a ten-year retrospective at Kingston, Jamaica in 1975. He was featured on US television in 1972 to 1973, painted murals in such diverse locations as San Francisco, Nova Scotia and Jamaica, and portraits of Fidel Castro, Duke Ellington and Dmitri Shostakovitch.

The relationship between music and painting held a fascination for Williams and is celebrated in the series of large canvases painted between 1960 and 1981 and inspired by the music of Shostakovitch, whom Williams particularly admired. Two of these paintings, hanging in the upper foyer of the Festival Hall, London, are the only works by him on permanent display in his adopted city. The Shostakovitch series, shown at the Commonwealth Institute in 1981 and at the Festival Hall in 1985 constituted one of two major solo exhibitions from Williams's later career, the other being *The Olmec-Maya and Now* at the Commonwealth Institute in 1985. In this series Williams explored the pre-Columbian Olmec and Maya cultures, which he viewed not only as intrinsic to his South American heritage but of relevance to modern civilization, and whose imagery and mythology form a leitmotif in his art.

It was only in the year of his death, however, that Williams's work was included in a major London exhibition: *The Other Story: Afro-Asian Art in Post-War Britain* at the Hayward Gallery. His status as a "Commonwealth" painter consistently caused him to be marginalized by the British art establishment, which has so far failed to recognize the contribution of its colonial heritage to the country's artistic evolution. It was to counteract the sense of cultural isolation experienced during his early years in London that he became a founder member, in 1966, of the Caribbean Artists Movement (CAM). Besides enabling Caribbean writers and artists to assert an indigenous aesthetic after centuries of European cultural domination, CAM provided a forum for British West Indians seeking contact with Caribbean literature and art. Williams was also instrumental in orchestrating Carifesta, the first Caribbean regional festival of the arts, held in Guyana in 1972. During the 1970s and 1980s he worked in the Caribbean, notably Jamaica, as much as in London.

Rhetorical, and deeply expressive of a wide range of powerful emotions, with its Pre-Columbian references, fiery colours and tropical atmosphere, Aubrey Williams's art possesses an exotic, foreign quality in British eyes. It nevertheless has a universality in its preoccupation with the relationship between man and nature, instilled in Williams by his experience in the Guyanese rain forest. "Inherent in my work since I was a boy", he said, "has been the human predicament, especially with regard to the Guyanese situation".

Born Aubrey Sendall Williams. **Father** Walter Williams. **Marriage** Eve. **Children** One daughter, Maridowa. **Education** St Martin's School of Art, London, 1952–53. **Emigration** Left British Guiana (now Guyana) for Britain, 1952. **Career** Agricultural officer, Guyana civil service; served two years with Warrau Indian tribe; founder, Caribbean Artists Movement, 1966; adviser, Guyana Festival of Art, 1972; US television series, 1972–73; member, Art panel, Arts Council, 1986. **Awards and honours** Commonwealth Prize for painting, 1964; Golden Arrow for Achievement, Guyana, 1970. **Works** (include) Murals: Park Forest, Illinois, Sligoville, Jamaica; portraits: Duke Ellington, Fidel Castro, Linden Forbes, Dr Eric Williams, Dmitri Shostakovitch. **Exhibitions** Archer Gallery, London, 1955; New Vision Art Gallery, 1956–66; *Commonwealth Art Today*, Commonwealth Institute, London, 1962–63; Expo '67; Saõ Paulo Biennale, 1967; San Francisco; Northwestern University, Chicago; retrospective, Olympia Art Centre, Kingston, Jamaica, 1975; *The Symphonies and Quartets of Dimitri Shostakovitch*, Commonwealth Institute, 1981, Royal Festival Hall, 1984; *Olmec-Maya and Now*, Commonwealth Institute, 1985; *The Other Story: Afro-Asian Art in Post-War Britain*, Hayward Gallery, London, 1990. **Collections** York Art Gallery, University of York; House of Assembly, Georgetown, Guyana; Colgrain House, Georgetown, Guyana; Timerhi Airport, Guyana. **Cause of death** Cancer, at age 63. **Further reading** Ann Walmsley, editor, *Guyana Dreaming*, 1990.

MAY

LUCY BOSTON

British Children's Writer

***Born* Southport, Lancashire, 10 December 1892**

***Died* Hemingford Grey, Cambridgeshire, 25 May 1990**

Lucy Boston, born Wood, was the fifth of six children. She grew up in the latter part of the Victorian era in a strictly pious Evangelical family. It was not long before the young Lucy showed signs of the fierce independence that guided her life. She rebelled against religion, and after only two terms at Somerville College, Oxford, she left university to train as a nurse. World War I had broken out, and she worked for a time at a French military hospital in Le Havre, before returning to England to marry her cousin, Harold Boston. The marriage ended after 18 years, leaving her with one son, Peter. For a while, shattered by the breakdown of her marriage, Lucy Boston pursued an artistic career in Austria, but returned again to England before the outbreak of World War II.

It was at this point in her life that a great love affair began — not with a man, but with the derelict Manor House she bought at Hemingford Grey near Cambridge. At first glance the house appeared to be Georgian, but when Lucy Boston first looked round it, she found she had bought a genuine Norman manor-house, with a Georgian façade. In her fascinating book, *Memory in a House,* the author writes: "Looking back now it is hard to know why I acted with such certainty and passion. It was like falling in love."

The house became her life's centre. With infinite patience and love, Lucy Boston and her son Peter began to uncover the wonderful secrets of the old house, and slowly to restore it to its former glory. Also transformed was the garden. Her roses were her pride and joy. Visitors to the house were sometimes invited to drink wine from a full-blown rose — an unforgettable experience. Also in the gardens was the topiary — yew trees cut into the shapes of birds, animals, crowns and orbs — there was even a chess set. She felt it vital to have a garden filled with fragrance, and her flowers were carefully chosen — honeysuckle, pinks, stocks, lilies. "Scent to me is very mysterious", writes the author. "It is the most immediate of the senses."

With her house and gardens emerging resplendent from their neglected state Lucy Boston began to feel the need to express in writing her strong and passionate feelings about her home. Well into her fifties she began to write her first books: *Yew Hall* and *The Children of Green Knowe.* Both books were accepted by Faber and Faber and published in 1954. *The Children of Green Knowe,* illustrated by her son, Peter, was the first of six novels set in the old manor-house at Hemingford Grey. Every corner and stone of Lucy Boston's home can be identified in her stories — the old Norman hall, her famous patchworth curtains, the gardens with the distinctive topiary and profusion of roses. The age of the house and the many generations who have inhabited it are reflected in the Green Knowe stories. In *The Children of Green Knowe* Tolly comes to stay with his grandmother, Mrs Oldknowe (who is, of course, Lucy Boston herself). He encounters the spirits of a past generation of children — Toby, Alexander and Linnet, together with their splendid horse, Feste. Real, yet elusive, these children reflect the author's preoccupation with time and the interweaving of past with present.

In 1961 Lucy Boston won the Carnegie Medal for *A Stranger at Green Knowe*. It tells of an escaped gorilla who finds refuge in the garden of Green Knowe. The gorilla is befriended, not by Tolly, the central character of the first books, but by Ping, a refugee Chinese boy, who feels as alien and dispossessed as the gorilla. The book says much about the concept of freedom, and it ends sadly. The gorilla chooses death rather than a return to captivity.

In *An Enemy at Green Knowe* Lucy Boston introduces evil in the form of Miss Melanie D. Powers, a present-day witch. Whereas all the other stories have a gentle, magical and subtle quality, and the supernatural elements are neither frightening nor malevolent, *An Enemy at Green Knowe* generates a feeling of fear and unease. The story has an unusual source. In *Memory in a House* the author describes how a local planning committee wished to erect a pavilion and a row of public toilets immediately overlooking the Manor. The author and her friends fought long and hard to get the decision reversed, and the struggle against the philistines of insensitive planning represented what is shown in *An Enemy at Green Knowe* as the fight of good versus evil. Luckily, both in the book and in real life, goodness and sensitivity prevailed.

In *The Stones of Green Knowe* Lucy Boston goes right back to the origins of the house, where twelfth-century Roger watches the building of a brand new manor house. It celebrates a whole history of Green Knowe and the people who lived there. It also echoes Lucy Boston's fear of a future where everything she loves and values is destroyed by overdevelopment and pollution. *The Stones of Green Knowe* was the last of the six novels, and is the least optimistic, as it offers no real hope for the future. Other shorter children's novels were *The Sea Egg* (set in Cornwall) and *The Castle of Yew,* which is an extension of the Green Knowe stories.

Three generations of children have enjoyed the Green Knowe books. Lucy Boston had a great affinity with children, for she never condescended to them, and regarded them as equals. "I would like to encourage children to use their senses", she wrote. "It is from direct sense stimulus that imagination is born."

Her favourite of her two adult novels, *Persephone* (published in America as *Strongholds*), never, to her sorrow, achieved the same degree of success as her children's books. When she was 85 her autobiography, *Perverse and Foolish,* was published. In this she returns to her childhood, whereas in *Memory in a House* she describes in detail her life's passion of later years — her careful, sensitive and loving restoration of the manor-house. She recalls her life there, the many friends who visited her — her American publisher was married from the house — and how this remarkable affinity she had with her home influenced her life and her writing.

Lucy Boston died at the age of 97 in her beloved Manor House, into which she had poured so much love. But, like the ghosts of Green Knowe, her spirit lives on. Her respect for the young, her love of freedom, beauty and all natural life, all can be found in the rich heritage of her books and within the walls of that Norman manor-house, deep in the Cambridgeshire countryside.

Born Lucy Maria Wood. **Parents** James, engineer, and Mary (Garrett) Wood. **Marriage** 1) Harold Boston, officer, Royal Air Force, 1917 (divorced 1935). **Children** One son, Peter. **Education** Downs School, Seaford, East Sussex; Somerville College, Oxford, 1914. **Career** Trained for Voluntary Aid Detachment, St Thomas's Hospital, London, served France, World War I; moved to Hemingford Grey, Huntingdon, 1939; first juvenile publication, 1954; first adult publication, 1954; first play published, 1970. **Awards and honours** Library

Association Carnegie Medal for *A Stranger at Green Knowe*, 1962; Lewis Carroll Shelf Award for *The Children of Green Knowe*, 1969. **Publications — juvenile** *The Children of Green Knowe*, 1954; *The Chimneys of Green Knowe*, 1958, published in US as *Treasure at Green Knowe*, 1958; *The River at Green Knowe*, 1959; *A Stranger at Green Knowe*, 1961; *An Enemy at Green Knowe*, 1964; *The Castle of Yew*, 1965; *The Sea-Egg*, 1967; *The House That Grew*, 1969; *Nothing Said*, 1971; *The Guardians of the House*, 1974; *The Fossil Snake*, 1975; *The Stones of Green Knowe*, 1976. **Publications — adult** *Yew Hall* (novel), 1954; (contributor) *The House of the Nightmare and Other Eerie Tales* (edited by Kathleen Lines), 1967; *Persephone* (novel), 1969, published in US as *Strongholds*, 1969; *The Horned Man; or, Whom Will You Send to Fetch Her Away?* (play), 1970; (contributor) *Young Winter's Tales I* (edited by M.R. Hodgkin), 1970; *Memory in a House* (autobiography), 1973; *Perverse and Foolish: A Memoir of Childhood and Youth* (autobiography), 1979. **Cause of death** Undisclosed, at age 97. **Further reading** Jasper Rose, *Lucy Boston*, 1965; *Twentieth Century Children's Writers*, 1989.

MARY BRUCE

British Sporting Pilot and Driver

Born **Coptfold Hall, Essex, 10 November 1895**

Died **Bradford-on-Avon, Wiltshire, 21 May 1990**

The years between the two world wars were the golden age of light aviation and motor racing. It was a time when "records" of every kind could be sure of headlines: the land-speed record at Daytona Beach, the fastest lap at Brooklands or the first solo crossing of the Atlantic could thrill a public which was not yet anxious about pollution or the ozone layer. The term "women's lib" had not then been coined, but women pilots such as Amelia Earhart and Amy Johnson demonstrated that being female was no barrier to record-breaking by land, sea or air.

Mary Bruce was of this company, but not content to confine herself to one element, she achieved fame in motor racing, in aviation and as a driver of speedboats. Already as a child she displayed a taste for adventure with horses and motorcycles, but it was her marriage to a keen motor-racing driver, Victor Bruce, which enabled her to satisfy her need for speed and excitement. She was soon racing at Brooklands, competing against famous male drivers such as Segrave and Malcolm Campbell, and establishing records for speed and distance round the Montlhéry track near Paris. The Monte Carlo Rally was another event which naturally attracted her; in the 1929 Rally she set off from Lapland only to have her car go out of control on a hill and end up badly smashed against rocks. This did not deter her at all; she had the car virtually rebuilt within 24 hours and was on her way again, to become the first competitor to reach Monte Carlo.

In the same year she was busy setting up speed records on water. Impatient with the slowness of cross-Channel steamers, she drove her motorboat from Dover to Calais and back, finally setting a record time of less than 80 minutes for the return journey.

She claimed to be afraid of flying, but when strolling in London one day in July 1930 she saw in a shop window a little two-seater Blackburn Bluebird aeroplane which bore a price ticket of 550 pounds and a sign "Ready to go anywhere". That evening she was poring over the atlas and decided to fly from England to her mother's birthplace in New Albany, Indiana. Next day she had bought the Bluebird and ordered maps ready for a departure in only eleven weeks' time, regardless of the fact that she had not yet learned to fly. She was soon working for her pilot's licence and studying navigation, while at its maker's works in Yorkshire the little Bluebird was having an extra 68-gallon tank installed, with mechanics working day and night. One of them, asked what the aircrafts's registration letters G-ABDS stood for, wearily replied "A Bloody Daft Stunt".

At dawn on 25 September 1930 she left Heston aerodrome, the little aeroplane loaded down with fuel, emergency rations, an emergency radio transmitter and a Dictaphone — ancestor of the modern tape-recorder — with which to record her impressions of the flight. There was much to record. She was forced down in the Syrian desert, and again in quicksand at the mouth of the Persian Gulf, this time breaking the propeller and having to fit the spare with unsuitable tools. Flying from Bangkok to Hanoi, she was above cloud for four hours and uncertain whether mountains lay below, so after breathing a tense last message into the dictaphone she closed the throttle and sank into the clouds, emerging by great good fortune right over a railway which led to Hanoi.

The little Bluebird did not have the range to cross the Pacific, so at Tokyo it had to be loaded aboard a liner and taken to Vancouver. Here it was reassembled and Mary Bruce was once more airborne for the flight across America. She successfully located her mother's old house in Indiana and dropped an American flag there, but before reaching New York she had two more crashes. During the repairs the old fabric had to be carefully restored to preserve the thousands of signatures which it had accumulated, including that of the notorious Al Capone of Chicago. The sea crossing to Le Havre was followed by a triumphant final flight across the Channel to Croydon, completing a journey of nearly 20,000 miles through 23 countries in less than five months.

She was now firmly "hooked" on aviation, and during the rest of the 1930s she carried out experiments in flight refuelling, set up a record for the longest distance covered over water in 24 hours, joined the British Hospitals' Air Pageant flying circus, and established a company called Air Dispatch offering a rapid delivery service for freight, which included gold bullion and early morning newspapers. This was extended to provide the fastest passenger service between London and Paris, and subsequently an aerial ambulance service. After the outbreak of war in 1939, her company operated an air ferry service to France, and then after the fall of France it moved to South Wales to undertake the repair of damaged military aircraft.

After such a life of adventure and danger, she settled in the attractive little Wiltshire town of Bradford-on-Avon, where she wrote her aptly titled autobiography, *Nine Lives Plus*. Even in extreme old age, however, her interest in mechanical things was undiminished. She owned a vintage Rolls-Royce and was to be seen testing high-performance cars on the track in her mid-seventies, and at 81, after 37 years away from aircraft, she took a flying refresher course and performed loops in a Chipmunk two-seater with the greatest delight.

There is a saying in aviation that there are old pilots and bold pilots, but no old, bold pilots. Mary Bruce, who died at 94 after a life packed with adventure and danger, is a distinguished exception to this rule.

Born Mildred Mary Petre. **Parents** Lawrence Petre, squire of Coptfold Hall, Essex, and Mrs Petre, Shakespearian actress. **Marriage** The Hon Victor Austin Bruce, motor-racing driver and fourth son of the second Lord Aberdare, 1926 (divorced 1941). **Children** One son, Adrian. **Education** Convent of Sion, Bayswater, London. **Career** Travelled furthest north by motor car into Lapland, 1927; broke 17 world records for motoring, Montlhéry, 1927; broke record for single-handed driving, longest distance covered by man or woman, 2164 miles in 24 hours, 1927; won Coupe des Dames, Monte Carlo Rally, 1927, 1929; broke 24 hour solo-driver record, Montlhéry, 1929; took up motor-boat racing, 1929; broke record for Double Channel Crossing by motor boat, Dover to Calais, 1929; took up flying, 1930; first person to fly solo from England to Japan, 1930; longest solo flight, 1930; record solo flight, India to French Indo-China, 1930; broke 24-hour record for motor boat, covering 674 nautical miles, single handed, 1932; British Air refuelling endurance flight, 1933; joined British Hospitals' Air Pageant flying circus, 1934; founded Air Dispatch, company for air transport of newspapers and passenger service to Paris, 1935; set up Inner Circle Line linking Heston, Hamworth, Gatwick and other places in the London area; contracted with Army for night flying to provide target practice for the Territorial Army, 1937; began show jumping, 1939, won first place, Royal Windsor Horse Show, 1939; air ferry service to France, World War II; opened factory to repair crashed Royal Air Force planes, World War II; test-drove Ford Capri, 1973; returned to flying, 1976. **Offices and memberships** Life member, British Racing Drivers' Club. **Awards and honours** Order of the Million Elephants and White Umbrella, French Indo-China; fellow, Ancient Monuments Society. **Publications** *Nine Lives Plus,* 1977; also: *Round the World by Air and Steam, The Peregrinations of Penelope, 9000 miles in Eight Weeks, The Woman Owner Driver, The Bluebird's Flight.* **Cause of death** Undisclosed, at age 94.

BOB DANVERS-WALKER

British Broadcaster

Born **Cheam, Surrey, 11 October 1906**

Died **17 May 1990**

Bob Danvers-Walker became an institution. He was a voice — a unique voice — and few would fail to recognize it, whether the speaker could be named or not. He received the imprimatur of the *Guinness Book of Records* as "The world's most durable commentator."

He was born near the beginning of the century, in commuter territory, south of London. His father, an accountant, soon transplanted the family halfway across the world to Tasmania, and set up a woollen mill there. Young Bob attended Launceston Grammar School, became a jackaroo (the local version of a cowboy), and survived the first Australian Grand Prix after his car caught fire. In 1925 he settled for a job with the Herald Broadcasting Station in Melbourne. This he managed to invest with his native enthusiasm and ability to convey excitement. He became noted for his gift of the gab, his outside broadcasts, and his pioneering "air to ground" commentaries from an aircraft in flight.

In the early 1930s Danvers-Walker returned to Europe as chief announcer of the International Broadcasting Company, as which he pioneered the transmission of commercial radio from various continental stations into the homes of British listeners. On the outbreak of World War II in 1939, he worked under the French Ministry of Propaganda in countering the German broadcasts masterminded by Goebbels. (He later discovered that this got him on the Nazis' list of those due for terminal retribution.) He also helped to entertain the British Expeditionary Force. Eventually he escaped from France, three weeks after the evacuation of Dunkirk.

Back in England, he began his 30-year association with the Pathé News organization. As a newsreel commentator and as an accredited war correspondent, he began to register the kind of talismanic qualities vital to the time, and his genial *brio* was welcomed wherever there were British servicemen and women. For some years after the war, Pathé News was the ballast in the British cinemagoer's diet; an ineluctable part of the "full supporting programme". Danvers-Walker's was the voice that related the big events of the day, week after week. Whether he worked at his talent or whether he was just lucky, he had a consummate way with the scripts; relentlessly upbeat, he could elevate their excruciating bathos or leaden facetiousness with an air of complete conviction. There were, too, occasions when he could be genuinely moving; his vivid description of the Farnborough air tragedy of 1952 (when a test pilot's plane exploded after breaking the sound barrier) is eyewitness broadcasting of the highest quality.

He turned his vocal ability to all sorts of projects; from commercial voice-overs to travelogues to BBC radio warhorses like *Housewives' Choice.* As British television developed, Danvers-Walker started a new career, binding his broadcasting skills to the sort of physical adventure he always found alluring. Enrolled by the BBC's *Now* programme (and backed by a considerable insurance policy), he jumped over a 100-foot cliff, escaped from a disabled ship and generally entertained himself and his public with similar pranks. He opened Independent Television's London Weekend service by walking a high wire above the Earls Court Road behind a professional artiste. (He later recalled that he "concentrated on the boil on the other chap's neck".) Stardom was finally conferred by the television quiz show *Take Your Pick* where, to popular delight, he intoned the list of prizes and hit a gong — a curiously poignant apotheosis.

The famous voice was clear, fruity and rich, with just the suggestion of raffishness. *The Daily Telegraph* thought that it "carried the unmistakably British flavour of, say, a roadhouse on the Kingston bypass" — a metaphor which defies explanation to those unfamiliar with the commuter-land of southern England.

By way of recreation, Danvers-Walker enjoyed studying The Bible. His enthusiasm for work remained unabated, and he was still in demand up until the time of his death. A "traditionalist", he deplored what he considered to be declining standards in modern broadcast speech, and frankly believed that the whole business was much too serious to admit the presence of women. With him passed, as one commentator put it, "the last dinosaur of newsreel commentators".

Born Cyril Danvers-Walker. **Father** Chartered accountant and woollen textile manufacturer. **Marriage** Vera White, 1933. **Children** One son and one daughter. **Education** Launceston Grammar School, Australia. **Emigration** Taken by father to Tasmania; moved to Europe, 1931; returned to England, 1940. **Career** Greaseboy, General Motors; jackaroo; Grand Prix driver; broadcaster, Herald Broadcasting Station, Melbourne, 1925; made first "air to ground" commentary from an aircraft in flight; chief announcer for continental Europe, International Broadcasting Company, 1931; broadcast for French Ministry of Propaganda, 1939–40; newsreel commentator, Pathé News, 1940–70, war correspondent, Pathé News; radio presenter on programmes including *Housewives' Choice*, *The Countryside*, *Film Time;* stunt man, *Saturday Night Out, Now;* television announcer/narrator: *Take Your Pick*; *A-Z of Television.* **Related activities** Entertained British Expeditionary Force, 1940–45. **Radio** Chief announcer: wedding of Princess Elizabeth, 1947, funeral of King George VI, 1952, World Cup, 1966. **Cause of death** Undisclosed, at age 83.

SAMMY DAVIS JR

American Entertainer

***Born* Harlem, New York, 8 December 1925**

***Died* Los Angeles, California, 16 May 1990**

When Sammy Davis Jr's autobiography, *Yes I Can,* was published in 1965, one reviewer called it, "the definitive documentary of the American Dream in America *now.*" The sequel, *Why Me?,* published 24 years later, revealed the ways in which the dream went sour. "The manic pursuit of success cost me everything I could love", he wrote. "And it cost me two or three fortunes which I might still have if during those desperate years I hadn't been so single-sighted that a million dollars was just three words."

A lot happened between the writing of those two books. Davis's marriage to May Britt broke up and he became estranged from their three children. His political allegiances changed. By the late 1970s and early 1980s, his excessive use of drink and drugs (two bottles of bourbon a day, and a bowl of cocaine he "kept filled next to the mixed nuts") led to such severe deterioration of his internal organs that a doctor told him that if he didn't stop drinking immediately, he would soon be dead. Finally, with an ashen face and excruciatingly painful stomach, Davis was rushed to hospital with advanced cirrhosis of the liver. Compelled to keep working, partly by his "need to excel", but mostly by his outstanding tax bill of 1.4 million dollars, his first show after leaving the hospital was a disaster. In Sydney, Australia, Sammy Davis Jr walked onto the stage with the aid of a stick and then found that his voice was gone. "I couldn't dance and I couldn't sing", he said later. "The nightmare had come to pass."

Talking about his drug and alcohol addiction, he once explained,

> I didn't like me. I just didn't like me. So it made all the sense in the world to me at the time that if you don't like yourself, you destroy yourself. And you don't do it quietly. You don't go into a room and turn on the gas so you don't bother anybody. You make sure that you create a lot of tumult before you go, and then you're going to bug everybody and drive them crazy, so you'll all die.
>
> ...I created a life-style, and I didn't want anyone to say I had been lying all the time, this isn't your life-style, so I had to play the game. I created a role I hated to play...I can't lie to you; there were times it was great fun...But most of the time, when I gave myself the moments to reflect, it wasn't fun. It wasn't fun to split up with May, to know that I had lost my kids and they had no respect for me. That wasn't fun...And the only way you can run away from it all is to make yourself so tired that you're never conscious of what you're doing.

Sammy Davis Jr's whole life consisted of making himself tired enough to block out unpleasant realities. Born in a Harlem tenement, his mother left when he was only two years old and he was raised on the road by his vaudevillian father and his uncle, Will Mastin. At the age of three, he began performing in his uncle's troupe, Holiday in Dixieland, as "Silent Sam, the Dancing Midget". Dressed in an exact replica of the clothes worn by his uncle and father, and with a fat cigar stuck between his teeth, he had to pretend to be an adult midget because of child labour laws. Sometimes his father would get a tutor for him, but he never went to school.

At the age of four, he played the title role in his first movie, *Rufus Jones for President,* in which the distinguished black American actress, Ethel Waters, played his mother. As he got older he got featured billing in the troupe. But vaudeville was beginning to decline and the troupe of a dozen performers became fewer and fewer in number until the act became "The Will Maston Trio, featuring Sammy Davis Jr".

Racism had always been part of the young man's experience; he couldn't eat at the same lunch counters as his white friends in other vaudeville acts, or stay in the same hotels, but his father and uncle had shielded him from the worst aspects of it: the undisguised hatred and violence. He was to meet that for the first time in the Army.

He was drafted into the US Army during World War II, at the age of 18. Assigned to infantry training and placed in a mixed barracks at Fort Francis E. Warren in Cheyenne, Wyoming, he was attacked repeatedly, both verbally and physically, by white GI's. His nose was broken several times, he was held down while the word "Coon" was painted across his forehead, and on one occasion he was offered a bottle of root beer that turned out to be urine. The only positive aspect of his time in Cheyenne was that a black sergeant taught him to read.

Davis transferred to Special Services, where he finally found acceptance. As a performer, doing shows in camps across the country, he finally found a way to "get to" the minds of those who had been so cruel to him. He once spotted a man who had beaten him up sitting in the audience and realized that for the first time, the man was looking at him in awe, without any trace of hatred. After that, he said that he always combed the audience for the "haters", and when he spotted one, he'd give his performance an "extra burst of strength and energy" because those were the ones he most wanted to reach. "I was dancing down the barriers between us", he said.

The army years definitely had a lasting effect on his psyche. Alan Ebert, a publicity man who later worked with Davis, wrote that "in Sammy's mind he still thinks of himself as the kid in the Army, the one who got stomped on, spat upon, and beaten", and that "Sam knocks himself out in a vain attempt to make the whole world love him and to erase from his mind those early years."

In a similar vein, Davis himself has written, "What have I got? No looks, no money, no education. Just talent...I want to be treated well. How do I get there? There's only one way I can do it with what I've got to work with. I've got to be a star! I have to be a star like another man has to breathe."

By the end of the war, vaudeville was dead. The trio had some lean years trying to break into Las Vegas, which was just beginning to be known as a show town. Eventually, though, they did a six-month tour with Mickey Rooney, and then they got a three-week booking to be on the same bill as Frank Sinatra.

The long-standing friendship and mutual admiration of Sammy Davis Jr and Frank Sinatra is legendary. Along with Dean Martin and Peter Lawford, among others, Sammy Davis Jr became one of Sinatra's famed "Rat Pack", a group of hard-drinking, fast-living hellraisers who were every bit as talented and hard-working as they were wild.

There were several Rat Pack movies, usually with a number in the title, like *Ocean's Eleven*, *Convicts Four*, and *Robin and the Seven Hoods*, and all great fun to watch. Davis made many films during his lifetime, but the one generally agreed to be his best was the 1959 film version of *Porgy and Bess,* in which he played Sportin' Life, the sleazy tempter who lures Bess away with a pocketful of "happy dust", and seduces a church-goers' picnic with a sinuous and sinister rendition of "It Ain't Necessarily So". Barry Crowther wrote in *The New York Times* that, "in every respect he is the sharpest and most insinuating character in the show". Yet he nearly didn't get the part. At the mention of Sammy Davis Jr, Sam Goldwyn is reported to have said "That monkey? You must be joking!"

Never a good-looking man (Robert Sylvester once wrote that "God made Sammy as ugly-looking as he could and then hit him in the face with a shovel"), he was badly injured in a 1954 car crash, giving his face a further battering and losing him one eye. Frank Sinatra visited him in the hospital and watched while Davis took a full five minutes to get a lighter flame to connect with his cigarette. "You're full of little party tricks, Charlie", Sinatra told him, to which Davis replied, "Stick around. For an encore I light my nose."

The child of a Baptist father and Catholic mother, Davis had never given much thought to religion until his near-fatal crash. Then Davis surprised the world, and surrounded himself with controversy, by converting to Judaism, saying that he felt there was a special affinity between Blacks and Jews, who have both "been oppressed for centuries". He once said in an interview that he had found strength and dignity in Jewish literature. "I wanted to know how a people could survive for so many years, being constantly persecuted. I wanted to know what gave them that inner strength, and when I found out, I found peace in it."

His religious conversion also served to give bigots even more ammunition against him, which he managed to joke about. Once, on a golf course, he was asked what his handicap was and he replied, "I'm a one-eyed coloured Jew."

There was further controversy when he married the Swedish actress May Britt in 1960, a time when inter-racial marriages were frowned upon and extremely rare. (An earlier relationship with actress Kim Novak is said to have resulted in a contract being put out on him by the head of her studio, who was rumoured to have connections with the Mafia.) Miss Britt, who also converted to Judaism, was asked if her parents in Sweden had any objections to her marriage. "Why should they?" she replied. "There is no anti-Semitism in Sweden."

Life was not easy for the couple. They were invited, and then uninvited to Kennedy's inauguration because the sight of a mixed couple might offend some southerners. There were many death threats. A hotel where they stayed in Washington, DC, was picketed by demonstrators waving banners that read, "Go back to the Congo, you Kosher Coon." A performance in England was interrupted by 14 brown-shirted neo-Nazis. The marriage ended eight years later, when May drove off, taking their three children (two of them adopted) with her, saying that they "had no family life" whatever.

He married the actress and dancer Altovise Gore in 1970. Davis admits that she "went through the tortures of the damned with me...I wouldn't have made it without her." In 1972, he found himself in the midst of controversy once more, this time alienating not the traditionally right-wing bigots, but the liberals and the Blacks. The reason? He hugged Richard Nixon. The fact that he had marched with Martin Luther King was temporarily forgotten. The work he had done for the National Association of Colored People was forgotten. The benefits he'd done for the United Negro College Fund, the family of Malcolm X and 1960s radical Angela Davis, all forgotten. Sammy Davis Jr was now accused of being an Uncle Tom. Author Truman Capote said, "When I saw him kissing Nixon, I thought he was the new Checkers", while others defended him by saying he was an emotional sort of person who would hug anybody. Davis would later let it be known that he regretted his support of Nixon; he said that Nixon had made promises he didn't keep, especially in the area of civil rights.

Always an ostentatious dresser, he took the style of the 1970s to its most extreme manifestation, appearing in high platform boots and wide, flapping flares. Not averse to a little self-parody, he played a charismatic and oh-so-hip evangelical preacher in the film of *Sweet Charity,* and made the theme from *Hawaii Five-O* his entrance music for stage shows. Unexpected appearances from Sammy Davis Jr were considered a major event, so he spent a large part of the 1970s walking onto talk shows unannounced, or interrupting a friend's act to join them on-stage. He was often referred to as "Mister Wonderful" (taken from the Broadway show of the same name in which he starred), "Mister Entertainment", or simply "Sammy". A talk-show regular who had filled in for Johnny Carson on *The Tonight Show,* he was given his own chat show in 1975, *Sammy and Company,* which ran for two years. Refusing to age gracefully, he started singing rock and pop, and had a number one hit in 1972 with "The Candy Man".

He was originally reluctant to sing one of the songs with which he is most identified, "Mr Bojangles", because it tells the story of an ageing dancer who becomes a has-been and is reduced to begging. Davis said he had seen too much of that in his lifetime, "performers who'd slid from headlining to playing joints, then toilets, and finally beer halls and passing the hat." He often said that one of his greatest fears was that he would die forgotten and penniless. "The song was my worst nightmare."

His health and tax problems of the early 1980s almost made it seem as if his nightmare might come true. But after a hip replacement operation in 1983 ("get well" telegrams usually ran along the lines of: "Wouldn't you know that if Sammy Davis had an operation it would be hip?") he was able to dance again. He fought his way back to health by quitting drugs and switching from bourbon to Strawberry Crush, and then embarked on a world tour with his old buddy Frank Sinatra, and Liza Minnelli, whom he'd bounced on his knee as a child. Unfortunately, he'd also been a heavy smoker for many years.

The throat cancer that killed him was diagnosed after his return from the tour. After two months of painful radiation therapy, the cancer was declared to be in remission. Then it made a comeback.

Knowing that he wouldn't be with them for very long, 26 of his fellow entertainers saluted him in a two-and-a-half-hour television special which was aired a couple of months before he died. The black superstar Michael Jackson let it be known that he was only where he is today because Sammy Davis Jr was there before him, paving the way. Davis, frail and close to death, unable to speak, kept up his long tradition of interrupting someone else's act. He got up on stage with Gregory Hines and, to a standing ovation, he did an impromptu tap dance.

He did not die alone and forgotten as he'd feared. In the weeks before his death, many of his friends, such as Lola Falana and Frank Sinatra, came to see him and say a final farewell. There were more than 1200 people seated inside the hall where his funeral service was held, while hundreds more stood outside. The pallbearers included Frank Sinatra, Dean Martin, Michael Jackson and Bill Cosby.

Davis was always modest about his achievements in the breaking down of racial barriers. "I'm not the Martin Luther King of nightclubs", he said in 1987. "I think I helped make conditions a little bit better for black performers. Somewhere down the line, I contributed — along with Lena (Horne) and Nat ("King" Cole) and 100 other people." But according to musician Quincy Jones, "He made it possible for the Bill Cosbys, the Michael Jacksons and the Eddie Murphys to achieve their dreams."

Liza Minnelli said that he was her inspiration. "He's the performer we all strive to live up to. I never saw anyone give so much." Jerry Lewis said that it was like losing a brother. There could be numerous quotes here from famous people, but perhaps the last word should go to Frank Sinatra: "I wish the world could have known Sam as I did...It was a generous God who gave him to us."

Born Sammy Davis Junior. **Parents** Sammy, entertainer, and Elvira (Sanchez), entertainer, Davis. **Marriages** 1) Loray White, singer, 1958 (divorced 1959); 2) May Britt, actress, 1960 (divorced 1968); 3) Altovise Gore, actress and dancer, 1970. **Children** Tracey, Mark (adopted), and Jeff (adopted), from second marriage; Manny (adopted), from third marriage. **Education** Calvert Correspondence School. **Military service** Infantry training, US Army, 1943; Special Services, US Army, 1943–45; wrote, produced, directed and performed in camp shows. **Career** Member, Will Mastin's "Holiday in Dixieland" troupe, 1930, The Will Mastin Trio, 1930–46, The Will Mastin Trio, featuring Sammy Davis, Jr, 1946; studied dance with Bill Robinson; solo night-club performer, 1945–90; first film appearance, *Rufus Jones for President,* 1929; first featured film role, *The Benny Goodman Story,* 1956; Broadway début, *Mr Wonderful,* 1956; toured Europe, 1966–67; United Service Organization tour, South Vietnam, 1972, Lebanon, 1983; command performance, White House, 1973; recording contracts: Decca Records, Twentieth Century Records, Warner Records, Motown Records, Reprise Records and others; world tour (with Frank Sinatra and Liza Minnelli), 1989. **Related activities** Vice-president, Tropicana Hotel, Las Vegas, Nevada. **Other activities** Chairman, Life Membership Committee, National Association for the Advancement of Colored People, 1966, chairman, Los Angeles membership committee; member, National Advisory Council on Economic Opportunity, 1971; associate: Operation PUSH (People United to Save Humanity), National Urban League, Southern Christian Leadership Conference. **Offices and memberships** Member: Actors Equity Association, Screen Actors Guild, National Association for the Advancement of Colored People, American Society of Magazine Photographers, American Guild of Variety Artists, American Federation of Television and Radio Artists, Negro Actors Guild, Urban League. **Awards and honours** *Metronome* magazine: record of the year award for "The Way You Look Tonight", 1946, most outstanding new personality of the year, 1946; best actor nomination, Antoinette Perry (Tony) awards, for *Golden Boy,* 1965; B'nai B'rith Man of the Year award, 1965; Emmy Award nomination, National Academy of

Television Arts and Sciences, for *The Sammy Davis Jr Show,* 1965, for *The Swinging World of Sammy Davis Jr,* 1966, special citation for contributions to television entertainment, 1974; Springarn medal, National Association for the Advancement of Colored People; Grammy Award nomination, National Academy of Recording Arts and Sciences, for "The Candy Man", 1973; honorary LHD, Wilberforce University, 1973; entertainer of the year, *Cue* magazine; personality of the year, New York Press Association; Cultural Achievement Award, Israel; citation of recognition: Police Association of America, League of Crippled Children; knighted by Ecumenical Knights of Malta, 1974; Kennedy Center honour for career achievement, 1987. **Stage** *Mr Wonderful,* 1956; *Golden Boy,* 1964; *Sammy on Broadway,* 1974; *Stop the World — I Want to Get Off,* 1978. **Films** *Rufus Jones for President,* 1929; *Season's Greetings,* 1930; *The Benny Goodman Story,* 1956; *Anna Lucasta,* 1958; *Porgy and Bess,* 1959; *Ocean's Eleven,* 1960; *Pipe,* 1960; *Sergeants Three,* 1962; *Convicts Four,* 1962; *Johnny Cool,* 1963; *Three Penny Opera,* 1963; *Robin and the Seven Hoods,* 1964; *Nightmare in the Sun,* 1965; *A Man Called Adam,* 1966; *Salt and Pepper,* 1968; *Sweet Charity,* 1969; *Gone with the West,* 1969; *Man Without Mercy,* 1969; *One More Time* (also executive producer), 1970; *Diamonds Are Forever,* 1971; *Save the Children,* 1973; *Sammy Stops the World,* 1979;*Cannonball Run,* 1981; *Heidi's Song,* 1982; *Cannon Ball Run II,* 1984; *Moon Over Parador,* 1988; *Tap,* 1989. **Television movies** *The Pidgeon,* 1971; *The Trackers* (also producer), 1971; *Poor Devil,* 1973; *Cinderella at the Palace,* 1978; *The Kid Who Loved Christmas,* 1989. **Television series and specials** (include) *The Sammy Davis Jr Show,* 1964; *The Swinging World of Sammy Davis, Jr,* 1965; *NBC Follies,* 1973; *General Electric Presents Sammy,* 1975; *Sammy and Company,* 1975–77. **Television guest appearances** (include) *GE Theatre,* 1958, 1961, 1963; *Lawman,* 1961; *Frontier Circus,* 1962; *Hennessey,* 1962; *Dick Powell Theatre,* 1962; *Ben Casey,* 1963; *The Patty Duke Show,* 1965; *Wild Wild West,* 1966; *I Dream of Jeannie,* 1967; *Mod Squad,* 1969, 1970; *Name of the Game,* 1970; *Wednesday Night Mystery Movie Special,* 1973; *All in the Family,* 1973; also: *The Eddie Cantor Show, the Ed Sullivan Show, The Jackie Gleason Show, Lucy Show, The Tom Jones Show, Tonight Show.* **Night-clubs, cabarets and concerts** (include) Slapsie Maxie's, Hollywood, 1945; Bill Miller's Riviera, Fort Lee, New Jersey, 1949; El Rancho, Las Vegas, 1953; Copacabana, New York City, 1954; Ciro's, Hollywood, 1956; Sands Hotel, Las Vegas, 1957–73; Prince of Wales Theatre, London, 1961; Olympia, Paris, 1964; Forrest, Philadelphia, 1966; Westbury Music Fair, Long Island, 1972; Alice Tully Hall, New York City, 1972; Elmwood Casino, Windsor, Ontario, 1972; Harrah's Lake Tahoe, 1972; Kennedy Center, Washington, DC, 1973; Front Row, Cleveland, Ohio, 1974; Grosvenor House, London, 1974; Nanuet Theatre Go-Round, New Jersey, 1974; Latin Casino, Philadelphia, 1975; Caesar's Palace, Las Vegas, 1975; Cafe Crystal, Diplomat Hotel, Hollywood, Florida, 1975; London Palladium, 1976. **Albums** (include) (all Reprise, unless otherwise indicated) *Starring Sammy Davis, Jr,* Decca, 1955; *Just for Lovers,* Decca, 1955; *What Kind of Fool Am I? and Other Show Stoppers,* 1962; *Sammy Davis, Jr, at the Coconut Grove,* 1963; *As Long as She Needs Me,* 1963; *Forget-Me-Nots,* Decca, 1964; *Sammy Davis, Jr, Salutes the Stars of the London Palladium,* 1964; *The Shelter of Your Arms,* 1964; *If I Ruled the World,* 1965; (with Count Basie) *Our Shining Hour,* Verve, 1965; *Nat Cole Song Book,* 1965; *Sammy's Back on Broadway,* 1965; *Try a Little Tenderness,* Decca, 1965; *The Best of Sammy Davis, Jr,* Decca, 1966; *The Sounds of '66,* 1966; *Laurinda Almeida Plays, Sammy Davis Sings,* 1966; *That's All,* 1967; *Dr Doolittle,* 1967; *I've Gotta Be Me,* 1969; *Sammy Davis, Jr, Steps Out,* 1970; *Let There Be Love,* Harmony, 1970; *What Kind of Fool Am I?,* Harmony, 1971; *Now,* Metro-Goldwyn-Mayer, 1972; *Portrait of Sammy Davis, Jr,* Metro-Goldwyn-Mayer, 1978. **Singles** (include) "The Way You Look Tonight", 1946; "Hey, There", Decca, 1954; "Something's Gotta Give", Decca, 1955; "Love Me Or Leave Me", Decca, 1955; "That Old Black Magic", Decca, 1955; "I'll Know", Decca, 1955; "Five", Decca, 1956; "Earthbound", Decca, 1956; "New York's My Home", Decca, 1956; "What Kind Of Fool Am I?", Reprise, 1962; (with Frank Sinatra) "Me And My Shadow", Reprise, 1962; (with Dean

Martin) "Sam's Song", Reprise, 1962; "As Long As She Needs Me", Reprise, 1963; "The Shelter Of Your Arms", Reprise, 1963; "Don't Blame The Children", Reprise, 1967; "Lonely Is The Name", Reprise, 1968; "I've Gotta Be Me", Reprise, 1968; "The Candy Man", Metro-Goldwyn-Mayer, 1972; "The People Tree", Metro-Goldwyn-Mayer, 1972. **Publications** (With Jane and Burt Boyar) *Yes I Can: The Story of Sammy Davis, Jr* (autobiography), 1965; *Hollywood in a Suitcase,* 1980; (with Jane and Burt Boyar) *Why Me?* (autobiography), 1989. **Cause of death** Throat cancer, at age 64.

CHARLES FARRELL

American Actor

Born **Onset Bay, Massachusetts, 9 August 1901**

Died **Palm Springs, California, 6 May 1990**

Singing in the Rain chronicles very well the powerful disturbing effect of the coming of sound on the movie industry. Budding careers were destroyed almost overnight as performing styles changed and audiences became increasingly sceptical of exaggerated, pantomimic actors, preferring in their place a new realism and naturalness. As in the film, a promising future in silent pictures was most often dashed by an actor's voice. Charles Farrell, at the time one of America's most popular film stars, suffered just such a fate as the audiences who had thrilled to his macho, rugged good looks, rapidly cooled as successive soundtracks revealed a thin, high-pitched voice which contradicted his athletic, authoritative exterior.

Born in Massachusetts, Farrell's original career plan was to become a psychologist, studying medicine and the arts at Boston University. A chance encounter with a member of a touring theatre company visiting the city changed his life, and he joined up with them as scene-shifter and business manager. He was soon performing in vaudeville, and arrived in Hollywood just one of a huge number of young hopefuls. His build and stature (well over 6 feet tall), coupled with an open, easy countenance and attractive smile, won him bit-part work on a number of films, including Cecil B. de Mille's epic, *The Ten Commandments.* These led eventually to a long-term contract with Paramount Studios, for whom he made a number of films.

It was his first feature for Fox, however, that catapulted him from the ranks of struggling actor to star when he was cast opposite the cute good looks of Janet Gaynor in *Seventh Heaven.* One of the most celebrated silent tear-jerkers, the film has Farrell as the upright, honest character that became his stock-in-trade, a sewer-worker with a heart of gold who returns nightly to his homely garrett, the "heaven" of the title. He saves Gaynor from moral degradation and a life of vice on the streets of a rather idealized, vaguely delineated Paris. In keeping with the spirit of the age, great care is taken to emphasize the purity of their relationship — separate bedrooms were *de rigeur* for unmarried characters, even in low-life areas of the world's romantic capital. This is encapsulated when Farrell becomes inordinately embarrassed at the sight of her stocking-top, but all proceeds smoothly and respectably until the war precipitates a wedding and immediate separation — before the marriage can be consummated. Farrell returns blinded, whereupon Gaynor "becomes his eyes" to the moistened pleasure of audiences all over the United States and Britain. Janet Gaynor's performance earned her the Oscar for Best Actress and Frank Borzage the prize for Best Director at the first ever Academy Awards ceremony. Some critics and film industry insiders felt at the time that Farrell had been hard done by.

Nevertheless, the film precipitated a sequence of a dozen more for Farrell in partnership with Gaynor, a romantic double act longer even than that of Fred Astaire and Ginger Rogers. Their's were the archetypal boy-with-the-girl-next-door love affairs that won them much affection with cinema audiences throughout the country. However, the coming of sound dealt a mortal blow to an actor called upon, as Farrell put it, "to play James Cagney with an accent like James Mason's." Despite the unwelcome efforts of studio voice coaches and diction experts, "America's Favourite Love Birds" parted company in 1934. Farrell's film career never really recovered, although Fox invited him back four years later to play Shirley Temple's penniless father in *Just Around the Corner.* Formerly one of the highest paid stars in the world, Farrell could see the writing on the wall and, rejecting the prospect of an ever-diminishing supply of supporting roles, he moved away from films and into the hotel business.

Exploiting his considerable native business acumen, Farrell bought up scrub land in the Californian desert at 30 dollars an acre, built two tennis courts and a hotel, and created the highly successful and lucrative Palm Springs Raquet Club — all planned and built before the Springs was even a city. (He subsequently sold it for 500 dollars an acre, reputedly making himself a millionaire in the process.)

His acting career was resuscitated in two very successful television shows of the 1950s, *My Little Margie* and the virtually autobiographical *The Charlie Farrell Show.* By the end of the decade, Farrell had had enough of the limelight, sold up his hotel and moved into a placid retirement in the California desert with his actress wife of 27 years, Virginia Valli. Looking back in an interview in the 1970s, Farrell could say with conviction that it had been "a hell of career and a hell of a good life".

Born Charles Farrell **Marriage** Virginia Valli, film actress, 1932 (died 1968). **Education** Studied medicine and the arts, Boston University. **Military service** United States Navy, World War II. **Career** Business manager and scene-shifter with touring troupe; in vaudeville; first film appearance, *The Cheat,* 1923; first film lead, *Seventh Heaven,* 1927; made 12 films with Janet Gaynor, 1927–34; retired with the advent of sound; owner/manager, Racquet Club resort hotel, Palm Springs, California, to 1959; mayor, Palm Springs, 1947–55; first television series, *My Little Margie,* 1952. **Films** *The Cheat,* 1923; *The Ten Commandments,* 1923; *Wings of Youth,* 1925; *Sandy,* 1926; *Old Ironsides,* 1926; *The Rough Riders,* 1927; *Seventh Heaven,* 1927; *Street Angel,* 1928; *The Red Dance,* 1928; *The River,* 1928; *Lucky Star,* 1929; *Sunny Side Up,* 1929; *City Girl,* 1930; *High Society Blues,* 1930; *The Man Who Came Back,* 1930; *Liliom,* 1930; *Delicious,* 1931; *Merely Mary Ann,* 1931; *Tess of the Storm Country,* 1932; *Aggie Appleby, Maker of Men,* 1933; *Change of Heart,* 1934; *Fighting Youth,* 1935; *Moonlight Sonata,* 1937; *Just Around the Corner,* 1938; *Tailspin,* 1939; *The Deadly Game,* 1942. **Television** *My Little Margie,* 1952–54; *The Charlie Farrell Show,* 1956, 1960. **Cause of death** Undisclosed, at age 88.

PAULINE FREDERICK

American News Commentator

***Born* Gallitzin, Pennsylvania, 1906**

***Died* Lake Forest, Illinois, 9 May 1990**

When Pauline Frederick made her first radio broadcast from Washington in 1939, she was one of the only woman commentators in the field of network news. Over the next 35 years, however, her pioneering work in radio and television news analysis earned her the admiration of journalists around the world. In addition to presenting her own news programmes on all three networks, she served for 21 years as NBC's United Nations correspondent and was the first woman to be elected president of the UN Correspondents' Association.

The second of three children, Pauline Frederick grew up in Harrisburg, Pennsylvania. While still in high school, she developed a knack for news, and in her spare time reported on school and social events for three city newspapers. Upon graduation, she was offered a job as a staff reporter, but opted for college instead. She went on to complete a BA degree in political science and an MA degree in international law at American University in Washington. Although she had originally intended to become a lawyer, a history professor advised her to pursue journalism instead. Washington, he believed, had lawyers enough to go around.

At the outset of her career, Frederick was relegated to covering what were generally regarded as "women's" stories — issues of light, domestic interest bearing little resemblance to real news. One of her first assignments, covering a forum for women on "How to Get a Husband", proved especially demeaning. "I don't think I learned anything from it, and I don't think the audience did either", she remembered. In the early 1930s, however, she used the "women's" angle to her own advantage. By conducting in-depth interviews with the wives of foreign ambassadors, she gained important insights into the hidden world of international diplomacy. The articles she produced earned her a regular weekly column in the *Washington Star*. Next, she was asked to cover the State, War, and Navy departments for the *United States News* (now *US News & World Report*), and shortly afterwards began a long and fruitful association with the North American Newspaper Alliance.

In 1938, after six years of newspaper experience, Frederick decided to venture into radio. She began slowly, with a part-time job helping commentator H.R. Baukhage prepare his scripts for broadcast, but soon gained a feel for the medium. Despite her enthusiasm, Baukhage was not optimistic. "Stay away from radio", he cautioned. "It doesn't like women." Frederick did not heed his advice, however, and before long had accepted an offer from the National Broadcasting Company to conduct occasional radio interviews from Washington. She remained there, alternating newspaper and radio work, until 1945, when the Newspaper Alliance posted her to Europe as a war correspondent.

Frederick's overseas assignment during the final year of World War II proved the chance of a lifetime. The only American correspondent sent to Kraków to cover the return of the stolen Wit Stowosz altar following the German occupation of Poland, she used the opportunity to observe and report on the tightening stranglehold of the Polish Communist Party and its effect on ordinary citizens. She also reported on the trials of Nazi war criminals in Nuremberg. By the end of her tour, she had visited 19 different countries.

In 1946, Pauline Frederick joined the news staff of the American Broadcasting Company. The first woman assigned to cover political events for the network, she joined commentator Gordon Fraser in reporting on developments at the United Nations. In 1947, she was the only woman among 135 journalists sent to Uruguay to cover the inauguration of that country's president. Other assignments in the late 1940s included the Democratic and Republican conventions — from which she made her first television broadcasts — the presidential campaign and inauguration; the trial of the eleven Communist leaders; the perjury trial of Alger Hiss; and the espionage hearing of Judith Coplon and Valentin Gubitchev. In May 1949, her quick manoeuvring and competent reporting enabled her to cover three momentous events: the negotiations leading to the lifting of the Berlin Blockade; Polish reaction to the capture of German Communist Gerhart Eisler; and the Paris meeting of the Council of Foreign Ministers.

During the early 1950s, Frederick appeared in a minimum of five morning radio broadcasts and three telecasts each week. In addition, on Saturday evenings she presented *Pauline Frederick's*

Guest Books, a non-news programme she had researched and written for ABC-TV. In 1951, an ABC biography described her as "the only network news analyst and diplomatic correspondent in American radio". Throughout the 1950s, she continued to blaze new territory in network news reporting, conducting the first radio interview with former King Michael of Romania and his mother, Princess Helen, and the first long-distance telephone interview with American minister to Hungary, Selden Chapin. She was also the only American woman commentator to cover the Korean crisis in the United Nations. Later she reported on UN efforts to restore peace in the Congo and on the Cuban missile crisis.

In 1953, Pauline Frederick returned to NBC as its UN-based correspondent, presenting a regular, daily programme, *Pauline Frederick Reporting,* as well as special news broadcasts and interviews. That same year she was the first woman to receive the eleventh Alfred I. DuPont award for "meritorious service to the American people". According to a report in *Variety,* the DuPont citation honoured Frederick for "exemplifying the best traditions of news commentary" and "avoiding the slickness, automatic orthodoxy and superficial sensationalism characteristic of much news commentary today...without making concessions to a vulgarization of either thought or style."

When she retired from NBC in 1974, Frederick joined National Public Radio as a foreign affairs commentator, returning to network television in 1976 to moderate the presidential debate between Gerald R. Ford and Jimmy Carter. She was the first woman ever chosen for such a role. Over the years she received a host of honours, including the coveted George Foster Peabody award, a Paul White award from the Radio-Television News Directors' Association, and a place in the Sigma Delta Chi Hall of Fame. She also earned honorary doctorate degrees in journalism, law, and the humanities from 23 colleges and universities.

The wife of former *Wall Street Journal* editor Charles Robbins, Pauline Frederick devoted her entire life to observing and analysing world affairs. International relations, she believed, are basically human relations, and policies geared towards achieving world peace must always consider the backgrounds and experience of the people "on the other side of the street".

Born Pauline Frederick. **Parents** Matthew P., Pennsylvania State Department of Labor official, and Susan (Stanley) Frederick. **Marriage** Charles Robbins, journalist (died 1989). **Education** American University, Washington, DC, BA in political science, MA in international law. **Career** Freelance journalist; feature writer, *Washington Star*; Department of State reporter, *United States News*; journalist, North American Newspaper Alliance; assistant to radio commentator, H.R. Baukhage, 1938; occasional interviewer, National Broadcasting Company, 1938–45; war correspondent, North American Newspaper Alliance, 1945, visited 19 countries, reported Nuremberg trials; news staff, American Broadcasting Company, 1946–53, United Nations reporter, 1947, reported from Berlin Blockade, 1949, wrote/telecast *Pauline Frederick's Guest Books*; broadcaster, National Broadcasting Company, 1953–74, United Nations reporter, 1953–74; foreign affairs commentator, National Public Radio, 1974–90; moderator, second Carter/Ford debate, 1976. **Other activities** Trustee, American University; council member: Save the Children, UN Association. **Offices and memberships** Fellow, Society for Professional Journalists; member, United Nations Correspondents' Association, president; member, Association of Radio and Television Analysts; member, Council on Foreign Relations. **Awards and honours** (include) Theta Sigma Phi National Headliner Award; American University alumni achievement award; International House citation, Alabama State Teachers College; Alfred I. DuPont Award, 1953; George Foster Peabody Award for contribution to international understanding, 1954; Golden Mike Award for outstanding woman in broadcasting, *McCall's*; Sigma Delta Chi Hall of Fame, 1975; Paul White Award for contribution to broadcast journalism, Radio and Television News Directors Association, 1980; radio woman of the year, *Radio-TV Daily* poll; University of Missouri

School of Journalism medal; special citation for United Nations coverage, National Federation of Women's Clubs; East-West Center Award; Journalism Achievement Award, University of Southern California; First Pennsylvania Journalism Achievement Award; Carr Van Anda Award, Ohio University School of Journalism; New York Professional Journalists Society Hall of Fame. **Broadcasts** (include) *Pauline Frederick's Guest Books; Pauline Frederick Reporting; Listen to the Witness;* panel member, *Citizen's Union Searchlight.* **Cause of death** Heart attack, at age 84.

SIR REGINALD GOODALL

British Conductor

***Born* Lincoln, England, 13 July 1905**

***Died* Canterbury, Kent, 5 May 1990**

Reginald Goodall's career had something of the Sleeping Beauty about it. A conventional beginning — a chorister at the Cathedral Choir School in the city where he was born, the study of piano and conducting at the Royal College of Music, London, organist and choirmaster at St Alban's church, Holborn, "where I learned to conduct" — an orchestra was assembled for feast-days. There, or in a similarly sheltered spot, he might have stayed indefinitely, but for the pilgrimages he made to Europe, to Vienna, and Munich sitting at the feet of Furtwängler, Knappertsbusch, and Krauss, while he covered his day-to-day expenses by playing the piano.

Always frail, he was invalided from wartime military service and joined Sadler's Wells Opera in 1944. He conducted them in much of the standard repertoire, and then was given what was to prove a major event in British musical history, the *première* in 1945 of Benjamin Britten's first major opera *Peter Grimes* (followed by *The Rape of Lucretia* at Glyndebourne the next year). It catapulted this already middle-aged, retiring figure (he was in his forties by then) into the limelight he so disliked and on to the staff of the Royal Opera House, Covent Garden. But they didn't really seem to know what to do with him, nor did he seem happy in the competitive atmosphere common to most such theatrical institutions. The Italian and French repertoire did not appeal, nor Berg, nor did even Britten's *Gloriana* leave any impression. Sir David Webster, the general administrator, was conscious that Goodall was not receiving the encouragement he needed, but wrote of problems caused by "many protests from artists of his conducting in terms of timing and accent." From the early 1950s performances in which he might have excelled were given to other resident and to guest conductors. "Pretty decent to excellent" was Webster's description of such performances — this faint praise, while Goodall's incandescence stayed unrevealed.

He retreated into his private world of a consistent and unremitting search for the truth of the operas he really loved most of all — Wagner's. This world was one he would willingly share with singers prepared to work at his pace, and the list of those he coached painstakingly and successfully is a role of honour: Anne Evans, Linda Esther Gray, Rita Hunter, Gwyneth Jones, James King, Donald McIntyre, Alberto Remedios, Amy Shuard, Josephine Veasey, Jon Vickers. Occasionally testy of temper if he felt someone was not really trying hard enough, he had the patience to make his "students" think for themselves, so that their progress came from within themselves rather than being imposed from outside — with what Goodall abhorred, domineering "conductoritis". In this his method was reminiscent of Klemperer in his latter years — a veteran he wellnigh worshipped, and spent some of his happiest hours in the late 1960s helping with recording sessions (another of

Walter Legge's acute choices). Klemperer's inscription in a score of *Fidelio* reads: "To my dear colleague Reginald Goodall, the *excellent* conductor. My very best wishes for a fulfilled life." From a man disinclined to be fulsome at any time this was a major tribute. Alberto Remedios has said "When you've learned something with Reggie for the first time it's not just in your voice or mind, it's in your soul." The small room where he did his coaching, way above the Amphitheatre at Covent Garden, acquired the name *Valhalla,* partly because it was "so bloody difficult to get to" and partly because Goodall demanded, and got, the highest standards of singing and interpretation... It also gave him the isolation he preferred. On bad days it was called *Nibelheim.* The current success of British and other singers at Bayreuth is just one proof of the virtues of his teaching.

One suspects that Goodall probably enjoyed the preparation more than the performance. Certainly 20 years passed without much in the way of either fame or complaints of neglect, but the occasional performance of Wagner which he was given, perhaps in a London suburb like Croydon or provincial Manchester, always caught the attention of the discerning, including of course critics like David Cairns, Peter Heyworth, Andrew Porter and Edmund Tracey. To Lord Harewood (a member of Covent Garden's staff) in 1948 his *Walküre* came as "a revelation". Even a couple of performances of *Die Meistersinger* had no effect on Covent Garden's management, which seems to have been unduly influenced by some incidents which, though unfortunate, were no worse than the sensitive reactions other artists are well known to produce. Goodall was indeed not a suitable stand-in for Sir George Solti at rehearsals (as anyone who knew him would have realized), nor is it surprising he did not welcome the suggestion that he rehearse *Die Meistersinger* but only conduct it if Kempe failed to turn up. Goodall hadn't Kempe's international reputation, but his intense shyness did not prevent his being fiercely uncompromising in such circumstances. The feeling prevailed that "Reggie" had a sympathy for Wagner which was exceptional; but the right moment for it to be manifested seldom arrived. His reactions were frequently not those desired by the Establishment. The post-war re-opening of the Bayreuth Festival saw Wieland Wagner's revolutionary approach to production, in which lighting effects and gauzes took precedence over the "old-fashioned" realism of scenery, a development alien to Webster's taste — it was too indefinite for him to copy with ease. He sent Goodall to sample it at Bayreuth, but to his dismay Reggie returned "enraptured" by Wieland Wagner's methods. His rapture was discounted, nevertheless, and even Wieland's offer to produce *Tristan und Isolde* at Covent Garden in 1953 was rejected. No wonder Goodall's obscurity threatened to become the habit of a lifetime.

Meanwhile Edmund Tracey had joined Stephen Arlen at Sadler's Wells Opera (which was to be renamed the English National Opera), then still based in its Islington theatre, and he was inspired to invite Goodall to prepare and conduct their new *Mastersingers,* for which he was promised all the rehearsal time he wanted. He coached the singers, rehearsed the orchestra section by section; Lord Harewood described the preparations as "unusually extensive, time-consuming, expensive, infinitely rewarding" — they were all these things, but the result after a year's devoted work justified it all, and received the appreciation that was Goodall's and the company's due. By 1970, when the company transferred to its present home, the much larger theatre of the Coliseum, his achievement had been recognized internationally, and he was acclaimed as being in the tradition of Furtwängler, Knappertsbusch, and among the greatest of Wagnerian conductors. The first English version for 40 years of *The Ring* followed in 1973 after equally meticulous groundwork, a line-by-line study which took five years to complete. It must be remembered that everyone involved was learning it from scratch. Rita Hunter, the Brünnhilde, studied her role for two years. A complete recording of this English *Ring* was issued with international success, earning the respect and admiration even of German opera lovers. Goodall when on to conduct *Tristan und Isolde* and *Die Walküre* for the Welsh National Opera, and *Parsifal* for one performance. (He conducted the latter at Covent Garden in 1971.)

His deep affinity with Wagner's idiom (in addition to the realization that it could not be acquired with superficial speed), was fundamentally a precise sense of proportion, of the correct balance of tempi, dynamics, orchestration, drama, vocal forces. Easy surface effects were eschewed like Kundry's kiss — the whole opera was allowed to flower slowly and gradually, and the purple patches had to take their proper place without undue prominence. Singers were taught the importance and significance of the text in relation to the action and music. Voices were not distorted but were enabled to hold their own against the most complex orchestral accompaniment because it was kept under control; not an oppressive control but one which ultimately produced the more vivid climaxes for their not being premature, but rather produced at the correct moment for maximum effect. The music was allowed to breathe and the long span of Wagner's phrases to stretch their appropriate length. This sense of dimension extended over the whole opera being performed, scenes and acts being balanced and shaped to produce a supremely satisfying whole. There being no sense of strain, the music still had a tension and grandeur, an expressive beauty seldom found in more hard-driven interpretations. And, because singers and instrumentalists had the opportunity to mature into their roles in advance, a Goodall first night was an accomplished event, with no need for the participants to settle down in their roles later in the run — security was established from the start.

It was typical of Goodall's self-effacement that all this late success indicated a triumph for Wagner rather than himself. This made curtain-calls an ordeal, not a pleasure. He regarded them as "an embarrassing irrelevancy" and his deportment in taking them was at best described as furtive; on one occasion he succeeded in completely escaping from a thwarted stage manager, leaving an empty jacket in his hands.

It could be said that Reginald Goodall's personality and artistry were of a kind destined to undergo a protracted development; that even had Covent Garden been able to provide the facilities he needed, he might not have been able to respond at that particular point. Maybe he should have stayed at Sadler's Wells rather than go to the larger house, but it must have seemed a correct choice at the time. Such speculation apart, there is no possible doubt that generations of operagoers, whether devoted Wagnerians or débutantes, were immeasurably fortunate to find themselves at Sadler's Wells or ENO during his ultimate triumphs, when his undeniable genius was the complete vindication of his methods.

Born Reginald Goodall. **Marriage** Eleanor Gibbs, 1932 (died 1979). **Education** Chorister, Lincoln Cathedral Choir School; studied conducting, violin and piano, Royal College of Music, London; studied independently in Munich and Vienna; played for Reinhold von Warlich's masterclasses, Lieder. **Military service** Ordnance Corps, World War II. **Career** Choirmaster and organist, St Alban's Holborn, London; assistant conductor, Royal Opera House, Covent Garden, 1936–1939, staff conductor, 1947–62; assistant conductor, Berlin Philharmonic, 1939; conductor, Wessex Orchestra; conductor Sadler's Wells (later English National) Opera, 1944–45, conducted first performance of Benjamin Britten's *Peter Grimes,* 1945; joined Royal Opera House, Covent Garden; invited to conduct *Die Meistersinger,* Sadler's Wells at the Coliseum, 1967, invited to conduct Ring Cycle, 1970–73; final appearance, conducted Act III, *Parsifal,* Promenade Concerts, London, 1987. **Related activities** Tutored many Wagner singers. **Awards and honours** Commander of the Order of the British Empire, 1975; knighted 1985; honorary Doctor of Music, Oxford University. **Operas conducted** (include) *Peter Grimes,* 1945; *The Rape of Lucretia,* 1946; *Die Walküre,* 1948, 1954; *Die Meistersinger,* 1967; *Parsifal,* 1971, 1986, 1987; *Tristan und Isolde,* 1979; also: *Manon, Wozzeck, Fidelio, Gloriana, Rhinegold, Siegfried.* **Recordings** (include) *Ring der Nibelungen; Parsifal; Tristan; Wagner; Rape of Lucretia.* **Cause of death** Undisclosed, at age 84. **Further reading** Montague Haltrecht: *The Quiet Showman: Sir David Webster and the Royal Opera House,* 1975; The Earl of Harewood, *The Tongs and the Bones: The Memoirs of Lord Harewood,* 1981.

ROCKY GRAZIANO

American Boxer and Actor

Born **Manhattan, New York, 1 January 1919 or 1922**

Died **New York City, New York, 23 May 1990**

Rocky Graziano's story was one that could have been invented in Hollywood. A tough streetwise kid who escaped the poverty and crime of the East Side of New York by literally fighting his way to fame and fortune; a crowd-pleaser who would throw punches until he dropped; a genial slugger with the heart of a lion; a lovable rogue who made a million. It is hardly surprising that his autobiography was called *Somebody Up There Likes Me.*

Graziano fought in the golden age of boxing. He might have lacked finesse, and did not trouble himself too much with defence. But in an eleven-year professional career he knocked out 52 opponents, winning 67 fights, sharing the spoils in ten, and losing only six.

An original juvenile delinquent-turned-boxer, Graziano grew up on the tough side of town and was as proud of his street fighting prowess as his professional record. "I was the best street fighter in history. Hell, I never lost a street fight", said the man who — with boyhood friend Jake LaMotta — was in constant trouble with the police.

Graziano never forgot his background, and in later life would protest: "I never stole anything unless it began with an 'A'...a piece of fruit, a watch, a pair of shoes, a bicycle." Similarly, he explained he was forced to leave school prematurely because of pneumonia: "not because I had it, but because I couldn't spell it".

His natural sense of humour nevertheless disguised the reality of a difficult upbringing. Born the son of a third-rate Italian-born boxer, Thomas Rocco Barbella was first arrested at 12 for breaking into a subway gum machine. On probation, he stole a bicycle and was sent for the first of his three trips to reform school. His wayward character emerged again on being drafted into the Army at the start of World War II, when he went AWOL from Fort Dix, New Jersey, after hitting a superior officer.

It was while he was on the run that he changed his name in a desperate bid to avoid detection. "But I later found that the original Rocky Graziano had a bigger police record than me", he joked.

Regular visits to the famous Stillman's Gym in New York began to channel his aggression towards a more positive end. He won the Metropolitan Amateur Athletic Union welterweight title, hocked the medal for five dollars (as he had sold everything he had stolen), and began to think along the lines that boxing "might not be such a bad racket after all. I think I'll give it a shake".

It proved to be the best decision of his life. In his first four years, he knocked out 32 opponents, including the highly regarded Billy Arnold. And by 1946, he was ready to challenge Tony Zale for the Middleweight Boxing Championship of the world.

All three fights which followed entered history as classics of brutal action — possibly the most brutal of any ever seen inside the ring. The first, at the Yankee Stadium, began with Graziano standing as 2–1 favourite to take the title. He put Zale down in the second round, but left himself open in the sixth and was knocked out by a fearsome blow which he later described graphically.

> It was a big left hook, and I see it coming but can't stop it. It was like the ground exploded up and hit me in the stomach. The lights spin in a circle and then dim down to a tiny spot. I try to yell, but I can't make a sound. I am deaf, I can't talk, I can't lift my arms and I am falling. For the first time in my life I know what it's like to be KO'd.

The second fight, the following year, was more like a war. Fought in the oppressive heat of the Chicago Stadium because the New York Boxing Commission had revoked Graziano's licence for failing to report the offer of a bribe he never accepted, the match saw Zale split Graziano's left eye wide open. But in the sixth round, "The Rock" finally stopped his opponent to become the champion of the world. "I wanted to kill him", admitted Graziano. "I like him, but I wanted to kill him." And, later, he added, "This was no boxing match. It was a war. If there had been no referee one of the two of us would have wound up dead." The third brutal encounter took place in 1948 when Zale regained the title with a knockout in the third round.

The former president of Madison Square Garden Boxing, Harry Markson, offered one of the best summaries of Graziano's boxing ability. "He was not a great fighter", he began, "but he was a good puncher and a tremendous competitor. He could knock you out with either hand. And when you knocked him down, he always got up."

Graziano had one more shot at the world title very late in his career when, against better judgement, he took on the great Sugar Ray Robinson. "I just wanted to see what it would be like to fight Sugar Ray", explained Graziano, who was knocked to the canvas in the third round, and who had just one more fight — against Chuck Davey, which he lost in a ten-round decision — before retiring.

A genuine folk hero, Graziano enjoyed a huge following and was loved as much for his sense of humour outside the ring as for his never-say-die endeavours in it. "He was a natural comedian", noted La Motta, who also held the middleweight title. "Anything he said cracked you up. It's why he was so popular for so many years."

Not surprisingly, Graziano turned to entertainment after leaving the ring at the age of 56, and first landed a role as the boyfriend of comedienne Martha Raye on her popular television show. Radio and television commercials for anything from yoghurt to foot powder, and from dog food to auto mufflers helped his healthy cash flow to such an extent that, 15 years after his retirement, he told a friend one day, "I just made the Big One. A million bucks. My accountant just told me. How about that?"

He never lost his heavy New York accent, never found the need to adopt any fancy airs, and never shook off that hoodlum-turned-prize fighter image. In later life, this once irresponsible, but always irresistible, character could be found visiting schools and colleges, lecturing about juvenile delinquency.

"You know, I'm so glad my father took the boat", he said, before taking the ultimate count at 71 years of age. "Because this is the best country in the world. And if there was another country like this one, I'd be jealous."

Born Thomas Rocco Barbella. **Father** Nicholas Barbella (Fighting Nick Bob), boxer. **Marriage** Norma Unber, 1943. **Children** Two daughters. **Education** Left school after sixth grade. **Military service** US Army, World War II, imprisoned for going absent without leave, Fort Leavenworth; dishonourable discharge. **Career** Began boxing, 1939; won Metropolitan Amateur Athletic Union welterweight championship, 1939; turned professional, 1942; fought three title bouts with Tony Zale, lost 1946, won 1947, lost 1948; world middleweight champion, 1947–48; licence revoked for failing to report an offered bribe, 1948; regained licence, 1949; lost title fight to Sugar Ray Robinson, 1952; retired from boxing, 1952; fought 83 fights, won 67 (52 knockouts), lost 10, drew 6; *Somebody Up There Likes Me* (autobiography) filmed, 1956; turned to acting; played Martha Raye's boyfriend, *The Martha Raye Show*; made many television and radio commercials. **Other activities** Three spells in Reform School as teenager. **Awards and honours** Elected to Boxing Hall of Fame, 1971. **Publications** *Somebody Up There Likes Me* (autobiography). **Cause of death** Cardiopulmonary failure, at age 68 or 71.

JIM HENSON

American Puppeteer

Born **Greenville, Mississippi, 24 September 1936**

Died **New York City, New York, 16 May 1990**

Forget Cleopatra and Mark Antony. Forget Cyrano and Roxanne. Wipe Romeo and Juliet from your mind. The romance that captured the imagination of 235 million people in 100 countries for at least five years, was between a green flannel frog and a blonde-haired pig with a mean karate chop.

Their creator, Jim Henson, always claimed he took up puppetry almost by accident. He'd belonged to a puppet club in high school, and when a puppeteer's job was advertised at a local station, he applied for it and got it. Years later, he recalled, "It was the early 1950s and I was between high school and college and needed a job...The job turned out to be perfect for me. I kept it all the time I was going to school and it served as the best possible training ground for the things I was to do later." With help from his future wife, Jane, and the earliest "Muppets" (a name coined by Henson, to refer to a cross between marionettes and puppets), *Sam and His Friends,* a five-minute puppet show, was so successful that Henson, already an Emmy-winner, rode to his college graduation in a Rolls-Royce.

Sam and His Friends was an opportunity for Henson to experiment and develop his own unique style. He once stated in an interview, "We'd try some really way-out things. I was convinced no one else at the station ever watched the show because there was never a complaint or any attempt at censorship of any kind."

There was an extremely significant development in 1955, though no one at that time could have guessed how important it was to be. It was this: Jim Henson took an old green coat that his mother had thrown away and a ping pong ball, which he cut in half. It was the birth of the character that was to become the superstar of Henson's muppets, the one he will always be remembered for and identified with: Kermit the Frog. Terry Jones, of *Monty Python* fame, wrote of the first time he saw the frog on television, "I was hooked. Kermit wasn't like any other puppet I had ever seen. He was simply a sketch of a creature with a couple of blobs for eyes and yet he had a personality and he was — in some magic way — alive." But that was many years later. Kermit is definitely the best known of the Muppets now, but he wasn't the first to become a household name.

The first Muppet "star" was designed by Henson's assistant, Don Sahlin, for use on a television commercial, and rapidly became a media celebrity. As George T. Miller reported in *The New York Times* on 5 April 1964, "I interviewed a rag dog the other day. The furry bit of show-business fantasy goes by the name of Rowlf. He is a bundle of foam rubber, artificial fur, and some of the most interesting tomfoolery to be seen around the American Broadcasting Company." Rowlf the dog was by then a regular on *The Jimmy Dean Show,* a network variety show which premiered in 1963 and ran for three seasons. Recalling those early days, Jimmy Dean once said, "I fell in love with that dang dog. Rowlf worked so beautifully, you would believe it was him and totally forget about Jim Henson and Frank Oz working him." An ABC executive of the time once stated that as he looked at Rowlf, "who at that moment was impaled on the deft left hand of Mr Henson...[his] brown eyes seemed to sparkle."

Like Kermit, Rowlf was a philosopher. Unlike Kermit, he was extremely laid-back and never lost his cool. It has been said of Henson that the only time he raised his voice was if Kermit was upset about something. And Kermit had a lot to be upset about. Throughout the 120 episodes of *The Muppet Show,* he was chased by a love-struck temperamental pig with a pronounced tendency towards violence, lumbered with the inept assistance of Scooter (the theatre-owner's nephew), heckled by two aged curmudgeons known as Statler and Waldorf, and faced with one disaster after another. No wonder he got upset now and then. After all, a frog is only human.

Henson had quite a bit of difficulty getting *The Muppet Show* on the air in the first place. He had been with *Sesame Street* since its *première* in 1969, and many of the Muppet characters, such as Kermit, were heavily associated with that show. *Sesame Street,* which is still being produced and is shown in syndication around the world, is an educational programme for small children, and so, in the eyes of American television producers, Jim Henson was a children's entertainer. As a result, when he approached them with the idea of a puppet show aimed at an adult audience, they turned him down flat. He was so disheartened that when Lord (Lew) Grade offered to produce the show in London, Henson didn't believe him. Lord Grade wrote after Henson's death, "I went down to the studios at Elstree and saw Jim Henson and his Muppets. I said to him that we would do 24 half-hour episodes with the Muppets. He replied that no one in the US was interested in the Muppets. I repeated that we would do 24 half-hour episodes." They ended up doing five times that many, and only stopped because Henson wanted to quit the series before it became stale.

There were three Muppet movies: *The Muppet Movie*, *The Great Muppet Caper* and *The Muppets Take Manhattan,* in which wedding bells ring and Kermit finally makes an honest pig of Miss Piggy. Henson also made the fantasy films, *The Dark Crystal* and *Labyrinth,* worked on the recent film of Roald Dahl's (q.v.) *The Witches,* and designed the computerized masks used in *Teenage Mutant Ninja Turtles.* His television work included *The Ghost of Faffner Hall*, *Fraggle Rock*, *The Muppet Babies*, *The Storyteller* (in which another Muppet star was born: the slightly exasperated dog that is the storyteller's sidekick), *The Jim Henson Hour* (an NBC special), and numerous appearances on variety and talk shows.

Jim Henson was constantly working, producing, creating. He was a major influence on American (and world-wide) culture. A large percentage of Americans under 20 learned to read and write and count with help from the Muppets on *Sesame Street.* In Britain, the creators of the satirical puppet show, *Spitting Image* credit Jim Henson with giving them the inspiration to work with puppets on television. According to *Spitting Image*'s Roger Law, "without Jim Henson there would have been no *Spitting Image.*" And there can't be many places in the world where they have never heard of *The Muppet Show*.

Jim Henson was one of those rare public figures everybody seemed to like. Perhaps this is because it was easy to feel that you knew not just the name and the reputation, but the man. Personally. On a first-name basis. And why? Because to millions of people around the world, Jim Henson was and always will be that lovable green frog with the ping pong ball eyes, Kermit. Love the frog, then you must love the man. That's certainly the case with children. When Henson used to go for walks in New York's Central Park, it was a common occurrence for children to shout, "Look, there goes Kermit!"

He was equally beloved by, and important to, adults. As Andrew Stephen reported from America in the British newspaper, *The Observer,* four days after Henson's death, "It was not the negotiations in Moscow about the future of the world that dominated this country last week. It was not racial tension in New York. It was not three executions within 24 hours, so commonplace have these become...What led the network television news bulletins and shocked the nation more than seems possible was the death of Jim Henson, the 53-year-old creator of the Muppets." He went on to relate how a Washington lawyer in her late thirties confided that she burst into tears upon hearing the news.

Jim Henson died of what the Victorians called "galloping pneumonia". He'd been complaining of flu-like symptoms on the Saturday, but a doctor he visited in South Carolina could find nothing wrong and prescribed no treatment beyond aspirin. By Tuesday morning, he was taken to New York Hospital, unable to breathe. He was dead within 20 hours.

Of course the Muppets will continue. Disney Productions recently purchased the rights to several of the Muppet characters for a sum reported to be somewhere between 100 and 150 million dollars. There are plans for a Muppets theme park. *Sesame Street* has 20 years' worth of tapes of Kermit, Ernie and Guy Smiley (all voiced by Henson) to fall back on. Eventually someone will be found to do Kermit's voice, and new segments will be taped. *Sesame Street,* and life, will go on as usual. But when Jim Henson died, a little of the child within all of us died with him.

Born James Maury Henson. **Father** Paul Henson, agronomist. **Marriage** Jane Nebel, puppeteer, 1959. **Children** Lisa, Cheryl, Brian, John and Heather. **Education** University of Maryland, BA, 1959. **Career** Joined a puppet club in high school; professional puppeteer (with Jane Nebel), *Sam and His Friends,* local NBC television station, Washington, DC, 1954; first Muppets developed; designed Kermit, 1956; designed Muppets for commercials; first Muppet appearances on variety shows, 1963; first Muppet regular role, Rowlf the Dog, *Jimmy Dean Show,* 1963–66; wrote, produced, directed and starred in non-Muppet short experimental film, *Timepiece,* 1965; designed muppets for *Sesame Street,* 1969–90; created *The Muppet Show,* 1976–81; designed muppets for *The Muppet Movie,* 1979; film directorial début, *The Great Muppet Caper,* 1981; Henson Associates acquired by Walt Disney Company, 1989. **Awards and honours** Local Emmy Award, *Sam and His Friends,* 1958; Academy Award nomination, best short film, *Timepiece,* 1965; National Educational Television award for outstanding children's television, for *Muppets on Puppets,* 1969; Emmy Awards: for outstanding achievement in children's programming, for *Sesame Street,* 1974, 1976, three awards for *The Muppet Show,* for *The Jim Henson Hour,* 1986, four for *The Muppet Babies;* Peabody Award for excellence in television programming; Grammy Award for a Muppets album. **Films** *Timepiece,* 1965; *The Muppet Movie,* 1981; *The Great Muppet Caper,* 1984; *The Muppets Take Manhattan,* 1984; *The Dark Crystal,* 1982; *Labyrinth,* 1986; *Teenage Mutant Ninja Turtles,* 1990; *The Witches,* 1990. **Television** *Sam and His Friends,* 1954; *The Jimmy Dean Show,* 1963–66; *Youth '68* (documentary), 1968; *Muppets on Puppets,* 1968; *The Cube* (drama), 1969; *Hey, Cinderella,* 1969; *Sesame Street,* 1969–1990; *The Muppet Show,* 1976–81; *Muppet Babies* (animated), six seasons; *The Jim Henson Hour,* 1986; also: *The Ghost of Faffner Hall, The Storyteller, Muppet Valentine Special, Out to Lunch, Fraggle Rock.* **Cause of death** Streptococcus pneumonia, at age 53.

JILL IRELAND

British Actress

***Born* London, England, 24 April 1936**

***Died* Malibu, California, 18 May 1990**

By the end of her life Jill Ireland, who had a long career as an actress, was probably best known as a writer and health campaigner who fought courageously and articulately against the cancer which eventually killed her, and against the drug addiction which afflicted one of her children.

Ireland was born in west London. Her father was the manager of a chain of grocery shops and, although not wealthy, the family was comfortably off. Ireland attended private schools and she was sent to ballet classes from the age of three. She was attracted to the performing arts from an early age and made it her goal in life to succeed in this competitive arena. She made her professional stage début at the age of 12 when she appeared as a ballet dancer in a musical comedy at the Chiswick Empire, London. She later appeared at the famous London Palladium and in her teens she danced with the Monte Carlo ballet.

Ireland, who was blonde and slight with classical "English rose" good looks, was soon spotted by the J. Arthur Rank film organization who offered her a contract and promoted her as one of their many up-and-coming young starlets. By the time she was 16, Ireland had won her first screen role as a singer and dancer in the Powell (q.v.) and Pressburger film, *Oh Rosalinda!*, which was a remake of the lighthearted opera *Die Fledermaus*. She made a success of this part and attracted favourable attention in the many fan magazines of the day with the result that she became well known to a large audience of film-goers.

Further film roles followed. In 1955 Ireland appeared in *Three Men in a Boat,* the movie version of Jerome K. Jerome's famous comic novel, with the actors Laurence Harvey and Jimmy Edwards. Two years later she played in *Robbery Under Arms*. This was not a particular success but for Ireland it had momentous consequences. She was cast opposite another young actor, David McCallum, and the couple lost no time in recreating their screen roles of young lovers in real life. They married just three weeks after their first meeting. Ireland continued with her film career and she had appeared in a total of 16 movies for the Rank Organization by the time she and her husband moved to Hollywood in 1962.

Ireland and McCallum's first child, Paul, was born in 1959. Two years later she suffered a miscarriage and was told by doctors that she would be unable to have any more children. She and McCallum adopted another son, Jason, the following year and shortly after this Ireland proved the medical profession wrong by giving birth a second time.

Although she continued to work, the demands of three young children resulted in Ireland putting the needs of her family first, which encroached on her acting to a certain extent. After moving to the United States in 1962, she switched from films to television work and made guest appearances in many series including *Ben Casey*, *Daniel Boone*, *Shane* and *The Man from U.N.C.L.E.* By contrast McCallum's career was flourishing. In 1963 he had a leading role in the highly successful film *The Great Escape* and Ireland accompanied him to Germany where part of the film was to be shot. It was here that she met Charles Bronson who was also in the film, and the couple fell in love.

Bronson too was married, and the next few years were fraught with difficulties as they both struggled to resolve the conflicting relationships. Eventually, they both obtained divorces and they married in 1968. The couple had one child, Zuleika, and they also adopted the teenage daughter of a close friend, who had died suddenly of a heart attack. With Ireland's three sons and Bronson's two children from his first marriage the household became large and somewhat chaotic.

By this time Bronson had become an international star and Ireland decided as a matter of expediency to accept parts only in her husband's films so as to minimize disruption to the family. This meant that she was often miscast in roles where she would play the gangster's moll to Bronson's outlaw. However, they enjoyed working together and Ireland appeared in a total of eleven of Bronson's films including *The Mechanic*, *The Valachi Papers* and *Breakheart Pass*.

In the turbulent world of film-making Ireland and Bronson stood out as a private and mutually devoted couple. But their tranquility was rudely shattered in 1984 when Ireland was diagnosed as having cancer and she had to undergo an emergency mastectomy. Ireland fought back and although she had to suffer a painful series of treatments which resulted in hair- and hearing-loss, she always remained optimistic.

During a period of recuperation Ireland wrote a book, *Life Wish,* in which she encouraged other cancer sufferers not to give up hope. The book became a best-seller and Ireland found herself much in demand to give talks and make appearances to raise money for cancer research. She threw herself into this new role with enthusiasm and became an influential advocate of increased government funding for pre-cancer screening. In 1988 she testified to the United States Senate Committee on Health and Welfare and was also awarded the Medal of Courage by President Reagan.

For a time it appeared that Ireland had made a full recovery, but early in 1989 it was discovered that the cancer had returned and had spread throughout her body. Shortly after this calamitous news Ireland received a further blow when her son Jason admitted to a serious drug problem. Ireland struggled to help him overcome the addiction but he subsequently died of an overdose. With characteristic fortitude Ireland turned to helping other families with drug-addicted children. She wrote *Lifelines* with the aim of encouraging parents to debate the painful issues involved openly and without shame.

For the last two years of Ireland's life Bronson abandoned his film career to care for her. When it became clear that she did not have long to live, Ireland's eldest son, Paul, brought his wedding forward by several months so that she could attend the ceremony. This was Ireland's last public appearance and she died at her Malibu home a few days later.

Born Jill Dorothy Ireland. **Parents** John Alfred, grocery chain manager, and Dorothy Connoll (Eborn) Ireland. **Marriages** 1) David McCallum, actor, 1957 (divorced 1967); 2) Charles Bronson, actor, 1968. **Children** Paul, Valentine and Jason (adopted, died 1989), from first marriage; Suzanne (adopted) and Zuleika, from second marriage. **Emigration** Left Britain for US, 1962. **Career** Professional début, dancer, Chiswick Empire, London, 1948; dancer, Monte Carlo Ballet; film début, *Oh Rosalinda!*, 1955; contract player, Rank Organization; moved to Hollywood, 1962; began appearing in television, 1962; after learning she had cancer, became spokeswoman for American Cancer Association. **Awards and honours** US Medal of Courage, 1988. **Films** *Oh Rosalinda!,* 1955; *Three Men in a Boat,* 1955; *Hell Drivers,* 1957; *Robbery Under Arms,* 1957; *Carry On Nurse,* 1959; *Raising the Wind,* 1961; *Twice Around the Daffodils,* 1962; *Villa Rides,* 1968; *Rider on the Rain,* 1970; *The Family,* 1970; *The Mechanic,* 1972; *Wild Horses,* 1973; *The Valachi Papers,* 1973; *Hard Times,* 1975; *The Streetfighter,* 1975; *Breakheart Pass,* 1976; *From Noon Till Three,* 1976; *Love and Bullets,* 1979; *Death Wish II,* 1982; *Assassination,* 1986. **Television** *Shane*; *Daniel Boone*; *Ben Casey*; *Mannix*; *Star Trek*; *The Man from U.N.C.L.E.* **Publications** *Life Wish* (autobiography), 1987; *Lifelines* (autobiography), 1989. **Cause of death** Breast cancer, at age 54.

LOTTE JACOBI

German/American Photographer

***Born* Thorn, West Prussia, 17 August 1896**

***Died* Concord, New Hampshire, 6 May 1990**

A strongly lit face against a dark background, an intense, concentrated gaze — Lotte Jacobi's self-portrait of 1930 seems to epitomize both her style, which placed the emphasis on the face of Jacobi's subjects, and her reflective, concentrated approach to her work. "I only photograph what I see," she once said, "my style is the style of the people I photograph. In my portraits I refuse to photograph myself, as do so many other photographers." By using her ability to observe, Lotte Jacobi has created portraits of members of the intellectual and artistic circles of the Berlin of the 1920s and early 1930s which are a fascinating documentation of Weimar culture.

Born into a family of photographers — her great-grandfather had learned the trade in Paris in 1839 from Daguerre himself — Lotte Jacobi took up the tradition and studied photography and art history in Munich. In 1927 she returned to Berlin where she worked in her father's studio. Jacobi also accepted commissions from magazines and newspapers which became increasingly interested in the new medium and reproduced photographs extensively.

Berlin had become the political and cultural capital of Germany after the establishment of the Weimar Republic under the Social Democrats in 1918. It attracted many artists who, in their search for novelty, moved there to be surrounded by a spirit that was receptive to their radical ideas. Against a background of political instability — of the imposition of the Versailles Treaty, the French occupation of the Ruhr, strikes, a soaring inflation, the failure to diminish the power of the Army and the aristocratic–industrial alliance, political assassinations and bloody street fights — the arts experienced an unprecedented period of bloom which led to the legend of "the golden 1920s". This atmosphere of experimental freedom, which oscillated between Expressionism, *Neue Sachlichkeit* and Dadaism, also had an influence on the avant-garde photographers who came to see their medium as the most suitable one to record the new industrial and social environment. Photographic technology was advanced rapidly and enabled the photographers to depart from the tradition. The experimental use of the camera on the one hand, and the commitment to realistic documentation on the other, created images which reflected the developments in the arts, the new scientific insights in the areas of time and matter, as well as social changes.

Drawn to Berlin's progressive circles, Lotte Jacobi captured the faces of many of those — such as the writers Thomas and Heinrich Mann and Karl Kraus, the composer Kurt Weill, the architect Erich Mendelsohn, the publicists Carl von Ossietzky and Egon Erwin Kisch and the theologian Martin Buber among many others — who took part in shaping the Weimar spirit. With her compact Ermanox camera, which permitted her to take photographs without a flashlight, Jacobi often produced close-ups. She rarely tried to capture fleeting events, but rather concentrated on still moments which revealed something about the character of her subject. The portrait of Käthe Kollwitz shows an expression shaped by both pain and strength, features which were the source of the whole of that artists's *oeuvre*. Jacobi's study of Ernst Block with questioning eyes behind dark-rimmed glasses, and a furrowed forehead, places the emphasis on the intellectual's critical mind. The writer Anna Seghers is shown in profile with a pensive, yet determined expression.

In spite of her commitment to observation, Jacobi did sometimes use theatrical means to stylize an image. In her famous portrait of Lotte Lenya she directed the light so as to suggest a mask over the actor's face. A dark shadow adds a dramatic element to Kurt Tucholsky's features.

Jacobi took part in *Das Lichtbild* (1930 in Munich), one of the numerous photographic exhibitions in Germany which placed the emphasis on new techniques and displayed photographs used for advertising, journalistic, technological, industrial and scientific purposes alongside creative works. She also undertook a trip to the USSR — arranged for her by the Communist leader Ernst Thälmann for whom she had worked in his election campaign — and brought back many photographs.

Germany's economic crisis, deepened by New York's stock-market crash in 1929, unleashed a political crisis which strengthened the Right. In effect, parliamentary democracy ended in 1930, three years before Hitler came into power. The campaign against Jews and against "progressing cultural Bolshevism" began. In order to escape persecution, Lotte Jacobi had to leave Germany in 1935.

She settled in New York and opened a studio with her sister Ruth, which they ran until 1955. She took portraits of German exiles, such as Klaus and Erika Mann, the publishers Kurt Wolff and Erich Reiss and Albert Einstein (the photograph of whom appeared in *Life* magazine). In course of time she also worked with American artists and intellectuals and her portraits of Eleanor Roosevelt, Alfred Stieglitz, the poets W.H. Auden, Marianne Moore and Robert Frost and the writer Theodore Dreiser among many others, appeared in newspapers and magazines. She had individual exhibitions and also took part in group shows.

In 1946 Lotte Jacobi began to experiment more and produced a series of abstract "photogenics". Unlike Man Ray's "photograms" which are made with recognizable objects, Jacobi's "photogenics" are compositions created by the movement of a light source on photo-sensitized paper. With the gradual changes in tone Jacobi explored concepts of light, depth and space.

She left New York in 1955 and settled in the countryside of New Hampshire where she opened a new studio in Deering and continued to take photographs. She was also involved in establishing the photographic department of the Currier Gallery of Art in Manchester, New Hampshire, and began to meet with young students. In order to develop her skills further she spent a period of study at Stanley Hayter's Paris studio in the early 1960s and had the opportunity to meet Albert Renger-Patzsch, one of the pioneers of experimental photography, during a trip to Europe.

Jacobi's works can be found in various museum collections in the United States and Germany and her archives, consisting of 47,000 negatives, are at the University of New Hampshire to which she donated them in 1981. They will always remain powerful reflections of a culture cut short, yet kept alive in exile.

Born Johanna Alexandre Jacobi. **Father** Photographer. **Marriages** 1) Fritz Honig, 1916 (divorced 1924); 2) Erich Reiss, publisher, 1940 (died 1951). **Children** One son, John Frank, from first marriage. **Education** Königliche Louisenschule, Posen, West Prussia, now Poland, 1902–12; Academy of Posen, studied art history and literature, 1912–16; studied photography, Bavarian State Academy of Photography and Art History, University of Munich, 1925–27; studied graphics, art history, French and literature, University of New Hampshire, Durham, 1961–62; studied etching and engraving with S.W. Hayter, Atelier 17, Paris, 1962–63. **Emigration** Left Europe for United States, 1935, naturalized, 1940. **Career** Film director, 1927; director Jacobi Studio of Photography, 1927–35; freelance photographer with own studio, New York, 1935–55; own gallery, New York, 1952–55; moved to Deering, New Hampshire, 1955; proprietor, Jacobi Studio and Gallery, Deering, 1963–70; a founder, department of photography, Currier Gallery of Art, Manchester, New Hampshire, 1970, honorary curator, 1972–78. **Awards and honours** Silver Medal, Royal Photography Salon, Tokyo, 1931; First Prize, British War Relief Photography Competition, *Life* magazine, New York, 1941; First Prize, New Hampshire Art Association, 1970; DFA: University of New Hampshire, Durham, 1974, University of Maryland, Baltimore, 1983, Rivier College, Nashua, New Hampshire, 1984; Doctor of Humane Letters: New England College, Henniker, New Hampshire, 1978, New Hampshire College, Manchester, 1982; New Hampshire Governor's Award for the Arts, 1980; LLD, Colby-Sawyer College, New London, New Hampshire, 1982; Erich Salomon Prize, West Berlin, 1983. **Individual exhibitions** (in New York, unless otherwise indicated) Jacobi Studio, 1937; Jacobi Studio, 1941; Direction Gallery, 1941; Norlyst Gallery, 1948; Ohio University College, Athens, 1952; University College of Education, 1953; Jacobi Gallery, 1955; Sharon Arts Center, Peterboro, New Hampshire, 1957; Currier Gallery of Art, Manchester, New Hampshire, 1959; Colby Junior College, New London, New Hampshire, 1962; 303 Gallery, 1964; Institute of Arts and Sciences, Manchester, New Hampshire, 1964; Templehof Art Gallery, Temple, New Hampshire, 1964; Middlebury College Library, Vermont, 1965; New England College, Henniker, New Hampshire, 1965; University of Chicago, 1965; Mr and Mrs Roger McCollester House, Irvington-on-Hudson, 1966; Community Church Art Gallery, 1967; New England College, Henniker, New Hampshire, 1968; Concord Public Library, New Hampshire, 1969; N.H. Belknap College, Center Harbor, New Hampshire, 1972; Staatliche Landesbildstelle, Hamburg, 1972; Folkwang Museum, Essen, 1973; University of New Hampshire, Durham, 1974; Light Gallery, 1974; Sharon Arts Center, Peterboro, New Hampshire, 1974; Washington Gallery of Photography, Washington, DC, 1974; University of New Hampshire, Durham; New England College, Henniker, New Hampshire, 1975; Photo-Graphics Workshop, New Canaan, Connecticut, 1976; Arts and Sciences Center, Nashua, New Hampshire, 1976; William Benton Museum of Art, Storrs, Connecticut, 1976; Danforth Museum, Framingham, Massachusetts, 1977; Kimmell-Cohn Gallery, 1977; Allan Frumkin Gallery, Chicago, 1977; Manchester Institute of Arts and Sciences, New Hampshire, 1977; University of Maryland, Baltimore, 1978; New Hampshire Art Association, Manchester, 1978; Studio 139, Portsmouth,

New Hampshire, 1979; Theater on the Sea, Portsmouth, New Hampshire, 1980; *Lotte Jacobi: Begegnungen,* Münchner Stadtmuseum, Munich, 1981; Gutenberg Museum, Mainz, West Germany, 1981; Westbrook College, Portland, Maine, 1981; Catskill Center for Photography, Woodstock, 1981; Lamont Gallery, Exeter, New Hampshire, 1982; The Plus Company, Nashua, New Hampshire, 1982; Dryden Galleries, Providence, Rhode Island, 1983; Galerie Taube, West Berlin, 1983; Associated Artists Gallery, Philadelphia, 1983; Currier Gallery of Art, Manchester, New Hampshire, 1984; Ledel Gallery, 1984; Carl Solway Gallery, Cincinnati, Ohio, 1984. **Group exhibitions** (include) *Das Lichtbild,* Munich, 1930; *Dance Photographs,* Brooklyn Museum, 1937; *In and Out of Focus,* Museum of Modern Art, 1948; *Subjektive Fotografie 2,* State School of Arts, Saarbrücken, 1955; *Subjektive Fotografie 3,* State School of Arts, Saarbrücken, 1958; *The Sense of Abstraction,* Museum of Modern Art, 1960: (with Marie Cosindas) *Two Photographers,* Gropper Galleries, Cambridge, Massachusetts, 1966; *Women of Photography,* San Francisco Museum of Art, 1975; *Recollections: 10 Women of Photography,* International Center of Photography, 1979; *Avant-Garde Photography in Germany 1919–39,* San Francisco Museum of Modern Art, 1980; *Fotogramme — die lichtreichen Schatten,* Fotomuseum im Stadtmuseum, Munich, 1983; *Photography and Art 1946–86,* Los Angeles County Museum of Art, 1987. **Collections** University of New Hampshire, Durham; Museum of Modern Art, New York; Metropolitan Museum of Art, New York: Massachusetts Institute of Technology, Cambridge; Wellesley College Museum, Massachusetts; Addison Gallery of American Art, Phillips Academy, Andover, Massachusetts; Currier Gallery of Art, Manchester, New Hampshire; Smithsonian Institution, Washington DC; Folkwang Museum, Essen; Staatliche Landesbildstelle, Hamburg. **Publications** *Portraits Before 1940,* 1978; *Portraits of Albert Einstein 1927–1938,* 1978; *Dance and Theater,* 1979; *Photogenics 1946–1955,* 1981; *Berlin, New York: Schriftsteller in den 30er Jahren,* with foreword by Ludwig Greve, 1982. **Film** *Portrait of an Artist,* 1927. **Cause of death** Pneumonia, at age 93. **Further reading** Robert W. Cooke, *Designing with Light on Paper and Film,* 1969; Patra Holter, *Photography Without a Camera,* 1972; *Lotte Jacobi: Menschen von Gestern und Heute — Fotografische Porträts, Skizzen und Dokumentationen* (exhibition catalogue), 1973; James A. Fasanelli, *Lotte Jacobi,* 1979; Margaretta K. Mitchell, editor, *Recollections: 10 Women of Photography,* 1979; Van Deren Coke, *Avant-Garde Photography in Germany 1919–1939* (exhibition catalogue), 1980; Weston J. Naef, *Counterparts: Form and Emotion in Photographs,* 1982; Floris M. Neususs, *Fotogramme — die lichtreichen Schattan* (exhibition catalogue), 1983; C. Traub, R. Silverman and G. Ackerman, *Figure della danza/Visions of the Dance 1959–1982* (exhibition catalogue), 1983; *Contemporary Photographers,* 1988.

JOHN KENDALL-CARPENTER

British Headmaster, Rugby Player and Rugby Administrator

***Born* Cornwall, England, 25 September 1925**

***Died* Wellington, Somerset, 23 May 1990**

Wellington School had already reconciled itself to the imminent retirement of its headmaster. But the sport of rugby suffered an enormous loss when the former England captain and chairman of the Rugby Football World Cup organizing committee died suddenly, aged 64. John Kendall-Carpenter was an inspirational figure in his professional career as a schoolmaster and as both a player and an administrator in the sport he loved. He gained the highest honours as a player and climbed to the very top of the administrative ladder, earning a CBE in 1989.

Both Oxford and England called on Kendall-Carpenter as a back-row forward. He captained both teams and always finished on the winning side at Oxford. On one particularly famous occasion, he single-handedly prevented arch rivals Cambridge from breaking that lucky streak when his last-minute tackle on an opposing winger saved the game and brought him fame. In time, he also wore the colours of the Barbarians, Cornwall, Bath, and Penzance and Newlyn. But the highlights of his playing career were set between 1949 and 1954, as he earned 23 "caps" for an England team which he first captained in 1954.

Kendall-Carpenter could always get the very best from the players around him. At a time when amateurism ruled supreme within the sport, he genuinely mirrored the "Spirit of Rugby Football", and was a stauhch supporter of amateurism throughout his life. A tough, energetic player, he always competed within the bounds of true sportsmanship; and, win or lose, he would always enjoy himself at the post-game receptions — gaining a reputation for being one of the first to arrive, and last to leave. He was in no sense of the word extrovert, but immensely friendly and hospitable in a quiet way.

Born a Cornishman, he remained a true and loyal west-countryman all his life. He left Truro School in 1943 to join the Fleet Air Arm, and from there moved on to Exeter College, Oxford. He entered the teaching profession in 1951, beginning as a geography master at Clifton College. Ten years later, he was appointed headmaster of Cranbrook School in Kent, where he remained for nine years, before spending a three-year spell as headmaster of Eastbourne College.

He made a huge impact wherever he went. At Cranbrook, a voluntary aided school (that is, one which derives its funding from various sources), for instance, he tried to build bridges between the local authority and full independence. As his obituarist in the London *Times* explained, "His desire to see such bridges between the independent and the maintained sectors of education led him to give much of his time and talents to the Boarding Schools Association, which he chaired between 1981 and 1983."

Wellington, one of Britain's most famous public schools, was the focus of his attention for the last 17 years of his life. He guided the institution through an extensive five-million-pounds rebuilding programme, helped it to gain a reputation for possessing one of the finest science centres in south-west England, and took full control as Wellington expanded in size from a 400 all-boys school to an 800 co-educational establishment.

A man of incredible energy and stamina, it amazed people that he could pursue such a full professional career while also devoting so much of his life to rugby. He served as president of the Rugby Football Union and was later elected president of the Schools Rugby Football Union. Election to the International Board — which controls the game world-wide — was inevitable, and after gaining the trust, respect and affection of most member countries, he was appointed chairman of both the International Board and the World Cup organizing committee.

The work took him all around the world, but he took all the inter-continental travel in his stride. The word jet-lag was simply not in his vocabulary; and he continued to inspire admiration for his ability to work as a headmaster *and* an international sports administrator, right up to his death

Planning to retire at the end of the school year, in order to channel all of his efforts into organizing the second World Cup in Britain, he would probably prefer to be remembered for what he did for the hundreds of school pupils who came under his influence, rather than for what he did on the field and behind the scenes for rugby.

Born John MacGregor Kendall Kendall-Carpenter. **Marriage** Iris Anson, 1955. **Children** Two daughters and three sons. **Education** Truro School, Cornwall; Exeter College, Oxford. **Military service** Fleet Air Arm, 1943–46. **Rugby career** Played rugby for Oxford, 1948–50, captain, 1950; played rugby for England, capped 23 times, 1949–54, captain, 1951–54; captained the Barbarians, Cornwall, Bath, and Penzance and Newlyn; president, Rugby Football

Union, 1980–81; chairman, Rugby Football Board, 1981–83; president, Schools Rugby Football Union; board member, International Rugby Football Union, 1984–90; chairman, World Cup organizing committee, 1985–90. **Professional career** Geography master, Clifton College, Bristol, Avon, 1951–61, housemaster, 1957–61; headmaster, Cranbrook School, Kent, 1961–70; headmaster, Eastbourne College, East Sussex, 1970–73; headmaster, Wellington School, Somerset, 1973–90. **Related activities** Chairman, Boarding Schools Association, 1981–83. **Awards and honours** Commander of the Order of the British Empire, 1989. **Cause of death** Undisclosed, at age 64.

BILL KEYS

British Trade Union Leader

Born **London, England, 1 January 1923**

Died **Thorpe Bay, Essex, 19 May 1990**

To those confronting him across a negotiating table, Bill Keys had the hide of an ox. To his colleagues around a committee table, he had a heart of gold. He was perhaps one of the last of the old-style trade union leaders. Self-taught, and a forceful and eloquent orator, he was a hard negotiator on behalf of his print union members. People he worked with speak of him as a warm, generous and compassionate man.

Maybe it was because he was a Londoner, born and raised not far from London Bridge, and worked most of his life in the print industry, that he imbibed their radical traditions. In the early nineteenth century London's print unions were in the forefront of those seeking to extend voting rights to working men and women and to abolish the widespread corruption in British parliamentary elections.

His strong political convictions were also shaped by his early experiences of growing up in the 1930s amid mass unemployment and poverty. He also witnessed the rise of fascist groups and their racist demonstrations in the East End of London. He sought to remedy these economic and social injustices by involving himself deeply in trade union activities and in the politics of the British Labour Party.

Bill Keys was elected as general secretary of the print union the Society of Graphical and Allied Trades (SOGAT) in 1974, and served in that capacity until he retired in 1985. The union has a long history dating back to the eighteenth century. It recruits members in the general printing trade, national and provincial newspapers, bookbinding and paper-making. At its peak in the 1970s, the union had about 200,000 members of whom about 35 per cent were women. The chief policy-making body is the biennial delegate council and it was there, on the eve of his death, that Keys watched as delegates voted in favour of a ballot on a merger with the other major British print union, The National Graphical Association. Such a merger, when approved by a ballot of the memberships of both unions, would produce a single union for the print industry in Britain — one of Keys's long-held dreams.

As a long-established craft union, SOGAT had made bargaining agreements with printing employers covering a wide range of employees' working conditions, such as recruitment, training and job manning. They also operated the "closed shop", a union-management agreement which requires all employees to become members of the union unless genuine religious objections can be shown. The existence of these agreements greatly increased Bill Keys's bargaining power with management. He would have argued that they were necessary to protect the jobs and pay of his members. In the 1980s he witnessed the gradual erosion of many of these agreements as they were effectively outlawed by the Conservative government.

Keys was always ready to take up the cudgels on behalf of other trade unions and on at least one occasion he found himself on the wrong side of the law. In one case, in 1977, a trade dispute existed between the *Daily Mirror* newspaper and the National Union of Journalists which resulted in a complete stoppage of production. The *Daily Express* decided to print more copies to cater for the increase in demand but Bill Keys told his members not to handle the additional copies. This instruction was in line with a "dog does not bite dog" agreement between unions and Fleet Street management. Despite this, the owners of the *Express,* Beaverbrook Newspapers, went to court seeking an injunction against the union — and won it. SOGAT were required to print the extra copies. The case is now enshrined in the text-books of labour law as *Beaverbrook Newspapers v. Keys* and provides an interesting example of how the British judges could effectively outlaw sympathetic industrial action even before the spate of anti-trade union legislation got under way in the 1980s.

Keys was not however always leading strikes. Often he was acting as a mediator in settling disputes involving other unions. His shrewd and sharp judgement was called upon to help resolve disputes in the steel and in the water industries, and in 1989 he acted as trouble-shooter in a long dispute affecting the London Underground. During the year-long coalminers' strike of 1984 to 1985, he acted as the main link between the miners' leaders, who trusted him, and the Trades Union Congress. He almost succeeded in producing a compromise solution but a combination of the determination of the Conservative government not to give way to the miners' union, and the intransigence of the miners' leader, Arthur Scargill, ruled out any negotiated settlement.

Perhaps the greatest challenge Bill Keys faced as a trade union leader was the introduction of new technology to the printing industry. Technology can be defined as the application of science to the solution of human, social or economic problems. Unfortunately it tends to create as many problems as it solves. It fell to Bill Keys to lead the union side of the print industry during the 20-year struggle to modernize the technology of the newspaper industry. It posed for him a cruel dilemma. He knew that the changes were inevitable. He also recognized that word-processors presented a major threat to his union's craft members. Because the level of skill required is much less than that needed for more traditional printing techniques, the printer's claim to craft status and high pay would be undermined. The need for certain types of print crafts could disappear altogether as the use of word-processors enables any trained typist to produce copy of an acceptable standard.

His strategy was to seek a gradual negotiated introduction of the new processes which he felt he could "sell" to his members. He needed all his skill and experience as a negotiator to engage in the gladiatorial combat on two fronts; with his members, and with the new breed of newspaper barons who were after quick results. His members were equally intractable. The result was that he had only recently retired from his leadership of SOGAT when one of the newspaper moguls, Rupert Murdoch, decided to impose the new technology without union agreement at a specially built printing plant in east London. At a stroke the jobs of 5000 printworkers were destroyed. These had to be added to the many thousands who had been made unemployed during the 1970s. Few had any prospects of ever finding another job.

Like most leaders of large trade unions in Britain, Bill Keys was in the public eye as a leading figure in the Trades Union Congress and in the Labour Party. At the annual conferences of these bodies he was able to speak to a national television audience on themes close to his heart. These included equal rights for women and racial equality. At the 1978 Congress he made an eloquent and passionate speech on these issues. He said, "our concern has long been for the dignity of labour, the right of all people to be treated as equals irrespective of race, colour or creed. British unions have campaigned for 80 years to achieve equal pay for women. Despite the 1970 Equal Pay Act passed by a Labour government, discrimination in pay against women has not been eliminated." As chairman of the TUC Employment Policy and Equal Rights committees he went on to announce that the TUC had drawn up a comprehensive list of changes that would be needed to make the Equal Pay Act "employer proof". He might have added that the act needed proofing against some male chauvinist trade unionists.

His speech was more than empty conference rhetoric. In his own union he encouraged and counselled women and young people to aim for the top positions. Brenda Dean, the present general secretary, can testify to this.

On racial equality he said in his speech to Congress "there is only one race, the human race". He warned politicians against stirring up racial prejudice and hostility. He went on to reveal that as a young soldier with the rank of sergeant-major during World War II he had witnessed the horrors of the Nazi concentration camps. This experience made a deep impression on him.

In politics he displayed the same energy and commitment as in his union work. He spearheaded a campaign in the early 1980s to persuade his union members to continue to support a union political fund. The campaign was brought about by new laws passed by the Conservative government compelling unions to ballot their members periodically on this question. The government clearly hoped that "ordinary sensible" trade union members would reject such funds which, among other things, could be used to help finance Her Majesty's loyal opposition, the British Labour Party.

Bill Keys won a resounding victory in his own union. He continued his campaign to ensure that political funds were maintained in every union which already had a fund, and set up anew in 17 additional unions.

Keys remained active in the politics of the British labour movement in his retirement and accepted the job of chairing a committee, Trade Unionists for a Labour Victory, set up before the 1987 British general election. Its aim was to smooth links between the party, the unions and rank-and-file members. He drove himself mercilessly in this role although his health was not good. He addressed countless meetings up and down the country, despite the fact that all the opinion polls showed that his cause was all but lost.

This was typical of a man whose simple political philosophy was to leave the world a better place than he had found it. In a speech in 1980 he said, "I want to hand down to my grandchildren a society that is based on social justice: a society where the word fear is removed from it — fear from want, fear from unemployment: justice for those who are sick, handicapped, old: a society that recognizes that all people stand equal irrespective of race, colour or creed." The hide of an ox did indeed obscure a heart full of golden ideals.

Born William Herbert Keys. **Marriage** Enid Gledhill, 1941. **Children** Ian and Keith. **Military service** Regimental sergeant-major, Rifle Brigade, World War II. **Career** Printer, *Daily Herald*; joined, Printing Bookbinding and Paper Workers Union, 1939, national organizer, 1953–61, London Secretary, 1961–70; general president, Society of Graphical and Allied Trades, 1970–74, general secretary, 1974–85 (from 1982, called SOGAT '82, after amalgamation with the National Society of Operative Printers, Graphical and Media Personnel); chairman, Trade Union Co-ordinating Committee, 1985–90. **Related activities** General council member, Trades Union Congress, 1974–85, chairman: Printing Industries Committee, Employment Policy and Organization Committee, Equal Rights Committee, Media Working Group, member, Finance and General Purposes Committee; Commission for Racial Equality, 1977–81; Manpower Services Commission, 1979–85; chairman, Trade Unionists for a Labour Victory. **Cause of death** Undisclosed, at age 67.

ASHLEY LAWRENCE

New Zealand Conductor

***Born* Hamilton, New Zealand, 5 June 1934**

***Died* Tokyo, Japan, 7 May 1990**

Ashley Lawrence may never have been a star conductor but he made an indelible mark on the musical world through his unique contribution to a neglected area of his profession — conducting for the ballet. He had an unerring sense of tempo and understanding of dancers' technical problems as well as a way of enthusing the musicians under his baton as they tackled *Swan Lane* for perhaps the five-hundredth time. This sense of commitment won him the respect and affection of audiences, dancers and orchestral players alike — traditionally a difficult combination to please. Choreographer Kenneth Macmillan said of him: "He understood the needs of dancers without ever compromising his fine musicianship and respect for the score. Dancers, choreographers and audiences throughout the world will miss him dreadfully, and I will miss a good friend."

As a schoolboy in Hamilton, New Zealand, physics and maths were his first love and he might have made science his career. But like many scientists, he had a great affinity for music, and while he was studying for his degree at Auckland University he realized that music was eclipsing his other interests. He decided to give music a try and travelled to England on a scholarship to study at London's Royal College of Music. While there, he took a part-time job which laid the foundations of his love of the ballet repertoire, as he told an interviewer later in life: "It began by chance through my being engaged to play the piano for a ballet class when I was still a student. It was a useful way of earning some money and I got on so well with it." Although he also had to do some part-time maths teaching, he now banished all thoughts of a career in science, especially when the opportunity arose to reinforce his music studies by attending a course in Switzerland to study with the conductor Rafael Kubelik.

Back in Britain in 1960 he shared a flat with Isobel Grundy, who remembers the days when he was struggling to become a conductor.

> I knew Ashley as a maths teacher sharing a Chelsea Flat which had the distinctive feature of a kitchen that doubled as a bathroom, the bath occuping a commanding position and wearing a wooden lid. It must have been the winter of 1960–61 when Ashley was invited to conduct at a Wigmore Hall concert of the New Zealand Music Society. Before and after the performance he put in a good deal of conducting in the kitchen striding mesmerisingly around the bath.

The concert brought good reviews and led to an invitation to conduct the Royal Ballet's touring company. There he met and made friends with Kenneth Macmillan who remembered his helpfulness: "[He was] not only a wonderful conductor but his contribution to finding new music for the ballet was informed and inspired. Any choreographer could call on him for advice when making a ballet and he was always more than generous with his vast musical knowledge." Later, in 1967, Kenneth Macmillan was appointed ballet director of Deutsche Oper Berlin, and invited Lawrence to join him there. In Berlin his work was regarded so highly that he was also invited to conduct the opera. But he declined, saying that he didn't want to give the impression that he regarded the Ballet as a poor relation. He felt a sense of mission both to improve the relationships between ballet companies and their orchestras and to raise the profile of ballet conductors in the profession.

Lawrence stayed in Berlin until 1972, also conducting for Stuttgart Ballet during the 1970–72 seasons. Meanwhile, in 1971, he was appointed principal conductor of the BBC Concert Orchestra, a duty he fulfilled with much enjoyment until 1989.

Berlin days over, Lawrence followed Macmillan again — to Covent Garden as conductor. He replaced another fine ballet conductor, John Lanchbery, as music director amid controversy in 1973, and this meant that he had to work hard to achieve the popularity and respect he enjoyed until he left the post in 1987. During this period, as well as continuing his commitment to the BBC Concert Orchestra, Lawrence also conducted the American Ballet Theater and the Ballet de L'Opera, Paris, on many occasions. Offers were coming in from New York City Ballet at the time of his death — during a tour of Japan with the Stuttgart Ballet.

Lawrence was no showman. He tended to arrive on the podium at a gallop, as if to suggest a desire to get on with the job. He painstakingly attended to the less glamorous tasks, such as taking part in planning meetings to allocate musicians across the different production requirements. He learned Benesch notation in order better to understand the choreographer's art and worked hard to adapt scores to suit the choreographer's needs, though, as Peter Wright, director of Sadler's Wells Royal Ballet says, "he would never agree to an unmusical request. Instead he always found an alternative approach to the problem and inspired the artist to proceed with confidence."

Those who worked with him will never forget his quiet, smiling authority on the conductor's stand, as he gave performances in which the music played a role equal to the movement, costumes and other components. And he gave his all — whether to a major ballet score by Tchaikovsky or Stravinsky, or to a relatively minor work.

Lawrence was a private character who never married, and who, as Peter Wright recalls, "led a solitary life, but had at the same time an enormous sense of fun and good humour and was a great 'bon-viveur', never happier than when joking and laughing with his musical and dancing friends after a performance over a good meal and a fine wine".

Born Ashley Macdonald Lawrence. **Education** Auckland University, BA in physics and mathematics; Royal Schools scholarship, Royal College of Music, 1956–59; studied conducting with Rafael Kubelik, Switzerland, 1960. **Emigration** Left New Zealand for England, 1956. **Career** Staff conductor, Royal Ballet, 1962–66, conductor, 1972–73, music director, 1973–87; music director, Deutsche Oper, Berlin, 1966–72; music director, Stuttgart Ballet, 1970–72; principal conductor, BBC Concert Orchestra, 1971–89. **Related activities** Guest conductor: Paris Opéra Ballet, American Ballet Theater. **Other activities** Mathematics lecturer, Wandsworth Technical College, 1956–59. **Cause of death** Failure to recover from heart surgery, at age 55.

LUIGI NONO

Italian Composer

***Born* Venice, Italy, 29 January 1924**

***Died* Venice, Italy, 8 May 1990**

There is a twelfth-century wall inscription in Spanish Toledo: *Caminantes no hay caminos hay que caminar* — "Travellers, you have no paths, only the travelling"; which was the basis for what was to be Luigi Nono's last project and an uncannily apt description of not only his own place in twentieth-century music but that of his peers. Whatever value our descendants give to the work of this generation may depend on a later and more general view, but Luigi Nono's consistency, sincerity and diligence made him a true pathfinder whose significance is great in his own country's music, and with comparable importance elsewhere.

His birth into an aristocratic Venetian family provided a background of artistic interests and sympathies, so that although he initially embarked on a career of law, studying at the University of Padua (where he graduated in 1946), when his musical inclinations began to surface his father was able to introduce him to Malipiero, the Italian musicologist and composer. After giving him two years' instruction in musical history and technique at the Venice Conservatory he in turn delegated his further education to Bruno Maderna, only four years older than Nono and one of the leading figures in post-war Italian composition. He endorsed Malipiero's teaching, but also brought in the element of the socio-historical place of music in the community. At the same time, Nono did not discard his knowledge of renaissance music, the fifteenth and sixteenth centuries, which were to continue to influence his work in the future, particularly with regard to vocal writing; and a natural lyricism always ran through his work, whether for voice or electronic device.

Italy for some time had experienced a resurgence of talent. At the end of a nineteenth century dominated by *verismo* opera, Casella, Malipiero and Petrassi had followed others in attempting to broaden the scope of Italian music to include instrumental compositions more in line with international style although based on a secure foundation of pre-Romantic Italian works such as those of Gesualdo, Monteverdi and Vivaldi; a form of neo-classicism resulted, a style which contrasted strongly with romanticism, impressionism and melodrama. Casella in particular was to spend much time travelling in Europe in an attempt to develop a new form of Italian musical language, but by his return to Italy in 1915 he had been won over by Schoenberg's atonalism. Ultimately (and not only because he met with a complete lack of understanding from the Italian public) he returned to a neo-classical style based on tonality and clarity, a progression in which he was accompanied by Nono's teacher Malipiero, and Ghedini. A different approach was taken by Pizzetti, whose music, though lyrical, was based strictly on dramatic inspiration. Petrassi left neo-classicism behind after 1932 with his *Partita,* and by 1951 had in the cantata *Noche oscura* demonstrated capable handling of serial construction. Dallapicolla's progress towards a dodecaphonic basis for composition was slow and difficult, but by the 1940s was beginning to be established. Two of his works are notable for their theme of the right to liberty: the 1938 *Canti di prigionia* and the 1944 opera *Il prigioniero.*

It will be seen from this very simplified sketch of the experiments in musical systems which so radically changed music in Italy (far more than the same period in England) that Nono was in an excellent position to take advantage of his compatriots' research and exploration. With the same speed as he caught up with acquiring musical theory in his late teenage years, he seems rapidly to have comprehended and assimilated the searchings of his forerunners; too quickly, on the whole, for musical Italy to keep pace. His was a generation of rebels unhampered personally by the exigencies of outright war, and able to benefit from the tolerant attitudes of western Europe. His compositions are essentially part of the prevalent social and political background, the latter always set in the context of humanitarian considerations. His hatred of Fascism and any form of oppression had led him to serve in the Italian Resistance movement.

After the war he met many who shared his interests (in particular Heinz Werner Henze), with them acknowledging Schoenberg's pre-eminence in advanced musical thought as exemplified by 12-tone theory. Taken to Darmstadt's summer school of music at the end of the 1940s by Bruno Maderna, he there met Stockhausen, and became a pupil of Hermann Scherchen, the German conductor and specialist in the avant-garde, who had assisted Schoenberg in the preparation of his *Pierrot lunaire* and conducted it in 1912. He was to be the conductor in 1960 of Nono's major opera *Intolleranza,* later revised in 1970, which illustrates his hatred of persecution in the forms of immigrant segregation, Nazism and the atomic bomb. Ironically the opera itself provoked a strong manifestation of intolerance in Venice, some of it Fascist-inspired. Throughout his life Nono refused to compromise, and his membership of the Italian Communist Party (which he and Maderna joined in 1952) did not blind him to the flaws of pure Marxism in relation to human values.

His single-minded approach meant that Darmstadt ceased to hold him after 1958 when the influence of John Cage, aleatory and structureless composition, came to the fore; Nono elected to continue the discipline of strict serialism.

He was equally possessed of a strong conviction that his music could not exist in a moral vacuum, but must arise from human reaction to social and political events. In 1960 he wrote that dodecaphony was "only a distribution of notes contrasting with one another and demonstrating what happens when democracy is carried on into the field of music." His first international success, after earlier recognition in Germany rather than Italy, was *Il canto sospeso,* a large-scale choral work for three soloists and orchestra, with a text taken from the letters of condemned European Resistance fighters. He was an eloquent proselytizer, and his belief in one of the basic principles of democracy, i.e. that artists such as he should be regarded as "of the people" made him enthusiastic about taking his music to them. He was very ready to engage in debate about it, particularly in Emilia Romagna, where two of his co-workers were the conductor Claudio Abbado and the pianist Maurizio Pollini. *La fabbrica illuminata* for soprano and tape (1964), a collage of workplace noises, must have provoked lively discussion. (Thanks to Abbado and Pollini he remained in the mainstream of musical performance, despite his declared contempt for the conventional media of opera house, orchestra and concert-hall. His second opera, *Al gran sole carico d'amore* was presented at La Scala, Milan in 1975, directed by the Russian Yuri Ljubimov, making his first appearance in western Europe.) Other outlets for his teaching ranged from Russia, where three visits failed to impress Communist audiences, to William Glock's Dartington Summer School of Music, where his appearances in 1959, 1960 and 1961 were of considerable importance to British and other nationalities.

He had become attracted to electronic music in the 1950s, increasingly so in the 1960s, and used taped or synthesized elements in many of his compositions. Eventually he found the RAI Milan Electronic Studio inadequate, and this was one of the factors influencing his decision to accept an invitation to become artistic director of the Experimental Studio of the Strobel Foundation attached to South West German Radio. He had also become more disappointed at lack of recognition in his own country, not only of his own personal contribution, but of the necessity for progress in musical education if Italy was to keep its place in the development of new music.

His last opera, the 1985 *Prometeo,* was presented in a totally unconventional way, with the principal performers placed centrally, the audience interspersed with chorus and orchestra, and the whole being enriched by computer sound banks. It was contained within a wooden shell specially designed by the architect Renzo Piano. This large-scale radicalism was balanced by the comparative delicacy and introversion of the 1980 String Quartet.

Just as music inspired by the love of long-forgotten human beauty lives on, so Nono's work is more temporally substantial than some of the political incidents it originally marked. His open but steadfast attitude towards new methods of composition is exemplary. It is summed up vividly in his exhortation to his audiences to "listen... this is a fundamental condition for life. One must listen to others, to their differences and diversity. Not to chase unanimity... but to work to understand diversity. Then there is the possibility of a new explosion." Nono was a skilful listener, and a composer and teacher whose originality has left its enduring mark on all who recognized it.

Born Luigi Nono. **Marriage** Nuria Schoenberg, 1955. **Children** Silvia and Serena. **Education** Studied jurisprudence, University of Padua, BA, 1946; studied composition with Malipiero, Venice Conservatory, 1941, 1943–45; studied advanced harmony and counterpoint with Bruno Maderna and Hermann Scherchen, 1946–50. **Career** First work performed, *Variazioni canoniche,* Darmstadt, 1950; first experimental electronic work, RAI Milan Electronic Studio, 1954; gained international recognition, *Il canto sospeso,* Cologne, 1956; first opera performed, *Intolleranza,* 1960. **Related activities** Lecturer, Darmstadt, 1959; lecturer, Dartington Summer

School, Devon, 1959, 1960, 1961; artistic director, Experimental Studio of the Strobel Foundation; South West German Radio; resident member, German Academic Exchange programme. **Other activities** In Italian Resistance movement, 1943–44; **Offices and Memberships** Member, Italian Communist Party, 1952–90, central committee member, 1975. **Compositions** (include) *Variazioni canoniche,* 1950; *Polifonica, Monodia, Ritmica,* 1951; *España en el corazón,* 1952; *Der rote Mantel* (ballet), 1954; *La Victoire de Guernica,* 1954; *Canti,* 1955; *Incontri,* 1955; *Il canto sospeso,* 1956; *Varianti,* 1957; *La terra e la compagna,* 1958; *Intolleranza* (opera), 1960, revised 1970; *Sarà dolce tacere,* 1961; *Sul ponte di Hiroscima,* 1962; *La fabbrica illuminata,* 1964; *Die Ermittlung* (occasional music), 1965; *Ricorda cosa ti hanno fatto in Auschwitz,* 1966; *A Floresta é jovem e cheja de vida,* 1966; *Per Bastiana,* 1967; *Non consumiano Marx,* 1968; *Voci destroying Muros,* 1970; *Y entonces comprendió,* 1970; *Ein Gespenst geht um in der Welt (A Spectre Rises over Europe),* 1971; *Coma una ola de fuerza y luz,* 1972; Piano Concerto, 1972; *Al gran sole carico d'amore* (opera), 1974; Piano Concerto, 1975; *... sofferte onde serene,* 1976; *Con Luigi Dallapiccola,* 1979; *Fragmente-Stille, an Diotima,* 1979–80; String Quartet, 1980; *Das atmende Klarsein*, 1980–81; *Quando stanno morendo,* 1982; *Di ario Polacci No 2,* 1982; *Prometeo — Tragedia dell' ascolto* (opera), 1981–85; *La lontananza nostalgica utopica futura,* 1988. **Cause of death** Liver ailment, at age 66.

CARDINAL TOMÁS Ó'FIAICH

Leader of the Roman Catholic Church in Ireland

Born **Crossmaglen, Northern Ireland, 2 November 1923**

Died **Toulouse, France, 8 May 1990**

A musician who played the fiddle and the accordion, who loved to drink and sing and recite Irish poetry into the small hours, there was always something of the jovial troubadour about Cardinal Tomás Ó'Fiaich. To his many friends and supporters his death from a heart attack while leading a diocesan pilgrimage to Lourdes seemed, if tragic, also wholly appropriate. The Cardinal was a priest who was always happiest among ordinary lay people, particularly those from his beloved County Armagh. And pilgrimage, especially pilgrimage to the sacred places of Europe, was in his blood.

Born in the "bandit country" of southern Armagh, just north of the Republican border, son of a local school teacher, Tom Fee was steeped from his youth in Irish history. In 1943 he took his first degree in Celtic studies at the national seminary of St Patrick's, Maynooth. After ordination at Wexford in 1948 he studied early Irish history at University College, Dublin, and then went on to the Catholic University of Louvain in Belgium where he perfected his knowledge of French and German and explored the Irish monastic sites of Europe.

As lecturer in Irish history and then president of the seminary at Maynooth, the future cardinal was to spend the first 25 years of his working life in academic work. Apart from a brief spell as curate in Moy, County Tyrone, in 1952, he had no direct parochial experience. While at Maynooth he wrote and lectured widely on the early Irish saints — missionaries like St Columbanus, St Killian and St Gall, who spread the Christian word to Europe in the seventh century. He became president of the Association of Irish-speaking priests and chairman of the government-appointed Commission on Restoration of the Irish Language.

Known as he was as a strong protagonist of Gaelic culture it is, perhaps, small wonder that the appointment of Tom Fee to replace his old friend Cardinal Conway as Archbishop of Armagh and

Primate of all Ireland in 1977 aroused some consternation in London. The fact that the new primate adopted the Gaelic form of his name, changing Tom Fee to Tomás Ó'Fiaich did little to reassure. Indeed it is suggested that the two-year gap between Ó'Fiaich's appointment as primate and his elevation to the rank of cardinal were the result of intense diplomatic activity in the Vatican.

"It would be unthinkable", Ó'Fiaich announced, "for me to use my position as Archbishop of Armagh to promote any political creed". Everyone knew, however, what that creed would be. There was no secret and, indeed, he repeated it often enough, that the new archbishop wanted the English out of Ireland and the country again united. Like his mentor Pope John Paul II Cardinal Ó'Fiaich was primarily a patriot. Like him, he was content to remain traditionally orthodox on most other controversial church matters — questions on divorce, abortion and the ordination of women, for example.

"Brotherly love, peace, harmony, reconciliation, mutual forgiveness, an end to past dissensions and a new beginning in the practice of justice and charity towards all", were what the new Archbishop prayed for and promised at his episcopal ordination in St Patrick's Cathedral in 1977. Adopting the motto *Fratres in Unum* — Brothers in Unity, he worked with the leaders of all the churches in Ireland to bring an end to the discord. He engineered the Papal visit to Ireland in 1978, and wrote for the pontiff the famous Drogheda speech in which the Pope begged "on bended knees" for the violence to cease.

Knowing which way his sympathies lay made the Cardinal's own denunciations of the violent methods of the IRA especially effective. Time and again and in the strongest language he was to deplore the terrorism: "No Catholic can join or remain a member of an organization which perpetrates such evil deeds" he said. And, on another occasion, "Only completely ruthless and heartless men, without any feeling for human rights or the sacredness of human life could do such a thing... under no pretext can such murderous attacks be excused or membership of the organization responsible be condoned."

For his critics the Cardinal's words were never quite enough. It even aroused hostility that he also condemned the violence of the Army and the RUC, that he visited "the boys" in Long Kesh and compared their prison conditions unfavourably with those in the slums of Calcutta (which he had seen with Mother Teresa), and that he worked for those, like the Guildford Four, he considered wrongfully imprisoned in England. The accusation was made that, in some way, Ó'Fiaich was still the "Provos' Cardinal".

Sadly, none of this seems in the long run to have made much difference. Indeed it is doubtful whether anything any one man, be he cardinal or not, could have done would have been more effective. Amazingly enough the Cardinal's Requiem Mass brought together under one roof the leaders of Sinn Fein and the Northern Ireland Secretary, Peter Brook. Tributes to his life and work poured in, moreover, from church leaders of all denominations and from many Protestant laymen as well. But the violence continues unabated and there still seems no hope of reconciliation in Ireland. Rumours of a new Papal initiative in Northern Ireland, which would have delighted the Cardinal's heart, will now have to be postponed until the installation of a new primate in Armagh.

Against this rather bleak background it is perhaps surprising that the things to which all Cardinal Ó'Fiaich's friends testify, are his happiness and the joy that he spread around him. It is for this quality of joy, rather than for his writings or his politics, that he seems to be remembered. The warmth, simplicity and honesty of his personality endeared him to many. Travelling around his diocese on a bicyle or leading a bus-load of pilgrims to Lourdes, Cardinal Ó'Fiaich was and remained a priest of the people, and it is for that that the people loved him.

Born Thomas Seamus Fee (later adopted Gaelic spelling). **Parents** Patrick, elementary-school teacher, and Anne (Caraher) Fee. **Education** Cregganduff Public Elementary School; St Patrick's College, Armagh; St Patrick's College, Maynooth, 1940–43, first-class honours in Celtic studies, BA, 1943; St Peter's College, Wexford; University College, Dublin, first-class honours in early Irish history, MA, 1950; Catholic University of Louvain, LicScHist, 1952. **Career** Ordained Roman Catholic priest, Wexford, 1948; curate, Moy, County Tyrone, 1952–53; lecturer in modern history, St Patrick's College, Maynooth, 1953–59, professor of modern history, 1959–74, president, 1974–77; Archbishop of Armagh and Primate of all Ireland, 1977–90, cardinal, 1979–90. **Related activities** Treasurer, Catholic Record Society of Ireland, 1954–74; president, Society of Irish-Speaking priests, 1955–67; chairman: Government Commission on Restoration of the Irish Language, 1959–63, Irish Language Advisory Council, 1965–68; senate member, National University of Ireland, 1964; member, Higher Education Authority, 1972–74; editor, *Seanchas Ard Mhacha* and other journals; president, Irish Episcopal Conference, 1977–90; member: Congregation for Catholic Education and Congregation for the Clergy, and Secretariate for Christian Unity, Vatican, 1979–90, Congregation for the Evangelisation of Peoples, 1984–90, Congregation for Bishops, 1980–90, Council for Public Affairs of the Church, 1984–90. **Awards and honours** Honorary doctorate: St Mary's, 1979, Notre Dame University, Indiana, 1979, Thiel College, Greenville, Pennsylvania, 1979, Boston College, 1981, College of St Thomas, St Paul, Minnesota, 1981, National University of Ireland, 1984. **Publications** *Gaelscrínte i gCéin,* 1960; *Irish Cultural Influence in Europe,* 1967; (with P. de Barra) *Imeacht na nIarlaí,* 1972; *Má Nuad,* 1972; *Art MacCumhaigh,* 1973; *St Columbanus in his Own Words,* 1974; *Oliver Plunkett: Ireland's New Saint,* 1975; *Olibhear Pluinceid,* 1976; *Aifreann Ceolta Tíre,* 1977; *Art Mac Bionaid,* 1979; *Gaelscrínte San Eoraip,* 1986; *The Irish College in France,* 1990. **Cause of death** Heart attack while on pilgrimage, at age 66.

WALKER PERCY

American Novelist

***Born* Birmingham, Alabama, 28 May 1916**

***Died* Covington, Louisiana, 10 May 1990**

Walker Percy is commonly dubbed a "novelist of the New South", but this is misleading. First of all, Percy's writing — by his own admission — is based on the tradition of European existentialists such as Sartre and Kierkegaard, a far cry from the stereotyped "southern" literary traditions of William Faulkner and Eudora Welty — also labelled as such by press and publishers alike. Why the world is quick to categorize authors as southern writers is itself a question open to debate. As any writer living in the supposed "New South" will tell you, contrary to public opinion, William Faulkner is not representative of any tradition other than his own. Thus, the only true definition of a "southern writer" is that one is a writer and one lives in the American South; if that is the case, then yes, Walker Percy can be described as a southern writer. Otherwise, he is best viewed as a modern American novelist, for his subject matter, style and tradition follows none of those the academics and journalists so gleefully like to label as "southern". (One wonders why there are no "north-western writers" or "eastern writers", and why so many would-be novelists who live elsewhere in the United States are so desperately trying to follow this ill-defined "southern" tradition.)

Now, don't be misled. The influence of the South on Walker Percy cannot be denied; however, one must be a southerner completely to understand it and its ramifications. In terms of "tradition", there is in the South — "New" or otherwise — a long history of oral and written story-telling that exists to a greater degree than it does anywhere else in America. That Percy grew up in such a society is bound to have fostered his own narrative abilities — especially given the "family" which cared for him until adulthood.

Percy's earliest years were traumatic, and this, too, is bound to have caused a good deal of introspection and soul-searching on his part. He was born in Birmingham, Alabama, the son of lawyer Leroy Pratt Percy and Martha Phinizy Percy. When the boy was ten or eleven, his father committed suicide. Two years later, his mother was killed in an automobile accident, and Percy and his two brothers were adopted by their father's bachelor cousin, William Alexander Percy, the man they came to call "Uncle Will". Albeit tragic, these turns of events could not have led to a better guardian for the boys, for W.A. Percy was to have a profound influence on them all.

"Uncle Will" lived in Greenville, Mississippi, and his story would make a book in itself. Indeed, he eventually published one about it, the charming series of autobiographical essays called *Lanterns on the Levee.* In this he extolled the paternal virtues of the southern landowners, while at the same time attacking the race-baiting activists who had cost his own father a seat in the Senate. Walker Percy would later write of his "uncle" that he was a "remarkable man" who almost single-handedly made "Greenville different from the rest of Mississippi". W.A. Percy was a man of many talents; he was a lawyer, a soldier, a community leader, a planter and a minor poet, and his house was always open to all kinds of people: William Faulkner often dropped in for tennis, and the black poet and activist Langston Hughes once came to stay. Years later, Walker Percy remembered what it was like to grow up in his "uncle's" house in an article he wrote for *Saturday Review/World.* The house on Percy Street, he said, was "visited regularly by other poets, politicians, psychiatrists, sociologists, black preachers, folk singers, itinerant harmonica players."

From W.A. Percy, the young Walker inherited a love of Shakespeare and the Romantic poets, an innate curiosity, a fondness for classical music, and an ambivalent attitude to tradition: although he had a profound respect for its power, Percy saw how it kept a man separated from the modern world.

As a boy, Walker Percy showed a no-greater-than-average desire to become a writer. He wrote sonnets for lazy fellow English students for 50 cents apiece, and produced a gossip column for the Greenville High School newspaper, but when he left to attend the University of North Carolina, Chapel Hill, Percy turned to science, convinced at the time, he recalled, "that scientific truth was the only truth worth pursuing". He received his undergraduate degree in chemistry in 1937, and went on to obtain his medical diploma from the College of Physicians and Surgeons at New York's Columbia University in 1941.

While he attended medical school, Percy had become greatly interested in psychology, undergoing three years of Freudian psychoanalysis himself in his quest for knowledge of the human mind and its desires. He also discovered a minor quirk in his own nature: while New York was filled with concert-halls and theatres, Percy found himself spending most of his leisure time at the cinemas in nearby Washington Heights. Years later, he would draw on this obsession and use it as a trait for the main character in his first novel, *The Moviegoer.*

In the meantime, however, the young doctor took a job in a pathology lab in New York's Bellevue Hospital. His work entailed doing autopsies, including working with bodies of down-and-outs who had died of chronic diseases. Soon, Percy himself was afflicted with tuberculosis — at that time still a very serious illness — and was forced to spend the next two years of his life in the Trudeau Sanitorium on Saranac Lake in the Adirondacks in upstate New York. His medical career had ended almost before it had begun.

Yet if his body was unfit for work, there was nothing at all wrong with Percy's mind. He put his enforced rest to good use, reading everything he could get his hands on, including a great deal of philosophy; the works of Camus, Kierkegaard, Heidigger, Sartre and Dostoevsky held a special fascination for him. Soon, the young man's ideas of life and what he wanted out of it had begun to change. As he wrote in an article in *Book Week* in 1966,

> What began to interest me was not the physiological and pathological processes within man's body, but the problem of man himself, the nature and destiny of man; specifically and more immediately, the predicament of man in a modern technological society...If the first great intellectual discovery of my life was the beauty of the scientific method, surely the second was the discovery of the singular predicament of man in the very world which has been transformed by science.

This statement could almost be taken as Percy's "signature tune", for the crux of each of his books focuses on man's "outsider" status in the modern world he has helped to create. During his time in the sanitorium, Percy's thoughts and interests turned seriously to writing. By the time he was released, Uncle Will had died, leaving him a legacy and with it, the freedom to change his career path. In his own words, Percy had decided to "think about the curiousness of man's condition and perhaps even to write about it." He left the North, moved to New Orleans where he embraced the Catholic faith, and eventually settled in Covington, Louisiana, a small town on the other side of Lake Ponchartrain, roughly 27 miles from New Orleans. He married Mary Bernice Townsend during 1946.

It was 20 years, however, before Percy's first book-length work appeared on the public shelves. He worked on his writing slowly and thoughtfully, at first producing articles for philosophical, psychiatric and literary journals; on the philosophical front, his work centred mainly on Kierkegaard. He *was* working on fiction, too, but only in so much as he wrote two manuscripts, considered them worthless, and abandoned them. According to Martin Luschei in *The Sovereign Wayfarer,* Percy's breakthrough occurred in the 1960s when he finally discovered his own voice, "a laconic tone that owes something to Camus". It was this style, Luschei states, that allowed the writer "to treat his recurring themes without Faulknerian or Wolfean excesses." The result of finding his voice was *The Moviegoer,* which Percy completed in slightly more than a year.

Percy himself explained the genesis of the novel: "One day I decided to write a novel about a young man who had all the advantages of a cultivated, old-line Southern family, a feel for science and art, a liking for girls, sports cars, and the ordinary things of the culture, but who nevertheless feels himself quite alienated from both worlds, the old South and the new America." Percy had sent this story to publisher Alfred Knopf, where editor Stanley Kauffman coached Percy through four additional drafts of the manuscript. When the published version finally appeared in 1961, it sent shock-waves through the publishing world by winning the prestigious National Book Award — an almost unheard-of feat for a first novel. Walker Percy had come late to writing, but the wait was worth it.

The Moviegoer tells the story of Binx Bolling, a young stockbroker who, although materially prosperous, is spiritually dead. He seeks solace in obsessive cinema-going and through womanizing, but eventually, when he falls in love with his cousin Kate, who is even more neurotic than he is, the two of them manage to find a type of peace and solace through caring for one another. The novel owes much to Albert Camus's *L'Etranger* (*The Stranger*), and essentially works through the question Percy had once proposed in an essay: "Why does man feel so sad in the twentieth century?" It was evidently a question bothering many people in the US at the time — at least in the eyes of Lewis Gannett, Herbert Gold and Jean Stafford, the judges for the National Book Award. When bestowing the prize on the book, they stated that *The Moviegoer* was "a truthful novel with shocks of recognition and spasms of nostalgia for every — or nearly every — American."

Despite the fact that his books are set in the South and deal in part with southern characterizations, it is this universal quality, these "national shocks of recognition" that place Percy outside the rather suspect label of a "southern writer" (Alfred Kazin dubbed him the "satiric Dostoevsky of the bayou"). Even as they struggle with universal problems, Percy's works are full of humour and social observation of all of contemporary America; they are also imbued with solutions — albeit imperfect — to many of his neurotic characters' problems. As the author himself put it, they are "chiefly diagnostic and therapeutic" novels.

The Last Gentleman, Percy's second (and many would say, his finest) novel appeared in 1966. Like *The Moviegoer,* the book centres on a neurotically disturbed individual — this time Will Barrett — who suffers from a strange mixture of amnesia and *deja vu,* qualities which suggest Percy's fundamental premise of simultaneous dislocation and familiarity. When Barrett re-emerges in *The Second Coming,* the sequel to *The Last Gentleman,* he is still disturbed and dislocated, since this time he is a victim of aphasia.

In his third novel, *Love in the Ruins* (which its author subtitled *The Adventures of a Bad Catholic at a Time Near the End of the World*), Percy deviated somewhat from his theme of misplaced man. Instead, he turned the theme on its head; his character, Dr Thomas Moore, is a fictitious descendant of the sixteenth-century British saint, and of him Percy declared: "It's the rest of the world that's alienated from him, and from what he knows is right. It's a question of 'who's crazy here?'"

Even so, critics such as the *New Republic*'s Jonathan Yardly noted the underlying, ever-present theme. "Walker Percy's third novel confirms once and for all what his first two strongly suggested: there is not a better comic writer around. That *Love in the Ruins* is also a deeply primed protest against modern vulgarity in all its forms, and a moving expression of cautious hope, gives breadth and power to the novel and emphasizes the persistent seriousness of its comedy." *Newsweek* agreed, describing Percy as "the chief diagnostician of our American *anomie.*"

Two later novels — *Lancelot* and *The Thanatos Syndrome* — were not so generally well received, although they, too, continue to explore the topic of dislocation. There is a subtle difference between them and their predecessors, however. As Andrew Rosenheim has written in London's *Independent* newspaper, "both [novels] seem to suggest an affection for a hierarchical segregationist south which Percy's younger self would have abhorred." In addition to numerous articles, the author also produced two non-fiction works on his philosophic meditations; these are *The Message in the Bottle* and *Lost in the Cosmos.*

Despite his fame, Walker Percy continued to live a quiet, secluded life in Covington, Louisiana, with his wife and two daughters. He eventually outgrew his cinematic obsession, but kept a habit of leaving the television on with the sound turned off. "I'm afraid the world will end when I'm not looking", he explained.

"He must be counted as one of the profoundest and most telling satirists of his time, and as a novelist whose work will always be highly valued and studied", surmised Percy's obituarist in the London *Times.* To this obituarist, that is a much better definition of Walker Percy than that of just another "southern writer".

Born Walker Percy. **Parents** Leroy Pratt, lawyer, and Martha Susan (Phinizy) Percy; on parents' death, adopted by William Alexander Percy, writer. **Marriage** Mary Bernice Townsend, medical technician, 1946. **Children** Mary and Ann. **Education** University of North Carolina, Chapel Hill, BA in chemistry, 1937; Columbia University, New York, MD, 1941. **Career** Intern, Bellevue Hospital, New York, 1942; contracted tuberculosis, 1943, treated at Trudeau Sanitorium, 1943–44; lecturer in pathology, Columbia Medical School, 1945; retired from medicine, 1945; converted to Roman Catholicism, 1946; published first novel, *The Moviegoer,* 1961. **Offices and memberships** Fellow, American Academy of Arts and Sciences; member, American Academy. **Awards and honours** National Book Award, for *The Moviegoer,* 1962; American Academy grant, 1967; National Catholic Book award, for *Love in the Ruins,* 1972; National Book Award nomination, for *The Second Coming,* 1980; *Los Angeles Times* award for non-fiction, 1983; St Louis Literary award, 1985. **Novels** *The Moviegoer,* 1961; *The Last Gentleman,* 1966; *Love in the*

Ruins: The Adventures of a Bad Catholic at a Time Near the End of the World, 1971; *Lancelot,* 1977; *The Second Coming,* 1980; *The Thanatos Syndrome,* 1987. **Other works** *The Message in the Bottle: How Queer Man Is, How Queer Language Is, and What One Has to Do with the Other,* 1975; *Lost in the Cosmos: The Last Self-Help Book,* 1983; *Novel-Writing in an Apocalyptic Time,* 1984; *Conversations with Walker Percy* (edited by Lewis A. Lawson and Victor A. Kramer), 1985. **Articles** (include) "Symbol as Need", *Thought,* 1954; "Symbol as Hermeneutic in Existentialism: A Possible Bridge from Empiricism", *Philosophy and Phenomenological Research,* 1956; "The Man on the Train: Three Existential Modes", *Partisan Review,* 1956; "The Coming Crisis in Psychiatry", *America,* 1957; "Semiotic and a Theory of Knowledge", *Modern Schoolman,* 1957; "The Act of Naming", *Forum* (University of Houston), 1957; "Metaphor as Mistake", *Sewanee Review,* 1958; "Symbol, Consciousness, and Intersubjectivity", *Journal of Philosophy,* 1958; "The Loss of the Creature", *Forum* (University of Houston), 1958; "Culture: The Antinomy of the Scientific Method", *New Scholasticism,* 1958; "The Message in the Bottle", *Thought,* 1959; "Naming and Being", *Personalist,* 1960; "The Symbolic Structure of Interpersonal Process", *Psychiatry: A Journal for the Study of Interpersonal Processes,* 1961; "From Facts to Fiction," *Writer,* 1967; "Notes for a Novel about the End of the World," *Katallagete,* 1967–68; "Toward a Triadic Theory of Meaning", *Psychiatry: A Journal for the Study of Interpersonal Processes,* 1972. **Manuscript collection** University of North Carolina, Chapel Hill. **Cause of death** Cancer, at age 73. **Further reading** W.A. Percy, *Lanterns on the Levee* (essays), 1941; Martin Luschei, *The Sovereign Wayfarer: Walker Percy's Diagnosis of the Malaise,* 1972; Robert Coles, *Walker Percy: An American Search,* 1978; Panthea Reid Broughton (editor), *The Art of Walker Percy: Stratagems for Being,* 1979; Jac Tharpe (editor), *Walker Percy: Art and Ethics,* 1980; Jac Tharpe, *Walker Percy,* 1983; Victor A. Kramer, *Andrew Lytle, Walker Percy, Peter Taylor: A Reference Guide,* 1983; L. Jerome Taylor, *Walker Percy's Heroes: A Kierkegaardian Self,* 1984; Patricia Lewis Poteat, *Walker Percy and the Old Modern Age: Reflections on Language, Argument, and the Telling of Stories,* 1985; *Contemporary Novelists,* 1986; John Edward Hardy, *The Fiction of Walker Percy,* 1987; Lewis A. Lawson (editor), *Following Percy: Essays on Walker Percy's Works,* 1988; Linda W. Hobson, *Understanding Walker Percy,* 1988.

PATRIARCH PIMEN

Russian Orthodox Priest

Born **Bogorodsk, Russia, 23 July 1910**

Died **Moscow, USSR, 3 May 1990**

His Holiness Patriarch Pimen of Moscow and all Russia was head of the Orthodox Church for 18 undistinguished years, during which he continued the policy of compromise with the atheist state adopted by his two immediate predecessors. Although there were no openly anti-religious attacks to match the fervour of those launched by Stalin and Khrushchev, during Pimen's patriarchate, priests who did not follow the party line still faced imprisonment, exile and incarceration in mental asylums. All aspects of church life including decisions of the Holy Synod and episcopal appointments were controlled by the state-run Council for Religious Affairs. Religious teaching was forbidden. KGB infiltration into the ranks of the priesthood was widely suspected.

Pimen generally maintained a low profile as patriarch. He travelled little, avoided public statements and, in audiences with foreign churchmen, always defended the Soviet government. In

1973 he angered many when he told the World Council of Churches of the "unquestionable merits" of the Soviet way of life. "The social evils so typical for the life of many people today just cannot occur within our social structure." As Solzhenitsyn complained in a "Lenten Letter" circulated a year after Pimen's appointment in 1971, "the Russian church has its indignant opinion on every evil in faraway Asia and Africa but on domestic ills, nothing, nothing at all."

Pimen's potentially greatest moment came in April 1988 with the beginnings of *glasnost* and an historic meeting between himself and the Soviet President in the Kremlin, ostensibly to prepare for the church's millenium celebrations the following year. But here, once again, those who had expected some plain-speaking from the patriarch were disappointed. Pimen had nothing but unqualified support to offer the "architect of *perestroika*" and praise for the hitherto obstructive Council for Religious Affairs in their efforts to ease the Church's difficulties. Father Gleb Yakunin, a dissident priest and former religious prisoner, who had called in March for the Patriarch's resignation on grounds of incompetence and ill-health, circulated in disgust a document entitled "Patriarchate or Matriarchate" accusing Pimen of having fallen totally under the domination of his secretary, Nadezhda Nikolaevna Dyachenko, "Nadezhda of Moscow and all Russia" as he mockingly named her.

To judge the Patriarch in this way is, however, just a little too easy. As Metropolitan Anthony of Sourozh, head of the Russian Orthodox Church in Great Britain asks: "How can we assess the men and women of this generation? We in the West have no notion of what it meant to grow up and live under the shadow of death, under the threat of arrest and torture."

Sergei Mikhailovich Izvekov, as Pimen was born, grew up during the worst of Stalin's "Terror". At the age of 17 he took the surely brave decision to become a monk and, three years later, to be ordained a priest. There is a gap in his official biography of some 13 years from 1932. During this time he is believed to have served in the Army and to have been arrested twice. He is thought to have spent around ten years in prison and labour camp and to have suffered greatly for the faith which it is clear he never lost. It also seems clear that, as patriarch, he became increasingly lonely and isolated, felt himself imprisoned behind the bars of a "golden cage" and that, by the time the changes heralded by *perestroika* were introduced he was too old and ill to handle them.

To judge the life of any priest solely in political terms is also inapposite and, in this case, is to fall into the Soviet trap of seeing all life in political and material terms. The task of the patriarch, Metropolitan Anthony insists, is "to intercede for the people before God". And to estimate the value of a life devoted primarily to prayer, fasting and intercession is, of course, impossible. Anyone, however, who attended any of the packed and moving services of the Orthodox Church during the Brezhnev era in Russia cannot fail to have been affected. Here, in the midst of the most openly atheist state of all time, was concrete, living evidence of the prevailing life of the spirit, of the triumph of faith against adversity. However compromised the church might have become, of the congregations' sincerity there could be no question.

Pimen was only the fourteenth patriarch the Russian church has had. He and his predecessors took the path of political compromise in the historic knowledge that the patriarchate, suppressed under Peter the Great in the eighteenth century and restored only in 1917, had also remained vacant under Stalin from 1927 until 1943. Nor should it be forgotten that the path chosen by Pimen, Alexi and Sergius was not supported by all Orthodox priests, many of whom chose instead to go underground, to hold forbidden services in the secret "catacomb churches" and to keep alive the spirit of dissidence and courage.

Those who have hoped for a change of direction in the patriarchate after Pimen's death seem likely, however, to be disappointed. The new patriarch, Alexi, enthroned in June 1990, is an Estonian of German origin, distinguished, like Pimen, by his unquestioning support for Brezhnev and his silence, even under *perestroika,* on all questions of religious persecution.

Born Sergei Mikhailovich Izvekov. **Father** Civil servant. **Military service** Russian Army, World War II. **Career** Monk, Russian Orthodox Church, 1927–32; deacon, 1931; ordained priest, 1932;

abbot, 1946; father superior: Pskov Monastery of the Caves, 1949–53, Archimandrite, 1950, Trinity-St Sergius Monastery Zagorsk, 1954–57; consecrated Bishop of Balta, 1957; head of patriarchate administration, 1959; archbishop, 1959; Archbishop of Tula and Belev, 1961; Metropolitan of Leningrad and Ladoga, 1961–63; Metropolitan of Krutitsky and Kolomna, 1963–71; Patriarch of Moscow and All Russia, 1971–90; elected to Congress of People's Deputies, 1989–90. **Related activities** Member, World Peace Council. **Offices and memberships** Honorary member, Academy Senate, Leningrad and Moscow theological academys. **Awards and honours** "Peace Fighter", Gold Medal, Soviet Peace Committee; Order of St Sergius of Radonezh, USSR, 1979; Order of Friendship of the Peoples, 1980; Order of the Red Banner of Labour, 1985. **Cause of death** Diabetes and cancer, at age 79.

EDWARD PIPER

British Painter, Photographer and Graphic Designer

***Born* 12 November 1938**

***Died* Frome, Somerset, 11 May 1990**

"Hard to come to terms with the cessation, far too young, of this vigorous and courteous man-for-all-seasons", wrote the novelist Fay Weldon on Edward Piper's death. Like his father, the distinguished painter John Piper, he was a late developer, attaining artistic maturity and critical recognition only in the last 15 years of his life. His death at 51 cut his career tragically short.

Growing up the son of a famous painter was, as Edward Piper later acknowledged, both a help and a hindrance. John and Myfanwy Piper provided a remarkable family background; Edward's earliest memories include his father and godfather, poet John Betjeman, discussing Anglican churches, and his mother talking on the kitchen telephone to Benjamin Britten about a libretto she was writing for him. Edward was passionately interested in life drawing from an early age and at eight had already resolved to become a painter. His schooling at Lancing College was followed by a year at the Bath Academy of Art, studying under Howard Hodgkin, after which he attended the prestigious Slade School of Art in London.

At the Slade, Piper was later to admit that he felt "depressed and repressed", unable to please his tutors. He noted that "Like many people since, they always inferred that my work was lightweight. 'Carry it further' they used to say, but where is this 'further'?". For Piper, joy and beauty had not been annihilated in the age of the bomb, but his innately lighthearted, even frivolous, approach was out of step with artistic fashion in the early 1960s. Suppressing his natural inclinations therefore, he painted in a "hard-edge" Pop style, exhibiting in 1965 at London's Institute of Contemporary Arts. His inherent love of life drawing was never wholly stifled, though, and was gradually to reassert itself.

To support himself and his young family Piper became a freelance graphic designer and photographer. His photographs appeared in a wide range of publications, from adverts and cookery books to the high-class magazine *The Tatler*. Most notable are those illustrating the Shell County Guides to Britain, co-edited by his father and Betjeman. Spanning some 20 years, they are poetic and evocative records of the country's topography which reflect his painterly vision. Edward Piper's stature as a photographer is still largely unrecognized, although in 1985 he had an exhibition at the Fox Talbot Museum in Lacock.

It was in the 1970s that Piper evolved a personal style in painting which finally brought him commercial success and the recognition not only of private collectors but of such public institutions as London's Tate Gallery. Between 1975 and 1987 he had 14 exhibitions, including three joint shows with his father. His lifelong love of the nude provided the inspiration for works in which voluptuous naked or semi-clothed young girls relax in sensuous poses amongst vases of bright flowers, before mirrors and open windows, in light-filled rooms. His second great love, landscape, stimulated by his work as a photographer, also found expression in his new style, whether the countryside of south-west England, where he lived, or Mediterranean France, Spain and Italy, which he visited increasingly in later years.

The light and fresh mood of Piper's paintings is partly the product of his exuberant vision and partly of his technique. The immediacy of his execution, the strength of his line and his free use of water-colour washes are traits inherited from his father. However, in its joy, vitality and brilliant colour Edward's work is the complete antithesis of the austere John's, and is often likened to that of Dufy and Matisse. He would commence by brushing on a loose water-colour wash onto which detail was then superimposed in bold, fluid black lines of varying thickness, while whites were created by areas of paper left blank. Piper possessed a quick and perceptive eye, and — like Rodin, another high priest of the female nude — used the inspiration of models moving around his studio to produce a succession of swift brush-drawings remarkable for their directness. Piper's ideal was what he called a "just-fallen-onto-the-page look". "Generally my work comes together like a jig-saw", he explained in an interview about a year before his death, "Each part coming together gradually and finally hoping that the last piece fits...[It] is ruined by reworking, the alterations seem so obvious...My work is unintellectual; it is a direct response to the subject."

The gentle hedonism which characterizes Piper's paintings extended to his life-style. With his wife Prue he created an idyllic home in the disused laundry-complex of an old Somerset manor-house, lovingly restored, with a garden in which new ideas were continually evolving, most recently for twin lakes with a John Piperish tower as a backdrop. For recreation, Piper, whose energy and talent were super-abundant, played jazz piano with friends in pubs and clubs. Blessed with a cheerful disposition, generosity, and optimism, he never resented his failure to equal his father in reputation, or his own tardy recognition by the art world.

Born Edward Piper. **Parents** John, artist, and Myfanwy, writer, Piper. **Marriage** Prue Mackillop, 1961. **Children** Luke and James. **Education** Lancing College, West Sussex, 1951–56; studied painting with Howard Hodgkin, Bath Academy of Art, Corsham, Wiltshire, 1956–57; Slade School of Art, London, 1957–61. **Career** Worked in the "Pop" style; first exhibition, Institute of Contemporary Arts, 1965; took up photography; photographer, Shell County Guides series, 1969–89; advertising photographer; first one-man show, Marjorie Parr Gallery, London, 1975; shifted to painting, especially nudes, flowers, landscapes and faces, from 1975; founded own jazz group, Edward Piper and His Friends. **Exhibitions** (include) Institute of Contemporary Arts, 1965; Marjorie Parr Gallery, London, 1975; Sherborne School, Dorset, 1981; Fox Talbot Museum of Photography, Lacock, 1985; Beaux Arts Gallery, Bath, 1985, 1987; Catto Gallery, Hampstead, 1987. **Paintings** (include) *Model and Vase of Flowers,* 1985; *Reclining Nude,* 1985; *Reflected Nude and Flowers,* 1986; *Jorox,* 1988; *Interior and Model,* 1988; *Standing Nude,* 1988; *Nude Reflected in Mirror,* 1988; *Malaga,* 1988. **Book illustrated** *Rings of Stone* by Aubrey Burl. **Cause of death** Cancer, at age 51.

DAVID RAPPAPORT

British Actor

***Born* London, England, 23 November 1952**

***Died* Los Angeles, California, 2 May 1990**

The creative temperament often appears to thrive best when faced with difficulty and the acting profession has attracted its fair share of those who have surmounted personal obstacles to achieve success. David Rappaport's "difficulty" was achondroplasia — a medical condition that caused him to stop growing when he was eight years old. His arrested height (3 feet, 11 inches) was to remain the bane of his life thereafter, but it was also to boost his career in directions he had never anticipated.

Born in the East End of London, the son of a Jewish taxi-driver turned schoolteacher, Rappaport himself went into teaching after gaining a degree in psychology from Bristol University. At the time of his "discovery" as an actor, he was working at a junior school in Halifax where most of his pupils were taller than him. A friend from his university days introduced him to the director Ken Campbell who was desperate to find a tiny actor for the role of Markoff Chaney in the 1976 production of the science-fiction epic *Illuminatus* in Liverpool. Rappaport got the part and was subsequently declared "a sensation". Sir Peter Hall, then director of the National Theatre, invited the production to the National's Cottesloe auditorium and later wrote in his diary: "Dave Rappaport's 20-minute turn on his own...is amazing. [In] his final self-phobia...he hurls himself around the stage trying to get away from his own diminutive body, his own tiny unwanted limbs."

Affliction had become attribute and Rappaport's acting career took off. Hall cast him as the dwarf in *Volpone,* in which he performed with John Gielgud and Paul Scofield, and the favourable reviews he received led to a constant supply of "quality" work. Major roles in *Doctor Faustus* and *Exit the King,* both at the Lyric Theatre in Hammersmith, London, followed and from then on he juggled a variety of commitments on stage and television. He was a popular performer on the children's programme *Tiswas,* a series that also found great favour with adults, he made a number of appearances opposite Spike Milligan on the anarchic comedy series *Not the 9 O'Clock News,* and he was the genial host of *Grapevine,* a community affairs series.

Like the other media, the cinema was not slow to recognize Rappaport's talent. His early films included *Cuba* and *Time Bandits,* but it was *The Bride,* released in 1985, in which he appeared with Jennifer Beals and Sting, that brought him to the attention of an international audience. Indeed, his numerous chat show appearances to promote the film in the US won him many new admirers. In typical self-effacing style, he made light of his diminutive stature. When asked, "Do you find any difficulties here with being, er, unusual?", he replied, "What, you mean my accent?"

In 1986 US television gave him his own 26-part series — *The Wizard* — in which he played a wacky scientist making high-tech inventions. Despite good reviews, the series did not catch on and, much to Rappaport's dismay, it was abandoned after only a short run. This was followed by perhaps his most famous role — that of "Mighty Mouth", a hard-hitting lawyer in the glossy series *LA Law.*

All appeared to be going well; work was steady, critical acclaim had been achieved and Hollywood was his oyster. None the less, David Rappaport was depressed. He wanted to be "a regular, boring, normal person" who did not have to suffer the tyranny of discrimination, but his lot was "to be unique". To add to his sadness, his marriage to a "full-sized" woman had foundered and he saw little of his "perfectly normal" son, Joseph. A first suicide attempt in early March was thwarted by police who found his comatose body in a fume-filled car and resuscitated him.

Unfortunately, the depression did not lift and Rappaport's second attempt to end his life was successful.

"The small man's Cary Grant", as he liked to describe himself, was a vivid and intelligent character actor who broke through the stereotyping that had always dogged people of his size. But even though he reached enviable heights in the acting profession, he could do nothing to achieve the height to which he truly aspired.

Born David Rappaport. **Father** Taxi-driver and school teacher. **Children** One son, Joseph. **Education** Bristol University, BA in child psychology. **Emigration** Left England for US, 1986. **Career** Junior-school teacher, Halifax; first stage appearance, *Illuminatus,* Liverpool, 1976; first television series, *Tiswas;* first film appearance, *Mysteries;* created one-man cabaret show, *Little Brother Is Watching You.* **Other activities** Founder, Free and Independent Republic of Frestonia, Notting Hill, minister of state for foreign affairs. **Stage** (includes) *Illuminatus,* Liverpool and London; *Dr Faustus,* London; *Volpone,* London; *Exit the King,* London; *The Secret Policeman's Ball* London, (also filmed). **Films** (include) *Cuba,* 1979; *Time Bandits,* 1981; *The Bride,* 1985. **Television** *The Wizard,* 1986–87; *LA Law,* 1988–89; *Opinions,* 1990; also: *Tiswas, Not the 9 O'Clock News, Grapevine, Unfair Exchanges, Robin of Sherwood.* **Cause of death** Suicide by shooting, at age 37.

MAJOR PAT REID

British Escape Officer, Engineer and Author

Born **Ranchi, India, 13 November 1910**

Died **Frenchay, England, 22 May 1990**

In 1973, BBC Television put on the series *Colditz.* It became one of their most popular ever shows, attracting audiences of around 19 million, and it was based on the wartime experience and later writing of Major Patrick "Pat" Reid — soldier, diplomat, author and civil engineer.

He was born at the end of the Edwardian era and educated in its traditions, at Clongowes Wood College, County Kildare, Ireland and Wimbledon College, London. He wanted to be an engineer and served a pupillage with a leading firm after gaining his Bachelor of Science degree at King's College, London. When World War II broke out in 1939, Reid joined the Royal Army Service Corps as an ammunition officer. His conventional military career was short; in May 1940 he was captured by the Germans and sent to a prisoner-of-war camp at Laufen, near the border between Austria and Germany. By September, he'd escaped, disguised as a woman, with several colleagues. Within a week however they were recaptured, and this time Reid was assigned to Oflag IVC, the maximum-security prison-camp at Colditz, in Saxony.

The camp was situated within a vast Gothic *Schloss* on a crag above a river and a village. This sounds story-book stuff; and in part, this is the area of Reid's imagination which was stimulated in what followed. By his own account, the "Boys' Own" tales of World War I, on which he'd been brought up, fired his imagination again. He became the prisoners' escape officer, whose job it was to scrutinize and assess any escape plans put forward, and to calculate their practicality and their probable impact on those who remained. Also he had to avoid clashes between plans and factions, as there were several nationalities among the detainees. These delicate arts he mastered, together with lock-breaking, key-making and other essential skills. By the end of 1942, eleven British officers had escaped to friendly or neutral countries (though pro-rata, the Dutch were the most successful fugitives). In October of that year, Reid and three companions left Colditz with *panache.* After getting into the German part of the castle, they crossed floodlit yards patrolled by sentries and made off under their jailers' noses. Within three days, they made the 400 miles to neutral Switzerland.

Reid stayed in Switzerland until the end of the war, nominally as assistant military attaché in Berne; in reality he was involved in intelligence work and in organizing other escapes. In recognition of his achievements, he was awarded the Military Cross and an MBE. After the war he was attached to the British embassy in Ankara, Turkey, as first secretary (commercial) and in 1949, he became a chief administrator with the Organisation for European Economic Cooperation in Paris, France.

His book, *The Colditz Story*, appeared in 1953. "The sympathetic style of his writing and his natural gift in recording dialogue made his books popular nationwide", as one friendly critic noted. A more astringent tone is heard elsewhere: "Reid's original mighty best-seller was a cross between *Tom Brown's Schooldays,* the outpourings of Frank Richards, and those war comics full of squareheads in coalscuttle helmets shouting *Schweinhund.*" It was certainly a successful formula, selling like hot cakes, spawning board games, "escaper" weekends in the country and a film in 1955. Reid followed it with a series of reminiscence-cum-adventure books around the Colditz theme, and encouraged his ex-adversary Hauptmann Reinhold Eggers, security officer at Colditz, to produce two books on the German side of the story (published only in Britain!)

Reid was now established as a house-builder and a consulting engineer, though frequently at Colditz-related lectures and publicity events. Interest reached a new crescendo with the television series (in which the escape officer was based directly on Reid) mentioned above. This in turn called forth opinion which accused Reid of capitalizing on experiences that some would prefer to forget, of marginalizing the achievements of other escapers, and of mythologizing the whole business. He refuted this: he had not published until a decade after the events he described, so anybody wishing to enter the lists had their sporting chance. Moreover there had been no word of direct criticism from his Colditz colleagues, and even in the closing years of his life, frail but still mentally alert, he would make a determined effort to attend the Colditz Veterans' reunion.

Until unification, Colditz was under East German government, which did not care to acknowledge some recent history. The local museum curator was told to destroy his collection of escape memorabilia, but true to the spirit of things, he hid it in the roof and it survived. At the time of writing, it is not entirely clear what will happen, but it is quite possible that the ancient pile from which Reid strove so hard to be free may yet become his monument.

Born Patrick Robert Reid. **Parents** John and Alice Mabel (Daniell) Reid. **Marriages** 1) Jane Cabot, 1943 (divorced 1966); 2) Mrs Mary Stewart Cunliffe-Lister, 1977 (died 1978); 3) Mrs Nicandra Hood, 1982. **Children** Three sons and two daughters, from first marriage. **Education** Clongowes Wood College, County Kildare; Wimbledon College, London; King's College, University of London, BSc, 1932. **Military service** Captain, Royal Army Service Corps, 2nd Division, ammunition officer, British Expeditionary Force, France, 1939–40; prisoner-of-war, Laufen, 1940, escape officer, Colditz, 1940–42, escaped, 1942; assistant military attaché, Berne, 1943–46. **Career** Pupillage, Sir Alex Gibb & Partners, 1934–37; first secretary (commercial), British Embassy, Ankara, 1946–49; chief administrator, Organisation for European Economic Co-operation, Paris, 1949–52; published first book, *The Colditz Story,* 1953; *Colditz* filmed, 1955; house-builder; director, Richard Costain (Middle East) Limited, 1959–62; W.S. Atkins and Partners, Consulting Engineers, 1962–63; *The Colditz Story* televised, 1973–74; managing director, Kem Estates Limited. **Other activities** Prospective Conservative Party parliamentary candidate, Dartford and Erith, 1953–55. **Offices and memberships** Associate member, Institution of Civil Engineers, 1936. **Awards and honours** Member of the Order of the British Empire, 1940; Military Cross, 1943. **Publications** *The Colditz Story,* 1953; *The Latter Days,* 1955; *Colditz* (omnibus edition of *The Colditz Story* and *The Latter Days*), 1962; (with Sir Olaf Caroe and Sir Thomas Rapp) *From Nile to Indus,* 1960; *Winged Diplomat,* 1962; *Economic Survey of Northern Nigeria,* 1962; *My Favourite Escape Stories,* 1975; *Colditz — The Full Story,* 1984. **Cause of death** Undisclosed, at age 79. **Further reading** Reinhold Eggers, *Colditz. The German Story* (translated and edited by Howard Gee), 1961.

BILL SOWERBUTTS

British Gardening Expert and Broadcaster

***Born* 1911**

***Died* Ashton-under-Lyne, Manchester, 28 May 1990**

Bill Sowerbutts, with his down-to-earth manner, northern English humour and his practical gardening wisdom, had a large and loyal following among British radio audiences as one of the most popular members of the team of gardening experts in the long-running Sunday afternoon BBC radio programme, *Gardeners' Question Time.* This ever-popular show began back in 1947 to help the public deal with the post-war food shortage and to continue the spirit of the wartime "Dig for Victory" campaign. From that very first show, Sowerbutts remained on its panel for 36 years, taking part in over 1500 broadcasts and answering an estimated 15,000 questions on gardening put to the team of experts by live audiences, as the travelling show moved around the country. Bill Sowerbutts always had bold and forthright advice to give, preferring to say "muck" rather than the more polite "farmyard manure" and "leaf" instead of "foliage" — and he often delighted in mispronouncing the plants' Latin names. He always relished a good constructive argument and radio listeners much enjoyed the lively banter between the three panellists, which sometimes drew in the questioner as well.

Like gardening itself, *Gardeners' Question Time* became a British institution, with its unchanging format and everyday conversational style, seeming to speak directly to the ordinary listener. Its countryman's subject matter seemed close to home and reassuringly safe compared with the changing world beyond the cosy confines of the garden. Perhaps this was especially so in the 1950s and 1960s before gardening, too, became controversial in its use of chemical fertilizers and pesticides and more linked with concerns about the environment in general. In the programme, questions would be asked by members of the audience, summarized by the chairman and then answered by panel members in turn. Questions ranged from the mundane to the exotic, including such subjects as "white mould on onions", "growing trees from fruit stones" and "orchids in unheated greenhouses". The programme appealed alike to passionate gardeners and to reluctant ones, to those who dutifully dug the garden or mowed the lawn at weekends, and to many who had no garden at all. The first show in 1947 had gone out from the Broad Oak Hotel at Ashton-under-Lyne, the town near Manchester where Bill Sowerbutts had grown up. Two of the programme's three regular panellists, Bill Sowerbutts and Fred Loads, took part in that first programme and were joined in 1950 by Alan Gemmell. Fred Loads was an immensely experienced and dedicated gardener with a deep knowledge of gardening folklore, Professor Alan Gemmell knew much about the scientific side of gardening and, aided by his academic training, was skilful at drawing information together into a coherent whole. Bill Sowerbutts, with his dry Manchester sense of humour and his homespun philosophy, had a shrewd business sense and thorough knowledge of how the horticultural world operated. The three men complemented each other admirably, broadcasting together for over 30 years. The deceptively easy manner of both team and chairman belied the fact that they were all excellent broadcasters. The two best-known chairmen over the years were Freddy Grisewood and Franklin Englemann, who steered the proceedings for nearly 20 years between them.

Despite his direct manner, Bill Sowerbutts was a man of some complexity. His father was a nurseryman and seedsman and young Bill grew up on the family market garden at Ashton-under-Lyne, absorbing gardening knowledge and tending a large flock of chickens, nursing all the while an ambition to be a journalist. His father's sudden death when Sowerbutts was 16 meant that he was needed to work on the smallholding and to sell the produce, along with gardening equipment, on nearby market stalls in Oldham, Ashton and Rochdale. Dreams of journalism put aside, his involvement in horticulture continued in the Ashton-under-Lyne area and he became a talented vegetable grower — later cultivating two-and-a-half acres at his home — and a good businessman, a skill much needed in the depressed years of the 1930s.

His interests were many and unlike Fred Loads, his colleague on *Gardeners' Question Time,* whose whole life was devoted to gardening, Sowerbutts had other hobbies, including a love of music. Despite enforced piano lessons in his teens, he came to love the piano and wherever that week's *Gardeners' Question Time* was being recorded, in village halls or Women's Institute meeting-rooms, he would search out the piano and could be heard playing Scott Joplin piano rags. He was also a cricket lover: a player in his younger days and then a supporter of the Lancashire and Derbyshire county teams, with weekends away for the radio programme providing the opportunity for long evening conversations on the sport. Sowerbutts was a golfer too and Geoffrey Smith, well known in British gardening circles and a later fellow-panellist on the radio, described the regular search for a good local golf course as the team travelled the country. Smith, a Yorkshireman, became a good friend, despite the older man's Lancashire background — the two counties being traditional rivals — and in later years acted as Sowerbutts's caddy on their golfing expeditions. Apparently Sowerbutts spent the last evening of his life watching the PGA Golf Championship from Wentworth on television. Smith got to know his friend's more ingrained habits on their travels, remembering: "He had his rituals...He always had a glass of two of beer in the evening and the last half-glass always went up to bed with him."

Smith remembered too Sowerbutts's acute mind, saying, "If you dropped your guard for a second and said something silly, he was on it like a terrier." Clay Jones, a later chairman of *Gardeners' Question Time,* said he never knew Sowerbutts to be at a loss when answering the audience's questions. He enjoyed playing up his Manchester accent and his bluff façade and as he rarely smiled, it was sometimes difficult to know whether or not he was joking. He once described how in the depressed 1930s, he used to be careful about choosing which bag to weigh tomatoes in, as some bags were that much heavier than others. On another occasion, when asked to name his favourite flower, he answered "cauliflowers" and when asked to explain his choice, replied that they made him a lot of money. One of his specialities was the loofah. Although he never had the opportunity to answer a radio question on that esoteric subject before his retirement in 1983, six years later, only six months before he died, he was asked to respond to a listener's question on loofahs while sitting in the audience, creating an opportunity for a final guest appearance. Sowerbutts also appeared on the television programme *Gardeners' Direct Line.* The public's fascination with his name and personality caused him to crop up in a popular children's story-book by Raymond Briggs, *Father Christmas Goes on Holiday,* in which he gives advice to Father Christmas as he tends his allotment.

When Bill Sowerbutts died, at the age of 79, his son Peter took over the family business, which includes florist shops. His voice and personality, as well as his knowledge, are much missed by the

British gardening public, for he was, as colleague Geoffrey Smith put it, "a thundering good gardener" and a "thoroughgoing professional both as a gardener and as a broadcaster."

Born William Edmund Sowerbutts. **Father** Nurseryman and seedsman. **Marriage** Doris. **Children** One son, Peter. **Career** Gardener and market trader; first radio appearance, *How Does Your Garden Grow?,* 1947; founder/member, *Gardeners' Question Time,* BBC Radio, 1947–83, final broadcast, 1989; contributor, *Gardeners' Direct Line* television programme. **Television** *Gardeners' Direct Line.* **Radio** *How Does Your Garden Grow?,* 1947; *Gardeners' Question Time,* 1947–83. **Publication** (With Ken Ford, Alan Gemmell and Fred Loads) *Gardeners' Question Time,* 1981. **Cause of death** Undisclosed, at age 79.

TED TINLING

British Dress Designer

***Born* Eastbourne, Sussex, 23 June 1910**

***Died* Cambridge, England, 23 May 1990**

Perversely it was Ted Tinling's own health problems that led to his becoming not only tennis's most famous dress designer but, ultimately, its wit, wisdom and guru.

Born the youngest child of a comfortably off but straitlaced chartered accountant and a free-thinking mother whose interests embraced socialism and birth control, Tinling developed interests unusual for a boy of his time. His hobby was lace-making and he owned the family sewing machine. Such pursuits did not endear him to the conventional heart of his father and there was considerable discord between his parents as a result. His tendency to asthma was probably exacerbated by the friction. Eventually he was taken to live on the French Riviera for the sake of his health.

Financial problems meant that he remained there with only his mother throughout his youth, enjoying a period that, in retrospect, proved a golden time: the era of Gatsby with the Depression yet to come. He developed an interest in tennis and at the age of 13, when he was already a formidable 6 feet tall, was invited to umpire a match for its 24-year-old French star, Suzanne Lenglen. He rapidly became part of the Riviera tennis circuit mixing, playing and umpiring with both the stars and royalty. His father disapproved because tennis was not a team game. His mother, on the other hand, encouraged her son's musical development.

Through music Tinling met and fell in love with a beautiful blonde contralto whom he invited, in 1928, to sing at his mother's funeral. His father's disapproval did not extend to his choice of female companionship. Within a few months Tinling's youthful love had become his stepmother. The idyll was virtually over and the 1929 Wall Street crash sealed its end.

His study of fashion design had already begun, however, and, in 1931, he set up his own design business in London, combining this with holidays of umpiring on both the British and French tennis circuits. Within a year he had premises in London's couturier quarter of Mayfair and a staff of five. This number rose rapidly as the business expanded until, by the time World War II was rumbling on the horizon, his reputation was on a par with those of designers to royalty such as Norman Hartnell and Hardy Amies. All were immensely original and innovative.

His war service was with the Intelligence Corps in which he rose to the rank of lieutenant-colonel but it was marred by an earlier rejection. A friend had arranged an introduction to a regiment. Being asked to join a regiment had more social cachet than conscription. However he was forced to withdraw his application because, as he later said, "I was told that if I didn't...I was going to be automatically accused of being a raging queer because I was a dressmaker." He never felt that his private life should be a public matter.

After the war he returned to designing but with a wider perspective. Then came the one incident which made his name a household word but which also led to a severing of his relationship with the British Lawn Tennis Championships at Wimbledon, in London's south-west, for many years. Nobody tells it better than Tinling himself.

> In 1949, out of the blue, I get a letter from this character we had all read about, Gussy Moran, who had been a sort of pin-up in California, a Forces sweetheart, the whole lot. She's got big Lana Turner tits and gorgeous long legs and she walks like she's walking on rubber balls, the whole bit. Yes, and she was a good player. She writes to me...So we made her a beautiful white dress with some satin on it that glittered along the bottom, which reflected her shimmering...And she said, "What am I going to wear underneath?" I said, "Well, it's nothing to do with me. It's not my area."

In the upshot Tinling allowed himself to be persuaded and produced some lace-trimmed briefs out of left-overs, only to learn that he had introduced vulgarity and sin into the game — he had "attracted the eye to the sexual area". As a result he received another stupendous rejection: he was barred from Wimbledon for 33 years. Only in 1982, after he'd proved himself as a master of almost all aspects of the game in the United States, was he welcomed back as head of Wimbledon's liaison committee. But the "Gorgeous Gussy" drama launched him into his new career of sports designer, the roots of which had been sown by his admiration for the soft silk frocks worn by his original heroine, Suzanne Lenglen.

"Really my dresses were designed to reveal in glimpses, as were Lenglen's", he said. "When she bent down for a low backhand her *décolleté* revealed things. She was a mistress of discovering just how far you could go on a suggestive basis."

Tinling gradually incorporated more from show business both into his creations and the sport as a whole, particularly in the US when he became official designer to the Virginia Slim's women's tournaments and where he will be remembered for dressing Rosie Casals in black sequins. Later he put the Wightman Cup players into bold dresses of Stars and Stripes. He had moved a long way from Wimbledon, where women may wear any colour providing it's white.

Gradually the United States became Tinling's home. He settled permanently in Philadelphia and, despite his sometimes failing health, continued with his unique career of diplomatic trouble-shooter on the international tennis circuit as well as the game's respected and amusing ambassador in the media. As was said at his memorial service in London, he was the historian, the measuring stick and the conscience of tennis.

Born Cuthbert Tinling. **Father** Chartered accountant. **Emigration** Left England for US, 1975. **Military service** Lieutenant-Colonel, Intelligence Corps. **Career** Suzanne Lenglen's personal umpire, from 1920; studied fashion design, London, 1927; liaison committee, Wimbledon, 1927–49, 1982–90, barred (for designing Gussy Moran's lace panties), 1949–82; dress designer, from 1931; amateur tennis player, 1935–50; designed first Wimbledon tennis dress, for Joy Gannon, 1947; official designer, Virginia Slims tour, from 1972; *chef de protocol,* International Tennis Federation, mediated dispute with Association of Tennis Professionals, 1973; promoter, Women's Tennis Association of America, 1980. **Awards and honours** Elected International Tennis Hall of Fame, 1986. **Exhibition** Victoria and Albert Museum, London, 1986. **Cause of death** Respiratory ailment, at age 79.

MAX WALL

British Comedian and Actor

***Born* London, England, 12 March 1908**

***Died* London, England, 22 May 1990**

"He was one of the last music hall comics. He was one of the brilliants" — and, on top of that he had "the additional bonus of a backlog of disaster: bankruptcies, broken marriages and a chilling display of ill-fitting false teeth." Thus is Max Wall remembered by musician George Melly and comedian Charlie Chester — high praise mingled with a recognition that, like so many of the world's finest comedians, under the laughter lay a trail of personal suffering.

Inspired by the wonderful circus-ring hilarity of Grock the clown, Max Wall was a comedian of the music-hall tradition who went on to gain great respect as a serious actor in such roles as Ubi in Jarry's *Ubi Roi* and Vladimir in Beckett's *Waiting for Godot*. He will probably be best remembered, however, by audiences young and old, for his favourite creation, Professor Wallofski, a crazy musician with the obligatory tails and waistcoat, but cavorting around in a balding long-haired wig, long black tights, white socks and huge boots. In true clown style Wall pranced around in the absurd "Max Wall Walk" — "Don't laugh" he would say, checking his audience in mid-giggles, "It's unkind" — and tried desperately to play Rachmaninov's Prelude in C sharp minor. Forever frustrated by the disappearance of his piano stool, Wall never got beyond the first few bars. Taking a cue from Grock, he raised uncontrollable laughter from his inability to cope with a world which persisted in baffling.

Born Maxwell George Lorimer in Brixton, south London — "I was born there because I wanted to be near my parents" — it was not an easy childhood. Wall's father was a noted Scots comedian and an alcoholic who drank himself to death. His mother, Stella Stahl, a music-hall dancer and singer, was a formidable and dominating figure whom Wall resented passively. During World War I his home was bombed, his brother and a baby were killed, and Wall himself lay buried in rubble. But, despite hardship, the entertaining tradition was in his blood and at the age of two Wall gave his first performance when he was carried on stage in a kilt. His first professional part was in *Mother Goose* in Devon and Cornwall at the age of 14. And out of pantomime a great Beckett actor rose.

It was during the 1920s that Wall first attracted attention as an eccentric and acrobatic dancer. He made his London début at the age of 17 in a revue at the Lyceum where he was billed as "the boy with the obedient feet" and, in 1932, he appeared in Earl Carroll's *Vanities* on Broadway. Wall later toured Europe with Maurice Chevalier and Mistinguet. "I really was a fine dancer", he said later in life. "It took me 15 years to learn to dance properly and from that has come all the funny walks I do. It made me very loose-limbed, you see."

In the days when if an actor spoke on stage he was paid more, Wall's act was restricted to non-verbal comedy. He harangued the management in vain and it was not until a few years later, in the heyday of radio, that that memorable Max Wall voice sounded out to his audiences. But first the sirens sounded across London. Wall joined the RAF in 1941, drilling airmen by day and entertaining them at night, until he was invalided out in 1944. It was after this, with his own show on radio, that Max Wall became a national figure, and with the arrival of television in the early 1950s he was one of the first to have his own series.

Flushed with success as a comedian, it was Wall's personal life which was to sound his downfall. Married to the dancer Marian Pola for 15 years — and with five children — Wall had an affair with the 24-year-old Miss Britain beauty queen, Jennifer Chimes. His marriage broke up and his children refused to see him. In those far less liberal times the press clamped down on Wall for his behaviour and ruined his career. The *Daily Mail* newspaper, for example, sent a carload of cuddly toys to Wall's house when he forgot his twins' birthday, "so they wouldn't be too disappointed", and the public responded harshly. Wall's popularity dropped off and, the limousines sold, Britain's favourite comedian retreated to a bed-sit in south London.

Having collapsed on stage and after a nervous breakdown, Wall was declared bankrupt in 1973 over a 20,000 pounds income tax bill. His marriage to Jennifer Chimes ended after 10 years, and they were later divorced. His third marriage, to a woman 33 years his junior, collapsed after less than a year. With one brief exception, it was 16 years before Wall appeared on a West End stage again.

Max Wall's return, however, is one of the success stories of the stage. The northern club circuit had kept Wall in money and in 1966 he was offered his first real part in *Ubi Roi.* What followed was a remarkable acting career to great critical acclaim. Michael Billington, chief theatre critic of the *Guardian* newspaper in London, wrote after his death, "Like many great comedians, Max Wall became a first-rate actor: his love of language, his comic melancholia, his genius for creating an indelible physical imprint were deployed in a wide variety of plays." One of Wall's greatest skills was with language. He relished the oddities of the English language, rolling simple words to delve into new meanings and images. As Wall himself observed, "I love the hard, sharp consonants in words like 'capital' and 'splendid', and like to play with rhetoric, giving it a sepulchral sound and generally out-Wolfiting Wolfit [actor Donald Wolfit]."

What this comic's passion for language meant was that Wall could give new insight to the great lines of Shakespeare and Beckett. Michael Billington recalled his performance in *Krapp's Last Tape*: "as the old man listening to the voice of his middle-aged hopeful self, Max would cry 'Revelled in the word spool', and then pause before dwelling lovingly on 'spoo-o-o-l', giving Beckett's vowels their full weight."

Alongside his ability with language, Wall also brought all his skill in comic timing to his acting roles. Just as he knew how to spin out his jokes to win the greatest laughs, so he paused in the middle of lines to wring from them the maximum dramatic effect. It was perfect timing learnt from the music-halls of Britain, and such skill will die as that tradition fades.

Max Wall is remembered with high praise by his fellow comedians, but praise which also recognizes the realities of his own confession, "My act is the debris of a life dredged up from disaster." As Ernie Wise said after Wall's death, "He was an original and there will never be another one like him. He didn't suffer fools gladly. He was very much his own man. Max was a melancholy kind of comedian, more depressive than optimistic."

But it was the melancholy and the depression which informed Max Wall's ability as a straight actor as much as his years as a comedian. Michael Billington put it best when he wrote, "He brought to every role he played fastidious timing and his own ingrained sense of life's cruelty. As Osborne's Archie Rice in *The Entertainer,* he was almost too funny; but in his final despairing address to the audience, the character and the actor became almost one. What moved us, as so often in Max Wall's acting, was the sense that the performance was invested not only with a lifetime's theatrical skill but with a wealth of human experience."

Born Maxwell George Lorimer. **Parents** Jack, comedian, and Maud Clara (Mitcherson), dancer and singer, Lorimer (Mother's stage name: Stella Stahl.) **Marriages** 1) Marian Pola, dancer, 1942 (divorced 1956); 2) Jennifer Chimes, beauty queen, 1956 (divorced 1969); 3) Christine Clements, 1970 (divorced 1972). **Children** Four sons and one daughter, from first marriage. **Military service** Royal Air Force, 1941–43. **Career** First stage appearance, 1910; acrobatic dancer; acting début, *Mother Goose,* 1922; first London appearance, *The London Revue,* 1925; toured Europe; first New York appearance, *Earl Carroll's Vanities,* 1932; appeared in variety and broadcasting,

1948–50; alternated between variety and legitimate theatre, from 1950; career declined after divorce from first wife, 1956; toured Australia in variety, 1958; toured South Africa, 1960; returned to prominence in legitimate theatre, 1972; bankrupted, 1973; one-man show, *Aspects of Max Wall,* 1975. **Awards and honours** Portrait by Maggi Hambling exhibited, National Portrait Gallery, 1983. **Stage** (includes, in London, unless otherwise indicated) *Mother Goose,* Devon and Cornwall, 1922; *The London Revue,* 1925; *Merely Molly,* 1926; *One Dam Thing After Another,* 1927; *Silver Wings,* touring, 1930; *Bow Bells,* 1932; *Earl Carroll's Vanities,* New York, 1932; *Mother Goose,* 1936; *Tune Inn,* 1937; *In Town To-Night,* 1937; *Tops Everything,* 1938; *Black and Blue,* 1939; *Band Wagon,* touring, 1939; *Present Arms,* 1940; *Funny Side Up,* 1940; *Panama Hattie,* 1943, 1945; *Hoopla!,* Blackpool, 1945; *Make It a Date* (also co-wrote), 1946; *Jack and the Beanstalk,* 1947; *Robinson Crusoe,* Swansea, 1950; *The Pyjama Game,* 1955–57; *The Gypsy Warned Me,* 1958; *Once Upon a Mattress,* 1960; *Ubi Roi,* 1966; *The Old Ones,* 1972; *Cockie,* 1973; *The Entertainer,* 1974; *Aspects of Max Wall,* 1975; *Krapp's Last Tape,* 1976–77; *The Great Wall,* 1976–77; *Fair Slaughter,* 1977; *Buster,* 1977; *Twelfth Night,* 1977; *The Caretaker,* 1977; *Aspects of Max Wall,* 1979, *Waiting for Godot,* Manchester and London, 1980. **Films** (include) *Jabberwocky,* 1977; *The Hound of the Baskervilles,* 1977; *Little Dorrit,* 1988. **Television** (includes) *Waiting for Godot; Emmerdale Farm; Born and Bred; Coronation Street; Crossroads; Minder; Jane in the Desert; Educating Marmalade; Shelley; Zastrozzi; Mrs Capper's Birthday Party; Earthstars; An Evening with Max Wall; Comic Asides.* **Radio** (includes) *Petticoat Lane; Variety Bandbox; Variety Playhouse; Mid-Day Music Hall; Workers' Playtime; Our Shed.* **Publication** *The Fool on the Hill* (autobiography), 1979. **Cause of death** Fractured skull after a fall, at age 82.

ELLIOT WILLENSKY

American Writer, Architect and Conservationist

***Born* Brooklyn, New York, 11 July 1933**

***Died* Brooklyn, New York, 25 May 1990**

Run-of-the-mill guidebooks make every city seem the same. So long as you had the appropriate number of the series, you could "do" Amsterdam one day and New York the next and hardly notice the change: what you're looking for, be it shop, church or bus station, will always be in the same place in the book. The disadvantages of this mass-produced approach outweigh the advantages. Reassuring though it may be to know instantly where your favourite breed of hotel, restaurant or museum is to be found, it doesn't make for an interesting read for the armchair traveller. Nor does it stimulate a desire to see for oneself.

The American Institute of Architects' guide to New York, *AIA Guide to New York City,* is not that kind of guidebook. From its shape — tall, narrow but chunky, like many of the buildings described inside — to the idiosyncratic views and quirky anecdotes it contains, it's a unique book. It's a great read, and it invites the reader to go and look.

This award-winning book, first published in 1968, was written by Elliot Willensky in collaboration with fellow-architect and educator Norval White. Willensky was a New Yorker through and through — to be specific, a Brooklynite. He was born in Brooklyn and attended Brooklyn Technical High School. Later, he lived and worked in Brooklyn Heights, and was from 1979 the official Brooklyn borough historian. He published a history, *When Brooklyn Was the World, 1920–1957.* And he died in Brooklyn.

Not surprisingly, the AIA guide is full of affection for New York. It takes you on a conducted tour of the city, which architects and lay readers alike can enjoy. There are illustrations and descriptions, and praise where praise is considered due. But there are no sacred cows. While Frank Lloyd Wright's astonishing building for the Guggenheim Museum is described as "one of the greatest modern interiors in the world, a museum more important as architecture than for the contents it displays", the authors add that the exterior "has not aged happily. And the side-street addition [not by Wright] is a labored affair."

Although it isn't a conventional tourist guide, interesting restaurants and museums are pointed out along the way, as are more *recherché* items such as the area described as the Belly Dancing Center of the Western World.

Willensky was a local historian, and the book doesn't stop at describing what's to be seen today, but also gives details of important vanished buildings: some are included in a necrology section, others in the text. It wryly laments the disappearance of such items as the nineteenth-century cast-iron buildings in Lower Manhattan which were dismantled, then stolen as the pieces lay awaiting reconstruction.

One doesn't have to be in New York to enjoy this evocative and generously illustrated book. Buildings like the 800-foot high, neo-Gothic Woolworth Building in Broadway merit everyone's attention: the authors comment, "Horace Walpole...who wrote *The Castle of Otranto* could have set his action here."

New Yorkers are known for speaking their minds and the guide does not mince words in dealing with eyesores. One modern skyscraper is described thus: "A behemoth. A thousand interior decorators' picture frames form an unhappy facade for this office building." A reviewer likened the authors' condemnations to a wrecking ball, demolishing the buildings of which they disapproved.

As a member from 1979 of the New York City Landmarks Commission, Willensky adopted the same forthright approach to discussing the conservation of the buildings in the Commission's charge. His frankness and insistence on knowing the full facts of every enquiry led to ructions at times, but since his views were founded not just on a passion for New York but on an unrivalled familiarity with that city, his fellow-commissioners held him in high regard. One described his as the perfect appointment, recalling his "unmatched and intimate knowledge of the architecture, people, history, neighborhood and culture of the city". Willensky was vice-chairman of the Commission from 1985 onwards.

Willensky's strongly held views had a solid basis in architectural theory and practice. He was an architect registered in New York and elsewhere. After training at Cooper Union, where he gained a certificate in architecture in 1953, and at Yale, where he graduated with a Master's degree in 1955, he worked in architectural design and administration for ten years. During this period he became involved with architectural education, from 1963 to 1968 directing the New York City Program for Cornell University College of Architecture, where he was an associate professor.

He had a substantial track record in conservation and civic affairs even before joining the Landmarks Commission. Between 1968 and 1970, he had been first director of design and then deputy administrator for development of New York City Parks, Recreation and Cultural Affairs, where he won an award from *Industrial Design Magazine* for his Urban Outdoor Graphics Program. He was director of the High Rock Park Conservation centre on Staten Island from 1971 to 1976, winning an award of merit from the Municipal Art Society of New York.

At the time of his death, he was working on a history of the mid-town area of Manhattan. Also in progress was a long-term project, an intriguing sounding book on "hidden" New York which was to reveal and tell the stories of points of interest so high or so low that they escape attention, or are otherwise concealed. Few people could have been as well qualified to write it.

A New Yorker *par excellence,* Willensky has a fitting memorial in the *AIA Guide to New York City*. Every city should have a guide like this.

Born Elliot Willensky. **Parents** Morris, merchant, and Fannie (Eisenstein) Willensky. **Marriage** Kathryn Rubeor (dissolved). **Children** Marc and Diana. **Education** Brooklyn Technical High School, New York; Cooper Union, New York, 1950–53; Yale University, New Haven, Connecticut, MArch, 1955. **Career** Architect, New York and other states; architectural designer and administrator, architectural firms, New York City, 1955–65; associate professor of architecture and director, New York City Program, College of Architecture, Cornell University, 1963–68; director of design, New York City Parks, Recreation and Cultural Affairs Administration, New York City, 1968, deputy administrator for development, 1968–70; director, High Rock Park Conservation Center, Staten Island, New York, 1971–76; executive director, Thirty-fourth Street Midtown Association, until 1989. **Related activities** Arts consultant, On-Site Urban Communications Program for New York City, 1970–72; consultant: Frederick Law Olmstead 150th Anniversary Exhibition feasibility study, 1971 and Young Film-makers/Video Arts-Film Forum feasibility study for Mediacenter, 1977; commissioner, New York City Landmarks Commission, 1979 onwards, vice-chairman, 1985 onwards; borough historian, Brooklyn, New York, 1979 onwards. **Offices and memberships** Secretary, New York chapter, American Institute of Architects, 1964–65; member: American Association of Museums, Society for Industrial Archaeology, Long Island Historical Society, director, 1974 onwards, Frederick Law Olmstead Association, vice-president, 1972 onwards. **Awards and honours** Award of merit, Municipal Art Society of New York for *AIA Guide to New York City,* 1969, and for High Rock Park Conservation Center programs, 1976; Design Award, *Industrial Design Magazine* for Parks, Recreation and Cultural Affairs, Urban Outdoor Graphics Program, 1969; Arnold W. Brunner Scholarship, American Institute of Architects, New York chapter, 1975. **Publications** (Editor with Norval C. White), *AIA Guide to New York City,* 1967; *Guide to Developing a Neighborhood Marker System,* 1972; *An Urban Information System for New York City,* 1972; *When Brooklyn Was the World, 1920–1957,* 1986. **Cause of death** Heart attack, at age 56.

GEORGE YOUNG

British Intelligence Officer, Journalist and Banker

***Born* Moffat, Scotland, 8 April 1911**

***Died* London, England, 9 May 1990**

A rugged, red-haired Lowland Scot, with all the austere traditions of the Covenanters and the United Free Church in his upbringing and the intellectual honesty and fierce individualism of the best of Scottish education, George Kennedy Young was in some ways the ideal Secret Service officer. But at the same time he was a difficult man to mould into any kind of bureaucratic team. The story goes that on one occasion in Cairo, after receiving a particularly indecisive instruction from London, he replied tersely "Yes, repeat No". In 1962, after he had left the service, he castigated the indecision of Whitehall in his book, *Masters of Indecision*. And he was fond of telling how a report from MI6's Tangier station about "a flaming pansy, one Guy Burgess" had elicited a governess-y reply from the Foreign Office's chief personnel officer that he was "not prepared to listen to tittle-tattle about members of His Majesty's Foreign Service" — only two years before the notorious spy fled to Moscow with Donald Maclean. Such pussy-footing was not for Young. Throughout his long career he saw things clearly in black and white, sometimes in his later years literally and disastrously.

Young's upbringing summed up all that was best in the Scottish tradition. He was educated at Dumfries Academy and St Andrew's University where he obtained a double first in modern languages, followed by study at the Universities of Giessen and Dijon and a Master's degree in political science at Yale. Active politics attracted him, but not the politics of appeasement of the late 1930s. Instead, he moved into journalism with the leading Scottish paper, *The Glasgow Herald.* This introduced him to the hard facts of the city's life in the era of the Great Depression, and his politics were inevitably those of the left-wing social reformer.

The outbreak of World War II vindicated his anti-Chamberlain stance. He immediately joined the regiment of his homeland, the King's Own Scottish Borderers, where he served with distinction, being mentioned in despatches in 1941. His facility with languages and his interest in politics inevitably drew him into Military Intelligence. In 1943 he joined the "specially employed list", first in Italy where he became involved in an unsuccessful attempt to engage the Vatican in a move to halt the persecutions in Nazi-occupied Europe. He wrote up the account of his dealings with Monsignor Montini, later to become Pope Paul VI, in his book *Who Is My Liege?,* published in 1972.

At the end of the war, and after helping to supervise the dismantling of the Abwehr, Young returned for a time to journalism, as Berlin correspondent for the British United Press. But the intelligence service was loath to lose a man of his calibre. He officially joined the Foreign Service in 1946 when he was offered the post of head of the MI6 station in Vienna. This was the Vienna of the "Harry Lime" period at the start of the cold war, and Young found himself controlling a network of agents and double agents in the Soviet bloc. No wonder, then, that on his return to London three years later his nose for the double agent soon sniffed them out in the MI6 operations in the Baltic states — an exposure which did not endear him to his superiors in the service. Young never suffered fools — or ditherers — especially when he knew he was right. But this single-mindedness made him a difficult colleague and was perhaps the reason why he never achieved the heights to which his brilliant intellect entitled him.

No matter; at this stage in his career he was still on the way up. In 1951 he was appointed controller, Middle East, just as the newly elected Iranian prime minister, Mohammed Mussadeq, had nationalized the Anglo-Iranian Oil Company. Young was the master mind behind Operation Buccaneer to seize back the company's assets and overthrow the Mussadeq government. Despite a change of government in London and a temporary loss of nerve in the US State Department, Young acted without London's authorization to keep the operation going with CIA help, in the process arranging to delay CIA communications to Tehran until Mussadeq had been overthrown and the Shah reinstated. He returned to London expecting to be dismissed, but quite unrepentant. "You and I both know that I was right and I'll do it again if need be", he told his superiors.

Young was convinced that he would be appointed chief of the service, especially as the then chief wished to retire early. Instead, Sir Dick White was moved over from the Security Service. Young remained as vice-chief, his next job being to obtain US collaboration once again, this time in the attempt to topple Nasser. This time he was to fail, as was the whole undertaking. Young was scathing in his condemnation of the government's handling of the Suez fiasco. "We consistently underestimated the emotional force behind extremists and nationalist movements throughout the Middle East" was his verdict — a judgement which could stand the test of more recent events! He was to get his own back a few years later, after he had left the service, when he was approached by the Israeli secret service to find a British agent capable of organizing a guerrilla war against the Nasser-backed puppet regime in Yemen. The Scotsman he supplied succeeded in rallying support for the Imam and Nasser was forced to withdraw his troops.

But by this time Young had resigned from the Foreign Service, a disappointed man, and had taken up a directorship in the merchant bank, Kleinwort Benson. He was good at this too and within a few years had written an authoritative book on banking. But the City seemed child's play to a man of Young's adventurous cast of mind. He turned increasingly to politics, but now of the far Right, not the Labour Left. He agreed to stand as the Tory candidate in the 1974 election for the safe Labour seat of Brent East. He was already disillusioned with the then Tory leader, Edward Heath, for his abandonment of the austere economic policy on which he had come into office, and he campaigned hard for Mrs Thatcher's election as leader in 1975. He continued to take a leading part in Tory Action, a right-wing Thatcherite group, and also joined Unison, one of several groups set up to counter what they saw as the unacceptable degree of civil and industrial unrest in the dying days of the Labour government.

This was the time when Young's public life took on a less attractive tone. He became a member of the right-wing Monday Club and chairman of the Society for Individual Freedom, which by its very name indicated the idiosyncracy of his views — especially on the compulsory repatriation of non-white immigrants and, later on, in his 1984 book *Subversion and the British Riposte,* on the danger of Communist cells within the very highest reaches of the British Establishment. Such opinions brought down on him condemnation as being both fascist and racist — condemnation which was perhaps not entirely deserved. Young was in essence a supreme individualist. A man of strong views and the highest principles, he spoke out for what he believed was right for his country and its traditions. It was his judgement as to what was reasonably feasible that was at fault.

Born George Kennedy Young. **Parents** George Stuart and Margaret (Kennedy) Young. **Marriage** Géryke Harthoorn, 1939. **Education** Dumfries Academy; University of St Andrews, double first in modern languages, BA; University of Giessen; University of Dijon; Yale University, New Haven, Connecticut, MA, first-class honours in modern languages, 1934, MA in political science, 1936. **Military service** Commissioned King's Own Scottish Borderers, 1940; mentioned in despatches, East Africa, 1941; specially employed list, Italy and western Europe, 1943–45. **Career** Editorial staff, *The Glasgow Herald,* 1936–38; editorial staff, British United Press, 1938–39, Berlin correspondent, 1946; British Secret Service, 1943–61, Department of Requirements, vice-chief, 1959–61, Her Majesty's Foreign Service, 1946–61, Vienna, 1946, Economic Relations department, 1949, British Middle East Office, 1951; Ministry of Defence, 1953–61, under-secretary, 1960–61; banker, Kleinwort Benson Limited, 1961–76; president, Nuclear Fuel Finance SA, 1969–76. **Other activities** Unsuccessful Conservative parliamentary candidate, Brent East, 1974. **Offices and memberships** Member, Monday Club; chairman, Society for Individual Freedom; member, Tory Action; member, Unison. **Awards and honours** Commonwealth Fund Fellowship, 1934–36; Medal of Freedom (Bronze Palm), 1945; Member of the Order of the British Empire, 1945; Companion of the Order of St Michael and St George, 1955; Companion of the Order of the Bath, 1960. **Publications** *Masters of Indecision,* 1962; *Merchant Banking,* 1966; *Finance and World Power,* 1968; *Who Goes Home?,* 1969; *Who Is My Liege?,* 1972; *Subversion,* 1984. **Cause of death** Undisclosed, at age 79.

JUNE

MICHAEL ANNALS

British Stage Designer

***Born* London, England, 21 April 1938**

***Died* London, England, c. 29 June 1990**

The stage designer is all too frequently the unacknowledged party in a theatrical production. Designers spend hours working with the director, discussing the text, assessing exactly the atmosphere they want the production to evoke, and finally creating a whole world on stage which reflects and enhances the work of the playwright, director and actors alike. And yet rarely are their praises sung. Michael Annals was one of those few designers whose work was recognized and praised by the audiences as much as those within the profession. His remarkable talent ensured early success — but perhaps also contributed to his disillusionment with the theatre in later years.

While still in his teens Annals was invited by Michael Benthall to work at the Old Vic theatre, and by the age of 23 he had already designed *Doctor Faustus* for the company's production at the Edinburgh Festival. It was during these early years with the Old Vic that Annals also had the opportunity to design the costumes and sets for *Macbeth* — a production which subsequently toured the Soviet Union. Such a record of success while still in his twenties meant that Annals's future career was secured.

Annals's greatest triumph came when he was only 25. On the basis of the sets he had designed for *St Joan,* John Dexter invited him to design the set for Peter Shaffer's *The Royal Hunt of the Sun* which was to be produced for the National Theatre at the Chichester Festival. It is Annals's work for this production which is remembered with such admiration today. The play contains the infamous stage direction "They climb the Andes" — but this was tackled with total confidence. Director, Michael Blakemore, recalling this production in London's *The Independent,* writes of Annals's design, "*The Royal Hunt of the Sun*... could claim to be the most visually exciting British production of the Sixties."

Blakemore is not alone in his judgement. David William, former artistic director of the National Theatre of Israel, wrote after Annals's death, "Michael's most unquestionable personal triumphs were the set and costumes for *The Royal Hunt of the Sun*... Rarely can a play have been so magnificently served by director and designer." This is high praise indeed for the work of a 25-year-old, and the question is begged — where does such a young success turn next?

Broadway was the next step for Annals and he mixed stage design with the position of associate professor of scenic design at Yale University. The majority of his work, however, continued to be London-based and Annals went on to do work for the National Theatre and the Royal Shakespeare

Company. After the success of *The Royal Hunt* work also continued with the Old Vic, and in the dozen or so productions on which Annals worked he revealed the scope of his talent as a stage designer.

Michael Blakemore, who worked closely with him on a number of projects described, in *The Independent,* the way in which Annals worked. "Annals was a designer of great flair and speed, attributes which can, of course, be double-edged. Sometimes, as in Hecht and MacArthur's *The Front Page* (1973, at the National), he would offer a first model so well-researched, inventive and effortlessly right that our work was virtually over. With other plays we would go through model after model before arriving at a solution."

Among his best-remembered work at the National is Annals's set for Eugene O'Neill's *Long Day's Journey into Night* with Laurence Olivier, and in view of the critical praise which he met, it seems surprising that Annals was never involved in a new production after the National moved to the South Bank (although a couple of his plays transferred to the Lyttleton auditorium).

Perhaps it was his early success in the medium of the theatre which prompted Annals to delve into other art forms, revealing a certain restlessness and impatience with his first chosen field. In his work with ballet Annals's design for *Shadowplay* in 1967 was possibly his best, and after this he moved over to opera and designed for Glyndebourne. It was in his production with John Cox of *Ariadne auf Naxos* that Annals showed his wit and humour. The two men decided that the plot of *Ariadne* — an entertainment put on in a grand house for the enjoyment of its rich proprietor — reflected perfectly Glyndebourne itself and an entirely realistic set was devised for the production. There was no doubt that Annals enjoyed mocking the more "aristocratic" elements of life at Glyndebourne!

During the 1980s Annals worked on the set designs for three plays by Michael Frayn. One of these, *Noises Off,* which played in New York in 1984, earned him enough money to retire to Devon and the seclusion of life in the country. Exactly why Annals left his active life in the theatre has never been clear, but those who knew and worked with him believe that his very early success is to blame. If one looks at Annals's career as a stage designer one can plot the path of a man who triumphed in his early twenties, and who is still remembered for a production he designed at the age of 25. In a sense Annals achieved too much too soon and was left wondering what to do next. In addition to this it appears that Annals found the continually changing face of the British theatre hard to accept. Great productions were forgotten and what was praised at one time lay dusty and unvalued as the fashion of the theatre moved on.

Deep in the west country it seems that Annals's final years were those of a disillusioned man. However, whatever his personal judgement of his life's achievements, the world of the theatre remembers Michael Annals as one of the most innovative and visually exciting of twentieth-century stage designers. His work showed imagination mingled with shrewd technical knowledge of the capabilities of the stage, and though times and fashions move on, the record of his work has much to teach the stage designers of the future.

Born Michael Annals. **Parents** Henry Ernest and Constance Anne (Walter) Annals. **Education** Harrow Weald County Grammar School, London; Hornsey College of Art, London. **Career** Designed *Macbeth,* Old Vic Soviet Union tour, 1961; first West End production designed, *St Joan,* 1963; associate designer, National Theatre at the Old Vic, 1963–1977; first opera designed, *Il Tabarro,* 1964; first Broadway production designed, *The Royal Hunt of the Sun,* 1964; staff designer, Royal Shakespeare Company, 1974–78. **Related activities** Associate professor of scenic design, Yale University, 1966–67; instructor, Wimbledon College, London. **Productions designed** *Dr Faustus,* 1961; *Macbeth,* 1961; *Jackie the Jumper,* 1963; *Saint Joan,* 1963; *Love's Labour's Lost,* 1964; *The Royal Hunt of the Sun,* 1964, 1965; *Il Tabarro* (opera), 1964; *Macbeth,* 1964; *The Chinese Prime Minister,* 1965; *Samson Agonistes,* 1965; *The Crucible,* 1965; *A Bond*

Honoured, 1966; *Iphigenia in Aulis,* 1967; *Shadowplay,* 1967; *Prometheus Bound,* 1967; *Staircase,* 1968; *St Joan,* 1968; *Her First Roman,* 1968; *Morning, Noon, and Night,* 1968; *The Importance of Being Earnest,* 1968; *H,* 1969; *The Satyricon,* 1969; *The Seagull,* 1969; *Beggar on Horseback,* 1970; *Captain Brassbound's Conversion,* 1971; *Hamlet,* 1971; *Long Day's Journey Into Night,* 1972; *Lorenzaccio,* 1973; *Richard II,* 1973; *Ariadne Auf Naxos* (opera), 1973; *The Front Page,* 1973; *Macbeth,* 1973; *The Visit of the Old Lady* (opera), 1974; *Design For Living,* 1974; *Chez Nous,* 1974; *Prodigal Son* (ballet), 1974; *Dr Faustus,* 1974; *Heartbreak House,* 1975; *Shadowplay* (ballet), 1975; *The Clandestine Marriage,* 1975; *Engaged,* 1975; *Plunder,* 1976; *Frontiers of Farce,* 1976; *The Ghost Train,* 1976; *Joseph Andrews* (film), 1976; *Privates on Parade,* 1977; *Die Schweigsame Frau* (opera), 1977; *Pillars of the Community,* 1977; *The Lady from Maxims,* 1977; *Barmitzvah Boy,* 1978; *Rookery Nook,* 1979; *Make and Break,* 1981; *Noises Off,* 1983; *Benefactors,* 1984. **Cause of death** Undisclosed, at age 52.

ERIC BARKER

British Actor and Comedian

Born **Thornton Heath, Surrey, 20 February 1912**

Died **England, 1 June 1990**

It has always been recognized that, despite their *sang froid* and stiff upper lip, the British have a wonderful ability to laugh at themselves. And it is precisely those most guilty of that stiff-upper-lip, bespectacled, jolly-good-fellow Britishness which Eric Barker delighted in portraying. His was a fine touch. He did not ham up his roles to attract the maximum laughs possible. As Gilbert Adair expressed it in London's *The Independent,* "He simply donned his ministerial suit, removed his umbrella from the umbrella stand, placed his newspaper under his arm, and set off to catch the 6.23 from Waterloo." That was all it needed for his audiences to roar with laughter.

Though perhaps best remembered as a comedian, Barker began his career as a writer. After school he joined his father's wholesale paper business and 18 months later began to be recognized as a writer. His early work consisted of short stories and prolific contributions to the fiction magazines of the 1920s and 1930s. Even at this stage Barker showed a clear comic inclination and one of his early stories is included in the anthology *A Century of Humour.* During this time Barker also wrote novels, perhaps his best known being *The Watch Hunt* and *Day Gone By.*

With successful publication behind him, Barker moved into the theatre. Starting out at the repertory theatre in Birmingham in the days of Sir Barry Jackson, Barker proceeded along the typical path of "filling in" and taking bit parts in a number of productions. His new-found love of acting did not, however, kill all inspiration to write in the young Barker. While still in his late teens and early twenties, two of his plays were performed in the south — *Now In Town* at the Oxford Playhouse, and *Silver Moon* at the old Croydon Greyhound Theatre.

It was in 1933 that Barker's talent as a comedian really came into its own. It was in this year that he started working with the Windmill Theatre and he soon established himself as their main comedian, both in the role of gag-writer and impressionist. It was the particular slant of Barker's comic sketches which singled him out at the time. As Gilbert Adair explains,

> Within the tradition of British comedy there exist basically two categories of clowns: those (e.g. the Maxes Miller and Wall [q.v.]) who clamorously flaunt their vocation... alerting us,

even before anything funny has either been said or done, to their determination to make us laugh; and those (e.g. Barker, John Cleese) who make us laugh precisely because of their uncanny gift for mimicking the tics and tropes of a social or professional class which in life tends to be — or rather, is perceived to be — chronically devoid of a sense of humour.

It was this, Barker's ability to observe and to reveal gently the humour in characters, which led to his brilliant portrayal of the ordinary chap battling against the odds. This particular line took Barker to Australia as a member of Fol de Rols, the seaside entertainment company under George Royle and Greatrex Newman which nurtured such comedians as Arthur Askey and Norman Wisdom. And it was through the work of this company that Barker was discovered as a natural talent for the radio, making his "wireless" début in *First Time Here* in 1933.

After World War II Barker's radio work grew, and his reputation easily kept abreast of his achievements. As the radio reached its height of popularity in the 1940s and 1950s, Barker was there as one of the medium's best-loved and most-listened-to entertainers. What singles out Barker's career is that, far from simply establishing himself as a comedian, he also created figures and catch-phrases which have gone down in the history books of comedy. "Oh, I say! I rather care for that!" and "Steady, Barker!" passed into the language of the day, and his creation of the old park-bench philosopher caught the imagination of his thousands of listeners. Kept alive for 12 years in the programme entitled *Just Fancy,* it was this figure which best stood for Barker's life-long belief that comedy writers should not underestimate their audiences. Indeed it was in relation to this firm belief — "Think high" — that Barker created a stir by accusing his fellow practitioners of writing down to their listeners.

Barker was an intelligent man who applied that intelligence to his comedy. His was not the humour of countless forgotten *risqué* sketches. Instead his satirical revue, *Howdy Folks,* created the characters of Lord Blockhead and the liftman with the catch-phrase "Olive Oil and tinketty-tonk, eh, old man?" — both still admired today.

Barker left this show to join the Navy, and he soon became responsible for writing (and frequently starring in) the forces' programme *Merry-Go-Round.* Such was its success that the show continued for several years after the war, regularly attracting audiences of 12 million. But as the 1950s gave way to the 1960s and television and film increasingly became more popular than radio, Barker made sure he moved with the times. In 1957 he joined the Boulting Brothers, winning a British Film Academy Award for his part in the comedy film *Brothers in Law,* and his other film and television credits read like a list from the best-remembered comedies of the day — *Carry On Sergeant, Carry On Constable, Blue Murder at St Trinian's, Doctor in Clover...* Not, of course, forgetting his own highly popular show *The Eric Barker Half Hour.*

In the 1960s Barker showed his versatility as an actor by performing straight roles in *Z Cars, Compact,* and the north-country detective series *Cluff.* And throughout his working life Barker's actress wife, Pearl Hackney, appeared as his partner in his radio and television shows. Eric Barker was a talented writer, actor and comedian. He was a man who triumphed in the hey-day of the wireless, and then showed the determination to make a success of a career in television and film. The totally British, totally respectable "Man at the Ministry" which Barker perfected, paved new roads for the course of British comedy, and in looking back over his career one can only cry " Oh, I say! I rather care for that!"

Born Eric Leslie Barker. **Parents** Charles, wholesale paper merchant and Maude Barker. **Marriage** Pearl Hackney, actress and comedienne, 1936. **Children** One daughter, Petronella. **Education** Whitgift School, Croydon, London. **Military service** Lieutenant, Royal Navy Voluntary Reserve, 1940–45. **Career** In father's paper business; short-story writer; first play performed, *Now in Town,* Oxford Repertory Company, 1932; member, Birmingham

Repertory Company, 1931; comedian, sketch and lyric writer, Charlot revues, Windmill Theatre, Prince of Wales Theatre, 1933–38; comedian, Fol de Rols Company Australian tour; radio début, *First Time Here,* 1933; first television appearance, 1935; wrote and appeared in Royal Navy contribution to Forces programming, *Merry-Go-Round;* broadcaster, BBC Radio Kent. **Awards and honours** British Academy Award for *Brothers in Law,* 1957, for *Left, Right and Centre,* 1959. **Films** (include) *Carry on London,* 1937; *Concert Party,* 1937; *On Velvet,* 1938; *Brothers in Law,* 1957; *Happy is the Bride,* 1958; *Blue Murder at St Trinian's,* 1958; *Carry On Sergeant,* 1958; *Left, Right and Centre,* 1959; *Carry On Constable,* 1960; *Dentist in the Chair,* 1960; *Raising the Wind,* 1961; *Heavens Above,* 1963; *The Bargee,* 1965; *Those Magnificent Men in Their Flying Machines,* 1965; *Doctor in Clover,* 1965; *The Great St Trinian's Train Robbery,* 1966; *Maroc 7,* 1967; *There's a Girl in My Soup,* 1970. **Television** *The Eric Barker Half Hour* (also wrote), 1952–55; *Absolutely Barkers* (also wrote), 1963; also *Z Cars, Compact, Cluff, Father Dear Father, The Avengers.* **Radio** (includes) *First Time Here,* 1933; *Howdy Folks* (also wrote), 1939–40; *Navy Mixture* (also wrote), 1944–45; *Merry-Go-Round* (also wrote), 1945–49; *Just Fancy* (also wrote), 1950–62; *Passing Parade* (also wrote), 1957; *Barker's Folly* (also wrote), 1958; *Law and Disorder* (also wrote), 1960. **Publications** *The Watch Hunt* (novel), 1931; *Day Gone By* (novel), 1932; *Now in Town* (play), 1932; *Silver Moon* (play), 1934; *Steady Barker* (autobiography), 1956; *Golden Gimmick* (novel), 1958; (contributor) *A Century of Humour.* **Cause of death** Undisclosed, at age 78.

CEDRIC BELFRAGE

British Author and Journalist

***Born* London, England, 8 November 1904**

***Died* Cuernavaca, Mexico, 21 June 1990**

Most people are content with one career, but Cedric Belfrage had three careers, each distinct, yet determined by its predecessor. To begin with he was Samuel Goldwyn's press agent, and a movie critic on Beaverbrook's *Daily Express.* The economic depression of the 1930s put paid to this Hollywood career and turned Belfrage into a journalist of radical persuasion. This, in turn, led to him being deported from the United States during the cold war hysteria and to his emigration to Mexico. Here he became a Spanish translator and an expert on Latin American liberation movements, his last avatar.

Belfrage is best remembered as editor of the *National Guardian,* which he founded in 1948 "to keep alive the fundamentally democratic spirit of America — now almost obliterated from public life." In exile he continued to edit this weekly.

The son of a doctor, Belfrage was born into a well-to-do English family whose antecedents included clergymen and representatives of brewing interests. His rebellion against this solidly bourgeois background took the form of playing truant from the public school he attended in order to haunt the local movie palace. As an undergraduate at Corpus Christi, Cambridge, his enthusiasm for the cinema had not abated, and he left without taking a degree to head for Hollywood.

Belfrage later recorded his early impressions of Tinsel Town, the excitement of his first glimpse of an orange grove, of his first visit to a studio. To keep the wolf from the door he wrote for various fan magazines. To his surprise he was taken up socially by celebrities like Conrad Veidt, who no doubt found it amusing to include a Cambridge undergraduate with an upper-class English accent among their guests. "They gave me caviar when my stomach cried out for bread", was Belfrage's comment.

When Belfrage returned to London it was as Samuel Goldwyn's press representative, and then he joined Beaverbrook's *Daily Express.* He did not tarry long in his birthplace, but took off on a grand tour which ended in the South Pacific, and which yielded his first book, *Away From It All.*

The Hollywood to which Belfrage returned in the late 1930s was utterly changed. In the orange groves he had so admired growers were pouring kerosene over the oranges and burning them in order to keep prices up, and this while people went hungry. America was in the trough of its deepest depression. The film industry, like all others, was affected; Warner Bros. musicals now featured such songs as "Remember the Forgotten Man" and "Brother, Can You Spare A Dime?"

The Depression turned Belfrage into a radical, and for a few months he may even have dallied with the American Communist Party, a flirtation which was to cost him dearly when he came up against the House Un-American Activities Committee. But first the war intervened, and Belfrage was called to New York for service with British intelligence, then in 1944 to Allied headquarters, Paris, to work on a programme to de-Nazify the German press.

His work with the German press gave Belfrage the idea of launching an independent left-wing weekly, which he did in 1948. *The National Guardian* took on many of the inflamatory issues of the day. It opposed the Korean war, campaigned against the death sentence imposed upon Ethel and Julius Rosenberg, the so-called "atom spies". It was the first newspaper in the United States with a black history section. Inevitably Belfrage came to the notice of Senator Joseph McCarthy, then at the height of his witch-hunt.

Subpoenaed by the House Un-American Activities Committee, Belfrage invoked the American Constitution in refusing to answer questions about his personal beliefs or his professional activities. His deportation from the United States in May 1955 was a foregone conclusion, given the cold war hysteria which then prevailed.

Belfrage had always felt more at home in America than in England, and in 1959, after teaching himself Spanish, he emigrated to Latin America, eventually settling in Cuernavaca, Mexico. There he and his American wife Mary ran a guest-house, offering good food and stimulating political discussion to a wide circle of friends and admirers.

There also he wrote his most important book, *The American Inquisition,* a history of the McCarthyite witch-hunts in America. In 1973 the American State Department granted Belfrage a 30-day visa to attend the launch of his book in New York, and to go on a lecture tour to promote it. In 1981, after suffering a stroke, Belfrage translated from the Spanish the three-volume *Memory of Fire,* by the Uruguayan writer Eduardo Galeano.

After Belfrage's death rumours that he had been a Soviet spy were revived by Rupert Allason, who cited FBI files and the testimony of Elizabeth Bentley, a professional witness before witch-hunting committees. These rumours were denied by Malcolm MacEwen, a long-time friend of Belfrage, who pointed out that Bentley had been discredited as a liar, and that in 1984 when the London *Sunday Times* named Belfrage as a Soviet spy the latter demanded and got both an apology and damages.

Born Cedric Belfrage. **Parents** Sidney Henning, doctor, and Grace (Powley) Belfrage. **Marriages** 1) An actress, name unknown; 2) Molly Castle, journalist, 1936 (divorced 1952); 3) Josephine Martin, psychiatrist, 1955 (divorced 1959); 4) Mary Bernick, 1960. **Children** Sally, Nicholas and Anne. **Education** Gresham's School, Holt, Norfolk; Corpus Christi, Cambridge. **Emigration** Left England for US, 1927; returned to England, 1930–36; permanently settled US, 1936, ordered deported for subversive activities, 1955; settled Mexico, 1963. **Military service** British Intelligence, New York, 1941–43; Psychological Warfare Division, Supreme

Headquarters, Allied Expeditionary Force, France, 1944, reconstruction of press, Germany, 1945. **Career** Hollywood correspondent, British publications, *New York Herald Tribune*, *New York Sun,* 1927–30; public relations man for Samuel Goldwyn, London, 1930; film and theatre critic, waterfront reporter, roving correspondent, *Sunday Express*, *Daily Express*, London, 1930–36; published first novel, *Away From It All,* 1937; founder/editor, *The National Guardian,* New York, 1948–55, editor-in-exile, 1955–67; investigated for subversion, House Un-American Activities Committee, 1953, ordered deported by Department of Immigration, 1953, unsuccessfully appealed and deported, 1955; freelance reporter, 1955–67; freelance translator, 1967–90. **Awards and honours** Guggenheim fellow, 1947; Louis M. Rabinowitz Foundation award, 1968. **Publications** *Away From It All,* 1937; *Promised Land,* 1938; *Let My People Go,* 1940, published in US as *South of God,* 1941; *They All Hold Swords,* 1941; *A Faith to Free the People,* 1944; *Abide with Me,* 1948; *Seeds of Destruction,* 1954; *The Frightened Giant,* 1957; *My Master Columbus,* 1961; *The Man at the Door with the Gun,* 1963; *La inquisicion democratica,* 1971, published in US as *The American Inquisition,* 1973; *Something to Guard,* 1978. **Works translated** (include) *Guatemala: Occupied Country,* 1969; *We the Puerto Rican People,* 1971; *Open Veins of Latin America,* 1973; *Workers' Struggle in Puerto Rico,* 1976; *The Sugarmill,* 1976; *Sandino, General of Free Men,* 1980; *Memory of Fire* by Eduardo Galeano, 1985. **Cause of death** Undisclosed, at age 85.

ADMIRAL ROBERT B. CARNEY

American Naval Strategist

***Born* Vallejo, California, 26 March 1895**

***Died* Washington, DC, 25 June 1990**

Admiral Robert B. Carney enjoyed a long and distinguished naval career, spanning some five decades, and gained an outstanding reputation both as an operational commander and as a naval strategist. He secured his reputation in both fields during the Pacific campaigns of World War II where he served as captain of the light cruiser *Denver* before joining the staff of Admiral William "Bull" Halsey as, in his admiral's words, "the brains of the outfit". In the post-war period he was controversially appointed NATO's commander-in-chief, Allied Forces, Southern Europe and finally US chief of naval operations.

Robert Bostwick Carney was born in Vallejo, California, the son of a retired US Navy lieutenant-commander. Always set for a naval career, Carney attended the US Naval Academy at Annapolis in 1912 where he excelled both at sport and his studies, graduating with a BS degree and being commissioned as ensign on 3 June 1916. His first posting was to the *New Hampshire,* a battleship of the Atlantic fleet, before being transferred to the *Dixie,* a torpedo auxiliary ship based in Queenstown, Ireland. America's entry into World War I found him a lieutenant (junior grade) torpedo and gunnery officer on board the destroyer *Fanning,* again stationed in Ireland. Engaged largely in the protection of the sea lanes against the hostile intentions of marauding U-boats, Carney showed his mettle when his depth charges forced U-58 to the surface, resulting in the capture of its entire crew.

He returned to the US in July 1918, with a promotion to lieutenant, in order to supervise the fitting out of the destroyer *Laub* which he joined initially as torpedo officer but later commanded—a pattern he later repeated on board the USS *Reno* of the Pacific Fleet. Following a succession of operational and staff appointments, Carney was promoted to lieutenant-commander in 1927 while serving on the staff of the commander-in-chief, Battle Fleet. His next two-year appointment took him to Washington and the Navy Department before being transferred as gunnery officer to the light cruiser *Cincinnati* in 1930. Such varied postings gave considerable depth to Carney's knowledge of the workings of the Navy at both staff and operational level, expertise which was to prove invaluable during the Pacific campaign. The entry of the US into World War II in December 1941 found Carney serving as chief of staff to Admiral Bristol with the rank of commander, considering problems similar to those which he had encountered in World War I, that of submarine detection and convoy protection. He was awarded the Distinguished Service Medal in April 1942 for "exceptionally meritorious service in a duty of great responsibility" in a position which "with remarkable and distinctive skill, he prepared all operational plans preceding and during belligerent operations of the Force". More was yet to come. Promoted to the rank of captain in October 1942 he took command of the light cruiser *Denver* which he handled with consummate skill in operations in the south-west Pacific, notably off New Georgia and later off the Solomon Islands in March to July 1943, when he participated in the sinking of two enemy destroyers and acted in close support of the landings on various islands. For such actions he was awarded the Legion of Merit and Bronze Star.

Elevated to the rank of rear-admiral in the summer of 1943, Carney was posted chief of staff to Admiral William Halsey, commander of the South Pacific Force and, after June 1944, commander-in-chief of the Third Fleet, to form one of the most productive partnerships of the war. "Bull" Halsey, as he was known, provided the dash and drive and the instinctive brand of courageous leadership that US servicemen prized so highly: Carney, on the other hand, brought his analytical and incisive mind to bear upon the immense tactical and logistical problems that were part and parcel of maintaining a vast fleet at sea and conceiving and co-ordinating the many and varied offensive operations launched against the Islands. The partnership really came to fruition in October 1944 when Halsey's Third Fleet devastated the Imperial Japanese fleet at the Battle of Leyte Gulf. In order to break the support for the landings on Leyte, carried out on 20 October, the Japanese deployed the largest and most potent naval force they could muster, including several aircraft carriers and the two new 70,000-ton battleships — the most powerful afloat, armed with massive 18-inch guns — the *Yamoto* and *Musashi.* Had such force got within range of the large armada of transport and auxiliary ships off Leyte, the Americans would have suffered enormous losses of men and material and put the success of the invasion itself in severe jeopardy. Halsey and Carney decided to strike while the Japanese fleet was still a significant distance from the island by launching vast and repeated air attacks from the Third Fleet's carriers. By the time action was broken off on the evening of 25 October, the Japanese Navy had suffered a grave defeat from which it never fully recovered, having lost four carriers, three battleships, including the *Musashi,* ten cruisers and nine destroyers, mostly to air attack. In November 1944 in recognition of the "extraordinary heroism" he displayed while under attack and his "invaluable assistance in formulating the plans for a series of combat operations in which task forces of the Third Fleet engaged capital ships of the Japanese Fleet, waging devastating attacks on major Japanese combatant and carrier task forces in the vicinity of Mindora, the Sulu Sea, and in areas north-east of Luzon and off the central Philippines", Carney was awarded the Navy Cross. His work, however, was not yet over, for in the next ten months Carney played a leading role under Halsey in marshalling and deploying the Third Fleet — comprising some 16 carriers with some 1200 aircraft, eight battleships, 19 cruisers and more than 60 destroyers by the end of the war — in the remaining Pacific operations, for which he was awarded yet another Distinguished Service Medal. It was fitting that on 30 August 1945 Carney should have accepted the formal surrender of the large naval base at Yokosuka on the Japanese mainland.

In 1946 Carney was promoted to vice-admiral and posted to the Navy Department as deputy chief of naval operations (logistics), a position which capitalized upon his extensive experience in such matters and which he held for some four years. In 1950 he was placed in command of the Second Task Fleet in the Atlantic but only five months later was promoted to admiral by President Truman and appointed commander, US Naval Forces, Eastern Atlantic and Mediterranean, encompassing an area from the Azores to India and from the North Pole to the Equator. In the following year Carney became embroiled in a heated debate between Britain and the United States as to whether a Briton or an American would be in command of the newly formed NATO naval forces in the Mediterranean area. The British, mindful of the Mediterranean's importance to the Empire and perhaps mindful of the Americans', including Halsey and Carney's, apparently deliberate under-employment of the British Pacific Fleet during the war, opposed a US naval commander. But under pressure from Eisenhower, Britain accepted the compromise appointment of Carney as overall commander of Allied Forces, Southern Europe. It was during this early cold war period that the Warsaw pact branded Carney "the arch American pirate" which he took as a compliment commenting "Well, I guess that means I made the team". Indeed he did, for in 1953 he was appointed to the most senior US Naval position, chief of naval operations. He retired from the service at the expiry of that appointment in 1955.

Admiral "Mick" Carney, as he was widely known, excelled in the complex and dangerous scenarios of modern naval warfare. Capable of great resolve and daring personal leadership, Carney handled his individual commands with great skill and expertise. Perhaps his main strength, however, lay in his immense powers of tactical and logistical organization, an aptitude for which he displayed time and again during the long and diverse Pacific campaign and in his very senior post-war appointments.

Born Robert Bostwick Carney. **Parents** Robert Emmett, naval officer, and Bertha V.H. (Bostwick) Carney. **Marriage** Grace Stone Craycroft, 1918. **Children** Elizabeth and Robert. **Education** Central High School, Philadelphia, Pennsylvania; United States Naval Academy, Annapolis, BS, 1916. **Military career** Commissioned ensign, US Navy, 1916; served USS *New Hampshire,* 1916; served USS *Dixie,* 1916–17; promoted lieutenant junior grade, 1917; gunnery officer, USS *Fanning,* 1917–18; promoted lieutenant senior grade, 1918; supervised outfitting, USS *Laub,* Bethlehem Shipbuilding Corporation, Squantum, Massachusetts, 1918; torpedo officer, USS *Laub,* 1919, commanding officer, 1920; executive officer, USS *Reno,* Pacific Fleet, 1920, commanding officer, 1921; served USS *Rathburne,* Asiatic Station, 1921–23; served USS *Delphy,* 1923; navigation instructor, Naval Academy, 1923–25; plotting room officer, USS *Mississippi,* 1925; aide and flag secretary, Battle Fleet staff, USS *New Mexico,* 1925–28; promoted lieutenant-commander, 1927; served Division of Fleet Training, Office of the Chief of Naval Operations, Washington, 1928–30; gunnery officer, USS *Cincinnati,* 1930–33; commanding officer, Receiving Station, Washington Navy Yard, 1933–35; war plans officer, Naval Gun Factory, Washington Navy Yard and District, 1933–35; commander, USS *Buchanan,* 1935–36; supervised fitting out, USS *Reid,* Federal Shipbuilding and Dry Dock Company, Kearney, New Jersey, 1936, commander, 1936–37; commander, cargo ship *Sirius,* Naval Transport Service, 1937–38; served Shore Establishments Division, Office of the Assistant Secretary of the Navy, 1938–40; executive officer, USS *California,* 1940–41; assistant chief of staff and operations officer, Commander of the Support Force of the Atlantic Fleet, 1941–42, chief of staff, 1942; promoted captain, 1942; commanding officer, USS *Denver,* 1942–43; promoted rear-admiral, 1943; chief of staff to Admiral William Halsey (commander, South Pacific Force), 1943–45; accepted formal surrender, Yokosuka naval base, Japan, 1945; promoted vice-admiral, 1946; deputy chief, Naval Operations, 1946–50; commander, Second Fleet, 1950; promoted to full admiral, 1950; commander-in-chief, United States Naval Forces, Eastern Atlantic and Mediterranean, 1950–52; commander-in-chief, Allied Forces, Southern Europe (North Atlantic Treaty Organisation), 1951–53; chief of naval operations, 1953–55; retired 1955. **Related activities** Naval aide, crown prince Olaf of Norway,

US visit, 1939; senior naval member, Armed Forces Petroleum Board, 1949; president, United States Naval Institute, 1950–51, 1954–56. **Business career** Chairman, Bath Iron Works (Ship Building), 1956–67. **Awards and honours** World War I Victory Medal; American Defense Medal; Asiatic-Pacific Campaign Medal; Navy Occupation Medal; European-African-Middle Eastern Campaign Medal; Distinguished Service Medal, 1942; Legion of Merit, 1943; Bronze Star, 1943; Gold Star, 1944, 1946, 1955; Navy Cross, 1944; honorary Commander of the Order of the British Empire, 1946; World War II Victory Medal; Navy Occupation Service Medal; Philippine Liberation Ribbon with two bronze stars; commander, Royal Order of St Olaf, Norway; honorary LLD, Loras College, 1955. **Cause of death** Undisclosed, at age 95.

SIR JAMES CARRERAS

British Film Producer and Executive

***Born* England, 30 January 1909**

***Died* England, 9 June 1990**

Sir James Carreras, the head of Hammer Film Productions throughout most of its existence as a purveyor of Gothic horror, was one of the great entrepreneurs of British cinema. Taking little active part in the scripting and shooting of Hammer's films, he concentrated his considerable energies instead on the areas of finance and marketing. Here he quickly established himself as an innovative and apparently indefatigable producer-showman.

Carreras was always attracted more to the economic nuts and bolts of the film industry than to any notion of film as art. He was in fact born into the film exhibition business. His father, Enrique Carreras, owned a small cinema chain in London, and in 1935 Enrique and his business partner Will Hinds formed Exclusive Films, a distribution company which made the occasional venture into film production. It was here that James Carreras effectively began his career in cinema.

After serving in World War II, James Carreras took control of Exclusive — which would shortly become Hammer Films (named after Will Hammer, the stage name of Will Hinds, who was an ex-musical-hall performer) — and set about transforming it into a production company. It was at this time that he began to make his mark as a producer with a distinctive and original approach. One example of this was his development of the idea of the presold subject. Working as Hammer had to do on very low budgets, Carreras turned the company toward subject-matter already known to the general public, usually via radio and television, with this aiding the marketing of the films. So as the 1950s progressed, Hammer produced adaptations of *Dick Barton*, *PC 49* and *The Man in Black* (all well-known radio series) as well as their version of BBC TV's groundbreaking science fiction series *The Quatermass Experiment,* the success of which pointed the way to the later Gothic horrors. As far as the horror films themselves were concerned, Carreras would often raise production money for these using only a provocative title and poster, with the screenplay following on at a much later stage.

Throughout the 1950s James Carreras was also seeking to establish co-production and distribution agreements with companies in the United States. His first major breakthrough came with a deal signed with US distributor Robert Lippert in the early 1950s. One of the most visible results of this was the appearance of minor or fading American stars in Hammer's productions in the first half of the decade. Later, riding on the enormous box-office pull of Hammer horror, Carreras would sign deals with all the US major studios.

The full significance and extent of Carreras's achievements, particularly as he built up Hammer in the 1950s, only become apparent when placed alongside what was going on elsewhere in the British film industry. After a spectacularly unsuccessful attempt by British film mogul J. Arthur Rank to break into the American domestic market in the mid-1940s, relations between British cinema and Hollywood had become uneasy, with many British producers increasingly fearful of the power wielded by the US majors. Carreras's attempts to forge transatlantic alliances clearly went against the general feeling of the time, and in so doing they anticipated the heavy reliance of British cinema on American finance in the 1960s.

Carreras's building of alliances also took place at a time when cinema attendances were falling, with the increasing popularity of television generally seen as the main cause of this. Perhaps because of his keen sense of market trends, Carreras was one of the first British producers to notice that the focus of family entertainment was now the domestic household, and that, in order to retain an audience, cinema had to offer that which television could not — namely, adult entertainment. Hence Hammer's sustained exploitation of the "X" certificate (which had been introduced in the early 1950s as a way of denoting films that were for adults only). For example, Hammer's version of *The Quatermass Experiment* was initially sold under the title *The Quatermass Xperiment,* while a later science fiction film was entitled *X — The Unknown.*

Hammer's first world-wide box-office hit came with the release in 1957 of *The Curse of Frankenstein,* which starred Peter Cushing as Frankenstein and Christopher Lee as the Creature. This and subsequent horror films (which included versions of *Dracula*, *The Mummy* and *The Hound of the Baskervilles*) rapidly established Hammer as a market leader in the horror genre. Bearing in mind that Hammer at all times remained a relatively small independent concern (in all his deals Carreras ensured that he retained full control of the company), the extent of this success was quite extraordinary. It can be put down in part to the talented craftsmen who actually made the films (most notable amongst these being director Terence Fisher, screenwriter Jimmy Sangster and producer-writer Anthony Hinds as well as, of course, Cushing and Lee) but the lion's share must go to Carreras himself.

Carreras was unimpressed by those critics who accused Hammer horror of violence and tastelessness. For Carreras, the horror film was primarily an entertainment, something that needed to be sold to the public with gusto and wit. As he himself put it, "Showmanship — and I'll say that 'til I'm blue in the face — is still this industry's lifeblood, a fact that is too often ignored by many. When I see producers who are reluctant to bang the big drum about their product, it makes me wonder why they bother to make films at all."

During his reign at Hammer, Sir James Carreras banged the big drum extremely effectively. In 1972 he handed over effective control of the company to his son Michael and took up a job as special adviser to the EMI conglomerate. He also continued the charity work which had earned him a knighthood in 1970. But it is as the man who put horror into British cinema and the Britishness back into horror that he will be remembered.

Born James Carreras. **Parents** Enrique, cinema exhibitor and distributor, and Dolores Carreras. **Marriage** Vera St John, 1927 (died 1986). **Children** One son, Michael. **Military service** Commanded anti-aircraft regiment, World War II. **Career** Founder/chief executive, Hammer Film Productions, 1946–73, chairman, 1949–80; special adviser to the chairman, EMI, 1972. **Related activities** Trustee, Royal Naval Film Corporation, vice-chairman, 1961; council member/ trustee, Cinema and Television Benevolent Fund; chairman, Cinema Veterans, 1982–83; board member, Services Kinema Corporation. **Other activities** Trustee: Police Dependant's Trust, Attlee Memorial Foundation, Bowles Outdoor Pursuits Centre; vice-president, London Federation of Boys' Clubs, president; chairman, Variety Clubs International Board, 1965; chairman, Friends of the Duke of Edinburgh Award, consultant; governing body member, The Docklands

Settlement. **Offices and memberships** Chief Barker, Variety Club of Great Britain, 1954–55. **Awards and honours** Member of the Order of the British Empire, 1944; Knight of the Grand Band and Order of African Redemption, Liberia, 1968; knighted, 1970; Grand Order of Civil Merit, Spain, 1974; Knight Commander, Royal Victorian Order, 1980. **Cause of death** Undisclosed, at age 81.

MARQUIS CHILDS

American Journalist and Novelist

Born **Clinton, Iowa, 17 March 1903**

Died **San Francisco, California, 30 June 1990**

Marquis Childs, the Pulitzer Prize-winning journalist, was nearing 40 when he took up figure skating. At a time when other men approaching middle-age, and fearful of broken bones, were opting for badminton, Childs, one of the last of the political columnists of the pre-television era, was to be seen on a Washington, DC, skating rink. Cutting backward figure eights was hard to beat as a form of relaxation, he found. It took one's mind off the world's problems. It helped one to maintain a sense of balance.

Maintaining balance was one of the goals which Childs set for himself in more than half a century of journalism. That he succeeded is attested by his popularity as a pundit. At the height of his career the column Childs wrote for the *St Louis Post-Dispatch* was syndicated to more than 200 newspapers throughout America. These ranged from the *Washington Post* to small-town dailies in the boondocks. In 1969 he was awarded the Pulitzer Prize for his incisive political analysis and commentary.

Childs liked to boast that he had the ear of every American president from Franklin Roosevelt to Ronald Reagan, the exception being Richard Nixon, who, for some fancied slight, placed him on the White House black-list. It was the era before the television cameras zoomed in, and button-holing presidents was an important part of a journalist's business. Nor was Child's hobnobbing confined to Washington, DC. Among the leading statesmen he interviewed abroad were Pandit Nehru, Zhou Enlai, Konrad Adenauer, Anthony Eden, and the Shah of Persia. What he gleaned from them is recorded in his book *Witness to Power,* published in 1975.

Marquis William Childs who was born in the Mississippi river town of Clinton, Iowa, came from a long line of farmers that stretched back to Adam, he claimed, though his father left the family farm to become a lawyer.

After taking a Master's degree from the University of Iowa in 1925 Childs worked briefly for United Press International before joining the *St Louis Post-Dispatch,* which remained his home base for the rest of his career. Although he was never based abroad as a foreign correspondent, Childs travelled widely, spent time as a war reporter during the Spanish Civil War (he was anti-Franco and pro-Loyalist) and in Europe during World War II.

Although he was the confidant of generals and statesmen Childs never allowed this fact to go to his head. Nor did he forget that his job was to report world events, not to try to shape them, a mistake which other colleagues in his shoes might have made. Modesty was one of his most attractive traits.

Nearing his eightieth birthday, Childs completed a book of reminiscences about the Mississippi which he had started as a young man, then abandoned. *Mighty Mississippi,* the biography of that river, was intended to "reflect the vigour, the passion, the love of life" of that stream, according to the author.

"Mark Childs lived through the greatest period of American journalism", in the words of his colleague, James Reston, who added, "he did it all with a sense of history and a sense of humour."

Born Marquis William Childs. **Parents** William Henry, lawyer, and Lilian Malissa (Marquis) Childs. **Marriages** 1) Lue Prentiss, 1926 (died 1968); 2) Jane Neylan McBain, 1969. **Children** Prentiss and Malissa (deceased). **Education** University of Wisconsin, BA, 1923; University of Iowa, MA, 1925. **Career** Reporter, Chicago and Mid-West area, United Press International, 1923–25, New York, 1925–26; English composition teacher, University of Iowa, 1924–25; feature writer, *St Louis Post-Dispatch,* 1926–30, special correspondent, Washington, 1934–68; freelance writer, 1930–34; studied housing in Sweden, 1930; toured Europe, 1933–34; columnist, United Feature Syndicate, 1944–54; retired 1974. **Related activities** Eric W. Allen Memorial Lecturer, University of Oregon, 1950; lecturer, Columbia University School of Journalism; contributor: *Saturday Evening Post, Life, New Republic, Yale Review, Reader's Digest.* **Offices and memberships** Member: Sigma Delta Chi, Kappa Sigma, Century Club, Washington Press Club; member, Overseas Writers Club, president, 1943–45; member, Gridiron Club, president, 1957. **Awards and honours** Honorary LLD, Upsala College, 1943; Order of the North Star, Sweden, 1945; Sigma Delta Chi award for best Washington correspondent, 1945; Order of Merit, Federal Republic of Germany; Order of Aztec Eagle, Mexico; University of Missouri award for journalism, 1951; honorary LittD: University of Wisconsin, 1966, University of Iowa, 1969; Pulitzer Prize for commentary, 1969. **Publications** *Sweden: Where Capitalism Is Controlled,* 1934; *Sweden: The Middle Way,* 1936; *They Hate Roosevelt!,* 1936; *Washington Calling!* (novel), 1937; *This Is Democracy: Collective Bargaining in Scandinavia,* 1938; (with William T. Stone) *Towards a Dynamic America: The Challenge of a Changing World,* 1941; *This Is Your War,* 1942; *I Write from Washington,* 1942; *The Cabin* (novel), 1944; (critical editor) *America's Economic Supremacy* by Brooks Adams, 1947; *The Farmer Takes a Hand: The Electrical Power Revolution in Rural America,* 1952; (with Douglass Cater) *Ethics in a Business Society,* 1954; *The Ragged Edge: The Diary of a Crisis,* 1955; *Eisenhower, Captive Hero: A Critical Study of the General and the President,* 1958; (editor with James Reston) *Walter Lippmann and His Times,* 1959; *The Peacemakers* (novel), 1961; *Taint of Innocence* (novel), 1967; *Witness to Power,* 1975; *Sweden: The Middle Way on Trial,* 1980; *Mighty Mississippi: Biography of a River,* 1982. **Cause of death** Undisclosed, at age 87.

JUNE CHRISTY

American Jazz Singer

***Born* Springfield, Illinois, 20 November 1925**

***Died* Sherman Oaks, California, 21 June 1990**

It is possible to trace the styles of most pre-1960 jazz instrumentalists and vocalists back to the influence of Louis Armstrong (Miles Davis remaining a resolute exception). Despite the fact that there was no palpable trace of Armstrong in June Christy's singing, the influence was there just the same, distilled through Billie Holiday and Anita O'Day, the two singers from whom she was next in line of descent. It was the essence of Armstrong that made Shirley Luster (she became Sharon

Leslie before finally settling on June Christy) a jazz singer rather than a pop singer, and it was her delicate use of the inflections of timing and vibrato that go together with jazz which made her stand out from the flock of Holiday's descendants.

June Christy began singing with Benny Strong's society band in her home town of Springfield. Strong eventually decided that she didn't fit in and agreed with her that her future lay as a jazz singer. Christy left for Chicago where she joined the progressive orchestra led by Boyd Raeburn. After she had sung with the band for six months Raeburn decided to move his operations to New York. Christy recalled,

> I was fortunate enough — or unfortunate, depending on how you look at the outcome — to have scarlet fever at the time and so I was in quarantine when the band moved to New York. Had I gone with it, I would never have joined Stan Kenton.
>
> When I knew that Anita O'Day was leaving Stan's band, I called in every day at the agency for which Stan worked in the hope of seeing him.

The eccentric Anita O'Day didn't like the discipline of life with Kenton. "Stanley was a gentleman", O'Day said, "but working with him was like wearing a tight girdle. Working with Gene [Krupa] made you feel as relaxed as if you were lounging around in an old kimono."

June Christy's persistence paid off and she was able to give Kenton a test record she had made. He liked it and she joined the band in March 1945. But she hadn't told Kenton that she couldn't read music, and was horrified when, on the way to Indianapolis for their first job together, Kenton handed her a sheet of music and told her it was to be one of her numbers that night. She was saved by her musical photographic memory which enabled her to learn a piece after having it played to her only once.

At the time June Christy was still Sharon Leslie. Kenton didn't like the name and decided to change both it and his new singer's style. On the way to a job at Corpus Christi College someone in the band suggested "June Christy".

The fact that she was singing the numbers Anita O'Day had featured with the band emphasized her use of O'Day's methods. Kenton asked his arranger Gene Roland to work up a new library and persuaded Christy into a cooler style using little vibrato. She did not have a colossal range, but her sense of swing and her husky way with ballads, which won her the soubriquet "The Misty Miss Christy", brought her instant success with Kenton's audience.

Among the handful of numbers which Roland produced and Christy recorded with the band was "Tampico". This became an immediate hit only two months after she had joined the band. Christy was rightly disappointed that she had joined such a formidable jazz group and yet her first hit (it was the second of Kenton's records to sell more than a million copies) was not a jazz number.

Soon after her début with the band, Bob Cooper, who later became one of the finest jazz tenor saxophone soloists, joined the band and they eventually married, becoming one of the most popular couples in the West Coast jazz community.

In 1946 she won the first of what were to be regular awards as best female vocalist of the year but, by 1948, the ill health which was to dog her for the rest of her life had shown itself and she left the band when it broke up in 1948. Kenton had made her an international star and she began her successful solo career, breaking it often when Kenton asked her to return to the band for special concerts or tours. In August 1953 when Chris Connor (whom she had recommended as her replacement) became ill, Christy toured Scandinavia, Iceland, the Azores and Tripoli with the band.

She made her first recording under her own name for Capitol in 1949 and in 1954 recorded the album for which she will be best remembered, *Something Cool.* In 1955 she successfully recorded a set of songs with solo piano accompaniment by Kenton. She sang with Britain's Ted Heath band when it toured the United States in 1957. In 1960 she re-recorded *Something Cool* in a straight copy of the original, even using the same musicians and arrangements, in order to take advantage of the advent of stereo subsequent to the original recording. Despite the stereo, the second version was not quite as good as the first had been.

Much in demand, she and her husband toured Australia and Japan in 1965, but her health was not good and she eventually restricted herself to local West Coast engagements. She returned to Kenton for the 1972 Newport Festival and made her last recording in 1977.

Coming out of retirement she came to Europe in 1985 with Shorty Rogers' Giants and sang at the Nice Jazz Festival. Her poor health was obvious and she was not able to sing at her best.

On her return home June Christy's medical problems accelerated and she was forced to spend her last years on a dialysis machine. Bob Cooper, by then continually in demand for his most eloquent tenor playing, temporarily abandoned his career to take care of her in her last years.

Born Shirley Luster. **Marriage** Bob Cooper, saxophonist, 1946. **Children** One daughter, Shay. **Career** Vocalist (as Sharon Leslie), Benny Strong band; society band singer, Chicago; vocalist (as Sharon Leslie), Boyd Raeburn band; lead singer, Stan Kenton band, 1945–48; recording début, 1945; solo recording contract, Capitol Records, from 1949; toured, Kenton band, 1953; toured, Ted Heath band, 1957–58; toured Australia and Japan, 1965; appeared with Stan Kenton band, Newport Jazz Festival, Rhode Island, 1972; vocalist, Shorty Rogers' Giants, Nice Jazz Festival, 1985. **Awards and honours** Best Female Vocalist with a Big Band, *Down Beat,* 1946, 1947, 1948, 1950. **Recordings** (include, recorded for Capitol unless otherwise indicated) "Tampico", 202, 1945; "He's Funny That Way", B98, 1946; "Willow Weep For Me", 287, 1946; "I'll Remember April", 57774, 1949; *This is June Christy,* T1006, 1949–56; (with Shorty Rogers) *Shorty Rogers plus Kenton and Christy,* Pausa 9016, 1950–51; *Something Cool,* 1954, re-recorded 1960; *That Misty Miss Christy,* T725, 1955–56; *Fair and Warmer,* T833, 1957; *Gone for the Day,* T902, 1957; *Those Kenton Days,* T1202, 1959; *Cool School,* T1398, 1959; *Impromptu,* Inter. 7710, 1977. **Cause of death** Complications from kidney failure, at age 64.

WALTER DAVIS JR

American Jazz Pianist

***Born* Richmond, Virginia, 2 September 1932**

***Died* New York City, New York, 2 June 1990**

Then a teenager, Walter Davis Jr was at his most receptive to new ideas when the bebop revolution struck in the mid-1940s. He chose as his model the turbulent and erratic Bud Powell, a man who devised not only the best way of playing bebop on the piano, but also a jazz piano style which shows itself in the hands of most jazz pianists to this day. In 1959, by which time Powell's self-neglect had crippled the potency of much of his playing, the two men recorded together with Art Blakey's [q.v.] Jazz Messengers, Powell taking the piano chair for one side of an album and Davis for the other. In general Davis's playing was smoother than Powell's, and his technical ability was formidable.

Davis rode the end of the bebop tide and in the decades that followed stayed closer to the original feel of the period than most. Consequently he was a natural choice for the soundtrack of *Bird,* Clint Eastwood's film biography of the bebop giant Charlie Parker.

In 1946 the eccentric jazz singer Babs Gonzales formed his band Three Bips and a Bop in Newark, New Jersey and specialized in using embryo giants within its ranks. Sonny Rollins and trombonist Benny Green were amongst them and eventually Davis came in on piano for his first professional job.

By 1952 he was well enough established to move to New York to join Max Roach's first band which also included the noted tenor player Hank Mobley. The greatest accolade came when, that same year, Davis was hired by Charlie Parker himself. He also worked for the other high priest of bebop, Dizzy Gillespie, and when the US State Department commissioned world tours by the Gillespie big band in 1956, Davis was the band's pianist. He visited the Middle East and South America with the band and recorded on Gillespie's exciting *World Statesman* album. In the late 1950s Davis became a regular for the Blue Note label, recording with men like altoist Jackie McLean and trumpeter Donald Byrd. He worked with Byrd in Paris and in typical cross-fertilization at Blue Note recorded on albums by both Byrd and McLean. He replaced another great pianist, Bobby Timmons, in the 1959 version of Art Blakey's Jazz Messengers and travelled again to Paris to appear at the famous concerts at the Théâtre des Champs Elysées. Timmons returned to the band briefly in late 1960 but left again because of ill health and Davis once more replaced him.

Davis, who was also a painter and had worked as a costume designer, then retired from jazz to take up a career as a tailor. He returned to music in the late 1960s. In 1969 he travelled to India to play and to study and in 1973 joined Sonny Rollins's group for two years. He became a member of Art Blakey's Messengers yet again in 1975 and wrote some good pieces for the band. He used Blakey as a member of his trio when he recorded in 1977 and in the winter of 1979 he made an oustanding album under his own name backed by two younger giants, bassist Buster Williams and drummer Tony Williams.

In August 1989 Davis played in a tribute to Bud Powell at the Lincoln Center in New York and up until his death was much in demand on the jazz scene.

Born Walter Davis Junior. **Father** Walter Davis. **Children** Four daughters, Evin, Alana, Sareenah, Aisha, and one son, Rama. **Career** Played with Babs Gonzales's group Three Bips and a Bop; played with Max Roach, 1952–53; played with Charlie Parker, 1952; first recording, 1953; toured Middle East and South America with Dizzy Gillespie, 1956; played with Donald Byrd, Paris, 1958; played with Art Blakey's Jazz Messenger's, 1959; retired to become a tailor, costume designer and painter, 1960; joined band, New Jersey; produced records; wrote arrangements; played with Art Blakey; led own trio; studied music, India, 1969; played with: Sonny Rollins, 1973–74, Art Blakey, 1975; played Newport Jazz Festival, Rhode Island, 1974–75; appeared: Antwerp Jazz Festival, Naarden Jazz Festival, Toulon Jazz Festival; formed own group, recorded, 1979; played on film soundtrack for *Bird,* 1988. **Television** *Focus,* Washington DC. **Compositions** (include) "Ronnie's A Dynamite Lady"; "Backgammon"; "Uranus"; "Illumination"; "Gypsy Folk Tales"; "Greasy"; "Davis Cup"; "A Million Or More Times". **Recordings** (include) (With Dizzy Gillespie) *World Statesman,* Norg 1084, 1956; (with Jackie McLean) *New Soil,* BN 84013, 1959; (with Donald Byrd) *Byrd in Hand,* BN 4019, 1959; *Davis Cup,* BN 4018, 1959; (with A. Shepp) *Attica Blues,* Imp 9222, 1972; (with Sonny Rollins) *Horn Culture,* Mlst 9051, 1973; *Four Hundred Years Ago, Tomorrow,* Owl 020, 1979; *Bird,* 1988. **Cause of death** Liver and kidney disease, at age 57.

JOSÉ FIGUERES

Costa Rican Former President

Born **San Ramón, Costa Rica, 25 September 1906**

Died **San José, Costa Rica, 8 June 1990**

That Costa Rica is today a relatively prosperous island of peace and democracy in the war-torn turbulence of Central America is in no small measure due to the statesmanship of its three-times president, José Figueres Ferrer. Not that Figueres was always on the side of the powers that be. He first came to power at the head of a revolutionary junta and his first official candidacy for the presidency was declared invalid. "I was a guerrilla", he admitted when he took office for the third time, "but I have no sympathy nor use for the present-day guerrillas." And he was to prove it in what he achieved for his country.

The son of a doctor who had emigrated from Spain, Figueres studied engineering at the Massachusetts Institute of Technology and returned to Costa Rica to establish a highly successful agro-industrial enterprise growing coffee and making rope. Even in those early days he was no run-of-the-mill businessman. He called his farm *La Lucha sin Fin* (the unending struggle) and he soon introduced welfare measures including a profit-sharing scheme for his workers. His first venture into the political sphere was a broadcast attack in 1942 on the government of President Rafael Calderón for its alliance with the Costa Rican Communists. Obliged to leave the country, Figueres spent the next two years in Mexico where, together with other political exiles, he helped to form the Caribbean Legion dedicated to ending dictatorship in the region. Some four years later came the first test of this organization when the supporters of Calderón tried to annul the presidential election. Figueres and a small body of followers led a brief but bloody uprising against the Communist-backed government and he emerged victorious at the head of a revolutionary eleven-man junta.

The 1948 revolution was to be but a momentary aberration. On taking over power Figueres announced that the long period of dictatorship was over. To signal this, his first action was to abolish the Army. "The many hundreds of thousands of dollars saved from having no army will be used for public schools and education", he announced and handed over the keys of the main barracks to the education minister to be converted into a cultural centre. But even more important, he had done away with the strutting generals and the danger of military revolts. The move was a risky one in the turbulent region, and the new regime was soon put to the test by an invasion of exiles from Nicaragua seeking to reinstate the ex-president. "A people is much harder to conquer than an army", was Figueres's response, and the repulse of the invading forces established his junta more firmly than ever.

Abolishing the Army was only one of Figueres's sweeping reforms. The banks were nationalized, the tax system overhauled, and a comprehensive social security system initiated. Later he was even to nationalize United Fruit, Costa Rica's largest company. These radical policies inevitably alarmed the moneyed interests who saw him as a traitor to his class.

As the country returned to constitutional government, he was forced to give way to a more moderate political figure at the end of 1949. But Figueres was soon to bounce back, and this time at the head of a newly formed Party of National Liberation. In July 1953 he was duly elected president, largely as a result of the enfranchisement, for the first time, of Costa Rican women. Declaring his intention "to establish a regime of equal treatment for all", his first five-year term consolidated his social democratic programme. A third term in the early 1970s saw the social welfare system extended and the economy put on a sound footing. Figueres did not always see eye to eye with the United States — not least over its policy towards the Nicaraguan Sandinistas — but he welcomed US investment and was largely responsible for creating the favourable economic and political climate for it. His last term of office was marred, however, by his association with the fugitive US financier Robert Vesco whom he refused to extradite, and by controversy over his decision to establish diplomatic relations with the Soviet Union and his visits to Cuba. Any idea of a fourth term was quickly ruled out of court.

But Figueres's achievements in setting his country firmly on the democratic path cannot be gainsaid. A "farmer socialist", as he always called himself, he had the realism to face facts and know just how far to go, combined with a streak of idealism which made him an enlightened and stalwart reformer. "Don Pepe", as he was popularly known, was indeed the "father" of modern Costa Rica and of the political stability and tolerance which make it the cynosure of all its neighbours.

Born José Pepe Figueres Ferrer. **Parents** Father, a doctor; mother, a teacher. **Marriages** 1) Henrietta Boggs (dissolved); 2) Karen Olsen. **Children** José and one other, from first marriage; four, from second marriage. **Education** Universidad de Costa Rica; Universidad de México; studied engineering, Massachusetts Institute of Technology. **Career** Coffee planter and rope maker, to 1942; denounced President Rafael Calderón on radio, 1942; exiled to Mexico, 1942–44; member, Caribbean Legion, 1942–48; led successful revolution, 1948; minister in charge of foreign affairs, justice and public security, 1948; provisional president, 1948–49, president, 1953–58, 1970–74; worked on economic problems, 1949–52; founder/president, Partido de Liberación Nacional, 1951–90; founder/co-owner, Sociedad Agricola Industrial San Cristóbal; granted asylum to indicted American businessman Robert Vesco, 1972. **Related activities** Visiting professor, Harvard University, 1963–64. **Publication** *Cartas a un ciudadano: la pobreza de las naciones,* 1973. **Cause of death** Heart attack, at age 83.

JACK GILFORD

American Actor

Born **Manhattan, New York, 25 July 1907**

Died **Manhattan, New York, 2 June 1990**

Thanks to the legendary American comic, Milton Berle, a 26-year-old Manhattan cosmetics shop manager named Jacob Gellmann became Jack Gilford, the droopy-faced comic actor who would become one of the most enduring and endearing figures on the American show business scene. Gilford had won a few amateur talent contests but Berle, also 26, was already a show-business veteran able to offer Gilford a job as his sidekick in a touring revue. Jack Gilford spent the next four years as Berle's foil, mainly playing vaudeville and the so-called Borscht Belt: the resort hotels of New York's Catskill Mountains which cater for a predominantly Jewish clientele, and are still the traditional training ground for many of America's Jewish comics. Cabaret, Gilford once told an interviewer, "is the most difficult performing art. Audiences drink, chat and dance. It's a constant struggle, and if you're rejected, you're standing there all alone."

After leaving Berle, he became MC at Barney Josephson's Greenwich Village night-club, Café Society, one of the few places in the 1930s where Blacks and Whites could mix freely. According to Gilford, "It was the first place to let Negroes sit down at tables below 110th Street. Hazel Scott was the lull pianist between acts. A young girl named Helena Horne was the singer before she changed her name to Lena. Billie Holiday was there, too."

His first big break came in the topical revue, *Meet the People,* which opened at the Hollywood Playhouse in 1940, went on tour, and had several revivals. Other revues during the 1940s included *Count Me In* and *Alive and Kicking.* He toured extensively in vaudeville and also with the Paul Whiteman band and with the Tommy Dorsey Orchestra. He made his film début in 1944, in *Hey, Rookie,* and was in *The Reckless Age,* the same year, but through most of the 1950s he was unable to work in either film or television, a victim of McCarthy's witch-hunt. Brought before the House Un-American Activities committee, he was asked, "Do you believe in the overthrow of the United States government by force and violence?" "No", replied the jug-eared comic, "just gently". He was blacklisted, and didn't make another film until 1953. He found work on Broadway, however, appearing in such diverse productions as *The World of Sholom Aleichem*, *The Diary of Anne Frank*, *Once Upon a Mattress* (a musical take-off of the classic fairy tale, "The Princess and the Pea" — he also appeared in a later television version), *Cabaret* (for which he received a Tony nomination in 1967), and probably his best-known role as the slave Hysterium in *A Funny Thing Happened on the Way to the Forum.*

His portrayal of Hysterium not only earned him his first Tony nomination, in 1963, it brought him to world-wide attention when he repeated the role in the 1966 film version which featured one of the most wonderful collections of comics and character actors ever to appear together. The film is a delight from start to finish, with marvellous, energetic performances from the likes of Zero Mostel (also repeating his Broadway role), Phil Silvers, Michael Crawford, Michael Hordern and Buster Keaton. Yet many feel that despite such illustrious co-stars, Jack Gilford's nervous slave, blackmailed into posing (in full drag) as the corpse of a beautiful courtesan, completely stole the show.

Other films included *Enter Laughing*, *Who's Minding the Mint?* (with his old partner, Milton Berle), *Catch 22*, *Save the Tiger* (his portrayal of Jack Lemmon's business partner earned him an Oscar nomination), and most recently, both the *Cocoon* movies, in which he played the crotchety geriatric who decides to remain on Earth while his fellows go to another planet.

He first appeared on television in 1948, as a regular on NBC's *The Phil Silvers Arrow Show,* but thanks to Senator McCarthy's blacklist, he didn't return to the small screen again until the 1960s, when he won the heart of America as the man on the Cracker Jack (candy-coated popcorn) commercials who looked on woefully as a child ate all the candy. He guested on several variety shows, hosted his own special, and played various roles in programmes such as *All in the Family, Soap*, *Taxi*, *The Love Boat* and *The Golden Girls.* He had a recurring role in the 1960s spy spoof, *Get Smart,* which occasionally featured him as the thoroughly inoffensive and charming enemy agent, Simon the Likeable.

If the part of Simon the Likeable wasn't written especially for Jack Gilford, then it should have been. There has seldom been an actor who was so genuinely engaging. He was often the underdog who gains the audience's sympathy: the long-suffering, silent character in *The World of Sholom Aleichem* who upon reaching heaven is told that he can ask for *anything,* and replies, "In that case, if it's true, could I have please, every day, a hot roll with butter?", the hen-pecked silent king in *Once Upon a Mattress,* the old man sent away to die in the future youth-dominated society of *Them,* and of course, the slave Hysterium, with his secret collection of erotic pottery. Once in a great while, he was a villain, but always a charming one. Simon the Likeable was a villain you wouldn't mind sharing a cup of tea with.

Sometimes he played tragedy, bringing tears to the eyes of the audience, other times his puckish sense of humour would come to the fore and he'd do his impression of a day in the life of a golf ball. His career was long and varied. In 1982, Frank Rich of *The New York Times* wrote that "no Broadway season should lack Jack Gilford". The Broadway stage will certainly be poorer without him.

With his curly hair, sparkling eyes and mischievous smile, he was often described as looking like a "Jewish leprechaun", and somewhere he's still laughing and doing his old vaudeville routines — perhaps at the end of a rainbow.

Born Jacob Gellman. **Parents** Aaron and Sophie (Jackness) Gellman. **Marriage** Madeline Lee Letterman, producer and actress, 1949. **Children** Joseph, Lisa and Samuel. **Education** Commercial High School, Brooklyn, New York. **Career** Début as comedian, Bronx Opera House, New York, 1934; managed Manhattan cosmetics shop; toured in *Leavitt and Lockwood Revue,* 1934; toured in vaudeville, 1934–35; toured in *Milton Berle Revue,* 1935–38; toured US and Canada, *Ina Ray Hutton Revue,* 1937–38; New York début, *Frank Fay Vaudeville,* 1939; national tour, *Meet the People,* 1940; toured with *United Services Organization in the Pacific,* 1943; film début, *Hey, Rookie,* 1944; television début, *The Phil Silvers Arrow Show,* 1948; toured in vaudeville, 1950; blacklisted after McCarthy hearings; toured in *Anything Goes,* 1973; toured in *The Sunshine Boys,* 1974. **Awards and honours** Antoinette Perry (Tony) award nomination for: *A Funny Thing Happened on the Way to the Forum,* 1963, *Cabaret,* 1967; Academy Award nomination for *Save the Tiger,* 1972. **Stage** (includes) *Amateur Night,* 1934; *Frank Fay Vaudeville,* 1939; *Meet the People* (revue), 1940; *Tommy Dorsey Orchestra* (revue), 1941; *They Should Have Stood in Bed,* 1942; *Count Me In* (revue), 1942; *Meet the People,* 1943; *Alive and Kicking* (revue), 1950; *The Live Wire,* 1950; *Die Fledermaus* (opera), 1950, 1958–59, 1962–64, 1966–67; *The World of Sholom Aleichem,* 1953; *The Passion of Gross,* 1955; *Once Over Lightly* (revue), 1955; *The Diary of Anne Frank,* 1955; *Romanoff and Juliet,* 1957; *Drink to Me Only,* 1958; *Look After Lulu,* 1959; *Once Upon a Mattress,* 1959; *The Tenth Man,* 1959; *The Desert Song,* 1961; *Can-Can,* 1961; *Cinderella,* 1961; *The Beauty Part, 1961; The Policeman,* 1961; *A Funny Thing Happened on the Way to the Forum,* 1962; *Cabaret,* 1966; *Three Men on a Horse,* 1969; *The Price,* 1970; *No, No, Nanette,* 1971; *The Seven Year Itch,* 1975; *Sly Fox,* 1976; *The Supporting Cast,* 1981; *The World of Sholom Aleichem,* 1982. **Films** (include) *Hey, Rookie,* 1944; *The Reckless Age,* 1944; *Main Street to Broadway,* 1953; *Mister Budwing,* 1963; *A Funny Thing Happened on the Way to the Forum,* 1966; *Enter Laughing,* 1967; *Who's Minding the Mint?,* 1967; *The Incident,* 1967; *Harry and Walter Go to New York,* 1967; *Catch 22,* 1970; *They Might Be Giants,* 1971; *Save the Tiger,* 1972; *Cheaper to Keep Her,* 1980; *Wholly Moses,* 1980; *Cave Man,* 1981; *Cocoon,* 1985; *Cocoon: The Return,* 1988. **Television** (includes) *The Phil Silvers Arrow Show (aka The Arrow Show* and *Arrow Comedy Theatre)*; *Apple Pie; The Dean Martin Show; The Carol Burnett Show; The Defender; All in the Family; Get Smart; Rhoda; Soap; Taxi; The Loveboat; Trapper John, M.D.; The Duck Factory; Dinah's Place; The World of Sholom Aleichem; Once upon a Mattress; Of Thee I Sing; The Cowboy and the Tiger; The Very Special Jack Gilford Special; Anna to the Infinite Power; Hotel; The Golden Girls.* **Other appearances** (include) Café Society (cabaret), 1939; Café Society Uptown (cabaret), 1946. **Recordings** *A Funny Thing Happened on the Way to the Forum; Cabaret.* **Publication** (Contributor with Zero Mostel) *170 Years of Showbusiness.* **Cause of death** Stomach cancer, at age 82.

PEGGY GLANVILLE-HICKS

Australian/American Composer

***Born* Melbourne, Australia, 29 December 1912**

***Died* Sydney, Australia, 25 June 1990**

A book of successful women composers would be thin indeed. But one of its main features would be the versatile, talented and innovative Peggy Glanville-Hicks, who left a rich legacy of music for both voice and instruments and who was also a champion of new music, especially by young composers. It is a tragedy that she is not more widely known today. She was imaginative in her choice of subject-matter, and was particularly keen on unorthodox texts: who else would have set letters by the eccentric novelist Paul Bowles to music? Another favourite theme was the exploration of foreign musical heritages, and her own style blended East and West; she has even been described as "an early forerunner of orientalism". She did not only equal the achievement of male composers, she surpassed them: when two movements of her *Choral Suite* were heard at the Festival of the International Society for Contemporary Music in London in 1938 it was the first time that Australian composition had ever been heard at the event. Not bad for a 26-year-old.

She was a child prodigy, studying music at the Melbourne Conservatory at the age of 14 under the director, Fritz Hart. When she was 19 she took the route of many aspiring Australian musicians before and after her: she went to London. She was already composing, and the year she left her homeland she finished a number of song cycles to poems by A.E. Housman. The Carlotta Rowe Scholarship enabled her to study for four years at the Royal College of Music, where the eminence of many of her teachers is today astonishing: Ralph Vaughan Williams, doyen of British composers, taught her composition; Gordon Jacob, orchestration; Arthur Benjamin, piano; Constant Lambert and Malcolm Sargent, conducting.

Before her course in London was completed she had composed a Sinfonietta for orchestra and the opera *Caedmon,* already writing the words as well as the music. As soon as she had a Royal College training under her belt she set off around Europe to see what she could learn there, and the same year wrote her first ballet, *Hylas and the Nymphs.* This time the trip was financed by an Octavia Travelling Scholarship, and her composition teachers included Egon Wellesz in Vienna and Nadia Boulanger in Paris.

For Glanville-Hicks 1938 was a watershed as she enjoyed her first real success with the *Choral Suite* triumph, given by Adrian Boult and the BBC Symphony Orchestra. It was a piece for women's voices, oboe and string orchestra. Five months after her and Australia's début at the International Society Festival she married the English composer Stanley Bates.

Two years on, the couple founded Les Trois Arts ballet company, and Glanville-Hicks worked on everything from arranging and conducting to administration and publicity. They moved to the United States during World War II and settled in New York. Here Glanville-Hicks was a member of the League of Composers and helped arrange open-air concerts of modern music in Central Park. When the war ended she co-founded, with Dr Carleton Sprague Smith, the International Music Fund for displaced European musicians, which was operated through Unesco.

By 1946 her marriage was over. Glanville-Hicks remained in the US and in 1948 took American citizenship. The same year she returned to Europe as a delegate to the Festival of the International Society for Contemporary Music in Amsterdam, and her *Concertino da Camera,* composed five years previously, was performed there. When she got back home she was taken on as a music critic for the *New York Herald-Tribune,* a post she held for ten years. She got involved with the Museum of Modern Art, where she helped organize concerts of new and innovative music and worked with Yehudi Menuhin on a programme of Indian concerts. She wrote for numerous magazines and periodicals, and in 1958 founded the Artists' Company, which put on new American operas. As if all this wasn't enough, from 1950 to 1960 she was director of the Composers' Forum, which put on new work by young composers. She was always trying to help people get started.

Fortunately the grants kept coming: from the American Academy of Arts and Letters in 1953; two Guggenheim fellowships a few years later; a Rockefeller grant in 1960 with which she researched Middle Eastern music; and the following year a Fulbright research grant which sent her on the track of Hindu folk music and Greek island songs.

While all this was going on her composition was going from strength to strength. She was particularly skilful at creating dramatic tension in her operas and ballets. The Bowles-inspired piece, *Letters from Morocco,* for voice and orchestra, was first performed in 1953, in New York, with Leopold Stokowski conducting and William Hess as soloist. Paul Bowles was a composer himself, and Glanville-Hicks gave him a great deal of support, as she did with many others, for example Colin McPhee and George Antheil. She wrote a lot for percussion and harp at this time.

Glanville-Hicks had a great sense of humour: before she started at the *Herald Tribune* she composed five songs to the words of music reviews in the paper by a fellow composer, Virgil Thomson, and gave them to him as a birthday present with the title *Thomsoniana.* She was a livewire with what might today be called a "can-do" mentality, and people liked her.

An opera set in India, *The Transposed Heads,* came in 1953; thanks to a Rockefeller Foundation grant; it was the first opera ever commissioned by the Louisville Orchestra in Kentucky. She adapted the words from the Thomas Mann novella. It was subsequently performed in New York and Sydney, and went onto vinyl, courtesy of Columbia. It was by no means her only work to be recorded: there were dozens of others.

She was very articulate about her methods, and spoke of *The Transposed Heads* thus:

> It required no great amendment of my own writing method to plan the structure of the work so as to include Indian materials, for over a period of years I have gradually shed harmonic dictatorship peculiar to modernists, and have evolved a melody rhythm structure that comes very close to the musical patterns of the antique world. It was possible, therefore — with a certain selectivity in regard to the scales used — to incorporate Indian folk themes without doing any violence to their unique character, or without altering my own way of writing.

In 1954 *Sinfonia da Pacifica* received its *première* under the baton of Bernard Heinze in Melbourne. Soon came the Greek connection. Her opera *Nausicaa,* based on a novel by Robert Graves and dealing with the theme of Homer's epic poem *The Odyssey,* was performed at the Athens festival in 1961. Again she wrote the lyrics herself. The review in the *Frankfurter Allgemeine* newspaper trilled, "It is an opera with an individuality all its own — a work opening vistas to new modern roads in ancient spirit never trodden before." Another opera with a Greek theme, *Sappho,* this time from a Lawrence Durrell (q.v.) story, was written as a commission for the San Francisco Opera House.

She had bought a house in Athens and made Greece her home in 1959. Glanville-Hicks never married again, and had no children; her obituary in London's *The Daily Telegraph* said that she considered her music to be her offspring.

The ballets continued, too, for example *Masque of the Wild Man* in 1958, commissioned by the first Festival of the Two Worlds in Spoleto, Italy. She even wrote one for television, *Saul,* which was commissioned by CBS.

Then she got a brain tumour. In 1966 it was operated on and she was given three years to live; it didn't quite work out that way. As a result, however, her sight deteriorated. In 1976 she returned home to Australia for good, but, as ever, was not idle; she directed the Asian Music Studies programme in Sydney and as late as 1989 was working on a newly commissioned opera about Thomas A'Becket. Her work was often performed there, for example in 1980 her *Etruscan Concerto* for piano and chamber orchestra, a work she described as "one of my favourites", and in 1987 she was awarded an honorary doctorate from the University of Sydney.

Born Peggy Glanville-Hicks. **Parents** Ernest and Myrtle (Bailey) Glanville-Hicks. **Marriage** Stanley Bate, composer, 1938 (divorced 1948). **Education** Studied composition with Fritz Hart, Melbourne Conservatory, 1927; Carlotta Rowe Scholarship, Royal College of Music, London, 1932–36, studied composition with Vaughan Williams, 1935, studied orchestration with Gordon Jacob, studied piano with Arthur Benjamin, studied conducting with Constant Lambert and

Malcolm Sargent; studied with Egon Wellesz, Vienna, 1936–38; studied with Nadia Boulanger, Paris, 1936–38. **Emigration** Left Australia for US, 1940, naturalized, 1948; settled Greece, 1959–76; returned to Australia, 1976. **Career** First serious compositions, 1931; first major performance of her work, *Choral Suite,* International Society for Contemporary Music, London, 1938; (with Stanley Bate) founded Les Trois Arts ballet company, 1940; *Concertino da Camera* performed International Society for Contemporary Music, Amsterdam, 1948; (with Chandler Cowles) produced own opera *Transposed Heads,* 1958; commissioned to compose ballet score *Masque of the Wild Man,* Spoleto Festival, Italy, 1958; commissioned to compose ballet *Saul,* CBS-TV, 1959; commissioned to compose opera *Nausicaa,* Athens Festival, 1961; commissioned to compose opera, *Sappho,* Ford Foundation, San Francisco Opera, 1964. **Related activities** Founded (with Dr Carleton Sprague Smith) International Music Fund; music critic, *New York Herald-Tribune,* 1948–58; director, Composers' Forum; produced young composers' series, Connell Library Auditorium, Columbia University, New York, 1950–60s; (with Yehudi Menuhin) master of ceremonies, Indian music concerts, Museum of Modern Art, 1955; (as The Artists' Company) produced Lou Harrison's opera *Rapunzel,* 1959; contributor, *Grove 5*, *Musical Quarterly.* **Other activities** Adviser, Australian Ministry of Information, New York. **Offices and memberships** Member: League of Composers Committee, Contemporary Music Society, Junior Council of Museum of Modern Art. **Awards and honours** Octavia Travelling Scholarship, 1936–38; American Academy of Arts and Letters grant, 1953–54; Guggenheim fellowship, 1956–57, 1957–58; Rockefeller Travel Grant, 1960; Fulbright Fellowship, 1961; honorary doctorate, University of Sydney, 1987. **Compositions** (include) *Frolic* (vocal), 1931; *Rest* (vocal), 1931; Sinfonietta, 1934; *Caedmon* (opera), 1934; *Hylas and the Nymphs* (ballet), 1935; *Choral Suite,* 1937; *Concertino da Camera,* 1945; *Last Poems* (vocal), 1945; *Profiles for China* (vocal), 1945; *Ballade* (vocal), 1945; *Thirteen Ways of Looking at a Blackbird* (vocal), 1947; *Thomsoniana* (vocal), 1949; *Tulsa* (film score), 1949; *Tel* (film score), 1950; Sonata for Harp, 1951; *Letters from Morocco* (vocal), 1952; Sonata for Piano and Percussion, 1952; *Sinfonia da Pacifica,* 1953; *The Transposed Heads* (opera), 1953; *Etruscan Concerto,* 1956; *The African Story,* 1956; *Concerto romantico,* 1957; *The Glittering Gate* (opera), 1957; *The Masque of the Wild Man* (ballet), 1958; *A Scary Time,* 1958; *Saul* (ballet), 1959; *Sappho* (opera), 1964; also: *Gymnopédies*, *Jephtha's Daughter* (ballet), *Tragic Celebration* (ballet), String Quartet, Flute Sonatina, *Concertino Antico, Musica Antiqua, Dance Cantata* (vocal), *Pastoral* (vocal), *Carlos Among the Candles* (opera), Poem for Chorus and Orchestra, *Tapestry, Drama, Come Sleep* (vocal), *Be Still, You Little Leaves* (vocal), *Five Songs from A.E. Housman* (vocal). **Manuscript collection** Victorian State Library, Melbourne. **Cause of death** Heart attack, at age 77. **Further reading** *Virgil Thomson on Virgil Thomson,* 1966; R. Covell, *Australia's Music,* 1967; J. Murdoch, *Australia's Contemporary Composers,* 1972.

JAY GORNEY

Russian/American Composer

Born **Bialystok, Russia, 12 December 1896**

Died **Manhattan, New York, 14 June 1990**

Not everything Jay Gorney did was a success. During the 1920s, he wrote the music for several stage shows in New York. None of them was a big hit, but one of them will always be remembered — for all the wrong reasons. The show was *Hoopla,* and the minute the curtain went up, it was in trouble. First of all, Bernard Granville, who was supposed to do a two-minute prologue, came out drunk and stayed on stage for an hour. (This reportedly drove Gorney, known as the most easy-going and even-tempered composer ever to work the Great White Way, to stamp his foot.) Scene One was then delayed by a further 40 minutes because there were problems with the set. By the end of the first act, there were only ten minutes left before everyone would have to be paid overtime, and the audience had dwindled down to only seven die-hards. These seven were the lucky ones—they got their money back. "Cheer-up," Gorney told his producer, "we just set a record for the shortest run in the history of the theatre: one act." Harold Dietz, the lyricist, said that the showed deserved a better fate, "as it is impossible to conceive of a worse one."

Unlike many Tin Pan Alley composers, Jay Gorney had a profession to fall back on. He was a lawyer. He didn't have to make his living writing songs with the titles like "Zulu Lou" and "Bom-Bom-Beedle-Um-Bo", but even *Hoopla* didn't drive him back to the law. He and Dietz wrote another show, *Merry-Go-Round,* which included the song that made Libby Holman a star, "Hogan's Alley".

Ira Gershwin introduced Gorney to the lyricist who would collaborate on his most famous song. The lyricist was E.Y. ("Yip") Harburg, and the tune Gorney played for him had these lyrics:

> I will go on crying big blue tears
> Till I know that you're true.
> I will go on crying big blue tears
> Till all the seas run blue.

With those lyrics, the song seemed destined to go the way of *Hoopla.* But it was the height of the Depression, and the haunting, melancholy tune evoked a feeling of the times in Harburg. As he recalled,

> It was a terrible period. You couldn't walk along the street without crying, without seeing people standing in breadlines... begging, "Can you spare a dime?" That was for a cup of coffee. That's what the big thing was, a dime could keep you alive for a few days. When Jay played me the tune, I thought of that phrase, "Can you spare a dime?" It kept running through my mind as I was walking the streets. And by putting the word "brother" to the line I got started on it.

Thanks to Harburg, the highly forgettable, "I will go on crying big blue tears..." became the immortal:

> Once I built a railroad, made it run
> Made it race against time.
> Once I built a railroad, now it's done.
> Brother, can you spare a dime?

Though the song has always been (rightly) praised for its lyric, Harburg always gave credit to Gorney for providing a far better tune than most lyricists ever get to work with. His lyrics owe much of their impact to the tune. As Harburg said, "Words make you think a thought. Music makes you feel a feeling. A song makes you feel a thought." There was at least one occasion when the impact of the song was recognized by someone who had very little, if any, recollection of the lyrics. Lee Schubert, Broadway's leading producer, sent for Gorney and asked him if he had another song like "Mister, Will You Give Me Ten Cents?"

Gorney moved to Hollywood in 1933 to work for Fox, and along with his first wife, Edelaine, made one of the biggest discoveries in the history of the movies. He saw a little girl standing outside the theatre where *42nd Street* was playing, staring up at a photo of Ruby Keeler, humming to herself and tap-dancing. He stopped and asked his wife, "Have you ever seen a cuter child?" His wife's exact words were: "She's adorable." As Gorney said later, "I don't usually talk to strange little girls, but this one was just charming, so I went up to her. 'Hello', I said. 'What's your name?'" It was Shirley Temple. Gorney wrote the song, "Baby, Take A Bow" especially for her, and got her a part in *Stand Up And Cheer,* launching the career of the greatest child star Hollywood has ever produced.

His satirical revue, *Meet the People,* in 1940, launched the careers of several adult stars, providing a first big break for the likes of Jack Gilford (q.v.) and Nanette Fabray. Later productions introduced such names as Jan Clayton, Betty Garett, Joey Fay, June Haver and Virginia O'Brien. The show, with book and lyrics by Edward Eliscu and Henry Myers, lampooned the social, political and even musical issues of the times. Among the most memorable numbers were a parody of Latin songs, "In Chi-Chi-Castenango", a ballad called "The Stars Remain", and "The Bill of Rights" (the first ten amendments to the American Constitution set to music), which the Department of Education adopted as the official song for its Bill of Rights Day. (It can be assumed that the Bill of Rights would have a special significance to someone like Gorney, whose family had fled to America when he was only six, in order to escape the brutal pogroms in their native Russia.)

Gorney and his wife, Edelaine, were divorced in 1942. Her second husband just happened to be Gorney's ex-lyricist, Yip Harburg. As she put it, "I never married a man who didn't write 'Brother, Can You Spare A Dime?'" In 1943, Gorney married Sondra Karyl. After writing and producing several films, such as *Moonlight and Pretzels*, *The Gay Señorita* and *Hey, Rookie* (in which Ann Miller set a world record of 550 taps per minute), and working on a few more Broadway musicals, Gorney and his new wife were invited to create a new department at the Dramatic Workshop at the New School for Social Research in New York. The couple co-chaired the new Music-Play Department at the school for three years, beginning in 1948. In 1952, the Gorneys joined the faculty of the American Theatre Wing professional training programme. In 1962, Jay Gorney was awarded a special Tony (Broadway's equivalent of an Oscar) in recognition of his years of outstanding teaching in the musical theatre.

Born Daniel Jason Gornetzky. **Parents** Jacob, mechanical engineer, and Frieda (Perlstein) Gornetzky. **Marriages** 1) Edelaine Roden, 1922 (divorced 1942); 2) Sondra Karyl, magazine editor, 1943. **Children** Rod, from first marriage; Daniel and Karen, from second marriage. **Education** Cass Technical High School, Detroit; studied harmony, counterpoint and orchestration with Earl V. Moore, University of Michigan School of Music; studied law, University of Michigan, BA, 1917, LLB, 1919, JD. **Emigration** Left Russia for US, 1906. **Military service** Bandleader, Great Lakes Training Center, US Navy, 1918. **Career** Practised law, 1919–20; wrote songs, Tin Pan Alley, New York, 1920; first song in a Broadway musical, "I've Been Wanting You", *The Dancing Girl,* 1923; first complete musical score, *Vogues of 1924*; joined American Society of Composers, Authors and Publishers, 1925; first songs for cinema, 1929; musical consultant, Paramount Studios, New York, 1929–30, editorial board, 1931; moved to Hollywood, 1933; contract composer, Fox Studios, 1933–34; independent film songwriter/producer, Columbia Studios, 1944–45; contributor, Hollywood Writers Mobilization Committee, 1943–45; (with Sondra Gorney) founded Music-Play Department, Dramatic Workshop, New School of Social Research, New York, 1948; (with Sondra Gorney) joined faculty American Theatre Wing professional training programme, from 1952; composed incidental music, CBS-TV. **Offices and memberships** Board member: American Guild of Authors and Composers, American Society of Composers, Authors and Publishers. **Awards and honours** Special Antoinette Perry (Tony) Award for outstanding teacher of musical theatre, 1962; citation for creativity, Yale Drama School, 1965; outstanding song award, Songwriters Hall of Fame, 1976. **Chief collaborators** E.Y.

Harburg; Henry Myers; Edward Eliscu; Lew Brown; Sidney Clare; Howard Dietz; Walter and Jean Kerr. **Productions composed for** *Dancing Girl,* 1923; *Greenwich Village Follied,* 1924; *Artists and Models,* 1942; *The Ritz Revue,* 1924; *Earl Carroll Vanities — Third Edition,* 1925; *Miss Happiness,* 1926; *Stand Up and Cheer,* 1927; *Jimmy and Sally,* 1927; *Moonlight and Pretzels,* 1927; *Marie Galante,* 1927; *Redheads on Parade,* 1927; *Glorifying the American Girl,* 1929; *The Battle of Paris,* 1929–30; *Applause,* 1929–30; *Earl Carroll's Sketchbook,* 1929; *Roadhouse Nights* (film), 1930; *Ziegfeld Follies,* 1931; *Shot the Works,* 1931; *Americana,* 1932; *Moonlight and Pretzels* (film), 1933; *Jimmy and Sally* (film); *Romance in the Rain* (film), 1934; *Stand Up and Cheer* (film), 1934; *Meet the People,* 1940. **Complete scores** *Top Hole; Vogues of 1924; Hoopla; Merry-Go-Round; Sketch Book; Earl Carroll's Vanities; Meet the People; Heaven on Earth; Touch and Go; The Happiest Girl in the World; They Can't Get You Down* (film); *Mona and Lisa* (film); *Kris Kringle Rides Again* (television); *The Georgrafoof* (television). **Shows produced** (include) *Merry-Go-Round,* 1927; *Meet the People,* 1939; *They Can't Get You Down,* 1941; *Hey, Rookie* (film), 1944; *The Gay Señorita* (film), 1945. **Screenplays and stories** *College Holiday; Troubador in Trouble; Holiday Hotel* (television); *Mama* (television). **Songs** (include) "I've Been Wanting You", 1923; "Zulu Lou", 1924; "Bom-Bom-Beedle-Um-Bo", 1924; "Hogan's Alley", 1927; "Moskowitz, Gogeloch, Babblekroit and Svonk", 1927; "Kinda Cute", 1929; "Like Me Less, Love Me More", 1929; "When I'm Housekeeping With You", 1929; "What Makes My Baby Blue?", 1929; "What Wouldn't I Do For That Man?", 1929; "It Can't Go On Like This", 1930; "Brother, Can You Spare A Dime?", 1932; "You're My Thrill", 1933; "Love At Last", 1933; "Song Of A Dreamer", 1934; "It's Home", 1934; "Baby, Take A Bow", 1934; "Ah, But Is It Love?", 1933; "The Bill Of Rights", 1939; "In Chi-Chi-Castenango", 1939; "The Stars Remain", 1939; "You're The First Cup of Coffee", 1948; "You Are So Near (And Yet So Far)", 1948; "Funny Little Old World", 1948; "It Will Be All Right (In a Hundred Years)", 1948. **Cause of death** Parkinson's disease, at age 93.

SIR REX HARRISON

British Actor

Born **Huyton, Lancashire, 5 March 1908**

Died **Manhattan, New York, 2 June 1990**

Debonair rogue, ultimate polished Englishman — Rex Harrison perfected the type, in a career spanning 60-plus years (and over 30 films). Although he is best known internationally as the cardigan-clad, charming curmudgeon Professor Henry Higgins in *My Fair Lady,* he portrayed a variety of characters. Whether as Caesar, the Pope, a ghost or the King of Siam, he was considered a warrior of the two most demanding show-businesses: film and stage. Harrison appeared in these and other guises in nearly every theatre in Britain; in fact, despite the popularity he gained as a film star, he considered himself essentially a stage actor. Harrison was always the master of sharp timing, the epitome of "class". He was also a superb comedian.

In public and in private, Harrison had great presence. When Alan J. Lerner described him as "a human thermostat who changes the tempo of every room he enters, turning summer to winter or ice to steam in a matter of seconds" he was undoubtedly referring to his appearance on the boards every bit as much as on the domestic living room carpet.

Despite being born with the rather grand name of Reginald Carey Harrison, his beginnings were far from aristocratic; his father was a civil servant, and he attended Liverpool College. At 16 he joined the Liverpool Repertory Company, very much at the bottom: he rolled umbrellas for cast members until graduating to small parts. A decade spent touring the provinces provided a superb foundation for playing effectively to myriad kinds of audiences. His first stage appearance was in *Thirty Minutes in a Street.* Parts followed in *Charley's Aunt*, *A Cup of Kindness*, *Other Men's Wives*, *For the Love of Mike*, and many others. His first performance in London was at the Everyman Theatre in 1931 in *Getting George Married.* Between 1932 and 1936, eleven plays followed. His first New York role was in the 1936 production of *Sweet Aloes,* playing Tubbs Barrow. The play was dubbed by humorist Robert Benchley, then writing for the *The New Yorker* as "Sweet Alousy"; it closed after three dismal weeks. Not an auspicious beginning for the camel-coated, cigarette-holdered soon-to-be "Sexy Rexy", who was happily creating his own image. *Storm in a Teacup* with Vivien Leigh in London won him more favourable notices as did, the same year (1936), his portrayal of Alan Howard in Terence Rattigan's *French Without Tears.* The elegance and charm were there, of course, but now there was an added element: creative wit. The debonair juvenile lead was graduating, through a series of more mature roles, into a smooth eccentricity that was often petulant, always engaging. Between 1939 and 1941 his performances in Noel Coward's *Design For Living* and S.N. Behrman's *No Time for Comedy,* propelled his image into that of a matinée idol. Harrison was also developing one of his strongest attributes: a naturalism that hid the art behind it, as well as sureness born of precision of judgement — and certainty of effect.

Of Harrison's early work, *St Martin's Lane,* a pleasing film with sparky chemistry between co-players Vivien Leigh and Charles Laughton, stood out. It was his eighth film. Also noteworthy were his roles in *The Citadel* and *Night Train.* In 1941 he repeated his London stage hit with Wendy Hiller in the film of G.B. Shaw's *Major Barbara,* adding personality to Shaw's spirit. Continuing to zig-zag across the Atlantic, he played to good reviews in the films *I Live in Grosvenor Square*, *Rake's Progress* and, especially, *Blithe Spirit.*

Rejected for military service because of poor eyesight, Harrison was in the RAF Volunteer Reserve, and became commanding officer of a Home Guard unit. Thereafter he alternated film and stage work, taking on plays by Chekhov, Anouilh and Pirandello. Unlike Olivier, he chose urbane, properly-attired roles, preferring drama no later than Rattigan's. He declared himself a "theatrical conservative" yet, he said of his regrets, "not playing Shakespeare is not among them". In his one and only Shakespearian role (in *Richard III,* in 1930), he is said to have answered the question, "What is't o'clock?" by groping for his wrist-watch beneath the chain mail.

Harrison's *Anna and the King of Siam,* in 1946, with Irene Dunne (q.v.) and Lee J. Cobb was, as he acknowledged, "the kind of challenge actors like", and his acting was superb, both sensitive and swaggering. With *The Ghost and Mrs Muir* in 1947, co-starring Gene Tierney, there was an edge of rougher masculinity that was enormously attractive. Another favourite of his films was *Unfaithfully Yours* the next year, directed by Preston Sturges, who had been quick to notice the actor's facility for "manicured malice". Nevertheless, the ultimate English gentleman of Hollywood was relieved to return to the stage, in order to control his own career once more.

It was acknowledged that the New York theatre gave Harrison work of a more challenging variety than that normally offered to him in England. His Henry VIII in *Anne of a Thousand Days* gained him a Tony Award. Other plays included *Bell, Book and Candle,* Peter Ustinov's *Love of Four Colonels,* which he also directed, and Christopher Fry's *Venus Observed.*

In *My Fair Lady,* adapted from Shaw's *Pygmalion,* audiences saw their popular star at his most effective, most spellbinding. Even the rampant egotism and insensitivity of his Higgins was charming. Self-admittedly no singer, Harrison employed a rhythmic speech, a form of talking on key, and melody was airily dismissed. Lerner's lyrics had a kind of punch to their delivery never possible before. A dedicated Shavian, Harrison fought for every line of dialogue, never approving of the altered happy ending. "Shaw was very much a realist", he maintained. Lerner attributed any ingenuous creation of his own to some obscure passage in Shaw, so that Harrison would accept it.

The play originally ran nearly 1000 performances, and its revival in 1981 gathered in another appreciative generation. When Harrison was asked to do a screen test for the film version (Clark Gable was the original choice), he indignantly declined. Inevitably Harrison added another Best Actor Oscar to his trophy case. It seems difficult to ascertain whether Higgins fitted Harrison like a glove, or vice versa; at any rate, Harrison even used the character's name from time to time when booking theatre or restaurant seats, and reportedly worried that Higgins's character might devour him completely.

Harrison's later films were enjoyable, if not always distinguished; *The Reluctant Debutante* was a pleasing trifle directed by Vincente Minnelli, co-starring Kay Kendall (then wife number three), John Saxon and Sandra Dee. *Cleopatra,* the elaborately-dressed stinker with Richard Burton and Elizabeth Taylor, won Harrison an Oscar nomination. *The Yellow Rolls-Royce* was an endearing comedy with an all-star cast about the role of a car in romantic pairings. In *The Agony and the Ecstasy,* Harrison's Pope bullied Charlton Heston's Michelangelo; the jury was out as to whether the part was playing against character or a mastery of typecasting. *The Honey Pot,* with Maggie Smith and Susan Hayward, served up an upmarket, updated version of Jonson's *Volpone* in a sly blend of high comedy and whodunnit.

That same year (1967) Harrison reprised his complacent un-singsong delivery in *Dr Dolittle,* a colossal musical dud with Samantha Eggar, Anthony Newley and Richard Attenborough. The photography was superb, the heart in the right place but the charm of the original had flown. It almost ruined the studio; Eliza's surname did not carry the same luck, the second musical around.

In the 1970s Harrison revived more Shaw plays. "Shaw was my contemporary in thought and feeling, and I felt it was a duty to revive his plays for the next generation." By now his elegant urbanity seemed to many to have atrophied into a kind of jaded grandeur; nevertheless the veneration by his public continued. He wrote his first autobiography, *Rex,* in 1974, flawed by what writer Sheridan Morley has described as "a deep inability to care much about anything that did not personally concern him".

With failing eyesight, which meant difficulty in learning new lines, Harrison went back to the classics: Shaw, Barrie's *The Admirable Crichton,* Pirandello's *Henry IV,* Douglas-Home's *The Kingfisher* and Lonsdale's comedy, *Aren't We All?,* the last two co-starring Claudette Colbert.

Harrison had six wives, matching his Henry VIII's record. Three were respected actresses; Lilli Palmer (his second wife) starred with him on Broadway in several plays. To Kay Kendall, his third wife, he showed a sensitive side that was often hidden. When she was diagnosed with myeloid leukaemia, he kept the news from her on the advice of her doctors, and married her in 1957, ensuring the last two years of her life (and reportedly the best two of his) were as wonderful as possible. Years later he starred in Terence Rattigan's *In Praise of Love,* which had been written with Kendall's and Harrison's situation as inspiration.

Another example of the hidden side of Harrison's publicly disdainful self was provided by Dirk Bogarde. At Puffin Asquith's (who adapted *Pygmalion* to *My Fair Lady)* memorial in 1968, Harrison sat next to Bogarde who wrote of violinist Yehudi Menuhin stepping forward to play. "We sat there spellbound. We had just heard Olivier read that bit from *Corinthians* about charity and that had nearly unmanned us all...but this compounded the lumps in our throats. Fortunately Rex leaned toward me and touched my arm gently. 'Never could abide a fiddler!' he whispered, and sort of broke the grief, beautifully."

Although Harrison had the reputation — notoriously — of being impossible to work with; although he could be said to be guilty of the most ungentlemanly behaviour to men and women alike, it was undeniable that he was one of the more distinctive voices in the theatre. (Literally, as well; his barking tenor was an instrument on its own.) Add to that merrily, wickedly, mocking slit eyes and cunning smile, with a technique that a New York paper described as "shaping his lines with a fluid, cultured English drawl, coloring them with a smile that is both knowing and ingratiating, and tossing them off with a deceptive carelessness", and it is possible to forget that he was an extremely disciplined actor. Relaxed, seemingly casual from years of perfecting his craft, he maintained an air of insolent surprise that the world would not behave according to his terms. He was the last of the sophisticates. As actor Tom Conti said, "Who's left?"

Born Reginald Carey Harrison. **Parents** William Reginald, civil engineer, and Edith (Carey) Harrison. **Marriages** 1) Marjorie Noel Collette Thomas, French teacher, 1934 (divorced 1942); 2) Lilli Palmer, actress, 1943 (divorced 1957); 3) Kay Kendall, actress, 1957 (died 1959); 4) Rachel Roberts, actress, 1962 (divorced 1971); 5) the Honourable Elizabeth Rees Harris, 1972 (divorced 1976); 6) Mercia Tinker, 1978. **Children** Noel, from first marriage; Carey, from second marriage. **Education** Birkdale Preparatory School, Lancashire; Liverpool College, Lancashire. **Military service** Royal Air Force Volunteer Reserve, 1941–44. **Career** Début, Liverpool Repertory Theatre, 1924, member of the company, 1924–47; toured 1927; member, Cardiff Repertory Company; first film, *The Great Game,* 1930; first London appearance, *Getting George Married,* 1931; first New York appearance, *Sweet Aloes,* 1936; moved to Hollywood, 1945–47; acted in and produced *Bell, Book and Candle,* New York, 1951, London, 1954; acted in and directed *Love of Four Colonels,* 1953; produced *Nina,* 1955. **Awards and honours** Antoinette Perry (Tony) Award for Best Actor: *Anne of the Thousand Days,* 1948–49, *My Fair Lady,* 1956–57; *Evening Standard* Best Actor Award, *Platonov,* 1960; Academy Award for Best Actor, *Cleopatra* (nomination only), 1960, *My Fair Lady,* 1964; Commendatore, Order of Merit of the Republic of Italy, 1967; knighted 1989. **Stage** (includes, in London unless otherwise indicated) *Thirty Minutes in a Street,* Liverpool, 1924; *Charley's Aunt,* touring, 1927; *Richard III,* touring, 1930; *Getting George Married,* 1931; *The Ninth Man,* 1931; *After All,* 1931; *Other Men's Wives,* 1932; *For the Love of Mike,* 1932; *Another Language,* 1933; *Road House,* 1933–34; *Mother of Pearl,* 1933–34; *No Way Back,* 1934; *Our Mutual Father,* 1934; *Man of Yesterday,* 1935; *Short Story,* 1935; *Charity Begins —,* 1936; *Sweet Aloes,* New York, 1936; *French Without Tears,* 1936–39; *Design for Living,* 1939–41; *No Time for Comedy,* 1939–41; *Anne of the Thousand Days,* New York, 1948–49; *The Cocktail Party,* New York, 1950; *Bell, Book and Candle* (also produced), New York, 1951, 1954; *Venus Observed,* New York, 1952; *Love of Four Colonels* (also directed), New York, 1953; *My Fair Lady,* New York and London, 1956–59; *The Fighting Cock,* New York, 1959; *Platonov,* 1960; *August for the People,* 1961; *The Lionel Touch,* 1969; *Henry IV,* New York and London, 1974; *Perrichon's Travels,* 1976; *Caesar and Cleopatra,* New York, 1977; *The Kingfisher,* New York, 1978–79; *My Fair Lady,* 1981; *Heartbreak House,* 1983; *Aren't We All?,* 1984–87; *The Admirable Crichton,* 1988; *The Circle,* New York, 1990. **Films** *The Great Game,* 1930; *The School for Scandal,* 1930; *All at Sea,* 1934; *Get Your Man,* 1934; *Leave It to Blanche,* 1935; *Men Are Not Gods,* 1936; *Storm in a Teacup,* 1937; *School for Husbands,* 1937; *St Martin's Lane,* 1938; *The Citadel,* 1938; *Over the Moon,* 1939; *The Silent Battle,* 1939; *Ten Days in Paris,* 1939; *Night Train to Munich,* 1940; *Major Barbara,* 1940; *I Live in Grosvenor Square,* 1945; *Blithe Spirit,* 1945; *Rake's Progress,* 1945; *Anna and the King of Siam,* 1946; *The Ghost and Mrs Muir,* 1947; *The Foxes of Harrow,* 1947; *Unfaithfully Yours,* 1948; *Escape,* 1948; *The Long Dark Hall,* 1951; *The Fourposter,* 1952; *King Richard and the Crusaders,* 1954; *The Constant Husband,* 1955; *The Reluctant Debutante,* 1958; *Midnight Lace,* 1960; *The Happy Thieves,* 1962; *Cleopatra,* 1962; *My Fair Lady,* 1964; *The Yellow Rolls-Royce,* 1964; *The Agony and the Ecstasy,* 1965; *The Honey Pot,* 1967; *Doctor Dolittle,* 1967; *A Flea in Her Ear,* 1968; *Staircase,* 1969; *Don Quixote* (television), 1972; *The Prince and the Pauper,* 1977; *The Fifth Musketeer,* 1977; *Man in the Iron Mask,* 1977; *Ashanti,* 1978; *Shalimar,* 1978; *Anastasia* (television), 1986. **Radio** *Berkeley Square; Love Letters; This is Hollywood; Notorious Gentleman; Night Train.* **Publications** *Rex* (autobiography), 1974; *A Damned Serious Business: My Life in Comedy* (autobiography), 1990. **Cause of death** Pancreatic cancer, at age 82.

ELIZABETH HARWOOD

British Soprano

Born **Kettering, Northamptonshire, 27 May 1938**

Died **Fryerning, Essex, 22 June 1990**

Elizabeth Harwood leaves a memory of radiance, of voice, personality and appearance. The delicacy of English beauty does not always tell in the harsh context of the stage — lighting and make-up sometimes blur and coarsen — but Harwood's radiance was not simply a matter of blonde hair, blue eyes, flawless complexion and generous mouth (a standard description of chocolate-box beauty) all of which she certainly possessed, but of charm and warmth of personality. She was the ideal Bella in Tippett's *The Midsummer Marriage,* especially in one appearance when, pregnant with her son, she stepped in at short notice and made Covent Garden's stage glow with her effervescent happiness.

She was one of Britain's proud collection of northern singers, and though not born there was Yorkshire-bred. She trained on the other side of the Pennines at the Royal Manchester College of Music, with Elsie Thurston and Frederick Cox. Her family was musical, and throughout her life she retained an empathy with domestic music-making of the best sort, arranging an unconventional and successful mixture of professionals and amateurs for musical evenings at her and Julian Royle's home.

On graduation she won the Kathleen Ferrier memorial prize and a little later the international Verdi Voices competition at Bussetto, and went straight into opera with the small but important part of Second Boy in *Die Zauberflöte* at Glyndebourne, Sussex. Then in 1962 she went to Sadler's Wells Opera, London where she became and remained a favourite singer of Sir Colin Davis, its musical director. Transferring to the Royal Opera House, Covent Garden, she took parts such as Bella (which she also recorded with him), and Teresa in Berlioz's *Benvenuto Cellini* (a part which has technical difficulties not always appreciated). This production was also given at La Scala, Milan, and where in 1972 she played Mozart's Constanze.

Her performance of Elivira in *Don Giovanni* at the Aix en Provence Festival of 1969 attracted Karajan's notice, and he invited her to Salzburg to sing the Countess in *Le nozze di Figaro,* Fiordiligi (*Così fan tutte*), Constanze (*Il Seraglio*), Musetta in *La Bohème* and that other sparkling lady, Lehar's Hana Glawari in *Die Lustige Witwe,* a performance of which she was particularly proud and which Karajan recorded with her.

These casting details reveal something of the type and quality of her voice, which could cope equally with coloratura and lyrical passages, with an even, creamy tone. In 1963 she had been another memorable Countess, Adele in *Count Ory* at Sadler's Wells, and her agility in a high tessitura was obvious in that she toured Australia in 1965 alternating with Joan Sutherland in the parts of Lucia di Lammermoor, Adina (*L'elisir d'amore*) and Amina (*La somnambula*).

As well as being an ideal interpreter of Tippett's Bella she was an equally successful coloratura Tytania in Britten's *A Midsummer Night's Dream,* as can be heard in the composer's own recording. Another beautifully moulded interpretation appeared on disc in Meredith Davies's recording of Delius's *A Village Romeo and Juliet* in which she sang Vrenchen.

In 1966 she had married the publisher Julian Royle, taking on the additional responsibility of being a "business wife" and it may be that this began to assume equal importance with the dazzling career that still lay open to her. She was unluckily prone to illness in the form of throat infections, and was also not always heard at her best on first nights. She was not of the type to relish tougher aspects of either the music business or the extensive travelling (and thence absence from home and family) required of international singers today. In other words, she had a realistic sense of proportion not based on a blinkered wish for fame. Nonetheless, she made her début with the Metropolitan Opera New York, in 1975 (Fiordiligi) and again appeared there in 1978 and 1982.

One of her last operatic roles was the Marschallin in the Glyndebourne production of *Der Rosenkavalier* (with its unconventional sets and costumes by Erté [q.v.]) in 1980 and 1982, a subtle, moving interpretation cherished by all who saw it. Even after her courageous fight against cancer began she continued to sing, and appeared in *Messiah* in November 1989. (She had taken part in the recording of Sir Charles Mackerras's pioneering version some years earlier, and often sang in oratorio.)

Beauty, charm, glamour, sensitivity, an individual timbre and warmth of voice, perfect enunciation, humour and attractive characterization — all these gifts from the Good Fairy were there and made most of. If only they had included good health and iron confidence, she would have been unrivalled. However, she will remain for so many opera-lovers an ideal interpreter of those roles for which she seemed predestined.

Born Elizabeth Jean Harwood. **Parents** Sydney and Constance Harwood. **Marriage** Julian Royle, publisher, 1966. **Children** One son, Nicholas. **Education** Skipton Girls' High School, Yorkshire; Royal Manchester College of Music, 1960. **Career** Professional début, *Die Zauberflöte,* Glyndeborne, 1960; London début, *Semele,* London, 1961; Covent Garden début, *Arabella,* 1967; began regularly performing Mozart, Salzburg Festival, 1970; toured Australia, 1975; New York début, *Così fan tutti,* 1975; began to emphasize concert and recital performances, 1975; ABC recital and concert tour, 1986. **Awards and honours** Kathleen Ferrier memorial prize, 1960; joint winner, Verdi Competition, Busetto, 1965; fellow, Royal Manchester College of Music; graduate, Royal Schools of Music; licentiate, Royal Academy of Music. **Stage** (includes) *Die Zauberflöte,* 1960; *Semele,* 1961; *Rigoletto,* 1961; *Iolanthe,* 1962; *Count Ory,* 1963; *La sonnambula,* 1965; *L'elisir d'amore,* 1965; *Arabella,* 1967; *Così fan tutti,* 1967, 1975, 1982; *The Midsummer Marriage,* 1968; *Un ballo in maschera,* 1968; *Don Giovanni,* 1969, 1978; *Der Rosenkavalier,* 1971, 1980, 1982; *Le nozze di Figaro,* 1972; *Lucia de Lammermoor,* 1974; *Die Meistersinger,* 1976; *Benvenuto Cellini,* 1976; also: *Ariadne auf Naxos, Il Seraglio, La Bohème, Rosina, A Midsummer Night's Dream, A Village Romeo and Juliet, Die Fledermaus, Die Lustige Witwe, The Merry Widow, The Tales of Hoffman* (television). **Recordings** (include) *The Merry Widow; La Bohème; Rosina; A Midsummer Night's Dream; Der Lustige Witwe; Romeo and Juliet; The Midsummer Marriage; Messiah.* **Cause of death** Cancer, at age 52.

DOREEN HENRY

British Jazz Singer

***Born* Leeds, Yorkshire, 9 January 1906**

***Died* Leeds, Yorkshire, 9 June 1990**

"You sho' do sing, Gate!" wrote trombonist Jack Teagarden when sending his love to his friend Doreen Henry. Teagarden, unlike Europe's then comatose musical press, realized that one of the finest jazz singers of the time — the 1940s — was hiding her light under an English bushel. To their shame it is only the small stir caused by her death that made the British wake up to the fact that such an accomplished artist had ever existed in their midst.

To listen to the tapes of her broadcasts and the ridiculously few records that she made, is to hear any rivals fall away without a chance. Doreen Henry sang with such sensitivity and unerring technical grace that she was beyond local comparison. She had a light and warm swing and a more easy use of range than the better known but usually inflexible female vocalists in Britain at the time. Such subtlety tended to slip by an audience raised on the emotional overdose of the records of Vera Lynn.

Three things militated against an international career. She refused to give up Leeds, her comparatively obscure Yorkshire home, for the bright lights of London. "They didn't exploit people like her in those days", explained a contemporary entrepreneur. And she didn't have the arrogance and narcissism which passes for "star quality". The foundations of her style owed something to Mildred Bailey, another vocalist who also had a remarkable "musicality" in her singing.

Doreen Henry's awareness of the musical scene in the United States was heightened when her eldest sister, Vera, moved there in 1924 and she followed two years later. She seemed to land on her feet very swiftly and during the eight years she spent in the US she was given her own series of radio programmes on WPCH, a New York station, when she sang and accompanied herself at the piano.

Back in England in 1939 Doreen Henry married Richard Auty. Auty, who had played as an international in the England Rugby Union team against Scotland in 1935, was a wool merchant whose work was in the north of the country. The family business had to take precedence over Henry's musical career, but musicians who visited Leeds heard her sing and took back the news to London. She came to be respected by musicians throughout the country. During the war she worked on the BBC's Armed Forces Programme and generated a lot of fan mail when she later broadcast on the American Forces network in Germany. After the war she appeared regularly on BBC Radio, commuting the 200 miles to London for each broadcast. She was featured with the top British musicians of the day including George Chisholm, George Shearing and Billy Munn. She sang with violinist Stephane Grappelli and made her most distinguished recording with him, a version of "Sugar". After the war Henry and her husband travelled frequently to the States on Auty's business and to see sister Vera. It was at this time that the couple met and were befriended by Jack Teagarden. This was a lasting friendship, and Henry sang with Teagarden's band at New York's Famous Door club with backing from cornettist Bobby Hackett. It was on one of these business trips that Henry appeared as a guest with Henry Levine's Chamber Music Society of Lower Basin Street in New York.

In the late 1940s Richard Auty diversified by founding his own record company, Harmony. One of the first people to record for him was the American cornet player Jimmy McPartland, in London with the US Army. The pianist on that date was a young local girl, Marian Page, known today as one of the finest of contemporary jazz soloists and presenter of the eminent Public Radio series, *Piano Jazz,* Marian McPartland. Soon after the McPartland session, Ralph Sharon and his Boptet came to the label's studio to record two famous bebop anthems which had vocals by Doreen Henry, "How High The Moon" and "Euphoria". At this period the eminent English critic Steve Race wrote of Henry as "a singer of great talent and rhythmic subtlety" and "a singer unrivalled in the jazz world."

The Harmony venture lasted for two years and when the label went out of business Henry finally relinquished her career to raise her family. However, tapes of her singing which were recorded when she was 83 showed her still possessed of a remarkably young and accurate voice.

Born Doreen Henry. **Marriage** Richard Auty, wool merchant, 1939. **Children** Two sons. **Career** Began jazz career, USA, 1926; weekly radio jazz series, New York; returned to UK, 1939; guest artist, *Jazz Club,* BBC; recorded with Harmony Records, 1949; guest soloist, Chamber

Music Society of Lower Basin Street; sang with Jimmy Skidmore, Tommy McQuater, George Chisholm, Cliff Townsend, Eddie Taylor, Billy Ternant, Henry Hall, Billy Munn, Stephane Grapelli Quintet, Ralp Sharon and his Boptet, Bobby Hackett and Jack Teagarden. **Recordings** (include) "Sugar", 1945; "Can't We Be Friends"/"St Louis Blues", Harmony, A.1008, 1949; "How High the Moon", 1949; "Euphoria", 1949. **Cause of death** Undisclosed, at age 84.

SIR TOM HOPKINSON

British Writer

Born **Manchester, England, 19 April 1905**

Died **Oxford, England, 20 June 1990**

When Tom Hopkinson was nine years old his father, a lecturer in archaeology, asked his children's permission before embarking on a new career in the Church — as a curate on a minimal stipend of 200 pounds a year. Young Tom freely agreed with his decision. In later years he himself was to change direction. Like his father, he did so on grounds of principle; unlike his father, he chose the eminently secular field of journalism in which to make his mark.

Hopkinson was educated — courtesy of wealthy uncle, Austin Hopkinson, MP — at St Edward's School, Oxford. From there he won a classical scholarship to Pembroke College, Oxford. On graduation his first ambition was to find a job on the newsaper with which he grew up — the *Manchester Guardian* (now simply the *Guardian* and the only English quality national daily with a consistently left-of-centre approach). "I thought all *Guardian* leader writers wore tweed suits, smoked pipes and had terriers", he said later. "But I was prepared to undergo all those hardships if I could realize the height of my social and journalistic ambitions."

He never did. Instead he went to London, where he began selling paragraphs to the *Westminster Gazette.* After the paper folded he spent four years at Crawford's, the advertising agency, writing copy; this he regarded as a prison. His next job was in the publicity department of Odham's, the publishers. At this time the *Daily Herald,* jointly owned by the British trades union movement and by Odhams, was still a going concern and Hopkinson was given the unenviable task of seeking endorsements for a *Daily Herald* encyclopaedia which supposedly contained "The Sum Total of all Human Knowledge". On application to the Astronomer Royal he was told that he and the *Herald* ought to be prosecuted for fraud. "Thank God," responded Hopkinson, "you're the first one who's given a straight answer." Thus, even in these early days, in a menial position in the duplicitous world of the media, he voiced his principles. He continued to do so throughout his life.

In 1933 Victor Gollancz published Hopkinson's first non-fiction book, *A Strong Hand at the Helm,* an astringent photo-and-caption-and-quotation commentary on the incoherence of Britain's first Labour prime minister Ramsay MacDonald and his national government. The *Daily Herald* printed a leader on the book saying, "This is the way Labour Party publicity ought to be done", which inspired Hopkinson to approach the managing director of the Herald group with a request to become a journalist.

In 1934, at the age of 29, he was appointed assistant editor of the *Clarion* — a kind of youth-cum-cycling version of the *Herald.* And in 1938 he moved from Odhams to Hulton Press at the invitation of the brilliant Stefan Lorant who wanted Hopkinson to be his assistant editor with responsibility for all the writing in the about-to-be-born *Picture Post. Picture Post* was the medium through which Hopkinson first put his stamp — as a man of both principle and perception — on the world of journalism. And while he was there he also contributed short stories to the prestigious literary magazine *Horizon*.

Picture Post was launched by Edward Hulton in 1938. Hulton intended it to be a sixpenny Conservative paper; he watched impotently as Stefan Lorant and Hopkinson — after he assumed the editorship in 1940 — turned it into a hugely successful, but nonetheless pro-Labour magazine.

The list of photographers who worked on *Picture Post* under Hopkinson's editorship reads like a *Who's Who* of the craft: Bert Hardy, Bill Brandt, Kurt Hutton, Grace Robinson among them. Hopkinson, a fervent believer in giving maximum credit to the taste and intelligence of his readers, also encouraged distinguished minority writers such as Cyril Connolly, Louis MacNeice and Geoffrey Gorer to contribute. And he encouraged new writers of quality — Robert Kee, Jill Craigie and James Cameron were among the young reporters who first made their mark with Hopkinson.

But it wasn't simply the quality of the writing and of the photography which made *Picture Post* a huge success. It was the philosophy behind them and, as a consequence, the subject matter on which they focused. Said Hopkinson many years later,

> there were other picture magazines, but they were all aimed up-market at the huntin' fishin' and shootin' set. The real idea of the magazine was to bring to ordinary people something which had hitherto been the prerogative of the well-to-do. It also took seriously the achievements of ordinary life. We ran seven pages, for example, on a charwomen's outing to Southend. No-one had ever thought of photographing something like that.

There was another dimension to his leadership. "In the early days in Fleet Street...," wrote Bert Hardy after Hopkinson's death, "a journalist would not be seen in the company of a photographer. We were considered 'inferior'." But not on *Picture Post*; "It's the pictures that matter and your job is to help the photographer", Hopkinson would tell his reporters. He trained writers and photographers to link picture and words, and many of them went on to use this skill in the newly developing medium of television.

Hopkinson cared about the marriage of picture and words; he also cared deeply about standards in journalism. An editor, he believed, had three duties: to his readers, to his staff and to his proprietors — in that order.

Some of his campaigns brought him very creditable unpopularity. During World War II *Picture Post* was so critical of the government that its distribution to the troops was blocked by the Ministry of Information. But he would never shock for the sake of it. He recalled of one particularly harrowing shot: "It was a stunning photograph, but is was pointless horror because it told you nothing about the war."

Hopkinson's principles proved his downfall. When James Cameron and Bert Hardy brought back from the Korean war a devastating word-and-picture account of atrocities committed by South Koreans, Hopkinson published — and was fired.

After his departure, *Picture Post* lost its heart and its direction; circulation dropped, the advertisers moved to television, and in 1957 it closed. But Hopkinson, too, had suffered a severe blow — to his morale. He spent four years in the cold climate of the freelance world, then, from 1954, two uncharacteristically muted years as features editor of the *News Chronicle*. He resigned in 1956 because, in his view, the paper was determined to commit suicide and — at the suggestion of his third wife Dorothy — went to South Africa to edit *Drum*, a pioneering magazine for Blacks.

He spent three years at *Drum*, where he said that his staff could "always be relied on in a crisis, but for a lot of the time they were drunk or missing or both." He insisted that it must be a picture magazine above all — and, again, he discovered and launched quality photographers who in turn made campaigning news in his employ. Ian Berry's coverage of the Sharpeville massacre was the most notable scoop. Recalled Hopkinson later, "One picture in particular, showing a policeman on top of a tank reloading his weapon while his companions still fired into the fleeing crowd, effectively demolished the government case that the police had been forced to fire in self-defence."

Hopkinson travelled widely in Africa, an experience which he later recalled in his memoir *In the Fiery Continent.* And it was in Africa that he discovered his second career. He was asked to set up courses for African journalists in Lagos and Nairobi. He financed his move from South Africa with a legal settlement of 400 pounds obtained from a paper which had printed smears on his parentage following publication in the *Rand Daily Mail* of his characteristically honest series of articles entitled *A Word to the English-speaking People.* He went on to become director for Africa of the International Press Institute.

Leaving Africa at the age of 61, he returned to England where he taught at Sussex University, then in Minnesota and finally set up the one-year post-graduate course in journalism at Cardiff University, which he directed until his retirement in 1975. Writes Maggie Brown, now an established journalist, but then a student, "this endeavour was all part and parcel of a life dedicated to improving and raising the standards of British journalism."

He continued to write books, including two volumes of autobiography and *Shady City,* a novel set in Nigeria and published in 1987. In 1978 he was knighted and in 1989, at the age of 84, he was honoured during a 150th-anniversary-of-the-invention-of-photography conference in Bradford, where he held the stage for one and a half hours. Wrote newspaper editor Harold Evans of this occasion, "Here was a man of quiet conviction, sure of his values, with a brooding sense of honour. The many students of journalism he taught at Cardiff University in his later life will have learned much about the craft of journalism, but they will have been inspired most of all, I think, by his reverence for life."

Born Henry Thomas Hopkinson. **Father** J.H. Hopkinson, lecturer in archaeology and cleric. **Marriages** 1) Antonia White, novelist, 1930 (divorced 1938); 2) Gerti Deutsche, musician and photographer (dissolved); 3) Dorothy (Vernon) Kingsmill, performer, 1953. **Children** Lyndall, from first marriage; two daughters, from second marriage. **Education** St Edward's School, Oxford; classical scholarship, Pembroke College, Oxford, 1923–27, BA, 1927, MA, 1932. **Career** Freelance journalist, advertising copywriter and publicity agent, 1927–34; assistant editor, *Clarion,* London, 1934; assistant editor, *Weekly Illustrated,* London, 1934–38; co-founder, *Picture Post,* London, 1938, assistant editor, 1938–40, editor, 1940–50; editor, *Lilliput,* London, 1941–46; freelance journalist, 1950–54; features editor, *News Chronicle,* London, 1954–56; editor-in-chief, *Drum* magazine, Johannesburg, 1958–61; director for Africa, International Press Institute, Nairobi, Kenya, 1963–66; senior fellow in Press Studies, University of Sussex, Falmer, 1967–69; visiting professor of Journalism and Mass Communication, University of Minnesota, Minneapolis, 1968–69; director, School of Journalism Studies, University College, Cardiff, 1970–75. **Related activities** Journalism adviser, *This Week,* ITV, 1956; chairman, Photographers' Gallery, London, 1969–77, president, from 1978; chairman, National Press Awards, 1968–77; contributor, *The Daily Telegraph.* **Awards and honours** Commander of the Order of the British Empire, 1967; honorary fellow, Royal Photographic Society, 1976; honorary professorial fellow, University College, Cardiff, 1978; knighted 1978. **Publications** *A Wise Man Foolish* (novel), 1930; (as Vindicator) *A Strong Hand at the Helm; Being a Complete and Final Vindication of the Sincerity, Lucidity, Profundity and Penetration of Our Prime Minister, the Right Honourable J. Ramsay Macdonald,* 1933; (as Vindicator) *Fascists at Olympia: A Record of Eye-Witnesses and Victims,* 1934; (as Thomas Pembroke with Mileson Horton) *Photocrimes,* 1936; *The Man Below* (novel), 1937; *Mist in the Tagus* (novel), 1946; *The Transitory Venus* (short stories), 1948; *Down the Long Slide* (novel), 1949; *Love's Apprentice: A Handbook for Combatants in the War of the Sexes,* 1953; *George Orwell,* 1953; *The Lady and the Cut-Throat* (short stories), 1958; *In the Fiery*

Continent, 1962; (with the editors of *Life*) *South Africa,* 1964; (editor) *Picture Post 1938–1950,* 1970; (with Dorothy Hopkinson) *Much Silence: The Life and Work of Meher Baba,* 1974; *Treasures of the Royal Photographic Society,* 1980; *Of This Our Time* (autobiography), 1982; *Under the Tropic* (autobiography), 1984; *Shady City* (novel), 1987. **Cause of death** Undisclosed, at age 85.

RAYMOND HUNTLEY

British Actor

***Born* Birmingham, Warwickshire, 23 April 1904**

***Died* London, England, 15 June 1990**

Raymond Huntley was born in 1904, when Britannia ruled the waves and a great deal of dry land besides. The location of his arrival was Birmingham, snug in the heart of England, and known as "the workshop of the Empire". His date of arrival, 23 April, is the feast of Saint George, patron of England, and, traditionally, the birthday of William Shakespeare. You might then support the idea that an aura of confidence and certainty surrounded Huntley's beginning: it is apparently one which he took to his Thespian career. He knew what he wanted to do and he just go on with it.

After his education at King Edward's School, Huntley was accepted by the Birmingham Repertory Theatre company (the most prestigious in the country outside London), without any formal training. He remained there for two years learning the craft, and after a notable appearance in George Bernard Shaw's juggernaut *Back to Methusela,* at the Court Theatre, London, moved to the capital city. By 1927 he was stalking the boards in the title role of Dracula, which he also made a success on a subsequent two-year tour of the United States. It was an anomolous episode, however; he seemed to enjoy neither the part nor the travel, and henceforward became the most British of actors.

London's West End theatreland became his centre of operations. Huntley was a shrewd judge of a play, and of his own abilties. As Richard Bebb wrote in London's *The Independent,* "Being neither a natural aristocrat nor having any experience of life at the lower end of the social scale, he concentrated on becoming a master of depicting with the greatest subtlety the foibles and idiosyncracies of the English middle class." So it was that, throughout the 1930s, he ensured himself a series of substantial, tailor-made roles on the London stage. A casting director's delight, he was a natural for such types as civil servants, bank managers, senior policemen, businessmen, doctors and lawyers. The vehicle which best accommodated his talents was the middlebrow fare of J.B. Priestley. In *When We Are Married,* Huntley produced a wonderfully funny portrait of the meanest man in Yorkshire; in *Bees on the Boatdeck* he appeared alongside the collossi Ralph Richardson and Laurence Olivier, and in *Time and the Conways,* he brought to his performance as Alan that very English sense of "still waters running deep" which was exactly what the role demanded and which haunted those who saw him. He did undertake more socially elevated parts in the historical dramas *Clive of India* and *St Helena,* but apart from appearing as Lord Hastings in Shakespeare's *Richard III*, he engaged little with the classics.

Huntley's unflashy, though flawless, technique transferred beautifully to the big screen. He was a master of the curled lip and the raised eyebrow, with a quiet, authoritative voice and a concentrated mien that enabled him to suggest unexplored depths of character with a minimum of effort. Starting with Alexander Korda's *Rembrandt* in 1937, Huntley played character roles in dozens of films, many of the sort which now find their way to television screens in the early morning or at dead of night. One of his very best performances was in Carol Reed's wartime classic *The Way Ahead*; while in *Mr Perrin and Mr Traill,* his smooth, cruel headmaster "must have given schoolboys nightmares for months", according to one critic. Later on, film allowed Huntley to develop his considerable gift for comedy. Here he employed a dry, unsmiling delivery which mocked the pretensions to seriousness of those he represented. Good examples are to be seen in several post-war British cinematic monuments like *Passport to Pimlico* and *I'm All Right Jack*, and later, in 1962, *Only Two Can Play*.

On the small screen, he appeared as a bachelor uncle in his own series, *Uncle Charles,* and as an undertaker in the black comedy *That's Your Funeral.* One of his best-known television characters was the crusty family solicitor Sir Geoffrey Dillon in the extremely popular series *Upstairs, Downstairs*, which ran in Britain during the 1970s, and was set in the Edwardian England of Huntley's early childhood.

A shy and private man, repelled by displays of emotion, it was a puzzle even to his closest friends what Huntley was doing in the business at all, though his love of it was never in doubt and clearly, it was repressed and concentrated energy which enriched his performances. Conversely, just as there was no hint of the meretricious in his acting, he liked to play-act in real life. As a member of the most convivial Garrick Club, he cultivated and guarded his place as the institutional curmudgeon. A good grumble and a good meal were his pleasures there, later in life, and the observation of his "gimlet eyes" focusing on the food as it was placed before him was regarded by his clubmates, writes Richard Bebb, as "one of the great comic sights in London". In his eighties, Huntley was quietly delighted to find himself back in the London West End, and as the oldest performer working there, when he took over the role of the judge in Jeffrey Archer's thriller *Beyond Reasonable Doubt.* Shortly after opening, however, he took a fall and broke some bones. After due convalescence, he returned to the play, but not to his usual place at the Garrick lunch-table. His concerned fellows assumed that he was garnering his precious and diminishing resources for the evening's show. Not at all. After seven decades in the profession, Huntley knew well the prick of financial insecurity, and now in receipt of a regular wage for the first time in several years, was indulging himself daily in a small and extremely expensive French restaurant in the patrician neighbourhood of St James's.

Born Raymond Huntley. **Parents** Alfred and Fannie (Walsh) Huntley. **Marriage** June Bell (dissolved). **Education** King Edward's School, Birmingham. **Career** First stage appearance, *A Woman Killed With Kindness,* Birmingham, 1922; member, Birmingham Repertory Theatre company, 1922–24; first London appearance, *As Far As Thought Can Reach*, (Part V, *Back to Methusela),* 1924; toured with various plays, 1925–28; first US appearance, 1928; New York début, *The Venetian Glass Nephew,* 1931; member, Alexandra stock company, Birmingham, 1931; member, Reando stock company, Edinburgh and Glasgow, 1932; first film appearance, 1934; final appearance, *Beyond Reasonable Doubt.* **Stage** (includes, in London unless otherwise indicated) *A Woman Killed With Kindness*, Birmingham, 1922; *As Far As Thought Can Reach,* 1924; *The Farmer's Wife,* 1924–26, 1931; *Dracula,* London and US tour, 1927–30; *Interference,* touring, 1927–28; *The Venetian Glass Nephew,* New York, 1931; *The Dubarry,* 1933; *Clear All Wires,* 1933; *What Happened Then?,* 1933; *Clive of India,* 1934; *The White Guard,* 1934; *Cornelius,* 1935; *Richard III,* 1936; *St Helena,* 1936; *Bees on the Boat Deck,* 1936; *Follow Your Saint,* 1936; *Young Madame Conti,* London and New York, 1936–37; *The First Legion,* 1937; *Time and the Conways,* 1937; *Susannah and the Elders,* 1937; *Glorious Morning,* 1938; *When We Are Married,* 1938; *Rhondda Roundabout,* 1939; *Rebecca,* London and tour, 1940–42; *They Came to a City,* 1943; *Private Lives,* 1944; *Ah! Josephine,* 1945; *Fear No More,* 1946; *The Day of Glory,* 1947; *The Anonymous Lover,* 1947; *The Late Edwina Black,* 1949; *Black Chiffon,* 1950; *And This Was Odd,* 1951; *Lords of Creation,* 1952; *No Sign of the Dove,* 1953; *The Bombshell,* 1954; *The Shadow of*

Doubt, 1955; *Double Image,* 1956; *Any Other Business?,* 1958; *The Woman on the Stair,* 1959; *Caught Napping,* 1959; *The Landing Place,* 1961; *Difference of Opinion,* 1963; *A Family and A Fortune,* Guildford and tour, 1966; *An Ideal Husband,* 1966; *Getting Married,* 1967; *Soldiers,* 1968; *Separate Tables,* 1977; *Beyond Reasonable Doubt,* 1988. **Films** (include) *Rembrandt,* 1937; *Knight Without Armour,* 1937; *Dinner at the Ritz,* 1937; *Night Train to Munich,* 1940; *The Ghost of St Michael's,* 1941; *The Way Ahead,* 1944; *School for Secrets,* 1945; *Mr Perrin and Mr Traill,* 1948; *So Evil My Love,* 1948; *Passport to Pimlico,* 1949; *Trio,* 1950; *The Long Dark Hall,* 1951; *Room at the Top,* 1959; *Carleton-Browne of the FO,* 1959; *I'm All Right Jack,* 1960; *Only Two Can Play,* 1962; *Rotten to the Core,* 1965; *Hostile Witness,* 1967. **Television** *Upstairs, Downstairs*; *Uncle Charles*; *That's Your Funeral*; *Destiny of a Spy.* **Cause of death** Undisclosed, at age 86.

RONALD ILLINGWORTH

British Paediatrician and Writer

Born **Harrogate, Yorkshire, 7 October 1909**

Died **Bergen, Norway, 4 June 1990**

Ronald Illingworth pioneered a new libertarian approach to child rearing, which today we all take for granted. He put paid to the old Victorian tradition, while encouraging a far more sympathetic and flexible attitude.

He was a highly esteemed paediatrician as well as a writer of great clarity and naturalness. Apart from writing several hundred learned articles for medical journals, he wrote 14 books, most of which were best-sellers and have been through many editions and been translated into an astonishing number of different languages, including one in Farsi.

His books cover a wide range of topics. The best known is *The Normal Child,* which went into nine editions. He also wrote *Babies and Young Children* and *Lessons from Childhood* in collaboration with his wife, also a paediatrician. In the first of these, they drew upon their own close family life, and in the second, they examined the childhoods of various notorious figures. Other books covered the problems of common disease in children and child development generally.

In *The Normal Child* Illingworth's writing is crisp and down to earth. Above all he concentrates on the common illnesses of children. He couldn't see the point of teaching student doctors about rare conditions when they were unlikely to come across them in their working life. In fact, it annoyed him to see time wasted in this way.

Also in *The Normal Child,* instead of writing about children in isolation, he examines them within the context of their relationship to others: parents, brothers and sisters, relatives and so on. He wonders how, if the parents' behaviour is questionable, they expect obedience from their children. Often parents demand a higher standard from their children than they themselves are capable of. Parents should, for example, apologize for bad behaviour, just as a child should. This is obviously a far cry from the Victorian tradition where children were seen and not heard, and the behaviour of the parent was never called into question.

Illingworth goes on to suggest that there should be no set rules for feeding, for bedtime, for crying: let a child eat when it is hungry, sleep when it is tired, and be comforted when it cries. Failure to do these things will create a whining child with no confidence in either itself or its parents.

Love is also important, and he says it should be the first law of parenthood. He writes, "It is of prime importance that parents should not only love their children, but should show it and try to ensure that the children learn to know it." How can a child learn to know love? Illingworth suggests that through actions, expressions, even tone of voice, a child can recognize love. Children need loving all the time, and this will make them normal children and later loving parents themselves. A happy, loving home is of key importance to a child's well-being.

The attitude of hospitals towards children was revolutionized by Ronald Illingworth. He insisted that a good children's ward, well-managed, should be messy. Parents should be allowed unrestricted contact with their children, staying overnight if necessary. He even promoted the idea of parents accompanying their children into the operating theatre. He was compassionate towards parents with sick children and endeavoured to help them through their pain and fear by offering hope and comfort.

Illingworth made it a principle of his life that the health and well-being of a child should never be left to unspecialized doctors. During his early career, many established physicians were all-powerful and felt themselves competent to cover all ages, from the cradle to the grave. Illingworth helped introduce specialization, particularly in the paediatric area.

Although Illingworth loved Yorkshire, where he was born and raised, and attended Bradford Grammar School and later Leeds University, his work often took him further afield. Before World War II, he worked in both London, at Great Ormond Street Hospital for Sick Children, and Oxford, where he took up a Nuffield Research Studentship. Following this, he took up a Rockefeller Fellowship in the US and worked under Arnold Gessell. He was greatly influenced by Gessell, who measured the physical and social achievements of children at different ages, and who moved the subject of child development into a clinical science.

It was as professor of child health at Sheffield University that Ronald Illingworth was able to make his greatest impact in the field of paediatrics. He was professor from 1947 until his retirement in 1975; in those years he drew upon all his past experience both in England and America, and was influenced by the work of James Spence and Donald Court, who were working in Newcastle on a programme of child development. He set up a highly organized department with a first-class clinical service: children were observed directly, assessed objectively and subsequently helped. Over the years his department gained world-wide prestige, and he showed himself to be very talented at teaching other paediatricians. He encouraged all those who worked for him, but he never forced his own views on them. Many, nevertheless, were influenced by him and are today professorial heads of paediatric departments scattered across the globe.

Just as he was totally committed to his work, always striving for perfection, so he pursued his interest in photography and philately. He was a talented photographer, winning over 70 awards in various competitions. In 1936, he was elected a fellow of the Royal Photographic Society. At the "Illingworth 80" celebrations, held in October 1989, he held his audience spellbound in the presentation of 120 colour slides of the Swiss Alps. He also enjoyed outdoor pursuits. As a student, he did a lot of cycling, financing his trips through the sale of photographs to newspapers. Later he took up skiing and skibobbing.

Ronald Illingworth was a modest, unassuming person, who did not like the pomp and formality of public ceremonies. He was shy, but those who knew him well found him warm and caring. His retiring personality meant his great qualities and achievements almost went unhonoured. He influenced the medical care of children more than anyone in his generation, and with his liberal and innovative views, helped move the study of child health out of the dark, Victorian period into the new enlightened era of today.

Born Ronald Stanley Illingworth. **Father** Herbert Edward, architect, and Ellen (Brayshaw) Illingworth. **Marriage** Cynthia Redhead, paediatrician, 1947. **Children** Andrea, Robin and Corinne. **Education** Clifton House School, Harrogate, Yorkshire; Bradford Grammar School, Yorkshire, West Riding County Major Scholar, 1928; Leeds University, MB, ChB, 1934, MRCS,

LRCP, 1934, MD, 1937, MRCP, 1937, Diploma in Public Health, with distinction, 1938, Diploma in Child Health, Royal College of Physicians, 1938; Nuffield Research Studentship, Oxford University, 1939–41; Rockefeller Research Fellowship, 1939 and 1946; fellow, Royal College of Physicians, 1947. **Military service** Medical specialist, officer in charge of Medical Division, Royal Army Medical Corps, 1941–46, became lieutenant-colonel. **Career** Resident assistant, Hospital for Sick Children, Great Ormond Street, London, 1938–39; assistant to professor of child health, University of London, 1946–47; professor of child health, University of Sheffield, 1947–75. **Offices and memberships** Fellow: Royal Photographic Society, 1936, Royal Society of Medicine, British Medical Association. **Awards and honours** Medal, University of Turku, Finland, 1974; honorary DSc, University of Baghdad, Iraq, 1975, Leeds University, 1982; honorary MD, Sheffield University, 1976; Aldrich Award, American Academy of Paediatrics, 1978; Spence Medal, British Paediatric Association, 1979; Dawson Williams Prize, British Medical Association, 1981; Freedom of the City of Sheffield, 1982; honorary member: British Paediatric Association, Swedish Paediatric Association, Finnish Paediatric Association, American Academy of Paediatrics, Academy of Paediatricians of the Union of Soviet Socialist Republics. **Publications** *Some Aspects of Child Health,* 1949; *The Normal Child: Some Problems of the First Three Years and Their Treatment,* 1953, second edition published as *The Normal Child: Some Problems of the First Five Years and Their Treatment,* 1957; (with C.M. Illingworth) *Babies and Young Children: Feeding, Management and Care,* 1954; *Children and Sleep,* 1956; *Recent Advances in Cerebral Palsy* (editor), 1958; *Common Ailments in Babies,* 1959, also published as *Common Ailments in Toddlers,* 1960; *Development of Infant and Young Child, Normal and Abnormal,* 1960; *An Introduction to Developmental Assessment in the First Year,* 1962; *Your Child from Five to Twelve,* 1962; *The Normal Schoolchild: His Problems, Physical and Emotional,* 1964; (with C.M. Illingworth) *Lessons from Childhood: some aspects of the early life of unusual men and women,* 1966; *Common Symptoms of Disease in Children,* 1967; *Development at Screening,* 1969; *Treatment of the Child at Home: a guide for family doctors,* 1971; *Basic Development Screening,* 1973; *The Child at School: a Paediatrician's Manual for Teachers,* 1974; *Your Child's Development in the First Five Years,* 1981; *Infections and Immunisation of your Child,* 1981. **Cause of death** Undisclosed, at age 80.

WOLFE KELMAN

Austrian/American Rabbi

Born **Vienna, Austria, 27 November 1923**

Died **New York City, New York, 26 June 1990**

Wolfe Kelman will be remembered as the rabbi who did more than anyone else to put Conservative Judaism on the map of America in the past 40 years. As vice-president of the Rabbinical Assembly since the year after his ordination in 1950, he worked tirelessly from his office in the New York Jewish Theological Seminary to promote the cause of Conservative rabbis. He helped to train and counsel many hundreds of students, he organized retreats for working rabbis, he struggled to ensure that all rabbis received a competitive salary and benefits such as pensions and insurance. He was the man to whom rabbis brought their troubles, congregations their needs; "the king-pin and king-maker" as one commentator described him "of the Conservative movement". When Rabbi Kelman began his work there were only 300 Conservative rabbis in the United States. At his death they numbered 1200, but Kelman himself would have been the last to claim credit for the increase.

The man whom everyone describes as "the rabbi's rabbi" came from a family of Polish Hasidic rabbis and, though he eschewed the strict Orthodoxy of his forbears, was something of a modern-day Hasidic master himself. Kelman's father was a Viennese rabbi who fled from Nazi persecution to Canada; Kelman's son is a rabbi as are his two brothers.

Perhaps the most formative influence in Kelman's life was, however, his mother. Kelman was only 13 when his father died. His mother brought up the six children of the family alone while becoming at the same time an active community leader in Toronto. "It was her example", Kelman said, "that made me believe women could function as rabbis".

The decision to allow women rabbis, made by Conservative Judaism in 1985, illustrates the particular philosophy of the Conservative movement. Its great strength lies in its ability to adapt to changes in society and in the world while maintaining reverence for the Jewish Law. In the 1840s Zacharias Frankel broke with the more radical members of the Reform movement at a series of conferences in Germany. His respect for historical scholarship and his insistence on the sacredness of the Law and the Sabbath remain central to the movement today, and were very much a part of Wolfe Kelman's thinking.

Like many Conservative Jews Kelman also supported the growth of secular Zionism and the establishment of the state of Israel. He spent a year as visiting professor at the Hebrew University in Jerusalem, and afterwards wrote a book on *Judaism in Israel.* Like others, he voiced severe doubts at some of Israeli policy, particularly in the occupied territories. "It's a pity", he said sadly, "we can't march on Jerusalem" — as in 1963 he and his seminary teacher Rabbi Abraham Joshua Heschel had joined with other rabbis to take part in Martin Luther King's great civil rights march in Alabama.

Wolfe Kelman's positive sense of pride in his Jewish heritage was apparent in all he did, both in helping caring organizations such as Concern and HIAS (Hebrew Sheltering and Immigrant Aid Society) and in the field of cultural activities. As president of the Hebrew Arts Foundation and chairman of the American section of the World Jewish Congress he promoted Jewish writers and artists as well as working to improve relations between the different branches of Judaism and between Christians and Jews.

To those Jews more inclined to self-deprecation and historical *Angst* he was fond of quoting Samuel's rebuke to Saul, "Though thou be little in thine own sight, art thou not head of the tribes of Israel?" "Be strong and of good courage" was the text he chose to preach from to Soviet Jews during a visit to Moscow in 1968. The Israelites, he would remind his listeners, were excluded from the Promised Land not because of any sin of the Golden Calf but because they listened too eagerly to the reports of their spies.

Kelman was a large, genial, bearded figure. He described himself as nothing but a "wild, colonial lad", and certainly had much of the colonial's outspoken frankness and brutal honesty — as some aspiring rabbis found to their discomfort. He himself felt that most of his ideas and attitudes owed more to his Canadian upbringing than to his eastern European origins. "The synthesis", Kalman wrote, "between Anglo-Saxon emphasis on personal liberty and the supremacy of conscience and the hallowed Jewish traditional emphasis on justice tempered by compassion and great reverence for tradition have shaped my perceptions and, hopefully deeds."

Born Wolfe Kelman. **Parents** Hersh Leib, rabbi, and Mirl (Fish) Kelman. **Marriage** Jacqueline Levy, 1952. **Children** Levi, Naamah and Abigail. **Education** University of Toronto, BA, 1946; Jewish Theological Seminary of America, MHL, 1950. **Emigration** Left Austria for Canada; settled US, 1946, naturalized 1962. **Military service** Royal Canadian Air Force, 1943–45. **Career** Rabbi from 1950; executive vice-president, Rabbinical Assembly, 1951–90; director, joint placement commission, Rabbinical Assembly, United Synagogue of America and Jewish Theological Seminary of America, 1951–66; member, governing council, World Jewish Congress,

1968–90, chairman, cultural commission, 1975–77, co-chairman, interreligious affairs, 1979–86, chairman, committee on small communities, 1986–90. **Related activities** Visiting rabbi, West London Congregation of British Jews, 1957–58; visiting professor of homiletics, Jewish Theological Seminary of America, 1966–73, adjunct assistant professor of history, 1973–90; visiting professor, Hebrew University, Jerusalem, 1984–85. **Offices and memberships** President, Committee of Neighbors Concerned for the Elderly, Their Rights and Needs, 1971–90; on board of directors, executive committee, Hebrew Shelter and Immigrant Aid Society, 1974–90; president, Hebrew Arts Foundation. **Awards and honours** Honorary DD, Jewish Theological Seminary of America, 1973. **Publications** *The Future of the American Synagogue,* 1962; *Judaism in Israel,* 1965. **Cause of death** Melanoma, at age 66. **Further reading** *Perspective on Jews and Judaism: Essays in Honor of Wolfe Kelman,* 1978.

RAANA LIAQUAT ALI KHAN

Pakistani Politician and Ambassador

Born **Almora, India, 13 February 1905**

Died **Karachi, Pakistan, 13 June 1990**

Raana Liaquat Ali Khan was one of the more extraordinary women of this century. The daughter of a senior government official, she received a degree in economics from Lucknow University. She became a lecturer in economics at Delhi, where she stayed until her marriage in 1933.

Together with her husband, Liaquat Ali Khan, she helped work toward the founding of the Muslim state of Pakistan. On their honeymoon in London they met and persuaded Muhammad Ali Jinnah to return to India and lead the Muslim cause. Jinnah complied. He returned home to wrestle with the British and to found Pakistan as a nation and separate entity from India.

The partition of Pakistan in 1947 was accompanied by much bloodshed. Fierce fighting broke out between the Hindus and Muslims in India and millions of Muslims flooded into Pakistan to escape the massacre. Begum Raana was the first to come to the aid of the refugees. She mobilized the rich into donating money and food to the camps. She personally saw to the feeding of the hungry and the housing of the destitute. She became known as the Florence Nightingale of the refugee camps. Her selfless devotion shamed those around her into action, and the All Pakistan Women's Association was formed. This organization would help millions escape poverty and worse.

However, harder times and personal tragedy were soon to follow for Begum Raana. In 1948 Jinnah died and in 1951, her husband, the then prime minister, was assassinated. In her grief she turned to social work, founding the Pakistan Cottage Industries in Karachi, industrial and health centres for women, the Health and Nutrition Association and the colleges of home economics in Karachi, Lahore and Dacca. She also established the Federation of University Women and the International Women's Club and became the chief patron of the Nurses Association and the Liaquat Memorial Hospital. She also sat on the management committees of numerous social organizations, wrote articles and gave impassioned speeches.

In 1949 she was appointed a brigadier and formed the Women's National Guard which was later disbanded by the mullahs. As her obituarist in London's *The Independent,* Ahmed Rashid, expressed it, "She had little time for the mullahs unless they respected women's rights." Throughout her life she opposed laws that she saw as discriminatory against women, and became an inspiration for younger generations.

In 1952 she became only the second Muslim woman delegate to the United Nations. From 1954 to 1966 she served as the first woman ambassador to Holland, Italy and Tunisia. In 1973 she became the first woman governor of Sind Province. In 1979, after years of dedication to the welfare of others, she received the Human Rights Award of the United Nations.

Raana Liaquat Ali Khan (known affectionately as Begum Sahiba) was widely beloved. She had a magnetic charm that could melt the heart of the most cynical. Nonetheless, the last years of her life were difficult. She did not support the government of General Zia ul-Haq, who tried to undermine women's rights. She often attacked what she saw as the discriminatory and bigoted Islamic laws passed in the 1980s. To her these laws were against the spirit of democracy and integrity upon which her country was founded.

Born Raana. **Father** Government official. **Marriage** Sahib Zada Liaquat Ali Khan, prime minister of Pakistan, 1933 (assassinated 1951). **Children** Ashraf and one other son. **Education** Lucknow University, MA in economics. **Career** Professor of economics, Delhi, to 1933; worked for Pakistan Movement against British rule, 1933–47; mobilized aid to refugee camps during Partition, 1947; husband assassinated, 1951; concentrated on social work, 1951–52; delegate, United Nations, 1952; ambassador: Holland, Italy, Tunisia, 1954–66; governor, Sind Province, 1973–76. **Related activities** Appointed brigadier, formed Women's National Guard, 1949; founder, All Pakistan Women's Association, 1949; founder, Pakistan Cottage Industries, Karachi; founder, Health and Nutrition Association; founder, colleges of home economics, Karachi, Lahore, Dacca; founder, Federation of University Women. **Other activities** Chief patron, Nurses Association; patron, Liaquat Memorial Hospital. **Offices and memberships** Member, International Labour Organization. **Awards and honours** Human Rights Award, United Nations, 1979. **Cause of death** Undisclosed, at age 85.

VASILIY KUZNETSOV

Soviet Politician

Born **Sofilovka, Russia, 13 February 1901**

Died **Moscow, USSR, 5 June 1990**

One way of surviving in the long term as a politician in the Soviet Union is to tell each party with whom you are connected exactly what they want to hear, and to be sincere about it. One man of such talents was Vasiliy Kuznetsov whose career spanned the Stalin era through the first years of Gorbachev — a feat by anyone's standards.

Born into a Russian peasant family, Kuznetsov joined the Red Army in 1919, becoming involved in the revolution and the civil war that followed. Greatly influenced by these dramatic times, he became an enthusiastic Bolshevik and upon leaving the army he was sent to Leningrad Polytechnical Institute, the better to take his place in the new society.

He began work in Donbass where he quickly climbed the career ladder in the huge metallurgical works at Makeyevka. In the same year (1927) he joined the Communist Party. The combination of technical competence and political zeal thrust him into the chance of a Soviet lifetime, for he was sent to the United States in 1931 to improve his professional qualifications. He studied at the Carnegie Institute of Technology in Pittsburgh, Pennsylvania, while holding down a job with the Ford Motor Company.

Two years later he returned to the Soviet Union to work at the Elektrostal plant where he introduced high-quality steel production. During Stalin's terror, when Kuznetsov's experience of foreign travel might have worked against him, he was once again saved — probably because of his fervent belief in the Party. For his efforts at the plant as well as his political activities, he was named deputy chairman of the State Planning Commission and received a Stalin prize.

During World War II he was attached to the State Committee for Defence, and in 1943 began to become involved in the Soviet trade union movement. The trade unions were strictly pawns of the government and Kuznetsov was appointed chairman of their council. During the last year in that office he was a member of the Central Committee.

After Stalin's death in 1953 Kuznetsov served as Soviet ambassador to China and worked at the Ministry of Foreign Affairs as deputy foreign minister until 1955, when he became first deputy foreign minister.

During the two decades in which he served in this office, Kuznetsov tackled several tough diplomatic assignments. In 1962 he was sent to New York to negotiate the removal of Soviet bases in Cuba after the famous Cuban missile crisis. He was the Soviet delegate to the Geneva talks which led to the 1963 test-ban treaty.

It was also in that office that Kuznetsov played an important role in sorting out the difficulties the Soviet Union was having with the leaders of the "Prague Spring". He was sent to Prague, invested with special powers by the Soviet Communist Party, in 1968, and conducted long and skilful interviews with each individual member of the Czechoslovak party leadership. After the interviews he was able to identify those who would be loyal to the Party.

It was widely reported by those who dealt with him that he was business-like, accomplished and skilled at his job. The key to his diplomatic success was that he had learned to show outward cordiality, while presenting an unyielding stand on the Soviet point of view.

In 1977 he reached the height of his career by becoming first deputy chairman of the Presidium of the Supreme Soviet. In this capacity he often relieved President Brezhnev from onerous ceremonial tasks. He was also elevated by Brezhnev to candidate membership in the Politburo.

He was able to hold onto his high office throughout the Andropov and Chernenko general secretaryships, but at the first party congress of Gorbachev's presidency he was dropped from his Politburo candidate membership. At the time he was 85 and out of step with the new order that Gorbachev hope to initiate.

Born Vasiliy Vasilyevich Kuznetsov. **Parents** Peasants. **Marriage** Zoya Izumnova. **Children** Three children. **Education** Studied engineering, Leningrad Polytechnical Institute, 1921–26; exchange student, Carnegie Institute of Technology, Pittsburgh, Pennsylvania, 1931–33, MS, 1933. **Military service** Red Army, 1920–21. **Career** Began working, 1916; joined Communist Party, 1927; engineer, Makeyevka Iron and Steel Works, 1927–31; worked for Ford Motor Company, Detroit, while exchange student in US, 1931–33; engineer, Elektrostal plant, 1934–37; engineer, Chief Administration for Special Steels, 1937, chief engineer, 1937–40; deputy chairman, State Planning Commission, 1940–44; chairman, central committee, Ferrous Metallurgical Workers' Union, 1944–53; worked to create World Federation of Trade Unions, 1945, vice-president, chairman, 1949–53; deputy, Supreme Soviet, 1946–90; chairman, Council of Nationalities, 1946–50; full member, Central Committee, 1952–90, presidium, 1952–53; ambassador to People's Republic of China, 1953; deputy minister of Foreign Affairs, 1953–55; first deputy minister, 1955–57; delegation leader, United Nations General Assembly, 1954; first deputy chairman, Presidium of Supreme Soviet, 1977–86; member, Politburo Central Committee, 1977–86; retired, 1986. **Related activities** Deputy member for metallurgical questions, State Defence Commission, 1941–45; chairman, All-Union Central Council of Trade Unions, 1944; chief, Soviet delegation, British Trades Union Congress international meeting on post-war labour policy, 1945, vice-president; delegate, UN organizing conference, San Francisco, 1945. **Awards and honours** Stalin prize, 1941; Three Orders of Lenin; Order of Red Banner of Labour; Order of Red Star; Badge of Honour. **Cause of death** Undisclosed, at age 89.

JOE LOSS

British Bandleader

***Born* London, England, 22 June 1909**

***Died* London, England, 6 June 1990**

Joe Loss was one of the last surviving figures from an era of British popular culture which still exercises a powerful nostalgic pull on an entire generation. He was one of those wartime entertainers whose status took on the trappings of legend.

Loss was the most popular and successful bandleader in Britain's peculiar but enduring big band swing craze, a dance-hall music refined — some would say watered down — from its origins in the great American big bands of the 1920s and 1930s. His career spanned 60 years and multi-million sales, and where contemporaries such as Geraldo, Ambrose and Henry Hall had long passed from the public eye Loss was still working until shortly before his death.

A much-liked figure of stage, television and, in recent years, winter cruises aboard the QE2, Loss is the man who symbolizes a particularly potent flashpoint between American and British culture. An early exponent of the white big band swing popularized by Glenn Miller and his Orchestra, Loss made his name in the thriving dance halls and *palais de danse*. He consolidated that appeal later with BBC radio broadcasts, prior to and during World War II. His fellow wartime legend, Vera Lynn, made her first radio broadcasts with the Loss Orchestra, although Loss liked to joke that she never appeared live with his big band, "because I could never afford her". Almost an entire generation grew up to the sound of the Joe Loss Orchestra and its counterparts, and the sound became synonymous with a certain era, and a certain shared experience.

Loss's parents, Russian Jewish émigrés, wanted him to become a classical violinist, but like many of his generation he was captivated by the swing music he heard leaking from cinemas and dance-halls in the London of the 1920s. He trained as a classical violinist, even entering London's prestigious Trinity College of Music, but by the age of 16 had already formed his own group, the Magnetic Dance Band. The almost Futurist name is resonant of the period, when jazz still had associations with artists and Bohemians, although Loss was to make his name in the unpretentious dance-halls of London and the provinces.

His first paid job was as a violinist accompanying silent films for 30 shillings a week at a cinema in the small home counties (that is, neighbouring London) town of Ilford. He soon moved on to play at two major London cinemas, the Rialto and the London Pavilion, and began playing in the dance orchestra of the Wimbledon Palais.

At the age of 21 he formed his own dance orchestra, and was shortly one of the roster of bands playing at the prestigious Astoria Ballroom in London's West End. By the early 1930s he was playing in fashionably rakish London night-clubs like the Kit-Kat Club, favoured by Edward, Prince of Wales, and his set. This was the first of many encounters with royalty, an acquaintance which would be pursued in earnest by one of his greatest fans, Elizabeth II, in regular command performances over the decades at Buckingham Palace and Windsor Castle.

By the mid-1930s the Joe Loss Orchestra was broadcasting on the radio regularly, and in 1936 Loss had his first hit record with "Begin The Beguine". In 1938 he had his biggest hit so far with a cover version of Glen Miller's popular "In The Mood", which sold over a million copies and became the Joe Loss Orchestra signature tune for the next 50 years.

At the outbreak of war Loss threw himself into the war effort, becoming a favourite on the daily *Music While You Work* radio show, touring munitions factories and military establishments here and abroad, even travelling with his orchestra as entertainers to the British Expeditionary Force when it landed in France.

It was this period that undoubtedly sealed Loss's popularity with the British public for the next half century, and it is perhaps because of the conditions of the times that he remained a mainly British phenomenon. Large numbers of American armed forces personnel may, in the media parlance of the time, have been "Over-paid, over-sexed, and over here", but they had also brought with them the vibrant culture of swing and jive music; and not just the music, but the trappings — clothes, accessories, drinks and cigarettes, language, life-style — that came with it. This was seized by a young and young-ish populace eager for a respite from the privations of wartime Britain. Decades before the arrival of pop music, but acting in much the same way, Loss's music became the soundtrack to countless thousands of wartime romances, and, presumably, not a few wartime mishaps.

Following the war, Loss continued to build his reputation in the dance-halls, in radio broadcasts, and in the popular music charts, where he would eventually record over 1000 different recordings for EMI Records. While swing and its English branch in particular were supplanted in the popular sector by the advent of pop and rock music, Loss and his orchestra survived — because, observers have said, of his innate ability to "read" a dance-hall audience, and to vary his repertoire accordingly. Loss scored his last significant chart hit in 1964 with "March Of The Mods", a response to the burgeoning youth cult of the time and itself a sign of his professional adaptability. The Joe Loss Orchestra was still recording million-selling albums for EMI in the mid-1970s, although perhaps understandably Loss drew the line at punk.

Loss's popularity made him a natural for television, in particular on the perennially successful ballroom dancing competition show, *Come Dancing*. He also composed the theme music to the popular television comedy, *Steptoe and Son,* as well as for the crime thriller series, *Maigret.* Loss was awarded the dancing world's version of the Oscar, the Carl Alan Award, no less than 14 times. It is not surprising that grander, or at least more formal, awards followed. As well as being given the Freedom of the City of London, an important if nominal civil award, he was also made an Officer of the British Empire and lieutenant of the Royal Victorian Order by Queen Elizabeth II.

His career was doubly remarkable in its longevity and in Loss's own stamina. He was still arranging bookings for his big band shortly before being diagnosed with the kidney illness that proved fatal. He was, by his own admission, an entertainer, and had no pretensions to innovation or showmanship. At the time that Loss was popularizing swing, jazz itself was already assuming the wild modernist angles of bebop in the hands of people like Charlie Parker. Yet for all his blatant populism, and the increasing nostalgia which buoyed Loss's career in the later decades, his achievement is particularly notable.

Born Joshua Alexander Loss. **Parents** Israel, cabinet maker, and Ada Loss. **Marriage** Mildred Blanch Rose, 1938. **Children** David and Jennifer. **Education** Jewish Free School, Spitalfields, London; scholarship Trinity College of Music, London; London College of Music. **Career** Silent film accompanist, Coliseum, Ilford, 1926, Tower Ball Room, Blackpool, 1926; formed own orchestra, Astoria Ballroom, London, 1930; first broadcast, 1934, then broadcast weekly; joined Regal Zonophone, 1936; first hit record, "Begin The Beguine", 1936; toured Commonwealth; toured in variety; toured overseas, 1939–45; resident orchestra leader, Hammersmith Palais, from 1945; joined Mecca, 1959; 50-year contract, EMI; first dance band to appear in China, Dairen, 1979; orchestra leader, *Queen Elizabeth II* World Cruises; appeared at Buckingham Palace and

Windsor Castle; orchestra leader, pre-wedding ball, Princess Margaret, Princess Alexandra, Princess Anne; orchestra leader, Queen's fiftieth birthday celebration; orchestra leader, Queen Mother's eightieth birthday celebration; Royal Variety Performance, 1980; retired 1989. **Awards and honours** 14 Carl Alan awards; *Musical Express* Top Big Band Award, 1963, 1964; Top Musical Personality Award, *Weekend Magazine,* 1964; outstanding personality, Music Publishers' Association, 1976; Queen's Silver Jubilee Medal, 1978; Officer of the Order of the British Empire, 1978; Freeman, City of London, 1979; liveryman, Musicians' Company, 1983; lieutenant, Royal Victorian Order, 1984. **Television** (includes) *Come Dancing; Bid for Fame; Home Town Saturday Night; Holiday Parade; This Is Your Life* (twice); panel member, *New Faces.* **Recordings** (include) "Begin The Beguine", 1936; "I Only Have Eyes For You"; "In The Mood", 1938; "Wheels Cha Cha", 1961; "Sucu Sucu", 1961; "The Maigret Theme", 1962; "Must Be Madison", 1964; "March Of The Mods", 1964; "The Steptoe Theme", 1960s; also: *Joe Loss Plays Glenn Miller, Joe Loss Plays The Big Band Greats.* **Cause of death** Kidney illness, at age 80.

ANGUS McBEAN

British Photographer

Born **Newbridge, Wales, 8 June 1904**

Died **Ipswich, Suffolk, 9 June 1990**

In his own words, Angus McBean was "stagestruck and camera-mad", but his career as a photographer came about by chance rather than design. Given the haphazard nature of his rise to fame, it is perhaps not surprising that the photography establishment should have regarded his work with disapproval, if not outright disdain. McBean, however, was phlegmatic about this attitude; he loved what he did and adverse comment merely spurred him on to greater heights.

Although of Scottish extraction, McBean was born in a mining village in south Wales, the son of a mines surveyor. It was here, during his unexceptional career at Monmouth Grammar School, that he bought his first camera and began to make masks and props for local dramatic societies. However, it would be many years before his twin interests would combine to make his name.

After the early death of his father and a short time as "the world's worst bank clerk", McBean moved to London where he worked for seven years at Liberty's department store. Here, he chafed against the strict dress code and when a snooty customer reprimanded him for wearing a coloured shirt, he contrived to catch her a blow across the rear with a bolt of cloth and was promptly sacked for assault.

Someone of more neurotic temperament might well have felt anxious at becoming unemployed during the Depression years. Not so McBean. He grew a beard to demonstrate his indifference to the job market and spent an enjoyable year at home making masks and taking photographs. The fruits of his labours were exhibited in a north London teashop, which happened to be next door to Hugh Cecil's photographic studio. The two men met at the exhibition and McBean was invited to become the great man's assistant. A year later, in 1934, McBean branched out on his own, opening his first studio in Victoria, a stone's throw from Buckingham Palace. Having no clients, he made money by photographing theatre shows free of charge and selling the resulting prints to such magazines as *The Sketch.* During this time he met and photographed all the stage stars of the day: Laurence Olivier, Vivien Leigh, Ralph Richardson, Peggy Ashcroft... In fact, were it not for McBean's obsession with the theatre there would be no photographic record of the many outstanding productions that were mounted during the 1930s.

Many stars, having noticed McBean's sensitivity to lighting and that he always made them look good, began to insist that he alone should take their photographs. Now his twin passions could unite. Inspired by surreal art, particularly that of Salvador Dali, he positioned his famous subjects in strange landscapes with oddly juxtaposed props he had made himself. Often only part of the body would be featured; indeed, in one especially memorable shot the disembodied head of the model was shown lying on the floor beside a kitchen chair and looking "like an animated boiled egg". Nothing, it seemed, was too bizarre for his sitters to endure. They knew that he could catch the soul behind the mask.

The artifice involved in creating such shots outraged purists and led to the *British Journal of Photography* denouncing him as a "charlatan". McBean, however, took the criticism in his stride, later recalling that there was only one area in which he took liberties:

> it was with my Christmas cards that I let myself go, using every device known to me — even the adamantly forbidden "mucking about in the darkroom". [The cards] went out for 30 years in great numbers, but it was only about five years ago when one of them came up at Christie's saleroom and sold for £240 that I realized that all those vintage prints in a drawer upstairs were worth a lot of money.

On the strength of his published work, he was eventually appointed official photographer to many theatre companies, including the Old Vic, Sadler's Wells, Stratford-upon-Avon, Glyndebourne and H.M. Tennent's commercial theatre empire. Theatre photography remained his passion for the next 30 years, and when that area of work became increasingly rare, he turned to shooting covers for record albums. His first, and probably most famous, was for *Please, Please Me* by the Beatles, a project for which they had specifically requested him.

By now, of course, McBean was a household name, but there had been times of great unhappiness in his life. When work dried up on the outbreak of World War II, he volunteered for active service but was declared unfit. This prompted him to move to Bath and it was here in 1942 that he was arrested for a homosexual offence for which he served two and a half years in prison. According to friends, the ordeal was patiently borne and never appeared to embitter him.

In 1945 he opened a studio in London's Covent Garden and resumed his theatre photography with vigour, although he now made more use of multiple exposures and cut-outs than elaborately contrived sets. Perhaps sensing that he needed to diversify his talents, he later began to establish a reputation as an interior designer, restoring houses to mock Regency splendour, designing the tented interior of the Pavilion Restaurant and taking on other commissions as they appealed to him.

McBean retired from professional photography in 1969 and spent most of his time restoring various historic properties he had bought in Suffolk. Five years later he sold his huge collection of glass negatives to Harvard University, no British institution having declared any interest in preserving them. In one of those ironic twists of fate, the 1980s saw a surge of interest in his work and various exhibitions were belatedly organized. He was also persuaded to take his first ever fashion photographs for some French magazines.

Variously described as "peppery", "bohemian" and "bold", Angus McBean inspired affection and loyalty in all who knew him, not least Vivien Leigh whom he photographed so strikingly over a period of 30 years. Despite his many achievements, he remained disarmingly modest about his success: "I make no claims for my work...[I have merely] produced many amusing and some good compositions."

Born Angus Rowland McBean. **Father** Pit surveyor. **Marriage** Helena Wood, school teacher, 1923 (divorced 1924). **Education** Monmouth Grammar School, 1915–21. **Career** Bank clerk,

Midland Bank, Newport and Brynmawr, Monmouthshire, 1923–26; shop assistant, antiques department, Liberty's department store, London, 1926–33; theatrical mask maker; photographic assistant, Hugh Cecil studio, London, 1934–35; freelance photographer, from 1935; established own studio, London, 1935–66, Eye, Suffolk, 1966–90; freelance stage photographer, 1935–65; imprisoned for homosexuality, 1942–45; official photographer: Old Vic, Sadler's Wells, Royal Shakespeare Company, National Theatre, Glyndebourne, H.M. Tennent; contributor: *Sketch, Picture Post;* interior designer. **Awards and honours** Fellow, Royal Institute of British Photographers. **Individual exhibitions** Pirates Den Tea Shop, London, 1934; *Shakespeare's Plays,* Kodak Gallery, London, 1964; *Thirty Years of Opera,* The Maltings Opera House, Snape, Suffolk, 1971; *A Darker Side of the Moon* (retrospective), Impressions Gallery, York, 1976, toured UK, 1976, National Theatre, London, 1978; *Photographs 1934–1960,* Rex Irwin Gallery, Sydney, 1980. **Group exhibitions** (include) *Hundert Jahre Photographie 1839–1939,* Folkwang Museum, Essen, 1959, toured Cologne and Frankfurt; *Modern British Photography 1919–1939,* Museum of Modern Art, Oxford, 1980, toured UK. **Collections** National Portrait Gallery, London; Victoria and Albert Museum, London; Theatre Museum, London; Royal Photographic Society, London; Kodak Museum, London; Australian National Gallery, Canberra; Harvard University, Cambridge, Massachusetts (photographic archives). **Publications** *Shakespeare Memorial Theatre* (contributor to biannual publication), 1948–64; (with Adrian Woodhouse) *Angus McBean,* 1982; *Vivien: A Love Affair in Camera,* 1989. **Cause of death** Undisclosed, at age 86. **Further reading** *Contemporary Photographers,* 1988.

FREDERICK MELLINGER

American Underwear Designer and Retailer

Born **New York City, New York, 1914**

Died **Los Angeles, California, 2 June 1990**

He was a purveyor of fantasy, openly admitting that he was "in the business of deceiving men like crazy". Men didn't mind being deceived, apparently. Frederick Mellinger used to boast that he received dozens of letters every week, thanking him for products which resulted in "a wonderful evening I'll never forget", or that "kept our marriage young and alive". Just what were these wonderful products that prompted so many to write letters of effusive gratitude? Inflatable bras, calf pads and edible panties, to name just a few. Yes, Frederick Mellinger was none other than Frederick of Hollywood, the man who introduced the crotchless panty to suburban America.

Born on the Lower East Side of New York City, Frederick Mellinger lied about his age (he was 14) to get a clerical job at a firm that specialized in "intimate apparel". There he learned the art of mail-order merchandising, and began to develop his own ideas about style. It occurred to him that "there simply was not enough romance in the way of clothes. I was always making notes saying more bust here, more fanny there, less waist here." He spent World War II stationed in the American Midwest, asking his fellow soldiers about the way they preferred women to dress. Surprise, surprise, the soldiers said they liked women in skimpy, tight-fitting clothing made from diaphanous material.

With his army buddies' tastes in mind, he opened his first mail-order business, Frederick's of Fifth Avenue, in 1946, not only designing clothes, but writing all the catalogue copy himself. One year later, he moved the business to the bright purple Art Deco building on Hollywood Boulevard which would become not only his headquarters, but a genuine Hollywood landmark. Girdles with padding ("for unrivalled curves"), girdles without bottoms ("the living end"), bras with holes for the nipples to peek through ("a Hollywood favorite"), see-through night-gowns ("elastic straps and neckline are made to G-I-V-E with the action"), and panties with embroidered messages such as: "Eeny meeny, miny, moe, this is as far as you can go", were all big sellers. Frederick's branched out from strictly mail-order, and began to open shops across America, in ordinary places like Dayton, Ohio and Omaha, Nebraska. The weekly trip to the local mall became transformed; along with the groceries and shoes for the kids, Mom could pick up a leopard-print G-string or a pair of sparkling pasties.

Feminists were (and still are) outraged at Frederick's "passion fashions". There can be little doubt that they are designed to appeal to male chauvinists, and they promote the idea of woman as sex-object. Yet Frederick's clients include the likes of Jerry Hall and Kathleen Turner, who would certainly describe themselves as modern, independent women, buying for *themselves*.

Ideology aside, *Frederick's of Hollywood* is one of those archetypal American success stories: boy from the Lower East Side makes good. The business went from a small mail-order catalogue of items designed and marketed by one man, to a nation-wide franchise traded on the New York Stock Exchange, in less than 25 years. At the time of Frederick Mellinger's death, there were 160 Frederick's stores, and the previous year's sales had topped 80 million dollars. As Frederick Mellinger said many times, "Sex never goes out of fashion."

Born Frederick Mellinger. **Marriage** Harriett. **Children** One son and one daughter. **Military service** US Army, World War II. **Career** Clerical assistant, mail-order intimate apparel firm, New York, from 1928; designed exotic lingerie for his company Frederick's of Fifth Avenue mail order business, New York, 1946, moved to Hollywood, 1947; Frederick's of Hollywood, traded on the American Stock exchange, expanded to 160 shops nationwide by 1990. **Cause of death** Pneumonia, at age 76.

ROBERT NOYCE

American Inventor and Businessman

***Born* Burlington, Iowa, 12 December 1927**

***Died* Austin, Texas, 3 June 1990**

Computers are getting everywhere these days. Even those who have made a conscious decision to exclude the beasts from their lives are likely to be unwittingly harbouring miniature versions in their washing-machines, watches or cars. And while there's no one invention which is solely responsible for the evolution of computers, there is little doubt that it's the microchip which has made them so pervasive.

The praise or blame for the invention of the microchip is by general consensus shared between two men, Jack Kilby and Robert Noyce, who came up with similar ideas more or less simultaneously. In 1989 both men were awarded the Draper Prize, the engineering world's equivalent of a Nobel Prize, with a citation for the single most important invention that helped to usher in the Information Age.

That invention was based on semiconductors, a group of substances including silicon which can be made to conduct electricity, like metals, or to insulate, like rubber. Semiconductors had for some years been used to manufacture transistors, invented in 1947 as a smaller, cheaper and more reliable substitute for valves in electronic circuits. Noyce and his colleagues made it possible to put not just one component but a whole circuit, and later large numbers of circuits, on a single piece of silicon, called a microchip. As a result, the power of a computer which would once have occupied a space the size of a house can be put on to a pinhead, and sold for pennies.

Noyce was distinguished not only as inventor but also as a businessman. The unofficial mayor of Silicon Valley, he was to a large extent responsible for bringing that prosperous Northern Californian enclave of hi-tech firms into being. As well as founding Intel, one of the biggest names in microchip manufacture, Noyce became an industry spokesman and, in the last years of his life, a leading participant in a research consortium set up to safeguard the US semiconductor industry from Japanese inroads.

Despite being the son of a Congregational preacher in Iowa, Noyce was not a saintly youth — he was once expelled from college for a term for stealing a pig. After losing a couple of model planes which flew too successfully and didn't come back, he applied himself to building a radio-controlled version, and in so doing acquired a passion for electronics.

Noyce first studied semiconductor technology while reading for a degree in physics and mathematics at the local Grinnell College, where he was lucky enough to have a teacher who was well up in the subject of semiconductors through a friendship with one of the pioneers of transistors. Noyce went on to obtain a PhD in physics at the Massachusetts Institute of Technology, where he got top grades in all but one subject. Graduating in 1953, he joined Philco Corporation in Philadelphia, a company which was developing new ways of etching the surface of semiconductors.

After three years with Philco, Noyce was head-hunted on the strength of a couple of his papers by William B. Shockley, formerly of AT&T where he had been one of the inventors of the transistors. Shockley was setting up a semiconductor Laboratory at Mountain View, California, and recruited the cream of the experts in this area, including, besides Noyce, Gordon Moore, who was to be one of Noyce's most important collaborators.

Shockley was a distinguished technologist but his management skills seem to have been lacking. He alienated his staff by such techniques as accusing one of them of sabotage and forcing him to take a lie-detector test. More fundamentally, he made his team work on a device called a four-layer germanium diode rather than the silicon transistors which they believed had the most potential. A year after joining, Noyce and Moore, together with half a dozen colleagues, resigned *en masse* and went to form the semiconductor division of Fairchild Camera and Instruments Corporation. After their time with Shockley, the group made sure that their Fairchild division was a pleasant place to work.

When their general manager left after a year to set up his own firm, Noyce was persuaded to step into the breach and found he had a flair for management. In his spare time, he invented the microchip.

As early as 1952, the British engineer G.W.A. Dummer had been expounding "the monolithic idea". He thought that with the advent of semiconductors it should be possible to produce electronic equipment with no connecting wires, overcoming the limitations to speed and reliability imposed by the laboriously wired and soldered circuits of the time. But although Dummer had a clear theoretical concept of an integrated circuit, he did not know how to overcome the practical problems, and failed to find the financial backing to progress his idea.

It was at Fairchild that Noyce came up with the method of making integrated circuits which, in essence, is still used today. The breakthrough came in 1959 when Noyce realized that instead of cutting the transistors out of the silicon wafers on which they were made, they could be left mounted on the wafer, forming a miniature circuit board. He also came up with a technique for isolating the transistors and adding other circuit components such as resistors and capacitors. The chip could be built up by printing successive layers of components on to a base.

Jack Kilby at Texas Instruments was coming up with a similar design at around the same time. The superiority of Noyce's solution lay in the method of wiring the components together. Whereas Kilby connected them with minute gold wires, Noyce found a way of depositing a metal layer on the surface of the chip to replace the wires, a much neater and less labour-intensive solution.

There ensued a 10-year patent battle between the two inventors. Most of the acrimony was on the part of the corporate lawyers, rather than the protagonists. Noyce emerged victorious, but by that time the two companies had adopted the pragmatic strategy of licensing one another to use the invention and jointly licensing any other would-be manufacturers.

As Fairchild employees gradually left to set up their own companies, the "Fairchildren" peopled Silicon Valley. The year 1968 saw Noyce selling his stake in Fairchild Semiconductor to the parent company for 250,000 dollars. Noyce, Gordon Moore and a few colleagues now founded an independent company, Intel. Noyce and Moore enjoyed working together, Moore's calmness complementing the dynamism of Noyce, and this time Moore and Noyce were in joint charge. They set Intel a target of 100 million dollars' turnover in its first ten years; in the event it reached four times that amount.

As the technology improved, circuits were becoming smaller and it was possible to put increasing numbers of interconnected circuits on a silicon chip. These advances and the improvements in production techniques meant that in the early 1970s memory chips were becoming the preferred medium for storing information inside commercial mini and mainframe computers.

A major part of Intel's success came from a revolutionary new type of chip. Employee Marcian Hoff realized that the entire central processing unit of a computer could be put on a chip: Intel announced the first such in 1971. These microprocessors were the advance that made personal computing possible; since then many millions of personal computers have been built around Intel chips.

In maturity Noyce was described by T.R. Reid, the author of a history of the Microchip, as "exuding the easy self-assurance of a jet pilot". Reid also described him as a fashionable dresser — an unusual attribute in an information technologist — and found him affable, gregarious and a natural leader. His attractive personality and unrivalled combination of technical and business expertise made him the ideal ambassador for the electronics industry.

And, to the admiration of his associates, Noyce was prepared to shoulder a sizeable burden of responsibility on behalf of the industry as a whole rather than concerning himself with the profitability of his own company, which he left others to run. He became instrumental in the setting up of the Semiconductor Industry Association and was its first president.

Sematech, of which Noyce was president and chief executive from its foundation in 1988, was a research consortium set up by the American computer industry to combat the threat from the other side of the Pacific basin. Japan now has more than half of the semiconductor market, and three quarters in the case of certain important memory chips.

Noyce believed that the US had a good deal to learn from the co-operative ventures between Japanese firms and government, and advocated a national policy for the management of the US industry. He strove with a surprising degree of success to smooth over rivalry and petty disputes among other industry executives. Not everyone agreed with his strategy, however: some saw the idea of government intervention as unwarranted interference with market forces. Without Noyce, the future of Sematech looks uncertain to some commentators.

His invention, however, is here to stay. Now ten million transistors can be held on a single chip, and electronics has become the world's largest manufacturing industry with an estimated value of 270 billion dollars. Noyce is due a fair share of the credit. But he was modest about his achievement, commenting: "I'm lazy. I invented the integrated circuit because I saw all these people putting wires on these gadgets and I thought it was terribly wasteful." The same creative laziness underlies many of the world's great inventions.

Born Robert Norton Noyce. **Parents** Ralph B., Congregational minister, and Harriet (Norton) Noyce. **Marriage** Ann S. Bowers, 1975. **Children** William, Pendred, Priscilla and Margaret. **Education** Grinnell College, Iowa, BA, 1949; Massachusetts Institute of Technology, PhD, 1953. **Career** Research engineer, Philco Corporation, 1953–56; research engineer, Shockley Semiconductor Laboratory, 1956–57; founder, Fairchild Semiconductor, 1957–59, director of research, 1957–59, vice-president/general manager, 1959–65; (simultaneously with Jack Kilby) invented integrated circuit microchip, 1959, granted patent, 1969; group vice-president, Fairchild Camera and Instrument, 1965–68; founder/president, Intel Corporation, 1968–75, chairman, 1968–75, vice-chairman, 1979–90; president/chief executive, Sematech Incorporated, 1988–90. **Related activities** Director, Diasonics Incorporated; president, Semiconductor Industry Association. **Other activites** Trustee, Grinnell College, 1962–90; regent, University of California, 1982–90. **Offices and memberships** Fellow, Institute of Electrical and Electronics Engineers; member: National Academy of Engineering, American Association for the Advancement of Science, National Academy of Science. **Awards and honours** Stuart Ballentine Award, Franklin Institute, 1967; Harry Goode Award, AFIPS, 1978; National Medal of Science, USA, 1979; Cledo Brunetti Award, 1978, Medal of Honour; 1978, Faraday Medal, 1979; Harol Pender Award, University of Pennsylvania, 1980; National Medal of Technology, USA, 1987; Draper Prize, 1989. **Cause of death** Heart attack, at age 62. **Further reading** Stan Augarten, *Bit By Bit: An Illustrated History of Computers,* 1984; T.R. Reid, *Microchip,* 1985.

LORD O'NEILL of the MAINE

Former Prime Minister of Northern Ireland

***Born* County Antrim, Northern Ireland, 10 September 1914**

***Died* Lymington, Hampshire, 12 June 1990**

An aristocrat in every sense of the word — he was descended from the ancient Irish High Kings of the Ui Neill dynasty, the oldest traceable family in Europe — Captain Terence O'Neill (as he was known throughout his political career) represented the best in the "Big House" Protestant Irish tradition of public service. The tragedy of his career was that he was not sufficiently charismatic a personality to carry through his own enlightened ideas — or, perhaps more true, he was too eclectic a personality to stoop to the level of the rough tough characters with whom he had to deal and the dirty games they played. For Northern Irish history has always been a murky business and, since Terence O'Neill bowed out, a bloody one.

Terence Marne O'Neill (his second name was a reference to the battle raging at the time of his birth) had the typical upper-class Anglo-Irish upbringing, educated at Eton and serving with distinction in the Irish Guards throughout World War II in which both his elder brothers were killed. It was inevitable that he should follow his father — the first Westminster MP to be killed in World War I — into politics, this time the politics of his native Ulster, and that he should make steady, if unspectacular, progress up the Stormont ladder. Of particular significance was his period as housing minister, trying to tackle what was to prove one of the fundamental problems beneath the later unrest.

When the time ultimately came for Lord Brookeborough to retire after his 20-year stint as Ulster's prime minister, O'Neill, by this time minister of finance, was an obvious successor, not least because his rival for the job was suspect in many Unionist eyes for being far too interventionist in his thinking and over-sympathetic to trade union interests. Throughout his parliamentary apprenticeship, O'Neill had become a forceful exponent of the need for Ulster to pull itself together and stand on its own feet. As he took over the premiership in March 1963, he set about creating a new image of the ailing Province. He embarked on attracting new investment for the shipbuilding and linen industries and forging new links with the trade union movement. He inspired the Ulster weeks in towns throughout Britain and inaugurated promotional campaigns. But his prime determination was to cut through the sectarianism that had poisoned the atmosphere ever since the turbulence of partition. The only hope was to bring the two sections of the Northern Ireland community — Protestant and Catholic — into a working relationship which would end the long injustice of Protestant rule. (O'Neill well remembered how, on his entry into politics, he had had to join the Orange Order in order to obtain the Unionist nomination for the constituency he was to represent from 1946 to 1970.) He became the first Unionist prime minister to visit Catholic schools and other institutions, shaking hands instead of the traditional cold-shouldered approach.

O'Neill also saw the importance of trying to improve relations with the Irish Republic. Perhaps his most courageous initiative as prime minister was his historic invitation to the Irish prime minister, Sean Lemass, to visit Belfast in January 1965 — the first such meeting since partition.

But in all these reforming moves O'Neill met with opposition, predominantly from within his own party. His overtures to the Catholics were seen as undermining the Protestant ascendancy, while at the same time being suspect in many Catholic eyes as well; the Unionist administrative machine continued to steamroller its way over all minority complaints, and the new factories, new roads, and even the new university of Coleraine, tended to be built in Protestant areas. His *démarche* towards Dublin was taken without previous cabinet consultation — typical of his autocratic habit of leading from the front, though perhaps also necessary for security reasons. The move inevitably provoked division within the government and the party; O'Neill supporters saw it as *de facto* recognition by Dublin, while the hard-liners condemned it as a sell-out to the enemy. Even in his efforts to revive the economy O'Neill came up against the resentments of long-standing party rivals, who felt they could have done the job better. And, of course, over and above all these party factions, there was the loud-mouthed harassment of Ian Paisley — a rising star in the entrenched opposition to any concessions to the Catholic community. Ironically enough, Paisley was to succeed O'Neill in his Bannside constituency.

O'Neill's six-year term of office was punctuated by a series of confidence motions, culminating in a marathon meeting of the party in 1966 after the Prime Minister complained of a conspiracy against him. He was to win them all, but with diminishing authority. He was to be more cautious, for instance, in his dealings with the next Irish Taoiseach, Mr Jack Lynch, whom he did not meet until the latter had been in office for more than a year.

The outbreak of the civil rights campaign in October 1968 — at first a peaceful demonstration in support of the sectarian reforms which O'Neill had long championed — marked the end of an era. Outrage at the hard-liners' stand against any move to end the discrimination in jobs and housing and the injustice of local elections broke into violence on the streets, with Paisley and his supporters staging counter-demonstrations. Undaunted, O'Neill took a strong line with his rebellious backbenchers and cabinet colleagues and announced a five-point liberalization programme. In the face of a deteriorating situation he called what came to be known as the "cross-roads" snap general election in February 1969, campaigning that Ulster was at the cross-roads and demanding endorsement of his reforms. But no mandate for reform emerged. As was to prove true for the next 20 years or so, Ulster was to remain ever more torn between those who shared his hopes of healing the sectarian wounds and those who insisted on opening them still wider. O'Neill resigned soon afterwards, his active political career at an end.

He retired to a quiet country life in England, occasionally contributing to debates on Northern Ireland in the House of Lords of which he was made a life peer in 1970. His administration at

Stormont can be seen as the last hope of a peaceful solution to what has since become the increasingly bloody situation of Northern Ireland. Even at the time, many saw him as a liberal before his time, the leader of a party which had little sympathy for his ideas and with many of whose members he himself had little patience. He lacked that essential characteristic of a twentieth-century politician — the common touch. A courageous and an honest man, he persisted in pressing on with the reforms in which he passionately believed, but he totally failed to understand the gut reactions of his Protestant hard-liners and their Catholic opponents, and would have scorned them if he had.

Born Terence Marne O'Neill. **Parents** Captain the Honourable Arthur O'Neill, member of parliament, and Lady Annabel Crew-Milnes. **Marriage** Katherine Jean Whitaker, 1944. **Children** Patrick and Penelope. **Education** Eton College, Berkshire. **Military service** Irish Guards, 1939–45. **Career** Aide-de-camp, governor of South Australia, 1939; Unionist member of parliament for Bannside, Parliament of Northern Ireland, Stormont, 1946–70; parliamentary secretary, Ministry of Health, 1948; deputy speaker, 1953; chairman, Ways and Means Committee, 1953; joint parliamentary secretary, Home Affairs and Health, 1955; Home Affairs minister, 1956; Finance minister, 1956; prime minister of Northern Ireland, 1963–69. **Related activities** Member, Hansard Society Commission on Electoral Reform, 1975–76. **Other activities** Director, Phoenix Assurance, 1969–84; director, Warburg International Holdings Limited, 1970–83; trustee, Winston Churchill Memorial Trust; governor, National Gallery of Ireland. **Awards and honours** Deputy Lieutenant, County Antrim, 1948; High Sheriff, County Antrim, 1953; Privy Councillor, Northern Ireland, 1956; honorary LLD, Queen's University, Belfast, 1967; created life peer, Baron O'Neill of the Maine, of Ahoghill, County Antrim, 1970. **Publications** *Ulster at the Crossroads,* 1969; *The Autobiography of Terence O'Neill,* 1972. **Cause of death** Undisclosed, at age 75.

LEONARD SACHS

South African Actor and Director

***Born* Roodeport, South Africa, 26 September 1909**

***Died* London, England, 15 June 1990**

The actor Leonard Sachs, who was fond of studying theatrical history, assured himself of a niche in it. By a pleasant paradox, he arrived from South Africa to revive a unique if moribund form of English entertainment, restore it to glory, and become a, if not *the*, leading exponent.

He was born at Roodeport, in the state of Transvaal, in 1909. After Jeppe High School, he attended Witwatersrand University, and thereafter decided on the actor's life. At his Majesty's Theatre in Johannesburg, making his first stage appearance as Jim Hawkins in *Treasure Island,* he had the good fortune to catch the eye of Sybil Thorndike. The *grande dame* of British theatre was touring South Africa and, deciding that she'd spotted a "promising young actor", provided him with introductions to various managers in London. So, to the hub of Empire he came, a colonial boy with little in his pocket. For the next seven years, he paid his dues in suburban repertory. He stage-managed, understudied Laurence Olivier, got bit parts in films and, eventually, in the West End, though still down the bill. To supplement income and broaden experience, Sachs would work in the late evening at the tiny Grafton Theatre, doing what he called "high brow variety". This form of entertainment, akin to revue, was a creature dear to Sachs and one for which he nursed ambitions; it is doubtful that he would have predicted quite what form they were about to take.

In 1936, together with his friend, writer Peter Ridgeway, Sachs founded the Players' Theatre under some undistinguished, crowded railway arches leading down to the Thames at Charing Cross. In fact, one of its earliest productions was a piece of social realism called *Heaven and Charing Cross,* but shortly after this came the crucial idea of a Victorian music-hall programme. The formula was one which had died about 35 years before: stand-up comedians, male impersonators, female impersonators, chorus singers, conjurers, jugglers — acts following each other at a hectic sort of pace, with audience participation encouraged. An indispensable member of the dramatis personae was therefore a chairman; to serve up the acts, to stir a tepid audience or quell a rumbustious one, to set and adjust the pace. Sachs was It. His style from the chair was urbane with an occasional touch of waspishness, and the audiences loved him. When Ridgeway died in 1938, Sachs acquired the added responsibilities of running the theatre and booking the acts. As a director in the genre, he developed an exceptional nose for "artistes" and material, and the felicitous ability to imbue the whole with a sense of period (although, as the present chairman, Dominic Le Foe, has pointed out, he had engendered "a milieu which in truth existed nowhere other than in his own creative mind"). Sachs had an eye for talent, and many of those given early opportunities at The Players' went on to do great things — examples are Peter Ustinov, Bernard Miles and Patricia Hayes. By the time war came in 1939, Sachs and the show were living in a state of institutional symbiosis. As the 1400 theatre members expressed it, "No Sachs, No Theatre".

But after wartime service in the Army, Sachs determined to get out and do some "serious" theatre around the country. In 1951, however, came the Festival of Britain, designed to rouse a tired nation, and Sachs found himself back in harness with Mr Sachs's Song Saloon, whose style and content may be guessed from its title. This in turn led him north to the City Varieties Theatre in Leeds and a television show called *The Good Old Days,* which was broadcast from there. Again he acceded to the chairmanship, and again he was an enormous success. With false (though impeccable) moustache and whiskers, with stiff shirt and white gloves, he cut a dapper figure for the screen, and this time he devised an extra embellishment. Banging a gavel, he would commend the entertainment in a storm of prolixity, especially alliteration and hyperbole. Thus "The pyrotechnical proliferation of the permutative possibilities of corporeal pliability" meant acrobats. Audiences would cheer, groan, gape and hope to pluck his meaning which, he cheerfully admitted, was not always present. Matching Sachs's flamboyance they came to the theatre in period costume; the show ran for 32 years, and when it closed with the Christmas edition of 1983, there were still 20,000 on the waiting list for tickets.

Meanwhile, Sachs had done good stage work elsewhere, including the classics. Notably, he played the Chorus in Shakespeare's *Henry V,* and Peter Stockman in Ibsen's *An Enemy of the People;* for television he was a "very convincing" Shylock, and he showed well as Tom Conti's father in the prestigious series *The Glittering Prizes.* His last television play, *Lost for Words,* was recorded shortly before his death.

In the professional realm, Sachs was considered a reliable actor and a perceptive director. He was also a campaigner for racial equality and a worker for charity. Possibly, as Le Foe speculated, "he was underestimated not only by the world at large but by himself as well." It may indeed be the case that he had qualified respect for the role which occupied him so much, but he brought enormous pleasure to vast and sometimes unlikely audiences. *The Good Old Days* was shown in eleven countries, was particularly popular with the Scandinavians (for reasons we have been unable to ascertain), and it was reported from a remote village in Portugal that the fishermen down there were singing "Down At The Old Bull And Bush". This, however, might be taken with a pinch of the proverbial condiment. Audaciously apochryphal anthropology, as your chairman might say.

Born Leonard Sachs. **Parents** Jacob and Bessie (Channoch) Sachs. **Marriage** Eleanor Summerfield, actress and comedienne, 1947. **Children** Two sons. **Education** Jeppe High School;

Witwatersrand University. **Emigration** Left South Africa for England, 1929. **Military service** Served in Army, 1941–45. **Career** Stage début, *Treasure Island,* Johannesburg, 1926; London début, *The Circle of Chalk,* 1929; toured 1931; member, Windsor Repertory Company, 1932; member, Croydon Repertory Company, 1933; (with Peter Ridgeway) founded Players' Theatre, 1936, directed and produced, 1936–47; film début, 1936; performed in Mr Sachs's Song Saloon, 1951, master of ceremonies, *The Good Old Days,* BBC, 1953–83; toured 1962; final appearance, *Follies,* 1987. **Stage** (includes) *Treasure Island,* 1926; *The Circle of Chalk,* 1929; *Highbrow Variety,* 1930; *Street Scene,* 1930; *Bright Star,* 1936; *Professor Bernhardi,* 1936; *Girl Unknown,* 1936; *The Witch of Edmonton,* 1936; *Georgia Story,* 1948; *La Jalousie,* 1948; *Caligula,* 1949; *The Golden Door,* 1949; *Misery Me,* 1955; *Enter Solly Gold,* 1962; *Three Men for Colverton,* 1966; *Henry V,* 1968; *An Enemy of the People,* 1969; *Country Matters,* 1969; *Follies,* 1987. **Television** *The Good Old Days,* 1953–83; also: *A Family at War, Coronation Street, The Man from Haven, Crown Court, The Glittering Prizes, Lost for Words.* **Cause of death** Undisclosed, at age 80.

HUGH SINCLAIR

British Nutritionist

Born **Edinburgh, Scotland, 4 February 1910**

Died **Oxford, England, 22 June 1990**

The connection between our illnesses and what we eat is universally accepted these days. Health food stores flourish in most towns; bran is liberally sprinkled on breakfast cereals; milk is bought skimmed and semi-skimmed; wholemeal bread is used rather than white, and shoppers study food packages to see what additives have been used. The changes in eating habits have been demonstrated to have cut the incidence of heart disease in the USA significantly, and no doubt the same is happening elsewhere.

The importance of nutrition has entered the public consciousness now, but it has taken a long time. For decades some scientists proclaimed it without effect. Hugh Sinclair, in particular, preached it consistently and with great force, but he was ignored except by a select few, and his research on the subject starved of funds.

Recognition took a very long time coming. When he wrote to friends shortly before his death, memory of the long years when his message was ignored made him say he felt his life had been wasted. But his achievements were great, and the effect he had as tutor on generations of students at Oxford will continue to bear fruit. He was a historian of medicine, and a remarkably successful book collector. And his early work, as one of the architects of the balanced diet of the British during World War II and of Holland and Germany just afterwards, was of paramount importance.

Humble about his own achievements, he was proud of those of his forebears, for he claimed descent from ancient Viking kings and the St Clair cousins who came with William the Conqueror. More recent members of the line included Sir John Sinclair, perhaps the greatest British agriculturist.

He was educated at Winchester College, where he won the senior science prize but also studied classics, and from there he went to Oriel College, Oxford, where he gained first-class honours in animal physiology as well as several university prizes.

It was while he was a second-year undergraduate that his life's interest in human nutrition began. He was reading William Farr's book, *Vital Statistics*, and noticed that the life expectancy of a middle-aged man had hardly changed since 1841, when the main "killer diseases" had been pneumonia and tuberculosis. Since medical advances had wiped out or weakened many of the former causes of death, why were people not living longer? The answer, he reasoned, must be connected with the change in diet, and particularly the fatty acids, including hydrogenated oils, which had come in with manufactured foods. The next 50 years of his life were largely devoted to investigating the diseases of civilization and their causes.

While he was still a medical student he began his collection of books covering the history of medicine. He also bought at this time, extremely cheaply, a 19-bedroom mansion at Sutton Courtenay near Oxford. He did this even though he was a bachelor, and he remained unmarried, losing two fiancées through early deaths.

In 1937 he was elected to a teaching fellowship at Magdalen College, Oxford, which he retained until 1980, and he became a lecturer in physiology and biochemistry.

When war started in 1939, Britain's dependence on food brought in through the U-boat blockade meant nutrition was of crucial importance. After working for a short time on defence against poison gas, Sinclair formed the Oxford Nutrition Survey to help the government by monitoring the wartime food policy. He organized teams to take full biological samples of normal diets around the country. He more or less invented this method of surveying — an extraordinary achievement for a man in his early thirties — and it was a crucial indicator for the government during the war, and for parts of Europe after it. One interesting finding at the time concerned meals served at the Oxford municipal restaurants. Lunches served at 2 pm had six times as much vitamin C as those served at noon. It transpired that the noon meals had been cooked at 9 am and kept hot for three hours while the 2 pm lunches were freshly cooked.

With his experience and knowledge, Sinclair and some of his team went to northern Holland after the war to advise on recovery from the severe famine there, and then they were asked to advise on nutrition in the British sector of Germany.

In 1946 Oxford University allowed Sinclair ten days to raise 25,000 pounds to found a department of human nutrition. He managed it with a day to spare, but the University then decided not to accept the money on the grounds that within ten years the department would have nothing left to study. For Sinclair the decision was devastating.

Worse was to come. Due to reorganization he even lost his laboratory, so little faith did the authorities have in his work. His own conviction never wavered. He was absolutely convinced that it was the substitution of the fatty acids put into foods to give them long shelf life, instead of the essential fatty acids (EFAs) the body requires, that causes very many ailments. His long list included coronary thrombosis, hypertension, skin diseases, some cancers, multiple sclerosis and diabetes. Possibly in desperation, or possibly as an act of bravado, he wrote a long letter to the medical journal, the *Lancet* pressing his point, a letter now hailed as a "Citation classic".

At the time the letter failed to have the desired effect. His seniors could not believe that so many diseases could result from a single cause. But Sinclair recognized that deficiency of any nutrient essential to every tissue would lead to abnormal function of every tissue. Secondly not all tissues would be affected in the same way, so which symptoms would appear in which person suffering dietary deficiency depended on that person's genes.

Where the letter was effective was in stimulating many other workers to initiate research on the lines he suggested, but for Sinclair the isolated years had begun. He continued as a tutor, and an extremely successful one. Generations of students were inspired by this very tall, large, eccentric man, with his scruffy clothes and worn-out ties. He wore only two ties — the Old Wykehamist showing he had been at Winchester, and the MCC tie (the Marylebone Cricket Club is the premier club in Britain).

He had an extraordinary capacity for work, for he regularly continued into the small hours, and expected a lot from his research students. He clearly cared very much about their progress while expecting them to get on with their own work. But they saw the warm side of him as well: not only did they enjoy sherry in his rooms at Oxford, but they frequently joined him for weekends at his mansion, the invitation always saying "The oldest clothes are worn in Sutton Courtenay". He was also a legendary speaker, using precise syntax, and often spicing his remarks with his own adaptations of the works of authors such as Longfellow, Tennyson and Lewis Carroll.

Sinclair had very little money during those difficult years, the fellowship at Magdalen being his only income. In 1965, to avoid insolvency, he sold most of his 7000 volumes of books on medical history for 90,000 pounds. Nevertheless he was determined to set up a foundation for the study of human nutrition. In 1972 he dedicated his house, garden and other resources to the International Nutrition Foundation, which he founded and directed.

The recognition he deserved came at last. Lord Wyatt was to say of him, "One of the most remarkable men in England is Dr Hugh Sinclair, the brilliance of whose lifetime work is now world-recognized." He was widely acknowledged as probably the most original, possibly the greatest, living dietary food nutritional scientist.

Two aspects of his work in particular have left lasting impressions on those who followed him. First his insistence that human nutrition was a fit subject for study, at least as important as laboratory animal nutrition which was the commonly recognized object for research. Secondly, since human beings have to be used for investigation in this subject, he believed in conducting experiments on himself. These included hilarious experiments trying to give himself chilblains as a student, depriving himself of thiamin in 1938, similarly reducing intake of vitamin A in 1942, and, in his seventieth year, living for 100 days on Eskimo food, consuming nothing but seal, fish and water, very many important observations being made of changes in his condition.

The third and probably most lasting memorial he has left is the recognition of the importance of the EFAs to human health. His work, and that of others following him, has changed the eating habits of very many, and there is the hope that heart disease and various other "western diseases" will be looked back on by the next generations in the same way as we regard consumption, polio and other scourges of the past.

Born Hugh Macdonald Sinclair. **Parents** Colonel H.M. and Rosalie (Jackson) Sinclair. **Education** Winchester College, Hampshire; Oriel College, Oxford, first-class honours in animal physiology, BA, 1932, senior demy, Magdalen College, Oxford, 1932–34; University College Hospital Medical School, London, 1933–36, BM, BCh, 1936; BSc in biochemistry, 1934. **Career** University lecturer in physiology and biochemistry, Oxford University, 1937–47, reader in human nutrition, 1951–58, director, Laboratory of Human Nutrition, 1951–58; fellow, Magdalen College, Oxford University, 1937–80, lecturer in physiology and biochemistry, 1937–76, vice-president, 1956, 1957, emeritus fellow, 1980; founder/director, Oxford Nutrition Survey, 1941–46; honorary nutrition consultant (with rank of brigadier), Control Commission, Germany, 1945–47; founder/director, International Institute of Human Nutrition, 1972. **Related activities** (include) Memorial lectures: Cutter, Harvard University, 1951, Schuman, Los Angeles, 1962, Golden Acres, Dallas, 1963, Bergami, Pisa, 1985; editor-in-chief, *International Encyclopedia of Food and Nutrition*, 24 volumes, from 1969; visiting professor in food science, University of Reading, 1970–80. **Offices and memberships** (include) Member: Biochemical Society, Medical Research Society, Society for Experimental Biology, Société Philomathique; treasurer, Physiological Society; president, McCarrison Society, 1983–90. **Awards and honours** (include) Senior Science Prize, Winchester; Gotch Prize, Oxford University, 1933; Gold and Silver Medals for Clinical Medicine, University College Hospital, Radcliffe Scholarship in Pharmocology, 1934, Radcliffe Travelling Fellow, 1937–38, Rolleston Prize, 1938; licentiate in Medicine and Surgery, Society of Apothecaries; US Medal of Freedom with Silver Palm; Officer of Order of Orange Nassau, Holland; fellow: Royal College of Physicians, Royal Society of Chemistry, Institute of Biology, American Public Health

Society, Hollywood Academy of Medicine; Master of the Apothecaries Company, 1967–68; honorary DSc, Baldwin-Wallace, USA, 1968. **Publications** (include) "Use of Vitamins in Medicine", in *Whitla's Pharmacy, Materia Medica and Therapeutics,* 1939; "Nutrition", in *Treatment in Modern Therapeutics,* 1941; (with A.H.T. Robb-Smith) *A Short History of Anatomical Teaching in Oxford,* 1950; "Nutrition", in *Aspects of Modern Science,* 1951; (editor) *The Work of Sir Robert McCarrison,* 1953; (with Sir Robert McCarrison) *Nutrition and Health,* 1953; (with Professor Jeliffe) *Nicholls's Tropical Nutrition,* 1961; (with F.C. Rodger) *Metabolic and Nutritional Eye Disease,* 1968; (with D. Hollingsworth) *Hutchinson's Food and Principles of Nutrition,* 1969; (with G.R. Howat) *World Nutrition and Nutrition Education,* 1980. **Cause of death** Undisclosed, at age 80. **Further reading** Mary Gale and Brian Lloyd, editors, *Sinclair* (in series published by McCarrison Society), 1990.

PETER THROCKMORTON

American Nautical Archaeologist

Born **New York, USA, 30 July 1928**

Died **Newcastle, Maine, 5 June 1990**

> At the turn of the century a Greek sponge boat captain named Demetros Kondos demonstrated the potential rewards awaiting under the Aegean for archaeologists, by raising a cargo of classical statuary… Returning from a sponging cruise off North Africa, Kondos had decided to wait out a Southerly gale in the Antikythera Channel between Crete and the Pelopennesus. Rather than sit idle, he despatched a diver to a depth of 30 fathoms, or 180 feet. Minutes later the diver was back on board, babbling almost incoherently about horses and naked men and women he had seen below. Kondos went over the side, and soon sent up the sand-filled, bronze right hand of a man. (Peter Throckmorton, *Shipwrecks and Archaeology: the Unharvested Sea*).

It is no exaggeration to say that without the efforts and the enthusiasm of Peter Throckmorton, the discipline of nautical archaeology might never have come into being. There have been few people whose personal vision and determination have had such an astounding impact upon the study of the past. As a result of his pioneering work, which has guided and inspired excavators and divers all over the world, millions of people can now marvel at the treasures of lost vessels, not as isolated items of "salvage", plundered without thought for what their sites might reveal about earlier times, but as part of a rich tapestry of knowledge and understanding of human history.

Unlike many of the pioneers of land-based archaeology, Peter Throckmorton was not a man of letters, nor an educated romantic in love with the legends of ancient civilizations. Born in New York, he spent much of his childhood moving between his divorced parents. He escaped to the sea at the age of 15 and took a variety of jobs in American ports, ending up in a salvage yard in Honolulu. There he was taught to dive by a former US Navy diver, and it was there, too, that he discovered the excitement of exploring wrecked ships. He recalled vividly the feelings he experienced investigating his first wreck, an old minesweeper in the harbour at Honolulu: "I had been caught by something harder to kill than any of the fabled beasts that storytellers put in sunken ships. That minesweeper crystallized the interest in shipwrecks which I had always had, and my interest in seamen, ships and voyages."

In 1948, short of money and ideas for what to do next, he joined the US Army Transportation Corps and was sent to work in a shipyard at Yokohama. He found the Japanese a fascinating people and longed to learn more about their culture and history. He lacked the necessary academic skills to do so, however, until he left the Army in 1951 to take advantage of the "GI Bill" which provided American servicemen with the opportunity to pursue a university education. Throckmorton enrolled at the University of Hawaii to study anthropology. He continued to work in the harbour, running a salvage business which was to furnish him with invaluable practical experience of surveying and raising wrecked vessels. He spent some time in Mexico City and finished his studies at the Institute of Ethnology in Paris in 1955.

In the year he started his studies a very important breakthrough in diving became available commercially. The "Aqualung" developed by the French Navy diver Jacques Cousteau was put on the market. Throckmorton did not instantly take up underwater exploration, but instead became a freelance photographer, travelling all over the world looking for stories and people to photograph, and learning the business of documentary film-making. It was while he was returning home from a filming project in India that he heard about an ancient bronze statue of the Greek Goddess Demeter, found on the seabed by Turkish sponge divers near Bodrum. He talked with the divers, swimming and diving in the area where they had found the statue, looking for the ship which had been carrying it. He did not find that wreck but he was able to learn about other possible sites from the Turkish divers. These sites were usually marked by *amphorae,* the most common container used by ancient merchants for their cargoes.

It was the sponge divers who first located the ancient wreck which set Throckmorton on his way as an archaeologist. In deep water, off a treacherous rocky cape called Gelidonya, on the southern coast of Turkey, Captain Mustafa Kemal had found a wreck which contained copper ingots, shaped like ox-hides. These ingots were from a ship which was wrecked no later than 1200 BC, making it the oldest shipwreck yet discovered. It was Throckmorton who realized that such an important vessel needed proper investigation. Wrecks had recently been dived on and explored all over the Mediterranean, with the help of the Aqualung, but their contents had been sold off to museums or art dealers, and the opportunity to excavate an entire site, in the manner of terrestrial archaeology, had not been taken.

In 1959 Throckmorton managed to convince George Bass, a young archaeologist from the University of Pennsylvania Museum, to come to the site. Bass learned to dive himself and, with the help of a team of dedicated divers and archaeologists, they conducted the first proper excavation of an underwater archaeological site. By proving to the world that such a project was possible, the Gelidonya team effectively founded the science of nautical archaeology. They meticulously drew and photographed everything they found, cleaning and preserving the finds for future study. Also by publishing his reports quickly and fully, George Bass set an example for others to follow.

Peter Throckmorton now devoted most of his time to archaeology. He dived in many parts of the Mediterranean and wrote a series of books and articles on the subject. He was a tireless advocate of properly organized scientific study of wrecks, showing people that there is much more to be obtained from this method than from mere "treasure hunting", which destroys more than it reveals. He spoke to politicians and to pleasure divers all over the world, encouraging them to recognize the importance of their underwater heritage, to protect it and exploit it in the best possible way.

The achievements associated with Throckmorton's labours and their inspirational effects are considerable. In Bodrum, with the help of George Bass, he was able to set up a working museum of nautical archaelogy. Texas A & M University created an Institute of Maritime Archaeology which now, under the direction of Professor George Bass, carries out work all over the world. Even the University of Oxford has recently appointed a professor of nautical archaeology. More importantly, amateur divers are learning to care for ancient (and modern) wrecks as part of their common heritage, thanks to the wealth of films, articles and books which have appeared on the subject, many of them written or edited by Peter Throckmorton. As the diver and draughtswoman Honor Frost put it, in her book *Under the Mediterranean:* "The conflict between journalism and archaeology, or rather, the balance which had to be struck between the two, is something which Peter Throckmorton has achieved, but that is his own story."

Born Edgerton Alvord Throckmorton. **Parents** Edgerton Alvord and Lucy Norton (Leonard) Throckmorton. **Marriage** Joan Henley, writer, 1964. **Children** Lucy and Paula. **Education** University of Hawaii, 1951–54; University of the Americas, Mexico City, 1954; Institute of Ethnology, University of Paris, 1954–55. **Military service** Sergeant, US Army, Transportation Corps, 1948–51, served in Far East. **Career** Tanker engineer, deep-sea fishing boat operator, diving and salvage businessman, Hawaii, 1951–54; undersea archaeology program research associate, University of Pennsylvania Museum, Philadelphia, 1960–69; freelance writer, television documentary maker and photographer, 1969–90. **Related activities** Underwater archaeological consultant: University of Chicago, Villa Guilia Museum, Hellenic Institute of Nautical Archaeology; curator, National Maritime Historical Society; contributor: *Expedition*, *Greek Heritage*, *Archaeology*, *National Geographic*, *Journal of Nautical Archaeology*, *Atlantic Monthly*, *Argosy*; advisory board member, *Argosy*. **Offices and memberships** Member: US Naval Institute, American Society of Magazine Photographers. **Awards and honours** Honorary DMH, Sea Research Institute, 1973; honorary degree, University of Florida. **Publications** (with Henry Chapin) *Spiro of the Sponge Fleet* (juvenile), 1963; *The Lost Ships,* 1964; (with others) *Surveying in Archaeology Underwater,* 1969; *Shipwrecks and Archaeology: The Unharvested Sea,* 1970; *The Sea Remembers,* 1987. **Cause of death** Undisclosed, at age 61. **Further reading** Honor Frost, *Under the Mediterranean*, 1963.

DAME EVA TURNER

British Opera Singer

***Born* Oldham, Lancashire, 10 March 1892**

***Died* London, England, 16 June 1990**

Eva Turner, the leading English opera singer of her generation, was a diamond-sharp soprano who achieved international recognition in the mid-1920s when it was most unusual for British singers to be engaged by first-rank opera houses. Her long life could be neatly divided into two sections: three decades as one of the finest dramatic sopranos of the century and 40 years of a remakably energetic retirement, spent promoting opera as a teacher and as an enthusiastic member of numerous committees.

Her final appearance in opera was in February 1948 at the Royal Opera House, Covent Garden, in the role most associated with her, Turandot. She had sung in Puccini's unfinished opera for the first time in 1926 in Brescia when Franco Alfano, who completed the score, thought her "ideal". Almost 60 years later, in a gesture rare in Britain, after the *première* of a new production in September 1984, she was brought on to the Covent Garden stage by her pupil and successor as the icy Princess, Gwyneth Jones. No one present could mistake the deep affection in which Dame Eva was held: the house rose to give a most dearly-loved "personality" a resounding ovation.

For a woman so small of stature (she was under five feet tall), Eva Turner had a surprisingly large voice with a brilliant top. From a delicate pianissimo, she could always expand it to a full-chested fortissimo, always targeting it with the accuracy of a laser beam. When asked whose voice was the most powerful of the many he had heard, the producer Walter Legge said that Eva Turner's was capable of going right to the back of the gallery at Covent Garden, boring a hole through the wall and sailing out into Bow Street. Nowhere are her vocal qualities more evident than in her famous recording of the sadistic Turandot's aria "In questa reggia". The seamless crescendo she pulls out as she ascends to the top C never fails to thrill. While perfectly cast as Puccini's eponymous heroine, a lack of ardour in the fabulous voice may well have been the reason why she was never engaged by the Metropolitan in New York or by several other leading houses, yet in Italy, where critics could be so devastating, she was a great favourite. The sheer dramatic thrust of her voice, which could negotiate the most technically challenging runs, was almost unrivalled this century. Only Birgit Nilsson and Kirsten Flagstad have ever approached its commanding authority.

Eva Turner was born in the Lancashire cotton town of Oldham where her father was chief engineer at a local mill. Although the family moved to Bristol when she was ten, she never lost the indomitable Lancastrian spirit or the distinctive accent of her native county. She made her decision to become an opera singer as a girl, after she had been to hear the Carl Rosa Company perform *Il trovatore.* "I came home that night announcing to the family that I was going to be an opera star, and the vocation was born, irrevocably". In this ambition, she was fortunate in having the support of her parents, especially her father who had given her her first music lessons. Clara Butt's teacher, Dan Rootham, became her mentor and between 1911 and 1915 she studied at the Royal Academy of Music in London. She joined the Carl Rosa Company and toured Britain with them, singing small roles such as one of the Boys in *The Magic Flute* before graduating to Kate Pinkerton, Micaëla, Arline in *The Bohemian Girl* and the title role in *Maritana.*

In November 1920, Eva Turner made her Covent Garden début in the Carl Rosa season as Santuzza, and followed with Musetta, Leonora (*Il trovatore),* Antonia and Butterfly. She came back the next year, her repertoire by then encompassing Freia, Elsa, Brunhilde, Nedda and Tosca, and in the company's 1992 Covent Garden season she sang her first Aida in the house.

Her Cio-Cio San at London's Old Scala Theatre in 1924 attracted Ettore Panizza, Arturo Toscanini's assistant at La Scala, who came round to her dressing room to ask if she would audition for the great conductor. Though she knew only one aria in Italian (she was later to pride herself and be praised for her excellent Italian), she went to Milan with her coach, Richard Broad, and was engaged by Toscanini to sing Freia in *Das Rheingold,* with Vittorio Gui conducting. At that time considerable prejudice towards Anglo-Saxon singers existed and the invitation to sing Freia in Italian, and later Sieglinde, was all the more remarkable since Eva Turner steadfastly resisted attempts to Italianize her name. Such was her success and popularity, she settled in a house she built on the edge of Lake Lugano and travelled to all the principal Italian houses. She also toured Germany, sang Minnie in *La faniculla del West* in Lisbon and went to Buenos Aires and Rio de Janeiro to sing Leonore in *Fidelio.*

Her return to London in 1928 was a triumph. Her overseas acclaim had assured her celebrity status. There were ten performances in the international season at Covent Garden. She sang Turandot, Aida and Santuzza. Of the former, one critic wrote "there was not a blemish, not a qualm" and *The Times* noted that her voice "was more like a superb instrument, not a human organ".

Her American début was also in 1928, with the Chicago Opera, to which she returned many times over the years. Throughout the 1930s, she sang all over Europe, and at Covent Garden where she added a memorable Agathe, Amelia in *Un ballo in maschera* and an impassioned Isolde to her repertoire. At a performance of the latter in October 1938 she took 17 curtain calls — only one less than Kirsten Flagstad at her London début. There had, however, been an inexplicable slight the previous year. On Coronation night, though invited to sing the National Anthem, with Sir Thomas Beecham conducting, she was not asked to take the title role in *Aida,* one of her foremost parts. She did, however, repeat her Turandot that season with her beloved Giovanni Martinelli singing his first Calaf.

During the war years, there were many performances at the Henry Wood Promenade Concerts and concerts for the forces. She was always a great favourite at the Proms, especially on Wagner nights, and she never lost her enthusiasm for the annual summer festival of music. Until the end of her life, she was a regular attender and, on the famous Last Night, Dame Eva's voice could be heard soaring above 8000 promenaders, a huge chorus and the BBC Symphony Orchestra. On occasions when one of her pupils was singing, it was not unusual for her to sit silently mouthing the words, gently beating time and, in the interval, offering pertinent comments to neighbours who often had no idea the tiny, lively, beautifully coiffeured old lady sitting beside them was a teacher who had been one of the world's greatest opera singers.

Her retirement, when it came in 1948, passed almost unnoticed. She slipped away to teach voice at the University of Oklahoma, initially for a year but, in the event, she stayed for nine. She sometimes recalled, with an infectious sense of fun, that the local newspaper had announced she was coming as Professor of Vice. "That's why I was such a success and stayed so long."

On her return to London, she went back to her Alma Mater, the Royal Academy of Music. While she was a strict disciplinarian, she was always unfailingly kind and helpful to pupils, and many — such as Amy Shuard, Rita Hunter and Gwyneth Jones — achieved international prominence.

Dame Eva Turner worked tirelessly for the Friends of the Royal Opera House, the Friends of English National Opera and in her ninety-third year was still serving on over 30 committees. She chaired the opera panel for the Society of West End Theatre awards, lectured in music schools and was an indefatigable attender at opera and theatre performances in London, the provinces and abroad. She went to New York for the opening night of the Metropolitan season in 1977 and at 94 was lecturing in Rome, where she attracted considerable attention on television and radio. It was more than 45 years since she had sung in Italy but she was feted by enthusiasts who came to honour her. She was given a luncheon at the Royal Opera House on her ninetieth birthday and four nights later a packed house at a celebratory concert, during which she sat in the royal box, heard personal tributes from, among others, Sir John Gielgud, Tito Gobbi, Lord (Bernard) Miles and world-famous opera stars, and a cascade of messages from Placido Domingo, Joan Sutherland and Birgit Nilsson to Gina Cigna and Leontyne Price was delivered. Her national memorial service in Westminster Abbey, attended by 2000 illustrious colleagues and friends, would have given her even greater pleasure.

Dame Eva never married, though she had been engaged briefly during World War I. Her immense personal charm assured her a large circle of devoted admirers and friends, the greatest of whom was her companion and secretary for over 30 years. Ann Ridyard was a fellow Lancastrian and her descent into senile dementia and death were a burden and blow.

Eva Turner was a handsome woman whose *joie de vivre* was expressed in her strikingly well-cut, brightly coloured frocks, her evening attire invariably rounded off with a mink cape or coat, just as her day-time suits were often topped with an elegant fur hat. Her most remarkable asset was, of course, her singing voice, but for those who never heard her in an opera house, her speaking voice was also unforgettable: distinctive deep, modulated tones, the slow enunciation of every syllable and the long-rolling Rs retained from her sojourn in Italy. A small body of her work was preserved on record, the most memorable being extracts from a "live" performance of *Turandot* in 1937 with Martinelli. In 1989, this and a number of her old records were transferred to CD and she introduced the reissue, speaking in her inimitable, precisely articulated way about her career and hoping that future generations would take pleasure in hearing her with improved sound quality.

Born Eva Turner. **Father** Cotton mill chief engineer. **Education** Royal Academy of Music, London, 1911–15. **Career** Joined Royal Carl Rosa Opera Company, 1915; Covent Garden début, 1920; La Scala, Milan début, 1924; toured Europe, South America and US with Chicago Civic Opera; first sang *Turandot,* Brescia, 1926; special performance to commemorate Bolivar Centenary; farewell performance, *Turandot,* Covent Garden, 1948; professor of voice, University of Oklahoma music faculty, 1949–59; professor of voice, Royal Academy of Music, London, 1959–66. **Related activities** British Council lecture tour, Italy, 1982. **Offices and memberships** (include) President, Wagner Society, 1971–85; member, National Association of Teachers of Singing, US. **Awards and honours** (include) Fellow, Royal Academy of Music; honorary international member, Sigma Alpha Iota, 1951–90; honorary international Soroptomist, 1955–90; Dame Commander of the Order of the British Empire, 1962; honorary member, Guildhall School of Music, 1968; fellow, Royal College of Music, 1974; fellow, Royal Northern College of Music, 1978; honorary fellow, Trinity College of Music, London, 1982; honorary citizen, State of Oklahoma, 1982; first freeman, Metropolitan Borough of Oldham, 1982; honorary DMus: University of Manchester, 1979, Oxford University, 1984; honorary fellow, St Hilda's College, Oxford University, 1984; honorary licentiate, Western Ontario Conservatory of Music, Canada, 1986. **Stage** (includes) *The Magic Flute,* 1916; *Tannhaüser,* 1916; *Aida,* 1916, 1922, 1928, 1939; *Tosca,* 1922; *Das Rheingold,* 1924–25; *Die Walküre,* 1924–25; *Turandot,* 1926, 1928, 1937, 1947, 1948; *Fidelio,* 1927; *Un ballo in maschera,* 1935, 1937; *Die Freischütz,* 1936; *Tristan and Isolde,* 1938; *Serenade to Music* (at Sir Henry Wood's Jubilee), 1938. **Recordings** (include) *Tannhaüser* (CD issue of 1933 recording); *Turandot* (CD issue of 1937 recording). **Cause of death** Undisclosed, at age 98.

IRVING WALLACE

American Author

Born **Chicago, Illinois, 19 March 1916**

Died **Los Angeles, California, 29 June 1990**

You may well ask why Irving Wallace is described above as an "author" rather than as a novelist. There is a simple reason for it: Wallace was a creator of popular fiction based on widely reported news events and as such, one cannot call him a novelist in the same way one speaks of a Steinbeck or a Hemingway. Popular fiction, however, *is* popular, and during his lifetime, Irving Wallace sold more than 120 million copies of his works — both fiction and sensationalist non-fiction — commanding an international audience of more than 900 million readers. In addition, he also wrote or collaborated on nine Hollywood screenplays and assisted his daughter and son in the compilation of almanacs and other books of lists. Thus, whether one classes Wallace's works as "art" or not — which is, after all, only in the eye of the beholder — one cannot deny that the man was, in the end, outrageously successful. As critic John Leverence put it, "You can't understand Irving Wallace's books if you try to relate them to a long tradition of élite, classical American literature. But if you relate them to the traditions of American popular writing, particularly journalism and film writing, then they make sense."

Perhaps his works make sense because Wallace took them so seriously, despite the fact that many critics lumped them under the generic titles of "junk" or "formula" fiction (largely, it may be added, because of Wallace's ability to make large sums of money out of them).

He once explained,

> I believe in telling a story as stories were told in wayside inns or around fires before men could read or had bound books. You tell a tale to adults as you might tell a different one to your child

> curled in bed at night, so that the listener or reader will exclaim, "But what happened next?" or "What happened to her?" If I write a book because I love it, to satisfy my own curiosity in the characters or its subject, then perhaps thousands of other people, too wise to live by dreams, but with the same common interests I have, may want to buy or borrow some of my make-believe.

It was most likely this attitude which enabled Wallace to work as a successful screenwriter as well as a successful journalist, both areas in which he served a long apprenticeship.

Born in the Chicago of 1916, Wallace was the son of Alexander and Bessie Wallace, two Russian Jews who had emigrated to the United States. A year or so later, the little family moved to Kenosha, Wisconsin, where Alexander Wallace took a job as a department store clerk; a few years later, he had opened his own business with his brother. Both parents were hard-working, literate people; Wallace recalled his mother's love and admiration for writers, and it was perhaps due in part to this influence that, even as a small boy, he made up his mind to become a writer. Typically, he threw himself towards his ambition: at the Washington Junior High School, he became the mainstay of the school newspaper, and at 15, he sold a magazine article — the first of an eventual 500-plus articles and short stories he marketed to national magazines. During his high-school years, his editorial work on the school newspaper won him two national journalism prizes; since sport was another interest of his, the young Wallace also served as a sports stringer for Milwaukee's *Wisconsin News*.

Wallace graduated from high school in 1934, and continued to work as a freelance writer, but not in any tame sense of the word. That summer, he and two other aspiring young journalists embarked on an expedition to Central America where they hoped to discover the Fountain of Blood, a legendary fountain said to be located somewhere in the dense vegetation of Honduras. For four months the trio travelled, backed by various newspapers, and sent accounts of their adventures back to the US; eventually, they did indeed discover the illustrious fountain — only to discover that it ran red because of mineral deposits carried by the waters.

The stories Wallace created during this time, however, were enough to bring him to the attention of various scholastic bodies, including the Williams Institute, a small college in Berkeley, California, which offered him a scholarship to its exceptional writing programme. Not surprisingly, Wallace remained there only a few months. He was already a published writer, after all, and decided that he could learn more about writing simply by doing it rather than learning theoretical practices in a classroom. Thus in 1936, he migrated to Los Angeles to scrape a living from article and playwriting, and here he made his first contact with the world of show business by ghostwriting several articles for such stage and screen personalities as Bob Hope, Boris Karloff and W.C. Fields.

When World War II broke out, Wallace enlisted in the Army, and spent most of the conflict working on training films with the likes of John Huston and Frank Capra. In 1943, he earned his first credit for a film idea when his name appeared in conjunction with the film *Jive Junction*, produced by PRC Pictures. Following his discharge in 1946, Wallace returned to the world of freelancing, but since, from 1941, he had been a married man (his wife was Sylvia Kahn, editor of one of the film magazines to which he contributed), Wallace found that family life demanded greater responsibility and more regular payments. Consequently he turned his hand to the more lucrative field of screenwriting and, during the 1950s, he wrote for virtually every major film company Hollywood had to offer. His screen credits included *The West Point Story* (Warner Brothers), *Meet Me at the Fair* (Universal) and *The Big Circus* (Columbia).

Despite the money, however, Wallace was not at all happy working on films. "It was a plush hell," he recalled years later, "an infernal region dominated by double-dealing, politics, feuds, pettiness, thievery, cretinism, where the writer suffered indignity, disrespect, disdain, and where he could make more money than he could possibly make in any other salaried medium of writing."

To keep his self-respect, Wallace managed to churn out three moderately successful non-fiction books during these years. These were followed by his first book-length work of fiction, *The Sins of Philip Fleming,* published in 1959, which dealt with a young writer's efforts to establish his literary career. The book almost sank without a trace, but for the fact that it brought its author to the attention of the New American Library, a paperback house, which offered him a 25,000-dollar advance for two books. The money was enough to keep Wallace and his family financially stable for a while, so the unhappy filmwriter was able to flee the world of Hollywood and its dirty deals.

His next novel was loathed by the critics: "sophomoric, outrageously contrived" were just some of the adjectives used to describe *The Chapman Report* in 1960, yet readers took no notice: the novel, based on the impact of a sex survey on the lives of some suburban women, remained on the American best-seller lists for 30 weeks, and did equally well abroad. Darryl F. Zanuck bought the movie rights to the story for 170,000 dollars, and the subsequent film, starring Jane Fonda and Shelley Winters, became a box-office sensation when it was released two years later. *The Prize* followed in 1962. A story based on the awarding of the Nobel Prize, it, too, jumped to the best-sellers' lists, despite the fact that it deeply offended the Swedes and was banned in Scandinavia. Like many Wallace novels, it was also made into a film.

"More fiction dealing with sexual detail followed," stated the London *Times,* "most of it filmed or televised, and if Wallace did not bring delicacy to this subject, he certainly brought it to a crude gusto, for which many people were apparently grateful." Among these sex-orientated stories were *The Three Sirens,* about an anthropological study of a sexually permissive society, and *The Seven Minutes,* about the censorship trial of a bookshop owner (the title refers to a woman's thoughts during the seven minutes she is engaged in sexual intercourse). From sex, Wallace jumped to religion in *The Word,* which deals with the discovery and impact of a new gospel on Christian society. The list of his novels goes on and on, but as *The Times* put it, "Wallace's collections of facts (and some were facts) were really his most original contributions to commerce...*The Intimate Sex Lives of Famous People* (1981), which with its garish and boldly delineated collection of facts, proved to be compulsive reading even for those who could not admit it. Other volumes of this type include *The Nympho and Other Maniacs* (1971), *The Book of Lists* (1977), and *The People's Almanac* (1975)." From which one can gather the reasons Wallace was slammed time and again for being nothing more than a writer of sensationalism.

While this is certainly true — gratuitous sex is, after all, just that — it cannot be denied that Irving Wallace worked diligently at his stories. When writing a novel, for example, he spent six days a week at his ancient Underwood typewriter that his parents had given him for his thirteenth birthday; a novel usually took between four to six months to write, but many (unlike the *Times* writer) considered his attention to facts and details to be on the mark. "As a writer", Wallace explained, "any modest success I've had has not been entirely accidental. I've never ceased trying to improve. I'm always studying books by other authors, often with admiration at how they achieve their effects and with dismay at my own shortcomings. I've never stopped reading books about writing. Since the day I was born, it sometimes seems, I've been reading." And for that matter, it seems that readers have been reading his works for just as long.

Perhaps he would be better defined as a great entertainer, but whatever the case, Irving Wallace will be missed by his fans. "His novels", states Lawrence Lafore, "have been hugely popular, in both senses of the word. They skillfully combine the most alluring features of the headline, the exposé, the editorial and the mystery story."

Born Irving Wallace. **Parents** Alexander, salesman and auctioneer, and Bessie (Liss) Wallace. **Marriage** Sylvia Kahn, author and editor, 1941. **Children** David and Amy. **Education** Washington Junior High School, Kenosha, Wisconsin; Kenosha Central High School, 1931–34; Williams Institute, Berkeley, California, 1935; Los Angeles City College. **Military service** Staff sergeant, US Army Air Force, 1942–46, writer, First Motion Picture Unit, Signal Corps Photographic Corps. **Career** Sports stringer, *Wisconsin News;* sports columnist, *Kenosha Bulletin;* sold first article, *Horse and Jockey* magazine, 1931; sold first short story, *Challenge,* 1933; foreign correspondent to Japan, *Liberty* magazine, 1940; first screen credit, *Jive Junction,* 1943; first screenplay filmed, *The West Point Story,* 1950; first non-fiction book published, *The Fabulous Originals,* 1955; first novel published, *The Sins of Philip Fleming,* 1959; published over 500 short stories; first novel chosen for Book-of-the-Month Club selection, *The Prize,* 1962; covered Democratic and Republican National Conventions, *Chicago Sun-Times/Daily News* Wire Service, 1972; contributor: *For Men Only, Ken, Modern Mechanics, Thrilling Sports, Modern Screen, Coronet, Liberty, Saturday Evening Post, Reader's Digest, Esquire, Collier's, American Mercury, Cosmopolitan, Pageant.* **Offices and memberships** Member: Authors Guild, Authors League of America, Writers Guild of America, Manuscript Society, Society of Authors, London; member, Poets, Playwrights, Editors, Essayists, Novelists. **Awards and honours** Two national journalism prizes, Kenosha Central High School, Grand Gold Cup of Medill School of Journalism, first place, national feature writing contest of International Quill and Scroll; top ten young public speakers of America, National Forensic League, 1933; Supreme Award of Merit and honorary fellow, George Washington Carver Memorial Institute, for *The Man,* 1964; silver medal, Commonwealth Club, 1965; *Bestsellers* magazine award, for *The Man,* 1965; Paperback of the Year Award, National Bestsellers Institute, for *The Seven Minutes,* 1970; Popular Culture Association award of excellence, for distinguished achievements in the popular arts, 1974; Venice Rosa d'Oro Award, for contributions to American letters, 1975. **Novels** *The Sins of Philip Fleming,* 1959; *The Chapman Report,* 1960; *The Prize,* 1962; *The Three Sirens,* 1963; *The Man,* 1964; *The Plot,* 1967; *The Seven Minutes,* 1969; *The World,* 1974; *The R Document,* 1976; *The Pigeon Project,* 1979; *The Second Lady,* 1980; *The Miracle,* 1983; *The Seventh Secret,* 1986; *The Celestial Bed,* 1987. **Screenplays** (With John Monks, Jr and Charles Hoffman) *The West Point Story,* 1950; *Meet Me at the Fair,* 1953; (with Lewis Meltzer) *Desert Legion,* 1953; (with William Bowers) *Split Second,* 1953; (with Roy Huggins) *Gun Fury,* 1953; (with Horace McCoy) *Bad for Each Other,* 1954; (with Gerald Adams) *The Gambler from Natches,* 1954; *Jump into Hell,* 1955; *Sincerely Yours,* 1955; *The Burning Hills,* 1956; *Bombers B-52,* 1957; (with Irwin Allen and Charles Bennett) *The Big Circus,* 1959. **Plays** *And Then Goodnight; Because of Sex; Hotel Behemoth; Speak of the Devil; Murder by Morning;* (with Jerome Weidman) *Pantheon.* **Other publications** (include) *The Fabulous Originals,* 1955; *The Square Pegs,* 1957; *The Fabulous Showman: The Life and Times of P.T. Barnum,* 1959; P.T. Barnum biography, *Collier's Encyclopedia,* 1960, *American Oxford Encyclopedia, Encyclopaedia Britannica; The Twenty-Seventh Wife* (biography), 1961; *The Sunday Gentleman* (collection), 1965; *The Writing of One Novel,* 1968; *The Nympho and Other Maniacs,* 1971; (compiler, with David Wallechinsky) *The People's Almanac,* 1975; (compiler with David Wallechinsky and Amy Wallace) *The Book of Lists,* 1977; (with David Wallechinsky) *The People's Almanac 2,* 1978; (with Amy Wallace) *The Two* (biography), 1978; (with David Wallechinsky, Amy Wallace and Sylvia Wallace) *The Book of Lists 2,* 1980; *The Second Lady,* 1980; *The Book of Predictions,* 1981; *The Intimate Sex Lives of Famous People,* 1981; *The People's Almanac 3,* 1981; *The Almighty,* 1982; *The Book of Lists 3,* 1983; *Significa,* 1983. **Manuscript collections** University of Wyoming; University of Texas, Austin. **Cause of death** Pancreatic cancer, at age 74. **Further reading** John Leverence, *Irving Wallace: A Writer's Profile,* 1974.

ELSIE WATERS

British Entertainer and Comedienne

***Born* London, England, 19 August 1884**

***Died* Steyning, West Sussex, 14 June 1990**

Elsie Waters played Gert to her sister Doris's Daisy in one of the most famous British stage and radio acts ever. The sisters were inseparable professionally and personally, living together until Doris died in 1978. Their double act began in the 1920s; at first they performed at seaside concert parties, singing humorous songs to Elsie's piano accompaniment. They appeared at dinners, concerts and masonic functions with these routines eventually forming their own concert party — The Enthusiasts — in 1927. Towards the end of the decade they began to take part in radio broadcasts, and it was through this medium that as Gert and Daisy they became a national institution. This comic duo of gossiping Cockney housewives was to remain popular from the early 1930s until the early 1970s. They included Winston Churchill among their fans, had a pair of elephants at the London Zoo named after them and, as indefatigable morale-boosters during World War II, were the subject of a radio warning from Nazi Germany (delivered by "Lord Haw-Haw") that the British people could not expect Gert and Daisy to protect them from attacks by the *Luftwaffe*!

Elsie's early days were hardly conducive to comedy. Born in London's East End, she was the daughter of a funeral furnisher who made coffin linings and shrouds. He was, however, a keen amateur musician who encouraged all of his six children to learn to play an instrument. Elsie took up the violin, and joined the family orchestra. Doris learned the piano, and the two sisters eventually studied at the Guildhall School of Music and Drama in London. Their brother Horace also became a professional entertainer. He shared Elsie's and Doris's flair for comedy, and also made a reputation as a straight actor on radio, screen and television, using the name of Jack Warner.

Elsie was the more creative of the sisters and the brains behind many of their routines and promotional campaigns. In their pre-Gert and Daisy days she wrote the following mock rueful announcement for the *Sunday Referee,* a theatrical journal: "Elsie and Doris Waters, all last week, first turn, three times daily, at the London Alhambra — thereby disproving the old saying: 'You can only die once.'" It was she who devised at very short notice the first Gert and Daisy sketch. The sisters were recording some of their comic songs for Parlophone, and were suddenly asked for extra material for the B side of one of their discs. Elsie rapidly wrote a song called "Wedding Bells" and improvised a dialogue between two Cockney women who were watching a "posh" marriage celebration. Soon afterwards Oscar Preuss, the recording manager of Parlophone, asked for more Gert and Daisy dialogues because the first had become a best-seller. Elsie was able to meet this demand and managed to breathe a sense of realism as well as extraordinary robustness into her sketches for many subsequent years in radio, stage and film contexts.

It was their proud boast that they never used the same script more than once. Certainly to music-hall, variety and radio audiences throughout the 1930s and 1940s it seemed as if Gert and Daisy were real friends, sharing the daily frustrations and aspirations of ordinary people, and expressing a genuine home-spun philosophy as well as pinpointing the humour of awkward husbands, nosy neighbours, petty bureacracy, or of simply being hard-up. Resilience was the keynote of their patter, and each of the sisters was blessed with a rich, warm, speaking voice which conveyed the eternal vitality of the Cockney (even though purists would claim that, despite being born in Bow, Elsie and Doris were not genuine Cockneys because they were too far away to hear the bells of the church of St Mary-le-Bow in Cheapside — the qualifying factor of true Cockneyism!).

Nevertheless the British nation took Elsie and Doris to its heart. During World War II especially, they came to symbolize almost as vividly as Winston Churchill, the pugnacious bulldog and John Bull, the wry humour and bloodymindedness of the British with their backs to the wall. They entertained the troops and the munition workers. On radio they were frequent stars of *Workers' Playtime,* a long-running, wartime-originated series which was devised to raise the morale of factory-workers and listeners at home during the days of blackouts and bombing. When Lord Woolton, as wartime minister of food, recruited their services, they gave these without remuneration, regularly and persuasively broadcasting hints on recipes, and how to improvise these according to current shortages.

They played leading roles in three films and a revue called *Pay the Piper* at a London West End Theatre. They took part on several occasions in Royal Variety performances. Possibly, however, the crown of their success in their own eyes was when in 1943 they played with tremendous zest and expertise in a radio production of Shakespeare's *The Merry Wives of Windsor.* Elsie portrayed Mistress Ford and Doris Mistress Quickly.

They were the greatest of the female double acts of their era, although the Houston Sisters and Elsie Revnell and Gracie West offered strong competition. Both were appointed OBE in 1946. Forty years later, several years after Doris had died, Elsie received the Burma Star at the Burma Star Association reunion for entertaining the troops there during World War II. To her delight, Doris was posthumously included.

Born Elsie Waters. **Father** Funeral furnisher. **Education** Guildhall School of Music and Drama, London. **Career** First appearance, 1923; appeared with Will C. Pepper's "White Coons"; formed own concert party, "The Enthusiasts", 1927; radio début, 1927; played Gert in "Gert and Daisy" double act with sister Doris Waters as Daisy, from 1920s; appeared in Variety, to 1973; recorded first "patter" record, "The Wedding", Parlophone Records, 1930; appeared "Henry Hall's Guest Night", BBC, 1934; first Royal Variety Performance, 1934; made *Feed the Brute* radio programme, Ministry of Food, from 1939–45; toured with Entertainment National Service Association, 1939–45; first film, *Gert and Daisy's Weekend,* 1941; first radio programme, *Floggit's,* 1946; final appearance, 1978. **Awards and honours** Officer of the Order of the British Empire, 1946; Burma Star, 1986. **Stage** (includes) *Pay the Piper* (revue). **Films** (include) *Gert and Daisy's Weekend,* 1941. **Radio** (includes) *The Merry Wives of Windsor,* 1943; *Floggit's,* 1946; also: *Workers' Playtime*, *Gert and Daisy's Working Party*, *Petticoat Lane.* **Recordings** (include) "The Wedding", 1929. **Publication** *Gert and Daisy Cookery Book.* **Cause of death** Undisclosed, at age 95.

JULY

JOE APPIAH

Ghanaian Lawyer and Politician
Born **Kumasi, Ghana, 16 November 1918**
Died **Accra, Ghana, 9 July 1990**

The only high political office Joe Appiah ever held was as roving ambassador for the repressive military regime of General Acheampong in 1970s Ghana. In England he was best known for his marriage to Peggy, daughter of Sir Stafford Cripps, the former socialist chancellor of the exchequer. But he was, nonetheless, a continuing force for change during the years before Ghana (then the Gold Coast and a British colony) achieved independence and he was equally instrumental in the country's subsequent struggle to achieve internal democratic freedom.

Joe Appiah (he was christened Joseph Emmanuel, but always used "Joe" in public life) distinguished himself in other ways; he was a tireless campaigner for the rights of the Ashanti people of Ghana and a leading member of the Methodist Church.

These last are hardly surprising, given his background. He was born in Kumasi into a prominent Methodist family. His father was an important figure at the court of Asantehene, the traditional leader of Ashanti, and an expert on customary law. After an education at Mfantsipim Secondary School the young Joe left — in 1943 — for London, where he followed in his father's footsteps in yet another respect — he studied law.

Like future African statesmen Kwame Nkrumah and Jomo Kenyatta, Appiah became immersed in British Labour Party politics. He grew close to Nkrumah who sometimes came to his Hampstead (north London) rooms to share a meal. They went together to the Pan-African Conference in Manchester in 1945. And when Nkrumah returned to his own country and his Convention People's Party (CPP) won the first free elections in 1951, Appiah, with his ebullient personality and acute legal mind, was the obvious choice as the new president's personal envoy in London.

It was in this capacity that he met Peggy Cripps. Their wedding in 1953 was a great social event, attended by Labour shadow-cabinet members and the delight of the gossip columnists of the day. At the marriage ceremony itself the very English brocade gown of the bride contrasted with the dress of the groom — who arrived in the tribal ceremonial robes of an Ashanti chief.

In 1954 Appiah was called to the Bar and then returned to the Gold Coast with his new wife. It was a matter of course that Appiah should join Nkrumah's CPP; in the following general election in 1954 he won a seat for them as one of the party's rising stars alongside Victor Owusu and R.R. Amponsah of the newly enfranchised people of Ashanti.

But it soon became obvious that those in the forefront of the movement for independence harboured two very different socialist ideologies which could not work together for long once they got down to the details of government. Back in England Nkrumah had been closely associated with left-wing socialists and with the British Communist Party; Joe Appiah and other leaders of the West African Students Union went home aiming to build classical but more equitable democracies for their people. The issue came to a head in 1955. Saying that he was disgusted with the corruption and authoritarianism of the CPP, Joe Appiah split with Nkrumah and joined the new Ashanti-based party, the National Liberation Movement (NLM).

In 1965 he was elected to parliament as NLM member for one of the Ashanti constituencies. Throughout the late 1950s he continued to voice his opposition to Nkrumah's government. At the time of Ghana's independence in 1957 he joined the United Party of Dr Busia when it absorbed the NLM and became one of the most active and outspoken of Nkrumah's critics. In 1958 he became deputy leader of the Opposition United Party.

He was a vigorous campaigner, in particular, against the notorious Preventive Detention Act of 1958 and a severe critic of the measure once it had been passed. Ironically, just three years later, the legislation was used against him and he was detained without trial for 15 months. His imprisonment left him a legacy of health problems: and, it seems, of disillusionment. He gave up politics and spent the next four years practising law in the city of Kumasi; though he still often represented opposition figures.

In 1966 Nkrumah's government was overthrown in a coup and replaced by the National Liberation Council (four soldiers and four policemen, with a lieutenant-general as the chairman). The NLC presented itself as having saved Ghana from Communism under Nkrumah's dictatorship and was therefore eager to be seen to be liberal and to support local interest groups who felt they had been robbed of their inheritance. It was at this point that Joe Appiah returned to the political stage in a characteristic role — as a member of the national committee set up by the military to prepare for the return of civilian government.

He clearly hoped that he would play a prominent role in the next regime. Splitting with Dr Busia, he formed his own party; but it did not do well. At the 1969 election it won only two seats and Appiah's — in Kumasi, among his own Ashanti people — was not one of them. But he was chosen as party leader outside parliament of the Justice Party — a tribute to the esteem and affection in which he was held in spite of the contradictions of his political make-up.

Appiah remained steadfast in his opposition to the Busia government. In 1972 that government was overthrown — again by a coup but this time led by Colonel Acheampong. After being "liberated" in 1966, Ghana now found itself being "redeemed" by Acheampong's National Redemption Council; and Joe Appiah, in the most controversial move of his political career, played a major part in that process. Shortly after the coup he emerged as a close adviser of Acheampong's regime and for the next five years he served as its roving ambassador. Acheampong's "Union Government" perhaps deserved more than any other the outspoken criticism of a Joe Appiah. Its basic message was that by maintaining a ban on "divisive" political parties, stable government would result, with some police and military intervention. The most violent means were used to propagate this view — from police brutality on a massive scale to the murder of those who voiced dissenting views. The end was inevitable; in 1978 the hated Acheampong regime was in turn removed.

Joe Appiah was again detained. This experience finished both his involvement in politics and his health. He retired to devote the last ten years of his life to his family and his religion. And to the Ashanti. His political career was erratic, but he retained throughout it a commitment to civil liberties, to democracy and, above all, to his own people.

Born Joseph Emmanuel Appiah. **Father** Chief Secretary, Ashanti Confederacy Council and expert on customary law. **Marriage** Peggy Cripps, 1953. **Children** Three daughters and one son: Isobel, Adowa, Abena and Anthony. **Education** Mfantisipim Secondary School, Cape

Coast; Richmond College, Kumasi; read law, London, 1943–54. **Career** Trainee manager, United Africa Company; British representative, Convention People's Party, Fifth Pan African Conference, Manchester, 1945; called to Bar, Middle Temple, 1954; returned to Ghana, 1955; private secretary to Kwame Nkrumah, 1955, broke with him to join National Liberation Movement, 1956, member for Atwima-Amansie, Ashanti, 1956; joined United Party, 1957; deputy leader, Opposition United Party, 1958; imprisoned 1961–62; returned to private law practice, 1962–66; vice-chairman, committee to guide Ghana's return to civilian rule, Busia government, 1966; goodwill ambassador, US and UK, 1966; defeated in general election, 1969; leader outside parliament, Justice Party, 1969–72; roving ambassador, National Redemption Council, 1972–77; permanent representative, United Nations, 1977–78. **Other activities** Lay preacher. **Offices and memberships** President, Ghana Bar Assocition. **Publications** (include) *Autobiography of an African Patriot*, 1990. **Cause of death** Cancer of the mouth, at age 71.

RICHARD BERNSTEIN

American Physical Chemist

***Born* Long Island, New York, 21 October 1923**

***Died* Helsinki, Finland, 8 July 1990**

Advertisements from car manufacturers on television show in slow motion what happens to their models when they collide or crash. We can witness in slow motion how the impact is absorbed, the collapse of the steering wheel, and how someone sitting in a driving seat would be saved from injury.

Similar detailed series of "snapshots" of chemical reactions are crucial in studying what happens when individual molecules collide, and how the energy transforms one chemical compound into another. But whereas the collapse of the car takes a moderate fraction of a second, the chemical reactions take place in *femtoseconds*, where a femtosecond is a quadrillionth of a second, the time light would take to travel a millionth of a metre.

Studies of collisions of molecules in reactions is now called *femtochemistry*, and it is of crucial importance in examining explosions, engine fuel combustion and many other chemical processes. It depends on being able to control the speed, direction and orientation of single molecules and atoms accelerated in beams, and the way to do this, using very rapid laser pulses, was developed by Dr Richard ("Dick") Bernstein and was his main scientific achievement.

Graduating with honours in chemistry and mathematics from Columbia University, New York, in 1943, he joined the Manhattan Project responsible for developing the atomic bomb and worked on uranium isotope separation. He became a member of the US Army Corps of Engineers and helped in measurements of radioactive fallout from the Bikini Atoll tests.

In 1948 he gained his doctorate from Columbia, and in 1953 moved to the University of Michigan as assistant professor. Here he began the quest which involved him for the rest of his life. He determined to find out how individual molecules arrange themselves prior to chemical reactions and what happens to the energy released. But to find that out, he had to observe individual collisions in isolation. And he realized that the tool for doing this was the molecular beam. He designed apparatus to control the speed, direction and orientation of the molecules in a beam, and then observed what happened when two such beams met, exchanging energy, breaking their electronic bonds and forming new products.

Other important developments for which he was responsible were in laser chemistry, and he initiated the first study by the US National Academy of Sciences which demonstrated the way chlorofluorocarbons are destroying the ozone layer. For his achievements he was to be awarded many honours and distinctions, and only months before his death was awarded the National Medal of Science by President Bush.

His successful research moved with him as he went to be a professor in turn at the universities of Wisconsin and Texas, then back to Columbia, and finally UCLA. In addition to being an outstanding experimentalist and theorist, Bernstein was a remarkably effective teacher, and at each institution left a core of inspired followers. Nor was it only in the lecture room he passed on his knowledge and enthusiasm. He was a prolific author of scientific papers, wrote two books with R.D. Levine of the Hebrew University of Jerusalem — *Molecular Reaction Dynamics* and *Molecular Reaction Dynamics and Chemical Reactivity* — and was editor for a number of years of *Chemical Physics Letters*. He often visited Britain and gave an influential series of Hinshelwood Lectures in Oxford in 1981, later published as *Chemical Dynamics via Molecular Beam and Laser Techniques*.

Scientific conferences provided another medium for him to share his ideas and enthusiasm. Always elegantly dressed, he used the occasions not only to suggest experiments to others but to learn from what they were doing. It was while he was attending a Soviet-American conference on laser chemistry in the Soviet Union that he had a heart attack. This led to complications and he was rushed to Helsinki for treatment, but his life could not be saved.

Born Richard Barry Bernstein. **Marriage** Norma Olivier. **Children** Neil, Minda, Beth and Julie. **Education** Columbia University, New York, BA, 1943, MA, 1944, PhD in chemistry, 1948. **Military service** US Army Corps of Engineers, 1944–46. **Career** Chemist, SAM Labs, Columbia University, 1943–44, Manhattan District, 1944–46; assistant professor of chemistry, Illinois Institute of Technology, 1948–53; associate professor to professor, University of Michigan, 1953–63; professor, University of Wisconsin, Madison, 1963–66, W.W. Daniells professor, 1966–73; W.T. Doherty professor of chemistry, University of Texas, Austin, 1973–77; Higgins professor of natural science and chemistry, Columbia University, 1977–82, chemistry department chairman, 1979–81; senior vice-president, Occidental Research Corporation, 1982–83; professor of chemistry, University of California, Los Angeles, 1983–90. **Related activities** Chairman, Office of Chemistry and Chemical Technology, National Research Council, 1974–79; visiting professor, Physical Chemistry laboratory, Oxford University, 1981; editor, *Chemical Physics Letters*, 1979–81, 1986–90; editorial board member, *Journal of Physical Chemistry*, *Journal of Chemical Physics*, *Chemical Physics*, *Accounts of Chemical Research, International Review of Physical Chemistry*, *Advances in Chemical Physics*. **Offices and memberships** (include) Fellow: American Academy of Arts and Sciences, American Association for the Advancement of Science, American Physical Society; member: National Academy of Sciences, American Chemical Society, Sigma Xi. **Awards and honours** Sloan fellow, 1956–60; senior fellow, National Science Foundation, 1960–61; Peter Debye Award, American Chemical Society, 1981; Robert A. Welch Award for Chemistry, 1988; Wolf Prize for Chemistry, 1989; Willard Gibbs Medal, American Chemical Society, 1989; National Medal of Science, 1989. **Publications** (with R.D. Levine) *Molecular Reaction Dynamics*, 1974, *Molecular Reaction Dynamics and Chemical Reactivity*, 1987; *Chemical Dynamics via Molecular Beam and Laser Techniques*. **Cause of death** Heart attack, at age 66.

HAROLD BROOKS

British Literary Scholar

Born **Halifax, Yorkshire, 1 May 1907**

Died **Canterbury, Kent, 23 July 1990**

Harold Brooks's first experience of the theatre, at age seven, was a matinée of Granville Barker's famous 1914 production of *A Midsummer Night's Dream*. Taken by his aunts, Brooks later sat round their Christmas hearth and they read the play through, all taking parts. This experience secured a place for the theatre in Brooks's heart and resulted in a lifetime of scholarly work on the great plays and works of literature of our time.

Born the only son of a Methodist preacher, Brooks was educated in Blackburn and Newcastle-upon-Tyne. His mother's family included public figures associated with the town of Jarrow — indeed Brooks's grandfather had been mayor of the town twice — and it was in the Unitarian chapel in Jarrow that Brooks first preached at the age of 16. Brooks had always been profoundly influenced by his father's preaching and throughout his life he described himself as a "socialist and Unitarian". What was also apparent was the extent to which Brooks had embraced his parents' pacifism, tee-totalism and their support for working-class radicalism.

In 1926 Brooks went up to Merton College, Oxford to read history, and it was here that his academic ability really started to develop and expand. After completing successfully his history degree, Brooks then went on to read English, not stopping until he had secured a BLitt and a DPhil. It was not until 1939, when Brooks was 32, that he finally completed his studies.

The following year Brooks was offered his first post as an English lecturer at Queen's College, Belfast, and five years later he left Ireland to embark on his 29-year career at Birkbeck College, London. Though much published Brooks took longer than most writers to complete his work because of his devotion to teaching and supporting his students.

Those who were students over those years recall a man selflessly dedicated to his work. He was one of the most thorough of lecturers, always at pains not simply to lecture about the text at hand, but to offer a full and detailed overview of the historical, social and cultural backdrop surrounding any given text. This meant that his research was consistently extensive, and when delivered in the lecture hall revealed an intense and passionate enjoyment of his work. Those who recall his lectures describe them as "delivered with a seriousness, wit, and warmth which could be deeply affecting." Wrote Raman Selden in the London *Independent*, "As a student at Birkbeck in the early 1960's I was deeply impressed by the range of Harold Brooks's lecturing; from Chaucer, Langland and medieval drama and ballad to Hardy, Yeats and T.S. Eliot. His attention to students' essays was renowned: his annotations were frequently as long and thorough as the essays themselves."

The *magnum opus* of Brooks's life was his textual and biographical research into the work of the Restoration poet John Oldham. Several publications appeared during his extensive research, but it was not until 1987, in his eightieth year, that Brooks's long-awaited edition of Oldham's work was finally published. The "Life and Works of Oldham" are currently waiting for publication.

Brooks is perhaps best known for his work on the Arden Shakespeare series. From 1952 to 1958 he worked as textual adviser, and from 1958 to 1984 he was general editor. His knowledge and advice helped the content of 30 or so volumes in the series, and his own thorough and scholarly contribution was the extensive and detailed introduction to *A Midsummer Night's Dream*. It seems more than fitting that he should have chosen this particular play with which to reveal both his love of the theatre and his scholarly ability. In his preface to his 50,000-word-strong introduction Brooks makes the simple observation "I have tried never to lose sight of performance as the end for which

Shakespeare designed the piece." Though simple it is an observation which often escapes the work of other theatre scholars, and by including it Brooks clearly revealed his love of the theatre and the great texts of the theatre as alive, open to interpretation, and able to move and inspire their audience.

Among his contemporary scholars and his students it is felt that Brooks's greatest achievement was his work on the Restoration period of English literature. The doctoral thesis Brooks wrote while still in his twenties so impressed the Regius Professor of Modern History, Sir Charles Firth, that he was invited to work as his literary assistant; and in 1949 Brooks wrote an essay on the history of "Imitation" in verse satire which still remains the authority in its field.

Aside from his academic achievements Brook was also a man who inspired affection. His devotion to his teaching proved him to be a man of the people as well as a literary scholar, and he is remembered with affection and respect by fellow teachers and pupils alike. Brooks always used to joke that his tombstone should read "Interrupted", and this is a sentiment reflected by those at Birkbeck who worked with him for so long.

Born Harold Fletcher Brooks. **Parents** Joseph Barlow, Methodist minister, and Jenny Brooks. **Marriage** Jean Rylatt Lee. **Education** Queen Elizabeth's Grammar School, Blackburn, Lancashire; Royal Grammar School, Newcastle-upon-Tyne, Tyne and Wear; Merton College, Oxford, BA in modern history, 1929, BA in English language and literature, 1931, MA, 1934, BLitt in English, 1934, DPhil in English, 1939. **Career** Lecturer, Worker's Educational Association; Assistant lecturer in English, Queen's University, Belfast, 1940–45; lecturer in English literature, Birkbeck College, University of London, 1945–61, senior lecturer, 1961–62, reader, 1962–70, professor of English literature, 1970–74; retired 1974. **Related activities** Textual adviser, Arden Shakespeare, 1952–58, general editor, 1958–84; Council of External Students, London University; English subcommittee, London University Faculty of Education. **Offices and memberships** Member: Association of University Teachers, English Association, Shaw Society, Sunday Shakespeare Society, president. **Publications** (With others) *Librarianship and Literature*, 1970; (with others) *Restoration Literature: Critical Approaches*, 1972; (editor) *A Midsummer Night's Dream*, 1979; (editor) *Major Barbara*, 1985; (editor, with the collaboration of Raman Selden) *The Poems of John Oldham*, 1987. **Cause of death** Undisclosed, at age 83. **Further reading** Antony Coleman and Antony Hammond, editors, *Poetry and Drama, 1570–1700: Essays in Honour of Harold F. Brooks*, 1981.

EDITH BÜLBRING

German/British Physiologist and Pharmacologist

Born **Bonn, Germany, 27 December 1903**

Died **Oxford, England, 5 July 1990**

Edith Bülbring had a love of music, and a talent for it. Everyone expected her to become a concert pianist, so when she chose medicine as a career, it came as somewhat of a surprise. But she approached the study of medicine with the same vigour she applied to everything else in her life. She was already a musician, a dancer, a skier, and proficient in several languages (her father had been a professor of English at Bonn University), but in the field of physiology she would excel herself, becoming known (in later years) as the "grandmother" of a new generation of medical researchers.

Professor Bülbring did post-graduate work in pharmacology at Berlin University, and then she spent a year working as a paediatrician in Jena. She returned to research at the university in 1932, but was expelled in 1933 for one reason and one reason only: her mother was Jewish. She went to stay with relatives in Holland for a brief period, and then she came to England, which became her adopted homeland.

She worked for Professor J.H. Burn in the laboratories of the Pharmaceutical Society. When Professor Burn moved to Oxford University, she went with him. In 1949, she went to America for a year on a fellowship to Johns Hopkins University, and then she returned to Oxford, where she was to make the discoveries that would ensure her place in scientific history. She was the first to record the electrical activity of smooth muscle, which is the muscle responsible for the contractions of hollow viscera such as the intestines, the stomach, and the uterus, as well as controlling the calibre of blood vessels. With the use of micro-electrodes, she was able to show that tension within muscle tissue is proportionate to the frequency of discharge of action potential.

In the late 1960s, Professor Bülbring discovered a fundamental difference between the action potential of smooth muscle and that of skeletal and cardiac muscle: smooth muscle action potential is due to the influx of calcium ions; the action potential of skeletal and cardiac muscle is due to sodium ions.

By this time she was drawing scientific collaborators to her from around the world: Ceylon, Taiwan, Japan, Europe, the Ukraine and the United States. Professor Bülbring never married; these young collaborators became her family, and of their many achievements together she said modestly, "I am doing nothing. I just listen. They do the work." These junior collaborators went on to become eminent scientists in their own homelands, training the next generation: Professor Bülbring's "grandchildren".

Busy as she was in her department at Oxford, she maintained her interest in music and the arts. She owned two grand pianos, and hosted frequent musical soirées, where she would delight her guests with her musical ability. She was a great fan of the opera, and of the paintings of her favourite artist, Rembrandt.

Tuesday evenings were set aside for sherry and congenial conversation in either the garden or the sitting room of her Oxford home. This was a time her colleagues looked forward to, when they could relax and discuss their ideas with kindred spirits.

Professor Bülbring's left leg was amputated while she was in her late seventies. In her indomitable style, she made a spectacular recovery and taught herself to walk on a false leg, without the aid of a stick. She kept on walking, with a clear head and a lively spirit, until the age of 86.

Born Edith Bülbring. **Parents** Karl Daniel, professor of English, and Hortense Leonore (Kann) Bülbring. **Education** Bonn University, MD; Munich University; Freiberg University; post-graduate work in pharmacology, Berlin University, 1929–31. **Emigration** Left Germany for England, 1933. **Career** Paediatrician, University of Jena, 1932, Virchow Krankenhaus, University of Berlin, 1933; Pharmacological Laboratory of Pharmaceutical Society of Great Britain, University of London, 1933–38; pharmacology department, Oxford University, 1938–71, university reader, 1960–67, professor of pharmacology, 1967–71, emeritus professor, 1971–90; professorial fellow, Lady Margaret Hall, 1960–71. **Awards and honours** Rockefeller Fellowship at Johns Hopkins University, 1949; honorary member: Pharmaceutical Society, Torino, Italy, 1957, British Pharmacological Society, 1975, Deutsche Physiologische Gesellschaft, 1976, Physiological Society, 1981; fellow, Royal Society, 1958; honorary fellow, Lady Margaret Hall, 1971; Schmiedeberg-Plakette der Deutschen Pharmakologischen Gesellschaft, 1974; honorary doctor of medicine: University of Groningen, Netherlands, 1979, University of Leuven, Belgium, 1981, University of Homburg-Saar, Germany; Wellcome Gold Medal in Pharmacology, 1985. **Cause of death** Undisclosed, at age 86.

ALAIN CHAPEL

French Chef and Restaurateur

Born **Lyon, France, 30 December 1937**

Died **Avignon, France, 10 July 1990**

Alain Chapel, who was one of the most outstanding chefs of his generation, was born appropriately enough in the gastronomic heartland of France. His parents ran a restaurant in Lyon but with the outbreak of World War II in 1939 they moved to Mionnay, a village 12 miles away, where they purchased a small bistro. Chapel's father was industrious and ambitious. The bistro soon became noted for the excellence of its food and in 1957 it was awarded one star by the prestigious Michelin Guide to restaurants.

Chapel flourished in this atmosphere and when he failed his school leaving examination in 1952 his father encouraged him to develop his natural talents by training as a chef. Chapel began a four-year apprenticeship with the famous restaurateur, Jean Vignard, in Lyon. Following this he was employed by another celebrated chef, Fernand Point, at his restaurant in Vienne.

Chapel returned to the family restaurant in 1967 where he took charge of the kitchens. He worked hard and within two years, in 1969, the restaurant was awarded a coveted second Michelin star. Shortly after this Chapel took over the restaurant totally following the death of his father. He continued to introduce innovative culinary ideas and in 1973 his diligence paid off when he won Michelin's top award, a third star. At the time this was a distinction which Chapel shared with only 16 other restaurants in the whole of France; at the age of 35 he was the youngest ever recipient of this accolade.

By this time Chapel's reputation had spread and his restaurant became a place of pilgrimage for serious gastronomes. Chapel's meals were elaborate affairs often consisting of seven courses. Ever the individualist, he spurned the vogue for the *nouvelle cuisine* style of cooking which swept through France in the 1970s, preferring the technique he had perfected of taking traditional recipes and investing them with his own particular genius. Chapel tended wherever possible to use local produce in his cooking, buying chickens from poulterers he knew well and relying on the extensive Lyon food market for the choicest vegetables.

Chapel himself described his cooking as "turn-of-the-century *cuisine bourgeois*" and his restaurant became famous for such dishes as *Poulette de Bresse en vessie* (chicken stuffed with truffles and cooked in a pig's bladder), stuffed calves' ears with fried parsley, and *gâteau de foies blonds*. This latter dish which consisted of a mousse of puréed chicken livers cooked in beef marrow and served with a lobster and cream sauce, became his trademark and inevitably provoked extravagant praise. Writing in *The New York Times* in 1977, Craig Claibourne described the dish as Chapel's "ultimate triumph and one of the absolute cooking glories of this generation". Henri Gault of the prestigious Gault Millau restaurant guide likened the experience of eating it to that of listening to a Mozart quartet, saying that in both cases "the same *frisson* ran through my body, the same tears formed in my eyes".

Chapel's dedication to cooking and his quest for perfection were total and because of this he was often perceived as being reserved and rather aloof. At his restaurant he presented a formidable figure, immaculately turned out in a high starched chef's hat with an old-fashioned apron reaching to his ankles. Often he did not appear to warm towards his customers, particularly newly-weds or lovers of whom he remarked "their minds are on other things than food."

However, to his friends Chapel showed a cordial and generous nature. He was on good terms with Europe's leading chefs, many of whom were among the 120 friends invited to his restaurant for his fortieth birthday celebrations. Chapel excelled himself in cooking them a truly memorable dinner. Years later the French chef Michel Roux fondly recalled this event saying "this meal remains with me today as though it were yesterday". Chapel was also well regarded by the elderly inhabitants of Mionnay for whom he provided a top-class buffet meal every year as a Christmas present.

To relax, Chapel would go for long walks in the countryside round his home. He also loved music and theatre and often visited the Salzburg and Aix-en-Provence festivals. He enjoyed travel and had made many trips to the United States over the years. At the time of his death he was planning to open a restaurant in Florida.

Born Alain Germain Gustave Chapel. **Parents** Roger and Eva (Badin) Chapel, restaurateurs. **Marriages** 1) Danielle Girard, 1965; 2) Suzanne, 1981. **Children** David and Romain, from second marriage. **Education** École de la Salle et Institution des Lazaristes, Lyons. **Military service** French Army. **Career** Apprentice chef: to Jean Vignard, Chez Juliette, Lyon, 1952–56, to Fernand Point, Lyon, 1956–57; chef, Restaurant Chèz la Mère Charles, 1967–90, inherited 1969, renamed Restaurant Alain Chapel, 1970, earned three-star Michelin rating, 1973–90. **Offices and memberships** Member: Tradition et Qualité, Grande Cuisine française, Maîtres-cuisiniers de France, Académie culinaire. **Awards and honours** Chevalier de l'ordre national du Mérite; Officier du Mérite agricole; Meilleur Ouvrier de France, 1972. **Publication** *Cooking is more than Recipes*. **Cause of death** Stroke, at age 52.

ANDRÉ CHASTEL

French Art Historian

***Born* Paris, France, 15 November 1912**

***Died* Paris, France, 18 July 1990**

André Chastel was the most important and influential art historian of his generation in France. A Renaissance scholar and something of a Renaissance man himself, he brought the fruits of his scholarship to bear on the state of modern art history in France and found it sorely lacking. In 1984 he wrote a report for the government which turned into a polemical attack on the narrow-minded chauvinism of contemporary French scholars, contrasting post-war developments in his own country unfavourably with those in Britain and America. This did not just shake up the art establishment. It also led to the foundation in 1989 of a national art library in Paris, bringing together material from all over France.

For the last 30 years of his life André Chastel was professor of the history of modern art at the Sorbonne and then at the Collège de France. His own field of studies, however, was primarily concerned with the Italian art of the Renaissance. His books on Botticelli, on the Age of Humanism and on the Sack of Rome in 1527 have been widely translated, as have the two volumes on Italian art he contributed to the Larousse series. The publishers Thames and Hudson also commissioned texts from Chastel for some of their art books. All agree that the depth of his scholarship is apparent even in the most popular of his books.

Distinguished, almost diplomatic in appearance, André Chastel was fluent in Italian and English, equally at home in America as in Europe. He had been a visiting fellow at Yale University, a lecturer at the Washington National Gallery, and a corresponding fellow at the British Academy.

Respect for his columns of art criticism in *Le Monde* led to his being the only foreigner ever invited to sit on the jury of the John Moores exhibition in Liverpool, England. In Italy they published a *Festschrift* for him entitled, *Il se rendit en Italie*.

The clue to André Chastel's own philosophy can best be sought in his most important early work, *Marsile Ficin et l'art* published in 1954. Cosimo de' Medici's appointed leader of the Florentine Academy, Marsilio Ficino was the most important Platonic scholar of his day and the first to produce a full translation of Plato's writings in a western language. Ordained a priest, his own works on Platonic Theology and on the Christian Religion developed Plato's ideas about the journey of the human soul towards God through knowledge, love and contemplation.

Chastel drew on Marcel's biography of Ficino and on the commentaries published by Kristeller in the 1930s. His later work, *Art et humanisme à Florence au temps de Laurent le Magnifique*, shows his continuing interest in Renaissance thinking about the place of the individual human soul in the pattern of Creation.

Born André Adrien Chastel. **Parents** Adrien, banker, and Marie-Isabelle (Morin) Chastel. **Marriage** Paule-Marie Grand, 1942. **Children** Louis, Arnaud (deceased) and Laurent. **Education** Collège Notre Dame, Paris; Lycée Louis-le-Grand, Paris; École Normale Supérieur, Sorbonne, Paris, agrégé des lettres, docteur ès lettres. **Military service** French Army, 1939–40. **Career** Lycée instructor: Havre, 1938–39, Henri IV, Paris, 1943–44, Chartres, 1944–45, Marcelin-Berthelot, 1948–49, Carot, 1949–51; assistant instructor, history of art, Sorbonne, Paris, 1945–48, chair of modern art history, 1957–70; director of studies École Pratique des Hautes Études, 1951–58, director of teaching, 1955; chair of Italian Renaissance Art history, Collège de France, 1970–85. **Related activities** Art critic, *Le Monde*, 1950–90; member, Historical Monuments Commission, 1958; scientific secretary, International Committee on Art History, 1961–69, vice-president, 1969–90; director, *Revue de l'Art*, 1968; president, French Committee on the History of Art, 1970–77; president, National Commission to inventory the art treasures of France, 1978; administrative council member, Academy of France and Rome, from 1973; contributor, *Médecine de France*. **Offices and memberships** Corresponding member, Academy of Lincei, Rome, 1976; corresponding fellow, British Academy 1976. **Awards and honours** Croix de Guerre, 1939–45; Focillon fellow, Yale University, 1949; Prix des Ambassadeurs, for *Le Mythe de la Renaissance: 1420–1520*, 1969; member, Institute of Arts and Letters, 1975–90; officer, National Order of Merit; commander, Academic Palm of arts and letters; Andrew Mellon lecturer, National Gallery, Washington, DC, 1977; grand prix national, Arts and Letters, 1978; Commandeur de la Légion d'honneur, 1986. **Publications** (include) *Vuillard*, 1946; *Léonard de Vinci par lui-même*, 1952; *Marsile Ficin et l'art*, 1954; *L'Art Italien*, 1957; *Art et humanisme à Florence au temps de Laurent le Magnifique*, 1959; (with Robert Klein) *L'Age de l'humanisme*, 1964; *La Renaissance méridionale, le Grand Atelier d'Italie: 1460–1500*, 1965; *La Crise de la Renaissance: 1520–1600*, 1968; *Le Mythe de la Renaissance: 1420–1520*, 1969; *Fables, formes, figures* (two volumes), 1978; *L'Image dans le miroir*, 1980; *Chronique de la peinture italienne (1280–1580)*, 1983; *Le Sac de Rome, 1527*, 1984; *Le Cardinal Louis d'Aragon*, 1986; *L'illustre incompromise: Mona Lisa*, 1988; *La Grotesque*, 1988. **Cause of death** Undisclosed, at age 77.

ALAN CLARKE

British Television and Film Director
***Born* Liverpool, Lancashire, 28 October 1935**
***Died* London, England, 25 July 1990**

Along with Ken Loach, Alan Clarke was one of the few directors to have made a distinctive, personal, visual stamp on what, in the UK at least, is still generally considered to be primarily a writer's medium — television, and, more especially, television drama. He was a genuine *auteur* in a way that very few British television (or for that matter, film) directors are but, sadly, he was a prophet largely unrecognized in his own country. As BBC television drama chief Mark Shivas put it: "if his name had been Clarkovsky or even Clarkski he would have been very famous; he was much held back by being plain Clarke". There were, of course, a few who recognized Clarke's remarkable talents — for example David Hare, whose first television play, *Man Above Men*, a critical study of the legal system, was directed by Clarke, whom he called "one of the few really individual directors in television drama's short and uneven history."

Clarke was also acknowledged abroad: after the release of the powerful cinema version of his film *Scum*, set in a borstal (juvenile offenders' institution), he was courted by producers in the US but was unable to hit upon a mutually satisfactory project, and was also scouting for suitable subjects there shortly before he was taken ill. In Europe his skinhead drama *Made in Britain*, starring Tim Roth, won the Prix Italia whilst *Contact*, an almost wordless account of an army patrol in Northern Ireland, won the Prix Locarno.

At home, however, Clarke had to put up with an uncomprehending and hostile BBC banning the television version of *Scum*, a sustained attack on Channel 4 by self-appointed guardian of public morality, Mary Whitehouse, when it had the temerity to show the film version late one night and after ample warnings about the content, and much swiping and griping from the Conservative press (climaxing in a sustained attempt by Murdoch's *The Sun* to bedevil the production of his hard-hitting football-hooliganism drama, *The Firm*, starring Gary Oldman) for daring to show the alleged Wonderland of Mrs Thatcher's Britain in a less-than-flattering light.

Clarke first came to notice (among the few who cared about television drama, at least) in the seminal Wednesday Play slot on BBC television with the 1969 *The Last Train Through Harecastle Tunnel*, written by Peter Terson. If this gentle comedy seems, in retrospect, somewhat uncharacteristic of Clarke's work it's also interesting to note that another early comedy, Douglas Livingstone's seaside postcard-style *I Can't See My Little Willie* seems to look forward to the anarchic, lubricious *Rita, Sue and Bob Too*, probably the first British film whose soundtrack features the squelch of a used condom hitting the deck. (Sadly, its young writer, Andrea Dunbar, died two months after Clarke, aged 29.) Nor should one forget that, although Clarke is known primarily as a director of harsh, gritty, naturalistic dramas, his *oeuvre* also includes David Rudkin's *Penda's Fen*, a daring, visonary, mystical, truly romantic work which, one fears, it would be quite impossible to produce in today's television environment. Curiously, it was repeated on Channel 4, after years of oblivion, just a few days before Clarke's death.

As David Hare put it, Clarke's urgent, governing conviction was that "the lives of working-class people should be afforded on television the same depth and passion which is usually given to middle-class subjects." This is apparent even in such early works as Tony Parker's prison drama, *A Life is For Ever*, Don Shaw's tough study of army life, *Sovereign's Company*, and David Yallop's reconstruction of the Craig-Bentley case, *To Encourage the Others*. Other notable writers with whom Clarke worked included Colin Welland (*The Hallelujah Handshake*), Ted Whitehead, Brian

Clark and Alun Owen. He also formed a particularly valuable partnership with Roy Minton (not only *Scum* but also *Horace, Fast Hands* and the mental hospital drama, *Funny Farm*), and David Leland (*Made in Britain*, as well as *Beloved Enemy* and *Psy Warriors*, this last about the tough training of an anti-terrorist squad).

Although Clarke's career had not been without its controversial moments prior to the television version of *Scum*, the banning of this play by the BBC brought him a degree of notoriety. At the time Clarke spoke out angrily about BBC managing director Alasdair Milne and BBC1 Controller Bill Cotton: "what appals me is that Cotton and Milne really believe that they know what they're doing. They're sure they know what the public wants and *needs*, and what the public would object to. It's a shame that the particular taste and opinion of two men like that — with such narrow vision — should filter down to millions of people ... They're self-protective and careerist." According to the BBC, one of the problems with *Scum* was lack of "balance"; Clarke countered by saying that

> what they mean by balance is to show it as nice 50% of the time and corrupt the other 50%. Be 50% critical, 50% uncritical. Otherwise they say you're distorting the picture. The implication was of course that we were actually telling lies, or inventing it all, or sensationalising the issue. That I do object to. Our aim wasn't to give the prison service a bad name. But it still remains to be said that something is dreadfully and awfully wrong with the borstal system in this country.

It might also be said that it's extremely difficult, if not impossible, to square demands for "balance" with the requirements of drama, except of the most anodyne variety. In all, it's hard not to agree with David Hare's judgement that "It was ... Alan's misfortunue to make his best work at a time when the people who ran the BBC showed no interest in the views of those who created their programmes." Certainly the ITV company, Central, was a great deal more supportive over the equally controversial *Made in Britain*, and it has to be said that when Clarke made his last film for the BBC (or for anybody else, for that matter), *The Firm*, he again ran into what one might call "editorial difficulties".

Hardly surprisingly, Clarke was drawn towards the subject of Northern Ireland, not only in *Contact*, but also in the bleak domestic drama, *Christine*, and in the extraordinary and highly controversial *Elephant*. Here, Clarke pares down the violence in the province to a series of wordless, uncontextualized, elliptical killings — never before has the brutal arbitrariness of random sectarian murder been so chillingly presented, or the realities of life lived in a tradition of violence and schism so effectively hammered home. Almost inevitably, transmission of *Elephant* was delayed by the BBC.

Like so much of Clarke's work, *Elephant* was marked by an intensely physical, almost visceral, feel, in which his characteristic use of Steadicam played a key dramatic role. Indeed, on the basis of *Made in Britain*, *The Firm*, *Rita, Sue and Bob Too*, and his version of Jim Cartwright's play *Road*, where his use of Steadicam is integral in achieving the original play's remarkable sense of intimacy, the device might have been invented for him. It enabled him to really get in amongst his characters, speak for them, and communicate a lived sense of *their* reality. As one critic put it, "most of his work was a series of extreme and vivid provocations showing the undeserving poor in uproar, violence and despair", and Clarke developed a kinetic, explosive style to match, a style a million miles removed from the bloodlessness and academicism of too many of his contemporaries. And in a cinema and televison industry notoriously reliant on over-wordy and "literary" scripts, Clarke cut his scripts to the bare bone in order to let the images speak for themselves.

In the UK, however, discussion of Clarke's work tended to be dominated by the "problem" of violence to the exclusion of virtually everything else. That being the case, however, it's perhaps important to know what he had to say about it. Thus in a discussion on the BBC arts programme *The Late Show* in the wake of the screening of *The Firm* Clarke stated,

I think it's important that we're very honest about violence. If people are violent you show the violence to be violence. You don't try to make it palatable and acceptable by trimming it and diminishing it. But you've also got to be very careful that you don't take what's supposed to be a very authentic documentary situation and take the violence from it and exploit it with close-ups, crank up the music, and all that kind of stuff. There's no lingering; we don't want people to admire the violence. But if you're going to do something truthfully and honestly, if you're going to portray malevolence, whether it's verbal, physical or emotional, then you've got to portray it as graphically and honestly as you possibly can.

How Clarke would have survived in the changing environment of British television, and the increasingly depressed state of the British film industry, is an interesting question. Maybe he would eventually have found congenial work in the US, although his remark that "I wouldn't make a film with the edge written out", makes one doubt that he would have had any easier a time there than with the mandarins of the British broadcasting system. But then again, at least films like *Made in Britain* actually got *made* in that system, numerous difficulties notwithstanding. The main worry about the brave new world of de-regulated broadcasting is that there will simply be no room and no money for the bold, uncompromising, uncomfortable films typified by the work of Alan Clarke. As critic and producer W. Stephen Gilbert ruefully put it, "no director now building a television career can hope to enjoy the opportunities that Clarke's generation took for granted."

Born Alan Clarke. **Father** Bricklayer. **Marriage** Jane Kinsey. **Children** One son and one daughter. **Career** Junior stage manager; directed first play, *The Last Train Through Harecastle Tunnel*, BBC, 1969; *Scum* banned, BBC, 1977, later reversed; directed final film, *The Firm*, 1990. **Awards and honours** Prix Italia for *Made in Britain*; Prix Locarno for *Contact*. **Films** *Rita, Sue and Bob Too; Billy the Kid and the Green Baize Vampire*. **Television** *The Last Train Through Harecastle Tunnel; Sovereign's Company; I Can't See My Little Willie; A Life is For Ever; To Encourage the Others; The Hallelujah Handshake; Penda's Fen; Man Above Men; The Love Girl and the Innocent; Danton's Death; Horace; Funny Farm; Fast Hands; Scum*; *Beloved Enemies; Psy Warriors; Made in Britain; Christine; Contact; Elephant; Road; The Firm*. **Cause of death** Cancer, at age 54.

BILL CULLEN

American Game Show Host

***Born* Pittsburgh, Pennsylvania, 18 February 1920**

***Died* Los Angeles, California, 7 July 1990**

Bill Cullen was the quintessential quizmaster and game show host. With bright eyes that flashed behind thick spectacles and a head sporting a choppy crewcut, he may today seem like a rarity if compared to the smoothed-and-polished deliveries of current masters of ceremony. His quick, often biting, wit and fresh performance signified all that was both temporal and great in TV's Golden Age. Said his manager, George Spota, of him, "He certainly created the yardstick of professionalism by which all other emcees could follow."

Fate played a hand in the formation of his future. At the age of 18 months he was stricken with infantile paralysis. It left him with a permanent limp, to which he credited his career. "Polio", he said, "moved me out of physical effort and into a mental manner of living." This "mental manner of living" transported him from being an unpaid announcer at a small radio station in Pittsburgh, to earning 250 dollars a week by the age of 24. But not wanting to find himself in the same rut that he saw informing the lives of his Pittsburgh colleagues, he opted to move to New York to try his luck.

The opportunities were there, as the war effort had dispersed a large number of men overseas, and radio stations were terribly short-staffed. Cullen easily found work as a staff announcer at Columbia Broadcasting Service. When the emcee for a quiz show, *Winner Take All* suddenly resigned due to an illness, he was made a temporary host. He did so well he was hired full time.

Radio might have remained a safe haven for him. For one thing, no one could see his limp. For another, his style quickly made him popular on a variety of shows such as *The Arthur Godfrey Show* and *This is Nora Drake*. As he told a reporter, radio "was the one place a ham like me — and believe me, I'm a ham — could limp and still get a job." For that reason, he did not make his first television appearance until 1952 — as a panellist on *I've Got a Secret* — where he would only be seen sitting down.

He had little to worry about, though. Television rapidly became a medium of fantasy, and the camera work in all of Cullen's shows left viewers with no hint of his disability. This enabled him to achieve an admirable niche in broadcast history — the master of ceremonies for one of the all time great game shows, *The Price is Right*. Unlike the hyper-excited delivery of his successor, Bob Barker, Cullen perfected a style somewhere between gushy and caustic — "the man in the middle", as he termed it.

"Bill was the ultimate host", said Dick Clark, who hosted the day-time version of a game show that Cullen emceed at night. "He had this great humor, intelligence, and humanity. Most of all, he had the great talent of making his job look easy."

Cullen once said of his own life, "Mostly, I try not to take myself too seriously because when I do, I get sad. I've got no beefs. I'm just a guy who's on a good-luck kick and I hope it lasts."

Born William Lawrence Cullen. **Father** Garage owner. **Marriage** Ann Roemheld. **Education** University of Pittsburgh, Pennsylvania, BA in fine arts. **Career** Struck with polio and left with permanent limp, 1921; radio station announcer, WWSW, Pittsbrugh, 1939–43; master of ceremonies, KDKA, 1943–44; patrol pilot/civilian instructor, Civilian Air Defense, Allegheny County, Pennsylvania; staff announcer, CBS, 1944–46; hosted first radio game show, *Winner Take All*, 1946; panellist, *I've Got a Secret*, 1952–67; hosted first television game show, *Give and Take*, 1952; hosted more than 35 game shows; retired 1988. **Television** (includes) *I've Got a Secret; Give and Take; The Price is Right; Break the Bank; Stop the Music; Name That Tune; Professor Yes 'n' No; The $10,000 Pyramid; Three on a Match; Pass the Buck; To Tell the Truth; The Joker's Wild; Eye Guess; Blockbusters; Place the Face; Chain Reaction; Pass the Buck; Quick as a Flash; Hit the Jackpot; Down You Go.* **Radio** (includes) *Winner Take All; The Arthur Godfrey Show; Skyline Roof; Sing Along; Waitin' for Clayton; Crime Photographer; Give and Take; This is Nora Drake; The Bill Cullen Show.* **Cause of death** Lung cancer, at age 70.

STANLEY EDGE

British Automobile Engineer

***Born* Old Hill, Staffordshire, 5 August 1903**

***Died* Oswestry, Shropshire, 24 July 1990**

Profit motive and market-place philanthropy have always been inextricably interwoven and will continue to be so. Entrepreneurism is the exploitation of the one for the benefit of the other.

Commercial history is strewn with innovations to bring within the reach of the "man or woman in the street" those assets from which the more wealthy have benefited for some time. The motor industry, in its broadest definition, has not been excluded. When traffic congestion means literally hours of wasted time, frayed tempers and the inhalation of toxic exhaust fumes from hundreds of ill-tuned motors, the inevitable thought occurs, however fleetingly, that perhaps this is something of a mixed blessing.

Accessibility of the British "common man" to his own motor car is due largely to Stanley Edge. True it was Herbert Austin, later to become Sir Herbert, who had the vision, the resources and the business acumen, but it was Stanley Edge who had the design genius and judgement. It is arguable whether Austin was interested in making the working classes mobile or whether this was the only route he could see to stave off impending bankruptcy. The receivers were already showing an interest in the company and the Austin Seven project was kept as secret as was practicable. It is reported that Austin received little support or encouragement from his fellow directors and it is possible that he financed the project from his own pocket.

Stanley Edge considered that he had gained little benefit from school and persuaded his father to let him leave at the age of 14 and become apprenticed in the drawing office at "The Austin". He was keen, good at his work, always the first to arrive each day and quickly became very knowledgeable. These qualities brought him to the attention of his employer. At the age of 18 he was removed from the drawing office and located at the home of Herbert Austin to work exclusively on the new project. His drawing board was the billiard table and his working day long. Often he would stay overnight in the lodge at Lickey Grange.

Even at 18, Edge must have been very persuasive as he was able to change Austin's mind over very significant features of the project. Austin's vision was in essence an upgrading of the motor cycle combination but Edge persuaded him that the new vehicle should be a "proper car" with a four-cylinder engine and brakes on all four wheels. The final product was truly Edge's creation. At its launch in 1922, the Austin Seven was greeted with scepticism and derision from sectors of the motor industry and dismissed as "merely a toy". Nevertheless, it proved to be highly successful and by the time production ceased in 1939, over 300,000 had been sold, some assembled under licence in Germany, France, Japan and America. It was clearly the forerunner of several new cars including the Morris Minor and the Ford Eight. Some have claimed it was the inspiration for the Volkswagen (people's car) in the 1930s.

History repeats itself, or so we are told, and there are certainly parallels to the Austin Seven story in more recent memory. It is a strange paradox that when we get used to amenities which we were previously denied, we become critical of them and demand they be improved, to the point where we can no longer afford them. This is certainly true of cars. Few "basic models" are really basic any more and as their value increases so a fresh demand is created for something cheaper. So, in the early 1950s, a new type of vehicle emerged on the roads of Britain, and presumably elsewhere in Europe, at least in Germany and Italy whence they originated. These were affectionately known as "bubble-cars", the commonest being the Heinkel Messerschmidt and the Isetta. Other less imaginative three-wheeled vehicles should not be overlooked, if only because they can still be found on British roads, usually at the head of a slow-moving convoy. But for the influence of Stanley Edge, perhaps Austin's new vehicle would have been such. Ironically, long after the demise of the Austin Seven, its engine was still used by the Reliant Company in its three-wheeled "Robin".

The next cheap British car (although of Italian design), was the "Mini", which took the motoring fraternity by storm and cut short the lifetime of the bubble-cars. Edge himself hailed this as a true successor to the Austin Seven. In fact his last car was a Mini. It wasn't long before the cycle of affluence repeated itself and up-market versions of the Mini appeared. Soon it was to become not so much the inexpensive economical car for the lower paid as the second family car and runabout for the wives of the affluent. It became a cult vehicle valued more for its liveliness, guaranteed by the production of a Cooper version, and its ease of parking in the crowded shopping streets.

The 1980s brought a strange new, but inexpensive, vehicle onto the streets of Britain. The objectives of the creator were similar to those of Herbert Austin but more so, in that the Sinclair C5 personal transporter was intended to give power-assisted transport to people who did not even hold a driving licence. It was little more than a partially enclosed tricycle with a washing machine electric motor for assistance. It truly earned the epithet which had unfairly been given previously to the Austin Seven. If only Clive Sinclair, now Sir Clive, had a Stanley Edge to call on we might now have a new generation of inexpensive vehicles.

It is surprising that only three years after his success at Austin, or perhaps because of it, Edge moved away from the company he had helped save from liquidation. He worked at Clayton Wagons Company in Lincoln and then moved to Triumph Motor Company to work, among other things, on a competitor to the Austin Seven.

Post-war events in Britian saw the successive swallowing up of individual motor companies, including both Austin and Triumph, into the large conglomerate, named successively as British Motor Corporation (BMC) and then British Leyland. More recently it has re-fragmented with parts of it being sold off as separate companies. For over 30 years, the names on many cars have been attempts to keep them alive although in fact they had no real separate identity. The same models existed under brand names of Austin, Morris, MG, Wolseley, Riley and Vanden Plas, although the accoutrements differred to appeal to a different section of the market. Many of these names have long since been buried. Until recently the name Austin was kept alive in the Austin-Rover Company but seems now finally to have been buried also. The current version of the Mini is marketed as the Rover Mini, which is a pity since its origins were totally independent of the Rover Company. This brings us back where we started — business ethics. Stanley Edge would have learned that there is no sentiment in business. It would be nice, however, to believe that although the greatest achievement in his life was a business venture, that he at least thought he was helping the "common man".

Born Stanley Howard Edge. **Father** Employee, Austin Motor Company. **Marriage** Rachel. **Children** One son. **Education** Halesowen Grammar School, West Midlands. **Career** Studied mechanical drawing on own, 1916–17; trainee draughtsman, Austin Motor Company, 1917; designed Austin Seven motor car, 1921–22; left Austin, 1925; chief engineer, Clayton Wagons, 1925–27; chief engineer, Triumph Motor Company, from 1927–39; chief, fighting vehicles test department, Ministry of Supply, 1939–45; consultant engineer, from 1945. **Cause of death** Undisclosed, at age 86.

BISHOP FLEMING

British Priest

***Born* Edinburgh, Scotland, 7 August 1906**

***Died* Dorset, England, 30 July 1990**

The Right Reverend William Launcelot Scott Fleming, KCVO, had a remarkable career as bishop, Antarctic Explorer, rowing coach and, finally, domestic chaplain to the Queen. But it was never the position he held, always the personality he brought to that position that friends and colleagues valued. He had, they say, a quite exceptional gift of friendship noticeable wherever he went. What made him important, one clergyman thought, was "his integrity and the sense of commitment to every single listener", something about, "the undimmed quality of his attention", what the Archbishop of Canterbury described as his particular mixture of "holiness and humanity".

Given Bishop Fleming's background — Rugby, Cambridge, a father who was one of Edinburgh's most prominent physicians — his first job as chaplain to his old college, Trinity Hall, would seem to have been tailor-made. He made a great success of it, becoming an enthusiastic rowing coach, entering into the life of the undergraduates with zest, convinced of "the personal and creative possibility of truly priceless worth" of each and every one of them. Among each group of new entrants were always to be found some of those known to the other tutors as "Launcelot's lambs" — "young men he had met on railway trains or football touchlines or playing squash" and persuaded to come to Cambridge.

It was during Fleming's Cambridge years that the Graham Land expedition to the Antarctic took place. Fleming took part as geologist and as chaplain. There was a long sledge journey with dog-teams down the George VI Sound which took them to the farthest point south yet reached. His geological reports were an important contribution as was his advice on the Fuchs expedition in 1958.

World War II, in which Fleming served as a naval chaplain, put an end to the Cambridge idyll, or maybe his talents would in any case have sought a wider sphere. At all events he was offered in 1949 the bishopric of Portsmouth, a surprising appointment in view of his age (he was only 43) and of his lack of previous parochial experience. That this self-named "L-plates bishop" managed to master the intricacies of diocesan diplomacy was made clear when, ten years later, he was elevated to the second largest diocese in the country and made Bishop of Norwich.

Norwich then was more of a challenge than it perhaps sounds today. Known as "the dead see" it had more than 60 unfilled benefices, countless large, empty, isolated, mediaeval churches, mostly in a shocking state of disrepair, and a disillusioned and ill-paid clergy. Fleming responded as best he could. He raised the clergy's stipends, introduced group ministries and organized compulsory refresher courses. More at home on the site of the new University of East Anglia, he pressed for the creation of the present "chaplaincy centre" at the heart of the campus open to people of all religious faiths, Christian and non-Christian alike.

Perhaps the work at Norwich wore him out. In 1967 he suffered a rare spinal failure which lost him the use of one leg, and a few years later he and his wife moved to a quieter life at Windsor, where he worked as dean and domestic chaplain to the Queen. It is said that the friendship between Bishop Fleming and the royal family was valued by both sides and that the conferences he held at St George's House on the political, economic and social problems of the day, seen in a Christian context, were lively and stimulating. In the running of St George's Chapel, however, Fleming was not a success. He inherited a chapter of four canons, already divided between reformers and traditionalist — divisions which all Fleming's Cambridge charm and gifts of friendship seem not to have been able to heal. It must have been a sad disappointment.

Born William Launcelot Scott Fleming. **Parents** Robert Alexander, physician, and Eleanor (Holland) Fleming. **Marriage** Jane Agutter, 1965. **Education** Rugby School, Warwickshire; Trinity Hall, Cambridge, first-class honours, Natural Science Tripos, Part II, BA, 1928, MA, 1932; Westcott House, Cambridge, 1931–33; Yale University, MS, 1931; Lambeth, DD, 1950. **Military service** Chaplain, Royal Navy Voluntary Reserve, HMS *King Alfred*, 1940, HMS *Queen Elizabeth*, 1940–43, HMS *Ganges*, 1943–44; director of Service Ordination Candidates, 1944–46. **Career** Deacon, 1933; priest, 1934; examining chaplain to: Bishop of Southwark, 1937–49, Bishop of St Albans, 1940–43, Bishop of Hereford, 1942–49; fellow and chaplain, Trinity Hall, Cambridge University, 1933–49, Dean, 1937–49; director, Scott Polar Research Institute, Cambridge

University, 1947–49; Bishop of Portsmouth, 1949–59; Bishop of Norwich, 1959–71; Dean of Windsor, 1971–76; domestic chaplain to Queen, 1971–76; retired 1976. **Related activities** Chairman, Church of England Youth Council, 1950–61; chairman of governors, Portsmouth Grammar School, 1950–59; chairman of governors, Canford School, 1954–60; governing body member, United World College of the Atlantic; visitor, Bryanston School; council member, University of East Anglia, 1964–71; chairman, Archbishops' Advisers for Needs and Resources, 1963–73; vice-chairman, parliamentary group for World Government, 1969–71, chairman, associate members, 1971–76; member, Royal Commission on Environmental Pollution, 1970–73; Register, Order of the Garter, 1971–76; trustee, Prince's Trust, 1976–90. **Other activities** Expedition to Iceland, 1932; expedition to Spitzbergen, 1933, chaplain and geologist, British Graham Land Expedition to the Antarctic, 1934–37. **Offices and memberships** President, Young Explorers Trust, 1976–79; Trident Trust. **Awards and honours** Commonwealth Fund Fellow, Yale University, 1929–31; Polar Medal, 1935–37; honorary chaplain, Royal Naval Reserve; honorary fellow, Trinity Hall, Cambridge, 1956; honorary vice-president, Royal Geographical Society, 1961; honorary DCL, University of East Anglia, 1976; Knight Commander, Royal Victorian Order, 1976. **Cause of death** Undisclosed, at age 83.

MADGE GARLAND

British Fashion Editor

Born **Melbourne, Australia, 12 June 1898**

Died **London, England, 15 July 1990**

Madge Garland, who devoted herself to the ephemeral world of fashion, must seem an unlikely candidate to be counted amongst the ranks of feminists. However, growing up as she did in an age when young ladies of her class were expected to conform meekly to a restrictive code of behaviour, her achievements in breaking out of a rigid family background to live life on her own terms and become a career woman who influenced the course of British fashion history and the training of designers, makes her a pioneer. She ranks alongside the suffragettes as a role model for sexual equality.

Garland was born in Australia but she was brought up in London. Her father was a successful international businessman and the family were well off and occupied a good social position. However they did not share Garland's love of books and the arts and she described them as being stolid, unimaginative and totally philistine. As a young child she suffered long periods of ill health and it was during these times that she amused herself by reading the whole set of the *Encyclopaedia Britannica* from cover to cover. This gave her a thirst for knowledge which never left her. Garland was education privately in London before attending the International School in Paris, and it was in France that she discovered the joys of travel, art and French fashion. She had hoped to continue her education at a German finishing school but this ambition was dashed by the outbreak of World War I in 1914 and, reluctantly, she returned home to London.

Garland's next aim was to go to university. She won a place at Newnham College, Cambridge, which was a considerable achievement, but her father refused to allow her to take it up as he considered the academic life was unsuitable for a well brought up young lady. Garland was allowed to take some courses at Bedford College, University of London, but again her family intervened before she could take a degree and insisted that she left to accompany her father on a business trip.

Not surprisingly, given these restrictions, Garland was not a fan of family life and she left home as soon as she came of age at 21. Deciding to become a journalist, she approached methodically every newspaper editor in London's Fleet Street, until finally she got taken on to run errands and make the tea. She rented a room in the bedsitter district of Earls Court, took an evening course in typing and prepared to make a success of her new life.

Within three years Garland was well on her way to achieving her ambitions. In 1922 she joined the staff of the fashion magazine *Vogue* and she soon became assistant to Dorothy Todd, the formidable editor. Todd was impressed with Garland's work and took her under her wing. Under Todd's guidance, *Vogue* had built up a reputation as an avant-garde magazine and the leading literary figures of the day, such as Virginia Woolf, Aldous Huxley and Edith Sitwell, were regular contributors. Garland thrived in this atmosphere and she developed a talent for spotting good books and pictures. Many of the writers and artists with whom she came in contact became personal friends. She was painted by Edward Wolfe and Marie Laurencin and photographed by Cecil Beaton.

In the late 1920s the Conde Nasté Company, owners of *Vogue*, changed the focus of the magazine and it reverted to being a glossy fashion periodical. Garland left to become a freelance writer contributing to the American magazine *Women's Wear Daily*, and to the *Illustrated London News*, *Britannia* and *Eve* in England. In 1932 Garland returned to *Vogue* as fashion editor and she specialized in writing about French *haute couture*. She visited the Paris fashion collections regularly and as she was blessed with a model's figure, she was able to buy her own clothes from such luminaries as Chanel, Faith and Schiaparelli at a fraction of the usual retail prices. According to her friends and colleagues, Garland was never less than immaculately turned out and although she was a great socialite she was always at her desk by 8.30 every morning.

Garland's life changed again with the outbreak of World War II. The fall of Paris in 1940 put paid to her trips to the French fashion shows. Ever resourceful, she changed direction and became merchandising manager for the London department store of Bourne and Hollingsworth, where she proved to be an extremely successful businesswoman. After the war Garland visited the United States to study the ready-to-wear market for the British fashion industry. She was also commissioned by the Council for Industrial Design to acquire accessories from Paris so that British designers could copy the "New Look" which, led by the designer Christian Dior, was sweeping the Continent.

In 1947 Garland was invited to found the first British School of Fashion at the Royal College of Art, London. This was a huge undertaking as she had to pioneer a degree course in a totally new area of study. Garland boldly involved an unlikely cross-section of people in the exercise. Art teachers worked alongside professionals from the fashion trade and Manchester textile manufacturers provided designs and materials. The project was a great success and Garland continued to lead the course as professor until 1956, by which time the school was well established. Her successor, Professor Janey Ironside, wrote tellingly of her first encounter at the school with Garland whose formidable appearance "terrified me so much that my lips stiffened and came apart with a 'guk' sound when I had to answer a question". Although she never felt at ease with her, Ironside considered herself fortunate to have worked with Garland, whom she dubbed "the complete fashion expert lady".

Following her retirement from the Royal College in 1958, Garland wrote several books on fashion which were well received. She also continued to travel extensively until she was in her eighties, and to take a keen interest in gardening. In her last years Garland's sight failed and she became so fragile that she had to give up her home and move into a convent where she was cared for by the nuns. However, she never lost her immense zest for life and would continue, when the opportunity presented itself, to give parties in friends' houses. Finally she became bedridden, but she still managed to entertain her friends with her customary sharp wit and lively anecdotes always, of course, immaculately dressed.

Born Madge McHarg. **Parents** Andrew, shipper, and Henrietta Maria (Aitkin) McHarg. **Marriages** 1) Captain Ewart Garland, 1922 (dissolved); 2) Sir Leigh Ashton, director, Victoria and Albert Museum, 1953 (divorced 1962). **Education** International School, Paris, 1912–14; Bedford College, University of London, 1916–19. **Career** Errand girl; receptionist/teagirl, *Vogue*, London, 1922–26, fashion editor, *Vogue*, London, 1932–41; freelance writer, *Women's Wear Daily*, New York, 1926–28; editor, women's section, London Illustrated Newspapers group, 1928–32; merchandising manager, Bourne and Hollingsworth, 1941–45, founding professor, School of Fashion Design, Royal College of Art, London, 1949–58. **Related activities** Stylist/fashion designer, Terylene (Dacron) fibre, 1949–53; contributor: *Vogue*, *Harper's Bazaar*, *Britannia*, *Eve*, *Scotsman*, *Spectator*, *Saturday Book*, *Architectural Review*, *Connoisseur*, *Apollo*, *Country Life*. **Offices and memberships** Founder/member, Contemporary Arts Society. **Publications** *The Changing Face of Beauty*, 1957; *Fashion*, 1962; *The Changing Face of Childhood*, 1963; *The Indecisive Decade: The World of Fashion and Entertainment in the Thirties*, 1968; *The Changing Form of Fashion*, 1970; *The Small Garden in the City*, 1973; (with J. Anderson Black) *A History of Fashion*, 1975. **Cause of death** Undisclosed, at age 92.

MAURICE GIRODIAS

French Publisher

Born **Paris, France, 12 April 1919**

Died **Paris, France, 3 July 1990**

Maurice Girodias died in Paris of a heart attack after being interviewed on French radio about his recently published autobiography, *Une journée sur la terre*. Girodias was 71 and his memoirs were the swansong of a remarkable personality who had pursued a career of unremitting opposition to the censorship of books and the arbitrary control of morals — what is thought to be proper language and sexual behaviour — through religion and the state. He was regarded by some as the man who made society safe for pornography.

Girodias preferred to call the erotica he published "DBs" — dirty books. He lived to see some of his most daring publications established as lucrative, respected classics of twentieth-century literature. Among these were Vladimir Nabokov's *Lolita*, Henry Miller's *Tropic* books, (as well as *Sexus* and *Quiet Days in Clichy*); J.P. Donleavy's *The Ginger Man*, Terry Southern's *Candy*, Samuel Beckett's *Watt and Molloy* and Pauline Reage's *The Story of O*. Other writers he published included Jean Genet, Lawrence Durrell (q.v.), William Burroughs and Georges Bataille.

Without any great intellectual pretensions — his education had stopped after his Paris lycée — Girodias, through his personality and commitment, had a significant part in shaping the attitudes and development of the "Swinging Sixties", particularly among the students and teachers of the new universities in Britain and the United States. He was, in some sense, one of the midwives of the Age of Aquarius, President Kennedy's new Camelot, the London fashion revolution of Carnaby Street and John Lennon, The Beatles and pop music.

Girodias went into the pornography business through his father, Jack Kahane, a man from a wealthy Manchester textile family who had settled in Paris after 1918 and married Marcelle Girodias, a French woman from the Auvergne. Kahane set up the Obelisk Press in 1931 and published Frank Harris's *My Life and Loves* and, after much hesitation, Henry Miller's first title, *Tropic of Cancer*. Maurice Girodias started up on his own in 1953 with the Olympia Press. It was promoted as "an outlet for banned books of literary quality in English". Girodias also went for the lower end of the market, setting up an alternative press called Ophelia, publishing works like *Who Pushed Paula?* by Akbar del Piombo, *House of Joy* by Wu Wu Meng and *Until She Screams* by Faustino Perez.

It became known in Paris in the 1950s and 1960s, that struggling writers could always pick up a bit of money by writing dirty books for Girodias. He kept his string of ghostwriters under close control, writing strictly to his instructions. He paid about 500 pounds a book and chose the pseudonyms himself. Many well-known writers have admitted acting as ghostwriters for Girodias.

In 1964, Girodias was, however, coming under increasing government pressure both in France and Britain. Nearly 70 of 200 books published by Olympia had been declared "unsuitable" in France, which meant that they could not be displayed or advertised. On one occasion, Girodias had also been ordered not to publish for 80 years, though the ban was subsequently reduced to three years. In total, he had been indicted and acquitted 25 times by the French courts.

There were grounds for believing that the British government had been exerting increasing pressure on France to close Girodias down. It had become known that he intended to publish the diaries of Sir Roger Casement, a former British colonial official who had been hanged for treason in 1916 after being captured smuggling guns from Germany to the Irish nationalist revolt under James Connolly. Casement's diaries contained frank accounts of his homosexual relations as British pro-consul in the Congo, and had been secretly circulated among privileged journalists and politicians at the time of the trial, to prejudice the jury. For more than 30 years, the British government refused even to acknowledge the existence of the diaries. Even after publication, the Home Office claimed that they were forged. In fact, their authenticity had been established beyond dispute by independent historians.

British pressure on the French police to suppress Girodias's output continued after publication of the diaries. In May 1972, the police raided the Girodias warehouse and seized nearly 40,000 books, 90 per cent of the stock. Girodias was on the way to bankruptcy.

Girodias had also been having trouble with authors, notably Nabokov and Donleavy. Nabokov had moved to an allegedly "more respectable" publisher and there was litigation over the control of rights to *Lolita* once the American customs had indicated they would not seek to ban the book. Girodias was outsmarted and settled for less than he might have expected. He also underestimated the full potential of *Lolita*'s commercial value by insisting that "Hollywood will never make a movie out of *that*!"

There were other difficulties in 1970 when the Olympia Press was forced into liquidation. The company was put up for auction and, to the everlasting *chagrin* of Girodias, the bidder who frustrated his efforts to buy it back was Donleavy.

Girodias had come under pressure in the United States after leaving France in 1964, and ten years later he was forced to leave America after trying to publish a novel in which Henry Kissinger, the former secretary of state, was thinly masked as the principal character. The turbulent career of a notable "porn" publisher was coming to its close.

Born Maurice Kahane. **Parents** Jack, publisher, and Marcelle (Girodias) Kahane. **Marriages** Two marriages; 1) In 1945, name unknown; 2) Leila Cabot, 1978. **Children** Two daughters, from first marriage. **Education** Lycée Pasteur, Paris. **Emigration** Settled US, 1964, expelled, 1974. **Career** Designed book cover for Henry Miller's *Tropic of Cancer*, 1934; took over Obelisk Press on father's death, 1939; founded Edition du Chêne, 1941; founded Galerie Vendôme, 1944; founded Olympia Press, 1953; commissioned Travellers Companions sex fiction, 1953; with Vladimir Nabokov's *Lolita* began publishing "banned" literature, 1953; prosecuted for publishing "unsuitable" literature, briefly jailed, then banned from publishing for 80 years, later reduced to three years, Paris, 1964; transferred publishing operation to US, 1964, but expelled after trying to publish novel including Henry Kissinger as character, 1974; Olympia Press liquidated, 1970, bought by J.P. Donleavy. **Related activities** Established underground Paris theatre, 1960, closed by police for pornographic performances, 1964. **Publications** (With Peter Singleton-Gates) *The Black Diaries*, 1959; (contributor) *To Deprave and Corrupt*; *Une journée sur la terre* (autobiography), two volumes, 1990. **Cause of death** Heart attack, at age 71.

IAN GOW

British Politician

***Born* London, England, 11 February 1937**

***Died* Hankham, East Sussex, 30 July 1990**

"Murder most foul" is the only way to describe the car-bomb explosion which brought to a brutal end one of Britain's outstanding Conservative politicians and a staunch supporter, and one-time member, of the Thatcher government. Like his mentor and patron, Airey Neave, who was murdered in similar fashion just before the 1979 election, Ian Gow was the victim of a terrorist campaign by the Irish Republican Army which has struck at targets throughout the United Kingdom over the last 20 years, most notably the (then) British Prime Minister herself in the 1984 bombing of the Grand Hotel at Brighton during the Conservative Party conference. Both Gow and Neave were obvious IRA targets, for both were devoted to the cause of maintaining Ulster within the United Kingdom — in Gow's case a cause for which he was prepared to jeopardize his political career by resigning in protest at the Anglo-Irish Agreement of November 1985.

Ian Gow's association with Northern Ireland was not one of birth. He was the son of a consultant physician at St Bartholomew's Hospital in London and was brought up near London and educated at Winchester, where as president of the school debating society he showed signs of his later prowess as a public speaker. His attachment to Ulster originated with his service there in County Tyrone in the mid-1950s during his national military service. This interest was fostered later on when he entered Parliament by two strong Unionist supporters — Enoch Powell and then Airey Neave, who brought him on to the Opposition front bench and was said to be planning to make him a minister in the Northern Ireland Office if the Conservatives won the general election. A solicitor by profession, Gow had aspired to a political career from the 1960s and contested several unwinnable seats until he was elected for Eastbourne in 1974 — a constituency which was to cherish him thereafter.

His promotion to ministerial rank did not come till some four years into the Thatcher administration, but he had been a stalwart and outspoken supporter of Margaret Thatcher from the start, making quite clear his opposition to Edward Heath and his vehement support for Thatcher in the 1975 leadership election. This candour was typical of the man. Not for him the hole-in-corner, bet-hedging policy of some politicians; what Ian Gow believed in he spoke up for, without fear or favour.

Such unreserved support drew the attention of Mrs Thatcher who, when she took office after winning the 1979 election, appointed Gow to the key position of her parliamentary private secretary. This was a delicate job, as the eyes and ears of the Prime Minister among the grass roots of the parliamentary party. It was a job which some people thought would never suit the blunt outspokenness of Gow, but which he fulfilled superbly, earning the nickname of "Supergrass" among his fellow MPs and his prime minister's gratitude and admiration. Hobnobbing with all sorts and conditions of backbenchers was not Gow's natural milieu. A sociable man in congenial company, he was nevertheless not one to suffer fools, or bores, gladly — but in a deserving cause he could discipline himself. And he was devoted to Mrs Thatcher and regarded her as the best hope for Britain in the aftermath of the disastrous "winter of discontent" — a devotion which was to continue throughout his parliamentary career, surviving even his disagreement with her over the Anglo-Irish treaty.

In 1983 Gow was promoted to ministerial rank as minister for housing and construction and two years later as minister of state in the Treasury. Doubtless membership of the cabinet would have followed had his opposition to the Anglo-Irish treaty not intervened. To his mind the arrangement gave far too much power to Dublin to interfere in what he saw as strictly UK affairs. In a minority of one he resigned from the government in protest and a few weeks later published the text of an alternative agreement under the aegis of the Friends of the Union, an organization which he founded to campaign for understanding of the Ulster cause and which he continued to promote up to the time of his death. He never failed to express his hatred and condemnation of the IRA, though he must have known from the example of Airey Neave that there was a very real risk that he would also be a target. But this weighed nothing in the balance. Gow's belief in the integrity of the United Kingdom, shown also in his opposition to the Labour government's earlier proposals for devolution for Scotland, was all important. It was worth losing office for, and was in the end to cost him his life.

In the words of his fellow MP, Nicholas Budgen, "Ian Gow was a romantic. He was a romantic about Northern Ireland, a romantic about Mrs Thatcher, a romantic about the House of Commons and about his friends." A man of immense integrity, he in no way exploited his contacts after he had left office. He straightforwardly returned to serve the House from the back benches and to enliven its debates with his trenchant and witty speeches. In this he retained the respect of his fellow Conservatives and of his party's leader. Indeed, it is interesting to speculate what might have happened had he still been there during the leadership crisis of November 1990; he might have been able to alert Mrs Thatcher earlier to the fragility of her position and might perhaps have been the one man whose warning she would have heeded. Three main features sustained him throughout his life: his deep Christian faith (he had been a lay reader in one of his places of residence and had seriously thought of becoming ordained if he ever left the House of Commons); his pride and good fortune in his happy family life; and his gift of friendship and loyalty to his wide circle of friends. It is tragic that a man who so greatly enjoyed life should have met such an untimely and cruel end.

Born Ian Gow. **Father** Alexander E. Gow, doctor. **Marriage** Jane Elizabeth Packe, 1966. **Children** Charles and James. **Education** Winchester College, Hampshire. **Military service** Commissioned officer, 15th/19th Hussars, 1956–58, reserve officer, 1958–74. **Career** Solicitor, 1962; partner, Joynson-Hicks, 1962; Conservative parliamentary candidate: Coventry East, 1964, Clapham, 1966, Conservative member of parliament, Eastbourne, 1974–90; parliamentary private secretary to prime minister, 1979–83; minister for housing and construction, 1983–85; treasury minister, 1985. **Related activities** Chairman, back bench committee on Northern Ireland. **Other activities** Founder, Friends of the Union, 1985; chairman, Airey Neave Memorial Trust, 1989–90. **Awards and honours** Territorial Efficiency Decoration, 1970. **Cause of death** Assassinated by Irish Republican Army car bomb, at age 53.

JAMES D. HART

American Scholar, Author and Librarian

***Born* San Francisco, California, 18 April 1911**

***Died* Berkeley, California, 23 July 1990**

It was 1934 and James D. Hart, a 23-year-old Harvard graduate student, was in Manhattan, browsing through secondhand bookshops. His mind was on his date for the evening; but it was also on the books. For it suddenly occurred to him that there was no American counterpart to *The Oxford Companion to English Literature* which had been published for the first time two years before.

He left the bookshops and, acting on impulse, went into the New York offices of the Oxford University Press to tell them of the omission and to ask why such a volume did not exist. Said editor Margaret Nicholson, "We've been looking for someone to do that", and took him to meet Sir Geoffrey Cumberlege, director of the press. Sir Geoffrey asked to see samples of the young man's work, explaining that he was sailing for Europe next day.

Hart had, of course, no samples. He returned to his hotel room, cancelled his date — which he later claimed was the most difficult part of the entire experience — and sat up all night composing entries on Emerson, Richard Henry Dana and other literary figures. In the morning he delivered his efforts; and in a few months he had a contract to produce the volume which he had suggested and which was to become his major work.

In the 1930s the study of American writing was in its infancy; academics looked to England for authors worthy of historical and critical scrutiny. So James D. Hart, in turning his attention to the literature of the US, was a pioneer in his field.

Hart studied for his doctorate at Harvard; but he spent the greater part of his life in his beloved home state of California. Born in San Francisco, he took his first degree there in 1932, at Stanford University. And, after only four years in the East, he returned — with his precious contract — to become an instructor at the University of California in Berkeley.

There he continued to work on his *Companion*; but with a difference. Unlike the vast majority of editors of such compilations, Hart did not assign essays to a team of scholars; he attended to every single entry himself. The final result appeared in 1941 and immediately established itself as the standard authority on the subject.

Shortly after Hart's death, critic Alfred Kazin recalled that the *Oxford Companion* had been on his desk for almost half a century and was "the most valuable handbook I know on our literature". The *Companion* went into five editions (1948, 1956, 1965 and 1983) and finally into the *Concise* version in 1986. It is readable as well as informative; and it contains an astonishing amount of background material. In its current edition it is an 896-page compendium of biographical, historical and literary information on American authors and their works: from Thomas Jefferson to J.D. Salinger, from Woody Allen to Ralph Waldo Emerson.

But the first *Companion* was only the beginning of Hart's achievements. He was a Californian through and through; and at that time the literary history landscape of California was even more barren than that of the nation as a whole. So he had plenty of pioneering work ahead. As he climbed the academic tree — becoming assistant professor at Berkeley in 1941, associate professor in 1947, professor of English in 1951, chairman of department in 1955 and vice-chancellor of the university in 1957 — he also (with others of his generation) established the premises and many of the interpretive classics of the literary study of California and of the West.

After the *Companion to American Literature*, his most important book (and the next to be published) is *The Popular Book: A History of America's Literary Taste* which is a combination of social and cultural history and is concerned with "the dynamic interplay of writer, reader and the times in which they live." In it he analysed the often obscure reasons why best-sellers appealed to the public.

He went on to produce scores of books and articles on California, on western American history, on Robert Stevenson and on Frank Norris. He co-wrote (with Clarence Ghodes) *America's Literature*, edited a collection of descriptions by eleven Californian writers of their first appearances in print, and his *Companion to California* was published — again by the Oxford University Press — in 1978.

For 21 years, from 1969, Hart was also the director of the Bancroft Library at Berkeley. The Bancroft is the principal source of historical material on western America (particularly California), Mexico and central America. Hart made it the major source of documents relating to Mark Twain. He acquired Twain's manuscripts; he also acquired the papers of William Saroyan and Henry J. Kaiser, two personalities who have California — if little else — in common. In short, he did not simply put California firmly on the cultural map, he — according to Professor Kevin Starr — "centered the world on the Bancroft, reached out to gather its ecumenical riches, and greeted the world when it came to call." He also proved himself a great librarian; the directorship of the Bancroft Library is now endowed in his name.

Hart was a fine scholar; he had an equally fine talent for administration. As chairman of the Berkeley English department, as vice-chancellor of the university and as director of the Bancroft, he notched up over 30 years of administrative work. And — a rare quality in a scholar — he enjoyed administration and was able to combine it with teaching and with his own studies.

Hart's studies of popular and western American culture blew a refreshing breeze through the then Anglophilic groves of American literary academe. But though a humanist, he was hardly a man of the people. Among the qualities which had first impressed Margaret Nicholson — the editor who made his masterwork possible — was his upper-crust San Francisco accent. Throughout his adult life he dressed impeccably; his idea of camping out was a weekend at a hotel; he was polished and urbane; he loved rare books; and he established — and stuck to — his own personal traditions.

This is how Kevin Starr (in the School of Urban and Regional Planning at the University of Southern California), recalls him:

> Each working day, for more than 50 years, James D. Hart would lunch at Bernard Maybeck's superb Faculty Club, a building so quintessentially representative of that finer California which he always cherished. His guest might be an eminent poet (W.H. Auden, perhaps, or Stephen Spender), or the writers he was currently collecting (Joan Didion, Alice Adams), or an aspiring graduate student pushing hard against that first important research project. That was how I met James D. Hart. He stopped by my table at the Bancroft as I was struggling to piece together *Americans and the Californian Dream*, and he asked me to lunch. We talked, and he guided me, and this happened again and again over the ensuing 20 years of our association.

For Hart, though elegant and patrician in person, was not a scholar of the reclusive, ivory-towered ilk. According to another commentator, he was "invariably good humoured and exceptionally positive in his approach" — as befits a man who brought popular, western American and above all Californian culture firmly onto centre-stage in the American academic world.

Born James David Hart. **Parents** Julien and Helen (Neustadter) Hart. **Marriages** 1) Ruth Arnstein, 1938 (died 1977); 2) Constance Crowley Bowles, 1985. **Children** Carol and Peter, from first marriage. **Education** Stanford University, California, BA, 1932; Harvard University, Cambridge, Massachusetts, MA, 1933, PhD, 1936. **Military service** Officer of Strategic Services,

World War II. **Career** Instructor, University of California, Berkeley, 1936–41, assistant professor, 1941–47, associate professor, 1947–51, professor of English, 1951–90, department chairman, 1955–57, 1965–69, university vice-chancellor, 1957–60, acting director of Bancroft Library, 1961–62, director, 1969–90. **Related activities** Editorial board member, *American Literature*, 1952–55, 1964–67; western US chairman, Marshall Scholarship Committee, 1959–63, 1979–86; visiting professor, Harvard University, 1964, visiting Phi Beta Kappa scholar, 1980–81; contributor: *American Heritage*, *American Literature*. **Other activities** Trustee, Mills College, 1970–78, 1979–90, president of the board, 1973–76; trustee, Fine Arts Museum, San Francisco, 1983–90. **Offices and memberships** Member: Modern Language Association of America, American Studies Association, Pacific Coast Philological Association, Book Club of California, president, 1956–58; fellow: American Antiquarian Society, American Academy of Arts and Sciences, California Historical Society. **Awards and honours** Commander of the Order of the British Empire, 1963; honorary LHD, Mills College, 1978. **Publications** *The Oxford Companion to American Literature,* 1941, 1948, 1956, 1965, 1983; *The Popular Book: A History of America's Literary Taste*, 1950; (with Clarence Gohdes) *America's Literature*, 1955; *American Images of Spanish California*, 1960; (editor) *My First Publication: Eleven California Authors Describe Their Earliest Appearances in Print*, 1961; (editor) *The Oregon Trail* by Francis Parkman, 1963; *The Private Press Ventures of Samuel Lloyd Osbourne and R.L.S.*, 1966; (editor) *From Scotland to Silverado: "The Amateur Emigrant: From the Clyde to Sandy Hook", "Across the Plains", "The Silverado Squatters"* and *"Four Essays on California"* by Robert Louis Stevenson, 1966; (editor) *A Novelist in the Making: A Collection of Student Themes and the Novels "Blix"* and *"Vandover and the Brute"* by Frank Norris, 1970; *New Englanders in Nova Albion: Some Nineteenth-Century Views of California*, 1976; *A Companion to California*, 1978; *Fine Printing: The San Francisco Tradition*, 1985; *The Oxford Concise Companion to American Literature*, 1986. **Cause of death** Brain tumour, at age 79.

BRUNO KREISKY

Austrian Politician

Born **Vienna, Austria, 22 January 1911**

Died **Vienna, Austria, 29 July 1990**

His countrymen called him "The Sun King" and "Kaiser Bruno", due to his habit of treating a democratic office — the chancellorship of Austria — more like the realm of a monarch than that of a democratic leader. His personality was, at best, difficult; he suffered other strong individuals badly, whether they belonged to his party or to the opposition. He was arrogant, domineering and deeply upset by criticism. For all his faults, however, history will remember Bruno Kreisky as the man who did the most towards putting Austria back on her feet after the ten-year four-power occupation which followed the devastation of two lost world wars. His policy of "active neutrality" managed to forge bonds between East and West, as well as between North and South, long before it was deemed fashionable to take up the olive branch of *détente*. As a socialist in a conservative country and as a Jew in an anti-Semitic environment, such achievements were certainly no mean feat.

Bruno Kreisky was born in 1911, the son of Max and Irene Felix Kreisky. Although his parents belonged to the wealthier, upper-class echelons of Vienna's Jewish society, their son exhibited an early love for socialism. As the London *Times* has stated, "While his friends were learning how to waltz, he was at Socialist youth movement meetings." And, when the party was declared illegal in 1934, the young Kreisky went underground along with it. Predictably, he was soon arrested, and sentenced to 16 months in prison on charges of "high treason" (he was released a few weeks later). The experience did not deter Kreisky from his political beliefs, however, and he continued his associations with the Socialists while finishing his law degree at the University of Vienna.

Shortly after his graduation, Kreisky was arrested once more, in March 1938, two days after the *Anschluss*. Once again, he was released, but all too aware of the fate his Jewish origins would bring him if he stayed in Austria — despite the fact that he was never a practising Jew — the young socialist fled to Sweden at the invitation of that country's Socialist movement.

Kreisky spent the war years working in Sweden as a foreign correspondent and aiding other Austrian refugees who managed to escape the clutches of Hitler's Gestapo. One of these, Vera Fuerth, became his wife in 1942. In 1946, Kreisky took his first steps in the realms of diplomacy when he was appointed secretary of the newly established Austrian legation in Stockholm. It is generally accepted that the long years in Sweden, a country where government took the form of a parliamentary democracy within which revolved a socialist movement, had a profound influence upon Kreisky's own views of government and politics; despite the fact that in later years he would "rule like a king", the Austrian always maintained a deep respect for democratic principles, while at the same time retaining many of the socialist ideals of his youth.

Kreisky remained in Sweden as a member of the Austrian embassy staff until 1951, when he returned to his homeland. There, in an Austria which had been economically shattered and politically demoralized by World War II, he quickly began his own political rise to power. His first appointment was as the political adviser to an ageing federal president, Koener. Just two years later, Kreisky became secretary of state for foreign affairs, a post which involved him deeply in the lengthy negotiations which lead to the signing of the Austrian state treaty in 1955, thus ending the era of four-power occupation and providing Austria with a new neutral status.

Kreisky was elected to Parliament in 1956, and in 1959 he became the minister for foreign affairs in the country's new coalition government — as well as being elected, in the same year, as deputy chairman of the Socialist Party. It was during this period as foreign affairs minister (1959–66) that Kreisky, as Paul Lendvai put it in the London *Independent*, "shaped more than anyone else the foreign policy priorities of the new Austria." In 1967 he was elected chairman of the Austrian Socialist Party, and as such, leader of the Opposition. When the next general election was held in 1970, Kreisky became chancellor of Austria in a minority government; a year after that, the Socialists achieved a majority, and the next two elections saw Kreisky remain as chancellor. For 13 years, then, Austria witnessed what has since become known as the "Kreisky era".

It was an era of great change — particularly within the field of international relations and recognition. "His influence in East–West relations was at its peak during his long tenure as federal chancellor", stated Paul Lendvai. "In one way or another, this 'social democratic great bourgeois' (*Le Monde*), speaking fluent English, Swedish and French, met during three decades everybody who was anybody on the international stage from East and West." Among Kreisky's achievements: he was the first western foreign minister after World War II to visit Hungary, Bulgaria and Romania; the first prime minister to visit officially East Germany; he also helped to pave the way for Austria's association with the European Community. As Henry Kissinger recalled in his memoirs:

> Shrewd and perceptive Bruno Kreisky had ... parlayed his country's former neutrality into a position of influence beyond its strength, often by interpreting the motives of competing countries to each other. That he could bring off this balancing act was a tribute to his tact, his intelligence and his instinct for the scope — and the limits — of indiscretion. He had a great

> sense of humour and far more geopolitical insight than many leaders from more powerful countries. One of the asymmetries of history is the lack of correspondence between the abilities of some leaders and the power of their countries.

For all his skill, however, Bruno Kreisky upset almost as many people as he inspired. By being the first western leader to receive — and even embrace — the PLO's leader Yassir Arafat, as well as the Libyan leader Colonel Gaddafi, Kreisky generated howls of protest from both Israel and the American and Austrian Jewish communities. In addition, his first Socialist cabinet included four former Nazis, and all these elements, combined with ill-thought-out statements concerning terrorist attacks, added fuel to the fire which eventually blew up over the wartime past of federal president and former UN secretary-general, Kurt Waldheim, in the late 1980s. Although at that time no longer chancellor, Kreisky could not resist pairing late criticism of Waldheim with a nasty outburst about the "vile intervention of the World Jewish Congress into internal Austrian affairs."

Yet despite this inability to keep his mouth shut, no one could doubt the positive side of Kreisky's legacy to Austria. Under his rule, both unemployment and inflation stayed at low levels (although there was a rise in the national debt); the Austrian schilling revived to become one of the hardest of the world's currencies; social reforms were carried out; and by and large the nation's new-found stability became a signpost for others. For all his irascible nature, the Chancellor remained a man of the people. His address and telephone number were always listed in the public telephone directories, and he was constantly available to the press. "I am a partner who is not always pleasant", Kreisky admitted, "but indispensable for journalists, because I always try to say something which is newsworthy." A legacy from his own journalistic days, perhaps?

"Political ability", he said, "is the ability to foretell what is going to happen tomorrow, next week, next month, and next year — and to have the ability afterwards to explain why it didn't happen." After the loss of an absolute majority in the elections of 1983, Kreisky stepped down from politics, "explaining" himself by saying, "It's time for a change." He remained honorary chairman of the Socialist Party until 1987, but could not be content to be honorably silent. Ageing and not in the best of health (he had undergone a kidney transplant in 1984), he continued to give vindictive and often irrational comments to the press at interviews, mostly to do with his successors, Fred Sinowatz and Franz Vranitzky; like Bavaria's Franz-Josef Strauss, he never knew when to quit, and these outbursts and increasing irritability probably resulted in the fall in his reputation during his last years.

Nonetheless, Bruno Kreisky remains the first social democratic leader to have reconciled his party's interests with those of such diverse groups as the Catholic Church, former Nazis, the youth movement and intellectuals. It was once said that he was "too big for Austria". The fact that his broad vision reached beyond Austria's parochial borders, however, remains the reason that Austria is "big" today in the eyes of the world.

Born Bruno Kreisky. **Parents** Max and Irene Felix Kreisky. **Marriage** Vera Fuerth, 1942 (died 1989). **Children** Peter and Susanne. **Education** Law degree, University of Vienna. **Career** Member, Austrian Social Democratic Party; arrested/imprisoned, 1935, 1938; escaped to Sweden, 1938; member, scientific staff, Stockholm Co-Operative Society, 1939–46; joined Austrian Foreign Service, 1946; Austrian legation, Stockholm, 1946–51; returned to Austria, 1951; Austrian Federation President's Office, 1951–53; state secretary for foreign affairs, Federal Chancellery, 1953; elected to parliament, 1956; minister of foreign affairs, 1959–66; chairman, Socialist Party of Austria, 1967–83, honorary chairman, 1983–87; federal chancellor of Austria, 1970–83; resigned office, 1983. **Offices and memberships** Founder/vice-president, Theodor Körner Fund for Promotion of Arts and Sciences; board vice-chairman, Institute for Advanced Studies and Scientific Research, Vienna; president, Vienna Institute for Development. **Awards and honours**

Gold Grand Cross of Honour; Freedom Award, 1975; Jawaharlal Nehru Award for International Understanding, 1985; Martin Luther King, Jr International Peace Award 1989. **Publications** *The Challenge: Politics on the Threshold of the Atomic Age*, 1963; *Aspects of Democratic Socialism*, 1974; *Neutrality and Co-existence*, 1975; *The Times We Live In: Reflections on International Politics*, 1978; *Between the Times: Memoirs from Five Centuries*, 1986; *In the Stream of Politics: Memoirs*, 1988. **Cause of death** Heart disease, at age 79.

MARGARET LOCKWOOD

British Actress

Born **Karachi, India, 15 September 1916**

Died **London, England, 15 July 1990**

The British feature film *The Wicked Lady* was the nearest thing to *Dynasty* in 1945. A piece of period-costumed nonsense aimed at helping its public temporarily forget the war, it featured an outrageous central character conceived specifically to out-Scarlett Scarlett O'Hara. It was Margaret Lockwood who played this central role, compelling the audience to believe in the amoral Restoration noblewoman and her secret life of seduction, highway robbery and murder.

Lockwood overcame dubious characterization and frequently ludicrous dialogue by the sheer lip-smacking gusto of her performance. Equipped with an immaculate *maquillage*, luxuriant crinolined costumes leaving little to the imagination in the bosom department, and gleaming canine teeth which suggested the fangs of a predator, she endowed the evil Lady Barbara Skelton with a curiously camp allure.

It's not surprising that the public remember her as the Wicked Lady. But the glamorous, raven-haired star was only one aspect of Margaret Lockwood. In real life a likeable woman with a restrained way of life, she was a genuine actress, highly respected for her professionalism. No less a director than Carol Reed described her as "the most efficient and the most versatile actress I have ever worked with."

She had always wanted to act, since seeing her first Charlie Chaplin film at the age of three, newly arrived in England from Karachi, India (now Pakistan) where she had been born. The rest of her childhood was spent in Sydenham, south London were she lived with her brother and mother. Her father, a railway official, stayed on in India. The children were at the mercy of their domineering mother, who fostered young Margaret's talents — up to a point.

Her flair for singing and dancing soon made themselves apparent. She took piano and dance lessons and began to get engagements. Even at a tender age, she was very much a professional. In 1929 she appeared in a pantomine, *The Babes in the Wood*. Initially brought in to replace the female Babe who was ill, she bore her relegation to the chorus with relative fortitude when the invalid recovered in time for the opening.

Mrs Lockwood chaperoned Margaret to her shows and pocketed half of the proceeds. But she drew the line at praise: "It was terrible!" was her verdict on *Cavalcade* in 1931. Lockwood had been selected for a walk-on part by the playwright, Noël Coward, in person, but was forced by her mother to relinquish her part in mid-run when she innocently enquired the meaning of a four-letter word learned from a fellow-member of the cast.

In 1933 she enrolled at the Royal Academy of Dramatic Art (RADA), the most prestigious of England's drama schools. At her audition, the principal, Kenneth Barnes, was struck by what he later called "the feeling that she was out for business, not just pleasure." The course took her only a year to complete instead of the usual two. Despite resisting attempts to teach her the affected accent then favoured, she did well: she tied for a scholarship, won a diction prize and took a starring part in the 1934 RADA diploma performance, where she was "spotted" by Herbert de Leon, who became her agent. This relationship lasted throughout her career.

Soon de Leon had helped her to her first minor role in a West End play; the reviewer in *The Times* already discerned "the sparkle of truth" in her performance. De Leon also arranged a screen test, which cost her her eyebrows (the cameraman refused to shoot until they had been shaved off and new ones pencilled in) but led to a part in a film of *Lorna Doone*. Another actress having dropped out, she was hurriedly promoted from her minor part to that of the second female lead, Annie Ridd.

British film-making in the 1930s was stimulated by legislation forcing cinemas to show a stipulated quota of British-made films. Many of the films were low-budget B-movies, but not necessarily the worse for it. Lockwood appeared in several such "quota quickies" after she was signed up for a three-year contract with British Lion. Though most of the films were unmemorable, they brought her into contact with people she could learn from.

Working on *Lorna Doone* she had made friends with the assistant director, Carol Reed. When he directed *Midshipman Easy*, Lockwood became his leading lady. Later she worked with Douglas Fairbanks Jr, who said she was "shy but very well disciplined, and seemed to all of us to have spent a good amount of time studying her craft."

By the age of 19 Lockwood had already made eight films and was described by critics as likely "to become a personality in British films", and as "a delightful heroine". In 1936 she made *The Beloved Vagabond* with Maurice Chevalier. The film was a disappointment but Lockwood was repeatedly singled out by reviewers for "beauty and natural ability" as one of them put it. In the US, too, she came in for attention: *Variety* commended her personality and her voice which was "less British than the average"! Profiles began to appear in fan magazines. Stardom was on the way.

The process was accelerated when, nearing the end of her British Lion contract, she was signed up for three years by Gainsborough Pictures, who offered the then fabulous basic salary of 3000 pounds per annum. The studio decided to make her into Britain's first home-grown, Hollywood-style screen goddess, insisting, for instance, that Lockwood, until then inconspicuous off the set in raincoat and beret, should dress as a star on social occasions. She made more films, notably Hitchcock's perennially enjoyable spy-thriller *The Lady Vanishes*. The attention of the press started to focus on her more and more, and it was one of the more diligent reporters who uncovered, and revealed to her mother, Margaret Lockwood's guilty secret.

Some months before, just after her twenty-first birthday, she had been quietly married to Rupert Leon (no relation to the agent), a man she had known for years and one her mother detested. The ceremony had taken place in a registry office on the way to a day's filming. Lockwood had been unable to pluck up the courage to tell her mother even after the event, and so things had continued much as before, with various subterfuges allowing the couple to spend a little time together.

Their secret out, they set up home together. But soon they were separated again: with war looming, few films were being made in Britain, and Gainsborough soon sent Lockwood to Hollywood to work on a late, ill-starred Shirley Temple film, *Susannah of the Mounties*. More enjoyable for her was a second Hollywood film, *Rulers of the Sea*. Her husband came out to join her and it looked as if she might stay to make more films. However, the threat of war made her anxious to get back home.

Carol Reed encouraged her to return, wanting her for his next project, *The Stars Look Down*. Lockwood was outraged when she discovered that she was cast as a prostitute, and one without a heart of gold at that. She was talked into it, and the role is agreed to be one of her most successful. The film was completed just as Britain declared war.

Her daughter Julia ("Toots") was born in 1940. Lockwood returned to work at Gainsborough, now under the Rank umbrella, to make *Alibi*, in which she was, for the first time, paired with James Mason. Then came *The Man in Grey*, and her first "evil" role, as a woman who murders her best friend in order to steal the latter's husband. It foreshadowed *The Wicked Lady* in other ways too: described by the *London Evening Standard* as "spectacle and sex, a dash of sadism, near-the-knuckle lines and an end where virtue is rewarded", it received a critical panning but was a box-office hit, like much of Gainsborough's, and Lockwood's, output over the next few years.

The anti-heroine of *The Wicked Lady* seduces and marries her cousin's fiancé, then, bored with married life, takes to impersonating the local highwayman. She bumps into the real highwayman (James Mason) when they both arrive to hold up the same coach. After a suitably torrid affair, she finds he's been unfaithful and shops him. His friends cut him down from the gallows. He rapes her, she shoots him, and she ends up being shot herself by another of her lovers.

Frankly, it doesn't sound like the sort of thing your grandma would enjoy, yet a surprising number of today's grandmas remember the film, and its star, with affection. Eighty-seven-year-old Queen Mary, present at the *première*, enjoyed it too, much to everyone's relief. Lockwood's biographer suggests that her performance owed some of its *panache* to a love affair which she was enjoying at the time, after a two-year estrangement from Rupert Leon. Her own comment was, "It may have been rubbish, but we took it seriously and it showed." Others have discerned a feminist subtext to please the post-war woman.

Whatever the secret of its appeal, the film overcame the derision of the critics to become an unprecedented world-wide hit. British offerings tended to be too insipid for the American palate, but this erred in the opposite direction: the US censor insisted that several of Lockwood's scenes be shot with less *décolletage*.

It represented the pinnacle of Lockwood's popularity: she was named the top money-making star of 1945 and 1946 and won three *Daily Mail* readership polls for the most popular actress. A string of *Wicked Lady* clones and other mediocre films came next, and Lockwood tended to bear the brunt of critical opprobrium, though she still had a loyal following among the public. There were repeated rows with Rank, to whom she was now directly under contract, as she became bored with the trivial and repetitious nature of the roles they offered. Her screen forays into comedy, such as *Cardboard Cavalier*, were disappointing. By 1951 she had had enough, and parted company with Rank with 18 months of her contract still to run.

The year 1951 was a low point not only in her screen career but also in her personal life. She was divorced from Leon, and at a custody hearing over their daughter, Lockwood's own mother, perhaps out of pique at not being allowed to bring up her granddaughter herself, gave evidence that Lockwood was not a fit mother. In spite of this testimony the court awarded her custody. The two women never met again.

With exemplary fortitude, Lockwood now bounced back to build a successful new career in the theatre, to which she had returned in the late 1940s with a sell-out tour of Coward's *Private Lives*. During the 1950s and 1960s, she made numerous stage appearances, including Shaw's *Pygmalion*; several *Peter Pans*, in some of which she played Peter to her daughter Julia's Wendy; *Spider's Web*, which Agatha Christie wrote specially for her; and Wilde's *An Ideal Husband*, which established her as a comedienne.

As well as a rapturous reception from audiences, her acting was attracting favourable attention from the critics once more. A return to the cinema in 1957 at Dirk Bogarde's request, for a supporting role in *Cast a Dark Shadow*, was also a critical success.

On television she appeared with her daughter in a 1960s television series *The Flying Swan*, which ran for two years. In the 1970s she played a barrister in three series of *Justice*, which also featured John Stone, with whom she had lived since the late 1950s. She made a final film appearance as the stepmother in *The Slipper and the Rose*, a version of Cinderella, in 1976, and a final stage appearance in *Motherdear* in 1980. Her last public engagement, also in 1980, was to collect a CBE from Buckingham Palace.

The departure of Stone to marry somebody else, the death of her lifelong agent Herbert de Leon, and the onset of a chronic ear problem bringing deafness and loss of balance, conspired to cause her to retire from professional life for her last ten years. Living in a privacy that was guarded by loyal neighbours at her home in Kingston-on-Thames near London, she politely declined offers of work and requests for interviews alike. She was visited only by a select few, including her daughter Julia and her old colleague and friend, actress Phyllis Calvert.

With an excellent memory for lines, a complete absence of prima-donna-ish behaviour and a belief that "the show must go on" in spite of personal sadness or inconvenience — she cancelled a holiday to return to *Spider's Web* when her replacement died — Margaret Lockwood demonstrated the advantages of acting tackled as a craft, as opposed to an art. It's true that regard for her "image" made her turn down opportunities such the film of Orton's *Entertaining Mr Sloane*. But perhaps those who complain that she could have done more if she had risked more are missing the point. She was loved by generations of fans.

Born Margaret Mary Lockwood Day. **Parents** Henry, British railway official in India, and Margaret Evelyn (Waugh) Lockwood Day. **Marriage** Rupert W. Leon, businessman, 1937, (divorced 1950). **Children** One daughter, Julia. **Education** Sydenham Girls' High School, London; Italia Conti School, London (one term only); Royal Academy of Dramatic Art, London, 1933. **Career** Stage début, *A Midsummer's Night Dream*, 1928; West End début, *Family Affairs*, 1934; film début, *Lorna Doone*, 1934; contract player, British Lion, 1934–37; contract player Gainsborough 1937–39; contract player, Twentieth Century-Fox, Hollywood, 1939; contract player, Gainsborough (merged with Rank), 1943–51; returned to stage; last film performance, *The Slipper and the Rose*, 1976; final stage appearance, *Motherdear*, 1980. **Awards and honours** British National Film Award, *Daily Mail*, 1946, 1947, 1949; *Daily Mirror* Television Award, 1961; Best Actress Award: *TV Times*, 1971, *The Sun*, 1973; Commander of the Order of the British Empire, 1980. **Stage** *A Midsummer Night's Dream*, 1928; *The Babes in the Wood* (pantomime), 1929; *Cavalcade*, 1932; *House on Fire*, 1934; *Family Affairs*, 1934; *Repayment*, 1936; *Miss Smith*, 1936; *Ann's Lapse*, 1937; *Private Lives*, 1949; *Peter Pan*, 1949, 1950, 1957; *Pygmalion*, 1951; *Spider's Web*, 1954–55; *Subway in the Sky*, 1957; *Murder on Arrival*, 1948–49; *And Suddenly It's Spring*, 1959; *Milk and Honey*, 1961; *Signpost to Murder*, 1962; *Every Other Evening*, 1964; *An Ideal Husband*, 1965, 1966; *The Others*, 1967; *On a Foggy Day*, 1969; *Lady Frederick*, 1970; *Relative Values*, 1972, 1973; *Double Edge*, 1975; *Quadrille*, 1977; *A Suite in Three Keys*, 1978; *Motherdear*, 1980. **Films** *Lorna Doone*, 1935; *The Case of Gabriel Perry*, 1935; *Some Day*, 1935; *Honours Easy*, 1935; *Man of the Moment*, 1935; *Midshipman Easy*, 1935; *Jury's Evidence*, 1936; *The Amateur Gentleman*, 1936; *The Beloved Vagabond*, 1936; *Irish for Luck*, 1936; *The Street Singer*, 1937; *Who's Your Lady Friend?*, 1937; *Dr Syn*, 1937; *Melody and Romance*, 1937; *Owd Bob*, 1938; *Bank Holiday*, 1938; *The Lady Vanishes*, 1938; *A Girl Must Live*, 1939; *The Stars Look Down*, 1939; *Susannah of the Mounties*, 1939; *Rulers of the Sea*, 1939; *Night Train to Munich*, 1940; *The Girl in the News*, 1940; *Quiet Wedding*, 1941; *Alibi*, 1942; *The Man in Grey*, 1943; *Dear Octopus*, 1943; *Give us the Moon*, 1944; *Love Story*, 1944; *A Place of One's Own*, 1945; *I'll Be Your Sweetheart*, 1945; *The Wicked Lady*, 1945; *Bedelia*, 1946; *Hungry Hill*, 1946; *Jassy*, 1947; *The White Unicorn*, 1947; *Look Before You Love*, 1948; *Cardboard Cavalier*, 1949; *Madness of the Heart*, 1949; *Highly Dangerous*, 1950; *Trent's Last Case*, 1952; *Laughing Anne*, 1953; *Trouble in the Glen*, 1954; *Cast a Dark Shadow*, 1957; *The Slipper and the Rose*, 1976. **Television** *An Ideal Husband*, 1965; *The Flying Swan*, 1965; *Justice*, 1971–74. **Publication** *Lucky Star* (autobiography), 1955. **Cause of death** Undisclosed, at age 73. **Further reading** Hilton Tims, *Once a Wicked Lady, A Biography of Margaret Lockwood*, 1989.

KARL MENNINGER

American Psychiatrist

***Born* Topeka, Kansas, 22 July 1893**

***Died* Topeka, Kansas, 18 July 1990**

Psychiatrists are often accused of doing more harm than good. However, it's difficult to see what harm could be done by Dr Karl Menninger's prescription of a friendly and ordered environment in which patients can develop their potential. Often called a father, if not *the* father, of American psychiatry, Menninger through his writing and clinical work liberalized the way in which mental illness, crime and behavioural abnormalities were viewed.

In contrast with the Victorian view of insanity, compounded of hostility and fear, and still popular in the early twentieth century, Menninger and his collaborators felt that the "insane" could usually be treated to good effect. Their condition, he felt, was due not to psychic deformity but to social factors, in particular a lack of parental love. A colleague said that he saw patients as "human beings, somewhat isolated from their fellow men, harassed by faulty techniques of living and making awkward manoeuvers to keep themselves emotionally intact."

Menninger came from a family of pioneer settlers in Topeka, Kansas. His father, a general practitioner, had been impressed by a visit to the Mayo clinic in Rochester, Minneapolis, a group practice where patients could be treated by specialists from a number of different disciplines. From then onwards he cherished an ambition of setting up a similar operation in Topeka, with his sons. His dream was to come true, on a scale he can hardly have imagined.

Having studied first at the University of Wisconsin, Menninger graduated from Harvard Medical School *cum laude* in 1917. After completing his clinical training as a doctor, and a brief period of war service, he taught neuropathology at Harvard, at the same time working with Dr Ernest Southard of the Boston Psychopathic Hospital, one of the mentors to whom he later felt he owed the most. Menninger was interested in Southard's simplification of the nosology, or classification, of mental illnesses. Southard advocated an arrangement of eleven classes of mental illness according to syndrome. Later Menninger was to espouse an even simpler system of five levels of dysfunction within a unitary concept of mental illness, as described in *The Vital Balance*, with the comment: "our concern now is not so much what to call something as what to do about it".

On Southard's death in 1920, Menninger returned to Topeka where he practised alongside his father. In 1925 they instituted a 13-bed psychiatric centre in an old farm-house. Menninger's younger brother William joined them shortly afterwards. In 1926 they started the Pearson School, later renamed the Southard School, for the treatment of disturbed children.

All these establishments were centres for research and training as well as for treatment, and in 1941 they were all brought under the umbrella of the Menninger Foundation, with Karl Menninger as its first president. The foundation has grown to the point where its employees number almost 1000. It has a 29-million-dollar annual budget, with 39 buildings spread over two sites. Menninger saw that the clinics could have the secondary function of a resource bank for scientific exploration and learning, and so the foundation came to embrace training facilities for not only psychiatrists and clinical psychologists, but also nurses, social workers, occupational therapists and auxiliary staff. Many psychiatric establishments came to be modelled on the Menninger idea.

Psychoanalysis had been originated by Freud decades before, but Karl Menninger was among the first US doctors to undergo psychoanalytic training and to apply psychoanalytic theory to psychiatric patients. Menninger was fond of describing himself as "more Freudian than Freud" —

in old age he described Freud as one of his life heroes, along with Shakespeare, Dickens and Franklin D. Roosevelt.

He briefly met the great man in 1934, and though the meeting was too short to be satisfactory he remained an enthusiastic admirer. Later he came to know Freud's daughter Anna well, through a shared interest in child psychiatry. He was particularly interested in Freud's concept of *Thanatos*, the death instinct, and its influence on suicides. But he was not always an orthodox Freudian, and was more interested in the practicalities of psychiatry than the theory. He continued to keep in touch with theoretical developments, but distanced himself from the often acrimonious debates that raged among his European colleagues.

Somewhat to the surprise of their contemporaries, Menninger and his brother had supplemented their professional training and research by undergoing psychoanalysis themselves. But rather than the traditional analysis sessions on the couch over a protracted period, Menninger's own approach to treatment favoured residential care in an atmosphere of emotional warmth and security to supply some of what the patients had lacked and allow space in which they could understand their own potential.

A family atmosphere and an orderly routine with physical work provided a background to the various types of therapy which patients were offered. "It should be a help for any people to be getting three square meals a day and to know that there is opportunity ahead — things to be done, land to be turned, things to build", said Menninger.

His was what would nowadays be called a holistic approach to the well-being of patients, with no exclusive commitment to any single form of therapy. Progress should be rigorously monitored — "What do we know? How can we be sure?" he would ask his clinical colleagues at case conferences — and different approaches tried where necessary. Menninger was a religious man, who had been brought up as a Presbyterian, and he and his mother conducted optional Bible classes for patients.

Menninger was convinced that childhood experiences were the key to emotional stability in adulthood, and that early emotional deprivation accounted for a wide range of mental problems and criminal behaviour. Effective teachers, he said, should be promoted from senior classes to junior ones, since their influence could do the most good in the youngest children. Damage done to children was hard to put right: "it is much easier to help a child grow up with love and courage than it is to instill hope in a despondent soul", he said. Among the Menningers' ventures was The Villages for the care of homeless children.

The Menninger establishments would take on patients rejected by other hospitals on the grounds of their intractable behaviour. For Menninger, this behaviour was a sign not of aggression but of inner frustration, which could be ameliorated by better understanding. A common-sense approach to dispelling delusions was advocated: a case history in *The Vital Balance* tells of an elderly woman patient who was disabused of the conviction that her son was outside the hospital and being kept from her by the staff, simply by being taken to look for him in the grounds.

The incarceration of criminals (except when their extreme violence rendered it unavoidable) was a *bête noire* of Menninger's. *The Crime of Punishment* denied the value of prison, either as a means of reforming criminals, as a deterrent, or as a moral response to crime. He was strongly opposed to the death penalty and gave evidence against it at hearings where its reintroduction in the state of Kansas was being discussed.

His ideas didn't arise from a woolly-minded view of crime — he wrote that murder was "so hideous a spectacle that one's horror and alarm are apt to destroy one's scientific detachment". On the contrary, he stressed how abnormal must be the state of mind of anyone who would carry out such an abhorrent act. For Menninger, crime and mental illness were closely linked.

Alongside the moral repugnance of the death penalty, he put forward the somewhat sinister-sounding argument that it is "a terrible waste ... of perfectly good laboratory material". He wanted to investigate and treat, rather than experiment on, the criminals: Menninger was always aware of the learning opportunities that are a byproduct of treatment.

Though many felt that Menninger's assimilation of criminal behaviour with mental illness was overstated, all but the most conservative agreed that his approach gave valuable insights to the state of mind of at least some criminals; to a large extent the reforms he wanted to see in the penal system came to be adopted.

Menninger at one time taught criminology at the Washburn University of Topeka. Education and training were a major interest of his and the Menninger Clinic together with Topeka State Hospital established the Karl Menninger School of Psychiatry and Mental Health Sciences, later a division of the Institute of Psychological Medicine.

One of Menninger's talents was for exposition. An admirer described him as "not a popularizer, but an enlightener": he could render ideas accessible to the lay person without diluting them. In 1930 he wrote *The Human Mind*, a primer of Freudian ideas intended for medical students, but read by a large lay audience. Later he was to write columns for the national magazines *Household* and *The Ladies' Home Journal*. By describing mental illness in plain English, he did much to dispel the fear surrounding the subject in the mind of the public, and to present patients as human beings rather than menaces to be put out of sight and out of mind. His writings had a somewhat hortatory tone and were occasionally criticized as vague.

Outside the main thrust of his work, Menninger lent his weight to a wide range of liberal causes, among them American Indian Defence, Planned Parenthood and the Council on Freedom from Censorship. He campaigned for the Anti-Nuclear lobby. In 1938, writing of war, he said: "The same body politic which believes in us as medicine men, as saviours of the people, as prolongers of life, encourages the manufacturing of instruments that can deal more destruction in a day than all the doctors in the country could repair in a year."

Perhaps ironically, family relationships within the Menninger family weren't always harmonious. Menninger was always full of ideas and energies which at times made him difficult to live with. A journalist described him as "one of the can't-sit kind". He was at times scathing towards those whose views he found unpalatable. His brother William was a much calmer personality, and the two were sometimes thought to avoid one another. In 1941 Karl Menninger was divorced from his first wife after a marriage of 25 years, but his second marriage the same year lasted for the rest of his life, almost half a century.

"I have always liked the idea ... that mental sickness is not hopeless, that most of its victims recover", wrote Karl Menninger, echoing his father's insistence that "no patient is untreatable". Society seemed to be persuaded. In the half-century from 1920, Menninger's views came to dominate the practice of psychiatry in the USA: according to one estimate, 80 per cent of psychiatrists and psychologists engaged in the field of mental health during the 1950s were Menninger-trained.

Since the 1970s, however, the emergence of other schools, together with new theories such as biological psychiatry, have diluted the Menninger influence on treatment methods. And, while the standards of patient care which he set are still respected throughout the US and beyond, sadly, the loving care of the mentally ill has been circumscribed by many countries' increasingly tight restrictions on social expenditure.

Born Karl Augustus Menninger. **Parents** Charles Frederick, doctor, and Flora (Knisely) Menninger. **Marriages** 1) Grace Gaines, 1916 (divorced 1941); 2) Jeanetta Lyle, 1941. **Children** Julia, Robert and Martha, from first marriage; Rosemary, from second marriage. **Education** Washburn College, Topeka, Kansas, 1910–12; Indiana University, 1910; University of Wisconsin at Madison, BA, 1914, BS, 1915; Harvard Medical School, Cambridge, Massachusetts, MD (cum laude), 1917. **Military service** Lieutenant, US Naval Reserve, 1917–18. **Career** Rotating internship, Kansas City General Hospital, 1917–18; assistant physician, Boston Psychopathic Hospital, 1918–20; assistant lecturer in neuropathology, Harvard Medical

School, 1918–20; assistant in neurology, Tufts Medical School, 1919–20; founder (with father and brother) Menninger Clinic, 1925, chief of staff, 1925–90; founder (with father and brother) Pearson School (later Southard School), 1926; founder, Menninger Foundation, 1941, president, 1941–43, director, department of education, 1946–62, board chairman, 1954–90; founder, Menninger School of Psychiatry and Mental Health Sciences, 1946. **Related activities** Staff member, Stormont-Vail Hospital and St Francis Hospital, Topeka, Kansas, from 1919; editor-in-chief, *Bulletin of the Menninger Clinic*, from 1936; manager, Winter Veterans Administration Hospital, Topeka, Kansas, 1945–48; clinical professor of psychiatry, University of Kansas Medical School, Kansas City, 1946–62; consultant in psychiatry, State of Illinois Department of Welfare, 1953–54; consultant in psychiatry, governor of Illinois, 1953–54; consultant, Office of Vocational Rehabilitation, Department of Health, Education, and Welfare, 1953–55; consultant, Bureau of Prisons, Department of Justice, from 1956; trustee, Albert Deutsch Memorial Foundation, 1961; trustee, Aspen Institute for Humanistic Studies, 1961–64; distinguished professor of psychiatry, Chicago Medical School; professor, Loyola University, Chicago; member, National Council on Crime and Delinquency; member, Open Lands Project; editorial board member: *Archives of Criminal Psychodynamics*, *Psychoanalytic Quarterly*, *Excerpta Criminologica*, *Academic Achievement;* contributor: *Nation, New Republic, Ladies' Home Journal.* **Other activities** On board of overseers: Lemberg Center for the Study of Violence, Brandeis University; on board of directors: Chicago Boys Club, John Howard Association of Chicago, W. Clement and Jessie V. Stone Foundation, Chicago; founder, The Villages, Incorporated, Topeka, board member. **Offices and memberships** Secretary, Central Neuropsychiatric Association, 1922–32, president, 1932–33; secretary, American Orthopsychiatric Association, 1926–27, president, 1927–28; counselor, American Psychiatric Association, 1928–29, 1941–43; life member, American Psychoanalytic Association, president, 1941–43; member, American Association for Physical and Mental Rehabilitation; vice-president, American League to Abolish Capital Punishment; national committee vice-chairman, American Civil Liberties Union; member, American Correctional Association; fellow, American Medical Association, 1978; life fellow, American College of Physicians; life member, American Medical Writers Association, second vice-president, 1957–58, first vice-president, 1958–59; member: American Association for the Advancement of Science, World Medical Association for the Advancement of Science, World Medical Association, American Academy of Child Psychiatry; honorary member: American Association Suicidology, International Association for Suicide Prevention, Sigmund Freud Archives; joint founder Central Neuropsychiatry Association; member: Central Psychiatric Hospital Association, Medical Association for Research into Nervous and Mental Diseases, American Assocation for Child Psychoanalysis, American Society of Criminology, Illinois Academy of Criminology, Association for Psychiatric Treatment of Offenders, American Academy of Psychiatry and Law, American Justice Institute, Association of Clinical and Pastoral Education, Illinois Commission on Family Law, International Psychoanalytic Association, Kansas Medical Society, Sigmund Freud Society, Vienna, World Society of Ekistics, National Congress of American Indians, American Humanics Foundation; co-chairman, national Commission for Prevention of Child Abuse, honorary board member; chairman, Save the Tallgrass Prairie, Incorporated. **Awards and honours** Honorary DSc, Washburn University, 1949, University of Wisconsin, 1965, Oklahoma City University, 1966; honorary LHD: Park College, 1955, Saint Benedict's College, 1963, Loyola University, 1972, DePaul University, 1974; honorary LLD: Jefferson Medical College of Philadelphia, 1956, Parsons College, 1960, Kansas State University, 1962, Baker University, 1965, Pepperdine University, 1974, John Jay College of Criminal Justice, 1978; Isaac Ray Award, American Psychiatric Association, 1962, first distinguished service award, 1965, first Founders Award, 1977; T.W. Salmon Award, New York Academy of Medicine, 1967; American Foundation of Religion and Psychiatry International Service Award, 1968; Good Samaritan Award, Eagles Lodge, 1968,

1969; annual service award, John Howard Association, 1969; Good Shepherd Award, The Lambs, Chicago, 1969; American Academy of Psychiatry and Law award, 1974; Roscoe Pound Award, National Council of Crime and Delinquency, 1975; special award, Kansas Department of Corrections, 1976; Sheen Award, American Medical Association, 1978; Presidential Medal of Freedom, 1981. **Publications** (Contributor) *Why Men Fail*, 1918; *The Human Mind*, 1930; (co-editor with Nelson Antrim Crawford) *The Healthy-Minded Child*, 1930; *Man Against Himself*, 1938; (contributor) *America Now*, 1938; (with Junius Flagg Brown) *Psychodynamics of Abnormal Behavior*, 1940; (with Jeanetta Lyle Menninger) *Love Against Hate*, 1942; *A Guide to Psychiatric Books*, 1956; *Theory of Psychoanalytic Technique*, 1958; *A Psychiatrist's World*, 1959; *A Manual for Psychiatric Case Study*, 1962; *The Vital Balance*, 1963; (with Seward Hiltner) *Constructive Aspects of Anxiety*, 1963; *The Crime of Punishment*, 1968; (with Lucy Freeman) *Sparks*, 1973; *Whatever Became of Sin?*, 1973; *The Selected Correspondence of Karl A. Menninger, 1919–1945* (edited by Howard J. Faulkner and Virginia D. Pruitt), 1989. **Cause of death** Abdominal cancer, at age 96. **Further reading** Flora Menninger, *Days of My Life*.

LOIS MORAN

American Actress

***Born* Pittsburgh, Pennsylvania, 1 March 1909**

***Died* Sedona, Arizona, 13 July 1990**

There are numerous actors, male and female, whose names are hardly known to anyone other than a frenzied cinema enthusiast, but who are nevertheless responsible for supplying beauty, sparkle and dashes of talent that flit across the silent screen. No less a literary figure than F. Scott Fitzgerald was impressed by the beauty of Lois Moran; he allegedly patterned his character Rosemary Hoyt in his novel, *Tender is the Night*, after her. According to him, she "had magic in her pink palms and her cheeks lit to a lovely flame, like the thrilling flush of children after their cold baths in the evening."

Born Lois Dartington Dowling, she was to begin her career somewhat glamorously: after being taken to Paris as a child in 1918, when her father was killed in the war, she made her first stage appearance as a dancer with the Paris Opera House's *corps de ballet* four years later. She remained there for two more years, during which time her mother noticed an advertisement placed by Samuel Goldwyn (then in town). Actresses were needed for his production of *Romeo and Juliet*. Although the plans fizzled out, he eventually used her in *Stella Dallas*, in 1925. "Her work in that film", according to film historian Kevin Brownlow, "stands among the most remarkable and most poignant of the entire silent era."

Her beauty also impressed French film director Marcel L'Herbier, who cast her in the 1924 *La Galerie des monstres*, and with international star Ivan Mosjoukine in *Feu-Mathias Pascal*, a year later. (The film was not released until 1926.) Back in the US, she was discovered once again — this time by playwright Marc Connelly, who cast her in his play *The Wisdom Tooth*, in 1926, with which she went on tour. That same year, she played in the film *The Road to Mandalay*, directed by Tod Browning, by then a respected name in the field, starring with Henry B. Walthall and Lon Chaney. It was a fairly standard potboiler concerning two eastern coffee planters who quarrel over a young girl, but performances were impressive — as was Miss Moran.

After *Stella Dallas*, the offers poured in. Moran accepted a long-term contract with Fox. She did not complete the Connelly tour, but she developed a taste for musicals, and began singing and dancing lessons. After filming *Reckless Lady*, an indifferent piece which produced few ripples, she made her Broadway début in *This is New York* at the Music Box Theater in Manhattan, in 1930. The following year she was in another film: George S. Kaufman's *West of Broadway*, with John Gilbert. Although their paths crossed, she and Gilbert were going in different directions, for Gilbert's career had been on the wane, while hers was rising steadily. More success followed with Kaufman and George Gershwin's Pulitzer Prize-winning musical *Of Thee I Sing*, which ran on Broadway, and the 1933 *Let 'Em Eat Cake*, in San Francisco. The year 1936 found her back in Hollywood, although her star had, with the certain lack of rationale that the Dream Machine has always possessed, lost some of its sheen. Her part in Archie Mayo's *The Petrified Forest*, from the play by Robert Sherwood, was small, though she played beside Leslie Howard, Bette Davis and Humphrey Bogart. The story, which focused on a group of travellers held up by gangsters, did not spotlight her individual talent, and several mediocre films followed, including *Padlocked, Whirlwind of Youth* and *The Men in Her Life* (a rags-to-riches drama by Gregory Ratoff, starring Conrad Veidt and Dean Jagger).

Moran shelved her career temporarily in the mid-1930s after she married Colonel Clarence Young, a former assistant secretary of commerce under Herbert Hoover. A pioneer aviator, he was later to become vice-president of Pan-Am Airlines. After moving to Palo Alto, Moran became periodically involved in Stanford University's stage productions, as she was artist-in-residence on the campus. Later, she co-starred with Robert Preston in the TV series, *Waterfront*, but she officially retired in 1954.

Born Lois Dartington Dowling. **Parents** Roger, doctor, and Gladys (Evans) Dowling. **Marriage** Colonel Clarence M. Young, assistant secretary of commerce, 1935. **Children** One son. **Career** Stage début, Paris Opera Corps de Ballet, 1922–24; film début, Paris, 1924, US, 1926; New York stage début, *The Wisdom Tooth*, 1926; contract player, Fox Studios, 1926; studied singing; Broadway musical début, 1932; retired, 1935; returned to acting, *Waterfront* television series, 1950s. **Stage** (includes) *The Wisdom Tooth*, 1926; *This is New York*, 1930; *Of Thee I Sing*, 1932; *Let 'Em Eat Cake*, 1933; *The Petrified Forest*, 1935. **Films** (include) *La Galerie des monstres*, 1924; *Stella Dallas*, 1925; *Feu-Mathias Pascal*, 1926; *The Road to Mandalay*, 1926; *West of Broadway*, 1931; *The Men in Her Life*, 1941; also: *Reckless Lady, Padlocked; Whirlwind of Youth*. **Television** *Waterfront*, 1950s. **Cause of death** Undisclosed, at age 81.

BRENT MYDLAND

American Rock Musician and Composer

Born **Germany, 21 October 1952**

Died **Lafayette, Los Angeles, 6 July 1990**

Musician and composer Brent Mydland, a lynchpin of rock group The Grateful Dead for a decade, was the band's third keyboards player, and its third keyboards player to die in unusual circumstances — in this instance, a heroin overdose, a fatality due in all probability to the drug culture overtones that have surrounded the group since their involvement in the LSD experiments on the West Coast in the early 1960s.

Mydland joined the group in 1979, replacing the late Keith Godchaux, who had joined the group in 1973, replacing original keyboards player Ron "Pigpen" McKernan. The "Grim Reaper" figure who has been the band's emblem or trade mark over the decades would appear to have a special interest in people who play piano, organ or synthesizer for The Grateful Dead.

Mydland was born into a services family — his father was an army chaplain — on a US Army base in Germany in the early 1950s. He grew up on Long Island, New York, and in the San Francisco Bay area. He began to study piano at the age of seven, and while too young to witness the birth of rock 'n' roll he was born in perhaps the best year to experience the revolutionary 1960s as a teenager.

Mydland became an amateur rock musician in high school, and began playing in a number of local rock groups. In his early twenties he left San Francisco for Los Angeles, where he joined and made a name for himself as keyboardsman with local rock band, Silver.

It was in Los Angeles that Mydland met Grateful Dead guitarist and singer Bob Weir. Weir, co-founder of "The Dead" with guitarist Jerry Garcia, was working with a spin-off group, Bobby and The Midnites, just one of the many part-time projects of members of this mammoth workhorse-cum-institution of a group. Weir invited Mydland to join the Midnites and, on the death of Godchaux, The Grateful Dead.

In the "long strange trip" that is the career of The Grateful Dead, the band has proved a rather strange but wonderful institution, immune to the whims of fashion and perversely committed to its own aesthetic. It evolved from an early 1960s San Francisco blues, R and B and bluegrass group, Mother McCree's Uptown Jug Champions. Renamed The Grateful Dead by Garcia during an LSD hallucination, it came to dominate the West Coast "acid rock" culture alongside bands such as Jefferson Airplane. The group has remained faithful to the journeyman ethic of its blues grounding, and has carried with it a huge and growing following of "Deadheads", fans, some of them younger than the group itself, who follow the group from city to city and even country to country. The group refuses to follow the common rock ploy of reproducing album tracks on stage, and is renowned, in fact notorious, for its lengthy improvisations on songs, a technique more common in jazz and some experimental music. A typical Grateful Dead concert can last hours, even part of a day. Some of their classics, such as "Dark Star" (inspiration of sorts for the John Carpenter film of that name), can while away a happy hour or two themselves alone.

Mydland is credited as the Grateful Dead member who truly understood electronics, and timing; critics have identified him as the musician who, in amid the discursive and wayward improvisatory performances, signalled and introduced shifts and changes in the music. In most bands this would be a matter of counting notes and bars and perhaps keeping an eye on the band's leader; in the case of "The Dead" it is more a matter of mindreading.

More concretely, Mydland made a number of significant contributions to the vast repertoire of Grateful Dead songs, among them "Far From Me", "I Will Take You Home", a lullaby written for his two daughters, and, as co-writer, "We Can Run (But We Can't Hide)", an environmentally concerned ballad which was used by the Audubon Society in a video promoting ecological awareness.

Perhaps most notably, of all the three keyboard players in The Grateful Dead Mydland worked with the band the longest, and paradoxically during a decade when the group achieved greater commercial success than ever before. Part of that must be credited to Brent Mydland.

Born Brent Mydland. **Father** A chaplain, United States Army. **Marriage** Lisa. **Children** Two daughters. **Career** Keyboards player, rock 'n' roll bands, San Francisco area as a teenager; recorded with Silver, Los Angeles, early 1970s; with Bobby and the Midnites, led by Bob Weir; keyboards player, The Grateful Dead, with Jerry Garcia, Bob Weir, Phil Lesh, Bill Kreutzmann and Mickey Hart, 1979 onwards. **Compositions** (include), "Far From Me"; "I Will Take You Home"; (co-writer) "We Can Run (But We Can't Hide)". **Recordings** (include) *The Grateful Dead Go to Heaven*, 1980; *Dead Reckoning*, 1980; *Dead Set*, 1980; *In The Dark*, 1987; *Built To Last*, 1989. **Cause of death** Drug overdose, at age 37.

MAXWELL NEWTON

Australian Journalist

***Born* Perth, Western Australia, 28 April 1929**

***Died* Boca Raton, Florida, 23 July 1990**

Maxwell Newton was a brilliant financial journalist who enjoyed more successes and suffered more failures than most people in his profession and whose roistering life-style undoubtedly played a substantial part in his comparatively early death.

He was born into a working-class family at the time of the Depression when Perth was a deprived and depressed area, very much isolated from the rest of Australia. But his parents, immigrants from England, were keen that their children should do well in life and, with that encouragement, his vast intelligence was allowed to shine. He won a scholarship to Perth Modern, a school run by the government for able children. It certainly had an excellent selection policy. Amongst several classmates later to achieve success was future prime minister, Bob Hawke. They did not however like each other. Hawke regarded Newton as an intellectual snob and Newton referred to Hawke as "that bumptious little bastard".

Following school Newton's scholastic achievements continued. He won more scholarships, first to the University of Western Australia and then on to Clare, one of the colleges of England's prestigious Cambridge University. (Bob Hawke went to its rival, Oxford, as a Rhodes Scholar.) At Cambridge Newton was awarded a Wrenbury Scholarship as the university's outstanding economics graduate of the year. He was also made an honorary scholar of Clare College. He was subsequently offered a junior fellowship. He also spent time at the Sorbonne in Paris.

Newton decided to eschew the offer of academic life in favour of the world of finance. He joined the Australian Reserve Bank, working first in London and then in the Australian capital, Canberra, where he supplemented his salary with a car battery business based in his backyard. He said it was for the money — he didn't want to be beholden to an employer — but it was just as likely a part of his flamboyant and slightly outrageous life-style. He had already developed a dependency on alcohol.

His career in journalism took off when, at the age of 28, he was appointed Canberra political correspondent for the staid *Sydney Morning Herald*. He was an instant success, his natural writing ability enabling him to achieve an authoritative and readable blend of fact and opinion, the latter mostly his own. His intellect, natural flair and enthusiasm for tilting at the Establishment brought him to the attention of others and, within three years, he was offered the post of managing editor of an ailing weekly, *The Australian Financial Review*. Despite his complete ignorance of the business and decidedly unorthodox methods of conducting the paper's affairs — which included clearing his desk on Monday mornings into the bin on the premise that "if it is [important] the bastards will write again!" — he tripled its circulation and increased its frequency of publication: first to a bi-weekly and, ultimately, a daily. His staff adored him and he was tipped as successor to the organization's chief executive. But, by 1964, Maxwell had caught the eye of another proprietor, the rising Rupert Murdoch, now a major and sometimes controversial proprietor in the UK itself. He was lured away to found Australia's first general circulation national newspaper, *The Australian*, in 1964.

From the beginning there were clashes between the two. Murdoch had originally envisaged *The Australian* as a semi-parochial Canberra newspaper but allowed Newton's vision and aspirations to take over. Within a year, however, they were at logger-heads, primarily over editorial direction and escalating costs. Newton left and founded his own Canberra newsletter, *Incentive*, rapidly to be known as "Invective", which proved a great success though and formed the base for his own excursion into proprietorship with Maxwell Newton Publications. He acquired trade and country journals but over-reached himself with the launch of *The Sunday Observer* in Melbourne. In an effort to boost circulation he took the paper right into gutter journalism, which was far from his forte although Newton, as usual, found the excursion fun. This led to his total downfall. He was declared bankrupt with liabilities of over six million Australian dollars and assets of just 100 dollars.

His battle with alcohol, which had started soon after he left school, had been lost for some time. He was now popping pills as well. His disastrous lack of business sense had led him to pour increasing sums of money into his ailing newspapers and journals and, meanwhile, he was being vigorously pursued by the Australian tax authorities for money he simply didn't have.

Both his marriages had failed. His first had ended in divorce in 1974 after 22 years and three children, one of whom died tragically at the age of 20. A second marriage brought him three more daughters but lasted only four years. Newton was in obscurity and despair when he was offered a life-saving rope by Rupert Murdoch.

He fled to New York and Murdoch's offer of a job with the *New York Post*. He joined Alcoholics Anonymous, married for the third time, and soon was also a regular correspondent for *The Australian* (again), the London *Times*, the *Boston Herald* and the *Chicago Sun Times*. His writing and insight were still good and his columns highly respected but his opinions had now solidified into right-wing conservatism. His health was damaged irreparably and he was plagued by serious illness from then on.

Newton, however, was a man of considerable humour and apparent cheerfulness who obviously aroused good feelings as well as alien in those who knew him. And, despite all his excesses and disasters, he never lost his clarity of vision and depth of perception concerning the world of economics. Like many another brilliant mind, he simply couldn't get the hang of ordinary life.

Born Maxwell Newton. **Parents** George William and Norah (Christian) Newton. **Marriages** 1) Anne Kirby Robertson, 1952 (divorced 1974); 2) Diane Austin, 1975 (divorced 1979); 3) Valerie Olivia Waldron, 1981. **Children** Sarah, Anthony, and Penelope, from first marriage; Natasha, Sally and Emma, from second marriage. **Education** Perth Modern School; University of Western Australia, Perth, BA in economics; Clare College, Cambridge, BA; Sorbonne, Paris. **Emigration** Left Australia for US, 1980. **Career** Australian Reserve Bank, London, Canberra; political correspondent, *Sydney Morning Herald*, 1957–60; managing editor, *The Australian Financial Review*, John Fairfax Limited, Sydney, 1960–64; founding editor, *The Australian*, News Limited, Sydney, 1964–65; managing director, Maxwell Newton Publications, Melbourne, 1966–79, editor, *Incentive* financial newsletter, 1966; founder, *The Sunday Observer*, declared bankrupt, 1979; syndicated financial columnist, *New York Post*, *The Australian*, *The Times*, London, *Boston Herald*, *Chicago Sun Times*, 1980–90; president, Maxwell Newton's Financial Network, Wilton, Connecticut, 1983–85. **Awards and honours** Wrenbury Scholarship, Cambridge University, 1953; honorary scholar, Clare College, Cambridge, 1953. **Publication** *The Fed*, 1983. **Cause of death** Stroke, at age 61.

SERGEI PARADJANOV

Soviet Film Director

***Born* Tbilisi, Georgia, 9 January 1924**

***Died* Yerevan, Armenia, 20 July 1990**

Few film directors are remembered with such profound respect, from relatively few produced works; Jean Vigo was one — Paradjanov was another. The latter cinematic genius actually directed more than a dozen films, including shorts. Only four have had limited screening in the West. He was the object of such political harassment that it's surprising his output was as extensive as it is; certainly admiration for his adherence to his creativity increased.

Sarkis Paradjanian (as he was christened) was born of Armenian parents, and grew up in an artistic, comfortable environment. After studying music and violin, he moved to Moscow in 1946 and enrolled in the VGIK, the State Institute of Cinematography. After graduating in 1951, he worked briefly directing feature films at the renowned Dovzhenko Studio, Kiev, a year later. Films such as *Moldavskaia skazka* (*Moldavian Fairy Tales*), a short, *Andriesh*, *Dumka* (*The Ballad*), *Natalya Ujvii* and *Golden Hands* (both shorts), Paradjanov considered failures, "albeit justified failures". However, it's obviously difficult to make a judgement on his own opinion, since very little critical notice was taken of these films, and they have never been screened outside the Soviet Union.

Little is known about the director's life in the late 1950s and early 1960s. Films produced then were *Pervyi paren* (*The First Fellow*) in 1958/59, *Ukrainskaia rapsodiia* (*Ukrainian Rhapsody*) in 1961, and *Tsvetok na Kamne* (*Flower on the Stone*) in 1962; already Paradjanov's love for the traditional tale is the main interest. However, it was his *Teni zabyrykh predkov* (*Shadows of Our Forgotten Ancestors*) in 1965 which finally established his international reputation; it gathered in not only applause from critics but 16 festival awards. It's an unconventional, indeed rare work by any criterion, but especially so when seen in the context of the Soviet film industry. The film was reported by the official press as having been "laughed off the screen by audiences" in Moscow. But it achieved immediate international acclaim, earning for the director the inherited "mantle of Sergei Eisenstein" from western critics — more a token of superior honour, less a direct comparison of style.

Shadows was adapted from the work by nineteenth-century Ukrainian writer M. Kotsiubinsky. Set in a small Carpathian village, it tells of a blood feud between two families; Ivan and Marichka are the Romeo and Juliet here. But the plot, a folktale of sorcery, is, as in most of Paradjanov's films, of secondary importance. "We intentionally gave ourselves up to the material, its rhythm and style, so that literature, history, ethnography and philosophy could fuse into a single cinematic image, a single act", according to Paradjanov. His structure is cyclical, with multiple parallel incidents, liquid camera movement, and development of the narrative via rituals, colours, folk songs and dancing. The result is a film spinning with exoticism and sensuality, but there is a disciplined hand behind all the lyrical extravagance. It is not self-indulgent.

There was no Communist ideology, either. At that time, each film had to be vetted by a commissioned panel of executives from Goskino, the State Film's Big Brother. They were also nettled by a mid- to long shot of a pre-pubescent unclothed Marichka, shot within tree branches, as she ran down to a stream with an equally naked Ivan. Soviet comment was surprisingly puritanical; this, according to the Soviet press, was nothing less than "degradation as a result of western influence". Although distribution was accordingly limited, houses were packed, queues long. But the investigation and harassment programme began; it was to be some years before the West got wind of it.

In 1968 Paradjanov joined Aremenfilm Studios; through them, the following year, he directed his other "best film". *The Colour of Pomegranates* is an icon-made-flesh work, which depicts events (factual or imagined) in the life of Armenian poet Arutiun Sayadin (1712–1795), known as Sayat Nova, the "King of Song", who rose from carpet-weaver's apprentice to court minstrel to archbishop. Like *Shadows*, it was highly coloured by Paradjanov's passion for folk and religious ritual, with a kind of pagan beauty utterly devoid of the officially, even traditionally, approved styles. Weaving in references to Armenian poetry, painting, history and symbolism, everything related to the poet's three professions. The film was shelved, then re-edited (although not by the director), and finally given a limited release in the Soviet Union in 1972, when copies were also smuggled to the United States. It was restored to its proper length after *Shadows* was released to the West.

Paradjanov made his actors' gestures symbolic, emblematic; movements (like many of the theme's concepts) were formalized within a static frame. While many symbols are not easily decipherable (such as the pomegranate juice forming a bloodlike stain in the shape of the Armenian region), the aesthetic impact still overwhelms.

His mature works had drawn much of their power from local roots; however, Moscow did not appreciate the regional film scene. "Ethnic" films, according to the Communist Party opinion, "provoked nationalism and defied authority". Paradjanov's next film, *The Frescoes of Kiev*, was banned and destroyed. It described the annihilation by Soviet authorities of the oldest frescoes in Russia, dating back to the tenth century. There were three cumulative events bringing about this deliberate destruction: the 1918 Revolution, and the vicious anti-religious campaigns of 1934 to 1936 and 1941. His 1972 film *Achraroumès* (*Return to Life*) was shot, but never saw the light of day. Official disapproval climaxed; in autumn 1973, Paradjanov was arrested. Trumped up charges included "spreading venereal disease, illegal currency dealings, incitement to suicide, trafficking in art objects, dealing in anti-Soviet legislation." The trial was closed to the public. In the end, he was sentenced to five years in a hard labour camp, having been convicted solely of homosexuality, still a crime in the USSR. In fact, Paradjanov was bi-sexual. According to Jeanne Vronskaya, "He loved equally men and women but only special ones — with dazzling talents." He was released in late 1977, due to the international outcry, although officials had threatened to extend his sentence by ten years.

Although out of jail, Paradjanov remained "under supervision" in his home in Tbilisi, which meant he was unable to work in film. Scripts were prepared, but always rejected by the authorities. In 1982 he was arrested once more, this time for unspecified crimes, but was able to avoid prison. Between arrests, he filmed a short, *Sign of the Times*, showing himself among his friends, within his family home, and surviving the upheaval.

In 1984/5 he directed *The Legend of the Suram Fortress* which was, thanks to an improved political climate, officially selected for the Moscow Film Festival. It was a sumptuous recreation of a Georgian legend, and a celebration of Georgian culture and history. Like *Colour*, it was divided into chapters, each embodying a religious concept depicted in striking tableaux. The overall experience, while often intellectually mystifying, was typically Paradjanov: unique, sensuous.

In 1988 he completed *Ashik Kerib*, with a nod to Lermontov's tale. It related in tableaux form the adventures of an impoverished wandering minstrel; like many of the director's heroes, something of a symbol for his own position. Filmed in Azerbaijan, it followed a young man's journey to seek his fortune and marry the woman he loves. On the way he plays at weddings for the blind and deaf-and-dumb, is imprisoned by an evil sultan, and rides a flying horse before he finds his loved one. The end has a white dove settling on a black film camera, dedicated to Andrei Tarkovsky, who had recently died of cancer.

Paradjanov had the same kind of cancer — of the lung — and the shooting of *Ashik Kerib* was complicated by his heart attack, after one lung was removed. But the film was completed. He was stubborn in his creative duties, as well as in following his vision — rightfully so, despite a career laced with ill luck, blatant harassment and financial hardship. He managed to sculpt a small body of cinematic work that has been the most singularly beautiful in film history. No one else has blended so effectively a loving respect for traditions with a spiritual vision of the aesthetic, the formal — and the pagan. As critic Ronald Bergan said, "His films are not about how things are, but how they would have been, had he been God."

Born Sarkis Iosifovich Paradjanian. **Marriage** Svetlana (dissolved). **Children** One son, Syrenchik. **Education** Kiev Conservatory of Music, 1942–45; State Institute of Cinematography, Moscow, 1946–51. **Career** Director, Kiev Dovzhenko Studio; reached international audience with *Shadows of Our Forgotten Ancestors*, 1965; ten films written and rejected, 1966–74; joined Aremenfilm Studios, 1968; indicted for several crimes, 1972, convicted of homosexuality, 1974, served hard labour, 1974–77, released after international protest, 1977; returned to Tbilisi; banned from film work; re-arrested, 1982; returned to feature film-making; *The Legend of the Suram Fortress* selected for Moscow Film Festival, 1985. **Awards and honours** *Shadows of Our Forgotten Ancestors* awarded: British Film Academy Award, 1966, Mar del Plata Grand Prize, and 14 others. **Films** *Moldavskaia skazka/Moldavian Fairy Tale* (short), 1951; (co-director) *Andriesh*, 1954; *Natalya Ujvii* (short), 1957; *Golden Hands* (short), 1957; *Pervyi paren/The First Fellow*, 1958/9; *Ukrainskaia rapsodiia/Ukrainian Rhapsody*, 1961; *Tsvetok na kamne/Flower on the Stone*, 1963; *Dumka/The Ballad*, 1964; *Teni zabytykh predkov/Shadows of Our Forgotten Ancestors*, 1965; *Sayat nova/The Colour of Pomegranates*, completed 1969, released 1972; *The Frescoes of Kiev* (destroyed), 1971; *Achraroumès/Return to Life* (short), 1978; *The Legend of the Suram Fortress*, 1985; *Ashik Kerib*, 1989; also: *Sign of the Times* (short) **Cause of death** Cancer, at age 66. **Further reading** *International Dictionary of Films and Filmmakers*, volume two, 1991.

SIR ALAN PARKES

British Physiologist

***Born* Purley, Surrey, 10 September 1900**

***Died* 17 July 1990**

Outspoken, controversial and passionate, Sir Alan Parkes actually achieved that staple of science fiction: suspended animation. The breakthrough came in 1949, when his discovery of glycerol made the long-term survival of frozen living cells possible. This was initially applied to animal spermatozoa, and was a great advance for the field of agriculture, making the artificial insemination of farm animals easy and practical, and was later applied to human sperm, giving rise to the now ubiquitous "sperm banks" that everyone has heard of. But Alan Parkes took it further than test tubes full of microscopic cells; he froze small animals then revived them, seeming to "bring them back to life".

He and his associates managed to cool small rodents such as rats and mice to deep body temperatures 15 degrees centigrade below the level at which the heart beat and respiration are arrested. They kept these animals in this frozen state for periods of up to 90 minutes before reviving them. These revived animals suffered no visible impairment, either physically or psychologically. Parkes was able to demonstrate that they suffered no loss of memory or learning capacity.

Ninety minutes is not a long time, but these findings gave hope to a generation of human cryopreservationists, who hope to be frozen and revived in later centuries, like Woody Allen in the film *Sleeper*. Or perhaps it might be more accurate to say that findings like these gave hope to what many would see as a new style of con-man, offering an essential service: refrigeration for those with hopes of immortaility (and lots of money). The less affluent can opt to just have the head frozen — takes up less freezer space, hence less cost — and by the time they revive you, they should have the means to give you a brand-new body. You pay your money and you take your chance. It is doubtful that Parkes approved of any of this, but he definitely saw it coming. As he stated at the time of his experiments, "Little imagination is required to see where this development could lead."

If suspended animation isn't controversial enough, how about Eugenics — the selective breeding of human beings? Parkes was president of the Eugenics Society, and he spoke of "taking action against low-grade individuals who are irresponsibly indifferent to both the quantity and quality of their offspring."

Parkes was greatly concerned with the problem of over-population, and he believed in attacking the problem from both ends. He advocated both abortion and voluntary euthanasia, arguing on the former that doctors should not "seek refuge behind their conscience" and deny a woman her legal right to abort, and on the latter that it was a gross violation of individual liberty to force a continued existence on anyone whose life had become burdensome to himself or to others.

In some ways he was a mass of contradictions. His pioneering work had made the preservation of sperm, red blood cells, and organs for transplant possible, but he didn't like it, calling it the "squandering of immense resources" on a small minority. He bemoaned the fact that advances in medical science (in which his own contributions had been invaluable) had interfered with the process of natural selection. He also strongly believed that with such massive over-population in the world, it was ridiculous to spend more time and money on curing infertility than on the control of fertility. Yet he was the one who invited Professor Robert Edwards to Cambridge to carry out his research in *in vitro* fertilization.

His career began in the 1920s, and he continued writing, travelling, and editing well after his retirement. He was working on a third biographical book at the time of his death. Possessing a keen sense of humour and a caustic tongue, he managed to delve deeply into his subject without limiting himself to a narrow field of specialization. Genetics, cryopreservation, reproductive physiology, endocrinology and pheromones were among the many subjects researched by Parkes and his colleagues. He liked to say that people should "change their spots like leopards", and he did it a few times himself.

Born Alan Sterling Parkes. **Father** Ebenezer T. Parkes, bank manager. **Marriage** Ruth Deanesly, endocrine histologist, 1933. **Children** Two daughters and one son. **Education** Willaston School; Christ's College, Cambridge, BA, 1921, MA, 1925, ScD, 1931; University of Manchester, PhD, 1923; University College, London, DSc, 1927. **Military service** British Army, 1918. **Career** Honorary lecturer, University College, London, 1929–31; staff member, National Institute for Medical Research, London, 1932–61, Mary Marshall Professor of the Physiology of Reproduction, Cambridge University, 1961–67, professor emeritus, 1968–90; fellow, Christ's College, Cambridge University, 1961–69, honorary fellow, 1970; chairman, Galton Foundation, 1969–85; consultant, Cayman Turtle Farm Limited, Grand Cayman, British West Indies, 1973–80. **Related activities** Foulerton Student, Royal Society, 1930–34; Memorial lectures: Sidney Ringer, University College Hospital, 1934, Ingleby, University of Birmingham, 1940, Galton, Eugenics Society, 1950, Addison, Guy's Hospital, 1957, Darwin, Institute of Biology, Robert J. Terry, Washington University School of Medicine, 1963, Ayerst, American Fertility Society, 1965, Dale, Society for Endocrinology, 1965, Dick, University of Edinburgh, 1969, Cosgrave, American College of Obstetricians and Gynaecologists, 1970, Tracy and Ruth Storer, University of California, Davis, 1973; Biology and Medicine committee member, Royal Commission on Population, 1944–46; secretary, Journals of Reproduction and Fertility Limited, 1960–76;

executive editor, *Journal of Biosocial Science*, 1969–78; consultant, International Planned Parenthood Federation, 1969–79; contributor: *Journal of Physiology*, *Proceedings of the Royal Society*, *Journal of Endocrinology*, *Journal of Reproduction and Fertility*, *Journal of Biosocial Science*. **Offices and memberships** Chairman, Society for Endocrinology, 1944–51; president, Royal Society of Medicine endocrinology section, 1949–50, comparative medicine section, 1962–63; chairman, Society for the Study of Fertility, 1950–52, 1963–66; president, Section D, British Association for the Advancement of Science, 1958; president, Institute of Biology, 1959–61; president, Association of Scientific Workers, 1960–62; breeding policy committee chairman, Zoological Society of London, 1960–67; on scientific advisory committee, British Egg Marketing Board, 1961–70; chairman, Nuffield Unit of Tropical Animal Ecology, 1966–69; Medical Research advisory committee member, World Health Organisation, 1968–71; president, Eugenics Society, 1968–70. **Awards and honours** Sharpey Scholar, University College, London, 1923–24, Beit Memorial Research Fellow, 1924–30, Schafter Prize in Physiology, 1926, Julius Mickle Fellowship, 1927; fellow, Royal Society, 1933; Commander of the Order of the British Empire, 1956; Cameron Prize, 1962; Sir Henry Dale Medal, Society for Endocrinology, 1965; knighted 1968; (with Dr A.U. Smith and Dr C. Polge) John Scott Award, City of Philadelphia, 1969; Marshall Medal, Society for the Study of Fertility, 1970; Oliver Bird Medal, Family Planning Association, 1970; honorary fellow, University College, London. **Publications** *The Internal Secretions of the Ovary*, 1929; (editor) *Marshall's Physiology of Reproduction* (third edition), 1952; *Sex, Science and Society*, 1966; *Patterns of Sexuality and Reproduction*, 1976; *Off-Beat Biologist*, 1985; *Biologist at Large*, 1988. **Cause of death** Undisclosed, at age 89.

MANUEL PUIG

Argentinian Novelist

***Born* General Villegas, Argentina, 28 December 1932**

***Died* Cuernavaca, Mexico, 22 July 1990**

Manuel Puig's novels are most commonly seen as part of the wave of South American "magical realist" writing which enjoyed popularity with fashionable English-speaking readers during the 1970s and 1980s. He has often been discussed alongside such imposing and influential figures as his fellow-Argentinian Jorge Luis Borges, or the Nobel Prize-winning Colombian novelist Gabriel Garcia Marquez. Taken together with yet further writers like Maria Vargas Llosa, Julio Cortazar, and Carlos Fuentes, Puig may be understood as a skilful experimental writer, exploring the technical resources of the novel, and bringing another idiosyncratic yet representative South American voice to new readers. Such an approach may be initially appropriate and useful, but it can seriously obscure Puig's distinctiveness. For unlike many of those other writers, Manuel Puig is essentially a playful and whimsical author, relatively unconcerned with weighty political or aesthetic matters, and, it must be said, his work has been much less influential. His most characteristic technique is the incorporation into his fiction of pastiche forms of popular culture. He is plainly saturated in soap opera, popular song, pulp fiction, and, most markedly, the Hollywood cinema of the 1940s and 1950s. In his best novels, the influence of the great Hollywood studios and their stars far outweighs any more orthodox literary precedents.

Puig was always an avid moviegoer — at least four times a week in his youth — and the cinema seems to have meant more to him than a simple avenue of entertaining escapism. In his own words, "for me literature was a secondary thing ... All my expectation, all my attention, was on movies." Puig always claimed that the films he saw when growing up in his home town of General Villegas in rural Argentina became his necessary and therapeutic substitute for the unattractive reality of small-minded pampas life around him — "That which was reality changed into a class Z movie in which I had been stuck by mistake." Although Puig later went on to study directing and screen-writing in Italy, the attraction the cinema continued to hold for him lay not in its technical dexterity or its capacity for narrative drive, but in its luxuriant glamour and its opulent fantasy. The influence of movies on Puig the writer can be seen much more in his liking for a racy style and glossy surface than in any attempt to imitate the cinema's urgency or verisimilitude.

In his first, and for many readers his best, novel, the narrative carefully imitates the objectivity and unblinking intimacy of the camera, while also incorporating an extended homage to one of the great Hollywood stars. *Le traición de Rita Hayworth* (published in 1968, and later translated as *Betrayed by Rita Hayworth*) describes the lives of a rootless immigrant provincial family through the fantasy world of their small son, Toto. His emotional and imaginative life is lived through reconstruction of the films he has seen at the local cinema, presented in extended interior monologue. By his concentration on the great female stars, Toto finds an alternative to the aggressive manly world he sees more immediately around him, and his fabrication of legends to communicate with his mother is touchingly and intelligently created, if intermittently over-sentimental. By avoiding overt novelistic intrusion, Puig creates fruitful uncertainties of perspective in the novel, leaving readers torn between a satirical condemnation of the imaginative paucity of the characters and a more indulgent celebration of the inspiring qualities of popular culture.

Betrayed by Rita Hayworth brought its author to the public's notice, but Puig's next two novels received more mixed responses. *Boquitas pintadas* (translated as *Heartbreak Tango*) is a sequence of stream-of-consciousness imaginings, introduced by lyrics from popular tangos and boleros, covering the daily lives of citizens of Buenos Aires between the 1940s and the 1960s. They see the world through ideas derived from radio serials, and although each episode is colourful and engaging, and although the figures emerge with some dignity and charm, the book as a whole lacks narrative pace and tension. Similarly, *The Buenos Aires Affair* exploits the form of the detective story and accumulates a whole range of story-telling techniques to enliven the mundane lives of its characters, an art critic and a sculptor. Despite the well-handled array of modernist styles, the book lacks a real sense of engagement, and eventually substitutes style for substance.

After these less successful works, Puig achieved his greatest success with *El beso de la mujer araña* in 1976 (translated as *Kiss of the Spider Woman*). This remarkable novel is set in a prison cell, shared by a revolutionary and a homosexual window-dresser. To pass the time, the window-dresser, Molina, recounts the ridiculous romantic plots of films he has seen. Eventually, a kind of grudging respect grows between the two men, and in the end, the apparently vacuous Molina achieves the most drastic kind of integrity. The claustrophobic setting allows Puig to construct his work almost entirely through dialogue — always his greatest skill — and even if the rather unsettlingly clinical footnotes about homosexuality are disturbing, and the portrayal of the political figure is not wholly convincing, the novel achieves great breadth of vision and wit through its presentation of Molina's fantasies.

With this book, Puig emerged in the forefront of Latin American writing, and the 1985 film version gave his name much wider currency than it had previously enjoyed. Fittingly, given Puig's love for the cinema, the film version gained much from a taut screenplay by Leonard Schrader, and from the sensitive direction by Hector Babenco, but it will always be remembered for its bravura star performance from William Hurt.

After *Kiss of the Spider Woman*, Puig's only extended fiction was *Pubis angelical*, and his other main project was a proposed musical version of his best-known book. Sadly, the play never reached the stage, and Puig died without further publication.

Born Manuel Puig. **Parents** Baldomero, merchant, and Maria Elena (Delledonne) Puig. **Children** Two sons: Javier Labrada and Agustin Garcia Gil. **Education** Facultad de Filosofia; Centro Sperimentale di Cinematografia. **Emigration** Travelled in Europe, 1956–63; worked in New York, 1963–73; moved to Brazil, 1973–80; settled Mexico, 1980–90. **Career** Translator, Spanish/Italian teacher, London, Rome, 1956–57; dishwasher, London, 1958–59, Stockholm, 1958–59; assistant film director, Rome, Paris, Buenos Aires, 1957–60; film subtitle translator, Rome, 1961–62; clerk, Air France, New York, 1963–67; writer, 1967–90; *Kiss of the Spiderwoman* filmed, 1985. **Related activities** Visiting lecturer in creative writing, Columbia University, New York. **Awards and honours** Best script award for *Boquitas pintadas*, 1974; San Sebastian Festival, jury prize for *El luga sin limites*, 1978. **Publications** (include) *La traición de Rita Hayworth*, 1968, published in US as *Betrayed by Rita Hayworth*, 1971; *Boquitas pintadas*, 1969, published in US as *Heartbreak Tango*, 1973; *The Buenos Aires Affair*, 1973; *El beso de la mujer araña*, 1976, published in US as *The Kiss of the Spider Woman*, 1979; *Pubis angelical*, 1979. **Screen adaptations** *Boquitas Pintadas*, 1974; *El lugar sin limites*, 1978. **Cause of death** Complications after gallbladder operation, at age 57.

MITCH SNYDER

American Political Activist

Born **Brooklyn, New York, 1944**

Died **Washington, DC, 5 July 1990**

During the last decade the plight of the homeless has been the focus of campaigns for many a charitable organization, but no voice was louder or more insistent than that of Mitch Snyder. Following in the footsteps of India's Gandhi, Snyder's actions incorporated the use of non-violent action, and fasting.

Born in the Flatbush section of Brooklyn, Snyder faced difficult times from early childhood. His father abandoned his family when he was only nine years old and he turned to petty thievery in his teenage years. For his crimes he spent time in a reform school in upstate New York. Eventually he married and had children, but like his father abandoned his family.

After this separation in 1970, Snyder was arrested for auto theft in Las Vegas. He was sent to federal prison in Danbury, Connecticut. It was here that he met Daniel and Philip Berrigan, the two anti-war priests who were arrested for destroying draft records. Under their influence, Snyder took on a type of radical Catholicism.

Upon his release he focused his attention on a number of causes using various dramatic tactics (later to be dubbed "guerrilla theatre") to attract the attention of both politicians and the media. On one occasion he fasted for eleven days in order to try and force the United States Navy to change the name of a submarine from Corpus Christi to City of Corpus Christi. The reason, he claimed, was because no arms-bearing vessel should take the name of the son of God. Surprisingly the Navy gave in.

The submarine incident was to be the first of many attention-getting and anger-causing incidents staged by Snyder. He seemed to have the knack of impeccable timing and the ability to drive officials to distraction. He, by now, had moved to Washington DC and joined the Community for Creative Non-Violence, an organization founded by followers of Dorothy Day, the Catholic socialist of the 1930s. It was on behalf of this organization that most of Snyder's protests were staged.

Once in Washington, Snyder carried a wooden coffin up the main staircase of the city council and threw blood over the walls. He was protesting against the lack of programmes for the homeless. "You have to make people angry to make people think", he claimed.

His most famous protest came about in 1984 during the presidential elections. Snyder fasted for 51 days, a few days over the maximum for average bodies, in order to wrest from President Reagan shelter for the city's homeless. Two days before the election, Reagan gave in, handing to the Community for Creative Non-Violence a derelict federal building and six million dollars with which to rehabilitate it. But Snyder's energetic campaigning did not stop there. He continued to push and goad people into action, constantly keeping the plight of the homeless in view.

A television movie was made about his life entitled, *Samaritan: The Mitch Snyder Story*. The movie not only brought in royalty money which Snyder donated to his organization, but it brought the support of the rich and famous to his cause. He was able to stage an event with several Hollywood celebrities in which they spent a night sleeping in the streets in protest against federal policies towards the homeless.

The late 1980s brought a series of serious defeats for Snyder. The Internal Revenue Service began to investigate his personal taxes, auditing the royalties he was paid for the TV movie. His disdain for the IRS had gone on for years. He refused to make the Community for Creative Non-Violence a tax-exempt organization because it would limit his engagement in political activity, and political protest was the mainstay of Snyder's diet.

It was also a time of great indifference. People were becoming accustomed to seeing the homeless on the streets, and all the anger and protest that Snyder could muster was not making any difference. Eleven days before his death he failed to stop the Washington DC city council from slashing spending on the destitute. "We're ready to take a deep breath and let it go," Snyder said, "start pounding away at that wall head first and see what's hardest, our head or their wall."

It would seem as though "their wall" might have held through the onslaught, for he was found dead, apparently a suicide, in a room at the shelter he fought so hard to obtain. He left a note attributing his death to a failure in his love affair with Carol Fennelly, his companion for the last 15 years. His friends seem to think it was due to the strain he had been under for some years. The more cynical claim he was suffering from a disease associated with the "upwardly mobile" — burnout. His tireless campaign had lasted for 17 years.

Born Mitchell Darryl Snyder. **Father** Robert Snyder. **Marriage** Ellen Kleiman, 1963. **Children** Ricky and Dean. **Education** Reform school **Career** Salesman for household appliances; job counsellor; construction worker; arrested for auto theft, Las Vegas, and imprisoned, 1970; conducted first hunger strike, against treatment of prisoners in Vietnam, in prison; joined Community for Creative Non-Violence, 1973; lived in plastic box, on street, to dramatize homelessness, 1974; fasted to force US Navy to change name of submarine Corpus Christi to City of Corpus Christi, fasted for 51 days to force President Reagan to fund shelter for the homeless, 1984; life dramatized in *Samaritan: The Mitch Snyder Story*, CBS-TV, 1986; continued fight for homeless in face of declining public support, 1986–90; audited by Internal Revenue Service, 1990. **Cause of death** Apparent suicide by hanging, at age 46.

ARTHUR STEWART-LIBERTY

British Businessman

***Born* 11 January 1916**

***Died* 11 July 1990**

To Londoners, Liberty's seems less a shop than an institution. Many Liberty-print fabrics are instantly recognizable. The Tudor-ish building in Great Marlborough Street (adjoining a less remarkable sibling on Regent Street) stands as a bastion of tradition against the tide of ephemera from nearby Carnaby Street. It represents luxury, but approachable luxury, its 1920s half-timbered building an unintentional but friendly echo of countless suburban housing estates. Liberty's status as national treasure was underlined by a centenery exhibition held in its honour by the Victoria and Albert museum in 1975.

Despite appearances, it is in fact a department store, not a national monument, and as such has to run at a profit. Keeping up with changing tastes and economic conditions while maintaining a shop's individual character poses a challenge which has defeated several of Liberty's equally well-established neighbours. That Liberty's is on course for celebrating its one hundred and twenty-fifth anniversary with its identity intact is much to the credit of Arthur Stewart-Liberty, or "Mr Arthur" as his staff called him, following the somewhat Dickensian tradition of British family firms.

The great-nephew of John Lasenby Liberty, the merchant who had founded the shop back in 1875, "Mr Arthur" was educated at Winchester College and Oxford University, where he graduated in history and forestry. It was a conventional rich man's education, but somewhere along the line he acquired the seeds of a sharp design sense and considerable business acumen. Perhaps they were in his blood; they must have grown rapidly during the few years when, after serving in World War II with the Bucks Yeomanry, he worked his way round the departments of the family firm to gain an insight into its running. On his father's death in 1952 "Mr Arthur" was ready to step into the job of chairman, a position he would hold for nearly 30 years.

The post-war years saw the sleeker styles of Scandinavia and Italy challenging English flounces and flowers. Stewart-Liberty had to reconcile the slightly Olde Englishe image which was Liberty's stock-in-trade with these newer influences.

There was no reason why Liberty's should not play an active part in disseminating the newer looks. After all, the Liberty's empire had been founded on imported oriental textiles and artefacts, both satisfying and further stimulating a public appetite for exotica aroused by the 1862 International Exhibition at Kensington, London. In the same way, Stewart-Liberty began to respond to the latest trends by importing and retailing Scandinavian furniture, and Liberty's did its bit in popularizing this fashion.

Faithful to its origins, Liberty's offers to this day an Aladdin's cave of carpets, ceramics and decorative arts from the Far East. By the 1950s, though, it was a long time since these had been the company's only, or even its primary, *raison d'être*. Soon after its foundation, Liberty's had been unable to import enough fine fabrics from the East to satisfy demand, and had begun to create its own textiles for both furnishing and clothes, to such effect that in the public mind "Liberty's" had long been synonymous with these "Liberty prints".

Now, fabric was Stewart-Liberty's special interest and he applied himself to rejuvenating the ranges, while respecting the timeless lines, such as flowered Tana lawns and Paisley prints, which were beloved of the American visitors flocking to London during the 1950s.

There was a business reorganization: he set up Liberty of London Prints, a company in its own right, to sell the fabrics wholesale, giving some autonomy to the branch of the operation with perhaps the greatest growth potential. There was also the establishment of a design committee. Convening regularly, this had a dual brief: on the one hand it was to commission new designs from the best talents of the day, and on the other hand it was to scour the archives for old designs which might be revived.

From the archives came, most notably, the 1960 Art Nouveau "Lotus" range, named after an early trade-mark of the company. There was already a resurgence of interest in Art Nouveau. The Lotus fabrics were launched at an event in the crush bar of the Royal Opera House Covent Garden, where they were displayed by some of the best-known models of the day. Much column-space was devoted to the launch, helping to secure Liberty's place on the fashion map. A 1920s collection the next year drew on Bakst's designs for Diaghilev's Ballets Russes.

For Stewart-Liberty, however, commissioning contemporary designers was at least as absorbing as reviving and adapting history. He often encouraged his committee to stick its neck out in making design decisions, and was himself adept at talent-spotting. Many a distinguished designer has acknowledged a debt to Liberty's, among them Jean Muir, who once said that Liberty's had been her "art school" in the 1950s. But there was selectivity as well as open-mindedness: Liberty's stood out against the youth cult of the 1960s, preferring to stick to classics rather than seize on passing trends.

Under Stewart-Liberty, this quintessentially English company began to put out shoots, licensing other retailers or opening outlets as joint ventures, until Liberty products were available in continental Europe, North America and the Far East. The latter, from having supplied Liberty's merchandise in the early days, now became one of its best customers. Stewart-Liberty also superintended the opening of branches throughout the British Isles, always with an eye to maintaining a consistent corporate image. His achievement in overseeing these expansionary activities was the more remarkable, coming as it did at a time when he had been confined to a wheelchair.

A fall while fox-hunting in 1964 had permanently paralysed him in both legs. But there were few things which intimidated the man who had won the Military Cross for bravery under Japanese attack during World War II. One night during the 1950s he had surprised a burglar about to avail himself of Mrs Stewart-Liberty's jewellery, and, armed only with a shillelagh, had briskly seen the intruder off the premises. Now the same courage brought him through his illness with a speed which surprised his friends and doctors.

The accident put paid to the sporting activities he loved — not only hunting but also golf, tennis and walking. Perhaps it was to compensate for these losses that Stewart-Liberty seemed to redouble his efforts on behalf of the company. He made a point of visiting its outposts, particularly those in the USA, and continued to act as chairman until his retirement in 1981.

Retirement allowed him to devote most of his considerable energies to running his Buckinghamshire estate, where he specialized in breeding cattle and growing cereals. But he continued to play an active part on the Liberty's board up until his death. Stewart-Liberty's two sons now continue to wield the family influence in the family firm, Mr Richard as merchandising director and Mr Oliver as managing director of Liberty of London Prints.

Born Arthur Ivor Stewart-Liberty. **Marriages** 1) Rosabel Fynn, 1941 (dissolved); 2) Liz Stuart, 1955. **Children** Richard, Oliver and one daughter, from first marriage; one daughter, from second marriage. **Education** Winchester College, Hampshire; Christ Church, Oxford. **Military service** Buckinghamshire Yeomanry, 1939–45, posted to India, 1943–45. **Career** Joined Liberty, 1945, chairman, 1952–81; instituted revival of classic Liberty's fabrics, from 1960; paralysed in a hunting accident, 1964; retired (but stayed on board) 1981. **Awards and honours** Military Cross, 1944. **Cause of death** Undisclosed, at age 74.

JOE TURNER

American Jazz Pianist

***Born* Baltimore, Maryland, 3 November 1907**

***Died* Paris, France, 21 July 1990**

When Fats Waller was asked in 1932 by Hugues Panassié, the French jazz critic, which pianists were his favourites, he replied James P. Johnson and Joe Turner. Perhaps later he might have added Art Tatum to this list, but it demonstrates the high esteem with which Joe Turner was regarded by his fellow stride pianists.

Stride piano is the New York-based derivative of ragtime current from the end of World War I, and pioneered by Johnson, Luckey Roberts, Willie "the Lion" Smith and Waller. The style is based on a strong left-hand technique that developed from the simple "oompah" alternation of bass note and chord common in ragtime, to a highly sophisticated series of patterns involving suspended beats ("turning the beat around" as it was called) and the superimposition of countermelodies played by the left thumb striking the keys momentarily in advance of the bass notes at intervals of a tenth or more (so-called "backward tenths"). The right hand, in addition to carrying the melody of most tunes, is required to perform a series of setpiece patterns of great intricacy and detail, which are strung together in formulaic series. Stride piano playing fuses improvisation with composition in a most intriguing manner.

Almost all the great pianists worked out their own setpieces, which were considered a challenge to other players in the "cutting contests" and rent parties of 1920s Harlem. These pieces were performed intact, with the minimum of individual improvisation. Typical among them were Waller's "Handful of Keys," Johnson's "Carolina Shout," Smith's "Echoes of Spring". Joe Turner contributed "The Shout" (co-composed with Kirby Walker) and his own breathtaking arrangement of Gershwin's "Liza" to this canon — the latter immortalized in the recording by Art Tatum.

Equally important to the style, however, was the ability to improvise on almost any tune, inserting the characteristic motifs or clichés of stride, and doing so in a manner where the more audacious the sequence of phrases, the better. In addition to assimilating this style perfectly in the years after he arrived during the winter of 1924/5 in New York with a few dollars and a cardboard suitcase, Turner made two contributions to jazz history that mark him out as unique. Firstly, he was no jealous guardian of his own skills. He worked hard to communicate his technique to others. By his own account, he helped such other pianists as Teddy Wilson and Marlowe Morris develop their left hand styles, and both men were keen to acknowledge his support. "I always had much admiration for the great stride pianists I heard when I came to New York ... and it was Joe Turner who gave me the best pointers to get familiar with that style" (Wilson). "I've never denied that my left hand stems right from Joe Turner" (Morris).

Secondly, however, Turner had an uncanny ability to apply critical judgement to the playing of others. He would talk knowledgeably about stride pianists who were not, perhaps, in the first rank: Seminole, Abba Labba, "Beetle" Henderson, Clarence Profit and Donald Lambert. In a remarkable interview in 1953 with the Swiss researcher Johnny Simmen (whom Turner had known since 1939) Turner recounted his views on "The Pianists in My Life". Working from a list of almost 100 musicians, Turner gave thumbnail critical accounts of a large number of them showing an astute critical judgement often present but seldom so well expressed in a world-class pianist.

If Turner is relatively obscure in terms of American jazz history, it is because he chose to spend the majority of his career in Europe. In the US, he made relatively few records: a handful with Louis Armstrong in 1930 (on which he doesn't solo) and a number of exciting (if ragged) 1935 jam sessions with musicians drawn from Adrian's Tap Room — the bar beneath New York's President Hotel, run by multi-instrumentalist Adrian Rollini. For some years, it was thought that Turner was not present on all these sides (some issued under Freddie Jenkins's name, some under Bernard Addison's), but Johnny Simmen scotches that theory in his impressive profile of Turner written for *Storyville* magazine in 1986. Aural evidence is enough to prove Turner's presence — his strong stride style contributing to Addison's "Toledo Shuffle" amongst other tracks.

By 1936, Turner was in Paris, where he recorded a couple of piano solos and also travelled to Prague to make some undistinguished records with Joe Sima. It was his second trip to Europe, Turner having crossed the Atlantic first in 1931 as accompanist to singer Adelaide Hall. His 1936 solos include a track named after his European wife, Lonci. World War II led to an enforced separation for Turner and his family. He returned to the US, leaving his Hungarian-born wife and daughter behind. He enlisted in a service band, playing under Sy Oliver at Camp Kilmer, New Jersey. After the war, Turner returned to Hungary to retrieve his family, and settled in Switzerland as he negotiated their release from the East after what had, by 1949, become a ten-year separation. Successfully reunited with his family, Turner stayed in Switzerland until 1962, when he moved to Paris, opening at the Club Calvados, which, by and large, was the setting for the rest of his life's work. He travelled from time to time, and recorded occasionally — less frequently, certainly, than a man of his talents should have, or would have had he been in the USA where he would have been virtually the sole survivor of the Harlem "stride" school. Instead, Turner was content to spend night after night at the keyboard, entertaining patrons with his own individual blend of vocals and virtuoso piano playing, becoming, in the process, something of a Parisian institution. His own thoughts about the place, quoted often in interviews, werc to come true: "I'm not refused any place. I like the freedom. In fact, I think this is where I'm gonna die."

Born Joseph H. Turner. **Father** Furniture mover. **Marriage** Lonci. **Children** One daughter, Rita. **Emigration** First travelled in Europe, 1931–39; returned 1945, settled permanently in France, 1962. **Military service** Sy Oliver's Army Band, Camp Kilmer, New Jersey, US Army, 1944–45. **Career** Learned piano from mother, 1912; moved to New York, 1925; played Baron Wilkin's Club, Harlem; played with: June Clark, 1927–28, Benny Carter, 1929, Louis Armstrong, 1930; accompanist for Adelaide Hall, toured (with Frances Carter), 1931; earliest recording, Oriole Records, 1931; toured as soloist, Europe, 1931–39, US, 1939–44; tap-dancer, from 1936; first solo recording, Sima Records, 1936; played with Rex Stewart; returned to Europe, 1948; toured Hungary, 1948, Switzerland, 1949–62; played at La Calvados, Paris, from 1962; appeared Newport Jazz Festival, 1973. **Recordings** (include) "Lonci", 1939; *Stridin' in Paris*, Vogue 947, 1952; *Joe's Back in Town*, BB 33064, 1974; *Another Epoch: Stride Piano*, Pablo 2310763, 1975–76; (with P. Francis) *Effervescent*, BB 33102, 1976; **Cause of death** Undisclosed, at age 82.

JOHNNY WAYNE

Canadian Comedian

***Born* Toronto, Canada, 28 May 1918**

***Died* Toronto, Canada, 11 July 1990**

As one half of the famous comedy duo, Wayne and Shuster, Johnny Wayne was an uncrowned king of Canadian comedy. Many well-known American comedians and comic actors are actually from

Canada: Dan Ackroyd, Martin Short, John Candy and Rick Moranis are just a few examples. The comedy clubs and theatres of Toronto are bursting with aspiring talent, and as soon as these talented performers get any recognition, they get snapped up south of the border. Johnny Wayne and his partner, Frank Shuster, were no exception. From the 1950s onwards, the American entertainment industry wooed them with irresistable offers (they were even offered complete control of their US programming) — all they had to do was move south — but they resisted. Toronto was their home, and they weren't going to leave it.

The two met at Toronto's Harbord Collegiate, where they both wrote and performed in an annual revue. They then went on to the University of Toronto, where they continued their partnership. Canadian songwriter Ruth Lowe saw them while they were still students and recommended them to a talent agency. They started performing on radio, first in a fundraising show for the Boy Scouts, and then on their own series *Wife Preservers*, a programme of humorous household hints.

World War II caused a temporary interruption to their careers. They both enlisted in the Canadian Army. However, they were re-united when impresario Jack Arthur arranged for both of them to be transferred to Montreal so they could headline the weekly *Canadian Army Radio Show*.

They were a hit, and they were sent on tour, first throughout Canada, and then to Britain, France, Belgium and Holland. They were in the first group to entertain the troops in Normandy after D-Day. Johnny Wayne once jokingly described these travelling shows as a "toughening-up process" for the soldiers. "If they could survive us, they could survive anything."

After the war, they were given a regular show on CBC (Canadian Broadcasting Company) radio, with a live audience. The live audience was an essential element of the programme; Wayne and Shuster threatened to quit if they were forced to play to canned laughter.

They began appearing on American television in the early 1950s, eventually racking up a record 67 guest appearances on *The Ed Sullivan Show*. Their humour, described as "an amiable mixture of slapstick, pantomime, visual tricks, sheer corn and sometimes ingenious twists on classic situations", was enduringly popular, despite occasional sniping from the critics, who are notorious for sneering at anything unashamedly corny. But Wayne and Shuster were lively and zany, with a repertoire of ridiculous characters like the Brown Pumpernickel, Professor Waynegartner and Tex Rorschach, and from 1954 onwards, they had their own show on Canadian TV, so who cared what the critics thought anyway?

Leonard Starmer, executive producer of the Wayne and Shuster CBC-TV show since 1970, and who is working on a new show about the first 50 years of the duo's partnership, said that to know Johnny Wayne "was to be challenged by his sense of humour and his general being."

Born John Louis Wayne. **Father** Clothing manufacturer. **Marriage** Bea (died 1982). **Children** Three sons. **Education** Harbord Collegiate School, Toronto; University of Toronto, BA in English. **Military service** Canadian Army. **Career** Began working with Frank Shuster while at Harbord Collegiate School, wrote, sang and acted in annual revue; developed *Wife Preservers* radio programme; entertained troops: Canada, Britain, France, Belgium and Holland, World War II; first regular CBC radio programme, 1947; first appearance, US television, 1950; initiated CBC-TV programme, 1954; 67 appearances, *Ed Sullivan Show*, CBS-TV. **Television** (includes) *Wayne and Shuster* programme, CBC; *Ed Sullivan Show*, CBS-TV. **Radio** (includes) *Wife Preservers; Canadian Army Radio Show; Wayne and Shuster* radio show. **Cause of death** Cancer, at age 72.

BERNARD WEX

British Engineer

***Born* 24 April 1922**

***Died* 31 July 1990**

The Humber Bridge, which connects Hull and Grimsby in eastern England, is the longest, single span suspension bridge in the world. It was built as a political sop, for in 1966 the Labour government were in a position where they had to win the by-election at Hull to retain power, and the surprise announcement that the government would build the bridge was made at a by-election meeting. The government was committed, and the bridge which could never pay its way — by 1989 its accumulated debt was 350,000,000 pounds — was constructed.

Regardless of its political beginnings and its financial losses, the bridge itself is a masterpiece. Its single span of 4625 feet is longer than the Golden Gate Bridge in San Francisco by 426 feet, and the whole is a structure of great beauty and a triumph of engineering. It stands as the finest memorial to Bernard Wex, its designer and engineer-in-chief.

Wex did not intend to be an engineer when young. Leaving school in 1940 when the war was going badly for Britain, his ambition was to be a pilot, and it was a great disappointment to him when he was refused for the RAF because of a minor eye defect. He had to join the Army instead, but planes, flying and aeronautical history remained absorbing interests throughout his life.

He was demobilized in 1947, having been a tank commander, and went to Imperial College in London University to study civil engineering. In 1950 he graduated top of the class list, with first-class honours and the Unwin Medal.

The consultant engineers Freeman, Fox and Partners recruited him at once, and he joined a team working under Gilbert Roberts and Oleg Kerensky, two experts in the design of steel structures, with international reputations. With them he helped design bridges in India, Africa and New Zealand, as well as the Severn and Forth suspension bridges in Britain.

By 1960 he was himself responsible for some large design projects, usually bridges but also power stations. Some of the bridges were for transporting oil and gas, with the pipes also acting as structural parts of the bridge. In Britain his success with a twin steel box structure, carrying the M5 motorway high across the River Avon near Bristol, led to his being made a partner of the firm.

Following this he completed several other projects, and when the Humber suspension bridge had been promised by the Labour government, Wex was chosen to design it and be responsible for the building.

Suspension bridges provide one of the oldest ways of crossing a gap. Primitive peoples have constructed them for centuries, using vines to suspend them from until the fourth century AD when cables of plaited bamboo were introduced in India making them much stronger. In modern times the cables have been spun from steel wires. The cables hang symmetrically from high towers to give them their strength.

The River Humber site provided a complication, as the railway on the north side meant the approach span had to be shortened, thus spoiling the symmetry. The tension in the cables, each spun with 15,000 wires of 5 milimetres (0.2 inches) diameter, is about 19,000 tonnes, or nearly 21,000 US tons. Because of this asymmetry the construction was complicated, and forces could easily have developed bending the towers sideways.

The practical complications were only part of the difficulties with which Wex had to contend. The bridge was built during a time of labour unrest, as well as spiralling inflation caused partly by the oil crises. The utmost diplomacy and patience was required to keep the contractors and the clients satisfied, but Wex kept his calm confidence and sense of humour throughout. When the bridge was completed he was awarded an OBE for his services.

In building bridges Wex's unusual combination of theoretical and practical ability was fully used. He introduced advanced analytical methods into structural design, but he never allowed his theoretical leanings to take precedence over his engineering experience and common sense. As anyone concerned with design must, he had a strong aesthetic sense, and his structures are things of considerable grace and beauty as well as functional objects. He was a first-class speaker, and could deliver opinions and make polished speeches impromptu. All these attributes made him an outstanding founding chairman of the Steel Construction Institute, and he also served on many other technical committees.

In company, his remarkable sense of humour and ability to tell amusing stories were helped by a great ability to mimic accents and dialects. He was a keen swimmer, and swam outdoors daily summer and winter unless there was ice on the pool. In his private hobbies he also combined his artistic, theoretical and practical abilities, for he was a very good amateur photographer, and his keenness always made his site visits unusually long, for he frequently made his team wait while he climbed to the top of the nearest structure to take photographs. Lastly he was a very skilled maker of beautiful furniture.

Born Bernard Wex. **Marriage** Sheila (Thompson) Lambert, 1945. **Children** Two sons. **Education** Acton Grammar School, London; Imperial College, University of London, first-class honours in civil engineering, BA, 1950. **Military service** Volunteer for Royal Air Force, 1940; transferred to Royal Armoured Corps, commissioned tank commander, 23rd Hussars, 1940–47. **Career** Associate, Freeman Fox and Partners, 1950–69, partner, 1969–87, supervised construction/design of: Avonmouth Bridge, 1969, Foyle Bridge, Auckland Harbour Bridge, Volta River Bridge, Myton Bridge, Humber Suspension Bridge, 1981. **Related activities** Chairman, Moor television mast committee of inquiry, 1969–76. **Offices and memberships** Member, International Association for Bridge and Structural Engineering, chairman, British division; founding chairman, Steel Construction Institute, 1986–90. **Awards and honours** Unwin Medal, Imperial College, University of London, 1950; Officer of the Order of the British Empire, 1982; City and Guilds Institute fellowship, 1982; Telford medal, Institution of Civil Engineers, 1985. **Cause of death** Undisclosed, at age 68.

YUN PO-SUN

South Korean Former President

***Born* 15 July 1899**

***Died* Seoul, South Korea, 18 July 1990**

Perhaps it was his time as a student of archaeology at Edinburgh University in the late 1920s/early 1930s which inspired in Yun Po-Sun, the briefly elected president of the Second Republic of South Korea from 1960 to 1962, his love of democratic freedom. His long career was to be a constant witness to his belief in the democratic process, which had so short a flowering but which he was to defend in so stalwart a fashion.

Born into a wealthy landowning family, which had distant connections with the last Korean monarch, Queen Yun, Yun Po-Sun's public spiritedness led him, after his student days, to become a member of the Consultative Assembly of the Provisional Government in exile in Shanghai against Japanese control of his country. But the irresponsible feuding of the exiles disillusioned him with politics and led to a period first as a post-graduate student in Scotland and then as a manager in his family's business affairs. It was only with the end of Japanese rule in 1945 that he returned to politics, this time as a protégé of the nationalist strong man, Syngman Rhee, who appointed him mayor of Seoul in 1948 and minister of commerce and industry the following year.

It did not take long, however, for Yun to become increasingly critical of Rhee's strong-arm, and frequently corrupt, style of government, and by the mid-1950s he became one of the founders of the Democratic party, whose chief objective was to counter the Rhee regime. The moment came with the student demonstrations of 1960, which forced Rhee to resign. Yun was swept to office as president of the Second Republic, only to find his every move stymied by the internecine rivalries of his party which imposed on him an inefficient prime minister, not of his choosing. Within less than a year an army *coup d'état* presented him with a new government led by Major-General Park Chung-Hee. Yun was persuaded to stay on as president but the ruthless purges of the Park military government inevitably led to his resignation in March 1962.

With the resumption of political activity a year later, Yun stood again in the presidential election, losing only narrowly to Park. There still seemed a chance of better things, but Yun's opposition to the 1965 treaty with Japan led to his splitting from his own party to form the New Korean party. Once again in May 1967 he stood as presidential candidate of a now united New Democratic party, this time to be defeated more trenchantly by Park. From then on his active political career came to an end, though he was to continue as an adviser of the New Democratic party and an outspoken critic of Park's increasingly repressive regime. This inevitably brought a number of charges against him of attempting to overthrow the Park government, and he was twice brought before a military tribunal and sentenced to periods of imprisonment, in each case suspended. Park's assassination in October 1979 seemed to offer new hope, and despite his age Yun began campaigning again for a return to civilian rule. But to no avail; again he was to be put on trial by the new regime and effectively silenced.

South Korea's remarkable economic achievements since the war of the early 1950s have been won at the price of repressive regimes which have crushed all attempts at political reform. And none has paid that price more heavily than Yun Po-Sun. A man of firm Presbyterian principles and staunch devotion to what he believed to be right for his country, he was fated to have his one chance to put those beliefs into practice condemned to be sandwiched between prolonged periods of corrupt repressive government. As hopes began to burgeon again in the late 1980s, it was too late. Yun Po-Sun had retired from active politics to devote his last years to more rewarding religious and cultural interests.

Born Yun Po-Sun. **Children** Two sons. **Education** Studied political economy, public law and archaeology, Edinburgh University, MA, 1930. **Career** Member, Consultative Assembly, Provisional Korean Government in exile, Shanghai; Family business, 1932–45; mayor of Seoul, 1948; minister of commerce and industry, 1949; elected National Assembly, 1954; founder, Democratic party, 1955; elected president, Second Republic, 1960–62; resigned in protest after military coup, 1962; ran for president, but narrowly defeated, 1962; split Democratic party to form New Korean party, 1965, recombined to form New Democratic party, 1967, adviser from 1967; charged with financing student opposition groups, 1974, given five-year suspended sentence; tried for responsibility for unauthorized mass rally for reform, 1979, given two years suspended sentence; retired from politics. **Cause of death** Diabetes, at age 91.

AUGUST

PEARL BAILEY

American Entertainer

***Born* Newport News, Virginia, 29 March 1918**

***Died* Philadelphia, Pennsylvania, 17 August 1990**

"I'm more of a philosopher than a jazz singer", Pearl Bailey told a *New York Times* interviewer shortly before her death. This was not a new sentiment on her part; *Time* printed something similar in 1978, saying that Miss Bailey described herself as "more of a philosopher than an entertainer". According to those who knew her, her "philosophy" could be boiled down to just one word: love. Cab Calloway, her co-star in the hit all-black Broadway production of *Hello, Dolly!* has said of her, "Pearl was love. Pure and simple love." Her husband of 38 years, jazz drummer Louis Bellson called her, "a person of love. She believed 'show business' was 'show love'."

"Show love" as a description of the highly competitive, cut-throat world of "show-biz" seems so romantic and rose-tinted a view as to be ridiculous. But in the case of Pearl Bailey, it's a pretty accurate assessment of her career. Of course, she was unique. There is no other actress of whom a critic would write, "The audience would have elected her governor if she'd only name the state." There is no other performer who would make a comment like, "If audiences take away a part of me each night, they're welcome", and mean it. What other actress could be nominated by a president (Richard Nixon) as "The US Ambassador of Love to the World" and actually be taken seriously in the role? Who else, on noticing the then-president, Lyndon Johnson, in the audience, would refer to him as "this child" and bring him up on stage to sing a chorus with her? How many American jazz singers have been awarded Jordan's Hussein Ben-Ali Freedom Medal? How many comediennes have received the First Order of Arts and Science of Egypt? How many dancers have a degree in theology? How many special representatives to the American delegation to the United Nations work in cabaret? As Cab Calloway said, "Pearl Bailey was something you'll never see again."

She was born in Newport News, Virginia, also the birthplace of another great singer, Ella Fitzgerald, who'd been born one month earlier. Bailey's father was an evangelical minister, of whom she said, "From him I got the wisdom, the philosophizing, the soul." She credited her mother as the source of her acting ability. "Mama, she could say more with a flick of a wrist... than any words." Young Pearl began singing and dancing at the age of three, in her father's church.

Her parents divorced while she was still a child. Her mother took her to Washington, DC, and eventually to Philadelphia. Bailey's ambition was to be a schoolteacher, but that came to an abrupt end when she won a talent contest at the age of 15. She left school and became an entertainer. She did a few stints as a chorus-girl and speciality dancer, and then she entered the rough-and-tumble world of Pennsylvania's coal-mining towns, singing and dancing in cafes for 15 dollars a week, plus tips. From that, she moved on to singing with big bands, such as Count Basie and Cootie Williams. She also worked with Cab Calloway and toured with the USO (United Service Organizations) during the war. She developed her line of playful patter while working as a solo artist in New York night-clubs. She got her first job in cabaret at the Village Vanguard. From there, she went to the prestigious Blue Angel Club, originally filling in for singer Helen Humes, who asked Pearl to take her place while she went home on a visit. It turned out to be her big break. As Helen Humes said later, "She moved in and took over, and from that moment she never looked back."

She made her Broadway début in 1946, in the Johnny Mercer – Harold Arlen all black-musical, *St Louis Woman*. On 1 April 1946, Harold Barnes wrote in the *New York Herald Tribune* that "Pearl Bailey pulls the show up by its shoestrings every time she makes an entrance." She won the 1946 Donaldson Award as the best newcomer on Broadway.

She made her film début in 1947, in a Paramount showcase called *Variety Girl*. She appeared in another Paramount film, *Isn't It Romantic?*, and then returned to Broadway. In 1952, she went to London and married the white jazz drummer, Louis Bellson, at Caxton Hall. He celebrated the event by writing and recording the song, "Caxton Hall Swing". Bellson would be her husband and her musical director for 38 years — and he was with her when she died.

One of her most memorable Broadway performances was in the Truman Capote – Harold Arlen musical *House of Flowers*. Her portrayal of Madame Fleur, the madame of a West Indian bordello, was praised by the *New York Herald Tribune*'s Walter Kerr as "easily raffish, demonically secure, justifiably confident." In the same year, 1954, she came to national attention in *Carmen Jones*, the Otto Preminger-directed screen version of Oscar Hammerstein's up-dated, Americanized, all-black version of Bizet's opera, *Carmen*. In this version, the bull-fighter is instead a champion boxer. Dorothy Dandridge played Carmen, and Pearl Bailey played Frankie, a flashy woman living the high-life as a member of the champ's entourage. A reviewer for *Time* magazine noted how "superbly" Bailey lolled around in feather boas, "dragging her weight in rhinestones". Another notable film was *Porgy and Bess*, in 1959, again directed by Otto Preminger, with her co-star from *Carmen Jones*, Dorothy Dandridge, again in the female lead (Bailey played Maria).

She mostly devoted herself to night-club engagements throughout the early 1960s. It was during that period that she first began to have heart trouble, which she referred to as "heart strain". She admitted in an interview back in 1965, "Singing does bring out the soreness." She continued working despite her health problems, and her greatest triumph was yet to come.

The all-black version of the hit musical *Hello, Dolly!* opened at New York's St James Theatre on 12 November 1967, starring Pearl Bailey and her old friend, Cab Calloway. The critics were unanimous in their unreserved praise. According to *Newsweek*, "Dolly is the highest office to which the American woman can aspire, and Miss Bailey has been elected to it by acclamation." Clive Barnes wrote in *The New York Times*, "For Miss Bailey this was a Broadway triumph for the history books... She took the whole musical in her hands and swung it around her neck as easily as if it were a feather boa. Her timing was exquisite, with asides tossed away as languidly as one might tap ash from a cigarette". (This is the review that went on to suggest that the audience would have elected her governor.)

For Bailey, it was a dream come true. "All this has been worth waiting for. At last I can sing, dance, say intelligent words on stage, love and be loved and deliver what God gave me", she told an interviewer for *Newsweek*, adding with her typical humour, "...and I'm dressed up besides." She said she wanted to take *Dolly* around the world, because, "It could bring such joy." Though the Broadway production closed after two years because of her ill-health, she did eventually tour with the show, and she toured again with a revival in 1975.

Meanwhile, she went back to playing cabaret, and was a big hit at London's Talk of the Town, where she won over the English audiences with her throw-away style of singing, husky patter, and feigned amnesia whenever she came to a bit of *double entendre*, playing it up for all it was worth. She was often dismissive about her brand of performance, "I have no style. I just sing songs." Songs like "Bill Bailey, Won't You Please Come Home" delivered in a throaty growl, liberally peppered with mumbled asides. No style, indeed.

She joked to her London audiences that she was too old to move, and then she would do a bit of old-style hoofing. The jokes never stopped, even when the situation was serious. Compared to Britain, the cost of medical treatment in America is very high, and she explained to an English reporter that at one stage she had to inhale oxygen and, "They wanted about five dollars a sniff for that stuff. Believe me honey, for two weeks I didn't breathe."

She referred to herself as "Pearlie Mae", and everyone, absolutely *everyone* else was "honey". And in 1975, Gerald Ford appointed Pearlie Mae to the UN, honey. She travelled extensively throughout Africa and the Middle East, visiting the Gulf as recently as 1988.

In 1978, although she had been made a special representative to the United Nations and written six books without even having a high-school diploma, she decided to go back to school. So, at the age of 59, she enrolled as a student at Georgetown University, and like any other student was duly awarded a book of coupons entitling her to free hamburgers. She graduated in 1985 with a Bachelor's degree in theology.

She kept working right up to the end. She died shortly before she was scheduled to deliver an address at the UN. More than 2000 people filled the Deliverance Evangelistic Church in North Philadelphia for her funeral, while scores more stood outside. At a private memorial service two days earlier, hundreds of people had queued outside in the rain to get a glimpse of her body. Her husband referred to the hundreds in the rain as "an outpouring of love", saying, "That's the way Pearl was."

She confirmed this in her autobiography, *The Raw Pearl*, in which she wrote: "All the things that seemed ugly have been washed away by the beauty I've found in living with humanity."

Born Pearl Mae Bailey. **Parents** Joseph James, minister, and Ella Mae Bailey. **Marriages** 1) John Randolph Pinkett Jr, 1948 (divorced 1952); 2) Louis Bellson Jr, jazz drummer, 1952. **Children** One son and one daughter, Tony and DeeDee, both adopted. **Education** Joseph Singerly School, Washington, DC; William Penn High School, Washington, DC; Georgetown University, Washington, DC, BA, 1985. **Career** Actress and singer, 1933 onwards; début in vaudeville, Pearl Theater, Philadelphia, 1933; in vaudeville and cabaret, often with Noble Sissle's society orchestra, Cootie Williams and Count Basie, 1930s; toured with United Service Organizations entertaining forces, World War II; Broadway début, as Butterfly in *St Louis Woman*, 1946; film début, *Variety Girl*, 1947; London début, at The Talk of the Town, 1972. **Other activities** Special representative, American delegation to the United Nations, 1975–90. **Awards and honours** Donaldson Award for *St Louis Woman*, 1946; special Antionette Perry (Tony) award for *Hello, Dolly!*, 1968; Woman of the Year award, United Service Organizations, 1969; Hussein Ben-Ali Freedom Medal, Jordan, 1975; First Order of Arts and Science of Egypt, 1975; honorary degree, Georgetown University, 1978. **Principal appearances** Pearl Theater, Philadelphia, 1933; Village Vanguard, 1941; Blue Angel, 1942; La Vie en Rose, 1945; *St Louis Woman*, 1946; *Arms and the Girl*, 1950; *Bless You All*, 1950; *House of Flowes*, 1954; *Call Me Madam*, 1966; *Hello, Dolly!*, 1967–70; *Festival at Ford's*, 1970; *Hello, Dolly!*, 1971; Coconut Grove, Los Angeles, 1971; Royal Box, 1972; Empire Room, Waldorf-Astoria, 1973; Talk of the Town, London, 1972, 1973; Madison Square Garden, 1973; *The Pearl Bailey Show*, 1973; *Hello, Dolly!*, 1975, 1976. **Films** *Variety Girl*, 1947; *Isn't It Romantic?*, 1948; *Carmen Jones*, 1954; *That Certain Feeling*, 1955; *Saint Louis Blues*, 1957; *Porgy and Bess*, 1959; *All The Fine Young Cannibals*, 1960; *The Landlord*, 1969; *Norman, Is That You?*, 1976; *Fox and The Hound* (voice only). **Television** (includes) Appeared with Carol Channing, 1969; *The Pearl Bailey Show*,

1971. **Recordings** (include) "Tired"; "Legalize My Name"; "Takes Two To Tango"; *The Bad Old Days*; *Pearl Bailey Sings for Adults Only*. **Publications** *The Raw Pearl* (autobiography), 1968; *Talking to Myself* (autobiography), 1971; *Pearl's Kitchen*, 1973; *Duey's Tale*, 1975; also: *Hurry Up* and *America and Spit*. **Cause of death** Apparent heart attack, at age 72.

GORDON BUNSHAFT

American Architect

***Born* Buffalo, New York, 9 May 1909**

***Died* Manhattan, New York, 6 August 1990**

"I eat and sleep architecture, but I don't like to talk about it. I prefer that it speak for me."

A sickly child, Gordon Bunshaft spent long periods bedridden. During this time he made, as children will, many drawings. These, it seems, were usually of houses or other buildings. His doctor, a Russian *émigré* like Bunshaft's mother and father, commented when he saw the drawings that the little boy should become an architect when he grew up. The idea took hold. Bunshaft decided at a very early age — said to be seven — that he *would* become an architect and pursued the idea diligently.

At high school Bunshaft did not participate in the sporting side of the curriculum, but he did take classes in manual training. This was to stand him in good stead eventually, when he came to the consideration of actual construction of buildings. Much later, he said that his idea of a really good time was buying new Stanley tools for his workshop.

Bunshaft studied at the Massachusetts Institute of Technology (MIT). He made his choice of university as a result of finding that his music teacher, "a wonderful charming Englishman", had two sons who were students there. When Bunshaft discovered that MIT had an architecture school his mind was made up. He enrolled in 1928, graduating BArch in 1933 and MArch in 1935.

Although architectural teaching at MIT was traditional, based on the French *atelier* system, Bunshaft read the books coming from Europe about the new architecture. Le Corbusier's *Vers une architecture*, for instance, was first translated into English in 1927. Other titles followed while Bunshaft was still a student. Bunshaft called Corbusier's books the "alphabet of young architects all over the world" and later commented that there are "only a few architectural geniuses who ever lived — in our time; Mies, Corbu, and maybe Wright" [Mies van de Röhe, Le Corbusier, Frank Lloyd Wright].

On graduation, Bunshaft worked for Harold Field Kellogg for nine months. Kellogg was so impressed at his young pupil's diligence and industry that he was prepared to help him with securing his next objective. Kellogg wrote a reference which said that Bunshaft had worked for a full year. This meant that Bunshaft was eligible to compete for the Rotch travelling fellowship, the most prestigious MIT architectural award. He was duly awarded the fellowship, which he used to make a trip to Europe and, briefly, to North Africa.

Bunshaft returned to the US and came to New York in 1937. He was fresh from his 15-month scholarship trip and set about looking for work in the offices of previous Rotch fellowship winners. He had a short stay in the office of Edward Durrell Stone, who had no work for a junior in those Depression days. Stone recommended him to Louis Skidmore.

Skidmore had set up an office in New York as an offshoot of a Chicago architectural practice. Nathaniel Owings continued to run their original office in Chicago. John Ogden Merrill, an engineer, joined the partnership in 1939. The firm became Skidmore, Owings and Merrill, or SOM. Skidmore had worked on the Chicago exhibition of 1933–34, so he was approached to design some of the buildings for the New York World's Fair of 1939. It was for this commission that he took on Bunshaft. The Fair provided the opportunity for what Bunshaft called his "first real building", the Venezuelan Pavilion.

After the World's Fair, which had kept Skidmore and Owings in business, World War II intervened. Bunshaft went to join up. He served in the Army Corps of Engineers until 1946. During the latter part of the war he worked for the American Army in London, England and Paris, France. He was designing camps to be built in Europe for the invading armies. Bunshaft did not encounter Mies van der Röhe at this time, but he did meet Walter Gropius, who was living in London, working in partnership with Maxwell Fry.

After the war Bunshaft returned to SOM. The practice had been ticking over, doing solid work for the US government, nothing too exciting, until the commission for Lever House came along at the turn of 1950. Bunshaft had been made a partner the year before but the name and acronym of the firm did not change.

The "international style" had been labelled as such by Henry-Russell Hitchcock and Philip Johnson when they curated their exhibition at the Museum of Modern Art in New York in 1931. They were, perforce, referring solely to small-scale domestic work. Corporate architecture remained, until after the war, resolutely stone-clad and semi-historical. Discounting the maverick work of Frank Lloyd Wright in the 1940s and 1950s, there was no new vision in American post-war business architecture. With the Lever Building, completed in 1952, the *real* "international" style came to New York. Slick, urban, "cool" twentieth-century, anonymous and, most important of all, perceived in economic terms as highly efficient. It was described by Lewis Mumford (q.v.) as "an impeccable achievement".

From the date of the design of the Lever Building, the initials SOM became practically synonymous with GB for Gordon Bunshaft. Bunshaft was the designer, the *eminence grise*, of SOM. The two senior partners were the businessmen, out at their clubs, oiling the wheels, getting jobs, keeping the clients sweet. Bunshaft had seen the way that architectural commissions were handed out at the time, by businessmen meeting architects socially in their clubs. Thus, he considered that one "had to be a club man — socially prominent" to get work. He was well aware that his personality was very different from this type. Worried that he would never succeed on his own, he was content to make a career for himself with SOM.

Buildings like the Vinegar Plant at Pittsburgh for H. J. Heinz (1952) now seem astonishingly forward-looking and sophisticated for their time. His work for institutions, like the great universities or art museums, was always daring and fresh, never a shallow concession to the existing architecture.

The Beinecke Rare Books library at Yale (1963) is a highly original conception of panels of translucent marble, framed in granite. The interior is thus bathed in an eerie glow, even on a dull day. Enough light is provided to see one's way, but not sufficient to damage the books. Architect, Kenzo Tange, called Bunshaft's additions to the Albright-Knox Gallery of Art, Buffalo (1962), "the most beautiful building in the world for an art museum." This praise must have been especially welcome as Buffalo was Bunshaft's home town and he wanted to provide the best for the local art gallery.

Among the last buildings that Bunshaft designed are a group of works in Saudi Arabia. The airport buildings came first, followed by the National Commercial Bank. The latter is a triangular prism-shaped structure of stone, not glass, built over a lagoon in the old Arab quarter of the city.

When the story of America's post-war building boom is written, the name of Gordon Bunshaft will be brought out from the shelter of the umbrella of Skidmore, Owings and Merrill. Not for Bunshaft the relative fame of other architects, who almost invariably graduate from working *for* someone else to working *with* someone else, then to working for themselves.

Unlike his many imitators, Bunshaft had a wide-ranging imagination, always proposing new and different solutions for the commissions he received. The other partners in SOM had their input to the work, but the "house style" of the partnership was seen as Bunshaft's.

Born Gordon Bunshaft. **Parents** David and Yetta Bunshaft. **Marriage** Nina Elizabeth Wayler, 1943. **Education** Lafayette High School, Buffalo, New York, 1924–28; Massachusetts Institute of Technology, Cambridge, 1929–35, BArch, 1933, MArch, 1935; on Rotch travelling fellowship in Europe and North Africa, 1935–37. **Military service** United States Army Corps of Engineers, 1942–46, became major. **Career** Worked for Harold Field Kellogg, Boston, 1935; worked briefly for Edward Durrell Stone, New York, 1937; chief designer, Skidmore, Owings and Merrill, New York, Chicago, San Francisco, Portland, Oregon, 1937–42, 1946–49, partner, 1949–83. **Related activities** Visiting critic: Massachusetts Institute of Technology, 1940–42, Harvard University, Cambridge, Massachusetts, 1954–60, Yale University, New Haven, Connecticut, 1959–62; member, President's Commission on the Fine Arts, 1963–72. **Other activities** Art collector. **Offices and memberships** Trustee: Museum of Modern Art, New York, 1975 onwards, Carnegie-Mellon University, Pittsburgh, Pennsylvania, 1977 onwards; Academician, National Academy of Design; fellow: American Institute of Architects, American Academy of Arts and Sciences. **Awards and honours** Brunner Award, National Institute of Arts and Letters, 1955; Medal of Honor, New York chapter, American Institute of Architects, 1961; DFA, University of Buffalo, Buffalo New York, 1962; honorary member, Buffalo Fine Arts Academy, Buffalo, New York, 1962; Chancellor Norton Medal, University of Buffalo, 1969; honorary professor, Universidad Nacional Federico Villareal, Lima, Peru, 1977; Gold Medal, American Academy and Institute of Arts and Letters, 1984; Pritzker Prize, 1988. **Works** Hostess House, Great Lakes Naval Training Center, Illinois, 1943; Lever House Corporate Headquarters, Park Avenue, New York, 1952; H. J. Heinz Company Vinegar Plant, Pittsburgh, Pennsylvania, 1952; United States Consular Housing, Bremen, West Germany, 1952; Manufacturers Hanover Trust Bank Branch Headquarters, Fifth Avenue, New York, 1954; United States Consulate, Dusseldorf, 1954; Hilton Hotel, Istanbul, 1955; Connecticut General Life Insurance Company Office Building, Bloomfield, 1957; Karl Taylor Compton Laboratories, Massachusetts Institute of Technology, Cambridge, 1957; Reynolds Metals Company Building, Richmond, Virginia, 1958; Pepsi Cola Building, New York, 1960; First National City Bank, Houston, Texas, 1961; Chase Manhattan Bank, New York, 1961; Union Carbide Corporation Building, New York, 1961; Albright-Knox Art Gallery addition, Buffalo, New York, 1962; Emhart Corporation Building, Bloomfield, Connecticut, 1963; Beinecke Rare Book and Manuscript Library, Yale University, New Haven, Connecticut, 1963; Banque Lambert Office Building and Bank, Brussels, 1965; H. J. Heinz and Company Limited, Headquarters and Research Buildings, Hayes Park, Middlesex, England, 1965; American Republic Insurance Company Building, Des Moines, Iowa, 1965; Marine Midland Building, 140 Broadway, New York, 1967; No. 1 Main Place, Dallas, Texas, 1968; American Can Company Suburban Corporate Headquarters, Greenwich, Connecticut, 1970, Lyndon Baines Johnson Library and Sid W. Richardson Hall, University of Texas at Austin, 1971; W. R. Grace Building, 1114 Avenue of the Americas, New York, 1973; Office Building, 9 West Fifty-seventh Street, New York, 1974; Hirshhorn Museum and Sculpture Garden, Washington, DC, 1974; Philip Morris Cigarette Manufacturing Plant, Richmond, Virginia, 1974; Jeddah International Airport, Saudi Arabia, 1975–85; National Commercial Bank, Jeddah, Saudi Arabia, 1979–83. **Exhibition** *Three Skyscrapers*, Museum of Modern Art, New York, 1983. **Cause of death** Cardiovascular arrest, at age 81. **Further reading** Henry-Russell Hitchcock (introduction), *Architecture of Skidmore, Owings and Merrill 1950–62*, 1962; Arthur Drexler (introduction), *Architecture of Skidmore, Owings and Merrill 1963–73*, 1974; *Contemporary Architects*, 1977.

MORLEY CALLAGHAN

Canadian Novelist, Short Story Writer and Memoirist

***Born* Toronto, Canada, 22 September 1903**

***Died* Toronto, Canada, 23 August 1990**

Morley Callaghan belonged in the company of the outstanding Roman Catholic writers of this century. Yet although he was highly esteemed by his readers, Callaghan's works were generally neglected by the critics except in his own country. Edmund Wilson, one of the few critics to recognize Callaghan's contribution to literature, described him as "the most unjustly neglected novelist in the English-speaking world" and as "a writer whose work may be mentioned without absurdity in association with Chekov's and Turgenev's".

Callaghan himself attributed this critical neglect to the brief period which he spent among American expatriate writers in Paris in the late 1920s. He declared once that "Hemingway and Fitzgerald became like a millstone around my neck... I became almost a peripheral being". The association of Callaghan with F. Scott Fitzgerald and Ernest Hemingway in popular memory turns upon Callaghan's and Hemingway's participation in a sparring session in a boxing ring. Before Callaghan's arrival in Paris, he had served as a cub reporter on *The Toronto Star*, for which Hemingway was also working as a reporter. Hemingway recognized the younger writer's talent and arranged for the publication of his work in one of the literary little magazines produced by expatriates in Paris. He also brought Callaghan's work to the notice of Maxwell Perkins, the all-powerful editor at his own publisher's, Scribner's, in New York. In 1928 Scribner's issued Callaghan's first novel, *Strange Fugitive*, which was an immediate popular and financial success. Encouraged by Hemingway, Callaghan decided to become a full-time writer and in 1929, he left for Paris with his bride, Lorette Florence Dee. During his stay there, he fraternized not only with Hemingway and Fitzgerald, but also with Ezra Pound and James Joyce.

While in Paris, Callaghan and Hemingway participated in the famous boxing bout, the "Long Round". Fitzgerald, who was supposed to be arbitrating, was so fascinated by the beating his idol Hemingway was receiving that he forgot to call time. Callaghan, much the lighter man, defeated Hemingway, who never forgave Fitzgerald and whose affection towards Callaghan soured. Hemingway created a rather malicious portrait of Callaghan in his account of the episode in *A Moveable Feast*, but Callaghan, who was universally liked and admired for his modesty and for his sympathetic nature, was more generous in his recollections of their association, recorded in his memoirs, *That Summer in Paris*. As writer William Saroyan remarked in his review of the book, "Each of the three writers was waging a fight of some kind that the others did not know about, could scarcely guess about, and could not help with. Callaghan's fight seems to have been the easiest — simply to write well and to go on writing well".

Yet although this period, and the friendships formed during it, marked a transition in Callaghan's career as a writer, to give it too much significance distorts the development of an artist who, committed to finding a way of representing the Canadian environment, began his career as a naturalist writer and progressed to a more symbolic and complex style. In his works Callaghan mapped out important areas of the Canadian *terrain inconnu*. Apart from the year in Paris and a brief period spent living in New York and Pennsylvania on his way back to Canada, Callaghan spent his life in his native Toronto. He attended St Michael's College at the University of Toronto, from which he graduated in 1925, and trained as a lawyer at Osgoode Hall Law School, Toronto, obtaining his law degree in 1928. He was admitted to the Ontario Bar in the same year, and practised the law sporadically during the 1930s. During World War II, Callaghan worked with the

Canadian Navy on assignment for Canada's National Film Board and travelled across Canada as chairman of the radio forum *Of Things to Come*.

Callaghan spent most of his adult years as a full-time writer, producing 14 novels, three plays, the commentary for a book, *Winter*, of evocative photographs by John de Visser, and over 100 short stories. His works exemplify several of the main trends of Canadian writing from the 1920s through to the late 1970s. His early short stories, which were first published in such magazines as *The New Yorker*, the *Saturday Evening Post* and *Esquire* and which then appeared in the collections *A Native Argosy* and *Now That April's Here*, show the influence of writers such as Sherwood Anderson, Katherine Mansfield, Ernest Hemingway, Erskine Caldwell and William Faulkner. Most noticeably, they bear witness to Callaghan's desire to write about economic and social conditions in Canada at the time. There are stories about the Depression and the ideological debates which surrounded it, and they articulate Callaghan's protest against the rottenness of the social and political structures of the day. Callaghan's restrained and controlled style, through which he creates exact descriptions of persons and places, is realistic, as he explores the effect of the environment and heredity upon characters from the lower echelons of society.

A significant turning point occurred for Callaghan when, in the winter of 1933, he came to know the French Catholic philosopher Jacques Maritain, with whom he held long conversations at the Institute of Medieval Studies in Toronto. Callaghan, of Irish descent on both sides, had been educated as a Catholic, but in his early works his religious beliefs are in conflict with his naturalism, with the influence of Marxist ideas in the 1920s and 1930s, and with his experimentation with Freudian ideas about the self. In novels such as *It's Never Over* and *A Broken Journey* Callaghan explores human suffering, suggesting that only pity can mitigate the futility of human existence. A transitional work is *Such is My Beloved*, which Callaghan dedicated to Jacques Maritain. The novel tells of the relationship between a priest and two young prostitutes. Father Dowling's attempt to save the souls of the prostitutes is in conflict with society and the Church, and in earthly terms his quest fails since the young women are driven from the city by the police, and Father Dowling is housed in a mental asylum. The bleak endings of Callaghan's novels have been criticized for implying too much of a judgement on the "sinners" concerned, but through his exploration of self-sacrificing love, Callaghan evokes the triumph of spiritual values over corrupt social structures.

The theme of Christian suffering, which recurs in *They Shall Inherit the Earth* and *More Joy in Heaven*, receives a more complex development within a contemporary Canadian setting in *The Loved and the Lost* and *The Many Coloured Coat*. In *The Loved and the Lost*, which was a landmark in Canadian writing, Callaghan portrays Montreal, with its unyielding black mountain, home of the rich Whites, and the snow-covered whiteness of the lower town, home of Blacks and paupers. In this setting, Callaghan places the unpredictable Peggy Sanderson, a wilful innocent who refuses to recognize colour-bars of any kind. But the novel shows how institutions finally crush individuals who flout their rules. In *The Many Coloured Coat*, which is regarded as one of Callaghan's finest novels, he reworks the biblical story of Joseph, the gifted and beloved young man, setting it in the life of the streets. The novel depicts urban life as being both squalid and ugly and full of beautiful moments, moments of human vitality and communication.

Callaghan was still prolific in the last years of his life, producing works such as the collection of short stories, *No Man's Meat, and The Enchanted Pimp* and the novels *A Time for Judas* and *Our Lady of the Snows*. He received several Canadian honours, including the Governor-general's Award in 1952, and in 1983 he was made a Companion of the Order of Canada.

Born Morley Edward Callaghan. **Parents** Thomas and Mary (Dewan) Callaghan. **Marriage** Lorette Florence Dee, 1929 (died 1984). **Children** Michael and Barry. **Education** St Michael's College, University of Toronto, BA, 1925; Osgood Hall Law School, Toronto, LLB, 1928. **Career** On *The Toronto Star* while a student; full-time writer 1928 onwards; first publication *Strange Fugitive*, 1928. **Other activities** Admitted to Ontario Bar, 1928; with Royal Canadian Navy on assignment for National Film Board, World War II. **Awards and honours** Governor-general's Award, for *The Loved and the Lost*, 1952; *Maclean's* award, 1955; Lorne Pierce Medal, 1960; DLitt: University of Western Ontario, London, 1965, University of Windsor, Ontario, 1973; LLD, University of Toronto, 1966; Canada Council Medal, 1966, prize, 1970; Molson Prize, 1970; Royal Bank of Canada award, 1970; Companion of the Order of Canada, 1982. **Novels** *Strange Fugitive*, 1928; *It's Never Over*, 1930; *A Broken Journey*, 1932; *Such Is My Beloved*, 1934; *They Shall Inherit the Earth*, 1935; *More Joy in Heaven*, 1937; *The Varsity Story*, 1948; *The Loved and the Lost*, 1951; *The Many Coloured Coat*, 1960; *A Passion in Rome*, 1961; *A Fine and Private Place*, 1975; *Close to the Sun Again*, 1977; *A Time for Judas*, 1983; *Our Lady of the Snows*, 1986. **Short stories** *A Native Argosy*, 1929; *No Man's Meat*, 1931; *Now That April's Here and Other Stories*, 1936; *Stories*, 1959; *An Autumn Penitent*, includes *In His Own Country*, 1973; *No Man's Meat, and The Enchanted Pimp*, 1978. **Uncollected short stories** "Lady in a Green Dress", in *Scribner's*, 1930; "The Chiseller", in *Scribner's*, 1932; "Emily", in *Household Magazine*, 1933; "Northern Summer Twilight", in *Household Magazine*, 1933; "The Bridegroom", in *Esquire*, 1934; "The Girl Who Was Easy", in *Esquire*, 1934; "She's Nothing to Me", in *Story*, 1934; "The Intellectual", in *Literary America*, 1935; "In the Big Town", in *Esquire*, 1936; "An Enemy of the People", in *Scribner's*, 1936; "A Pair of Long Pants", in *Redbook*, 1936; "The Fiddler on Twenty-Third Street", in *John O'London's Weekly*, 1936; "Rendezvous with Self", in *Esquire*, 1937; "This Man, My Father", in *Maclean's*, 1937; "Evening in Madison Square", in *Esquire*, 1937; "A Little Beaded Bag", in *Harper's Bazaar*, 1937; "A Night Out", in *Household Magazine*, 1937; "A Boy Grows Older", in *Esquire*, 1937; "The Fugitive", in *North American Review*, 1938; "The Consuming Fire", in *Harper's Bazaar*, 1938; "The Sentimentalists", in *Harper's Bazaar*, 1938; "The New Coat", in *Esquire*, 1938; "The Thing That Happened to Uncle Adolphe", in *John O'London's Weekly*, 1939; "Hello America", in *John O'London's Weekly*, 1940; "Big Jules", in *Yale Review*, 1940; "The Importance of Henry Bowman", in *Good Housekeeping*, 1945; "Lilacs for Catherine", in *Seventeen*, 1946; "Night of the Fire", in *Cosmopolitan*, 1946; "I Knew Him When", in *American Magazine*, 1947; "The Mexican Bracelets", in *Maclean's*, 1947; "This Man Couldn't Find a Fresh Angle on Xmas but He Did Find Peace and Good Will", in *New World*, 1947; "With an Air of Dignity", in *Maclean's*, 1948; "All Right, Flatfoot", in *Maclean's*, 1948; "All the Doors Were Open", in *National Home Monthly*, 1948; "The Indulgent Lady", in *Mademoiselle*, 1948; "One Stormy Night", in *National Home Monthly*, 1948; "The Bachelor's Dilemma", in *Maclean's*, 1950; "On the Edge of the World", in *Esquire*, 1951; "Keep Away from Laura", in *Maclean's*, 1952; "The Way It Ended", in *Canadian Home Journal*, 1953; "Something for Nothing", in *Canadian Home Journal*, 1954; "We Just Had to Be Alone", in *Maclean's*, 1955; "The Doctor's Son", in *Ten for Wednesday Night*, edited by Robert Weaver, 1961; "The Meterman, Caliban, and Then Mr Jones", in *Exile*, 1973. **Plays** *Turn Again Home*, adaptation of his novel, *They Shall Inherit the Earth*, produced New York, 1940, produced as *Going Home*, Toronto, 1950; *To Tell the Truth*, produced Toronto, 1949; *And Then Mr Jones* (for television), 1974. **Other publications** *Luke Baldwin's Vow* (juvenile), 1948; *That Summer in Paris: Memories of Tangled Friendships with Hemingway, Fitzgerald, and Some Others*, 1963; *Winter*, photographs by John de Visser, 1974. **Cause of death** Undisclosed, at age 86. **Further reading** Brandon Conron, *Morley Callaghan*, 1966; Victor Hoar, *Morley Callaghan*, 1969; Fraser Sutherland, *The Style of Innocence: A Study of Hemingway and Callaghan*, 1972; Brandon Conron (editor), *Morley Callaghan*, 1975; Patricia Morley, *Morley Callaghan*, 1978; David Staines (editor), *The Callaghan Symposium*, 1981; Judith Kendle, *The Annotated Bibliography of Canada's Major Authors 5* (bibliography), edited by Robert Lecker and Jack David, 1984; *Contemporary Novelists*, 1986; *Reference Guide to English Literature*, 1988.

JIMMY CARRUTHERS

Australian Boxer

***Born* Sydney, Australia, 25 July 1929**

***Died* Sydney, Australia, 16 August 1990**

Jimmy Carruthers found a place in sporting history for becoming the first Australian fighter to win a world title at any weight. But, happily, it is not the fact, so much as the manner, of that victory, 40 years ago in Johannesburg, for which he is best remembered today.

No one gave the spindly southpaw from the Sydney suburb of Paddington much chance against the compact and heavily muscled champion, Vic Toweel, who was noted for his immense punching power. Odds of 5–1 had been given against the Australian, and the 28,000 South African fight fans who had gathered at the stadium on 15 November 1952, confidently expected to see their man brush his challenge aside.

Carruthers, however, was equally confident. He had learned his trade at his local Police Boys' Club, and had made rapid progress through the amateur ranks, becoming the Australian bantamweight amateur champion in 1947. Only a cut eye in the final had prevented him from achieving Olympic glory in London, in 1948. More crucial still, was that he had seen Toweel in action. Returning to Australia with no real ambition to make money from the fight game, he was eventually persuaded to turn professional in 1950, after learning that Toweel had become the world's bantamweight champion.

Jimmy Carruthers became the Australian bantamweight champion after his ninth professional fight, when he beat the tough and highly rated Aborigine, Elly Bennett. Five bouts later, he had reached the point where he was able to challenge for the world crown.

At 5 feet, 6½ inches, many felt he was too tall for his weight of 8 stone, 4 pounds, and that he would be no match for Toweel. Carruthers, however, knew better. Having seen Toweel fight in London four years earlier, he was convinced he had his measure. Possessing a surprising degree of power for someone so slender, the wispy left-handed Australian also had the attributes of speed and courage, and was nothing short of ferocious once he stepped into the ring. He went for Toweel from the bell, and a left hook had the champion on the defensive from the very first moment. In the second minute, a stream of left hooks and uppercuts sent Toweel through the ropes. He returned to the ring only long enough for a right to the jaw to send him spiralling out again after just two minutes and 19 seconds of the fight.

It was an astonishing win, but a return bout brought a similar result; and the new world champion went on to defend successfully his title against the American, Henry "Pappy" Gault, and the Thai champion, Chamrern Songkitrat.

The fair-haired fighter became a folk hero in his native country, and as his popularity grew, so too did his generosity. More than half of the money he made from his defence against Pappy Gault — fought in front of some 32,500 fans in Sydney — found its way to the Woolooloolo Police Boys' Club in Paddington.

Prone to cuts, Carruthers was wise to the fight game, and took the sport by surprise by announcing his retirement in March 1954, after beating "the man with the atomic punch", Chamrern Songkitrat, in a tough fight in Bangkok. It was made even tougher by the fact that both men had to fight in bare feet after being drenched in a tropical rain-storm.

Just 24 years of age, Carruthers had nevertheless invested his winnings from 19 undefeated professional bouts wisely, and supplemented his income as a boxing referee as the sport enjoyed a boom period in Australia. He was tempted to make a brief return to fighting in 1961, but his reflexes and sharpness had deserted him, and after losing a few bouts, he was quickly persuaded to hang up his gloves for good.

During the time he was a docker, he was an active trade unionist, and was even investigated by the Australian Security Intelligence Organization (ASIO), which, during the paranoid 1950s, regarded many of their own nationals as possible subversives.

Ironically, boxing not only provided him with an escape from the docks, but also elevated him to national-hero status.

The man who ruled the world from 1952 to 1954 enjoyed life after boxing as the publican of a Sydney hotel and, later, as proprietor of a fresh juice bar.

Born James William Carruthers. **Father** J. W. Carruthers. **Marriage** Myra Hamilton, 1951. **Children** Two sons and two daughters. **Education** Paddington Technical College, Sydney. **Career** Australian bantamweight champion, as an amateur, 1947; docker; member, Australian Olympic team, 1948; professional boxer, 1950–54, 1961; referee, mid 1950s; later became a publican, then proprietor of a juice bar, Sydney. **Championships** World Bantamweight Champion: against Vic Toweel, Johannesburg, 1952, against Pappy Gault, Sydney, 1953, against Chamrern Songkitrat, Bangkok, 1954; 13 knockout wins; eight wins on points. **Cause of death** Cancer and Parkinsons's disease, at age 61.

HENRY CROWN

American Industrialist

***Born* Chicago, Illinois, 13 June 1896**

***Died* Chicago, Illinois, 14 August 1990**

A business associate once said of Henry Crown, "When the Colonel gets into a deal, he knows the size of your underwear." A long-time supporter of the Boy Scouts of America, Crown seemed to heed their motto, "Be Prepared", in all his business affairs. He went from rags to riches, lived the American dream, and died at the age of 94 with a fortune estimated at over two billion dollars.

Born Henry Krinsky, the third of seven children of a Lithuanian immigrant sweatshop worker, and his wife, Ida, Crown dropped out of school in the eighth grade to take a four-dollar a week clerical job at the Chicago Firebrick Company. His initial flirtation with big business ended abruptly, however, when he dispatched the wrong mixture of sand and gravel to a construction site.

In 1912, at the age of 16, Crown took a job with the Union Drop Forge Company, where he learned the art of wrought iron and metal working. He supplemented on-the-job experience with night-school business classes, and impressed instructors with his grasp of figures, and his ambitious financial models.

Still only 19, Crown went into partnership with his older brothers, Sol and Irving, establishing a steel brokerage firm with 10,000 dollars, most of it borrowed. Soon after, the fledgling company diversified into sand, gravel, lime and coal, and became known as the Material Service Corporation.

By keeping a tight rein on costs as the company's treasurer, Crown was able to convince local bankers to extend him steady credit and unsecured loans. He was named company president in 1921, and helped the Material Service Corporation win a stream of government contracts through the 1920s and 1930s.

During this period of phenomenal growth — in which the company became one of the largest construction concerns in the Midwest — allegations were made that Crown had bought influence in City Hall. These charges were never substantiated, however, and the company went on to help construct some of Chicago's landmarks, including the Loop Elevated Train system, the Merchandise Mart and the Civic Opera House.

By the 1950s, Material Service Corporation was the world's largest building supply firm and Crown was expanding into real estate, acquiring commercial properties throughout Illinois, California and New York.

In 1951, Crown led a syndication in buying the Empire State Building — then jokingly referred to as the "Empty State Building" — for 51.5 million dollars. He bought out the other stockholders almost immediately. Then, through extensive modernization, Crown was able to fill the previously under-occupied property with a roster of prestigious tenants. In 1961, he sold the Empire State Building for 65,000,000 dollars.

When Material Service Corporation became a tempting takeover target in 1959, Crown merged the company with General Dynamics of St Louis for convertible stock worth 120 million dollars. Crown was appointed a director of the defence contracting giant, and later served as chairman of its executive committee.

Although Crown helped General Dynamics overcome difficulties associated with its venture into commercial aviation, he was unable to centralize operations, and therefore incapable of reversing sliding profits. In 1966 the corporation bought him out for 100,000,000 dollars. This enormous cash sum enabled Crown to buy up large blocks of General Dynamics stock, and announce four years later that he held effective control of the company. To avoid a proxy fight, General Dynamics appointed Crown to the board of directors. He had the privilege of naming the company's new chief executive in 1971.

Referred to as the "Colonel" for his service in the Army Corps of Engineers during World War II, Crown was respected not only for his imposing demeanor and business savvy, but for his philanthropy. Self-effacing and modest in his life-style, he said in a 1971 interview: "My goal since the end of World War II, and I think I've attained it, is to have less money at the end of the year than I had at the beginning of the year."

In the last 20 years of his life, Crown gave at least 100,000,000 dollars to charity. The Crown family has contributed to universities including Northwestern, Stanford, and the University of Chicago. They have also invested in Chicago culture, establishing the Henry Crown Space Center at the Chicago Museum of Science and Industry, and the Arie Crown Theater at McCormick Place.

More than 1000 people attended Henry Crown's funeral. Chicago mayor, Richard Daley, was quoted as saying, "in his family life and in the business community as well, [Mr Crown] gave something back to Chicago, to culture and to education."

Born Henry Krinsky. **Parents** Arie, sweatshop worker, and Ida (Gordon) Krinsky. **Marriages** 1) Rebecca Kranz, 1920 (died 1934); 2) Gladys Kay. **Children** Robert (died 1969), Lester and John. **Education** Public schools, Chicago, Illinois. **Military service** Lieutenant-colonel, US Army Corps of Engineers, World War II. **Career** Clerk, Fire Brick Company, 1910–12; traffic manager, Union Drop Forge Company, 1912–16; partner, S. R. Crown & Company, 1916–19; treasurer, Material Service Corporation, 1919–21, president, 1921–41, chairman of the board, 1941–59; director and member, executive committee, General Dynamics Corporation, 1959–66, 1970–86, honorary chairman, board of directors, 1986 onwards; chairman of the board, Henry Crown & Company, 1967; also, director, Hilton Hotels, Waldorf Astoria Corporation, Rock Island and San Francisco railroads. **Other activities** Advisory member, board of trustees, De Paul University; member, citizens board: University of Illinois, Loyola University, Chicago. **Offices and memberships** Chicago Civil Defence Corps; trustee: Syracuse University, University of

Chicago, Chicago Boys' Clubs; member, Northwestern University Association; fellow, St Joseph's College, Rensselaer, Indiana; associate fellow; Brandeis University; member, Reserve Officers Association. **Awards and honours** (include) Legion of Merit, United States; Chevalier de la Legion d'honneur; Gold Cross, Royal Order Phoenix, Greece; Order Ruben Dario, Nicaragua; Horatio Alger Award, American Schools and Colleges Association; Damen Award, Loyola University, Chicago; Humanitarian Service award for industry, Eleanor Roosevelt Cancer Research Foundation; Julius Rosenwald Memorial Award, Jewish Federation and Welfare Fund, Chicago; Education for Freedom award, Roosevelt University, Chicago; Meritorious Public Service award, United States Navy; honorary vice-president, Illinois council, Boy Scouts of America. **Cause of death** Undisclosed, at age 94.

HEDLEY DONOVAN

American Editor and Journalist

***Born* Brainerd, Minnesota, 24 May 1914**

***Died* Manhattan, New York, 13 August 1990**

When Hedley Donovan succeeded founder Henry Luce as editor-in-chief of Time incorporated in 1964 the consensus was that it was a hard act to follow. Luce was the majority share-holder of an empire which he had co-founded in 1923, and which included *Time*, *Life*, *Fortune* and *Sports Illustrated*. Compared to him Donovan was a johnny-come-lately.

Luce's politics had been grounded in the Republican Party, whereas Donovan favoured a more middle-of-the-road stance ("I am a political independent with conservative leanings", the new editor had announced early on). Donovan, an ex-Rhodes scholar, enjoyed the company of intellectuals (he once boasted that he had sat through 93 different operas without falling asleep during a single performance) whereas Luce was more at home in the smoke-filled corridors of power.

Donovan was cool, calm, unflapable. Luce was inclined to fly off the handle with subordinates. Their personality differences were reflected in their approach to the news, Luce's outlook tending towards the parochial, whereas Donovan extended overseas coverage, particularly of Asian news. Under his aegis *Time* magazine became "more thoughtful and fair-minded", in Donovan's words. When Donovan retired in 1979 after a 15-year tenure as top editor his authority was as absolute as that of his predecessor.

From the beginning Donovan had interpreted his appointment as a mandate for change, and had proceeded accordingly. That change was given dramatic emphasis when during the 1964 presidential campaign *Life* endorsed the Democratic incumbent, President Lyndon B. Johnson, thereby breaking its long-standing ties with the Republicans. During his tenure Donovan also founded two new magazines, *People* and *Money*, to add to the existing stable, which had a total circulation of more than 12 million copies per week.

Vietnam and Watergate were Donovan's two biggest headaches. Convinced that the Vietnam war was a just one, and winnable, he lined up the magazine empire at his command solidly behind the American war effort. Nor was he content simply to listen to his cronies in the Pentagon; Donovan made extended trips to Vietnam, talked to the generals who gave the orders and to the "grunts" who carried them out. And when he finally concluded that the war could not be won at reasonable cost he said so publicly.

Before that *Life* had appeared with a memorable story entitled "One Week's Dead" that had presented yearbook-style portraits of all the Americans killed in action during a single week's combat. The feature, which devastated readers, had Donovan's full approval.

As for Watergate, *Time*, which had supported President Richard Nixon originally, called for his impeachment after the break-in. Donovan's reputation for integrity was not confined to America. In 1968 Alexei Kosygin, the Soviet premier, opted to be interviewed by him, this despite the fact that *Life* had recently published excerpts from the memoirs of Svetlana, Stalin's daughter.

Hedley Williams Donovan was born in Brainerd, Minnesota, the son of a mining engineer. A graduate of the University of Minnesota, he won a Rhodes scholarship to Hertford College, Oxford, where in 1936 he took a BA in history.

Donovan spent five years with *The Washington Post*, starting as a cub reporter, and later covering the State Department and the White House beats. During World War II he served in US Naval intelligence, ending with the rank of lieutenant-commander. After the war Donovan joined *Fortune*, and by 1953 was its managing editor. In 1959 he was chosen by Luce to become editorial director of *Time* and, by implication, his "heir apparent".

A handsome six-footer with greying brown hair, Donovan's quiet-spoken manner was often mistaken for weakness, but managing editors knew they were in for a rocketing if he summoned them with the words, "I have a few bothers here." Those "bothers" could entail endless revisions. Nor was Donovan easily persuaded from his point of view. Whereas Luce was content to win half his arguments, Donovan settled for two out of three.

Yet the tall Minnesotan who bore a slight resemblance to film star James Stewart could be warm and friendly outside office hours, according to those who knew him well. He had a dry sense of humour, and was fond of telling anecdotes, often at his own expense.

Aside from opera, American football was one of his major passions. His bets on Super Bowl games were not confined to which team would win, but he would bet on what would be the longest punt return, how many field goal attempts would be made, what would be the longest completed pass.

When Donovan retired in 1979 as editor-in-chief he was appointed senior adviser to President Jimmy Carter with the brief to provide "substantive advice on the full range of matters before the President". Donovan was more modest concerning his duties. "The President just wants to be able to talk about almost anything freely with somebody who has some grey hair."

Born Hedley Williams Donovan. **Parents** Percy Williams, mining engineer, and Alice (Dougan) Donovan. **Marriage** Dorothy Hannon, bacteriologist, 1941, (died 1978). **Children** Peter, Helen and Mark. **Education** West High School, Minneapolis; University of Minnesota, AB, magna cum laude, 1934; Hertford College, Oxford, Rhodes scholar, BA, 1936. **Military service** United States Naval Reserve, engaged in editorial work for Naval intelligence, 1942–45, became lieutenant-commander. **Career** Reporter, *The Washington Post*, 1937–42; writer, editor, *Fortune* magazine, New York City, 1945–51, associate managing editor, 1951–53, managing editor, 1953–59; editorial director, Time Incorporated, 1959–64, editor-in-chief, 1964–79, director, 1962–79, consultant, 1979–84. **Related activities** Economic adviser, State Department, 1958; member, Council of Foreign Relations, director, 1969–79; senior adviser to the President of the United States, 1979–80; fellow, faculty of government, Harvard University, 1980 onwards; visiting residential fellow, Nuffield College, Oxford 1986; director, Aerospace Corporation. **Offices and memberships** Trustee: National Center for Humanities, ASIA Society; fellow, American Academy of Arts and Sciences; member: Phi Beta Kappa, Delta Upsilon. **Awards and honours** Outstanding Achievement award, University of Minnesota Alumni, 1956; Loeb Journalism award, 1978; honorary fellow, Hertford College, Oxford, 1978; Gallatin Medal, New York University, 1979; Leslie Moeller Distinguished Lectureship, University of Iowa, 1985; LittD: Pomona

College, Boston University, Mount Holyoke College; Doctor of Humane Letters, Southwestern at Memphis, Rochester University, Transylvania University; LLD: Carnegie-Mellon University, Leligh University, Allegheny College. **Publications** *Roosevelt to Reagan: A Reporter's Encounters with Nine Presidents*, 1985; *Right Places, Right Times: 40 Years in Journalism*, 1989. **Cause of death** Lung infection, at age 76.

NORBERT ELIAS

German/British Sociologist

***Born* Breslau, Germany, 22 June 1897**

***Died* Amsterdam, Holland, 1 August 1990**

Norbert Elias, although born in the nineteenth century, was possibly the first of the new men in Europe, with a truly European background and a vision which integrated many of the human sciences (from history and sociology to biology and psychology) into a synthesis of understanding valued throughout the continent.

Of Jewish origin, he was born in Breslau, now the Polish city of Wroclaw, and after service in World War I he studied medicine, later moving to philosophy in which he took his doctorate. By the mid-1920s he was pursuing sociology and, in 1929 at the age of 32, he moved to the University of Frankfurt as assistant to Karl Mannheim. His career was interrupted however when the Nazis seized power in 1933. Thus, at a crucial age for an academic, he found himself exiled in France where, although he had a good grasp of the language, he was unable to find work.

Two years later he went to England where, with the aid of a modest grant, he was able to pursue his studies and write his remarkable two-volume work, *The Civilising Process*, which was published just after the commencement of World War II by a small *émigré* publishing house in Switzerland. Although highly regarded, it was read by comparatively few because it was not to be translated into English for nearly 40 years.

The Civilising Process started from the thesis that by the nineteenth century the manner in which Europeans used the word "civilization" demonstrated that they had forgotten its process. Assured of their own superiority they went about trying to impose their own, acquired, standards on "lower orders" and the native populations of their empires as if they were innate and absolute. They had forgotten the many centuries of history during which these standards had developed.

To bring back awareness of the process Elias traced this history. He looked at the development of what may be called European manners: such matters as the socially acceptable methods of dealing with eating, nose-blowing, spitting, urination and defecation, undressing and so on. He noted that more elaborate codes set in after the Renaissance, leading to greater self-restraint.

Violence, *per se*, also became hidden but gradually rulers came to make accepted and acceptable claims on its legitimate use. People were thus forced to live peacefully together—a new morality—and over generations personality became moulded differently. Changes in social structure were mirrored by changes in the psychological structure of individuals.

This theory, that social and individual development are inextricably linked, can also be seen as a development of those of the French sociologist, Emile Durkheim. In *The Division of Labour in Society*, first published in 1893, Durkheim demonstrated how different types of society produce different types of morality, with a two-level theory running on a continuum. As one moves from a "primitive" society of low population and with little division of labour towards a "modern" one with a large population and a high division of labour, so one also moves along a moral continuum of behaviour to others. In simpler societies there is stress on moral behaviour to others *because* people are alike — everyone is in the same boat and doing very similar things. In a more complex society morality is required precisely *because* of the complexity; everyone does different things and people are far more interdependent. This aspect played a large part in Elias's theory. As society changed its structure so the chains of social interdependence grew and the constraints on them became ever more complex. It was the growth of the state and its gradual taking over the means of violence that changed the people.

The Civilising Process was not without its dissenters. The eminent British social anthropologist, Edmund Leach (who was later to be knighted) pointed out that, at the time Elias was writing, "Hitler was refuting the argument on the grandest scale." But this is to discount the basic anthropological concept — that what *matters*, in any society, is what is taken for granted and accepted as the norm. And it is not unusual to find oppressed or "uncivilized" people actually colluding in the support of such norms. Thus many people from other races have attempted to make their appearance more European: their hair straighter, their skins paler, even their eyes rounder. The refusal to collude in racism, in particular, is a very recent phenomenon.

In 1954, and at an age when most academics are beginning to reflect on formal retirement, Elias moved back into university life. He was appointed to a post at the new University of Leicester where, in partnership with the foresighted Ilya Neustadt, he helped build its renowned department of sociology and where later colleagues took his many interests further, particularly in looking at the roles of sport and violence in European life today.

Elias left England in his later life, spending some time in Germany and his last years in Amsterdam. He continued writing prolifically — his last book was published only a year before his death. In addition these last years brought him the recognition he had been denied earlier because his work was not then available in English. He received many honours including, on his ninety-first birthday, the Premio Europeo Amalfi for his book *Die Gesellschaft der Individuen* as the best sociology book of the year.

It has been said that Elias represented one of the last links with the classical age of German sociology. He also represented his truth in clearly understood language. Another of his later books was *The Loneliness of the Dying* in which he said, "Death hides no secret. It opens no door. It is the end of a person. What survives is what he or she has given to other people, what stays in their memory."

What stays of Elias is his commitment, his breadth of understanding and his brilliance of mind. All are immortalized in his works which will long stimulate the reader.

Born Norbert Elias. **Education** Studied medicine and philosophy, Breslau, Germany, PhD in philosophy; studied sociology, Heidelberg, mid-1920s. **Emigration** Left Germany for France, 1933, left France for England, 1935, naturalized, left England for Germany, 1975, finally settled in the Netherlands. **Military service** German Army, World War I. **Career** Sociologist, University of Frankfurt, 1929–33; author, researcher, Paris, 1933, England, 1935; first publication, *Über den Prozess der Zivilisation* (*The Civilising Process*), 1939; senior lecturer, Leicester University, 1954, reader, professor, 1962; founder, sociology department, University of Ghana, 1962; guest lecturer, German and Dutch Universities. **Awards and honours** Premio Europeo Amalfi, for *Die Gesellschaft der Individuen*, 1988; Commander, Order of Orange-Nassau, Netherlands, 1988; Grosskreuz der Bundesverdienstordens, West Germany, 1988; also, honorary degrees, decorations and prizes, Germany and the Netherlands. **Publications** *Über den Prozess der Zivilisation*, 1939, published in English as *The Civilising Process* (translated by Edmund Jephcott), 1978; *The Loneliness of the Dying* (translated by Edmund Jephcott), 1985; *Die Gesellschaft der Individuen*, 1987; *Studien Über die Deutschen*, 1989. **Cause of death** Undisclosed, at age 93.

MAURICE GENDRON

French Cellist

Born **Cannes, France, 26 December 1920**

Died **Grez-sur-Loing, France, 20 August 1990**

"I've always said there were only three cellists in the world worth listening to: me, myself and Gendron!" Maurice Gendron may not have been the world's most modest, let alone the world's best cellist but he was certainly entitled to be proud of his achievement as his friend Yehudi Menuhin testified: "his playing was both romantic and deeply serious. A typically French talent, he brought style, elegance, warmth, possessing the profound musicality that we have come to expect from the great school of French cellists."

Gendron often declared that a cellist sounded the same whether playing on a "Strad" or an orange box. Whether that accounts for the beauty of tone that characterized his own playing, or whether credit for that should also go to the fine Stradivarius cello he played, he certainly knew how to make his instrument sing. That this most aristocratic of cellists should have had such a priceless instrument in his hands at all is a measure of the length of his career's journey from rags to riches.

During Gendron's childhood in Cannes, his mother, a fiddle player in the cinema, was deserted by his father and left to bring up her son alone. His earliest memories of music were of his mother playing in a performance of Schubert's *Unfinished Symphony*, used as background music to a silent Hollywood movie. His own talent proclaimed itself early on — by the age of three he could read music and began violin lessons. But he soon asked to change to the cello and then became truly converted at the age of ten when hearing Emmanuel Feuermann play at the Cannes Casino: "I knew I would never be satisfied until I could play like him". By the age of 14 Gendron was giving concerts but then came the talkies which put his mother out of a job. Young Maurice was reduced to scrubbing floors and taking in ironing to help keep the family.

From the age of 12 he had attended Nice Conservatoire and his professor there helped him move on to Paris to study with the distinguished Conservatoire professor, Gerard Hekking. He arrived there aged 18 with a pauper's free ticket from Cannes municipality and protested to Hekking that he would not be able to afford the lessons. "Have I asked you for any money?", Hekking asked. Gendron won the Conservatoire's top prize within one year (1938) and was all set for a brilliant career when war came. Unfit for Military Service, he joined the Resistance movement, was decorated for bravery, and where possible gave charity recitals and played for wounded servicemen.

One day a neighbour overhead him practising and invited him to play to a few friends, after which his career took off. He soon made his name playing in salons before artists and writers like Picasso (who painted on one of his cellos), Sartre, Camus and Cocteau — who once said that Gendron was so musical that he almost became his cello as he played. Through this circle, he also came to know Mauriac and Poulenc and the composer Jean Françaix, with whom he enjoyed a long musical partnership.

After the war, Gendron quickly began to be noticed by the major orchestras. Before the end of 1945 he had already been invited to make his London début with a performance of Prokofiev's concerto. While in England he also gave two recitals with Benjamin Britten who immediately invited him to Aldeburgh for the first year of the Festival in 1948. After that he visited Aldeburgh regularly, gave concertos under Menuhin at the Bath Festival, played at the Proms and fulfilled many other British engagements.

In 1970, Gendron took up conducting and worked for a season with the Bournemouth Sinfonietta. Meanwhile he also gave masterclasses and became the most highly prized professor at the Conservatoire.

An injury to his shoulder sustained in a car accident in the mid 1970s removed Gendron from concert life for nearly a decade. But in an act of tremendous courage he returned to the platform at the age of 63. He had spent three years teaching himself to hold the bow and control it, and then several more to get back both confidence and technique. When the time came to face the Paris audience once more he spurned the offer of a shared recital, saying he would "play solo Bach to whoever wants to hear me". The event was sold out.

He died in the village of Grez-sur-Loing, where Delius also lived and died, and there Gendron kept art treasures of Chagall, Braque and Picasso and a drawing by Cocteau of himself with the cello. "Maurice was the most enchanting of companions," Menuhin said, "with a divine gift for comedy — a natural actor as well as a musician [he enjoyed conjuring and puppetry]. To every occasion one was sure that Maurice would bring his particular brand of humour and glorious sense of the absurd. He was also intensely proud of his family — his wonderful wife, Monique, and his two devoted children." His art lives on in a number of recordings, particularly of solo Bach and French music of his own generation and he even made recordings of Haydn and Boccherini cello concerti under the baton of Pablo Casals.

Born Maurice Gendron. **Parents** François and Jeanne (Lemarchand), violinist, Gendron. **Marriage** Monique Nérot, 1947. **Children** Caroline and François-Eric. **Education** Conservatoire de Nice, 1938; studied under Gerard Hekking, top prize-winner, Conservatoire national supérieur de musique, Paris. **Military service** French Resistance, World War II. **Career** Concert début, at age of 14; employed in various menial jobs, Nice; London début, western *premiére* of Prokofiev's Cello Concerto, with London Philharmonic, 1945; cellist, Paris Symphony Orchestra; performed frequently at festivals of Aldeburgh, Gstaad and Bath, from 1948; professor, violincello masterclass, Conservatoire d'Etat de Sarrebrück, 1954–70; US début, with National Orchestral Association, New York City; professor: Conservatoire national supérieur de musique, 1970 onwards, Yehudi Menuhin School, Surrey, England, 1976 onwards; member, trio with Yehudi and Hepzibah Menuhin; assistant conductor, Bournemouth Sinfonietta, 1970; gave first performance since accident in mid-1970s, Paris, 1985. **Awards and honours** Chevalier de la Légion d'honneur; Officier de l'ordre national du Mérite. **Recordings** (include) Haydn and Boccherini concertos, directed by Casals; Bach suites; Mozart and Schubert piano trios with Yehudi and Hepzibah Menuhin, twentieth-century French music. **Cause of death** Cancer of the oesophagus, at age 69.

MAX GORDON

South African Architect

***Born* Cape Town, South Africa, 10 June 1931**

***Died* London, England, 23 August 1990**

The art lover's architect: that was Max Gordon. His well-deserved fame derived almost exclusively from the art galleries he designed, nearly all of them conversions, and absolutely all of them perfect spaces for the exhibition of works of contemporary art. His peers said that he could do it because he knew and understood so well what contemporary art was all about.

His architectural studies began in England in 1949 when he started at Christ's College, Cambridge. Three years later he moved on to the Architectural Association in London for a year, and then went to the United States to attend a post-graduate course at the Harvard School of Design under José Louis Sert (1955 to 1956). It was there that he received his Master of Architecture degree.

Then it was real work, and he began it at Skidmore, Owings and Merrill in New York. One of his major projects there was to work as associate architect to Gordon Bunshaft (q.v.) on the Chase Manhattan and Union Carbide buildings. But England was pulling him back, and by 1962 he was a partner at Chapman, Taylor and Partners in London, where he stayed for seven years, moving on to become a senior partner with Louis de Soissons for another 12.

During all of this Gordon has been nourishing his passionate interest in contemporary art. He was friendly with such rising stars as Howard Hodgkin and Richard Smith in London, and with Joel Shapiro and many others on the other side of the Atlantic. He was on the International Council of the Museum of Modern Art in New York for 20 years, and from 1978 to 1985 on its Trustee Committee on Architecture and Design. In London he was a founding committee member of the Patrons of New Art at the Tate Gallery and a trustee of the Whitechapel Art Galley. He was really international: the Spanish Ministry of Culture later signed him up on an advisory committee.

It was natural, then, that when, in 1981, the moment came for him to take the plunge and set up on his own, it would be as an architect and consultant devoted to art-related architecture. Just at the right moment, in 1984, Doris and Charles Saatchi found a disused paint factory in north London and wondered if it might do for their extensive collection of contemporary art. Gordon was game, threw himself into the task of a major conversion, and when it was opened one critic said it was, "one of the most blissful spaces of its kind".

It was his finest hour. He had painted the concrete floors of the six interconnecting ground floor rooms grey, and the walls white, which provided a good contrast to the jungle of metal and glass that formed the original roof. The ceiling in the main room was terribly low, so Gordon quite simply lowered the floor. He lit the place with trays of fluorescent tubes along the metal struts of the roof, so the light was thrown back down. Innovative, understated, harmonious: the Max Gordon style.

This *tour de force* meant that people ran after him to design their art galleries. He went all over the place. In Madrid in 1986 he advised on the conversion of an eighteenth-century Charles III hospital in the centre of the city: it became the Centro d'Arte Reina Sofia. He did galleries in New York, Helsinki, Los Angeles, Athens, and London — his last one in the latter was the new Annely Juda gallery. When he died he had been one of four architects to be invited to submit a design for a new public museum in Stuttgart.

Simplicity was always the key to his art-gallery work, to leave room for the art on display to express itself. He also designed numerous private residences for art collectors. He was actually a shrewd and respected collector himself, too.

He was tremendously gregarious, very witty, and he knew how to enjoy himself. He knew thousands of people, never played the prima donna despite his success, and his finger was always on the art world's fast-beating pulse. But he had his reserved side: Doris Saatchi, in an appreciation in London's *Guardian* newspaper, said he rarely spoke of his personal life: he had, she said, "secret pleasures".

Born Max Gordon. **Parents** Shalom and Tanya Gordon. **Education** Studied architecture, Christ's College, Cambridge, 1949–52; Architectural Association, London, 1953-54; Harvard School of Design, MArch, 1956. **Career** Architect, Skidmore, Owings and Merrill, New York, 1956–62; partner, Chapman, Taylor and Partners, 1962–69; senior partner, Louis de Soissons, 1969–81; established own architectural practice and consultancy, 1981. **Related activities** Art collector; member, International Council of the Museum of Modern Art, New York, for 16 years; foreign member, Museum of Modern Art's Trustee Committee for Architecture and Design, 1978–

85; founding committee member, Patrons of New Art, Tate Galley, London; consultant, Reina Sofia Museum, Madrid, 1986; member, international committee advising Spanish Ministry of Culture. **Offices and memberships** Trustee, Whitechapel Art Gallery, London. **Works** (include) Development of Butler's Wharf, London: Saatchi Gallery, London, 1985; conversion of Reina Sofia Museum, Madrid, 1986; Annely Juda Gallery, London; 12, Cork Street, London, gallery and library underneath; 16 Clifford Street, London; also, numerous art galleries, museums and private residences for collectors, in New York, Los Angeles, London, Athens, Helsinki, Chicago, Philadelphia. **Cause of death** Liver failure, at age 59.

COLONEL ELSPETH HOBKIRK

British Soldier and Prison Governor

Born **Trellech, Wales, 17 May 1903**

Died **21 August 1990**

Elspeth Hobkirk, who was to become a social reformer in the mould of Elizabeth Fry, was born into a military family. Her father was Brigadier-General Clarence Hobkirk and he was to have an immense influence on her choice of career, which encompassed the Army and subsequently the prison service. However in early life Hobkirk appeared to be treading a traditional path for the daughter of an upper-middle-class family in turn-of-the-century Britain. She was privately educated at Sandecotes in Dorset before attending the London School of Art. Although she did not become a professional painter, she was to enjoy landscape painting for the rest of her life.

The outbreak of World War II in 1939 was to have a profound effect on Hobkirk's life. She joined the First Aid Nursing Yeomanry, known as FANY, and subsequently enlisted in the Auxiliary Territorial Service (ATS), the women's section of the Army. Hobkirk served with distinction throughout the course of the war, in increasingly responsible positions.

Hobkirk thrived on the military life and when the war ended in 1945 she elected to remain in the Army. In 1947 she was appointed deputy director of the Women's Royal Army Corps at the War Office and she subsequently served as vice-president of the Regular Commissions Board from 1950. She retired from the Army in 1952.

For many years Hobkirk had also served as a magistrate and it was perhaps her experience of the courts and the legal system which prompted her next career. After two years as head warden of Bristol Royal Hospital in England's west country, she was appointed governor of Duke Street women's prison in Glasgow, Scotland, in 1954. Hobkirk had the distinction of being the first woman to be appointed as a governor, previous incumbents having been known as lady superintendents.

The following year the women's prison was moved to Greenock, an industrial town a few miles out of Glasgow. This institution already housed a girls' borstal (juvenile offenders' institute) and it also held a section of untried male prisoners. In addition Hobkirk was given some difficult prisoners from Scotland's notorious Peterhead gaol to take care of, the hope being that she might have a calming influence on these disturbed men. Hobkirk's formidable task was to convert the forbidding Victorian prison into a modern establishment and introduce some kind of training plan for her charges. She threw herself into this new job with characteristic enthusiasm and energy, often working an 18-hour day.

Under Hobkirk's direction the fortress-like institution was humanized. The halls were painted white and primrose. The women's cells were rechristened "rooms" and painted in pastel shades.

Hobkirk created gardens in the austere grounds. She had a laburnum avenue planted and she raided the gardens of her friends for roses and other plants for the borders. On one occasion she persuaded her brother, who was a bailiff of the Queen's Royal Parks, to let her have a sack of bulbs remarking, "After all, we are on Her Majesty's property." Hobkirk opened up the prison to the outside world, making it an integral part of the local community. She created opportunities for the inmates to receive education and professional advice, whilst at the same time informing and interesting local people in the running of the prison. As a result the Greenock prison became well known to the local populace, with the Provost being a regular visitor who bought his socks at the annual sale of work.

Hobkirk was respected by the prisoners and staff alike for her policy of building up relationships of mutual trust between the disparate groups, rather than relying simply on a disciplined and hierarchical structure. She introduced a system of individual talks with the women which gave them the opportunity to discuss their problems with her in private, and in this way she got to know them well. Although she came from a vastly different background she had the ability to relate to the women in her charge without being patronizing. Hobkirk found the work endlessly fascinating. She wrote "This work never stops being interesting, it is often exhausting and sometimes tragic, but the percentage of success is very high and there is no work that is more worthwhile."

Hobkirk's ability was recognized early on. She was appointed woman adviser to the Scottish Home and Health Department's committee on the conditions of detention of women and girls in Scotland. She was also a member of the Government Advisory Committee on Drug Dependence and later chairman of the Civil Service Commission Panel of Interviewers. In 1976 Hobkirk was awarded an honorary degree of Doctor of Laws by Glasgow University. The accompanying citation described how "In a service almost totally dominated by men she fought for recognition of the distinctive needs of the women's service."

Elspeth Hobkirk retired from the prison service in 1969 but for many years she still sat on a multitude of influential committees. She remained active until well into her eighties and continued to enjoy her hobbies of painting, music, gardening and travel.

Born Elspeth Isabel Weatherley Hobkirk. **Parents** Brigadier-General Clarence and Nora Louisa Hobkirk. **Education** Sandecotes, Dorset; London School of Art. **Career** First Aid Nursing Yeomanry, 1938; senior commander, Auxiliary Territorial Service, 1939, 1942, chief commander, 1945, controller and deputy director, headquarters, London District, 1946, deputy director, War Office, 1947–49; commissioned, Women's Royal Army Corps, 1949, deputy director, War Office, 1949, deputy director, headquarters Eastern Command, 1950–52, vice-president, Women's Royal Army Corps Regular Commissions Board, retired, 1952; head warden, Bristol Royal Hospital, 1952–54; governor, Her Majesty's Prison, Duke Street, Glasgow, 1954–55, Greenock, 1955; governor, Her Majesty's Prison and Her Majesty's Borstal for Girls and Her Majesty's Young Offenders Institute, Greenock, 1955–69. **Related activity** Justice of the peace, Monmouthshire, 1938–49; woman adviser, Scottish Home and Health Department, on conditions of detention of women and girls in Scotland, 1956; member, Government Advisory Committee on Drug Dependence, 1967–70; on parole board for Scotland, 1970–73; chairman, Civil Service Commission Panel of Interviewers, 1969–73; adviser, Council on Social Work, Scotland, 1970–72; Emslie Committee on Penalties for Homicide, 1970–72. **Offices and memberships** Member: Edinburgh Appeals Committee, Campaign for Cancer Research, 1970–73, Catholic Social Work Centre Executive Committee, 1974–77, Abbeyfield Edinburgh Executive Committee, 1975–76, chairman, Extra Care House; on board of governors and executive committee, St Columba's Hospice, 1976–80; on council, Scottish Soldiers', Sailors' and Airmen's Housing Association and member, House committee, 1979–84. **Awards and honours** Commander of the Order of the British Empire, 1951; Territorial Efficiency Decoration, 1952; Royal United Kingdom Beneficent Association, honorary secretary, 1974–75; LLD, Glasgow University, 1976. **Cause of death** Undisclosed, at age 87.

B. KLIBAN

American Cartoonist

***Born* Norwalk, Connecticut, 1 January 1935**

***Died* San Francisco, California, 12 August 1990**

Kliban's cats were nothing like Garfield, the lovable lasagne-eater. Though Kliban referred to the cat as "one hell of a nice animal, frequently mistaken for meatloaf", his drawings of cats were slightly sinister, inspiring a sense of unease, like his drawing of a man in a fish-shaped tie warily eyeing a cat perched on the arm of his chair. Even when the animal looked outwardly harmless, like his famous guitar-strumming cat, perched on the generic wooden stool found at any folk-club with eyes closed and a mellow expression, the caption still had the power to jar:

Love to eat them mousies,
Mousies what I love to eat.
Bite they little heads off...
Nibble on they tiny feet.

After the publication of his first book, *Cat*, Kliban's cats were everywhere. They could be seen on calendars, greeting cards, bedding, aprons, umbrellas, mugs, you name it. To Kliban's surprise, they made millions. In 1976, he said he was amazed he was actually making money from something he liked to do. "When I was in art school, I was nowhere near the top. So much of success is perseverance."

He didn't just do cats. He published ten books with marvellous titles like *Never Eat Anything Bigger Than Your Head* and *Whack Your Porcupine*. His non-cat cartoons were strange and wonderfully surreal, in a similar vein to Gary Larson's *The Far Side*. They might feature an empty pair of shoes with the caption: "Due to the convergence of forces beyond his comprehension, Salvatore Quanucci was suddenly squirted out of the Universe like a watermelon seed and never heard from again", or a drawing of a Mongol warrior with his arm around a middle-aged woman in a polyester pantsuit, titled: "Genghis and Sylvia Khan".

"Hap" Kliban (real name: Bernard — which he preferred to keep secret) hated school, where "the whole trip was to be a conformist". He flunked out of Pratt Institute and Cooper Union, and worked at a variety of menial jobs. He moved to California in 1959, and as he told an interviewer, "I knew I was home immediately." He became a freelance advertising illustrator, and then he started selling cartoons to *Playboy*. His agent suggested that he specialize in cats, and the rest, as they say, is history.

Those who knew him say he was shy but charming and hospitable. Obviously, he had a great sense of humour. His usual attire was jeans and sandals, and when he wasn't cartooning, he spent most of his time painting water-colours of San Francisco Bay. They were his insurance for the future. "If the cartoon thing ended tomorrow, I would have a craft to fall back on and not have to work for some corporation", he once said. "I could just take one of these paintings and trade it to some farmer for a chicken."

It never came to that; he was only 55 when he died.

Born Bernard Kliban. **Father** Manufacturer. **Children** One child. **Education** Pratt Institute, New York, Cooper Union, New York. **Career** Freelance advertising illustrator; cartoons published *Playboy* magazine; first book published, *Cat*, 1975. **Publications** *Cat*, 1975; *Never Eat*

Anything Bigger Than Your Head, and Other Drawings, 1976; *Whack Your Porcupine, and Other Drawings*, 1977; *Tiny Footprints, and Other Drawings*, 1978; *Playboy's Kliban*, 1979; *Two Guys Fooling Around the Moon*, 1982; *Luminous Animals*, 1983. **Cause of death** Heart disease, at age 55.

NORMAN MALCOLM

American Philosopher

***Born* Selden, Kansas, 11 June 1911**

***Died* London, England, 5 August 1990**

An ideal for any sphere of human achievement is that of the devoted pupil of a great teacher — a pupil who goes on to important work with a lasting sense of affection and respect for his tutor. For Norman Malcolm that teacher was the eccentric and enigmatic philosopher Ludwig Wittgenstein. Malcolm played an important part in introducing generations of students to Wittgenstein's work. He also interpreted and elaborated it, for Wittgenstein's style was compact and highly thought-provoking. Even where Professor Malcolm pursued his own insights the aura of his mentor was often evident.

It was at Cambridge University, England, that the two men first met, in 1938. There Malcolm also worked under G. E. Moore and John Wisdom. By that time he had already spent five years on post-graduate studies at Harvard after taking his first degree at the University of Nebraska. Remaining in England for a year and a half on a travelling fellowship, Malcolm attended Wittgenstein's classes and they became good friends, maintaining a correspondence subsequently when Malcolm was teaching at Princeton, and later through the war. Amongst the mail were Street and Smith detective-story magazines, much appreciated by Wittgenstein.

During the war, Malcolm served with the US Navy as executive officer of a destroyer escort on convoy duty in the North Atlantic, of which time he was later inclined to recall the comic incidents more than any other. But soon after the war he was back in Cambridge at Wittgenstein's classes, this time on a Guggenheim fellowship. Malcolm's first and highly acclaimed book, *Ludwig Wittgenstein: A Memoir*, recounts with great sensitivity these long hours spent together and tells of Wittgenstein's extraordinary personality, which was always caught in a love-hate relationship with the world of academia.

Returning to the US in 1947, Malcolm took up a teaching post at Cornell University, where he later became Susan Linn Sage Professor of Philosophy. Together with the philosopher Max Black, he transformed the department there, turning it into an important centre for the introduction of Wittgenstein's ideas to America. Central to these ideas was the theme of philosophical therapy, a process of liberation from mistakes embedded in the tradition as invisible assumptions in the very formulation of questions. At the same time, Malcolm was pursuing his own development of Wittgensteinian thinking and first caused a stir in the philosophical world with his book *Dreaming*, which appeared in 1959.

This book argued for the very counter-intuitive idea that what makes it true that someone has had a dream is their giving a sincere report of a dream, and that any talk of mental processes going on in them while they sleep, is spurious. That is, there is no fact about their having dreamt over and above the sincerely delivered report. Malcolm marshalled subtle arguments for this thesis, which so offends the popular modern idea that there are mental processes and that they are to be identified somehow or other with what goes on in people's heads. This area is now even more problematic to philosophers than ever. Malcolm's arguments, involving the analysis of meaning, have had an important part to play in creating current perplexity.

In philosophical discussion, Norman Malcolm was temperamentally fully in tune with Wittgenstein's dictum that the first law should be "take your time". In a lecture once, a student complained to the Professor that he was too slow; "You think I'm slow?" Malcolm replied, "And you think that's a *fault*?" His careful but relentless deliberation was accentuated by the gravelly Nabraska drawl which he always retained; but he was not ponderous, there was a composed but high-spirited energy to his delivery. There was also a composure about his general approach to life and handling of personal tribulation — composure seemingly founded on a religious faith that was for him beyond discussion.

Religion, he argued, like science, was language embedded in action. And the groundlessness of religious belief is no different from the groundlessness of the principles of science — something that many philosophers have found themselves forced to admit, albeit reluctantly, Bertrand Russell, for example, never found himself able to justify the best science as against the ravings of "the man who thinks he is a poached egg", yet he retained a faith in science. Malcolm wrote of religion and science, that "neither stands in need of justification, the one no more than the other". Three months before he died he completed an article on Wittgenstein's remark that he saw his own philosophical work "from a religious point of view".

It was in the sphere of religion that Malcolm was again to stimulate a flurry of philosophical controversy, with his publication in 1960 of an article on St Anselm's ontological arguments for the existence of God. Malcolm maintained that the statement "God is the greatest of all beings" is a logically necessary truth and that such a conception of God is an intrinsic part of our language through the influence of Judeo-Christian religion. This is a novel approach to an old debate. Suddenly, the proposition is not just lying on the logician's slab for careful dissection, it is incorporated into the social and linguistic practice in which we have our being. The move opens a metalevel of argument.

Throughout the 1960s and 1970s Malcolm worked and published on the theory of knowledge and philosophy of mind. He became particularly interested in memory, characteristically resisting the increasing tendency to equate memory with the recording processes being discovered by psychologists and invented by computer scientists. His stand here has been an important element in maintaining the tension which will one day, perhaps, give rise to a theory of mind subtle enough to explain the materialist intuitions, without succumbing to them in a simplistic and ultimately nonsensical way.

In 1978 Malcolm retired from Cornell to become visiting professor to the Department of Philosophy at King's College, London. He enjoyed living in England and found a new happiness in his second marriage, to Ruth Riesenberg. They lived in north London's Hampstead, where they regularly entertained visiting academics and old friends from around the world. At King's, Norman Malcolm remained active until close to his death. He held a weekly post-graduate seminar, regularly attended staff seminars and maintained a rigorous critical engagement with contemporary issues, corresponding with such well-known philosophers as David Armstrong, Saul Kripke, Thomas Nagel and Jerry Fodor.

In 1984 he published with Armstrong a discussion of the nature of mind entitled *Consciousness and Causality*. In 1986 came an analysis of Wittgenstein's philosophy, *Nothing is Hidden*, for which Malcolm was much praised by Wittgenstein scholars. The book was the fruit of a long career of revisiting again and again the ideas of the man whom he had found personally and intellectually so captivating.

Born Norman Malcolm. **Parents** Charles Claude and Ada (Wingrove) Malcolm. **Marriages** 1) Leonida Morosova, 1944 (dissolved); 2) Ruth Riesenberg, 1976. **Children** Christopher and

Elizabeth, from first marriage. **Education** University of Nebraska, BA, 1933; Harvard University, Cambridge, Massachusetts, MA, 1938, PhD, 1940; Cambridge University, 1938–40, 1946. **Military service** Executive officer, United States Navy, North Atlantic, 1942–45, became lieutenant. **Career** Instructor in philosophy, Princeton University, Princeton, New Jersey, 1940–42, 1946; assistant professor, Cornell University, Ithaca, New Jersey, 1947–50, associate professor, 1950–55, professor of philosophy, 1955, Susan Linn Sage Professor of Philosophy, 1965–78; Visiting Flint Professor of Philosophy, University of California, Los Angeles, 1964; Center for Advanced Study in the Behavioural Sciences fellow, 1968–69; visiting professor, King's College, London, 1978–90. **Offices and memberships** Member, American Philosophical Association, president, Eastern Division, 1972; member: American Association of University Professors, American Academy of Arts and Sciences. **Awards and honours** Guggenheim fellow, 1946–47; Hibbern research fellow, Princeton University, 1952; Fulbright research fellow, University of Helsinki, Finland, 1960–61. **Publications** *Ludwig Wittgenstein: A Memoir*, 1958; *Dreaming*, 1959; *Knowledge and Certainty*, 1963; *Problems of Mind*, 1971; *Memory and Mind*, 1977; *Thought and Knowledge*, 1977; *Wittgenstein: The Relation of Language to Instinctive Behaviour* (lecture), 1981; (with D. M. Armstrong), *Consciousness and Causality: A Debate on the Nature of Mind*, 1984; *Nothing is Hidden: Wittgenstein's Criticism of His Early Thought*, 1986. **Cause of death** Leukaemia, at age 79. **Further reading** Carl Ginet and Sidney Shoemaker, editors, *Knowledge and Mind: Philosophical Essays* (bibliography), 1983; *Thinkers of the Twentieth Century*, 1987.

REAR-ADMIRAL SIR DAVID MARTIN

Australian Naval Officer and Former State Governor

***Born* 15 April 1933**

***Died* Sydney, Australia, 10 August 1990**

The pomp and circumstance of a vice-regal position might well seem anachronistic in this day and age, and especially in an egalitarian country like Australia. But in the hands of the right man, even such a hang-over from colonial days as the position of governor of New South Wales, can be used to popular advantage. And such a man was Rear-Admiral Sir David Martin. A genuine Australian of Australians—he was descended on his mother's side from an army officer who sailed to New South Wales with the First Fleet in 1788 and on the way met and married one of the earliest batch of convicts—Martin took on the ceremonial post determined to be a "people's governor". During his brief period of office—only 17 months—he did much to break down the normally stuffy image of the Queen's representative. He was available to all and ready to visit every kind of organization and institution. All sorts and conditions of people were invited to Government House (schoolchildren were particularly welcome), and the Governor was to be seen not only at investitures and other ceremonial occasions, but down coalmines, at sewage plants and waste disposal works, wherever people wanted to meet him. In his own words at his untimely resignation through ill-health; "We had so much to do, so many people on the list we wanted to meet, so many coalmines, mental homes and sheltered workshops we wanted to go back to and so many people we wanted to bring to Government House."

David James Martin was born into a naval family. His father was executive officer of HMAS *Perth* and went down with her when she was sunk by the Japanese in action in the Java Sea in 1942. Educated at the Scots College, New South Wales, there was no question but that the 13-year-old

David should follow the family tradition. When asked once if his father's death had put him off the Navy, Admiral Martin replied "I think it put me on". After the Royal Australian Naval College at Flinders, he specialized as a gunnery officer and saw action in the Korean war, the Cyprus Emergency and the Icelandic "cod wars". He ended up as flag officer, Naval Support Command, and in this capacity was responsible for organizing the Royal Fleet Review in Sydney harbour in 1986 to commemorate the seventy-fifth annniversary of the Royal Australian Navy.

On retirement in 1988 he was an obvious popular choice for appointment as governor of New South Wales, and was sworn in as the thirty-fourth holder of that office on 1 January 1989. Despite his unstuffy attitude, he took his duties very seriously. His mixture of dignity and informality struck a happy note with the Australian public; he will long be remembered for his personal comfort to the victims of the Newcastle earthquake and other disasters. His own life was to be cut short by a mesothelioma — an incurable chest cancer associated with asbestosis which may well have come from his service career in ships lagged with asbestos. Though greatly debilitated by his illness, he hung on for as long as possible. His farewell parade was one of smiles and gestures to the crowd which gave no inkling of his critical condition. Within three days of leaving office he was dead. A man of wide interests and with an enormous circle of friends, he summed up the best in his country's character. As he said in his farewell speech: "What we have come to realize is that Australians are looking for decent standards and ethics and are reaching out for guidance and example." They could not find a better example than David Martin.

Born David James Martin. **Father** Commander W. Harold Martin. **Marriage** Suzanne Millear, 1957. **Children** One son and two daughters, William, Sandy and Anna. **Education** The Scots College, New South Wales; Royal Australian Navy College, 1947. **Career** Officer, Royal Australian Navy, 1947–88; served in HMAS *Sydney*, Korea, 1951–52; in HMS *Battleaxe*, 1959–60; gunnery officer, HMAS *Voyager*, 1963; naval attaché, Royal Australian Navy Liaison Staff, Australian High Commission, United Kingdom, 1964–65; executive officer, Royal Australian Navy College, 1967–68; in HMAS *Vampire*, 1967; commanding officer, HMAS *Queensborough*, 1969, *Torrens* and Third Destroyer squadron, 1974, *Supply*, 1978, *Melbourne*, 1979; fleet operations officer, 1969–71; director-general, Naval Reserves and Cadets, 1973; Royal College of Defence Studies, 1980; director-general of Manpower, 1981–82; chief of naval personnel, 1982–83, flag officer, Naval Support Command, 1984–88, retired as admiral; Royal Australian Navy Emergency List, 1988; governor of New South Wales, 1989–90. **Offices and memberships** Fellowship of First Fleeters; member: Australian Naval Institute, Australasian Pioneers Society; patron, Captain A. Phillip Bicentennial Committee; chairman, Sydney-Portsmouth Sister City Association; trustee, Variety Club of Australia. **Awards and honours** Officer of the Order of Australia, 1985; Knight Commander of the Order of St Michael and St George, 1988. **Cause of death** Mesothelioma, at age 57.

ETTORE MASERATI

Italian Automobile Engineer

***Born* 1894**

***Died* Bologna, Italy, 4 August 1990**

Orsi was so impressed with the spark plugs, it bought the car (apologies to Remington). Ironically, anybody with little or no interest in motor cars will at least know the name but who would associate Maserati with a sparkplug?

There were six Maserati brothers: Carlo, Mario, Alfieri, Bindo, Ettore and Ernesto. Alfieri was responsible for setting up the sparkplug company in Milan towards the end of World War I. Initially these were used in aero-engines, and in peacetime there was expansion into the car market. Ettore, the fifth of the six brothers, together with Carlo, Alfieri and Ernesto, set up business in Bologna. They prepared customers' cars for the racetrack, being especially involved in the design and production of a racing car for the Diatto car company. After a year, Diatto withdrew and the Maserati brothers took control. Ettore's contribution was largely as motor engineer and mechanic, making good use of his previous experience working on racing cars for Isotta Fraschini. To Ettore fell responsibility for tuning and testing of the vehicles, which he accomplished, not without occasional mishap. Responsibility for the business and managerial aspects of the company were largely vested in his brothers.

The Maserati company was launched with a bang, Alfieri driving the car to victory in its 1926 début in Targa Florio. The following four years saw a succession of Grand Prix victories for the car with the trident motif.

Following the deaths of both Carlo and Alfieri Maserati, the Orsi industrial concern purchased the company in 1937. The remaining brothers signed ten-year contracts but this was the beginning of the end of the family influence on the vehicles which still bear their name. There were a few more wins, notably the 500 Mile Race in America in 1939 and 1940, but the inevitable rationalization was already under way. Ettore was to concern himself with the electrical side of the business in Modena.

In 1947, the brothers broke free and established a new motor company, OSCA, in Bologna. Ettore was production engineer, primarily making sports racing cars but OSCA could not compete with Ferrari (to whom Ettore was a technical adviser for a short time), Lotus, Porsche and the continuing Maserati. OSCA was sold and by 1967 it had ceased to exist.

The original Maserati company grew in strength and reputation, sadly without any involvement of the Maserati brothers. Its golden years were in the 1950s with Fangio and Stirling Moss in the cockpit.

Ettore was the last surviving member of the brothers, most of whom had been obsessed with motor racing. He must have reflected with mixed feelings on the success and reputation of the company he had helped to establish. Had the family not relinquished ownership, no doubt lack of investment would have starved it to death and it would have met the same fate as OSCA. The name lives on, now the property of the Fiat empire.

What of the sparkplugs? They may have fired the engines of one the world's greatest cars but they hardly fire the imagination.

Born Ettore Maserati. **Father** A racing driver. **Career** Test driver for Isotta Fraschini, Milan; founder, director, with brothers Carlo, Alfieri and Ernesto, Maserati factory, firstly for the production of sparkplugs, later of racing cars, Bologna, 1914–26; first Maserati car, 1926; founder, director, car tuner and tester, with brothers, Officine Alfieri Maserati, Bologna, 1926–38; manager, Maserati, under ownership of Orsi industrial combine, Modena, 1938–47; founder, director, production engineer, Officina Specializzata Costruzione Automobili, Bologna, 1947–63; company taken over by MV, motorcycle manufacturers, 1963–66; retired, 1966. **Related activities** Technical adviser to Ferrari, briefly. **Championships** (include) Targa Florio, 1926; Indianapolis 500, 1939, 1940; Sebring 12-hour race, Florida, 1954. **Cause of death** Undisclosed, at age 96.

HAROLD MASURSKY

American Space Scientist and Geologist

***Born* Fort Wayne, Indiana, 23 December 1923**

***Died* Flagstaff, Arizona, 24 August 1990**

In the two decades since a spacecraft first escaped from the earth's gravitational pull — the Russian Lunik in January 1959 — the range of geologists has expanded similarly. Close-up photographs of the surfaces of planets, and better still soil samples brought back from the moon by astronauts, have injected the excitement of a completely new territory to the subject that no one could have imagined before World War II. Harold Masursky was in the forefront of this new exploration, firstly working on lunar projects with the US National Aeronautics and Space Administration, then leading the team that brought back images of the surface of Mars, and finally participating in the Voyager Project obtaining pictures of planets in the outer solar system.

Harold Masursky, or Hal as he always liked to be called, was a teacher's son, and he graduated from Yale University in geology and civil engineering in 1943. After two years with the Army Corps of Engineers in India he returned to Yale for his Master's degree in 1951.

For the next decade he worked with the US Geological Survey in the western United States, where he worked on uraniferous coal deposits. At the time Lunik left the Earth, he was discovering a zone of rocks rich in minerals which led to a resurgence in prospecting and eventually a significant gold deposit.

In 1962 he joined the Astrogeology branch of the US Geological Survey to work on lunar exploration. He was quickly recognized as a superb communicator to the public as well as his scientific colleagues: he was informally known as "The Golden Voice". At the same time the work used his great administrative talents. He believed in "using people for what they're good at, not trying to change them."

By 1966 the craters on the Moon's surface had been well photographed. Some scientists felt they were the result of meteoric impacts, others of volcanic activity both recently and in the distant past. Masursky studied over 200 miles of film from the unmanned probe Orbiter 1 and came to the conclusion that both theories were correct — it depended which crater you were studying. "The geological evolution of the Moon is going on now", he said. "It looks very nearly as dynamic as the Earth.

"There are many processes going on — the 'faulting' or uplifting of material, the distribution of material by meteor impacts, and the construction of features by volcanic processes."

In 1967, when the unmanned lunar probe Surveyor 5 analysed lunar soil, Masursky showed that it contained the same minerals as the basalt which comprises about a fifth of the Earth's crust, demonstrating the two are very similar bodies, even though the Moon has no air, and no water in any form has yet been detected there. Masursky also helped choose the landing sites for the manned lunar landings of Apollo 16 and 17.

After completing his work on the lunar programme, Masursky led the Mariner 9 Imaging Experiment to map the surface of Mars. As Mariner 9 arrived there it encountered a gigantic dust storm engulfing the entire planet, making observation impossible. This storm was a complete mystery and no other Martian storms have been seen in the 19 years since it was observed. Some experts think it may have been caused by a gigantic meteorite crash. As the storm began to clear, three large, circular features became visible. Many of the imaging team thought they had been caused by impact, but Masursky instantly and correctly identified them as enormous volcanic craters. His interest in Mars and especially in the possibility of a wet climate in the Martian past led him to play an important role in the selection of landing sites and the search for life.

As early as the 1960s Masursky was pressing for the mapping of Venus, which is always covered with clouds, by radar. He was a major participant in the Pioneer Venus Mission, and fought long and hard for the Magellan Project, determined to get the best instruments possible for revealing the planet's geological secrets. The Pioneer Mission penetrated below the thick carbon dioxide atmosphere which is caused by a "runaway greenhouse effect" from volcanic eruptions raising the surface temperatures to above 900 degrees Fahrenheit, hot enough to melt lead. The surface was even more battered and craggy than Earth's, with a mountain 8000 feet higher than Everest and a plateau bigger than the plateau of Tibet. The Magellan probe began taking pictures shortly before he died.

In the 1980s Masursky contributed to the exploration of the outer solar system and was a key figure in the Voyager Project. He championed the geological exploration of Jupiter's bizarre moons and was engaged in Voyager 2's encounter with Neptune and its moon Triton, then the most distant known objects from the Sun in our planetary sytem.

As author or co-author of countless publications and a member of innumerable scientific committees, Masursky's influence in planetary exploration was very wide. Popular with his fellow-scientists in the US he also worked very closely with Russian colleagues — he was "Uncle Hal" to many of their families — and this resulted in many joint efforts which would not have been possible otherwise.

The one battle that Masursky fought for most of his life — the struggle with diabetes — was the one he finally lost. He always considered that his work was infinitely more important than his health. Because so many of his days were spent on aeroplanes or in airports the world over, many people in many countries knew when he was going into insulin shock. He was saved from disaster on countless occasions.

It is especially poignant that just before his death, his 25-year dedication to the exploration of Venus had started to bear fruit: Magellan was just beginning its orbital mapping of Venus. When he was told of the startling detail of the Magellan images, his response was a broad smile, which probably showed his satisfaction at a job well done and a life well spent.

Born Harold Masursky. **Parents** Louis, teacher, and Celia (Ochstein) Masursky. **Marriage** LesLee Alexander. **Children** Lisa, Danielle, Leo and Noah. **Education** Yale University, New Haven, Connecticut, BS in geology and civil engineering, 1943, MS, 1951. **Military service** Army of the United States, Coast Artillery and Corps of Engineers, 1943–46. **Career** Joined United States Geological Survey, 1947, began work on lunar exploration, Astrogeology branch, Flagstaff, Arizona, 1962, chief scientist, 1971–75, senior scientist, 1975 onwards; surveyor of projects, lunar orbiter, United States Geological Survey, 1965–67; team leader, principal investigator, first team to map Mars, 1971; co-investigator, Apollo field geological team, Apollo 16, Apollo 17, also, member, Apollo orbital scientific photographic team, Apollo site selection group; leader, Viking landing site staff, deputy team leader, orbiter visual imaging systems, Viking Mars, 1975; team member, Voyager, Jupiter, Saturn, Uranus, 1977; chairman, mission operations group, Pioneer Venus Mission, 1978; co-chairman, mission operational group, Galileo Mission, 1981; mission operations leader, radar team, Magellan mission, Venus orbiting imaging radar mission, 1981 onwards; member, camera team, Mars observer, 1986; as team member, Voyager Project, engaged in Voyager 2's encounter with Neptune and Triton, 1989. **Related activities** Member: Space Scientific Advisory Committee, 1978–81, solar systems exploration committee, 1980–83, Space Scientific Board, 1982 onwards; president, Working Group for Planetary Systems Nomeclature, International Astronomical Union; secretary, Coordinating Committee of Moon and Planets; associate editor: *Icarus*, bulletin of the Geological Society of America; author of over 200 publications, dealing mostly with the geological evolution of the Moon, Mars and Venus. **Offices and memberships** (include) Fellow, Geological Society of America, president, planetary geological division; member: American Association for the Advancement of Science, American Geophysical Union, International Astronomical Union, American Astronomical Association. **Awards and honours** National Aeronautics and Space Administration awards for exceptional scientific achievement, 1972, 1973, 1977, 1980, 1988; honorary doctorate, Northern Arizona University, 1981; National Award for Achievement in Lunar and Planetary Exploration, Smithsonian Institution, 1988. **Cause of death** Illness associated with diabetes, at age 66.

JOE MERCER

British Football Player and Manager

Born **Ellesmere Port, Cheshire, 9 August 1914**

Died **Manchester, England, 9 August 1990**

A cartoonist at the time when Joe Mercer managed the national team, in the 1970s, drew him sitting beside the post-match bath, sharing fried potatoes — "Give us a chip, son" — with his players. There have been few, if any, such genial and avuncular spirits since then in the harsh world of professional soccer.

He was born in 1914, at Ellesmere Port on the estuary of the River Mersey, and emerged at school as a footballer to watch. The Ellesmere Port team gave him six pennies and a bag of vegetables for his first appearance with them; by the age of 17, he was getting five pounds, "and I counted it a dozen times on the way home." This was with Everton, the giants on the other side of the Mersey. Leading the forward line here was the formidable Dixie Dean, who, built like a brick outhouse himself, didn't fancy the new boy much: "You've got a pair of legs that wouldn't last the postman his morning round." Mercer's spindly, bandy legs were a regular source of amusement to other players and the public, though appearances can be deceptive of course. Playing at left half (in what is now covered by the catch-all Midfield) he was a scientific tackler, a quick passer and a tireless runner in support of the attacks he could thus set up. In 1939, Everton won the Football League Championship, and Mercer was selected by England for all international matches that season.

World War II denied Mercer what should have been the prime of his playing life, though he did win unofficial England honours during the years of fighting. He served meanwhile with the Army Physical Training Corps, and valued his years as a soldier, being particularly pleased with his later appointment as an honorary vice-president of the Army Football Association. In 1946 there was peace again; the national soccer programme was rejuvenated but, alas, Mercer was not. Now aged 32, and suffering knee-trouble, he was rejected by Everton and, hurt not only in his spiral legs, considered retirement. To general surprise, his services were requested by the London club Arsenal. Though he no longer had boundless energy, his sound technique, tactical sense and warm personality did wonders for an ailing side. Mercer enjoyed an Indian summer of seven seasons, captaining Arsenal to a Football Association Cup, and two League Championships. He was voted footballer of the year aged 35; after breaking a leg at the age of 38 — a ripe one for an outfield player — he decided to call it a day.

Mercer's second career, as a team manager, did not have a very bright start. He could not keep Sheffield United away from relegation, and his consequent determination to succeed at Aston Villa (another club in the doldrums) took a toll on his health: Villa won promotion and the League Cup, Mercer suffered a nervous breakdown. The fun began in 1965, when he took over at Manchester

City. Unabashed by the vast shadow of glamorous Manchester United, he guided his new team through the most successful period of its history: a League Championship, the FA Cup, the League Cup and the European Cup-Winners Cup. A shrewd judge of players and men, he bought wisely and, as always, fostered *esprit de corps*. The young tearaway Malcolm Allison was established as coach. Of the brilliant partnership that resulted, Derek Hodgson writes "Allison had 10 good ideas a day, nine of which were ridiculous, one of which was brilliant. Mercer was sage enough to spot the one idea that could be adapted to serve footballers, not all of whom were nuclear physicists." Allison himself said "I charged into situations like a bull...Joe came behind me, picking up the pieces, soothing the wounded and the offended with that vast charm." They fell out in 1972. Mercer lost the ensuing power struggle and moved away to become general manager of Coventry City.

Two years later, the Football Association sacked Alf Ramsey as manager of England. Mercer, now in semi-retirement, accepted the position of caretaker manager, on the understanding that he did not want the job on a permanent basis. He was in charge for seven matches and produced some memorably sophisticated soccer and although, allegedly, Mercer could not always recall the names of individuals in his squad, the atmosphere in the dressing room heightened perceptibly on his arrival. A grimmer era was coming with the next incumbent — Don Revie, the "tight-lipped dossier king".

Mercer represents the best of the old-style professional sportsman, being much more than a gifted player. He was wise and humorous — Allison said he could "cut through the pompous like a knife". With his enormous, horsey smile, it was unmistakable that he liked life, and he liked people: others seem always to have felt better for meeting him.

Born Joseph Mercer. **Father** A professional footballer. **Marriage** Nora. **Military service** Instructor Army Physical Training Corps, Aldershot, also, representative for the Army, Aldershot Football Club, World War II. **Career** Footballer, Ellesmere Port; wing-half: Everton, 1931–46, Arsenal, 1946–54; first division début, 1933; manager, Sheffield United, 1955, Aston Villa, 1958, Manchester City, 1965, Coventry City, 1972, also director; caretaker manager, England team, 1974. **Statistics** As footballer: England International, five times, 1939, plus 27 wartime and Victory games; Inter-league games, 1; league championship, 1938–39, 1947–48, 1952–53; FA Cup championship, 1950, runner-up, 1952; as manager: Aston Villa, League Cup win, 1960–61; Manchester City, League Cup win, 1967–68, Division One title, 1969–70, European Cup-Winners Cup, 1969–70, Football League Cup, 1969–70. **Awards and honours** Three championship medals; Football Association Cup winner's medal; five full and 22 war-time international caps; Footballer of the Year, 1950; honorary vice-president, Army Football Association; Officer of the Order of the British Empire, 1976. **Cause of death** Undisclosed, at age 76.

BRUCE NORMAN

British Writer, Editor and Producer

Born **Northampton, England, 2 November 1936**

Died **16 August 1990**

Bruce Norman will be greatly missed by historians and archaeologists as well as by his colleagues in the world of documentary television. To the scholars and the excavators he was the man who brought their work to the widest possible audience, to the TV professionals he was a master of his art, able to make excellent, enthralling programmes about such unlikely subjects as nautical archaeology, or World War II code-breaking.

Although he was educated in England, and studied at Nottingham University, he gained his early experience of broadcasting in the United States, working for radio stations as a writer. Only in 1965 did he return to England to embark on a career in television with Granada, an independent company based in Manchester. Bruce wrote and researched for news and current affairs programmes and even spent some time as a scriptwriter for *Coronation Street*, Britain's longest running TV soap opera. It was in the imaginative presentation of real drama, however, that he excelled, his most notable achievement in the late 1960s being a study of the effects of prolonged bombardment on the inhabitants of Leningrad, Berlin and London during World War II. *Cities at War* was a sympathetic, emotional and even humorous look at the lives of ordinary people in difficult times, carefully researched and beautifully written. It showed that he was expert in the most difficult side of documentary work: writing a script that is entertaining and absorbing for a large and varied TV audience, whilst still being accurate and informative.

In 1970 he went freelance, combining the roles of writer, producer and editor on a variety of projects which used dramatic presentation to deal with historical themes. He worked for the BBC as part of their Scientific and Features Department, for several years, writing scripts for documentaries which featured well-known actors playing celebrated scientists of the past. These included Arthur Lowe, a renowned comedy actor, who starred as Louis Pasteur in *Microbes and Men* and Edward Fox as Sigmund Freud in *The Rat Man*. During this time he also researched into the early days of television in Britain, making a programme called *The Birth of Television* to celebrate the fortieth anniversary of the BBC. This work resulted in a book called *Here's Looking at You*. Another project which produced a successful book was his acclaimed dramatization of the story of how the Allies broke the Nazi code systems in World War II, learning the secrets of the famous "Enigma" machine.

Bruce's growing reputation, and a string of successful productions, brought him the coveted post of editor on the BBC's science programme, *Horizon*. In one extended season he achieved a pair of nominations for awards from the British Academy of Film and Television Arts (the British equivalent to the Oscars), and won the award for the Best Documentary Series in 1974. Two years later he was made head of the History and Archaeology Unit at the BBC. It was the perfect place for him to make the most of his talents as a writer and editor. He travelled widely and explored all sorts of possible themes for the two main programmes which fell within his area, *Chronicle*, which had an established format, and the magazine-style history programme, *Timewatch*, which was his own creation.

He loved the challenges and adventure of researching for his programmes, even if there might also be a certain amount of danger involved. On one occasion, while investigating the desert trails of the Yemen, he was kidnapped and held in custody by some local nomadic tribesmen. It was his ability to bring something of the excitement of studying the past to an audience sitting comfortably at home which earned him the eternal respect of his fellow workers.

The editor's role in television is made even more crucial when a particular event is being covered live. On the face of it there was little to make people's pulses race about the recovery of an old wooden wreck from the muddy waters of the English Channel in 1982. The raising of the *Mary Rose*, Henry VIII's short-lived flagship, was a painfully slow and delicate manoeuvre. The sodden timbers were cradled in a mass of brightly painted steel, and the fascinating combination of everyday items and "buried treasure" which had made the wreck so important were already on the surface and in the hands of the conservationists and art historians. Yet skilful editing, coupled with imaginative presentation of the circumstances of the initial wreck and the subsequent underwater excavation, produced an enthralling spectacle for the watching millions as they saw the vessel being slowly brought to the surface after almost 500 years underwater.

The television documentary field is a difficult one, especially for a writer and editor, whose work is perhaps best appreciated when it passes almost unnoticed by the audience. Bruce Norman's contribution to history and archaeology, as well as to television, was recognized in 1990 when he was made a fellow of the Royal Television Society. It was an appropriate acknowledgement of his professional excellence, which has set the standards for other programme-makers to aim for in the next century.

Born Bruce Norman. **Marriage** Psyche. **Children** One son and one daughter. **Education** Nottingham University. **Career** Teacher, briefly; broadcaster, US radio, early 1960s; writer, broadcaster, 1965 onwards; scriptwriter, researcher, Granada Television, 1965–70; freelance writer, producer, British Broadcasting Corporation, 1971, television editor, Science and Features Department, Kensington, 1972–76, head, Archaeology and History Unit, 1976–89. **Offices and memberships** Fellow, Royal Television Society, 1990. **Awards and honours** British Academy of Film and Television Arts Award for Best Documentary Series, 1974; three nominations, British Academy of Film and Television Arts, one for Best Outside Broadcast for *Mary Rose*, 1982. **Television** (as editor, unless otherwise indicated) *Coronation Street* (scriptwriter), 1965; *Cities at War* (scriptwriter), 1967; *Omnibus* (scriptwriter/producer), 1971; *Horizon*, 1972–74; *Chronicle*, 1976–89; *Timewatch* (also instigator), 1982 onwards; *Mary Rose*, 1982; also: *The Case of the Midwife Toad* (scriptwriter), *Microbes and Men* (scriptwriter), *The Codebreakers* (scriptwriter), *The Birth of Television* (scriptwriter), *Tigris*, *Six English Towns*, *Footsteps*, *Discoveries*, *Underwater*. **Publications** *Secret Warfare*, 1973; *The Inventing of America*, 1976; *Here's Looking at You*, 1984. **Cause of death** Undisclosed, at age 53.

RICHARD LITTLE PURDY

American Literary Scholar

Born **Middletown, New York, 21 April 1904**

Died **Chatham, New Jersey, 7 August 1990**

"A PURE WOMAN": that's the sub-title Thomas Hardy gave to one of the most famous and most heart-rending of his novels, *Tess of the d'Urbervilles*. According to Richard Purdy, Hardy added the sub-title, "at the last moment, after reading the final proofs, as being the estimate left in a candid mind of the heroine's character — an estimate that nobody would dispute. It was disputed more than anything else in the book." For, by the standards of Hardy's nineteenth-century England, Tess was also a "fallen woman".

On the niceties of when and what Hardy wrote, Purdy was an expert — indeed, he was *the* expert. It was his life's work to shed light, through careful study, on the character and the writing of Thomas Hardy. His own character remains elusive.

Richard Little Purdy's first scholarly work was an edition of *The Rivals*, by the eighteenth-century Irish dramatist, Sheridan. Other than this, his life and career centred on Hardy to a quite extraordinary degree: and on Yale University. He went to Yale in 1922 as an undergraduate and stayed as a post-graduate, then as a teacher, until his retirement nearly 50 years later in 1970. There he was trained in bibliography by Chauncey B. Tinker, an exacting task-master. It was Tinker's influence which led him to the study of books as physical objects.

Thomas Hardy died in January 1928. It fell to Purdy to organize an exhibition of the writer's books and papers; in the same year — at the age of 24 — he approached Hardy's widow with his proposal for the bibliography which was to take him nearly 30 years to complete. It was his association with the Yale exhibition — not matched, as Florence Hardy said, by anything done in England — that especially recommended him to her. In the summer of 1929 he visited he for the first time.

Hardy's widow — his second wife — had remained in Max Gate, the house her husband had designed. The house stands about a mile outside the county town of Dorchester (which features as Casterbridge in Hardy's *Mayor of Casterbridge* and other novels) and is in the heart of the English countryside which the novelist brought to life as "Wessex" in his fiction. When Purdy arrived, the house itself and — undoubtedly more important to him — the study, were exactly as Hardy had left them.

Ill and lonely, with a great burden of responsibility as her husband's literary custodian, Florence Hardy took a liking to the young American scholar and began to turn to him for advice. He in turn became attached to her. "It is probably not too much to say", wrote Hardy scholar and colleague Michael Millgate after Purdy's death, "that Florence Hardy's friendship...became and remained the central experience of Purdy's life."

In 1933 Purdy visited Florence Hardy again and continued to do so periodically thereafter. He made friends with several Hardy enthusiasts including the poet Henry Reed who also knew Florence Hardy. She told Purdy and Reed more about her husband than she told anyone else. Purdy was told the most and the notes he made of these conversations were so precious to him that when he decided to make them available to Michael Millgate for biographical purposes, he "could not bear to surrender them entirely but sat and read them aloud." Thus it was that Purdy was able to reveal (three years after Florence Hardy's death in 1937) that her so-called *Life* of her husband had in fact been written by Hardy himself and she had merely finished it off from his notes.

Back at Yale Purdy continued working on the bibliography. He also built up a private Hardy collection (now destined for the university) which was remarkable for its wealth of letters and annotated volumes from Hardy's own library.

His attachment to Yale endured; but his trips to Dorset had made him a committed Anglophile. After World War II he visited London almost every year. He loved English traditions and soon fell into a routine of staying at the old-established Brown's Hotel and eating at the gentlemen's club, the Athenaeum, of which he was a member. He also loved opera — Wagner particularly — and paid regular visits to the Met in New York and to Glyndebourne in Sussex.

In 1954 *Thomas Hardy: a bibliographical study* was finally published by the Oxford University Press. It has been kept in print ever since and remains a bible for Hardy scholars. It was an outstanding work — meticulous, scholarly and informative. It also had a substantial influence on bibliography generally; it was very much ahead of its time in its handling of material and its methods.

Purdy was a shy man. He was also a modest one. After the publication of the bibliography he was content to work behind the scenes. He shared his special knowledge of Hardy with Michael Millgate which enabled the English scholar to produce the best and fairest Hardy biography — published in 1982 and dedicated to Purdy. From 1978 until 1988 Purdy collaborated with Millgate on the seven-volume *Collected Letters*, also published by Oxford University Press.

Purdy's thoroughness, exactness and fastidiousness made him a superb bibliographer. In his personal life the same qualities made him an isolated man. He was a stickler for the conventions of dress and for the niceties of correct pronunciation. He was extremely conservative, adhering rigidly to the habits he established and the places he knew. He hated being photographed and — although he lectured at Yale throughout his adult life — he did not shine as a teacher.

The novels and poems of Thomas Hardy, though set mainly within the confines of rural Dorset, brook no limits in their portrayal of extremes of human passions — of love, of death, of guilt and of betrayal. It is a matter of speculation whether chance or choice led Richard Little Purdy to make the systematic study of the origins of these tempestuous creations his life's work. Only his continuing devotion to the majestic operas of Wagner gives any suggestion of the feelings his dry and scholarly manner concealed.

That and his behaviour towards his closest friends. To those who shared his interests, to serious scholars and Hardy enthusiasts, he was, according to Professor J. L. Bradley whom he taught at Yale, "a charming companion and a good friend". To Michael Millgate with whom he worked over so many years, he was, above all, a generous man: "an amusing companion, a concerned and kindly host, an eager sharer both of the resources of his collection and of his own vast knowledge, and the most generous of collaborators."

Born Richard Little Purdy. **Education** Yale University, New Haven, Connecticut, 1922, BA, PhD. **Career** Lecturer in nineteenth-century poetry, Yale University, associate professor, professor emeritus, 1970 onwards. **Related activities** Organizer, exhibition on Hardy, Yale, 1928; collector, Hardy manuscripts, letters. **Offices and memberships** Fellow: Berkeley College, Yale University, 1933 onwards; chief marshall and mace bearer, Yale Commencement Exercises. **Publications** *The Larpent Manuscript of "The Rivals"*, 1935; *Thomas Hardy: a bibibliographical study*, 1954; Thomas Hardy, *Our Exploits at West Poley* (editor), 1952; Thomas Hardy, *Far from the Madding Crowd* (editor), 1957; (co-editor with Michael Millgate) *The Collected Letters of Thomas Hardy*, volumes i-vii, 1978–88. **Cause of death** Undisclosed, at age 86. **Further reading** Michael Millgate, *Thomas Hardy: a biography*, 1982.

ROBERT REID

British Editor and Writer

***Born* Bradford, Yorkshire, 20 April 1933**

***Died* Hamstead Marshall, Berkshire, 17 August 1990**

The range and quality of television programmes on science in Britain is probably unsurpassed, and this stems to a large extent from a brilliant team in the British Broadcasting Corporation between 1964 to 1973. An important member of that group was Robert Reid, and he went on to lead it through a crucial stage in its development.

The son of a Yorkshire miner, he studied chemistry at Christ Church, Oxford before joining the Royal Tank Regiment with a commission for his National Service. Part of that time he was in Hong Kong. A proficient guitarist, he became an "uncle" on a forces' radio programme for children. When out of the Army he went to Cambridge, to Queens' College, where he received his doctorate in chemistry.

With such qualifications industry would have been the natural target, but instead he joined the BBC Television Talks Department as a general trainee, and he was attached to the *Tonight* programme, which involved him with an average of two filmed stories each week.

In April 1964 BBC 2, BBC's second television channel, came on the air. The programmes were intended to be more intellectual, and in the wave of recruitment of suitable staff, Reid joined the Science and Features Department.

His three years' experience with television, together with his scientific background and analytical mind, made him a success from the beginning, and his first documentary, *The Building of the Bomb*, was widely praised. It was 75 minutes long, and told the story of the Manhattan Project, the building of the first atomic bomb. Bob Reid included in it an interview with Robert Oppenheimer, who led the project, and he described later how he had sat by the cameraman appalled at the mumbled, incoherent responses of Oppenheimer to the interviewer's questions. He thought the sequence was a disaster. But when he looked at the rushes, he realized how the film had captured the anguish of the physicist haunted by his conscience, and in fact was the most memorable sequence from the programme.

A filmed biography of Einstein followed, and documentaries on the hydrogen bomb and autistic children. His scientific honesty, narrative art and skill as a director enhanced greatly the reputation of science on television. The initial public response had been ostracism and distrust, but this swung to an enthusiastic awareness of its power for informing and educating.

In 1966 Reid was given the programme *Horizon* to manage, and he steered it through from being a barely surviving, fortnightly magazine programme in black and white to a thriving weekly filmed documentary in colour with quadrupled audiences, and it soon gained a number of awards. The series has run for 24 years without a break.

In 1969 Reid was promoted to head of science and features. Now he was responsible for *Tomorrow's World*, James Burke's "specials" and many Tuesday documentaries as well as *Horizon*. He also helped initiate and edit Dr Jacob Bronowski's *The Ascent of Man*. In those programmes Bronowski said, "The most far-reaching change our century has set in motion is, I believe, a shift in our view of Nature and of man's place in it." Reid helped to portray that shifting view, the new awareness of the environment and the effect of it on man and man on it.

In 1973 he resigned from the BBC after a disagreement over management policy, and formed his own company under the umbrella of Video Arts. John Cleese was one of the founding directors, and the subjects of the videos made included how to run a company, how to conduct selection interviews, how to negotiate and how to run meetings. Reid wrote several of these and was responsible for a number of commissioned films as well.

Writing held his interest now, rather than production, and although he still produced as well as wrote prize-winning documentaries for the BBC, including the script for the dramatized series *The Life of Charles Darwin*, books occupied more of his time. His first one, *Tongues of Conscience*, asked whether the scientist working in the laboratory should be involved with the moral outcome of his work. Should he publish the truth that could damage the world or keep quiet about it?

His books were remarkably good. With far more science knowledge than most authors, he was much more skilled in communicating than most scientists. He kept in touch with scientific developments through the Royal Institution, of which he was a vice-president, and he was also a director of the Committee on the Public Understanding of Science.

His work brought him a fortune if not fame, and he had the money to live as a country gentleman with a 500-acre farm. He always dressed like one, and was a fine horseman. He became joint Master of the Vine and Cravan Foxhounds. He was friendly, but not easily an intimate friend for he was a very private person.

His success made him very wealthy, but others gained immeasurably as well, particularly television viewers. The tradition of BBC science productions which he helped found has educated as well as entertained millions, and will continue to do so.

Born Robert William Reid. **Father** A miner. **Marriage** Penelope MacKay, 1965. **Children** One son and one daughter. **Education** Heckmondwike Grammar School, Bradford, West Yorkshire; Christ Church, Oxford, scholar, BS in chemistry, 1956; research student, Queen's University, Kingston, Ontario; Queens' College, Cambridge, PhD in chemistry, 1959. **Military service** Commissioned, Royal Tank Regiment, served in Hong Kong, also broadcast on forces' radio children's programme, 1956–58. **Career** General trainee, British Broadcasting Corporation Television Talks Department, 1961; producer, BBC Science and Features, department, 1964–

67; first documentary, *The Building of the Bomb*; editor, *Horizon*, 1967–69; head, BBC Science and Features Department, 1969–73; author 1973 onwards; founder member with John Cleese, Sir Antony Jay, Peter Robinson and Michael Peacock, Video Arts, 1974, director, 1974–89. **Related activities** Collaborator, adviser, *Nova*, WGBH, Boston; director, Committee on the Public Understanding of Science. **Offices and memberships** Vice-president, Royal Institution; master, Vine and Cravan Foxhounds. **Television** (includes) *The Building of the Bomb*; *Horizon*; *Tomorrow's World*; *Ascent of Man*; *The Voyage of Charles Darwin* (scriptwriter). **Publications** *Tongues of Conscience*, 1969; *Marie Curie*, 1974; *Microbes and Men*, 1974; *Land of Lost Content: the Luddite revolt 1912*, 1986. **Cause of death** Undisclosed, at age 57.

DAVID ROSE

American Composer

***Born* London, England, 15 June 1910**

***Died* Burbank, California, 23 August 1990**

There are no lyrics, only a slow, suggestive melody that literally bumps and grinds. There has never been a song that was so totally identified with its title, and with the image conjured by that title. And anyone can hum the tune. It was a number-one song in 1962, staying in the American charts for 17 weeks. It's been heard in movies, in stage shows, in television comedies, and even commercials, such as the 1960s advertisement for a men's shaving product, in which a sultry blonde cooed, "Take it off, take it all off." (She was referring to a man's facial hair, of course.) The song is "The Stripper", and it was written by David Rose.

"The Stripper" was by no means his only accomplishment. He wrote and conducted the music for more than 50 albums, scored 36 films, including *Texas Carnival*, *Rich, Young and Pretty*, *Jupiter's Darling* and *Port Afrique*, and wrote the theme tunes for 24 different television series, such as *Sea Hunt*, *Highway to Heaven*, *Little House on the Prairie* and *Bonanza*. He won a total of four Emmys and five Grammys. He was nominated for an Oscar for the song, "So In Love", sung by Frank Sinatra in the film, *Wonder Man*.

His family emigrated from England to America when he was four years old. He grew up in Chicago, where jazz has always been a pervasive influence. He studied at the Chicago College of Music, and went on to make several 78 rpm recordings with the C-Melody saxophonist, Frankie Trumbauer. By 1933, Rose was arranging for jazz trombonist Jack Teagarden, and soon after that, he was playing piano as part of a group called the Hotcha Trio, and working as a staff arranger on local radio.

He moved to Hollywood, scored a hit record for Benny Goodman's orchestra, and then in 1938, he married the well-known actress and comedienne, Martha Raye. He was still married to Raye when he met the 19-year-old Judy Garland. It was one of those accidental meetings — they were working on different shows along the same corridor, and the first time he saw her, Garland, who'd just finished her fifteenth film and was totally exhausted, was crying. They fell in love, but Louis B. Mayer, the head of MGM, did not approve.

Mayer had several reasons for his objections. First, the fact that Judy Garland was involved with a married man would not be good for her image. Rose got divorced. Then, Mayer's plan was to get a few more years out of Garland as a teenage singer; he couldn't do this if she was a married woman. When Rose became engaged to Garland, Mayer summoned him to his office and threatened to have him barred from every studio and radio station in the country unless he agreed to postpone the wedding for at least 12 months. The couple defied him and were married in 1941. The marriage was over within 18 months, and Rose went into the Army, thus sparing MGM any embarrassment about their young star's marital difficulties. They didn't get divorced until 1945, one week before Judy Garland married Vincente Minnelli.

While still in the Army, Rose composed and arranged the music for *Winged Victory*, a propaganda show that was filmed in 1944 by Twentieth Century-Fox, with George Cukor directing. After the war, he worked on several MGM musicals (including *The Unfinished Dance* which featured another of his tunes which was to become a standard, "Holiday For Strings"), and also in their record division. He got married again, in 1948, to Betty Bigelow. This time it lasted the rest of his life.

He arranged hit recordings for Jane Powell and Connie Francis, he collaborated with André Previn, he conducted, he wrote hits, and he gave concerts. He had a long and fruitful career working in television. Louis Mayer's threat to bar him from every studio and station in the country had obviously come to nothing.

Born David Rose. **Marriages** 1) Martha Raye, actress and singer, 1938 (divorced 1941); 2) Judy Garland, actress and singer, 1941 (divorced 1945); 3) Betty Bigelow, 1948. **Children** Melanie and Angela. **Education** Chicago College of Music. **Emigration** Left England for United States, 1914. **Military service** US Army Air Forces, sergeant, World War II. **Career** Pianist, for Ted Fiorito's dance band, Chicago, at age of 16; pianist for NBC Radio, while still a student; first recordings as pianist with Frankie Trumbauer; staff arranger, Chicago radio stations; founder, musical director, the David Rose Orchestra for the Mutual Broadcasting System's twice weekly show, *California Melodies*, Hollywood, 1938; music director, *The Tony Martin Show*; conductor, composer and arranger, 1940s onwards; theatre début, 1943, film début, 1944, both with *Winged Victory*; television début with Red Skelton's Show, 1947. **Awards and honours** Four Emmys: for *Little House on the Prairie* (two), for *Bonanza*, for *An Evening with Fred Astaire*; five Grammys: for "Holiday for Strings", "Our Waltz", "The Stripper", for two André Previn albums, *Like Young* and *Like Blue*; six gold records: "Holiday for Strings", "Calypso Melody", "The Dance of the Spanish Onions", *Like Young*, *Like Blue*; Oscar nomination for "So In Love" from film *Wonder Man*, 1945. **Stage** (includes) *Winged Victory*, 1943; *Pasadena Pops Concert*; *David Rose* concerts, Hollywood Bowl. **Films** (include) *Winged Victory*, 1944; *Texas Carnival*, 1951; *Rich, Young and Pretty*, 1951; *Jupiter's Darling*, 1954; *Port Afrique*, 1956; *Please Don't Eat the Daisies*, 1960. **Television** (includes) *Bonanza*; *Highway Patrol*; *Sea Hunt*; *Highway to Heaven*; *Little House on the Prairie*; *Red Skelton Show*; *Fred Astaire Show*; *Jack Benny Show*; *Bob Hope Show*. **Radio** (includes) *California Melodies*; *Red Skelton Show*. **Compositions** (include) "It's Been So Long"; "Melancholy Mood"; "Our Waltz"; "So In Love"; "Holiday For Strings"; "Manhattan Square Dance"; "One More Time"; "True Love"; "My Happiness"; "The Stripper"; "Waukegan Concerto"; "Calypso Melody"; "The Dance Of The Spanish Onions"; Concerto for Flute and Orchestra. **Cause of death** Complications from heart disease, at age 80.

RAYMOND ST JACQUES

American Actor and Director

Born **Hartford, Connecticut, 1 March 1930**

Died **Los Angeles, California, 27 August 1990**

Like that of many black actors, Raymond St Jacques's talent in the film and theatre industries was never fully appreciated; yet at 6 feet, 3 inches, lean and elegant, the vibrant-voiced actor rarely failed to make an impression, however insignificant the role. He was neither the "obliging" black figure (as in the 1930s and 1940s) unlike Hattie McDaniel or Step 'n Fetchit, nor the reasonably homogenized role model (as in the 1950s), such as Dorothy Dandridge or Harry Belafonte. He did not enter the strong 'n sassy jivers' circle, such as Eddie Murphy, Sidney Poitier or Whoopi Goldberg, more recently.

Born James Johnson, he "borrowed" his name from a white French boy who, according to St Jacques, is now a "milkman in New Haven". Although he was a Yale psychology major, the lure of the stage proved irresistable after he replaced an actor in a college production of Shakespeare's *Othello*. After doing a series of casual jobs in New York — the dues most aspiring actors have to pay — he won his first role in the 1954 Off-Broadway production of *High Name Today*, which dealt with the Korean war. When told, "We have no parts for Negroes", St Jacques retorted, "You've got soldiers, haven't you? And there are Negro soldiers in Korea!" He was hired. He then appeared, at the age of 30, in a major Off-Broadway production of Jean Genet's *The Blacks*, with a starry cast: Cicely Tyson, James Earl Jones and Godfrey Cambridge.

St Jacques studied under Lee Strasberg at the New York Actors Studio, gathering further experience at the American Shakespeare Festival (including being a fencing master and fight-arranger) at Stratford, Connecticut for three seasons, as well as more Shakespeare in San Diego and New York. A reasonable role in another Off-Broadway production, *The Man With the Golden Arm* followed.

St Jacques's first film role was, like his first major theatrical one, in a play "specifically designed" — in this case, *Black Like Me*, with James Whitmore. Adapted from the novel, it told the story of a man who takes pills which darken his skin, in order for him to experience what it's like to live as a black man. Although dated and possibly naïve now, it came at a time (1964) when the growing civil rights movement in America was beginning to force social changes, including, to a limited degree, the way Blacks were represented in the media. St Jacques's name was more firmly established that same year, when he portrayed an unsavoury character in Sidney Lumet's powerful film, *The Pawnbroker*, with Rod Steiger.

However, his roles did not increase in dignity; 1965 found him portraying a jealous witchdoctor's son in *Mr Moses*, with Robert Mitchum and Carroll Baker. But he made TV history, also in 1965, when he landed a part in *Rawhide*, the successful Western series. "All I amounted to on that show was tokenism", he bitterly recounted later.

> When the hero and I rode into town, we got off our horses and were ready to go into the bar. Then the director yelled, "Cut!" He told me to go into the stall in back of the bar and take care of the horses. I couldn't believe it. I told him no intelligent black of that period was going into a bar and snatch one of those blondes and start dancing with her. But there was no reason in the world why he couldn't go up to the bar and have a drink with the boys. The best thing that could have happened was that that show went off the air!

Other films followed, including *The Comedians*, with Richard Burton, *Madigan*, directed by Don Siegel and *The Boston Strangler*, with Tony Curtis. The parts were small. When John Wayne's nauseating glory-of-war film, *The Green Berets*, was produced at the height of the Vietnam war protest, St Jacques was a member of the cast. "I thought the fact I was integrating it was justification enough. But when I saw the preview, I wanted to join the picket line, downstairs!" Many in the audience agreed; the film was not a great success.

An antidote, perhaps, was *Uptight*, Jules Dassin's tough remake of *The Informer* — ghetto-style. St Jacques had top billing, along with Ruby Dee, as a junior-high-school teacher who is also a militant leader. The film sank without a trace, as did *If He Hollers, Let Him Go*, where he played the victim of a false rape-murder charge. In 1970's *Cotton Comes to Harlem*, by Ossie Davis, he was a cop who suspects that a preacher's back-to-Africa campaign is a swindle. The film was a nice blend of comedy and action, with good use of the Harlem locale. "There are ethnic minorities on both sides of the camera and there weren't before", he said at the time. "Black producers, directors and technicians. That's a notable change from when I first arrived, believe me." The film was one of the first black thrillers, hardly another in the spate of "blaxploitation" films, but it was nevertheless lumped in with the rest.

St Jacques appeared in other films, including *The Book of Numbers*, which he also wrote and directed, about two black confidence men during the Depression, *Eyes of Laura Mars*, with Faye Dunaway, *Glory*, where he portrayed the abolitionist Frederick Douglass in the story of the first Negro regiment in the Civil War. His last role was in John Carpenter's *They Live*, a tawdry movie mess, as a grizzled blind man preaching revolution who gets beaten up by the police. There is a slight irony here, considering that the "black Lee Marvin", as he was sometimes called, had a career that was rather more respectable than distinguished because of his being beaten by the system of an industry, one that is necessarily a reflection of society. Many of his roles are, with hindsight, dated and possibly a poor model for black audiences; his professionalism and seriousness as an accomplished actor surely isn't.

Born James Arthur Johnson. **Mother** A domestic, then a medical technician. **Education** Studied psychology, Yale University, New Haven, Connecticut; New York Actors Studio. **Career** Stage début, title role in *Othello*, while still a student; spent three seasons with American Shakespeare Festival Academy; film début, *Black Like Me*, 1964; television début, *Rawhide*, 1965; début as writer, director, *The Book of Numbers*, 1973. **Related activities** Fencing director, American Shakespeare Festival, Stratford, Connecticut and various films including *Eyes of Laura Mars*. **Stage** (includes) *Othello*; *High Name Today*; *The Blacks*; *The Man With the Golden Arm*; *Romeo and Juliet*; *Raisin in the Sun*; *Julius Caesar*; *Seventh Heaven*. **Films** (include) *Black Like Me* 1964; *The Pawnbroker*, 1965; *Mr Moses*, 1965; *Mr Buddwing*, 1966; *The Comedians*, 1967; *Madigan*, 1968; *The Boston Strangler*, 1968; *If He Hollers, Let Him Go*, 1968; *The Green Berets*, 1968; *Uptight*, 1968; *Cotton Comes to Harlem*, 1970; *The Book of Numbers*, 1973; *Lost in the Stars*, 1973; *Change of Mind*, 1977; *The Private Files of J. Edgar Hoover*, 1978; *Born Again*, 1978; *Sweet Dirty Tray*, 1981; *They Live*, 1988; *Glory*, 1989; *Eyes of Laura Mars* (fencing director). **Television** (includes) *Rawhide*, 1965. **Cause of death** Cancer, at age 60.

GENERAL LEMUEL SHEPHERD

American Marine Commander

Born **Norfolk, Virginia, 10 February 1896**

Died **La Jolla, California, 6 August 1990**

General Lemuel Shepherd was a dedicated soldier, a tough and uncompromising commander who exemplified the virtues traditionally associated with the US Marine Corps. A "leatherneck" through and through he served with the Marines for over 40 years, seeing distinguished service in Europe in World War I, the arduous Pacific campaigns of World War II and in the bitter war in Korea, being awarded well over 30 medals and decorations along the way. He retired having earned an outstanding combat reputation and with the distinction of being the first Marine to sit on the Committee of the Joint Chiefs of Staff.

Born in Norfolk, Virginia, the son of a respected doctor, Lemuel Cornick Shepherd Jr enjoyed a comfortable childhood in the surroundings of Fauquier County. Although not lacking in academic ability — he obtained a BS degree from the Virginia Military Institute in Lexington — his heart was not in it; even in the services he could not escape the frustrations of the classroom but, graduating only thirty-fourth in a class of 58, Shepherd nevertheless achieved his long held ambition on 11 April 1917 when he was commissioned as a second lieutenant in the US Marine Corps. Within two months Shepherd found himself in the trenches of France as a lieutenant in command of a platoon of the Fifth Marine Regiment during the major Aisne-Marne Allied offensive. Here, at the sharp end of the war, Shepherd's straightforward courage and determination quickly marked him out as a gifted combat leader. Although wounded twice in a sharp engagement at Belleau Wood, his citation for the Navy Cross reads, "he declined medical treatment...and continued courageously to lead his men". Back in the line only a month later, he took part as a company commander in the bloody Meuse-Argonne offensive where his bold leadership from the front caused him yet another wound. Promoted to captain in July 1918 Shepherd followed the war with a tour of duty with the Army of Occupation in the unsettled post-war Germany.

Returning to the United States in 1920 Shepherd found himself appointed an aide-de-camp to the commandant of the Marine Corps and, more interestingly, to President Harding in the White House. With the end of the war came a slump in the fortunes of the Marine Corps: with relatively little call or enthusiasm for their hard-hitting and uncompromising philosophy, the Corps at one point was reduced in manpower to a level below that of the New York Police Department. Shepherd hung on and held a succession of appointments within the US and abroad but had to wait until April 1932 for his promotion to the rank of major. Elevated to lieutenant-colonel in 1935 he took up command of the Second Battalion of the Fifth Marine Regiment following his graduation from the Naval War College, Rhode Island, in May 1937. The outbreak of war in Europe in September 1939, however, found him back in a non-operational role, posted to the Marine Corps School in Quantico, Virginia. There he was employed in a variety of senior administrative and supervisory capacities, gaining a useful understanding of the value of training, until March 1942, some four months after the US entry into the war. Shepherd was given command of the Ninth Marine Regiment, attached to the Third Marine Division serving in the Pacific. Now, at last, Shepherd was able to put into action his own particular, stern brand of Marine philosophy, honing his command into an eager and efficient fighting force and earning his much cherished nickname of "Combat Ready". Although posted as assistant divisional commander of the First Marine Division, he continued in his pugnacious approach to training and combat, earning him the affection and respect of his Marines in the difficult Cape Gloucester operations on New Britain from December 1943 to March 1944. His demanding approach paid off again three months later when, as commander of the First Provisional Marine Brigade, he secured a bridgehead against ferocious Japanese opposition in the invasion of Guam, an action for which he was awarded the Distinguished Service Medal. Shortly afterwards he was posted to Guadalcanal where the "Striking Sixth" Marine Division was undergoing training. Once again Shepherd quickly stamped his personality and unique brand of fearsome paternalism (it was said that each Marine received a talk from him on duty and self-discipline) upon the unit and impressed upon it the need for perfection in combat preparation. Considered over-zealous in this respect by some, his point was proved emphatically as he led his well-prepared men with great success — and relatively light casualties — in one of the bloodiest battles of the Pacific War: Okinawa.

At only 350 miles from the Japanese mainland, the Japanese were well aware of Okinawa's immense strategic importance and resolved to defend this hilly and heavily wooded island to the last man. The Japanese pulled out all the stops in resolute fanaticism with, for example, over 350 kamikaze attacks being launched against the supporting US fleet and the suicidal deployment of the world's largest and most powerful battleship, the *Yamoto*. The struggle for the island, only some 60 miles long by just eight miles wide, was to cost the Japanese almost 130,000 men and the US some 12,000 dead and 36,000 wounded.

On 1 April 1945, after a fortnight of heavy bombing and bombardment, the first waves of some 170,000 US troops hit the beaches of Okinawa. Surprisingly casualties were light and remained so as the Americans swiftly moved inland: such advances came to an abrupt and bloody end as the soldiers came across an elaborate and virtually impenetrable network of Japanese defensive systems, built deep into the limestone hills. As other divisions bogged down Shepherd skilfully pushed his men onward into the Motobu peninsula, inflicting casualties at the rate of ten to one as he did so. Fortunately for the Americans the nightmare came to a premature end when the Japanese commander, General Ushijima, rashly turned to the offensive and was quickly routed by the superior US forces. In the subsequent mêlée it was the rugged Sixth under Shepherd's determined control that captured the capital Naha, after a campaign of some 82 days of hard fighting. With scarcely time to draw breath, Shepherd and the Sixth found themselves posted to China where in October 1945, acting on behalf of Chiang Kai-shek, he received the surrender of the Japanese forces at Tsingtao.

Shepherd parted company with the Sixth in December 1945 and, as major-general, took up, in March 1946, the Troop Training Command of the amphibious forces of the Atlantic Fleet at Little Creek in his home state of Virginia. From here, following a short spell at Marine Corps Headquarters, he was appointed commandant of the Marine Corps School at Quantico in April 1948. His days of active service, however, were far from over: the outbreak of war in Korea in 1950 put Shepherd, then as lieutenant-general commander of the Fleet Marine Force at Pearl Harbor, back in the front line. In spite of the varying fortunes of the largely American-backed international force in this bitter war, Shepherd successfully maintained his reputation as a tough front-liner on his frequent visits to Korea, taking part, for example, in the landings at Inchon. On another occasion when Chinese and Communist forces threatened to surround the Marines stationed near the Yalu river, Shepherd specially flew by helicopter into the danger area to stiffen the morale of the Marines. For as General Ruffner recalled later, "When our troops were heading up towards the Yalu we had lots of VIPs. But when we got hit by those seven Chinese Divisions...the only VIP we had was General Shepherd. And he was there all the time." In January 1952 he was appointed commandant of the US Marine Corps as a full four-star general, taking over from General Clifton B. Cates, and was "charged with and is responsible for the procurement, discharge, education, training, discipline and distribution of the officers and enlisted personnel of the Marine Corps, including the Reserve" (*US Government Organization Manual*). Shepherd then applied his forthright tactics to the long debated question of the inclusion of a Marine officer on the Joint Chiefs of Staff and the creation of the Marines as a separate entity, particularly important with the Marine Corps still playing a leading role in the campaigns in Korea. After persistent and vocal pressure by Shepherd, notably, among others, on 28 June 1952 President Truman signed a bill which gave the Marines' commandant co-equal status with other chiefs of staff and ended the Marines' traditional dependence upon the US Navy. Shepherd retired from the Marines in 1956 at the age of 60 but was recalled to the Corps only two months later for a further three-year period.

Lem Shepherd was a man of undeniable personal courage and resolute character. A stern task-master, he always worked his men very hard but won their respect by sparing himself no more than them. A determined and skilful commander, he knew how to get the best from the men under his command and indeed never lost touch with them or their points of view. Each night his boots were daubed with a mixture of vaseline and boot polish to be burnished in vigorous fashion the following morning. A Marine by adoption, temperament and outlook, he, perhaps, epitomized the virtues and high standards of the Corps. As one of his officers once remarked: "Life under General Shepherd is very uncomplicated. All he is going to stress is combat readiness — today, tomorrow, next year and four years later."

Born Lemuel Cornick Shepherd Junior. **Parents** Lemuel C, doctor, and Emma Lucretia (Cartwright) Shepherd. **Marriage** Virginia Tunstall Driver, 1922 (died 1989). **Children** Lemuel III, Wilson and Virginia. **Education** Norfolk Academy, Virginia; Virginia Military Institute, BS, 1917; on field officers' course, Marine Corps Schools, 1929–30; Naval War College, Newport, Rhode Island, 1936–37. **Career** Second lieutenant, United States Marine Corps, 1917, captain, 1918, major, 1932, lieutenant-colonel, 1935, colonel, 1940, brigadier-general, 1943, major-general, 1944, lieutenant-general, 1950, general, 1952; second-lieutenant, Fifth Marines, France, 1917–19; aide-de-camp to commandant of Marine Corps, 1920–22; junior aide-de-camp to President Harding; commander, Marine detachment, United States Ship, *Idaho*, 1922–25; commander, Sea School detachment, Marine Barracks, Norfolk, Virginia, 1925–27; regimental adjutant, Fourth Marines, attached to Third Marine Brigade, China, 1927–29; district and department commander, Gendarmerie d'Haiti, Dartiguenave Barracks, 1930–34; executive officer and registrar, Marine Corps Institute, 1934–36; commander, second battalion, Fifth Marine Regiment, Fleet Marine Force, 1937; director, correspondence school, chief of operations section, assistant commandant and commandant of Marine Corps School, Quantico, Virginia, 1939; commander, Ninth Marine Regiment, Pacific, 1942; assistant divisional commander, First Marine Division, 1943–44; commander, First Provisional Marine Brigade, 1944; commander, Sixth Division, 1944–45; commander, Troop Training Command, amphibious forces, Atlantic fleet, Little Creek, Virginia, 1946; assistant to the commandant of the Marine Corps and chief of staff, Marine Corps headquarters, 1946–48; commandant, Marine Corps Schools, Quantico, 1948; commanding general, fleet Marine forces of the Pacific, Pearl Harbor, 1950; staff member, General MacArthur's personal staff, Korea; commandant of the Marine Corps, 1952–56; retired, 1956; recalled to active duty, 1956–59. **Awards and honours** Distinguished Service Cross; Navy Cross; Silver Stars (two); Croix de Guerre with Gilt Star and Fourragère; Purple Heart with two Oak Leaf Clusters; World War I Victory Medal with four bronze stars, defensive sector clasp; Occupation of Germany medal; Expeditionary Medal with one bronze star, for service in China and Haiti; Yangtze Service Medal; American Defense Medal; American Campaign medal; Legion of Merit; Distinguished Service Medal; Bronze Star; Presidential Unit Citation with one bronze star, for Okinawa; Navy Unit Commendation with one bronze star, for Guam and Cape Gloucester; Asiatic-pacific Campaign medal with four bronze stars; China Service Medal; World War II Victory Medal; Navy Occupation Medal; Silver Medal for Bravery, for Montenegro; Order of Honour and Merit; Distinguished Service Medal, Haiti; Order of Cloud and Banner, second grade, China; Bronze plaque with special commemorative diploma, Brazil. **Cause of death** Bone cancer, at age 94.

B. F. SKINNER

American Psychologist

Born **Susquehanna, Pennsylvania, 20 March 1904**

Died **Cambridge, Massachusetts, 18 August 1990**

After his death, as in his lifetime, B. F. Skinner was the focus of vehement debate within the world of psychology and beyond. Some commentators have vilified him as a stubborn, obsessional and fanatical man whose intellectually sterile theories had bleak consequences for human welfare. Others have placed him as one of the most influential psychologists of the twentieth century whose insights had a revolutionary impact on educational practice and the treatment of mental illness.

Skinner became the most famous and single-minded advocate of the behaviourist approach to psychology — an approach based on the blindingly simple premise that mental processes are entirely subjective and cannot be observed directly. According to behaviourist theory, "mentalistic" concepts such as motivation, feeling and thought are invalid when used to explain human behaviour scientifically. The only observable data are the environmental stimuli to which the person is exposed and the behavioural responses that he or she makes. Skinner, in a career that embraced professorship at the universities of Minnesota, Indiana and Harvard, argued that the aim of psychology was to investigate "how behavior was maintained and shaped by its consequences". Desirable consequences such as rewards would lead to an increased probability of a specific behaviour being repeated (positive reinforcement). Negative reinforcement would encourage behaviour which led to the removal of undesirable consequences. Punishment formed a third category of reinforcement whereby behaviour would be discouraged by its unpleasant consequences.

Skinner is often mistakenly associated with the idea that punishment has an important role in modifying behaviour. He demonstrated through his animal experiments that the only way to encourage novel behaviour patterns was by negative or positive reinforcement. Punishment could only be employed to extinguish (perhaps temporarily) unwanted behaviour. Consistently, he opposed the use of punishment for criminals and errant children as ineffective for modifying their behaviour.

Born into a close-knit family in the railroad town of Susquehanna, Pennsylvania, he was raised in an atmosphere of moralistic righteousness that some commentators have identified as a major influence on his later didactic approach to social issues. He was not a model child, however. A comment from his school report might well double as a pithy epitaph: "Annoys others".

After graduating in English from Hamilton College, New York, at the age of 22, he returned to live with his parents, intending to launch his career as a writer. Encouraged in his ambitions by the poet Robert Frost, Skinner wrote several short stories but gave up after a year, realizing that his imagination was not up to the task. He later described this as his "dark year", and reflected, "I discovered that I had nothing to say." His life's work demonstrated, however, that he very much wanted to say something significant. He acknowledged that this was why he was drawn to the budding science of psychology, with its wealth of unexplored subject-matter and its exciting new scientific approach advocated by the controversial psychologist John B. Watson, author of the seminal text, *Behaviorism*.

He began graduate study of psychology at Harvard in 1928 and gained his doctorate three years later for research into the impact of gravity on ant behaviour. During this time he was inspired by the opening section of Bertrand Russell's book, *An Outline of Philosophy*, in which the arguments for behaviourism are explored. As the eminent philosopher was later to discover with some astonishment, Skinner did not go on to read the rest of the book in which the theory of behaviourism is cogently demolished.

He stayed on at Harvard after his doctorate and devised an experimental device that became the behaviourist's trademark, the Skinner Box. The animal (usually a rat) placed within the box is faced with a lever or panel that when pressed will deliver a reinforcing stimulus, such as a food pellet or an electric shock. This apparatus had the advantage of automatic recording of the frequency and timing of the animal's responses. Using this technique, Skinner made the important and counter-intuitive discovery that irregular and unpredictable rewards were more effective at maintaining behaviour than rewards given in a consistent pattern. Compulsive gambling was seen as a human example of this phenomenon. The Skinner Box has come under fire from many psychologists who have argued that the sensory deprivation experienced by the caged animal inside it is the nearest thing to removing its cerebral cortex without actually killing it. The animal, they argue, is in such an artificial environment that its normal responses are not exhibited. During

World War II Skinner pursued enthusiastically the application of his theories to the war effort. He was convinced that pigeons could be trained to guide missiles to their target. They were to be placed in a reinforced glass compartment on the missile's nose cone and trained to peck at the image of the target on the glass. This information would be fed back to the missile's guidance system. Although the US government initially invested 25,000 dollars in the project, the Pentagon later rejected the idea as totally impractical, much to Skinner's dismay.

Skinner's faith in the validity of behaviourist theory for humans led him to apply its principles to himself and his family. He once said, "I work on the environment to get my own behaviour out in ways that are reinforcing to me." For instance, he employed a moving pen device to give him graphical feedback of the amount of time he had spent working at his desk. He also invented a system for training his two-year-old daughter to spend less time on the toilet seat. A simple detector in the pan activated a musical box as soon as urine hit it. In future the hard-pressed professor would not have to fritter his time by the toilet giving his child the positive reinforcement of her father's company.

As with many eminent animal psychologists such as Konrad Lorenz and Desmond Morris, Skinner wished to extend his theories to the human sphere. In 1971 he published *Beyond Freedom and Dignity*, in which he laid out the behaviourist manifesto for curing what he saw as the social and moral malaise of the modern world. He proposed that human freedom was illusory and that we were like puppets operated by the reinforcing contingencies of the environment. Socially desirable behaviour could be conditioned by devising a society that consistently rewarded it. Violence, jealousy and competitiveness could be eliminated by manipulating child-rearing practices, education and the media. His difficult task was to make the idea of authoritarian behavioural engineering acceptable. The successful use of such social control techniques in totalitarian societies such as Nazi Germany had given Skinner's vision an unfortunate image in many people's eyes. Nevertheless, he argued congently that there was no reason to suppose that these methods could not be as useful in the pursuit of humane goals vital to the survival of the planet. He had already explored this thesis in his commercially successful and controversial Utopian novel, *Walden Two*, published in 1948.

Some indication of the difficulties of applying behaviourist principles to society as a whole comes from the experimental community set up in Twinoaks, Virginia, founded roughly on Skinnerian principles. Despite Skinner's vision of universal happiness in such a group, it was clear that it was not a complete success. It had a high turnover of inhabitants, some of whom, in Skinner's words, were not "good behaviourists".

Skinner was prompted to explore the application of behaviourist theory to education after a visit to an arithmetic class at his daughter's elementary school, where he saw "minds being destroyed". His animal experiments, many years earlier, had shown that the most efficient way to teach a skill was by building it up gradually through a series of small discrete steps, each of which would be rewarded when successfully mastered. This technique of "shaping" had been used in one of his most famous experiments to train two pigeons to play a passable version of ping-pong. He applied the principle behind shaping to help design mechanical teaching machines (now largely superseded by computer software) which led the child through a topic, rewarding him or her at regular intervals with the achievement of getting a "correct" answer. Through a process of elimination, every child would get there eventually.

Although Skinner claimed to have evidence that such methods were more effective in promoting students' learning than traditional classroom practices, his theories were regarded with scepticism by a teaching profession mindful of the more subtle influences on the learning process. Undoubtedly, though, his ideas have had an impact, albeit diffuse, on changing established teaching methods. The modern teacher's careful use of rewards to encourage learning and modify disruptive behaviour is partly attributable to Skinner's influence. The design of much current educational computer software owes a debt to the system first established by Skinner's teaching machines.

Skinner's idea of shaping is now a keystone of behaviour therapy for the treatment of both mentally ill and mentally handicapped people; for example, in the rehabilitation of institutionalized chronic schizophrenics and in the socializing of autistic children. However, many therapists doubt the lasting value of behaviour modification that leaves the underlying psychological conflicts within the patient unresolved.

For most of us, our problem with Skinner's theories is that we like to think there is more to a human than there is to a rat. As scientist and philosopher Jacob Bronowski expressed it in *The Ascent of Man*, "There must be something unique about man because otherwise the rats would be writing papers about B. F. Skinner."

Born Burrhus Frederic Skinner. **Parents** William Arthur, lawyer, and Grace Madge (Burrhus) Skinner. **Marriage** Yvonne Blue, 1936. **Children** Julie and Deborah. **Education** Susquehanna High School, Susquehanna, Pennsylvania, 1922; Hamilton College, Clinton, New York, Hawley Greek Prize-winner, BA, 1926; Harvard University, Cambridge, Massachusetts, MA, 1930, PhD, 1931. **Career** Research fellow, National Research Council, 1931–32; junior fellow, Harvard Society of Fellows, 1933–36; instructor in psychology, University of Minnesota, Minneapolis, 1936–37, assistant professor, 1937–39, associate professor 1939–45; professor and chairman, Department of Psychology, Indiana University, Bloomington, 1945–48; William James Lecturer, Harvard University, 1947, professor of psychology, 1948–57, Edgar Pierce Professor, 1958–74, professor emeritus, 1974 onwards. **Related activities** War researcher, Office of Scientific Research and Development, 1942–43. **Other activities** Writer, novel, *Walden Two*, 1948. **Offices and memberships** Member: National Academy of Sciences, American Academy of Arts and Sciences, American Philosophical Society, American Psychological Association; fellow, Royal Society of Arts, London. **Awards and honours** Harry Crosby Medal, 1942; Guggenheim Fellowship, 1944; Career Grant, National Institute of Mental Health; Honorary doctorate: Ripon College, Wisconsin, 1957, North Carolina State University, Greensboro, 1960, University of Chicago, 1967, University of Michigan, Ann Arbor, 1968, Alfred University, New York, 1969, University of Exeter, England, 1969, Indiana University, Bloomington, 1970, McGill University, Montreal, 1970, Ohio Wesleyan University, Delaware, 1971, C. W. Post Center, Long Island University, New York, 1971, Rockford College, Illinois, 1971, Hobart and William Smith Colleges, Geneva, New York, 1972, Dickinson College, Carlisle, Pennsylvania, 1972, Framingham State College, Massachusetts, 1972, University of Baltimore, 1973, Lowell Technological Institute, Massachusetts, 1974, New College, Hofstra University, Hempstead, New York, 1974, Nasson College, Springvale, Maine, 1976, Western Michigan University, Kalamazoo, 1976, University of Louisville, Kentucky, 1977, Tufts University, Medford, Massachusetts, 1977, Johns Hopkins University, Baltimore, 1979, Keio University, Tokyo, 1979; Distinguished Science Contribution Award, American Psychological Association, 1958; National Medal of Science, 1971; Joseph P. Kennedy Jr Foundation Award, 1971; honorary fellow, British Psychological Society; Phi Beta Kappa. **Psychology publications** *The Behavior of Organisms: An Experimental Analysis*, 1938; *Science and Human Behavior*, 1953; *Verbal Behavior* (lectures), 1957; (with C. B. Ferster) *Schedules of Reinforcement*, 1957; *Cumulative Record* (essays), 1959; (with James G. Holland) *The Analysis of Behavior: A Progress for Self-Instruction*, 1961; *The Technology of Teaching*, 1968; *Contingencies of Reinforcement: A Theoretical Analysis*, 1969; *Beyond Freedom and Dignity*, New York, 1971; *About Behaviorism*, 1974; *Reflections on Behaviorism and Society*, 1978; *Skinner for the Classroom: Selected papers*, edited by Robert Epstein, 1982. **Other publications** (Editor, with William A. Skinner) *A Digest of Opinions of the Anthracite Board of Conciliation*, 1928; *Walden Two* (novel), 1948; *Particulars of My Life* (autobiography), 1976; *The*

Shaping of a Behaviorist: Part Two of an Autobiography, 1979; *Notebooks*, edited by Robert Epstein, 1980; (with M. E. Vaughn) *Enjoy Old Age*, 1983; *A Matter of Consequences: Part Three of an Autobiography*, 1983. **Cause of death** Leukaemia, at age 86. **Further reading** Terry J. Knapp, compiler, *A Comprehensive Bibliography of Published Works by and Concerning B. F. Skinner from 1929 through 1973* (bibliography), 1974; Finley Carpenter, *The Skinner Primer: Behind Freedom and Dignity*, 1974; John A. Weigl, *B. F. Skinner*, 1977; Robert D. Nye, *Three Views of Man: Perspectives from Sigmund Freud, B. F. Skinner, and Carl Rogers*, 1975, second edition published as *Three Psychologies: Perspectives from Freud, Skinner, and Rogers*, 1981; Richard I. Evans, *B. F. Skinner: The Man and His Ideas*, 1978; Robert D. Nye, *What Is Skinner Really Saying?*, 1979; Paul T. Sagal, *Skinner's Philosophy*, 1981; Mark P. Cosgrove, *B. F. Skinner's Behaviorism: An Analysis*, 1982; *Thinkers of the Twentieth Century*, 1987.

JACQUES SOUSTELLE

French Anthropologist and Politician

Born **Montpellier, France, 3 February 1912**

Died **Paris, France, 6 August 1990**

France has always been a country to produce unusual politicians but Soustelle was one of the most unusual of all. Once tipped as successor to premier General Charles de Gaulle, he was later involved with a group who envisaged assassinating the General. From being in the forefront of political influence, with a seat as deputy for Lyon, he went into exile chased by a warrant for his arrest. He was seven years in the wilderness before a law of amnesty was passed and he was welcomed back to France to enter politics once again and to receive many accolades for his academic work.

Jacques Soustelle was born into the Protestant working class and although his parents were not particularly interested in education, he came early to the notice of his teachers who observed a keen intelligence. With their encouragement he gained himself a first-class education purely by winning through on merit. He went to the elitist École Normale Supériere at 17 and three years later came out as the best philosophy student. Three more years and he obtained his doctorate in sociology. By the age of 25 he was assistant director at the Musée de l'Homme. He also became the youngest professor ever to hold the Chair of American Antiquities at the Collège de France in Paris.

His first love and expertise was the Aztec civilization and his Latin American studies and writings made him possibly France's foremost ethnologist but, from the time he joined the museum, he was also developing an interest in politics and became an active member of the Anti-Fascist League of Intellectuals.

The outbreak of World War II, when he was still only 27, took him to London where he joined the Free French movement set up by General Charles de Gaulle in exile. De Gaulle appointed him to the foreign service section and sent him back to South America on a mission to several countries. Later in the war he became commissioner of information and, when the Allies moved into North Africa, moved with them to a base in Algiers.

After the war he became part of de Gaulle's first cabinet, holding several posts in succession, and was also involved in the organization of the Gaullist party. He became its first secretary, a post he held for five years until 1952, just one year after his election as the Lyon deputy to the National Assembly. Early in 1952 Soustelle was asked to form a cabinet but de Gaulle was not encouraging.

When asked again at the end of the year de Gaulle apparently agreed but Soustelle failed to get support from the other parties.

In 1955 Premier Pierre Mendès-France appointed Soustelle as governor-general of Algeria in, it was said, an attempt to placate the Gaullists. But Soustelle remained implacably opposed to a free Algeria although the nationalist movement was making the French position increasingly untenable and, in 1958, civil war threatened. Having brought down successive governments he welcomed, in 1958, the return of de Gaulle who agreed to take over the premiership on his own terms. When these were overwhelmingly accepted by the people and he began to get to grips with the problem of Algeria, Soustelle was devastated to realize that his political hero was actually in favour of a free Algeria. In addition he was also setting up channels of communication with the Soviet Union, another anathema to Soustelle.

He talked to de Gaulle and told him his friends were not happy. De Gaulle told him to change his friends. Total disaffection followed. Soustelle became actively involved in the Secret Army Organization (OAS) which was dedicated to the cause of a French Algeria and was responsible for a great amount of violent action towards its ends. There was also a plot to assassinate de Gaulle. Soustelle vigorously denied his involvement for many years but later admitted to membership of the CNR (the Conseil National de la Résistance). When the difference between the two was examined, it was found that the OAS had been renamed.

By 1961 he had left the government and was in severe trouble but he escaped secretly from Paris and went to Algiers. He may not have suspected it at the time but it was the beginning of an unhappy seven-year exile from France. He spent most of the time moving around Europe unable to return home because of an arrest order which had been issued in 1962. In 1968, however, this was rescinded under an amnesty law and he went back, somewhat older, greyer and staider, as the prodigal son, apparently totally forgiven and allowed to start again with a new political party, Progress and Liberty, which he launched in 1971. Two further years found him back in the National Assembly in his old deputy's seat.

Forgiveness spread and he received many honours, most notably being elected to the Académie française which is perhaps the summit of achievement for French intellectuals. But, despite his substantial and honoured wartime services he was, significantly, never made a Companion of the Liberation.

Above all Soustelle was a man swayed more by his feelings than his supreme intellect. Experience may well have taught him, as he once admitted, "to be prudent", but he always hoped for too much. He was basically caught by the conflict between his background and experience. His birthright gave him the vision of the oppressed fighter for opportunity whereas his academic life taught him the value of order and the beauty of symmetry. These he never reconciled but, although in retrospect it may be said that he squandered his talents on the attempt to maintain colonialism in Africa, the world has a valuable legacy in the form of his anthropological writing. His study of the Aztecs, their language, society, art, architecture, rituals and beliefs is outstanding.

Born Jacques Emile Soustelle. **Parents** Jean, railway worker, and Germaine (Blatiere) Soustelle. **Marriage** Georgette Fagot, anthropologist, 1931. **Education** Lycée du Parc, Lyon; Faculty of Letters, Lyon; École Normale Supérieure, Paris, MPhil, 1932; PhD, Sorbonne, Paris, 1937. **Career** Anthropological researcher, Central America, 1932–39; assistant curator, Musée de l'Homme, 1937–39; professor of American Antiquities, Collège de France, 1938–39; lecturer, applied sociology, École Normale; member, Free French Forces under General de Gaulle, London, 1940; national commissioner of information, Free French National Council, 1942; director-general, Special Services, Algeria, 1943–44; regional commissioner of the Republic, Bordeaux, 1944; minister of information, 1945; minister of the colonies, 1945; deputy, Mayenne department, 1945–46; professor of sociology, l'École pratique des Hautes Études, 1951, director of studies, social sciences department, 1969 onwards; deputy from Lyon, Rhone, National Assembly, 1951–58, 1973–78; governor-general, Algeria, 1955–56; minister of information, 1958–59; minister for Sahara and Atomic Questions, 1959–60; municipal councillor, Lyon, 1971–77; vice-president, Rhone Alps Regional Council, 1975–77; Zaharoff lecturer, Oxford University, 1988. **Related activities** Member, Comité de vigilance des intellectuels antifascists, 1930s; Free French delegate, Latin America and Caribbean, 1940–42; secretary-general, Rally of the French People, 1947–51; delegate, United Nations, 1957; member, Central Committee of the Union for the New Republic, 1958; president, Centre of Information on the problems of Algeria and the Sahara, 1960; political director, *Voici pourqoui*, 1960; charged with subversive activities, 1962; in exile, 1962–68; leader, Conseil National de la Résistance; founder president, national movement for Progress and Liberty, 1970; French representative, Council of Europe, 1973; founder, France-Israel Association. **Offices and memberships** Académie des Sciences d'outre-mer; Académie française, 1983. **Awards and honours** Commandeur de la Légion d'honneur; Rosette of the Resistance; honorary Commander of the Order of the British Empire; Commandeur de Polonia Restituta; Commandeur de l'ordre de l'Aigle azteque, Mexico; Alfonso Reyes Prize, 1981. **Publications** *La Vie quotidienne des Aztèques a la veille de la conquete espagnole*, 1955, published in English as *The Daily Life of the Aztecs on the Eve of the Spanish Conquest*, 1961; *Envers et contre tout*, 1962; *Aimée et souffrante Algérie*, 1962; *L'Espérance trahie*, 1962; *Sur une route nouvelle*, 1965; *La Page n'est pas tournée*, 1965; *L'Art du Mexique ancien*, 1966; *Les Quatre Soliels*, 1967, published in English as *The Four Suns*, 1971; *La Longue Marche d'Israël*, 1968; *Vingt-huit ans de gaullisme*, 1968; *Lettre ouverte aux victimes de la decolonisation*, 1973; *Archéologie et Anthropologie*, 1976; *L'Univers des Aztèques*, 1979; *Les Olmèques*, 1980; *La Civilisation des Maya*, 1982. **Cause of death** Undisclosed, at age 78.

PATIENCE STRONG

British Author of Popular Verse

***Born* London, England, 4 June 1907**

***Died* 28 August 1990**

Patience Strong is to popular verse what Barbara Cartland is to romantic fiction, what Frank Richards is to the British school story or Agatha Christie is to the sleuthing tale. Astoundingly prolific, and an undisputed master of her chosen genre, she defied the censure of critics and wrote verses which were inspirational to millions of readers from all over the world, tackling a vast range of subjects from roses, robins, babies and butterflies to bereavement, religion and patriotism. Her work appeared in countless cards and calendars; she produced well over 70 books, and many booklets of verse and religious comment. She has been condemned for sentimentality and blandness, and certainly there is nothing revolutionary or challenging about her easy-flowing reflections on life. Her main purpose was to offer comfort to her readers, and there is no doubt that she was highly successful in bringing them a sense of warmth and well-being.

Born Winifred Emma May at Forest Hill in south London, she seems to have mastered the piano and written copious rhymes from the age of four. Apparently hardly a day of her life went by after that on which she did not produce some verses. Her first work was published when she was only ten years old, and as a teenage office girl working for the London music publishers Lawrence Wright, she soon demonstrated her flair for quickly creating lyrics. One of her first was to become famous:

when her boss, Lawrence Wright, was battling to find appropriate words for an intense and catchy tune, she dashed off a lyric that became a best-seller. The song was "Jealousy", and her long-standing success with this sensuous tango was to be repeated when she later wrote the words for "The Dream of Olwen".

It was through her interest in music that she met her first husband, Frederick Williams, when, in her late teens, she was playing the piano at a Welsh hotel during a regatta week in which he took part. They did not marry until she was in her late twenties. Around this time she sent some of her verses to the London newspaper, the *Daily Mirror*. She was inspired to do so by the death of Wilhelmina Stitch, who had been the versifier *par excellence* for a rival paper, the *Daily Sketch*. The editor of the *Mirror* wondered whether Winifred, despite her obvious facility for producing rhyming aphorisms, could keep her compositions in full flood over a sustained period. He demanded 18 further poems straight away and gave these a trial run in a feature called "The Quiet Corner". This proved so popular that her verse was run regularly by the Mirror group for 40 years. For the same length of time the weekly magazine *Woman's Own* published her work.

As soon as she started writing for the *Daily Mirror*, its editor suggested that she should find a new and appropriate name. She stumbled on this immediately, being lent by a friend a book by Mrs A. D. T. Whitney about New England family life. It was called *Patience Strong*, which seemed ideally suggestive of the quietly cosy and doggedly uplifting tones of her work. Once she had adopted her new name she used it privately as well as professionally.

Patience Strong's poems were in even greater demand during the period of World War II, when many servicemen carried clippings of her verses into action with them, and parted lovers found consolation in her emphasis on the "God's in his heaven, all's right with the world" approach. Patience Strong was absolutely sincere in everything that she wrote; she loved Nature and what might be described as very English country life. Her views were conservative about most issues, and two of her most intense dislikes were the European Common Market and the Channel Tunnel which she said would "fill Kent full of foreigners on motor-cycles". Nevertheless her religious convictions were enhanced by a spirit of enquiry which ranged from Anglicanism to Christian Science and the British Israel World Federation.

It is easy to make Patience Strong's verse the subject of send-up, but one suspects that many of her critics were in fact somewhat jealous of her easy skill and immense popularity. Amongst her vast legacy of poems several stand out as absolutely typical of her inimitable blend of appreciation of the natural scene and simplistic spiritual uplift. One of the best known of these begins:

> If you stand very still in the heart of a wood
> You will hear many wonderful things,
> The snap of a twig and the wind in the trees
> And the whirr of invisible wings...

Patience Strong was married and widowed twice; her second husband was Guy Cushing. She had no children. Despite her success she liked living in a country cottage — in Kent during the 1940s and later in Sussex. For the last 20 years of her life her poems appeared regularly on the back cover of *This England*, a nostalgic, rustically inspired magazine which seems to have provided a perfect setting for them.

Born Winifred Emma May. **Pseudonym** Patience Strong. **Marriages** 1) Frederick Williams, late 1920s (deceased); 2) Guy Cushing, architect (deceased). **Career** Author of verses from childhood onwards; also, lyricist; office worker, Lawrence Wright music publishers; verse writer for "The Quiet Corner", *Daily Mirror*, the *Sunday Pictorial*, later to become the *Sunday Mirror* and *Woman's Own*, 1934–1970s; also wrote verses for quarterly, *This England*; publisher, greetings cards. **Lyrics** (include) "Jealousy"; "The Dream of Olwen". **Publications** (include) *With a*

Poem in my Pocket (autobiography), 1981; *The Patience Strong Omnibus*, 1982. **Cause of death** Undisclosed, at age 83.

RICHARD STROUT

American Journalist

Born **Cohoes, New York, 14 March 1898**

Died **Washington, DC, 19 August 1990**

For six decades, from the administration of President Warren G. Harding to that of Ronald Reagan, Richard Strout observed and commented upon the world of American politics. "If you live long enough", the journalist quipped in 1978 (the occasion of his eightieth birthday), "people confuse ability with longevity. I'm not a whizbang; I'm just an analytical writer with some color." Readers of his articles, however, would — and did — disagree. His style, wit, common sense and liberal indignation led to Strout's being dubbed "the journalist with the Proustian eye". It also led to a Pulitzer Prize citation in 1978.

Richard Strout was born in the small town of Cohoes, New York, in 1898, the younger of two sons. His parents were descended from a line of long-lived New Englanders; his father, George Morris Strout, an English teacher and sometime poet, and his mother, Mary Susan Lang Strout, both lived well into their nineties. Shortly after Richard's birth, the little family left Cohoes for Brooklyn's Flatbush district where Strout *père* took a teaching job at Erasmus Hall High School. It was here that young Richard went to school, and where he made up his mind to become a journalist.

Strout graduated from high school in 1915 and began his higher education at New Hampshire's Dartmouth College, where he studied English and liberal arts. World War I interrupted his studies in 1917 when he enlisted in the Army, but his duties kept him stateside for the duration: because he had joined the Student Training Corps in college, he was quickly commissioned as a second lieutenant in the infantry and "posted" to the faculty of the military school at Norwich Academy in Northfield, Vermont. After the war's end, the young officer went to Harvard to continue his studies, working at various odd jobs to support himself. Needless to say, while at the university he served as a writer on both the *Harvard Crimson* and the *Harvard Advocate*, two collegiate publications. Strout graduated from Harvard in 1919, with a Bachelor of Arts degree.

His military duties had not taken him abroad and, at the age of 21, the lure of other countries proved too much for Richard Strout: the graduate signed up as a seaman on a transatlantic grain ship, and when it landed, he found himself in England. There, after some searching, he landed a job as a "confidential assistant" to the editor of the *Sheffield Independent*, the provincial daily newspaper of the town in south Yorkshire. His salary as "CA" was two pounds a week, but Strout soon became the paper's "sub" or copy-editor. After two years in England, the young journalist returned to the US where he worked briefly for *The Boston Post*, and took freelance assignments for the New York *Globe* before joining the staff of *The Christian Science Monitor* in 1921. There he would stay — first as a reporter in the Boston office, then as a member of the Washington bureau — for the next 63 years, until his retirement in 1984.

The Christian Science Monitor was and remains a highly regarded daily newspaper of national scope. During his first years on the staff, Strout's writing skills were polished and tempered under what the other *Monitor* staff-members called the "Deland School of Journalism". This phrase referred to the paper's hard-driving city editor, Paul Deland who, though an uncompromising taskmaster, was largely responsible for instilling the traits of objectivity and precision (among others) into the writing of his underlings, Richard Strout included.

For three years, Strout worked in the paper's Boston office; at the same time, he was adding to his educational qualifications by completing a Master's degree in economics and political science at Harvard, which he received in 1923. It was in that year that he drove his beloved Model T Ford (about which he would write a popular elegiac-type article) to the *Monitor*'s Washington bureau. Richard Strout's years of political reporting had begun.

For the next 20 years, Strout's byline appeared on many articles — front-page and otherwise — which ran the gamut from political scandals to presidential campaigns and party conventions, from the Depression to the flight of the first cross-country passenger plane. In addition to his work at the *Monitor*, Strout sold the occasional freelance article and, in 1939, he edited the diary of a young girl which had been written during the middle of the Victorian era. The young girl had grown up to become Strout's mother-in-law, Isabella Maud Rittenhouse Wilke, and *Maud*, as the book was eventually called, became an overnight best-seller. The royalties proved enough to buy a new house for his growing family.

During the early 1940s, however, it was not for *Maud* but for his political writing that Strout's reputation became solidified. In 1943, Richard Strout succeeded Kenneth Crawford as the anonymous author of the *New Republic* weekly political column. Then as now, the magazine was a stronghold of liberal political reportage, and its infamous "TRB" column had always been viewed as *the* expression of the nation's liberal political opinion. The initials actually stood for the Brooklyn Rapid Transit system spelled backwards, a hangover from the days when the magazine had been published in New York, and its editor, Bruce Bliven, had been forced to carry copy to the printer by subway.

Under Crawford, "TRB" had been respected; under Strout it became revered. "When I took the job," Strout recalled in 1968, "I was advised that the column was easy to write: just get mad at someone once a week and spit in his eye." In Strout's first column, published in March 1943, his anger was directed against the US Congress and its attitude towards the war effort. "The war needs a shot in the arm," Strout proclaimed, "a moral tonic... the announcement of specific, idealistic, postwar aims, or some approach to it...When a man dies", the journalist concluded, "he wants to die for something important."

Throughout his years as "TRB", Congress caught a great deal of Strout's verbal flak, and realized the anonymous journalist was not one to mince words. It was the "inefficient", "parochial" "troglodytes" of the 78th Congress, Strout declared, who had dried up his "inner juices of geniality, like the blight of those unfortunate Manhattan trees that continually gather in another kind of exhaust miasma." Congress, however, was not the only faction to come under fire. Strout called Dwight D. Eisenhower's presidency a "government by sedative"; the paranoid Communist-hunter Senator Joe McCarthy was described as "as hard to catch as a mist that carries a lethal contagion". Then came Strout's premonitory description of the then vice-president, Richard Milhouse Nixon: "Every move is charted, every effort planned", TRB wrote in 1958. "There are unwritten rules in the great game of politics, but the lethal young Nixon does not accept these rules. He is out for the kill and the scalp at any cost." Only a few years later, TRB was noting that the "cost" was the Watergate Scandal; it was, he stated, "a special kind of corruption without greed. No sex, no dollars. Just power. It didn't strike at oil leases, it struck at democracy".

Other TRB columns took on different causes. "The rich stay rich in the US," one column began, "and the poor, poor, and the gulf between them hardly changes. America's disparity of income is the single most significant and sinister social fact in the nation. Everything comes back to that." His last column, published in 1983, dealt with Soviet-American relations. "Presidents come and presidents go", Strout wrote. "You can measure the passage of time, I think, by counting things we knew couldn't happen". He went on to list events like the election of a Catholic President (ie Kennedy) and issues such as school desegregation, ending with, "And there was another absolute: America couldn't lose a war." A collection of his unhappy views of presidents past was published in 1979 under the title *TRB: Views and Perspectives on the Presidency*.

Cynical he may have been, but then Richard Strout had a bird's eye view of America's president. His old roll-top desk in the *Monitor*'s Washington bureau office was just two blocks from the White House. There he worked for the paper and there he composed his *New Republic* columns, trying, as he said, "to cram too many ideas into 800 words, like the coats bulging in a closet at a cocktail party". The 6 foot, 1 inch journalist clearly enjoyed his political observation, no matter how incensed it made him. "The pay in Washington ain't much", he explained, "but the show's swell" — the *political* show, that is; Strout avoided the DC social scene like the plague, preferring to spend his leisure hours in gardening, walking and most importantly, reading. "You can't read enough", he once told a fellow journalist. "You can't know enough."

Like his parents before him, Richard Strout lived a long life; the grey-eyed, white-haired newspaperman died at the age of 92 — appropriately, in Washington, DC.

Born Richard Lee Strout. **Parents** George Morris, teacher, and Mary Susan (Lang) Strout. **Marriages** 1) Edith R. Mayne, 1924 (died 1932); 2) Ernestine Wilke, 1939. **Children** Alan, Phyllis and Nancy, from first marriage; Elizabeth and Mary, from second marriage. **Education** Erasmus Hall High School, New York; Dartmouth College, Hanover, New Hampshire, 1915–17; Harvard University, Cambridge, Massachusetts, BA, 1919, MA, 1923. **Military service** Second lieutenant, US Army, 1917–18. **Career** Staff reporter and subeditor, *Sheffield Independent*, Sheffield, England, 1919; reporter, *The Boston Post*, Boston, Massachusetts, 1921; reporter, *The Christian Science Monitor*, Boston, 1921–23, Washington bureau reporter, 1923–84; political columnist "TRB From Washington", *New Republic*, 1943–84. **Related activities** War correspondent, World War II; contributor: *Harper's*, *New York Times Magazine*. **Offices and memberships** Member: National Press Club, Overseas Writers Club. **Awards and honours** George Polk Memorial Award for National Reporting, Long Island University, 1958; Journalism award, University of Missouri, 1974; Sidney Hillman Award, 1974; Fourth Estate Award, National Press Club, 1975; Pulitzer Prize citation, 1978; honorary DLitt, Brown University, 1980; Population Action Council award, 1983; Federation for Immigration Reform award, 1983; honorary fellow, Sigma Delta Chi. **Publications** (With E. B. White) *Farewell to the Model T*, 1936; (editor) *Isabelle Maud Rittenhaus: Maud*, 1939; *TRB: Views and Perspectives on the Presidency*, 1979. **Cause of death** After a fall, at age 92.

SIR ALEXANDER TURNBULL

British Obstetrician

***Born* Aberdeen, Scotland, 18 January 1925**

***Died* Oxford, England, 18 August 1990**

Alexander Turnbull, knighted in 1988, was internationally renowned for his research work into the mechanism of women's labour in childbirth and, in particular, for the "Cardiff pump", an induction technique he pioneered together with his colleague, Dr Anne Anderson, when occupying the Chair of Obstetrics and Gynaecology at the University of Cardiff.

He was educated at Aberdeen Grammar school and Aberdeen University from which he graduated in 1947 and, following his national service with the Army, he returned to Scotland for his training in 1950 where he came under the influence of Dugald Baird, regius professor of midwifery at Aberdeen and who also was knighted in due course.

Turnbull remained in Scotland until his move to Cardiff in 1966. He was first a senior lecturer in Queen's College, Dundee — then an outpost of the University of St Andrews on the southern side of the River Tay — and, in 1961, moved back to Aberdeen as a senior lecturer. Throughout these years he was still perfecting his MD thesis which was not awarded until 1966 also. This was partly because of his personal search for perfection both in terms of research and the thesis itself. When the award came it was with honours and a major prize. The long delay, however, had very positive fallout for all those undertaking later research in his vicinity. He was able to spot developing snags and iron them out almost before others were aware of them.

It was also at Aberdeen that he met and commenced his long working relationship with Dr Anderson, one that continued until her own early death in 1983. She moved with him to Cardiff and then, in 1972, to Oxford. And it was she who, more often than not, took Turnbull's original ideas, moulded them into solid research projects and then sought the funding — usually successfully. The other woman closely involved with his work, especially in the early days, was Elizabeth Bell, another of Dugald Baird's able students. They married in 1953 and she collaborated in much of his work. Throughout his life, Turnbull always acknowledged "Elsie's" role in his success.

The "Cardiff pump" was a safe means by which labour could be induced. It supplied a regular dose of a hormone normally produced by the pituitary gland, oxytocin, to which the uterus is sensitive towards the end of pregnancy. Once contractions were properly established nature tended to take over.

The technique was immensely valuable in delivering babies who were at risk, for whatever reason, and Turnbull was given due international recognition for this work. However over time it seemed that in many cases women were being induced simply to suit their doctors' choice of working hours, whereas there is a biological tendency for the human infant, like many another primate, to be born during the hours of darkness. In the natural order of things, it is probably safer then. The development of the natural childbirth lobby during the 1970s brought many voices of female dissent towards induction for the sake of intervention and Turnbull came in for particularly harsh criticism in a BBC television documentary, *Horizon*. Not all the criticism was warranted but Turnbull, nevertheless, took a serious look at what was happening and decided to intervene less. At an international medical conference in 1976 he announced that although the technique caused no harm he was moving away from it because it was not helpful in reducing perinatal mortality.

In 1972 he was invited to become Nuffield Professor of Obstetrics and Gynaecology at the University of Oxford. He also became a fellow of Oriel College but his working base was at the large, acute Radcliffe Hospital on the outskirts of the city's historic centre. It was from the John Radcliffe that he encouraged young doctors to undertake research into such matters as: the early onset of labour; serum screening for spina bifida; new techniques of foetal monitoring; development of *in vitro* fertilization; and heavy menstrual bleeding was treated by means of a new technique in which part of the womb lining is removed rather than the entire organ.

Sir Alec, as he became, was also an adviser to the Welsh Hospital Board and, later, consultant adviser to the country's chief medical officer. Thus he was closely involved in the development of gynaecological and obstetrical provision throughout England and Wales.

His tremendous influence at home and abroad brought him many awards and accolades. One he valued greatly was the Eardley Holland Medal, the highest honour possible from the Royal College of Obstetricians and Gynaecologists, together with an honorary fellowship. He was also very touched to be known as the "obstetricians' obstetrician". It would be less than fair however if one omitted the fact that his primary concern was always his patients. He cared for them as fellow human beings rather than as repositories of certain ailments and problems, as has too often been the case.

One young woman who had lost three babies in mid-term pregnancy recalled her first consultation with him as follows, "We were impressed not so much by his medical expertise but more by his sympathy for our previous distress, an attitude we had not previously experienced." In the upshot she produced a healthy son after six and a half months in hospital supported not just medically but also emotionally by the "Prof".

Sir Alec will be remembered not only for his charm, warmth, and generosity of spirit, but also for his immense courage — personal and professional.

Born Alexander Cuthbert Turnbull. **Parents** George Harley and Anne (White) Turnbull. **Marriage** Elizabeth (Elsie) Bell, doctor, 1953. **Children** One daughter and one son. **Education** Robert Gordon's College; Merchant Taylors' School, Crosby; Aberdeen Grammar School, 1942; Aberdeen University, MB, ChB, 1947, MD with honours and Thursfield Prize, 1966; member, Royal College of Obstetricians and Gynaecologists, 1947; Medical Research Council Research Scholar. **Military service** National service, Royal Army Medical Corps, Malaya and India. **Career** House posts; senior lecturer and honorary consultant obstetrician and gynaecologist with Professor J. Walker, University of Dundee, 1957–61; senior lecturer and honorary consultant obstetrician and gynaecologist with Sir Dugald Baird, University of Aberdeen, 1961–66; professor of obstetrics and gynaecology, Welsh National School of Medicine, Cardiff, also honorary consultant gynaecologist and adviser in obstetrics and gynaecology, Welsh Hospital Board, 1966–73; honorary consultant obstetrician and gynaecologist, Oxfordshire Health Authority, 1973 onwards; fellow, Oriel College, Oxford and Nuffield Professor of Obstetrics and Gynaecology, 1973 onwards. **Related activities** Member: Clinical Research Board, Medical Research Council, 1969–72, Lane Commission, 1971–73, Medical Educational Sub-committee, Universities Grant Committee, 1973–83; adviser in obstetrics and gynaecology to chief medical officer, Department of Health and Social Security, 1975–86; council member, Royal College of Obstetricians and Gynaecologists. **Offices and memberships** Fellow, Royal College of Obstetricians and Gynaecologists, 1966, junior vice-president, 1982–83, senior vice-president, 1984–86. **Awards and honours** Honorary MA, Oxford University, 1973; Blair-Bell Medal, Royal Society of Medicine, Section of Obstetrics and Gynaecology, 1984; Commander of the Order of the British Empire, 1982; knighted, 1988; honorary fellow and Eardley Holland Medal, Royal College of Obstetricians and Gynaecologists, 1990. **Publications** (Co-editor) *The Oxygen Supply to the Human Fetus*, 1960; *The Scientific Basis of Obstetrics and Gynaecology* (chapters), edited by R. R. Macdonald, 1969; (joint author) *Confidential Enquiries into Maternal Mortality in England and Wales*, 1973–75. **Cause of death** Cancer, at age 65.

STEVIE RAY VAUGHAN

American Rhythm and Blues Musician and Producer

Born **Dallas, Texas, 3 October 1954**

Died **(near) East Troy, Wisconsin, 27 August 1990**

Guitarist Stevie Ray Vaughan was a child prodigy who found renown late — only to have it snatched away in an air crash at the age of 35. All the pointers suggested that Vaughan, a recovering alcoholic and drug user who had achieved a superheated cult status in the last decade, was on the verge of joining friends such as Eric Clapton in the superstar league. A growing army of fans considered him a member already. Vaughan's life and career followed such a classical rock 'n' roll model that presented as fiction the details would look like cliché. Inspired by an older brother, Jimmy (later of the much-respected Fabulous Thunderbirds), Vaughan began to learn guitar at the age of eight, and was soon playing in amateur groups formed by older boys in his home town, Dallas. Music, specifically rhythm and blues, dominated his childhood, and at the expense of school work. It is said the he used music to escape a home life made problematic by his father's alcoholism.

By the time he reached his teens he was already playing in local semi-professional and professional bar bands. He dropped out of high school at the age of 18 and moved to Austin, Texas, where he began to pursue his career in earnest.

In 1975 he joined Austin rock-blues band The Cobras, and it was here that the Stevie Ray Vaughan reputation began. The Cobras won a fine reputation for their rock, blues and R & B repertoire, especially because of the fleet and dramatic style of their guitarist. Vaughan was one of those honorable journeyman R & B musicians, who acknowledge and respect their teachers in the blues pantheon, unlike those musicians who consider rock music a white invention. He was also an accomplished and passionate stylist, with an originality that soon began earning him the comparison with Jimi Hendrix which would increase as his career progressed.

Emboldened by the response to his work, Vaughan left The Cobras in 1977 to form his first band as leader, Triple Threat. For four years, Vaughan paid his dues with this rhythm and blues revue band, allegedly sleeping on bar floors when times were hard. He disbanded Triple Threat in 1981, looking to incorporate his blues and R & B style into a more straightforward, contemporary rock format.

The unit he returned with was Double Trouble, a "power trio" in the mould of Texan compatriots ZZ Top. The name came from the title of a song in the repertoire of one of his heroes, blues singer Otis Rush. Even now Vaughan's reputation was still only parochial, but as word spread beyond Texas opportunities began to present themselves. Quite crucially, Double Trouble was invited to perform at the annual Montreux Blues Festival in Switzerland. Like its equivalent Montreux Jazz Festival, the blues festival is an important annual event in the world music market, and attracts many important artists and business people. Vaughan was already beginning to collect a number of big-time fans — The Rolling Stones and legendary CBS talent-spotter John Hammond among them — and a particularly electrifying performance at Montreux caught the attention of sometime Swiss resident David Bowie. Bowie asked Vaughan to play guitar on his 1983 album, *Let's Dance*, one of Bowie's biggest late-career successes and, tellingly, his début on a new American label. The Montreux performance also won Vaughan and band an invitation from Jackson Browne to record at his Los Angeles studios.

The result was Double Trouble's début album,*Texas Flood*, released on CBS subsidiary Epic Records. The record reached the top 40 in *Billboard* magazine, and eventually went gold. Both group and members began to score in a variety of music magazine readers' polls, winning nominations for the coveted Grammys, but this prize would elude them until 1985 when a contribution to an Atlantic Records blues compilation, *Blues Explosion*, won them the Grammy Award for Best Traditional Blues Recording.

By this time Vaughan's career as musician and bandleader was truly under way. He was writing more and more original material for Double Trouble's rock-blues repertoire, and beginning to enjoy a reputation comparable perhaps to that of white blues guitarist Johnnie Winter in the late 1960s. The 1984 Double Trouble album, *Couldn't Stand the Weather*, saw Vaughan expanding his style to encompass jazz and contemporary rock styles. It also showcased an improvisatory version of Hendrix's "Voodoo Chile", which for most bands would be at worst folly and at best hubris, but Vaughan's technique brought if off.

Despite increasing problems with drink and drugs — in particular an affection for bourbon and cocaine, sometimes mixed as a cocktail to debilitating effect — Vaughan set about a series of albums, and an accompanying, not to mention punishing, tour schedule, which saw Double Trouble scoring bigger sales and attracting bigger audiences. In 1986 their double live album, *Live Alive*, was their fifth consecutive gold album. The year proved to be a watershed, however; combined alcohol and drug intake caused Vaughan to collapse during a European tour. Evidently Vaughan stopped to take stock of his life, for he retreated to heal himself before returning with 1989's *In Step*, a collection of often painfully autobiographical songs which is regarded as the masterpiece of his career. It won his second Grammy. A follow-up album, *Family Style*, produced with brother Jimmy Vaughan, was released posthumously, just months after Vaughan died in a helicopter crash, when he and members of his entourage were travelling from a concert in Wisconsin to Chicago. Vaughan had played to a 25,000-strong crowd as a support to Eric Clapton.

While conferring a form of legend on Vaughan — when his helicopter crashed in dense fog, killing passengers and crew outright, Vaughan was immediately admitted to that morbid rock élite of Buddy Holly, Big Bopper, Otis Redding, Richie Valens, Jim Croce, Rick Nelson and other stars who died in air crashes — it is a particularly bitter irony that this should happen precisely at the time when he was returning to consolidate his career. In the 1980s he got to play alongside many of his blues heroines and heroes, among them Big Mama Thornton, Albert King, Bobby "Blue" Bland, Albert Collins and B. B. King. He never made the superstar league, but leaves behind a body of work that should endure and perhaps even improve with time.

Born Steven Ray Vaughan. **Mother** Martha Vaughan. **Career** Guitarist with bands such as the Chantones, Blackbird, Night Crawlers in Dallas area while still at high school; with The Cobras, Austin, 1975–77; lead guitarist, own band, Triple Threat, 1977–81; member, trio, Double Trouble with bass guitarist Tommy Shannon and drummer Chris Layton, 1981; début at Montreux Festival, 1982; lead guitarist for David Bowie in album, *Let's Dance*, 1983; recording début with own band, *Texas Flood*, Epic, 1983; also, record producer, mid 1980s onwards. **Awards and honours** "Rude Mood", nominated as Best Rock Instrumental, 1983; *Texas Flood* nominated Best Traditional Blues Recording, 1983; *Texas Flood* named Best Blues Album, *Guitar Player* magazine, 1983; named Best New Talent and Best Electric Blues Guitarist, *Guitar Player* magazine, 1983; Grammy nomination for *Couldn't Stand the Weather*, 1984; Grammy Award for Best Traditional Blues Recording, for track on *Blues Explosion*, 1985; Grammy Award for Best Contemporary Blues Recording, for *In Step*, 1989. **Recordings** *Let's Dance* with David Bowie, 1983; *Texas Flood*, Epic, 1983; *Couldn't Stand the Weather* (also producer), 1984; *Soul to Soul* (also producer), 1985; *Strike Like Lightning* (producer only) by Lonnie Mack, Alligator, 1985; *Live Alive*, 1986; *In Step*, 1989; *Family Style*, 1990. **Compositions** (include) "Empty Arms", 1985; "Life Without You", 1985; "Ain't Gone 'N' Give Up On Love", 1985; "Walk Of Denial", 1989; "Tight-rope", 1989. **Cause of death** Helicopter crash, at age 35.

CHARLES MARQUIS WARREN

American Writer and Director

***Born* Baltimore, Maryland, 16 December 1912**

***Died* West Hills, California, 11 August 1990**

Charles Warren considered himself an author of dramatic history, rather than a Western story-teller. While that opinion might be respectfully debatable, the fact is, he did begin his career in a more lofty literary vein. When a play he had written in Baltimore College — *No Sun, No Moon* — was produced at Princeton University, then optioned by MGM studios in 1933, Warren moved to Hollywood. In hand was an introduction from F. Scott Fitzgerald who, after a rather boozy afternoon, had semi-adopted Warren as a godson, of sorts. After a treatment he had worked on for *Tender is the Night* had not proved attractive enough to sell to the moguls of Tinsel Town, Warren turned to book-writing (between loan-outs for other treatments). In 1940 he wrote *Wilderness* and a book on dental history. He then returned to New York and carved a career writing Western stories for magazines. He began with the "pulps", but quickly established himself at the *Saturday Evening Post*; three of his stories for them, "Bugles are for Soldiers", "Only the Valiant", which was turned into a film starring Gregory Peck, and "Valley of the Shadows", became best-sellers.

After World War II, where he was bedecked with honours, Warren returned to Hollywood and churned out routine scripts for Paramount, Republic and other studios. His first, *Beyond Glory*, a paean to West Point Military Academy, proved to be a good vehicle for Alan Ladd. Despite erratic cutting, his next, *Streets of Laredo*, spotlighted a young William Holden. His niche was now secure. The year 1951 proved to be a fruitful one. Warren scripted *Oh Susanna*, *Woman of the North Country* and *Little Big Horn*, which he also directed, after persuading his distributor to give him a chance. In 1953 he formed a film corporation with John Champion to produce *Hellgate*, a stark Western prison drama with Sterling Hayden and Joan Leslie, following with *Pony Express* with Charlton Heston as Buffalo Bill, and *Arrowhead*, with Heston, Jack Palance and Katy Jurado. In 1953 Warren directed *Seven Angry Men*, about the abolitionist John Brown (with Raymond Massey, in one of his stormier roles), and wrote the screen plays *Flight to Tangier* and *Ride a Violent Mile* (filmed in 1957 with Warren as director). In 1955, he wrote (and directed 39 episodes of) one of the most popular television series in the medium's history, *Gunsmoke*, and was credited with the successful transfer of the formula Western. Starring James Arness as lawman Matt Dillon, it ran for 18 seasons — unusual by TV standards even today. Reruns are still being shown around the world.

A series of mediocre films followed, including *Tension at Table Rock* in 1956, one of the few productions Warren did not direct — and one that made little impact. The titles began to sound formula: *Black Whip*, *Blood Arrow*, *Copper Sky* — all written and directed in 1957, all low-budget. Warren realized that the Western genre had made the full switch to television, and was dying at the movie theatres. So, turning again to TV, he gave a young Clint Eastwood his first starring role as Rowdy Yates in the 1958 series, *Rawhide*, also successful. *The Virginian*, in 1962, brought James Drury to the small screen as a mysterious law — unto himself — man in 1890s Wyoming. Warren's conception came from the much-filmed Owen Wister novel, the most famous being the 1929 version in which Gary Cooper deadpanned, "When you call me that, smile." The last film Warren directed was *Charro!*, a disastrous Elvis vehicle, which proved to be an anti-climactic finish to his career.

The 1953 film *Arrowhead*, with Charlton Heston, on which Warren was as usual writer/director, was emphatic in its anti-Indian sentiment. This was one characteristic of his writing. Another was an action-filled rhythm that pleased a particular breed of reader: the Western adventurist. His simple plot-lines translated well into low-budget, undemanding films, as they described a black-and-white world. The hero, graduate of the "strong-and-silent" school, was not portrayed with depth; that dimension was left for the particular actor to mine for himself. The most severely criticized aspects of Warren's story-telling have been — admittedly common faults of the times — his portrayals of both Indians and women.

While the Indian is given credit for cunning (in order to provide a credible foil, crucial to a story), he is portrayed as cruel, primitive and usually murderous. The many examples (and ones more historically accurate) of his ill-treatment by the white man, including broken treaties, land-stealing, cultural destruction and the systematic wiping out of families, were never mentioned. The women watched, cooed and fluttered — honourably, purely, quietly. It can be said that Warren's cowboy bore little resemblance to the truly unglamourized figure in the 1800s American West. However, if the reader/viewer accepted Warren's world as a stylized, action-packed place of heroism, honour and good old American values—after all, cinema's role was not always to reproduce reality—then there were few better for spinning yarns in a particularly American genre than Warren.

Born Charles Marquis Warren. **Parents** Charles and Beatrice (Porter) Warren. **Marriages** 1) Anne Crawford Tootle, 1941; 2) Mildred Lindeberg. **Children** Anne, Jessica and Victoria, from first marriage. **Education** Baltimore High School, Maryland; Baltimore City College, Maryland, specialized in law of the American West. **Military service** United States Naval Reserve, Navy photographic unit, 1942–46, became commander. **Career** All-Mayland halfback; sports correspondent, *Baltimore News Post*; first play, *No Sun, No Moon*, produced at Princeton University; collaborated with F. Scott Fitzgerald on screenplay of *Tender is the Night*, 1934; freelance writer, mostly of Westerns in *Blue Book*, *Argosy* and *Saturday Evening Post*; first novel, *Only the Valiant*, 1943; first screenplay, *Beyond Glory*, 1948; film-directing début, *Little Big Horn*, 1951; first television creation, *Gunsmoke*, 1955. **Related activities** President: Commander Films Corporation, Beverly Hills, California, 1951 onwards, CMW Productions, Beverly Hills, 1960 onwards, Emirzu Productions, Beverly Hills, 1962 onwards, CMW Incorporated, Los Angeles. **Offices and memberships** Member: Academy of Motion Picture Arts and Sciences, Screen Directors Guild, Writers Guild of America, Screen Producers Guild. **Awards and honours** Purple Heart, 1946; Bronze Star, 1946; five battle stars, 1946; award nominee, Academy of Motion Picture Arts and Sciences, 1949; British Critics Award, 1956; Western Heritage Award, 1959. **Publications** *History of American Dental Surgery*, 1941; *Only the Valiant* (Western), 1943; *Valley of the Shadow* (Western), 1948; *Bugles are for Soldiers*; *Deadhead*, 1949. **Uncollected short stories** "Forward into Battle", in *Argosy*, 1941; "Lo, the Tattooed People", in *Argosy*, 1941; "This Is Not Gettysburg", in *Saturday Evening Post*, 1943; "The Cowboy Quoted Keats", in *Saturday Evening Post*, 1947. **Screenplays** (With Jonathan Latimer and William Wister Haines) *Beyond Glory*, 1948; (with Louis Stevens and Elizabeth Hill) *Streets of Laredo*, 1949; *The Redhead and the Cowboy*, 1951; (with Kenneth Gamet) *Fighting Coast Guard*, 1951; *Oh Susanna*, 1951; (with Harold Shumate) *Little Big Horn*, 1951; (with Norman Reilly Raine and Prescott Chaplin) *Woman of the North Country*, 1952; (with Frank Davis and Sloan Nibley) *Springfield Rifle*, 1952; (with John C. Champion) *Hellgate*, 1952; (with Frank Gruber) *Pony Express*, 1953; *Arrowhead*, 1953; *Flight to Tangier*, 1953; (with Eric Norden) *Ride a Violent Mile*, 1958; (with Endre Bohem) *Desert Hell*, 1958; (with Eric Bercovici) *Day of the Evil Gun*, 1968; (with Frederic Louis Fox) *Charro*, 1960. **Films** (as director) *Little Big Horn*, 1951; *Hellgate*, 1952; *Arrowhead*, 1953; *Flight to Tangier*, 1953; *Seven Angry Men*, 1955; *Tension at Table Rock*, 1956; *The Black Whip*, 1957; *Trooper Hook*, 1957; *Back from the Dead*, 1957; *The Violent Unknown*, 1957; *Copper Sky*, 1957; *Ride a Violent Mile*, 1957; *Desert Hell*, 1958; *Cattle Empire*, 1958; *Blood Arrow*, 1958; *Charro!*, 1969. **Television** (includes) *Gunsmoke*, 1955; *Rawhide*, 1958; *The Virginian*, 1962; *The Iron Horse*, 1966. **Cause of death** Complications after surgery for an aneurysm, at age 77.

ROY WILLIAMSON

British Folk Musician

***Born* Edinburgh, Scotland, 25 June 1936**

***Died* Forres, Scotland, 12 August 1990**

Singer and multi-instrumentalist Roy Williamson may well have rued what many will consider his finest hour: the adoption, in the 1970s, of his folk song, "Flower Of Scotland", as a nationalist anthem. The song, written for his folk group The Corries in the 1960s, contains the plaintive lines,

O Flower of Scotland,
When will we see
Your like again?

This sentiment, which Williamson considered to be a purely personal and private philosophical observation, was siezed upon by Scots nationalists, and, in particular, patriotic rugby fans, especially on the terraces of home games against foreign teams.

Born in Edinburgh and educated at Gordonstoun, Williamson studied at Edinburgh Art College in the late 1950s, and was of the precise age to fall in with the then-burgeoning traditional jazz and skiffle music of the nascent "teenage" culture. He experimented with a number of musicial styles, but was finally captured by the folk revival that swept through Britain in the early 1960s. In 1962 he joined up with fellow musicians Bill Smith and Ronnie Browne to form the Corrie Folk Trio — "corrie" being, at least according to Chambers, a mountain recess, in the manner of a caldera, taking its name from the Gaelic for cauldron. The group soon encountered young Belfast singer Paddie Bell, whose sweet voice greatly enhanced what was now the Corrie Folk Quartet.

The group began to build a reputation on the folk circuit, most notably for a fresher, robust and more authentic folk than the twee fairies and elves/barking yokels image that dogged much English folk. This "authentic" style would in later years come under attack from purists who accused such performers of behaving like actors in a theme park, but for its time and in its context it was quite radical.

In the early 1960s the group was still only semi-professional, with Williamson and Browne working as art teachers to support themselves. In 1963 the group was invited to appear on a new television show dedicated to folk music, called *The Hootenanny Show*. *Hootenanny* made their name and enabled the group to become fully professional. This was not without its problems; Paddie Bell left the group shortly afterwards, and Bill Smith departed in 1966, but the stint on *Hootenanny* had established The Corries, as they were now simply known, to work on as a duo for the next two decades. By now, they were the most popular folk performers in Scotland.

The duo recorded a number of albums for EMI Records, and later for the independent Dara label, mixing traditional Gaelic material with their own modern-day observations on the Scottish heritage — a subject of fierce pride and debate among Scots everywhere. The duo also established a routine of touring Britain or the Continent once or twice a year. The folk circuit is a far-flung and complex network, and is comprised of fans as tenacious as their heroes. The music may ebb and surge in fashionability, and it entirely lacks the chances of fame and fortune afforded by pop, but it is sturdy enough to support performers such as The Corries, who became perennial figures on the folk scene. While the material may vary, indeed while the size of the audience may vary, such performers become timeless.

The Corries' abiding association with "Flower Of Scotland" reached its peak in 1990, when the Scottish Grand Slam rugby team adopted it as their pre-match anthem, the team singing it on the field. It reached its absolute apogee in March, when a 50,000-strong crowd crammed Murrayfield stadium to sing the song as a prelude to a rugby game in which the Scotsmen trounced the English. Williamson and Browne, both keen rugby fans and, in earlier years, players, had hoped to lead the crowd in the singing, but Williamson was too ill from the effects of cancer to attend.

Williamson often expressed bemusement at the way people responded to his most famous composition, but it would appear to have earned him a niche in the Gaelic tradition which he and The Corries did so much to perpetuate.

Born Roy Murdoch Buchanan Williamson. **Marriages** Two. **Children** Two daughters from first marriage. **Education** Gordonstoun School, Moray, Scotland; Edinburgh Art College, 1955–

59. **Career** Coastguard; member, mountain rescue teams; art teacher; with Bill Smith, Ronnie Browne and singer Paddie Bell formed Corrie Folk Trio, 1962; member, duo, The Corries with Ronnie Browne, 1966 onwards; recorded first with EMI, later on Dara label. **Compositions** (include) "Flower Of Scotland", 1966–67, recorded, 1969. **Cause of death** Cancer, at age 54.

SEPTEMBER

JOHN BOWLBY

British Psychiatrist
Born **London, England, 26 February 1907**
Died **Isle of Skye, Scotland, 2 September 1990**

John Bowlby was the western world's most influential psychiatric figure on the effects of maternal deprivation of this century. His work has had a profound effect on both the treatment of children in institutions, particularly hospitals, and politically, in terms of how his findings have been indirectly employed in the "control" of women.

Bowlby was born into a medical family but was originally destined for a naval career to which end he went to the Royal Naval College at Dartmouth. However, partly because of naval cutbacks in the 1920s, he moved to Cambridge University to read medicine. He realized his primary interest lay in the psychopathology of human relationships at a very early stage and opted for psychoanalytical training under the supervision of Melanie Klein. By 1937 he had joined the London Child Guidance Clinic where his own lifelong research work began.

He noted a series of children who had been referred following theft, all of whom had previously experienced prolonged separation from their mothers. This led to his first work on the topic, *Forty-four Juvenile Thieves: Their Characters and Home Life,* published in 1946 following his war service as an Army psychiatrist.

After the war he began his work with the Tavistock Clinic in London's Hampstead district where he was to remain for the rest of his life. He took over the department for children which he rapidly renamed as being for children *and parents,* thus proving himself also a pioneer in the now fully accepted field of family therapy. Until this time an individual with problems had been dealt with in isolation. Bowlby was the first to appreciate that people do not so much develop their own difficulties as have them thrust upon them by circumstances and other people.

By the end of the 1940s he had been invited to join the World Health Organisation to research one aspect of the aftermath of World War II: what to do with the immense numbers of homeless youngsters throughout Europe — not solely refugees but also those left alone in their own homelands. Originally supposed to be a 15,000-word report, Bowlby produced his internationally acclaimed monograph, *Maternal Care and Mental Health* in 1951. This he subsequently rewrote for a more general audience under the title *Child Care and the Growth of Love,* which was published two years later and has been selling ever since as the seminal work on maternal deprivation throughout the world.

Bowlby's thesis, which now goes almost without saying, was that infants form affectional bonds with the primary caretaking figure in their lives and that if those bonds are broken serious problems may ensue, in some cases leading to those infants themselves being incapable of parenting in adult life. In those early days much reliance was placed on the idea of "instinct" and there were those who doubted the mechanisms involved, but as time went by and Bowlby discovered the emerging body of work from the field of ethology he found an ever-increasing amount of support for his theories. Studies of animal behaviour by Europeans such as Konrad Lorenz and Niko Tinbergen all added grist to his mill and he found especial back-up from the Harlows' work with young rhesus monkeys in the United States. Orphans given the choice of two dummy mothers, one made of wire with a milk supply, the other covered in clutchable cloth, were seen to choose the wire mother only when hungry. Comfort under threat was always sought from the more cuddly model. The "cupboard love" theory of infant affection was finally destroyed.

Bowlby's life work was the full documentation of his findings in his trilogy *Attachment and Loss*. The first volume, *Attachment,* came out in 1969 and dealt with the processes involved in the creation of affectional bonds and the role of those bonds as a survival mechanism for all forms of mammalian life. Volume Two, *Separation,* followed four years later and covered the fear, anxiety and anger involved in separation — real and imagined — and the behavioural effects it can have on the child. The final volume, *Loss,* dealing with the depression that can result from bereavement or similar total and irreparable loss, appeared in 1980 and completed one of the greatest contributions to psychoanalytic theory since its beginning. Bowlby had completely rethought Freud's original theory, based on a nineteenth-century understanding of neurophysiology, with one based on innate behavioural patterns, stimuli and feed-back.

The impact of Bowlby's work came swiftly. The most immediate change came with the hospitalization of children. Hard though it may be for younger people to appreciate, a child going into hospital in the UK for any reason was not allowed to receive any visitors whatsoever in the 1940s. This was because children often cried when their mothers left and, so the experts ruled, upset other children. Some kindly nurses did permit parents to peek around the ward door but the physical separation was meant to be absolute. By the mid-1950s it was possible actually to visit one's children in hospital and by the mid 1960s a "pushy" mother could be allowed to stay with a young child. Spin-offs came in other directions as primary schools began to realize that parents were not necessarily a hindrance to the education of children. Both mothers and fathers came also, by the time of Bowlby's death, to be as welcome in the classroom as they were on the ward.

Institutional care changed too, although by the nature of the bonds broken for those requiring it and the difficulty of creating affectional bonds between its charges and those employed to care for them, it had proved a harder nut to crack. There has been, however, a much stronger move to the avoidance of institutional care if at all possible: poor parenting being seen as better than no parenting and resources being deployed more extensively in fostering. It also has to be noted that the loss of stigma attaching to illegitimacy has meant that virtually no child has natural parents capable of caring for it who fail to do so.

There was, inevitably, a backlash against Bowlby's views from the more extreme members of the women's liberation movement who saw them as a means to prevent women achieving for themselves, and his theory as a "plot" against the female sex. There was also, as mentioned earlier, misrepresentation of his work by political forces interested, for example, in the preservation of a totally fictitious view of "the family", with all women chained to domestic tasks, so that unemployment might appear less of a social problem than was the true case. In addition there were those who failed actually to read his books and assumed maternal deprivation meant that mothers were supposed to be propping up their infants 24 hours a day with never a break for anything else. This was far from the case. Bowlby's message was really quite simple: that infants need the opportunity to form good bonds with a caretaking figure or figures; that they need to *know* those figures are available when they are distressed or afraid; that they can sense a true security. Bowlby himself did actually believe that mothers ought to do their own mothering but he did not regard this as an absolute necessity for a child's ultimate mental health.

Although his work was mainly research-based, Bowlby continued to spend about one third of his time as a psychotherapist at the Tavistock and even after his formal retirement from the Department for Children and Parents in 1968 he continued his association with the clinic, both as teacher and senior research fellow.

Although widely travelled and acclaimed Bowlby was himself devoted to his own family both in their London home on the fringes of Hampstead's famous heath land and the holiday home on the Isle of Skye where he spent his last days. He derived much pleasure from being close to his own children and grandchildren, some of whom grew up as neighbours. He was, in some respects, rather quiet and stern, but in fact his life was as full as he had expected it to be. He often reflected that the most inadequate child care derived from the richest countries of the world and caused vast amounts of mental ill health, the resultant loneliness and depression even leading to suicide, whereas the poorest countries could often be seen giving their children the best possible emotional start in life. A paradox, yes, but as he said, "It is not my job to change this. But I can't pretend that I think it a sensible way to live." In his life as in his work Bowlby set his own example and standards.

Born Edward John Mostyn Bowlby. **Parents** Anthony Alfred, surgeon, and Maria (Mostyn) Bowlby. **Marriage** Ursula Longstaff, 1938. **Children** Mary, Richard, Pia and Robert. **Education** Royal Naval College, Dartmouth; Trinity College, Cambridge, BA, 1928, MA, 1932; University College Hospital Medical School, London, MD, 1933. **Military service** Psychiatrist, Royal Army Medical Corps, 1940–45, retired lieutenant-colonel. **Career** Staff psychiatrist, London Child Guidance Clinic, 1937–40; consultant psychiatrist, Tavistock Clinic, 1946–72, chairman, Department for Children and Parents, 1946–68, honorary consultant, senior research fellow and teacher, 1972–90. **Related activities** Mental health consultant: World Health Organisation, from 1950, National Institute of Mental Health, Bethesda, Maryland, 1958–63; fellow, Center for Advanced Studies in Behavioral Sciences, Stanford, California, 1957–58; part-time member, external scientific staff, Medical Research Council, 1963–72; visiting professor in psychiatry, Stanford University, 1968; H.B. Williams Travelling Professor, Australia and New Zealand College of Psychiatrists, 1973; Freud Memorial visiting professor, University College London, 1980. **Offices and memberships** Fellow, British Psychological Society, 1945; President, International Association for Child Psychiatry and Allied Professions, 1962–66; fellow, Royal College of Physicians, London, 1964; fellow, Royal College of Psychiatrists, 1971, honorary fellow, 1980; honorary member, American Academy of Arts and Sciences, 1981–90; honorary fellow, Royal Society of Medicine, 1987; member, British Psychoanalytic Society. **Awards and honours** Honorary DLitt, Leicester University, 1971; Commander of the Order of the British Empire, 1972; Sir James Spence medal, British Paediatric Association, 1974; G. Stanley Hall Medal, American Psychological Association, 1974; honorary ScD, Cambridge University, 1977; Distinguished Scientific Contribution Award, Society for Research in Child Development, 1981; Salmon Medal, New York Academy of Medicine, 1984. **Film** (Associate) *A Two-Year-Old Goes to Hospital,* 1952. **Publications** (With E.F.M. Durbin) *Personal Aggressiveness and War,* 1938; "The Influence of Early Environment in the Development of Neurosis and Neurotic Character", 1940; *Personality and Mental Illness,* 1940; *Forty-Four Juvenile Thieves: Their Characters and Home Life,* 1946; *Maternal Care and Mental Health,* 1951, also published as *Child Care and the Growth of Love,* 1953; "A Two-Year-Old Goes to Hospital", 1952; "The Nature of the Child's Tie to His Mother", 1957; *Attachment and Loss,* Volume One: *Attachment,* 1969, Volume Two: *Separation: Anxiety and Anger,* 1973, 1978, Volume Three: *Loss: Sadness and Depression,* 1980; *The Making and Breaking of Affectional Bonds,* 1979; *A Secure Base: Clinical Applications of Attachment Theory,* 1988; *Charles Darwin: A New Biography,* 1990. **Cause of death** Stroke, at age 83.

LORD CARADON

British Colonial Administrator and Diplomat

***Born* Plymouth, Devon, 8 October 1907**

***Died* Plymouth, Devon, 5 September 1990**

By his own definition Hugh Foot, Lord Caradon, was "one of the last of an almost extinct species" — the British colonial governor. Or, as Baroness Jeger was later to write, he was "a Colonial Governor who ran out of colonies". And the fact that he did so was in no small part a testimony to his own efforts to prepare those self same colonies for independence.

Hugh Foot was born into the Radical, Nonconformist tradition of a family remarkable for its distinction in politics, literature and the championship of human rights. He was the second son of the scholarly Isaac Foot, Liberal MP, solicitor and devout Methodist lay preacher. In later years he always acknowledged the debt to his family and to the home where books seemed to "breed in their plenitude".

He was educated at Leighton Park, a Quaker school, and at St John's College, Cambridge where he earned an honours degree in history and law and in 1929 he joined the Colonial Service. Like others of his time he believed that preparing nations for self-government combined unique opportunities for putting liberal ideas into practice with an out-of-doors, overseas career.

His first post was as an administrative officer to the Palestine government. He soon found himself in an overwhelmingly Arab area where he would ride on horseback, unarmed and unaccompanied, into "his" villages; and he demonstrated an almost endless capacity for hard work plus the physique to stand it. During this appointment he realized the impossibility of fulfilling the hopes of both Jews and Arabs. Many Arabs had fought with Britain against the Turks in World War I and felt they had earned their freedom. On the other hand, the Jews invoked the Balfour Declaration of 1917, promising a National Home in Palestine.

Hugh Foot remained in Palestine until 1937, then returned to London for two years at the Colonial Office, followed by a spell as assistant British resident in Trans-Jordan. In 1943, at the early age of 36, he was appointed colonial secretary in Cyprus; for it was already clear that his abilities and personality would soon take him to the top. In 1947 he became chief secretary in Nigeria where he found 40 million people, over 200 languages, no central parliament and no Nigerian participation in the making of central policy. He also found a welcome among the horsemen of the North, for polo was their favourite sport and Foot was a fine player. But the appointment was not without its dangers; in 1950 he narrowly escaped assassination — the assailant's dagger actually grazed his cheek.

He first achieved real prominence in his next post — as governor of Jamaica. His six years there (from 1951) were fruitful and happy; he grappled successfully with local unrest: he was a popular figure and widely judged a good governor. Michael Manley, now prime minister of Jamaica, later wrote of "the deep personal interest he took in the development of the political process in Jamaica", and continued, "there is no doubt that the political maturity we now enjoy was based on the principles he helped to formulate and the preliminary constitutional foundations he laid while he was Governor."

Hugh Foot was an idealist with an optimistic belief in post-imperial self-determination. He took his duties seriously, being fond of quoting the poet Milton's words, "Let not England forget her precedence in teaching the nations how to live." And he took the view that the only way to teach people responsibility was to give it to them. So it is hardly surprising that many hoped he would stay as chief of the West Indian Federation created in 1957. But he had already been earmarked for another, more challenging trouble spot in the Empire — for Cyprus.

His predecessor as governor of the island, Field Marshal Sir John Harding, had had the difficult task of stabilizing the political and military situation; Foot's job was to guide the warring Turkish and Greek factions to independence.

He began, characteristically, with a number of tours — on foot and, of course, on horseback — in order to show himself freely to the Greek and Turkish communities to try to win their respect and confidence. He also walked, unescorted, along the notorious "murder mile" in Nicosia, chatting with the shopkeepers. And he proposed a truce in hostilities while the British, the Greek generals and the Turkish Cypriot leader Archbishop Makarios conferred in Athens.

As both Greece and Turkey were in Nato it was important to reach agreement; but Foot's attempt to placate and make friends with the Greek Cypriots infuriated the Turks. In 1958 serious Turkish protest riots erupted on the island. Following the murder of British soldiers, Foot was obliged to restore the death penalty. Fighting between the two communities reached its peak in July of that year when he was forced to impose a curfew and ordered the arrest of more than 1000 Greek and Turkish Cypriots to prevent civil war.

Meanwhile, he continued to attend talks and to develop and present proposals for a solution. Eventually a settlement was reached by direct negotiation between the Greek and Turkish governments and the British government — and an agreement was signed in London in 1959.

At last, on 16 August 1961, independence was declared. Foot, in his traditional governor's plumed helmet, was a splendid sight; and he left the island with high hopes for its peaceful future. A citation from the British government hailed his "wisdom, courage and humanity, and his unwearying efforts in negotiations." But years later he was to speak of his shame that the treaty he had signed had not been honoured after the Turkish invasion of Cyprus in 1974.

Hugh Foot was 53 when he left Cyprus; but he was not a retiring man. In the following year he was made Britain's representative on the United Nations trusteeship council with the rank of ambassador. A mere 15 months later he resigned — on a matter of principle. The trusteeship council was calling for the release of Joshua Nkomo by the Southern Rhodesian authorities and for the ban on his Zimbabwe African People's Union to be lifted; but, although Rhodesia was then a British colony, the Conservative government in London made no attempt to intervene on Nkomo's behalf. Wrote Hugh Foot at the time, "I do not feel able to speak in the UN or elsewhere in defence of our position in this matter. I simply cannot do it."

However, his standing at the United Nations was such that he was soon afterwards appointed as a consultant to the special fund for African development and named as one of the international experts to inquire into apartheid in South Africa.

In 1964, with the return of a Labour government in England, he was made a life peer as Lord Caradon and appointed by Prime Minister Harold Wilson as permanent United Kingdom representative at the United Nations with the rank of Minister of State at the Foreign Office. For the next five years he was in the thick of controversies and conflicts over Rhodesia and South Africa. He acquired a considerable reputation for the tenacity and skill with which he handled these often explosive situations and when the Conservative Party won the elections in Britain in 1970 he was asked to stay on as consultant to the United Nations Development Programme.

For, in spite of his period as a member of the Labour government, Hugh Foot was an old-fashioned idealist rather than a party politician. Writes George Ivan Smith in the London *Independent* newspaper: "In Africa and the United Nations I was able to witness how the essence of his genuine concern for human beings was like the balm and skill of a midwife at times when vast human societies across the world were writhing with violence and labour pains, when old empires were dying and giving birth to new nations." To this natural concern Hugh Foot added the skills of a diplomat — and the all-important quality of caution. In an interview, he said he never smiled when journalists were nearby: "You never know when there may be a stray photographer around and, in a newspaper alongside a headline saying '100,000 people dead', there is a picture of you smiling all over your face."

Hugh Foot was born into a family whose members had campaigned long and ably for human rights. Two of his brothers, Dingle and Michael, achieved political distinction and a third became a Liberal life peer as Lord Foot. He himself achieved equal distinction in his chosen field and nobly upheld his family's tradition in times — and places — of great political turmoil. Hardly surprising then, that in 1970, when Harold Wilson was asked on television, "Which appointment now gives you the most pride in retrospect?" he replied, "Hugh Foot".

Born Hugh Mackintosh Foot. **Parents** Isaac, Liberal member of parliament, and Eva (Mackintosh) Foot. **Marriage** Florence Sylvia Tod, 1936 (died 1985). **Children** Paul, Sarah, Oliver and Benjamin. **Education** Leighton Park School, Reading, Berkshire; St John's College, Cambridge, BA, 1929. **Career** Entered Colonial Service, 1929; administrative officer, Palestine, 1929–37; in Colonial Office, London, 1937–39; assistant British resident, Trans-Jordan, 1939–42; chief colonial secretary and acting governor-general, Cyprus, 1943–45; colonial secretary and acting governor, Jamaica, 1945–47; chief secretary, Nigeria, 1947–51; governor-in-chief and captain-general, Jamaica, 1951–57; governor and commander-in-chief, Cyprus, 1957–60; retired from Colonial Service, 1960; adviser and ambassador, UK mission to United Nations, 1961–62, resigned, 1962; Minister of State for Foreign Affairs, 1964–70; permanent representative to United Nations, 1964–70. **Related activities** Consultant, United Nations Special Fund, 1962–64. **Awards and honours** Officer of the Order of the British Empire, 1939; Commander of the Order of St Michael and St George, 1946; Knight Commander of the Order of St Michael and St George, 1951; Knight Grand Cross, 1957; Knight of the Order of St John of Jerusalem, 1952; Knight Commander, Royal Victorian Order; fellow, St John's College, Cambridge University, 1960; created life peer, Baron Caradon, 1964; International Planned Parenthood award. **Publications** *Constitutional Reform: A New System of Government for Jamaica — Three Broadcast Talks,* 1953; *Empire Into Commonwealth,* 1962; *A Start in Freedom* (autobiography), 1964; (with Charles Coulson and Trevor Huddleston) *Three Views on Commitment,* 1967; *Southern Africa in International Relations,* 1970. **Cause of death** Undisclosed, at age 82.

MARCUS CUNLIFFE

British Historian

Born **Rochdale, Lancashire, 5 July 1922**

Died **Washington, DC, 2 September 1990**

Marcus Cunliffe belonged to a generation of British academics whose lives were profoundly influenced by their experiences in World War II. He served in the Royal Tank Regiment as an intelligence officer, and in his case it was the novel experience of close contact with America's military might which captured his interest: "We had driven in American vehicles and fired American guns. I had seen Flying Fortresses spiral into formation at dawn over East Anglia."

He returned to his history studies at Oxford University — interrupted by the war — in 1946, and began research into English military history. But the lure of the United States was strong and in 1947 he obtained a Commonwealth Fund fellowship at Yale University. After two years in the US he returned to Britain to become a lecturer at Manchester University in a new and exciting academic discipline — American studies.

Marcus Cunliffe was to become the leading British writer on the history and literature of the United States, producing a succession of excellent books and attracting numerous graduate students who followed in his footsteps. His first book was a regimental history of the Royal Irish Fusiliers, published in 1953, but the following year Pelican Books published *The Literature of the United States,* a work which explored the unique character of America through its literature. With this authoritative study Cunliffe showed how an interdisciplinary approach could yield far better results than the traditionally separate branches of history and literature. He followed this up with several major works, including a biography of George Washington.

In 1965 he moved south to the new University of Sussex, outside Brighton. There he continued to produce excellent academic work and, with his first wife Mitzi, an American sculptor, he gathered a circle of friends and colleagues who made his house a centre of Anglo-American cultural exchange.

Marcus Cunliffe was a witty, charming man, always ready to laugh at himself and to encourage others to do the same. He was born and brought up in the north of England, attending the Royal Grammar School in Newcastle-upon-Tyne, an institution which has produced many fine scholars, and continues to do so. His childhood love of the picturesque northern English countryside never waned, although he spent most of his life away from the area. Many people have called him a "transatlantic" man but it would be truer to say that he was a British person, who saw the Americans through European, or English, eyes.

He was never one to lose himself entirely in the university world, disliking administrative tasks and those who preferred to further their careers through such means. Novelist and academic Malcolm Bradbury was a post-graduate student of Cunliffe's and, as fellow-academic and critic, Frank Kermode, delicately put it in the *Guardian* newspaper, "Cunliffe, as some believe, was implicated in certain stormy political events, later reflected in Malcolm Bradbury's *The History Man*". Certainly, it seems to have been a growing disillusionment with the British university establishment which caused Cunliffe to take up a post in Washington in 1980.

In many ways it was the logical step for him to take. He had visited the United States frequently in an academic capacity since the 1950s, and in 1976 he was awarded an honorary doctorate by the University of Pennsylvania in recognition of his contribution to American historiography. He was comfortable among Americans, although he retained a very English wit and academic style. Unfortunately, shortly after taking up his post as professor of American history at the George Washington University, he became ill with leukaemia, the disease that was eventually to claim his life.

Marcus Cunliffe did much to make American studies a popular subject in Britain, and to establish the basis of its pursuit for the next generation of academics, many of whom he taught as undergraduate or post-graduate students. His clear, unpretentious writing and his keen analytical mind, backed by a limitless curiosity and an almost encyclopaedic knowledge, marked him as one of the foremost scholars of American history and literature.

Born Marcus Falkner Cunliffe. **Parents** Keith Harold and Kathleen Eleanor (Falkner) Cunliffe. **Marriages** 1) Mitzi Solomon, sculptor, 1949 (divorced 1971); 2) Lesley Hume, journalist, 1971 (divorced 1980); 3) Phyllis Palmer, historian, 1984. **Children** Antonia, Shay and Jason, from first marriage. **Education** Royal Grammar School, Newcastle-upon-Tyne; Oriel College, Oxford, BA, 1944, MA, 1946, BLitt, 1947. **Emigration** Left England for US, 1980. **Military service** Lieutenant, British Army, 1942–46, intelligence officer, Royal Tank Regiment. **Career** Commonwealth Fund fellow, Yale University, 1947–49; lecturer in American studies, University of Manchester, 1949–56, senior lecturer, 1956–60, professor of American history and institutions, 1960–64; professor of American studies, University of Sussex, 1965–80; University Professor, George Washington University, 1980–90. **Related activities** Fellow, Center for Advanced Study in the Behavioral Sciences, Stanford, California, 1957–58; visiting professor: Harvard University, 1959–60, City College of the City University of New York, 1970, University of Michigan, 1973, Mercer University, Macon, Georgia, Mount Holyoke College, Washington State

University, University of California, Berkeley; fellow, Woodrow Wilson International Center, Washington, DC, 1977–78. **Offices and memberships** Member: American Historical Association, Massachusetts Historical Society, Society of American Historians, British Association for American Studies. **Awards and honours** Honorary DHL: University of Pennsylvania, 1976, New England College, 1979. **Publications** *The Royal Irish Fusiliers, 1793–1950,* 1953; *The Literature of the United States,* 1954, 1967, 1986; *History of the Royal Warwickshire Regiment, 1919–1953,* 1958; *The Nation Takes Shape, 1789–1837,* 1959; (editor) *Life of Washington* by M.L. Weems, 1962; (with R.B. Morris) *George Washington and the Making of a Nation* (juvenile), 1966; *The Presidency,* 1968; (with others) *The American Heritage History of the Presidency,* 1968; (with others) *The Making of America,* 1968; *Soldiers and Civilians: The Martial Spirit in America, 1775–1865,* 1968; *American Presidents and the Presidency,* 1969; (editor with Robin Winks) *Pastmasters: Some Essays on American Historians,* 1969; (editor) *The London Times History of Our Times,* 1971, published in England as *The Times History of Our Times,* 1971; *The Ages of Man: From Savage to Sew-age,* 1971; *The Age of Expansion, 1848–1917,* 1974; (editor) *Sphere History of Literature* volumes eight and nine: *American Literature,* 1975; (editor) *The Divided Loyalist: Crèvecoeur's America,* 1978; *Chattel Slavery and Wage Slavery,* 1979; *In Search of America.* **Cause of death** Leukaemia, at age 68. **Further reading** Brian Halden-Reid and John White, *American Studies: Essays in Honour of Marcus Cunliffe,* 1990.

DAN DAVIN

New Zealand/British Writer and Publisher

***Born* Invercargill, New Zealand, 1 September 1913**

***Died* Oxford, England, 28 September 1990**

Dan Davin was an Irish New Zealander who spent his adult life in Britain, and it shows in the novels. Poet Louis MacNeice said that Davin was an expatriate of two countries. He was something of a Renaissance Man, excelling in scholarship, soldiering, intelligence work, academic publishing and making friends in pubs. People liked him. He was tall, good-looking, sincere and a charmer with a dry sense of humour. Davin was known as a gifted raconteur but, more unusually, he was a good listener too.

His father, Patrick, was a Roman Catholic labourer from Tonygurrone near Galway, Ireland, who had emigrated to the bottom of New Zealand's South Island and become a railwayman. Young Daniel Marcus, the fourth child, went to a school in Invercargill run by the Marist Brothers, and won a scholarship to the Sacred Heart College in Auckland. From there he proceeded to Otago University in Dunedin and took a First in both English and Latin; he said, later, that this was "the most important of all my rites of passage".

In 1936 he was awarded one of the two New Zealand Rhodes Scholarships, and arrived at Balliol College, Oxford to read classics, again achieving a First. He was also a keen rugby player. Davin did the kind of things you might expect literary-minded new arrivals in Britain to do, like visiting Paris, and, liberal that he was, he suffered considerable *Angst* at this time over the fact that he was not doing his bit for the Spanish Civil War.

In 1939 (also the year of his marriage to a fellow student from Otago, Winifred Gonley), he volunteered for the Army. He served in the Warwickshire Regiment for a short while and was then commissioned into the Second New Zealand Expeditionary Force, with whom he was wounded in

Crete and evacuated to Egypt. But he went on to work as an intelligence officer in GHQ in Cairo and, after a period with the "J" Service, later called Phantom, was appointed to General Freyberg's divisional intelligence staff. Finally he served as a corps commander at Cassino in Italy. Davin was something of a hero, mentioned in despatches three times and adorned with a military MBE.

Another New Zealander and Rhodes Scholar, Kenneth Sisam, hired him as junior assistant secretary at the Clarendon Press in Oxford as soon as the war was over. He was to spend his entire professional career with the Oxford University Press, moving up to become deputy secretary to the delegates in 1970, a job which changed its name to academic publisher while he was doing it.

Davin was a fine publisher. At the Clarendon Press he commissioned great numbers of books, from monographs to dictionaries. An essential ingredient of his success was his skill at getting his own way with the delegates at their fortnightly meetings; colleagues still talk about his use of the time-honoured tactic of presenting books he wanted to publish but suspected that they might not just before lunch. He would have hated the contemporary business ethos that has overtaken publishing, and yet he was an astute businessman, in his own way. Above all, he had a good eye.

Davin was always perceived as an academic. From 1965 he had a professorial fellowship at Balliol and was made an emeritus fellow on his retirement in 1978. For 30 years he reviewed books from New Zealand for *The Times Literary Supplement,* and he was a fellow of the Royal Society of Arts. The University of Otago bestowed on him an honorary DLitt in 1984.

He realized that he wanted to write when he was a student, keen to say his piece as a poet, novelist and historian. Poetry seems to have gone by the board at a fairly early stage, and the only history book he ever wrote was *Crete,* an excellent volume in the Official New Zealand History of the Second World War. But in fiction he found his *métier.* He wrote seven novels, beginning with *Cliffs of Fall,* which appeared in 1945, and a number of short stories.

Unsurprisingly, New Zealand is a vital element of his work, in particular the Irish Catholic minority. He drew on his war experiences, too, for example his second novel, *For the Rest of Our Lives,* in 1947, was about the NZ Division in Crete and the Western Desert. But the personal material did not limit him: he used it all as a starting point for a wider exploration of universal issues — an exploration that he often pursued too vigorously, in fact, as although he used the interior monologue effectively to that end, the plot and characters sometimes suffered. Davin said that *Not Here, Not Now* concluded, more or less, a sequence of novels he had had in mind since 1939; the war and his career had brought in "new themes and substances", with the result that *Not Here, Not Now* was the book he had originally intended to write first. His last novel, *Brides of Price,* was more sophisticated in style and content, as he himself recognized. The books didn't sell particularly well. Davin was most popular in New Zealand.

He also produced some fine non-fiction, for example in 1975 he wrote *Closing Times,* a collection of tributes to writers he had known, from Enid Starkie to Dylan Thomas. He was an authority on the most well known of all New Zealand writers, Katherine Mansfield.

Like so many writers he enjoyed sitting around in bars talking, and like so many creative types he needed nicotine — until his later years he was rarely seen without a cigarette-holder between his fingers. One of the Davins' closest friends was the neglected British novelist Joyce Cary (Winnie Davin was Cary's literary executor). Davin was also a keen member of the Johnson Club, a male dining society inspired by the eighteenth-century man of letters, Samuel Johnson.

Davin shared the tragic experience of so many people who leave their country and don't share in the process of its rapid social change: when he went home to New Zealand on his last visit he said it wasn't the country he wanted to remember. But in his obituary in the London *Independent* newspaper, Professor Vincent O'Sullivan said, "If one may speak of an intellectual landscape, however, it was Davin himself who helped New Zealanders shift their bearings to more expansive views." As a writer, you can't get a much greater tribute than that.

Born Daniel Marcus Davin. **Parents** Patrick, railwayman, and Mary Davin. **Marriage** Winifred Kathleen Gonley, 1939. **Children** Three daughters. **Education** Marist Brothers' School, Invercargill, New Zealand; Sacred Heart College, Auckland; Otago University, Dunedin, MA in English (first class), DipMA in Latin (first class), 1935; Balliol College, Oxford, BA in classics, 1939 (first class), MA, 1945. **Emigration** Left New Zealand for England, 1935. **Military service** Private, Royal Warwickshire Regiment, 1939–40; Major, New Zealand Division, 1940–45; served in Greece and Crete, wounded 1941; Intelligence, General Headquarters, Middle East, 1941–42; North Africa and Italy, 1942–45; mentioned three times in despatches. **Career** Junior assistant secretary, Clarendon Press, Oxford, 1946–48, assistant secretary, 1948–69; deputy secretary to the delegates, Oxford University Press, 1970–78, academic publisher, 1974–78; retired 1978. **Offices and memberships** Fellow, Royal Society of Arts. **Awards and honours** Rhodes Scholar, 1935–39; Member of the Order of the British Empire, 1945; professorial fellow, Balliol College, Oxford University, 1965–78, emeritus fellow, 1978–90; honorary DLitt, Otago University, 1984; Commander of the Order of the British Empire, 1987. **Novels** *Cliffs of Fall,* 1945; *For the Rest of Our Lives,* 1947, revised 1967; *Roads from Home,* 1949; *The Sullen Bell,* 1956; *No Remittance,* 1959; *Not Here, Not Now,* 1970; *Brides of Price,* 1972. **Short stories** *The Gorse Blooms Pale,* 1947; *Breathing Spaces,* 1975; *Selected Stories,* 1981; "When Mum Died", in *The Summer Book: A New Zealand Miscellany* edited by Bridget Williams and Roy Parsons, 1982. **Other publications** (With John Mulgan) *An Introduction to English Literature,* 1947; *Crete* (history), 1953; (editor) *New Zealand Short Stories,* 1953; (editor) *Selected Stories,* by Katherine Mansfield, 1953; (with W.K. Davin) *Writing in New Zealand: The New Zealand Novel* (two volumes), 1956; (editor) *English Short Stories of Today* (second series), 1958; *Katherine Mansfield in Her Letters,* 1959; *Closing Times* (memoirs), 1975; *Snow upon Fire: "A Dance to the Music of Time": Anthony Powell* (lecture), 1976; (editor) *Short Stories from the Second World War,* 1982; (joint editor) *From Oasis to Italy, 1983; The Salamander and the Fire: Collected War Stories,* 1987. **Cause of death** Undisclosed, at age 77. **Further reading** James Bertram, *Dan Davin,* 1983; *Contemporary Novelists,* 1986.

SAMUEL DOE

Liberian President

***Born* Tuzon, Liberia, 6 May 1952**

***Died* Monrovia, Liberia, 10 September 1990**

"They that take the sword shall perish with the sword." So says the Bible, and never was the saying to be proved more true than in the case of President Samuel Doe of Liberia. In 1980, when a lowly sergeant-major, he led a bloody *coup* on behalf of the ranks and non-commissioned officers in the Liberian army against the long-time oligarchy of the Americo-Liberians, and was reported to have himself bayoneted to death the then president, William Tolbert. Then years later, after many attempts to overthrow his dictatorship, he was himself trapped into an ambush by one of the rebel groups in the accelerating civil war and brutally done to death. Thereafter his country plunged ever deeper into military and economic chaos.

Sergeant Doe's rebellion originally had some justification as a tribal revolt against an urban élite, popularly known as "the Congo". The prosperity which Liberia had long enjoyed as one peaceful haven in a troubled continent rested on the country's lack of a colonial history and its long domination by the returning freed American slaves who had founded the country in 1847. But, in turn, this rested on the suppression of the ethnic tribal majority of indigenous Liberians, "the country people", whose resentment of the privileges of the ruling party had been growing ever since President Tubman's abolition of opposition parties in 1955. The trade and foreign investment which the stability of the oligarchical regime attracted to the country failed to spread their benefits over the tribal divide, and by the end of the 1970s the greed and corruption of the ruling Americo-Liberian class were leading to riots and growing unrest. This was the moment that master-sergeant Doe seized.

Doe himself was a member of the native Krahn tribe, the son of a small farmer in the east of the country and typical of the under-dogs of Tubman's Liberia. After a rudimentary education he took the one avenue of possible advancement and enlisted in the Liberian armed forces, where by 1980 he had progressed to the rank of master-sergeant or sergeant-major. He had also developed close ties with the incipient Marxist movement growing up in the country. Quite how his *coup* was planned is not known. The Marxist leaders were already arrested after riots over proposed food price increases, and numbers of demonstrators had been killed. But a small group of soldiers from the National Guard invaded the presidential palace in the early hours of 12 April 1980 and within days the entire Tolbert government had been put to death.

The *coup* was initially welcomed by the mass of the people, and by the outside world, as the end of a long tyranny. Within two years Doe, as the head of the People's Redemption Council, found himself being received in Washington by President Reagan (unfortunately as "President Moe") and benefiting from more US aid than was given to any other black African government. But the rest of Africa waited to see how things would develop. Doe meanwhile was enjoying the fruits of power, now promoted to the rank of a five-star general and commander-in-chief of the armed forces. The early hopes of social reform were soon dashed, however, as his regime became increasingly repressive. By 1984 he had been forced by US pressure to promise a return to civilian rule, but his election as president the following year was blatantly rigged. At the same time the army was transformed into an ethnically reliable instrument of political repression and the press was muzzled. Meanwhile, general incompetence and mismanagement, coupled with blatant corruption, led to the ruin of what had been a thriving economy. In 1987 the country's arrears on its external debt led to the cutting off of all aid from the International Monetary Fund and the World Bank.

Not even US aid, itself diminishing, could save Doe. He had managed to survive innumerable attempts to overthrow his increasingly repressive regime. But in the end it was tribalism which overthrew him just as it had brought him to power. Rival tribesmen advanced on the capital during 1990 and, despite promises of further elections and a broader-based regime, Doe was gradually forced to retreat into his presidential palace. He was ultimately gunned down in an ambush as he tried to negotiate a ceasefire, leaving his wrecked country in utter turmoil.

Born Samuel Kanyon Doe. **Parents** Matthew G.K., farmer, schoolmaster and military man, and Anna Doe. **Marriage** Nancy. **Children** Four children. **Education** R.E.B. Richardson Baptist Junior High School, 1967–69; Ministry of National Defence Radio and Communication School, Monrovia, 1971; University of Liberia, BS in political science, 1988. **Career** Private, Liberian Army, 1969, acting first sergeant, 1973–75, first sergeant, 1975–79, master-sergeant and adjutant, 1979–81, general, 1981–90, commander-in-chief of armed forces, 1981–90; overthrew President William Tolbert in coup, 1980; Head of State, 1980–90; chairman, People's Redemption Council, 1980–85; president, Interim National Association, 1985–90; founder/head, National Democratic Party of Liberia, 1984–90; overthrown in coup, 1990. **Cause of death** Assassination, at age 38.

IRENE DUNNE

American Actress

Born **Louisville, Kentucky, 20 December 1898**

Died **Los Angeles, California, 4 September 1990**

Irene Dunne was as versatile as they come. She was not only the "queen of the weepies", she was, according to Hollywood gossip columnist Louella Parsons, "one of the most sought-after comedy players in filmdom". The apparently effortless way she could switch back and forth between hanky-soaking melodrama and screwball comedy baffled many. "How can a woman with the aplomb of a duchess act the madcap so faultlessly?" is the way one writer put it. The answer to this question is really very simple: Irene Dunne was a professional. According to her co-star in *The Joy of Living,* Douglas Fairbanks Jr, "She was fun to work with but wonderfully concentrated... one of the most professional women I've ever known. Nothing is instinctive, everything she does is carefully thought out, she knows every movement, every intonation, every nuance. She's a first-class craftswoman."

After a convent education, she won a scholarship to the Chicago College of Music, where she studied to be an opera singer. She auditioned for New York's Metropolitan Opera, but said she was rejected for being "too young, too inexperienced, too slight, too everything". She turned instead to musical comedy, playing the lead in the touring production of *Irene* and appearing in several minor Broadway musicals.

In 1929, she got on the same elevator as Flo Ziegfeld, the producer best known for his "Follies". The story goes that he was so struck by her beauty, he asked her to audition for his touring production of *Show Boat.* She got the part of Magnolia, and played to "standing room only" crowds in a 72-week tour that visited almost every large city east of the Mississippi River.

She signed a contract with RKO studios and moved to Hollywood in 1930, leaving her dentist husband behind in New York and beginning a nine-year period of "long-distance" marriage. She tested for and won the female lead opposite Richard Dix in Edna Ferber's *Cimarron.* The role required her to age half a century, winning her her first Academy Award nomination and some unlikely admirers, such as the notoriously anti-women-in-politics Will Rogers, who declared, "If women like Irene Dunne would run for Congress, I'd vote for them."

She was then cast in a string of "weepies", such as *Symphony of Six Million* (she played a crippled schoolteacher), *Back Street* (a long-suffering mistress), and *Magnificent Obsession* (a blinded widow). "So for my career I cry", she once said. These tear-jerkers may have been box-office smashes (*Back Street* raked in record-breaking amounts of money for the studio), but they weren't always appreciated by the critics. James Agate wrote that "as a rule she makes my skin crawl".

Most critics, however, were full of praise for her work in screwball comedy. Comments such as "No other star can be so nicely naughty as Irene Dunne", or "combined the naivete of Cinderella and the devastating wit of a Dorothy Parker charmingly", were typical of the notices she received.

Cary Grant, her co-star in *The Awful Truth*, *Penny Serenade*, and *My Favorite Wife*, said, "Her comedy timing was impeccable. She played it straight, instead of playing it for laughs as some comediennes do." Dunne herself once said, "The best way to be funny is to be cold-blooded and purely mental about it."

Several of the films she appeared in are now considered classics: *The White Cliffs of Dover*, *Anna and the King of Siam*, *Life with Father*, to name just a few. And of course, *I Remember Mama.* Many consider her portrayal of the Norwegian immigrant matriarch the high point Bof her career, but Irene Dunne's personal favourite was the romantic comedy, *Love Affair,* which co-starred

Charles Boyer, "not only because it was so well done, but also because we had such a good time making it."

It seems odd that such a fantastically successful career could come to an abrupt end because of one picture, but that's what happened. She was cast as Queen Victoria in *The Mudlark,* released by Twentieth Century-Fox in 1950. There was much criticism of the fact that an American had been given the part. There was much criticism of the fact that Miss Dunne was unrecognizable and ineffective beneath heavy make-up. There was much criticism of everything. The film flopped. It didn't matter that only two years had passed since her triumph in *I Remember Mama,* her career was finished. After a minor, unsuccessful comedy, she retired.

She didn't fade into obscurity upon her retirement, though. She still made occasional television appearances and became active in charities and also in politics. She was a staunch Republican and supporter of President Dwight D. Eisenhower, who appointed her as a delegate to the United Nations. She often spoke to journalists and students about her career, and (amazingly for Hollywood) managed to stay married to the same man for nearly 40 years, until his death in 1965.

She never won an Oscar, despite five nominations, but in 1985 she was awarded the Kennedy Center Honors in the performing arts. She hadn't made a film in over 30 years, but she hadn't been forgotten.

Born Irene Marie Dunne. **Parents** Joseph John, US government steamship inspector, and Adelaide Antoinette (Henry), musician, Dunne. **Marriage** Francis D. Griffin, dentist, 1928 (died 1965). **Children** One adopted daughter, Mary. **Education** Loretta Academy, St Louis, Missouri; scholarship, Chicago Musical College, diploma 1919. **Career** Stage début, touring company, *Irene,* Chicago, 1920; Broadway début, *The Clinging Vine,* 1922; final Broadway appearance, *Luckee Girl,* 1929; toured in *Show Boat,* 1929; contract player, Radio Keith Orpheum films, 1930; film début, *Leathernecking,* 1930; final film performance, *It Grows on Trees,* 1952. **Related activities** Board member, Technicolor Incorporated, 1965. **Other activities** Member, Defense Advisory Committee, to advise on welfare matters in women's services, 1951; alternative delegate, United Nations General Assembly, 1957–58. **Awards and honours** Academy Award nominations for best actress: *Cimarron,* 1930–31, *Theodora Goes Wild,* 1936, *The Awful Truth,* 1937, *Love Affair,* 1939, *I Remember Mama,* 1948; honorary DMusic, Chicago Musical College, 1945; Laetaere medal, University of Notre Dame; Kennedy Center Honors, 1985. **Stage** (includes, all New York unless otherwise indicated) *Irene* (tour), 1920; *The Clinging Vine,* 1922; *Lollipop,* 1924; *The City Chap,* 1925; *Sweetheart Time* (tour), 1926; *Yours Truly,* 1927; *She's My Baby,* 1928; *Luckee Girl,* 1929; *Show Boat* (tour), 1929. **Films** (include) *Leathernecking,* in England as *Present Arms,* 1930; *Cimarron,* 1930; *Bachelor Apartment,* 1931; *Consolation Marriage,* in England as *Married in Haste,* 1931; *The Great Lover,* 1931; *The Stolen Jools,* in England as *The Slippery Pearls,* 1931; *Symphony of Six Million,* in England as *Melody of Life,* 1932; *Back Street,* 1932; *Thirteen Women,* 1932; *No Other Woman,* 1933; *The Secret of Madame Blanche,* 1933; *The Silver Cord,* 1933; *Ann Vickers,* 1933; *If I Were Free,* in England as *Behold We Live,* 1933; *This Man Is Mine,* 1934; *Stingaree,* 1934; *The Age of Innocence,* 1934; *Sweet Adeline,* 1935; *Roberta,* 1935; *Magnificent Obsession,* 1935; *Show Boat,* 1936; *Theodora Goes Wild,* 1936; *High, Wide and Handsome,* 1937; *The Awful Truth,* 1937; *Joy of Living,* 1938; *Love Affair,* 1939; *Invitation to Happiness,* 1939; *When Tomorrow Comes,* 1939; *My Favourite Wife,* 1940; *Penny Serenade,* 1941; *Unfinished Business,* 1941; *Lady in a Jam,* 1942; *A Guy Named Joe,* 1943; *The White Cliffs of Dover,* 1944; *Together Again,* 1944; *Over 21,* 1945; *Anna and the King of Siam,* 1946; *Life with Father,* 1947; *I Remember Mama,* 1948; *Never a Dull Moment,* 1950; *The Mudlark,* 1950; *It Grows on Trees,* 1952. **Television** (includes) Hostess, *Schlitz Playhouse of Stars,* 1952; *Ford Theatre,* 1954–56; *Loretta Young Show,* 1955; *Perry Como Show,* 1956; *June Allyson Show,* 1959; *Diamond Jubilee Plus One special,* 1960; *G.E. Theatre,* 1962; *Saints and Sinners,* 1962; presenter,

Academy Awards Special, 1967. **Cause of death** Heart failure, at age 91. **Further reading** *International Dictionary of Films and Filmmakers,* volume three, 1986.

LAWRENCE D. HILLS

British Horticulturist

Born **Dartmouth, Devon, 2 July 1911**

Died **Ryton-on-Dunsmore, Warwickshire, 20 September 1990**

Lawrence Hills was a man whose own experience and vast study of history and other cultures led him to his personal vision of horticulture in which organic methods predominate and in which man should actively explore the variations provided by nature.

His childhood was restricted by coeliac disease in which an inability to absorb fats leads to chronic diarrhoea and subsequent malnutrition. As a result he was educated at home by his mother and, on medical advice, took up a career in horticulture, starting as an apprentice and then moving on as improver and journeyman in some of Britain's leading nurseries. He specialized in Alpines and his first of four books on the topic was published in 1944.

But it was his war service with the RAF that made him think about organic methods. He had been in charge of landscaping camp sites which also entailed the provision of sanitation for several hundred people. He realized that valuable fertilizing material was, literally, being wasted while scarce funds were spent on chemical substitutes.

After the war, in between serious relapses into ill health (often spending time in hospital or a wheelchair), he studied the subject and realized it was not just a matter of waste — it was also a matter of damaging the environment. He became an advocate of alternative methods. In particular he came to study comfrey, a fast-growing perennial fodder crop which could make a substantial difference to the protein problems of the Developing World and be a provider of high potassium compost at home which would speed up the growth of vegetable protein.

In the nineteenth century Henry Doubleday had introduced a hybrid comfrey into Britain. Hills wrote a book chronicling both the man and his work. *Russian Comfrey,* published in 1953, created such interest that the Henry Doubleday Research Association (HDRA) was set up in Essex with Hills as its unpaid secretary.

His publishers, Faber and Faber, had invited him to become their horticulture and agriculture editor shortly after the war. In 1958 he also became the weekly gardening correspondent for the Sunday newspaper *The Observer,* writing a column for eight years before moving on to *Punch,* the humorous weekly magazine, for four more, but it was the HDRA that really absorbed him until his retirement in 1985.

His interests widened to encompass almost everything relating to the "natural way". He became concerned about the mutation effects on plants of the nuclear tests carried out in the late 1950s. He was appalled at the loss of hundreds of traditional British vegetable and fruit varieties brought about by the "harmonization" legislation as Britain became more involved in the European Community. But through his campaigning a number of seed bank and library schemes were set up to protect the British concern for flavour and prevent these varieties from becoming extinct.

Hills married late in life. His wife, known as Cherry, was a physiotherapist who was the first actually to recognize his illness and to establish him on a gluten-free diet. Not only did she enable him to enjoy prolonged periods of good health for the rest of his life but also was immensely supportive in editing his letters and prolific output of books. Always aware of his tremendous debt to her, Hills retired when her own health began to fail as she approached her nineties. He survived her by only a few months.

Hills was one of those very fortunate men who sow the seed of a new idea and live to see it embraced by the highest in the land. Before he died he had the satisfaction of knowing that his research centre was moving on to ever greater things in its new home near Coventry. He also had the satisfaction of knowing that the Prince of Wales was farming organically. His only regret was that he never did solve the problem of slugs!

Born Lawrence Donegan Hills. **Parents** William Donegan and Mabel Annie Hills. **Marriage** Hilda Cherry (Fea) Brooke, 1964 (died 1990). **Military service** Royal Air Force, 1940–44. **Career** Horticultural worker, 1927–40; published first book, *Miniature Alpine Gardening,* 1945; founded Henry Doubleday Research Associates, 1954, managing director, 1954–85, retired 1985, president, 1986–90; horticultural editor, Faber and Faber publishing house. **Related activities** President, international body of gardeners and farmers without chemicals, 1954–86; gardening correspondent: *Observer,* 1958–66, *Punch,* 1966–70, *The Countryman,* 1970, *Garden News,* 1981; associate editor, *Ecologist,* 1973; contributing editor, *Organic Gardener,* 1988–90. **Publications** *Miniature Alpine Gardening,* 1944; *Rapid Tomato Ripening,* 1946; *Propagation of Alpines,* 1950; *Alpines Without a Garden,* 1953; *Russian Comfrey,* 1953; *Alpine Gardening,* 1955; *Down to Earth Fruit and Vegetable Growing,* 1960; *Down to Earth Gardening,* 1967; *Lands of the Morning* (archaeology), 1970; *Grow Your Own Fruit and Vegetables,* 1971; *Comfrey — Its Past, Present and Future,* 1976; *Organic Gardening,* 1977; *Fertility Gardening,* 1981; *Month by Month Organic Gardening,* 1983; also: *Comfrey the Herbal Healer, Fighting Like the Flowers* (autobiography). **Cause of death** Undisclosed, at age 79.

ROBERT HOLMES à COURT

Australian Financier

***Born* Johannesburg, South Africa, 27 July 1937**

***Died* Perth, Western Australia, 2 September 1990**

During the 1980s a handful of Australian entrepreneurs put their country on to the world's financial map by a wave of company acquisitions distinguished more for their rapidity and ruthlessness than for any benefits which they brought to the businesses which they took over. In his stock-market dealings, Robert Holmes à Court was as ruthless as any of them, and yet, as a cultivated and reticent personality, cut a very different figure from certain of his compatriots.

By their share-dealing tactics, men such as Holmes à Court contribute to the short-termism which forces managers in countries like the UK to run their enterprises with one eye on the day-to-day vagaries of the stock market. (This contrasts with, say, West Germany where companies tend to be in the more stable hands of banks and other financial institutions, which are motivated by long-term profitability rather than the hope of an overnight killing.) Rather than producing goods and services, the Holmes à Courts of the world create their wealth by the buying and selling of paper. Consequently they are especially vulnerable to upsets in the stock exchanges to whose very instability they themselves contribute.

To do Holmes à Court justice, though, he could manage firms as well as shuffle paper. He was able, on occasion, to turn round the ailing businesses he acquired and contribute sensible advice to those others in which he had an interest. The chairman and CEO of Standard Chartered Bank, of which Holmes à Court was a non-executive director and former deputy chairman, said that he had made a "major contribution" with his "wise counsel". In contrast with some of his competitors who were, like him, brought low by the stock-market crash of 1987, Holmes à Court had put his business on the road to recovery when he died at 53.

Australia was his country only by adoption; he was born in South Africa of British parents and brought up in Rhodesia (now Zimbabwe). At boarding school he gave a hint of where his talents lay, providing a commercial taxi service for his fellow-pupils at the end of term. His family then moved to New Zealand, where Holmes à Court studied agricultural science at Massey University. Next he trained as a lawyer at the University of Western Australia in Perth. While still at university, he foreshadowed certain aspects of his entrepreneurial career once again by buying the wreck of a crashed plane and selling its parts at a tidy profit.

On completing his studies, he was articled to a firm of lawyers. When the senior partner indicated he would be paid eight pounds per week, Holmes à Court retorted, "If that's all you can afford you may as well keep it." Soon he had opened his own commercial law practice, undercutting the competition and so gaining droves of customers.

Despite the success of his law firm, Holmes à Court shortly abandoned it to enter the world of commerce. One of his clients, the West Australian Worsted and Woollen Mills, was on the verge of bankruptcy in 1969, when Holmes à Court decided to buy 21 per cent of it. Six months later the company was in an even more parlous state. Holmes à Court took a month off the law to rescue his investment — and never returned.

Fortunes were to be made at this period from nickel, giving rise to the brief stardom of shares in mining companies like Poseidon. Holmes à Court took WA Worsted and Woollen Mills company into nickel, and was shortly able to sell a million shares for 1.5 million Australian dollars. In 1973 he bought another troubled company, Bell Brothers Holdings, which included transportation and engineering interests. Renamed the Bell Group, the company became the instrument Holmes à Court used to build a business empire which spanned three continents.

He acquired a reputation as a corporate raider, buying up shares in companies with a view to launching a takeover, whether the management liked it or, as more often, not; at one point he was said to be the world's most active stock-market participant, though he remained one of the least conspicuous. His methods were unusually stealthy: during an attempt to buy Melbourne's Broken Hill Proprietary Ltd (BHP), a mining corporation which was the largest industrial concern in Australia, he operated through a small company, itself newly acquired. He was patient, waiting sometimes for years for the right moment for a raid.

Sometimes the takeover bids were successful — hence Holmes à Court's nickname "The Great Acquirer" — sometimes not. But even when a bid failed, it would often have stirred up market interest in the company, and caused friendly players to start buying up its shares in competition with Bell, resulting in a price rise which could be as high as 300 per cent. Then the shares could be sold again at a satisfying profit. A number of such ventures gained Holmes à Court the alternative name "The Profitable Loser".

It was often unclear whether the motive of a particular raid was to buy the company or to realize a profit on the shares, but either way, in the bull market prior to the 1987 crash, he could not lose. He was also known to act as a white knight on occasion, foiling hostile takeover bids of companies, such as when he helped prevent Lloyds from taking over Standard Chartered, of which he became joint deputy chairman.

Holmes à Court was based in Perth but had from the first had his sights on prizes much further afield. He was determined to penetrate the closed circle of East Australian commerce, and did so to a great extent, but failed to take over BHP, the prize which he particularly coveted. Holmes à Court was also one of the many who attempted to buy the Herald and Weekly Times media group.

Bell Group did not by any means confine its activities to Australia: before the stock-market crash it looked as if it might be going after American companies, including Texaco. Often in his overseas dealings Holmes à Court would come up against his compatriots; he attempted, for example, to acquire the UK Times newspaper group, which subsequently became part of Rupert Murdoch's News International. A stunningly successful takeover on the part of Bell had been that of Britain's Associated Communications Corporation in 1982. Holmes à Court was accused of having used his charm to gain the confidence of Lord Grade, who owned an almost-but-not-quite controlling interest, before "putting the boot in" and forcing him to sell. Once again Holmes à Court was successful in turning round the fortunes of an ailing company.

But then came the October 1987 crash. Holmes à Court, by now the richest man in Australia, saw his personal fortune, estimated at 1.5 billion Australian dollars, reduced to one-third of that, and the value of his company's assets, once worth around 6 billion Australian dollars, reduced by around 60 per cent. Once again Holmes à Court broke the records: Bell's loss in a single day's trading on "Meltdown Monday" was Australia's largest ever. With a lot of its purchases financed by borrowing, the decimation of the value of its shares could have bankrupted Bell. But the Australian government stepped in, believing that Holmes à Court's financial demise could set the country's economic development back 20 years, and bought a large proportion of his holdings. Holmes à Court was shortly to surrender control of the Bell Group to Alan Bond. His remaining shares were subsumed under the family firm of Heytesbury Holdings.

"Hacca", as he was called by the Australian popular press, kept an even lower profile after the crash than before; the public in Australia was less sympathetic to the doings of their home-grown plutocrats during the economic crises of the late 1980s. But by the time he died he was back among the tycoons: his personal fortune, now an estimated 700 million Australian dollars, was only exceeded by that of Kerry Packer. He had bought a controlling interest in Sherwin Pastoral, a major Australian cattle ranching company, which meant that he owned about one per cent of Australia; he had also acquired a racehorse stud.

In the UK, Holmes à Court had bought back the London theatres which he had had to sell to Bond, and at his death owned 13 theatres in the West End including the Coliseum, home of the English National Opera, and the Stoll Moss Group. He also had a stake in Andrew Lloyd Webber's Really Useful Group. Holmes à Court's raid on the latter foiled the British composer of *Cats* in his plan to regain control of all the shares in his company. Holmes à Court attempted shortly before his death to prevent Lloyd Webber making large severance payments to ex-employees including the former Arts minister Lord Gowrie, who had been chairman.

It was more or less by default that Holmes à Court's wife Janet took over the running of the firm on his death. He was said to have given no consideration to the question of his successor; a serious oversight, but then he cannot have expected to die from a heart attack at only 53.

Unlike some other empire-building Australian tycoons, Holmes à Court struck most of those who met him as a retiring, civilized and even a likeable character. He was a distinguished and knowledgeable collector of fine art who had an important collection of paintings including French Impressionists and Rodin sculpture. He also had a great interest in Aboriginal art. For a rich man, he could be very generous; he provided accommodation for the British Theatre Library together with a sizeable contribution towards its running costs. It's doubtful, though, how much consolation it was to those he outmanoeuvred in business to know that they were actually dealing with quite a pleasant chap.

Born Michael Robert Hamilton Holmes à Court. **Parents** Peter Worsley and Ethnée Celia Holmes à Court. **Marriage** Janet Lee Ranford, 1966. **Children** Peter, Catherine, Simon and Paul. **Education** Michaelhouse, Natal, South Africa; studied agricultural science, Massey University, New Zealand; University of Western Australia, Perth, LLB, 1965. **Emigration** Left South Africa for New Zealand, settled Australia, 1962. **Career** Barrister and solicitor, Supreme Court of Western Australia, 1965–70; acquired West Australian Worsted and Woollen Mills, 1970;

acquired Bell Group Limited, Australia, 1970; acquired Associated Communications Corporation, 1982; chairman, Bell Group International Limited, 1982–88; chairman, Bell Group International Limited, Australia, 1983–88; director, Standard Chartered Bank, 1986–90, joint deputy chairman, 1987–90; chairman, Heytesbury Company. **Cause of death** Heart attack, at age 53.

ERIC HOLTTUM

British Botanist

Born **Linton, Cambridgeshire, 20 July 1895**

Died **London, England, 18 September 1990**

If you fancy an extended sojourn on this mortal coil, here is a tip, gratis, to all readers of *The Annual Obituary:* get yourself made director of the Botanic Gardens, Singapore. The first of these gentlemen died at the age of 100, the second made 94, and their successor, Eric Holttum, possessed of enormous energy and a phenomenal memory, lived to be 95.

He was born into a Quaker family in 1895, at the Cambridgeshire village of Linton, and went first to the Friends School at nearby Saffron Walden, and then to Bootham School in York. His entry with a scholarship to St John's College, Cambridge coincided with the outbreak of World War I, and in 1916 he broke off his undergraduate career to serve with the Friends Ambulance Unit in Flanders and on the Somme. Only in 1920 was Holttum able to graduate, with a first-class degree in botany, and the Frank Smart Prize. He stayed on to take the university teachers' diploma, and seemed destined for a career in palaeobotany. However, after a visit to West Greenland, in search of fossil plants, his life and work took a sudden and contrasting change of course.

In 1922 the British Colonial Office sent Holttum to its then possession, Singapore, right at the tip of the Malay peninsula, where he was to become assistant director of the Botanic Gardens. Once in post, it was suggested that he concern himself with "putting the fern herbarium in order". So began the study of ferns, orchids, gingers and bamboos which was to dominate the rest of his scientific life. Holttum was captivated, and with his famous powers of memory, set about the mammoth task of identifying and classifying the species which surrounded him. Meanwhile, he assumed full directorship of the Singapore Botanical Gardens in 1926, and also nurtured the Malayan Orchid Society. When the Würtzburg professor Hans Burgeff showed Holttum how to grow orchid seedlings in a test tube, Holttum passed this on to his fellow growers, and himself began to produce large number of hybrid varieties. This was the start of Malaya's orchid industry.

The years of World War II produced the most peculiar circumstances for Holttum. When the Japanese swept over Singapore in 1942, his Quaker principles moved him to share the hardships of the many internees. However, the occupant of the Chrysanthemum Throne was himself something of a botanist: the Emperor Hirohito's agent commanded Holttum to continue the administration of the gardens until a Japanese director took over. Thus, for three-and-a-half years, isolated from the rest of the scientific world and relieved of extraneous duties, Holttum was left to organize his cornucopia of field notes, and prepare papers and books for publication. As the *Guardian* newspaper put it, with admirable succinctness, "he must have been one of the few Britons who emerged from the Japanese Occupation with health, integrity and the respect of the enemy — and outstanding scientific work." The blossoms of these years were *Ferns of Malaya*, *Orchids of Malaya*, *Plant Life in Malaya* and *Gardening in the Lowlands of Malaya*. "Each volume", in the opinion of one learned commentator, "would be considered by a lesser scientist as their life's work."

In 1949, Holttum joined the newly created University of Malaya as the only teaching member of its Department of Botany. To the position he brought a wealth of experience from his travels in Malaya, Borneo and Indonesia and of course, his unparalleled knowledge of the region's flora. He is remembered as an inspirational teacher, not patient with stupidity, but assiduous in the encouragement of promising students. Within five years, he had established a flourishing department, and returned to England.

He settled close to the Royal Botanic Gardens at Kew, by the River Thames, west of London. Here he frequented the library and the herbarium, and continued to publish copiously on the classification of ferns. The Rijksherbarium at Leiden, in the Netherlands, made him an honorary research associate in 1955, and from 1960 to 1963, he was president of the British Pteridological Society. Honorary doctorates arrived from Cambridge and Malaya, followed by the Linnean Gold Medal, the Royal Horticultural Society Victoria Medal of Honour, and the American Orchid Society Gold Medal.

At the age of 75, Holttum suffered complete deafness, but immediately addressed himself to learn lip-reading, and then won a clear speech competition run by the British Association for the Hard of Hearing. For those who knew him, this was not a surprising display of resourcefulness; he was still very much an active member of the Society of Friends, and an enthusiastic contributor to the *Friends Quarterly* journal, writing on a range of subjects from scientific and religious truth to metaphysics and mysticism. His loss, felt as it was by the botanic community, was alleviated by the magnitude of the contribution he had made to the discipline. The Orchid Society of South East Asia awards the Eric Holttum Medal each year for the best locally produced hybrid, and still more enduring monuments are the plants named for or after him, which is maybe the way he'd most like to be remembered.

Born Richard Eric Holttum. **Father** Richard Holttum. **Marriage** Ursula Massey, artist, 1927 (died 1987). **Children** Two daughters. **Education** Friends School, Saffron Walden, Cambridgeshire; Bootham School, York: foundation scholar, St John's College, Cambridge, natural science tripos, part two, Botany, first-class honours degree, 1920. **Emigration** Left England for Singapore, 1922, returned 1954. **Career** Junior demonstrator in botany, Cambridge University, 1920–22; assistant director, Botanic Gardens, Singapore, 1922–25; director, 1925–49; professor of botany, University of Malaya, 1949–54; retired 1954. **Related activities** Editor, Series Two (Pteridophyta), *Flora Malesiana,* from 1959. **Other activities** Served with Friends Ambulance Unit, 1916–18. **Offices and memberships** President: Singapore Gardening Society, 1937–39, 1947–53; Singapore Rotary Club, 1939–41, British Pteridological Society, 1960–63, Section K (Botany), British Association for the Advancement of Science, 1961, International Association of Pteridologists, 1981. **Awards and honours** (include) Croix de Guerre, 1918; Frank Smart Prize, Cambridge University, 1920; honorary DSc, University of Malaya, 1949; honorary ScD, Cambridge University, 1951; honorary research fellow, Rijksherbarium, Leiden, 1955; American Orchid Society Gold Medal, 1963; Linnean Gold Medal, 1964; Victoria Medal of Honour, Royal Horticultural Society, 1972; Robert Allerton Award for excellence in tropical botany, Pacific Tropical Garden, Hawaii, 1975; clear speech competition prize, British Association for the Hard of Hearing, 1977; honorary research associate, Royal Botanic Gardens, Kew, 1977–90; fellow, Linnean Society; namesake of the annual medal of Orchid Society of South East Asia. **Publications** *Orchids of Malaya,* 1953; *Gardening in the Lowlands of Malaya,* 1953; *Plant Life in Malaya,* 1954; *Ferns of Malaya*, 1955; (co-editor/co-author) *Flora Malesiana. Series II, Pteridophyta, Ferns and Fern Allies* Volume One, Parts 1–5. **Cause of death** Undisclosed, at age 95.

SIR LEN HUTTON

British Cricketer

***Born* Fulneck, Yorkshire, 23 June 1916**

***Died* Kingston-upon-Thames, Surrey, 6 September 1990**

There are those who'd claim more intellectual satisfaction and physical excitement from a long wait at a wet bus stop than from the idea of watching cricket. And fair enough. But of all sports attended by the English language, cricket has attracted the most polished writing and the most eloquent commentary. So, if you are of the bus-stop persuasion, we hand you over to the experts. Here is the music critic Neville Cardus on Len Hutton: "[he has] a strength that is generated effortlessly from the physical dynamo, through nerve and muscle, so that we might almost persuade ourselves that the current of his energy, his life-force, is running electrically down the bat's handle into the blade." Or the poet, Edmund Blunden: "His body and his bat were as truly one as love itself". Cricket history also reflects the English addiction to class distinction, and Hutton's career marked a leap in the game's progress away from the more ludicrous manifestations of this. Into this widened perspective may be introduced one of the greatest batsmen that cricket has ever produced.

Leonard Hutton was born at Fulneck, South Yorkshire. The village was largely formed by the Protestant Nonconformist Moravian sect in the previous century, and in this religious atmosphere the young man grew up. His ancestors were Scots, his father a joiner by trade. Yorkshire takes its cricket very seriously, and the Hutton males were keen players. Young Len showed ability early but also enjoyed football; when a consortium of aunts considerately burned his boots after he'd injured a knee, any heretical doubts about choice disappeared.

At the age of 12 he was playing for the neighbouring adults at Pudsey. Two years later he witnessed a piece of cricket history to which he was numinously bound — the Australian batsman Donald Bradman made a record 334 runs against England at the Headingly ground, Leeds. (The corollary comes later.) Meanwhile Len Hutton turned up for practice with a thriving and powerful Yorkshire County team, where the coach declared that he could teach him nothing. Accordingly, he entered the side, only to make opening scores of 0 and one. That was an apparent hiccup; after a series of impeccable performances with the bat, he was capped for England at the age of 21, only to make 0 and one in his opening game against New Zealand. Maybe it was less of a hiccup than a peculiar psychological necessity; again he collected himself, made 100 in the next game, and played the rest of the season with distinction. In 1938 he made 12 centuries, and in the England team faced the Australians, captained by the invincible Don Bradman. At the London Oval ground, Hutton batted for 13 hours and 20 minutes, over a period of three days, and found himself approaching Bradman's record 334. Hutton had been able to sleep little during his term of trial; numbed with fatigue and exhaustion, he drooped over his bat. Bradman piled fielders around him and forced the attack, "glaring", as Hutton remembered, a few feet away. This time The Don did not prevail. Hutton was at last out for 364. (The record stood until the West Indian Garfield Sobers made 365, 20 years later.) After that, until World War II broke out in September 1939, Hutton seemed to make runs at will in England, the West Indies and South Africa, always opening the batting and taking the brunt of the bowling attack.

"Ah yes — everybody remembers 1938 but I was actually better in 1939. I was nearly as good as Bradman. After the war, of course, I was a different man. I'll never know how good I might have become in those lost years. I might not have got any better at all. The trouble is you see, I'll never know." Hutton had good cause for this philosophical reminiscence. Serving in the Army as a physical training instructor, he broke his left arm very badly in a gymnasium incident. The healed limb was weakened and about two inches shorter than its fellow. For a right handed batsman, the left arm and hand provide most of the power and control; when peace and cricket returned after 1945, Hutton had to adjust his technique and use a smaller bat.

Technique and concentration had been the keystones of his success hitherto, and neither failed him in the second half of his career. No one has ever matched the 1294 runs he made in June 1949. In those lean years, the England team had to rebuild; the bowling was weakened, and on Hutton's slight shoulders fell the main responsibility of batting. Still the opener, he was always looked to for the innings' foundation. (Only Denis Compton, with a contrasting cavalier style came near Hutton as an aggregator of runs.) Hutton alone fathomed the mysteries of the West Indian Sony Ramadhin's spin bowling, and Hutton alone was England's buttress against the Australian pace bowlers, Ray Lindwall and Keith Miller.

In 1952, the year of his thirty-sixth birthday, Len Hutton became the first professional cricketer appointed to the England captaincy. The post had previously been haunted by the conglomerate spirits of *bon viveur* gentleman amateurs, and it is the case that cricket grounds retained one entrance for these people, and another for "players", meaning those paid to appear. The *New Statesman and Nation* journal hailed the event: "Henceforth the selectors will pick England's captain not because he is the best available cricketing amateur but because he is the best captain available for the best eleven cricketers who could represent England. That is a revolution both in cricket and social history". Hutton duly sent the nation into raptures by recapturing the Ashes (winning a Test series against Australia) for the first time in nearly 20 years, celebrating himself with "one of the most regal centuries ever seen at Lord's", and maybe pleasing Queen Elizabeth, whose coronation year it was. In the winter of 1954–55, Hutton's England team, with a handful of burgeoning young players responding brilliantly to his now rather careworn disposition, toured Australia and retained the Ashes. But success had finally taken its toll. The game at Sydney was his last Test match and within four months, he played his last game for Yorkshire. He announced his retirement that same year. Hutton had never been physically very strong, and his powers of concentration were of themselves exhausting. Now almost 40, he suffered lumbago, the control of which required large quantities of pain-killers.

But there was plenty of life after cricket. Hutton enjoyed his family, worked as a commentator for BBC radio, and in collaboration with a ghost writer, produced three books. He moved south to Kingston-upon-Thames, in order to take up a permanent position with London's *Evening News,* and he also wrote for *The Observer.* From 1975 to 1977, he was an England selector, though he resigned with characteristic discretion when it became apparent that these duties were clashing with his business interests — he now had a seat on the board of J.H. Fenner, a power transmission company. Honour followed fame: Hutton was only the second man (after Jack Hobbs) to be knighted for his services to cricket, Marylebone Cricket Club created a precedent by electing him a member before his playing career had finished, and the University of Bradford conferred on him an honorary degree in 1982. He was never, though, given the Yorkshire captaincy. There are some who believe that he would have played on for two or three years had he been appointed, but the Byzantine affairs of Yorkshire County Cricket Club are a law and a world unto themselves, as is well known. Eventually, Hutton was elected the club's president.

It is hard to sum up Hutton's character. Various accounts suggest a combination of naïvety and shrewdness, a whimsical sense of humour, and a certain vulnerability. On the field he was the definitive master-craftsman, in defence or attack, "mentally as tough as teak" as one commentator put it, and always suiting his game to the occasion.

Hutton did not offer advice where it wasn't sought, but those who chose to consult him might be rewarded with the oracular. "Don't say too much", was one such. Possibly even better is "My advice to you...is just keep buggering on."

Born Leonard Hutton. **Father** Henry Hutton, joiner. **Marriage** Dorothy Mary Dennis, 1939. **Children** Richard and John. **Education** Pudsey School, Yorkshire. **Military service**

Physical training instructor, Royal Artillery, Army Physical Training Corps, sergeant, 1939–45. **Cricketing career** First played for Yorkshire, 1934, capped 1936; first played for England, 1937; scored record Test score, 364, 1938; played Test Matches against: New Zealand, 1937, Australia, 1938, South Africa, 1938, West Indies, 1939, India, 1946; record total scored in single month, 1294, June 1949; first professional to captain England, 1952; captained England against: India, 1952, Australia, 1953, 1954, Pakistan, 1954; captained Marylebone Cricket Club against West Indies, 1953–54; retired, 1956; selector, Marylebone Cricket Club, 1975–77. **Related activities** Commentator/columnist: *Evening News*, *The Observer*; President, Yorkshire Cricket Club, 1989–90. **Statistics** First-class career: 40,140 runs (averaged 55.51), 129 centuries, 173 wickets, 387 catches; Test match career: played 79, captained 23, 6971 runs (averaged 56.67), 19 centuries, 3 wickets and 57 catches. **Business career** Director, Fenner International (Power Transmission) Limited, 1960–84, board member, 1973–84; retired 1984. **Awards and honours** Honorary member, Marylebone Cricket Club, 1955; knighted 1956; honorary MA, Bradford University, 1982. **Television** *Maestro: Sir Leonard Hutton,* television portrait by Donald Trelford, BBC, 1988. **Publications** (all with others) *Cricket is My Life,* 1950; *Just My Story,* 1956; *Fifty Years in Cricket,* 1984. **Cause of death** Ruptured aorta, at age 74.

MARYA MANNES

American Journalist, Poet and Novelist

***Born* Manhattan, New York, 14 November 1904**

***Died* San Francisco, California, 13 September 1990**

In a long and wide-ranging literary career, Marya Mannes is best remembered for her outspoken and contentious essays on American culture and society and for her stinging, satirical verse. A staunch defender of the written word against the ineluctable onslaught of television — a powerful perpetrator of what she described as "verbal anarchy and faddist distortion" — Mannes strove throughout her life to "communicate clearly and honestly what I see and what I believe about the world I live in". Few subjects escaped her sharp and critical eye.

The daughter of violinist David Mannes and pianist Clara Damrosch, founders of New York's Mannes College of Music, Marya Mannes grew up in a music-filled apartment on Manhattan's Upper West Side. Her grandparents, one uncle, and brother, Leopold, were also musicians, but Mannes did not inherit the family talent. "A love of language took priority", she remembered. "I turned to words instead of notes." She developed a voracious appetite for reading and writing, which the faculty at Miss Veltin's School for Girls — just a block from her home — did much to encourage. She later credited the school with having given her "whatever tools and disciplines I acquired as a writer, along with an abiding respect for language, native or foreign".

When she graduated from Miss Veltin's in 1923, Mannes was offered the choice of attending college or travelling to Europe. She picked the latter, and with the help of a modest inheritance, spent a year in England studying sculpture and learning, as she put it, "a number of things not in books". She returned to the United States determined to launch a career as a dramatist, and over the next few years wrote ten playscripts. Three caught the eyes of producers, and one, *Café,* made it to Broadway, but closed four days later. An early attempt at acting was equally unsuccessful. She turned to journalism and fiction-writing instead. During this period she also met and married the first of her three husbands, set designer Jo Mielziner, but the union lasted only four years.

Following her divorce, Mannes went to work as an editor for *Vogue* magazine, where she remained until 1936, when her second husband, artist Richard Blow, persuaded her to follow him to Florence. Over the next three years, while Blow painted, Mannes turned her energy from writing to portrait sculpture. While in Italy, she also gave birth to a son. At the outbreak of World War II, the family returned to the United States, and from 1941 until 1945 — with the exception of one four-month stretch in 1944, when she travelled overseas to report on the belligerent neutrality of Spain and Portugal for *The New Yorker* — Mannes worked as an intelligence analyst for the Office of Strategic Services.

At the end of the war Mannes joined the staff of *Glamour* magazine, but left in 1947 to write her first novel. *Message from a Stranger,* which focuses on the idea that the dead live on in the memory of the living, sold well, but received mixed reviews. Diana Trilling of *The Nation* called it "the best compendium I know of the most approved social, political, sexual, and domestic attitudes of modern educated women", while a critic from the *New York Herald Tribune* dismissed it as "elementary, over-simplified political talk and a somewhat naïve metaphysic". Her second novel, *They,* published 20 years later, was also uneven in execution, if ambitious in conception. *They* centres on the discussions of a group of ageing intellectuals banished — because of their age — to a remote beach house. One critic identified its tone as one of "embittered nostalgia", while another dismissed the characters as "mere spokesmen for the author's complacent and muddled defense of her generation's values and achievements as against the inhumanity and philistinism of the young."

Following the publication of *Message from a Stranger,* Mannes worked as a freelance writer. She also met and married her third husband, British Civil Air Attaché Christopher Clarkson, and moved with him to Washington, DC. She spent four years as an embassy wife before returning to New York. In 1952 she joined the staff of *The Reporter,* the liberal, influential journal that helped to make her name. She remained there for the next 12 years, producing television and theatre criticism, feature articles, social satire and satirical political verse, much of it under the pen-name "Sec". The critical essay soon emerged as her most powerful and effective vehicle, and it is from her *Reporter* essays that she drew much of the material for her book *More in Anger,* published in 1958. While Harry Golden of *Saturday Review* described the book as "a series of gripes" about American complacency and criticized Mannes for her failure to probe the reasons behind the problems, William du Bois of *The New York Times* praised her for her energy and daring. "Whether or not you can accept all she says without a sudden rush of blood to the brain," he wrote, "this book is guaranteed to shock you into awareness of its author as an original thinker."

In addition to two novels, several collections of essays, and countless magazine articles — besides *The Reporter* she wrote for *The New Yorker,* the *Literary Digest*, *McCall's*, and *The New York Times* — in 1959 Marya Mannes published a collection of poems under the title *Subverse*. The book received glowing reviews. "It is brilliant and dogmatic and partisan and intensely clever", critic S.R. Davis enthused. T.F. Houlihan went even further. "Those seeking some indication of sanity in this world apparently gone mad will find much solace, and many a wry laugh, in Mannes's pungent comments", he wrote. In 1959 she hosted her own television programme, *I Speak for Myself,* but left after only 13 weeks, convinced that, as she put it, "It was impossible to be a TV 'personality' and remain a serious writer." She made her views known at a gathering of the American Society of Newspaper Editors. "No picture on a screen can ever be an adequate substitute for the reporting of a trained observer and an honest writer", she told them.

Nevertheless, Mannes continued to appear as an occasional guest and commentator on a variety of TV programmes. Her powerful persona won her the admiration of The *New York Times*'s television critic Jack Gould, who wrote, "Her sustained acerbity is one of the attractive adornments of contemporary criticism." She also lectured, and continued to produce books. Among these were *Out of My Time,* her autobiography; *The New York I Know,* a collection of bittersweet essays comparing the city of her childhood and the troubled New York emerging in the post-war period; and *Uncoupling: The Art of Coming Apart,* a candid look at the dissolution of three marriages (her own), which she described as a "guide to sane divorce". An anthology of her writing, *The Best of Marya Mannes,* was published in 1986.

Mannes always considered Manhattan her home, but spent the last seven years of her life in San Francisco, near her son, David Blow. Though she published no more books, she continued to be a keen observer of the American scene. She described her favourite recreations as swimming and beachcombing, and her loves — in addition to poetry and drama — as "human warmth, animals, the ocean, food, drink, and music."

Born Marya Mannes. **Parents** David, violinist, and Clara (Damrosch), pianist, Mannes. **Marriages** 1) Jo Mielziner, scenic designer, 1926 (divorced 1931); 2) Richard Blow, artist, 1937 (divorced 1943); 3) Christopher Clarkson, British Civil Air Attaché, 1948 (divorced 1966). **Children** One son, David, from second marriage. **Education** Miss Veltin's School for Girls, New York, 1923. **Career** First publication, *Theatre Arts* magazine, 1926; reviewer, *Creative Art;* first play performed, *Café,* 1930; feature editor, *Vogue* magazine, New York, 1933–36; intelligence analyst, Office of Strategic Services, 1942–45; writer, *Glamour* magazine, 1945–47; freelance writer, 1947–52, 1963–83; staff writer, *The Reporter,* New York, 1952–64; television host, *I Speak for Myself,* 1959. **Related activities** Monthly columnist, *McCall's* magazine, 1965–67, movie critic, 1968; monthly columnist, *The New York Times,* 1967; television commentator, WNET-Channel 13, New York, 1967–70; columnist, United Features Syndicate, 1971–83; contributor: *International Studio*, *New York Times Magazine*, *Esquire*, *Harper's*, *New York Herald Tribune Book Week*. **Other activities** Trustee, Mannes College of Music, New York. **Offices and memberships** Member: Authors League, Dramatists Guild, Newspaper Guild, American Federation of Television and Radio Artists. **Awards and honours** George Polk Memorial award for magazine criticism, 1958; honorary LHD, Hood College, 1960; achievement award, Federation of Jewish Women's Organizations, 1961; award of honor, Theta Sigma Phi, 1962. **Publications** *Message from a Stranger* (novel), 1948; *More in Anger: Some Opinions, Uncensored and Unteleprompted* (essay), 1958; *Subverse: Rhymes for Our Times* (satirical verse), 1959; *The New York I Know* (essays), 1961; *But Will It Sell?,* 1964; *They* (novel), 1968; *Out of My Time* (autobiography), 1971; (with Norman Sheresky) *Uncoupling: The Art of Coming Apart,* 1973; *Last Rights,* 1974; *The Best of Marya Mannes* (anthology edited by Robert Mottley), 1986. **Cause of death** Stroke, at age 85.

ALBERTO MORAVIA

Italian Novelist, Playwright and Journalist

Born **Rome, Italy, 28 November 1907**

Died **Rome, Italy, 26 September 1990**

It has been said by more than a few that Alberto Moravia's life was dominated by three obsessions: sex, boredom, and money. Not for nothing was he considered a *scrittore scomodo* in his native Italy; that is, "an awkward writer", awkward in the sense that throughout his literary career he continually outraged the public's sense of morality — to the point that his work was placed on the Vatican's Index of Forbidden Books (before the Index was discontinued in the mid-1960s). Not that this fact bothered Moravia: "I don't know if I believe in God", he wrote in his memoir, *The*

Life of Alberto Moravia. "I never thought seriously about it." Whatever his ethics, what Moravia *did* think seriously about was literature and, regardless of whether one agrees with his views of sex and sexual politics, his literary talent was enough to ensure the grudging admiration of his contemporaries; he remains the most widely read Italian author of this century and his works, which have been translated into 30 different languages, have sold millions of copies throughout the world.

Moravia was not his real name. He was born Alberto Pincherle, the son of an Austro-Hungarian countess (maiden name de Marsanich) and a Venetian architect and painter. Thus, his life as a child was one played out within the comfortable confines of the well-off European middle classes. Yet Moravia's childhood differed greatly from most: at the age of eight or nine, he came down with tuberculosis of the bone, a disease which necessitated approximately ten years of hospital treatment and one which left him with a permanent and awkward limp. Despite the fact that his illness kept him out of schools, Moravia received a remarkable literary education with the help of a succession of governesses; he became precociously familiar with the literature of France, Germany and England, in addition to that of his native Italy.

Unlike Robert Louis Stevenson, who also spent most of his childhood bedridden, Moravia seemed never able to shake off a sense of bitterness at his lot. "To understand my character," he would write in his memoirs, "you must keep in mind that I was ill in infancy, and because of it I was alone, completely alone, until I was 18. I never went to school. I never had other children to play with. Solitude entered my soul so deeply that even today I feel a profound detachment from others." Detached or not, it was through his enforced solitude that Moravia discovered another writer who was to have a profound impact upon hs own creativity, the French author and poet Charles Baudelaire. Baudelaire wrote of both boredom and sex — boredom as a distressing symptom of the rich, and sex as a means of illustrating the power struggle between two individuals. Moravia began his own exploration of these two themes when he was sent, at age 16, to a sanatorium at Cortina d'Ampezzo in the Italian Alps.

It was here that he began his first novel, *Gli indifferenti* (*The Time of Indifference*) and he continued to work on it for three years after his release from the sanatorium in 1925. In the meantime, however, he had already seen his name in print as the contributor of literary criticism to a series of avant-garde reviews. Eventually, the young writer completed his novel, but found that no company would risk publishing it. *Gli indifferenti* eventually came into print during 1929, but only after its author had paid 5000 lire to a vanity publisher.

The reasons behind the book world's reluctance to touch the novel become clear when one places the work in its historical context. In the middle of Mussolini's Fascist regime, the story seized on the corruption of the opulent middle classes, attacking the Fascist-fostered cult of exaggerated mother-worship by charting the interrelationships of one particular family. In addition, the novel also portrays sex as the basic psychological motivation of modern humanity. The characters of *Gli indifferenti* — a widow, her son and daughter, and a ruthless man who seduces both mother and daughter — use sex, money and politics (and even the last two factors are seen in the ways they relate to sexual obsession) as a means of striving towards happiness. That happiness, if such it can be called, is of course doomed, precisely because their sexual relations are completely devoid of love. Because the novel was written from within the society itself, it hardly supported or complemented the current regime, whose official ideology was supposed to have fostered strength in and a regeneration of the Italian people.

The critics loved the novel and the Fascist censors became highly suspicious of its author — to the point that, when his next novel, *Le ambizioni sbagliate* (*Mistaken Ambitions*) was published in 1935, the newspapers were forbidden to review it. In 1941, the same year in which he married his first wife Elsa Morante (who would later become a novelist in her own right), Moravia struck at Mussolini again with the publication of *La mascherata* (*The Masquerade Party*) which was nothing more than a thinly disguised lampoon of the Italian dictatorship. Thereafter, the censors came down with a crash: Moravia was forbidden to publish *any* type of writing, including newspaper and magazine reviews. This did not stop the obstreperous Moravia; he simply adopted a variety of pseudonyms and continued to produce film scripts and articles in Italy, or else he travelled outside the country and wrote what he wanted under his own name.

When the Germans invaded Italy during the autumn of 1943, however, Moravia was forced to flee for his life. He and his wife endured nine months of cold and hunger in the mountains outside Rome, waiting for the arrival of the Allied forces. This experience produced what is probably Moravia's best-known work in the United States and Britain, *La ciociara* in English: *Two Women.* First published in 1957, the novel tells the story of a Roman mother and daughter who, seeking shelter from the Allied bombs which are falling on the city, hide in the mountains and experience hardships similar to that experienced by Moravia and his wife. The women's plight is worse, however: when Moroccan soldiers arrive, supposedly to rescue the mountain village's inhabitants, the daughter is brutally raped by them and subsequently turns to prostitution for a living while her mother engages in thievery. "It is the tragic burden of Moravia's story that the war that destroys Fascism degrades the innocent even while it roots out the guilty", wrote John K. Hutchens in the *New York Herald Tribune,* "that its impersonal cruelty finds victims in the remotest corners." *Two Women* was given an even wider audience when it was made into a film of the same name starring Sophia Loren.

Before embarking on this novel, however, Moravia's pen had been flowing almost non-stop since the end of the war. Travel diaries, criticism and short stories were produced in addition to the novels, and the author even found time to help found a periodical review. Prior to *Two Women,* Moravia had also written *La romana* (The Woman of Rome) in 1947. This novel, also among his best, traces without sensationalism the career of a Roman prostitute and examines her relationships with a steady succession of lovers. It was a departure for Moravia, for in the work he resorted to a first-person narrator, a device many critics said gave him the power to delve deeply into the woman's psychology; others, though, were disturbed by the thoughts he placed there.

It was during the 1960s — the days of the so-called sexual revolution — that sales of Moravia's work, not surprisingly, rocketed. At least eleven film versions of his novels appeared between 1960 and 1970, but most of them were admittedly less than great, depicting actresses who were usually semi-clothed (if at all). The author claimed that his literary influences were those of Proust, Balzac, Dostoevsky, and Conrad — in short, the "Old Masters" of literature, but this claim came under deep suspicion when, in 1971, Moravia produced *Io e lui* (*The Two of Us*), a supposed semi-black comedy consisting of a man's conversations with his penis. As the decade progressed, lesbianism, sodomy and group sex cropped up more and more frequently in his writings, and many considered Moravia to be slipping into the depths of quick-selling high-class pornography. Even when, in the 1980s, he created a novel dealing with the horrors of a nuclear holocaust, the plot was laden with sexual symbolism — despite the fact that he was serving in the "respectable" European parliament at the time.

"I have been a writer, and that's it", Moravia maintained. "I have taken literature seriously above all else; the rest has been subordinated" — and, to an extent in the best of his works, critics will agree with him. "Of Alberto Moravia's 30 novels", wrote critic Ian Thompson in *The Independent*, "*Agostino*, *La ciociara* and *La noia* will secure him a solid reputation in contemporary Italian fiction. *Gli indifferenti,* though, deserves a place of prominence in twentieth-century literature as a whole. At his best, Moravia wrote as a moralist genuinely troubled by human turpitude, and as a man who has enriched, albeit in a sometimes militant fashion, the civilisation of Italy."

Moravia's facial features and general personality seemed to reflect his outlook on the world. Every popular photograph of him shows a disdainful, frowning, older man, his eyes overshadowed by a pair of bushy white eyebrows. "His mien was that of the sourest of men", wrote George Armstrong. "One might have thought he had no sense of humour and, in fact, in his writings humour tended to be confined to his short stories." His view of life seemed at best to be despairing and Freudian, given the views of sex recorded in his memoirs: "There can be sex without love, but there can be no love without sex. That is to say, that you can very well have a quick sexual relationship, even a very happy one, without love. However, the opposite is not possible. It is like a match thrown away in a forest. The forest bursts into flame and the match is lost, but at the beginning there was that match."

As for his own love-relationships, Moravia separated from his first wife in 1962; shortly afterwards he started a long love affair with Dacia Maraini, another writer, but in 1986 he married Carmen Llera, a 32-year-old Spanish advertising executive.

For all that, Alberto Moravia was considered more or less a national institution in his native Rome. "He could be cranky and not always the most pleasant companion", wrote Clyde Haberman of *The New York Times.* "But always he remained Moravia, quotable and free with opinions."

Born Alberto Pincherle. **Parents** Carlo, architect and painter, and Teresa (de Marsanich), Austro-Hungarian countess, Pincherle. **Marriages** 1) Elsa Morante, writer, 1941 (dissolved); 2) Carmen Llera, advertising executive, 1986. **Career** First book published, *Gli indifferenti,* 1929; foreign correspondent: *La Stampa,* Milan, *Gazetta del Popolo,* Turin; fled to mountains to escape Nazis, 1943–44; film critic, *La Nuova Europa,* 1944–46; editor (with Alberto Carocci), *Nuovi Argomenti,* Milan, from 1955; film critic, *L'Espresso,* Milan, from 1955. **Related activities** Visiting lecturer, Columbia University, 1934–35; US state department lecturer, 1955; president, International Poets, Playwrights, Editors, Essayists, Novelists, 1959. **Other activities** Member, European parliament, 1984–90. **Awards and honours** Corriere Lombardo prize, 1945; Strega prize, 1952; chevalier de la Légion d'honneur, France, 1952, commandeur, 1984; Marzotto prize, 1954; Viareggio prize, 1961; honorary member: American National Academy of Arts and Letters, American National Institute of Arts and Letters. **Publications** *Gli indifferenti,* 1929, in English as *The Indifferent Ones,* 1932, and as *The Time of Indifference,* 1953; *Le ambizioni sbagliate,* 1935, in English as *The Wheel of Fortune,* 1937, and as *Mistaken Ambitions,* 1955; *La bella vita,* 1935; *L'imbroglio,* 1937; *I sogni del pigro,* 1940; *La mascherata,* 1941, in Engish as *The Fancy Dress Party,* 1947; *L'amante infelice,* 1943; *L'epidemia: Racconti surrealistici e satirici,* 1944; *Agostino,* 1944; *Due cortigiane: Seratudi Don Giovanni,* 1945; *La romana,* 1947, in English as *The Woman of Rome,* 1949; *La disubbidienza,* 1948, in English as *Disobedience,* 1950; *L'amore coniugale e altri racconti,* 1949, selections published in English as *Conjugal Love,* 1951, and in *Five Novels,* 1955; *Two Adolescents: The Stories of Agostino and Luca,* 1951; *Il conformista,* in English as *The Conformist,* 1951; *I racconti,* 1952, in English as *Bitter Honeymoon and Other Stories,* 1954, 1956, and as *The Wayward Wife and Other Stories,* 1960; *Racconti romani,* 1954, in English as *Roman Tales,* 1956; *Il disprezzo,* 1954, in English as *A Ghost at Noon,* 1955; *Five Novels,* 1955; *La ciociara,* 1957, in English as *Two Women,* 1958; *Nuovi racconti romani,* 1959, in English as *More Roman Tales,* 1963; *La noia,* 1960, in English as *The Empty Canvas,* 1961; *L'automa,* 1963, in English as *The Fetish and Other Stories,* 1964; *Cortigiana stanca,* 1965; *L'attenzione,* 1965, in English as *The Lie,* 1966; *Una cosa è una cosa,* 1967, in English as *Command and I Will Obey You,* 1969; *Il paradiso,* 1970, in English as *Paradise and Other Stories,* 1971, and as *Bought and Sold,* 1973; *Io e lui,* 1971, in English as *Two: A Phallic Novel,* 1972, and as *The Two of Us,* 1972; *Un'altra vita,* 1973, in English as *Lady Godiva and Other Stories,* 1975; *Boh,* 1976, in English as *The Voice of the Sea and Other Stories,* 1978; *La vita interiore,* 1978, in English as *Time of Desecration,* 1980; *1934,* 1982; *La cosa e altri racconti,* 1983; *Storie della preistoria Favole,* 1983; *L'uomo che guarda,* 1985, in English as *The Voyeur,* 1987; *The Friday Villa,* 1990. **Plays** (With Luigi Squarzini) *Gli* *indifferenti,* 1948; *Il provino,* 1955; *Non approfondire,* 1957; *Teatro,* 1958; *Il mondo è quello che è,* 1966; *Il dio Kurt,* 1969; *La vita è gioco,* 1970. **Screenplays** *Un colpo di pistola,* 1941; *Zazà,* 1942; *Ultimo incontro,* 1951; *Sensualità,* 1951; *Tempi nostri,* 1952; *La provinciale* (*The Wayward Wife*), 1952; *Villa Borghese,* 1953; *La donna del Fiume,* 1954; *La romana* (*The Woman of Rome*), 1955; *Racconti romani* (*Roman Tales*), 1956; *Racconti d'estate* (*Love on the Riviera*), 1958; *Il delfini* (*The Dauphins*), 1960; *La giornata balorda* (*From a Roman Balcony*), 1960; *Una domenica d'estate,* 1961; *Agostino,* 1962; *Ieri oggi domani* (*Yesterday, Today and Tomorrow*), 1963; *Le ore nude,* 1964; *L'occhio selvaggio* (*The Wild Eye*), 1967. **Other publications** *La speranza: Ossia cristianesimo e comunismo,* 1944; *Opere complete* (17 volumes), 1952–67; *Un mese in U.R.S.S.,* 1958; (with Elemire Zolla) *I moralisti moderni,* 1960; (editor with Elemire Zolla) *Saggi italiani,* 1960; *Women of Rome* (photographs by Sam Waagenaar), 1960; *Un'idea dell'India,* 1962; *Claudia Cardinale,* 1963; *L'uomo come fine e altri saggi,* 1964, in English as *Man as an End: A Defence of Humanism,* 1965; *La rivoluzione culturale in Cina ovvero il convitato di pietra,* 1967, in English as *The Red Book and the Great Wall: An Impression of Mao's China,* 1968; *A quale tribù appartieni?,* 1972, in English as *Which Tribe Do You Belong To?,* 1974; *Al cinema: Centoquarantotto film d'autore,* 1975; *La mutazione femminile: Conversazione con Moravia sulla donna* by Carla Ravaiola, 1975; *Intervista sullo scrittore scomodo* edited by Nello Ajello, 1978; *Quando Ba Lena era tanto piccola,* 1978; *Cosma e i briganti,* 1980; *Lettere del Sahara,* 1981; *The Life of Alberto Moravia* (edited by Alain Elkann), 1990. **Cause of death** Stroke, at age 82. **Further reading** Giuliano Dego, *Moravia,* 1966; Donald W. Heiney, *Three Italian Novelists,* 1968; Joan Ross and Donald Freed, *The Existentialism of Moravia,* 1972; Jane E. Cottrell, *Moravia,* 1974; Ferdinando Alfonsi, *An Annotated Bibliography of Moravia Criticism in Italy and in the English-Speaking World (1929–1975),* 1976. *Contemporary Foreign Language Writers,* 1984.

LAWRENCE O'BRIEN

American Political Strategist and Sports Executive

***Born* Springfield, Massachusetts, 7 July 1917**

***Died* Manhattan, New York, 26 September 1990**

O'Brien was not the type who took centre stage in historical events, but he nevertheless played an important role in them. "The New Frontier" is something we associate with presidents Kennedy and Johnson, but it was O'Brien who put Kennedy in the White House, and it was he who ensured the passage of the bulk of New Frontier legislation. The Watergate scandal is synonymous with Richard Nixon, but it was the bugging of O'Brien's office and the suit he filed which started the affair. He was always behind the scenes, and from there he changed the shape of the Democratic Party and US politics. As a campaign organizer in the 1950s and 1960s, he was a master of grassroots techniques. As chairman of the Democratic National Committee (DNC), he modernized the party with a new emphasis on the media. His ability to persuade and compromise earned him the reputation as "the Democrats' most professional political operator". In tribute to him, current DNC chairman, Ronald H. Brown, said O'Brien was a progressive leader who laid the foundations of the modern Democratic Party.

O'Brien's parents emigrated to Massachusetts from County Cork. His father, Lawrence Sr, became a local businessman and hotelier in Springfield. Lawrence Jr was born in the Roland Hotel, one of his father's concerns, and grew up surrounded by politics and politicians. The Roland Hotel was something of a clubhouse for local Democrats, where mayors and senators often gathered. O'Brien's father was a loyal party member, and O'Brien once explained that "the anti-Irish bigotry he encountered made him that way. It was a place for him to go. He wasn't wanted elsewhere, and he became a Democratic Party fighter in a Republican stronghold."

O'Brien was interested in sports as well as politics, especially basketball, but he was not a particularly gifted nor a successful athlete. He did have a talent for political organization, however. From his early teens he was petitioning, distributing leaflets, and later speaking at rallies. He studied law at Northeastern University, tending bar at his father's restaurant and taking night classes, and received his degree in 1942. During this time, O'Brien was elected president of the Hotel and Restaurant Employees Union. However, his talents were at the organizational level, and this would be his only elective office.

After the war, which he spent in Massachusetts because of his poor eyesight, O'Brien began to develop and perfect his talents. His first campaign was on behalf of his boyhood friend, Foster Furcolo, running for a seat in the House of Representatives. In the first campaign, Furcolo lost by a mere 3500 votes. Two years later, in 1948, O'Brien and Furcolo turned that deficit into a 15,000-vote victory. O'Brien joined Furcolo in Washington, but returned to his home in 1950 for undisclosed reasons. At this time, Massachusetts was represented in the House by John F. Kennedy, a young progressive Democrat, and in the Senate by Henry Cabot Lodge, a pillar of the state's conservative establishment. As a rising star in politics, a face-off between Kennedy and Lodge was inevitable, and Kennedy turned to O'Brien for help.

Kennedy and O'Brien had a lot in common politically, and they shared their Irish heritage. Socially, they were poles apart. The Kennedys were the patricians to the O'Briens' plebeians. In a sense, Kennedy was just as much "Establishment" as Lodge, but the Democratic Party leaders were reluctant to support him. So, he turned to O'Brien's extensive local contacts and popular approach. O'Brien had learned from his father all the means of challenging the Establishment: "My father would say, 'All right, now we'll get the signatures.' It was organizational politics, signatures on petitions, door-to-door canvassing. He was a great one for planning."

Lawrence Jr was every bit as able as his father. So as not to offend the entrenched party leaders, who thought Lodge was unbeatable, he drafted 340 volunteers, calling them "Kennedy secretaries", to run the campaign. They went door-to-door, winning one vote at a time. In the course of the campaign, O'Brien perfected his own political methods, which he codified in *The O'Brien Manual,* a 68-page handbook that he re-issued at every race he organized. It stressed the importance of voter registration, encouraging women to participate, telemarketing and good press relations. It combined the best of classical and contemporary methods, and it worked wonders: despite Dwight Eisenhower's landslide victory in 1952, Kennedy defeated Lodge by 70,000 votes. Six years later, O'Brien's organization returned a record 874,608 votes (in Massachusetts) to keep Kennedy's seat.

The Democratic National Convention of 1960, held in Los Angeles, was another major success for O'Brien. He had already recruited volunteers nationwide, and Kennedy had carried the seven state primaries he had entered. To secure a first-ballot victory at the convention, O'Brien assigned a liaison to each state delegation and maintained constant communication via walkie-talkies. So accurate was his planning that his prediction of the tally came within one vote of the actual result.

After the election, O'Brien became Kennedy's special assistant for congressional relations, gaining support for the long list of the president's "New Frontier" legislation. This list included proposals for economic and manpower redevelopment, health care and civil rights; and O'Brien was not above twisting arms and granting favours to secure passage. Still, he had a tough time making the members of Kennedy's coalition work together. Before Kennedy's death in Dallas, bills were coming down from Capitol Hill at a trickle.

O'Brien was with Kennedy on that day in November 1963, and it was he who bore the bad news. "I remember standing in the hospital with Ken O'Donnell for a half-hour, refusing to tell the world he was dead — because we couldn't accept it." It was the first of three great blows to O'Brien's political optimism. He was going to leave Washington, but Lyndon Johnson, taking over for Kennedy, persuaded him to stay.

It was a fortunate decision. More bills were passed between 1964 and 1966 than in any other period in US history, except during the New Deal of the 1930s. Moreover, O'Brien was the motivating force behind the activity. As Johnson became more preoccupied with the Vietnam conflict, O'Brien was allowed to make whatever changes he thought were needed to get the bills passed. In 1965, 84 of the 87 bills sent to Congress were passed; in 1966, the figure was 97 of 113. Among these were such landmark bills as the Peace Corps, Medicare, the nuclear test ban treaty and the Civil Rights Acts.

Once again, O'Brien was ready to leave government service, but Johnson managed to keep him on. In 1965, O'Brien became Postmaster General, and while continuing the legislative *tour de force,* managed to revamp the ageing postal system. It took Congress two years to approve his plans, but O'Brien devised schemes to replace the Post Office Department with a non-profit government corporation, introduced a long-overdue office of planning, and succeeded in completing a major mechanization programme.

Finally, O'Brien left the Johnson administration in 1968. Johnson had decided not to seek re-election, and O'Brien went to co-ordinate the campaign of Kennedy's younger brother and former attorney-general, Robert Kennedy. Thus began O'Brien's second race with catastrophe, which ended on 5 June 1968, when Robert Kennedy was assassinated. "At that moment," O'Brien recalled, "I became fatalistic." "With nothing to do, and nothing [he] wanted to do", O'Brien was prepared to leave politics and return to Springfield. Instead, he co-ordinated the campaign of the other Democratic hopeful, Hubert Humphrey. Humphrey appointed O'Brien chairman of the DNC in the hope of holding the party together through the 1968 election. But the Democrats were bitterly divided over Vietnam, their annual convention in Chicago was a shambles, and Humphrey was defeated by Nixon.

Nevertheless, O'Brien had learned some important lessons. When he returned to the DNC in 1970, he oversaw sweeping reforms in delegate selection, staff organization, and he re-addressed himself to "cracking the TV nut". The Republican media blitz had made the difference in 1968 and, as the 1972 election neared, the Democrats were so debt-ridden they could not afford to buy air-time. To prevent a repetition of 1968, O'Brien petitioned the Federal Communications Commission for equal time on television, and in May of 1970 launched a series of broadcasts attacking Nixon's "blind pursuit of a military solution" in Indochina. The first, on ABC-TV, aired one week after the invasion of Cambodia. The second, on CBS, was called *The Loyal Opposition,* and was the most damaging. It showed clips of Nixon's campaign promises, followed by a factual rebuttal. So alarmed were the Republicans, Nixon's Committee to Re-Elect the President (ironically known as CREEP) set out to discredit the Democrats. Specifically, their target was O'Brien.

They arranged three separate audits of O'Brien's income tax returns and authorized the bugging of his offices. The agents were caught replacing some of the listening devices on 17 June 1972. In his autobiography, O'Brien said "I've been a politician most of my life, and I've never dreamed of bugging an opponent's telephone or breaking into his office." Believing that "if a generation of Americans becomes convinced that burglary and wire-tapping are 'politics as usual', then there is not much hope for our political system", he filed a million-dollar damages suit against CREEP. It became the most notorious political scandal in the nation's history, and led to Nixon's resignation in 1974.

O'Brien's own involvement in politics came to an end shortly after the break-in. The summer leading up to the 1972 election were "the worst three months of my life", O'Brien said. The battles beween the Democratic aristocracy and minority delegates continued to rage, money problems were endemic and the party, under George McGovern, suffered a humiliating defeat. O'Brien left politics for good and moved to New York.

He had one more major contribution to make, however. In 1975, he began a nine-year tenure as commissioner of the National Basketball Association. It, like the Democratic Party, was in trouble. Disputes between players and owners, falling attendance, and widespread drug abuse threatened the league and the sport. As he had done for the Democrats, O'Brien managed to solve these problems. He settled the long-standing "Oscar Robertson suit" and allowed players to become free agents after two years. He also negotiated the merger of the failing American Basketball Association with the NBA, put a cap on players' salaries, initiated the most comprehensive drug and alcohol abuse policy in professional sports and introduced the popular three-point shot. The league expressed their gratitude by naming their championship trophy after him in 1984.

"He was a giant in American politics and sports", said one of his colleagues. And although his name and his face are not immediately recognized by the general public, Lawrence O'Brien has left an indelible mark on the institution and the game.

Born Lawrence Francis O'Brien Junior. **Father** Lawrence Francis O'Brien, hotelier and restaurant owner. **Marriage** Elva Brassard, 1945. **Childen** One son, Lawrence. **Education** Northeastern University, Boston, Massachusetts, LLB, 1942. **Military service** Sergeant, US Army, 1942–45. **Career** President, Hotel and Restaurant Employees Union, 1939; manager for Foster Furcolo congressional campaign, 1946, 1948, administrative assistant, 1948–52; aide, John F. Kennedy senatorial campaign, 1952, manager, 1958; manager, John F. Kennedy presidential campaign, 1960; special assistant for Congressional relations, Kennedy and Johnson administrations, 1960–65; political adviser, Lyndon Johnson presidential campaign, 1964; US Postmaster General, 1965–68; co-ordinator, Robert Kennedy presidential campaign 1968; director, Hubert Humphrey presidential campaign, 1968; Democratic Party national chairman, 1968, 1970–72; office burgled by Watergate conspirators, 1972. **Related activities** Commissioner, National Basketball Association, 1975–84; president, Basketball Hall of Fame, Springfield, Massachusetts, 1984–90. **Other activities** Founder/director, O'Brien Associates public relations and management firm, 1968–70, 1972–75. **Publications** *The O'Brien Manual* (handbook), 1952; *No Final Victories: A Life in Politics from John F. Kennedy to Watergate* (autobiography), 1974. **Cause of death** Cancer, at age 73.

HERMES PAN

American Dancer and Choreographer

Born **Memphis, Tennessee, 10 December 1910**

Died **Los Angeles, California, 19 September 1990**

Hermes Pan graced the art form of dance. He was also a superb example of those talented souls who were responsible for making the stars sparkle, but who were rarely seen themselves, either on stage or on camera. As the man who helped make Fred Astaire, Ginger Rogers and other dancers dazzle, he was responsible for some of the best choreography and dance direction to be found on Broadway or in Hollywood.

Pan's inventive and structured sequences had their roots not in formal classes but from imitating the styles of the Blacks in his home town. The son of an American mother and the Greek consul in

Memphis, Hermes Panagiotopoulos danced for tips in speak-easies when the family moved to New York upon his father's death. School ended then; before long Broadway bit-parts beckoned, and his talents were expanded and honed. During a stint in the show *Top Speed,* in 1929, he met a young Ginger Rogers; they met again at the Marx Brothers stage show of *Animal Crackers* the same year. Both ended up in Hollywood soon after, Pan while on a touring revue.

When he became dance assistant to Dave Gould on the film *Flying Down to Rio* in 1933, he met Astaire. "Gould couldn't dance, so he asked me if I could be of assistance to Mr Astaire", remembered Pan, who had impressed Gould immediately with his inventiveness. After offering a few steps to the star, who had been snagged on a particular routine (which was incorporated into the film), Astaire was also impressed — enough to make him his dance director on the spot. Pan was the only man, Astaire was to say later, who could dance the way he could. Pan was then only 28.

Pan considered *Flying Down to Rio,* which had paired Astaire and Rogers for the first time, as the first film where full-length dance numbers were seen on the screen; that is, a complete dance sequence that truly commanded the viewer's attention from beginning to end, not merely the backdrop for vocal numbers which dance had been up until that point. A tradition was shattered (the film's producers had had their doubts) and an important dimension to the Hollywood musical had been created — one of Pan's most important contributions, in team with Astaire. The dance was finally *part* of the plot, involving technically demanding and creative duets, solos and chorus work. It was no longer "hoofing". And audiences were delighted with an art form that had been jazzed up, glamorized and energized.

Pan choreographed not only the memorable scene of girls cavorting on the wing of a plane, but also the forehead-to-forehead romp of the "Carioca". He went on to choreograph the rest, save one, of the Astaire-Rogers films, including *Roberta*, a film that was saved by the exuberance of the dance numbers; *Gay Divorcee,* which included the Oscar-winning "Continental" and the seductive "Night And Day" Cole Porter tune-to-dance; *Top Hat* — in which Pan displayed his versatility from the gracefully sweeping rainstorm courtship of "Isn't This A Lovely Day" to the energy of "Top Hat, White Tie And Tails", and *Follow the Fleet,* with "Let Yourself Go" and the lyrically stylish "Let's Face The Music And Dance".

In the 1936 *Swing Time,* Pan and Astaire created the Astaire-Rogers duo's most breathless footwork as a team, which saved the practically non-existent plot and rather forced ending. The dances to an excellent score, with numbers such as "The Way You Look Tonight" and "Pick Yourself Up", made the film one of their finest. The "Bojangles" production number was a taste of Pan's unique imagination; Astaire danced (with bold adaptations of modern and jazz styles) in front of three huge shadows of himself projected on a wall behind him. The inventiveness continued in 1937's *Damsels in Distress,* in "Fun House", a sequence using distorting mirrors, revolving treadmills and barrels and slides. It won an Academy Award.

In *Carefree,* the next year, musical comedy took on an edge of wackiness as Rogers went to psychiatrist Astaire — Pan adapted to the tone. In "The Yam" number, he created swooping lifts, where Astaire props his legs on each of two tables and swings Rogers over; Pan was adding a touch of athleticism to Astaire's more formal style. Both adapted well to period moods and period steps in the bio-musical, *The Story of Vernon and Irene Castle,* about the American dance team in the early 1900s.

After more than ten years Astaire and Rogers re-teamed for *Barkleys of Broadway,* in 1949, about the battle of a popular theatrical couple when one of them decides to try serious drama. The wistful "They Can't Take That Away From Me" was married with Pan's gentle lyricism in the production piece.

Pan not only provided ideas, inspiration and constructive criticism, he also dubbed the taps themselves on the soundtrack. The audiences never realized that while they saw Astaire, they *heard* Pan. It was enormously difficult to match the visuals, except that both artists thought uncannily alike; often talk was completely unnecessary. The two men communicated their ideas by movement. Both were also perfectionists and even walked similarly. Their physical resemblance was also remarked upon; both were slight, lean and high-foreheaded. And when Rogers couldn't rehearse, it was Pan who stepped in; Astaire could continue creating and refining without a hitch. The two men remained close friends until Astaire's death. The partnership was represented by two dancing shoes (one worn by Rogers, one by Astaire) that were perched upon the piano at Pan's home.

Together Pan and Astaire changed the face of the film musical, dispensing with the accepted practice of frequent cutting during numbers, and creating routines so meticulously for the camera that the dances gave the impression of being filmed in a continuous take. (*Swingtime*'s last eight bars alone for "Never Gonna Dance" took 47 takes — along with the immense fatigue, Rogers's bleeding feet and the rest which both the perfectionists had to ignore!) Pan would always emphasize Astaire's movements, minimizing those of the background chorus, and constantly strove for smooth integration of plot and dialogue with the dancing. The seductive duets they created for the team (such as in "Cheek To Cheek", "Night And Day" and "Smoke Gets In Your Eyes") have proved to be real dance masterpieces. Their livelier numbers such as "Pick Yourself Up", "They All Laughed" and "Let Yourself Go" have a spontaneity and wit rarely found elsewhere. Pan fitted the Astaire screen persona perfectly — and added to it, on the screen. As he said, simply, "It sort of blended into a beautiful thing."

After the Astaire era, Pan continued to choreograph stage musicals which had transferred to screen; notable work was done with Kathryn Grayson, Howard Keel and Ann Miller in *Kiss Me Kate,* in *Porgy and Bess,* in *Can-Can* (with Juliet Prowse, a Paris discovery, in her first Hollywood film), and in *My Fair Lady,* where he was at his most elegant. The scene had changed; he worked now with technically trained dancers, not self-taught hoofers. He showed further versatility when he was requested to choreograph and direct the entry of Cleopatra into Rome in the 1963 Liz Taylor potboiler by the same name. On screen he performed his own dance-steps in films such as *Moon Over Miami* (with Betty Grable), *My Gal Sal* (with Rita Hayworth) and *A Life of Her Own* (with Lana Turner).

Pan's choreography wasn't limited to the hard floor; he created dances on water (for Esther Williams) and ice (for Sonja Henie), as well. But the dancer/actor who, he felt, expressed his ideas the best was Cyd Charisse (*Silk Stockings*). With the decline in Hollywood musical productions, Pan returned to Broadway and TV work, achieving an Emmy Award for *Astaire Time: An Evening With Fred Astaire. Finian's Rainbow,* in 1968, was his last musical. At Astaire's insistence he was hired, then fired, by director Francis Coppola who, in Pan's words, "interfered with my work, even Fred's" — a not unusual accusation, given Coppola's infamous egotism. The picture proved to be an unhappy event all around.

Pan received a National Film Award for Achievement in Cinema in 1980 and a special award from the Joffrey Ballet six years later. As a primarily self-taught "hoofer", the irony had not escaped him. Pan had been open to and had perfected for the media of stage and screen an enormous variety of dance styles and sources. Each dance was a complete, unique and creative experience using techniques of ballet, jazz, modern, tap, ballroom and ethnic styles. He blended technical skill with the fire and energy drawn from within — forces rarely demanded from others, but which Pan usually inspired. He was in a league with the Busby Berkeley and the Stanley Donen/Gene Kelly group. "He was a great dancer and a wonderful, wonderful man", said Ginger Rogers.

Born Hermes Panagiotopoulos. **Parents** Pantelis, Greek consul to Memphis, Tennessee, and Mary (Huston) Panagiotopoulos. **Children** One daughter, Michelene. **Career** Laboratory assistant, Edison Company, 1925; saloon dancer; stage dancer and singer, 1927–30; chorus singer: *Top Speed,* 1929, *Animal Crackers,* 1929; touring dancer, 1929–33; went to Hollywood as part of dance team with sister, Vasso Meade, 1933; assistant dance director, *Flying Down to Rio,* 1933; introduced to Fred Astaire, 1933; first chief choreography job, *Roberta,* 1935; staff choreographer, Radio Keith Orpheum films, 1935–38; staff choreographer, Fox Studios, 1939–48; choreographed *As the Girls Go,* Broadway, 1948; staff choreographer, Metro-Goldwyn-Mayer studio, 1948–57; freelance choreographer, from 1957; choreographed *Astaire Time: An Evening with Fred Astaire* television special, 1961. **Awards and honours** Nominated for Academy Award for dance direction, 1935–37, won for *Damsel in Distress,* 1937; Emmy Award for *Astaire Time: An Evening with Fred Astaire,* 1961; National Film Award for Achievement in Cinema, 1980; special citation, Joffrey Ballet, 1986. **Films choreographed** *Flying Down to Rio,* 1933; *The Gay Divorcee,* 1934; *Roberta,* 1935; *Top Hat,* 1935; *Old Man Rhythm,* 1935; *I Dream Too Much,* 1935; *In Person,* 1935; *Follow the Fleet,* 1936; *Swing Time,* 1936; *Shall We Dance,* 1937; *A Damsel in Distress,* 1937; *Carefree,* 1938; *Radio City Reels,* 1938; *The Story of Vernon and Irene Castle,* 1939; *Second Chorus,* 1941; *That Night in Rio* 1941; *Moon over Miami* (also danced), 1941; *Sun Valley Serenade,* 1941; *Rise and Shine,* 1941; *Week-end in Havana,* 1941; *Song of the Islands,* 1942; *Footlight Serenade,* 1942; *My Gal Sal* (also danced), 1942; *Springtime in the Rockies,* 1942; *Coney Island,* 1943; *Sweet Rosie O'Grady* (also danced), 1943; *Hello, Frisco, Hello,* 1943; *Pin Up Girl* (also danced), 1944; *Irish Eyes are Smiling,* 1944; *Billy Rose's Diamond Horseshoe,* 1945; *All-Star Musical Review,* 1945; *Blue Skies,* 1946; *I Wonder Who's Kissing Her Now,* 1947; *The Lady in Ermine,* 1948; *The Barkleys of Broadway,* 1949; *Let's Dance,* 1950; *Three Little Words,* 1950; *Texas Carnival,* 1951; *Kiss Me Kate,* 1953; *Excuse My Dust,* 1953; *Sombrero,* 1953; *The Student Prince,* 1954; *Hit the Deck,* 1954; *Jupiter's Darling,* 1955; *Meet Me in Las Vegas,* 1956; *Silk Stockings,* 1957; *Pal Joey,* 1958; *Porgy and Bess,* 1959; *Can-Can,* 1960; *The Pleasure of His Company,* 1961; *Flower Drum Song,* 1961; *Cleopatra,* 1963; *The Pink Panther,* 1963; *My Fair Lady,* 1964; *The Great Race,* 1965; *Finian's Rainbow,* 1968; *Darling Lili,* 1970; *Lost Horizon,* 1972. **Cause of death** Undisclosed, at age 79.

EDWIN REISCHAUER

American Scholar and Diplomat

Born **Tokyo, Japan, 15 October 1910**

Died **San Diego, California, 1 September 1990**

Edwin Reischauer devoted a lifetime to promoting better understanding between western and eastern nations, notably Japan. He did so by means of numerous books on the subject, which are regarded as models of scholarship; and by helping to make Harvard University, with which he was associated for 50 years, a world centre for East Asian studies.

But it is as American ambassador to Japan in the turbulent 1960s that Reischauer's reputation largely rests. When President John F. Kennedy chose him as envoy in 1961 Reischauer was the very opposite of the career diplomat usually picked to fill such a post. For one thing, Reischauer was born in Tokyo, where he spent the first 17 years of his life. For another, he not only spoke their language, but he had a profound knowledge of the Japanese people and their history. He was widely regarded as the right man in the right place at the right time.

The son of an American missionary in Tokyo, Reischauer was educated at the American School there, and at Oberlin College, Ohio. When Reischauer arrived at Harvard in 1932 there were only two graduate students interested in East Asian studies, he and his elder brother, as he later recalled.

On a fellowship from the Harvard-Yenching Institute of Oriental Studies, Reischauer spent the years 1933 to 1938 pursuing his studies in France, Korea, Japan and China. In 1938, with a colleague, he devised a phonetic system for transliterating the Korean language into the Latin alphabet. In 1939 he received his PhD from Harvard.

Reischauer was teaching at Harvard when war broke out between Japan and the United States. Thereafter for the duration of the war he served as adviser first to the State Department, then to the War Department, being discharged from the latter's intelligence service with the rank of lieutenant-colonel and the Order of Merit. After the war Reischauer returned to Harvard to teach, his popular survey course in Asian history being known on campus as "rice paddies".

Reischauer's arrival in Tokyo to take up his ambassadorial post was awaited with curiosity by the Japanese. The fact that the lanky, blue-eyed professor brought with him a Japanese wife merely added to the interest. Haru Matsukata, whose grandfather had been a prime minister, was Reischauer's second wife, his first wife having died in 1955.

The seat which Reischauer filled was a hot one. The year before his arrival there had been anti-American riots in Tokyo over amending the US-Japanese security treaty. Outweighing other factors in dispelling distrust was the fact that the new ambassador was a *sensei*, or teacher, a profession highly respected in Japan.

In the following years Reischauer more than fulfilled the expectations of President Kennedy. He staffed his embassy with experts on Japan. He established good working relations with both the ruling party and opposition leaders. He travelled the length and breadth of the land until his face became as well known through public appearances as that of the latest television celebrity. "How wonderful it is", remarked a newspaper editor, "to write an editorial and know that the American ambassador will actually be able to read it."

Reischauer paid the price of celebrity when, in March 1964, he was stabbed in the thigh by a mentally deranged youth in Tokyo. Premier Ikeda formally apologized to President Johnson, while the Japanese minister for home affairs resigned claiming the attack was his responsibility. From his hospital bed Reischauer begged his hosts not to blame themselves. President Kennedy's assassination had occurred four months earlier, he reminded them.

Looking back over his five and a half years as ambassador, Reischauer had reason for quiet satisfaction. He had managed to stem the tide of anti-American feeling, which had run high over American involvement in Vietnam (Reischauer later changed his mind about the Vietnam war, spoke of it as a "disastrous mistake").

Above all, the scholarly ambassador had been able to reassure and to encourage the Japanese at a moment of identity crisis when they were hesitant about assuming their new international role. "I was sent here", he said, "to re-establish communications with the Japanese people on a broad scale. That has been accomplished, and the problem is now of a different nature."

Having enjoyed the public limelight Reischauer at first found it hard to adjust to academic life. However he continued to teach at Harvard for another 15 years until his retirement in 1981. They were seminal years insofar as his writings were concerned. In articles and speeches he continued to play an active role in Asian affairs, urging the diplomatic recognition of China, an end to American occupation of Okinawa. He also travelled extensively in the United States to raise money for the oriental studies centre of his beloved Harvard.

Harvard and Japan were Reischauer's two loves. Commenting on the definitive work which Reischauer published in 1977 under the title *The Japanese*, *The New York Times* described him as the master builder of an "intellectual arch between the two countries", a description which might well have pleased him.

Born Edwin Oldfather Reischauer. **Parents** August Karl, missionary and philosophy professor, and Helen Sidwell (Oldfather), teacher of the deaf, Reischauer. **Marriages** 1) Adrienne Danton,

1935 (died 1955); 2) Haru Matsukata, foreign correspondent, 1956. **Children** Ann, Robert and Joan, from first marriage. **Education** American School, Tokyo; Oberlin College, Ohio, BA, 1931; Harvard University, Cambridge, Massachusetts MA, 1932, PhD, 1939; travelling fellow: University of Paris, 1933–35, University of Tokyo, 1935–36, University of Kyoto, 1937–38. **Military service** Lieutenant-colonel, US Army Military Intelligence, 1943–45. **Career** (With George M. McCune) developed phonetic method for converting Korean into the Latin letters, 1938; instructor, Harvard University, 1938–42, associate professor, 1946–50, professor of Far Eastern languages, 1950–61, director, Harvard-Yenching Institute, 1956–61, board chairman, 1969–83, university professor of Japanese history, 1966–81; senior research analyst, War Department, 1942–43; chairman, Japan-Korea Secretariat, Department of State, 1945–46, special assistant to director of Office of Far Eastern Affairs, 1945–46; US ambassador to Japan, 1961–66. **Related activities** Member, Cultural Mission to Japan, 1948–49. **Offices and memberships** Member: American Historical Association, Japan Society, Phi Beta Kappa, Japan-United States Committee on Cultural and Educational Exchange, American Oriental Society, Association for Asian Studies, president, 1955–56. **Awards and honours** Harvard-Yenching Institute travelling fellowship, 1933–38; Legion of Merit, 1945; honorary doctorates: Nihon University, Japan, Rikkyo University, Japan, University of Maryland, Harvard University, University of Michigan, Yale University, Brandeis University, and Oberlin College, 1957; Grand Cordon of the Rising Sun, Japan. **Publications** (Compiler with Elisseeff and Yosihash) *Elementary Japanese for University Students* (two volumes), 1941; (compiler with Elisseeff) *Selected Japanese Texts for University Students* (three volumes), 1942–47; (compiler with others) *Elementary Japanese for College Students,* 1944; *Japan, Past and Present,* 1946; *The United States and Japan,* 1950; (compiler and translator with Joseph Yamagiwai) *Translations for Early Japanese Literature,* 1951; (with others) *Japan and America Today,* 1953; *Wanted: An Asian Policy,* 1955; (translator) *Diary: The Record of a Pilgrimage to China in Search of the Law* by Ennin, 1955; *Ennin's Travels in T'ang China,* 1955; "The Broken Dialogue", *Foreign Affairs,* 1960; (with John K. Fairbank) *East Asia: The Great Tradition,* 1960; (with Fairbank and Craig) *East Asia: The Modern Transformation,* 1965; *Beyond Vietnam: The United States and Asia,* 1967; *Japan: The Story of a Nation,* 1970; (with Fairbank and Craig) *East Asia: Tradition and Transformation,* 1973; *Toward the Twenty-First Century: Education for a Changing World,* 1973; *The Japanese,* 1977; *Looking Both Ways: My Life Between Japan and America* (autobiography), 1986. **Cause of death** Complications from chronic hepatitis, at age 79.

ATHENE SEYLER

British Actress

***Born* London, England, 31 May 1889**

***Died* London, England, 12 September 1990**

Athene Seyler had two great loves in her life. The first was Restoration comedy; the second was her second husband, Nicholas "Beau" Hannen. She remained true to both until the end of her life.

Her love of acting and comedy came early but theatrical aspirations were frowned on by her parents. After a somewhat unconventional, but nonetheless rigorous, schooling she went to Bedford College in London to study Restoration drama, disguised as literature, but shortly afterwards went into a Victorian "decline". Parental concern overcame disapproval and she was allowed to apply to the Academy of Dramatic Art (now RADA) for "therapeutic reasons". She then won one of the Academy's first gold medals and thereafter gained enough awards to finance all her tuition fees. Fifty years later she became president of the Academy.

She moved straight into the theatre and was never out of work, except from choice, for the whole of her life. Already established by the outbreak of World War I, an overview of her work can best be gathered by breaking it into decades. In the 1920s she was playing in revivals of her beloved Restoration comedies, in which she excelled — works by Congreve, Dryden, Wycherley and Sheridan. In the 1930s she added Wilde, Maugham, and Shaw to her repertoire. With the 1940s came roles by Chekhov, Hellman and Lonsdale but by the 1950s she was playing in more modern roles — by Rattigan, Ayckbourn and Douglas-Home, now less interspersed with her old favourites. They were going out of fashion. But Shakespeare was a constant throughout and she also produced some memorable performances on film, particularly in *Pickwick Papers* and *Nicholas Nickleby*, *Dear Octopus* and the *Inn of the Sixth Happiness*.

Her special ability with all roles was her intelligent approach to the work. She did not impose an external characterization until she had met her fellow players. Although, in later life, the role of the Nurse in *Romeo and Juliet* became a favourite she could not know, she said, whether to slap or cajole until she had looked into the eyes of Juliet.

She has been compared to some of the other grand old ladies of the British theatre — such names as Sybil Thorndike and Edith Evans spring to mind. But she lacked a sense of her own grandeur. What she believed in was honing the professionalism of her craft and encouraging others to do the same. This may be why she never came to be regarded as a star although she could, and sometimes did, act all the others off the stage.

Her first marriage lasted only a few years and by 1920 she had met Nicholas Hannen (called "Beau" because of his gentle and courteous Edwardian manners) with whom she toured extensively abroad. Both were Roman Catholics and had other marriages from which they could not extricate themselves but, defying the rigorous conventions of the times, they lived happily together for 40 years until they were both free to marry in 1960. Hannen, nine years her senior, died 12 years later at the age of 91, and Seyler, by the time she reached her own nineties, really wanted little more than to join him in the afterlife.

She felt that during her life acting had improved quite considerably in the British theatre but this was not apparent generally because the standard of new plays was low. She could not endure the plays of Harold Pinter; she maintained that they had quite put her off the theatre.

Her most lasting contribution was made in the form of a small book, first published in 1944, called *The Craft of Comedy*. It arose from a series of letters exchanged with fellow actor Stephen Haggard, who was killed in action shortly before publication. Over the years it has come to be regarded as the seminal work on the subject and has twice been reissued.

During her long life Athene Seyler was able to recognize many emerging talents coming along in her wake. Two of those she was encouraging in their student days were John Gielgud and Laurence Olivier. So why, particularly in view of her longevity, was she not made a Dame of the British Empire? When asked this by her friend, actor Marius Goring, two years before her death, she gave a bewitching smile and said, "Darling, one can't live in sin *and* be a Dame."

Born Athene Seyler. **Parents** Clarence H. and Clara (Thies) Seyler. **Marriages** 1) James Bury Sterndale-Bennett, newspaper editor, 1914 (separated 1920, died 1941); 2) Nicholas James Hannen, actor, 1960 (died 1972). **Children** One daughter, Jane, from first marriage. **Education** Coombe Hill School, Westerham, Kent; school in East Grinstead, Sussex; Bedford College, London; Royal Academy of Dramatic Art, London, 1908. **Career** First stage appearance, *The Truants,* Kingsway Theatre, 1909; first comedy appearance, *The Double Dealer,* 1916; toured Africa and US; film début, *This Freedom,* 1922; toured Egypt; member of the company, Old Vic/

Sadler's Wells, 1933, 1952; directed *Dandy Dick,* 1958; final stage appearance, *Arsenic and Old Lace,* 1966; final public appearance, reading *The Craft of Comedy,* Royal National Theatre, London, 1990. **Related activities** President, Theatrical Ladies' Guild of Charity; drama panel, Council of the Encouragement of the Music and the Arts, 1943; honorary treasurer, British Actors Equity Association, 1944; member, Arts Council of Great Britain; president, Royal Academy of Dramatic Arts, 1950; president Theatrical Ladies Guild. **Awards and honours** Gold medal, Royal Academy of Dramatic Art, 1908; Commander of the Order of the British Empire, 1959. **Stage** (includes, all London unless otherwise indicated) *The Truants,* 1909; *Making a Gentleman,* 1909; *The Double Dealer,* 1916; *Marriage à la Mode,* 1920; *As You Like It,* 1920; *Love for Love,* 1921; *The Dover Road,* 1922; *The Country Wife,* 1924; *A Midsummer Night's Dream,* 1924; *The Importance of Being Earnest,* 1929–30; *Twelfth Night,* 1933; *The Cherry Orchard,* 1933; *Macbeth,* 1933; *The School for Scandal,* 1937; *Watch on the Rhine,* 1942; *Harvey,* 1949; *Who is Sylvia?,* 1950; *Bell, Book and Candle,* 1954; *Breath of Spring,* 1958; *The Chances,* Chichester, 1962; *Arsenic and Old Lace,* 1966; also: *Much Ado About Nothing*, *Othello*, *Romeo and Juliet*, *Lady Windermere's Fan*, *A Woman of No Importance*, *The Rivals*, *Candida*, *The Corn is Green*, *Pygmalion*, *Too True to Be Good.* **Films** (include) *This Freedom,* 1922; *The Perfect Lady,* 1932; *The Citadel,* 1938; *Quiet Wedding,* 1940; *Dear Octopus,* 1943; *Nicholas Nickelby,* 1947; *Queen of Spades,* 1948; *Young Wives' Tale,* 1951; *The Beggar's Opera,* 1953; *Pickwick Papers,* 1953; *Yield to the Night,* 1956; *Doctor at Large,* 1957; *Campbell's Kingdom,* 1958; *The Inn of the Sixth Happiness,* 1958; *Make Mine Mink,* 1959; *Two and Two Make Six,* 1961; *Nurse on Wheels,* 1963. **Publication** (With Stephen Haggard) *The Craft of Comedy,* 1944 (republished 1990). **Cause of death** Undisclosed, at age 101.

LORD SWANN

British Administrator and Biologist

Born **Cambridge, England, 1 March 1920**

Died **23 September 1990**

When Sir Michael Swann was made chairman of the governors of the BBC in 1973 it was a surprise appointment, since up until then his career had pointed in quite other directions: fellow of Gonville and Caius College, Cambridge; professor of natural history at the University of Edinburgh; principal and vice-chancellor of the same institution, and a member of numerous committees including the Medical Research Council and the Committee on Manpower Resources.

As a research biologist, his main interest had been in cell physiology, and in particular fertilization, mytosis and cell division. Most of his experimental work was done with Victor Rothschild (q.v.) and Murdoch Mitchison. In a tribute in the London *Independent,* Mitchison wrote, "Swann was an excellent cell biologist but he also had a wider and longer influence on biology as a whole... His interest in biology and support for it continued all his life".

Swann's predecessor at the BBC, Lord Hill, had been an active interventionist, and this had tipped the all-important balance between the director-general and the chairman of the governors very much in the latter's favour. Constitutionally the governors *are* the BBC, but they also have the responsibility of representing the public interest *vis-à-vis* the corporation, and this dual role has been a source of misunderstanding and conflict with senior management — most strikingly during the *Real Lives* (a controversial documentary series) affair of 1985. Swann's tenure, however, was a happy one — not least, perhaps, because when Prime Minister Edward Heath appointed him it was made clear that one of his first tasks was to re-establish the position of the director-general. As Swann himself put it, "the Director General will be doing the driving and the Governors and I will be reading the map, deciding where we are going". He worked with two director-generals — Charles Curran and Ian Trethowan (q.v.) — and enjoyed an excellent relationship with both.

At the time of Swann's appointment, it was suggested in *The Economist* magazine that "Mr Heath is perhaps giving the BBC a last chance to prove that the old system worked", and in some respects Swann's tenure marked the last days of the "old system", which did indeed work well under him. Its problems were to multiply alarmingly after his departure in 1980, though this had less to do with his absence than with the arrival in 1979 of the Conservative government, which rapidly made clear its impatience with and hostility to "old systems" of any kind.

Though he never sought the limelight, Swann successfully saw the BBC through several difficult licence-fee negotiations at times of high inflation, the renewal of its Charter, and the Annan Committee's review of its performance. He also defended the corporation against government pressure and interference — usually over the ever-vexed question of the coverage of Northern Ireland, which gave rise to some notable hard tactics from the then Labour secretary of state for Northern Ireland, Roy Mason. More specifically he saw off the 1977 recommendations of the Central Policy Review staff, which would have severely curtailed the operations of the External Services, and a 1978 Labour proposal that the BBC's three services — radio, television and external — should be run by Service Management Boards, half of whose members would be appointed by the home secretary. This would have had the effect of reducing the power of the governors and, by widely extending quango patronage, increasing the influence of the government over the corporation.

After leaving the BBC, Swann became provost of Oriel College, Oxford but missed the buzz of the BBC and left after a year, greatly to the benefit of his other interests and activities. He published a respected report on the education of children from the ethnic minorities, and was first a member and then, after 1983, chairman of the governors of the Royal Academy of Music. He was also a trustee of the National History Museum and the Council for Science and Society. He was a frequent and committed contributor to Lords debates on broadcasting and scientific matters.

Born Michael Meredith Swann. **Parents** M.B.R., doctor and academic, and Marjorie (Dykes) Swann. **Marriage** Tess Gleadowe, musician, 1942. **Children** Two sons and two daughters. **Education** Exhibitioner, Winchester College, Hampshire; Gonville and Caius College, Cambridge, BA, MA, PhD. **Military service** Lieutenant-colonel, served in various scientific capacities, 1940–46, radar research, Arctic Warfare School, operational research, mentioned in despatches, 1944. **Career** Fellow, Gonville and Caius College, Cambridge, 1946–52, university demonstrator in zoology, 1946–52, professor of natural history, University of Edinburgh, 1952–65, faculty of science dean, 1963–65, principal and vice-chancellor, 1965–73; chairman, BBC, 1973–80; provost, Oriel College, Oxford, 1980–81; chancellor, University of York, 1979–90. **Related activities** Member: Advisory Council on Education in Scotland, 1957–61, Fisheries Advisory Committee, Development Commission, 1957–65, council, St George's School for Girls, 1959–75, Edinburgh University Court, 1959–62, Medical Research Council, 1962–65, Committee on Manpower Resources, 1963–68, Council for Scientific Policy, 1965–69, Science Research Council, 1969–73, Advisory Council, Civil Service College, 1970–76, Council, St George's House, Windsor, 1975–84, Scientific Foundation Board, Royal College of General Practitioners, 1978–83; chairman: Nuffield Foundation Biology Project, 1962–65, Joint Committee on Use of Antibiotics in Animal Husbandry and Veterinary Medicine, 1967–68, Scottish Health Services Scientific Council, 1971–72, Joint Committee of Inquiry into the Veterinary Profession, 1971–75, Council for Science and Society, 1974–78, Council for Applied Science in Scotland, 1978–80, Technical

Change Centre, 1980–87, Committee of Inquiry into education of Children from Ethnic Minority Groups, 1981–85, County Pensions Informations Centre, 1984. **Other activities** Director: Inveresk Research International, Midlothian, 1969–72, New Court Natural Resources Limited, 1973–85, Charities Investment Managers Limited, 1981, M & G Group, 1981; member, board of trustees, Wellcome Trust, 1972; governor, Ditchley Foundation, 1975; member, Royal Academy of Music, 1980–90, chairman, board of governors, 1983–90; chairman, Cheltenham Festival, 1983; trustee, British Museum of Natural History, 1982–86; president, Association for Information Management, 1982–84; chairman, committee of management, London School of Hygiene and Tropical Medicine, 1982–90. **Offices and memberships** Fellow, Institute of Biology; fellow, Royal Society, 1962; fellow, Royal Society of Edinburgh, 1952. **Awards and honours** Honorary fellow, Royal College of Surgeons of Edinburgh, 1967; honorary LLD, Aberdeen University, 1967; honorary DSc, Leicester University, 1968; honorary DUniv: York University, 1968, Edinburgh University, 1983; honorary DLitt, Heriot Watt University, 1971, knighted 1972; honorary fellow, Royal College of Physicians of Edinburgh, 1972; honorary associate, Royal College of Veterinary Surgeons, 1976; honorary fellow, Gonville and Caius College, Cambridge, 1977; honorary fellow, Winchester, 1979; created life peer, Baron Swann, 1981; honorary associate, British Veterinary association, 1984. **Reports published** (include) *Antibiotics* 1968; *Veterinary Profession,* 1975; *Education of Ethnic Minority Children,* 1985. **Cause of death** Undisclosed, at age 70.

A.J.P. TAYLOR

British Historian and Journalist

Born **Birkdale, Lancashire, 25 March 1906**

Died **Barnet, Hertfordshire, 7 September 1990**

In one of Kipling's *Just So Stories,* "How the Whale Got His Throat", the 'Stute Fish describes to the Whale what it would be like to eat Man: "Nice, but nubbly." The same could be said of A.J.P. Taylor's qualities as an historian.

As this writer can testify, Taylor was something quite unusual in the historical profession, a serious scholar who could nevertheless make one laugh out loud at what was on the printed page, and whose style was always full of the unexpected and the stimulating. To anyone coming fresh to the study of history, he was proof that it need not be boring.

At the same time Taylor's style had its drawbacks, and his work was by no means above serious criticism. Even on first reading his conclusions could appear bewilderingly paradoxical, to the point where the desire to be witty seemed to outweigh his concern for accuracy.

Among historians he will always be remembered for the almighty row he provoked with his *The Origins of the Second World War* in 1961. The controversy was the greater because Taylor's reputation already rested on a number of books, the academic merits of which could hardly be disputed.

On balance it is hard not to conclude that he was one of the greatest British historians this century. But this was mainly because of his ability to reach the widest possible audience, as a journalist and television personality, rather than as an academic historian.

Alan John Percivale Taylor was heir to a tradition which perhaps predisposed him to orneriness. Although his father, Percy Lees Taylor, was a prosperous Lancashire cotton merchant, both Taylor's parents were Nonconformist Liberals, who later switched their support to the Labour

Party and socialism. Political radicalism, which had strong roots in Lancashire, was also part of the Taylor family history. An ancestor had been one of those killed at the Peterloo Massacre in 1819.

In his 1983 autobiography, *A Personal History,* Taylor described himself as "always a 'loner', a solitary only child, out of step in all sorts of ways, rarely influenced by others and learning by the painful process of trial and error." He spent his first school years at a local institution, but in the middle of World War I, when he was ten, his pacifist mother removed him because she objected to the school's links with the Officer Training Corps. Taylor was sent for two years to Downs School at Colwall, a Quaker establishment, where he does not appear to have been happy. Then he won a scholarship for the more prestigious Bootham School in York.

Schooling at Bootham gave him a love of medieval architecture, and introduced him to Shaw, Butler and, perhaps most significantly, H.G. Wells's *Outline of History.* He also boasted of having read Gibbon's *Decline and Fall of the Roman Empire* in a fortnight. Before he had left school his father, who had an especially strong influence on him, committed himself to the Independent Labour Party or, as Taylor put it, "turned himself politically into a working man". The son followed suit at the age of 15.

In 1924 he won a Bootham scholarship to study history at Oriel College, Oxford. Although he also immediately joined the Labour Club at Oxford, there was a brief period in which he showed an interest in the Communist Party. He was later to say that he had tried to be a Communist, but "common sense kept breaking through". During the General Strike of 1926 he left no doubt as to where his sympathies lay, being one of the few undergraduates to support the strikers.

He completed his degree in 1927, taking a First in modern history. His studies had included medieval history but he seemed to have no idea of becoming an historian at this stage. Instead he spent the next few months in a London solicitor's office, evidently with a legal career in mind.

It was the Regius Professor of History at Oxford, H.W.C. Davis, who advised Taylor to continue with historical research. Davis recommended some time at the feet of the Austrian specialist in Cromwell, A.F. Pribram. Taylor accordingly moved in 1928 to Vienna, where he spent the next two years. Pribram, as it turned out, had lost interest in Cromwell and was now immersed in nineteenth-century diplomatic history, so by this quirk Taylor's research was deflected into the area that became his own speciality.

Pribram was one of the two major academic influences on Taylor. A firm believer in liberal institutions, he nevertheless regretted the passing of the Habsburg Monarchy, which in his view had provided a supranational framework for the development of those institutions. The Vienna-trained Pribram was also free of the heavy intellectual traditions of German historiography, although he shared the German tendency to concentrate on the primacy of foreign policy and international relations in history. From him Taylor imbibed both an enduring interest in central and east European history, and his relative disinterest in economic and social history.

On Pribram's recommendation Taylor obtained in 1930 a lecturer's job at Manchester University, where he remained for eight years. Here he not only perfected the technique of lecturing without notes, but also had as his head of department his second great mentor, Lewis Namier. Namier, like Pribram, was an Austrian Jew, but Polish, not German, and of a fundamentally different outlook. Whereas Pribram stressed the progressive elements in the old Monarchy, Namier saw mainly its repressive nature, a vehicle for intolerant German and Hungarian nationalism. Namier's conservatism also assigned a greater role to the accidental in history, a viewpoint which strongly shaped Taylor's own interpretations.

Taylor's two years' work in the Austrian archives provided the basis for his first book, *The Italian Problem in European Diplomacy 1847–49,* published in 1934. This was a conventional study based on primary sources, as was his *Germany's First Bid for Colonies 1884–85,* which came out in 1938.

While at Manchester Taylor became actively involved in the anti-appeasement movement, and was a ready speaker at public meetings urging action against Hitler's Germany. He later claimed that it was the reoccupation of the Rhineland in 1936 which finally "brought me to my senses". He also established a connection with the *Manchester Guardian* which was to prove the passport to much subsequent journalistic work. Under the editorship of A.P. Wadsworth he wrote a constant stream of reviews and, during World War II, contributed to the leader columns. According to Taylor it was Wadsworth who taught him to write copy that people could read "on the way to work". Whatever the occasional lapses into which this facility might have led Taylor subsequently, it remains a pity that more of his fellow academics have not also acquired the knack.

In 1938, with Namier's assistance, he became a fellow of Magdalen College, Oxford, a connection which was to last until his formal retirement in 1976. During his first year at Magdalen Taylor completed the text of one of his most influential books, *The Habsburg Monarchy 1809–1918,* which did not however come out until 1941.

This first edition of *The Habsburg Monarchy* was noticeably different in tone from the second edition of 1948, which is the one most students have come to know. It represented a balancing act between the positive views of Pribram and the negative views of Namier, on the subject of whether the nations of eastern Europe could ever have continued living within the same state, and on what basis. Taylor was later to describe his first version as the product of "liberal illusions". Whereas in the first edition the Germans and Hungarians are referred to as "historic" or "ruling" peoples, by 1948 they had become the "master nations", and the inevitability of the Monarchy's collapse starkly portrayed.

This change in Taylor's view of the Habsburg Monarchy reflects the impact which World War II had upon him generally. It would not be too much to say that most of his subsequent work revolved around the "German question" in European history. For Taylor the war against Hitler was unquestionably a just one, although he also followed with keen interest the power-political realities to which it gave rise, with the emergence of the United States and the Soviet Union as superpowers at the expense of Europe.

He remained at Oxford throughout the war, while serving in the Home Guard, and gave innumerable lectures and radio broadcasts on war aims. Much of this was in direct support of the eastern European nationalities, the justice of whose fears of German aggression was now so apparent.

Taylor's preoccupation with the German problem, however, led him to overlook the possibility of the Soviet Union stepping into the post-war vacuum in eastern Europe. "Soviet policy looks eastward", he wrote (somewhat inaccurately) in 1945. "It desires security, not domination." His wartime work also gave rise to what by common consent is his least attractive book. In 1944 he was asked to give a series of lectures on German history to British personnel, the tone of which was so vitriolically anti-German that the talks were called off by the government. The result was their publication as *The Course of German History* in 1945.

In Taylor's view the war was the product, not so much of Hitler and Nazism, as of the German people's own inveterate belief in their mission to dominate Europe. This "fundamental poison" of German nationalism, moreover, was an element of continuity in German history from the nineteenth century onwards. The Namierite legacy was particularly strong in this analysis; it meant that Taylor continued to regard the post-war division of Germany as convenient and, to a considerable extent, justified.

The corollary, which Taylor developed three years later in his extensive revision of *The Habsburg Monarchy,* was the absolute entitlement of the east European successor states to exist independently. Ironically, this postulated not only Soviet indulgence, but also the nationalities' willingness to tolerate one another. Forty years on, both these assumptions are unhappily still in question.

Taylor found himself in something of a dilemma as the cold war developed, since he could hardly approve of Soviet hegemony in eastern Europe. On the other hand, as a lifelong sympathizer with the Soviet Union, especially during the war, it was easier for him to condemn the United States for the tensions of the post-war period.

Not that he was ever a fellow traveller. In 1948 he accepted an invitation to attend a conference at Wrocław in Poland, an occasion stage-managed to present the new east European order in a favourable light. Speaker after speaker rose to do so; but when Taylor's turn came, he made a speech of what one western observer described as "died-in-the-wool conservatism". Sitting down in an offended silence, he whispered to his companion, "I've been dying to make a speech like that for ages!"

In the 1950s his activity seemed Protean. Apart from his lecturing at Magdalen, which regularly packed the hall even early in the morning, he wrote for an immense range of newspapers and magazines, including *The Observer*, *New Statesman*, *Sunday Pictorial* and *Daily Herald.*

Most controversial in the academic world was his connection from 1956 on with Lord Beaverbrook's mass circulation tabloid, the *Sunday Express,* and later the *Evening Standard.* This was distinctly raffish company for an academic historian at the time, although Taylor was setting a fashion: nowadays quite a few academics write for the popular press. The *Sunday Express* also brought Taylor into contact with Beaverbrook himself, the beginning of a remarkable friendship. It was remarkable because of the element of hero-worship Taylor showed for the man who, by all accounts, was one of the most ruthless pirates of the press world. Both men, though, in their different ways, were dissenters from Establishment viewpoints, and it seems that each recognized this in the other.

What really made Taylor a national figure was his exploitation of the new medium, television. In August 1950 he began to appear as a regular member of one of the early "chat shows", BBC's *In the News.* Against the other three panellists, all MPs, he proved a sparkling weekly debater; and when *In the News* was wound up after a couple of years he was soon invited back to a similar format on the programme *Free Speech,* which was broadcast from 1955 to 1959.

These television appearances, like some of Taylor's journalism, were considered rather vulgar by professional historians, but their impact on public consciousness can hardly be overestimated. As the first "telly don", Taylor was addressing, and apparently holding the interest of, millions of people — an audience no historian had ever reached before.

Taylor was always subsequently in demand as a media commentator, but perhaps the high point of his television stardom was the series of lectures he delivered, starting in 1957. Anyone who has watched one of these half-hour performances can only be amazed at the fact that they were invariably delivered without notes, looking directly into the camera, and equally invariably finished, all themes and arguments tidily wound up, exactly on time. Taylor claimed that he developed this ability giving wartime radio propaganda broadcasts to Germany, but even more astounding was the fact that he only made the decision on each programme's topic in the ten minutes or so that it took him to arrive at the studios by taxi.

All this productivity by no means hindered Taylor's academic output. In 1954 he published what many still agree is his most substantial and perhaps most enduring work, *The Struggle for Mastery in Europe 1848–1918.* This was a standard diplomatic history, which even today remains a useful quarry for insights into its period. Considering the imbalance which had marred *The Course of German History,* Taylor's even-handedness was commendable, although he had certainly not abandoned his belief in the tendency of Germany to dominate the European continent. In this *The Struggle for Mastery in Europe* was essentially a more sober attempt to underpin the central thesis of Taylor's previous book.

His biography of Bismarck, which appeared in 1955, was part of the same general effort, trying to place the nineteenth-century statesman within this context of continuity in German history. While acknowledging the clear difference between Bismarck and the likes of Hitler, Taylor made clear his conviction that the mere fact of German unification, coming when it did, was a destabilizing factor.

One of the most explicit keys to Taylor's view of himself was *The Trouble Makers,* in 1957. This was the published form of his 1956 Ford Lectures on the Radical critics of British foreign policy. In discussing the ideas which motivated men like Tom Paine, Cobden and Bright, Taylor was identifying strongly with such awkward outsiders. *The Trouble Makers* remained his own favourite among his works, and exerted a considerable influence on a younger generation of historians.

Taylor's record and reputation were such, by 1957, that there was general astonishment when Prime Minister Macmillan appointed not him, but his colleague Hugh Trevor-Roper (later Lord Dacre) as Regius Professor of History at Oxford. Speculation at the time naturally assumed that it was Taylor's down-market journalism and televison connections which made him ineligible in the eyes of the Establishment. Namier, who advised Macmillan on the appointment, reportedly told Taylor he would support him if he gave up writing for the *Sunday Express,* which led to a breach between the two men.

Taylor himself later said that he would not in any case have accepted an appointment from someone, like Macmillan, "stained with the blood of Suez". But the most probable explanation for overlooking Taylor was that he was a notorious Labour supporter and advocate of nuclear disarmament.

Despite being elected to the British Academy in 1956, Taylor's radicalism was in fact still very much in evidence in the late 1950s. He was, as indicated, a passionate critic of the Suez intervention of 1956. His most heartfelt political involvement at this time, however, was with the Campaign for Nuclear Disarmament (CND), which he helped launch. At the founding meeting in the Central Hall, Westminster in 1958, Taylor was one of the key speakers, alongside Bertrand Russell, Michael Foot and others. He gave his audience a graphic account, in his best lecture-hall manner, of the devastation wrought by an H-bomb. "Is there anyone here who would want to do this to another human being?" he asked, to a hushed silence. "Then why are we making the damned thing?"

Three years later Taylor produced his most controversial book, *The Origins of the Second World War.* The storm this provoked was understandable in view of the interpretations some critics placed on it, but much of this was mistaken. The book's basic, radical claim is summed up tersely enough in the statement that "the war of 1939, far from being premeditated, was a mistake, the result on both sides of diplomatic blunders." Hitler is portrayed as "an ordinary German statesman in the tradition of Stresemann and Brüning", who did not possess a "blueprint for aggression", but instead seized upon events with brilliant opportunism. His aim throughout was revision of the Versailles settlement of 1919, and the logical outcome of this revision would be German hegemony in Europe.

Some of the reactions to *Origins* verged on the hysterical. Historian and critic A.L. Rowse denounced its "frivolity", and more than one reviewer warned that it would bring comfort to neo-Nazis with its "whitewash" of Hitler. The most damaging criticism to begin with came from Trevor-Roper, who pointed to the standard proofs of Hitler's long-term aggressive intent, such as *Mein Kampf.* Trevor-Roper also took Taylor's references to the "inevitability" of German hegemony in the inter-war period as a justification of Soviet hegemony in the post-war period.

None of these immediate attacks stuck. Taylor was patently not trying to whitewash Hitler, indeed the charge in view of his published record was ludicrous. Nor was he entirely ignoring the traditional evidence for Hitler's aggression. What he was doing was to put Hitler in context, by pointing out that, in foreign policy as opposed to domestic affairs, Hitler was more rational than had hitherto been admitted, and more representative of German opinion than was generally accepted by 1961. Hitler was part of the continuity of German history, but he was also an actor on the historical stage, obliged to deal with emergent circumstances.

Where Taylor was more vulnerable was in his reluctance to consider the ideological, social and economic imperatives behind Hitler's foreign policy. As much recent research has shown, this played its part in the calculations of the National Socialist leadership as much as traditional power-political considerations.

The Origins of the Second World War, while brilliantly presented, also exhibited Taylor's weaknesses. It was epigrammatic to a fault, and many of its paradoxes, as the subsequent uproar showed, were all too easily misunderstood. It seems appropriate to apply to Taylor the criticism he himself once levelled in an essay at the philosopher Nietzsche: "As he exposes himself to perversions, he has the air of the elderly woman anxiously demanding of the enemy officer: 'When does the raping begin?'"

Nevertheless, the fact that so much debate and so much wide-ranging and novel research has been prompted by this one book is perhaps sufficient tribute to its value. It remains the ultimate vindication of Taylor as Trouble Maker. The controversy may or may not have influenced the termination of his appointment as a lecturer in 1963, but he stayed on as a fellow of Magdalen College.

Critics have differed widely as to the merits of his last major academic work, *English History 1914-1945.* While some consider it his best, others voted it too much a personal account of Taylor's own era, although it was as usual a beguiling introduction to the period.

In 1972 appeared his biography of Beaverbrook, a labour of love in which many who had known the press magnate failed to recognize him. Taylor had been made honorary director of the Beaverbrook Library in 1967, a post he held until 1975. He continued to produce a wide variety of work, much of it aimed at a decidedly popular market, such as the magazine series on the twentieth century, and a number of illustrated potted histories.

In 1980 he resigned his membership of the British Academy in protest at the explusion of Anthony Blunt, the exposed Soviet spy. Taylor's robust view, which was echoed by many, was that it was Blunt's achievement as an art historian, and not his political background, which ought to determine his status within the Academy.

Taylor's private life rather mirrored the controversies of his academic career. He was three times married, and had six children by two of his wives, but only seems to have achieved lasting happiness with the last of the three, the Hungarian historian Eva Haraszti. His essential shyness, which contrasted so sharply with his public personality, ensured that not much is known about his personal life behind what he and a few friends have chosen to reveal.

The real test of Taylor's importance as an historian is not which of his books will be still read 50 or a hundred years from now. Few historians pass that test, since every generation writes its own history. What made Taylor a great historian was rather his ability to communicate his own interest in history to vastly greater numbers of people than most academic historians ever dream of. That some of the conclusions pointed to were misleading cannot detract from the magnitude of that achievement.

Born Alan John Percivale Taylor. **Parents** Percy Lees, cotton merchant, and Constance (Thompson) Taylor. **Marriages** 1) Margaret Adams, 1931 (divorced 1951); 2) Eve Crosland, 1951 (divorced 1974); 3) Eva Haraszti, historian, 1978. **Children** Giles, Sebastian, Amelia and Sophia, from first marriage; Crispin and Daniel, from second marriage. **Education** Downs School, Colwall, 1917–19; scholarship, Bootham School, York, 1919–24; scholar, Oriel College, Oxford, first-class honours in modern history, BA, 1927, MA, 1932; studied with A.F. Pribram, University of Vienna, 1928–30. **Military service** Home Guard, 1939–45. **Career** Lecturer in history, Manchester University, 1930–38; book reviewer and editorial writer, *Manchester Guardian,* from 1931; tutor in history, Magdalen College, Oxford, 1938–53, fellow, 1938–76, university lecturer in international history, 1953–63; first radio broadcast, 1942; first television appearance, *In the News,* BBC, 1950 first television lecture series, 1957; honorary director, Beaverbrook Library, 1967–75. **Related activities** Memorial lectures: Ford, Oxford University,

1955–56, Raleigh, British Academy, 1959, Leslie Stephen, Cambridge University, 1961–62, Creighton, University of London, 1973, Andrew Lang, St Andrews University, 1974, Romanes, Oxford University, 1981; visiting professor of history, Bristol University, 1976–78; columnist: *Sunday Pictorial,* 1951–53, *Daily Herald,* 1953–56, *Sunday Express,* from 1956; contributor: *The Observer*, *New Statesman*, *Guardian*, *The Times Literary Supplement*, *New York Review of Books*, *The Listener*, *London Review of Books*. **Offices and memberships** President, City Music Society; member, Historical Association; founder/member, Campaign for Nuclear Disarmament, 1957. **Awards and honours** Commemorative scholarship, Bootham School, 1924; Rockefeller fellowship in social sciences, 1929–30; fellow, British Academy, 1956–80, resigned in protest, 1980; honorary DCL, New Brunswick University, 1961; honorary DUniv, York University, 1970; honorary fellow: Magdalen College, Oxford, 1976, Oriel College, Oxford, 1980; honorary DLitt: Bristol University, 1978, Warwick University, 1981, Manchester University, 1982; honorary doctorate, University of East Anglia; foreign honorary member, American Academy of Arts and Sciences, 1985; honorary member, Yugoslavian Academy of Sciences, 1985; honorary member, Hungarian Academy of Sciences, 1986. **Television** (includes) *In the News,* 1950; *Free Speech,* 1955–59; *The Russian Revolution* (script), 1959; *The Twenties,* 1962; *Men of the 1860s,* 1963; *The War Lords,* 1976; *How Wars Begin,* 1978; *Revolutions and Revolutionaries,* 1978; *How Wars End.* **Publications** *The Italian Problem in European Diplomacy, 1847–1849,* 1934; (editor) *Struggle for Supremacy in Germany, 1859–1866* by Heinrich Friedjung, 1935; *Germany's First Bid for Colonies, 1884–1885,* 1938; *The Habsburg Monarchy, 1815–1918,* 1941, revised as *The Habsburg Monarchy, 1809–1918,* 1949; *The Course of German History,* 1945; (editor with R. Reynolds) *British Pamphleteers,* volume two, 1948–51; (editor with Alan Louis Charles Bullock) *A Select List of Books on European History, 1815–1914,* 1949; *From Napoleon to Stalin,* 1950; *Rumours of Wars,* 1952; *The Struggle for Mastery in Europe, 1848–1918,* 1954; *Bismarck: The Man and the Statesman,* 1955; (editor with Richard Pares) *Essays Presented to Sir Lewis Namier,* 1956; *The Trouble Makers; Dissent Over Foreign Policy, 1792–1939,* 1957; *Lloyd George,* 1961; *The Origins of the Second World War,* 1961; *The First World War,* 1963, in US as *An Illustrated History of the First World War,* 1964; *Politics in Wartime,* 1964; *English History, 1914–1945,* 1965; *From Sarajevo to Potsdam,* 1966; *From Napoleon to Lenin,* 1966; (editor) *The Abdication of King Edward VIII* by Lord Beaverbrook, 1966; *Europe: Grandeur and Decline,* 1967; (author of introduction) *1848; The Opening of an Era* edited by F. Fejto, 1967; (with others) *Churchill Revised: A Critical Assessment,* 1969; *War By Timetable,* 1969; (editor) *Lloyd George: Twelve Essays,* 1971; (editor) *Lloyd George: a Diary by Frances Stevenson,* 1971; *Beaverbrook,* 1972; (editor) *Off the Record: Political Interviews, 1933–43* by W.P. Corzier, 1973; *The Second World War: An Illustrated History,* 1975; (editor) *My Darling Pussy: The Letters of Lloyd George and Frances Stevenson,* 1975; *Essays in English History,* 1976; *The Last of Old Europe,* 1976; *The War Lords,* 1977; *The Russian War,* 1978; *How Wars Begin,* 1979; *Revolutions and Revolutionaries,* 1980; *Politicians, Socialism and Historians,* 1980; *A Personal History* (autobiography), 1983; *An Old Man's Diary,* 1984; *How Wars End,* 1985. **Cause of death** Parkinson's disease, at age 84. **Further reading** Martin Gilbert (editor), *A Century of Conflict, 1850–1950: Essays for A.J.P. Taylor,* 1966; W. Roger Louis (editor), *The Origins of the Second World War: A.J.P. Taylor and his Critics,* 1972; Alan Sked and Chris Cook, *Crisis and Controversy: Essays in Honour of A.J.P. Taylor,* 1976; *Journal of Modern History,* March 1977; Chris Wrigley, *A.J.P. Taylor: A Complete Annotated Bibliography and Guide to His Historical and Other Writings,* 1980; Eva Haraszti, *A Life with Alan,* 1987.

DENYS WATKINS-PITCHFORD

British Writer and Illustrator

***Born* Lamport, Northamptonshire, 25 July 1905**

***Died* Oxford, England, 8 September 1990**

Denys Watkins-Pitchford, known as "BB", wrote and illustrated almost 60 books, the majority for children. He was also the author of sporting books such as *Confessions of a Carp Fisher,* and of books on shooting, such as *Tide's Ending* and *Dark Estuary,* all of which are considered to be classics in their field.

Watkins-Pitchford spent his childhood and most of his adult life in Northamptonshire, a largely unspoilt rural county. Both his love of nature and his artistic skill were evident from an early age. At 15 he entered Northampton School of Art from where he won a travelling scholarship to Paris. He completed his studies as a post-graduate at London's Royal College of Art. A long-standing teaching post (1930–47), at Rugby School for boys, allowed the young author to develop without financial constraint. Long school holidays also gave this enthusiastic sportsman and naturalist time to pursue his main hobbies of wildfowl shooting and fishing.

As a children's author he achieved fame with the delightfully original story about gnomes, *The Little Grey Men,* published in 1942, and winner of the Carnegie Medal the following year. The author recalls in his memoirs, *A Child Alone,* that as a little boy he definitely saw a "Being" or a gnome: "It had a round, very red bearded face about the size of a crabapple". The illustrations in this book and in his many others (he also illustrated over 30 works by other authors), demonstrate his ability to suggest diversity of nature in fairly simple black-and-white images. He employed the scraperboard technique which involves creating a picture from scraping a white surface to reveal black lines.

Among the author's other successful children's books are two earlier works, *Wild Lone,* about a fox surviving in hunting country, and *Sky Gipsy: The Story of a Wild Goose,* the very evocative tale of a bird's life and travels. Watkins-Pitchford was particularly fascinated by wild geese, indeed his pseudonym, BB, is taken from the type of shot used to kill these birds. It is perhaps contradictory, especially to the city-dweller, that this sensitive man could admire the beauty and skill of a creature and yet enjoy shooting it down. However, Watkins-Pitchford saw no conflict here, believing man's rightful role to be that of hunter; for him, sporting and wildlife interests were interlinked. Indeed, he steadfastly worked to preserve the Purple Emperor butterfly from near extinction.

Watkins-Pitchford made no distinction in his writing style for children or for adults. His writing is always full of enthusiasm for all aspects of the natural world, managing to be informative as well as poetic — his illustrations particularly convey the romantic and mysterious side of nature. Some of his most exciting and evocative passages appear in books for the younger reader. For example, in *The Pool of the Black Witch* he describes the excitement felt by a young boy as he pursues the elusive trout: "There, cuddled close under the overhanging ledge, was a monstrous fish! He could see the little dark dots on its silver side, the round staring eye, the gently working gills which shone palely as they went in and out like bellows."

Watkins-Pitchford writes like an artist painting his subject. His books also convey this author's obvious pleasure in his chosen career, indeed he said, "I write because I find it an intensely rewarding thing, and it is fun to illustrate my own books." This is a typically modest statement from one of the twentieth century's most successful sporting and children's writers in the English language.

Watkins-Pitchford's private life was generally happy and fulfilled. However, his otherwise idyllic childhood was overshadowed by the death of his elder brother and later he and his wife Cecily (whom he had married in 1939) suffered the ultimate blow when their son Robin died when only seven. It appeared that he had fallen heir to the family curse, which had been laid upon his father when the latter was a young unmarried clergyman. The Reverend Watkins-Pitchford had refused alms to a beggar when travelling in the Holy Land, the beggar swore that his first-born son would die young and that his second son's first male child would also die. Watkins-Pitchford bore this hideous heritage — and the loss of his wife in 1974 — with stoicism. Little of this personal grief ever came to the surface either in his writing or in his manner.

Watkins-Pitchford always found comfort in his love of nature and he was always delighted by the popularity of his work, welcoming visitors to the end of his days. He always prefaced his books with the following Celtic gravestone inscription: "The wonder of the world, the beauty and the power, the shapes of things, their colours, lights and shades; these I saw. Look ye also while life lasts." No other words could better describe this man's outlook and beliefs. He was loved and admired by all those close to him and although official recognition came late in life (he received the MBE in 1989) he will surely be remembered and enjoyed through his delightful books.

Born Denys James Watkins-Pitchford. **Pseudonyms** BB; Michael Traherne. **Parents** Walter, cleric and composer, and Edith Elizabeth (Wilson) Watkins-Pitchford. **Marriage** Cecily Mary Adnitt, 1939 (died 1974). **Children** Angela and Robin (deceased). **Education** Northampton School of Art, 1920; travelling scholarship to study in Paris, 1924; Royal College of Art, 1924–25; associate, Royal College of Art, 1926–28. **Military service** City of London Yeomanry Royal Horse Artillery, 1926–29; captain, Home Guard, 1939–45. **Career** Art master, Rugby School, 1930–47; first book published, *The Sportsman's Bedside Book,* 1937; freelance author and illustrator, from 1947; *The Little Grey Men* adapted for television, 1975; *Brendon Chase* adapted for television, 1980. **Related activities** Contributor: *Country Life, Field, Shooting Times.* **Offices and memberships** Fellow, Royal Society of Arts. **Awards and honours** Library Association Carnegie Medal, 1943; honorary MA, Leicester University, 1986; Member of the Order of the British Empire, 1989. **Juvenile fiction publications written and illustrated** (As BB) *Wild Lone,* 1938; *Sky Gipsy: The Story of a Wild Goose,* published in US as *Manka, The Sky Gipsy,* 1939; *The Little Grey Men,* 1942; *Brendon Chase,* 1944; *Down the Bright Stream,* 1948; *The Forest of Boland Light Railway,* 1955, published in US as *The Forest of the Railway,* 1957; *Monty Woodpig's Caravan,* 1957; *Ben the Bullfinch,* 1957; *Wandering Wind,* 1957, published in US as *Bill Badger and the Wandering Wind,* 1981; *Alexander,* 1957; *Monty Woodpig and His Bumblebuzz Car,* 1958; *Mr Bumstead,* 1958; *The Wizard of Boland,* 1959; *Bill Badger's Winter Cruise,* 1959; *Bill Badger and the Pirates,* 1960; *Bill Badger's Finest Hour,* 1961; *Bill Badger's Whispering Reeds Adventure,* 1962; *Lepus the Brown Hare,* 1962; *Bill Badger's Big Mistake,* 1963; *Bill Badger and the Big Store Robbery,* 1967; *The Whopper,* 1967; *At the Back o' Ben Dee,* 1968; *Bill Badger's Voyage to the World's End,* 1969; *The Tyger Tray,* 1971; *The Pool of the Black Witch,* 1974; *Lord of the Forest,* 1975; (with A.L.E. Fenton and A. Windsor-Richards) *Stories of the Wild,* 1976; (with A. Windsor-Richards) *More Stories of the Wild,* 1977; *Bill Badger and the Secret Weapon,* 1983. **Other juvenile publications** *Meeting Hill: BB's Fairy Book,* 1948; *The Wind in the Wood,* 1952; *The Badgers of Bearshanks,* 1961; *The Pegasus Book of the Countryside,* 1964. **Adult publications written and illustrated** (As BB, unless otherwise indicated) *The Idle Countryman,* 1943; *The Wayfaring Tree,* 1945; *A Stream in Your Garden,* 1948; (as Michael Traherne) *Be Quiet and Go A-Angling,* 1949; *Confessions of a Carp Eater,* 1950; *Tide's Ending,* 1950; *Letters from Compton Deverell,* 1950; *Dark Estuary,* 1953; (with others) *Five More Stories* (short stories), 1957; *A Carp Water: Wood Pool and How to Fish It,* 1958; *The Autumn Road to the Isles,* 1959; *The White Road Westwards,* 1961; *September Road to Caithness and the Western Sea,* 1962; *The Summer Road to Wales,* 1964; *A Summer on the Nene,* 1967; *Recollections of a 'longshore Gunner,* 1976; *A Child Alone: The Memoirs of BB* (autobiography), 1978; *Ramblings of a Sportsman-Naturalist,* 1979;

The Naturalist's Bedside Book, 1980; *The Quiet Fields,* 1981; *Indian Summer,* 1984; *The Best of BB,* 1985; *Fisherman's Folly,* 1987. **Publications edited** *The Sportsman's Bedside Book,* 1937; *The Countryman's Bedside Book,* 1941; *The Fisherman's Bedside Book,* 1945; *The Shooting Man's Bedside Book,* 1948. **Works illustrated** *Sport in Wildest Britain* by H.V. Prichard, 1936; *Winged Company* by R.G. Walmsley, 1940; *England is a Village* by Clarence H. Warren, 1940; *Southern English* by Eric Benfield, 1942; *Narrow Boat* by L.T.C. Rolt, 1944; *Red Vagabond* by Gerald D. Adams, 1946; *It's My Delight* by Brian V. Fitzgerald, 1947; *Philandering Angler* by Arthur Applin, 1948; *A Sportsman Looks at Eire* by J.B. Drought, 1949; *Landmarks* by Arthur G. Street, 1949; *Fairy Tales of Long Ago* edited by Mabel C. Carey, 1952; *The White Foxes of Gorfenletch* by Henry S. Tegner, 1954; *The Secret of Orra* by Elfrida Vipont, 1957; *The Long Night* by William Mayne, 1958; *Thirteen O'Clock* by William Mayne, 1960; *Vix* by Arthur Richards, 1960; *Birds of the Lonely Lake* by Arthur Richards, 1961; *Beasts of the North Country* by Henry S. Tegner, 1961; *Prince Prigio and Prince Ricardo* by Andrew Lang, 1961; *The Rogue Elephant* by Arthur Catherall, 1962; *The Cabin in the Woods* by Arthur Richards, 1963; *Red Ivory* by Arthur Catherall, 1964; *The Wild White Swan* by Arthur Richards, 1965; *To Do With Birds* by Henry S. Tegner, 1965; *Jungle Rescue* by Arthur Catherall, 1967; *Granny's Wonderful Chair* by Frances Browne, 1963; *King Todd* by Norah Burke, 1963; *The Lost Princess* by George MacDonald, 1965; *Where Vultures Fly* by Gerald Summers, 1974. **Cause of death** Undisclosed, at age 85. **Further reading** *Twentieth-Century Children's Writers,* 1989.

PATRICK WHITE

Australian Writer

***Born* London, England, 28 May 1912**

***Died* Sydney, Australia, 30 September 1990**

After Patrick White died, few of the Australian news outlets dared report the fact for several hours. His executors were no help; his will forbade them to tell the media of his death until he was safely six feet under.

No doubt the frequently cantankerous novelist would have enjoyed the spectacle of journalists and broadcasters rushing around trying to confirm his demise. For although Patrick White is publicly recognized worldwide (and publicly acclaimed through the award of the Nobel Prize in 1973) as one of Australia's greatest novelists, he remained throughout his life an outsider, an eccentric — and a man of many contradictions.

The manner — or at least the place — of his birth was the first of these. Although a fourth-generation Australian, he was born, "by chance" as he put it, in London during his parents' two-year wedding journey to Europe. They returned to Australia when he was six months old and he spent the next dozen years mainly on sheep and cattle ranches in New South Wales. "Whatever has come since," he wrote in an early autobiographical sketch, "I feel that the influences and impressions of this strange, dead landscape predominate." In 1925 he was sent back to England, to Cheltenham College, "that expensive prison", where he spent four years, "learning very little, except from my own private reading, and detesting everything to do with the educational system". When he returned to Australia — he preferred "the harsh, burnt-out quality of the Australian landscape to the lush greenery of England" — he found he had become a stranger there: "I had acquired too much European veneer, and was too young and inexperienced to practise tolerance." This sense of being an outsider in his own country remained with him; he was always a "colonial" in England and a "Pom" in the Australian sheep stations on which he worked for the next few years.

During this period he began on what he later described as his immature novels. Then he returned to England, to King's College, Cambridge, as an undergraduate and here, for the first time, he made "human contacts". He also acquired a taste for the theatre and wrote both revue material and sketches.

Indeed, Patrick White's first ambition was to be a playwright; and he had considerable success in this field. Two of his comedies were staged in Sydney in the 1930s and *The Ham Funeral* (1948) was produced in Australia in 1961. Three plays were written in 1961 to 1962 — *The Season at Sarsaparilla*, *A Cheery Soul* and *Night on Bald Mountain* — all turning a savage, satirical eye on suburbia. These were followed by four later plays: *Big Toys*, *The Night the Prowler* (a screenplay), *Netherwood* and *Signal Driver,* which portray the hypocrisies of modern Australian society. His plays were often boldly experimental; and their themes were close to the subjects he explored at greater length and with greater complexity in his novels. They have been of central importance in the development of Australian drama since the 1950s.

But it was a novel that launched his literary career in 1939, and it is, of course, as a novelist that he achieved the greatest international recognition. *Happy Valley* was a caustic story of the solitariness in social relationships of a small community in the isolated outback: and it won the Australian Literature Society's Gold Medal. He followed it with *The Living and the Dead,* an equally bitter (though considerably less successful) study of degradation and despair in London's Bloomsbury.

By the time *The Living and the Dead* was published, White was serving in the RAF in World War II. For a time he was stationed in Greece — a country in which he developed a special interest through his long friendship with Manoly Lascaris, a Greek. This interest only added to his ambiguous sense of nationality. "I'm a mongrel", he declared later. "I'm part Australian, part European, with a soft spot for England." Nonetheless, after the war and a short spell in America, he decided to settle in New South Wales. Here, on a former duck farm, and in the company of Manoly Lascaris, he bred goats and dogs, cultivated olives and citrus fruits and lived "more or less" off his own produce. He was also writing his first major novel, *The Aunt's Story.* This met with a mixed reception, but most critics recognized White's ability to evoke the mental processes of inarticulate and "abnormal" people — the kind of people who were to continue to fascinate him and to recur over and over in his work. The novel is an account, half-surrealistic and visionary, of the painful flowering of Australian maiden aunt Theodora Goodman, who pursues Reality: "I shall strip myself, the onion-folds of prejudice, till standing naked though conscious I see myself complete or else consumed."

The Tree of Man established more firmly his unique fictional territory — a blend of realistic detail and symbolic character. The book is a saga of Australian pioneering days in which ritual trials of fire, flood, storm and drought shape the lives of Stan and Amy Parker, as do the seasons and the normal cycle of youth and old age. White wanted to suggest, "every possible aspect of life, through the lives of an ordinary man and woman. But at the same time to discover the extraordinary behind the ordinary and the mystery and poetry which alone could make bearable the lives of such people." Stan Parker, like all White's main characters, is a visionary searching for the meaning and the unity of life; he is granted his vision, but at the price of isolation and loneliness.

Voss, published in 1957, takes his epic theme further. It is ostensibly an historical fiction based on the life of the German explorer, Leichardt, who was lost in the centre of Australia in 1848. But, for the eponymous central character, the realm explored turns into one of religion and the voyage itself becomes a modernistic investigation into the heart of darkness. A man of overweening pride and ambition, Voss eventually approaches a sense of divinity only when humbled through suffering; he finds that "true knowledge only comes of death by torture in the country of the mind."

By this point White was recognized as Australia's leading novelist. He had also begun his painful search for what he called "some meaning and design". Although it baffled many readers, his next book, *Riders in the Chariot,* was generally considered a probing study of mystical experience. It had four highly eccentric central characters: an epileptic spinster living in a decrepit mansion called Xanadu; a Jewish refugee from Nazism; an Aboriginal artist; and a compassionate washerwoman married to an alcoholic. It contained, too, a scathing, satirical attack on the folk of Sarsaparilla (based on a suburb of Sydney) and was not, therefore, an easy novel for the Australian public to accept.

As White's disillusionment with the present grew and his faith in his country's future diminished, he portrayed more and more the pursuit of integrity as the occupation of the fringe-dwellers of society. *The Solid Mandala* was again set in the vapid and malicious town of Sarsaparilla. In this novel it is the "defective" one of two twin brothers who is given insight into the totality symbolized by the mandala.

Riders in The Chariot had introduced Alf Dubbo, the Aboriginal artist, and in White's later years he became an outspoken advocate of Aboriginal rights. He was also a collector of both Aboriginal and modern Australian art. He was fascinated by painting — he said that he wanted to give his novels the texture of music and the sensuousness of paint. So it was inevitable that he should at some time choose to write a novel about a painter; but his savage view of the artist in *The Vivisector* as a voyeuristic cause of suffering in others was the subject — as increasingly with his writing — of much controversy.

As has been indicated, White was never an easy writer for Australians to come to terms with. But the technical brilliance of *The Eye of the Storm,* together with its deeply moving insights into the final days of an elderly woman, consolidated his achievement as a writer. This was recognized by the award of the Nobel Prize for Literature in the same year. In awarding the prize, the Academy said he had wrestled with the English language to take it almost beyond the limits of its expressive power. It added that he had given Australia "an authentic voice that carries across the world".

Characteristically, White later said of the Nobel Prize, "I was really rather horrified. I would have liked to refuse it because of all the publicity it made in this childish country." For — when he was not fulminating about the ghastliness of modern Australian life — White was a reclusive person, spending his time cooking and housekeeping and gardening.

A Fringe of Leaves, about a woman who discovers herself through living with the Aborigines, and *The Twyborn Affair* continued to develop his theme of the integrity of the outcast and the artist coupled with a savage attack on the West's consumer society.

White said that he saw his task as that of civilizing Australia. In the 1970s he took a more overt approach to this goal, becoming increasingly involved in left-wing politics and local Sydney affairs. When the Governor General dismissed the elected Federal Labour government of Gough Whitlam in 1975 he became a convinced republican. In 1976 he returned his Order of Australia Award and campaigned vigorously for a new Constitution. Though a supporter of the Labour Party for many years, he made, in 1984, an outspoken attack on Mr Bob Hawke's Labour government which he stigmatized as hypocritical and cynical — and began voting Communist instead. In 1988 he made headlines with some decidedly uncomplimentary remarks on television about a visit to Australia by the Prince and Princess of Wales on the occasion of Australia's bicentenary celebrations. He then boycotted the celebrations, describing the organizers as "vulgar Philistines" and demanded that "quite a bit" of Australia should be returned to the Aborigines. Indeed, his politics and his open homosexuality made him something of a cult figure among radical young Australians.

They also confirmed his reputation as an eccentric. In his personal life he was equally outspoken and equally irascible. Wrote his second cousin, Peggy Garland, "He endeared himself to people without effort, always very friendly up to the point of disillusionment — when he became bitter and often quite bitchy. (When he once suggested that he ought to move from Sydney to Adelaide, 'the nicest town in Australia', he was told: 'There's no point — there would not be enough people for you to quarrel with.')"

More and more Patrick White concerned himself with exposing the shortcomings of society — and with self-revelation. His autobiography, *A Flaw in the Glass,* explains many of his difficulties, including his coming-to-terms with his homosexuality and is, according to one critic, "merciless", and "mean": to another a "woeful, if revealing affair". Yet in spite of this public airing of his private affairs he perversely expected "that newspapers should sit up and take notice when he was talking about books and should ignore him at other times."

But there was another side to this cantankerous and argumentative old man. He gave away the Nobel Prize money to endow an annual Patrick White Prize for authors who had received less attention than they deserved and was equally generous in his encouragement of young writers. According to Peggy Garland, "He once said to me in quite an angry voice, 'I am not a good man, but I do know about goodness': I think this was a predominant subject of all his writing. Some critics have seen him as being in search of God. I think he was agnostic but in search of the Good, of 'goodness'."

In the course of this quest — across an imaginative and symbolic landscape of epic proportions and through an almost schizophrenic impression of conflicting cultures — Patrick White brought a visionary, poetic and profoundly original power to the modern Australian novel.

Born Patrick Victor Martindale White. **Parents** Victor Martindale, landowner, and Ruth (Withycombe) White. **Education** Tudor House, Moss Vale, Australia, 1919–25; Cheltenham College, England, 1925–29; King's College, Cambridge, BA, 1935. **Emigration** Travelled in Europe and the US, lived in London, 1935–40; returned to Australia, 1948. **Military service** Intelligence officer, Middle East and Greece, Royal Air Force, 1940–45. **Career** First poems published, 1930; wrote sketches for Herbert Farjeon's Gate revues; first novel published, *Happy Valley,* 1939. **Related activities** Contributor, *Australian Letters,* Volume One, 1958. **Awards and honours** Australian Literature Society Gold medal, 1939, 1956; Miles Franklin award, 1958, 1962; W.H. Smith Literary award, 1959; National Conference of Christians and Jews Brotherhood award, 1962; Nobel Prize for Literature, 1973; Companion, Order of Australia, 1975, returned 1976. **Novels** *Happy Valley,* 1939; *The Living and the Dead,* 1941; *The Aunt's Story,* 1948; *The Tree of Man,* 1955; *Voss,* 1957; *Riders in the Chariot,* 1961; *The Solid Mandala,* 1966; *The Vivisector,* 1970; *The Eye of the Storm,* 1973; *A Fringe of Leaves,* 1976; *The Twyborn Affair,* 1979; *Memoirs of Many in One,* 1986. **Short stories** *The Burnt Ones,* 1964; *The Cockatoos: Shorter Novels and Stories,* 1974; *A Cheery Soul and Other Stories,* 1983; *Three Uneasy Pieces,* 1987. **Plays** *Bread and Butter Women,* 1935; *The School for Friends,* 1935; *Return to Abyssinia,* 1947; *The Ham Funeral,* 1961; *The Season at Sarsaparilla,* 1962; *A Cheery Soul,* 1963; *Night on Bald Mountain,* 1964; *Four Plays,* 1966; *Big Toys,* 1977; *The Night the Prowler* (screenplay), 1977; *Signal Driver: Play for the Times,* 1983; *Netherwood,* 1983; *Shepherd on the Rocks,* 1983. **Verse** *Thirteen Poems,* 1930; *The Ploughman and Other Poems,* 1935. **Other** *Flaws in the Glass: A Self-Portrait* (autobiography), 1981; *Credo,* 1988. **Cause of death** Undisclosed, at age 78. **Further reading** Geoffrey Dutton, *Patrick White,* 1961; Robert F. Brissenden, *Patrick White,* 1966; Berry Argyle, *Patrick White,* 1967; Janette Finch, *A Bibliography of Patrick White,* 1966; G.A. Wilkes, *Ten Essays on Patrick White Selected from Southerly,* 1970; Patricia A. Morley, *The Mystery of Unity: Theme and Technique in the Novels of Patrick White,* 1972; Alan Lawson, *Patrick White,* 1974; Peter Beatson, *The Eye in the Mandala: Patrick White: A Vision of Man and God,* 1976; Ingmar Bjorksten, *Patrick White: A General Introduction,* 1976; William Walsh, *Patrick White's Fiction,* 1977; Ron E. Shepherd and Kirpal Singh (editors) *Patrick White: A Critical Symposium,* 1978; Manly Johnson, *Patrick White,* 1980; Brian Kiernan, *Patrick White,* 1980; A.M. McCulloch, *The Novels of Patrick White,* 1983; Mari-Ann Berg, *Aspects of Time, Ageing and Old Age in the*

Novels of Patrick White, 1939–1979, 1983; Peter Wolfe, *Laden Choirs: The Fiction of Patrick White,* 1983; John Colmer, *Patrick White,* 1984; John A. Weigel, *Patrick White,* 1984; *Contemporary Novelists,* 1986; *Contemporary Dramatists,* 1988; *Reference Guide to English Literature,* 1991.

OCTOBER

LOUIS ALTHUSSER

French Philosopher
Born **Birmandreis, Algeria, 16 October 1918**
Died **Yvelines, France, 22 October 1990**

The later career of Louis Althusser, although highly personal and idiosyncratic, and marred by a tragic conclusion, has frequently been taken as representative of the vicissitudes of Marxist thinking in European intellectual life since the mid–1960s. During his most productive period, represented by the theoretical and philosophical essays collected in *For Marx*, *Reading Capital* and *Lenin and Philosophy*, Althusser offered a reinvigoration of the traditional, orthodox, virtually moribund Marxism of the French Communist Party (of which he was a prominent member), in line with the comparable "structuralist" developments in other fields associated with Roland Barthes and Michel Foucault. Althusser's self-proclaimed "return to Marx" was profoundly influential on the French Left, and it soon discovered an intellectual following in Britain and the United States. Although some were suspicious that it might simply be a version of Stalinism revisited, Althusser's philosophical project remained at the centre of political and theoretical debate on the international Left for some time.

In a 1974 essay (in *Essays in Self-Criticism)*, he defined his central thesis as follows: "Marx founded a new science, the science of History...this scientific discovery is a theoretical and political event unprecedented in human history...this event is irreversible". The emphasis on "theory" and "science" here is highly characteristic, as is the confident intellectual excitement. Althusser forcefully rejected what he called "humanist" interpretations of Marx in favour of an altogether more rigorous and objective account. He argued that Marx's own thinking showed a decisive "epistemological break" around 1845, when he was working on *The German Ideology*. Whereas his earlier work had remained within the broad philosophical outlines laid down by Hegel and Feuerbach, thinking always of individualized human experience and relying on empirical analytic procedures, his later work showed a more austerely "scientific" approach, concerned with the functioning of society in the abstract. In *Capital* and in the Introduction to the *Grundrisse*, Althusser argued, the "real" Marx could be found, more concerned with the relations of production than with the lives of the producers; more concerned with the functioning of societies as a whole than with the alienated existence of the proletariat. Althusser's Marx is thus anti-humanist, anti-empiricist, anti-positivist, and anti-historicist. And yet amid all these disquieting negatives emerged a Marxist validation of theoretical procedures, and an opportunity for a purely rational and philosophical enquiry into the nature of society — an enquiry to become known as "structural Marxism".

Althusser's belief that knowledge was produced within theory led to his suggestive writings on ideology, most notably the 1969 essay "Ideology and Ideological State Apparatuses", an influential starting point for many left-wing literary critics of the 1970s. However, his idealist presentation, his reluctance to define his central terms, and his highly convoluted method of argument also attracted hostility from many more interventionist Marxists, who were less than happy with the dehumanizing features of Althusser's analysis, as well as by his apparent indifference to the more urgent questions of *praxis*. The account of his thinking in Leszek Kolakowski's *Main Currents of Marxism* is almost wholly dismissive, and in a powerful and provocative essay called *The Poverty of Theory* the British empiricist historian E. P. Thompson produced a devastatingly caustic and damaging critique of Althusser's pretensions to knowledge.

In Britain at least, Thompson's analysis was highly influential, and Althusser's intellectual reputation quickly began to decline. Not long after came the news that he had been confined to an asylum after confessing to killing his wife, the sociologist Hélène Rytmann. It had long been known that Althusser had suffered from depression, but this mental collapse signalled the end of his immediate influence. In retrospect, his attempt to provide a purely theoretical or philosophical justification for Marxist commitment seems brave and intense, but there can be no doubt that it remained excessively divorced from the sphere of everyday political activity. By providing an intellectual Marxism pure enough for academic respectability, Althusser lost touch with the humanist intensity and sense of injustice which all left-wing thought must retain. As a result, the occasion of his death allowed many commentators on the Right to see him as yet another idolator of the god that failed. However, even if the "Althusserian moment" has undoubtedly passed, the problems which he strove to encompass with theory cannot be dismissed, and his discussions of ideology and the state will come to be fruitfully re-examined.

Born Louis Althusser. **Marriage** Hélène Rytmann, sociologist (strangled by Althusser, 1980). **Education** École Normale Supérieure, Paris, Diplome d'Agrégé en Philosophie, 1948. **Military service** French Army, 1939–40; captured 1940, prisoner of war, 1940–45. **Career** Maître assistant agrégé, École Normale Supérieure, Paris, 1948–82; strangled his wife, Hélène Rytmann, 1980, homicide charge dropped due to insanity, 1981; inmate, psychiatric hospital, 1981–84. **Related activities** Director, Collection "Théorie", Editions Maspero, Paris, 1965–82. **Publications** *Montesquieu: La politique et l'histoire*, 1959, published in English as "Montesquieu: Politics and History" in *Politics and History: Montesquieu, Rousseau, Hegel and Marx*, 1972; "Contradiction and Overdetermination", 1962; (with E. Balibar and others) *Pour Marx*, 1965, published in English as *For Marx*, 1969; *Lire le Capital*, 1965, published in English as *Reading Capital*, 1970; *Lénine et la philosophie*, 1969, published in English as *Lenin and Philosophy and Other Essays*, 1971; *Eléments d'autocritique*, 1974, published in English as "Elements of Self-Criticism" in *Essays in Self-Criticism*, 1976; *Philosophie et philosophie spontanée des savants*, 1974. **Cause of death** Heart failure, at age 72. **Further reading** Miriam Glucksmann, *Structuralist Analysis in Contemporary Thought: A Comparison of the Theories of Claude Lévi-Strauss and Louis Althusser*, 1974; Leszek Kolakowski, *Main Currents of Marxism*, 1978; E. P. Thompson, *The Poverty of Theory*, 1978; Simon Clarke and others, *One-Dimensional Marxism: Althusser and the Politics of Culture*, 1980; William C. Dowling, *Jameson, Althusser, Marx: An Introduction to the Political Unconscious*, 1984; Steven B. Smith, *Reading Althusser: An Essay on Structural Marxism*, 1984; *Thinkers of the Twentieth Century*, 1987; Gregory Elliott, *Althusser: The Detour of Theory*, 1988; Alison Assiter, *Althusser and Feminism*, 1990.

JILL BENNETT

British Actress

Born **Penang, Straits Settlements, 24 December 1931**

Died **London, England, 4 October 1990**

Before she succeeded in committing suicide from a lethal dose of sleeping pills mixed with alcohol, Jill Bennett left written instructions that her friends should attend a party after her cremation at her own house in Britten Street, Chelsea, where cases of champagne would be waiting ready for them. Her explicit orders were that every drop should be drunk and nobody should be in a condition to leave the party, other than on their knees.

Jill Bennett, remembered as an "inimitable talent", was an unforgettable character for her audiences and friends. Described once as "immensely articulate, acidly funny and infinitely elegant", she was also someone who admitted to melancholy. Champagne was a staple anti-depressant to which she was addicted. "It deadens the pain", she said and once kept half-bottles refrigerated at the foot of her bed. Many people have tried to root out the cause of her periods of depression and appallingly low self-esteem but director Lindsay Anderson, with whom she worked since the 1960s, has said, "One of the most important things to remember is that she was an actress. There is a tendency to get tangled up in psychological debate, forgetting there is such a thing as an actress temperament. She had it."

Her extraordinary quality as an actress has been expressed by another friend, playwright Sean Mathias.

> She was an artist who needed to build slowly from within. The people she connected most deeply to were writers, painters and dancers whose dedication and isolation she understood. As I found when I directed her in Geraldine Sherman's *Expectations* at the New End [Theatre], she could express a passive sort of suffering with more compassion than any other actor alive today. Like her fashion mentor, Jean Muir, she was a craftsman; her work, when it was right, hung beautifully. She could carry words in the way she wore clothes, with finesse and simplicity.

Was her life tragic? She was born in Penang, an only child, to wealthy Scottish parents. Her father was taken captive by the invading Japanese, imprisoned and tortured so brutally that his health never recovered after the war. Young Jill escaped with her mother to England where she was expelled from the exclusive girls' school, Roedean, as she claimed, "for seducing a prefect". She attended the Royal Academy of Dramatic Art (RADA) in London, from which she was also expelled after two years, and then began her career as an actress. In 1949 she joined the company at the Shakespeare Memorial Theatre at Stratford-upon-Avon to play small parts, the best of which were Fleance in *Macbeth* and Bianca in *Othello*. The leading man in both plays was the tremendous star, Godfrey Tearle, 40 years her senior. Midway through the season she and Tearle began a passionate friendship which lasted until his death, four years later. In many respects this was the central relationship of her life. In her touching memoir about him, *Godfrey: A Special Time Remembered*, she wrote, "I know it was the easiest relationship I have ever had... He was one of the few men in my life who did not make me feel anxious." After appearing in productions at the St James Theatre at the invitation of Laurence Olivier, during 1950 and 1951, she struck out on her own and made a number of films including leading roles in *Moulin Rouge*, *Hell Below Zero* and *Lust for Life*. Director John Huston is reported to have specially made room for her in an already fully cast *Moulin Rouge* because he was so fascinated by her looks that he "wanted to put her face on the screen". She appeared at the Lyric Theatre, Hammersmith, in 1959 in a double bill by Willis Hall whom she later married; and it was he who introduced her to the world of the Royal Court Theatre where she was to do much of her best work. In 1964 she appeared as the Countess in John Osborne's *A Patriot for Me*, and in 1968 Osborne wrote *Time Present* for her which was largely based on her early relationship with Godfrey Tearle. This was the role of her career and her performance duly won her the *Evening Standard* Best Actress of the Year Award.

In 1968 she married John Osborne. It was her second marriage and his fourth. She appeared in several more of his plays as well as scoring an immense success in 1972 in his adaptation of *Hedda Gabler*. The role of Hedda, as one critic wrote, "exactly suited her talent for expressing a quivering sense of insecurity disguised by outwardly invincible aggressiveness. She was quite simply the most convincing Hedda I have ever seen." Her marriage to Osborne came to a bitter end in 1977 and she never married again. She was quoted as saying, "Never marry a man who hates his mother, because he will end by hating you."

The failure of this marriage meant a great personal loss for Jill Bennett. Among other things she was forced to live alone again, which she never liked, and without children (she had had two miscarriages during her marriage to Osborne). The future must have looked very bleak. However, she eventually recovered her essential toughness and courage and went on to give many more brilliant performances in the theatre, on television and in films. She had just completed her best part for many years in Bernardo Bertolucci's film of Paul Bowles's *The Sheltering Sky* in which she gave a very remarkable performance, before she died.

Her death prompted a chorus of admiration and numerous recollections of her own pithy sayings in attempts to recapture the irreplaceable sparkiness of her character. The roles for which she will be remembered most particularly are those she created in the Osborne plays of the 1960s and 1970s, though her mannered elegance on television and in film will also have a lasting place. The last word on Jill Bennett should come from Sarah Bernhardt, Queen of the nineteenth-century French stage. This quote from *Advice Particular* was found typed on a crumpled scrap of paper in Jill Bennett's handbag, after she had died,

> You should live for those who know and appreciate you, who judge and absolve you and for whom you have love and indulgence. The rest is merely the CROWD from whom one can only expect fleeting emotions, good or bad, which leave no grace. One should hate very little because it's extremely fatiguing. One should despise much, forgive often, but never forget. Pardon doesn't bring with itself forgetfulness. At least not for me.

Born Nora Noel Jill Bennett. **Parents** James Randle, rubber planter, and Nora Adeline (Beckett) Bennett. **Marriages** 1) Willis Hall, playwright, 1962 (divorced 1965); 2) John Osborne, playwright, 1968 (divorced 1977). **Education** Tortington Park, Surrey; Priors Field; Roedean School, Brighton, East Sussex; Royal Academy of Dramatic Art, London, 1944–46. **Career** London stage début, *Now Barabbas*, 1947; repertory player, Croydon, 1948, Eastbourne, 1949; company member, Memorial Theatre, Stratford-upon-Avon, 1949–50; joined Laurence Olivier's company, 1950; film début, *Moulin Rouge*, 1953; first major role, Masha in *The Seagull*, 1956; Chichester season, 1979; co-founder, Off The Avenue, 1986. **Awards and honours** Best Actress Award for *Time Present*, *Evening Standard*, 1968, Variety Club, 1968. **Stage** (includes, all London unless otherwise indicated) *Macbeth*, Stratford-upon-Avon, 1949; *Othello*, Stratford-upon-Avon, 1949; *Captain Carvallo*, 1950; *Antony and Cleopatra*, 1951; *Caesar and Cleopatra*, 1951; *The Night of the Ball*, 1955; *The Seagull*, 1956; *The Bald Prima Donna*, 1956; *The Touch of Fear*, 1956; *Dinner with the Family*, 1957; *Last Day in Dreamland*, 1959; *A Glimpse of the Sea*,

1959; *Breakfast for One*, 1961; *The Showing-Up of Blanco Posnet*, 1961; *Androcles and the Lion*, 1961; *In Camera* (*Huis Clos*), Oxford, 1962; *Castle in Sweden*, 1962; *The Sponge Room*, 1962; *Squat Betty*, 1962; *The Love Game*, 1964; *A Patriot For Me*, 1965; *A Lily in Little India*, 1965; *Trelawney of the Wells*, 1966; *The Storm*, 1966; *Time Present*, 1968; *Three Months Gone*, 1970; *West of Suez*, 1971; *Hedda Gabler*, 1972; *Private Lives*, 1973; *The Letter*, 1973; *The End of Me Old Cigar*, 1975; *Loot*, 1975; *Watch It Come Down*, 1976; *Separate Tables*, 1977; *The Aspern Papers*, Chichester, 1978; *The Eagle Has Two Heads*, Chichester, 1978; *The Man Who Came to Dinner*, Chichester, 1979; *Hamlet*, 1980; *The Little Foxes*, Nottingham, 1981; *Dance of Death*, Manchester, 1983; *Advice*, 1985; *Infidelities*, 1986; *Mary Stuart*, Edinburgh, 1987; *Exceptions*, 1988. **Films** (include) *Moulin Rouge*, 1953; *Hell Below Zero*, 1954; *Lust for Life*, 1956; *The Criminal*, 1960; *The Skull*, 1965; *The Nanny*, 1965; *Inadmissible Evidence*, 1968; *The Charge of the Light Brigade*, 1968; *Julius Caesar*, 1970; *I Want What I Want*, 1971; *Mister Quilp*, 1975; *Full Circle*, 1977; *For Your Eyes Only*, 1981; *Britannia Hospital*, 1982; *Lady Jane*, 1985; *Hawks*; *The Sheltering Sky*, 1990. **Television** (includes) *The Heiress*; *The Three Sisters*; *Design for Living*; *The Parachute*; *Rembrandt*; *Almost a Vision*; *The Old Crowd*; *Poor Little Rich Girls*; *Paradise Postponed*. **Publication** (With Suzanne Goodwin) *Godfrey: A Special Time Remembered*, 1983. **Cause of death** Suicide by drug overdose, at age 58.

LEONARD BERNSTEIN

American Conductor and Composer

***Born* Lawrence, Massachusetts, 25 August 1918**

***Died* Manhattan, New York, 14 October 1990**

"Thank you for that fortepiano! I thank you, Sibelius thanks you! Now, Brasses, don't kill us. We're not deaf. You're grown up boys and girls..." There are thousands of musicians alive who'd admit it was often hard to keep a straight face when Bernstein stood before them on the podium. But they laughed with him and not at him. He had the ability to take liberties with the score; to distort it to the limits of self-indulgence and yet to convince the listener that that is how the music should sound. He said: "A conductor must make the orchestra love the music as much as he loves it." He was a figure of uninhibited emotional energy. He coaxed, he pleaded, he demanded. He looked to the skies for inspiration. He leapt into the air — when these tricks worked he elicited a response denied to all but the very greatest. His uninhibited character found natural expression above all in the works of Mahler, Shostakovitch and Beethoven at which he excelled. And when he conducted Stravinsky's *Symphony of Psalms*, he drew from the composer the single word "Wow!".

Conductor, pianist, composer, teacher, television host and celebrity, Bernstein was one of the outstanding musical figures of his age. Born Louis Bernstein to Russian-Jewish immigrant parents, Lenny, as he became universally known, had a prestigious education at the Boston Latin School and Harvard. The loan of a piano at the age of ten was crucial, and as a child he was moved to tears by the synagogue music and thought of becoming a rabbi. But it was the music that meant most and against parental opposition he decided to make it his career. His father's attempts to persuade him into the family hairdressing supply business were fruitless; Lenny would literally play the piano all night to make his point — the sort of exaggerated behaviour that was to become legendary.

At Harvard University he studied with Walter Piston. "There wasn't much to teach him", said Piston, "He knew it all by instinct." He also went to Philadelphia Curtis Institute to study conducting with the disciplinarian Fritz Reiner. But it was to his friend, the composer Aaron Copland (q.v.) that he felt he owed most. "I thought Aaron Copland was about the most sensational human being I'd ever come across...Whatever I wrote I showed Aaron. And that's the closest I came to studying composition with anyone."

Copland's represented a native American art music that had not really existed before and Bernstein became one of his most devoted followers and interpreters. Woe betide anyone who served that composer ill. He once wrote a review of a middle-aged lady pianist's attempt at Copland's *Piano Variations*, saying the piece was executed "with a butcher's lack of sensitivity, with the tone of a Woolworth xylophone and the half-heartedness of a professor in his 24th year of reading the same lecture."

Few conductors have enjoyed as meteoric a rise to stardom as Bernstein. Early in the 1940s he impressed Koussevitsky at the Tanglewood Summer Schools, and became his assistant. This gave him the chance to conduct in New York. Then in 1943 the conductor Rodzinski named Bernstein his assistant at the New York Philharmonic. "I asked God who to take and God said Bernstein." God was right, for Bernstein was an overnight sensation, as musicologist Peter Dickinson related in an obituary in the London *Independent*:

> At the time, Bernstein was looking forward to his first New York hearing as a composer. This was his song cycle called — of all things — *I Hate Music*. The family came to New York for the performance and there was a wild party, not including the family, after the successful recital. In spite of a warning that Bruno Walter might be too ill to conduct the next day and Rodzinski was snowbound the party went on til dawn. Soon after he got to bed, the telephone rang and Bernstein learnt that he did indeed have to conduct the concert that day at 3pm without rehearsal. He went to see Walter in bed, but was too much in the throes of a hangover to absorb much of what he said. Then he told his family to stay in town. It was front-page news that the unknown Leonard Bernstein had stood in brilliantly for Walter in a concert broadcast live to the whole country.

But he did not choose to dedicate himself to the life of the international star conductor. He would never listen to those who advised him to concentrate on one field — composing or conducting, serious music or popular. "I don't want to spend my life", he said, "as Toscanini did, studying and restudying the same 50 pieces of music. It would bore me to death. I want to compose, I want to play the piano. I want to write for Hollywood. I want to write symphonic music. I want to keep on trying to be, in the full sense of that wonderful word, a musician."

Many close to him believed that his real vocation was that of composer. His earlier works aroused excitement. The *Jeremiah Symphony* was chosen by the New York music critics as Best New American Orchestral Work of the season. In the same year he wrote his popular ballet, *Fancy Free*, which was choreographed by Jerome Robbins. That scenario developed into the musical *On the Town*, which ran on Broadway for more than 450 performances. This was followed by *Trouble in Tahiti*, the second symphony, *The Age of Anxiety*, *Candide*, *On the Waterfront* and of course, the sensationally successful Sondheim musical, *West Side Story*. An update of *Romeo and Juliet*, *West Side Story* was set in contemporary New York to tell a modern tale of racial gang warfare between the Puerto Rican "Sharks" and American "Jets". It deservedly became acknowledged as one of the greatest American musicals ever written — on a level with Gershwin.

In 1959 he became the first American to hold the post of sole conductor and music director of the New York Philharmonic, giving the orchestra the most exciting eleven years in its history. During his tenure, which lasted until 1969, the Philharmonic enjoyed a golden age, selling millions of recordings and holding a status among American ensembles it has never recaptured. He also had what he called a love affair with the Vienna Philharmonic, which will be remembered above all for some splendid recordings. When he resigned from the New York Philharmonic he was created laureate conductor for life.

In his later compositions Bernstein's ideas seemed to lack the intensity of the earlier works. Perhaps this came from his confused response to the works of the 1960s modernist composers. Certainly, Copland's decision to write in 12-tone serialism counted almost as a betrayal. Bernstein was now attempting to redress the balance from the popular idiom to the serious art work, often by treating religious themes, especially the reconciliation of Judaism and Christianity. This resulted in works like *The Chichester Psalms* and *The Mass* — a controversial attack on the Vietnam war and upholding of 1960s values, which was written for the opening of the John F. Kennedy Center in Washington, DC. Then came the *Kadish Symphony* of 1963 and *Halil*, of 1971, written in memory of a young Israeli flautist killed in Sinai that year, and the *Jubilee Games*, written for the fiftieth anniversary of the Israel Philharmonic, in 1986. While the emotional sincerity of the works is not in doubt there was a thinness about some of these later serious works — a lack of invention perhaps — that couldn't go unremarked. Perhaps his most enduring work, apart from *West Side Story*, will prove to be his last opera, *A Quiet Place*. A flop at its *première* in Houston in 1983, it has had several successful revivals. Its plot, like Strauss's *Intermezzo*, is thought to be a slice of autobiography.

A powerful communicator, Bernstein also instructed America with great imagination and flair in the *Omnibus* and *Young People's Concerts* on television in the 1950s and 1960s, and with his Harvard lectures broadcast on television and published as *The Unanswered Question* in 1976. From 1951 to 1956 he was on the staff of Brandeis University where he conducted the first performance of his one-act opera, *Trouble in Tahiti*. He was a tireless teacher, even, perhaps, at his best passing on his knowledge late at night, in company, with a glass or two of whisky.

It was always hard to separate the man from the showman. His politics were ostentatiously liberal and he supported civil rights, but this led to accusations of "champagne socialism". The opulent fund-raiser held for the Black Panthers in his New York flat in 1966 was sharply and famously lampooned by Tom Wolfe in his book *Radical Chic*. He was generally criticized for his flamboyant manner, his open bisexuality, the dandelions behind the ear. Yet when the Berlin Wall fell in 1989, Bernstein was on the scene straight away, leading heroic performances of Beethoven's *Ninth* and characteristically substituting *Freiheit* (freedom) for *Freude* (joy) in the choral finale.

His schedule was permanently ludicrously tight. During one stretch he conducted 25 concerts in 28 days. This reflected his breathless race through life. Far from slowing down as age advanced, he seemed to accelerate. But eventually the emphysema, from which he had suffered for decades, intervened, "God knows, I should be dead by now", he had said a couple of years earlier, "I smoke, I drink, I stay up all night. I'm overcommitted on all fronts. I was told if I didn't give up smoking I'd be dead by the age of 35. Well, I've beaten the rap." More than twice that age, at 72, death claimed him only five days after he announced his retirement. A few weeks earlier Ian Ball had met Bernstein for the first time in the cancer radiation centre, just after the great musician had learnt his disease was terminal. "He asked me what I was doing in those sterile halls and I put the same question to him. The reply, delivered with a dynamic upward thrust of the arms, was pure Bernstein: 'I'm involved in a new experiment with life!'"

Born Louis Bernstein. **Parents** Samuel J., hairdressing supplies wholesaler, and Jennie (Resnick) Bernstein. **Marriage** Felicia Montealegre Cohn, actress, 1951 (died 1978). **Children** Jamie, Nina and Alexander. **Education** Boston Latin School; studied piano with: Helen Coates, 1935, Heinrich Gebhard, 1935; studied with Walter Piston, Edward Burlingame Hill, and A. Tillman Merritt, Harvard University, Cambridge, Massachusetts, BA, 1939; studied music with: Fritz Reiner, Isabelle Vengerova, Randall Thompson, Curtis Institute of Music, Philadelphia, Pennsylvania, 1939–41; studied with Serge Koussevitsky, Berkshire Music Center (Tanglewood), 1940–41. **Career** Assistant conductor to Serge Koussevitsky, Berkshire Music Center, 1942;

music arranger (as Lenny Amber) Harms-Remick music publishing company, 1942; conducting début, New York Philharmonic Orchestra, 1943, assistant conductor, 1943–44, co-conductor, 1957–58, musical director, 1958–69, toured: South America, 1958, Europe, 1959, the Near East, 1959, Soviet Union, 1959, US, 1960, West Berlin, 1960, US, 1961, Japan, 1961, Canada, 1961, Bicentennial tour, US and Europe, 1976; first dance score performed, *Fancy Free*, 1944; first Broadway musical, *On the Town*, 1944; conductor, New York Symphony Orchestra, 1945–48; conductor, Israel Philharmonic, 1948–49, music adviser, 1948–49; television début, conductor and lecturer, *Omnibus*, CBS-TV, 1952; first American to conduct at La Scala, Milan, 1953; first film score, *On the Waterfront*, 1954; composed fanfare for John F. Kennedy presidential inauguration, 1961; conducted Israel Philharmonic concert at end of Six Day War, 1967; conducted Israel Symphony round-the-world "Jubilee" tour, 1986; conducted Beethoven's Symphony No. 9 to celebrate the fall of the Berlin Wall, Berlin, 1989; retired, 1990. **Related activities** Conductor, *Facsimile*, Ballet Theatre, 1946; guest conductor, International Music Festival, Prague, 1946; professor of music, Brandeis University, 1951–56; Norton lecturer, Harvard University, 1973; visiting lecturer, Massachusetts Institute of Technology, 1974. **Offices and memberships** Member, American Society of Composers Authors and Publishers, 1944–90; member, Berkshire Music Center, faculty, 1948–90; member, National Institute of Arts and Letters. **Awards and honours** New York Music Critics' Circle award, Symphony No. 1 *(Jeremiah)*, 1944; Antoinette Perry (Tony) Award for *Wonderful Town*, 1953; Academy Award nomination for best score, *On the Waterfront*, 1954; New York Theatre Critics Award for *Candide*, 1956; Emmy Award for: *The Music of Johann-Sebastian Bach*, 1957, *Leonard Bernstein for Omnibus*, 1958, *Bernstein and the New York Philharmonic*, 1960, *Bernstein and the New York Philharmonic in Japan*, 1962, *Young People's Concerts*, 1960, 1964, 1965, *Beethoven's Birthday (A Celebration in Vienna)*, 1972, *Bernstein and the New York Philharmonic*, 1976, Outstanding Individual Achievement, 1987; Christopher Award for *The Joy of Music*, 1959; Grammy Award for best: classical choral performance, *Beethoven: Missa Solemnis*, 1961, recording for children, *Prokofiev: Peter and the Wolf- Saint-Saens: Carnival of the Animals*, 1962, recording for children, *Saint-Saens: Carnival of the Animals- Britten: Young Persons' Guide to the Orchestra*, 1962, recording for children, *Bernstein Conducts for Young People*, 1963, classical album, *Bernstein: Kaddish, Symphony No. 3*, 1964, classical album, *Mahler: Symphony No. 8*, 1967, opera recording, *Bizet: Carmen*, 1973, classical album, *Concert of the Century*, 1977, classical orchestral recording, *Beethoven: Symphony No. 9*, 1980, classical orchestra performance, *Shostakovich: Symphony No. 5*, 1980, Lifetime Achievement Award, 1985; Page One Award and Citation, Newspaper Guild of New York; Peabody Award; Alice M. Ditson award; Sonning Prize, Denmark; Order of Merit, Chile, 1964; Order of the Lion Commander, Finland, 1965; Chevalier de la Légion d'honneur, France, 1968, Commandeur, 1986; Cavaliere, Italy, 1969; laureate conductor, New York Philharmonic, 1969; Austrian Honorary Distinction in Science and Art, 1976; Albert Einstein Commemorative Award in the Arts, Einstein College of Medicine; International Education Award; honorary doctorate: Northwestern University, Dartmouth College, Brandeis University, Temple University, Hebrew Union College, University of Michigan, Ohio State University, Westminster Choir College, Rockford College, Brown University, Yale University, Warwick University, England; Gold Medal, American Academy of Arts and Letters, 1985; Gold Medal, Royal Philharmonic Society, 1987; Great Merit Cross of the Order of Merit, Federal Republic of Germany, 1987. **Orchestral scores** Symphony No. 1 *(Jeremiah)*, 1942; Symphony No. 2 *(The Age of Anxiety)*, 1944; *Hashkivenu*, 1945; *Yidgal*, 1950; Serenade for Violin Solo, Strings and Percussion, 1952; *Harvard Choruses*, 1957; *Fanfare* (for presidential inauguration), 1961; *Fanfare* (for twenty-fifth anniversary of the High School for the Performing Arts, New York), 1961; Symphony No. 3 *(Kaddish)*, 1964; *Chichester Psalms*, 1965; *Songfest*, 1977; *Slava! A Political Overture for Orchestra*, 1977; *CBS Music*, 1977; *Divertimento*, 1980; *A Musical Toast*, 1980; *Halil*, 1981; *Olympic Hymn*, 1981; *Jubilee*

Games, 1986; *Opening Prayer*, 1986. **Chamber music** Piano Trio, 1937; Music for Two Pianos, 1937; Piano Sonata, 1938; *Music for the Dance*, 1938; *Scenes from the City of Sin*, 1939; Violin Sonata, 1940; *Four Studies*, 1940; Sonata for Clarinet, 1941; *Seven Anniversaries*, 1942–43; *Four Anniversaries*, 1948; *Brass Music*, 1948; *Elegy I, II and III*, 1950; Prelude, Fugue and Riffs for Jazz Combo, 1950; *Five Anniversaries*, 1954; *Shivaree*, 1969; *Touches*, 1981. **Songs** *Psalm 148*, 1932; *I Hate Music (5 Kid Songs)*, 1943; *Lamentation*, 1943; *Afterthought*, 1945; *La Bonne Cuisine* (*4 Recipes for Voice and Piano*), 1945; *Two Love Songs*, 1949; *Silhouette*, 1951; *Get Hep!*, 1955; *So Pretty*, 1968; *Piccola serenara*, 1979. **Theatrical scores** *The Birds* (incidental music), 1938; *The Peace* (incidental music), 1940; *On the Town*, 1944; *Peter Pan*, (incidental music including lyrics), 1950; *Trouble in Tahiti*, 1952; *Wonderful Town*, 1953; *Salome* (incidental music), 1955; (with others) *Candide*, 1956, revised, 1973; *The Lark*, 1955; (with Stephen Sondheim) *West Side Story*, 1957; *The First-Born*, (incidental music), 1958; (with Stephen Schwartz) *Mass*, 1971; *By Bernstein* (trunk songs), 1975; (with Alan Jay Lerner) *1600 Pennsylvania Avenue*, 1976; *The Madwoman of Central Park West*, 1970; *A Quiet Place*, 1984. **Film scores** *On the Town*, 1949; *On the Waterfront*, 1954; *West Side Story*, 1961. **Dance scores** (include) *Fancy Free*, 1944; *Facsimile*, 1946; *The Age of Anxiety*, 1949; *The Dybbuk*, 1974. **Operas conducted** (include, all New York unless otherwise indicated) *Medea*, Milan, 1953; *La Sonnambula*, Milan, 1955; *Falstaff*, 1964, Vienna, 1966; *Kaddish Symphony*, 1964; *The Cradle Will Rock*, 1964; *Chichester Psalms*, 1965, Chichester, England, 1965; *Der Rosenkavalier*, Vienna, 1968; *Fidelio*, Vienna, 1970; *Cavalleria Rusticana*, 1970; *Carmen*, 1974. **Television appearances** (include) Musical conductor and director, *New York Philharmonic Young People's Concerts*, CBS-TV, 1957–71; *The Unanswered Question*, 1976. **Recordings as composer** (include, all Columbia unless otherwise indicated) *On the Town*; *Peter Pan*; *Wonderful Town*, Decca; *Candide*; *West Side Story*; *Mass*; *Trouble in Tahiti*; *Serenade for Violin Solo, Strings and Percussion*; *Chichester Psalms*; *Dybbuk*; *Symphony No. 1*; *Symphony No. 2*; *Symphony No. 3*; *Prelude, Fugue and Riffs*; *On the Waterfront: Symphonic Suite*; *Fancy Free*; *Facsimile*; *Sonata for Clarinet*; and many others. **Recordings as conductor** (include) *Marc Blitzstein's "Symphony: The Airborne"*; *Carmen*; *Der Rosenkavalier*; *Beethoven: The Nine Symphonies*; *Tchaikovsky: Symphonies 1, 2 and 3*; *Bernstein Conducts Wagner*; *William Tell — Favorite Overtures*. **Publications** *The Joy of Music*, 1959; *Leonard Bernstein's Young People's Concerts*, 1962; *The Infinite Variety of Music*, 1966; *Six Talks at Harvard: The Unanswered Question*, 1976; *Findings*, 1982. **Cause of death** Heart attack caused by progressive lung failure, at age 72. **Further reading** David Ewen, *Leonard Bernstein: A Biography for Young People*, 1960; A. Holde, *Leonard Bernstein*, 1961; J. Briggs, *Leonard Bernstein: The Man, His Work and His World*, 1961; M. Cone, *Leonard Bernstein*, 1970; E. Ames, *A Wind from the West: Bernstein and the New York Philharmonic Abroad*, 1970; J. W. Weber, *Leonard Bernstein* (discography), 1975; Jack Gottlieb, *Leonard Bernstein: A Complete Catalogue of His Works, Celebrating His Sixtieth Birthday*, 1978; P. Robinson, *Bernstein*, 1982; Joan Peyser, *Bernstein: A Biography*, 1987; Peter Gradenwitz, *Leonard Bernstein*, 1988; *Contemporary Composers*, 1991.

ART BLAKEY

American Jazz Drummer and Bandleader

Born **Pittsburgh, Pennsylvania, 11 October 1919**

Died **New York, 16 October 1990**

To have had Art Blakey's talent as a jazz drummer would have made any modern jazz musician remarkable, but to combine this with what became an unerring eye for spotting and developing talented new musicians meant that he was the single most influential drummer in modern jazz.

Along with Elvin Jones and Max Roach, Blakey developed a coherent style of bebop drumming that built on the foundations laid by Kenny Clarke into what became known as "hard bop". In the late 1940s, Roach, Clarke and Blakey recorded in turn with most of the pioneers of the new jazz and each made a distinct contribution to the development of jazz drumming. While Clarke moved the beat from bass drum to ride or hi-hat cymbal, using the drum pedal to add individual accentuations or "drop bombs", Roach experimented with Latin and other rhythms to move the beat around from the conventional four-four of 1930s swing. Blakey, in many ways, was a more conventional swinging drummer, never losing sight of the dance origins of much of his music, but he also experimented with the timbre of the drums. His heavy press roll and strong off beats on the snare drum had their origins in early jazz and military drumming, but Blakey was also successful in getting a range of pitches and tones from the kit, and (after trips to Africa in the early 1950s to study traditional percussion) employing "talking drum" techniques. His best work in this genre is preserved in a set of trio recordings made in London in the early 1970s with Thelonious Monk where he responds to Monk's idiosyncratic piano by "talking back", changing the pitch of the heads of his tom-tom and snare drums using finger pressure in a manner firmly rooted in the music of Africa.

Blakey had grown up in Pittsburgh, receiving piano lessons, and working from an early age as a semi-professional musician even when financial necessity drove him into the steel mills. Well before his twentieth year (prompted, he recalled, by the presence of the teenage Erroll Garner in his group) he had switched to drums, which he played in an aggressive swing style. He came to New York in 1942, where he worked with Mary Lou Williams and then Fletcher Henderson, in a late edition of his swing orchestra. During a tour in the South, with Henderson, Blakey was injured in a racial attack.

The most important band with which he was to work in the mid–1940s was Billy Eckstine's, that had grown out of Earl Hines's orchestra and also contained (at various times) Dizzy Gillespie, Charlie Parker, Dexter Gordon (q.v.) and Miles Davis. Although Eckstine's group played swing, it was a melting pot for the ideas of the young beboppers, and after it broke up in 1947, Blakey was to make seminal recordings with Thelonious Monk, Miles Davis and Fats Navarro. Few players suited the probing, aggressive style of Blakey's drums better than Monk, whose stark compositional lines and atonalities needed such support.

The name "Messengers" first appeared as the title of Blakey's rehearsal big band, which he led in 1947 after Eckstine's group broke up. Blakey also used the name for a small-group recording that year, but the "Jazz Messengers" did not surface prominently again until 1955 when the name was applied to a co-operative quintet containing Blakey, pianist Horace Silver, saxophonist Hank Mobley and trumpeter Kenny Dorham. The association with Silver was forged in the early 1950s, after Blakey had visited Africa and begun his involvement with Islam. (He took the name Abdullah ibn Buhaina.)

With Horace Silver, the Jazz Messengers pioneered a style of small-group bop that combined elements of gospel music (such as Silver's composition "The Preacher") with the harmonies and rhythms of the new jazz, over a pulsing, driving dance beat. Blakey combined effectively with Silver's repetitive ostinato left-hand playing to underpin the group's rhythm. Their first records came out over Silver's name, but in 1956 Blakey took over leadership of the band. As time went on, his leadership was confined to his on-stage role, and a succession of fine musicians became "musical directors" of the Messengers, also taking over much of the administrative and financial management.

Blakey led the Messengers for the rest of his life, although he took time out to work with other groups including the Giants of Jazz (1971–72), in which (spurred on by Dizzy Gillespie, Sonny Stitt and Thelonious Monk) he reached great creative heights as a drummer.

Blakey appeared often as a drum soloist, and had a commitment to teaching percussion techniques.

For over three decades Blakey's bands launched the careers of a succession of fine jazz musicians. In the 1950s Lee Morgan and Wayne Shorter played with him, as did Donald Byrd and Johnny Griffin. Keith Jarrett and Woody Shaw both spent time in Blakey's groups, and more recently Wynton Marsalis played trumpet in the Messengers, a role taken over by Terence Blanchard. When Blakey toured internationally, he singled out new talent to appear with the band, welcoming the young British saxophonist Courtney Pine to play with him on a late 1980s visit to London. This was typical of his constant search for new voices with an original contribution to make. It is testimony to Blakey's skill as a leader and a drummer that virtually all the musicians who played with him paid tribute to his ability to support their playing in the best possible way, spurring them on to more creative invention. If he appeared domineering, it was in part due to an unerring instinct to sense a falling off in attention of soloist or audience and to lift the performance back to a high creative plane. At the time of his death, particularly in Europe, his best work from the 1950s and 1960s was once more in vogue with the jazz disco audience.

Born Arthur Blakey. **Marriage** Four marriages. **Children** Twelve children, five adopted. **Career** Played with James Murray, Pittsburgh; joined Mary Lou Williams, Kelly's Stable, New York, 1942; Fletcher Henderson Orchestra, 1943–44, toured US South; joined Billy Eckstine's band, St Louis, 1944–47; first recording, 1944; visited Africa, 1947; took the Muslim name, Abdullah ibn Buhaina, 1947; played with Lucky Millinder, 1949; joined Buddy DeFranco Quartet, 1951–53; organized rehearsal band, Jazz Messengers, 1947, reformed and led, 1955–90; world tour with Giants of Jazz, 1971–72; appeared Newport Jazz Festival, 1972–74; led septet including Delfayo Marsalis and Benny Green, 1987. **Awards and honours** *Down Beat* New Star Award, 1953; Grammy Award for best jazz instrumental performance group, 1984. **Recordings as leader** (include) "Message From Kenya"/"Nothing But Soul", BN 1626, 1953; *A Night at Birdland*, BN 5037–9, 1954; *Drum Suite*, Col.CL1002, 1956–57; *A Message from Blakey: Holiday for Skins*, BN 4004, 1958; *Art Blakey with the Jazz Messengers*, 1958; *Des Femmes Disparaissent*, Fon.660224, 1958; *The Freedom Rider*, BN 84156, 1961; *Buttercorn Lady*, Lml.86034, 1966; *Jazz Messengers '70*, Cat.7902, 1970; *Anthenagin*, Prst.10076, 1973; *Recorded Live at Bubba's*, Who's Who in Jazz 21019, 1980; *Album of the Year*, Tim.155, 1981; also: *Backgammon*, *Child's Dance*, *Buhaina*, *Gypsy Folk*, *In My Prime* (volume one), *Like Someone in Love*, *Roots and Herbs*, *In This Korner*, *Keystone 3*, *Night in Tunisia*, *Reflections in Blue*, *'S Make It*, *Straight Ahead*, *Thermo with Hubbard, Shorter, Fuller*. **Recordings as sideman** (include) Billy Eckstine: "Blowin' The Blues Away", De Luxe 2001, 1944, *Together!*, Spot.100, 1945; Thelonious Monk, "Who Knows", BN 1565, 1947; Miles Davis, "Weirdo", BN 45–1650, 1954; Horace Silver, *Horace Silver and the Jazz Messengers*, BN 5058, 1954; also: *Giants of Jazz*, *Newport in New York: The Jam Sessions, Volumes 3 and 4*, *Sonny Stitt with Art Blakey and the Jazz Messengers*. **Cause of death** Lung cancer, at age 71.

JORGE BOLET

Cuban/American Pianist

***Born* Havana, Cuba, 15 November, 1914**

***Died* Mountain View, California, 16 October 1990**

Jorge Bolet was one of the world's greatest pianists and one of the last exponents of the great romantic tradition of pianism. From his early days as a boy wonder at the Curtis Institute in

Philadelphia there was never any doubt about his phenomenal talent. He studied with Saperton, Godowsky, Hofmann and Rosenthal. When he made his professional début at the age of 16, playing Tchaikovsky's first piano concerto, under Reiner, sitting in the audience were Heifitz, Horowitz and Rachmaninov — whom Bolet worshipped. An auspicious beginning, and yet Bolet was not to achieve international fame until he was in his sixties.

In 1937 he won the Naumburg Piano Competition and then came World War II. He was recalled to Cuba to join the Army and later sent to Washington as military attaché, and to Tokyo in the post-war period where, in addition to his military duties, he found time to conduct the Japanese *première* of *The Mikado*. Returning to civilian life Bolet played for many of the world's greatest conductors: Koussevitsky, Furtwängler, Szell and others, to considerable acclaim, but in the 1940s and 1950s these engagements were few and far between and he later referred to this period as one of "half starvation".

The turning point in his career came in 1960 when he recorded the sound track for *Song Without End*, a biopic in which Dirk Bogarde starred in the role of Liszt. But Bolet's real break came with the Carnegie Hall recital he gave in 1974 at the age of 60; this was a triumph and brought fame at last. Decca signed a major recording contract with him and he increased his concert schedule dramatically. Those who had kept the faith over the years felt that his playing had entered a new phase, but Bolet confessed himself puzzled by the late recognition. "Why now?" he asked a *New York Times* journalist. "I've been told by many people that my playing has undergone a transformation in the last few years...but I'm not sure this is something I can feel myself."

In reality what had undergone a transformation was musical taste. In Bolet's youth, musical opinion was largely anti-romantic and Liszt, in particular, was considered meretricious — a show-off. Consequently pianists were taught to turn their backs on tradition, let the notes speak for themselves and keep additional expressive devices to a minimum. To these musicians, Bolet's playing, linked strongly to the traditions of his heroes, Rachmaninov and Hoffman, seemed anachronistic. The purists accused him of taking too much licence, but according to Bolet he was following the great romantic pianists who did not show off but merely employed what he called "flexibility within the pulse of the music". When, in the 1970s, a new generation rehabilitated Liszt and the Romantics, Jorge Bolet came into his own.

He was one of about a dozen pianists who could bring a convincing interpretation to bear on romantic music. He had a colossal technique which he never used for its own sake. At all times his playing had elegance and refinement, and while he also had titanic power, he never hammered. His statuesque looks, reminiscent of a dusky, moustached bandit, brought an element of glamour to the concert-hall that had been missing for a long time.

Bolet believed he should pass on his knowledge to the next generation, and did a great deal of teaching. He held posts at Indiana University and at the Curtis Institute, where he eventually succeeded Rudolf Serkin as head of the Piano Department, 50 years to the day after he had gone to audition there as a child. "I have received knowledge and experience from the great masters", he once said, "and it's now my responsibility to pass it on to the next generation." This he extended to a wider audience by giving televised masterclasses.

By the end of his life Bolet was giving more than 100 concerts a season and was preparing a world tour to mark his seventy-fifth birthday, when ill health forced him to give up the concert platform.

Over a 13-year recording career Bolet made 25 recordings, including eight solo records of Liszt, winning the Grand Prix du Disque three times. According to record producer, Peter Wadland, he did not really care for the recording process, although he felt that he should preserve his performances for the future and acknowledged that he had his recordings to thank in part for his fame. "During recording playbacks, he would sip huge amounts of coffee and smoke cigarettes incessantly (these he gave up a few years before his death on his doctor's advice) uttering very few comments, except what became a familiar phrase, 'Could be worse', which usually meant that he was pleased."

As a person Jorge Bolet was reserved and courteous, although in the company of friends he would become "unbuttoned" and tell hilarious jokes and stories. He was not a drinker — apart from the occasional glass of wine — but he always took pleasure in food, and especially looked forward to the dessert course.

Born Jorge Bolet. **Education** Studied with David Saperton and Fritz Reiner, Curtis Institute of Music, Philadelphia, Pennsylvania, 1928–32, MusB, 1932; studied piano with: Leopold Godowsky, 1932–33, Mortiz Rosenthal, 1935, Rudolf Serkin, 1937–38, Abram Chasins, 1947. **Emigration** Left Cuba for US, 1928, settled permanently, 1944. **Military service** Assistant military attaché, Cuban embassy, Washington, DC, 1943–45; US Army, 1944–46, musical director, US Army General Headquarters, Tokyo, 1946. **Career** Professional début, New York, 1930; European début, Amsterdam, 1935, toured, 1935–36; instructor, Curtis Institute, 1938–42, assistant to Rudolf Serkin, 1939–42, head of Piano Department, 1977–86; musical director, Japanese *première*, Gilbert and Sullivan's *The Mikado*, Tokyo, 1946; performed piano soundtrack of film *Song Without End*, 1960; professor of music, Indiana University School of Music, 1968–77. **Related activities** Recording contracts with CBS, Decca-London, Ensayo, Fidelio and Vox. **Awards and honours** First prize, Naumburg Piano Competition, 1937; Josef Hofmann Award, 1938; Caballero, Order of Carlos Manuel De Cespedes; *Gramophone* Instrumental Award for *Liszt's Années de Pélerinage Book One*, 1984; Grand Prix du Disque (three times). **Recordings** (include) *Prokofiev's Second Piano Concerto*, 1952; *Song Without End*, 1960; *Liszt's Années de Pélerinage Book One*, 1984. **Cause of death** Heart failure, at age 75.

NORMAN BUCHAN

British Politician and Poet

***Born* Sutherland, Scotland, 27 October 1922**

***Died* Glasgow, Scotland, 23 October 1990**

Norman Buchan read the works of Marx, Lenin and Trotsky and, according to his close associates, fully understood them. This is no mean achievement. Some able people on the British political Left, such as Sydney Webb, admitted that they found Marx's three-volume *Capital* beyond their comprehension.

In his lifetime Buchan disproved the hoary old dictum attributed to Bernard Shaw, no doubt with his tongue in cheek, that if you are not a socialist by the time you are 20, there is something wrong with your heart, and if you are still a socialist by 30, there is something wrong with your head. Like many of his generation who witnessed the extreme misery caused by the great capitalist Depression of the 1930s, Buchan joined the Communist Party. As a member he would have had to accept the harsh discipline and the mental self-denying ordinances imposed by this relatively new and ruthless kind of "religious" order. In his thirties he defected to join their arch-enemies, the British Labour Party and remained a socialist of the democratic Left for the rest of his life. Political friends and foes alike testify that he had one of the keenest intellects in British politics and that from his heart always emanated compassion and kindness.

His break with the Communist Party came when Soviet tanks rolled into Hungary in 1956 to suppress the popular uprising. He had began even earlier to be troubled by the transparent ambiguities of the word "socialism". He recognized the great gulf that had been created between

Marx's theory of liberation of the working class and the Stalinist dictatorship of the Soviet Union. True to his roots, he saw that humanity and the rights of individuals to freedom were higher goals than an abstract political theory.

In his long career as a member of the British parliament, 1964–90, his integrity of mind was much in evidence. He opposed the official party line on a series of issues. He was against US action in Vietnam, supported the Campaign for Nuclear Disarmament and was against any compromise with the white minority government in Rhodesia. He was always available to help and sustain the anti-apartheid cause in South Africa.

His outstanding abilities were recognized by the party chiefs who sought to channel them more along official party lines by appointing him to a succession of ministerial jobs. He was too much of a non-conformist to compromise his principles for the sake of party or personal advancement. He resigned as minister of agriculture in 1974 in a row over Britain's entry into the European Community, which he vehemently opposed. In the 1980s when he was official spokesman for the arts, including broadcasting, his concern was for the rights of broadcasters to make programmes based on events as they saw them, and not as dictated by a government ministry. The party leader, Neil Kinnock, decided to leave broadcasting to the Home Office, the law and order department, rather than include it in a new ministry for the arts which is what Buchan wanted. Characteristically he stuck to his principles and resigned his post, sacrificing a life-long ambition to become a minister for the arts in a future Labour government.

His departure was a great loss to the arts in Britain. He was one of the few members of parliament with a concern for and an understanding of the visual arts, and a genuine desire to help the institutions in any way he could. He supported the case for public financial backing and argued that national museums and galleries were institutions worthy of being preserved and enhanced.

The Edinburgh International Festival had a marked effect on Buchan. Started in the late 1940s, the festival was supported financially by the canny burghers of the city partly no doubt from commercial motives, but also to proclaim their proud boast that Edinburgh was truly the Athens of the North. After all, they had a partly built replica of the Parthenon to prove it.

During a visit to the festival in its early years Buchan met theatre director, Joan Littlewood, who was looking for a venue for an anti-nuclear play by her Theatre Workshop. He also met the poet Hamish Henderson who was staging an evening of Scottish folk songs. These encounters had a profound influence on his attitude to the relationship between arts and politics. "I genuinely was not aware that that kind of music existed," he explained, "a popular form of art, direct and full of social content." From then on he got very much involved in the whole folk revival and he became one of Scotland's best known writers of folk songs.

He became also an archivist, historian and popularizer of the folk song, and went on to edit the best-selling collection, *101 Scottish Songs*, and *The Scottish Folksinger*. For him the folk song was about the history and aspirations of ordinary people, about protest and dissent. The kind of songs about the skirl of the bagpipes did not appeal to him. His lyrics were made of much sterner stuff celebrating, for example, such popular heroes as Johnny Ramensky, a safebreaker who spent most of his life in prison.

It is interesting to note that the politics of dissent, not unlike the religions of dissent, involve a lot of singing. Perhaps the song acts both as a transmitter of the message in an enjoyable and easily understood form and as a safety valve for the feelings of the protesters.

Buchan's discovery of the rich potential of Scottish folk music coincided with and contributed to the revival of Scottish nationalism. Through his songwriting he helped to popularize one of the folk heroes of the "red Clydeside" era of the early 1900s. John McLean was a fiery orator and teacher from Glasgow who led a Marxist-based revolutionary group, the Social Democratic Federation, and acted as Lenin's consul in Glasgow. In making him into a cult figure to young Scots, Buchan helped to foster McLean's dream of an independent socialist republic for Scotland. But as a passionate supporter of international working-class solidarity, Buchan rejected any form of narrow nationalism.

His influence can be seen in the growth of folk song groups in Scotland today. But his disciples have taken the master's message of international brotherhood and turned it inwards to promote the cause of Scottish independence.

Buchan's commitment to the Campaign for Nuclear Disarmament never faltered. He helped rally the Scottish CND in its opposition to the USA nuclear submarine base at Holy Loch. This produced another collection of songs and ballads. Only months after his death, a decision to close the base was taken as part of the peace dividend.

Buchan worked with other Scottish poets to create the folk music revival of the 1950s through countless musical events and gatherings. They all wrote ballads about freedom and independence which have passed into the popular repertoire. It is perhaps a tribute to their influence that Scottish football fans chant, among other things, songs about ancient victories over medieval English monarchs, whereas English fans parody their national anthem and invoke their deity to save their team. Mostly the English prayers are answered.

As a poet with a self-deprecatory wit, he preferred to write in a satirical vein and in 1977 wrote a lengthy polemic on the Scottish nationalist movement, *The MacDunciad*, in the style of Alexander Pope. Among his targets were the well-heeled middle-class nationalists whom he regarded as tartan Tories.

In politics as in folk music he was well aware of the distinction between patriotism and nationalism. He viewed Scottish nationalism as a mixture of sentimental attachment to the past and political opportunism; a kind of exclusive "wee frees". His patriotism was based on a respect for his country's long independent history, its unique culture and its separate educational and legal traditions. He was in effect stressing the inter-dependence of nations within the wider international community.

Yet strangely his internationalist outlook fell short of embracing Britain's closest neighbours in Europe. Like many on the Left and also, for different reasons, those on the extreme Right of British politics, he was implacably opposed to Britain's membership of the European Community. It seems clear from this brief summary of his life that his opposition was not based on any insular British nationalism. He took the view that the common European market was an alliance between capitalist interests and the agricultural community, which would prevent the attainment of socialism in the member countries. He also believed that true internationalism meant that ordinary people throughout the world should be free to unite to shape their own destinies.

This is an admirable but unrealistic view to take in a world full of nation states noisily proclaiming their national independence and sovereignty. A limited but achievable internationalism had been set up in western Europe by 1960. The European Community sought to modify the worst manifestations of aggressive nationalism which had devastated Europe three times in 100 years. By unifying and harmonizing the economic and social systems it was hoped that wars in Europe would become not only unthinkable but impossible.

Norman Buchan lived to witness the Marxism of his early youth become discredited and rejected by most Communist bloc countries. He had long been aware of its defects in theory and practice. Within the British Labour Party he sought to combine his fierce faith in individual freedom with a burning zeal for social justice. He recognized the vital role of art and music in enriching the lives of people. As a politician he had the distinction of being loved by his friends and respected by his political enemies. He was even more unique in the fact that he possessed many of the Christian cardinal virtues, including that of resignation. A fitting swan-song for this intrepid internationalist, poet and folk song writer might have been: people of the world unite in song, the devil does not have all the best tunes.

Born Norman Findlay Buchan. **Father** John Buchan. **Marriage** Janey Kent, member, European parliament, 1945. **Children** One son. **Education** Kirkwall Grammar School; University of Glasgow. **Military service** Royal Tank Regiment, British Army, 1942–45, served North Africa, Sicily and Italy. **Career** English and history teacher: University of Glasgow extramural department, 1950–60, Rutherglen Academy; Labour member of parliament for: Renfrewshire West, 1964–83, Paisley South, 1983–90; parliamentary under secretary, Scottish Office, 1967–70; opposition spokesman on: agriculture, fisheries and food, 1970–74, 1980–81, social security, 1980–81, the arts, 1983–87; minister of state for ministry of Agriculture and Fisheries, 1974, resigned 1974; shadow minister for agriculture, 1981. **Related activities** President, Rutherglen District Educational Institute of Scotland; chairman of the board, *Tribune*, 1985–90; contributor, *New Statesman*. **Offices and memberships** Member, Scottish Association of Labour Teachers. **Publications** (Editor) *101 Scottish Songs*, 1962; (editor with Peter Hall) *The Scottish Folksinger*, 1973; *The MacDunciad* (verse pamphlet), 1977. **Cause of death** Undisclosed, at age 67.

AVIS BUNNAGE

British Actress and Entertainer

***Born* Ardwick, Lancashire, 22 April 1923**

***Died* Thorpe Bay, Kent, 4 October 1990**

Forceful, acerbic, bossy and brassy in many of her roles, Avis Bunnage was a familiar face in British theatre, films and television, although not always at the forefront. Tending to be typecast as a slatternly landlady or a grittily anarchic north country working-class woman, she nevertheless excelled in a variety of unstereotyped parts, particularly during her long involvement with director Joan Littlewood's challenging and anti-Establishment Theatre Workshop.

Her confidence as a performer began in childhood with parents who both had a passion for music and entertaining. Her father, William Bunnage, was a dentist by profession but also a drummer with an orchestra; her mother, as Evaline Ward the Dainty Soubrette, had been one of the famous Tiller girls, and continued to sing and dance as a solo act, appearing on the same music-hall bills on occasions as Stan Laurel and Charlie Chaplin. The juvenile Avis soon learned to sing, dance and play the piano at home, and to form her own concert-party from local children to give shows in the Bunnages' garden.

Most of her childhood was spent at Chorlton-cum-Hardy near Manchester and, after leaving Chorlton Central School, she became first a telephonist and then a nursery teacher. However, responding to the thespianism which was in her blood and background, she was active in amateur theatricals during this period. In 1947 she played Tabitha in *The Brontës*, her first professional performance, at the Chorlton Repertory Theatre, and stayed with the company for several years.

She joined the Theatre Workshop in 1952 when its company was touring the north of England, and appreciating its innovative and radical approach, she then seemed to have found her professional niche. Remaining with it until the end of the 1960s, she was to become its leading performer. Her first Theatre Workshop assignment was in several parts in Ewan McColl's *Uranium 235* which transferred to London's Embassy Theatre in May 1952. Her most notable roles with the company were in two plays which became landmarks: in 1958 she played the part of Helen, the mother, in Shelagh Delaney's *A Taste of Honey* and of Meg Dillon in Brendan Behan's *The*

Hostage. Both were originally staged at the company's base at the Theatre Royal in Stratford, east London. Bunnage's first appearance in New York was at the Cort Theater, where she recreated her original role in *The Hostage* in 1960, then toured Canada in the play.

Her part in *A Taste of Honey* seems to have been more than an actor's interpretation of a writer's character. When Joan Littlewood, the Theatre Workshop's founder and producer, received Delaney's play, both she and Avis Bunnage had some doubts about aspects of it. Howard Goorney's book *The Theatre Workshop Story* reports Bunnage's typically forthright initial response: "My first reaction was that whoever wrote this needs a swift kick up the arse. We did a lot of improvisation. When we came to bits that didn't seem to work we ad-libbed around the ideas, made it up as we went along." Joan Littlewood considered that "The young author understood her heroine and her black lover, but the 40-year-old mother only came to life through the wit and art of the actress — Avis." Shelagh Delaney, in a footnote to the London *Daily Telegraph*'s obituary of Bunnage, generously endorsed this by commenting that the role of the mother was "created out of her [Bunnage's] own wicked, sophisticated wit and wisdom".

During her long association with the Theatre Workshop Avis Bunnage appeared in a truly wide range of plays by authors as different in time and talent as Shakespeare, Shaw and many new writers. Her most notable performances were possibly in *Fings Ain't Wot They Used T'Be* (when it transferred to London's West End in 1961) and in Joan Littlewood's memorable musical satire, *Oh, What a Lovely War!* in 1963.

The climax of her contributions to the work of the Theatre Workshop came in 1967 when, in *The Marie Lloyd Story*, she ebulliently portrayed the eponymous British music-hall star. Joan Littlewood decided to stage this as a tribute to Bunnage "which would show her gifts to advantage", and Bunnage belted out Lloyd's Cockney songs with a freshness and robustness which almost brought the house down, night after night.

Avis Bunnage was able to adapt her broad and extroverted stage style for film and television work. She appeared with great success as the sleazy landlady in The *L-Shaped Room* in 1962 and, in the same year, as the mother of the leading character, played by Tom Courtenay, in *The Loneliness of the Long Distance Runner*. Her most recent film part was in the 1990 film *The Krays*, in which her portrayal of the grandmother of the notorious East End brothers was much acclaimed.

She also became a familiar face and personality on television, particularly when starring with Thora Hird in the series *In Loving Memory* and during an eight-week exposure in the long-running, north country soap, *Coronation Street*. Other impressive television roles were in an adaptation of Walter Greenwood's *Love on the Dole* and Dennis Potter's adaptation of Thomas Hardy's *The Mayor of Casterbridge*.

It is typical of this strong-natured and many-faceted actress that in *Who's Who in the Theatre* she listed her "favourite parts" as "All", and that when replacing Miriam Karlin in 1968 in *Fiddler on the Roof* she diluted cosy Jewish sentimentality with north country British astringency; according to some critics "she seemed to be itching to take over as the dominant member of the family and give them all a good Lancastrian wigging."

Born Avis Bunnage. **Parents** William, dentist and musician, and Evaline (Ward), variety artiste, Bunnage. **Marriage** Derek Orchard (dissolved). **Education** Chorlton Central School, Manchester. **Career** Telephonist; nursery teacher; professional début, *The Brontës*, Chorlton Repertory Theatre, Manchester, 1947; London début, *Uranium 235*, 1952; member, Theatre Workshop Company, Theatre Royal, Stratford East, 1952–68; television début, *Probation Officer*, 1959; New York début, *The Hostage*, Cort Theater, 1960, Canadian tour, 1960–61; directed *The Big Rock Candy Mountain*, 1972. **Stage** (includes, all London unless otherwise indicated) *The Brontës*, Manchester, 1947; *Uranium 235*, 1952; *The Dutch Courtesan*, 1954; *An Enemy of the People*, 1954; *The Good Soldier Schweik*, 1954; *The Midwife*, 1955; *The Legend of Pepito*, 1955;

Mother Courage and Her Children, Devon Festival, Barnstaple, 1955; *The Sheep-Well*, 1955; *The Italian Straw Hat*, 1955; *The Good Soldier Schweik*, Paris, 1955, London, 1956; *Edward II*, 1956; *Captain Brassbound's Conversion*, 1956; *The School for Wives*, 1957; *The Playboy of the Western World*, 1957; *Macbeth*, London, Zürich and Moscow, 1957; *And the Wind Blows*, 1957; *Man, Beast and Virtue*, 1958; *Unto Such Glory*, 1958; *A Taste of Honey*, 1958; *The Hostage*, 1958; *A Christmas Carol*, 1958; *Ned Kelly*, 1960; *The Hostage*, New York, 1960, Canada, 1960; *They Might Be Giants*, 1961; *Fings Ain't Wot They Used T'Be*, 1961; *Oh, What a Lovely War!*, Paris, 1963, London, 1963; *Merry Roosters' Panto*, 1963; *Henry IV*, 1964; *Sweet Fanny Adams*, 1966; *The Marie Lloyd Story*, 1967; *Fiddler on the Roof*, 1968–69, 1970, South African tour, 1969; *Slip Road Wedding*, 1971; *Stringer's Last Stand*, 1972; *Costa Packet*, 1972; *Is Your Doctor Really Necessary?*, 1973; *Sweeney Todd*, 1973; *The Rivals*, 1973; *Billy*, 1974; *Lionel*, 1977. **Films** (include) *The L-Shaped Room*, 1962; *The Loneliness of the Long Distance Runner*, 1962; *Sparrers Can't Sing*, 1962; *Tom Jones*, 1963; *The Whisperers*, 1966; *Gandhi*, 1982; *No Surrender*, 1985; *The Krays*, 1990. **Television** (includes) *Probation Officer*; *In Loving Memory*; *Coronation Street*; *Love on the Dole*; *My Lords, Ladies and Gentlemen*; *The Mayor of Casterbridge*; *Yesterday's Dreams*; *Inspector Morse*. **Cause of death** Undisclosed, at age 67. **Further reading** Howard Goorney, *The Theatre Workshop Story*, 1981.

LORD CACCIA

British Diplomat

***Born* Pachmarhi, India, 21 December 1905**

***Died* Builth Wells, Wales, 31 October 1990**

"The briskest man I ever worked for" was the verdict of the present British foreign secretary, Douglas Hurd, on Lord Caccia, one of the principal British diplomats during the troubled times when Britain was losing an empire without having yet found a new role. It was in such times that the polished diplomatic skills, the bustling energy, the never-failing cheerfulness and robust good sense of a man like Caccia were needed to represent his country abroad.

Harold Anthony Caccia was born in India where his father was a member of the forest service, who himself served with distinction in the secretariat of the Paris Peace Conference in 1919. The family had originally come from Italy in the mid-nineteenth century, and this was to serve the rising diplomat in good stead when he worked with Macmillan during the Allied Italian campaign in 1943. But Harold was more British than many of those of older native stock. Always keen on games — he won a rugby Blue at Oxford (a rare feat for an Etonian) — and with a ready supply of sporting metaphors tripping off his tongue, a good shot, always fighting fit, and with plenty of good sound commonsense, he was "the very model of a modern" British public servant. After scholarships to Eton and Trinity College, Oxford and a Laming Travelling Fellowship at Queen's College, Oxford, his aptitude for languages naturally attracted him to the diplomatic service, where his first posting in 1929 was to the British Legation in Beijing. On his return home after a five-year stint, he had his first stroke of luck in being appointed assistant private secretary to the then foreign secretary, Anthony Eden. This brought him to the notice of the men at the top, and was to be repeated in his wartime service with Macmillan and again after the war when Ernest Bevin personally chose him for the important job of helping to carry through the post-war unification of the foreign service from its many hierarchical levels.

Caccia's first ambassadorial post was to Vienna in the tricky period of the early 1950s, when the neutral status of Austria was being hammered out between the cold war adversaries. He enjoyed his bouts with the Russians whom he often beat at their own game, and he became increasingly popular with the Austrians, not least for his hunting prowess. His most difficult assignment was his appointment to Washington in 1956, where he arrived a few days after the start of the ill-starred Suez campaign. Though appointed by Eden, his main task was in mending fences with the Americans on behalf of his long-standing mentor, Harold Macmillan. Caccia travelled the length and breadth of the United States during his five-year stay, and was particularly instrumental in maintaining the "special relationship" during the early months of the Kennedy administration and the Bay of Pigs fiasco. Caccia reassured the British government by his personal confidence in Dean Rusk and the young President. Some may have seen his faith in America as exaggerated and as having laid the basis for an over-ardent view of the "special relationship", which perhaps diverted Britain from its European interests. He was certainly an Atlanticist first and foremost. But then he served under governments which had not yet abandoned Britain's world role.

In 1962 Caccia returned to London to become permanent under-secretary at the Foreign Office and head of the unified Diplomatic Service. He was created a life peer on his retirement in 1965 and thereafter made a number of contributions to debates on foreign affairs from the cross-benches in the House of Lords. But essentially his view of the world had come to an end with the Labour governments of the 1960s and Britain's withdrawal from east of Suez. Caccia's public career was by no means over, however. On leaving the diplomatic service he was immediately appointed provost of Eton College, again at a critical time when his old school was to undergo a major change of direction. Here again his management skills were of great benefit. Some might criticize him for spending so much of his time on other ploys in London — he was inevitably in great demand in the City, and as chairman of the Ditchley Foundation for Anglo-American understanding, as president of the Anglo-Austrian Society, and as Lord Prior of the Order of St John of Jerusalem, among other positions — but he was a great delegator. His faith in the headmaster he had appointed led him to leave the educational affairs of the College in his hands and get on with what concerned his job as chairman of the governors. In this, as in his other spheres of duty, he showed great good sense, energy and enthusiasm. At the end of a long and happy life — saddened towards the end by the untimely death of his only son — he could look back on many achievements, not least his wide circle of friends.

Born Harold Anthony Caccia. **Father** Anthony Caccia, dendrologist. **Marriage** Anne Catherine Barstow, 1932. **Children** Two daughters and one son (deceased). **Education** Eton College, Windsor, Berkshire; Trinity College, Oxford, BA, 1927; Laming Travelling Fellowship, Queen's College, Oxford, 1928. **Career** Entered foreign service as third secretary, Foreign Office, 1929; posted to Beijing, 1932, second secretary, 1934; Foreign Office, 1935, assistant private secretary to foreign secretary, 1936; posted to Athens, 1939, first secretary, 1940; Foreign Office, 1941; seconded for service with resident minister, North Africa, 1943; appointed vice-president, political section, Allied Control Commission, Italy, 1943; political adviser, General Officer Commanding-in-Chief Land Forces, Greece, 1944; Minister local rank, Athens, 1945; assistant under-secretary of state, 1946, Foreign Office, deputy under-secretary of state, 1949; British high commissioner, Austria, 1950–54; British ambassador in Austria, 1951–54; deputy under-secretary of state, Foreign Office, 1954–56; British ambassador at Washington, 1956–61; permanent under-secretary of state, Foreign Office, 1962–65; head of Diplomatic Service, 1964–65; retired, 1965. **Other activities** Provost, Eton College, 1965–77; director, Westminster, later National Westminster Bank, 1965–75; director, Prudential Assurance Company, 1965–80; director, F & C Investment Trust, 1965–78; chairman, Gabbitas-Thring Educational Trust, 1967–73; member, advisory council on Public Records, 1968–73; chairman, Standard Telephones and

Cables, 1968–79; director, Orion Bank, chairman, 1973–74; director, F. & C. Eurotrust Ltd, 1972–84; member, advisory council, Foseco Minsep, 1972; chairman, ITT (UK) Limited 1979–81. **Offices and memberships** President, Anglo-Austrian Society; president, Marylebone Cricket Club, 1973–74. **Awards and honours** Companion of the Order of St Michael and St George, 1945; Knight Commander of the Order of St Michael and St George, 1950; Knight Commander, Royal Victorian Order, 1957; Knight Grand Cross of the Order of St Michael and St George, 1959; Knight Grand Cross of the Royal Victorian Order, 1961; honorary fellow, Trinity College, Oxford, 1963; created life peer, Baron Caccia of Abernant, 1965; Lord Prior of the Order of St John of Jerusalem, 1969–80; honorary fellow, Queen's College, Oxford, 1974; golden ring of Styria (Austria), 1990. **Cause of death** Undisclosed, at age 84.

XAVIER CUGAT

Spanish/American Bandleader

Born **Barcelona, Spain, 1 January 1900**

Died **Barcelona, Spain, 27 October 1990**

Xavier Cugat was the "rumba king", the man who introduced the rhythms of Latin America to their northern neighbours. "You know," Cugat once said, "this music is important in the efforts to create Pan-American friendship. The people down there are learning the United States has a human side. After all, the rumba created thousands of friends for Cuba. And I think the United States has learned more about Brazil from Carmen Miranda than they would from ten ambassadors." Of course there were other Latin bands, but as Cugat put it, "They all switched to something else when times for Latin-American musicians were bad. I knew it would click for good some day so I never changed."

He didn't always play Latin music, though. He started out as a classical violinist. Born near Barcelona on the first day of the century, his family emigrated to Cuba when he was either three or five (accounts vary). He started playing the violin at about the age of five, and studied music in Berlin, Paris and New York. He played with Havana's Grand Opera Company, the Berlin Symphony Orchestra, and the Los Angeles Philharmonic. His earnings financed his family's move to the United States, where they settled in Brooklyn, New York.

He toured with the great opera singer, Enrico Caruso, for more than five years, beginning when Cugat was only 15 years old. During long train journeys, he and Caruso often passed the time drawing caricatures. According to Cugat, "Caruso was a marvellous amateur at caricature." Cugat himself had quite a talent for it. When a lukewarm critical reaction caused him to become disillusioned with his career prospects as a concert violinist, he spent a year working as a cartoonist on *The Los Angeles Times* before he returned to music, and to his roots: the rhythms of Latin America.

In those days, Latin-American music was referred to as "gigolo music", so Cugat called his band the "Gigolos". The silent screen heart-throb Rudolph Valentino got them their first job: the relief band at Hollywood's Coconut Grove night-club. It was 1928, and as Cugat later explained to a Spanish interviewer, "Americans knew nothing about Latin music. They neither understood it nor felt it. So they had to be given music more for the eyes than the ears. Eighty per cent visual, the rest aural."

The visual side of the band was always a striking one: the men wore flaming red jackets and the singers and dancers were always extraordinarily beautiful women, such as Rita Hayworth, who danced with the band when she was only 13. Cugat (affectionately known as "Coogie") was known for surrounding himself with beautiful women, and he married five of them. Four of his wives were singers: Carmen Castillo, Lorraine Allen, Abbe Lane, and Charo. None of the marriages produced children.

Though Cugat and his band had already appeared in several films for Vitaphone and Paramount, they reached a peak of popularity in the 1940s, making musicals for Columbia, United Artists and MGM. The outbreak of war meant that neither American tourists nor Hollywood films were making the trip to Europe, so the attention of both turned to South America. The tourists headed south, where according to Cugat, "under the influence of tropical skies and a couple of daiquiris" they developed a taste for the local music. Meanwhile, South America became Hollywood's main market for overseas distribution. (Also, a 1941 dispute over fees between the radio networks and the American Society of Composers, Authors and Publishers resulted in a ban on ASCAP songs, leaving most bands with nothing to play but standards in the public domain while Cugat, with a library of more than 500 non-ASCAP Latin tunes, got maximum radio exposure.) This combination of circumstances was perfect for Cugat. Latin music was what Hollywood demanded, and with the national following he'd won during the ASCAP dispute, he was the one to provide it. Clutching the pet chihuahua which was his trademark, he logged in more screen time than any other bandleader, even playing small acting roles, such as Carmen Miranda's sweetheart in *A Date with Judy*.

Cugat's admirers included Cole Porter, whom he met at New York's Waldorf-Astoria Hotel, where his band played for many years, and Fred Astaire. In 1933, Porter heard the band rehearsing and asked them to play his new song, "Begin The Beguine". Cugat later recorded it, and several other Porter songs. Astaire had initially despaired at hearing that Cugat would be working with him on *You Were Never Lovelier*, objecting that he didn't want to be accompanied by "a mere rumba band". During the filming, however, he came to admire Cugat's musicianship so much that he dropped a dance number written by Jerome Kern and replaced it with a medley of Latin-American tunes. When the shooting was finished, Astaire presented Cugat with a silver baton.

In later years, Cugat would occasionally appear on television with whoever was his current wife. While still married to Abbe Lane, he was given his own show on Italian television, *Casa Cugat*, but his wife's dance movements reportedly upset Pope Pius XII so much that the cameramen were ordered not to film her below the waist (the same treatment was currently being given to Elvis Presley on American television). The show was finally taken off the air after it was decided that Miss Lane was probably not wearing a bra. With his fifth wife, Charo (otherwise known as the "coochie-coochie girl"), he became a frequent guest on American television chat-shows. He would usually lean back, stroking a chihuahua and smiling in indulgent amusement as his young Spanish wife babbled on in her incoherently fractured rendition of the English language. They were a great comedy double-act.

He suffered a stroke in 1971 and went into semi-retirement. He announced in 1986 (at the age of 86) that he would be recreating some of his 1930s hits with a new band, but his health was failing and it never happened.

In the 1990s, everyone's talking about "World Music". Latin and African rhythms have been rediscovered. During the 1980s, groups such as The Talking Heads (a former "New-Wave" rock group headed by David Byrne) popularized the traditional music of countries like Brazil by combining it with modern American dance-music, making it accessible to the young of North America and Europe. That's exactly what Xavier Cugat did four decades earlier, when he was voted the most popular bandleader among American college students.

Born Francisco de Asís Javier Cugat Mingall de Brue y Deulofeo. **Parents** Juan and Mingall (de Bru) Cugat. **Marriages** 1) Rita Montaner; 2) Carmen Castillo, singer, 1929 (divorced 1945); 3)

Lorraine Allen, singer, 1946 (divorced 1950); 4) Abbe Lane, singer, 1952 (divorced 1963); 5) Charo Baeza, singer, 1966 (divorced 1978). **Education** Studied violin with Franz Kneisel. **Emigration** Left Spain for Cuba, c. 1903, settled US, 1921, naturalized. **Career** Violinist, Havana Symphony, 1912; Concert violinist, Caruso's US tour, 1921; radio début, 1921; featured violinist, Los Angeles Philharmonic; organized dance orchestra, Coconut Grove, Los Angeles, 1928; first film appearance, Vitaphone short, *Xavier Cugat and his Gigolos*, 1928; bandleader, Hotel Astoria, New York, from 1933; featured on *Let's Dance* US radio programme, 1934; orchestra leader, *The Camel Caravan* US radio programme, 1935; invented congat (cross between bongos and conga); first feature film appearance, *Go West Young Man*, 1937; featured artist, Metro-Goldwyn-Mayer Films, 1944–49; *Casa Cugat* television programme, RAI, Italy, 1954; entered semi-retirement, 1971. **Other activities** Cartoonist, *The Los Angeles Times*, 1927. **Awards and honours** Orden de Honor y Mérito de la Cruz Roja Cubana, 1941. **Films** (include) *Go West Young Man*, 1937; *You Were Never Lovelier*, 1942; *The Heat's On*, 1943; *Stagedoor Canteen*, 1943; *Two Girls and a Sailor*, 1944; *Bathing Beauty*, 1944; *Weekend at the Waldorf*, 1945; *Holiday in Mexico*, 1946; *No Leave, No Love*, 1946;*This Time for Keeps*, 1947; *A Date with Judy*, 1948; *Luxury Liner*, 1948; *Neptune's Daughter*, 1949; *Chicago Syndicate*, 1955; *The Monitors*, 1969; *The Phynx*, 1970. **Compositions** (include) "My Shawl"; "Rain in Spain"; "Night Must Fall". **Publications** (Editor and illustrator) *Other Americas*, 1938; (illustrator) *Best I Know* by E. B. Smith, 1941; *The Rumba is My Life* (autobiography), 1949. **Cause of death** Heart failure, at age 90.

JACQUES DEMY

French Film Director

***Born* Pont Château, France, 5 June 1931**

***Died* Paris, France, 27 October 1990**

It says something quite remarkable about a film-maker's reputation that it can rest primarily upon a few early works. The creator of *Les Parapluies de Cherbourg* (*The Umbrellas of Cherbourg*) and *Les Demoiselles de Rochefort* (*The Young Girls of Rochefort*) had an achievement that proved even more considerable, given that it was spun out of a chilly, intellectual climate dominated by the French New Wave — a movement he ignored, preferring instead the pastel romance and the American style of musical comedy, all fused into a kind of modern fairy-tale.

Jacques Demy's background was a solid one; after studying art in Nantes, he moved to Paris in 1949 to learn film-making at the École Nationale de Photographie et Cinématographie. In 1952 he became assistant to the animator Paul Grimault, with whom he made several animated commercials. Two years later, having dropped animation as lacking potential (sadly, the scene is not vastly improved today), he worked with documentarist Georges Rouquier.

Demy had not therefore cut his cynic's teeth by starting as a film critic — an occupation which can jade one faster than prostitution — as did Godard and Truffaut. The latter, it can be said, did not suffer from the learned dissection. Demy was later courted by both Truffaut and Eric Rohmer to write for the periodical bible, *Cahiers du Cinéma*, but declined. "It wasn't my role to criticize" he said.

His first short film gave a taste of a style to come; *Le Sabotier du Val de Loire*, under Rouquier's eye, drew heavily on youthful memories and more than a degree of stylization. His first feature film, *Lola*, displayed a marked assurance. It carried several influences one would see in his other films, such as that of Max Ophuls and Jean Cocteau — and those of MGM musicals. It also had Anouk Aimée and a wider distribution. In it a man returns to Nantes to "reclaim" a cabaret dancer he deserted seven years earlier. It was well received by the critics. After this film, Demy developed melodramatic patterns of coincidence, with more emphasis on arrivals and departures, and less on plots. *La Baie des Anges* was an excellent showcase for Jeanne Moreau; in fact, it was structured around her. The story, concerning a gambler who arouses the love of a bank clerk on holiday, barely touched upon the difficulties of addiction to gambling — seen as a spontaneous response, not a disease. Instead, the film focused on the miracle that love brings. However, the rhythm had vivacity and it did reasonably well at the box office.

Les Parapluies de Cherbourg sealed Demy's style and reputation as a refreshing young French talent. The story, again, was flimsy: a love affair is broken by war and by parental disapproval. Once more, Michel Legrand's excellent music created a curious revival of the operetta tradition, as every line of dialogue was sung, every word set to music. The formula won Demy the Golden Palm at Cannes. The film starred Catherine Deneuve as a daughter of an umbrella shop loved by a garage mechanic — and had been criticized by the film's backers as "having no presence". While there was an obvious need for an antidote to the intellectual analysis of the *nouvelle vague*, not all the critics were kind. It was called by Bosley Crowther "a cinematic confection so shiny and sleek and supersweet, so studiously sentimental, it comes suspiciously close to a spoof." Others remarked that the sacharine sing-song style grew monotonous. But it put the stamp of Demy's pastel balletic world on celluloid. *Les Demoiselles de Rochefort*, also in song, was another homage to the American musical; this time, three pairs of lovers, in yet another seaside town, spun the simple plot. Unfortunately, the inclusion of the supremely talented Gene Kelly did not, for many, add the substance the film needed. Demy's respect for the genre was not enough. "He doesn't understand the mechanism of the American musical and what makes them move", said critic Pauline Kael. The lack of texture to the characters, once again, had taken its toll. Critics found Demy's world either enchanting or embarrassing. But the addition of Françoise Dorleac and Catherine Deneuve (sisters in real life), as the bell-bottomed Pierrots, brought enormous grace. The 1969 film *The Model Shop* (or, in a sense, *Lola* transported to Los Angeles) concerned an affair with a Vietnam draftee; the backdrop was the underside of the city. But the formula of romance and melodrama remained, a curious distillation of genre through French sensibility.

Peau d'âne (*Donkey Skin*), was taken from the classic Perrault fairy tale — with a slightly more Freudian slant. Despite a sterling cast, with Deneuve and the superb Jean Marais (Cocteau's stalwart), it suffered beside Cocteau's *Beauty and the Beast*. Nevertheless, it was one of the few films that made a good profit; it was luminous and lovely in its celebration of the domain of happily-ever-after. In 1971 Demy followed with another fairy-tale, *The Pied Piper of Hamelin*, which was shot in England, but this time the sweetness gave way to an unwieldy mixture of dark and light; the curious casting of pop singer Donovan was ineffectual, instead of innocent and inspired.

Demy's *naif* style was not suited to the tougher atmosphere of the 1970s, and his popularity, which had brushed the mainstream level, plummeted. He had, perhaps, stayed too long at the fair. After several other insignificant films, Demy directed *L'Evénément le plus important depuis que l'homme a marché sur la lune* — its ungainly title shortened to *A Slightly Pregnant Man*. Deneuve once more starred, as if her magic could lift his popularity. It didn't. Demy's last film of critical, if not fiscal, note was 1982's *Une chambre en ville* (*A Room in Town*), with the musical format of *Umbrellas*. It was a fantasy of social conflicts with a gloomier tone. He called it a "musical tragicomedy": "Since *Parapluies*, things have changed. My story is more violent, more passionate, and has become more funny." The film became a *cause célèbre* when, with the strength of a revitalized French industry bolstering them, critics denounced what Ginette Vincendeau has described as "the discrepancy between the poor level of marketing of the film, compared with the obscene amount of money poured into the release of a run-of-the-mill Jean-Paul Belmondo blockbuster" — the French *auteur* cinema stifled by mass commercialism.

Demy had stayed constant to his particular vision of film-making, whether it proved successful or not. For three decades he seemed oblivious to the more abrasive demands of the fashion — there was simply no other way to explore his combination of fairy-tale, pop music and Hollywood film genre to create a world properly proportioned in both realism and artifice.

Born Jacques Demy. **Parents** Raymond and Marie Louise (Leduc) Demy. **Marriage** Agnès Varda, film director, 1962. **Children** One son, Mathieu. **Education** Collège de Nantes; École des Beaux-Arts, Nantes; École Nationale de Photographie et Cinématographie, Paris. **Career** Assistant to animator Paul Grimault, 1952; assistant to Georges Rouquier, 1954; directed first short film, *Le Sabotier du Val de Loire*, 1955; began association with editor Anne-Marie Cotret, 1955; first feature film, *Lola*, 1960; first international success, *Les Parapluies de Cherbourg* (*The Umbrellas of Cherbourg*), 1963; first US film, *The Model Shop*, 1969; directed theatrical productions, Salzburg and Paris. **Awards and honours** Prix Louis Delluc for *Les Parapluies de Cherbourg*, 1964; Palme d'Or for *Les Parapluies de Cherbourg*, Festival de Cannes, 1964; Officier des Arts et des Lettres; Officier, Ordre Nationale du Mérite; Grand Prix National for *Une chambre en ville*, 1982. **Films directed and written** (include) *Lourdes et ses miracles* (assistant only), 1954; *Arthur Honegger* (assistant only), 1955; *S.O.S. Noronha* (assistant only), 1956; *Le Sabotier du Val de Loire*, 1957; *Le Bel Indifférent*, 1957; *Le Musée Grévin*, 1958; *La Mère et l'infant* (co-directed), 1959; *Ars*, 1959; *Lola*, 1961; "La Luxure (Lust)" segment of *Les Sept Péchés capitaux* (*Seven Deadly Sins*), 1962; *La Baie des Anges* (*Bay of the Angels*), 1963; *Les Parapluies de Cherbourg* (*The Umbrellas of Cherbourg*), 1964; *Les Demoiselles de Rochefort* (*The Young Girls of Rochefort*), 1967; *The Model Shop* (also produced), 1969; *Peau d'âne* (*Donkey Skin, The Magic Donkey*), 1971; *The Pied Piper of Hamelin*, 1972; *L'Evénément le plus important depuis que l'homme a marché sur la lune* (*A Slightly Pregnant Man*), 1973; *Lady Oscar*, 1978; *La Naissance du jour*, 1980; *Une chambre en ville* (*A Room in Town*), 1982; *Parking*, 1985; *Trois places pour le Vingt-six*, 1988. **Film appearances** (include) *Les Quatre Cents Coups*, 1959; *Paris nous appartient*, 1960. **Cause of death** Leukaemia, at age 59. **Further reading** *International Dictionary of Films and Filmmakers*, volume two, 1985.

AIR COMMODORE SIR JAMES EASTON

British Air Force and Intelligence Officer

Born **Winchester, Hampshire, 11 February 1908**

Died **Grosse Pointe, Michigan, 19 October 1990**

Air Commodore Sir James Easton was one of the leading RAF intelligence officers during World War II, before going on to demonstrate his intellectual and administrative skills in MI6, rising to become its deputy director. It was at MI6 that Easton played a notable role in the exposure of the traitor and Soviet double agent Kim Philby, a role which, amid controversy, he revealed publicly in 1988.

James Alfred Easton was born in Winchester and brought up there, attending the local Peter Symonds' School. His academic ability and agile mind soon revealed itself and it was no surprise when he later passed out top of the civil service examination for Sandhurst, Cranwell and

Woolwich. Easton was tempted by the junior but high-profile service and joined the RAF in 1928. After graduating successfully from Cranwell the following year, Easton was posted to 101 Squadron on the North West Frontier of India, flying Boulton-Paul Sidestrand biplane bomber aircraft, before transferring two years later to 31 Squadron, flying Westland Wapitis in the same region. After completing his tour of duty in India, Easton served in several areas, most notably in Egypt. It was significant in terms of his later career that he also specialized as an armaments officer before being seconded in 1937 to the RCAF as an air armaments adviser at the Department of National Defence in Ottawa.

Early in 1939, with the storm clouds of war gathering rapidly, Easton was brought back to the United Kingdom to join a Blenheim light bomber squadron where he earned a mention in despatches. Shortly afterwards, like many other regular officers over the age of 32 with specialist skills, Easton, now a squadron-leader, was withdrawn from flying duties and posted again as an armaments adviser to the Air Ministry, where he helped set up and took command of the first RAF Technical Intelligence Unit, then known as A12G. Drawing heavily upon both civilian and RAF specialists Easton welded together a skilled and highly motivated unit to track the progress of German aerial technical development, particularly with regard to navigational aids and codes, by a variety of means including the interrogation of prisoners, the sifting of field agents' reports, aerial photography and examination of downed German aircraft. One such aircraft that came to Easton's attention proved particularly rich in valuable information. In May 1942 a night fighter version of the highly versatile Junkers 88 had been forced down undamaged near Aberdeen by two Canadian Spitfire pilots, later mentioned in despatches for their actions. The aircraft was fitted with the Germans' latest and highly effective Lichtenstein radar equipment and, after preliminary examination of the aircraft, Easton thought it necessary to call in Professor R. V. Jones who was able to analyse the new equipment and begin to attempt counter-measures against it. Easton's talent for incisive organization was recognized by his superiors and rapid promotion followed; in 1943 he became an Air Commodore at the early age of 35 and director of Intelligence (Research). The directorate controlled operations in diverse and varied areas, still controlling A12G but also the Special Service Squadrons which catered for the specialized and ever-increasing requirements of the Special Operations Executive and other British Intelligence operations in occupied Europe. In 1944, when the V1 and later V2 menace began to make itself felt in London and south-east England, Easton was a valuable member of the hastily formed Crossbow Committee set up by Churchill to evaluate the new threat, investigate the technical complexities of these deadly weapons — the first, if crude, surface fired missiles — and to advise on possible counter measures.

At the end of hostilities Easton was attached to the Foreign Office and posted to the RAF Delegation in Washington. However, the resignations of the two senior officers in MI6, Air Commodore L. G. S. Payne and Group Captain F. W. Winterbotham (q.v.) enabled Easton to join MI6, where he rapidly became a close adviser to its chief, Major-General Stewart Menzies, who appreciated his cool-headed and logical approach to the rapidly changing peace-time role and structure of the organization. In the austere atmosphere of post-war Britain and the nascent but rapidly developing cold war, changes had to be made and new policy goals decided; to such problems Easton brought a vigorous and clear-sighted objectivity and, as an eloquent advocate of the service, fostered close relations with the USA and Commonwealth countries. Indeed by 1949 he was in charge of the section dealing with the FBI and the recently created CIA with which he was keen to forge strong ties. It was at this time that he came into close contact with Kim Philby, then based in Washington, who came under his command. Anglo-American relations became particularly strained after the abrupt defections of Burgess and Maclean, and Easton, well known for his pro-American views, was sent to join Philby in Washington in July 1951 to smooth down the ruffled feathers of the FBI and CIA chiefs. While in Washington Easton confirmed his suspicions about the loyalty of Philby, doubts already shared by MI5. On his return from the US, Easton later stated "I encountered a document . . . I realized when I read it that this man was an accomplished liar and therefore capable of anything. The more I read, the more certain I became that Philby was a traitor." Philby was subsequently recalled and although it was not Easton's main task to interrogate him, he was a moving force behind the procedure and, under questioning, he later stated, "Philby attempted to answer each point but he did so too cleverly. He looked and behaved like a rat in a trap." But, unfortunately, suspicion, however well founded, was not enough. Philby was asked to resign and given a 4000-pound handshake but, under increasing suspicion and ever closer scrutiny, fled to the Soviet Union from Beirut where he had been working as a journalist for *The Observer* newspaper.

The details of Easton's role came to light in an interview with Antony Cave Brown, the author of a biography of Sir Stewart Menzies, entitled *The Secret Servant.* Although he received much criticism for his detailed revelations in the wake of action taken by the British government over books by Peter Wright and Anthony Cavendish, Easton, while accepting the absolute need for secrecy in such matters, maintained that he had spoken so as to give a correct and authoritative account which he hoped would set to rights the many uncorroborated and often highly speculative and damaging accounts already published. Philby, of course, had already published his highly distorted and unreliable account of the events in his book *My Secret War.* For his part, he certainly remembered with admiration and horror Easton's "rapier" style of questioning and noted that Easton "gave the impression of burbling and bumbling but it was dangerously deceptive. His strength was a brain of conspicuous clarity yet capable of deeply subtle twists".

In 1952 Menzies retired, to be succeeded by his deputy, Major-General John Sinclair. Easton was appointed his deputy with the clear implication that he would in due course be raised to the top post. Unfortunately for Easton the capricious hand of fate intervened. At the height of the cold war, Bulganin and Khrushchev visited Britain aboard the new Soviet cruiser *Ordzhonikidze.* The prime minister, Sir Anthony Eden, made it clear that whatever the military significance of surveying the vessel at close quarters, no form of action was to be taken by any of the services. MI6, however, took a gamble and sent an ex-Navy frogman Commander "Buster" Crabb to inspect the cruiser's hull; unfortunately he was discovered and some time later his headless body was found in Portsmouth harbour. Given the delicacy of the political situation, Eden was understandably furious and promptly sacked Sinclair and, in an attempt to curb direct military influence, appointed Sir Richard White, the civilian head of MI5, to the top job of MI6. Easton, meanwhile, was in Malaya, assessing the Communist-inspired insurgency there; upon his return he found that although White was keen for him to retain his position as deputy chief of MI6, he would not be succeeding White upon his retirement. Easton accepted the situation with characteristic good grace but two years later, in 1958, he took up the post of consul-general in Detroit.

Quite at home in the US, Easton held this post for an uncommon ten years before leaving the British Diplomatic Service. By now 60 years of age, Easton decided to stay on in Michigan and took up a number of high-level business appointments, although still able to find time to write a speculative study entitled *The Transportation of Freight in the Year 2000* in 1970, and four years later he was deputy chairman of the World Energy Conference. Easton finally retired from business in 1981 to devote himself to his local Grosse Pointe golf and bridge clubs.

Jack Easton, as he was known, was a man of rare intellectual ability and distinction. A gifted administrator, he had a clear grasp of technical and engineering detail and served with distinction in the field of Air Intelligence. From here it was a natural step for him to apply his decisiveness and clarity of purpose to the realms of MI6 at a time when its role and structure was changing and confidence in it was at a low ebb. Easton did much to restore that damaged confidence and, as part of MI6 and later as consul-general in Detroit, played a significant role in the cementing of Anglo-American relations.

Born James Alfred Easton. **Father** W. C. Easton. **Marriages** 1) Anna Mary McKenna, 1939 (died 1977); 2) Jane (Leszynski) Walker, 1980. **Children** One son and one daughter, from first marriage. **Education** Peter Symonds' School, Winchester, Hampshire; Royal Air Force College, Cranwell, Lincolnshire. **Career** Joined Royal Air Force, 1928; served: North West Frontier, India, 1929–32, Egypt 1935–36; served as air armament adviser to Department of National Defence, Canada, 1937–39; joined Air Staff Branch Directorate of Intelligence, Air Ministry, 1939, deputy director, 1941–43, director, 1943–45; mentioned in despatches, 1940; Group Captain, 1941; Air Commodore, 1943; member, Royal Air Force Delegation, Washington, 1945; retired, 1949; attached to Foreign Office, 1945–58; deputy director, MI6, 1953–58; consul-general, Detroit consulate, 1958–68; resident consultant on trade development of Great Lakes Area, 1968–71; deputy chairman, Host Committee for 1974 World Energy Conference, 1972–75; associate member, Overseas Advisory Associates Incorporated, Detroit, 1975–82; retired 1981. **Awards and honours** Officer, Legion of Merit, US 1945; Commander of the Order of the British Empire, 1945; Companion of the Order of the Bath, 1952; Knight Commander, Order of St Michael and St George, 1956. **Publications** *The Transportation of Freight in the Year 2000*, 1970. **Cause of death** Undisclosed, at age 82. **Further reading** Kim Philby, *My Secret War*, 1968; Antony Cave Brown, *The Secret Servant*, 1988.

DOUGLAS EDWARDS

American Broadcaster

***Born* Ada, Oklahoma, 14 July 1917**

***Died* Sarasota, Florida, 13 October 1990**

Broadcasting was Douglas Edwards's life. He wrote in *The New York Times*, "I virtually grew up in broadcasting. As a kid, I listened to a crystal set in a place called Silver City, N.M. What an experience that was, transfixed by broadcasts from faraway places." That transfixed child grew up to become network television's first news anchorman.

He began his career at the age of 15, as a junior announcer on a 100-watt radio station next door to a Methodist church in Troy, Alabama. According to his obituarist in *The New York Times*, the station was "put together with rubber bands". Edwards's job was to announce the selections played by the church organist.

He later combined his college studies with work at several different radio stations, then moved to Detroit to work at station WXYZ, alongside another up-and-coming young newscaster, Mike Wallace.

He joined CBS in 1942. He was part of Edward R. Murrow's renowned London staff during the final days of World War II, and later served as Paris bureau chief. The turning point in his career came when he joined Murrow and Quincy Howe in covering the presidential conventions of 1948. "We did very well, the three of us, on those conventions", Edwards recalled later. "Afterwards, CBS asked me to go into television, and I did it with some fear and trepidation, not because I was nervous about being on television — I had done quite a bit of it — but radio was the power".

Radio may have *been* the power, but that was about to change, thanks to Douglas Edwards. According to Don Hewitt (associate director of Edwards's nightly newscasts and now executive producer of America's acclaimed weekly television news programme, *60 Minutes*), "Doug ushered in the television era. ...Whatever is good and right about TV news today, Doug Edwards can claim a lion's share of the credit."

Douglas Edwards with the News will always have a place in history as the first nightly network television news programme. The show went coast-to-coast in 1951, and was watched by 34 million viewers. In its time, the programme was the world's largest single news medium.

Winston Churchill, Eleanor Roosevelt, Herbert Hoover, John F. Kennedy — these are just a few of the people Edwards interviewed. He was one of the first television reporters to work on location; in 1954 he gave an on-the-spot report when five congressmen were shot by Puerto Rican nationalists, and two years later, he gave an exclusive eyewitness account of the sinking of the *Andrea Doria*. That same year, he won the Peabody Award for television news.

He anchored the nightly news for 14 years, and was succeeded by Walter Cronkite. He stayed with CBS until his retirement in 1988. He had been with the network for 46 years. When he made his last television broadcast in April 1988, this was his farewell: "A deep bow of gratitude, love and respect to the men and women of CBS News and to the company for which they stand. To you out there, thank you for honoring me with your presence in my audience."

They were gracious words from a gracious man, a man fellow CBS anchor Charles Kuralt referred to as "an old-fashioned journalist of the best kind".

Born Douglas Edwards. **Marriage** May. **Children** Lynn, Donna and Robert. **Education** University of Alabama; Emory University, Atlanta, Georgia; University of Georgia, Athens. **Career** Junior announcer, Troy, Alabama, 1932; freelance announcer, 1932–42; announcer, WXYZ radio, Detroit; joined CBS radio, 1942, London staff, 1944–46, Paris chief of staff, 1947, presidential reporter, 1948; became first television regular news anchorman, *Douglas Edwards with the News*, CBS-TV, 1948–62; retired from CBS, 1988. **Awards and honours** George Foster Peabody Award for best television news, 1956; Lowell Thomas Award, Marist College, 1986; Paul White Award, Radio and Television News Directors Association, 1988. **Cause of death** Cancer, at age 73.

MAJOR HOLLEY

American Bass Player

Born **Detroit, Michigan, 10 July 1924**

Died **Maplewood, New Jersey, 25 October 1990**

The hilarious combination of bowed bass and voice invented by Slam Stewart had only one other exponent — Major "Mule" Holley. The sound became each man's trade mark and remained unique to them because it was so hard to create. Stewart hummed an octave above what he was playing on the bass, while Holley hummed, growled and grunted in unison with his bow. Although Stewart's work in the style was more sophisticated, Holley's interpretation in later years was funnier. The two friends eventually recorded an album of duets but alas it suffered from overkill and became rather tedious.

"I've never had any true employment", he claimed proudly in 1987. "I've been a freelance all of my life." This was true, and the hard work which he put into establishing his reputation in the post-war years paid off when eventually he was able to pick and choose from the best jobs available. The fact that he was fluent in any of the styles from traditional jazz to bebop and that he could switch from being a star turn to a modest but brilliant accompanist made him the perfect jazz chameleon.

"Everybody in my family played something or sang", he said. "My father was a great bass singer and my mother was a pianist." When he was six his parents sent him to study with a German violin teacher. "Eventually I went on to join the orchestra led by LeRoy Smith, *the* black classical director of music in Detroit." Holley first worked professionally as a violinist when he was 14.

In 1942 he was called into the Navy and assigned to a military band. "I switched from violin to bass. What made me decide to take up the bass? I didn't decide — the United States Government decided for me! I would have been comfortable as a violin player, but since I'd had some experience with the tuba and the bass horn, I was obliged to play the bass. They said that if I didn't play bass then I'd be sent to dig the garbage pits."

While in the Navy Holley met and worked with jazz stars of the future, like trumpeters Clark Terry, Gerald Wilson and Ernie Royal. He roomed with the great alto player Willie Smith. It was Clark Terry who first called him "Mule" when he saw Holley carrying both his instruments at once, a tuba and a double bass. The nickname stuck.

After his war service Holley went first to San Diego and there made his professional début as a jazz player with saxophonists Wardell Gray and Dexter Gordon (q.v.). He soon moved to a hotel on Fifty-second Street, scene of most of the contemporary jazz action, and let it be known that he was available 24 hours a day. His appetite for work paid off, and he was soon accompanying the cream of the best musicians in the Street, including Charlie Parker, Coleman Hawkins and Al Haig. During this time he worked with some of the "popular" jazz stylists like Earl Bostic and the singer-guitarist T Bone Walker. In 1950 he worked with Oscar Peterson and recorded with him as a duet, but by then Holley had become disenchanted with New York and had decided to live abroad. Fortuitously he was offered a chance to tour Britain with the pianist-singer Rose Murphy. He took the job, liked Britain and stayed there when the tour was over.

Despite the rigours of post-war Britain (rationing was still in force) he loved the country and managed somehow to evade the tightly-enforced laws which forbade foreign musicians to work in the country. He worked with every kind of jazz musician during his five-year stay. "My first job in London was at the Astor Colony restaurant. I played for the Queen when she was a princess — in fact I played for both of the princesses at the Astor Colony."

The British jazz musicians were more than impressed by Holley, and he recorded with Sid Phillips, Kenny Graham and Tubby Hayes. He also worked with Humphrey Lyttelton, Chris Barber, Sandy Brown and Mick Mulligan's Magnolia Jazz Band on the more traditional side.

He worked for the BBC as a studio musician and took up the same work when he finally returned to New York in 1956. But to play jazz he had to stay on the move, and in 1958 he joined Woody Herman to tour South America. On his return he joined the group led by the two tenor players Al Cohn and Zoot Sims. He taught at the Berklee College of music for three years — an unusually stable period in his life — but kept up his jazz connections by working at this time with Art Tatum, Teddy Wilson, Ella Fitzgerald, Earl Hines, Coleman Hawkins and, in 1964, Duke Ellington. He joined the Westchester Symphony Orchestra and in 1974 returned to Europe with an all-star band called the Kings of Jazz. His classical experience enabled him to turn his feature number on that tour, "Angel Eyes", into a miniature grand opera which was both musically dextrous and enormously funny.

Holley began to visit Europe annually and also toured in Japan and the Soviet Union. In 1986 Quincy Jones invited him to record an album with Frank Sinatra and he continued to be busy until his death, returning from work in Germany only a week before he died.

Born Major Quincy Holley Junior. **Parents** Father, minister and singer; mother, pianist. **Education** Cass Technical High School, Detroit, Michigan; Groth School of Music. **Military service** Played tuba and double bass, US Navy band. **Career** Played with: Dexter Gordon, Wardell Gray, California; recorded with Oscar Peterson band, 1950; toured Britain; studio musician, BBC orchestra, London, 1954–56; Woody Herman State Department tour, South America, 1958; Al Cohn-Zoot Sims band, 1959–60; studio musician, from 1960; played with: Kenny Burrell, Coleman Hawkins, Duke Ellington; faculty member, Berklee College of Music, 1967–70; toured Europe with Kings of Jazz; recorded with Roy Eldridge, 1975, Lee Konitz,

1975, Roland Hanna, 1979, Frank Sinatra, 1986. **Recordings** (include) (With Oscar Peterson) "Robbins Nest"/"Exactly Like You", Clef 8930, 1950; (sideman) *Woody Herman*, Ev.5010, 1958; (sideman to T. Wilson) *And Then They Wrote*, Col.CS8238, 1959; (sideman to Al Cohn and Zoot Sims) *You 'N' Me*, Mer.60606, 1960; (sideman to Coleman Hawkins) *Today and Now*, Imp.34, 1962; (sideman to Lee Konitz) *Chicago 'n' all that Jazz*, GM 3306, 1975; (solo) *Mule!*, BB 33074, 1974; also recorded with Michel Legrand, Dickie Wells, Vic Dickenson and Ella Fitzgerald. **Cause of death** Heart attack, at age 66.

REAR-ADMIRAL SIR EDMUND IRVING

British Naval Officer

Born **British North Borneo, 5 April 1910**

Died **1 October 1990**

Rear-Admiral Sir Edmund Irving was an outstanding naval and maritime specialist. Innovative, industrious and far-sighted, Irving spent almost the whole of his long and distinguished naval career improving techniques and equipment available for surveying the oceans. No armchair expert, he was twice mentioned in despatches for his actions in World War II and spent many of his years in the Navy at sea, putting into practice what he preached. In retirement Irving was active in a number of naval and maritime research councils and associations.

Born in British North Borneo, Edmund Irving was educated at St Anthony's, Eastbourne before enrolling as a cadet at the Royal Naval College, Dartmouth in 1924 and being posted as midshipman on the 29,150-ton battleship *Royal Oak* (sunk in Scapa Flow on 14 October 1939) in 1927. Promoted to sub-lieutenant in December 1931, he joined HMS *Kellett*, a ship of the Surveying Service, in which he was to remain throughout his career. Irving spent the rest of the decade almost continually at sea, serving in a number of survey ships in all quarters of the globe. Although one of the least well known and glamorous arms of the navy, the Surveying Service can and does undertake vital and indeed dangerous tasks in times of war.

In 1941 Irving, as the navigation officer aboard HMS *Scott*, found himself in the harsh and potentially hostile seas off the coast of Iceland laying marker beacons to identify the correct positions for minefields. In recognition of the dangers and pin-point accuracy of navigation involved, he was mentioned in despatches. In the following year, now a lieutenant, serving on the elderly coal-burning survey ship HMS *Endeavour*, Irving carried out a swift series of surveys in difficult conditions of possible harbours east and south of Port Sudan that might be used if, as seemed likely, Rommel's Africa Corps forced a British withdrawal beyond the Nile Delta. With the successful completion of Operation Husky, the invasion of Sicily, attention turned to the preparations for the invasion of the Italian mainland. In this Irving played a key role and was again mentioned in despatches for his operational ingenuity. Although the Straits of Messina are quite narrow, the sheer size of the seaborne invasion force made navigational accuracy both difficult and vital. Just prior to the invasion in early September 1943, Irving surveyed the three main landing areas upon the mainland and fixed them accurately by arranging for a battery of searchlights to be stationed on the Sicilian shoreline to act as a pin-point navigational aid and beacon.

Irving's war was by no means over and in 1944 he took command of HMS *Franklin*. As the Allied forces moved through, he systematically surveyed the heavily damaged channel ports which fell throughout September 1944 (although Dunkirk held out until the close of hostilities) with a view to getting them into action as quickly as possible. Such was the damage, however, that there was little hope of swift repair and clearance, and the supply of the Allied ground forces in Europe became an increasingly great problem for the Allied commanders, even threatening to halt the advance itself as demands increased and supply lines from the Normandy beacheads lengthened. The key to the problem was felt to be the great port of Antwerp. Although the port itself fell in October, the Scheldt estuary was still resolutely and fiercely defended by the German 15th Army under General Gustav von Zangan, and its approaches dominated by the fortress island of Walcheren and its powerful gun batteries. Even after the reduction of Walcheren and the clearance of the estuary area in Operations Switchback and Vitality, themselves bitter and bloody campaigns fought by British and Canadian troops, the approaches to Antwerp remained closed owing to mines and block ships.

Rather than waste time waiting for the channel to be swept of mines, Irving, ordered to survey the port, persuaded the Army to carry his survey boats overland on tank transporters to Bruges, where they joined the canal system, sailing to Terneuzen on the Scheldt where he began work at once. Throughout November a fleet of nearly 200 vessels swept the 75-mile length of the channel no less than 17 times. It was not until 26 November that the minesweepers completed their dangerous task and, thanks to Irving's ingenious short-cut and the early completion of his work, the first ships were able to dock in Antwerp the same day, thereby beginning a process which much eased the Allied supply problems. Soon after VE Day Field Marshal Montgomery visited HMS *Franklin* to thank Irving personally and to thank the ship's company for their vital role in opening the port, though his unprecedented order to splice the mainbrace found little favour in the Admiralty.

After the war, Irving remained in the Hydrographic Department with shore postings alternating with sea commands of HMS *Sharpshooter*, HMS *Dalrymple* and HMS *Vidal*. Both on land in theory and in practice at sea, Irving helped to pioneer new techniques of marine position fixing and navigation by modified forms of radar under the inspired guidance of Admiral Day, Hydrographer of the Navy from 1950 to 1955. In 1960 Irving was appointed Hydrographer of the Navy and at once brought his enthusiasm and firm belief in the importance of his department's work to bear on staff, service chiefs and politicians alike. His first task was to persuade Lord Carrington, then First Lord of the Admiralty, to relocate the chart compilation office from unsuitable quarters in Cricklewood to Taunton, where the Naval printing works had been built in 1940. Moreover, he succeeded in overturning the practice — one which dated back to the days of Captain Cook — of converting old warship hulls into survey vessels, a method of construction which patently had failed to keep pace with technological change and requirements. By his drive, enthusiasm and hard-headed reason, he won the case for the building of a specially designed and equipped oceanographic fleet which, in modified form, is still in service with the Navy. Irving long maintained his commitment to this fleet and was actively opposed to the withdrawal of the Antarctic patrol and survey vessel HMS *Endurance* from the Southern Atlantic in 1981, thereby limiting British scientific activity and the British military presence in the area with, as he predicted, tragic results.

After his retirement from the Navy in 1966, Irving took up a post with his former technological partners, Racal, where he promoted new and ever more sophisticated survey systems to hydrographers and maritime agents. He continued to press for further exploration, being an active member of NERC's Research Vessel Committee which oversaw the construction of the RRS *Challenger*. He was also the much-respected founder president of the Society for Underwater Technology which aims to bring together scientists, engineers and maritime laymen to promote and further the development and exploration of Britain's offshore resources. After a lifelong interest in natural phenomena, Irving was elected president of the Royal Geographical Society in 1969, and in 1976 received the rare distinction of its Patron's Medal for his continued enthusiastic support of and commitment to exploration. Moreover, he was equally keen to preserve Britain's extensive martime heritage, serving for nine years as a trustee of the National Maritime Museum, and for ten as acting conservator of the River Mersey. One further institution which he was especially happy to help and support was the Royal National Lifeboat Institution, serving on its management committee and as chairman of the Boat Committee for a period in which he oversaw the design and construction of new types of rescue craft. Indeed, only four days before his death, Irving was in Ramsgate, Kent, for the naming ceremony of a new lifeboat.

Sir Edmund, or "Egg" as he was almost universally known, was a highly talented scientific naval officer with a firm grasp of both technological and maritime matters. An imaginative thinker and enthusiastic, bustling figure, he had a reputation for warmth, approachability and fairness among his staff and colleagues. A practical seaman, he made a significant contribution to naval surveying and navigational techniques and was a tireless supporter of numerous maritime causes.

Born Edmund George Irving. **Parents** George Clerk and Ethel Mary Frances (Poole) Irving. **Marriages** 1) Margaret Scudamore Edwards, 1936 (died 1974); 2) Esther Rebecca Ellison, 1979. **Children** One son and one daughter, from first marriage. **Education** St Anthony's, Eastbourne, East Sussex; Royal Naval College, Dartmouth, Devon, 1924–27. **Career** Midshipman-cadet, HMS *Royal Oak*, Royal Navy, 1927; sub-lieutenant's courses, 1930–31; entered surveying service, 1931; HMS *Kellett* Surveying Service, 1931; mentioned in despatches, 1941, 1944; commander, HMS *Franklin*, 1944; Hydrographics Department, 1946–48, 1949–50, assistant hydrographer, 1954–56, 1956–59; commander, HMS *Sharpshooter*, 1948–49; commander, HMS *Dalrymple*, 1950–53; commander, HMS *Vidal*, 1953–54, 1956–59; aide-de-campe to the Queen, 1960; Hydrographer of the Navy, 1960–66; retired, 1966. **Related activities** Management committee, Royal National Lifeboat Institution, 1960–90, boat committee chairman, 1969–78; consultant, Decca (Racal), from 1966; trustee, National Maritime Museum, 1972–81; acting conservator of the River Mersey, 1975–85; member, South West Atlantic group. **Offices and memberships** Fellow, Royal Geographical Society, president, 1969–71; fellow, Royal Institution of Chartered Surveyors; fellow, Royal Society of Arts; founder president, Society for Underwater Technology. **Awards and honours** Officer of the Order of the British Empire, 1944; Companion of the Order of the Bath, 1962; Knight Commander of the Order of the British Empire, 1966; Patron's Medal, Royal Geographical Society, 1976. **Cause of death** Undisclosed, at age 80.

FREDA JACKSON

British Actress

***Born* Nottingham, England, 28 December 1907**

***Died* 20 October 1990**

"Classically repellent" is how Freda Jackson was described by one critic as Mrs Voray in *No Room at the Inn*, her greatest success, source of fame and typecasting. While Kenneth Tynan coined an equally memorable phrase, calling her "about as warm as a key dropped down one's back", those who knew her as a person characterized her as "full-blooded: a warm and generous friend", although one remarked that "in real life she could be a bit scary too".

Freda Jackson was a railwayman's daughter who won a place at Nottingham University and trained to be a teacher. She even worked as one for a couple of years before making her acting début in 1934 at Northampton Rep. — a theatre with which she had a long and happy association. Her London début was in a revival of Somerset Maugham's play *The Sacred Flame* at the Q Theatre.

Two actor-managers took a great interest in forwarding her career. The first, Emlyn Williams, invited her to tour with his company as Nurse Libby in his own play, *Night Must Fall*, before giving her a leading role in Elmer Rice's *Judgement Day*. At a second, and perhaps more critical juncture, Anthony Hawtrey feted her, and after he had directed her in *No Room at the Inn*, staged Strindberg's *The Father* for her, to play opposite Michael Redgrave. Hawtrey's sudden and early death was to leave a large gap in her professional life.

By 1940 she had already gained much experience in the younger "character roles" of the classics, working with Edith Evans in *The Country Wife* and *As You Like It*, and in 1941 she joined Barry Jackson's RSC company at Stratford-upon-Avon for a season. Her Mrs Malaprop in *The Rivals* was hailed as "brilliant" by one critic, while she was judged a sardonic Kate in *The Taming of the Shrew*. She also took the roles of the Nurse in *Romeo and Juliet* and Mistress Quickly in *The Merry Wives of Windsor*, a part she was to play again in Laurence Olivier's film version of *Henry V*. It was obvious from these roles that Freda Jackson's distinguished rather than pretty face would win her only a narrow band of work on screen in Britain. On stage, at least, she revealed a determination to work in the best possible plays and venues.

Her intelligence and also her classical training in the theatre, were to stand her in excellent stead for the role she was to repeat in more than one play, if in a slightly different guise, that of the sadistic harridan, Mrs Voray, in Joan Temple's *No Room at the Inn*. Freda Jackson added a coarse social realism and a measure of twisted gentility to a play which could have been described as a crossbreed between thriller and melodrama. Mrs Voray was a woman who took in evacuees for money, keeping them in terror in a house which was little more than a brothel. The play struck a bitter note of recognition in post-war Britain, forcing some people to recognize some of the social problems which had been swept under the carpet during the war. The play ran for a year, and in the intervening period of three years between it and Ivan Foxwell's film version, there was a notorious court case in Britain involving the mistreatment of evacuees. From the film, a more sentimental version of the play, Freda Jackson's face became familiar to a wider audience. Kenneth Tynan described her as "swift of movement, tart, and venomous on a scale which Hogarth would have recognised as and claimed for his own: a twentieth century rat-wife."

As David Quinlan, author of *Wicked Women of the Screen* wrote: "[for Freda Jackson] of shadow face and jagged smile there was little respite from villainy." However, on stage this was not quite the case, although she did triumph in one of the nastiest classical roles, Goneril in *King Lear*, in 1952, "as fierce as a she-wolf". In Northampton, she took her favourite role, Marguerite Gautier in *La Dame aux camélias*, at the age of 48. On the less flattering large screen, she played more broadly comic roles: from Mrs Gargery in David Lean's *Great Expectations* in 1946 to Mrs Seagrim in Tony Richardson's *Tom Jones* in 1963. Her return to Northampton allowed her to spend time with her husband, Henry Bird, a painter and art teacher, whom she had married in 1937. Together they enjoyed the company of other artists and actors, and Jackson divided her time between supporting roles in London and major roles in excellent repertory companies, such as *Mother Courage* at Bristol in 1961.

In 1960 she joined the cast of the Hammer Horror film *Brides of Dracula*, soliciting a description of her "unalloyed evil, as she crooned endearments to bring 'dead' girls scrabbling through the earth from their coffins." Five years later, she was the "terrifyingly disfigured" wife of Boris Karloff in *Die Monster Die* (*Monster of Terror*).

Some critics have remarked that she was too unwilling to compromise on roles, and that she would not sell her talent short. Although this may have been true, she achieved a remarkable variety of work in a long career and impressed a number of people with her sometimes ferocious talent. John Cowper Powys, author and poet, was once heckled by Freda Jackson, at great length, whilst giving a lecture on "Shakespeare as a Welshman". In a letter written to her husband the following day, he described her as "the most wonderful woman I have ever met".

Born Freda Jackson. **Father** A railway foreman. **Marriage** Henry Bird, painter and art teacher, 1937. **Children** One son. **Education** High Pavement School, Nottingham; University College, Nottingham University. **Career** Schoolteacher; stage début, Northampton repertory company, 1934; London début, the nurse in *The Sacred Flame*, Q Theatre, 1936; Old Vic début, Lucy in *The Country Wife*. **Theatre** (includes, in London, unless otherwise indicated) With Northampton repertory company, 1934–36; *The Sacred Flame*, 1936; *Night Must Fall*, on tour; *The Country Wife*, *As You Like It*, *Trelawny of the Wells*, *Hamlet*, all with Old Vic Company, 1936–39; *Judgement Day*, *The Taming of the Shrew*, *Twelfth Night*, *The Merry Wives of Windsor*, *The Rivals*, *Romeo and Juliet*, all Stratford-upon-Avon, 1940–41; *No Room at the Inn*, 1945; *No Room at the Inn*, Bournemouth, 1946; *The Father*, 1949; *They Walk Alone*, 1949; *Women of Twilight*, 1952; *King Lear*, 1952; *Anna Christie*, Dublin, 1953; *La Dame aux camélias*, Northampton, 1955; *Camino Real*, 1957; *Duel of Angels*, 1958; *Sergeant Musgrave's Dance*, 1959; *Intimate Relations*, Oxford, 1960; *Mother Courage*, Bristol, 1961; *John Gabriel Borkman*, 1961; *When We Are Married*, 1970; *Uncle Vanya*, 1982. **Films** (include) *Henry V*, 1944; *A Canterbury Tale*, 1944; *No Room at the Inn*, 1948; *Women of Twilight*, 1952; *Bhowani Junction*, 1956; *Brides of Dracula*, 1960; *Tom Jones*, 1963; *Monster of Terror* (US title, *Die Monster Die*), 1965. **Television** (includes) *She Fell Among Thieves*; *The Kilvert Diaries*. **Cause of death** Undisclosed, at age 82. **Further reading** David Quinlan, *Wicked Women of the Screen*, 1987.

LE DUC THO

Vietnamese Politician

Born **Tonkin Province, French Indo-China, 14 October 1911**

Died **Hanoi, Vietnam, 13 October 1990**

Le Duc Tho was one of the dominant figures in the Vietnamese Communist Party for some 60 years. A hard-liner in the Stalinist mould, he played a key role in establishing party supremacy in North Vietnam, winning North Vietnamese independence from France, defeating the United States and unifying North and South Vietnam.

A shadowy figure for most of his life, Tho achieved an uncharacteristic public profile as the North's chief negotiator in the four years of Paris peace talks which led to American withdrawal from Vietnam. The result was the controversial joint award of the Nobel Peace Prize to Tho and Henry Kissinger, and Tho's equally controversial rejection of the award on the grounds that peace had not yet been reached in Vietnam.

Le Duc Tho was a pseudonym. He was born Phan Dinh Khai, one of several sons of a middle-ranking administrative official in what is now Nam Ha Province, then the French colony of Tonkin. Tho's personal background always remained obscure, but his family appear to have been well enough off to have him educated in French-run schools.

Vietnam at the time of Tho's birth was divided into the three provinces of Tonkin in the north, around Hanoi; Annam in the central coastal strip; and Cochin-China to the south. Together with Cambodia and Laos the entire area was generally referred to as French Indo-China, and had been a colony since the 1880s.

Tho's education gained him a job as a post office telegrapher, but the decisive factor in his early development was his involvement with left-wing political agitation. Before he was 20 he had, with Ho Chi Minh, helped found the Indo-Chinese Communist Party in 1930.

Given Tho's privileged origins, his identification with the Communist movement is something of a mystery. As with many other Asian Communists, nationalist resentment of a colonial regime played its part, and the fact that Tho's own father was a symbol of this hated colonial presence suggests some inner tension.

The immediate results of Tho's political commitment were discouraging. Having participated in a large-scale revolt against French rule in 1930, he spent the next six years in the penal settlement of Poulo Condore (Con Son). Conditions were cramped and unpleasant, but a number of Tho's political soulmates were also at Poulo Condore, including Le Duan, later Party secretary-general, and Phan Van Dong, a future prime minister. The prisoners were able to continue their education, and on one occasion even put on a production of Molière.

Released in 1936, Tho immediately returned to work as a press and propaganda activist. Already a dour, seemingly humourless personality, the years of imprisonment, and what were referred to by the Party as "semi-open activities", made him increasingly secretive and self-effacing, an ideal organizer of subversion. Subversion had its risks, and Tho was again imprisoned in 1939, where he remained for most of World War II, and where he revealed a taste for political poetry. Whatever its artistic merit, the political preoccupation of Tho's muse is clear, as in "Cell of Hatred":

> Rage grips me against those barbaric imperialists,
> So many years their heels have crushed our country...

While Tho languished behind bars, the situation in French Indo-China was changing radically. France's defeat in 1940 left the French colonies isolated and vulnerable, and despite a brief British occupation that year, Vietnam was effectively dominated by Japan throughout the war. By raising the banner of resistance to both Vichy France and Japanese occupation, Ho Chi Minh was able to establish a much broader-based, more specifically nationalist movement, the so-called Viet Minh. Towards the war's end the Viet Minh emerged as the principal political force in Tonkin and most of Annam, but not in the South.

By the time Tho was released from prison in 1944 (according to one source this was to forestall a massacre of prisoners by the departing Japanese), the Viet Minh were poised to take over from the French authorities in North Vietnam. Tho threw himself into the preparations for an uprising. The revolt culminated in the "August Revolution" of 1945, at the end of which, on 2 September, Ho Chi Minh proclaimed Vietnamese independence from Hanoi. Tho's reward was appointment to the Party's Central Committee.

France's post-war government, however, was not yet ready to accept the situation in Indo-China, and late in 1946 war broke out between the new North Vietnamese regime and the French forces in the South. Organizing resistance in the South became a prime objective of the Hanoi government, and in 1949 Tho was made chief delegate for South Vietnam, exercising administrative and political control over the fighting.

The struggle against the French, which lasted until the colonial power's withdrawal in 1954, was mirrored by political infighting between Tho and his former fellow prisoner, Le Duan. Not much is known about this, but Tho's apparent victory, in securing Le Duan's recall to Hanoi, seems in the end to have given Le Duan the chance to consolidate his hold on power. In 1960 it was Le Duan, not Tho, who emerged as Party secretary-general.

By the Geneva Conference decision of July 1954, Vietnam was partitioned into North and South along the 17th Parallel in Annam. Ho Chi Minh's Communist movement, reconstituted as the Lao Dong or Workers' Party of Vietnam, was left in control of the North. South Vietnam, under a non-Communist, pro-western regime, began to receive significant backing after 1955 from the United States, which stepped into the vacuum created by French withdrawal.

Le Duc Tho was clearly one of the Party's leading lights by now, with a position on the secretariat of the Central Committee, and specializing in Party organization and ideology. His status was confirmed by his attendance as a North Vietnamese representative at the Twentieth Congress of the Communist Party of the Soviet Union in 1956.

In 1957 North Vietnam launched a guerrilla war against the South, working through its proxy irregular army, the Viet Cong, to overthrow the government of Saigon. Tho was at the centre of this effort, as secretary-general of the Party Training School. This instructed the Party cadres who in turn directed Viet Cong operations, a network over which Tho exerted a close personal control.

As the war intensified, Tho's influence in the Party hierarchy appears to have increased, although he never attained supreme power. He was instrumental in bringing in a new Party constitution in 1960, and was reported to have ruthlessly "purified" the Party, thousands of whose members were alleged to have been executed.

American involvement in the war, an acknowledged fact after 1962, at first seemed to doom the Communist insurgency to failure, but events proved otherwise. Despite a massive commitment of manpower and technology the United States found first the Viet Cong, and then North Vietnam's own regular troops, a resilient enemy. Tho's role in the war with the United States continued to be that of directing Viet Cong operations, allegedly as "Chairman for the Supervision of the South". He was undoubtedly one of the most stubborn advocates of all out resistance in what was, for him, both an ideological and a national struggle.

By early 1968 public discouragement with the war in the United States was so strong that President Johnson had effectively conceded the pointlessness of further involvement, by agreeing to negotiate with the North Vietnamese for a ceasefire. That it took four years to arrange an armistice, followed by American withdrawal, was due in large part to the obduracy, as well as the negotiating skills, of Le Duc Tho. Talks began in Paris in May 1968, and although Tho participated throughout only as a "special adviser" to the North Vietnamese delegation it was well understood that he, as a Politburo member, was the driving force.

Between the North Vietnamese and the American positions there was inevitably a wide gap, which took years of haggling to bridge, against a background of continued fighting in Vietnam itself. The Americans began by stipulating a mutual withdrawal of US and North Vietnamese forces, followed by the exchange of prisoners and a peaceful negotiation of South Vietnam's status. Tho, in the name of the North Vietnam government, demanded America's unconditional withdrawal, leaving North Vietnam's forces where they were, and a new South Vietnam government including members of the Communist Party.

In the end both sides had to compromise, but in any such test of diplomatic endurance, Tho had an advantage over his American opponents. For political reasons the American government *had* to disengage, eventually, from Vietnam, and the North Vietnamese leadership not only knew this but were also prepared to accept high losses on the ground in pursuit of their goal. Time was on Tho's side.

Matters began to inch forward after the first secret meetings between Tho and Henry Kissinger, President Nixon's special adviser. Beginning in August 1969, the two men continued to meet on an irregular, *ad hoc* basis for the next two years, so that, while the public talks remained apparently stagnant, behind the scenes a deal was being painfully worked out. It was in these negotiations that Tho revealed the qualities that earned him the grudging respect of even the arch-Machiavellian Kissinger. Capable of sitting motionless at the table for hours on end, Tho was dubbed "Iron Pants" by the exasperated Kissinger, who found him "difficult to come to terms with". It was a measure of how frustrating Kissinger found the Vietnamese delaying tactics that on one occasion he was goaded into characterizing the entire delegation as "Tawdry, filthy shits". Tho, for his part, does not appear to have reciprocated this involuntary accolade. In his eyes Kissinger was representative of everything hateful in the West and the capitalist world, the diplomatic embodiment of American arrogance and brutal power.

In the meantime the pressure on both sides for a settlement slowly mounted. The war was more unpopular than ever in the United States by 1972, which was presidential election year. The North

Vietnamese were also aware that Russian and Chinese support for them was less defensible in an age of dawning superpower *détente*.

In October 1972 Tho and Kissinger, whose talks were by this time a matter of public record, reached a nine-point provisional agreement. This gave Kissinger the pretext for his famous pronouncement, on the eve of the elections, that "peace was at hand". There were last-minute objections on both sides, principally over the Nixon government's determination to consult the South Vietnamese before finalization. Only after the Christmas bombing of Hanoi could the North Vietnamese opposition to this provision be overcome.

The agreement signed in January 1973 was far more of a North Vietnamese triumph than an American one. On the crucial issue of withdrawal it was the United States alone which pulled out its troops, leaving the North Vietnamese in possession of the ground they had won in ten years of war. In return, Tho had been obliged to accept the continued existence of Nguyen Van Thieu's pro-western government in Saigon. A "National Council of Reconciliation and Concord" was eventually to supervise elections for a unified Vietnam, although the machinery for implementing this provision was left unspecified.

Behind these pious bromides Tho had not conceded much of substance. Once United States forces were out of Vietnam there was little likelihood of their return, as Tho instinctively must have known. Nor was there anything to inhibit a recommencement of hostilities between North and South Vietnam, and this time there could not be much doubt of the outcome. The announcement, in October 1973, that Tho and Kissinger had been nominated for a joint Nobel Peace Prize consequently created something of a furore.

To his critics, Kissinger had devoted most of his diplomatic talents to the pursuit of war rather than peace; while Tho was a Communist who had been fighting an ideological war all his life. They seemed improbable candidates, despite the achievement of the ceasefire. Kissinger accepted, whereas Tho rejected the award. Tho publicly gave as his reason the fact that "Peace has not yet really been established in Vietnam". Another reason was a genuine distaste for sharing such an award with someone who, in Tho's eyes, was at least partly responsible for inflicting so much suffering on the Vietnamese people. That he himself had not scrupled to inflict comparable suffering in the past would not have seemed a valid objection to Tho.

Tho played a leading part in the final offensives against the Thieu regime in 1974 to 1975. In January 1975, as the high command in the south were debating where to attack in the central highlands, the debate was settled by the arrival of Tho, who made it clear he thought a major offensive was necessary. As so often with Tho's interventions, the political insight was the key to military success. The "Ho Chi Minh Campaign" of 1975 drove everything before it, and Saigon had fallen by April. Tho's report to the Party leadership in Hanoi, on 1 May, took the form of one of his poems:

> Finished forever, our days
> Of hunger, misery and great pain...

To journalists he spoke of his "indescribable emotions" at this culmination of 45 years of personal struggle.

In the post-war period Tho continued to function as the *éminence grise* of the united Vietnam. He never held a ministerial portfolio, but instead was responsible for Party organization. Between 1983 and 1986 he was the deputy chairman of the National Defence Committee of the Party. He was also reportedly entrusted, in 1978, with the campaign against the Pol Pot regime in neighbouring Cambodia, when the latter provoked Vietnam into invading, and oversaw the formation of the Heng Samrin government there.

When Tho's old rival Le Duan died in July 1986, there were rumours that Tho might succeed him as secretary-general. That this key post went instead to Truong Chinh was an indication that Tho's standing in the Party hierarchy was less secure than hitherto. This perhaps reflected dissatisfaction within the Party over Vietnam's disastrous economic record since the conclusion of the unification war. Tho was of course closely identified with the attempt to impose a classic Communist command economy on the South.

To be fair, Vietnam's economic situation was not helped by the perceived need to intervene in Cambodia, and by the subsequent short war with China. Vietnam's continued victimization by the United States, which obstructed post-war reconstruction aid, was another debilitating factor. But it is also clear that in such straitened circumstances Tho's hard-line Stalinist views on collectivization were not appropriate, in particular the persecution of many southerners tainted, in the eyes of such as Tho, with the virus of capitalism. All these factors heightened the immiseration of the country, of which the spectacle of the "boat people" has in recent years been the most poignant evidence.

In December 1986 Tho was persuaded to "retire", and spent the last four years of his life as a mere "adviser" to the Politburo. He was naturally profoundly out of sympathy with the Gorbachev-style reforms and openness lately affected by the leadership. Even in retirement, however, Tho was apparently not entirely bereft of influence. One of his brothers, Mai Chi Tho, was interior minister and hence in charge of the East German trained security apparatus. And Tho was naturally revered as one of the great wartime leaders.

In March 1990 a leading reformer, Tran Xuan Bach, who had gone so far as to advocate a multi-party system, was abruptly dismissed. This was said to have followed an attack on him at the Party plenum by Tho. It was a possible indication of an impending or intended crackdown in a regime which remained very much the creation of Tho and his generation.

Born Phan Dinh Khai. **Father** A civil servant. **Marriages** Two. **Career** Radiotelegrapher; founder, with Ho Chi Minh, Indo-Chinese Communist Party, 1930; imprisoned for anti-French activities, on island, Poulo Condore, now Con Son, 1930–36; director, Communist propaganda organization, Nam Dinh, 1936–39; imprisoned, Nam Dinh jail, 1939, later at Son La, until 1944; in charge of organizational work, Central Committee, 1944; member, Central Committee and Standing member, Indo-Chinese Communist Party, 1945–55; member, Communist Party Central Committee, Bac Ty, Tonkin; in charge of Party Organizational Work, 1945–48; deputy secretary, Party Central Office, South Vietnam, 1948–52, secretary, 1952–55; member, Politburo, Lao Dong party of Vietnam, North Vietnam, 1955–86; member, General Organizational Department, 1957–68; deputy secretary, Party Central Office, Vietnam, 1968; member, secretariat, Central Committee of the Communist Party, 1960–86; Chairman for the Supervision of the South, 1967; head, South Vietnam Communist Central Committee participation in commanding Ho Chi Minh campaign, 1975; deputy representative of Communist Party and Government Committee, South Vietnam after liberation, 1975–76; head, South-West War Front, 1977–79; deputy chairman, National Defence Committee of Communist party, 1983–86; retired from Central Committee, 1986, adviser, Politburo, 1986 onwards. **Related activities** Viet Minh government delegate for South Vietnam, 1949, head, Reunification Committee, 1955–56; North Vietnamese representative, Twentieth Congress of the Soviet Communist Party, 1956; member, Military Commission, 1967–82; special adviser, North Vietnamese delegation, Paris Conference and peace talks with Henry Kissinger, 1968–73; adviser, formation of Heng Samrin regime, Phnom Penh, Cambodia, 1978. **Other activities** Poet. **Awards and honours** Refused Nobel Prize for Peace, awarded jointly with Henry Kissinger, 1973. **Cause of death** Cancer of the throat, at age 78. **Further reading** Henry Kissinger, *Years of Upheaval*, 1982; Stanley Karnow, *Vietnam: A History*, 1983; Robert Shaplen, *Bitter Victory*, 1986.

GENERAL CURTIS LeMAY

American Air Force Officer and Strategist

Born **Columbus, Ohio, 15 November 1906**

Died **March Air Force Base, California, 1 October 1990**

Curtis LeMay will be forever famous for two things. Most notorious was his suggestion, during the Vietnam war, that North Vietnam should be bombed "back into the Stone Ages". And in the presidential elections of 1968 he was the running-mate of the segregationist George Wallace, a combination which enhanced the reputation of neither man.

Everything in LeMay's record and public utterances, particularly on nuclear weapons, tended to reinforce the popular image of Pentagon generals as overweight brutes, in love with the Bomb and glorying in their ability to inflict technocratic slaughter.

Behind the deplorable image, however, there was a genuine historical significance. LeMay played a leading role in the strategic bombing of both Germany and Japan during World War II, and was responsible for executing President Truman's order to drop the atomic bomb. In the post-war period, he organized the Berlin airlift of 1948, and was the executive power-house in the creation of America's front-line defence in the nuclear age, the Strategic Air Command.

Curtis Emerson LeMay was brought up in Columbus, Ohio, where his father, of French Canadian descent, was an ironworker. As a boy he hunted, and dabbled in amateur radio sets.

He wanted to attend West Point Military Academy, but could not secure the necessary recommendation from his congressman. Determined to pursue a military career, he then started a degree course at the Ohio State University's School of Engineering, and joined the Reserve Officers' Training Corps at the same time.

This back-door approach paid off, in 1928, with a commission in the Field Artillery Reserve. LeMay was then appointed to the 62nd Field Artillery Brigade at Camp Knox in Kentucky. He completed his engineering degree in 1932, as a result of a service posting back to Columbus.

In the meantime he had become a pilot. Lindbergh had made his historic flight from New York to Paris in 1927, and LeMay was one of many young people to be inspired by this with an ambition to be an aviator.

He applied for a place in the Air Corps Flying School, then based outside Los Angeles, in September 1928, and graduated in June 1929. By January 1930 he was a regular commissioned lieutenant in the Air Corps. Postings followed to air bases in Michigan, Ohio, Virginia and Hawaii, where LeMay served as pilot, engineer and operations officer, and studied advanced navigation.

In 1937 he received the appointment which was to shape his subsequent career, as operations and intelligence officer for the 49th Bombardment Squadron at Langley Field, Virginia. He was thus one of the first navigator-pilots for the new B-17 heavy bomber, the so-called Flying Fortress. The B-17s were sent on a flight to Buenos Aires that year for what, in navy jargon, is generally called showing the flag. LeMay, as navigator, established a record for plotting a course 600 miles out to sea and then coming in directly on course through overcast skies. A similar tour the following year won LeMay's bomber group a trophy for the excellence of their navigation. By 1939 LeMay was commanding his own B-17.

In 1940 came promotion to captain, and a succession of assignments to different bomber squadrons. The next year LeMay, by now a major, was chosen to make experimental long-range flights to Britain and Africa. Landing heavy bombers on fields not built for them, after a gruelling transatlantic flight, was a risky business, and earned LeMay the Distinguished Flying Cross.

With American involvement in World War II, LeMay was posted to active service in Europe in the autumn of 1942, as a colonel in command of 305th Bombardment Group. His unit was one of the first United States bomber groups to see action.

His style became terrifyingly apparent, to his own men as much as to the enemy, in a series of bombing raids from Britain in 1942. Zigzagging to avoid enemy ground fire, many of the B-17s had strayed off course on their first missions, and had dropped their bombs off target. For the next raid, on the French port of St Nazaire, LeMay therefore decreed that there was to be no zigzagging. He led his group straight in, a cigar clenched between his teeth, through seven minutes of "ack-ack" fire, before releasing his bombs on target. It was a pattern adhered to with unwavering determination from then on. Every time, LeMay seemed so indifferent to the flak coming up that his crews nicknamed him "Old Ironpants".

Such tactics were criticized at the time, but there was no denying that they were the surest way of bombing efficiently. LeMay also introduced a combat formation of 18 bombers, so grouped that their defensive firepower could be used against fighter attack to maximum effect. Despite this innovation, losses in bombing raids were severe, to the point where Eighth Air Force, of which 305th Group was a part, had to be temporarily withdrawn from combat duty at one point to rebuild its strength.

In August 1943 LeMay led a major raid against the Messerschmidt plant at Regensburg in Bavaria. Because of the distance involved it was decided, for the first time, to shuttle the bombers to North Africa after delivering their payloads, another long-distance achievement, for which LeMay received the Distinguished Service Cross.

Promoted to brigadier shortly after, and to major-general in March 1944, LeMay took over the 3rd Bombardment Division, within Eighth Air Force. This was one of the units used to bomb German positions in Normandy in support of the D-Day landings.

In August 1944 LeMay was transferred to the Far East, where long-range bombing of Japanese targets was finally becoming feasible. At first he was based in India and China, at the head of 20th Bomber Command, made up of the new and formidable B-29 Superfortresses.

There were three raids against industrial centres in Japanese-held Manchuria in the autumn of 1944, but it soon became apparent that the range was simply too great for effective bombing. When the Mariana Islands fell to the Americans, however, the picture altered. The B-29s were now within easy range of the Japanese mainland, and a raid on Tokyo itself was mounted as early as November 1944. Nevertheless the initial results of mainland bombing were disappointing.

LeMay, now in charge of 21st Bomber Command in the Marianas, was convinced that high altitude bombing was not the way to knock Japan out of the war. Accordingly he stripped his force of B-29s down to the bare minimum of equipment, to increase their bomb-load, and flew a low-level raid over Tokyo on 9 March 1945, with incendiary bombs. The result was one of the most horrifying Allied successes of the war. With each of the 300 B-29s releasing 1500 incendiaries, 16 square miles of the Japanese capital were razed to the ground and an estimated 100,000 people killed. For nine days the raids went on, devastating other major population centres of Japan. They were only halted, after some 10,000 tons had been dropped, because Bomber Command had exhausted existing stocks of incendiaries.

Resumed in the early summer of 1945, the fire-bombing was stepped up in ferocity. Japan's industrial production ground to a halt, 1.25 million tons of shipping were lost, 8 million people rendered homeless. The destruction had reached such proportions by mid-summer that Japan's ability to carry on fighting much longer was seriously in question. LeMay himself was convinced that a surrender could have been forced by conventional bombing alone, without resort to the atomic bomb.

Certainly the casualties caused by the nuclear bombing of Hiroshima and Nagasaki, which was done by a bomber under LeMay's command, were dwarfed by those of the first raid on Tokyo alone. This may explain LeMay's willingness, in subsequent years, to contemplate the use of what, in his view, was just another bomb. Nor can there be any question that, as far as LeMay was concerned, he was just obeying orders. "We went ahead and dropped the bombs because President Truman told me to do it", he explained matter-of-factly in 1985.

After the war, having flown back to Chicago non-stop from Japan in one of his bombers, LeMay took up an appointment as deputy chief of Air Staff Research and Development. Shortly after his return he was invited to run for Ohio senator, but indicated no interest in a political career at this stage.

In 1947 to 1948 he was the United States Air Force commander in Europe, which meant that when the Russian blockade of Berlin began, in June 1948, LeMay was the man called upon to organize the airlift. There was some initial confusion when the American commander-in-chief, General Clay, asked LeMay over the telephone for planes which could carry coal. "We must have a bad connection", said LeMay. "It sounds as if you are asking if we have planes for carrying coal." Assured this was the case, he recovered swiftly: "The Air Force can carry anything."

It was the beginning of a massive operation which, by the time the blockade was lifted in May 1949, had delivered more than 2 million tons of supplies in some 300,000 flights. LeMay flew some of the aircraft in himself.

In the middle of this, however, he was recalled to head a new organization, for which he was uniquely fitted. The Strategic Air Command (SAC), set up in 1948, was to consist of a force of long-range bombers, permanently on alert, for the delivery of nuclear bombs. LeMay headed SAC until 1957, and gave chilling reality to the concept of massive retaliation. By using the latest generation of heavy bombers, as well as the now standard technique of aerial refuelling, SAC acquired a truly global potential. Planes were kept in the air night and day, and LeMay had his own personal bomber in constant readiness at SAC's Nebraska command centre, so that he could lead a nuclear strike himself.

As befitted a man in such a position, LeMay's political views by now were those of the coldest of Cold Warriors. He was reported to have said that Communism could best be handled from a height of 50,000 feet.

In 1957 he was made vice-chief of staff to the Air Force, and in 1961 chief of staff. As a bomber, however, he was perhaps bound to come into conflict with the new strategic thinking at the end of the 1950s, which saw the future nuclear deterrent as missile-launched. To LeMay it was axiomatic that manned bombers would continue to play a role equal at least to the new ICBMs.

At the heart of his disagreement with Robert Macnamara, President Kennedy's defence secretary, was the retention of enough bombers to maintain "first strike capability". Politically this was unacceptable. During the Cuban missile crisis, LeMay was for an immediate air attack on Cuba, regardless of the probable Russian response. As Kennedy remarked, "If you have to go, you want LeMay in the lead bomber. But you never want LeMay deciding whether or not you have to go."

By the time he was eased out by the Johnson administration, on 1 February 1965, LeMay was already fundamentally at odds with the prosecution of the war in Vietnam. Even when, shortly after his "retirement", the United States started bombing raids on North Vietnam, he thought it was not enough. "We are swatting flies when we should be going after the manure pile", he complained.

In March 1965 President Johnson authorized what was called "Rolling Thunder", a systematic, long-term bombing of the North, using B-52s. It was aimed at cutting off supplies to North Vietnam's forces in the south, but accomplished little in this respect, apart from stiffening Hanoi's resistance and provoking world outrage. To LeMay, fuming now on the sidelines, it was all wrong, and inspired his most notorious bomb-blast. That year he brought out his book, *Mission with LeMay*. "My solution to the problem," he wrote, "would be to tell them [the North Vietnamese] frankly that they've got to draw in their horns and stop their aggression or we're going to bomb them back into the Stone Ages."

His unhappiness at the conduct of the war was undoubtedly LeMay's principal reason for coming out in support of Governor Wallace's American Independent Party in 1968. It was the action of a political *naïf*, which also got him sacked from the electronics executive job he had occupied since leaving the Air Force.

Observers pointed out at the time that Wallace and LeMay were ill-matched running-mates. LeMay had actually promoted racial integration while Air Chief of Staff; and Wallace was to find LeMay's views on the Bomb an electoral Hiroshima. At their very first press conference to introduce LeMay as "a man of peace", the General went into self-destruct. The nuclear bomb, he told the world, was "just another weapon in the arsenal. There may be occasions when it would be most efficient to use nuclear weapons." He went on to claim that if he had a choice between being killed "with a rusty knife" in Vietnam, or using nuclear weapons, "I'd lean towards the nuclear weapon."

Americans, in other words, needed to overcome their "phobia" about the Bomb, which in any case did not mean the end of the world. As proof, he cited the allegedly flourishing state of the flora and fauna on Bikini Atoll, 20 years after nuclear tests there.

It was not a message, by the late 1960s, that was likely to go down well with any but the most conservative Americans, and LeMay's political career was over almost before it had begun.

Born Curtis Emerson LeMay. **Parents** Erving, ironworker, and Arizona Dove (Carpenter) LeMay. **Marriage** Helen Estelle Maitland, 1934. **Children** One daughter, Patricia Jane. **Education** South High School, Columbus, Ohio; School of Engineering, Ohio State University, Columbus, 1928, BCE, 1932; Air Corps Primary Flying School, March Field, California, 1928–29; Air Corps Advanced Flying School, Kelly Field, Texas, 1929; studied advanced navigation, Langley Field, Virginia, 1933; Air Corps Tactical School, Maxwell Field, Alabama, 1939. **Career** Member, Reserve Officers' Training Corps; second lieutenant, Field Artillery Reserve, 1928; joined Regular Army, 1928; second lieutenant, Air Reserve, 1929; second lieutenant, Air Corps, Regular Army, 27th Pursuit Squadron, Selfridge Field, Michigan, 1930–34; also, assistant engineer, and operations officer, Norton Field, Columbus, Ohio, 1931–32; with 18th Pursuit Group, Schofield Barracks, Hawaii, 1934; became first lieutenent, 1935; operations and intelligence officer, 49th Bombardment Squadron, Air Force General Headquarters, Langley Field, Virginia, 1937–39, commander B-17 airplane, 1940; became captain, 1940; operations and intelligence officer, 41st Reconnaissance Squadron, Langley Field, 1940; commander, 34th Bombardment Group, Langley Field, 1941, group operations officer, Westover Field, Massachusetts; became major, 1941; became lieutenant-colonel, 1942; became colonel, 1942; commanding officer, 305th Bombardment Group, in California, then England, 1942; became brigadier, 1943; commanding general, Third Bombardment Division, 1943–44; became major-general, 1944; commander, 20th Bomber Command, Pacific, 1944–45; commander, Mariana-based 21st Bomber Command, 1945; deputy chief, Air Staff Research and Development, 1945–47; commander, United States Air Force in Europe, 1947–48; commander-in-chief, Strategic Air Command, 1948–57; vice-chief of staff, United States Air Force, 1957–61, chief of staff, 1961–64. **Other activities** American Independent Party candidate for vice-president of the United States, 1968. **Offices and memberships** Life trustee, National Geographic Society. **Awards and honours** With members of group, awarded Mackay Trophy for superior achievement in aviation, 1938; Distinguished Flying Cross with two Oak Leaf Clusters; 1941; Distinguished Service Cross, 1943; Silver Star, 1943; Air Medal with three Oak Leaf Clusters, 1943; Distinguished Service Medal, 1944, with one Oak Leaf Cluster, 1945; Medal for Humane Action, 1948; Distinguished Flying Cross, Great Britain; Commandeur de la Légion d'honneur, France; Croix de guerre with Palm Leaf, France; Belgian Croix de guerre with Palm Leaf; Brazilian Order of the Southern Cross; Commander, Moroccan Order of the Ouissam Alaouite Cherifien; Russian Order of Patriotic War; Argentine Order of Aeronautical Merit; General Mitchell Memorial Trophy, American Legion, 1954; several honorary degrees. **Publication** *Mission with LeMay*, 1965. **Cause of death** Heart attack, at age 83.

BERTHA LINDSAY

American Religious Elder

***Born* Massachusetts, USA, 1897**

***Died* Canterbury, New Hampshire, 3 October 1990**

There would come a time, prophesied their founder, Mother Ann Lee, when the number of the Shakers would be counted on the fingers of one hand. By her death at the age of 93 Eldress Bertha Lindsay, the last surviving Shaker eldress, has almost brought that prophecy to pass. At her once thriving community in Canterbury only one elderly sister now remains. In Maine the Shakers at Sabbathday Lake now include only four covenanted members and a further four who follow their teaching.

An illiterate textile worker from Manchester, England, Mother Ann Lee became a member of the Shaking Quakers in the mid–1750s. The sect was a radical branch of the English Quakers, so called because of the ritual practices, borrowed from the French Camisards, of shaking, shouting, dancing, whirling and singing in tongues when overtaken by religious fervour. After losing several babies in childbirth Ann Lee had a vision sometime in the early 1770s in which she saw Adam and Eve engaged in carnal intercourse. She awoke convinced that it was sex itself that was the root of all evil in the world, the cause of Man's first Fall. Believing herself charged with the task of spreading the message in the New World, she and eight followers crossed the Atlantic in 1774 where they set about building up the United Society of Believers in Christ's Second Coming.

Shaker communities, their members committed by vows to lifelong celibacy and productive labour, spread throughout New England. By 1826, 18 Shaker villages had been set up in eight states. Throughout the nineteenth century many more followers had visions which confirmed Mother Ann Lee's own conviction that she herself represented the female spirit of God, Christ's second incarnation on earth. While some visitors, among them the writer Charles Dickens, were shocked by the head-to-toe mystic shaking that ritually took place during Shaker services, others could not fail to be impressed by the beauty and simplicity of the Shaker way of life.

Mother Ann Lee's insistence upon total celibacy made her belief in the eventual demise of her sect almost a self-fulfilling prophecy. It was, moreover, an issue of the first importance. "Brothers" and "sisters" who were suspected of forming attachments to one another were either separated or encouraged to return to the world to live together as couples. And of course this meant that the communities could only survive by attracting converts or by taking in — as they did frequently throughout the nineteenth century — orphans and abandoned children.

Bertha Lindsay, who came to Canterbury in 1905 when the community was already beginning to decline, was herself an orphan, adopted at the age of five on the death of her parents. In her demure old age she would recall with a smile the kindness of the Shaker sisters who took her in and the beauty of the apple orchard which was then in bloom. At the age of 21 she chose to sign the Shaker covenant and become a sister: "I felt that I could give as much here as I could anywhere else in the world and could have more friends, both men and women. If I had gone into the world and married, I wouldn't have had that."

The older Bertha Lindsay was a walking advertisement for the way of life she chose. In 1965 when the sect was formally closed to new members, she helped to set up a museum at Canterbury dedicated to telling the world about the Shaker way of life. In her starched white bonnet and apron she was herself a fount of stories — many of which she recorded on tape after she lost her eyesight at the age of 90. "I want people to know", she said, "we did have fun and plenty of it".

Shaker brethren are known for their skills in carpentry — they were early pioneers in machining wood and produced the famous and austere Shaker chair. Less well known are the many tools invented by the Shakers, tools which include everything from an automatic pea-sheller, a turbine water wheel and rotary harrow, to the circular saw and common clothes peg. Had they been more mercenary these inventions alone could have made them millionaires, but taking out patents was never part of Shaker mythology, nor did they believe in harnessing "the gifts of the spirit" for worldly gain.

Bertha Lindsay's own gifts of the spirit were mainly fulfilled in the kitchens at Canterbury and in the vegetable garden which she started in 1942, growing all kinds of fruit, salads and vegetables. In 1987 she published a book of her own recipes, *Seasoned with Grace*, in which each chapter is preceded by stories of Shaker life. What she said about apples will give some kind of idea of the flavour of her writing.

> We used Talman Sweets for baking in the summer and yellow Transparents and Maiden's Blush in the spring. In the fall, we used Jonathans for boiling. The Winesaps were also a favorite at that time of the year. The Nonesuch, Sheep's Nose, and Turkey Egg apples were used for mincemeat pies. The Chenango, or Virgin apple, was a very dry apple when cooked, so we were very fond of using it when making the famous Shaker hand pies.

When asked if she was sad about the demise of the sect in which she had lived so happily, Bertha Lindsay was apt to remind her questioner of the other half of Mother Ann Lee's prophecy. When the number of the Shakers could be counted on less than the fingers of one hand, she said, then "there would be a revival of spirit in the world" and the Shakers as such would no longer be needed. This, Bertha Lindsay believed, was now in some sense coming about. If one considers this an age of spiritual revival then perhaps one can understand her optimism. Certainly such central tenets of Mother Ann Lee's teaching as pacifism, the importance of the good life and the central concentration on the complete spiritual equality of men and women are doctrines which find a wide echo in the world today.

Born Goldie Ina Ruby Lindsay. **Education** Shaker Community School, Canterbury, New Hampshire. **Career** Member, United Society of Believers in Christ's Second Appearing, or The Shakers, Canterbury, New Hampshire, 1905, second elder, 1967–70, elder 1970 onwards; caterer to business leaders of community; manager, community's fancywork trade, 1944–58. **Publication** *Seasoned with Grace: my generation of Shaker cooking*, 1987. **Cause of death** A stroke, at age 93.

SIR BEN LOCKSPEISER

British Scientist and Administrator

***Born* London, England, 9 March 1891**

***Died* 18 October 1990**

One of World War I's top "boffins", Sir Ben Lockspeiser continued to play a vital part in scientific development in Britain after the war. Known by his colleagues as "the genius of very uncommon common sense", he backed a very wide range of projects varying from aircraft structures and armaments to nuclear weapons and cosmic rays. A gentle, chubby, kindly man who was a good listener, he had an unusual gift for spotting good ideas and talents. "Scientific men with first-class judgement and originality of mind," wrote Sir Henry Tizard, "who are also good administrators and men of the world, with political wisdom and a sympathetic understanding of their fellow men are — if they exist at all — so rare that, for practical purposes, they may be ruled out of account." Sir Ben Lockspeiser was one of the few men who came a long way towards that ideal.

Born into an industrious and devout Jewish family, he started as a physicist, and graduated at Sidney Sussex College, Cambridge. In 1914, when World War I broke out, he was studying at the Royal School of Mines, but he enlisted in the Royal Army Medical Corps and was with the Friends' Ambulance Unit at Gallipoli. Invalided out, he spent some time in recuperation before joining the scientific civil service.

In 1920 he moved to the Royal Aircraft Establishment (RAE) at Farnborough, and for 17 years he worked with relatively low pay, in poor working conditions, in the armaments and aerodynamics section. He recalled later how at times buckets had to be placed in his dilapidated laboratory to catch the raindrops. Here he was recognized as an original and outstanding physicist who was also blessed with remarkable common sense. An all-round personality, he was a keen cellist and pianist, and formed the excellent RAE orchestra.

In 1937 he was promoted to be head of the RAE's Air Defence Department, and at last his great gift for administration blossomed. Under his leadership, the defence of important targets by barrage balloon was created, and in the war the accuracy of *Luftwaffe* raids on Britain was to be reduced considerably by the clusters of wire-tendered balloons which hovered over British cities. He was also responsible for inventing a method for de-icing aircraft which proved most effective and considerably reduced the number of bombers forced to crash in the war.

When hostilities began, he moved his department to Exeter where they worked on electronic fuses for bombs, but after a time he left to join the Air Ministry as assistant director of scientific research. Next he moved to Lord Beaverbrook's Ministry of Aircraft Production, where by 1943 he was director of scientific research.

Wing Commander Guy Gibson consulted him there for help with the idea of the Dambuster raids. No one could find a way of flying a Lancaster bomber accurately at 150 feet over the surface of water in reservoirs. In Gibson's words, Lockspeiser "thought an old idea might work: spotlights placed on either wing, pointing towards the water where they would converge at 150 feet. The pilot could see the spots and when they merged into one he knew the exact height. Within a week everyone could fly within a few feet of the water with amazing consistency."

In 1943 Lockspeiser saw the need to investigate the unknowns of supersonic flight, and for some reason gave the contract to the small Miles Aircraft Company which had only built small wooden aircraft up to that time. With inadequate resources the firm built a prototype, the M52, powered by a Whittle W2 jet engine. Shortly after the war Lockspeiser visited a German research establishment near Brunswick, and reckoned that swept-back wings were vital for supersonic flight. He therefore cancelled the contract for the M52, for which he was criticized, and unfortunately went on to say that "the impression that supersonic flight is just around the corner is quite erroneous. We intend to tackle these new problems by use of rocket-driven models, radio-controlled because we have not the heart to ask pilots to fly such high-speed aircraft." Could the fact that his son became a test pilot indicate a cause of his caution? The rocket-powered models were disastrous. Only 15 months later the piloted American rocket-powered Bell X-1 was flown faster than the speed of sound (Mach 1.06) by Captain Charles "Chuck" Yeager, and it was not for seven years that the first English Electric P1 Lightning broke the sound barrier. Lockspeiser was criticized for his caution, but by 1958 the Lightning was flying at better than Mach 2, and Concorde is still unmatched in crossing the Atlantic daily with commercial loads at twice the speed of sound.

By the end of the war Lockspeiser was widely recognized as not only a "good scientist" but an "industrious and sympathetic manager". By 1949 he had risen to be permanent secretary of the Department of Scientific and Industrial Research. Shortly afterwards a young man called Bernard Lovell came to plead for support. Drawing "a squiggle" on a piece of paper, he said this represented radio waves which had travelled through space for millions of years, and he requested a thousand pounds to build a radio telescope to investigate them. Recalling the visit later Lockspeiser said, "After he had explained about his idea, I realised that he was proposing a very promising line of enquiry and he got his 1000." Lockspeiser continued to back Sir Bernard Lovell over the years with hundreds of thousands of pounds, building very large steerable dish aerials, the largest in the world for many years. In 1956, when Lockspeiser retired from his post, Lovell felt the full force of the Public Accounts Committee and the Treasury, and was very aware of how valuable an umbrella Lockspeiser had been for his research.

Lockspeiser held many other posts, and was on the Council of the European Organization for Nuclear Research from 1955 to 1957. He was on the boards of a number of companies, making them give much more thought to research and development. Sympathetic, humorous and solid, his knowledge of government circles was invaluable, and having learnt to deal with all sorts from imperious ministers to scientific recluses, high-ranking officers in the services to sharp manufacturers, he was able to get his way when few others could.

During his time in ministries, very many projects received his backing, but the radio telescope system dominating the Cheshire plain is perhaps the most visible monument to Lockspeiser's great faith in young scientists with good ideas.

Born Benjamin Lockspeiser. **Parents** Leon and Rose Lockspeiser. **Marriages** 1) Elsie Shuttleworth, 1920 (died 1964); 2) Mary Alice Heywood, 1966 (died 1983). **Children** One son, David, and two daughters by first marriage. **Education** Grocer's School, London; scholar, Sidney Sussex College, Cambridge; Royal School of Mines, MA. **Military service** Royal Army Medical Corps, Friends' Ambulance Unit, Gallipoli, World War I. **Career** Researcher, armaments and aerodynamics section, Royal Aircraft Establishment, Farnborough, 1920–37, head of Air Defence Department, 1937–39; assistant director of scientific research, Air Ministry, 1939; deputy-director of scientific research and armaments, Ministry of Aircraft Production, 1941, director of scientific research, 1943, director-general of scientific research, 1945; chief scientist to Ministry of Supply, 1946–49; permanent secretary to Committee of Privy Council for Scientific and Industrial Research, 1949–56; retired, 1956. **Related activities** President, Council of European Organization for Nuclear Research, 1955–57. **Offices and memberships** Fellow of the Royal Society, 1949; fellow: Fellowship of Engineering, Institute of Mechanical Engineers, Royal Aeronautical Society; president: Engineering Section of British Association, 1952, Johnson Society, 1953–54. **Awards and honours** Knighted, 1946; Medal of Freedom, Silver Palms, United States, 1946; Knight Commander of the Order of the Bath, 1950; honorary member, Parly and Scientific Committee, 1960; honorary fellow, Sidney Sussex College, Cambridge; DSc, Oxford; DEng, Witwatersrand; DTech, Haifa. **Cause of death** Undisclosed, at age 99.

BERTHOLD LUBETKIN

Russian Architect

***Born* Tiflis, Georgia, 14 December 1901**

***Died* Bristol, Avon, 23 October 1990**

In 1931 Berthold Lubetkin, a young Russian architect steeped in the continental *avant garde*, swept into England and, in the brief span of less than a decade, established modernist architecture in

Britain. He rapidly became a legendary figure, international in stature, the hero of architecture students in the 1930s and 1940s. His retirement from the architectural scene in the early 1950s, as sudden as his emergence onto it, did not diminish his legendary status.

Born in the south Georgian town of Tiflis, with a cultivated home background which explains his deep-rooted awareness of classic art-historical values, Lubetkin began his architectural training in the stimulating ambience of revolutionary Moscow, under the Constructivist and socialist influences of Tatlin, Rodchenko and Melnikov. Oppressed, however, by Lenin's directives on art, he left Russia in 1922, to study first in Berlin, then in Warsaw, and finally in Paris, the "finishing school" for young architects of the day. Arriving in Paris in 1925 he trained under Auguste Perret, receiving a thorough grounding in geometric form and reinforced concrete, the aesthetic and technical requisites of the modern architect's repertoire. Making a living as site supervisory architect for Melnikov's dynamic Soviet pavilion for the Paris Expo of 1925, he mixed with such *avant garde* artistic figures as Ehrenberg, Braque, Léger and Picasso. He formed a partnership with his fellow-exile Jean Ginsburg and in 1927 designed his first major building, an apartment block at 25 Avenue de Versailles, Paris, which caused a storm. With rhythmic horizontals inspired by the flow of passing traffic, it typifies the poetry underlying Lubetkin's functional aesthetic.

Attracted to England by memories of "the beautiful flat green aesthetic of the playing fields" seen on a childhood visit, he felt it on his arrival in 1931 to be "the spearhead of human knowledge" and hoped that here he would at last find the freedom from bureaucracy without which he could not practise as an architect. In 1932 he set up Tecton, a young architects' co-operative formed with graduates from the Architectural Association, of which he was unofficial leader. Tecton, which survived until 1948, rapidly gained a reputation for building in the revolutionary continental style, and became a training ground for the new generation, notably Denys Lasdun.

With Tecton, Lubetkin designed a succession of buildings during the 1930s which represent the supreme achievement of modern British pre-war architecture. They include a number of zoo buildings, of which the most famous is the Penguin Pool at the London Zoo. Sculptural, white and unadorned, possessing — in Lubetkin's words — "the simplicity of a Brancusi", it reads like a manifesto of modernist themes. Its design, dictated by the acrobatics of the birds, produced a flawlessly elegant double helix comprised of two interlocking cantilevered spiral ramps around an oval pool, possibly inspired by the form of a penguin's white chest. The Penguin Pool was followed by commissions from the London Borough of Finsbury, notably for a revolutionary Health Centre, and by two private apartment blocks — Highpoint One and Two — on London's Highgate Hill. Highpoint One merits comparison with the best work of Le Corbusier, who himself praised it as "an achievement of the first rank, and a milestone that will be useful to everybody".

Lubetkin's pre-war buildings were undoubtedly the most influential of their day, although regrettably much of the post-war architecture they inspired is mere pastiche, lacking the philosophical rigour of his conceptual imagery. Lubetkin's own post-war career (the war itself he spent farming the Gloucestershire estate he had bought in 1937) failed to live up to expectations, either his own or the public's. In 1948 he was appointed architect-planner of Peterlee New Town, County Durham, a project which was designed for miners and therefore appealed to his socialist principles. However, his ambitious Soviet-inspired design for a compact, high-rise city core with a centralized layout was at odds with the suburban-type plans for other post-war new towns, and fell victim to political and economic disputes. Disillusioned, feeling that the bureaucracy that had driven him from Russia was now closing in on Britain, he resigned in 1950 and gave up practising architecture soon afterwards.

Retiring to his Gloucestershire home at Upper Kilcott, Lubetkin again took up farming and lived a virtual recluse with his wife and three children. In 1936 he had married Margaret Church, the youngest student ever to enrol at the Architectural Association. It was a deep and lasting relationship, cut short in 1978 by her death after a long illness, which had caused them to move to a flat in Bristol overlooking the Clifton Gorge, where Lubetkin himself continued to live alone.

After his wife's death he emerged somewhat from his seclusion, sought out by students as a sage, taking a few advisory commissions and occasionally speaking up for the architectural convictions he had never ceased to hold. He was very much the grand old man of British architecture, as was belatedly recognized when in 1982 the RIBA awarded him the Royal Gold Medal for Architecture, other recipients of which have included Lutyens, Frank Lloyd Wright, Le Corbusier and Mies van der Röhe. His acceptance speech, a furious attack on what he called "transvestite post-modernism", showed him still very much alive to contemporary architectural issues, and the passionate champion of modernism. On a subsequent occasion he defended modern architecture against the criticisms of the Prince of Wales.

For Lubetkin, modernism was not so much a style as a method of using reason and logic in the design of buildings. His approach to architecture, grounded in the functional ethos common to his generation, was tempered with theoretical and philosophical insights. Like others in the 1930s, he was committed to the vision of the new society which he believed was in the making, and was especially concerned with what he termed "human betterment" and the role to be played in this by architecture. Thus in 1933 he joined in the formation of the Modern Architecture Research Group (MARS), but soon grew frustrated with its inability to address social issues, and set up a counter-movement, ATO (the Architects and Technicians Organization), which was actively concerned with inner-city housing and other aspects of "social engineering".

As a personality Lubetkin was complex, possessed of a distinguished intellect, vitality and exuberance, profound in his beliefs and original in thought. An amusing and fascinating companion, he was nevertheless deemed difficult by his critics. His untimely retirement from the architectural scene may be construed as the truculent act of an individualist incapable of compromise, or that of an idealist who possessed the courage of his convictions. Either way, given what he had previously achieved, it constituted a monumental loss to British architecture.

Born Berthold Lubetkin. **Father** An industrialist. **Marriage** Margaret Church, architect, 1936 (died 1978). **Children** Two daughters and one son, Sasha, Louise and Steven. **Education** Tenishevskaya Gymnasium, St Petersburg (now Leningrad) and Miedvendikoy Gymnasium, Moscow, 1910–17; studied under A. Rodchenko, V. Tatlin and A. Vesnin, at the Vkhutemas, Moscow, and the Svomas, Petrograd, 1920–22; studied under Professor Fleming, Textile Academy, Berlin, and under Professor Kersten, Building School, Berlin-Charlottenburg, 1922–23; Warsaw Polytechnic School of Architecture, 1923–25; École Spéciale d'Architecture, Paris, 1925; École des Beaux Arts, Paris, 1926–27; École Supérieure de Béton Armé, Paris, 1927; Institut d'Urbanisme, Sorbonne, Paris, 1927–29. **Emigration** Left Russia for Europe, 1922, emigrated to England, 1931. **Military service** Reservist, Red Army, Moscow, 1919–20. **Career** Worked with Bruno Taut, Berlin, 1922–23; worked with Ernst May, Frankfurt, 1924; architect and designer in private practice for Union of Soviet Socialist Republics Trades Delegation, Paris, 1926–29, with Jean Ginsberg, Paris, 1928–30; partner, with Anthony Chitty, Lindsay Drake, Michael Dugdale, Valentine Harding, Godfrey Samuel, Francis Skinner, Tecton Group of architects, London, 1932–48; partner with Skinner and Douglas Bailey in Skinner Bailey and Lubetkin, London, 1948–52. **Related activities** Editorial board member, *L'Architecture d'aujourd'hui*, Paris, 1930–31; founder member, MARS, Modern Architecture Research Group, London, 1933; founder, with others, ATO, the Architects and Technicians Organization, 1935. **Other activities** Farmer, Upper Kilcott, Gloucestershire, 1952–69. **Awards and honours** Royal Gold Medal, Royal Institute of British Architects, 1982. **Exhibitions** *Lubetkin and Tecton*, Arnolfini Gallery, Bristol, 1981; *La Modernité — un projet inachevé*, Centre Georges Pompidou, Paris, 1982; *Berthold Lubetkin: un moderne en Angleterre*, Institut Français d'Architecture, Paris, 1983. **Works** Dacha (project), Russia, 1920–22; Dacha (project), Russia, 1920–22; Studio House (project), Russia, 1920–22; (with C. M. Da Costa and L. Ituralde) Polytechnic of the Urals, near Sverdlovsk, Union of Soviet Socialist Republics (competition project), 1925; Collective housing (project), Paris, 1925–29; Monsieur P. apartment interiors, Paris, 1925–29; Dismountable USSR Trades Pavilions, France, 1926–29; Club Trapèze Volant (warehouse conversion), 1927–28; Rue de Volontaires, Paris, 1927–28; Centrosoyuz Building, Miasnitzkaia, Moscow (project), 1928; (with Jean Ginsberg) Apartments, Avenue de Versailles, Paris, 1928–31; Harrari House, Hampstead, London, (project), 1930; (with Blum and Sigalin) Palace of the Soviets, Moscow (project), 1931; Tuberculosis Clinic, East Ham, London (project), 1932; Gorilla House, London Zoo, Regent's Park, London, 1932–33; (with Pilichowski) Houses, Genesta Road, Plumstead, London, 1932–34; House, Heath Drive, Hare Street, Gidea Park, Essex, 1933; "Beach House", Bay Walk, Aldwick, Bognor, Sussex, 1933–34; Highpoint One flats, North Hill, Highgate, London, 1933–35; Two houses, Whipsnade Zoo Estate, Bedfordshire, 1933–36; Venesta display stand, Building Exhibition, Olympia, London 1934; Penguin Pool, London Zoo, Regent's Park, London, 1934; Egypt End house (now Gordonbush), Farnham Common, Buckinghamshire, 1935; Six Pillars House, Crescentwood, Dulwich, London, 1935; Houses, Sunnywood Drive, Haywards Heath, Sussex, 1935; Giraffe House, Elephant House, restaurant and kiosks, Whipsnade Zoo, Bedfordshire, 1935; Working-Class Flats, London (competition project), 1935; Finsbury Health Centre, Pine Street, Finsbury, London, 1935–38; House alterations, Mill Hill, London, 1936–37; Refreshment Bar, London Zoo, Regent's Park, London, 1936–37; Dudley Zoo, Dudley Castle, Worcestershire, 1936–37; Highpoint Two flats, North Hill, Highgate, London, 1936–38; Studio of Animal Art, London Zoo, Regent's Park, London, 1937; *News Chronicle* School (competition project), 1937; Elephant House, London Zoo, Regent's Park, London (not completed), 1937; Lubetkin Penthouse in Highpoint Two, Highgate, London, 1937–38; Air Raid Shelter Plan, Finsbury, London, 1937–39; Priory Green Housing Estate, Finsbury, London, 1937–51; Spa Green Housing Estate, Finsbury, London, 1938–46; "Joldwynds" house (now "The Wilderness"), Holmbury St Mary, Abinger, Surrey, 1939; Lenin Memorial, Holford Square, Finsbury, London, 1942; Hallfield Housing Estate, Bishop's Bridge Road, Paddington, London (completed by Lasdun and Drake), 1947–55; Peterlee New Town Plan, County Durham (project), 1948–50; New Docks Development, Karachi, Pakistan (project), 1952; Lubetkin Farmhouse interiors, Upper Kilcott, Gloucestershire, 1953; Holford Square Housing Development, Finsbury, London, 1954–56. **Publications** *Opening of Finsbury Health Centre*, 1938; *Planned A.R.P.*, 1939; *Report to Finsbury Borough Council on Structural Protection for People Against Aerial Bombardment*, 1939; *Spa Green Estate*, 1952; *La Modernité — un projet inachevé* (exhibition catalogue), 1982. **Cause of death** Undisclosed, at age 88. **Further reading** Dennis Sharp, editor, *The Rationalists: Theory and Design in the Modern Movement*, 1978; Alastair Service, *The Architects of London*, 1979; John S. Allan, *Lubetkin and Tecton: the Modern Architecture of Classicism*, 1981; Lionel Esher, *A Broken Wave: The Rebuilding of England 1940–1980*, 1981; Peter Coe and Malcolm Reading, *Lubetkin and Tecton: Architecture and Social Commitment*, 1981; William J. R. Curtis, *Modern Architecture since 1900*, 1982; Peter Coe, Malcolm Reading, Jean-Louis Cohen and others, *Berthold Lubetkin: un moderne en Angleterre* (exhibition catalogue), 1983; *Contemporary Architects*, 1987.

JOEL McCREA

American Actor

***Born* South Pasadena, California, 5 November 1905**

***Died* Woodland Hills, California, 20 October 1990**

Occasionally, in Tinseltown, life imitates art. Joe McCrea, one of the most believable of Western heroes, had a strong Western background: his maternal grandfather, a major in the Army, came to

California during the Gold Rush in a covered wagon; his paternal grandfather, another major, was a veteran of skirmishes with the American Indians, as well as a stagecoach driver. In addition, the young McCrea learned a preference for the roles he would later portray by working on a ranch, along with members of his family. They were frontier people, "and that's why my heart was in it" he would explain later in his career. After acting in close to 90 films over three decades, he retired to his first love, ranching, and enjoyed the fruits of smart investments in both land and livestock.

McCrea's slow-talking and easy-going manner and tall, rugged looks were almost typecast for the cowboy suit, yet he fitted a tuxedo as well; some of his finest performances were in other genres such as the sharp-edged social comedies of Preston Sturges and other directors.

McCrea's family moved to Hollywood when he was nine; later he studied drama at Pomona College. After working his way through odd jobs, he graduated from movie wrangler to stuntman to bit player. His first feature part was in the 1929 film, *The Jazz Age* (starring Douglas Fairbanks Jr), after being picked from the crowd. Several months later Cecil B. De Mille (who was to become something of a mentor as well as a friend) gave him the juvenile lead in *Dynamite*. McCrea played the nice guy — typed from the beginning, with his strong, homespun and honest face — with whom married Kay Johnson had a fling. In *The Single Standard*, in an uncredited part, he even danced with Garbo (q.v.) — and into an MGM contract, which was unusual for an actor of his minor (as yet) stature. His first leading role was in 1930's *The Silver Horde* — he was 24 — and the instructions given to him by a co-star were remembered 50 years later. "He used to tell me how mentally lazy I was", said McCrea. "'You've got to think, not act', he'd say. 'Your face is expressive enough. When you think, I can read your thoughts. So, if you want to show you're mad, don't scowl: just think mad and you'll act mad!'"

In the 1930s McCrea acted in 40 films: action-adventure to melodrama to romance to comedies. In *Girls About Town*, a sophisticated comedy directed by George Cukor, he portrayed a young decent fellow who softened gold-digger Kay Francis's heart. (This was a common role for McCrea in the early days, and audiences adored it.) In *The Silver Cord*, with Irene Dunne (q.v.), he met co-star and future wife Frances Dee, while playing a husband in the midst of a wife's battle to free him from a possessive mother. His role was innocent, almost to an irritating degree in the film; however, the script is to be blamed more than his artless portrayal.

In *Chance of Heaven*, he turned petrol-station owner who marries a socialite but ends up with his home town sweetheart. The partnership between McCrea and Ginger Rogers had a sparkling chemistry. He starred with the great Edward G. Robinson in *Barbary Coast* directed by Howard Hawks. The storyline was run-of-the-mill: a naïve prospector loves a woman gambler and takes her away to a better life. But *These Three* (also known as *The Loudest Whisper*), directed by William Wyler, gave McCrea one of his better roles. Ironically, producer Goldwyn's first choice was Leslie Howard, who was unavailable. The story of the damage done by the gossip of a malicious schoolgirl — McCrea's teacher is loved by two others, portrayed by Merle Oberon and Miriam Hopkins — was powerful, the script more than literate as it was taken from Lillian Hellman's play, *The Children's Hour*.

McCrea's first Western, *Wells Fargo*, co-starred his wife Frances Dee. That was followed by the epic *Union Pacific*, the De Mille film about the construction of the first transcontinental railroad. It starred a favourite leading lady, Barbara Stanwyck (q.v.), and the superb Robert Preston. By this time McCrea had more than cemented his reputation as a professional, dependable player; his only drawback was his rather monotone voice. (When Sturges mentioned this to him later, he replied, "Well, the way I look at it, Rubenstein [meaning Arthur] and those other guys are looking for their one note — I've already found mine.") Goldwyn had lent McCrea out — profitably, as McCrea was sought after — but when he put Gary Cooper under contract, McCrea asked to be released. His conviction that he only got roles turned down by Cooper, whom he actually admired, meant that he went after the role in *Union Pacific*...when Cooper refused it.

The 1940s brought the actor some of his best work. In Hitchcock's thriller *Foreign Correspondent* (which Cooper had kicked himself for turning down) he played one of his finest, best-defined roles as an American wartime journalist with a brash innocence, caught up in events he could not control. With typical bluntness, he blurts out to Laraine Day, "I'm in love with you and I want to marry you." Her response, appropriately; "I'm in love with you and I want to marry you." "That cuts down our love scene quite a bit, doesn't it?" he answers with relief. The passion is saved for the stirring radio speech he makes from London to the US. As the bombs plummet, he pleads earnestly,

> Don't tune me out! Hang on — this is a big story, and you're part of it. It's too late now to do anything except stand in the dark and let them come. It feels as though the lights are all out everywhere except in America. Keep those lights burning! Cover them with steel, ring them with guns, build a canopy of battleships and bombing planes around them. Hello, America! Hang on to your lights. They're the only lights left in the world!

McCrea's delivery made the words shine with a devout sincerity — and Hitchcock had complained to Truffaut that the actor was "too easy-going in the role"...

Although for many people McCrea was best known for his cowboy roles, he impressed others more in his social comedies, with his gentle style and excellent timing. Preston Sturges brought out his feel for comedy, as the innocent inevitably surrounded by chaos; people and situations simply happen to him. McCrea was Sturges's favourite leading man; they made three films together, including the witty *Palm Beach Story*, with Claudette Colbert and Mary Astor. *Sullivan's Travels*, with Veronica Lake, was another of McCrea's best roles. He played a successful Hollywood director who, disillusioned with his string of featherweight films such as *So Long, Sarong* and *Ants in their Pants of 1939*, decides to make a searing drama about human suffering. He becomes a tramp for first-hand experience of social deprivation and research for *Brother, Where Art Thou?*. At the climax, as a member of a chain-gang (the result of a tragic mistake), he is allowed to watch a creaky Mickey Mouse cartoon and realizes the enriching value that comedy has to offer. McCrea was reassuringly masculine; there's an easy kind of sexuality that wasn't always noticed before.

More wisecracking showed off McCrea to excellent effect in *The More the Merrier*; co-star Jean Arthur was a particularly good screen match in George Stevens's comedy of wartime Washington manners. In one scene he takes a shower while beating his arms against his chest and looking like a seal uttering a primeval mating call.

McCrea took time off to entertain the troops in World War II. His success in 1946's *The Virginian* was the beginning of his string of Western roles. He played Cooper's old role in a remake of that film — the straight solid man in the saddle. This sort of role suited him best, he said, although most of them were of the double-bill variety; the generally unambitious actor was more interested in making money for his dream ranch than in promoting his career. But he turned in good performances in *Four Faces West* and *Colorado Territory*, in the latter playing a villain for a change, and in *Wichita*, playing Wyatt Earp. *Ride the High Country* pulled him out of semi-retirement in 1962. Also known as *Guns in the Afternoon*, it was directed by Sam Peckinpah. He and Randolph Scott, also semi-retired, also ending his career in the saddle, played ageing gunslingers hired to transport gold from a mine to the bank; one of them succumbs to greed. The actors amiably flipped a coin to decide who was to play which part — Scott ended up as the villain. The film was a perfect final curtain for the two veteran stars, a poignant demonstration of the "unchanged men in a changing land" theme. They were a winning team for a nostalgic salute to a dying genre.

A brief appearance in 1977 for *Mustang Country*, an offbeat little film, was to be his last. He said of it, "I liked the story, because it was decent kind of adventure, outdoor". He then happily and completely retired to his acres and his ranch. The best tribute came from a superb actress of a younger generation, Maureen Stapleton: "There are men you dream of, there are men you fall in love with, there are men you marry and there is real life — and that s.o.b. Frances Dee got it all." *And* he rode off into the sunset, the way heroes often do.

Born Joel Albert McCrea. **Father** Thomas McCrea, utility executive. **Marriage** Frances Dee, actress, 1933. **Children** Three sons, Jody, David and Peter. **Education** Hollywood High School, Los Angeles, California; Pomona State College, Claremont, California, 1928. **Career** Variously employed on ranches and as a lifeguard; film extra, mid–1920s; on stock contract with MGM, 1928; on contract with RKO, 1929; featured film début, *The Jazz Age*, 1929; first leading role, Boyd Emerson in *The Silver Horde*, 1930; worked with Paramount and Samuel Goldwyn. **Other activities** Rancher. **Films** *The Fair Co-Ed*, 1927; *The Enemy*, 1927; *The Jazz Age*, 1929; *Single Standard*, 1929; *Dynamite*, 1929; *So This Is College*, 1929; *The Silver Horde*, 1930; *Lightnin'*, 1930; *Once a Sinner*, 1931; *Kept Husbands*, 1931; *Born to Love*, 1931; *The Common Law*, 1931; *Girls About Town*, 1931; *Business and Pleasure*, 1932; *The Lost Squadron*, 1932; *Bird of Paradise*, 1932; *The Most Dangerous Game* (*The Hounds of Zaroff*), 1932; *Rockabye*, 1932; *The Sport Parade*, 1932; *The Silver Cord*, 1933; *Scarlet River*, 1933; *Bed of Roses*, 1933; *One Man's Journey*, 1933; *Chance of Heaven*, 1933; *Gambling Lady*, 1934; *Half a Sinner* (*Alias the Deacon*), 1934; *The Richest Girl in the World*, 1934; *Private Worlds*, 1935; *Our Little Girl*, 1935; *Woman Wanted* (*Manhattan Madness*), 1935; *Barbary Coast*, 1935; *Splendor*, 1935; *These Three* (*The Loudest Whisper*), 1936; *Two in a Crowd*, 1936; *Adventure in Manhattan*, 1936; *Come and Get It*, 1936; *Banjo on My Knee*, 1936; *Interns Can't Take Money* (*You Can't Take Money*), 1937; *Woman Chases Man* (*The Woman's Touch*), 1937; *Dead End*, 1937; *Wells Fargo*, 1937; *Three Blind Mice*, 1938; *Youth Takes a Fling*, 1938; *Union Pacific*, 1939; *They Shall Have Music* (*Melody of Youth*), 1939; *Espionage Agent*, 1939; *He Married His Wife*, 1940; *The Primrose Path*, 1940; *Foreign Correspondent*, 1940; *Reaching for the Sun*, 1941; *Sullivan's Travels*, 1941; *The Great Man's Lady*, 1942; *The Palm Beach Story*, 1942; *The More the Merrier*, 1943; *Buffalo Bill*, 1944; *The Great Moment*, 1944; *The Unseen*, 1945; *The Virginian*, 1946; *Ramrod*, 1947; *Four Faces West* (*They Passed This Way*), 1948; *South of St Louis*, 1949; *Colorado Territory*, 1949; *Stars in My Crown*, 1950; *The Outriders*, 1950; *Saddle Tramp*, 1950; *Frenchie*, 1950; *Hollywood Story*, 1951; *Cattle Drive*, 1951; *The San Francisco Story*, 1952; *Lone Hand*, 1953; *Shoot First* (*Rough Shoot*), 1953; *Border River*, 1954; *Blackhorse Canyon*, 1954; *Stranger on Horseback*, 1955; *Wichita*, 1955; *The First Texan*, 1956; *The Oklahoman*, 1957; *Trooper Hook*, 1957; *Gunsight Ridge*, 1957; *The Tall Stranger*, 1957; *Cattle Empire*, 1958; *Fort Massacre*, 1958; *The Gunfight at Dodge City*, 1959; *Ride the High Country* (*Guns in the Afternoon*), 1962; *Cry Blood Apache*, 1970; *The Great American Cowboy* (narrator, television documentary), 1974; *Mustang Country*, 1977. **Television** *Wichita Town* (series), 1959–60. **Cause of death** Pulmonary complications, at age 84. **Further reading** *International Dictionary of Films and Filmmakers*, volume three, 1986.

KENNETH MAIDMENT

British Classical Scholar and University Administrator

Born **England, 29 October 1910**

Died **Oxford, England, 3 October 1990**

A decade of classical scholarship in the cloistered environment of England's Oxford University is hardly the most obvious qualification for the administrator of a new and expanding university in the more informal, egalitarian climate of New Zealand. Yet for Kenneth Maidment, the study of Greek democracy held practical lessons for the present — and informed many of his decisions about the future of the institution over which he came to preside.

Maidment began his classical education at Bristol Grammar School and continued it at Merton College, Oxford, where he won the Craven Scholarship and took a double First. He stayed on at Merton as a junior research fellow, was elected a fellow and tutor at Jesus College and then returned to Merton where — with a break for service in Military Intelligence in World War II — he held a tutorial fellowship until 1949.

In this fairly brief and interrupted time as a researcher and tutor he produced a critical Greek text of the Athenian orators Antiphon and Andocides, with an English translation. Published in 1940, this classic remains in print and in use after half a century. For Kenneth Maidment possessed one of the sharpest and ablest academic minds of his generation; but his life led away from scholarship and towards administration when in 1950 and at the age of 39 he went out to New Zealand as principal of Auckland University College.

Maidment was soft-spoken, donnish, witty and friendly in conversation, yet showed self-confidence and strength. He needed all these qualities in his new post, for there were plenty of storms to be endured before the college achieved the status of an independent university. When he arrived, Auckland was a miscellany of three permanent buildings amid assorted prefabs and corrugated iron structures. Its 2800 students mostly attended lectures part-time and could rarely discuss them with lecturers, because they spent the rest of their days earning their living in offices and workshops. The college had had no principal before. Professors had chaired the Board in rotation, quarrelling incessantly with the Council, which was presided over by an autocratic president supported by a tiny administrative staff. But Maidment was more than equal to the challenge. *Fluctuat nec mergitur* was a motto he liked to apply to himself, translating it as, "he has certainly managed to weather a crisis or two."

In 1957 the college became the University of Auckland and Maidment became its vice-chancellor. There followed a difficult period of controversies over admissions policies and opposition to new subjects such as sociology and, less understandably, Maori studies and the anthropology of the Pacific. For a decade — the length of the Trojan War — the "Homeric Battles" over the university's future site brought conflict with town councillors and became a national issue. They delayed the hoped-for expansion until the 1960s. But Maidment was an effective administrator who achieved policy aims without stress to his colleagues and maintained good relations with his staff. His appointment of bright and able academics enabled Auckland to take its place among the world's emerging universities.

Maidment did not merely weather storms. Once his Homeric Battles were over, a grand building programme was launched and a wide range of new studies developed, from art history and Chinese, to medicine and theoretical physics. Maidment also strengthened the Professorial Board of the university and promoted student representation on the Senate — again, his knowledge of the democracy of ancient Greece was applied in practice and to good effect.

By the time Maidment retired, Auckland University was well on the way to achieving world status, with nearly 10,000 full-time students, a fine campus, a range of new departments and a library which had grown from 50,000 books to 500,000. But he had not wanted expansion for its own sake. Drawing a parallel with Aristotle's definition of the proper size for a Greek city, he warned against a university with a staff so numerous as to fall apart into fresh communities, each intent on its own interests and indifferent to those of its neighbours.

Through all his years in administration Maidment never lost his enthusiasm for teaching. Two of his four return visits to Auckland after his retirement were to give tutorials and classes in Greek. He was steeped in Herodotus, Thucydides, Plato and Aristotle; and he continued to put the lessons he learned from them to practical use. Committees were sometimes taken aback at being presented with a parallel from an ancient writer which turned out to be sharply relevant to the issue in hand.

In one respect Maidment differed from the Ancient Greeks; he was not desperate for fame. The University Arts Centre was named after him by student demand, "but", he commented, "it might be even better to be sold tickets there at half-price."

After his retirement, he returned to Oxford where Merton College elected him to an emeritus fellowship. He was immensely hospitable and in old age was an engaging conversationalist with a fund of stories from his earlier Oxford and New Zealand days.

He assessed his fellow classicists critically to the very end. And when he died one of the readings for his funeral service was, of course, from the classics — William Cory's rendering of Callimachus:

Still are thy pleasant voices,
  thy Nightingales, awake
For death, he taketh all away,
  but them he cannot take.

Born Kenneth John Maidment. **Parents** Francis George and Jessie Louisa (Taylor) Maidment. **Marriage** Isobel Felicity Leitch, 1937. **Children** One son and three daughters. **Education** Bristol Grammar School, Avon; Merton College, Oxford, Hertford Scholar, 1929, first-class Classical Honour Moderations, 1930, Craven Scholar, first-class Litterae Humaniores, 1932. **Military service** Oxford and Buckinghamshire Light Infantry, 1940; seconded, War Office, 1941; on liaison duties, United States, 1942–45; became lieutenant-colonel. **Career** Junior research fellow, Merton College, 1932; fellow and classical tutor, Jesus College, Oxford, 1934–38; fellow and classical tutor, Merton College, 1938–49, sub-warden, 1945–49, university lecturer in Greek literature, 1947–49, emeritus fellow, 1971 onwards; principal, Auckland University College, 1950–57; vice-chancellor, University of Auckland, 1957–71. **Offices and memberships** Governor, Bristol Grammar School, 1972–79. **Awards and honours** LLD, Auckland. **Publications** Critical edition and translation of *Antiphon and Andocides*, 1940; contributor to classical journals. **Cause of death** Undisclosed, at age 79.

DENIS MITCHELL

British Television Documentary Producer

***Born* Cheshire, 1 August 1911**

***Died* Great Massingham, Norfolk, 1 October 1990**

One of the very few television documentary makers to become virtually a household name even in the early days of the medium, Denis Mitchell was a pioneer of *télé-vérité* or what came to be known as the "observational style". "I don't plan films", he once said. "I've never used a script in my life. I just hope for the best and sometimes it works." His real forte was his ability to record, both visually and aurally, the vivid actuality of ordinary, everyday people and places, and his films are marked by their deep concern for those at the bottom of the social pile. In particular Mitchell let people speak for themselves, something all too rare in the medium then as now. As he put it: "I've fallen in love with the human voice."

Mitchell's fascination with people talking about their daily lives and experiences began when he was working for the South African Broadcasting Corporation after World War II. The SABC had picked up some primitive wire-recording equipment from the US Army and Mitchell decided to use it to record various interviews on location. In the event the SABC thought the sound quality too poor to broadcast, and anyway had a policy about not transmitting unscripted material. "However", Mitchell said, "it dawned on me that the ability to record people talking at their jobs and in their homes was not a mere novelty but a most important new means of communication".

When Mitchell returned to Britain he soon found an ideal niche as a features producer in radio at BBC Manchester, which had already established a strong reputation for programmes with "social" content. Before too long the all-important portable disc recorder and then a tape-recorder were at his disposal and he was able to get down to his own distinctive method of work. Today, of course, it might seem quite extraordinary that such basic equipment was not there in the first place, but as Philip Purser explained in an early profile of Mitchell:

> Tape was still suspect in orthodox BBC circles. The proper place to interview a member of the public was in the studio, and the proper way to record the outcome was on a twelve-inch disc. Mitchell experimented with a portable recorder, taking it into the streets and pubs and revivalist chapels of the North and bringing back hour upon hour of random talk. Edited, shaped and presented as a regular feature, *People Talking*, it lent a flavour and spontaneity to the spoken word undreamed of by Lord Reith.

In the mid–1950s Mitchell was temporarily attached to Television Talks at BBC Lime Grove where he was initiated into film-making by Norman Swallow, whom he had replaced in Manchester. Apart from Swallow, the other seminal figures there were Leonard Miall and Grace Wyndham Goldie. At this time in British television, sound cameras and even location filming were still relatively rare, but Mitchell was determined to use the unscripted conversations from his recordings as opposed to the standard format of dubbed narration and added sound effects. His first documentary was a programme about teenagers for the *Special Enquiries* series, which was so successful that some of the material was re-used in the one-off *On the Threshold*. In 1958 he transferred completely to Television Talks as producer and scriptwriter, remaining there until 1962 and turning out a remarkable body of work which included *Morning in the Streets*, *Night in the City*, *In Prison* (the first film to be made in Manchester's Strangeways, where Mitchell lived in a cell for three weeks), *Soho Story*, the South African trilogy *Wind of Change*, and *Chicago*. Like *Morning in the Streets* this last won the Prix Italia, but it was not popular with American correspondents in London, the Hearst press, nor the city's Mayor Daley, who threatened to punch Mitchell if he ever returned! Mitchell's crime was not to have flinched from the sleazier side of city life, and by means of both aural and visual montage to have made some pretty pointed comments on the social inequalities evident in the Windy City.

Mitchell became one of the very first of television's independent producers when he left the BBC in 1962. He was joined by Norman Swallow, and the two were fortunate enough to receive a large number of commissions from Granada and to work there for the enlightened Denis Forman. By this time Mitchell, always in search of new refinements in the manner of capturing his subjects, was experimenting with recorded video tape. To this period belong *A Wedding on Saturday* (another Prix Italia winner), *Only Believe*, half a dozen segments of the pioneering *World in Action* series, an unforgettable portrait of Quentin Crisp (which begins with film of the arrival of the TV crew and the setting up of the equipment), various stages of René Cutforth's *European Journey*, *Private Lives* ("surely no interviewer has extracted more by saying less", as one critic noted), and the altogether characteristic *This England* series, which presented the lives of ordinary people without narration or commentary (and which included early directional stints by Michael Apted and Richard Eyre, among others). Almost inevitably Mitchell's unflinching eye got him into trouble with the Independent Television Authority (forerunner of the Independent Television Commission) when, for *The Entertainers*, he rented an empty house in Manchester, installed an assortment of club artistes, set up cameras and microphones, and monitored the results from a van outside: the ITA took exception to the fact that two of the performers were strippers.

One of Mitchell's very last films was made for Granada, *Never and Always*, shot around Great Massingham in Norfolk where he lived. It is also one in which the dark streak present in much of his work is most noticeably to the fore, and an illustration of his thesis that Britain's watchwords are "closed shop, closed mind, and closed". Given Mitchell's clear sympathies in his films it is hard not to see this warning of the coming of what he called a new "Dark Age" in Britain as a portent of the dawn of Thatcherism. But whatever the case, the film, like so many of its predecessors, is clear proof of Norman Swallow's judgement that Denis Mitchell possessed "a vision of the world that is as personal and as intense as the creations of the most serious poet or painter".

Born Denis Holden Mitchell. **Father** A Non-conformist minister. **Marriages** 1) Dorothea Bates, actress, 1938 (dissolved); 2) Betty Horne, 1953 (dissolved); 3) Linda Webster, 1965. **Children** Two daughters by first marriage, one deceased; one son by second marriage. **Education** On scholarship, drama school, London. **Military service** Artillery officer, South African Army, 1939; entertainments officer, Cairo, became captain. **Career** Employed variously as a bank clerk, journalist, shop assistant, actor; writer-producer, South African Broadcasting Corporation, 1945–49; freelance producer, BBC Features Department, London, 1949–50; features producer, North Region British Broadcasting Corporation, Manchester, 1950–58; first television documentary for series *Special Enquiries*, 1955; television documentary producer, British Broadcasting Corporation, *(Television Talks)*, 1958–62; independent producer, Denis Mitchell Films Limited, 1962 onwards. **Awards and honours** Prix Italia: 1959, 1961, 1965; Desmond Davis Award for Outstanding Creative Contribution to Television, 1975. **Films** (include) *On the Threshold*, 1955; *In Prison*, 1957; *Night in the City*, 1957; *On Tour*, 1958; *A Soho Story*, 1959; *Morning in the Streets*, 1959; *The Wind of Change*, comprising *Main Street, Africa*, *A View From the Farm*, *Between Two Worlds*, 1960; *Chicago*, 1961; *Ed and Frank*, 1961; *The Entertainers*, 1964; *The House on the Beach*, 1965; *A Wedding On Saturday*, 1965; *Quentin Crisp*, 1970; *Pigs*, 1971; *European Journey*, 1972–73; *Never and Always*, 1977; *Maryport*, 1979; also: *Only Believe*; *Private Lives*; *This England*. **Cause of death** Undisclosed, at age 79. **Further reading** Michael Wharton, *The Missing Will*, 1984.

SETH MORGAN

American Novelist

***Born* New York City, New York, 1949**

***Died* New Orleans, Louisiana, 17 October 1990**

In an obituary piece written in the style of its subject, Jocelyn Targett called Seth Morgan an auto-vivisectionist, which is an admirable summing-up. Born into the literary establishment, he rejected it with spectacular determination, was reclaimed, and died like a burnt out meteor, as if to say, sucks to you — told you so. Though he wouldn't have used those words, exactly.

Morgan was the son of a wealthy East Coast family. His father, Frederick, founded the literary magazine, *The Hudson Review*, and his mother died of alcohol abuse when he was six years old. His childhood recollections include sampling the left-over drinks while "literary jawboning" went over his head in the family's Park Avenue apartment. Sexual misdemeanours and extortion activity led to his dismissal from several exclusive schools (accounts vary as to the exact number), including one in Switzerland, and he furthered the most liberal of educations in Mexico. After more experiments with drink and drugs, he enrolled in the University of California at Berkeley.

Ostensibly studying English literature, Morgan, complete with Harley Davidson, was running a drug shuttle between San Francisco and New York, trading grass for cocaine. Whilst trying to get rid of a shipment of the latter, he met another self-destructor, the rock singer Janis Joplin. "We went off to a Mexican Restaurant and got into a guacamole fight. I won Janis's heart by throwing food at her. That was it. I pretty much moved into her place in Marin County. After that I didn't have to sell any drugs. I was fixed up." The talk of marriage never occurred. Within three months Joplin died from a toxic overdose and Morgan was a heroin junkie.

Morgan continued through the 1970s in overdrive. He was twice married; the first time, allegedly to prevent his girlfriend from suing after a motorcycle accident, the second time to a Sausalito stripper named Laura George. After running through his inheritance, a house and cars, Morgan ended up pimping for his wife, working as a night-club barker and peddling drugs in San Francisco's Tenderloin red light district. To supplement the unpredictable earnings, and to finance his heroin habit, he took to armed robbery, pulling off 20–30 by his own account before being arrested in 1977 and sentenced to three years in Vacaville prison, near Sacramento.

The prison, Morgan said, was like an ashram, providing physical rehabilitation and some semblance of peace. He began voluminous reading and turned out a short (autobiographical) story called "Pink Cocaine", which won a PEN American Prisoners' writing award in 1978. He also telephoned his father (who had no idea where his son was) and told him that he'd begun writing a novel. And so he had, but it was a long time in gestation. After release, Morgan returned to San Francisco, took up with another prostitute and became an alcoholic. Then, he wrote "on my last legs, I hiked down to New Orleans to quietly drink myself to death, and I nearly did, but something awoke in me and I wrote a book instead."

The novel was *Homeboy*; thinly veiled autobiography. Morgan handed the manuscript to his father and returned to New Orleans and the bottle. The manuscript was passed on to Norman Mailer's editor Jason Epstein, and published in May 1990, to rapturous reviews. Deborah Mason, writing in *The New York Times Book Review* called it a "savagely comic and often brilliant" look at "the teeming San Francisco nether world of junkies, pimps, drag queens and hookers". David Browne, in London's *The Independent*, described it as "Rolling with syncopated rhythms, the language of the streets, the bravado of bars and prison yards". It sold 25,000 copies, an unusually high number for an unknown writer.

Morgan and his father enjoyed a brief reunion in promoting *Homeboy*. Jocelyn Targett describes them at literary parties: "They were a happy sight, the stocky writer with short, badger features, little limbs and a jagged capacious grin, and the gentle old man...his bald head flushed with pride and publishers' claret." Early in the morning of 16 October 1990, Seth Morgan was arrested in New Orleans and charged with driving his motorcycle while intoxicated. Early the next morning, he and his passenger were thrown from the motorcycle when it struck a dividing post on a New Orleans bridge. Both were pronounced dead at the scene. Morgan's second book, *Mambo Mephista*, was eagerly awaited. Published extracts show another relentless performance at the top of his form, sensuous writing, seemingly crafted and reckless at the same time.

Morgan's life reads like pulp fiction, and it is hard to resist the conclusion that, right up to and including the death, it was the way that he wanted it. He was apt to quote F. Scott Fitzgerald: "In the real dark night of the soul it is always three o'clock in the morning, day after day."

Born Seth Morgan. **Father** Frederick Morgan, poet, editor and publisher. **Marriages** 1) A waitress, name unknown; 2) Laura George, stripper. **Education** Private schools in United States, Mexico and Switzerland; University of California at Berkeley, dropped out. **Career** Writer, 1977 onwards. **Other activities** Drug dealer and addict, pimp, armed robber, night-club barker; inmate, Vacaville State Penitentiary, California, for armed robbery, 1977–80. **Awards and honours** American Prisoners' Writing Award, Poets, Playwrights, Editors, Essayists and Novelists association, 1978. **Publications** "Pink Cocaine" (short story), 1978; *Homeboy*, 1990. **Cause of death** Motorcycle accident, at age 41.

RICHARD MURDOCH

British Actor and Comedian

***Born* Keston, Kent, 6 April 1907**

***Died* Walton Heath, Surrey, 9 October 1990**

A household voice and face in Britain for over 50 years, Richard Murdoch deftly combined charm, comedy and charisma in his performances. He was a fireside familiar from the fairly early days of radio, a stylish song and dance man in the theatre, and an actor of subtlety in films and television. Most of all he will be remembered for his radio work both before World War II, and during it when, as an officer in the Royal Air Force, he took time out from his official duties affectionately to "send up" his branch of the service and various aspects of British bureaucracy.

The second of three sons of a tea merchant, Richard Bernard Murdoch was born in Keston, Kent, at a time when it was still a countrified village within fairly easy reach of London. He was educated privately at Charterhouse, and then at Pembroke College, Cambridge. At university, however, he showed more interest in performing with the Cambridge Footlights than in his academic progress, and inevitably graduated to a stage career. His first role was in the chorus in a musical called *The Blue Train* at the Prince of Wales Theatre in the West End of London.

It seemed that he had all the requisites of the matinée idol — height, good looks, elegance, a light but appealing singing voice, acting and dancing ability. Arthur Askey, who was to become his partner in *Band Waggon* (one of the most popular of all British radio series) felt that Murdoch could have gone right to the top as a theatre performer. He saw him as essentially someone with "natural class", and with a flair for this type of entertaining that was on a par with that of Jack Buchanan.

In fact, the outbreak of World War II curtailed Murdoch's stage career just as he was about to star in a new musical which, because of the threat of bombing, never actually opened. He had during the run-up to the war already established a formidable reputation in radio and the early days of television, in which he was something of a pioneer. He had appeared on the small screen in a short Noël Coward piece called *Red Peppers* (which led to further theatrical parts) and teamed up with Arthur Askey for *Band Waggon* in 1938. The combination of the suave, dapper and cultured Murdoch with Askey, the exuberant Liverpudlian stand-up comic, was a stroke of genius on the part of *Band Waggon*'s producers. "Big" (Big-hearted Arthur) and "Stinker" (Murdoch, as nicknamed by Askey) seemed to become part of everyone's life. They were supposed to live together in a flat on the top of the BBC's Broadcasting House, and their imaginary ménage included a rather mothy goat (Lewis) as well as some feathered friends, and a charlady whose daughter, Nausea Bagwash, was supposed to be Arthur's fiancée. The strength of *Band Waggon* in radio terms is well illustrated by the fact that although Nausea's voice was never heard, her personality (largely through Murdoch's chats with Askey about her) became extremely firmly established.

Band Waggon was British radio's first situation comedy; the techniques of sound broadcasting were brilliantly exploited in it by Murdoch and Askey, and the fusion of their differing talents was tremendously effective. The show was the basis of a successful film of the same name in 1939, and the duo made several further pictures together, of which the most memorable was the 1941 remake of Arnold Ridley's *The Ghost Train*.

In the same year, Richard Murdoch joined the Royal Air Force as an intelligence officer. He was flight lieutenant at a bomber station in Norfolk, from which he was able to travel occasionally to London to take part in various broadcasts. Making a guest appearance in a forces show called *Mediterranean Merry-Go-Round* he met Squadron Leader Kenneth Horne, a peace-time business executive who had become a popular radio quiz-master during the war. Murdoch and Horne formed a long-lasting friendship; they shared a similar approach to humour, with emphasis on wit, wordsmanship and the debunking of pomposity. When Horne had been promoted to wing-commander and posted to the Air Ministry, he managed to have Murdoch transferred there, as a squadron leader.

Their collaboration was to be not only a service one; apparently their duties allowed them time and opportunity to devise radio gags and scripts, which culminated in the creation of a fictional Royal Air Force station, Much-Binding-in-the-Marsh. *Much-Binding*, as it became popularly known, was to run — with some "rests" — for eight years on radio. Murdoch and Horne wrote the show, including their signing-off *Much-Binding* song for which new and topical lyrics had to be provided every week. They were the main performers, transposing their real-life ranks so that Murdoch was the station's commanding officer with Horne as his assistant. The series survived the change of mood from hostilities to peace-time with the aerodrome being refitted as a country club in which the pair could carry on with their muddling through, with their "flaps" and their sometimes schoolboyish and sometimes sophisticated humour. Said to be the favourite radio programme of King George VI, *Much-Binding* provided the nation with a host of quips and catch-phrases which are still in current use.

By the end of the 1950s Richard Murdoch was, of course, a seasoned broadcaster. He appeared in a variety of shows, both in England and Australia, as well as stage performances which ranged from serious drama to revue to pantomime (in which he occasionally played the Dame). However, radio provided the peak of his career with another long-running series, *The Men from the Ministry*, which, perfectly suited to Murdoch's talents, featured him as a civil servant battling against "red tape" and a highly irascible boss. This ran for 15 years, after which Murdoch was to make several television appearances, most notably as Uncle, the bumbling, ageing barrister who rarely got a brief in *Rumpole of the Bailey*.

There was a universality of appeal about Murdoch, which is evidenced by the fact that his career spanned so many decades and his broadcasts, through the BBC World Service, were appreciated by immense and far-flung audiences, despite what one might have categorized as their quintessential Englishness!

Born Richard Bernard Murdoch. **Parents** Bernard, tea merchant, and Amy Florence (Scott) Murdoch. **Marriage** Peggy Rawlings, actress, 1932. **Children** One son and two daughters. **Education** Charterhouse, Godalming, Surrey; Pembroke College, Cambridge. **Military service** Intelligence officer, Royal Air Force, 1941–45, became squadron leader. **Career** Teacher, briefly; stage début, in chorus of *The Blue Train*, King's Theatre, Southsea, 1927; London début, *The Blue Train*, Prince of Wales Theatre, 1927; film début, 1934; television début, 1930s; début as scriptwriter, with Arthur Askey, *Band Waggon*, 1938. **Offices and memberships** Captain, Stage Golfing Society, 1953, 1965. **Stage** (in London unless otherwise indicated) *The Blue Train*, 1927; *Oh, Letty!*, on tour, 1929; *The Five O'Clock Girl*, 1929; *Cochran's 1930 Revue*, 1930; *Stand Up and Sing*, 1931; *Ballyhoo*, 1932; *Mother of Pearl*, on tour, 1933; *Charlot's Char-a-Bang!*, 1935–36; *The*

Sleeping Beauty, 1935–36; *The Town Talks*, 1935–36; *Gay Divorce*, on tour, 1936; *Over She Goes*, 1936; *Band Waggon*, on tour, 1938; *Band Waggon*, 1939; *Merry-Go-Round* (forces show, scriptwriter also), 1940s; *Strike a New Note*, on tour, 1946; *Little Miss Muffet*, 1949; *Cinderella*, 1952; *As Long As They're Happy*, Blackpool, 1953; *Tax Free*, on tour, 1961; *Happy Returns*, Coventry, 1962; *The General's Tea Party*, Harrogate Festival, 1966; *Tons of Money*, 1968; *You Never Can Tell*, on tour, United States and Canada, 1973; *Not in the Book*, on tour, South Africa, 1974; *Birds of Paradise*, on tour, 1976; *Lloyd George Knew My Father*, on tour, 1977; *Bedroom Farce*, Plymouth, 1979. **Films** (include) *Over She goes*, 1937; *Band Wagon*, 1939; *Charlie's Big-Hearted Aunt*, 1940; *The Ghost Train*, 1941; *I Thank You*, 1941; *It Happened in Soho*, 1948; *Golden Arrow*, 1952; *Not a Hope in Hell*, 1959; *Strictly Confidential*, 1961. **Television** (includes) *Red Peppers*; *Hazel*; *Rumpole of the Bailey*; *Winston Churchill — the Wilderness Years*; *The New Avengers*; *In the Looking Glass*; *The Three Kisses*; *Mr Majeika*; *Never the Twain*. **Radio** (includes) *Band Waggon*; *Much-Binding-in-the-Marsh*; *The Men from the Ministry*; *A Slight Case of Murdoch*. **Cause of death** Undisclosed, at age 83.

HANS NAMUTH

German/American Photographer

***Born* Essen, Germany, 17 March 1915**

***Died* East Hampton, New York, 13 October 1990**

Hans Namuth was one of those rare individuals who are not only true artists in their own right but are also able to interpret the act of artistic creation for the benefit of others. He was therefore also a witness to the art of his time, most notably that of the abstract expressionists working in New York following the end of World War II which had, of course, temporarily closed the great European cities as centres of creative excellence.

Originally his interest lay in the theatre but the rise of Nazism made him leave Germany and the radical youth movements of the continent set him travelling with his Leica. By the age of 18, he was working as a photographer in Paris. His work was taken by the French magazine, *Vu*, and soon after he left for Spain as its photojournalist for the Spanish Civil War. The violence of the images and sounds of war were quickly brought home to him. On his first morning in Madrid he watched a young guard shot and photographed his death. He later recalled that before he could put his camera down a bullet smashed into the window frame beside him. It had been taken for a gun.

When the war began in 1939 Namuth was interned and subsequently spent a period with the French Foreign Legion. By 1941, however, he had managed to escape to the United States where he was later granted citizenship. He then joined the US Army Intelligence Service in Europe, where he served until 1945. He was awarded both the French *Croix de Guerre* and the Purple Heart.

When the war ended Namuth decided that photography was to be his career. To that end he spent a year at the New School for Social Research in New York. There he renewed contact with a former mentor, Alexey Brodovitch, the famed art director of *Harper's Bazaar*. He then freelanced, working for *Life*, *Look*, *Time*, *Newsweek* and *Vogue*. In 1950 he opened his own, renowned, New York Portrait Studio and began the film-making that made his name.

During a summer on Long Island he decided to make a study of neighbour Jackson Pollock, the rising star of abstract expressionist painting in the USA. Although there were initial problems

Pollock eventually co-operated fully, reworking a canvas he had previously declared finished. The interesting part of this was the Pollock technique. His canvases were stretched across the floor and he would surge across their massive expanses dripping, splattering and whiplashing the paint.

Over that summer Namuth had unlimited access to the studio and shot film upon film ending up with over 500 frames. These played a substantial part in establishing Pollock's very great reputation. The strong relationship that emerged from this work firmly established both men in their respective fields, but a later movie Namuth made of Pollock was fraught with difficulties. He resented taking direction and felt he had devalued himself and his work by performing on cue for camera. As a result he blamed Namuth for driving him back to alcohol after two years "on the wagon".

Namuth, however, went on to document the creative processes of other painters of the school, notably Willem de Kooning and sculptor Alexander Calder, best known for his intricate and elaborate mobiles.

Namuth's interests were also wide and it was with great love that he took up the photography of early American tools, formerly a neglected field. His book on the subject, published in 1975, shows a deep reverence for the simple beauty of objects created for a purpose.

This reverence also extended to people. In 1943 he had married Carmen Herrera with whom he visited, in 1946, her native Guatemala. He became entranced by the people of the remote northwestern village of Todos Santos Cuchumatan. He was enchanted by its feeling of medieval mystery and explored it with his Rolleiflex. Thirty years later he returned, this time with a better understanding of how to gain the trust of its people. He found little had changed, set up a makeshift studio and invited the inhabitants to come to him but, to obviate any sense of a society trapped in a time warp, he asked each to bring a prized possession. Villagers arrived with sewing machines and typewriters — their youngsters with footballs. One brought her pet pig. His portraits were a blend of ravages from cataracts, rotting teeth and stunted growth, with the dignity and joy of a people also resplendent in their heritage and the richness of their colourful clothes. It was a true record.

Namuth, fashioned by the upheavals of his European youth, held to one key imperative throughout his work: the need to seize the spirit, the essence and truth of the present. He was always aware, as he wrote in later life, that "Delving into other people's lives and souls can be an indiscretion." Courageously he recalled two occasions where he felt, in retrospect, he had perhaps overstepped the mark. Two portraits, of de Kooning and Edward Hopper, retained the power to pull him up, each seeming to ask, "Why can't you leave me alone?"

But photography is a two-way process. No matter how skilled the eye behind the camera, a human subject needs to participate in portraiture. When, as in the case of Pollock, there was later regret, it should be remembered that the subject does have a choice as to how far he chooses to participate and how much he chooses to reveal. An artist with the integrity of Namuth is unlikely to have intruded without permission.

Born Hans Namuth. **Parents** Adolph and Anna (Weiskirch) Namuth. **Marriage** Carmen P. de Herrera, 1943. **Children** Tessa and Peter. **Education** Humboldt Oberrealschule, Essen, Germany, 1925–31; studied under Joseph Breitenbach, Paris 1937–38; New School for Social Research, New York, studied under Breitenbach and Alexey Brodovitch, 1946–47. **Emigration** Left Europe for the United States, 1941, naturalized, 1943. **Military service** French Foreign Legion, 1939–40; United States Army Intelligence Service, Europe, 1943–45. **Career** Freelance photographer for *Vu*, *Life* and other magazines in Paris, France, Majorca, Spain, 1935–36; covered Spanish Civil War for *Vu* and other magazines, 1936–37; in New York, 1946 onwards; established own studio, New York, 1950; also, freelance film-maker, 1951 onwards. **Offices and memberships** Member, American Society of Magazine Photographers. **Awards and honours** Purple Heart, 1945; Croix de Guerre, 1945; Médaille du Maroc, 1945; Merit Award, Film Council of

Greater Boston for *Calder's Universe*, 1952; Association of Business Publishers Award, 1955; Art Directors Club of New York Award, 1956, 1959; Public Service Award, United States Department of State, 1958; special citation for film *Image from the Seas*, 1958; Art Directors Club of Philadelphia Award, 1959; Red Ribbon Award, American Film Festival for *Alfred Stieglitz, Photographer*, 1983. **Individual exhibitions** (in New York unless otherwise indicated) *Guatemala: The Land, The People*, Museum of Natural History, 1949; *Guatemala: The Land, The People*, American Federation of Arts; 1955; *17 American Painters*, at the *World's Fair*, Brussels, 1958; *17 American Painters*, Stable Gallery, 1959; *Pollock*, Museum of Modern Art, 1967; *American Artists*, Castelli Gallery, 1973; *American Artists*, Corcoran Gallery, Washington, DC, 1974; *Early American Tools*, Castelli Gallery, 1975; *The Spanish Civil War*, Castelli Graphics, 1976; *Living Together*, Benson Gallery, Bridgehampton, Long Island, 1976; *Small Retrospective*, Himelfarb Gallery, Water Mill, Long Island, 1978; *Todos Santos*, Castelli Graphics, 1979; *Jackson Pollock*, Museum of Modern Art, Oxford, 1979; *Jackson Pollock: 63 Prints*, Musée d'Art Moderne de la Ville, Paris, 1979; *Pictures from the War in Spain 1936–37*, Galerie Fiolet, Amsterdam, 1980; *Pollock Painting*, Castelli Graphics, 1980; *Artists 1950–1981: A Personal View*, Pace Gallery, 1981; Leo Castelli Gallery, 1982; Catskill Center for Photography, Woodstock, 1982; Mercer County Community College, Trenton, New Jersey, 1982; Carl Solway Gallery, Cincinnati, Ohio, 1982; Hunter College, 1982; Phoenix II Gallery, Washington, DC, 1982; Modernism Gallery, San Francisco, 1984; Städtische Galerie, Munich, 1986. **Group exhibitions** (include, in New York, unless otherwise indicated) *The Photographer and the Artist*, Sidney Janis Gallery, 1975; *Self-Portraits*, Center for Creative Photography, University of Arizona, Tucson, 1979; *Counterparts: Form and Emotion in Photographs*, Metropolitan Museum of Art, 1982; *Die fotografische Sammlung*, Museum Folkwang, Essen, 1983; *Portraits of Artists*, San Francisco Museum of Modern Art, 1984. **Collections** Metropolitan Museum of Art, New York; Museum of Modern Art, New York, Virginia Museum of Fine Arts, Richmond; Tulane University, New Orleans; Cleveland Art Museum; Center for Creative Photography, University of Arizona, Tucson; Los Angeles County Museum of Art; Fondation de la Photographie, Lyons; Museum Folkwang, Essen. **Publications** *52 Artists*, 1973; *American Masters*, text by Brian O'Doherty, 1973; *Early American Tools*, 1975; *L'Atelier de Jackson Pollock*, text by Rosalind Krauss and Francis V. O'Connor, 1978; *Pollock Painting*, 1980; *Artists 1950–1981: A Personal View*, 1981; *Der Krieg in Spanien 1936*, 1986; *Todos Santeros*, 1988. **Films** (with Paul Falkenberg) *Jackson Pollock*, 1951; *Calder's Universe*, 1952; *Willem de Kooning, the Painter*, 1958; *Image from the Seas*, 1958; *Joseph Albers: Homage to the Square*, 1969; *The Brancusi Retrospective at the Guggenheim*, 1970; *Centenniel at the Grand Palais*, 1971; *Louis I. Kahn, Architect*, 1972; *Alfred Steiglitz, Photographer*, 1982; *Balthus at the Pompidou*, 1984. **Cause of death** Road accident, at age 75. **Further reading** Weston J. Naef, *Counterparts: Form and Emotion in Photographs*, 1982; Douglas Davis, author of introduction, *The Library of World Photography: Photography as Fine Art*, 1982; Ute Eskildsen, author of introduction, *Museum Folkwang: die fotografische Sammlung* (exhibition catalogue), 1983; *Contemporary Photographers*, 1988.

GRIM NATWICK

American Film Animator

***Born* Wisconsin Rapids, Wisconsin, 1890**

***Died* Santa Monica, California, 7 October 1990**

The creator of Snow White and Betty Boop, not being British, did not receive the Queen's congratulatory telegram on his hundredth birthday, but was greatly honoured elsewhere.

He retired more than once, officially in 1968, when he went to Vienna with the goal of becoming a serious painter. Five years later he was lured to the London studio of Dick Williams where he animated, magically, the witch in *The Thief and the Cobbler*.

Born Myron Natwick in Wisconsin Rapids, nicknamed from childhood "Grim", he became revered as the grand-daddy of animators; as cultural historian Denis Gifford has said, "of the grand old men of animation, he was the grandest."

Natwick had a classical art training, in Chicago and New York, followed by his first visit to Vienna where he painted under the influence of Schiele and Klimt, during the 1920s. He had already worked as an animator from 1918 in the silent film era, starting with versions of newspaper strip-cartoons, including the noted Katzenjammer Kids (Americanized as the Shenanigan Kids to take into account post-World War I anti-German sentiment).

From the start, Natwick was an innovator, adding dimension to his cartoon animation, and then, in 1930, at the dawn of the talkies, creating Betty Boop with a vivid musical inspiration. Inspired by Helen Kane's hit song, "Boop-Boop-A-Doop", Betty Boop was the first cartoon character to be censored, in the mid 1930s.

Working for various studios, including Fleischer and Disney, Natwick was involved with such cartoon celebrities as Krazy Kat, Woody Woodpecker, Mr Magoo, Raggedy Ann, and Snow White herself. He was one of the animation directors for *Gulliver's Travels*, one of the first feature-length cartoons, and did the Mickey Mouse Sorcerer's Apprentice sequence in Disney's *Fantasia*. *Swing Symphonies*, in 1941, was another example of his musical flair.

Betty Boop's mini-skirt was a good quarter of a century before its fashionable time. But so was Grim Natwick, combining graphic qualities based on art traditions and skill, with a musical awareness translated into commercial effectiveness. It is not for nothing that he had Viennese mentors who were not only interested in the female form, but understood it. His early gift and originality in making his animated creations more fluid than any other examples, he attributed to his interest in athletics in high school:

> I was never a great sprinter, but I knew the form of running the hurdles, and form in animation is just as important. I notice that, among animators, there are either former athletes or athletic devotees. There's a physical feeling in animation. When I animate a scene I feel I know it perfectly. When I make one drawing I know exactly how that figure feels. I know exactly how it feels to stretch that leg forward and then I know how those "inbetweens" are going to feel.

His achievements cannot be over-estimated, since when Natwick started, the panoply of today's animation — designers, storymen and the rest, to say nothing of sophisticated technical aids — did not exist. On occasion, he could produce about a thousand drawings a week. He also became an inspired teacher.

Betty Boop was to return in the 1988 film *Who Framed Roger Rabbit?* Myron "Grim" Natwick's work will long outlive it.

Born Myron Natwick. **Children** One daughter. **Education** Chicago Institute of Art; National Academy of Design, New York; Vienna National Academy, 1925–28. **Career** Song sheet designer; animator: William Randolph Hearst animation studio, International Film Service, 1918–25, Ub Iwerks Studio, 1932–34, Disney Studio, 1934, Fleischer, 1938, Walter Lantz, 1939–45; supervising animator, United Productions of America, New York, 1950–56; freelance in partnership with Tissa David, 1956–67; tutor in residence, Richard Williams studio, London, 1973. **Awards and honours** Winsor McCay Award, 1975. **Films** (include) *The Rotisserie Brothers*, 1920; *Bringing Up Father*, 1928; *Dizzy Dishes*, 1930; *Flip the Frog*, 1931; *Any Rags*, 1932;

Mickey's Fire Brigade, 1935; *Musicland*, 1935; Cookie Carnivall, 1935; *Alpine Climbers*, 1936; *Mickey's Polo Game*, 1936; *Snow White*, 1937; *Mother Goose Goes Hollywood*, 1938; *Yip, Yip, Yippy!*, 1939; *Gulliver's Travels*, 1939; *Fantasia*, 1940; *Swing Symphonies*, 1941; *Enemy Bacteria*, 1945; *Trouble Indemnity*, 1950; *Gerald McBoing Boing*, 1950; *Willie the Kid*, 1952; *Rooty-Too-Toot*, 1952; *Raggedy Ann*, 1977; *The Thief and the Cobbler*, 1981; also *Krazy Kat*, *Happy Hooligan*, *Katzenjammer Kids*, *Swing You Sinner*. **Cause of death** Undisclosed, at age 100.

WILLIAM S. PALEY

American Broadcasting Executive

Born **Chicago, Illinois, 28 September 1901**

Died **Manhattan, New York, 26 October 1990**

In 1928, when William S. Paley invested 400,000 dollars of his family's cigar-manufacturing money in a fledgling radio network called United Independent Broadcasters, friends and acquaintances looked on in amazement. "[They] thought I was crazy to quit a sure-fire thing with my father", Paley remembered. Over the next 40 years, the man author Truman Capote described as "part visionary, part robber-baron" built the small string of struggling stations, renamed the Columbia Broadcasting System, into the most powerful communications conglomerate in the world. President and chairman of the board at CBS for more than half a century, Paley was "as much a pioneer in American broadcasting as Henry Ford was in the car industry", wrote W. J. Weatherby of England's *Guardian* newspaper.

The son of a Ukrainian-Jewish cigar manufacturer, William Paley grew up on the West Side of Chicago. During his high school years he studied at Western Military Academy in Alton, Illinois, then went on to the University of Chicago. In the early 1920s his father moved the family and the business to Philadelphia, and Paley transferred to the Wharton School of Finance and Commerce at the University of Pennsylvania. When he received his Bachelor of Science degree in 1922, he joined his father's firm, the Congress Cigar Company, first as a tobacco buyer, then as vice-president and secretary.

Paley first recognized the power and potential of radio in 1925, when his uncle left him temporarily in charge of the company's advertising budget. On a whim, he decided to commit 50 dollars a week to a sponsored music programme on Philadelphia's local station, WCAU. When his uncle returned, he was infuriated at what he regarded as a waste of funds, and ordered the sponsorship to stop. But Paley's father disagreed. After examining the books, he discovered that in the weeks following the broadcasts, cigar sales had sky-rocketed. The Congress Cigar Company's association with the station was quickly restored, and William Paley took over as supervisor of a new show, *The La Palina Smoker*, named after one of the enterprise's more successful cigar lines. Three years later, Samuel Paley urged his son to buy into the United Independent Broadcasters network and backed him with 400,000 dollars. At the age of 27, William Paley became president of the company and changed its name to Columbia Broadcasting. Shortly afterwards the family invested an additional 86,000 dollars, giving Paley full control of network operations.

Before long, Paley had moved to New York and increased the size of the network from 16 to 49 stations. He also introduced an important change in the company's relationship with its affiliates. Instead of charging the stations for unsponsored material, he got them to adhere to a network schedule wherein only the sponsored programmes were broadcast during peak listening hours.

This way, Columbia could sell time to advertisers with a guarantee that their commercials would be heard by the largest audiences.

Paley was equally daring in his creative endeavours. From the beginning, he had an uncanny knack for correctly reading — even anticipating — the public taste. In 1931, for example, he happened to hear the records of Bing Crosby, then an unknown singer. Recognizing Crosby's potential, he ordered CBS executives to sign him up. He was also one of the first to recruit performers — such as Will Rogers and Paul Whiteman — from other areas of entertainment, convincing them that radio exposure would advance their careers. Then, in the 1940s, he began what came to be known as the "Paley Raids", luring big-name talent, such as Jack Benny, Burns and Allen, Edgar Bergen and Red Skelton, away from competing networks.

But low-brow soaps and comedies were only part of Paley's repertoire. During the 1930s he pioneered educational and cultural programming, broadcasting New York Philharmonic concerts, the *Lux Radio Theater*, and the *American School of the Air*. He was equally committed to news. When newspaper publishers, fearful of competition, barred the wire services from providing news reports to broadcasters, CBS set up its own news-gathering unit. With the skill and commitment of distinguished journalists such as Edward R. Murrow, Howard K. Smith and Howard Shirer, CBS News quickly gained a reputation for quality. Network news reports during World War II helped to establish CBS — and Ed Murrow — as the voice of broadcast journalism.

During these early years, Paley basked in the power and glory of his thriving monarchy. "I used to do everything", he recalled. "I was the salesman. I made the news decisions. I knew every correspondent on a first-name basis. I'd call up in the middle of a radio programme and get them to change something. I'd go down to Broadway and catch a show, and if I saw someone I liked, I signed them up." Years later, his stubborn refusal to relinquish the reins led to bitter feuds with successors, some of whom he had considered his friends.

In the early 1930s, CBS was the first network to establish regularly scheduled television broadcasting. But America's entry into World War II ten years later brought all programming and development to a halt. In 1943, Paley went overseas to work for the Office of War Information, using his knowledge of radio broadcasting to aid Allied activities in North Africa and Italy. He was later to achieve the rank of colonel in the US Army, then served as deputy chief of the Psychological Warfare Division under General Eisenhower. Upon his discharge from active duty in November 1945, he returned to New York. Back at CBS, he began a massive reorganization. Frank N. Stanton, former head of the company's research department, ended up as president, and Paley became chairman of the board. Never personal friends, Stanton and Paley were nonetheless united in their devotion to CBS. Their association spanned four decades.

When, in 1931, CBS had begun the world's first regular television broadcasts, Paley's friends and advisers had cautioned him about the medium's limited appeal. It will never catch on, they told him. But Paley's pioneering spirit drove him on. "My imagination went wild contemplating the possibilities of it", he remembered. After the war, the time was ripe. Recognizing the importance of entertainment programming in generating revenue, he set his sights on NBC's top talent, and with the help of a 5 million-dollar bank loan, managed to manoeuvre many popular performers into the CBS fold. His overwhelming success then, at the dawn of commercial television, brought CBS into the ratings lead. It was a position the network held until 1976. Over the years, the company's programming successes ranged from *Gunsmoke* and *I Love Lucy* to *Playhouse 90* and *The Beverly Hillbillies*. With the 1970s came more sophisticated, socially conscious serials, such as *All in the Family* and *The Waltons*. Some of Paley's colleagues and associates, notably Ed Murrow, could not reconcile the CBS of mass entertainment with CBS the news pioneer. For, while Paley insisted upon quality, he also insisted upon popular appeal. "I think I was born with a sense of what was important to the American public", he once said. "I care about quality, but I also care about the bottom line . . . you have to know where to cut-off". Over the years, wrote Jeremy Gerard of *The*

New York Times, Paley was "quick to cancel shows whose popularity sagged and equally quick to anticipate changes in the public taste." Paley's former chief of programming, Mike Dann, put it more bluntly: "He wasn't the least bit interested in creating new forms. He believed in building the best mousetrap."

The power and influence of CBS did not end with radio and TV, however. In 1948, the company revolutionized the recording industry with the introduction of the long-playing record. Vladimir Horowitz, Leonard Bernstein (q.v.), Duke Ellington, Billie Holiday, Bob Dylan and Bruce Springsteen were among the company's top artists. Later, CBS moved into film-making, publishing and aerospace engineering, and also invested in a string of successful Broadway musicals. In a number of other ventures — its purchase of Hytron Radio and Electronics Corporation in the 1950s in an attempt to manufacture television sets; its investment in the development of an early electronic video recording system; and its brief ownership of the New York Yankees baseball team — CBS was less successful. But, despite these setbacks, it continued to prosper, moving into a host of new areas, including musical instrument manufacturing and cable television.

During this time, Paley and his second wife, glamorous socialite Barbara Cushing Mortimer, known as Babe — his first marriage to Dorothy Hart Hearst ended in divorce in 1947 — were the toast of the town, patronizing New York's finest restaurants and night-clubs, often in the company of celebrated writers and artists. They also played an active role in city charities and civic organizations. A long-term trustee of the Museum of Modern Art, Paley had a consuming passion for Post-Impressionist paintings. Priceless Picassos, Cézannes and Pollocks covered the walls of his Fifth Avenue apartment, his Manhasset, Long Island estate, and his luxurious office suite at CBS. In 1976, his desire to promote and preserve the media he had done so much to develop led him to found the Museum of Broadcasting in New York. It remained one of his favourite projects.

Despite Paley's philanthropy, friends described his relationships with his four children and two stepchildren as cold and often remote. They grew up on the family estate in Manhasset and saw their parents only on weekends. He also feigned indifference to Babe, but when she developed lung cancer, he devoted all of his power and energy to the search for a cure. When she died in 1978, he was shattered, and five years later stepped down as CBS chairman.

While CBS had established a compulsory retirement age of 65, William Paley made himself the single exception to the rule. More than a decade after most executives had hung up their hats, he was still reporting for work, providing final approval for all of the network's major policy decisions. He had handpicked, then rejected, three successors before finally passing the reins of power to Thomas Wyman in 1983. Then he insisted upon staying on as a consultant and founder chairman.

During the next few years, the news division at CBS was racked by a series of dramatic changes. Paley, dissatisfied with Wyman's leadership, joined forces with Laurence Tisch, chairman of Loew's Corporation, CBS's biggest stockholder, to retake control. But by this time, most of Paley's power had evaporated, and he could do little more than sit back and watch Tisch lay off news staff and cut back operations in a desperate bid to reduce costs and fight off predators. CBS News ratings had plummeted, cable TV had come to the fore, and the network's enfeebled entertainment schedule had dropped to third place. The golden age of the Columbia Broadcasting System had come and gone. In 1979 Paley published his memoirs, *As It Happened*. The book appeared at virtually the same time as *The Powers That Be*, David Halberstam's authoritative account of the growth of CBS, Time Inc., *The Washington Post* and *The Los Angeles Times*, the US's four media giants.

Despite his failing health, Paley never stopped travelling or appearing at stockholders' meetings, and continued to screen potential shows until 1988. "He was an enthusiast, whether over the purchase of a hot dog from a sidewalk vendor, a Picasso for his apartment, or a sitcom for his network", wrote Jeremy Gerard of *The New York Times*. "He cared little for the details of corporate management, but never lost his love of programming, suggesting schedule changes and offering his opinions of CBS shows until the last month of his life."

Upon hearing of Paley's death, Fred Friendly, former head of CBS News, described him as the "father of American television", adding that "a lot of the fun and the glory, the nobility that he possessed, has sort of vanished in the throes of profits."

Born William Paley (adopted "S" at age 12, did not stand for any name). **Parents** Samuel, cigar manufacturer, and Gold (Drell) Paley. **Marriages** 1) Dorothy Hart Hearst, 1932 (divorced 1947); 2) Barbara Cushing Mortimer, 1947 (died 1978). **Children** Jeffery and Hilary by first marriage; William and Kate by second marriage. **Education** Western Military Academy, Illinois; University of Chicago, 1918–19; Wharton School of Finance and Commerce, University of Pennsylvania, BS, 1922. **Military service** Supervisor, Office of War Information, 1943–44; chief of radio operations, Psychological Warfare Division, Supreme Headquarters Allied Expeditionary Forces, 1944–45; deputy chief, Information Control, 1945; colonel, United States Army, deputy chief of Psychological Warfare Division. **Career** Tobacco buyer, Congress Cigar Company, Philadelphia, Pennsylvania, 1922–28, vice-president, 1923–28, secretary, 1925–28; president, United Independent Broadcasters, later Columbia Broadcasting System, now CBS Incorporated, New York City, 1928–46, chief executive officer, 1928–77, chairman of board of directors, 1946–83, executive committee chairman, 1983 onwards. **Related activities** President and director, William S. Paley Foundation; founding member, Bedford-Stuyvesant D & S Corporation, 1967–72; partner, Whitcome Investment Company, New York City, 1983 onwards; director, International Executive Service Corporation; director, Thinking Machines Corporation, 1983 onwards; co-chairman of the board, *International Herald Tribune*, 1983. **Other activities** Chairman, President's Materials Policy Commission, 1951–52; executive committee member, Resources for the Future, 1952–69, chairman, 1966–69, honorary director, 1969 onwards; committee member, White House Conference on Education, 1954–56; chairman, New York City Task Force on Urban Design, 1967; chairman, New York City Urban Design Council, 1968–71; member of Commission of Critical Choices for America, Commission for Cultural Affairs, City of New York, 1973–77; founder and chairman, Museum of Broadcasting, 1976 onwards; founder member, on board of directors, Genetics Institute, 1980 onwards. **Offices and memberships** Trustee, Museum of Modern Art, 1937 onwards, president, 1968–72, chairman, 1972 onwards; member of board of directors, North Shore University Hospital, 1949–73, co-chairman, board of trustees, 1954–73; life trustee, Columbia University, 1950–73, trustee emeritus, 1973 onwards; life trustee, Federation of Jewish Philanthropies; member: France-United States Association, National Institute of Social Scientists, Pilgrims of the United States, Academy of Political Scientists, Economic Club, New York, Metropolitan Club, Washington, DC. **Awards and honours** (include) Medal of Merit; Legion of Merit; numerous foreign awards, including Croix de Guerre with Palm, France, Order of Merit, Italy; LLD: Adelphi University, 1957, Bates College, 1963, University of Pennsylvania, 1968, Columbia, Brown University, 1974, Pratt Institute, 1977, Dartmouth College, 1979; LHD, Ithaca College, 1979; Medallion of Honor of the City of New York, 1965; Gold Achievement Medal, Poor Richard Club; Keynote Award, National Association of Broadcasters; special award, Broadcast Pioneers; Concern Artist Guild Award; Skowhegan Gertrude Vanderbilt Whitney Award; gold medal, National Planning Association. **Publication** *As It Happened: A Memoir* (autobiography), 1979. **Cause of death** Pneumonia-induced heart attack, at age 89. **Further reading** Robert Metz, *CBS: Reflections in a Bloodshot Eye*, 1975; David Halberstam, *The Powers That Be*, 1979.

SHEIKH RASHID bin SAID al-MAKTOUM

Ruler of Dubai

***Born* In the desert, 1914**

***Died* Dubai, 7 October 1990**

Britain's decision in 1968 to withdraw her forces from east of Suez had nowhere a greater effect than on the small Trucial States of the Gulf "Pirate Coast" — "Trucial" because they had come under British protection after the Treaty of 1820 which pacified the notorious piracy of the warring coastal tribes of the southern Gulf. And for none of them was it more important than for the Emirate of Dubai whose strategic position on Dubai creek had made it the trading, and smuggling, centre of the region. No Trucial ruler was more conscious of the value of Britain's protection than Sheikh Rashid bin Said al-Maktoum, the ruler of Dubai since 1958, and none more anxious to build up an edifice to replace that protection. It is primarily for his part in the creation of the United Arab Emirates that Sheikh Rashid will go down in history.

But he had already done much for his small sheikhdom before that. He had assumed effective control of Dubai during the long dotage of his father, Sheikh Said. During World War II Dubai prospered as a trading centre, particularly with Iran, and with the discovery of oil its port came into its own. It was on Sheikh Rashid's initiative that the creek was dredged and a new major deep-water port constructed, and a modern airstrip laid to establish Dubai's pre-eminence as the aviation centre of the southern Gulf. The doubling and redoubling of oil income in the 1970s brought accelerated growth: heavy industry, an aluminium smelter, the most efficient port in the whole Middle East, banking and advanced communications facilities all bid fair to make Dubai the Hong Kong of the Gulf. And not even the Iran-Iraq war put paid to this economic boom. Dubai continued to trade with Iran throughout the hostilities, and it will not be forgotten that it was an Iranian airliner bound for Dubai which was shot down in the war's later stages.

This accelerating prosperity lay at the root of Sheikh Rashid's efforts to underpin the strategic situation when Britain's protection was removed. Here his superb diplomatic skills came into play. The old animosities of the "Pirate Coast", and in particular the rivalry between the two largest of the Trucial sheikhdoms, Dubai and Abu Dhabi, were still very much alive, and it required remarkable wisdom on the part of the two rulers to devise a federal constitution for the new union which preserved the internal independence of the individual member states. And even more skill to persuade the other four sheikhdoms to join what in July 1971 became the United Arab Emirates (UAE). The prime movers, Sheikh Rashid and Sheikh Zayed of Abu Dhabi, always maintained a healthy respect for, and an equally healthy suspicion of, each other. Sheikh Rashid always resisted suggestions of a unified command of the armed forces, and he was frequently accused by Sheikh Zayed, the President of the UAE, of defending too vigorously the smaller states' autonomy against the encroachments of the federal government. As a result, no permanent federal constitution was ever arrived at, though Sheikh Rashid was persuaded in 1979 to enlarge his vice-presidential powers by becoming the federal prime minister. In this capacity, he supported the setting up of the Gulf Co-operation Council in 1981 in an attempt to ward off any danger of an extension of the Iran-Iraq war.

Sheikh Rashid's natural business acumen — he had, after all, been born in the desert and had enjoyed little formal education — succeeded in transforming his small sheikhdom on a mud creek from an entrepot of the dhow smuggling trade into one of the leading commercial centres of the Middle East. And he did much to spread the benefits of that transformation among his people, allowing considerable freedom to the individual citizen and a remarkable freedom from restrictions to expatriates. This enlightened attitude undoubtedly underpinned his country's prosperity. Moreover, he personally retained much of his bedouin simplicity, and his modest way of life, and in particular his one wife, were a model of restraint for many other oil-rich rulers. His family's one great indulgence was in horse racing, and his sons have achieved worldwide fame as owners of some of the most renowned race horses.

Born Rashid bin Said al-Maktoum. **Parents** Sheikh Said al-Maktoum and Hissa. **Marriage** Latifa bint Hamdan al-Nahayan (died 1983). **Children** Four sons, Crown Prince Sheikh Maktoum bin Rashid al-Maktoum, Hamdan, Mohammed and Ahmed, and six daughters. **Education** Qur'anic schools. **Career** Deputy ruler, later regent, Dubai, 1938–58; became Sheikh, ruler of Dubai, 1958; vice-president, United Arab Emirates, 1971 onwards, federal prime minister, 1979 onwards. **Other activities** Endowed new library, Exeter University, England, 1980; founder: Oxford Diabetes Trust and Sheikh Rashid Diabetes Unit, Radcliffe Infirmary, Oxford, 1981. **Cause of death** Undisclosed, at age 76.

LORD REILLY

British Authority on Design

***Born* Liverpool, Lancashire, 29 May 1912**

***Died* London, England, 11 October 1990**

Although Lord Reilly, as he was to become, never set out to be a leading authority on design, his background was such that it became both inevitable and a consuming passion, which he pursued long after his formal retirement.

Both his grandfather and father were influential architects. His father was Sir Charles Reilly, the head of Liverpool School of Architecture whose great contribution in the UK was the promotion of modern building design. He took his young son on tours of the great European buildings. His mother was a painter who had studied at the Slade, the prestigious and academic art school based in London's Bloomsbury district, which was very much an intellectual centre in the earlier decades of this century. Lady Reilly never lost her enthusiasm for the study of human anatomy and, even after becoming an invalid, would spend many hours at a time drawing from life.

Reilly was educated at Winchester, one of England's leading independent schools where, like so many other youngsters from the upper middle classes, he was not happy. He later revealed that school had killed his self-confidence. But at university he fared better. At Oxford, after a shaky start, he developed his speaking skills and became widely respected.

Too overwhelmed by his father's eminence to risk a career in architecture and finding himself unable to get a foothold in industry in the difficult economic situation of the early 1930s, Reilly joined a plywood manufacturing firm called Venesta. He moved swiftly from commercial traveller to sales manager and was partly responsible for the firm's success in pioneering new uses for plywood, particularly in furniture design. The seeds of his eventual career had been sown.

Meanwhile, however, he moved sideways into the completely different field of journalism, having been offered a post with the *News Chronicle*, then a middle-brow British daily. Although not a news man by nature (when the story of Edward VIII and Wallis Simpson broke in the UK he authorized the publication of a large picture of the latter with a banner headline reading, "Welcome to Our New Queen"!) he distinguished himself both as editor of features and of the leader page.

After war service with the Army and, later, Naval Intelligence which involved some considerable travelling in Europe, he joined the staff of the New York magazine *Modern Plastics* and co-edited the *British Plastics Encyclopaedia*. Plastic was, he foresaw, a material of the future. During this time, however, he was not neglecting his early love. It was in 1948 that he published his first major book, *An Introduction to Regency Architecture*. And it was this combination of interests that led to another offer coming his way, this time to head the Information Office of the Council of Industrial Design. Set up just before the end of the war, the Council aimed to promote the improvement of design throughout British industry. There were therefore two joint prongs to the venture — to make both producers *and* consumers aware of good design. Within a year he had launched the magazine, *Design*, and was immediately closely involved in the selection of the best of British consumer goods for exhibition at the 1951 Festival of Britain, held on the South Bank of London's River Thames where today stand the National Theatre complex and the Royal Festival Hall (itself a tribute to the best of post-war architecture in the UK).

In 1956 the Council opened The Design Centre in London's West End where the general public was able to see the best of recent design in regularly updated exhibitions. In 1960 Reilly took over as the Council's director.

Reilly was a passionate crusader whose achievements were considerable. His skill with people and extremely wide connections enabled him eventually to get funding towards the pursuit of engineering design as an integrated and major field, to provide technical advice to industry and to ensure that design was to become part of the national school curriculum through a casual discussion of lamp posts with Margaret Thatcher when she was minister of education in the early 1970s. Having received a knighthood in recognition of his dedication in 1967 he was granted a peerage after his retirement as director of the Design Council.

But he did not retire from design itself. He continued as a consultant and director to a number of bodies including the Conran Foundation, of which he was president and in which capacity he helped launch a major exhibition on international industrial design at the Victoria and Albert Museum in London's fashionable district of Kensington.

Reilly was proud of his achievements and of his peerage which he took, rightly, as an honour for design but did not allow this to blind him to the fact that the British public still relished the "tyranny" of the three-piece suite (sofa and two easy chairs) and that manufacturers were still overly willing to pander to this taste. When Terence Conran produced a well-stuffed and comfortable sofa for his Habitat stores Reilly expressed his thorough disapproval with the comment, "That is exactly the sort of horrible and self-indulgent product that I have spent my life trying to abolish." He was only too well aware that he had been unable to abolish what he called the visual illiteracy of the British and likened the task to "helping to push a steamroller up a hill".

He did, however, push it quite a distance!

Born Paul Reilly. **Father** Professor Sir Charles Reilly, architect and head, Liverpool School of Architecture, and Lady Reilly, painter. **Marriages** 1) Pamela Wentworth Foster, dancer, 1939; 2) Annette Stockwell, cookery expert, 1952 (died 1990). **Children** One daughter, Victoria, by first marriage. **Education** Winchester College, Hampshire; Hertford College, Oxford; London School of Economics, London University. **Military service** Royal Armoured Corps; Royal Naval Volunteer Reserve, 1941–45, seconded by Naval Intelligence to Royal Patriotic School. **Career** Salesman and sales manager, Venesta Limited, 1934–36; leader page editor and features editor, *News Chronicle*, 1936–40; on editorial staff, *Modern Plastics*, New York, 1946; co-editor, *British Plastics Encyclopaedia*, 1947; chief information officer, Council of Industrial Design, 1948, deputy director, 1954; director, Design Council (formerly Council of Industrial Design), 1960–77; Crafts Advisory Committee, 1977–81, chief executive, 1971–77; chairman, Conran Foundation, 1981–86, trustee, 1986–90; director: The Building Trades Exhibition Limited, Race International

Design. **Related activities** Council member: Royal Society of Arts, 1952, 1962, 1963–70, British Tourist Authority, 1960–70, Royal College of Art, 1963–81; General Advisory Council, British Broadcasting Corporation, 1964–70; British National Export Council, 1966–70; member: British Railways Board Design Panel, 1966, Environment Panel, 1977–84; Greater London Council Historic Buildings Committee, 1967–82, Post Office Stamp Advisory Committee, 1967, Design Advisory Committee, 1970–84, British Council Fine Arts Advisory Committee, 1970–80, Conseil Supérieur de la Création Esthétique Industrielle, France, 1971–73, Advisory Council of Science Policy Foundation, 1971 onwards, British Crafts Centre Board, 1972–77, National Theatre Design Advisory Committee, 1974 onwards, Royal Fine Art Commission, 1976–81; president: Society of Designer-Craftsmen, 1976–84, Association of Art Institutions, 1977–80, World Crafts Council, 1978–80; chairman of trustees, Building Conservation Trust, 1977–82; design consultant, Courtaulds; member, British Telecom Design Committee, 1981–83. **Offices and memberships** Governor: Hammersmith College of Art and Building, 1948–67, Central School of Art and Design, 1953–74, Camberwell School of Art and Design, 1967–77, City of Birmingham Polytechnic, 1970–77; vice-president, International Council of Societies of Industrial Design, 1963–67, Modular Society, 1968–77, London Society, 1977 onwards, Institute of Contemporary Arts, 1979 onwards, Rye Conservation Society, 1980 onwards; on Court of Governors, London School of Economics, 1975–80. **Awards and honours** Honorary corresponding member, Svenskaslöjdforeningen, 1956; honorary fellow: Society of Industrial Arts, 1959, Royal Institute of British Architecture, 1965; knighted, 1967; honorary member, Art Workers Guild, 1961; Commander, Royal Order of Vasa, Sweden, 1961; Bicentenary Medal, Royal College of Art, 1963; honorary associate, Manchester College of Art, 1963; senior fellow, Royal College of Art, 1972; DSc: Loughborough, 1977, Aston, 1981, Cranfield, 1983; honorary Doctor of the Royal College of Art, 1978; created life peer, Baron Reilly of Brompton in the Royal Borough of Kensington and Chelsea, 1978; honorary liveryman, Furniture Makers' Company, 1980; Ornamo, Finland, 1981; honorary commissioner, Japan Design Foundation, 1983. **Publications** *An Introduction to Regency Architecture (Art and Technics)*, 1948; *An Eye on Design* (autobiography), 1987. **Cause of death** Undisclosed, at age 78.

ELLIOTT ROOSEVELT

American Writer and Businessman

***Born* New York City, New York, 23 September 1910**

***Died* Scottsdale, Arizona, 27 October 1990**

Elliott Roosevelt, second son of President Franklin Delano Roosevelt, had a varied career ranging from Air Corps general to mayor of Miami Beach, Florida, from breeder of Arabian horses to business executive. The irony is that probably he will best be remembered as the writer of who-dunnits featuring his famous mother, Eleanor Roosevelt, as an amateur detective.

His writing career took off in 1946 with the publication of *As He Saw It*, a best-selling account of the summit meetings President Roosevelt attended in the company of Churchill and Stalin. One reviewer likened Elliott Roosevelt in his role of observer to "a boy engaged in a man's work", but found the book engaging, if indiscreet, "history on its most intimate level".

Encouraged, Roosevelt went on to write 12 more books, including a trilogy about the behind-the-scenes life of the Roosevelt family which brought down the wrath of his sister and three brothers upon his head.

"Eleanor Snoops to Conquer", is the way one reviewer described the series of murder mysteries casting Eleanor Roosevelt in the role of a political Miss Marple. Best of these was *Murder in the Oval Office*, in which the First Lady single-handedly solves the closed-door murder of a southern congressman whose blood stains her best carpet.

His last non-fiction work, entitled *The Conservators*, published in 1983, indicates that Roosevelt in his seventies had exchanged his obsession with Oedipus for an interest in green matters, the survival of this planet, no less, being its subject.

In his younger days Elliott Roosevelt, 6 feet, 3 inches, blond and squarely built, bore a strong resemblance to FDR, a likeness which faded with the years. Like his brothers, he suffered from growing up in the shade of such a famous father, and reacted by kicking over the traces as best he could. For example, Elliott became "the Roosevelt who did not go to Harvard". Instead, he took a job as an advertising executive. Again, during World War II he broke a family tradition by enlisting in the Army Air Corps instead of in the Navy. Gossip that he had used family influence to obtain his commission as captain was soon laid to rest by his wartime record.

Young Roosevelt flew 300 combat missions and commanded the 325th Photographic Reconnaissance Wing which played an important role in the Allied invasions of North Africa and Sicily as well as the Normandy D-Day landings. He was decorated with the US Air Medal, the Legion of Merit, and the Distinguished Flying Cross with oak leaf cluster. In addition he was made a Commander of the Order of the British Empire, and was awarded the French *Croix de Guerre* with palm.

Roosevelt's post-war years were characterized by restlessness. He changed wives almost as often as he changed jobs: he was wedded four times before marrying in 1960 Patricia Peabody, with whom he remained the rest of his life.

Patricia and Elliott Roosevelt moved to Miami Beach, where Roosevelt was elected mayor. They travelled widely abroad, and lived in Portugal where Roosevelt raised Arabian steeds. After sojourns in Seattle and Palm Springs they finally came to roost in Scottsdale, Arizona.

Nothing in his earlier writing career prepared the reading public for *An Untold Story*, published in 1973, in which Elliott revealed Franklin Roosevelt's intimate relationship with his secretary, Marguerite (Missy) Lehand, in whose arms the President died. After the birth of their youngest son, John, in 1916, his parents "never again lived as husband and wife", according to Elliott. These "whistle-blowing" revelations caused his sister and brothers to "disassociate themselves completely from this book".

Born Elliott Roosevelt. **Parents** Franklin Delano, US president, and Anna Eleanor (Roosevelt), US ambassador to the United Nations, Roosevelt. **Marriages** 1) Elizabeth Donner, 1932 (divorced 1933); 2) Ruth Googins, 1933 (divorced 1944); 3) Faye Emerson, actress, 1944; 4) Name unknown; 5) Patricia Peabody, 1960. **Children** William, from the first marriage; Chandler, Elliott and David, from the second marriage; Gretchen, James and Ford, from later marriages. **Education** Groton Academy, 1923–29; Hun School, New Jersey, 1929 30. **Military service** Captain, Army Air Corps, 1940, aerial reconnaissance, 1942–44, retired brigadier-general, 1945. **Career** Assistant account executive, Albert Frank advertising agency, 1930; vice-president, Kelly, Nason and Roosevelt, 1931; account executive, Paul Cornell advertising agency, 1932; aviation editor, Los Angeles *Examiner*, 1933–35; vice-president, Young Democrats of Texas; vice-president, Hearst Radio, 1936, president/general manager, 1937–1939; owner, Frontier Broadcasting System, from 1937; commentator: Texas State Network, 1938, Emerson Radio and Phonograph for Mutual Broadcasting System, 1939; advisor, Transcontinental Broadcasting System, 1939–40; president, Empire Airlines, 1945; freelance writer; Arabian horse breeder, Portugal; published first Eleanor Roosevelt mystery novel, *Murder and the First Lady*, 1984. **Related activities** Vice-president, Aeronautical Chamber of Commerce of America, 1934; mayor, Miami Beach, Florida; delegate, Democratic National Party, committeeman. **Awards**

and honours Air Medal, 1945; Legion of Merit, 1945; Distinguished Flying Cross with oak leaf cluster, 1945; Commander of the Order of the British Empire, 1945; Officier de la Légion d'honneur, 1945; Croix de Guerre with palm, 1945. **Publications** *As He Saw It*, 1946; *An Untold Story*, 1973; *The Conservators*, 1983; *Murder and the First Lady*, 1984; *Eleanor Roosevelt, With Love: A Centenary Remembrance*, 1984; *The Hyde Park Murder*, 1985; *Murder at Hobcaw Barony*, 1986; *The White House Pantry Murder*, 1987; *Murder at the Palace*, 1988; *Murder in the Oval Office*, 1989; *Murder in the Rose Garden*, 1989; (editor) *Perfect Crimes: My Favourite Mystery Stories*, 1989; *Murder in the Blue Room*, 1990. **Cause of death** Congestive heart failure, at age 80.

IRENE SELZNICK

American Theatrical Producer

Born **Brooklyn, New York, 2 April 1907**

Died **Manhattan, New York, 10 October 1990**

Any portrait of Irene Selznick seems invariably to begin with a history of the making of Hollywood as personified by her father, Louis B. Mayer, and a catalogue of blockbuster films made by her husband, David O. Selznick. Though she acknowledged that Hollywood was her first home and never denied the impact of her famous parent and husband, it was in spite not because of Hollywood that she emerged as a talent in her own right, as a theatre producer on Broadway.

Born in New York, Irene Selznick passed her infancy outside Boston where her father had some cinemas. In 1919 the family moved to California where Mayer founded his film company which merged with two other companies in 1924 to form Metro Goldwyn Mayer. Young Irene went to the exclusive Hollywood School for Girls but her father didn't think women should have careers. "I'd pick up a book", she recalled, "and my father would say, 'She knows too much already.'" He refused to let her go on to college. He also forbade her to associate with actors. At 23 she married film producer, David O. Selznick, who is reported to have proposed to her in a memo. Mayer's initial dislike of Selznick (son of one of his bitterest enemies) was transformed to warm paternal affection when Selznick became Mayer's production supervisor and went on to make big pictures for MGM. The marriage was successful for some years and they had two sons. Though Irene Selznick made light of her influence on her husband's films, she claimed some credit for the realism of *A Star is Born*, which lifted the lid on life in Hollywood, and for the phenomenally successful *Gone with the Wind*.

During World War II the marriage foundered, and in 1948 Irene Selznick decided to file for divorce and to pursue a secret ambition. She moved to New York and surprised many who saw her only as Louis B. Mayer's daughter by becoming a perceptive and successful producer of Broadway hits. Her first production, *Heartsong*, was not a success, but with the second, Tennessee Williams's *A Streetcar Named Desire*, she became established. In this production as in others that followed, her involvement with author and actors in the early stages of the script went far beyond that of the usual Broadway impresario. She claimed that while working with Williams to find a more affecting ending for *Streetcar*, she rescued the play's most famous line, "I have always depended on the kindness of strangers", from the wastepaper basket. When Laurence Olivier, who, she felt, didn't understand *Streetcar*, was directing the West End production, she flew to London to save the script from cuts. She was described as "precise" in her editing of scripts. Later, voicing her opinion of Laurence Olivier as director of *Streetcar* she was nothing if not incisive — "How were we to know that he was a numbskull and that he had no understanding whatever of modern American plays?"

A Streetcar Named Desire opened in 1947 and stayed on Broadway for 855 performances. Selznick also worked with Williams to see that the film adaptation — which made Marlon Brando a star overnight — was done just as he wanted it. Further successes on Broadway included Enid Bagnold's *The Chalk Garden* and John Van Druten's *Bell, Book and Candle*. Selznick's last production was of Graham Greene's *The Complaisant Lover*. At this point she felt that Broadway theatre was no longer taking its plays as seriously as its musicals and she decided to retire, though only in her mid-fifties, saying, "With a little more luck, I'd like to grow very old as slowly as possible."

Described as "a slim woman with striking dark eyes", she herself claimed that she owed any success she had had to perseverance. She remained a formidable personality to the end. During her long retirement she persevered for over seven years in writing her memoirs, entitled *A Private View*, and published in 1983. In the memoirs she recalled how, as a young girl, she had overcome a stutter by persevering, how she had coped with a demanding father and an almost equally demanding husband and survived the hectic atmosphere of the inter-war years of Hollywood. Somewhat wistfully she wrote, "I've had three lives, one as the daughter of my father, another as the wife of my husband. The theatre furnished me with a third act, I'd have settled for so much less."

Born Irene Mayer. **Parents** Louis B., founder and chief executive of Metro Goldwyn Mayer, and Margaret (Shenberg) Mayer. **Marriage** David O. Selznick, film producer, 1930 (divorced 1948). **Children** Lewis and Daniel. **Education** Public schools, Massachusetts; Hollywood School for Girls, California. **Career** With Selznick-International Pictures Incorporated, Culver City, California, 1936–40; with Vanguard Films, California and New York City, 1941–49; managing director and producer, Irene M. Selznick Company, New York City, 1946 onwards. **Productions** (in New York unless otherwise indicated) *Heartsong*, Philadelphia, 1947; *A Street Car Named Desire*, 1947, London, 1949; *Bell, Book and Candle*, 1950; *Flight Into Egypt*, 1952; *The Chalk Garden*, 1955; *The Last Joke*, 1960; *The Complaisant Lover*, 1961. **Publication** A Private View (memoirs), 1983. **Cause of death** Breast cancer, at age 83.

DELPHINE SEYRIG

French Actress

***Born* Beirut, Lebanon, 10 April 1932**

***Died* Paris, France, 15 October 1990**

As much as the irony delighted her later in life, in hindsight, Seyrig proved to be the quintessential French lady of exoticism, cool elegance, intelligence and, above all, mystery. Despite the fact that the number of truly memorable films she graced was small, her persona and performances were arresting. It can be said, perhaps, that her early work did not allow her to display her dimensioned talents as a gifted actress; when she did, it was through experimental works by women directors which did not enter the crucial commercial mainstream. In the mid–1970s Seyrig gave up the portrayals of the male-ordered fantasies and iconographies and made her commitment to the Women's Movement in promoting female talent. Nevertheless, she remains best-known for her role in Alain Resnais's *L'Année dernière à Marienbad*. But she considered herself primarily a stage actress and was a notable interpreter of Pinter and Beckett.

Partly due to the fact that her father was an archaeologist, Seyrig spent her childhood in Lebanon, then Greece, Paris and, during World War II, in New York, where her father was a cultural attaché for de Gaulle. After training in Paris drama schools and taking several parts on the French stage, she moved back to New York to study at the Lee Strasberg Actors Studio. Her next stage role of note was a supporting one in Arthur Miller's adaptation of Ibsen's *An Enemy of the People*. Although she appeared in Robert Frank's 1958 minor cult film, the wretchedly named *Pull My Daisy*, it was her performance in *An Enemy of the People* which caught Resnais's eye. He had been looking for an "unnatural" casting of the sophisticated woman in Robbe-Grillet's screenplay for *Marienbad*. More irony: the playwright had wanted the less cerebral, more carnal Kim Novak. And Seyrig had hardly seemed the part, at least in appearance: "I had never been to a hairdresser, never worn heels in my life", she remembered. "The character was a disguise, like dressing up in my mother's clothes." Research involved watching silent films, where "the dresses of actresses were composed, and there was a certain reality to the actors' behaviour, which was not realistic."

Nevertheless, the choice was inspired. As the male character endeavours to create in a woman's mind a past that never was, in order to control her present (very Robbe-Grillet, very Resnais sort of time-and-memory theme), much of the dramatic energy and narrative tension relied on her psychic resistance. The film's mystery and tease proved to be a perfect vehicle for Seyrig's created persona and "fashion-plate" perfection. Little was demanded of her internal emotional life and external physicality. When she was posed like a model, a stylized representation of a woman, like the rest of the static set, her controlled emotional power merely suggesting itself through her face, Seyrig's beauty was perfect. Seyrig's manner *here*, mind *elsewhere*, produced an emotional tension that helped create *Marienbad*. Shot in black-and-white and in Cinemascope, every image was elegant, nearly surreal; no other actress could have become part of Resnais's architecture.

The film made her suddenly one of the most sought-after actresses in Europe. In Resnais's next film, *Muriel*, she scooped up the Best Actress prize at Venice because she *acted*; her study of a woman moving painfully between the present and the past was perceptive and haunting. The backdrop was the Algerian war, a major taboo in French cinema — then and now. In Joseph Losey's *Accident*, her brief, wordless liaison with Dirk Bogarde (almost a spoof of her rarified earlier image) was more intriguing than anything else; nevertheless she was not in front of the camera for long. As Losey also used a dislocated time structure, one might be forgiven for speculating upon the success of the film had more of it been wrapped around her.

Truffaut freed her from the time-warp frame and allowed her to reveal a natural warmth and an easy wit in *Stolen Kisses*. Seyrig played a stylish older woman who discreetly seduced Jean-Pierre Leaud. She allegedly prepared for her breathless strategy by running up two flights of stairs immediately before the scene was shot. In *Mister Freedom*, she was purposely cast by director William Klein to contradict everything she had been before; in this she was a sexy, 1960s Barbie Doll, complete with fuzzy orange wig and outrageously false lashes. She was anything but precious. In another questionable triumph of image-breaking, she also portrayed a streetwise vampire in the horror flick, *Daughters of Darkness*. One role she made deliciously her own was as the very voguish, malicious fairy godmother in Jacques Demy's (q.v.) *Peau d'âne* (*Donkey Skin*) in 1971, his enchanting reworking of the classic fairy-tale.

Seyrig played to good effect one of the middle-class set in Luis Buñuel's *The Discreet Charm of the Bourgeoisie* in 1972, condemned to a kind of moveable feast as their attempts to dine in each other's company were perpetually thwarted. It was here her gift for comedy was illuminated. The following year she entered the commercial mainstream with a small part in *The Day of the Jackal*.

By now she had become more closely associated with the feminist movement in France, and was prominent in the setting up of the Simone de Beauvoir Centre which produces audio-visual documentaries on women's issues, as well as fighting for French women's rights to abortion. Most of her last dozen films were experimental works by women directors. She shone under the direction of film-makers such as Chantal Akerman (*Jeanne Dielman 23 Quai du Commerce 1080 Bruxelles*) in 1975, involving the real, everyday life of a woman who turned to prostitution in order to keep her children. In Marguerite Duras's *India Song*, the same year, she was the embodiment of an upper-class pampered wife who was also a failed pianist. Her character employed both emotional and intellectual power in order to enslave men. The role required the illusive but commanding presence that Seyrig had tuned to a fine art: the quintessential Frenchwoman, but in the structure created by a brilliant feminist film-maker. There is no doubt that Seyrig's acting skills were never showcased better.

Her stage work was less well known outside France, although she also performed in England. She was known for her roles in Chekhov, Turgenev, Pirandello and contemporary playwrights. Notable were her performances in Turgenev's *A Month in the Country*, Stoppard's *Rosencrantz and Guildenstern Are Dead* and in Pinter's *The Lover* in both New York and London, which gave her the chance to indulge in Pinteresque comedy. She performed primarily for low-profile companies doing experimental work, or for companies which were not on the main theatrical circuits.

While Seyrig's career can be said to be patchy — from a few lead parts to supports to cameos to small experimental works — her ability to make the ordinary character extraordinary (and extraordinary ones accessible and absorbing) made her a superb actress. Her husky voice fed the cool, mysterious eroticism she was often celebrated for; yet her dry, ironic, comedic wit was as sharp, if not always properly showcased. Resnais, through only two films, helped to define her for an entire generation of cinephiles; she, through her other films, smaller ones, did the rest. But any film was lifted up by her very presence.

Born Delphine Claire Beltiane Seyrig. **Parents** Henri, archaeologist, and Hermine (de Saussure) Seyrig. **Marriage** Jack Youn-Germain (or Youngerman), painter, 1950 (dissolved). **Children** One son. **Education** Drama schools in Paris. **Career** Actor, 1952 onwards; member: Centre dramatique de L'Est, 1952, Comédie de Saint-Etienne, 1954; with Actors Studio, New York, 1956–59; film début, *Pull My Daisy*, 1958; film, *Aloise* selected for Cannes Film Festival, 1975. **Related activities** Director, video shorts: *Inès*, 1974, *Sois belle et tais-toi*, 1976; Guardian Lecturer, National Film Theatre, London, 1987. **Other activities** Signatee, "Charter of the 343 Sluts", 1974; founder, with others, Centre Audio-visuel Simone de Beauvoir, 1982. **Awards and honours** Lion d'or du festival de Venise for *L'Année dernière à Marienbad*, 1960; grand prix d'Interprétation féminine, Venice Film Festival, 1963; Gerard-Philipe Prize, 1963; Coupe Volpi, Venice Film Festival for *Muriel*, 1964; grand prix d'Interprétation féminine de l'Académie du cinéma for *La Musica*, 1967; grand prix national du cinéma, 1977; prize for the best actress, Syndicat professionel de la critique dramatique et musicale, 1983. **Stage** *Henry IV*, Philadelphia, 1950s; *The Enemy of the People*, New York, 1950s; *L'Amour en papier*, 1963; *Le Complexe de Philemon*, 1963; *Un Mois à la campagne*, 1964; *Cet étrange animal*, 1964–65; *La Collection*, 1965–66; *L'Amant*, 1965–66; *La Prochaine Fois je vous le chanterai*, 1966; *Se trouver*, 1966; *Rosencrantz et Guildenstern sont morts*, 1967; *L'Aide-mémoire*, 1968; *Le Jardin de délices*, 1969; *C'était hier*, 1971; *The Little Black Book*, New York, 1972; *La Chevauchée sur le lac de Constance*, 1973; *The Bitter Tears of Petra von Kant*, Hampstead, London, 1976; *Antony and Cleopatra*, London, 1976; *La Bête dans la jungle*, 1981; *Sarah et le cri de la langouste*, 1982. **Films** *Pull My Daisy*, 1958; *L'Année dernière à Marienbad* (*Last Year in Marienbad*), 1960; *Muriel*, 1963; *Qui êtes-vous, Polly Magoo?*, 1965; *La Musica*, 1967; *Accident*, 1967; *Baisers volés* (*Stolen Kisses*), 1968; *La Voie lactée* (*The Milky Way*), 1969; *Mister Freedom*, 1969; *Peau d'âne* (*Donkey Skin, The Magic Donkey*), 1970; *Les Lèvres rouges* (*Daughters of Darkness*), 1971; *Le Charme discret de la bourgeoisie* (*The Discreet Charm of the Bourgeoisie*), 1972; *Chacal* (*The Day of the Jackal*), 1972; *Le Journal d'un suicidé*, 1973; *Eulalie quitte les champs* (*The Star, The Orphan, and the Butcher*), 1973; *Maison de* *poupée* (*The Doll's House*), 1973; *Le Cri du coeur*, 1974; *Contre une poignée de diamants*, 1974; *Dites-le avec des fleurs*, 1974; *The Black Windmill*, 1974; *Le Boucher*, 1975; *Aloise*, 1975; *Le Jardin qui bascule*, 1975; *Jeanne Dielman 23 Quai du Commerce 1080 Bruxelles*, 1975; *India Song*, 1975; *Voyage en Amérique*, 1975; *Je t'aime, tu danses*, 1975; *Son nom de Venise dans Calcutta désert*, 1976; *Providence*, 1976; *Vera Baxter*, 1976; *Caro Michele*, 1977; *Repérages* (*Faces of Love*), 1977; *Der letzte Schrei*, 1977; *Le Chemin perdu*, 1979; *Chère inconnue* (*I Sent a Letter to My Love*), 1980; *Le Grain de sable*, 1983; *Letters Home* (video), 1986. **Television** (includes) *Le Troisième Concerto*, 1963; *Un mois à la campagne*, 1966; *Hedda Gabler*, 1967; *Le Lys dans la vallée*, 1970; *The Ambassadors*, 1976. **Cause of death** Undisclosed, at age 58. **Further reading** *International Dictionary of Films and Filmmakers*, volume three, 1986.

NOBUTAKA SHIKANAI

Japanese Businessman

Born **Hokkaido, Japan, 17 November 1911**

Died **Tokyo, Japan, 28 October 1990**

Militant trade unionism and Japan don't go together in the western mind; rather, we caricature Japan as a country of paternalistic employers marshalling ranks of dedicated, compliant staff to keep on performing the Economic Miracle. If this picture is not so far from the truth in the 1990s, things looked very different in the immediate post-war years, when powerful unions were gaining ground against a management in disarray.

The stemming of this tide was in large measure the work of Nobutaka Shikanai. In the late 1940s and early 1950s he headed the employers' association Nikkeiren, the Japanese Federation of Employers' Associations, and in this role, and that of employers' representative on the Central Labour Relations Commission, he presided over the emasculation of the Japanese union movement.

Shikanai had read politics and economics at Waseda University, Tokyo. After graduating in 1936 he became a pay officer in the Japanese Army. It was immediately after the war that he became involved with industrial relations.

President Truman had put General MacArthur in charge of the occupation and control of defeated Japan. MacArthur had tried to foster industrial democracy, but now things were getting out of hand. Industry-wide union federations had attained a position of unprecedented power, with workers sitting on management discussion councils which could determine personnel and financial policy. Unions were demanding secure jobs and "livelihood" wages based on family commitments, rather than the productivity-based wage deals management wanted.

Though Japan was facing hyperinflation and there was mass unemployment, management initially lacked the muscle to argue with the unions: there was no national management organization until 1947 when the Kanto Managers Association began to take on a national role. The following year this organization evolved into Nikkeiren. Shikanai, already an associate of many of Japan's senior businessmen, was instrumental in setting up Nikkeiren, and became its managing director. Nikkeiren ostensibly recognized the right of labour to organize itself, but wanted to restrict the power of the unions. It ended up crushing them.

A series of acrimonious and often violent disputes hit Japanese industry, culminating in the Nissan strike of 1953, which involved physical fighting around the car plant between strikers on one side and the police and hired heavies on the other. Nikkeiren helped arrange finance for Nissan and induced the firm's competitors not to take advantage of Nissan's plight while the strike was on. Then Nissan locked the strikers out of the plant and arranged for the formation of a Nissan-only union, which, after the arrest of the strike leader, the remaining employees were induced to join instead of the national car-workers' union. The new Nissan-only union rejoiced in the Orwellian slogan, "Those who truly love the union, love the company."

Shikanai, who had masterminded management tactics in the Nissan strike, said in later years that, like a dose of an infection which afterwards confers immunity, the industrial disputes of the post-war period had given the Japanese economy an immunity to industrial unrest, and so helped to position it for its dramatic recovery. There were more disputes after Nissan, but the writing was on the wall for the unions. Most were replaced by docile staff associations, on friendly terms with management, and thereafter days lost through strikes were minimal.

Wage bargaining became an annual ritual with a foregone conclusion. As some kind of a quid pro quo for their lost bargaining power, employees tended to be offered lifetime employment together with fringe benefits such as company housing and schools. And as Japan attained its unprecedented industrial success, the wage settlements became very good indeed.

In 1954 Shikanai, apparently as a reward for his efforts in Nikkeiren, was given the opportunity to create and run Nippon Broadcasting, a commercial radio network. This company became the foundation of his empire, the giant Fujisankei group, which grew to include almost 100 companies, including the popular Fuji television network, the largest private one in Japan. In 1958 Shikanai took over the ailing national newspaper *Sankei Shimbun*, whose fortunes he revived to some extent, though the paper reportedly continued to lose money, while Shikanai gained a reputation among his staff as a mean and exacting employer. He used the paper as a mouthpiece to propound his conservative views, to the derision of the other national papers which, however, lacked political content to the point of vapidity.

The Fujisankei group as a whole had an annual turnover of an estimated 700 billion yen, or 2.8 billion pounds, at the time of Shikanai's death; the largest media group in Japan and allegedly the largest but three in the world, it was still privately owned.

Shikanai had been succeeded by his son Haruo as head of Fujisankei in 1985, but when Haruo died, aged only 42, in 1988, he resumed the chair. The following year his son-in-law, Hiroaki, took over, assuming the name Shikanai in accordance with Japanese custom. Hiroaki began to lead the group into overseas ventures, such as investment in Britain's Virgin music group, of which Fujisankei is said to own a quarter-share, and news distribution via US cable television networks. There was also an investment of 10 million dollars in the film-making of British producer David Puttnam.

All this international enterprise must have enjoyed the approval of Nobutaka Shikanai. A recurrent theme of his later years was his desire that the voice of the Japanese nation be given a fair hearing by the West. He had been involved in various initiatives to attract some international limelight. He was, for instance, on the organizing committee of the 1964 Tokyo Olympics, which the Japanese used as an opportunity to display their economic and technological progress to the world.

Many of Shikanai's international enterprises attracted the wrong sort of attention. The year before his death saw the first round of the Praemium Imperiale awards for the visual arts, set up by Shikanai as chairman of the Japan Art Association, and funded by Fujisankei. The Japanese imperial family were enlisted as patrons of the scheme. Shikanai intended the awards to be in the same league as the Nobel prizes, and, doubtless, hoped that they would attract as much attention. But the plan backfired.

A judging panel consisting of Establishment figures such as Chancellor Helmut Schmidt of West Germany and former prime minister Edward Heath of the UK chose a list of prize-winners who included, in the first year of the awards, artist David Hockney and Pierre Boulez, the conductor. Since these beneficiaries of the 100,000-dollar awards were not exactly struggling unknowns, Shikanai came in for accusations of self-aggrandisement under the guise of philanthropy, and the awards failed to make the headlines in the West.

In 1989 Shikanai invited Ronald and Nancy Reagan to Japan, paying them a rumoured fee of 2 million dollars and parading them on his Fuji television network during their eight-day visit. Shikanai claimed that he and Reagan were kindred spirits as far as their view of the world and politics went. The visit attracted opprobrium from all sides: Americans, as some saw it, witnessed their first family prostituting itself for the Japanese yen, while Shikanai's competitors accused him of a publicity stunt, albeit an expensive one.

An initiative of more lasting value was Shikanai's patronage of the arts, particularly sculpture. Admittedly he adorned his group's offices with huge portrait busts of himself, but, more significantly, he was among the first Japanese to collect western art on a grand scale.

He created two art museums. The first was founded in 1969: this was the famous Hakone Open-Air Museum, which, against a landscape of the foothills of Mount Fuji, displays an astonishing collection of modern works from the West, including a pavilion-full of Picassos and the largest group of Henry Moore sculptures anywhere. This successful variant on the traditional Japanese sculpture garden has become a major tourist attraction. Later, in 1981, Shikanai was to establish, this time with the emphasis on experimental art, the Utsukushigara Museum. These museums will be Shikanai's monuments. Whether his political contribution can endure as well is less certain.

During the period of Japan's affluence, the system of tame trade unions has flourished. No doubt the meritocratic Japanese system whereby able workers can often get promoted from the shop floor to the ranks of management makes the lack of real industrial democracy more palatable. But those who are enjoying a comfortable standard of living are less inclined to be militant than those on the breadline. If the times of famine ever visit Japan again, there will be a question as to whether Shikanai's industrial edifice can remain standing, or whether the unions will grow teeth once more.

Born Nobutaka Shikanai. **Children** One son, Haruo (died 1988), and a daughter. **Education** Waseda University, Tokyo, studied politics and economics, 1936. **Military service** Pay officer, Japanese Army. **Career** Director of various companies, 1944–54; managing director, Nippon Broadcasting System, later with additions of nearly 100 companies, became chairman and chief executive, Fujisankei Communications Group, until 1989, except for 1985–88; created Fuji Television Network; proprietor, *Sankei Shimbun*, 1958 onwards. **Related activities** Employers' representative, Central Labour Relations Commission; founder, with others, and managing director, Japan Federation of Employers' Associations, Nikkeiren, late 1940s and early 1950s. **Other activities** Founder: Hakone Open-Air Museum, Tokyo, 1969, Utsukushigara Museum, 1981; art collector; head, organizing committee, Tokyo Olympics; chairman, Japan Art Association; founder, Praemium Imperiale, 1988. **Cause of death** Liver failure, at age 78. **Further reading** Andrew Gordon, *The Evolution of Labour Relations in Japan*, 1988; William Horsley and Roger Buckley, *Nippon, New Superpower: Japan since 1945*, 1990.

WILLIAM FRENCH SMITH

American Lawyer

***Born* Wilton, New Hampshire, 26 August 1917**

***Died* Los Angeles, California, 29 October 1990**

His mild manner caused some Washington observers to dismiss William French Smith, President Reagan's first attorney general, as a lightweight (journalists nicknamed him "The Somnambulist"). Nothing could have been more deceptive.

It was Smith's proud boast that during his three years at the Justice Department he made more changes in public policy than any previous attorney general had done in like time. They included a complete overhaul of the liberal legislation enacted over the previous 20 years — laws designed to redress racial inequality, to reinforce civil rights, and to break up corporate monopoly. Concerning the latter, Smith's remark in 1981 that "bigness in business does not necessarily mean badness" summed up his attitude towards anti-trust laws.

Civil servants and legislators on Capitol Hill soon learned that it was unnecessary to run to President Reagan for advice on every detail of government. His reaction was apt to be, "Have you checked this out with Bill Smith?" Smith enjoyed this unique position because he had once been Reagan's personal lawyer, had helped to elect the former film star first as governor of California in 1964, then in 1980 as the nation's chief executive.

Smith came from an old and well-connected New England family, he being born in Wilton, New Hampshire. One of the few times he ran contrary to type was when he went west to attend the University of California at Berkeley, where he graduated *summa cum laude* in 1939. He soon redressed the balance by taking his law degree from Harvard.

After World War II, during which he served in the Pacific with the United States Navy, Smith settled in California. "I decided my life was not going to be dictated by my ancestors", was his explanation for turning his back on New England. In 1946 he joined Gibson, Dunn & Crutcher, eventually becoming a senior partner of this blue-chip Los Angeles law firm which had 250 lawyers on its payroll.

Smith came to life politically when in 1964 he tuned in on a national broadcast by Ronald Reagan on behalf of the presidential aspirations of Senator Barry Goldwater. In his speech the future Great Communicator praised the free enterprise system, lambasted the "Washington bureaucrats" who had concentrated power in their hands, called for a lower level of taxation and an end to government intrusion in the private sector.

These were exactly the sentiments Smith and his wealthy Republican cronies voiced when they met in their clubs or on the golf course. In 1966 a group of these cronies — the "Kitchen Cabinet" as it came to be called — banded together and persuaded Reagan to make his successful bid for the governorship of California.

Smith's reward was to be appointed to the University of California's Board of Regents in 1968, the year of turbulence on campus. As regent he gave a preview of what he would be like as US attorney general. He took a hard line against anti-Vietnam war protestors on campus, backed Governor Reagan's cuts in education, and resisted demands that the university divorce itself from nuclear weapons research.

Surprisingly, he backed the university's stand in refusing to admit Allan Bakke, a White, to its medical school while accepting less qualified Blacks, an example of "positive discrimination", as it was called.

Smith, as attorney general, won feminine plaudits when he backed President Reagan's nomination of Sandra Day O'Connor to be the first woman justice appointed to the Supreme Court. His zeal in the war against drugs also earned him an international reputation.

The white-haired, soft-spoken ex-attorney general was a very private person, but he enjoyed Washington's black-tie dinners and cocktail parties. Over the years he worked on behalf of many philanthropic, civic and cultural causes.

Born William French Smith. **Parents** William French and Margaret (Dawson) Smith. **Marriages** Two marriages; 2) Jean Webb, 1964. **Children** William, Scott, Gregory and Stephanie, from first marriage. **Education** University of California, AB, summa cum laude, 1939; Harvard University, Cambridge, Massachusetts, LLB, 1942. **Military service** Officer, United States Naval Reserve, 1942–46. **Career** Member, Californian Bar, 1942 onwards; partner, Gibson, Dunn & Crutcher, Los Angeles, 1946–81, 1985 onwards; attorney general of the United States, Washington, 1981–85; also, director: Pacific Lighting Corporation, Los Angeles, 1967–81, Pacific Telephone and Telegraph Company, San Francisco, 1969–81, Pacific Mutual Life Insurance Company, Los Angeles, 1970–81, Crocker National Bank, Crocker National Corporation, San Francisco, 1971–81, Jorgensen Steel Company, 1974–81, Pullman Incorporated, Chicago, 1979–81, Radio Corporation of America, National Broadcasting Company, 1985 onwards, American International Group, New York City, 1985 onwards, Pacific Telesis Group, Pacific Bell, San Francisco, 1985 onwards. **Related activities** Member, Los Angeles Committee on Foreign Relations, 1954–74; chairman, Californian delegation to Republican National Convention, 1968, delegate and vice-chairman, 1972–76; on University of California Board of Regents, 1968, chairman, 1970–72, 1974, 1976; on board of directors, Los Angeles World Affairs Council, 1970 onwards, president, 1975–76; member, United States advisory commission on International, Educational and Cultural Affairs, Washington, 1971–78; member: Stanton Panel on International Information, Education and Cultural Relations, Washington, 1974–75, Mayor's Committee on City Finances, Los Angeles, 1975–81; United States delegate, East-West Center for Cultural and Technical Interchange, Hawaii, 1975–77; on advisory council, Harvard University School of Government, Cambridge, Massachusetts, 1977 onwards; advisory board member, Center for Strategic and International Studies, Georgetown University, 1978 onwards. **Offices and memberships** Fellow, American Bar Foundation; member: American Los Angeles County Bar associations, State Bar of California American Judicature, Society of American Law Institutions, California Chamber of Commerce, director 1963 onwards, president, 1974–75; on board of directors: Legal Aid Foundation, Los Angeles, 1963–72, Independent Colleges of Southern California, 1969–74, Center Theatre Group, Los Angeles Music Center, 1970–81, California Foundation of Commerce and Education, 1975–81; trustee: Henry E. Huntingdon Library and Art Gallery, 1971 onwards, Claremont Men's College, 1967–80, Cate School, 1971–77, Northrop Institute of Technology, 1973–75; national trustee, National Symphony Orchestra, Washington, 1974 onwards; executive committee member, California Roundtable, 1975–81; on board of governors, Performing Arts Council, Los Angeles Music Center, 1978–79; Phi Beta Kappa; Pi Gamma Mu; Pi Sigma Alpha. **Cause of death** Cancer, at age 73.

ELEANOR STEBER

American Soprano

***Born* Wheeling, West Virginia, 17 July 1914**

***Died* Langhorne, Pennsylvania, 3 October 1990**

Eleanor Steber was an extremely handsome, stylish and intelligent singer remembered above all as a leading soloist at New York's Metropolitan Opera House over a period of more than 25 years, giving 404 performances in 33 roles. During the 1950s there were opportunities to hear her in Bayreuth, Florence, Vienna and Salzburg and, at the first Edinburgh Festival, in 1947, Glyndebourne Opera presented Mozart's *Il nozze di Figaro* with Steber in tremendous voice as a memorable Countess. But apart from these and a few other appearances, Steber has mostly been known, outside America, through the many recordings that she made, immortalizing her in all her best roles: the Countess, Fiordiligi, Fidelio, Elsa, the Marshallin and the role she herself created — Vanessa, in Samuel Barber's opera of that name.

Eleanor Steber attended the New England Conservatory of Music, where she studied with William Whitney and made an unofficial début in 1936, at the age of 20, with the Commonwealth Opera, as Senta in *The Flying Dutchman*. She went on to New York to study with Paul Althouse and four years later won the Metropolitan Auditions of the Air. She made her début at "the Met" as Sophie in *Der Rosenkavalier* in December 1940, and the performance brought her praise for the security and sense of style in her singing.

It was a combination of vocal flexibility and strong dramatic talent that made the Wagnerian-figured blonde an immediate success with Met audiences. During her first season she was entrusted with some challenging roles for a young singer: a Rhinemaiden, the forest bird in *Siegfried* and Micaela in *Carmen*. Over the next four years she aimed higher and added Mozart to her repertoire, singing Donna Elvira, Pamina, The Countess, Fiordiligi and Constanze — a role she sang at the first Metropolitan production of *Il Seraglio* in 1946. Meanwhile she also acquired some Verdian roles: Violetta, Mistress Ford, Elisabeth de Valois and Desdemona. As her voice matured and the silver of her youthful soprano mellowed to gold, she was able to take on weightier roles, such as Leonore in *Fidelio* and the Marshallin in *Rosenkavalier*, Eva in *Die Meistersinger* and Elsa in *Lohengrin*, which she also sang in Bayreuth in 1953 — the first American singer to perform there after the war.

In 1948, in Boston, she commissioned and sang in the *première* of the American composer Samuel Barber's *Knoxville: Summer of 1915*. Ten years later she created the title role of Barber's *Vanessa*, also singing the role in the revival at Salzburg during the summer. Although the opera was cordially disliked, Steber herself was regarded as its redeeming feature — sympathetically portraying the woman who falls in love with a much younger man. The following year at the Met she added another very different role, that of Marie in the US *première* of Berg's opera *Wozzeck*.

In 1962 Rudolf Bing, then general manager of the Met, believing it was time for Steber to retire, decided not to renew her contract. "He told me I wouldn't miss the Met at all", Steber recalled in 1973. "I tell you I was knocked for a loop." But she did make one final appearance in 1966 standing in for a singer who was indisposed.

During the 1960s Steber's career took a different turn as she began to devote more and more time to the concert platform. She was the first singer to give a solo recital in the newly opened Philharmonic Hall in New York City. She also began to teach and was appointed head of the Voice Department at the Cleveland Institute, a position she held from 1963 to 1972. Later she taught at the Juilliard School of Music in New York, the New England Conservatory and Brooklyn College, New York. For 12 successive years she also gave masterclasses at the American Institute of Musical Studies in Graz, Austria, leading up to 1990.

Steber's last opera performance was in 1973, at Santa Fe, where she sang Miss Wingrave in the US *première* of Britten's *Owen Wingrave*. Two years later she founded the Eleanor Steber Music Foundation to help young professional singers.

Steber was much honoured as a classical singer, but she was not above a little popular culture either. In the 1960s she appeared in revivals at the New York City Center, playing Charley's Aunt in Frank Loesser's musical version of *Where's Charley?* and the Abbess in Rodgers and Hammerstein's *The Sound of Music*.

Born Eleanor Steber. **Parents** William Charles and Ida A. (Nolte) Steber. **Education** New England Conservatory of Music, studied under William Whitney, MusB, 1938; studied privately with Paul Althouse, New York. **Career** Unofficial operatic début, Senta, *The Flying Dutchman*, Commonwealth Opera, Boston, 1936; Metropolitan Opera house, leading soprano, 1940–66, Metropolitan début, as Sophie in *Der Rosenkavalier*, 1940; first solo recitalist, Philharmonic Hall, New York, 1962; head, voice department, Cleveland Institute of Music, 1963–72; also taught at the Juilliard School from 1971, New England Conservatory of Music from 1971, Philadelphia Music Academy from 1975 and Brooklyn College, City University of New York from 1980; lecturer, American Institute of Musical Studies, Graz, Austria, 1978 onwards. **Related activities** Founder/ president, Eleanor Steber Music Foundation, 1975. **Offices and memberships** Board member, Washington District Council Opera; director: Brooklyn Opera Company, Opera Society, Washington; Delta Omicron; Pi Kappa Lambda. **Awards and honours** Winner, Metropolitan [Opera] Auditions of the Air, 1940; took part in President Eisenhower's People-to-People Music Program; American Society of Composers, Authors and Publishers Award for outstanding service to American Music, 1944; honorary MusD: New England Conservatory of Music, Bethany College, University of West Virginia, Florida Southern College, Temple University, Ithaca College; Doctor of Humane Letters, Wheaton College, 1966; Doctor of Fine Arts, Oklahoma City. **Stage** (includes) *The Flying Dutchman*, 1936; *Der Rosenkavalier*, 1940; *Siegfried*, 1940; *Carmen*, 1940; *La traviata*, 1943; *Faust*, 1943; *Hoffmann*, 1943; *Falstaff*, 1943; San Francisco Opera Company, 1945; Central City Opera Festival, 1946; *Die Entführung aus dem Serail*, 1946; Edinburgh Festival, 1947; Glyndebourne, 1948; *Knoxville: Summer of 1915*, 1948; *Der Rosenkavalier*, 1949; *Don Carlos*, 1950; *Lohengrin*, 1953; *La fianculla del West*, 1954, 1966; *Arabella*, 1955; Vienna State Opera, 1956; *Tosca*, 1958; *Vanessa*, 1958; *Wozzeck*, 1959; Salzburg, 1959; *Where's Charley?*, 1960s; *The Sound of Music*, 1960s; *Owen Wingrave*, 1973. **Television** (includes) *TV's Voice of Firestone*. **Recordings** (include) *Ein Deutsches Requiem*, RCA; *Vanessa*, RCA; *Lohengrin*, Decca; *Fidelio*, HMV; *Così fan Tutte*, Columbia; *Faust*, Columbia; *Madame Butterfly*, Columbia; *Don Carlos*, Estro Armonico. **Cause of death** Congestive heart failure, at age 76.

NOVEMBER

SIR RICHARD ACLAND

British Politician and Teacher

Born **Killerton, Devon, 26 November 1906**

Died **Broadclyst, Devon, 24 November 1990**

Some men seem destined to dedicate their lives to lost causes. Such a one was Sir Richard Acland — the fifteenth heir to a baronetcy which was itself the reward for service to the lost cause of King Charles I during the English Civil War. Nevertheless, Acland's life spanned a period of great moment in his country's history and reached its peak in stands against appeasement to facism in the 1930s, against the Conservative-Labour consensus during World War II, and against nuclear weapons, and particularly the hydrogen bomb, in the 1950s.

Richard Acland was a west country man from a family with a long history of public service. There was never any question of his not following in that tradition, and of not taking his own line. Had not the Tory tenth baronet, "Great Sir Thomas", stood out against his party in favour of the repeal of the Corn Laws? The Aclands of Devon were known for their independent views; no toeing the line of the Tory squirearchy for them! Despite their large estates, they were liberal stock, and Richard's father had been one of Asquith's MPs and had held high office in the Lloyd George coalition government.

The conventional upper-class education of Rugby and Balliol College, Oxford was directed solely to preparing the young Richard for Parliament. But even at school he had earned the name of "the little Sinn Feiner" for daring to criticize the government's Irish policy — shades of things to come! After unsuccessfully contesting two elections for west country seats immediately after coming down from Oxford, he won the North Devon seat of Barnstaple for the Liberals in the 1935 election and remained its MP for the next ten years.

Acland entered Parliament as a staunch supporter of the Liberals, but his introduction to Keynes's *General Theory* and its prescriptions for dealing with the Depression of the 1930s, and the growing fascist threat on the continent of Europe, pushed him towards socialism, the Left Book Club and a Popular Front against Hitler and Mussolini and Chamberlain's policies of appeasement. The outbreak of war, which he saw as sounding "the death knell of private capitalism", drew him into a personal campaign for "common ownership" as enunciated in his best-selling book — a personal answer to Hitler — *Unser Kampf.* Acland was a brilliant orator and his millenarian vision attracted a considerable following in the troubled war years. After a second book, *The Forward March,* in 1941, he joined with a small dissenting group, including J.B. Priestley's 1941 Committee and Tom Wintringham, a Marxist veteran of the Spanish Civil War, to form the Common Wealth

Party. This was an attempt to break the political stalemate of the wartime coalition, and under Acland's leadership it succeeded in winning spectacular victories in three by-elections. But Acland's sally as a political gadfly was to suffer a crushing defeat when the realities of peace-time politics returned with the 1945 general election. Most of his 23 candidates, including Acland himself, lost their deposits and the Common Wealth Party was no more.

Acland then moved over to the Labour Party and in 1947 succeeded in winning, against all the odds, the by-election at Gravesend in Kent. There he followed an MP who had been expelled from the House of Commons, and for a time he was welcomed in the constituency for his outstanding moral uprightness and devotion to his Christian beliefs. But these were soon to bring him up against the official party line on Britain's decision to manufacture the H-bomb. Acland stood firmly against nuclear arms, in the days long before the official Campaign for Nuclear Disarmament had begun. "I have sinned", he told the House of Commons with characteristic evangelistic fervour. "I should have protested much more vigorously ... against the A-bomb." He resigned his seat and with it his parliamentary career.

What it must have cost him emotionally to abandon his favoured calling, no one knows. But Acland was not one to count the cost. "Do not ask 'Is it expedient?'", he had always exhorted his audiences. "Simply ask: 'Is it right?'" And this was the precept he followed throughout his career. Firmly disapproving of inherited wealth, he handed over his rich west country estates to the National Trust in 1943 (the largest bequest the Trust had ever received) — Common Wealth in practice! From 1959 he devoted himself to the west country and to teaching in Exeter, mainly at the University's College of Education (again in the family tradition — his grandfather had been minister of education in Gladstone's last government). An aristocrat and a man of wealth, he adopted unexpectedly radical causes. An ardent supporter of the under-dog, his political career upset those on both Left and Right. His personal life was kindly and unassuming; he was always "Dick" to all who knew him. A truly Christian socialist, he was a twentieth-century Don Quixote, but tilting at targets more substantial than windmills.

Born Richard Thomas Dyke Acland. **Parents** Sir Francis Acland, member of parliament. **Marriage** Anna Stella Alford, architect, 1936. **Children** Three sons, oldest son, John. **Education** Rugby School, Warwickshire; Balliol College, Oxford. **Military service** Royal Artillery, briefly, World War II. **Career** Parliamentary candidate, Torquay division, 1929, Barnstaple, 1931, Putney, 1945; Liberal member of parliament for Barnstaple, Devon, 1935–45; Labour member of parliament, Gravesend Division of Kent, 1947–55; senior lecturer, St Luke's College of Education, Exeter, 1959–74. **Related activities** Founder, Forward March Group; on amalgamation with 1941 Committee, became leader, the Common Wealth Party, 1942; founder, Council of Clergy and Ministers for Common Ownership. **Other activities** Succeeded father to become 15th baronet, 1939; donator, 16,000 acres of estate at Killerton and Holnicote, Devon, to National Trust, 1943; Second Church Estates Commissioner, 1950–51. **Publications** *Unser Kampf,* 1940; *The Forward March,* 1941; *What It Will Be Like,* 1942; *How Can It Be Done,* 1943; *Public Speaking,* 1946; *Nothing Left to Believe?,* 1949; *Why So Angry,* 1958; *Waging Peace,* 1958; *We Teach Them Wrong: religion and the young,* 1963; (with others) *Sexual Morality: three views,* 1965; *Curriculum or Life,* 1966; *Moves to the Integrated Curriculum,* 1967; *The Next Step,* 1974; *Hungry Sheep,* 1988. **Cause of death** Undisclosed, at age 83.

EVE ARDEN

American Actress

***Born* Mill Valley, California, 30 April 1908**

***Died* Los Angeles, California, 12 November 1990**

She was the wise-cracking career girl, the heroine's best friend, the one who'd been around and seen it all and just didn't care any more. Eve Arden's delivery was deadpan, her timing exquisite. She was a natural comedienne, totally relaxed, totally in control, and fortunate enough to have been given some of the most memorable lines in cinema history. In *Mildred Pierce* (for which she received an Oscar nomination) she makes this remark about Joan Crawford's ungrateful daughter: "Veda's convinced me that alligators have the right idea. They eat their young." In the same film, she proposes this toast: "To all the men we've loved... The stinkers", and also utters that poignant line so fitting for the type of woman she usually played, "I'm awfully tired of men talking to me man to man."

In a battle of wits, she'd always win. "You seem very superior. Just what have you done in the theatre?" Katharine Hepburn challenges her in *Stage Door,* to which she replies, "Everything but burst out of a pie at a Rotarian banquet." Hepburn doesn't give up, though. "It would be a terrific innovation", she tells Arden, "if you could get your mind to stretch a little further than the wisecrack." "You know I tried that once", Eve replies in a mock-serious voice, "but it just didn't snap back into place."

Despite the high standard of writing and direction in films such as *Mildred Pierce*, *Stage Door*, and *Anatomy of a Murder* (in which she warns her lawyer boss, James Stewart, who is defending an army lieutenant, "Don't let him pay you off in purple hearts"), most of her more than 75 films were a disappointment to her and she refused to watch them. Exceptions included her personal favourites, *The Doughgirls,* in which she played a Russian guerrilla leader, and *The Voice of the Turtle.* Her leading man in the latter film was Ronald Reagan, with whom she found it a great pleasure to work for the simple reason that he was taller than she. "It was the first film for many a month", she said later, "when I did not have to stand in a hole or take my high heels off."

Born Eunice Quedens, probably in 1908, although she gave her own date of birth as 30 April 1912, she was raised by her divorced mother (a former stage actress Arden described as "a great beauty"), and an aunt. Though her mother always said she wanted her to get married and have children, she didn't discourage her from a stage career, either. In fact, according to Arden, at the age of 16, "I was dumped by my mother and aunt at the Henry Duffy office in San Francisco and told to get a job acting, which I did."

By 1934, she was a showgirl in the *Ziegfeld Follies* on Broadway. It was around that time that she was told to change her name. Eunice Quedens studied the cosmetic jars on her dressing table for inspiration, and "stole my first name from 'Evening in Paris' and the second from Elizabeth Arden".

In 1935, the *New York Times* drama critic Brooks Atkinson wrote of her performance in *Parade,* "Count on the credit side Eve Arden's lorgnette humor which turns a song entitled 'Send For The Militia' into highly amusing satire." She was given a featured role in the *Ziegfeld Follies* of 1936, and understudied their top comedienne, Fanny Brice. In 1937, *Stage Door* propelled her toward stardom.

Despite her long and successful career in motion pictures, most Americans over 40 know Eve Arden best as Connie Brooks, the brash but beloved English teacher at mythical Madison High. *Our Miss Brooks* ran for four years on radio, moving to television in October 1952. The programme also featured Gale Gordon (later Mr Mooney on *The Lucy Show*) as the blustering high school principal, Osgood Conklin, and a young Richard Crenna as Walter Denton, Connie's devoted but nerdy student, who would say things like, "Greetings, fairest of all possible English teachers", to which she would reply, "Well, good morning, most observant of all possible pupils."

Our Miss Brooks had a large following among school teachers, and Eve Arden was even offered teaching jobs in real schools. Though she didn't accept any job offers (she was making about 200,000 dollars a year at the time), she did become a regular speaker at PTA (Parent-Teacher Association) meetings. The series ran until 1956 and won her an Emmy.

Another 1950s series, *The Eve Arden Show,* was short-lived, but she returned to television in 1967, co-starring with Kaye Ballard in *The Mothers-In-Law,* which ran until 1969. Ballard described her two years working with Arden as "the happiest I have had in show business".

She worked until about the mid-1980s, appearing in films such as *Grease*, *Grease II* and *Under the Rainbow*, and in various television programmes, such as Spielberg's *Amazing Stories*.

She said in a 1970 interview that she never regretted not being a raving beauty.

> I've worked with a lot of the great glamorous girls in the theatre. They would always give their last ounce to get where they wanted to be. And I'll admit I've often thought it would be wonderful to be a femme fatale; but then I'd always come back to thinking that if they only had what I've had — a family, real love, an anchor — they would have been so much happier during all the hours when the marquees and the footlights are dark.

She was too modest. Anyone can see from early photographs that she was a beautiful young woman: blonde hair, large eyes, full lips. She was a Ziegfeld showgirl, after all. But she made the choice (and it was a wise one) to go into comedy, where brains were what mattered, not looks. Her smart, cool and sardonic persona would prove to have a much longer-lasting appeal than looks alone ever could.

She was a unique and special actress. Milton Berle said of her, "She established a character I do not think will ever be duplicated." Bob Hope, who appeared in the 1936 *Ziegfeld Follies* with both Berle and Arden, had this to say: "I just loved her."

Born Eunice Quedens. **Parents** Charles Peter and Lucille (Frank), actress and millinery shopkeeper, Quedens. **Marriages** 1) Edward G. Bergen, literary agent, 1939 (divorced 1947); 2) Brooks West, actor and artist, 1951 (died 1984). **Children** Two adopted daughters, Liza and Constance with first marriage, one adopted son, Douglas and one son, Duncan, with second marriage. **Education** Tamalpais High School, California; trained for stage with Henry Duffy Stock Company, Alcazar Theatre, San Francisco, 1928–29. **Career** Acting début, with Henry Duffy Stock Company, Alcazar Theatre, 1928; film début, as Eunice Quedens, *Song of Love,* 1929; changed name to Eve Arden, 1934; New York début, *Ziegfeld Follies,* 1934. **Offices and memberships** Actors Equity Association; Screen Actors Guild; American Federation of Television and Radio Artists. **Awards and honours** Best Supporting Actress Academy Nomination for *Mildred Pierce,* 1945; Best Female Star of a Regular Series Emmy, for *Our Miss Brooks,* 1953; Actress of the Year, Sarah Siddons Award for *Hello, Dolly!,* 1967–68. **Stage** (in New York unless otherwise indicated) *Lo and Behold,* Pasadena Playhouse, 1932; *On Approval* on tour, 1933; *Private Lives,* on tour, 1933; *Ziegfeld Follies,* 1934; *Parade,* 1935; *Ziegfeld Follies,* 1936; *Very Warm for May,* 1939; *Two for the Show,* 1940; *Let's Face It,* 1941; *Over 21,* 1950; *Here Today,* Maryland, 1951; *Auntie Mame,* on tour, 1958; *Goodbye, Charlie,* on tour, 1960; *Marriage-Go-Round,* 1961; *Beekman Place,* on tour, 1965; *Hello, Dolly!,* Chicago, 1966; *Barefoot in the Park,* Atlanta, 1967; *Cactus Flower,* Miami, 1968; *Butterflies Are Free,* Los Angeles, also on tour, 1970; *Natural Ingredients,* on tour, 1971; *Silverplate,* on tour, 1971; *Under Papa's Picture,* San Diego,

1973; *The Most Marvelous News,* Chicago, 1977; *Absurd Person Singular,* Los Angeles, 1978; *Moose Murders,* 1983; also *She Couldn't Say No,* Los Angeles. **Films** (include) *Song of Love,* 1929; *Dancing Lady,* 1933; *Oh Doctor,* 1937; *Stage Door,* 1937; *Cocoanut Grove,* 1938; *Letter of Introduction,* 1938; *Having Wonderful Time,* 1938; *Women in the Wind,* 1939; *Big Town Czar,* 1939; *The Forgotten Woman,* 1939; *Eternally Yours,* 1939; *At the Circus,* 1939; *The Women,* 1939; *Slightly Honorable,* 1940; *Comrade X,* 1940; *A Child Is Born,* 1940; *No, No Nanette,* 1940; *Ziegfeld Girl,* 1941; *Whistling in the Dark,* 1941; *Obliging Young Lady,* 1941; *Bedtime Story,* 1941; *Manpower,* 1941; *That Uncertain Feeling,* 1941; *She Couldn't Say No,* 1941; *She Knew All the Answers,* 1941; *San Antonio Rose,* 1941; *Sing for Your Supper,* 1941; *The Last of the Duanes,* 1941; *Change of Heart (Hit Parade of 1943),* 1943; *Let's Face It,* 1943; *Cover Girl,* 1944; *The Doughgirls,* 1944; *Pan-Americana,* 1945; *Patrick the Great,* 1945; *Earl Carroll Vanities,* 1945; *Mildred Pierce,* 1945; *The Kid from Brooklyn,* 1946; *My Reputation,* 1946; *Night and Day,* 1946; *Song of Scheherazade,* 1947; *The Arnelo Affair,* 1947; *The Unfaithful,* 1947; *Voice of the Turtle,* 1947; *One Touch of Venus,* 1948; *Whiplash,* 1948; *My Dream Is Yours,* 1949; *The Lady Takes a Sailor,* 1949; *Paid in Full,* 1950; *Curtain Call at Cactus Creek,* 1950; *Tea for Two,* 1950; *Three Husbands,* 1950; *Goodbye My Fancy,* 1951; *We're Not Married,* 1952; *The Lady Wants Mink,* 1953; *Our Miss Brooks,* 1956; *Anatomy of a Murder,* 1959; *Dark at the Top of the Stairs,* 1960; *Sergeant Deadhead,* 1965; *The Strongest Man in the World,* 1975; *Grease,* 1978; *Under the Rainbow,* 1981; *Pandemonium,* 1982; *Grease II,* 1982. **Television** (includes) *Our Miss Brooks,* 1952–56; *The Eve Arden Show,* 1957–58; *Meet Cyd Charisse,* 1959; *The Mothers-In-Law,* 1967–69; *A Very Missing Person,* 1972; *All My Darling Daughters,* 1972; "Mother of the Bride", *ABC Afternoon Playbreak,* 1974; *For the Love of It,* 1982; "Secret Cinema", *Amazing Stories,* 1985; *Alice in Wonderland,* 1985. **Radio** (includes) *Village Store,* 1945; *Our Miss Brooks,* 1948–56. **Publication** *Three Phases of Eve,* 1985. **Cause of death** Heart failure, at age 82. **Further reading** James Parish, *Good Dames,* 1974; James Robert Parish and William T. Leonard, *The Funsters,* 1979; *International Dictionary of Films and Filmmaking,* volume three, 1986.

HERBERT BERGHOF

Austrian/American Actor, Director and Teacher

Born **Vienna, Austria, 13 September 1909**

Died **Manhattan, New York, 5 November 1990**

Herbert Berghof was an Austrian classical actor of some repute, who may never have had such a remarkable impact upon the acting styles of more than a generation through his teaching, had it not been for the decimation of his family and threat to his own life by Hitler in 1938. His idealism and energy was channelled by this loss, to which he never referred in public, and led him to become one of the most celebrated drama teachers in the United States.

Born in Vienna in 1909, the son of a railway stationmaster, Berghof began his studies as an actor at the Vienna State Academy of Dramatic Art. His teachers were Alexander Moissi and Max Reinhardt, the latter being the more formative influence upon him. Reinhardt produced almost every modern German play of any value and had the initial idea for the Salzburg festival, where Berghof was to play Death in *Everyman.* The Reinhardt seminar in the Castle of Schoenbrunn in Vienna was the first school in the world for producers/directors, where they were given the opportunity for practical work.

Berghof's stage début was in 1927 at the Deutsches Volkstheater, Vienna, in *Don Carlos*. His most noted roles over the next eleven years included Romeo in *Romeo and Juliet,* won through his handsome good looks and strong delivery; the title role in *Hamlet;* Oswald in *Ghosts* and Orlando in *As You Like It.* As a leading classical star he had the opportunity to travel to Berlin, Paris, Salzburg and Zürich, where he was a member of the St Gallen Repertory Company for several months. He began directing in 1929 at the Volles Theater, Vienna, a production called *The Melody That Got Lost.*

This success in northern Europe came to a violent end in 1938, when the Nazis wiped out his entire family. Berghof was smuggled to Britain and was immediately invited to work in the West End for the impresario Gilbert Miller, who even offered to pay for English lessons for him. Before he began work for Miller, however, Berghof was granted a visa for the US and decided to move to New York, even further away from his shattered former life.

Herbert Berghof's first work in New York was directing *From Vienna* for the Refugee Artists' Group at the Music Box Theater in 1939. In 1941 he played the Fool in *King Lear,* followed by the lead in *Nathan the Wise* and, in 1943, Hakim in *Oklahoma!*. He joined the Actors Studio, but found it restrictive and, with a confidence drawn from the backing of numerous actors and directors, he founded his own studio. The Herbert Berghof (HB) Studio opened in 1946, with the intention of giving free rein to experimental techniques for both students and professionals. Uta Hagen, the well-known actress and teacher who was to become his second wife, took an equal share in this enterprise, teaching students while also continuing to star in the plays Berghof directed. Other teachers joined them, including Eli Wallach, Mildred Dunnock, Mira Rostova and Lee Grant.

Hot-tempered but incisive, Herbert Berghof inspired his students not only to become actors and directors but also drama teachers. By creating a hot-house atmosphere, he gave actors an opportunity to reach a creative pitch of intensity that would be impossible in the commercial theatre. The fee for one class was a mere three dollars. His students, including Geraldine Page, Robert de Niro, Steve McQueen and Al Pacino were then able to carry their "method" of working into their film and stage roles.

In 1956 Berghof directed the US vaudeville comedian, Bert Lahr (best known on screen as the cowardly lion in *The Wizard of Oz*) in the first Broadway production of Samuel Beckett's *Waiting for Godot.* The play had received a unanimous "NO" from the "mink clad audience" in Miami where it made its US début. The director, Alan Schneider (who later called Berghof "too old, too foreign and too strange" as an actor, and chided him for his inability to handle the tape-editing scenes as Krapp in Beckett's *Krapp's Last Tape*), had many problems with the Miami version, and in particular with Lahr, whom he claimed wanted to be "top banana". The producer, Michael Myerberg, asked Berghof to direct in New York and only Lahr remained in the cast. After the disastrous opening in Miami, Myerberg took an advertisement in the New York press: "This is a play for the thoughtful and discriminating theater-goer. I respectfully suggest that those who come to the theater for casual entertainment do not buy a ticket to this attraction." One commentator surmised that Berghof "managed to induce an element of cerebration significant enough to counteract Lahr's clowning." Beckett, annoyed at not being invited (with expenses) to New York by Myerberg made one comment: "*Godot* has been playing on Broadway in what seems to be a dreadfully wrong and vulgar production." Lahr, at least, seemed grateful to Berghof for creating a still point in his character, Estragon, so that he was not bobbing and weaving, as in Schneider's production.

In 1958, the HB Studio moved to its present location on Bank Street, Greenwich Village. In 1964, the Playwrights Foundation was opened next door, a theatre that did not charge for entrance, but survived on donations. This was Berghof's dream realized: to relieve talented actors, playwrights and directors of the commercial pressures which he believed must stunt their promise and the potential for a great American theatre.

Born Herbert Berghof. **Parents** Paul, railway stationmaster, and Regina Berghof. **Marriages** 1) Alices Hermes, acting teacher (dissolved); 2) Uta Hagen, actress and acting teacher, 1951. **Education** University of Vienna; Vienna State Academy of Dramatic Art, studied under Alexander Moissi and Max Reinhardt. **Emigration** Left Europe for the United States, 1939. **Career** Actor, 1927 onwards; stage début, *Don Carlos,* Deutsches Volkstheater, Vienna, Austria, 1927; directing début, *The Melody That Got Lost,* Volles Theater, Vienna, Austria, 1929; Broadway début, as director, *From Vienna,* Refugee Artists' Group, Music Box Theater, 1939; acting teacher, New School for Social Research, American Theater Wing, Neighbourhood Playhouse, Columbia University, New York; founder and teacher, Herbert Berghof Studio, New York, 1946 onwards. **Related activities** Founder, Herbert Berghof Playwrights Foundation, 1964. **Offices and memberships** Member Actors Equity Association, American Federation of Television and Radio Artists, Screen Actors Guild. **Stage — as actor** *Don Carlos,* 1927; with St Gallen Repertory Company, Zürich, Switzerland, 1927–29; with Volkstheater, Vienna, 1929–30; at Salzburg Festivals, Austria, 1933–38; performed in Vienna, Zürich, Paris, Berlin, Salzburg, in numerous productions including *Romeo and Juliet, The Doctor's Dilemma, Hamlet, Everyman, Ghosts, As You Like It, Candida, Marius, The Unknown Soldier, Journey's End, All God's Chillun Got Wings, Crime for Crime, Six Characters in Search of an Author, An American Tragedy;* (as actor in New York unless stated): *Reunion in New York,* 1940; *Somewhere in France,* Washington, DC, 1941; *King Lear,* 1941; *The Criminals,* 1941; *Nathan the Wise,* 1942; *Winter Soldiers,* 1942; *The Russian People,* 1942; *The Innocent Voyage,* 1943; *Oklahoma!,* 1944; *Jacobowski and the Colonel,* 1944; *The Man Who Had All the Luck,* 1944; *Beggars Are Coming to Town,* 1945; *Dr Lazare's Pharmacy,* on tour, United States and Canada, 1945–46; *Temper the Wind,* 1946; *The Whole World Over,* 1947; *Hedda Gabler,* 1947; *Ghosts,* 1948; *Miss Liberty,* 1949; *Torquato Tasso,* 1949; *The Lady from the Sea,* 1950; *The Guardsman,* Buffalo, 1951; *Tovarich,* 1952; *The Deep Blue Sea,* 1952; *Michael and Lavinia,* Matunuck, Rhode Island, 1954; *Cyprienne,* Connecticut, 1955; *The Affairs of Anatol* (also director), Michigan, 1957; *The Andersonville Trial,* 1959; *Krapp's Last Tape,* 1960; *Enrico IV,* Washington, DC, 1964; *In the Matter of J. Robert Oppenheimer,* 1969. **Stage — as director** *The Melody That Got Lost,* Vienna, Austria, 1929; *Reunion in New York,* 1940; *The Key,* 1947; *Rip Van Winkle,* 1947; *Protective Custody,* 1956; *Waiting for Godot,* 1956–57; *The Affairs of Anatol,* Michigan, 1957; *The Infernal Machine,* 1958; *Twelfth Night,* Boston, 1959; *The Queen and the Rebels,* Pennsylvania, 1959; *Men, Women and Angels,* Vancouver, Canada, 1961; *Do You Know the Milky Way?,* Vancouver, later New York, 1961; *This Side of Paradise,* 1962; *The Sponsor,* Atlanta, 1975; *Poor Murder* (also translator), 1976; *Charlotte,* 1980; *Easter* (also actor), 1990; also for the Berghof Playwrights Foundation: *Tomorrow, Seize the Day, Democracy and Esther, Kaspar.* **Films** (as actor) *Assignment Paris,* 1952; *Diplomatic Courier,* 1952; *Five Fingers,* 1952; *Red Planet Mars,* 1952; *Cleopatra,* 1963; *Fräulein,* 1963; *Harry & Tonto,* 1974; *Those Lips Those Eyes,* 1980. **Television** (as actor) "For Whom the Bell Tolls", *Playhouse 90* (episode), 1959; "Chez Rouge", *Desilu Playhouse* (episode), 1965; *And the Bones Come Together,* 1973; *Kojak: The Belarus File* (film), 1985; also: *Producer's Showcase, Kraft Television Theatre.* **Radio** *Report to the Nation; The Goldbergs; Norman Corwin Presents.* **Publication** *Poor Murder* (translation), 1976. **Cause of death** Heart ailment, at age 81.

TOM CLANCY

Irish Singer and Actor

***Born* Carrick-on-Suir, Republic of Ireland, 1923**

***Died* Cork City, Republic of Ireland, 7 November 1990**

Together with his brothers, Tom Clancy was the original manifestation of what one comedian very rudely called "the singing sweater". Amongst *afficionados,* there is some debate about the quality of their contribution to folk music, but there can be no doubt about the power of their influence. There was a period during the 1960s when the scene was overwhelmed with crowds of hearty boys roaring at you out of their matching Aran pullovers.

Tom Clancy was born at Carrick-on-Suir, County Tipperary, in the south-east of the Republic of Ireland. He left school at the age of 14 to become a baker, and three years later, together with his elder brother Paddy, joined the Royal Air Force. During World War II he flew missions over Germany and North Africa as a radio officer. The idea of being paid to entertain appealed to all sons of the Clancy family, and after the war Clancy joined an Irish-based theatre company called Shakespeariana Internationale, before crossing the Atlantic with Paddy Clancy to find acting work in the United States.

Clancy paid his dues on and off Broadway, and attracted some praise, appearing with Helen Hayes in Eugene O'Neill's *Touch of the Poet,* Siobhan McKenna in George Bernard Shaw's *Saint Joan,* and Orson Welles in *King Lear.* Then Clancy and brother Paddy rented the Cherry Lane Theater in New York's Greenwich Village and started promoting folk concerts as a means of supplementing their income. (Paddy Clancy, meanwhile, had founded the Tradition record label.) For recreation, Tom, Paddy and little brother Liam Clancy, who'd arrived in 1956, used to frequent a certain White Horse Tavern, where they might sing for their suppers in such distinguished company as the blues virtuoso Josh White. Out of this ambience grew the Clancys' first record, "Rising Of The Moon", a mishmash of Irish rebel songs which, conveniently distributed by the Tradition label, took the folk scene by storm. It was followed up with a collection of drinking songs entitled "Come Fill Your Glass", and the Clancys decided to try performing for six months. There was a modification to the line-up with the introduction of Tommy Makem, a friend over from Ireland. When the new group was booked for Chicago's influential folk-club, the Gate of Horn, the proprietor started getting agitated while they tried to think up a name for themselves. While they dithered, a poster appeared, baldly announcing them as The Clancy Brothers and Tommy Makem, and that is what they stayed for approaching 30 years. Back home in New York they were booked at the Blue Angel, whence they were invited onto Ed Sullivan's television show. A hitch in the programme resulted in their three-minute slot running to 18 minutes, and as Liam Clancy said, "We found ourselves famous."

The Clancy Brothers and Tommy Makem toured internationally, played Carnegie Hall in New York, the Royal Albert Hall in London and, in 1965, topped the bill at the first Cambridge Folk Festival. In Great Britain and Ireland their imitators sprang up like mushrooms. As Bob Davenport remembers: "Wherever you went there at that time there were Clancy clones — we did an Irish concert in Bedford and there were four of them on the bill — all boosting the Aran sweater trade of course." None of the imitators threatened the supremacy of the genuine article though. Tommy Makem left in 1969, and Liam Clancy in 1975, by which time the group had made no less than 50 albums.

The material which brought them such fame and success was mostly Irish ballads, Dublin music-hall and rebel songs. And in those less troubled times, they could pick at will from both republican and loyalist sources without being contentious. The style in which they were delivered was four-square, uncomplicated, and guaranteed to plug straight into the formidable nostalgia of the deracinated Irish abroad. But there were critics — like Karl Dallas — who felt that the Clancys had done Irish traditional music a disservice, by "ironing out its sprung rhythms and ignoring the decorations which rival flamenco and the blues for their richness."

The Clancys now split into factions, so to speak. Liam and Bobby (yet another brother) continued performing, though in a more restrained manner, while Tom returned mainly to the theatre. He featured in 150 Broadway shows and several television series, like *Charlie's Angels, The Little House on the Prairie,* and the *Incredible Hulk.* In 1984 there was an informal reunion of the Clancy Brothers for a television film, and in 1985 they were invited back to Cambridge to celebrate the twenty-first folk festival. That same year, Tom Clancy returned to Ireland, making his home in County Waterford, and living there in semi-retirement up until the time of his death.

Tom Clancy was not the star vocalist of the quartet; what he provided was a grasp of the immaculate stagecraft which distinguished their performances. A good example is his recitation of the opening lines of James Joyce's *Finnegans Wake,* which a spectator described as "Pure magic...the most effective moments of their concerts were always theatrical." Once the Clancys were loved for putting a lusty boot under a moribund folk scene. Although it later became fashionable to disdain their simple balladeering, Tom Clancy, like his fellows, was a craftsman and a sensitive performer. Research has yet to reveal who had the idea of the matching Aran sweaters.

Born Thomas John Clancy. **Marriage** Blawnin. **Children** Raylin and Cait. **Emigration** Left Ireland for United States after World War II, returned to Ireland, 1985. **Military service** Radio officer, Royal Air Force, 1940–45. **Career** Baker, at age of 14; actor: with Shakespeariana Internationale theatre company, mid 1940s, at Playhouse, Cleveland, Ohio, early 1950s, also off-Broadway; Broadway début, *Touch of the Poet;* first folk concerts, with brother Paddy, Cherry Lane Theater, Greenwich Village, New York; Clancy Brothers folk group joined by younger brother Liam, 1956–75 and Tommy Makem, 1956–69; recording début, "Rising Of The Moon"; formed group with brother Bobby and cousin, Robbie O'Connell, 1980s; retired to Ireland, 1985. **Related activities** Helped brother Paddy found Tradition record label, 1956; also recorded with Columbia, CBS and Vanguard. **Stage** (includes) (As actor, all New York): *Touch of the Poet; King Lear; St Joan;* (as folk singer): Cherry Lane Theater, New York, 1956; Gate of Horn, Chicago; Blue Angel, New York; Carnegie Hall, New York; Royal Albert Hall, London; Cambridge Folk Festival, 1965, 1985. **Television** *Ed Sullivan Show,* 1956; *Incredible Hulk; Charlie's Angels; Little House on the Prairie.* **Recordings** (include) "Rising Of The Moon"; "Come Fill Your Glass". **Publications** Clancy songbooks. **Cause of death** Cancer of the stomach, at age 67.

NORMAN COUSINS

American Writer and Editor

Born **Union Hill, New Jersey, 24 June 1915**

Died **Los Angeles, California, 30 November 1990**

In an interview with Norman Cousins for *Publisher's Weekly,* Lisa See wrote, "Cousins has led a wonderful, if strangely related, series of overlapping lives. He is a complex meshing of science and letters. He is serious and silly, intellectual and maniacal." Considering that Norman Cousins was author of 25 books and hundreds of essays, editor of an influential magazine, a lecturer, foreign correspondent, humanitarian, presidential adviser, crusading activist for such causes as disarmament and world government, unofficial diplomat, health researcher, and (occasional) hoaxer, Lisa See seems to have summed him up pretty well.

He was frequently referred to as "the man who laughed his way to health". In 1964, he contracted ankylosing spondylitis, a degenerative, arthritis-like, crippling disease. He was almost completely paralysed and was given only months to live. He left the hospital and moved into a hotel room where he began his own highly unusual treatment. He took massive doses of Vitamin C to oxygenate his bloodstream and counter the inflammation, and relied on humour as a pain-killer. He read books by P.G. Wodehouse, Robert Benchley and James Thurber. He set up a movie projector and watched old Marx Brothers' movies. In his best-selling book about the experience, *Anatomy of an Illness as Perceived by the Patient,* he wrote, "I made the joyous discovery that ten minutes of genuine belly laughter had an anaesthetic effect and would give me at least two hours of pain-free sleep."

His regimen of laughter and Vitamin C worked. Instead of dying within months, he was back at work within months. Norman Cousins, who had absolutely no medical training, had cured himself. He said in an interview many years later, "I think people have been miseducated about health. We've been educated to be timid and fearful. We don't understand how beautifully robust the human body is... The fact is that 85 percent of all illnesses are self-limiting; the body will right itself if given the chance."

Cousins was only 25 when he became editor of the *Saturday Review.* It was called the *Saturday Review of Literature* and had a circulation of 20,000, which was barely enough to keep it going. The first thing Cousins did was to shorten the title. The second was to broaden the magazine's scope. He said he wanted to make it a "more inclusive cultural journal", encompassing all the arts, current events, science, travel, education and contemporary society. Under Cousins's leadership the magazine's readership steadily increased. By 1971, when the magazine was sold for a reported 5.5 million dollars, the *Saturday Review* had a weekly circulation of 650,000.

In August 1945, 12 days after the first atomic bomb was dropped on Japan, Norman Cousins published his most famous editorial, "Modern Man Is Obsolete". He wrote, "Man stumbles fitfully into a new age of atomic energy for which he is as ill-equipped to accept its potential blessings as he is to counteract or control its present dangers." He went on to argue for a centralized world government, saying that man must learn to live as a "world citizen" or die a "world warrior". It has been estimated that this essay (which was also expanded into book form with the same title) has been read by more than 40 million people.

His involvement with the victims of the Hiroshima blast didn't stop with the editorial. He arranged for 25 young Japanese women, known as the "Hiroshima Maidens", to come to the United States for medical treatment. Their trip was financed by *Saturday Review* readers. A few years later, the magazine initiated a similar programme for the "Ravensbruck Lapins", 35 Polish women who had been the victims of horrific medical experimentation in a Nazi concentration camp.

He undertook numerous diplomatic missions on behalf of Pope John XXIII and Presidents Eisenhower, Kennedy and Johnson. During the Kennedy administration, he negotiated a limited nuclear test ban treaty with Nikita Khrushchev. In 1972, he wrote a book about it: *The Improbable Triumvirate: John F. Kennedy, Pope John, Nikita Khrushchev.*

Despite his involvement in such serious matters, Cousins always had time for a joke. He loved to print fake letters to the editor, such as the one from "K. Jason Sitewell" complaining about proposed legislation to abolish golf. To their great embarrassment, *Golf World* were taken in. They published an editorial denouncing the anti-golf law. Cousins defended his little hoaxes, saying,

"Spoofing has been a tradition here. We like to laugh and share our laughter with others, especially in times when there's not much to laugh about."

Of course he was a great believer in laughter, it had saved his life, and he wanted to show it could save others. He spent a lot of time at the UCLA School of Medicine, where he became an adjunct professor in the Department of Psychiatry and Biobehavioral Science. He taught ethics and medical literature, and researched his theories about the link between mental attitude and health by working with cancer patients. According to L.J. West, professor and past director of psychiatry and biobehavioral science at UCLA, "He would talk to them and listen to them and help them understand that a diagnosis of cancer doesn't have to be a death sentence. The results were not only changes in their quality of life but changes in the progress of the disease itself." According to Dr Sherman Mellinkoff, professor emeritus and former dean of the UCLA medical school, "Mr Cousins was an inspirational leader in trying to understand the grandeur of the human spirit and its promotion of health and resistance to illness."

Like so many of his other accomplishments, his work with cancer patients was important and fulfilling, but his real love was the magazine he edited for nearly four decades. He once said, "Nothing in my life, next to my family, has meant more to me than the *Saturday Review*. To work with books and ideas, to have unfettered access to an editorial page which offered, quite literally, as much freedom as I was capable of absorbing — this is a generous portion for any man."

Born Norman Cousins. **Parents** Samuel and Sara Barry (Miller) Cousins. **Marriage** Ellen Kopf, 1939. **Children** Andrea, Amy, Candis and Sara, and one adopted daughter, Shikego. **Education** Teachers' College, Columbia University, New York. **Career** Educational editor, *New York Evening Post,* 1934–35; book critic, *Current History,* 1935–40, literary editor, managing editor; executive editor, *Saturday Review of Literature,* 1940–42, editor, *Saturday Review,* 1942–71; editor, *Saturday Review/World,* 1973–74; editor, *Saturday Review,* 1975–78; adjunct professor in Department of Psychiatry and Biobehavioral Science, University of California, Los Angeles, 1978–90. **Related activities** Editorial board member, Overseas Bureau, Office of War Information, 1943–45; co-chairman, national campaign board, Victory Book Campaign, 1943; editor, *U.S.A.,* 1943–45; chairman, Connecticut Fact Finding Commission on Education, 1948–52; US diplomat/lecturer, India, 1951, Pakistan, 1951, Ceylon, 1951; member, Commission to Study Organized Peace; board member, Freedom House; board member, Willkie Memorial Foundation; board member, Columbia University Conference on Science, Philosophy and Religion; founder/president, United World Federalists, 1952–54, honorary president, 1954–56; co-chairman, National Committee for a Sane Nuclear Policy, 1957–63; chairman, board of directors, McCall Corporation, 1961–70, editorial committee, 1961–70; vice-president/director, Brain Research Institute, McCall's Corporation, New York City, 1961–70; editorial board member, *Encyclopaedia Britannica;* board chairman, National Educational Television, 1969–70; board member, Charles F. Kettering Foundation; board member, Samuel H. Kress Foundation. **Offices and memberships** Member: American Council of Learned Societies, World Association of World Federalists, Council on Foreign Relations, National Press Club, Overseas Press Club, National Planning Association, National Academy of Sciences, international relations committee member; director, US division, United Nations Association; member, Poets, Playwrights, Editors, Essayists, Novelists, American section vice-president, 1952–55. **Awards and honours** Thomas Jefferson Award for the Advancement of Democracy in Journalism, 1948; honorary LittD: American University, 1948, Elmira College, 1957, Ripon College, 1957, Wilmington College, 1957, University of Vermont, 1957, Western Michigan University; Tuition Plan Award for outstanding service to American education, 1951; honorary LHD: Boston University, 1953, Colby College, 1953, Denison University, 1954, Colgate University, 1958; Benjamin Franklin citation in magazine journalism, 1956; honorary LLD: Washington and

Jefferson College, 1956, Syracuse University, 1957, Albright College, 1957; Wayne State University award for national service to education, 1958; honorary EdD, Rhode Island College of Education, 1958; New York State Citizens Education Commission Award, 1959; John Dewey Award for Education, 1959; Eleanor Roosevelt Peace Award, 1963; Publius Award, United World Federalists, 1964; Overseas Press Club Award, 1965; Distinguished Citizen Award, Connecticut Bar Association, 1965; New York Academy of Public Education Award, 1966; Family of Man Award, 1968; Annual Award, Aquinas College, 1968; national magazine award, Association of Deans of Journalism Schools, 1969; Peace Medal, United Nations, 1971; Sarah Josepha Hale Award, 1971; Carr Van Anda Award for contributions to journalism, Ohio State University, 1971; Gold Medal for literature, National Arts Club, 1972; Journalism Honor Award, University of Missouri School of Journalism, 1972; Irita Van Doren Book Award, 1972; award for service to the environment, Government of Canada, 1972; Henry Johnson Fisher Award as magazine publisher of the year, Magazine Publishers Association, 1973; Human Resources Award, 1977; Convocation Medal, American College of Cardiology, 1978; Encyclopaedia Britannica Achievement in Life Award, 1980; Author of the Year Award, American Society of Journalists and Authors, 1981; American Book Award nomination in paperback non-fiction, for *Anatomy of an Illness as Perceived by the Patient,* 1982; Albert Schweitzer Prize for Humanitarianism, 1990. **Recordings** "Betting One's Life on the Future of Print", Development Digest, 1973. **Publications** *The Good Inheritance: The Democratic Chance,* 1942; (editor) *A Treasury of Democracy,* 1942; *Modern Man Is Obsolete,* 1945; (editor with William Rose Benet) *An Anthology of the Poetry of Liberty,* 1945; (editor) *Writing for Love or Money: Thirty-Five Essays Reprinted from the Saturday Review of Literature,* 1949, 1970; (contributor) *Years of the Modern* edited by John W. Chase, 1949; (with Jawaharlal Nehru) *Talks with Nehru,* 1951; *Who Speaks for Man?,* 1953; *Amy Loveman, 1881–1955: A Eulogy* (pamphlet), 1956; *The Religious Beliefs of the Founding Fathers,* 1958; (editor) *In God We Trust,* 1958; (editor) *Thesaurus Dictionary* by Francis March, 1958; *The Rejection of Nothingness* (pamphlet), 1959; *Dr Schweitzer of Lambarene,* 1960, 1973; *The Last Defense in a Nuclear Age,* 1960; *In Place of Folly,* 1961; *Can Cultures Co-Exist?* (symposium), 1963; (with others) *...Therefore Choose Life, That Thou Mayest Live, Thou and Thy Seed,* 1965; (editor) *Profiles of Nehru: America Remembers a World Leader,* 1966; (editor) *Great American Essays,* 1967; *Present Tense: An American Editor's Odyssey* (autobiography), 1967; (with others) *Issues: 1968,* 1968; *Profiles of Gandhi: America Remembers a World Leader,* 1969; *The Improbable Triumvirate: John F. Kennedy, Pope Paul, Nikita Khrushchev, an Asterisk to the History of a Hopeful Year, 1962–1963,* 1972; *The Celebration of Life: A Dialogue on Immortality and Infinity,* 1974; *The Quest for Immortality,* 1974; (editor with Mary L. Dimond) *Memoirs of a Man: Grenville Clark,* 1975; *Anatomy of an Illness as Perceived by the Patient: Reflections on Healing and Regeneration,* 1979; *Reflections on Healing and Regeneration,* 1980; *Human Options: An Autobiographical Notebook,* 1981; *The Physician in Literature,* 1981; *Healing and Belief,* 1982; *The Healing Heart: Antidotes to Panic and Helplessness,* 1983; *The Trial of Dr Mesmer: A Play,* 1984; (editor) *The Words of Albert Schweitzer,* 1984; *Albert Schweitzer's Mission,* 1985; *The Pathology of Power,* 1987. **Cause of death** Full cardiac arrest, at age 75.

ROALD DAHL

British Writer

Born **Llandaff, Wales, 13 September 1916**

Died **Oxford, England, 23 November 1990**

In late November 1990, this notice appeared in the British national newspaper, *The Times:* "DAHL — peacefully in hospital, Roald, scrumdiddlyumptious husband of Felicity and wondercrump father of Tessa, Theo, Ophelia, and Lucy... there will be no rotsome memorial service by his request." The Big Friendly Giant, the children's champion, was dead.

Adults were often repelled and horrified by the crudeness depicted in his writing; they squirmed in discomfort as he went to great pains to describe bits of food stuck in a man's beard, or "whizzpopper" farts. Children loved it.

"I have a great affinity with children", Dahl said in an interview one month before his death:

> When you are born you are a savage, an uncivilised little grub, and if you are going to go into our society by the age of ten, then you have to have good manners and know all the do's and don'ts — don't eat with your fingers and don't piss on the floor. All that stuff has to be hammered into the savage, who resents it deeply. So subconsciously in the child's mind these giants become the enemy. That goes particularly for parents and teachers.
>
> When I wrote *Matilda* I based it on this theory. There are foul parents and a disgusting, barbaric teacher. Children absolutely warm to this. They think: "Well, Christ! He's one of us." I don't think you find many chaps or women in their mid-seventies who do think like I do and joke and fart around. They usually get pompous, and pomposity is the enemy of children's writing.

It never occurred to him to be a writer until *after* his first sale, to the US *Saturday Evening Post,* which earned him the princely sum (it was the early 1940s) of 1000 dollars. This accidental sale came about because he didn't want to spoil a nice luncheon by talking too much, so he offered to write some notes on his war experiences and send them to his dining companion, C.S. Forester. Forester, upon receiving them, declared them "the work of a gifted writer" and sent them to the magazine under Dahl's name. The magazine sent Dahl a cheque. He promptly lost the money in a poker game. But he had found a career.

The son of Norwegian immigrants, he was born near Cardiff, Wales. His early life was marked by tragedy: his elder sister died when he was three years old, followed a few weeks later by his father. His mother financed his education by selling her jewellery, but he hated the school he was sent to, Repton, calling his days there "torture".

"I'm afraid I was always something of a rebel", he told an interviewer. "I was much hated by teachers because they can only run their schools properly with boys who conform, the sort who become head prefects."

Declining his mother's offer to send him to university, he took a job with the eastern staff of the Shell Oil Company, a posting that eventually took him to Africa. He was in Africa when the war broke out in Europe. He joined the RAF and became a fighter pilot, flying Hurricanes in Greece.

After being injured in a plane crash, he was sent to Washington as an assistant air attaché. It was there he met C.S. Forester and had the luncheon that changed his life. He became a regular contributor to *The Saturday Evening Post,* and in 1946 his *Post* pieces were collected and published as a book entitled, *Over To You: Ten Stories of Flyers and Flying.*

He started selling short stories to that most prestigious of magazines, *The New Yorker,* in the days when writers were given the sort of attention that any writer starting out today would gladly die for; it must have been writers' heaven. "The way it worked was this", Dahl explained:

> The fiction editor would buy the story and he would then ask you to come in. In you'd go and he would sit you right beside him at the table and he would go through every line of the story. He would never ask you to alter the plot or anything like that, he was simply dealing with the English, making sure it was dead accurate and shortening a sentence here and there. It was very careful and meticulous work and I learnt a lot from it, everyone did.

Dahl's early works were usually macabre, blackly comic tales, written for adults, such as "The Visitor", in which a man fears that an unscrupulous seduction might have left him with a deadly disease (how appropriate today), or "Lamb to the Slaughter", in which a woman murders her husband with a frozen leg of lamb and gets a detective to eat the murder weapon. Twenty-two of these adult, twist-in-the-tale stories were televised by Britain's Anglia Television as *Tales of the Unexpected.*

He had this advice for other writers:

> The trick is to write it down at once, otherwise you'll forget it... I was once driving alone on a country road and an idea came for a story about someone getting stuck in an elevator between floors in an empty house. I had nothing to write with in the car. So I stopped and got out. The back of the car was covered with dust. With one finger I wrote in the dust the single word ELEVATOR. That was enough.

He married the actress Patricia Neal in 1953. They had five children, and he said that he started writing for them because most of the children's writing around at the time was "really crummy". His children's books, such as *James and the Giant Peach* and *Charlie and the Chocolate Factory* (later made into a film as *Willie Wonka and the Chocolate Factory*), were great successes, but Dahl's personal life was dogged by tragedy. In 1960, his son Theo suffered brain damage as the result of a road accident (he was two years old at the time), and two years later, his eight-year-old daughter Olivia died of complications following a bout of measles. Then, to cap it off, in 1965, Patricia Neal was debilitated by a series of three massive strokes.

Dahl's efforts to nurse his wife back to health are well documented (some say he "bullied" her back to health), so their 1983 divorce, and his second marriage to Felicity Crosland, came as a surprise to many.

Despite his many personal traumas and tragedies, he always maintained a consistent output, working in a shed at the bottom of his garden, behind Gipsy House in Buckinghamshire. "I distrust any writer who sits in a Chippendale chair", he told an interviewer. His shed was his favourite place, his "refuge", cluttered with such memorabilia as a silver ball made from chocolate bar wrappings, and a hip bone (his own, removed because of arthritis). "You can have terrific fun up here", Dahl said.

Quentin Blake, Dahl's illustrator for 15 years, was a regular visitor to the shed. Dahl was always deeply involved in the visual side of his children's books; his text would usually contain notes on his ideas for illustrations, and he and Blake met frequently to discuss the drawings. Blake wrote in London's *Evening Standard,* "I always drew as near as I could what Dahl had written, but if he was dissatisfied with the final effect, he was ready to rewrite the words to give me the brief for a new picture." And over 15 years, Blake had plenty of time to get used to Dahl's insistence on following an idea through, "It was not sufficient to see a lavatory pedestal flying through the air when thrown out a window; for full satisfaction, you have to see *it hitting the pavement.*"

Dahl was often controversial. He was accused of racism in *Charlie and the Chocolate Factory,* sexism in *The Witches,* and certain comments on Israel brought him charges of anti-Semitism. Asked about the gleeful way he went around putting people's backs up, Dahl replied, "I only do it to people I think are very in the wrong". As to what others may say of *him:* "I don't care what other people think. If I don't like what people say or write about me then I simply say they're wrong. Sod 'em."

He had a reputation for crustiness, and he lived up to it. But others remember him differently. In reply to the obituary printed in the London *Independent* newspaper, Spiv and Marius Barran wrote,

> For those who knew him well, the most important things were his fantastic enthusiasm and his great generosity.

> "Treats!" he would cry, displaying a dinner table laden with quantities of his favourite food: Norwegian prawns, or lobster, or caviar or scrumptious roast beef. Second and third helpings were pressed on his lucky guests... Excellent claret and the inevitable chocolates were essential parts of his enthusiasm for food, drink and conversation...
>
> Charitable giving may be expected from a rich man, and he certainly gave more than most, but he also gave tirelessly of himself. Recently, already ill, he drove across two counties to talk to a boy in a coma. His private, unrecorded generosity was as spontaneous and open-handed as his well-known work for various charities.

Quentin Blake wrote that he remembers, "the expectantly-raised eyebrows, the little smile of relish, the gleam of a sort of ageless enthusiasm." The last word comes from a fan, ten-year-old Eve Wilmott, quoted in Britain's *Observer* newspaper: "I like Roald Dahl because he's funny and a bit rude about adults. They don't act like normal grown-ups — they do disgusting things."

Born Roald Dahl. **Parents** Harald, shipbroker, and Sofie Magdalene (Hesselberg) Dahl. **Marriages** 1) Patricia Neal, actress, 1953 (divorced 1983); 2) Felicity Ann Crosland, 1983. **Children** Tessa, Theo, Ophelia, Lucy and Olivia (deceased), by first marriage. **Education** Llandaff Cathedral School, Cardiff; St Peter's Preparatory School, Weston-Super-Mare; Repton School, Derbyshire. **Military service** Temporary Army officer, 1939; Royal Air Force, 1939–45: in Nairobi and Habbanyah, 1939–40, with a fighter squadron in Western Desert, 1940, wounded, in Greece and Syria, 1941, assistant air attaché, Washington, DC, 1942–43, became wing-commander, 1943, with British Security Co-ordination, North America, 1943–45. **Career** Author, 1940s onwards; first story "A Piece of Cake", published in *The Saturday Evening Post,* 1941. **Related activities** Donor, rights of manuscript, *The Vicar of Nibbleswicke* to Dyslexia Institute, 1990. **Other activities** Member, Shell Company, London, eastern staff, 1933–37; member, Public Schools Exploring Society expedition to Newfoundland, 1934; member of staff, Shell Company of East Africa, Dar-es-Salaam, 1937–39; collector, avant-garde paintings. **Awards and honours** Mystery Writers of America Edgar Allan Poe Award, 1953, 1959, 1980; Federation of Children's Book Groups Award, 1983; Whitbread Award for *The Witches,* 1983; World Fantasy Convention Award, 1983; DLitt, University of Keele, Staffordshire, England, 1988. **Publications for children — fiction** *The Gremlins,* illustrated by Walt Disney Studio, 1943; *James and the Giant Peach,* illustrated by Nancy Ekholm Burkert, 1961; *Charlie and the Chocolate Factory,* illustrated by Joseph Schindelman, 1964; *The Magic Finger,* illustrated by William Pene du Bois, 1966; *Fantastic Mr Fox,* illustrated by Donald Chaffin, 1970; *Charlie and the Great Glass Elevator,* illustrated by Joseph Schindelman, 1972; *Danny, The Champion of the World,* illustrated by Jill Bennett, 1975; *The Wonderful Story of Henry Sugar and Six More,* 1977, also published as *The Wonderful World of Henry Sugar,* 1977; *The Complete Adventures of Charlie and Mr Willy Wonka,* illustrated by Faith Jaques, 1978; *The Enormous Crocodile,* illustrated by Quentin Blake, 1978; *The Twits,* illustrated by Quentin Blake, 1980; *George's Marvellous Medicine,* illustrated by Quentin Blake, 1981; *The BFG,* illustrated by Quentin Blake, 1982; *The Witches,* illustrated by Quentin Blake, 1983; *The Giraffe and the Pelly and Me,* illustrated by Quentin Blake, 1985; *Matilda,* illustrated by Quentin Blake, 1988; *Esio Trot,* illustrated by Quentin Blake, 1990; *The Vicar of Nibbleswicke* (manuscript); *The Mins Pins* (awaiting publication). **Verse** *Revolting Rhymes,* illustrated by Quentin Blake, 1982; *Dirty Beasts,* illustrated by Rosemary Fawcett, 1983; *Rhyme Stew,* 1989. **Publications for children — other** *Boy: Tales of Childhood* (autobiography), 1984; *Going Solo* (autobiography), 1986. **Publications for adults — novels** *Sometime Never: A Fable for Supermen,* 1948; *My Uncle Oswald,* 1979. **Short stories** *Over to You: 10 Stories of Flyers and Flying,* 1946; *Someone Like You,* 1953; *Kiss, Kiss,* 1960; *Twenty-Nine Kisses,* 1969; *Selected Stories,* 1970; (with others) *Penguin Modern Stories 12,*

1972; *Switch Bitch,* 1974; *The Best of Roald Dahl,* 1978; *Tales of the Unexpected,* 1979; *Taste and Other Tales, 1979; More Tales of the Unexpected,* 1980, also published as *Further Tales of the Unexpected,* 1981; *A Roald Dahl Selection: Nine Short Stories,* edited by Roy Blatchford, 1980; *Two Fables,* 1986; *A Second Roald Dahl Selection: Eight Short Stories,* edited by Helen Fawcett, 1987; also contributor to *The New Yorker, Harper's, Atlantic, Collier's, Playboy, Esquire, Town and Country and other magazines.* **Play** *The Honeys,* New York, 1955. **Screenplays** (With Harry Jack Bloom) *You Only Live Twice,* 1967; (with Ken Hughes) *Chitty-Chitty-Bang-Bang,* 1968; *The Night Digger,* 1970; *The Lightning Bug,* 1971; *Willy Wonka and the Chocolate Factory,* 1971. **Television play** *Lamb to the Slaughter, Alfred Hitchcock Presents* series, 1955. **Publication as editor** *Roald Dahl's Book of Ghost Stories,* 1983. **Cause of death** Undisclosed, at age 74. **Further reading** Barry Fawcett, *Pat and Roald,* 1969; Chris Powling, *Roald Dahl,* 1983; Twentieth-Century Children's Writers, 1989.

LAWRENCE DURRELL

British Poet, Playwright and Novelist

Born **Julundur, India, 27 February 1912**

Died **Sommières, France, 7 November 1990**

No doubt the critics will take pleasure in debating the exact position of Lawrence Durrell in the history of twentieth-century literature for many years to come. Those who grew up with his magical *The Alexandria Quartet,* published at the end of the dreary 1950s, will be more likely to remember him simply with that affection and gratitude earned by all writers who change people's lives.

From the opening words of *Justine,* the first novel of the quartet: "The sea is high again today, with a thrilling flush of wind. In the midst of winter you can feel the inventions of spring. A sky of hot nude pearl until midday, crickets in sheltered places, and now the wind unpacking the great planes, ransacking the great planes", it was clear that a new and exciting voice was speaking. Into the sad and puritan austerities of post-war Britain and before the sexual revolution that was to shake a million bourgeois bedsprings in the more swinging 1960s, erupted these four interlinking exotic novels, huge unwieldy chunks of poetic and often purple prose, tales of sex and death, of political intrigue and pagan mysteries, of Greeks and Jews and Copts and, mainly, of the city of Alexandria, "city of death" and the "obsessive rhythms of death".

Durrell at his best was always a poet of place. And if his *Quartet* had more impact than others of its kind — Olivia Manning's *Balkan* and *Levant* trilogies, Burgess's novels about Malaya, Frank Tuoy's *Ice Saints* — that may have something to do with his own almost obsessive love of the places that he wrote about. There was also a barely suppressed romantic allure that had a whole generation of aspirant diplomats modelling themselves upon the sombre Mountolive, of British teachers aping the life-style of the narrator, Darley.

Durrell's own early life was as romantic in its way as even he could have wished. Born in the foothills of the Himalayas of an Anglo-Indian colonial family and sent home to England in his teens for education, he failed the Cambridge entrance examination three times and eventually drifted off to London's Bloomsbury to become a writer. In 1935 he sent the text of his first serious novel, *The Black Book,* to Henry Miller in Paris, instructing him to throw it into the Seine after reading. Miller encouraged him to publish in France but not, because of British obscenity laws, in England.

The Black Book, published in 1938 by the Obelisk Press in Paris, was a savage diatribe against English gentility, spiritual death and "pudding" qualities. Having got it out of his system Durrell seems next to have thrown his considerable energy into the task of persuading his widowed mother and younger siblings to move from their damp, unhealthy house in Bournemouth to the sunny shores of Corfu, a move described in detail in his younger brother Gerald's book, *My Family and Other Animals* (in which Lawrence himself features as something of an intellectual snob, self-conscious aesthete and sanctimonious prig).

The Corfu idyll, which produced the first of Durrell's Greek island books (*Prospero's Cell*), ended with the outbreak of war. In April 1941 Durrell and his wife and ten-month-old daughter escaped from Navarone by caique to Crete and thence to Egypt. It is interesting that one year spent working with the British Information Office in Alexandria was enough to inspire the writing of *The Alexandria Quartet* almost 15 years later — as it was for Paul Scott who also wrote the *Raj Quartet* on only one year's experience of India during the war. Expatriates who complained that in Alex in the war "nothing ever happened" were perhaps not steeped as was Durrell in the poems of Constantine Cavafy, in T.S. Eliot's *Wasteland,* or in E.M. Forster's history of the city.

From Alexandria Durrell was posted to Rhodes (source of *Reflections on a Marine Venus*), to Argentina as a British Council teacher and then, in 1949, as press attaché to the British embassy in the newly Communist Belgrade (scene of the satirical sketches of diplomatic life published as *Sauve Qui Peut* and *Esprit de Corps*). When he went to Cyprus in 1952 to write about Egypt, the gentle island life he describes in the opening chapter of *Bitter Lemons* was only too quickly shattered by the eruptions of EOKA and an incipient civil war that was to drag Durrell back into the familiar dilemmas of government information work.

It was not until 1957 and the publication in one year of *Justine*, *Bitter Lemons* and *White Eagles over Serbia* (a book for children about the war in Yugoslavia) that Durrell's financial success as a writer finally brought him the independence he craved. It had been more than 20 years since T.S. Eliot greeted the publication of *The Black Book* as, "the first piece of work by a new English writer to give me any hope for the future of prose fiction". In the intervening years Durrell had published novels, short stories and several volumes of poetry. Only now was he able to retire to the south of France to the solitary life of the full-time writer and to obscurity.

For every ten people whose eyes light up at mention of *The Alexandria Quartet* or the island books, it is hard to find one who has read *Tunc* or *Nunquam* or even heard of the quincunx, Durrell's final ambitious five novels which make up *The Avignon Quintet* and which he published gradually over the years between 1974 and 1985. The critic Kenneth McLeish says the trouble was that Durrell began in his later years to take himself far too seriously. "He succumbed in print", McLeish wrote, "to the 'persona' he had assumed in life from adolescence onwards." Novelist and critic Anthony Burgess felt that it was Durrell's continuing adolescent tone which finally harmed so much of his fiction. Certainly both critics and readers have found it hard to deal charitably with books which abandon all attempt to hold together any kind of plot, narrative or characterization.

This is a pity because the themes on which Durrell wrote are serious. In later years his preoccupation was increasingly with mysticism and the teachings of Zen Buddhism, his anger turned not just towards the unspiritual English but widened to include the moral decline that he saw taking place throughout western civilization. *The Avignon Quintet* weaves a pattern in European history extending from the fourteenth-century sack of the Knights Templar to the experience of the German occupation of France in World War II. The quincunx itself is an ancient mystical figure formed by the pattern of dots on a domino, figures on a playing card. It is to be found in the Roman numeral X and in the Greek cross. It corresponds to the number of Tantric Chakras (energy centres) in the body and to the five senses. "The old force-field quincunx" Durrell tells us in *Quinx* is also to be found in sex — "the five-sided being with two arms, two legs and the kundalini as properties".

Somehow Durrell never lost that somewhat *jejune,* mocking attitude to sex. Even at the end of his last, posthumously published travel book about Provence, *Caesar's Vast Ghost,* he could not resist including an ode to Cunégonde, a large latex doll christened in honour of Voltaire's favourite niece. It is as though, after all these years, he was still trying to shock, still writing with one eye on the boarding-house biddies of Bournemouth, still secretly hoping someone would ban his books on grounds of obscenity laws long since rendered obsolete.

It does not seem that the older Durrell was particularly happy. Of his four wives three had left him and one died tragically and suddenly. His beloved daughter Sappho committed suicide in 1985. Visitors to his house in Sommières, near Nîmes, found him desperate to "keep the shades at bay" with wine, meditation and yoga. But perhaps we are still too close to the later work to see it clearly. Perhaps only future generations will be able to judge how much Durrell's later explorations into Buddhism, psychoanalysis and European history actually brought him closer to the truth and to himself.

Born Lawrence George Durrell. **Pseudonyms** Charles Norden, Larry Dell. **Father** A civil engineer. **Marriages** 1) Nancy Myers, painter, 1935 (divorced 1947); 2) Eve Cohen, 1947 (divorced); 3) Claude Forde (née Vincendon), writer, 1961 (died 1967); 4) Ghislaine de Boysson, 1973 (divorced 1979). **Children** Penelope, from first marriage; Sappho (died 1985), from second marriage. **Education** College of St Joseph, Darjeeling, India; St Edmund's School, Canterbury, Kent. **Career** Author, 1931 onwards; first publication, the poems, *Quaint Fragment: Poems Written Between the Ages of Sixteen and Nineteen,* 1931; lived in Corfu, 1934–40; (with Henry Miller and Alfred Perlès) editor, *The Booster* (later *Delta*), Paris, 1937–39; columnist, *Egyptian Gazette,* Cairo, 1941; (with Robin Fedden and Bernard Spencer) editor, *Personal Landscape,* Cairo, 1942–45; special correspondent in Cyprus for *The Economist,* London, 1953–55; editor, *Cyprus Review,* Nicosia, 1954–55; lived in France from 1957. **Other activities** Employed variously as jazz pianist, Blue Peter night-club, London, racing car driver, estate agent before 1934; teacher, British Institute, Kalamata, Greece, 1940; foreign service press officer, British Information Office, Cairo, 1941–44; press attaché, British Information Office, Alexandria, 1944–45; director of public relations for the Dodecanese Islands, Greece, 1946–47; director, the British Council Institute, Cordoba, Argentina, 1947–48; press attaché, British Legation, Belgrade, 1949–52; director of public relations for British government in Cyprus, 1954–56; Andrew Mellon Visiting Professor of Humanities, California Institute of Technology, Pasadena, 1974. **Offices and memberships** Fellow, Royal Society of Literature, 1954. **Awards and honours** Duff Cooper Memorial Prize, 1957; Foreign Book Prize, France, 1959; James Tait Black Memorial Prize, 1975. **Publications — novels** *Pied Piper of Lovers,* 1935; (as Charles Norden), *Panic Spring,* 1937; *The Black Book: An Agon,* 1938; *Cefalu,* 1947, also published as *The Dark Labyrinth,* 1958; *The Alexandria Quartet,* 1962, comprising: *Justine,* 1957, *Balthazar,* 1958, *Mountolive,* 1958, *Clea,* 1960; *White Eagles over Serbia,* 1957; *Tunc,* 1968; *Nunquam,* 1970; *The Avignon Quintet* comprising: *Monsieur, or, The Prince of Darkness,* 1974, *Livia, or, Buried Alive,* 1978, *Constance, or, Solitary Practices,* 1982, *Sebastian, or, Ruling Passions,* 1983, *Quinx, or, The Ripper's Tale,* 1985; *The Revolt of Aphrodite,* 1974. **Short stories** *Zero, and Asylum in the Snow,* 1946; *Two Excursions into Reality,* 1947; *Esprit de Corps: Sketches from Diplomatic Life,* 1957; *Stiff Upper Lip: Life among the Diplomats,* 1959; *Sauve Qui Peut,* 1966; *The Best of Antrobus,* 1974; *Antrobus Complete,* 1985. **Plays** *Sappho: A Play in Verse,* produced in Hamburg, 1959, Edinburgh, 1961, Evanston, Illinois, 1964, published, 1958; *Acte,* produced in Hamburg, 1961, published, 1964; *An Irish Faustus: A Morality in Nine Scenes,* produced in Hamburg, 1963, published, 1963; *Judith,* 1966. **Screenplays** (with others) *Cleopatra,* 1963; (with others) *Judith,* 1966. **Radio script** *Greek Peasant Superstitions,* 1947. **Television scripts** (With Diane Deriaz) *The Lonely Roads,* 1970; *The Alexandrians,* 1970; *The Search for Ulysses* (Canada); *Spirit of Place:* Lawrence Durrell's Greece, 1976; *Lawrence Durrell's Egypt,* 1978. **Verse** *Quaint Fragment: Poems Written Between the Ages of Sixteen and Nineteen,* 1931; *Ten Poems,* 1932; *Ballade of Slow Decay,* 1932; *Bromo Bombastes: A Fragment* *from a Laconic Drama by Gaffer Peeslake,* 1933; *Transition,* 1934; *Mass for the Old Year,* 1935; (with others) *Proems: An Anthology of Poems,* edited by Oswald Blakeston, 1938; *A Private Country,* 1943; *The Parthenon: For T.S. Eliot,* 1945; *Cities, Plains, and People,* 1946; *On Seeming to Presume,* 1948; *A Landmark Gone,* 1949; *Deus Loci,* 1950; *Private Drafts,* 1955; *The Tree of Idleness and Other Poems,* 1955; *Selected Poems,* 1956; *Collected Poems,* 1956; (with Elizabeth Jennings and R.S. Thomas) *Penguin Modern Poets 1,* 1962; *The Poetry of Lawrence Durrell,* 1962; *Beccaffico (Le Becfique),* French translation by F.J. Temple, 1963; *A Persian Lady,* 1963; *Selected Poems 1935–1963,* 1964; *The Ikons and Other Poems,* 1966; *Faustus: A Poem,* 1970; *The Red Limbo Lingo: A Poetry Notebook,* 1971; *On the Suchness of the Old Boy,* 1972; *Vega and Other Poems,* 1973; *Lifelines,* 1974; *Selected Poems,* edited by Alan Ross, 1977; *Collected Poems 1931–1974,* edited by James A. Brigham, 1980. **Published lyrics** (music by T.W. Southam): (as Larry Dell), *Walking in My Sleep,* 1945, *Nemea,* 1950, *Lesbos,* 1967, *Nothing Is Lost, Sweet Self,* 1967. **Other publications** *Prospero's Cell: A Guide to the Landscape and Manners of the Island of Corcyra,* 1945, with *Reflections on a Marine Venus,* 1960; *Key to Modern Poetry,* also published as *A Key to Modern British Poetry,* 1952; *Reflections on a Marine Venus: A Companion to the Landscape of Rhodes,* 1953, with *Prospero's Cell,* 1960; *Bitter Lemons,* 1957; *Art and Outrage: A Correspondence about Henry Miller Between Alfred Perlès and Lawrence Durrell, with an Intermission by Henry Miller,* 1959; *Groddeck,* 1961; (with Gustaf Grundgens) *Briefwechsel über "Actis",* 1961; *Lawrence Durrell and Henry Miller: A Private Correspondence,* edited by George Wickes, 1963; *La Descente du Styx,* 1964, also published as *Down the Styx,* 1971; *Spirit of Place: Letters and Essays on Travel,* edited by Alan G. Thomas, 1969; *Le Grand Suppositoire* (interview with Marc Alyn), 1972, also published as *The Big Supposer,* 1973; *The Happy Rock* (on Henry Miller), 1973; *The Plant-Magic Man,* 1973; *Blue Thirst,* 1975; *Sicilian Carousel,* 1977; *The Greek Islands,* 1978; *A Smile in the Mind's Eye,* 1982; *Literary Lifelines: The Richard Aldington-Lawrence Durrell Correspondence,* edited by Harry T. Moore and Ian S. MacNiven, 1981; *The Durrell-Miller Letters 1935–1980,* edited by Ian S. MacNiven, 1988; *Henri Michaux: The Poet of Supreme Solipsism,* 1990; *Caesar's Vast Ghost: Aspects of Provence,* 1990. **Publications as editor** (With Robin Feddeon and Bernard Spencer) *Personal Landscape: An Anthology of Exile,* 1945; *A Henry Miller Reader,* 1959, also published as *The Best of Henry Miller,* 1960; *New Poems,* 1963; *Poems* by Wordsworth, 1972. **Translations** *Six Poems from the Greek of Sekilianos and Seferis,* 1946; (with Bernard Spencer and Nanos Valaoritis) *The King of Asine and Other Poems* by George Seferis, 1948; *The Curious History of Pope Joan,* by Emmanuel Royidis, 1954, revised edition, published as *Pope Joan: A Romantic Biography,* 1960; (with others) *Selected Poems,* by Alain Bosquet, 1973; *Three Poems of Cavafy,* 1980. **Recordings** *The Love Poems,* Spoken Arts; *Ulysses Come Back: Sketch for a Musical,* author of story, music and lyrics, Turret Records. **Manuscript collection** University of California, Los Angeles; University of Illinois, Urbana. **Cause of death** Undisclosed, at age 78. **Further reading** Harry T. Moore, editor, *The World of Lawrence Durrell,* 1962; John Unterecker, *Lawrence Durrell,* 1964; John A. Weigel, *Lawrence Durrell,* 1965, G.S. Fraser, *Lawrence Durrell: A Study* (including bibliography by Alan G. Thomas), 1968; Hartwig Isernhagen, *Sensation, Vision, and Imagination: The Problem of Unity in Lawrence Durrell's Novels,* 1969; G.S. Fraser, *Lawrence Durrell,* 1970; Alan Warren Friedman, *Art for Love's Sake: Lawrence Durrell and The Alexandria Quartet,* 1970; Kari Sajavaara, *Imagery in Durrell's Prose,* 1975; Jane Lagoudis Pinchin, *Alexandria Still: Forster, Durrell, and Cavafy,* 1977; Walter G. Creed, *The Muse of Science and The Alexandria Quartet,* 1977; Guido Kums, *Fiction: or, The Language of Our Discontent: A Study of the Built-In Novelist in the Novels of Angus Wilson, Durrell, and Doris Lessing,* 1985; *Contemporary Poets,* 1985; Alan Warren Friedman, editor, *Critical Essays on Lawrence Durrell,* 1986; *Contemporary Novelists,* 1986; Ian S. McNiven and Carol Peirce, editors, *Twentieth Century Literature,* "Durrell Issue", vol. 33, nos. 3–4, 1987; *Contemporary Dramatists,* 1988; Frank Kersnowsky, editor, *Into the Labyrinth: Essays on the Art* *of Durrell,* 1989; Michael Begnal, editor, *On Miracle Ground: Essays on the Fiction of Durrell,* 1990; *Reference Guide to English Literature,* 1991.

ROWLAND EMETT

British Cartoonist and Inventor

Born **London, England, 22 October 1906**

Died **Hassocks, West Sussex, 13 November 1990**

Even if you have no belief in such things, it would be nice to know the precise astrological circumstances of Rowland Emett's birth. It is pleasing to imagine what zodiacal capering, what conjunction of this and that starry animal could produce such a character. Whatever the cause or influence, he was favoured by fate, amusing himself and others, being paid to do what he liked doing best. There's nothing very unusual about that, but he did it in a singular way.

Frederick Rowland Emett was born in London in 1906. His father was a journalist and an amateur inventor, and his paternal grandfather a court engraver to Queen Victoria. In the hope of becoming a landscape painter, Emett attended the Birmingham School of Arts and Crafts. The prestigious Royal Academy did accept one of his pictures, but this was the limit of his career as a fine artist; the Depression years of the 1920s and 1930s forced him to earn a living working for a commercial studio. In 1939, one of Emett's friends sent a story to the humorous magazine, *Punch,* and had it accepted. Feeling the prick of emulation, Emett countered with a cartoon, had it rejected, but received a "try again" note from the art director. (This, at the time, was the influential stylist Kenneth Bird, alias Fougasse.)

Emett tried again. Meanwhile, World War II broke out and he became a draughtsman working on the design of aircraft. Soon, though, his cartoons sidled onto the pages of the weekly *Punch*, and established themselves as great favourites. The central creation was the Far Twittering and Oyster Creek Railway, an obscure stretch of line which encompassed such stops as Abbots Grumbling, Friars Ambling and Wisteria Halt. These stations, the steam engines which plied between them, and the staff and passengers, were drawn in a spidery, filigreed style, cross-hatched with great delicacy. The ambience was both gentle and disturbing. The engines were particularly popular, and their authorship unmistakable. Emett's fascination with machinery and gadgetry ranged from the whimsical to images seemingly from the edges of consciousness. The Featherstone-Kite Openwork Basket-weave Mark 2 Gentleman's Flying Machine (to name but one) for example, brings to mind the work of Joan Miró and Paul Klee — particularly the latter's idea of "taking a line for a walk". The drawings were also records of their time. Produced throughout and immediately after the war, they refer to fuel shortages, accommodation difficulties, and reflect an anxious nation. Laughter is encouraged, but a chilly wind blows over the landscapes and the people look melancholy and malnourished. (Some commentators connect this to Emett's discovery of *The New Yorker*'s Saul Steinberg.) There was however another side to the Emett oeuvre. Together with his wife he produced the highly regarded children's story, *Anthony and Antimacassar,* and at the poet Walter da la Mare's request, Emett illustrated a collection of his verses entitled *Peacock Pie.* A natural application of his talent was the design of revues for London West End theatres.

In 1951 the nation was instructed to pep itself up with The Festival of Britain. Events and exhibitions of all sorts were organized across the land, with London as the centre-piece. At the Pleasure Gardens, by the Thames, Emett was invited to design a scaled-up working version of his famous railway. He duly set to work, with the help of a model railway building firm, using amongst other things, kettles, rum barrels and divers' helmets. Two million people came for the ride, and Emett was on his way to a second career. He now became a maker of — to use his own phrase —

Gothick-Kinetic Things. Industry was an eager sponsor. The Shell Company commissioned the Astroterramarre, which was propelled by a rocket and "vaguely held up" by sails, balloons and an umbrella. For Honeywell, Emett produced the elephant-shaped Forget-Me-Not-Computer, which (of course) did not compute, but could do many other things and featured a card-punch system run by electronic woodpeckers. His Exploratory Moon-probe Lunacycle, "Maud", came with Astrocat — "since cats always land on their feet, she is carried to establish which way up gravity is", and was used by the astronomer Patrick Moore to introduce his programmes on the Apollo 13 Moon landing. The Vintage Car, sponsored by Borg Warner, solved the problem of traffic prediction by the simple inclusion of a crystal ball. In 1968, Emett's genius was enshrined in the film *Chitty Chitty Bang Bang,* for which he devised several Things, notably an exquisitely irrelevant egg-boiler.

From the middle of the 1950s, Emett lived in the peace and beauty of a Sussex village, his workshop being a 200-year-old forge nearby. He was doubly blessed inasmuch as his wife was an astute business manager, allowing him to potter on to his heart's content. In 1974, his first permanent construction, The Rhythmical Time Fountain, was unveiled at the Nottingham Victoria Arts Centre, and in 1978 he was awarded the Order of the British Empire. The Victoria and Albert Museum and the Tate Gallery in London acquired some Emett drawings, but the Things are mostly treasured on the other side of the Atlantic — in Toronto, Chicago and in four galleries of Washington's Smithsonian Institute.

The most impressive thing about Emett's creativity is that he could convert the ethereal, feathery quality of his drawings into solid working models and still retain their soul. In this he constrasts rather than compares with William Heath Robinson, his rival fantasist in the realms of unlikely machinery and English whimsy. Where the latter's dreamings are stolidly plausible at first glance, and operated by rotund and earnest personnel, you never feel they are likely to stir at all from the printed page. Emett was once buttonholed at a trade fair in Philadelphia, and asked to defend his current Gothick Kinetic Thing, on display there: "What's the end product?" The considered answer was: "To bring the smallest smile to the eye of the beholder."

Born Frederick Rowland Emett. **Father** A journalist and amateur inventor. **Marriage** Mary, 1949. **Children** One daughter. **Education** Birmingham School of Arts and Crafts. **Career** Draughtsman, Siviter Smith Limited, Birmingham, England, late 1930s; engaged in aircraft design work, World War II; freelance artist, illustrator, cartoonist, inventor, writer, 1939 onwards; regular contributor to *Punch,* from 1939. **Offices and memberships** Fellow of the Society of Industrial Artists. **Awards and honours** Member of the Order of the British Empire, 1978. **Publications** (self-illustrated unless stated, include) (With Mary Emett) *Anthony and Antimacassar* (juvenile), 1943; *Engines, Aunties, and Others: A Book of Curious Happenings,* 1943; *Sidings and Suchlike, Explored by Emett,* 1946; *Home Rails Preferred,* 1947; *Saturday Slow,* 1948; *Far Twittering,* 1949; *High Tea, Infused by Emett,* 1950; *The Emett Festival Railway,* 1951; *Nellie Come Home,* 1952; *New World for Nellie,* 1952; *The Forgotten Tramcar, and Other Drawings,* 1952; *The Best of Rowland Emett,* 1953; *Hobby Horses* (illustrator only), 1958; *The Early Morning Milk Train: The Cream of Emett Railway Drawings,* 1976; *Alarms and Excursions and Other Transports Transfixed by Emett,* 1977; also, Walter de la Mare's *Peacock Pie* (illustrator only); also contributor to *Punch*, *Life*, *Vogue*, *Cosmopolitan*, *Mademoiselle*, *Harper's Bazaar* and other magazines. **Creations** (include) "The Far Twittering to Oyster Creek Railway", Festival of Britain, 1951; Edwardian inventions for film *Chitty Chitty Bang Bang,* 1968; "The Rhythmical Time Fountain", City of Nottingham Victoria Centre, 1974; "Exploratory Moon-probe Lunacycle, 'Maud'"; "Borg Warner Vintage Car of the Future", Museum of Science and Industry, Chicago; "SS Pussiewillow II", commissioned by and exhibited in National Museum of Air and Space, Smithsonian Institution, Washington, DC; "The Featherstone Kite Openwork Basket-weave Mark 2 Gentleman's Flying Machine" and seven other machines, Ontario Science Centre, Toronto; "Pussiewillow III", commissioned by Basildon New Town; "Forget-Me-Not-Computer", designed for Honeywell; "Hush-a-Bye Rocking Chair"; "Hog-muddle Rotary Niggler and Fidgeter"; "Astroterramarre", commissioned by Shell; "Dawn Flight: mist clearing, mallard rising", Tate Gallery, London; "Up Slow Surprised", Tate Gallery, London; stage set for *A Penny A Song*. **Exhibitions** Beetles Gallery, London, 1988; *Too Late for the Past, Too Early for the Future,* Washington, 1988; Ideal Home Exhibition, London, 1989. **Cause of death** Undisclosed, at age 84.

SIR FRANK FIGGURES

British Civil Servant

***Born* London, England, 5 March 1910**

***Died* Uppingham, Leicestershire, 27 November 1990**

It has always been the chief boast of Britain's senior civil servants that they are administrators, not specialists, and that they can administer anything. Never has this been more true than of Frank Figgures, whose public career took on many guises in all of which he excelled, making one wonder why he never reached the topmost pinnacle as head of the Home Service. Instead, he always seemed to be shunted off into a siding, just as the main action was ready to break out somewhere else. Nevertheless, he was a man who greatly enjoyed life, a hard worker who could still manage to get away from the office in time to watch the end of a Test match at Lord's or dash from Bonn to Düsseldorf to the opera, and an enthusiastic walker who always did his daily stint of exercise on Hampstead Heath.

Figgures had read history at New College, Oxford and his first job as a research student was to help the Warden, H.A.L. Fisher, to complete his *History of Europe.* At that time he was tempted to take up a singing career, but the need to earn a secure living in the days of the Great Depression led him to turn instead to the law and he was called to the Bar in 1936. For a short time before World War II he had his first taste of international work with the League of Nations in Geneva.

After war service in the Royal Artillery, Figgures joined the British civil service as a "mature" entrant in 1946. Here there was soon the ideal post waiting for him — as director of the trade and payments division of the Organisation for European Economic Co-operation, the body set up to administer the Marshall Plan of US aid to the war-torn continent. Multilateral trade, so soon after the end of the war, was virtually non-existent and international payments at a standstill with the lack of convertible currency. Figgures was to exercise his ingenuity and negotiating skills in helping to devise the European Payments Union to get round the difficulties. Who knows where events might have taken him, had Britain not decided to abstain from the Messina Conference on the closer integration of western Europe and the signing of the Treaty of Rome? Instead, Figgures was to be consigned to picking up the pieces that remained and negotiating the association of the "Outer Seven" — the European nations which did not join the European Economic Community — into the European Free Trade Association (EFTA) of which he was appointed secretary-general in 1960.

From this vantage point he had high hopes of reaching an overall settlement in the game of "sixes and sevens", but the incoming British Labour government's introduction of a surcharge on all imports in 1964 stymied these chances. Figgures was now the champion of the EFTA partners — an action which laid him open to Prime Minister Wilson's charge that he had "gone native". But Figgures was acting as the true international civil servant; he saw Britain's action as a serious breach of the EFTA Convention and he knew where his duty lay. What a superb president of the Commission of the European Community he would have made, had things turned out differently! But by the time of Britain's entry into the Community he had already reached the civil service age of retirement.

From then on, his international career was over. He was to play a further part on the national stage, however. From 1971 to 1973 he was director-general of the National Economic Development Office, and here again his negotiating skills were brought into play to persuade Vic Feather, general secretary of the Trades Union Congress, Campbell Adamson, director-general of the Confederation of British Industry, and Douglas Allen, head of the Treasury to join with him as "the four wise men" to revamp British industry and fight the rising tide of inflation. The Heath government soon had other ideas for him, however. His success at "Neddy" made him the obvious choice as chairman of the newly formed Pay Board in 1973 to tackle the key problem of wage restraint. The miners' pay claim and the subsequent defeat of the Conservative government killed off the new body within a little over a year, however, and brought Figgures's public career to a sad, and perhaps untimely, end.

In retirement, he continued with his various business directorships and was generous with his advice to younger colleagues in the European arena. In many ways he was a true European — enjoying good food and good wine, an avid lover of opera and a competent linguist. At the same time, he was a devoted British public servant. Not for nothing did he earn the nickname of "Reliable Figgures"!

Born Frank Edward Figgures. **Parents** Frank and Alice Figgures. **Marriages** 1) Aline Frey, 1941; 2) Ismea Barker (née Magill), school matron, 1975. **Children** One son and one daughter from first marriage. **Education** Rutlish School; New College, Oxford, first-class honours in modern history, 1931; Harmsworth Senior Scholar, Merton College, Oxford, 1931; Henry Fellow, Yale Law School, 1933. **Military service** Royal Artillery, 1940–46, became lieutenant-colonel. **Career** Called to the Bar, Lincoln's Inn, 1936; joined His Majesty's Treasury, 1946; director of trade and finance, Organisation for European Economic Co-operation, 1948–51; under-secretary, Her Majesty's Treasury, 1955–60; secretary-general, European Free Trade Association, 1960–65; third secretary, Her Majesty's Treasury, 1965–68, second permanent secretary, 1968–71; director-general, National Economic Development Office, 1971–73; chairman, Pay Board, 1973–74; director, Julius Baer Bank International Limited, 1975–81. **Related activities** Chairman, Central Wagon Company Limited, 1976; member, British Broadcasting Corporation General Advisory Council, 1978–82; member, advisory board, London Branch, Julius Baer, Zürich, 1982–84. **Awards and honours** Companion of the Order of St Michael and St George, 1959; Companion of the Order of the Bath, 1966; Knight Commander of the Order of the Bath, 1970; DSc, Aston University, 1975. **Cause of death** Undisclosed, at age 80.

SIR HUMPHREY GIBBS

British/Rhodesian Colonial Administrator and Farmer

Born **London, England, 22 November 1902**

Died **Harare, Zimbabwe, 4 November 1990**

The end of empire brings many problems, not least for its devoted public servants. And there were problems in plenty for Britain's last governor of Rhodesia as he maintained a beleaguered stand as the Queen's representative after the colony's unilateral declaration of independence in the midst of his governorship. Cut off physically and emotionally from all outside contacts, with no salary, official car, nor police guard, and for a time no public services of water, electricity and telephone, Sir Humphrey Gibbs and his devoted wife managed to keep the flag flying over Government House in Salisbury and the loyal toast to the Queen was drunk at the end of dinner every night — a symbolic gesture of defiance to the rebel Smith regime!

Humphrey Vicary Gibbs was not a Rhodesian by birth. Third son of the first Baron Hunsdon, he was a member of a distinguished banking family in the City of London. Educated at Eton and Trinity College, Cambridge, he might well have followed his brothers into the City. But the outdoor life was what appealed to him and in 1928 he went out to what was then Southern Rhodesia to become a well-known farmer and conservationist, and ultimately president of the Rhodesian National Farmers Union. Inevitably he was persuaded into politics and was elected to the Legislative Assembly in 1951. But a five-year term was enough for him and he returned with relief to his farm in 1956. As the then prime minister, Sir Godfrey Huggins, said: "He was far too honest a man to remain in politics for long".

Nevertheless, his outstanding qualities of character and his distinguished looks and manner — he stood out literally (at 6 feet, 3 inches tall) from all his fellows — made him a natural choice as the colony's first Rhodesian governor in 1959, an office which he accepted with some reluctance but which he filled with dignity and success during the first six years. But from 1964 on, with the premiership of Ian Smith, the anti-colonial struggle developed, and in November 1965 Gibbs found himself at the heart of a political and constitutional storm, with the Rhodesia Front government's unilateral declaration of independence. It was an awkward position for the Governor. He was constitutionally obliged to act on the advice of his ministers and sign the declaration of an act of emergency which preceded UDI, but at the same time his loyalty to the Queen made it impossible for him to recognize the validity of the declaration of independence. It was also a difficult position emotionally. Gibbs had become a Rhodesian citizen and Rhodesia was the land to which he now belonged and to which he was greatly attached. But he also had his sense of duty and loyalty to the Queen whose representative he was. There was never any doubt as to his choice. In the name of the Queen he dismissed Ian Smith from office, to be dismissed in turn himself and ordered to leave Government House. This he refused to do, despite all the hardships and indignities this brought upon him. He resolutely remained in post, and throughout the various attempts at negotiation between the British and Rhodesian governments he brought what little influence he had to bear on the situation.

The Smith government's decision in 1969 to make Rhodesia a republic evoked mixed feelings in the Governor: disappointment that no settlement had been reached, but at the same time relief that he could now abandon his post and return to his farm. But this was no longer the peaceful refuge of before; the mounting civil war turned his farmhouse increasingly into a fortress, and though things improved after independence, he was at last persuaded by his family to sell up and move into the capital. Here he continued to take an active part in business and in his various charitable interests, particularly in the education field and in support of the Anglican cathedral in Harare.

Some have seen Sir Humphrey's defiance of the Smith regime as a futile gesture. The efforts made to win him over to the rebel side and the indignities to which he was subjected when they failed, would gainsay this interpretation. Throughout, his steadfastness and courage earned him widespread admiration and respect for his integrity. It lies with future historians to judge how far his stand helped in the end to bring a Zimbabwean government to successful independence.

Born Humphrey Vicary Gibbs. **Father** First Baron Hunsdon. **Marriage** Molly Peel Nelson, 1934. **Children** Five sons. **Education** Eton College, Windsor, Berkshire; Trinity College, Cambridge. **Career** Farmer, Bulawayo, Southern Rhodesia, now Zimbabwe, 1928–83; united party member, legislative assembly for Wankie, 1951–56; governor of Rhodesia, 1959–69. **Other activities** Active supporter, charity, Beit Trust. **Offices and memberships** President, Rhodesian National Farmers Union. **Awards and honours** Officer of the Order of the British Empire, 1959; Knight Commander, Order of St Michael and St George, 1960; Knight Commander, Royal Victorian Order, 1965; Privy Councillor, 1969; Knight Grand Cross of the Royal Victorian Order, 1969; LLD, Birmingham, 1969; Doctor of Civil Law, East Anglia, 1969. **Cause of death** Complications from influenza, at age 87.

HOWARD HARTOG

British Impresario

***Born* London, England, 2 March 1913**

***Died* London, England, 27 November 1990**

The Svengali syndrome, the Diaghilev/Nijinsky relationship, haunts the popular concept of how an artist's agent operates. The public eye sees him as the all-powerful manipulator, assuming total control of the protégé's life, loves and art — usually in that order. Seldom is any thought given to exactly how this mythical manager-beast acquires the know-how to exercise its power, nor how the basic economics of the enterprise work. Ultimately every performer is judged on the basis of their own technique and musicianship. But the demands of acquiring and maintaining these attributes leave little time for the practicalities of life, and not everyone possesses that rare quality, personal insight. However high personal standards, it is unusual for artists to have sufficient detachment to make certain decisions vital for their careers, particularly at that crucial stage when — say — a soprano may feel she can do anything, regardless of whether it lies in the right part of her voice so it will develop without strain.

Ironically, Howard Hartog, one of the best of artists' managers and the guardian of so many outstanding careers, insisted that nothing in his own was actually planned by him — it only happened that way — "I just fell into it" he would insist. But what did not "just happen" was the way in which he exploited the chances presented him. This talent remained unguessed at until the catalyst of World War II and the often bizarre circumstances of its aftermath. After Harrow and Oxford he drifted into publishing at the suggestion of Herbert Read, the art historian, whom he acknowledged as a major influence. He spent a short period in Norway with Tanum in Oslo. But it was conscription in 1940 which was the unlikely gateway to his future obsession with music. He had already in his college days amassed a large collection of gramophone records, and had been able to experience all aspects of the lively atmosphere surrounding the arts in pre-war London, ranging from Lotte Lenya to Toscanini. His Dutch father and mother had chosen to live in England before World War I but were not in the least insular in outlook. They brought up Howard to have the same cosmopolitan attitude, and he was present at the first English performance of Alban Berg's *Wozzeck,* conducted by Sir Adrian Boult for the British Broadcasting Corporation in 1936. This opened Hartog's ears to the excitement of contemporary music — he later described it as "a complete revelation". It was the first sign of an interest which was to stand him in good stead. In 1940 he joined the British Army and exchanged a comfortable life in London for boredom in North Africa. He was trained in Signals, however, and was sent to pass on his knowledge of this technology of communications, then in its infancy, to the American Army in Italy, which he worked his way up attending opera *en route.* The San Carlo Opera House at Naples continued to function, usually with Captain Hartog in the audience (and on one occasion with two Captains Hartog, when his brother's unit arrived at the coast). At the end of the war in 1945 he was posted to Hamburg. He had a lot of spare time, and on discovering that the Army Education Centre had a hall and a grand piano he began to wonder what he could do to promote live music for the troops rather than routine gramophone recitals. It seemed to offer possibilities for chamber music. He found a string quartet only just released from a concentration camp, and a pianist — starved and with dreadful instruments, it was at least a start. He was introduced to James Gibb, a pianist attached to the British Forces (Radio) Network, of which the music section was run by the conductor Trevor Harvey. Some good recitals were the result, and their success came to the notice of one of the conductors of the Hamburg Opera. Ferdinand Leitner asked why Hartog did not use any German artists. The reason being that there were no official funds with which to pay them, Leitner pointed out that they were very short of food and would be happy to accept a decent meal or two in lieu of fees. Hartog had access to ample supplies of rations and the bargain was struck. Instead of gramophone records of Beethoven's Sixth Symphony played in the wrong order the troops were given a relatively broad selection of live artists, and the average audience increased from six to 200.

The news spread, and Hartog found himself offered a post he would not have dreamed of applying for — that of running the music department of Nord-West Deutsche Rundfunk, the German radio. It was a case of being in the right place at the right time, but he nevertheless felt inadequate. The outgoing music officer suggested he seek the opinion of Hans Schmidt-Isserstedt, director of the Radio Orchestra, who looked at him with his pale blue eyes and said drily, "If we don't get you, we might get somebody a bloody sight worse." Hartog decided there was nothing to lose — he was at least a few steps ahead in that he had been able to enjoy a wider experience of current music-making than they had at that time. He thus assumed charge of policy and administration for a full orchestra and chorus which gave public concerts as well as studio ones. Young and relatively inexperienced, they had never, for example, played Beethoven's Seventh Symphony.

By virtue of his appointment Major Hartog now had an allowance from the British government to enable him to promote British music abroad. He put on a performance of Michael Tippett's Double Concerto, and more surprisingly, the first performance of the choral cantata *A Child of our Time* — with a German choir singing a pacifist work in English — in 1946. It was a sensation, and brought Hartog to the composer's attention. Britten's *Sinfonia da Reguiem* was another unconventional work performed, and his *Variations on a Theme of Frank Bridge,* with its gentle but audacious mockery of established European styles.

He took advantage of other accidental circumstances which were to have repercussions on his future career. The Hamburg Opera lost its intendant, but almost immediately a friend of Schmidt-Isserstedt, Gunther Rennert, turned up in the city. Hartog introduced him to the British officer-in-charge, and he was appointed with a speed rarely achieved these days. Later he was to become a producer renowned throughout the opera-houses of Europe, including Britain's Glyndebourne, and a valuable friend to have in the eventual placing of Hartog's singers. At Hamburg he wanted to take a contemporary opera into the repertoire, and was persuaded by Hartog to put on Britten's *Peter Grimes,* a great success.

The British Foreign Office's allowance to enable Hartog to hire British music was generous, in fact more than he could use. He wheedled his way round the powers that be and obtained permission to divert some of it to music by non-British composers — Bartok, Stravinsky, Shostakovitch. Britten's music publishers had come over to Hamburg for the performances of *Peter Grimes,* giving Hartog the chance to ask them for the first performance in Germany of Richard Strauss's orchestral lament for the destruction of Germany — *Metamorphosen.*

Hartog was approached by the BBC with a view to an appointment with the Corporation, on condition that he serve a year in Graz in sole charge of the small radio station there. He was interviewed no fewer than three times in London by their Appointments Board, only to be ultimately rejected. Some say he was too much of an individualist for the Corporation. It was the BBC's loss. In fact events were — yet again — to turn to Hartog's advantage and give him as much influence on the musical world as he could possibly have wished.

Without a job to go to in 1949 he returned to London where he was visited by Schmidt-Isserstedt, who expressed a wish to see Michael Tippett. Hartog had not yet himself met him, but arranged a lunch — Tippett was equally pleased to meet the man who had championed his music in Germany, and suggested he contact his publishers, the London branch of the German-based house of Schott, where there was a very suitable vacancy. He was put in charge of the contemporary music list, then headed by Hindemith and Orff, with Tippett the only British composer. Hartog soon managed to change this emphasis, at least in London, and in the course of time Harrison Birtwistle, Peter Maxwell Davies, Peter Racine Fricker, Alexander Goehr, Ian Hamilton and Humphrey Searle joined the list. Constantly enlarging his knowledge of what was going on, he met Messiaen (the teacher of Pierre Boulez), Stockhausen, Henze, in fact anyone who was anyone. After a productive 12 years, however, Mainz decided to take a firmer hold on its British subsidiary, and Hartog found his activities curtailed, but not before he had become a conspicuous figure in Britain and the continent.

In 1961 Joan Ingpen invited him to join her music agency, which she had run singlehanded since 1946. He was the first person to share her philosophy, "the idea of putting the pursuit of ideal conditions for a singer, conductor or instrumentalist before the pursuit of a 10 per cent agency fee." Not a year had passed before he found himself in sole charge, Joan Ingpen having accepted a post at the Royal Opera House. Once again he took this stroke of luck in his stride. Some of her artists left, of course, but those who stayed included Joan Sutherland, David Ward, Rudolf Kempe, Donald McIntyre and Elizabeth Söderström. He himself had just "discovered" Alfred Brendel. It demonstrated his ability to convey a tremendous sense of security, a feeling that trust in him would reap its reward. He looked after Jessye Norman for several years, and other artists included Yvonne Minton, Jamis Martin, Heinz Holliger, various string quartets, and young conductors such as Richard Armstrong and Mark Elder. Of the older generation he represented Pierre Boulez and George Solti. Boulez's attitude to contemporary music, his own and that of others, accorded perfectly with Hartog's and he became a close personal friend.

Such friendships were not allowed to compromise artistic decisions. Hartog was always true to himself. He possessed an unerring perception of quality and an uncanny instinct for the right course of action. With an encyclopaedic knowledge of repertoire and performance, could marry the two with a speed and accuracy which would have left the latest generation of computers standing. He took the attitude that the truth never hurt anyone and he would not waste time, his own or anyone else's, in beating about the bush. Hence the matter-of-fact telephone calls, usually abruptly terminated (you had to be in training to put the receiver down before he did) and the shortest letters ever written — sometimes just "Yes", or "No". Airs and graces played no part in his life. Without any formal training in music he was seldom found wanting in judgement, having a knack of spotting the potential in a young artist and systematically developing it in the way best for that particular person without forcing either technique or personality at an unhealthy rate. In Joan Ingpen's words, he taught singers in particular "to guard the capital while spending the income of their musical talent". He kept a constant eye on their progress and no engagement was remote enough for him to miss it. Consequently his artists felt continuously supported, and that he knew as much as they did about themselves; his candour was welcomed as enlightening and constructive. The globe-trotting could have been some excuse for his rumpled appearance, redolent of cigar-smoke and ash, and while good food meant a great deal to him, quite a lot landed on his suits. What his invariably *soignée* mother thought of it has not been recorded, but while she was staying at the Hotel Scribe in Paris his tousled figure was announced to her thus: "Madame — il y a un individu que se *dit* votre fils..." [Madam, there is someone here who *says* he's your son.] Yet he had an acute visual sense as far as fine art was concerned, and a keen interest in Romanesque architecture. On a different plane, he delighted in discussing soccer tactics, and Chelsea Football Club lost an enthusiastic supporter when they dropped out of the First Division.

Undoubtedly he felt the most important theme of his life was the promotion of new music. It saddened him that current press opinion, with some honourable exceptions, seemed to have recoiled from what it called inaccessibility. People became discouraged too soon, and gave up the attempt to widen the scope of appreciation, instead of having the patience essential for the assimilation of new styles and sounds. It was a negative approach found in other branches of the arts, reminding him of the worst aspects of the 1930s with their admiration of the facile and gaudy — instant culture, swallowed too quickly and ill-digested. Taking the easy way out was not acceptable to Howard Hartog, and no one has ever done more for his artists, the maintenance of high standards and the cause of contemporary music. His was a major influence over four decades, and will have helped shape the attitudes of performers, conductors and administrators for some time to come.

Born Howard Hartog. **Parents** Simon, managing director of food importing company, and Elizabeth Amelia Hartog. **Marriages** 1) Simone Campeau, 1939; 2) Margaret Kitchin, concert pianist, 1951. **Children** One son, Simon, by first marriage. **Education** Harrow School, London; New College Oxford, read Roman history. **Military service** Served in North Africa and Italy, World War II, became major. **Career** Worked in publishing section, Tanum, Oslo; in charge of music programmes, Nord-West Deutscher Rundfunk, Hamburg, 1945–47; in charge of music programmes, radio station, Graz, Austria, 1948; promotions manager, Schott's, London, 1949–61; proprietor, Ingpen and Williams, 1961 onwards. **Offices and memberships** Chairman: Society for the Promotion of New Music, International Society for Contemporary Music. **Publication** (Editor) *European Music in the 20th Century,* 1957. **Cause of death** Cancer of the pancreas, at age 77.

ROBERT HOFSTADTER

American Physicist

***Born* Manhattan, New York, 5 February 1915**

***Died* Stanford, California, 17 November 1990**

Science advances at such a rate that it is not often a scientist gains a lead that lasts for years, but in the field of analysing the nuclei of molecules, Robert Hofstadter managed to do just that. Over almost a decade he, with the team he led, was able to bring out more and more precise measurements of the size and structure of nuclei and the protons and neutrons found in them, and no one else could catch him up. For his pioneering work he was awarded a Nobel Prize, the highest possible recognition of an outstanding achievement. Yet his work on another discovery, the inorganic transparent scintillator, he considered very much more important. It is still in use, and has led to discoveries of subatomic particles even smaller than protons and neutrons.

Robert Hofstadter was born and educated in New York, the third of four children of a salesman. He followed his very able brother to City College of New York, wanting, like him, to study literature and philosophy. "My earliest ambition as I entered", he said later, "was to be a literary figure, a writer, and my model at that time was Dostoevski." But he obtained a "C" in writing. He also considered philosophy. But an inspiring young physics teacher convinced him that "the laws of physics could be tested, and those of philosophy could not". So he concentrated on physics and mathematics, won the Kenyon Prize for outstanding work, and went on to Princeton to study for his PhD "because Albert Einstein was there".

When the USA entered World War II, Hofstadter joined the National Bureau of Standards, where he helped develop the "proximity fuse". This is a small radar set in the nose of an anti-aircraft shell which detects when it is passing near a target and detonates the shell.

In 1944 the first V1, Hitler's first "secret weapon", landed on Britain. The V1s were pilotless, jet-propelled aircraft, each carrying nearly a ton of high explosive. They caused a great deal of damage, and the threat carried by the sound of their engines, which cut out before they crashed to the ground, caused a lot of distress. Thousands of proximity fuses were sent to Britain, and they helped destroy many "buzz-bombs" or "doodlebugs" as the Londoners called them, making the attack much less effective.

Hofstadter's next post was assistant chief physicist at Norden Laboratories Corporation in New York. After three years, he returned to teaching and research at Princeton with an assistant professorship. This was where he invented the inorganic, transparent scintillator in 1948. The scintillator emits light when a charged particle crosses it, the amount of light being proportional to the energy lost by the particle through ionization. If the particle is stopped by the scintillator, the light is a measure of its total energy. It can even be used for neutral particles like X-rays and gamma rays which convert in the scintillator into charged particles. Hofstadter used sodium iodide, a crystal laced with thallium, for the purpose, and arrays of this crystal form the sensitive surfaces used in the "spectrometers" attached to particle accelerators up to the present day.

Hofstadter left Princeton to join Stanford University in 1950 as an assistant professor. While driving across to his new post he stayed with a friend in St Louis, who suggested he use his skill with detectors to find how electrons "bounce" off objects such as nuclei. Experiments of this sort have led to several of the most important advances in physics this century. It was by firing particles from disintegrating radioactive substances at thin sheets of gold that Lord Rutherford found that material is largely space, and that molecules, instead of being solid, have minute nuclei with electrons circling round them. The nucleus was tens of thousands of times smaller than the atom. What Hofstadter's friend was suggesting to him was that he should use a similar technique to see how solid the nucleus is.

By careful measurement of deflections, Hofstadter and his team were able to announce their first results in 1953. The nucleus, they had found, is not a solid point, but consisted of a densely packed core and gradually thinned out towards its boundary. The core was found to be 130 times denser than water. A drop of water as dense would weigh 2,000,000 tons. To discover this the team used the university's linear accelerator to fire electrons at targets containing the atomic nuclei being investigated. The electrons coming through were counted and their deflections measured using an enormous scattering machine developed by the team. In passing through the target the electrons had been deflected by the electrical fields of the particles within the nuclei. From the directions of the emerging electrons Hofstadter could distinguish the positions of the nuclear particles, so that he could construct a model of the nucleus.

To progress further, Hofstadter reckoned a much more powerful particle accelerator would be needed, and although at the time they were housed in large rooms, he astonished colleagues by arguing the need for one a mile long. As early as 1954 he pressed for a Stanford Linear Accelerator Facility (SLAC) to be built, but his ideas were disregarded for a time.

Methodical and independent, he chose his team carefully. They built a whole series of machines and instruments, increasing the sensitivity of the basic experiment. Over a period of years, Hofstadter and his team came to determine the size and shape of protons and neutrons for the first time. Both particles are about 7×10^{-14} centimetres in diameter, with a dense core. Hofstadter explained the structure and charges of these particles in terms of mesons, even smaller nuclear particles. As a result of all this work, Hofstadter was awarded a share of the Nobel Prize for Physics in 1961.

At Stanford, plans for the building of SLAC and its accelerator were now formulated, and they caused a difference of opinion. Hofstadter wanted it to be Stanford-dominated and therefore under his control, while others felt it should be a more community-orientated national laboratory. Hofstadter lost the argument. The accelerator was built — two miles long and called "The Monster" — and Hofstadter boycotted the ground-cutting ceremony. The split in the faculty was to last some time, but the building of SLAC was in itself a tribute to Hofstadter and his pioneering work.

Teaching was as important a part of his work as research, his courses varying from graduate level to a non-mathematical introductory physics course known as "Physics for Poets". He reckoned he taught over 10,000 students in his time.

Yet his interests were far broader than science. He had a wide taste in music, and enjoyed sports and photography. "I have always loved the outdoors," he said, "mountains, lakes and oceans, and in fact I do a little farming and ranching in Northern California. I might have made my way in any one of these activities, but of course I don't know how satisfying it might have been on a lifelong scale. But I have never regretted the academic life: a life of learning, teaching and research."

He continued at Stanford, and at the time of his death he was working on a project to launch a gamma ray detector in space. Many of his students have distinguished themselves, some doing pioneering work on the SLAC accelerator. The day before he died Stanford held a celebration in honour of Jerome Friedman, Henry Kendall and Richard Taylor, who shared the 1990 Nobel Prize for Physics for continuing at SLAC research opened up by Hofstadter's great work. Unfortunately he was unable to attend, spending the day in hospital, but he sent them his best wishes.

Born Robert Hofstadter. **Parents** Louis, salesman, and Henrietta (Koenigsberg) Hofstadter. **Marriage** Nancy Givan, 1942. **Children** Douglas, Laura and Mary. **Education** City College of New York, BS (magna cum laude), 1935; Princeton University, New Jersey, MA, PhD, 1938. **Career** Proctor Research Fellow, Princeton University, 1938–39; Harrison Research Fellow, University of Pennsylvania, 1939–40; instructor in physics, 1940–41, instructor, City College of New York, 1941–42; physicist, National Bureau of Standards, 1942–43; assistant chief physicist, Norden Laboratory Corporation, New York, 1943–46; assistant professor of physics, Princeton University, 1946–50; associate professor of physics, Stanford University, 1950–54, professor, 1954–71, director, high energy physics laboratory, 1967–74, Max H. Stein Professor of Physics, 1971–85, emeritus professor, 1985–90. **Related activities** Associate editor, *Physical Review,* 1951–53; co-editor, *Investigation in Physics,* from 1951; associate editor, *Review of Scientific Instruments,* 1954–56; editor, *Reviews of Modern Physics,* from 1958; on board of governors, Weizmann Institute of Science, 1967–90; consultant on laser fusion, KMS Fusion, 1972–80; associate, Linus Pauling Institute of Science and Medicine, 1974–90; on board of directors, Israel Institute of Technology, 1977–90. **Offices and memberships** Member: National Academy of Science, American Association for the Advancement of Science; fellow: American Physical Society, American Academy of Arts and Sciences, Physical Society of London, Italian Physical Society. **Awards and honours** Kenyon Prize, City College of New York, 1935; Coffin fellowship, General Electric Company, 1936; Proctor fellowship, 1937; Guggenheim fellowship, 1958–59, 1974–75; California Scientist of Year, 1958; (with Rudolf Mössbauer) Nobel Prize for Physics, 1961; honorary LLD, City College of New York, 1962; National Science Foundation fellowship, 1965–66; honorary DS, University of Padua, 1965; honorary DSc, Carleton University, 1967; honorary doctorate, University of Clermont-Ferrand, 1967; Humboldt fellowship,

1981. **Publications** (include) (With Robert Herman) *High-Energy Electron Scattering Tables,* 1960. **Cause of death** Heart disease, at age 75.

MEIR KAHANE

American/Israeli Rabbi and Politician

Born **Brooklyn, New York, 1 August 1932**

Died **Manhattan, New York, 5 November 1990**

Rabbi Meir Kahane, founder of the Jewish Defense League, was an ultra-Orthodox Zionist with fanatically right-wing views, a charismatic personality and a good deal of physical courage. The extreme violence of the policies he advocated made him seem to most, however, always more of a liability than an asset to the causes he espoused. And although at one time he attracted a certain amount of grass-roots support both in Israel and the US he had, in recent years, been cold-shouldered by the Establishment in both countries. It is therefore questionable whether the Arab assassin's bullet that finally killed him in Manhattan actually put a stop to anything more than a rather embarrassing side-show on the fringes of Jewish politics.

Born in the prosperous Jewish suburb of Flatbush in Brooklyn, Kahane's childhood was, in his own words, "very pleasant". He himself, it would seem, was not personally exposed to any overt anti-Semitism. Zionism, however, was in his bloodstream. He grew up among Zionists, nurtured by his father's stories and was later to boast that Ze'ev Jabotinsky — founder of Herut (the right-wing freedom movement) had been a house-guest in his youth. At the age of 15 Kahane was among a group of youths hurling eggs and tomatoes at the visiting British foreign secretary, Ernest Bevin, in protest at British policy on Jewish immigration to Palestine. In 1946 he joined the youth movement of Herut and, around this time, was seen by Flatbush neighbours parading a group of Jewish youths dressed provocatively in Nazi-type brown shirted uniforms. It was a presage of things to come.

"Copy thine enemy" was always to be one of the mature Kahane's most sacred precepts. Deeply affected by the fate of Europe's Jews in the Holocaust he determined on changing the attitudes of all who saw or accepted the role of the Jew as the victim. "No anti-Semitism was ever created", he maintained, "by a Jew who fought back". "I don't think", he told a *New York Post* interviewer in 1971, "the growth of Israel has made anti-Semites love us more, but it has certainly instilled in them a grudging respect — and perhaps fear. And I'd rather be respected, feared and safe, than loved, with eulogies."

In the meantime, however, Kahane pursued the studies expected by his parents, gaining a BA in political science at Brooklyn, and LLB at New York Law School and finally an MA in international affairs from New York University. He was ordained as a rabbi in the late 1950s and began work at the Howard Beach Jewish Center in Queens, New York. Finding, however, that his views were too Orthodox for his congregation he left, went to Israel for a few months and, on his return, embarked on a new career as a journalist writing for the *Jewish Press* (an English-language weekly published in Brooklyn) under the name of "Michael King".

As Michael King, Kahane led a strange and shadowy life during most of the 1960s, maintaining a number of different apartments and carrying on undercover assignments for both the US government and for Mossad, secret service branch of the Israeli government. He became a leading advocate of the war in Vietnam and in 1967 published a book, *The Jewish Stake in Vietnam,* urging all Jews to support the war effort. Appalled by the rising crime and anti-Semitism in the poorer, mainly black, suburbs of New York, he formed, in 1968, the Jewish Defense League, an armed self-defence movement based, he frankly admitted, on Black Panther tactics. In pursuit of the cause of Jews persecuted and denied rights of emigration from the Soviet Union, he organized a noisy series of anti-Soviet demonstrations in 1970 and 1971, which culminated in fire-bombs in Soviet offices and the much-publicized release of rats during a New York performance by the Bolshoi Ballet.

Being arrested on charges of breaking the peace was no new experience for Kahane but in 1971, after eight months in prison and a suspended prison sentence for the illegal manufacture of explosives, he suddenly announced his intention of moving to Israel to set up an international Jewish Defense League. The next shock event was his election to the Knesset in 1984 as leader of his Kach Party. "We will drive this country crazy, we will make this country Jewish again", promised an exultant Kahane.

The policies of Kach did, indeed, threaten for a time to drive Israel pretty crazy. Using the same clenched fist symbol and "Never Again" slogan adopted by the Jewish Defense League, Kach preached a policy of forcible "transfer", that is to say expulsion of all Arabs from Israel. Realizing that democracy could not work in favour of the Jewish minority Kahane decided that Jewishness was of much greater importance. In a solution described by the London *Times* as "chillingly reminiscent" of Hitler's Nuremberg Laws of 1935, he proposed a ban on sexual relations between Jews and Arabs and the confinement of non-Jews to ghettos lest they pollute "the authentic Jewish spirit". Alliance between Kach and other right-wing parties was clearly out of the question. The unacceptability of Kach policies, together with the suggestion from surveys conducted among Israel's youth that many of them were at least attracted by some of his ideas, shocked the ruling Likud party into banning Kach from the 1988 election on grounds of racism.

Kahane described himself as "a proud Jew who walked alone". He and his supporters suggest that his only crime was to say what others thought. Therein, of course, lay his danger. On the other hand it should be remembered that America imprisoned him as a law-breaker, Israel banned him as a racist and the Israeli press unanimously agreed to deny him all further publicity after 1988. "Copy thine enemy" was eventually seen to do nothing more than to reduce Kahane himself to the level of his enemies. What is more, as Michael Sheridan put it in the London *Independent*'s obituary, "for many Israelis his racial hatred, his bigotry and his exultation in violence were an affront to the memory of those who perished in Europe and his constant exploitation of their doom a dishonour to their sacrifice."

Born Martin David Kahane. **Pseudonym** Michael King. **Parents** Charles, rabbi, and Sonia (Trainin) Kahane. **Marriage** Libby Blum, 1955. **Children** Two sons and two daughters. **Education** Yeshiva of Flatbush, Brooklyn, New York; Talmudical high school; Yeshiva Mirrer (rabbinical school), Brooklyn; Brooklyn College, BA, 1954; New York Law School, LLB, 1956; graduate school, New York University, MA in international affairs, 1957. **Career** Ordained an Orthodox rabbi, began to use name Meir, 1957; rabbi: Howard Beach Jewish Center, Queens, New York, on kibbutz, Israel, 1963, Rochdale Village, Queens, New York, 1967–68; columnist under name Michael King, *Jewish Press,* 1963, editor until 1968; founder with Bertram Zweibon and Mort Dolinsky, Jewish Defense League, 1968, activist in United States, 1968 onwards, in Israel, 1971 onwards; member of one-man Kach Party, Knesset, Israel, 1984–88. **Related activities** Researcher, consultant, government agencies, mid–1960s; founder, with Joseph Churba, Consultants Research Associates, 1965; with Churba established Crossroads with Information Incorporated, 1967. **Publications** (With Joseph Churba) *The Jewish Stake in Vietnam,* 1967; *Never Again!,* 1971; *Time to Go Home,* 1972; *Our Challenge: The Chosen Land,* 1974; *Why Be Jewish?: Intermarriage, Assimilation, and Alienation,* 1977; *They Must Go,* 1981. **Cause of death** Assassination by shooting, at age 58.

RICHARD LEWIS

British Tenor

***Born* Manchester, Lancashire, 10 May 1914**

***Died* Old Willingdon, East Sussex, 13 November 1990**

There's no guarantee that the musical precocity of a boy treble will develop consistently into adulthood; vocal cords slacken, the throat enlarges and adolescence can close doors as well as open them. Richard Lewis, however, negotiated the obstacles on the road to maturity as skilfully as Tamino in *The Magic Flute,* a role he was subsequently to make his own. The boy Thomas Thomas (his real name) seems to have been the Aled Jones of his time — in 1930 alone he won 13 first prizes and one second out of a total of 14 festivals. Blessed with diligence and intelligence as well as an exceptional voice, he left school at the age of 16, but while working in the office of a Manchester cotton manufacturer obtained a scholarship to the Royal Manchester College of Music, the result of studying harmony and counterpoint in his spare time. There he worked with Norman Allin, himself the possessor of a beautiful and sonorous bass voice; but World War II intervened after only four terms at the College. Lewis spent a year with ENSA, the British wartime organization responsible for co-ordinating entertainment and education for the armed forces, and in 1941 fitted in his first experience of professional opera, two months with the indefatigable Carl Rosa Company, which continued to bring opera to some unlikely places and in often uncomfortable conditions. For them he sang Rossini's Almaviva, and Pinkerton in *Madame Butterfly,* but had to doff his make-believe naval uniform for the real one of the Royal Corps of Signals. The postponement of formal vocal training did not prevent his singing while in the Army, in Brussels, Antwerp, Liége, Copenhagen and Hamburg, and it was the capital of Norway rather than London which saw his début. Fortunately he was under the command of a sympathetic general who gave him every opportunity to exercise his talent. A report on the very favourable impression he made in Europe came to the notice of Rudolf Bing, then in charge of the Glyndebourne Opera Company, Sussex. It described Lewis as "a really excellent tenor who looks wonderful, has a very beautiful voice, is a superb musician and has absolute mastery of Mozart's style." Superlatives indeed, but entirely accurate, and they were to remain so for the rest of his career. The immediate result was to give him the chance to sing Ottavio in *Don Giovanni* with the Company, not in Sussex but at the Edinburgh Festival in 1948.

After the war he continued his studies, again with Norman Allin but at the Royal Academy of Music, London, and made his first British concert appearance at Brighton in 1947, in Britten's *Serenade for Tenor, Horn and Strings.* The fact that this was a comparatively new work, written in 1943, was a sign of the enterprise and versatility he was to display throughout his life. Of Welsh parentage and born in the north of England, he might have been expected to concentrate on oratorio, but a strong sense of drama and a very positive stage presence proved otherwise. Only a few months after his performance of the *Serenade* he stepped into Peter Pears's shoes as Britten's Peter Grimes, one performance at Covent Garden Opera House in November 1947 and others on the Royal Opera's subsequent provincial tour. He shared with Pears the ability to emphasize the poetic aspect of the uncouth fisherman's character (and some, indeed, preferred his acting to that of the role's creator). Be that as it may, it was in another Britten role, the Male Chorus in *The Rape of Lucretia,* that he made his first appearance at Glyndebourne itself in the same year.

Although he and Pears were equally suitable and successful in many works, there were certain differences between their voices and methods of vocal production. They both knew how to make the words work for them in facilitating a smooth legato line, and both possessed a clarity of tone which makes a high tenor or soprano sound even more elevated than the averagely endowed singer. Lewis's tone colour and the distinct quality of his diction revealed his Welsh origins. In the lower registers his voice was more robust than Pears's, and strongly projected. Although he was certainly not a "Heldentenor" in the strict Wagnerian sense, his voice had a ringing, heroic substance absolutely appropriate for Walton's Troilus and for Tippett's Achilles. At the same time he was the perfect Mozartian, with an even, mellifluous quality of great lyrical elegance as well as stamina. He was an ideal Idomeneo and in 1951 sang that title role in its first British professional presentation, which took place at Glyndebourne in the historical production by Carl Ebert, of which his recording under Sir John Pritchard gives a very good impression. The same year he sang Tamino in *The Magic Flute* at Covent Garden.

Oratorio and other concert opportunities were not disregarded, however, and there were many fine performances of Elgar's Gerontius, in the noble tradition of Gervase Elwes, John Coates and Heddle Nash. The passion he could display on stage was an important factor in his portrayal of Gerontius's progress towards his Maker, with its mixture of doubt and faith, humility and striving. But not only British music demonstrated his skill — he was among the best of those who could essay the taxing tenor line of Mahler's *Das Lied von der Erde,* and he was a notable Evangelist in Bach's *St Matthew Passion.*

His obvious musical intelligence brought him many of the most important *premières* of the time. Besides Achilles in Tippett's *King Priam* he created the part of Mark, the hero of the earlier opera of 1955, *The Midsummer Marriage.* Equally well taken was the role of Aaron in Schoenberg's *Moses and Aaron* at Covent Garden in 1965, Boston in 1966 and the Paris Opera in 1973. Other modern roles included the Captain in Berg's *Wozzeck* and Alwa in *Lulu.* Stravinsky chose him for the first performance of his *Canticum Sacrum* at Venice, in 1956. He had been an admirable choice for Tom Rakewell in Stravinsky's *The Rake's Progress* at Glyndebourne, where (after Hugues Cuenod) he holds the record for the singer who has sung there most often — over 350 performances. Once more, the range of his characterization and musical versatility was breathtaking, embracing Ferrando in *Così fan tutte,* Florestan in *Fidelio,* Nero in *Incoronazione di Poppea,* Bacchus in *Ariadne auf Naxos* and Admète in *Alceste.*

Another Britten role in which he excelled was Captain Vere in *Billy Budd,* an interpretation which was one of his finest, a combination of beauty, integrity and the human dilemma which he was to take all over the world. In the United States he sang in its American *première* with the American Opera Society at Carnegie Hall in 1966. He appeared frequently in concert and oratorio there, and had a long and happy association with the San Francisco Opera beginning with Troilus in 1955, and including the parts of Don José in *Carmen,* Pinkerton in *Madam Butterfly,* des Grieux in *Manon,* Eisenstein in *Die Fledermaus,* Jenik in *The Bartered Bride,* Offenbach's Hoffman and the Simpleton in *Boris Godunov* — another astonishingly diverse list which hardly seems feasible for one man. In England the extensive role call included Gilbert and Sullivan recordings for Sir Malcolm Sargent — he was a particularly beguiling Marco in *The Gondoliers.*

It is rare to find such variety of accomplishment achieved with such a breadth of intelligence, allied to a vocal instrument of graceful distinction. Even at the age of 65 he was able to fulfil the demanding, important role of Eumaeus, the old shepherd in Monteverdi's *Il ritorno d'Ulisse in patria,* with a slight dryness of tone but little diminution in strength, as can be heard on the recording of the Glyndebourne performance. It was a voice which lingers in the memory and, for anyone who heard it either on stage, in the concert-hall or on record, will not easily be effaced from the mind, however accomplished its successors may be.

Born Thomas Thomas. **Marriages** 1) Mary Lingard; 2) Elizabeth Robertson, soprano, 1963. **Children** Nigel from first marriage and Michael from second marriage. **Education** Royal Manchester College of Music, scholar, studied under Norman Allin; Royal Academy of Music,

London, studied under Norman Allin. **Military service** Entertainments National Service Association, 1939; Royal Corps of Signals, 1941–45. **Career** Boy soprano using name Thomas Thomas; clerk, cotton manufacturers; operatic début with Carl Rosa Opera Company, 1941; performed in Denmark and Norway, 1945, 1946; British concert début, Britten's *Serenade for Tenor, Horn and Strings,* Brighton, 1947; Glyndebourne début, Male Chorus in *The Rape of Lucretia,* 1947; Covent Garden début, title role in *Peter Grimes,* 1947; at Edinburgh Festival with Glyndebourne, Don Ottavio, *Don Giovanni,* 1948; leading tenor, Glyndebourne, 1948–58, appeared at Glyndebourne until 1979; début as Don José, San Francisco Opera, 1955, guest artist, 1962–68; teacher, Curtis Institute, Philadelphia, 1968–71; formed Richard Lewis Bach Ensemble c.1974; also sang with the Handel Opera Society. **Offices and memberships** President, Incorporated Society of Musicians, 1975–76. **Awards and honours** Commander of the Order of the British Empire, 1963. **Stage** (includes) *The Barber of Seville,* 1941; *Madame Butterfly,* 1941; *The Rape of Lucretia,* 1947; *Peter Grimes,* 1947; *Boris Godunov,* 1948; *Così fan tutte,* 1948, 1950; *Don Giovanni,* 1948; *Nemorino* (radio), 1948; *The Magic Flute,* 1950–51; *La traviata,* 1950–51; *Idomeneo,* 1951, 1974; *The Rake's Progress,* 1953; *Menna* (created role of Gwyn), 1953; *Troilus and Cressida,* 1954; *Carmen,* 1955; *The Midsummer Marriage,* 1956; *Canticum Sacrum* (tenor soloist, first concert performance), 1956; *Doktor Faust* (concert performance), 1959; *Alkmene* (created role of Amphitryon), 1961; *The Queen of Spades,* 1961; *King Priam* (created role of Achilles), 1962; *Billy Budd,* 1964, 1965, 1966, 1970, 1979; *Moses and Aaron,* 1965, 1972, 1973; *In coronazione di Poppea,* 1962; *Il returno d'Ulisse in patria,* 1979; *The Dream of Gerontius,* 1983. **Recordings** (include) *Poppea,* conducted by Pritchard; *Der fliegende Holländer,* conducted by Dorati; Gilbert and Sullivan (numerous operas), conducted by Sargent; *Troilus and Cressida,* conducted by Walton; *Gerontius:* conducted by Sargent, conducted by Barbirolli; History of Music in Sound (several records), HMV. **Cause of death** Undisclosed, at age 76.

HUGH MacLENNAN

Canadian Novelist and Writer

Born **Glace Bay, Canada, 20 March 1907**

Died **Montreal, Canada, 7 November 1990**

"After two unpublished books", Hugh MacLennan observed in 1972, "I discovered that I had, as a Canadian, a special technical problem. I was writing out of a country at that time unknown even to itself, to say nothing of the rest of the world." Even with voices such as his, voices which created works like *Barometer Rising* and *Two Solitudes,* much of Canada's history and culture — to say nothing of its literature — still remain unknown to the greater part of today's global society. As part of that culture, no matter how removed from it he felt at times, Hugh MacLennan, author, has suffered much the same fate. "Some fine writers are never fully appreciated abroad, and so it was with Hugh MacLennan", wrote the London and Manchester *Guardian*'s W.J. Wetherby. "He was a leading writer in his own country...But except for students of Canadian literature, his name meant little in Europe, not to mention the near-but-far literary circles in the US."

This may be a strange way to begin an essay about a person — particularly a fellow writer — but the facts speak for themselves: the name of Hugh MacLennan is not well known. There is a difference, however, between "not well known" and "unknown", and the latter MacLennan certainly wasn't. His many honorary degrees and awards, including three Canadian Governor-

General awards for fiction, and two for non-fiction, bear testimony to his literary skills. The reasons for his seeming anonymity, then, fall on two fronts. The first was his subject-matter: Canada itself is a nation still struggling to establish its own national identity, dragging itself slowly from a huge inferiority complex which has caused it to lie hidden in the shadows of both the United States and Britain.

Secondly, like his country, Hugh MacLennan did not believe in self-promotion. If he had wanted to attract attention and gain status in the massive US readership market to the south, he should, *Time* magazine advised, have made more of a display of himself and not "just quietly gone about his business which is to write good, solid novels about Canadians." Had he done so, of course, then the author probably wouldn't have been worth his salt, and his work would not have gained the serious, though limited, respect it so well deserves.

It is one of the "typical" Canadian traits that Hugh MacLennan rarely thought of himself as Canadian; one can understand such a statement more easily when considering his background. Born in the mining town of Glace Bay, Nova Scotia, MacLennan was the son of a doctor who spoke Gaelic at home and Highland-accented English in public. Dr Samuel MacLennan retained the Scotsman's pride in his heritage as well as his fierce religiosity; his son Hugh inherited both, though was not nearly as severe in the latter. The boy grew up in Halifax and took his schooling at Halifax Academy. After graduating from the town's Dalhousie University with a BA in 1928, he won a Rhodes Scholarship and spent the next three years at Oriel College, Oxford, studying modern and classical literature. These years in England, MacLennan would later recall, were among the happiest of his life and, in addition to his studies and university pursuits, the young scholar was able to tour Europe during his vacations. Only another North American who has lived through it can fully appreciate the effects caused by an extended stay in Europe, particularly in Britain. To a young Canadian with already strong British ties, the experience would have produced a peculiar mixture of recognition and alienation — the latter caused by the inability of one's fellow countrymen to comprehend the overseas ways of life. In many cases, as in MacLennan's, such a stay can also bring about a profound sense of nationalism; it is no coincidence that the novelist wrote that he never thought of himself as a Canadian until he went to Oxford.

After the scholarship came to an end, MacLennan returned to Canada, only to find himself unemployable in the midst of the Depression; although he applied for a teaching position at Dalhousie University, his Alma Mater, he was beaten out of it by an Englishman with identical qualifications. Fortunately, because of his scholastic talents, he was able to gain a graduate fellowship at America's Princeton University, where he obtained his PhD in 1935, and in the same year published his first book. Entitled *Oxyrhynchus,* the book told the story of a Roman colony in Egypt — unsurprisingly, in the light of its author's recent wanderings, the focus was on the Romans' separation from their country.

Despite feelings of alienation, however, both his American and English sojourns contributed to MacLennan's style as a novelist, what critic J.E. Morpurgo has called his "eloquent literary manner and his elegant literary manners". "Similarly", Morpurgo went on, "his writing of fiction was much influenced by his profound knowledge of Greek literature and, though more often than not he kept to Canadian settings and held to Canadianism themes, he seemed at times so determined to establish for Canada a mythology after the Greek pattern, that his Canadianism is submerged and all his ostensibly Canadian characters act, speak and think like characters out of Greek drama."

Whether that is indeed true remains a matter of opinion. What the critics do agree on, however, is the fact that MacLennan, as the London *Times* stated, "did more to help Canadians understand themselves than any writer of his generation." He did this perhaps most skilfully in *Barometer Rising* which appeared in 1941, after MacLennan had been teaching for some time at Lower Canada College. *The Times* calls the work "one of the finest novels in Canadian literature". The novel is set in 1917 Halifax, scene of a huge munitions explosion which the author had witnessed as a ten-year-old; he used the blast as a symbol of conscious Canadian independence as a nation, even though by claiming that sense of solidity so early, MacLennan was projecting a false hope. Canada will never come to be an integrated nation until it comes to terms with itself and with its culture, but at the very least MacLennan has contributed to that fact.

Even though critics consider *Barometer Rising* to be his finest work, *Two Solitudes* is probably the most talked about of MacLennan's seven novels, mainly because it dealt with the rift between Canada's French and English speaking populations. The title, which has so often been quoted in discussions about the "two Canadas", actually comes from a poem about love written by the German poet, Rilke, which defines the emotion as being "two solitudes...which protect and touch and greet each other" — the complete opposite of Canada's present situation. "One is more aware of loneliness and solitude in Canada where we are still creating our underpopulated country", MacLennan said in later years. "Now I would write about not two solitudes but a million."

The author was always trying in his work, he said, to make "as universal a statement as possible" and, although much of his later writing made didactic and even tedious reading, there were indeed universal themes to be found. In *Each Man's Son,* MacLennan turned the spotlight on his father's generation's adherence to puritan values and the plight of a rural people transplanted into an urban setting; in *The Watch that Ends the Night* a married couple struggles to come to terms with the wife's approaching death. The latter book, according to writer and critic Robertson Davies, had its roots in MacLennan's own grief.

After receiving a Guggenheim Award in 1943, Hugh MacLennan abandoned teaching for a while to write, then, in 1951, he took a post at McGill University in Montreal, where he lectured on English Literature. He eventually became a professor emeritus and made his home in Montreal, but he never really mastered the city's French. He remained, as it were, encased within his own particular type of solitude.

"One has a great sense of separation in contemporary Canada", MacLennan admitted in later life. "But this is not necessarily a spiritual state that older, more congested societies identify with. I have had a feeling of being a pioneer in the early days of a neglected literature."

"He had his full share of misfortune and he bore it with gallantry", wrote Robertson Davies. "Indeed, there was always about him something of the Highland Scot, although his ancestors had lived long in Canada. But in his personal flair, in his splendid conversational rhetoric, in his occasional sacrifice of fussy veracity to a fine flourish of language, he reminded everyone who knew him of the debt Canada owes to Scotland, not only for its enduring explorers but for its no less enduring writers."

One can only wonder now, after his death, whether many countries the world over will begin to lay claim to Hugh MacLennan, and whether one day, his native Canada will be among them. In any case, it will always be acknowledged that MacLennan was the first to give Canada — whatever it considers itself to be — a voice in fiction.

Born John Hugh MacLennan. **Parents** Samuel J., doctor, and Katherine (McQuarrie) MacLennan. **Marriages** 1) Dorothy Duncan, 1936 (died 1957); 2) Frances Walker, 1959. **Education** Halifax Academy; Dalhousie University, Halifax, BA, 1928; Rhodes Scholar, Oriel College, Oxford, BA, MA, 1932; Princeton University, New Jersey, PhD, 1935. **Career** Classics master, Lower Canada College, Montreal, 1935–45; full-time writer, 1945–51; associate professor, McGill University, Montreal, 1951–67, professor of English, 1967–79, professor emeritus, 1979 onwards. **Offices and memberships** Fellow: Royal Society of Canada, 1952, Royal Society of Literature, 1956. **Awards and honours** Governor-General's Gold Medal, 1928; Guggenheim Fellowship, 1943; Governor-General's Award, 1945, 1948, 1959, for non-fiction, 1949, 1954; Royal Society of Canada Gold Medal, 1951; Lorne Pierce Medal, 1952; Quebec Prize, 1952; DLitt: University of New Brunswick, Fredericton, 1952, University of Western Ontario, London, 1952,

University of Manitoba, Winnipeg, 1953, Waterloo Lutheran University, Ontario, 1961, McMaster University, Hamilton, Ontario, 1964, University of Sherbrooke, Quebec, 1967, University of British Columbia, Vancouver, 1968, University of Waterloo, Ontario, 1977; LLD: Dalhousie University, 1955, University of Saskatchewan, Saskatoon, 1959, University of Toronto, 1965, Laurentian University, Sudbury, Ontario, 1966, Carleton University, Ottawa, 1967, St Mary's University, Halifax, Nova Scotia, 1968, Mount Allison University, Sackville, New Brunswick, 1969; Critics Circle Award, 1959; Alberta Medal, 1960; Canada Council Grant, 1963; Doctor of Civil Law, Bishop's University, Lennoxville, Quebec, 1965; Molson Award, 1966; Companion of Literature, Royal Society of Literature, 1967; Companion, Order of Canada, 1967; Royal Bank of Canada Award, 1967, 1984; Canadian Authors Association Award, 1981; honorary degree, University of Montreal, 1983. **Publications — novels** *Barometer Rising,* 1941; *Two Solitudes,* 1945; *The Precipice,* 1948; *Each Man's Son,* 1951; *The Watch That Ends the Night,* 1959; *Return of the Sphinx,* 1967; *Voices in Time,* 1980. **Other publications** *Oxyrhynchus: An Economic and Social Study,* 1935; *Cross-Country,* 1949; *The Present World as Seen in Its Literature* (address) 1952(?); *Thirty and Three* (essays), edited by Dorothy Duncan, 1954; *The Future of the Novel as an Art Form* (lecture), 1959(?); *Scotsman's Return and Other Essays,* 1960; *Seven Rivers of Canada,* 1962; *The History of Canadian-American Relations* (lecture), 1963; *The Colour of Canada,* 1967; *The Other Side of Hugh MacLennan: Selected Essays Old and New,* edited by Elspeth Cameron, 1978; *Quebec,* photographs by Mia and Klaus, 1981; *On Being a Maritime Writer,* 1984. **Publication as editor** *McGill: The Story of a University,* 1960. **Manuscript collections** McGill University Library, Montreal; University of Calgary Library, Alberta; Fisher Library, University of Toronto. **Cause of death** Undisclosed, at age 83. **Further reading** Edmund Wilson, *O Canada,* 1965; Peter Buitenhuis, *Hugh MacLennan,* 1969; George Woodcock, *Hugh MacLennan,* 1969; Alec Lucas, *Hugh MacLennan,* 1970; Robert H. Cockburn, *The Novels of Hugh MacLennan,* 1971; Patricia Morley, *The Immoral Moralists: Hugh MacLennan and Leonard Cohen,* 1972; Paul Goetsch, editor, *Hugh MacLennan,* 1973; Elspeth Cameron, *Hugh MacLennan: A Writer's Life,* 1981; Elspeth Cameron, *Hugh MacLennan 1982: Proceedings of the MacLennan Conference at University College,* 1982; *Contemporary Novelists,* 1986; *Reference Guide to English Literature,* 1991.

MARY MARTIN

American Actress and Entertainer

Born **Weatherford, Texas, 1 December 1913**

Died **Rancho Mirage, California, 3 November 1990**

When Mary Martin was five years old, a silent screen version of J.M. Barrie's *Peter Pan* inspired her to test her own small wings by jumping off the roof of her garage. "I wanted to fly, and all I did was break my collarbone", Martin recalled. Some 40 years later, she was still playing Peter Pan, only this time, all of America was watching.

One of the leading stars of American musical theatre during the 1940s and 1950s, Mary Martin sang and danced her way through a host of popular Broadway shows, winning three Tony awards and captivating audiences with an irresistible blend of vivacity, warmth and wholesomeness. On stage, she is best remembered for her portrayals of Ensign Nellie Forbush in *South Pacific,* Maria Von Trapp in *The Sound of Music,* and Dolly Levi in *Hello, Dolly!* But it was the role of Peter Pan, a part she played on Broadway and then recreated for American television, that was closest to her heart. Forever youthful, upbeat and optimistic, Martin never lost her love of life — or of flying. "The secret, of course, is to keep moving and have no fear", she told an interviewer in 1989. "I've been hurt a few times, but never enough to keep me from flying."

The daughter of a lawyer and a violin teacher, Mary Martin grew up in Weatherford, Texas. She made her stage début at the age of five, singing at a local firemen's ball, and at 12, started formal vocal training. She spent her teenage years studying tap dancing and watching musical films. When she graduated from the Ward-Belmont School in Nashville at the age of 16, she went on to the University of Texas. Here she met her first husband, aspiring lawyer Benjamin Hagman. Her son, Larry, who later earned fame as J.R. Ewing in the television series *Dallas,* was born the following year. To make ends meet, Martin left college and opened her own dancing school for local children. The enterprise was successful, but she soon tired of teaching and, her marriage on the rocks, left Larry in the care of relatives and headed for Hollywood in hopes of pursuing a singing career. She left with a 500-dollar loan from her family and a promise to return when the money ran out. By 1935, she and Hagman had divorced.

Over the next few years, Martin attended so many auditions she earned the nickname "Audition Mary", but met with little success. To sustain herself, she ventured into radio and night-club work, making her professional début as a vocalist at the Trocadero in Hollywood. It was here, while singing with Phil Ohlman's band, that she was talent-spotted by producer Charles Schwab. He brought her east to New York to audition for a new Cole Porter musical, *Leave It To Me.*

While *Leave It To Me,* which opened on Broadway in 1938, featured a host of veteran stars, Martin's stunning rendition of "My Heart Belongs To Daddy", accompanied by a coy, mock-striptease routine, stopped the show. Hired as a replacement for actress June Knight, who had walked out over the insignificance of the role, Martin became an overnight sensation. Within three months she was given featured billing. According to David Ewen, author of *The Complete Book of the American Musical Theatre,* she became "at once one of the radiant stars of the American stage...[and] made herself the toast of Broadway." Successful though she was, her *naïveté* was real. She always maintained that the show's hit song had no unorthodox sexual implications, but was merely the lyric of a daughter to a father.

Martin's triumphant performance in *Leave It To Me* earned her a long and lucrative Hollywood contract. Over the next three years she appeared in nine Paramount films, including *The Rage of Paris*, *The Great Victor Herbert*, *Kiss the Boys Goodbye*, *Rhythm on the River* and *Birth of the Blues*. Despite a string of memorable songs, the films themselves were undistinguished, and her Hollywood career never quite caught hold. Martin, observed Tom Vallance of London's *Independent* newspaper, "was one of several Broadway stars whose compelling stage presence did not penetrate the camera lens... The studio tried to capitalize on her saucy "Daddy" image by inserting songs that went as far as the Hays Code would allow, but her elfin features resisted their attempts to make her a glamour girl". In Hollywood, however, she met and married Paramount story editor Richard Halliday, who returned with her to New York. He later became her manager.

By 1943, Mary Martin was back on Broadway, first in an overnight flop called *Dancing in the Streets,* and then in the musical fantasy *One Touch of Venus.* Originally chosen as a replacement for Marlene Dietrich, for whom the play was written, Martin enchanted audiences as the goddess who comes to life and falls in love with a mortal. *One Touch of Venus* was followed in 1946 by *Lute Song,* the show which brought Yul Brynner to Broadway.

Following a brief London appearance in an unsuccessful Noël Coward venture, *Pacific 1860,* Martin toured the United States as Annie Oakley in *Annie Get Your Gun.* Then, in 1949, she was chosen for the role of Ensign Nellie Forbush in Rodgers and Hammerstein's *South Pacific.* The play enjoyed one of the longest runs of any Broadway musical — 1925 performances — and warmed the hearts of thousands of theatre-goers, both in New York and at London's Drury Lane Theatre.

Harold Clurman of the *New Republic* described Martin as "our ideal, our dream, our faith... She sings, dances, flirts and acts with a bouncing naturalness that is the happy marriage of hard work and talent." Her portrayal of Nellie Forbush brought critic Kenneth Tynan to tears. "Skipping and roaming round the stage on diminutive flat feet," he wrote, "she poured her voice directly into that funnel to the heart which is sealed off from all but the rarest performers." It was the role with which she was most often identified.

In 1953, the year after *South Pacific* finished its final run, Martin appeared in a landmark television special opposite Ethel Merman. The highlight of the show, broadcast to commemorate the fiftieth anniversary of the Ford Motor Company, was a 35-song medley featuring the two leading ladies. The programme reached 60 million American viewers, and an album released shortly afterwards sold 200,000 copies in a single day. The following year Martin opened on Broadway in the title role in *Peter Pan.* Though it lasted only a short time on stage, in 1955 it was adapted for the small screen, and some 65 million television viewers watched her fly. Even on Broadway, Brooks Atkinson had praised her powerful performance, suggesting that, for Martin, the role and the reality of Peter Pan were indistinguishable. "Instead of using 'Peter Pan' as a vehicle, she acts it from the inside out with faith in the validity of Barrie's legend", he wrote. Thereafter, her name became synonymous with that of Peter Pan. Her TV performance in the role earned her an Emmy Award.

Though some critics dismissed Martin's next Broadway hit, *The Sound of Music,* as overly sweet and sentimental, her sterling performance as Maria Von Trapp did much to uplift it. "Martin", wrote Charles Wodruff of the *New York Republic,* is "a joy to see and hear throughout the evening, even when the show becomes embarrassing." Brooks Atkinson concurred: "Without her bright personality and guileless voice, the story... could become sticky", he wrote. "But the wonderful music and her candour give *The Sound of Music* an attractive and often affecting beauty in the theatre." Her performance also won her the coveted Tony and New York Drama Critics awards.

Over the next few years, Mary Martin appeared in a handful of musicals, including *Jennie*, *Hello, Dolly!* and *I Do, I Do,* but none of her performances had quite the sparkle of her earlier efforts. Towards the end of the 1960s she retired to Brazil with her husband, Richard Halliday, to begin what she once described as "a second exciting life" on their 15,000-acre ranch. In addition to producing an autobiography, *My Heart Belongs,* in 1976, and a best-selling book on needlepoint, she opened her own combination beauty and dress salon, where she sold her own designs. Following Halliday's death in 1973, she emerged from retirement for an occasional performance with Ethel Merman, and in 1987 toured briefly with Carol Channing in a comedy called *Legends.* Though the show was a resounding failure, her fans still flocked to see it.

In 1982, Martin and several friends, including the actress Janet Gaynor, were badly injured in an automobile accident in San Francisco. A year later, fully recovered and optimistic as ever, Martin organized a stage show to benefit the trauma center at San Francisco General Hospital, which she credited with saving her life. Though doctors had feared she would never walk again, in 1983 she was fit enough to fly. Clad in her trusty Peter Pan costume, and with the help of a special wire rigging suspended from the roof of the Davies Symphony Hall, she flew across the stage to the third balcony, crowing wildly and showering gold "fairy dust" on the audience below.

Though the exertion wore her out, Martin had no regrets. "I proved that you can do anything... if you try", she said. The secret, she once told reporters, is to "always have a good time. I love living. I love every minute of it. I guess it's my stubborn Texas determination to continue to the last breath." In 1989, she had planned to tour in a musical version of Thornton Wilder's classic, *Our Town,* but cancer forced her to withdraw.

Born Mary Virginia Martin. **Parents** Preston, lawyer, and Juanita (Pressley), violin teacher, Martin. **Marriages** 1) Benjamin J. Hagman, 1930 (divorced 1935); 2) Richard Halliday, literary agent, manager and producer, 1940 (died 1973). **Children** Larry from first marriage; Heller from second marriage. **Education** Ward-Bellmont School, Nashville, Tennessee; University of Texas; Fanchon and Marco School, Hollywood, California, studied dance. **Career** Proprietor, teacher, dancing school; night-club singer; actress, 1929 onwards; Broadway début, *Leave It To Me,* 1938; affiliated with Paramount Pictures, 1939–43; film début, *The Great Victor Herbert,* 1939; London début, *Pacific 1860,* Drury Lane, 1946. **Other activities** Boutique owner, needlepoint designer, Brazil, 1968; linen designer, Fieldcrest Collection, 1978, 1979. **Offices and memberships** Actors Equity Association; Screen Actors Guild; American Federation of Television and Radio Artists. **Awards and honours** Donaldson Award for best actress in musical comedy for *One Touch of Venus,* 1944; winner, *Variety* New York Drama Critics polls: for performance in *One Touch of Venus,* 1944, for performance in *South Pacific,* 1949, for performance in *The Sound of Music,* 1960; Antoinette Perry (Tony) awards, League of New York Theatre and Producers: for *Annie Get Your Gun,* 1948, for best actress for *Peter Pan,* 1955, for best actress for *The Sound of Music,* 1960; Emmy Award, National Academy of Television Arts and Sciences, for television performance of *Peter Pan,* 1955; Kennedy Center honoree, 1989; honorary member, Texas Rangers. **Stage** (includes) *Doctor Knock,* 1928; *Diamond Lil,* 1928; *Achilles had a Heel,* 1935; *Young Madame Conti,* 1937; *Empress of Destiny,* 1938; *Leave It To Me,* 1938; *Johnny 2x4,* 1942; *Dancing in the Streets,* 1943; *One Touch of Venus,* 1943; *Our Town,* 1944; *Lute Song,* 1946; *Pacific 1860,* 1947; *Annie Get Your Gun,* 1947, 1953; *South Pacific,* 1949, 1951, 1952; *Kind Sir,* 1953; *Peter Pan,* 1954; *The Skin of Our Teeth,* 1955; *Girl Crazy,* 1956; *Babes in Arms,* 1956; *Music With Mary Martin,* 1958; *Cinderella,* 1958; *Three to Make Music,* 1958; *The Sound of Music,* 1959; *Jennie,* 1963; *Hello, Dolly!,* 1965; *I Do, I Do,* 1966; *Do You Turn Somersaults?,* 1977; *Together on Broadway,* 1977; *Legends,* 1987 (on tour). **Films** *Shopworn Angel* (ghost singer); *The Rage of Paris* (singing coach, bit part), 1938; *The Great Victor Herbert,* 1939; *Rhythm on the River,* 1940; *Love Thy Neighbor,* 1940; *Birth of the Blues,* 1941; *Kiss the Boys Goodbye,* 1941; *New York Town,* 1941; *Star Spangled Rhythm,* 1942; *Happy Go Lucky,* 1943; *True to Life,* 1943; *Night and Day,* 1946. **Television** (includes) *Good News of 1938,* 1938; *Rudy Vallee Show,* 1939; *Good News of 1940,* 1940; *Jack Benny Show,* 1940; *Kraft Music Hall,* 1942; *Tex and Jinx,* 1947; *Bell Telephone Hour,* 1949; *America Applauds: An Evening for Richard Rodgers,* 1951; *Weekend,* 1953, 1954, 1955; *Ford Fiftieth Anniversary,* 1953; *Rodgers and Hammerstein Cavalcade,* 1954; *Christmas Program,* 1955; *Peter Pan,* 1955, 1956, 1960, 1963; *Monitor,* 1955; *Ford Star Jubilee,* 1955; *The Skin of Our Teeth,* 1955; *Biographies in Sound,* 1956; *Born Yesterday,* 1956; *Hungarian Relief Christmas Program,* 1956; *Annie Get Your Gun,* 1957; *Music With Mary Martin,* 1959; *Magic With Mary Martin,* 1959; *Mary Martin at Radio City Music Hall,* 1966; *This Is Your Life,* 1972; *The Fabulous Fifties,* 1978; *Valentine,* 1979; *Over Easy* (host) from 1981. **Publications** *Mary Martin's Needlepoint,* with photographs by Sol Mednick, 1969; *My Heart Belongs* (autobiography), 1976. **Recordings** *South Pacific,* Columbia, 1949, *Peter Pan,* RCA Victor, 1954; *Girl Crazy,* Columbia, 1956; *Babes in Arms,* Columbia, 1956; *Annie Get Your Gun,* 1957; *Adventures for Readers,* Harcourt, 1958; *Mary Martin Sings — Richard Rodgers Plays,* RCA Victor, 1958; *Three to Make Music,* RCA Victor, 1959; *Cinderella,* RCA Victor, 1959; *The Sound of Music,* Columbia, 1959; *Jennie: From the Broadway Musical "Jennie",* RCA Victor, 1963; *Hello Dolly: From the London Musical "Hello, Dolly!",* RCA Victor, 1965; *I Do, I Do: From the Broadway Production "I Do, I Do",* RCA Victor, 1967; *Cole Porter Sings and Plays Jubilee,* with Danny Kaye, Ethel Merman and others, Columbia, 1972; *Mary Martin in "The Sound of Music",* Columbia, 1973; *Together With Music,* with Noël Coward, AMR Records, 1976. **Cause of death** Cancer, at age 76. **Further reading** Daniel C. Blum, *Great Stars of the American Stage,* 1952; Jessie Clayton Adams, *More Than Money,* 1953; Cecil Walter Hardy Beaton and Kenneth Tynan, *Persona Grata,* 1954; *This I Believe: Two,* 1954; David Ewen, *The Complete Book of the American Musical Theatre,* 1959; Thornton Martin, *Pete Martin Calls on...,* 1962; Roddy McDowall, *Double*

Exposures, 1966; Shirlee Petkin Newman, *Mary Martin on Stage,* 1969; David Shipman, *Great Movie Stars,* 1970; George T. Simon, *Best of the Music Makers,* 1979.

RODRIGO MOYNIHAN

British Painter

***Born* Tenerife, Canary Islands, 17 October 1910**

***Died* London, England, 6 November 1990**

Perplexing, enigmatic, elusive, paradoxical: accounts of Rodrigo Moynihan's art tend to employ these and similar terms. Extraordinarily wide-ranging in his abilities and aims, he remained aloof from the artistic mainstream of which he was apparently part. While in no sense artistically unsure of himself, he was motivated both by an innate conservatism and a complete disregard for convention. This duality, combined with his intelligence and cultivation, a strong literary bent and a cosmopolitan background, produced a somewhat exotic artistic personality which, while among the foremost of its generation in Britain, defies classification. Unlike most artists, he did not follow a straightforward evolutionary course, but alternated between abstraction and figurative painting, and between the roles of successful Establishment artist and controversial pioneer of radical styles.

Moynihan was the son of an Irish fruit-broker and an aristocratic Spanish mother. He was born and spent his early childhood in Tenerife before being sent to school in England for six years, and subsequently to an American high school in Madison, New Jersey. At this age his inclinations were chiefly literary, but in 1927 he returned to Europe and, on a visit to Rome, saw the Sistine Chapel and became committed to painting. Artistic studies in Rome and the south of France were followed by entry to London's Slade School of Art in the autumn of 1928. Here, under the tutelage of the great Professor Tonks, he was among the most brilliant of a formidable generation of students which included William Coldstream, Antony Devas and Elinor Bellingham Smith, whom he married in 1931, the year of his graduation. His talent was recognized by Tonks, who intervened when Moynihan was withdrawn from the school by his parents to work in business, and awarded him a scholarship.

He emerged onto the London art scene as the most radical member of the short-lived Objective Abstraction Group, whose 1934 exhibition at Zwemmer's Gallery caused a sensation. Moynihan's thickly encrusted, creamy-coloured paintings, emphasizing the texture of the paint, baffled the critics, although they simply developed ideas from the then unfashionable art of Monet. Discouraged, and left with "a thick white painting that nearly killed me", in another radical move, Moynihan resumed figurative painting. He became involved with the realist Euston Road School of Coldstream and Victor Pasmore in the late 1930s, although he never embraced their social and political ideals, and despite doing some teaching there, he remained essentially an outsider.

In 1940, the year of his first one-man show at London's Redfern Gallery, Moynihan was called up. Rescued from uncongenial service in the artillery by Kenneth Clark and transferred to the camouflage section, in 1943 he was invalided out of the Army and appointed an official war artist. His masterpiece in this capacity was *Medical Inspection,* which powerfully expresses military subservience and official indifference. The majority of his war paintings were, however, portraits, mostly of high-ranking figures but also of lesser individuals, such as the poignant *Private Clarke, ATS*.

The post-war years were ones of immense success for Moynihan. His war portraits earned him new, prestigious commissions, notably for portraits of Princess Elizabeth and the prime minister,

Clement Attlee. As well as an ability to capture likeness, he demonstrated skill in handling large figure compositions in his group portraits, *After the Conference: the Editors of Penguin Books* and *The Teaching Staff of the Painting School, Royal College of Art.* The latter, regarded the supreme group portrait of its time, celebrates the revitalization of the Royal College's Painting Department, of which he had been appointed professor in 1948 and where he remained a presiding influence until 1957. In 1953 he was awarded the CBE and the following year was elected a Royal Academician. His home became a focus of London's artistic life and his future as an Establishment artist was assured.

At the height of his success, however, Moynihan performed an about-turn characteristic of his career. In 1957, under pressure from official duties, teaching commitments, portrait commissions and the break-up of his first marriage, he resigned from the Royal College and the Academy, and further distanced himself from all he had achieved by abandoning figurative painting and embarking on a new phase of abstraction. He moved to France, living in Paris and later Provence, and also spending time in New York. In 1960 he married his second wife, the painter Anne Dunn, with whom he edited the seminal 1960s review, *Art and Literature.* During this period his palette grew richer and he was influenced by contemporary American painting: abstract expressionism and the hard-edged style. He acquired a considerable reputation outside Britain, notably in the US, where he is among the few modern British painters represented in the Metropolitan Museum.

His career entered yet another phase in the 1970s, with a return to realism centred on a series of still-lifes of studio paraphernalia, still in progress at the time of his death, and hailed as significantly adding to the tradition of still-life painting. Like his earlier work, these are investigatory and sceptical in approach, yet imbued with an unprecedented melancholy and austerity of tone and colour, sophisticated and assured in their detachment.

Moynihan's critical rehabilitation in Britain was marked by a major retrospective in 1978 at the Royal Academy, to which he was re-elected the following year. He resumed the role of society portraitist — in which he will probably be best remembered — with portraits such as those of artist Francis Bacon and the then prime minister, Margaret Thatcher, the latter commissioned by the National Portrait Gallery in 1983. He had an unromantic attitude to his sitters, remarking that, "You must establish a relationship. Men want to look like types — generals all want to look like generals. But women all want to look the same... Oh, and academics — so timid. Such grey, unremarkable faces."

Gregarious and broad of outlook, widely travelled and well read, with a large quota of personal magnetism, Moynihan himself was anything but grey and unremarkable. He is evocatively characterized in her autobiography by Nicolette McNamara Devas, who was with him at the Slade: "His mind was continental, deeply civilised, old in the sense of antique furniture with the accumulation of mellow gloss... he was a man of subtleties, shades, inflection and innuendo." Only a few weeks before his death, Moynihan's eightieth birthday was celebrated with a dinner at the Royal Academy. He had a strong sense of artistic tradition, occasionally writing perceptive pieces on art, and was conscious of his debt to such figures as Manet and Monet, Goya and the seventeenth-century Dutch painter Pieter Saenredam. His own achievement is summed up by his friend and fellow-academician Sir Lawrence Gowing: "Moynihan had a capacity, which none of his friends shared, to paint near-masterpieces in either [the abstract or the realist] style. Looking back, one realises that his work included some dozen of the most memorable and individual pictures of the century."

Born Rodrigo Moynihan. **Parents** Herbert James, fruit-broker, and Maria (de la Puerta) Moynihan. **Marriages** 1) Elinor Bellingham Smith, painter, 1931 (dissolved); 2) Anne Dunn, 1960. **Children** Two sons, John and Daniel, one by each marriage. **Education** University College School, London; high school, Madison, New Jersey, United States, 1924–27; American

School and Povada Studio, Rome, 1928; Slade School, University College, London, 1928–31. **Military service** Artillery, 1940–43; official war artist, 1943–44. **Career** Exhibitor, London Group, 1932, member, 1933; member, Objective Abstraction Group, 1934; associated with Euston Road School, 1937–39; professor of painting, Royal College of Art, 1948–57; visiting professor, Slade School, 1980–84. **Related activities** On War Artists' Advisory Committee, National Portrait Gallery, Hirschorn College, Washington; editor, with second wife, Anne Dunn, *Art and Literature,* 1963–68. **Offices and memberships** Associate, Royal Academy, 1944; Royal Academician, 1954–57, 1979 onwards; fellow, University College, London, 1970 onwards. **Awards and honours** Commander of the Order of the British Empire, 1953; Honorary Doctor, Royal Academy of Art, 1969. **Exhibitions** (in London unless otherwise indicated) (With Geoffrey Tibble and Graham Bell) Zwemmer Gallery, 1934; Redfern Gallery, 1940, 1958, 1961; Leicester Gallery, 1946; Hanover Gallery, 1963, 1967; Egan Gallery, New York, 1966; Tibor de Nagy, New York, 1968; Fischer Fine Art, 1973, 1982; Royal Academy (major retrospective), 1978; Robert Miller Gallery, New York, 1980, 1983; Galerie Claude Bernard, Paris, 1984. **Collections** Chantry Bequest, London; Tate Gallery, London; Contemporary Art Society, London; Metropolitan Museum, New York. **Works** (include) *The Studio at Walberswick,* 1937; *Self-portrait,* 1938; *Medical Inspection* (Imperial War Museum, London), 1943; *Private Clarke, ATS* (Tate Gallery, London), 1943; *Princess Elizabeth,* 1946; *Rt Hon Clement Attlee MP,* 1947; *The Teaching Staff of the Painting School, Royal College of Art,* 1949–50; *After the Conference: the Editors of Penguin Books,* 1951; *Yellow Lake,* 1970–71; *Francis Bacon,* 1975; *Mrs Thatcher,* 1983; *Self Portrait,* 1984. **Publications** *The Attributes of Painting* (inaugural lecture), 1949; *Goya,* 1951. **Cause of death** Undisclosed, at age 80.

MALCOLM MUGGERIDGE

British Writer and Broadcaster

Born **Croydon, Surrey, 24 March 1903**

Died **Sussex, England, 14 November 1990**

Malcolm Muggeridge's life as a controversial but brilliant writer and broadcaster can also be seen as a quest, internal as well as external, for an absolute truth which, when put to the test, would not be found wanting. It took him a lifetime to find it.

He was born into an intellectual, left-wing family of modest means and educated at a grammar school. At home he absorbed from his parents an appreciation of the Marxist Utopia destined eventually to arrive. He went on to Cambridge University to read natural sciences, of which he did little, but sufficient to scrape a degree, and first became interested in Christianity through a friendship with Alec Vidler, an Anglican scholar-priest who tried to persuade him to read for Holy Orders. Muggeridge demurred, preferring to take a post teaching English at a Christian college in southern India where he remained a year, studying much of Indian life and writing for local newspapers. However he started as he went on, by telling the truth as he saw it and upsetting many people.

Back in the UK he continued teaching but after his marriage, in 1927, to Kitty Dobbs — herself related to the Fabians (a group of people who believe in the eventual triumph of socialism) Beatrice and Sidney Webb — he took a post at Cairo University where he remained for three years and began his writing association with the left-wing British newspaper, then called the *Manchester*

Guardian. He was later invited to join the staff as a leader writer, a job he was able to perform with ease, but his forthright approach earned him increasing disapproval from his editor-proprietor, C.P. Scott. It was a productive period for Muggeridge, however. In 1931 his play *Three Flats* was produced by the Stage Society and his first book *Autumnal Face* was published. But by the following year Muggeridge was less in favour with the paper and he volunteered for the post of correspondent in Moscow.

It is important to appreciate that for people imbued with the political background of Muggeridge, the image of Moscow in the 1930s conjured up dreams of the great new Bolshevik society in which all people are truly equal; all contribute what they can and are given what they need. They believed in the message brought back from Moscow in 1919, just two years after the revolution, by Lincoln Steffens: "I have seen the future, and it works."

So Muggeridge and his wife disposed of the bourgeois trappings of English life, such as their marriage certificate and evening clothes, and set off for their brave new world in which Muggeridge found disillusion. The appalling results of Stalin's collective farming in the Ukraine which produced an artificial famine of horrendous proportions together with difficult conditions, little money and his wife's sickness left him totally disenchanted. But he felt a greater sense of betrayal by the fact that he could not get his articles published in more than a watered-down version. This was not the result of USSR censorship but far more that other journalists and his superiors would not accept that Communism had failed.

On his return to the UK Muggeridge wrote two novels. The first, *Winter in Moscow,* was a bitter evocation of the experience and marked his break with socialism. The second, *Picture Palace,* marking his break from, and disaffection for, the *Manchester Guardian* remained unpublished for the next 50 years owing to its extremely libellous content, notably a portrait of his former boss as an irascible old man who, ultimately, turned out to bear quite a resemblance to Muggeridge himself in later years!

After leaving his wife and young family for a further spell in India, this time working on the *Calcutta Statesman* and writing a biography of Samuel Butler, Muggeridge returned to work on the London *Evening Standard.* But two years seemed to be his limit and he resigned to live in Sussex and work on what many consider his best novel, *In a Valley of This Restless Mind*, and *The Thirties*, a chronicle of the inevitable progression towards a second world war.

By the end of the decade he had joined the Army but was posted to the Intelligence Corps and, soon after, to MI6. Much of his time was spent as a spy in Africa where he ended up running a network on one coast while novelist Graham Greene was doing similar things on the other. At the end of the war he spent time in Paris investigating alleged collaborators. Here his most notable achievement was to rescue P.G. Wodehouse (of Jeeves and Wooster fame) and to speed him on his way to the USA.

After the war Muggeridge joined another Fleet Street paper, the right-wing *Daily Telegraph,* writing leaders once more. This enabled him to spend much of his time on other writing, this time editing the diaries of Mussolini's son-in-law. He was then posted as correspondent to Washington and later made deputy editor. But it was in 1953 when his career really took off. He was 50 and offered the editorship of *Punch,* a weekly journal of humour and considerable history.

Muggeridge was the first so-called "outsider" to become editor and it totally fitted his free-thinking and balloon-pricking style. He threw out all the pre-war jokes about servants, sharpened up the writing, brought it up to date and increased circulation. However he still managed to get into trouble, this time by publishing a cartoon of the great British war hero Winston Churchill, then still prime minister, showing him as an old man made senile by his strokes. As a result his contract was not renewed.

At the end of the 1950s he put himself completely out of favour with the British Establishment. An article he had written for the *Saturday Evening Post,* which was subsequently published in

Britain, embroiled him in a huge row. He was said to have attacked the Royal Family by likening them to a soap opera — now a very mild and entirely valid criticism. But one has to remember that this was only shortly after the Queen had come to the throne, that the memory of the abdication was still fairly fresh in the minds of the British people, and that there had been comparatively recent public and governmental concern about a relationship of Princess Margaret, then third in line of succession. By 1990 she had become twelfth in line and such things no longer mattered. But in the late 1950s they mattered very much indeed and Muggeridge was turned into a journalistic pariah.

It was America that, somewhat surprisingly, gave him the opportunity to shine in an entirely new and immediate way. He was interviewed on television in New York by Mike Wallace and offered trenchant comments also on Eisenhower and the American way of life. Back in Britain he was gradually embraced by the emerging demand for personalities on the small screen and slowly built up a whole new generation of admirers for his skill as an interviewer and his pithy wit which could produce such gems as, "Dull, duller, Dulles", and, "The trouble with kingdoms of heaven on earth is that they're liable to come to pass"!

Slowly, however, a more serious side developed and, by the end of the 1960s, a man who had also been known as being keenly enthusiastic about smoking, drinking and womanizing, gave up these pleasures and began speaking out against them. Contraception and abortion became anathema to him. Certain inconsistencies in his viewpoints were recognized by other satirists but there was little doubt that Muggeridge's opinions were genuinely and firmly held and slowly, too, he began his move towards accepting the authority of formal religion.

Despite refusing to believe in certain tenets of Christian faith such as the Resurrection, when he visited the Holy Land in 1968 to make a series of television programmes, he found his own certainty about the life and ministry of Jesus. And when, the following year, he was asked to make a film of Mother Teresa (which later helped her gain the Nobel Peace Prize) he found the experience profoundly affirming and spiritually enriching. He gave all the profits from a book he wrote about her to her cause.

In his seventies Muggeridge began easing up on television work, turning back to his own writing once more and, in particular, some autobiographical books, *Chronicles of Wasted Time,* and campaigning against what he saw as the "moral pollution" of modern society. In 1982, and shortly before his eightieth birthday, he was received into the Roman Catholic Church. His account of this, *Conversion,* was published in 1988.

Whether or not he found what he spent his life seeking does not perhaps matter. What is important is that his quest produced some of the finest modern writing in the English language and that above all, as an honest man, others have seen what it means to have the true courage of your convictions.

It might be asked why he received no award, except from the French in recognition of his war service, no knighthood, no Order or Merit. But "St Mugg", as he was called affectionately, would have known the answer: "A prophet is not without honour, save in his own country..."

Born Thomas Malcolm Muggeridge. **Parents** Henry Thomas, lawyer's clerk and Labour member of parliament and Annie (Booler) Muggeridge. **Marriage** Katherine Dobbs, 1927. **Children** Three sons and one daughter. **Education** Selhurst Grammar School, Surrey; Selwyn College, Cambridge, MA, 1923. **Military service** British Army, 1939–45, in Intelligence Corps, mostly in Lourenco Marques; became major. **Career** Teacher: Union Christian College, Alwaye, south India, later at a Birmingham state school, 1927; lecturer, Egyptian University, Cairo, Egypt, 1927–30; first newspaper articles published, 1930; editorial staff member, *Manchester Guardian,* Manchester, England, 1930–32, Moscow correspondent, 1932–33; affiliated with International Labour Office, Geneva, Switzerland, 1933–34; assistant editor, *Calcutta Statesman,* Calcutta, India, 1934–35; editorial staff member, *Evening Standard,* London, England; Washington

correspondent, *The Daily Telegraph,* London, 1946–47, deputy editor, 1950–52; television interviewer, *Panorama,* BBC, 1951; editor, *Punch,* London, 1953–57; rector, University of Edinburgh, Scotland, 1967–68. **Awards and honours** Legion of Honour, France; Croix de Guerre with Palm, France; Médaille de la Reconaissance Française; Christopher Book Award for *Something Beautiful for God,* 1972. **Publications** *Autumnal Faces* (novel), 1931; *Three Flats* (three-act play), 1931; *Winter in Moscow,* 1934; (translator) Maurice Bedel, *New Arcadia,* 1935; *The Earnest Atheist: A Study of Samuel Butler,* 1936, also published as *A Study of Samuel Butler: The Earnest Atheist,* 1937; (with Hugh Kingsmill) *Brave Old World,* 1936; (author of introduction) Galeazzo Ciano, *Hidden Diary,* 1937; (with Hugh Kingsmill) *A Preview of Next Year's News,* 1937; *In a Valley of This Restless Mind,* 1938; *The Sun Never Sets: The Story of England in the Nineteen Thirties,* 1940, also published in *The Thirties: 1930–1940 in Great Britain,* 1940; (editor) Galeazzo Ciano, *Ciano's Diary, 1939–1943,* 1947; (editor) Galeazzo Ciano, *Ciano's Diplomatic Papers: Being a Record of Nearly 200 Conversations Held During the Years 1936–42 With Hitler,* 1948; *Affairs of the Heart,* 1949; (with Hesketh Pearson) *About Kingsmill,* 1951; (author of introduction) Galeazzo Ciano, *Diary, 1937–1938,* 1952; (author of introduction) *Esquire's World of Humor,* 1965; *The Most of Malcolm Muggeridge,* 1966; *Tread Softly for You Tread on My Jokes,* 1966; *London à la Mode,* 1966; *Muggeridge Through the Microphone: BBC Radio and Television,* 1967; *Jesus Rediscovered,* 1967; (with others) *What They Believe,* 1969; *Something Beautiful for God: Mother Teresa of Calcutta,* 1971; (with Alec Vidler) *Paul: Envoy Extraordinary,* 1972; *Malcolm's Choice: A Collection of Cartoons,* 1972; *Chronicles of Wasted Time* (autobiography), Volume I: *The Green Stick,* 1973, Volume II: *The Internal Grove,* 1974; *Jesus: The Man Who Lives,* 1975; *A Third Testament,* 1976; *Christ and the Media,* 1977; *Things Past,* 1978; *A Twentieth Century Testimony,* 1979; *Like It Was,* 1981; *Picture Palace,* 1987; *A Spiritual Journey,* 1988; *Conversion,* 1988; contributor to *Ladies' Home Journal, Esquire, Christianity Today, Reader's Digest, The Observer* and other magazines and newspapers. **Television** (includes) *Twilight of Empire* (producer), 1964; *Ladies and Gentlemen, It is My Pleasure,* 1965; *Something Beautiful for God* (producer), 1971; also *Panorama.* **Cause of death** Illness from a stroke suffered three years previously, at age 87.

RAYMOND OLIVER

French Chef

Born **Langon, France, 27 March 1909**

Died **Paris, France, 5 November 1990**

Raymond Oliver was a chef who had no doubt that his was an art, not just a craft. He made no bones about comparing cooking with literature, painting and music, sometimes all in the same sentence.

Of all artefacts, those of cooking are the most ephemeral; there is as yet no known method of filming or photographing a flavour. Oliver is likely to be among the handful of chefs whose reputations survive their death. He has left dozens of books of recipes and essays on food. Two of his recipes, for lampreys à la Bordelaise and for cèpes (mushrooms) cooked with Bayonne ham and goose fat, are honoured with inclusion in Curnonsky's definitive *Cuisine et Vins de France.* But more durable than Oliver's writings, since recipes never turn out quite the same when you do them yourself, will be the mark he has left on the gastronomic heritage of France. He taught his own version of traditional cuisine to millions through the medium of television. And, though he would deny paternity, some gastronomes go so far as to credit him with begetting Nouvelle Cuisine.

Oliver was adamant that he was a traditionalist, a devout follower of Escoffier, and opposed to the Nouvelle. Certainly his dishes do not make any concessions to modern fads. Like most of France, his restaurant was no place for a vegetarian. Foie gras was ubiquitous, even appearing in his recipe for fried eggs, and most of his vegetable dishes seem to involve a splash of meat stock or a smidgeon of bone marrow.

But he admitted to personalizing or "liberating" the classic recipes and certainly experimented with unorthodox combinations of wine and food — such as vintage Sauternes with practically anything. He also simplified dishes, while insisting that cooking needed a "solid base" in the same way as a painting needs the foundation of good draughtsmanship.

Certainly his television demonstrations made many ambitious recipes accessible to his audience of amateur cooks — though other recipes, such as his hare à la Royale, involving eight days of preparation, a bottle of Sauternes and three bottles of Pomerol, sound far from simple. He lightened dishes and tried to make them easily digestible, and also pioneered cruises for gourmet slimmers (though the five-course menu, complete with alcoholic accompaniments, suggests that the gourmet aspect triumphed over the slimming).

Heredity and environment alike had destined Oliver for a career as a chef. He was born at his maternal grandmother's restaurant La Malle-Poste, at Langon in the Gironde region of south-west France. Even three years spent at school in England, where his chef father had once cooked at the Savoy Hotel, failed to dampen his enthusiasm for good cooking, though his only comment on British cuisine was that the tea was good. On returning to France, he was apprenticed to a Paris restaurant at 15, then worked for a period in a restaurant run by his father in the south-west. This regional background gave him a special interest in the preparation of game.

In 1948 he took over the famous but down-at-heel restaurant called le Grand Véfour, near Paris's Place Palais Royal. He restored its sumptuous *belle époque* décor and set about restoring its fortunes too. Only a dozen or so restaurants could boast three-star status in the Michelin restaurant guide in those days. Oliver obtained his three stars within five years of taking over the restaurant. He was to own le Grand Véfour for 35 years.

The restaurant had existed for two centuries. Earlier customers had included not only Napoleon, with his Joséphine, but also literary figures such as Lamartine and Alexandre Dumas. Under Oliver it continued the literary tradition. Customers included the writers André Malraux and Colette (who lived in the same building and would drop in for a cassoulet), as well as the writer and artist Jean Cocteau, who designed Oliver's menus and often entertained his friends to dinner in the restaurant. Simenon, the creator of Maigret, incorporated the restaurant into one of his novels.

As a practitioner of an art form which he considered as important as theirs, Oliver was not inhibited about dropping the names of his illustrious clientele. In his *Cuisine pour mes amis* (Cooking for my friends) he included two recipes for Vichyssoise: the one that Jean Cocteau liked and the one that he didn't. Cocteau for his part wrote in the introduction to the same book that Oliver had numbered among the genuises of the kitchen.

Unlike some contemporary chefs in London who are renowned for their rudeness to customers, Oliver was a courteous, though masterful, figure in his restaurant. He had firm views on the *contrat tacite* (unspoken contract) between chef and customer, and disapproved of a fellow-restaurateur who threw out a customer who had committed the admittedly grave *faux pas* of asking for appetizers. But he deplored as much customers who think they have the right to start finding fault the moment they cross the threshold. "The customer must know what he wants — even if that is advice from the restaurateur — and then, having been given what he asks for, he must get on with it. The role of the restaurateur is to give the customer what he asks for — and care, courtesy, psychology, discretion, skill and dispatch into the bargain."

The restaurant itself was exclusive, to say the least, but Oliver was a proselytizer, who spread the word through all the media at his disposal. Fame arrived with his pioneering television series, *Art et magie de la cuisine* (Art and magic of cookery), which started in 1953 and ran until 1968; Oliver, a persuasive and relaxed communicator, did not charge for his earliest appearances, but must have done well out of what would now be called "merchandising" of associated products: a book with the same title as the television series was an early spin-off in 1955.

Oliver went on to produce a total of 26 books, including several best-sellers. In addition, he recorded recipes and instructions on gramophone records, and undertook lecture tours, His ardour infected not only the French but many other nations including the Japanese, Australians and Americans. Not everyone was susceptible, though; at a cookery demonstration in 1950s London, the frugal British were said to have been appalled by his liberal ways with butter, and a British branch of le Grand Véfour, opened in 1971, was not a success.

Although he revered gastronomy — and his waiters were credited by one restaurant critic with the demeanour of bishops — Oliver was anything but abashed by the sensuous aspects of his calling. He would compare the demands of cooking with those of an insatiable mistress, sometimes in the same breath with which he likened it to painting and music. He pointed out resemblances between puddings and items of female anatomy. Such an unreconstructed view of the relationship between women and food once led him in an unguarded moment to allege that women could not be taken seriously as creative chefs. The challenge was quickly taken up by British television cook Fanny Craddock, who tried to outcook him in a contest at London's Café Royal. Oliver was declared the winner but conceded that his opponent's cooking was, indeed, creative.

Despite such frivolities, his approach to food was scholarly. He had a library of 3000 recipe books, the oldest dating from the fifteenth century; he drew on them, to the extent of reproducing what purported to be "prehistoric" recipes in his own books. All aspects of food interested him and he could discourse learnedly on obscure details such as the supposed aphrodisiac properties of different mushrooms (morilles are best, apparently).

He withdrew from the running of the restaurant in the late 1970s, and in 1983 sold it, after terrorists had bombed the building, doubtless seeing the place as a hotbed of conspicuous consumption. Oliver retained his personal following in retirement, and shortly before his death he was voted France's most popular chef. His son and grandson carry on the family tradition of *haute cuisine* and his son is also host of a television cookery show.

Born Raymond Guillaume Oliver. **Parents** Louis, restaurateur and chef, and Marie Cécile (Cavernes) Oliver. **Marriage** Mari, 1964. **Children** Michel, Dominique, Chantal and Sophie. **Education** Collège des Jésuites; École supérieure de Talence; also attended a school in Clapham, London, 1915–18. **Career** Apprentice, Paris restaurant at age 15; chef, restaurateur: La Réole at Langon, 1932, at l'Alpe-d'Huez, 1943–48, at Thèoule, 1946–47, at Croix-Valmer, 1947–48, le Grand Véfour, near Place Palais Royal, Paris, 1948–83. **Related activities** Editor, *Larousse de la cuisine;* collaborator, O.R.T.F. **Offices and memberships** President, Palais Royal committee; member, Number Ten Club, Institute of Directors. **Awards and honours** Officier de la Légion d'honneur, des Palmes académiques et des Arts et des Lettres; Commandeur du Mérite agricole; Officier du Mérite touristique; Gold Medal of the town of Bordeaux; Great silver medal of the town of Paris; Grand Véfour awarded three-stars, Michelin guide, 1953–83. **Television** (With Catherine Langeais) *Art et Magie de la Cuisine,* 1953–68. **Publications** (include) *Art et magie de la cuisine,* 1955; *The French at Table,* 1967; *La Cuisine,* 1969; *Cuisine pour mes amis,* with preface by Cocteau, 1976; *Adieu fourneaux,* 1984. **Cause of death** Undisclosed, at age 81.

LORD PEARCE

British Laywer and Painter

***Born* England, 9 February 1901**

***Died* Crowborough, East Sussex, 26 November 1990**

When Edward Pearce was a young, impoverished barrister he contracted tuberculosis. In those days there was no cure for the disease. But he did not give up. Instead he followed the regime prescribed by his doctor: "Supper and breakfast in bed — always eat something at lunchtime, have a pause — no theatres, no evening parties." And he followed it for 20 years, until he was finally pronounced healthy!

Such strength of character and determination were typical of a man who said of himself, "I do inherit from someone a capacity for trying very hard at things." He tried — and he succeeded: achieving high distinction in the British legal system, as a respected and fair-minded chairman of many public bodies — and as a painter.

The son of a headmaster, Edward Pearce attended Charterhouse school, then Corpus Christi College, Oxford. In 1925 he was called to the Bar by Lincoln's Inn in London and began his career as a barrister.

He was soon to embark on a very different pursuit which continued to claim his attention throughout his life. His illness forced him to spend several months in a sanitorium in Switzerland. There he bought artist's materials and taught himself to paint in oils.

Once back in London, Pearce built up a highly successful legal practice and soon advanced in his career. In 1948 he became a High Court judge in the Probate, Divorce and Admiralty Division. As a judge he was famed for his kindness and consideration particularly towards young barristers. In 1951 he became an influential member of the Royal Commission on Marriage and Divorce.

In 1954 he moved to the Queen's Bench Division, graduating to the Court of Appeal in 1957 and the House of Lords in 1962. Sir James Comyn recalls of Pearce's work as a judge, "the simplicity and common sense shown by him to litigant and lawyer and welcomed by both. He had the great ability to clarify what had hitherto been obscure or been obscured. He brought down to earth what had been too long lingering in the clouds."

These qualities proved invaluable when, in 1969, he became chairman of the Press Council, the official watchdog body for British newspapers. To the Council's deliberations he brought, according to a former director of the Council, "a constant reminder that humility and humanity need not sacrifice strength of character, resolution in performance of duty and courage in the face of formidable deterrents." In his opening speech as chairman, Lord Pearce proclaimed that it was for the press to see that democracy survived and that the voice of the individual was heard. The converse, he said, was that the press must behave responsibly and exercise restraint. It was a great disappointment to him that he did not achieve his ideal — that the editors of the British press should commit themselves to self-regulation of the conduct of their own papers.

It was in the early 1970s that Edward Pearce became a household name in England; he was appointed chairman of the commission to test Rhodesian approval of the proposed British-Rhodesian settlements. These proposals would have perpetuated white rule of the African colony (now Zimbabwe) under the regime of Ian Smith.

When Pearce visited Rhodesia in 1972 many Labour MPs were suspicious that his commission would prove a mere "rubber stamp" for Smith's regime. Smith himself believed that consultation with the people of the country was a formality and that Rhodesia would become independent under his leadership on the terms he had agreed with British foreign secretary, Sir Alec Douglas-Home.

In fact the commission provided the first genuine and independent outlet for African opinion that there had been for many years.

Pearce's task was undertaken in chaotic conditions, with riots, arrests by the Smith regime and intimidation of the black majority from both sides. Blacks in Rhodesia outnumbered Whites by nearly 5 million to 228,000; their opinions, as portrayed in the Pearce Report, clearly took white Rhodesians by surprise. "We are satisfied on our evidence", the report concluded, "that the proposals are acceptable to the great majority of Europeans. We are equally satisfied after considering all our evidence, including that on intimidation, that the majority of Africans rejected our proposals. In our opinion the people of Rhodesia do not regard the proposals as acceptable as a basis for independence." The proposals were shelved and settlement did not take place. In 1980 elections were held and the colony gained independence from Britain as the Black-ruled Republic of Zimbabwe.

Throughout his distinguished career Edward Pearce continued to paint. With characteristic modesty he described his role as "that lowest form of artistic life, the amateur artist. He cannot swim in the surging seas of true creation where the big fish live. He stays in the surf by the sea shore like a sandhopper." His achievements in this field belie his modesty. He was accomplished at landscapes, became a member of the Royal Society of British Artists in 1940 and eleven years later exhibited an oil in the prestigious Royal Academy Summer Exhibition — he was reputed to be the first High Court judge to have done so. He went on to enjoy successful one-man shows in private galleries as well as joint exhibitions with his painter wife, Erica. And he always found time to paint; even during his arduous spell in Rhodesia he managed a series of pictures of the Victoria Falls.

Indeed, in his spare time, nothing pleased him better than to escape to his Sussex home and to set up his easel: and to work in his garden. Between them, he and his wife created the garden. When she died in 1985 he founded a publishing company — The Sweethaws Press — and produced *The Permissive Garden,* the account she had written over 20 years before of how the garden came into being. And — resolute and determined to the last — he continued to garden until shortly before he died, using a three-wheeled scooter to carry him up and down the steep slopes in his pursuit of weeds. It is a fitting, final image for a man whose determined and courageous response to serious illness prefaced a life of equally hard work — and of high achievement.

Born Edward Holroyd Pearce. **Parents** John W.E., preparatory school headmaster, and Irene (Chaplin) Pearce. **Marriage** Erica Priestman, artist, 1927 (died 1985). **Children** Bruce (died 1987) and James (died 1985). **Education** Charterhouse, Godalming, Surrey; Corpus Christi College, Oxford. **Career** Called to Bar, Lincoln's Inn, 1925, bencher, 1948, treasurer, 1966; Queen's Council, 1945; deputy chairman, East Sussex Quarter Sessions, 1947–48; Judge of High Court of Justice, Probate, Divorce and Admiralty Division, 1948–54, Queen's Bench Division, 1954–57; Lord Justice of Appeal, 1957–62; Lord of Appeal in Ordinary, 1962–69; chairman, Press Council, 1969–74; chairman, Appeals Committee Takeover Panel, 1969–76; chairman, commission to test Rhodesian approval of proposed British-Rhodesian settlements, 1971–72; professor of law, Royal Academy of Arts, 1971–89. **Related activities** Chairman, Committee on Shipbuilding Costs, 1947–49; member, Royal Commission on Marriage and Divorce, 1951; chairman, committee on the organization of Bars and Inns of Court, 1971–73; independent chairman, Press discussions on Charter of Press Freedom, 1976–77. **Other activities** Governing body member, Charterhouse, 1943–64; governor, Tonbridge School, 1945–78; governor, Sutton's Hospital in Charterhouse; trustee, Chantrey Bequest; first appearance, Royal Academy Summer Exhibition, 1951; governor, Federation of British Artists, 1970–73; published *The Permissive Garden* by Erica, Lady Pearce, 1987. **Offices and memberships** Member, Royal Society of British Artists, 1940; member, Court of Company of Skinners, Master, 1946–47; president, Artists League of Great Britain, 1950–74. **Awards and honours** Knighted 1948; honorary fellow, Corpus Christi College,

Oxford, 1950; Privy Councillor, 1957; created life peer, Baron Pearce of Sweethaws, 1962; honorary fellow, Royal Society of British Sculptors; honorary senate member, Four Inns of Court, 1974. **Exhibitions** One man show, The Mall Galleries, 1971, with wife, 1973, 1976; Alpine landscapes show, Chur, Switzerland, 1977, Alpine Gallery, London, 1983. **Cause of death** Undisclosed, at age 89.

JACK PETERSEN

British Boxer

Born **Cardiff, Wales, 2 September 1911**

Died **Cardiff, Wales, 22 November 1990**

In Britain during the 1930s, the Welshman Jack Petersen was the most popular, and certainly one of the most admired, boxers of his era. He had great heart and an artful technique, but his relative slightness of build stopped him finally from challenging for world-class heavyweight honours.

Born in Cardiff in 1911, he laid aside the ambition to become a doctor when, at the age of 19, he won the Amateur Boxing Association's light heavyweight championship. A syndicate of businessmen thought that they'd found Britain's first world heavyweight champion since Bob Fitzsimmons in 1897, so, with their backing and his father's training, Petersen entered the professional ring. In the first eight months he made spectacular progress, cramming in 15 fights and taking the Welsh light heavyweight championship in one round. With supreme confidence, he challenged Harry Crossley for the British light heavyweight championship, and even before meeting him, agreed to fight the British heavyweight champion Reggie Meen, 50 days later. This was the kind of chutzpah to get bums on seats, certainly, but events proved it more than justified. Petersen was far too fast for Crossley, though the fight went the distance: Meen lasted only two rounds. In order to concentrate on the heavier division and its greater financial rewards, Petersen immediately relinquished the light heavyweight title.

The mountainous heavyweights taken for granted in these days were by no means so common then, but the 13-stone Petersen had some spectacular giant-killing exploits. In 1932 he despatched the 6 feet 6 inches, 17-stone Jim Campbell in 22 seconds, and the following year he knocked unconscious the Londoner Jack Pettifer, 6 feet 7 inches and 17 stones. Contemporary critics were now comparing Petersen with his upright style, speed, versatile punching and obvious courage, to the great Georges Carpentier. For his successful defence of the British Heavyweight title, Petersen was awarded outright one of the National Sporting Club's Lonsdale Belts. (In those days, the coveted trophy not only contained gold, but brought the owner a pension of one pound per week. Only the World War I cult hero Bombadier Billy Wells had been given the same honour before.) And then to most people's surprise, the west-countryman Len Harvey came to London at the end of 1933, took Petersen the whole distance, and went home with his title.

The following year, however, restored Petersen's fortunes; after four wins he met Len Harvey again and stopped him in 12, thus becoming what the British used to call the Empire Champion. This he remained for five years, making five defences, notably against the great black boxer Larry Gains, and the Australian George Cook. It was Ben Foord from South Africa who eventually took the title, pounding Petersen in only three rounds — though Petersen had once again given away over 20 pounds advantage in weight.

The closing episodes of Petersen's ring career had a doomed quality. He had enough left to beat Jock McAvoy (you could sense his nickname — The Rochdale Thunderbolt — lacked a certain conviction), but he was finished by a series of epic and bloody encounters with the German Walter Neusel. Again much the lighter man, Petersen attacked with ferocity, but sustained fearsome punishment, particularly from cuts above the eyes. Wisely, he decided to retire from boxing.

During World War II, he served with the Royal Air Force, and in the post war period became an active contributor to sports administration. He was a respected chairman of the Welsh Area Council of the Welsh Sports Council, and his 50 years' stewardship of the National Boxing Board of Control culminated with the presidency in 1986. Petersen comprehensively belied the notion that "boxers are thick of ear, mind and voice", working for BBC radio as an inter-round summarizer during boxing coverage, and obliging many as an after-dinner speaker. Described as "an intelligent, articulate man of good sense and impeccable manners", he was in fact a dignified and rather disconcerting advertisement for the hard way he had earned his living, giving the impression, as the London *Times* eloquently put it, that "a career in the ring might be had without unacceptable long term cost." Well... thanks, but no thanks.

Born Jack Petersen. **Military service** Royal Air Force. **Career** Winner, Amateur Boxing Association light heavyweight title, 1931; professional boxer, 1932–37. **Related activities** Steward, British Boxing Board of Control, for 50 years, president, 1986 onwards; radio "inter-round" summarizer, British Broadcasting Corporation, early 1940s; chairman, Welsh Area Council of the Welsh Sports Council. **Awards and honours** Officer of the Order of the British Empire. **Major titles** Amateur Boxing Association, light heavyweight champion, 1931; Welsh light heavyweight champion, 1931; British light heavyweight champion, 1932, against Harry Crossley; British heavyweight champion: 1932–33, 1934–36, fought against Reggie Meen, 1932, against Jack Pettifer, Jack Doyle, and Len Harvey, 1934–36; Empire heavyweight champion, 1934–36. **Cause of death** Undisclosed, at age 79.

ELIOT PORTER

American Photographer

***Born* Winnetka, Illinois, 6 December 1901**

***Died* Santa Fe, New Mexico, 2 November 1990**

When this writer was 14 years old and having to spend a good deal of time in bed recovering from an illness, a friend used to visit and to try and cheer her up. One day she brought with her a brightly wrapped package which she placed in the writer's hands; it proved to be Eliot Porter's *In Wildness Is the Preservation of the World.* Through its pages were discovered a photographer who not only understood the colours of nature, but one who knew intimately Nature herself. For inside this book are a myriad of natural treasures: autumn leaves drifting on the surface of a pond; dew-covered cobwebs in a grass glade; a small bunch of violets; a lichen-covered stone. These are not what could be called "spectacular" photographs, but to those who spend a great deal of their time in quiet walks among the woods and fields of North America, these natural portraits are as priceless as the Hope Diamond. "At last", thought this writer in her teenage wisdom, "someone else sees the outdoors the way *I* do." Years later, she discovered that the pictures had been taken by the man considered to be the father of artistic colour photography.

"I think he set the standard for color photography and he set that standard in a time when photography was considered a black-and-white art form", explained Steve Yates, curator of photography at the New Mexico Museum of Fine Arts. "There's not going to be a major collection of color photography in the world that's not going to have an Eliot Porter. In terms of depth and breadth of contribution in color photography, he's almost unparalleled."

In today's world of ever-new and more advanced aids to colour photography, such statements might seem anachronistic. Yet when one considers that only in the last 20-odd years has the colour photograph been regarded as an art-form — and even then the acceptance has been grudgingly given — and that Porter was exhibiting colour photographs as early as the 1940s, then the laurels heaped upon him are more understandable. His reputation is even more impressive in light of other facts: that Porter did not become a professional photographer until the age of 37; that Ansel Adams, the great black-and-white landscape photographer called him "impeccable"; that it was another photographic genius, Alfred Stieglitz, who encouraged him by offering the use of his An American Place gallery in Manhattan for Porter's first major exhibition. In some ways, perhaps, the roots of his extraordinary talents and success can be found in his family background.

Eliot Furness Porter was born in Winnetka, Illinois, the second of the five children of James and Ruth Porter. His father was an architect, camping enthusiast and amateur photographer; his younger brother Fairfield Wadsworth Porter became a well-known painter; thus it doesn't seem strange in the least that, with them, Eliot Porter should have shared a love of beauty, form, light and nature. After being given a Brownie camera as a child, Porter's first photographic attempts were of landscapes, in imitation of his father. It wasn't long, however, before he found his own particular love in the natural world: birds. "I soon discovered that the most satisfactory outlet for expressing my excitement over birds was the camera, rather than pencil or brush", Porter wrote in the introduction to his *Birds of North America,* another collection which has since become a classic. "The camera is an instrument for immediate results, and by focusing my attention on the subject, it offers a way of sublimating the indefinable longing that is aroused in me by close association with birds."

Not surprisingly, the Porter family spent their annual summer vacation on the islands off the coast of Maine, and there young Eliot could photograph gulls and other sea and land birds to his heart's content. This hobby, along with other facets of nature study, took up the majority of his free time during his school-days (which were spent at the Morristown School, Morristown, New Jersey). When the time came for him to attend college, however, Porter, who was accepted by Harvard, chose chemical engineering, graduating with a Bachelor of Science degree in the subject in 1924. From there he moved on to the Harvard Medical School, graduating in 1929, and entered the fields of bacteriological and general biological research, and eventually combined them with teaching at Harvard University and Radcliffe College.

Understandably, the years spent in medical school left little time for anything else except study, but when the rigours of his student days were over, Porter purchased a Leica camera. Soon his free hours were once again filled with photography — of birds, of course, but also of other natural and man-made objects. At some point he made the acquaintance of Alfred Stieglitz who encouraged the young researcher to turn his talents to art photographs and eventually organized an exhibition of his work in 1939. When he received enthusiastic comments from other notable photographers — Dorothea Lange and Ansel Adams among them — "Dr" Porter decided to abandon the world of medicine and devote his time to becoming a freelance photographer.

Birds were Porter's first subjects, but the young photographer was not happy with the existing standards he found in that field. "What was needed", he wrote, "was essentially to raise bird photography above the level of reportage, to transform it into an art." With these principles in mind, Porter set to work. Yet in 1941, when he approached a publisher with a collection of bird photographs, printed in the conventionally acceptable black-and-white medium of the day, he was told that identifications of his subjects were difficult because of the monochrome format. This reaction sent Porter scurrying off to the Eastman Kodak Company where, after obtaining advice on the (at that time) new Kodachrome colour film he set about compiling a colour collection of "bird-shots". World War II held him back for its duration while he worked on radar development at the Massachusetts Institute of Technology, but with the financial help of a Guggenheim Fellowship Award, Porter soon had his colour collection ready for publication — only to be told that it was all too expensive to reproduce! It wasn't until 1972 that his *Birds of North America: A Personal Selection* was published.

The first major book with which Porter overcame this colour prejudice in publishing was *In Wildness Is the Preservation of the World.* This effort represented years of work by Porter, who selected passages from the nineteenth-century naturalist and transcendentalist Henry David Thoreau, and illustrated them accordingly. After large publishing houses turned it down on the grounds of expense, Porter at last approached the American conservationist organization, the Sierra Club, which first mounted the works in the form of an exhibition, then produced a large-format, exhibition-type book. And here Eliot Porter had the last laugh, because *In Wildness* quickly became a best-seller.

The reason? Kenneth Poli says it best:

> A Porter photograph of a landscape (or detail of one) is, first of all, a contemplation. Typically, it is quiet. But it is the quiet of one who has shrugged off his backpack at trailside to rest a moment. The resulting quiet is not an exhausted but a studious one. The observer, we feel as we ourselves study the image, has looked hard at all within his field of view. He has seen the subtle shadings of different greens in trees and moss and grasses. He has noticed every ripple and reflection nuance on the surface of the quiet pool of water, the position of each leaf that floats on its surface. And from this raw material he has extracted something that is at once universal and yet highly personal.

The photographer, however, achieved much more than that. "Porter's book", wrote Peter Ride in the London *Independent* newspaper, "made a direct appeal for greater attention to be paid to ecology. The book was a milestone in photographic publishing." Such a "milestone" was an attitude Eliot Porter seems to have considered as natural all his life. "When I began to make color prints", he wrote in later years,

> it became apparent that almost infinite possibilities, contrary to the assertions of the disparagers of color, were available for interpretation and individual expression. Why, I wondered, was the remarkable attribute of color vision, not shared by all vertebrates, treated with such disdain by photographers, alone in all the field of art?... To say that because a photograph is in color it is less creative than one in black-and-white is to manifest a poverty of perception no less egregious than to condemn photography as a whole because it is the product of an optical instrument.

Porter's beliefs and subject-matter did more than simply earn him respect and admiration; *In Wildness* also gave the Sierra Club its own international reputation. But that isn't really surprising; ecology and conservation issues were always an intrinsic part of Porter's work, though perhaps not consciously. "I wanted to make people aware of the natural beauty, the unique features — both living and inanimate geologic and biotic — of the world around them", he told *Backpaper* magazine. "So I began other book projects with this in mind." These other projects included works such as *Baja California: The Geography of Hope* and *Galapagos: The Flow of Wilderness,* as well as *The Tree Where Man Was Born: An African Experience,* on which he collaborated with writer Peter Matthiessen.

Whatever his subject-matter, critics are united on the quality of Porter's work. "Porter has that kind of intuition which captures the moment of importance and conviction", wrote Ansel Adams in an article for *Modern Photography* magazine, and the *Albuquerque Tribune* agreed: "He left behind a body of work that sings a tribute to life itself." "He is, beyond a doubt, the father of color photography as an art form", said David Scheinbaum owner of the Scheinbaum and Russek Gallery of Photography in Santa Fe, New Mexico, Porter's home. "There is a whole generation of young photographers who are following in his footsteps." There certainly is, as well as a whole set of generations who will continue looking at his photographs and thinking, "Yes, I understand."

"Light and color and form are inseparable parts of this master's vision of the world", Steve Yates concluded. "What we gain by viewing his photographs is a special quality in the affirmation of life."

Eliot Porter took his last photograph in 1986, the same year in which he was diagnosed as having amyotrophic lateral sclerosis — better known as Lou Gehrig's disease. With over 20 publications and numerous collections and exhibitions to his name, however, a part of Eliot Porter will continue to live on in his work. "The essential quality of a photograph is the emotional impact that it carries, which is a measure of the author's success in translating into photographic terms his own emotional response to the subject", Porter wrote for his retrospective exhibition in 1987. Needless to say, he was profoundly successful.

Born Eliot Furness Porter. **Parents** James Foster, architect, and Ruth Wadsworth (Furness) Porter. **Marriages** 1) Marian Brown, 1927 (divorced 1934); 2) Aline Kilham, 1936. **Children** Eliot and Charles from first marriage; Jonathan, Stephen and Patrick from second marriage. **Education** New Trier High School, Kenilworth, Illinois, 1916–18; Morriston School, New Jersey, 1918–20; Harvard University, School of Engineering, Cambridge, Massachusetts, 1920–24, BS, 1924; Harvard Medical School, 1924–29, MD, 1929; self-taught in photography. **Career** First photographs, "Great Spruce Head Island", Maine, 1913; instructor in biochemistry and bacteriology, Harvard University and Radcliffe College, Cambridge, Massachusetts, 1929–39; first bird photographs, 1927; serious photographer, 1930 onwards; professional photographer, 1939 onwards; freelance photographer, Cambridge, Massachusetts, 1939–42; worked on development of radar, Radiation Laboratory, Massachusetts Institute of Technology, 1942–44; freelance landscape and wildlife photographer: Winnetka, 1944–46, Santa Fe, New Mexico, 1946 onwards. **Related activities** On board of directors, Sierra Club, San Francisco, 1962–68. **Offices and memberships** Associate fellow, Morse College, Yale University, New Haven, Connecticut, 1967; fellow, American Academy of Arts and Sciences, 1971; member: American Ornithological Union, Cooper Ornithological Society, Wilson Ornithological Society, National Audobon Society, Michigan Audobon Society, Wilderness Society. **Awards and honours** Guggenheim Fellowship: 1941, 1946; Silver Plaque, Wildlife Photography Award, *Country Life International Exhibition,* London, 1950; Conservation Science Award, United States Department of the Interior, 1967; Maine Commission on Arts and Humanities Award, 1969; Distinguished Son of Maine award, 1969; Doctor of Fine Arts, Colby College, Waterville, Maine, 1969; Newhouse Citation, Syracuse University, New York, 1973; LLD, University of Albuquerque, New Mexico, 1974; Governor's Award, New Mexico Arts Commission, 1976; Gold Medal, Academy of Natural Sciences, Philadelphia, 1978; DSc, Dickinson College, Pennsylvania, 1979; Kulturpreis Deutscher Gesellschaft für Photographie, 1982. **Individual exhibitions** Delphic Studios, New York, 1936; An American Place, New York, 1939; George Lingafelt Bookshop, Chicago, 1939; Museum of Art, Santa Fe, New Mexico, 1940; Katherine Kuh Gallery, Chicago, 1942; Bronx Zoological Society, New York, 1942; *Birds in Color,* Museum of Modern Art, New York, 1943; Academy of Natural Sciences, Chicago, 1943; Museum of Modern Art, New York, 1952; Art Institute of Chicago, 1953; Limelight Gallery, New York, 1955; Nelson Gallery, Kansas City, Missouri, 1959; *Seasons* (retrospective), International Museum of Photography, George Eastman House, Rochester, New York, 1960; San Francisco Museum of Modern Art, 1960; Baltimore Museum of Art, 1960; Museum of Science, Boston, 1960; Smithsonian Institution, Washington, DC, 1960; De

Cordova Museum, Lincoln, Massachusetts, 1962; Art Institute of Chicago, 1963; Museum of Fine Arts, St Petersburg, Florida, 1970; Amon Carter Museum, Fort Worth, Texas, 1973; University of New Mexico, Albuquerque (retrospective), 1973; Roswell Museum and Art Center, New Mexico, 1974; Witte Memorial Museum, San Antonio, Texas, 1974; Pensacola Center, Florida, 1975; *Intimate Landscapes,* Metropolitan Museum of Art, New York, 1979. **Group exhibitions** (include) *International Salon of Photography,* American Museum of Natural History, New York, 1940; *Images of Freedom,* Museum of Modern Art, New York, 1941; *Country Life International Exhibition,* London, 1950; (with Ellen Auerbach), *Madonnas and Marketplaces,* Limelight Gallery, New York, 1957; (with Laura Gilpin) Fine Arts Museum of New Mexico, Santa Fe, 1958; (with Laura Gilpin and Todd Webb) Fine Arts Museum of New Mexico, Santa Fe, 1962; *American Photography: The 60's,* University of Nebraska, Lincoln, 1966; *Photography USA,* De Cordova Museum, Lincoln, Massachusetts, 1967; *Aspects of American Photography,* University of Missouri, St Louis, 1976; *The Great West: Real/Ideal,* University of Colorado, Boulder, subsequently Smithsonian Institution travelling exhibition, toured United States, 1977; *Photographs: Sheldon Memorial Art Gallery Collection,* University of Nebraska, Lincoln, 1977; *Eliot Porter, Laura Gilpin, William Clift,* Horwitch Gallery, Santa Fe, New Mexico, 1977; (with Daniel Lang) Smithsonian Institution, Washington, DC, 1977; *Mirrors and Windows: American Photography since 1960,* Museum of Modern Art, New York, 1978, toured United States, 1978–80; *The Imaginary Photo Museum,* Kunsthalle, Cologne, Germany, 1980; *Ansel Adams, Eliot Porter, William Clift,* Cronin Gallery, Houston, 1981; *Photography in America 1910–83,* Tampa Museum, Florida, 1983. **Collections** Museum of Modern Art, New York; Metropolitan Museum of Art, New York; International Museum of Photography, George Eastman House, Rochester, New York; Library of Congress, Washington, DC; Art Institute of Chicago; University of New Mexico, Albuquerque; Santa Fe Museum of Art, New Mexico; Center for Creative Photography, University of Arizona, Tucson. **Publications** *American Birds,* with text by Amedon and Murphy, 1953; *In Wildness Is the Preservation of the World,* with text by Henry David Thoreau, introduction by Joseph Wood Drutch, 1962; *The Place No One Knew: Glen Canyon on the Colorado,* edited by David Bower, 1963; *Portfolio One: The Seasons,* 1964; *Summer Island: Penobscot Country,* edited by David Brower, 1966; *Forever Wild: The Adirondacks,* with text by William Chapman White, 1966; *Baja California: The Geography of Hope,* with text by Joseph Wood Krutch, 1967; *Galapagos: The Flow of Wilderness,* two volumes, with text by Kenneth Brower and Porter, 1968; *Down the Colorado: Diary of the First Trip Through the Grand Canyon,* 1969, with text by John Wesley Powell, 1969; *Appalachian Wilderness: The Great Smoky Mountains,* with text by Edward Abbey and Harry M. Caudill, 1970; *The Tree Where Man was Born: An African Experience,* with text by Peter Matthiessen, 1972; *Birds of North America: A Personal Selection,* 1972; *Iceland: Portfolio II,* 1972; *Portraits from Nature* (portfolio), with an introduction by Beaumont Newhall, 1973; *Moments of Discovery: Adventures with American Birds,* with text by Michael Harwood, 1977; *Antarctica,* 1978; *Seal Song,* with text by Brian Davies, 1979; *The Greek World,* with text by Peter Levi, 1980; *American Places,* with text by Wallace and Page Stegner, 1981; *All Under Heaven: The Chinese World,* with text by Jonathan Porter, 1983; *Eliot Porter's Southwest,* 1985; *Maine,* 1986. **Cause of death** Cardiac arrest, at age 88. **Further reading** Robert Doty, with an introduction by Minor White, *Photography in America,* 1974; Cecil Beaton and Gail Buckland, *The Magic Image: The Genius of Photography from 1839 to the Present Day,* 1975; Sandy Hume, Gary Metz and others, editors, *The Great West: Real/Ideal,* 1977; introduction by Norman A. Geske, *Photographs: Sheldon Memorial Art Gallery Collection, University of Nebraska* (exhibition catalogue), 1977; John Szarkowski, *Mirrors and Windows: American Photography since 1960,* 1978; Weston J. Naef, *The Collection of Alfred Stieglitz,* 1978; Lee D. Witkin and Barbara London, *The Photograph Collector's Guide,* 1979; Weston Naef, *Eliot Porter: Intimate Landscapes* (exhibition catalogue), 1979; Fritz Binder, Gert Koshofer, Rolf Sachsse and others, *Die Geschichte* *der Farbphotographie von 1861 bis 1981,* 1981; Helmut Gernhseim, Renate and L. Fritz Gruber and others, *The Imaginary Photo Museum,* 1981; Ian North, editor, *International Photography 1920–1980,* 1982; David Plowden and Ian Jeffrey, *The Library of World Photography: Landscape,* 1984; Robert A. Sobieszek, editor, *Masterpieces of Photography from George Eastman House,* 1985; *Contemporary Photographers,* 1988.

YANNIS RITSOS

Greek Poet

***Born* Monemvasia, Greece, 1 May 1909**

***Died* Athens, Greece, 11 November 1990**

There are not many Communist institutions outside the Kremlin, but there was one in Greece: the poet Yannis Ritsos. He was a hero in a country where poets are taken seriously, fulfilling a role handed down the generations, if not from Homer, as some would have us believe, certainly from the founding of the Greek nation in 1821. As for the really great poets of the world, no, Ritsos was not among them; but he was good, sometimes very good indeed, and he embodied the aspirations of a large segment of the Greek people.

Yannis Ritsos was born in Monemvasia in the Peloponnese to a well-off landowning family, but a series of appalling traumas entirely destroyed his childhood happiness and security. First his brother died of tuberculosis. Then his father, a gambler, was financially ruined in 1922, the year Greece suffered a catastrophic defeat in Asia Minor. When his mother died shortly after (also of tuberculosis) his father became insane and then one of his sisters did too.

The boy went to live with relations in Githion, not far from ancient Sparta, left school at 17, went to Athens and worked as a clerk in a law firm; he had to give up when he too developed tuberculosis. He was in and out of a sanitorium for four years. He subsequently found work as a dancer, an actor and a publisher. He often thought he was insane and he often thought of suicide. But poetry was there, as it had been since he first started writing at the age of eight, and it helped him keep going.

He had joined the Communist Party in 1934, and that kept him going too. He was committed to the struggle against tyranny and injustice, and there was plenty of the latter about. The country was filled with Greek refugees expelled from Asia Minor after the campaign. But in addition his personal experience of the decay of the family, which returned time and again in his poetry, was a paradigm of the Marxist notion of the collapse of bourgeois society.

The first of his 117 books (he was so prolific he could write poetry for 14 hours a day) was the collection *Trakter* (Tractor) in 1934, followed the next year by *Pyramides* (Pyramids), and the blending of personal and political was already an essential ingredient.

This was a fertile time for Greek letters, a time which has been labelled the "Generation of the Thirties"; the protagonists rebelled against the overblown lyricism of their predecessors. The really big guns in the world of poetry were George Seferis and Odysseas Elitis, but Ritsos was influenced more by Kostas Kariotakis, a poet who committed suicide in 1928 at the age of 32, which made him very fashionable (he was genuinely good, too).

In 1936 Ritsos wrote what has become, probably, his most famous poem, *Epitafios,* an extraordinary first-person lament by the mother of a striking tobacco worker murdered by the police. It was an expression of Ritsos's feeling for socialist revolution, and an impressive display of technical mastery as the whole thing was written as a *miroloi* (folk lament) in 15-syllable rhyming couplets. But it was not that which made the poem famous: it was Mikis Theodorakis, one of the few internationally known Greek cultural exports of our time, who set it to music in the 1950s. It became the anthem of the Greek Left, as did *Romiosini* (published under the same title in English) which Theodorakis also set to music.

Soon afterwards he published *To tragoudi tis adelfis mou* (Song of my Sister), lamenting his sister's insanity. As a complete contrast it was entirely in free verse, to which he stuck almost exclusively for the rest of his life. It was as if he had got the business of form out of his own system with *Epitafios*.

But dark days were upon him, and upon Greece. The Metaxas dictatorship came to power in the very year that *Epitafios* was published. The poem was publicly burned below the Acropolis, but the dramatic gesture was rather a damp squib as the edition had virtually sold out, so the authorities only had about 200 copies to burn. It was banned, and for almost 20 years Ritsos was not permitted to publish. He went on writing, of course, always writing.

During World War II and the Occupation critics have said that his poetic concerns became more humanitarian and less doctrinaire. When the Communist-inspired National Liberation Front collapsed, Ritsos was arrested without trial for his involvement (his health had not allowed him to fight, either in the war or in the Resistance, but he had done what he could, including helping in the organization of a People's Theatre) and exiled to the Aegean island of Limnos and then to the prison camp on Makronisos. The only novel he ever wrote was lost, along with other work. While he was a prisoner he buried poems in bottles, because his work was still banned.

He was freed in 1952, wrote a great deal, and married Falitsa Georgiadis in 1954; they soon had a daughter. Ritsos was officially recognized, finally, in 1956, when he was awarded the National Prize for Poetry with *I sonata tou selinofotos* (Moonlight Sonata). He used to recite it against a background of Beethoven. But more oppression was to come. The deadly dictatorship of the colonels was sprung upon Greece in 1967 and Ritsos was arrested and exiled to Samos.

He came back to Athens in 1971, and when the junta fell he often spoke at Communist rallies; the young literati of the Left came to him as to an oracle. Besides poetry, which he continued to write, publishing his last collection in 1988, he wrote essays, two plays and translated Blok and Mayakovsky from Russian as well as authors from Hungarian, Turkish and other languages. Throughout his work there is a great range of form, from short, imagistic pieces to almost epic-length poems on classical topics; he liked to be discursive sometimes, and at other times epigrammatic. He produced powerful dramatic monologues too. His language could be beautifully delicate. The author and critic Peter Levi once wrote, "One of the most brilliant gifts of this poet is the sheer abundance, the striking force and consequential rhetoric of his imagination."

Nominated for the Nobel Prize twice, in 1975 and 1986, he never won it, but he was awarded many others, such as the Grand International Prize for Poetry in Belgium in 1972 and the Lenin Prize in 1977. His work has been translated into 43 languages at the last count, including various selections in English. He died during the fall of Communism throughout the East Bloc; it must have broken his heart.

Both his parents bore the name meaning freedom, Eleftherios/Eleftheria, and Ritsos's daughter, of course, was named Eleftheria too.

Born Yannis Ritsos. **Parents** Eleftherios, land-owner, and Eleftheria (Vouzounara) Ritsos. **Marriage** Falitsa Georgiades, doctor, 1954. **Children** One daughter, Eleftheria. **Education** Athens Law School, Greece, briefly, 1925. **Career** Assistant librarian, Lawyers' Association, Athens, 1926; editor and proof-reader, Govostis, publisher, Athens, 1945–48, 1952–56; full-time writer, 1956 onwards. **Other activities** Law clerk, law firm Angelopoulos, Athens, Greece, 1925; clerk, Mitzopoulos-Oeconomopoulos, notaries for National Bank of Greece, 1925–26; confined to a sanatorium with tuberculosis, 1927–31; employed by a music theatre, 1930s; member, Chorus of Ancient Tragedies, National Theatre of Greece, Athens, 1938–45; also, actor and dancer, Lyriki Skini, Athens Opera House; arrested and exiled for political convictions, 1948–52; arrested by Papadopoulos dictatorship, 1967, imprisoned, 1968–71. **Offices and memberships** Member: Greek Communist party, 1934, National Liberation Front (EAM), 1940s, European Community of Writers, Society of Greek Writers, Society of Greek Dramatists, Comité des Gens de Lettres, Société des Ecrivains et Compositeurs Dramatiques Français, Academy of Meinz, Academy Mallarmé. **Awards and honours** State Award for Poetry, Greece, 1956; Grand Prix International de la Biennale de Poésie de Knokke, Belgium, 1972; International Prize "Georgi Dimitroff", Bulgaria, 1974; honorary doctorate, Salonica University, Greece, 1975; Grand Prix Français de la Poésie "Alfred de Vigny", 1975; nominated for Nobel Prize, 1975, 1986; International Prize for Poetry "Etna-Taormina", Italy 1976; International Prize for Poetry "Seregno-Brianza", Italy, 1976; Lenin Prize for Peace, 1977. **Publications — poetry in English** *Romiosyne,* 1966, translated by O. Laos, published as *Romiossyni,* 1969; *Dekaochto lianotragouda tes pikres patridas,* 1973, translated by Amy Mims, published as *Eighteen Short Songs of the Bitter Motherland,* 1974; *Diadromos kai skala,* 1973, translated by Nicos Germanacos, published as *Corridor and Stairs,* 1976. **Poetry collections in English** *Poems of Yannis Ritsos,* translated by Alan Page, 1969; *Romiossini and Other Poems,* translated by Dan Georgakas and Eleni Paidoussi, 1969; *Gestures and Other Poems, 1968–1970,* translated by Nikos Stangos, 1971; *Contradictions,* translated by John Stathatos, 1973; *Yannis Ritsos: Selected Poems,* translated by Nikos Stangos, 1974; *The Fourth Dimensions: Selected Poems of Yannis Ritsos,* translated and introduced by Rae Dalven, 1977; *Chronicle of Exile,* translated and introduced by Minas Savvas, 1977. **Other poetry** (English titles) "Tractor", 1934; "Pyramids", 1935; *Epitafios,* 1936; "The Song of My Sister", 1937; "Spring Symphony", 1938; "The March of the Ocean", 1940; "An Old Mazurka in the Rhythm of the Rain", 1942; "Trial", 1943; "Our Comrade", 1945; "The Man with the Carnation", 1952; "Vigil", 1954; "Morning Star", 1955; "Moonlight Sonata", 1956; "Chronicle", 1957; "Farewell", 1957; "The Urn", 1957; "Winter Limpidity", 1957; "Stony Time", 1957; "The Neighbourhoods of the World", 1957; "When the Stranger Comes", 1958; "Unsubjugated City", 1958; "The Architecture of the Trees", 1958; "The Old Women and the Sea", 1959; "The Window", 1960; "The Bridge", 1960; "The Black Saint", 1961; "Poems Volume I", 1961; "Poems Volume II", 1961; "The Dead House", 1962; "Beneath the Shadow of the Mountain", 1962; "The Prison Tree and the Women", 1963; "Testimonies I", 1963; "12 Poems for Cavafy", 1963; "Poems Volume III", 1964; "Playful Games of the Sky and the Water", 1964; *Philoktetes,* 1964; *Orestes,* 1966; "Testimonies II", 1966; *Ostrava,* 1967; "Stones, Repetition, Railings", 1972; "The Return of Iphigenia", 1972; "Helen", 1972; "Gestures", 1972; "Fourth Dimension", 1972; *Chrysothemis,* 1972; *Ismene,* 1972; *Graganda,* 1973; "The Annihilation of Milos", 1974; "Hymn and Lament for Cyprus", 1974; "The Soot-black Pot", 1974; "Belfry", 1974; "The Wall in the Mirror", 1974; "Papermade", 1974; "The Lady of the Vineyards", 1975; "The Last Century Before Humanity", 1975; "Circumstantial Verse", 1975; "The Postscript of Glory", 1975; "Diaries in Exile", 1975; *Mantatofores,* 1975; "Poems Volume IV", 1975; "Conciergerie", 1976; "Remote", 1977; "Becoming", 1977. **Other publications** *Pera ap'ton iskio ton Kyparission* (Beyond the Shadow of the Cypress Trees, three-act play), Bucharest, 1958; *Mia gynaika plai sti thalassa* (A Woman by the Sea, three-act play), Bucharest, 1959; *Meletimata* (essays), 1974; translations of work represented in anthologies, including *The Penguin Book of Socialist Verse,* edited by A.N. Bold, 1970, *Modern Greek Poetry: From Cavafy to Elytis,* edited by K. Friar, 1973; also translator of French, Romanian and Czechoslovakian poetry into Greek. **Cause of death** Undisclosed, at age 81. **Further reading** Kimon Friar, "Introduction: The Social Poets" in *Modern Greek Poetry,* 1973; Edmund Keeley, in an introduction to *Ritsos in Parentheses,* 1979; *Contemporary Foreign Language Writers,* 1984.

ANYA SETON

American Novelist

***Born* Manhattan, New York, 1904**

***Died* Old Greenwich, Connecticut, 8 November 1990**

There is more to Anya Seton's historical novels than "the thrill of the ripped bodice". But read on — seductive passion is an essential element. Her works are a fusion of popular romance and a serious and meticulously researched attempt to describe a historical period. She wrote, "I love to recreate the past, and to do so with all accuracy possible." A compelling story-teller, Anya Seton portrayed vividly and enthusiastically different eras in American and British history. Her books are "hard to put down" as they sweep the reader back to bygone ages which are conjured up not only by rich descriptions of pageantry and setting but by authentic everyday detail of a cruder and harsher way of life. Heralded as one of the leading romantic historical novelists of her generation, Anya Seton had a tremendous following on both sides of the Atlantic, although she never reached the stature of Margaret Mitchell or Daphne du Maurier, two novelists she at times emulated.

The offspring of two literary parents, Anya Seton was at first determined never to be a writer, claiming "the career had no glamour for me whatsoever". "I was thoroughly aware of the seamy side of the profession — the drudgery, the essential loneliness". Her father was Ernest Thompson Seton, the British-born naturalist and author of such outdoor classics as *Wild Animals I Have Known* and *The Biography of a Grizzly*. He was the founder of the Boy Scouts of America, a renowned wildlife artist and lecturer on the Great Outdoors. Anya Seton's mother, Grace Gallatin, a native Californian and suffragist, was also a writer, producing travel books on the Orient and Middle East. Anya Seton had, in her own words, "rather an unorthodox upbringing", centred mainly around her father's large estate in Connecticut. There, visiting Indians taught her woodcraft and dancing; one Sioux chief was even responsible for changing her name from Ann to the Indian "Anutiha", which was gradually modified by her family to Anya. She received much of her education at home from governesses, thus accommodating her parents' rather peripatetic existence.

Anya Seton's chosen escape route from her parents' overwhelming enthusiasm for the literary life was medicine — but her medical training had to end with her marriage when she was 18 years old and the birth in quick succession of two children. She never lost interest in medicine, however, later incorporating a historical view of the subject into her novels and also working as a medical aide and secretary. The Depression, offering little opportunity for outside employment, forced her into trying her hand at writing while at home. She, in her own words, at first "experimented rather drearily with short stories and verse". Perhaps still inhibited by her literary family, she did not find her niche until "I gave up trying to be a Nobel Prize-winner and was satisfied to be a story-teller." The year 1938 was a turning point, with the acceptance by a newspaper syndicate of one of her short stories. This gave Anya Seton the confidence necessary to tackle the first of her massive "biographical novels" (as she liked to call them). *My Theodosia,* published in 1941, the story of the hapless daughter of Thomas Jefferson's vice-president, Aaron Burr, set the ball rolling by its instant acclaim and a dozen or so historical novels followed. Two were made into successful films — *Dragonwyck,* a chilling gothic tale set in a nineteenth-century mansion along the Hudson River in upstate New York, and *Foxfire,* a story of Arizona in the 1860s. *The Winthrop Woman,* which appeared in 1958 and portrayed seventeenth-century Puritan Massachusetts, has the distinction of being one of America's all-time best-sellers.

Historic Britain was as likely a backdrop for Seton's novels as the United States: Anya Seton was proud of her British roots, through her father's side of the family, and maintained an interest in

Britain throughout her life. Her British novels include *Avalon,* set in tenth-century England, and *Devil Water,* a highly praised story of eighteenth-century Britain and Virginia. *Katherine,* published in 1954, is the tale of Katherine Swynford, the mistress and then wife of John of Gaunt, Duke of Lancaster, and is, perhaps, the best example of Seton's work. Unlike many other romantic historical writers who adopt one period and stick with it, Anya Seton selected a different era and place for each of her novels. She relished the enormous amount of research that was involved in becoming familiar with each period, a process that could take her up to three or four years. She would visit locations associated with her subject, study archival material and consider different historical interpretations of characters. She was successful in incorporating the fruits of her inquiries into a flowing and fascinating story, being careful to invent only within the framework of known historical fact.

In Anya Seton's novels we generally see the past through the eyes of women — some are fictional, others drawn from legend or history. For those heroines based on actual historical figures, which became the hallmark of her work, Seton chose women who were related to prominent men of their time but who, in themselves, have been deemed marginal by historians. Anya Seton rescued these women from obscurity by providing them with "biographies" which supplemented scant historical information about their personal lives with fiction and romance. Women's dependent status throughout history provided in itself a powerful element of romance for all Seton's novels. In addition, Seton frequently used the classic romantic formula of love between a woman of gentle birth and no fortune and a man of influence who is apparently superior, brooding and unobtainable.

Despite the limitations their society imposed on them, Seton's heroines are lively, intelligent and full of determination. As critic Kay Mussell points out, they often show a respect for love, marriage and family which would appeal to the sensibilities of Seton's mid-twentieth century readers. Although they have a tendency to be swept up into passionate relationships doomed to disaster, they eventually make amends by acts of contrition or a new start in life. Even though they may find themselves committed to an unfortunate marriage, they buckle down faithfully and resourcefully to make the best of their situation. "True love", when it is experienced, is unmistakable — compelling and almost overpowering; these are tales of seduction; however — there are no explicit descriptions of sex.

It seems appropriate to end an obituary of Anya Seton with thoughts of the hereafter. Anya Seton had a strong interest in mysticism which she inherited from her parents. Indeed, she believed that she possessed powers of extra-sensory perception which enabled her to receive messages from those she was writing about. Her last major novel, *Green Darkness,* which appeared in 1972, is a powerful work with strong supernatural overtones as contemporary characters in England redress evils that occurred in the mid-sixteenth century. In her introduction to the novel, Anya Seton states her belief in reincarnation which "still seems to me the only logical explanation for life's inequities".

Born Ann Seton. **Parents** Ernest Thompson, writer and naturalist, and Grace (Gallatin) Seton, writer. **Marriages** Two; 2) Hamilton M. Chase, investment lawyer. **Children** One son and one daughter, Seton and Forcey, from first marriage, one daughter, Clemency, from second marriage. **Education** Educated by governesses; Spence School, New York; L'Hotel Dieu, Paris. **Career** Worked as a nurse's aid and secretary before first marriage; author, 1941 onwards. **Related activities** Member, editorial board, *Writers Magazine.* **Offices and memberships** Member: Poets, Playwrights, Editors, Essayists, Novelists, Authors League, National League of American Pen Women, pioneer branch. **Awards and honours** Medal of Honor, Society of Colonial Wars, 1958; honorary member, Pen and Brush Club. **Publications — novels** *My Theodosia,* 1941; *Dragonwyck,* 1944; *The Turquoise,* 1946; *The Hearth and the Eagle,* 1948;

Foxfire, 1951; *Katherine,* 1954; *The Winthrop Woman,* 1958; *Devil Water,* 1962; *Avalon,* 1966; *Green Darkness,* 1972. **Other publications** *The Mistletoe and Sword: A Story of Roman Britain* (juvenile), 1955; *Washington Irving* (juvenile), 1960; *Smouldering Fires* (juvenile), 1975. **Cause of death** Heart failure, at age 86. **Further reading** Kay Mussell, *Women's Gothic and Romantic Fiction,* 1982; *Twentieth Century Romance and Historical Writers,* 1990; Virginia Blain, Isobel Grundy, Patricia Clements, *The Feminist Companion to Literature in English,* 1990.

DODIE SMITH

British Playwright and Novelist

Born **Whitefield, Lancashire, 3 May 1896**

Died **Great Dunmow, Essex, 24 November 1990**

As an entertainer, Dodie Smith gave more pleasure to the reading and playgoing public than it is reasonable to expect from a single pen. That her work has tended to go out of fashion is partly an effect of her fine attunement to her public at the time of writing. She believed that "successful plays originate at the intersection point of an author's desire to write the play with the public's desire to see it." As far as plays went, she could find no intersection between what she wanted to write and what the public wanted to see after World War II; she had no desire, for instance, to try her hand at kitchen-sink drama. She switched to novels, and while, with the possible exception of *I Capture the Castle,* her adult fiction has not lasted particularly well either, her children's novel, *The Hundred and One Dalmatians,* has become a classic.

Dodie Smith was born into a middle-class family in Lancashire, in the north-west of England. After her father's death when she was 18 months old, she and her mother moved in with Dodie's maternal grandmother in Old Trafford, outside Manchester. The house was a chock-a-block with grown-up aunts (two) and uncles (three), plus three pianos, and various pets including a cat so affectionate that it stole and ate the infant Dodie's tonsils after they had been removed by the family doctor. The household often included, too, Dodie's mother's suitors. All made much of the young Dodie.

Uncle Harold was a well-known amateur actor, and the family were keen theatre-goers. From an early age, Smith was stage-struck, and her desire to go on the stage seemed to encounter little opposition from her family and friends, even if it did not get much encouragement either. A maid, present at an early performance in which Smith represented "The Sleeping Beauty", was pressed to recall any compliments she had overheard from the audience, but the only one she could remember hearing was, "That girl's got strong teeth."

Professional acting wasn't an altogether accepted thing for a young lady to do in Edwardian England. But then the household was an odd mix of the bourgeois and the Bohemian. Attitudes to religion, for example, were unconventional. Her mother encouraged her to read most things but drew the line at the Bible saying there were "some very nasty things in it", a view with which Smith was forced to agree when she finally read it.

Soon Smith was not only acting in amateur dramatics, at school and with local societies, but also trying her hand at writing plays, though again not with any notable success: her mother, to whom she read an early effort, responded by falling asleep, to awaken with the apology, "Sorry darling, but it was very, very dull."

At 14, Smith was transplanted to London after her mother succumbed to the most persistent of her suitors. She wrote afterwards that this period of her life made her "introspective, self-conscious and far less self-confident". The new marriage was not a success, and Smith missed the lively and loving Manchester relatives. Nor did she derive much comfort from her new school, the academically distinguished St Paul's School for Girls in Hammersmith, where she found the singing master — the composer Gustav Holst — less interesting than her previous teacher, and her fellow-pupils "snooty little beasts" who prided themselves on cold-shouldering new girls. She admitted, though, that she had benefited from the fine teaching, particularly of English literature. And outside school hours, once she and her mother had rebelled against the parsimonious restrictions which her step-father attempted to impose on their excursions to the West End, they made the most of the theatres.

She went on to study acting at what is now the Royal Academy of Dramatic Art, then simply "the Academy", passing the entrance audition only by a whisker as she afterwards learned to her discomfiture. Her studies were disrupted by her mother's illness and death, and she showed workmanship rather than talent during her studies, though the principal of the Academy, Kenneth Barnes, commended her "sense of the stage". She went doggedly on to pursue a sporadic acting career between 1915 and 1922. An "elfin" figure, less than 5 feet tall, she was usually cast in juvenile bit-parts, which she played with indifferent success, frequently getting sacked. However, as she recalled in her memoirs, she could occasionally bring the house down unintentionally with a line like "We cannot choose, our faces *madden* men": her pictures show a face which, though amiable and even attractive, is irresistably suggestive of an amiable and attractive horse.

Though she refused to give up on acting, it seemed to be giving up on her. Lack of parts forced her into a stop-gap job at Heal's, the venerable furniture store in London's Tottenham Court Road, where she discovered a flair for business and stayed for the best part of a decade. At first put "under the China buyer" to the ribald amusement of her theatrical friends, she successfully ran her own gallery within Heal's and acted as a buyer herself. She became a good friend of the proprietor, Ambrose Heal.

But she did not forget about writing plays. As a schoolgirl she'd sold a screenplay *Schoolgirl Rebels* to a film company for three pounds, ten shillings; a subsequent effort had been turned down. Just before starting at Heal's she had written her first stage play as an adult: *British Talent* was given an amateur production by Smith's friends from the Three Arts Club, a hostel where she had often stayed as an impoverished actress.

Now, on a business trip to Austria, she had a new idea for a play. This story of love between an English schoolmistress and a Tyrolean inn-keeper was to be her first commercial hit, *Autumn Crocus,* which opened in 1931. Despite an inauspicious first night disrupted by rowdies in the audience, *Autumn Crocus* received enthusiastic notices, and was to be the first of half a dozen successes which together notched up 1800 West End performances before the outbreak of World War II. She gave up business for full-time writing.

Her acting experiences, unsatisfactory as they had been, combined with her playgoing to help her create plays which would be fun to act as well as pleasing audiences. Following the advice to write about what one knows, she drew heavily on her own life for subject-matter. *Service* was based on a department store not a million miles from Heal's. *Dear Octopus* was a family drama with echoes of her Manchester childhood — the octopus of the title being the numerous family. Most of her plays had starry casts, and *Dear Octopus* cannot have suffered from the presence of John Gielgud in the not-very-challenging role of the son who turns out at the end to have been in love with his mother's devoted companion for years, without realizing.

By the late 1930s Dodie Smith was a Rolls-Royce-owning celebrity, and was about to marry. At Heal's she had met Alec Beesley, seven years younger than herself, who became first her manager and then her husband. Beesley was a pacifist, a stance with which Smith was in agreement, and it was partly to avoid his getting called up that the couple spent the war years in the US, mainly in California where Smith became a close friend of the distinguished novelist Christopher Isherwood.

It was her idea to dramatize the Sally Bowles story from his *Goodbye to Berlin*; the play, *I Am A Camera,* eventually became the musical *Cabaret.* Dodie Smith herself acted as screenplay doctor for several Hollywood films, and also scripted one or two of her own, though she wasn't always impressed with the end product: when she saw what Hollywood did to her work on the adaptation of J.M. Barrie's *Alice Sit-by-the-Fire,* renamed *Darling, How Could You!,* she gave it another new name: *Bastards, How Could You!*

Smith was homesick for England throughout her 14-year stay in the US, though only intermittently so towards the end. Nostalgia added fervour to the many descriptions of English pubs, castles, and countryside in her novel *I Capture the Castle,* written during her self-imposed exile and published in 1949. Purporting to be the diaries of 17-year-old Cassie, who lives in penury in a derelict castle, it charts the fortunes of her eccentric family and the romantic entanglement of Cassie and her sister with two Americans. Cassie's father is an author whose ten-year writer's block is only cured when his children imprison him in a dungeon.

I Capture the Castle is richly peopled and full of incident, hard to put down. Dodie Smith reported that her friend, the playwright John Van Druten, said that the book was beautifully written but not "important", and wondered how an admirer of Proust and Henry James could write anything so trivial. She responded that she had just wanted to write it and had written it as well as she could. Trivial or not, it was a smash-hit on both sides of the Atlantic, and became standard reading for teenage girls, to the surprise of Dodie Smith who had intended it for an adult market.

She continued to write plays in the immediate post-war years but her later efforts never enjoyed the successes of *Autumn Crocus* and *Dear Octopus,* despite the best efforts of colleagues like Binkie Beaumont, the legendary theatrical manager. *Dear Octopus* with its large cast of well-differentiated characters remained a popular choice for amateurs and was revived in the West End as recently as 1967. But Smith had no desire to oblige the public with the type of realism which became popular during the 1950s. She concentrated on novel-writing with few regrets, though by entitling her four volumes of memoirs *Look Back With Love*, *Look Back With Mixed Feelings* and so on, some thought she was having a dig at John Osborne's play *Look Back In Anger,* a supreme example of the theatrical genre which displaced hers.

It was after Smith had stopped writing for the theatre that she produced her most perennially popular work. She had always adored animals of all kinds. In California she had a morning ritual of fishing out bees which had fallen into the swimming pool, and drying them out indoors in a specially constructed bee-cage before liberating them. But her ruling passion was for Dalmatians, of which she had anything up to nine at any one time. The dynasty of Dalmatians, their progenitor Pongo, and an unfeeling friend who 20 years before had remarked that Pongo would make a nice fur coat, inspired what is probably her best-remembered work, the 1956 children's classic *The Hundred and One Dalmatians,* on which the Disney cartoon *101 Dalmatians,* released in 1961, was based.

The fictional Pongo and his wife leave their "pet" humans to go and recover their family of 15 pups, which have been rustled by the fiendish Cruella de Vil who has designs on their pelts. As well as their own pups, they find a huge collection of puppies waiting to be turned into fur coats at Cruella's country lair. After many adventures, all are led back to the safety of Pongo's London home where they are adopted by the "pets". Although the anthropomorphism is rather repellent to an adult reader, and the suggestion of an animal freemasonry hard to stomach (the dogs are fraternizing with cows in one chapter and eating beef steaks in the next), the book and the cartoon continue to delight even 1990s children, who are accustomed to stronger fare. Cosiness and the certainty of a happy ending are not yet defects in the context of a children's book.

Dodie Smith and her husband spent their last 40 years living in the seclusion of their Essex home. She continued to write adult and children's fiction, and in 1974, at the age of almost 80, began to publish her four-volume autobiography. At times rambling, as the reminiscences of an octogenarian are entitled to be, they display a vigour and intellectual honesty which is not usually equalled by her fiction and plays, besides an astonishingly detailed recall of her early life.

It's easy to see why Dodie Smith's work was popular, and not hard to explain why she is unfashionable. She had imagination, lucidity, humour, and considerable descriptive power. And she had sympathy with her characters, to an excessive degree. If she had treated them with the same rigour she meted out to herself in her memoirs, then the results might have been less soft-centred and more long-lived.

It would be wrong to overstate the conventionality of her material, however. In *Dear Octopus* and elsewhere adulterous affairs are not off-limits, and, referring to another stage hit, *Call It A Day,* she boasted that she had slipped a homosexual character, camouflaged with distracting stage directions, past the Lord Chamberlain (who in those days censored plays before they were staged).

What is often called the anodyne quality of her work cannot be attributed to an over-sheltered life. Though she had been born into comparatively privileged circumstances, in her teens she had watched her mother pass her last few years in an unhappy marriage, for which Smith never forgave her step-father; she had then seen her die from cancer. There was the disappointment and poverty of her own failed career as an actress, and various unhappy love affairs before marriage. She could have drawn on these experiences if she had wanted to, but they would have detracted from what she was aiming for, which was escapism.

It's unfair to criticize someone for failing to do what they never attempted. Literary immortality was not on her agenda. Dodie Smith set out to divert herself and her public — and succeeded.

Born Dorothy Gladys Smith. **Pseudonyms** C.L. Anthony; Charles Henry Percy. **Parents** Ernest Walter and Ella (Furber) Smith. **Marriage** Alec Macbeth Beesley, 1939 (died 1987). **Education** Whalley Range High School, Manchester; St Paul's Girls' School, London; Royal Academy of Dramatic Art, London, 1914–15. **Career** Actress, 1915–22; buyer, Heal and Son, London, 1923–32; author, plays and screenplays using pseudonym C.L. Anthony until 1935; full-time author using own name, 1935 onwards. **Awards and honours** Novel *I Capture the Castle,* Literary Guild selection, 1948. **Publications for children** *The Hundred and One Dalmatians,* 1956; *The Starlight Barking: More about the Hundred and One Dalmatians,* 1967; *The Midnight Kittens,* 1978. **Publications for adults — novels** *I Capture the Castle,* 1948; *The New Moon with the Old,* 1963; *The Town in Bloom,* 1965; *It Ends with Revelations,* 1967; *A Tale of Two Families,* 1970; *The Girl from the Candle-lit Bath,* 1978. **Other publications — memoirs** *Look Back With Love: A Manchester Childhood,* 1974; *Look Back With Mixed Feelings,* 1978; *Look Back With Astonishment,* 1979; *Look Back With Gratitude,* 1985. **Plays** (As C.L. Anthony) *British Talent,* London, 1923; (as C.L. Anthony) *Autumn Crocus,* London, 1931, published, 1931; (as C.L. Anthony) *Service,* London, 1932, published, 1932; (as C.L. Anthony) *Touchwood,* London, 1934, published, 1934; *Call It a Day,* Glasgow and London, 1935, published, 1936; *Bonnet over the Windmill* (also co-director), Leeds and London, 1937, published, 1937; *Dear Octopus* (also co-director), Newcastle-upon-Tyne and London, 1938, published, 1938; *Lovers and Friends,* New York, 1943, published, 1947; *Letter from Paris,* Brighton and London, 1952, published, 1954; *I Capture the Castle,* Blackpool and London, 1954, published, 1955; *These People, Those Books,* Leeds, 1958; *Amateur Means Lover,* Liverpool, 1961, published, 1962. **Screenplays** (As Charles Henry Percy) *Schoolgirl Rebels,* 1915; (with Frank Partos) *The Uninvited,* 1944; (with Lesser Samuels) *Darling, How Could You!,* 1951. **Stage as actress** *Playgoers,* 1915; *Kitty Grey,* 1915; *Mr Wu,* 1915; *Ye Gods,* 1916–17; *Jane and Niobe,* 1916–17; *When Knights Were Bold,* 1917; *Telling the Tale,* 1919–20; *French Leave,* 1921; *The Shewing Up of Blanco Posnet,* 1921; *You Never Can Tell,* 1921; *The Pigeon,* 1922. **Stage as director** (With Murray Macdonald) *Bonnet over the Windmill,* 1937; (with Glen Byam Shaw) *Dear Octopus,* 1938. **Cause of death** Undisclosed, at age 94. **Further reading** *Contemporary Dramatists,* 1988; *Twentieth-Century Children's Writers,* 1989.

COLONEL SIR DAVID STIRLING

British Military Officer

***Born* Scotland, 15 November 1915**

***Died* London, England, 4 November 1990**

Who Dares Wins: like a *Boy's Own* story come true, David Stirling dreamt up the idea of a Special Air Service (SAS), chose this suitably daredevil motto, and, brilliantly, made it work. He always dared, but in later life he didn't always win.

He was born into a military and upper-class family: his father was Brigadier-General Archibald Stirling of Keir, and his mother was the fourth daughter of the thirteenth Baron Lovat. Young Archibald David (he dropped his first name) grew up in the Highlands of Scotland and was educated at Ampleforth, a well-known public school in Yorkshire. From there he proceeded to Trinity College, Cambridge, but he didn't stay the course — other things were more important to him than his degree, not least racing and gambling. He began learning to paint.

Stirling at this time had the idea that he would be the first man to climb Everest. He trained for it for five years, latterly in the Rockies, but was thwarted by World War II, so joined the Scots Guards Supplementary Reserve of Officers as an ensign instead. He didn't like it very much (too ordinary) and was soon recruited into Bob Laycock's Commandos. Once he got to the Middle East with them, however, they were disbanded so that the men could make up losses in the Western Desert. This was the beginning. Stirling and some companions learned to parachute, with such poor equipment that Stirling was inevitably injured, but that didn't matter. In July 1941, on crutches, he put a plan to General Auchinleck for a small, mobile unit that could work as a raiding force behind enemy lines in the desert.

He got his way, and the Special Air Service was born. To have persuaded his superiors was a tremendous achievement in itself, as they were short of men at that time, and Stirling was only 25 and hadn't yet done anything particularly impressive. He immediately got together a detachment of 60 men and six officers, called L Detachment, SAS Brigade (which didn't exist: it was to confuse the enemy) and he, as commanding officer, became a major. From the word go he picked people himself; it was all his own work. They trained very hard.

It got off to an inauspicious start with a disastrous parachute operation, but Stirling ploughed on. He asked the Long Range Desert Group, basically a reconnaissance and intelligence-gathering unit, to carry his team and their Jeeps, and so he was able to work behind enemy lines. This was a tremendous help. In addition, Stirling was brilliant at persuading people to give him equipment. He was soon to be nicknamed the Phantom Major by the Germans for his feats way behind their lines.

In just two weeks in December 1941 the SAS units destroyed 90 aircraft on the ground, many of them the latest and most important the Germans had. He was off. With permission to recruit more men he went from strength to strength, and in 1942 the SAS was officially designated a regiment. They destroyed, over the next 14 months, more than 250 aircraft and severely debilitated enemy communication lines by mining roads, as well as derailing trains, blowing up ammunition dumps and so on. Almost everything came out of Stirling's head. Once 18 of his Jeeps, each with four Vickers K-machine guns, drove straight down the central runway of Sidi Haneish airfield, destroying Junkers, Heinkels, Messerschmitts and Stukas, and finishing the job by driving round the perimeter.

But on 10 January 1943 Rommel's special unit captured Stirling in Tunisia, where he was reconnoitring behind enemy lines ahead of the Eighth Army towards the end of the North African

Campaign. Some Arabs gave him away, and 500 Germans surrounded the cave where he was sleeping. He escaped, but was recaptured, incarcerated in a prison camp in Italy where he escaped four times, and eventually they sealed him into Colditz until the war was over. (Both the First and Second SAS carried on till the end of the war though, and continued to be brilliantly successful.)

So the war was over. Stirling headed to Southern Rhodesia, and became deeply involved in developing African policy. In 1949 he formed the Capricorn African Society, which eventually grew to include the six Commonwealth countries of East and Central Africa; its aims were to create a non-political society based on common citizenship, free of racial discrimination. This was a difficult task indeed, and it didn't really work out.

So, back in the United Kingdom, he founded Television International Enterprises, a consortium providing capital loans for television stations in the emergent countries of Africa, amongst other things. It had the franchise for operating Hong Kong's television service.

In 1967 Stirling started Watchguard, a company based in Guernsey offering security services to foreign heads of state. In 1970 it was involved in a failed plot to free some political prisoners from a Libyan jail. Stirling often advised units dealing with terrorism. He resigned from Watchguard in 1972.

The projects seemed to be getting dodgier. In the unstable political climate of 1974, after the miners' strike had brought down Edward Heath's Conservative government, Stirling was convinced that the country was seriously threatened by extremist action. So he secretly founded GB (Great Britain) 75, which was supposed to be ready to take over essential services like power stations in the event of a general strike. He called it "an organization of apprehensive patriots", whatever that meant. But it clearly wasn't going to work, it was publicly condemned by the then defence secretary, Roy Mason, and Stirling disbanded it before it was properly made public, in 1975.

In a related field, Stirling was asked to support Truemid, the Movement for True Industrial Democracy, which was basically opposing left-wing extremism in the trade unions. He wrote the foreword in the organization's first pamphlet, *The Day of the Ostrich.* He also hatched an idea about putting working-class boys into public schools. A certain section of the press had it in for him, and suggested he was involved with mercenary or secret organizations.

During the last years of his life Stirling was based in London's South Audley Street — he must have enjoyed the joke of the address's initials. Bestowed with a DSO in 1942 and an OBE in 1946, he was awarded a knighthood the year he died: surprisingly late, considering his achievement in founding the SAS, but not so surprising given the activities in which he was subsequently involved.

The SAS was disbanded after the war, a decision strongly criticized by many in the military, but in the early 1950s, after a great deal of lobbying by Stirling and his supporters, it was revived, and still continues, with one regular and two Territorial regiments. Many countries have tried to imitate it.

Stirling was the archetypal dark horse. He never married. Although he had many friends, they often said that he was essentially a private man. He was distinguished to look at, and very tall. He was above all a man of great vision. What he did in 1941 was to see an opportunity that his seniors had missed: that the Sand Sea and Qattara Depression were territories for small-scale, well-equipped raiding parties. Then he had an apparently endless stream of ideas about how to cripple Rommel's Africa Corps. He used the desert well. And of course he was a born leader of soldiers.

Montgomery said of him, "That boy Stirling is quite mad. However, in war there is a place for mad people."

Born Archibald David Stirling. **Parents** Archibald Stirling of Keir, brigadier-general, and the Honourable Mrs Margaret (Lovat) Stirling. **Education** Ampleforth College, North Yorkshire; Trinity College, Cambridge, for one year; studied painting. **Career** Ensign, Supplementary

Reserve of Officers, Scots Guards, 1939–40; transferred to No 3 Commando, Brigade of Guards, Middle East, 1940–41; founder Special Air Service Regiment, 1941; prisoner-of-war, 1943–45. **Other activities** Founder Capricorn Africa Society, 1949, president, 1949–59; chairman, Television International Enterprises Limited, 1961; director, Watchguard, 1967–72; founder GB, (Great Britain) 75, 1975. **Offices and memberships** Movement for True Democracy (Truemid). **Awards and honours** Companion of the Distinguished Service Order, 1942; Officer of the Order of the British Empire, 1946; Officier de la Légion d'honneur; Officer, Orange Nassau; knighted 1990. **Publication** Author of foreword, *The Day of the Ostrich,* Movement for True Democracy. **Cause of death** Undisclosed, at age 74.

December

GEORGE ALLEN

American Football Coach

***Born* Detroit, Michigan, 29 April 1922**

***Died* Rancho Palos Verdes, California, 31 December 1990**

Some people are born winners. Hard-driving, uncompromising football coach George Allen was one of them. "When Coach Allen came in, you felt that winning atmosphere come with him", was how Hall of Fame wide receiver Charley Taylor paid tribute to the man who had the ability to make winners out of losing teams. And one of Allen's old adversaries, Miami Dolphins' coach Don Shula, added, "When you played a George Allen-coached team, you knew they always would be well-prepared and ready to play. He was a winner in all levels of coaching."

A magnificent motivator, his coaching career spanned an incredible six decades, beginning at Morningside College in Sioux City, Iowa, where his first year record of 3–6 proved to be one of only three times that he would end a season with a losing record. The only other blemishes were in the 1951 and 1954 seasons when he was coaching Whittier College.

It was 1957 when he first entered the National Football League, joining the Los Angeles Rams as offensive end coach. The following season he switched to the Chicago Bears, and became the defensive end coach under George Halas. A players' coach, Allen was paid the great compliment not only of being named the Defensive Coach of the Year in 1963, but of also being awarded the game ball after the Bears beat the New York Giants to claim that season's NFL Championship.

But things did not always run on rails for Allen, who succeeded in setting some sort of NFL record by being hired and fired as head coach by the Los Angeles Rams twice in ten years. First recruited as head coach in 1966, he created the Rams' "Fearsome Foursome" front line of Merlin Olsen, Lamar Lundy, Rosey Grier and Deacon Jones. Olsen himself would later eulogize: "He certainly had a major impact on my professional life. He turned around a losing team into a winner. I guess that was what he did best. He took some sad situations and injected his enthusiasm and confidence, and made things happen."

Allen rankled Rams' owner Dan Reeves, and was fired in 1968, but was reinstated as a result of the players' protests. It was almost a direct reversal of the situation which confronted him ten years later, in 1978, when nine of the players refused to suit-up for the stern disciplinarian in a pre-season game, and owner Carroll Rosenbloom fired him.

The records show, however, that Allen's tactics worked: he finished his NFL career with the third best winning percentage (71.2 per cent) of all coaches with 100 or more victories.

Of all the positions he held, it is perhaps as head coach of the Washington Redskins, from 1971 to 1977, that Allen is best remembered. His motto at Washington was "The Future Is Now", and he put that into practice by trading future draft choices for older and more experienced players other teams had given up on. Allen made more trades than any other coach in NFL history, and the Redskins acquired so many veteran players that they earned the nickname of the "Over The Hill Gang". This worried taskmaster Allen little. The team started winning; Redskin fever intensified, and the coach took them to their first Super Bowl appearance with an 11–3 regular season record, and play-off wins over Green Bay and Dallas. It was the closest that Allen would come to producing Super Bowl winners. But on the day, the "No Names" of Miami beat the "Over The Hill Gang" 14–7 in the packed Los Angeles Memorial Coliseum.

His work rate was as phenomenal as his record for producing winning teams. He wrote eleven books on football, took part in marathons, bike-a-thons and triathlons, and, under President Reagan, served as chairman of the President's Council on Physical Fitness and Sports. But one of the greatest tributes to his success as a head coach is the fact that a total of 14 of his assistant coaches went on to become head coaches in the NFL.

Allen coached two teams in the NFL's rival league, the United States Football League, before announcing his retirement in 1984. Five years later, however, he was back in the hot seat, this time as head coach to Long Beach State, which had not had a winning season for four years.

Associate athletic director Bob Donlan, who ran with fitness fanatic Allen every day at Long Beach, noted, "Certainly, we had heard about all the stories on how difficult he was to work with. But based on what he did for us this past year, I wish he had come into my life 20 years earlier." It was typical of the reaction of those who came into contact with Allen. His enthusiasm and will to win infected those around him. And it came as no real surprise that Long Beach State finished with a 6–5 record in what Allen described as his most gratifying season in 35 years of coaching. Ironically, six weeks before his death, he admitted he had not been feeling completely healthy since the players drenched him with ice water to celebrate their season-ending victory over Nevada-Las Vegas in November.

When George Allen had coached games in the NFL, they all kicked off at five minutes after the hour. It was fitting that the memorial service to one of the greatest football coaches in history was scheduled for a 2:05 start.

Born George Allen. **Parents** Earl, worker in Chrysler auto plant, and Loretta Allen. **Marriage** Etty Lumbroso, 1951. **Children** George, Greg, Bruce and Jennifer. **Career** Head coach, Morningside College, Sioux City, Iowa, 1948–50; head coach, Whittier College, California, 1951–56; offensive end coach, Los Angeles Rams, 1957, head coach, 1966–71, 1978; assistant coach/recruiter, Chicago Bears, 1958–62, defensive coach, 1963–66; head coach, Washington Redskins, 1971–77; head coach, Chicago Blitz, 1983; head coach, Arizona Wranglers, 1984; head coach, Long Beach State, 1989–90. **Related activities** Chairman, President's Council on Physical Fitness and Sports, 1981–88. **Career statistics** Third-best all-time winning percentage, National Football League, 118–54–5. **Other activities** Founder, Red Cloud Athletic Federation. **Awards and honours** Named Defensive Coach of the Year, 1963; honorary Sioux chief. **Publications** (include) *How to Scout Football*, 1953; *Encylopedia of Football Drills*, 1953; *The Complete Book of Winning Football Drills*, 1959; *How to Train the Quarter-back*, 1960; *Pass Defense Drills*, 1968; *Inside Football; Fundamentals, Strategy and Tactics for Winning*, 1970. **Cause of death** Undisclosed, at age 68. **Further reading** Bill Libby, *The Coaches*, 1972; William Gildea and Kenneth Turan, *The Future is Now: George Allen, Pro Football's Most Controversial Coach*, 1972.

JOAN BENNETT

American Actress

***Born* Palisades, New Jersey, 27 February 1910**

***Died* White Plains, New York, 7 December 1990**

It would be difficult to think of another actress whose image changed so drastically — and whose screen popularity changed so markedly — by virtue of changing her hair colour from blonde to brunette. Another happy accident in the naked city of Hollywood. Bennett went from sweet *ingénue* (who could be, when depending upon an ineffectual script, a trifle insipid) to treacherous *femme fatale* and the perfect *film noir* heroine, to screen mother — hardly of the self-sacrificing type, but personifying a level-headedness, and an understanding of a need for her child's independence. The lack of self-delusion was representative of the actress herself; of her 60-odd films, Bennett felt that only a half-dozen were of value. But her beauty and her ability to appear innocent and vulnerable on the surface, while concealing an icy evilness inside, kept audiences fascinated for years.

Bennett came from a starry family; her father was actor Richard Bennett, while her older sister Constance was already an established screen figure when young Joan began to act. She was educated in a Paris finishing school, from which she ran away and eloped with a millionaire when she was 16. The marriage lasted two years. In 1915, meanwhile, her father and sister joined her in *Valley of Decision*, a preachy film about birth control. Bennett made her début as "an unborn soul", dressed in diaphanous robes. She had a more auspicious Broadway début with her father in *Jarnegan*, in 1928.

Bennett's first major film role was across Ronald Colman in *Bulldog Drummond*; her second was across George Arliss in *Disraeli*, both in 1929. In these films she was a sweet little thing, with a pretty face and not much to do. A friend of the family, John Barrymore, rescued her by casting her opposite him in *Moby Dick*. The next year she signed a two-year contract with Fox Studios (later to be dropped after unsuccessful pairings with most of her male stars in an attempt to create the "sweetheart team" of which Fox was so enamoured). She played a personable waitress trading wisecracks with Spencer Tracy in *Me and My Gal*, teaming up with him again in another fluffy piece, *She Wanted a Millionaire*. When Fox turned down her request for *Bill of Divorcement*, with Barrymore — the film which made Katharine Hepburn a star — she walked out, in 1933. Ironically, that year she portrayed a pert sister to Hepburn in *Little Women*, directed by George Cukor; her good reviews brought her back to Fox, now joined with Twentieth Century Studios. Other unremarkable films followed, including *Two for Tonight* with Bing Crosby, *Private Worlds*, where her portrait of a psychiatrist's wife slipping into insanity allowed her to display her dramatic talent, *The Man Who Broke The Bank of Monte Carlo*, and *Wedding Present* (across Cary Grant), a feeble screwball comedy. Joan Bennett was the lovely blonde interest ...

> Let's talk of Lamarr, that Hedy so fair
> Is it true that Joan Bennett wears all her old hair?

What won her a verse in a Cole Porter song was a joke suggestion by the director of *Trade Winds* in 1938 that Bennett wear a long black wig in imitation of Hedy Lamarr, who had established the vogue for screen brunettes. (Walter Wanger, Bennett's producer and future husband/mentor, had, by another stroke of irony, directed Lamarr in *her* first high, *Algiers*.) Bennett's transformation proved to be so popular that she decided to remain dark-haired for good. It also helped her emerge from sister Constance's *soignée* shadow at last. Her sultry eyes and deep voice cemented the image.

Almost overnight, Bennett was cast as a *femme fatale*. In films for such illustrious European directors as Fritz Lang (for whom she did her best work), Jean Renoir and Max Ophuls, she was the quintessential sexual mischief-maker in *film noir*. Just before World War II, when audiences demanded more ambiguous, even "dirtier" screen heroines (and that term was never used so ... loosely), Bennett kicked into high gear. As her obituarist in London's *Daily Telegraph* concluded, "Few other Hollywood actresses ... made evil so attractive — or their victims seem so deserving."

Notable films of the 1940s included *House Across the Bay*, where she was a *chanteuse* wife of jailbird George Raft. In 1941 she made the first of her four Lang films, *Man Hunt*, surprising critics with her portrayal of a good-hearted Cockney streetwalker on the run with Walter Pidgeon. It was considered by many to be her finest performance thus far. In *Woman at the Window*, directed by Lang, she achieved the height of her fatal attraction as a mysterious model, opposite the excellent Edward G. Robinson, as the mild academic enamoured of her portrait, who gets involved in murder and chaos when he meets the original. Lang was able to exploit her explosive coarseness and sexual snakiness. In 1945 she was the epitome of predatory malevolence in *Scarlet Street* as Lazylegs, who drove Robinson again to murder. It was a production by the new team of Lang, Wanger and Bennett, as was *The Macomber Affair*, with an unusually good Robert Preston, a year later. Those were the only films for the team's short-lived Diana Productions.

Bennett played the deceptive female for Renoir in *Woman on the Beach* but failed to energize what was an atypically poor film for the French director. But in the following year, 1948, in Max Ophuls's *The Reckless Moment*, she was cast opposite James Mason in an excellent thriller where she discovers the body of her daughter's lover, and ends up in the clutches of a blackmailer. Bennett was a complex bitchy source, in her roles, of all that sexual energy required by the genre. Because of her, Mary Astor (*Maltese Falcon*), Rita Hayworth (*Lady From Shanghai*) and others, women's assertiveness and sexuality was happily out of the celluloid closet at last.

In 1950 (when, at only 40 years old, she was unusual among actresses her age in being willing to play screen mothers), Bennett easily shifted images once more. It is possible that she had grown tired of portraying women in what can be considered (with some justification) narrowly defined roles. She was an elegant, witty and nurturing mother in Vincente Minnelli's *Father of the Bride* with Spencer Tracy and Elizabeth Taylor (following with *Father's Little Dividend* in 1951, with the same cast). The timing was better than she might have imagined — or constructed in a script of her own. In 1951 her screen persona had come uncomfortably close to real life. She was the centre of a scandal when husband Wanger shot her agent in the testicles for, he said, "alienating my wife's affections and breaking up my home". She had insisted that there had been no sexual mischief, and blamed (again, with some reason) the shooting on Wanger's mental state. Plagued by debt, he had gambled and lost on his production of *Joan of Arc* with Ingrid Bergman, and the film market was beginning to change. Nevertheless, Bennett's relationships had been favourite fodder for the gossip columns; Errol Flynn was fortunately saved from Wanger's castrating bullet, thanks to the intervention of Flynn's good friend, actor David Niven. Wanger served 100 days in jail.

But Bennett's mentor *had* helped to damage her career. Glamour was the key to her popularity, but her style didn't translate to the more dimensioned characterization which would have been necessary to sustain her career. Later in life, she admitted to having had little interest in 1950s and 1960s films, but to pay off debts, she had been willing to continue acting — and the industry didn't want to know. Before the shooting, she had starred in over 60 films. After it, at the age of only 41, she was offered only a handful of roles. Outraged at the way she had been treated, friend Humphrey Bogart insisted on having her cast with him in *We're No Angels* in 1955. More roles followed — but only a few. In 1956 she played Fred MacMurray's boring wife whom he contemplates leaving for sassy Barbara Stanwyck (q.v.) in *There's Always Tomorrow*.

After 1956 Bennett worked chiefly in television and some radio to pay off further debts of her husband's. She was the leading lady for a cult TV series, *Dark Shadows*, which ran for five years, and has been rebroadcast often. Television was, according to Bennett, "summer stock in an iron lung". She did some stagework in the early 1960s, including a brief stint in London with *Never Too Late*, which she then took to Broadway. The subject, the pregnancy of a middle-aged woman, was not received ecstatically by the tough New York press. Her last film roles were in horror movies: *Suspiria* and *This House Possessed*. Although they were a far cry from her glamorous icon in 1940s films, she continued to personify self-possessed professionalism.

Born Joan Geraldine Bennett. **Parents** Richard, actor, and Adrienne Mabel (Morrison), actress, Bennett. **Marriages** 1) John Marion Fox, 1926 (divorced 1928); 2) Gene Markey, writer, 1932 (divorced 1937); 3) Walter Wanger, producer, 1940 (divorced 1965); 4) David Wilde, publisher, 1978. **Children** Diana, from first marriage; Melinda, from second marriage; Stephanie and Shelley, from third marriage. **Education** St Margaret's School, Waterbury, Connecticut; L'Hermitage, Versailles, France. **Career** Stage début, *Damaged Goods*, Chicago, 1914; film début, *The Valley of Decision*, 1915; film extra, 1928; Broadway début, *Jarnegan*, 1928; signed five-year contract, United Artists, 1929, released after two films; signed two-year contract, Fox, 1930; first successful film, *Little Women*, 1933; personal contract to Walter Wanger, 1933; signed contract with Columbia and Twentieth Century-Fox, 1941; first film with Fritz Lang, 1941; (with Fritz Lang and Walter Wanger) formed Diana Productions, 1945–48; television début, 1949; acting career halted by scandal after husband shoots agent, 1951; career revived, *We're No Angels*, 1955; London début, *Never Too Late*, 1963; member of the company, Bucks County Playhouse, New Hope, Pennsylvania, 1972–73; retired 1982. **Awards and honours** Mother of the Year, Perkins Children Service. **Stage** (includes, touring production unless otherwise indicated) *Jarnegan*, New York, 1928; *The Pirate, New York*, 1928; *Stage Door*, 1937; *Susan and God*, 1948, 1951; *Bell, Book and Candle*, 1952–53; *Best Foot Foward*, 1953; *Anniversary Waltz*, 1956; *Janus*, 1956–57, Palm Beach, Florida, 1975; *Love Me Little*, New York, 1958; *Once More With Feeling*, 1959; *The Pleasure of His Company*, 1960–61; *The Reluctant Debutante*, Chicago, 1962; *Never Too Late*, Miami, 1963, London, 1963; *Barefoot in the Park*, 1967. **Films** *The Valley of Decision*, 1915; *Power*, 1928; *The Divine Lady*, 1929; *Bulldog Drummond*, 1929; *Three Live Ghosts*, 1929; *Disraeli*, 1929; *The Mississippi Gambler*, 1929; *Puttin' on the Ritz*, 1930; *Crazy That Way*, 1930; *Moby Dick*, 1930; *Maybe It's Love*, 1930; *Scotland Yard*, 1930; *Many a Slip*, 1931; *Doctors' Wives*, 1931; *Hush Money*, 1931; *She Wanted a Millionaire*, 1932; *Careless Lady*, 1932; *The Trial of Vivienne Ware*, 1932; *Week Ends Only*, 1932; *Wild Girl*, 1932; *Me and My Gal*, 1932; *Arizona to Broadway*, 1933; *Little Women*, 1933; *The Pursuit of Happiness*, 1934; *The Man Who Reclaimed His Head*, 1934; *Mississippi*, 1935; *Private Worlds*, 1935; *Two for Tonight*, 1935; *She Couldn't Take It*, 1935; *The Man Who Broke the Bank at Monte Carlo*, 1935; *Thirteen Hours by Air*, 1936; *Big Brown Eyes*, 1936; *Two in a Crowd*, 1936; *Wedding Present*, 1936; *Vogues of 1938*, 1937; *I Met My Love Again*, 1938; *The Texans*, 1938; *Trade Winds*, 1938; *Artists and Models Abroad*, 1938; *The Man in the Iron Mask*, 1939; *The Housekeeper's Daughter*, 1939; *Green Hell*, 1940; *The House Across the Bay*, 1940; *The Man I Married*, 1940; *The Son of Monte Cristo*, 1940; *Confirm or Deny*, 1941; *Man Hunt*, 1941; *She Knew All the Answers*, 1941; *Wild Geese Calling*, 1941; *Girl Trouble*, 1942; *Twin Beds*, 1942; *The Wife Takes a Flyer*, 1942; *Margin for Error*, 1943; *The Woman in the Window*, 1944; *Colonel Effingham's Raid*, 1945; *Nob Hill*, 1945; *Scarlet Street*, 1945; *The Macomber Affair*, 1947; *The Woman on the Beach*, 1947; *Secret Beyond the Door*, 1947; *Hollow Triumph*, 1948; *The Reckless Moment*, 1949; *Father of the Bride*, 1950; *For Heaven's Sake*, 1950; *Father's Little Dividend*, 1951; *The Guy Who Came Back*, 1951; *Highway Dragnet*, 1954; *We're No Angels*, 1954; *Navy Wife*, 1956; *There's Always Tomorrow*, 1956; *Desire in the Dust*, 1960; *House of Dark Shadows*, 1970; *Suspiria*, 1977. **Television** *Danger*, 1950; *Somerset Maugham's TV Theatre*, 1950; *Nash Airflyte Theatre*, 1950; *Ford Television Theatre*, 1952; *The Best of Broadway*, 1955; *Playhouse 90*, 1956; *Junior Miss* (pilot), 1957; *Pursuit*, 1958; *Too Young to Go Steady* (series),

1959; *Dark Shadows* (series), 1966–70; *Gidget Gets Married*, 1972; *The Eyes of Charles Sands* (film), 1972; *Suddenly Love* (film), 1978; *This House Possessed* (film), 1980; *Divorce Wars* (film), 1981; *The Spencer Tracy Legacy* (special), 1986. **Publications** *How to Be Attractive*, 1951; (with Lois Kibbee) *The Bennett Playbill*, 1970. **Cause of death** Heart attack, at age 80. **Further reading** *International Dictionary of Films and Filmmakers*, volume three, 1986.

AARON COPLAND

American Composer

Born **Brooklyn, New York, 14 November 1900**

Died **North Tarrytown, New York, 2 December 1990**

Aaron Copland was the cowboy composer, the man behind those all-American ballets with a country feeling — real homespun hoedowns with titles like *Rodeo* and *Billy the Kid* and *Appalachian Spring*. Yet he was a Jewish boy from Brooklyn, the youngest of five children of eastern European immigrants. He never even saw the West until he was 28. But, he explained, "For me it was not necessary to have an experience in order to compose about it. I preferred to imagine being on a horse without actually getting on one."

Along with such greats as Irving Berlin and Leonard Bernstein (q.v.), Aaron Copland is generally considered to have defined "American" music. He wasn't afraid to sound American, to draw on American folklore and religion to speak to his audiences in their own natural cadences. Concert pianist Samuel Lipman once wrote that Copland "has succeeded in fixing in the mind of a large public an aural image of what America, and therefore American music, sounds like."

As Copland himself wrote in his book, *Our New Music,*

> I was born on Nov. 14, 1900, on a street in Brooklyn that can only be described as drab. It had none of the garish colour of the ghetto, none of the charm of an old New England thoroughfare, or even a pioneer street. I mention it because it was there I spent the first 20 years of my life. Also, because it fills me with mild wonder each time I realize that a musician was born on that street.

His first attempt at composition came at the age of eight, when he wrote a song for his mother, but he didn't decide he wanted to be a composer until his early teens, which he admitted was "rather late for a musician to get started". According to Copland, "My parents were of the opinion that enough money had been invested in the musical training of the four older children, with meagre results", so they refused to pay for music lessons for him. Though one of his older sisters tried to help him by teaching him to play the piano as well as she could, it wasn't enough. He worked and saved until he had enough to go to Paris, at the age of 20.

He stayed in Paris for four years, studying harmony with Nadia Boulanger. He returned to America in 1924, having been commissioned to write a major work for organ and orchestra for Boulanger to play on her first American tour. After the *première* performance of Copland's Symphony for Organ and Orchestra (later re-scored without the organ as his First Symphony), the conductor Walter Damrosch turned to the audience and said, "Ladies and gentlemen, I am sure you will agree that if a gifted young man can write a symphony like this at 23, within five years he will be ready to commit murder."

Copland followed this by experimenting with jazz, which met with some disapproval. When his Piano Concerto (1926) was premièred in Boston, some of the audience accused the conductor of insulting them. Copland followed the jazz experiment with an experiment in avant-garde dissonance. Pieces such as his *Piano Variations* (1930), *Short Symphony* (1932–33), and *Statements* (1933–35), were notably lean in texture and spare on sonority. Paul Moore wrote about these scores in *Theatre Arts*, "Dissonance abounded, along with nervous, irregular rhythms and angular, jagged, non-melodic thematic material." Though avant-garde critics praised these pieces for being "complex, and uncompromisingly austere", they were notoriously difficult to play, and well over the head of the average listener. Copland changed his style once more, and began to compose (as the title of one of his most frequently performed pieces, *Fanfare for the Common Man* suggests) for the man in the street. As he wrote in *Our New Music*, "It seemed to me that we composers were in danger of working in a vacuum. Moreover, an entirely new public for music had grown up around the radio and the phonograph. It made no sense to ignore them and to continue writing as if they did not exist. I felt it was worth the effort to see if I couldn't say what I had to say in the simplest possible terms." He expanded on this theme in 1976, when he stated, "It's nice to vary the attack, so to speak, by sometimes addressing a highly sophisticated audience ... and then to turn around and write something for school chorus or orchestra ... Not all composers are able to do that." Copland was.

An interesting aspect of his work is the way he incorporated established traditional tunes into his own work, transforming them in the process. In his *El Salón México* (1937), he used authentic Mexican tunes, cloaked in dazzling orchestrations. *Billy the Kid* (1938) incorporates genuine cowboy songs. *Appalachian Spring* (1944) features a number of variations on an old Shaker hymn, "The Gift To Be Simple". His *Lincoln Portrait* (1942) utilizes popular songs from Lincoln's time, such as "Camptown Races". (In that pre-electronic era of the 1930s and 1940s, it would seem that Aaron Copland was the first "sampler"!)

Among the young composers of his time, Copland was the acknowledged leader. He was actively involved in furthering the cause of modern music, organizing concerts and festivals to bring the new music to the public's attention. He also took an active interest in the careers of his fellow composers. According to Virgil Thomson, "all were to serve under his leadership as a sort of commando unit for penetrating one after the other the reactionary strongholds." Leonard Bernstein wrote of Copland, "He was the composer who would lead American music out of the wilderness. He was 'The Leader', the one to whom the young always came with their compositions." The list of composers nurtured by Copland through the early days of their careers is an impressive one, including such luminaries as Lukas Foss, David Diamond, Toru Takemitsu, David Del Tredici and of course, Leonard Bernstein.

His relationship with Bernstein was a special one. They met in 1937, and Bernstein was to recall his initial impression of Copland as someone tall and lithe and angular, "with buck teeth and a giggle and a big nose, of a charm not to be described". Copland was to become, according to Bernstein, "my master, my idol, my sage, my shrink". He said that Copland "always understood my music almost intuitively".

There was a brief period of tension between them when Copland embraced the Schoenberg 12-tone system of music. Bernstein chided him, "Of all people, why you — you who are so instinctive, so spontaneous? Why are you bothering with tone rows and with the rules of retrograde and inversion and all that?" Copland felt compelled to defend himself, and in an interview with Donal Henahan of *The New York Times*, he said of Bernstein, "I thought it was rather naïve of him to imagine that you can just happily go on doing what you always had been doing and get away with it. Going into 12-tone seemed to me to be giving myself possibilities I wouldn't otherwise have had, and it never occurred to me that by adopting a method that so many other people were working with that I was somehow betraying myself, my chosen path."

But the bond of friendship between them was too deep to be damaged by a disagreement over just one of Copland's many experiments with style. A photograph taken of the two of them in 1980 sums it all up: Bernstein, by now an old man himself, is leaning over the smaller, somewhat frail-looking Copland, holding his mentor's face gently in his hands. The warmth of that image is almost palpable. Sad though it may be for American music, it somehow seems right that they died within two months of each other.

Copland spent some time in Hollywood, writing background music for films, and winning an Oscar for the 1948 film, *The Heiress*. Surprisingly, he found Hollywood the perfect place for working on his masterpiece, *Appalachian Spring*. He wrote in *Our New Music*, "An air of mystery hovers over a film studio after dark. Its silent and empty streets give off something of the atmosphere of a walled medieval town. This seclusion provided the required calm for evoking the peaceful, open countryside of rural Pennsylvania".

The 1950s brought him a series of problems. A victim of the McCarthy witch-hunts, his *Lincoln Portrait* was cancelled as part of Eisenhower's inauguration ceremonies. He also lost his place as the acknowledged leader of younger composers. Bernstein recalled that the young "gradually stopped flocking to Aaron; the effect on him — and therefore American music — was heartbreaking."

By the 1970s he had stopped composing. Interviewed in 1980, he said, "I'm surprised I don't miss composing more than I do ... I must have expressed myself sufficiently." He may have retired from composition, but he certainly hadn't retired from life. He travelled the world as a self-styled ambassador of American music, and "luxuriated" in conducting. He was well into his seventies when he stated, "When somebody calls me and invites me to conduct, I don't ask where, or what the fee is, I just say 'yes' immediately." He was an incredibly energetic conductor; at the age of 80 he was still "literally leaping into the air in his exuberance".

His exuberant style of conducting was a natural outgrowth of his exuberant music. According to Paul Rosenfeld, Copland represented "American brass and momentum, all that's swift and daring, aggressive and unconstrained in our life."

To his fervent disciple, Leonard Bernstein, Copland was "this simple and great man in our midst". Virgil Thomson picked up on this particular quote of Bernstein's, saying, "The Copland catalogue has good stuff under every heading, including opera. He has never turned out bad work, nor worked without an inspiration. His stance is that not only of a professional but also of an artist — responsible, prepared, giving of his best. And if that best is also the best we have, there is every reason to be thankful for its straightforward employment of high gifts. Also of course, for what is the result of exactly that, 'this simple and great man in our midst.'"

Born Aaron Copland. **Parents** Harris Morris, department store owner, and Sarah (Mittenthal) Copland. **Education** Boys' High School, Brooklyn, New York; studied piano with: Leopold Wolfson, Victor Wittgenstein, Clarence Adler and Ricardo Vines; studied composition with: Rubin Goldmark, 1917–21, Nadia Boulanger, Fontainbleau School of Music, 1921, Paris, 1921–24. **Career** Published first composition, *The Cat and the Mouse*, 1920; first compositions performed publicly, 1924; lecturer on music, New School for Social Research, New York, 1927–37; founded Arrow Music Press; début, *Billy the Kid*, 1938; début, *Rodeo*, 1942; composed *Fanfare for the Common Man*, 1942; début, *Appalachian Spring*, 1944; last major composition, *Inscape*, 1967; farewell concert, *Appalachian Spring*, New York, 1983. **Related activities** Organizer, Copland-Sessions Concerts, 1928–31; founder, American Festival of Contemporary Music, Yaddo, New York, 1932; toured Latin America, 1941, 1947; lecturer in music composition, Harvard University, 1935, 1944, Charles Eliot Norton Professor of Poetry, 1951–52; faculty chairman, Berkshire Music Center, 1940–65, head of composition, 1942–65; vice-president, Koussevitsky Music Foundation; president, Edward MacDowell Association; director, Walter W. Naumburg Music Foundation,

American Music Center; founder, American Composers Alliance, 1939, president, 1939–45; advisory editor, *Perspectives of New Music.* **Offices and memberships** Member: National Institute of Arts and Letters, 1942, American Academy of Arts and Letters, American Society of Composers, Authors and Publishers, 1946; director: League of Composers, International Society for Contemporary Music; member: Royal Academy of Music, London, Royal Society of Arts, London, Accademia Nazionale di Santa Cecilia, Rome, Academia Nacional de Belles Artes, Buenos Aires; honorary fellow, University of Chile. **Awards and honours** Guggenheim Fellowship, 1925, 1926; RCA Victor Company 5000-dollar prize for *Dance Symphony*, 1930; Pulitzer Prize in music for *Appalachian Spring*, 1945; New York Music Critics Circle award for: *Appalachian Spring*, 1945, Third Symphony, 1946; Oscar for best musical score for *The Heiress*, 1950; American Academy of Arts and Letters Gold Medal for Music, 1950; honorary DMus: Princeton University, 1956, Oberlin College, 1958, Illinois Wesleyan University, 1958, Temple University, 1959, University of Hartford, 1959, Rutgers University, 1967, Ohio State University, 1970, New York University, 1970, Columbia University, 1971, University of York, England, 1971; honorary HHD: Brandeis University, 1957, Harvard University, 1961, Syracuse University, 1964, University of Rhode Island, 1964; Edward MacDowell Medal, 1961; Presidential Medal of Freedom, 1964; Howland Memorial prize, Yale University, 1970; Commander's Cross of the Order of Merit, Federal Republic of Germany, 1970; Gold Baton, American Symphony Orchestra League, 1978; Kennedy Center Award, 1979; Aaron Copland School of Music founded in his honour, Queens College, City University of New York, 1982. **Operas** *The Second Hurricane*, 1936; *The Tender Land*, 1952–54. **Ballets** *Grohg*, 1922–25; *Hear Ye! Hear Ye!*, 1934; *Billy the Kid*, 1938; *Rodeo*, 1942; *Appalachian Spring*, 1943–44; *Dance Panels*, 1959. **Film scores** *The City*, 1939; *Of Mice and Men*, 1939; *Our Town*, 1940; *North Star*, 1943; *The Cummington Story*, 1945; *The Red Pony*, 1948; *The Heiress*, 1948; *Something Wild*, 1961. **Orchestral compositions** Symphony, 1924; *Music for the Theatre*, 1925; Symphony for Organ and Orchestra, 1925 (without organ, Symphony No. 1); Piano Concerto, 1926; *Symphonic Ode* 1927–29; *Short Symphony* (Symphony No. 2), 1932–33; *Statements: Militant, Cryptic, Dogmatic, Subjective, Jingo, Prophetic*, 1932–35; *El salón México*, 1933–36; *Music for Radio (Prairie Journal)*, 1937; *An Outdoor Overture*, 1938; *Quiet City*, 1939; *From Sorcery to Science*, 1939; *John Henry*, 1940; *Fanfare for the Common Man*, 1942; *Lincoln Portrait*, 1942; *Music for Movies*, 1942; *Letter from Home*, 1944; *Jubilee Variation on Theme of Goossens*, 1944; *Danzón cubano*, 1944; Symphony No. 3, 1944–46; Clarinet Concerto, 1947–48; *Preamble for a Solemn Occasion*, 1949; *Orchestral Variations*, 1957; *The World of Nick Adams* (television score), 1957; *Connotations*, 1962; *Music for a Great City*, 1964; *Down a Country Lane*, 1964; *Emblems*, 1964; *CBS* (signature tune), 1967; *Inscape*, 1967; *Inaugural Fanfare*, 1969; *Three Latin American Sketches: Estribillo, Paisaje mexicana, Danza de Jalisco,* 1972. **Chamber compositions** *Capriccio*, 1916–21; *Poème*, 1916–21; *Lament*, 1916–21; *Two preludes*, 1916–21; Piano Trio, 1916–21; *Rondino*, 1923; *Lento molto*, 1928; *Lento espressivo*, 1923; *Nocturne*, 1926; *Ukelele Serenade*, 1926; *Vitebsk, Study on a Jewish Theme*, 1929; *Miracle at Verdun* (incidental music), 1931; *Elegies*, 1932; *Sextet*, 1937; *The Five Kings*, 1939; *Quiet City*, 1939; *Violin Sonata*, 1942–43; Piano Quartet, 1950; *Nonet*, 1960; *Duo*, 1971; *Threnody I: Igor Stravinsky, in memoriam*, 1971; *Vocalise*, 1972; *Threnody II: Beatrice Cunningham, in memoriam*, 1973. **Compositions for keyboard** *Moment musical*, 1917; *Danse Caractéristique*, 1918; *Waltz Caprice*, 1918; *Sonnets I and III*, 1918–20; Piano Sonata, 1920–21; *Sonnet II*, 1919; *Scherzo Humoristique: Le Chat et La Souris*, 1920; *Three Moods: Embittered, Wistful, Jazzy*, 1920–21; *Petit Portrait*, 1921; *Passacaglia*, 1921–22; *Sentimental Melody*, 1926; Piano Variations, 1930; *Dance of the Adolescent*, 1932; *Sunday Afternoon Music*, 1935; *Piano Sonata, 1939–41; Episode*, 1940; *Danzón cubano*, 1942; *Our Town*, 1944; *Two Piano Pieces: Midday Thoughts, Proclamation for the Piano*, 1944–82; *Four Piano Blues*, 1926, 1934, 1947, 1948; *Piano Fantasy*, 1952–57; *Preamble for a Solemn Occasion*, 1953; *Down a Country Lane*, 1962; *Rodeo*, 1962; *Danza de Jalisco*, 1963;

Dance Panels, 1965; *In Evening Air*, 1966; *Night Thoughts (Homage to Ives)*, 1972; *Midsummer Nocturne*, 1977. **Choral compositions** Four Motets, 1921; *The House on the Hill*, 1925; *An Immorality*, 1925; *Into the Streets May First*, 1934; *What Do We Plant?*, 1935; *Lark*, 1938; *Las Agachadas*, 1942; *Song of the Guerrillas*, 1943; *The Younger Generation*, 1943; *In the Beginning*, 1947; *Stomp Your Foot, The Promise of Living*, 1954; *Canticle of Freedom*, 1955. **Songs** *Melancholy*, 1917; *Spurned Love*, 1917; *After Antwerp*, 1917; *Night*, 1918; *A Summer Vacation*, 1918; *My Heart is in the East*, 1918; *Simone*, 1919; *Music I Heard*, 1920; *Old Poem*, 1920; *Pastorale*, 1921; *Alone*, 1922; *As It Fell Upon A Day*, 1923; *Poet's Song*, 1927; *Vocalise*, 1928; *Twelve Poems of Emily Dickinson*, 1944–50; *Old American Songs*, 1950; *Old American Songs: Set Two*, 1952; *Dirge in Woods*, 1954; *Laurie's Song*, 1954. **Publications** *What to Listen for in Music*, 1939; *Our New Music*, 1941; *Music and Imagination*, 1952; *Copland on Music*, 1960; (with V. Perlis) *Copland 1900–1942* (autobiography), 1984. **Cause of death** Complications from stroke and respiratory problems, at age 90. **Further reading** Arthur Berger, *Aaron Copland*, 1953; Julia Smith, *Aaron Copland: His Work and Contribution to American Music*, 1955; C. Peare, *Aaron Copland: His Life*, 1969; JoAnn Skowronski, *Aaron Copland: A Bio-Bibliography*, 1985; *Contemporary Composers*, 1991.

BOB CUMMINGS

American Actor and Television Personality

***Born* Joliet, Missouri, 10 June 1910**

***Died* Los Angeles, California, 2 December 1990**

In attempting to appraise the life and career of Bob Cummings, reviewers often fail to make the correct observations. First, Cummings was not really an actor in the sense that he desired to be in movies or remembered for his contributions to the cinematic arts. This mistake is made because the public mind wishes to perceive and even expects movie idols, like other artists, to "live for their craft". Secondly, Cummings himself used his career and the money, position, and freedom it could afford him in the pursuit of his real interest — aviation. As an interviewer for a popular aviation magazine put it, Cummings "was a flyer who also happened to act."

Many reviewers like to mention Cummings's adventurous *entrée* into the profession, comparing it to his later lack-lustre career. Having had no luck finding work as an actor on Broadway due to a trend among theatre producers to hire only British actors, Cummings cashed a life insurance policy and sailed for England. He stayed long enough to develop an accent and a persona he called Blade Stanhope Conway (or B.S. Conway) and returned to the Great White Way where he found parts waiting for him. He pulled the same scam when he went to Hollywood in 1935, posing as Texan Brice Hutchens to break into Westerns.

One reviewer wrote, "One looks in vain for more than traces of the rebellious zaniness in the likeable but finally one-dimensional romantic lead he played in so many light comedies". Yet Cummings only entered acting, after being convinced of the golden opportunities involved, in an effort to gain the means to continue his flying lessons, which lack of money during the Depression had impeded.

As a pilot, Cummings might have been remembered as something special. He held the very first federal flight instructor's rating ever issued. Rejected by the armed forces for combat prior to World War II, because of his age, Cummings helped originate California's first Civil Air Patrol. He even had an airport named after him and taught many of his Hollywood friends and family members how to fly.

As an actor, Cummings seldom soared. The role in which he continues to garner praise was the lead in *Princess O'Rourke*, not surprisingly, the story of an airline pilot. In most of his movies, Cummings was serviceable as a light comic lead. When cast in dramas, however, Cummings failed to command the screen like other actors. Hopelessly miscast in Hitchcock's *Saboteur*, Cummings eventually succeeded in the role of the man Ray Milland suspects of having an affair with his wife, Grace Kelly, in the Master's *Dial M for Murder*.

It is telling that he found a niche for himself on the burgeoning medium of television. First in the situation comedy, *My Hero*, in 1952 and then in his self-produced hit series, *The Bob Cummings Show*, Cummings proved the medium a perfect space for working actors. In a review of the syndicated version of the latter show, renamed *Love That Bob*, a reviewer called it "sexist and dumb". Yet the show was enormously successful, probably due to the fact that post-war American "innocence" valued ignorance and sexism (and other "isms" as well). It is duly noted that Cummings did receive an Emmy for the Studio One *première* of the realist play, *Twelve Angry Men*, yet it was for a character who was basically, though impassioned, a talking head.

Cummings kept a firm grasp on semi-stardom, partly due to his eternal youthfulness. He was a proponent of health foods, ran a vitamin business, and wrote a book, *How to Stay Young and Vital*. Upon his eightieth birthday, a few months before his death, he insisted to friends that he was only 40.

Born Charles Clarence Robert Orville Cummings. **Parents** Charles C., physician and tuberculosis sanitorium owner, and Ruth (Kraft), ordained minister, Cummings. **Marriages** 1) Vivian Janis, dancer, 1933 (dissolved); 2) Mary Elliott, actress, 1945; 3)Name unknown; 4)Regina Young; 5) Janie, 1989. **Children** Robert, Mary, Sharon and Laurel, from second marriage; Anthony, Charles and Michelle, from later marriages. **Education** Drury College, Springfield, Missouri; Carnegie Institute of Technology; American Academy of Dramatic Arts. **Military service** Flight instructor, US Air Force, 1941–45. **Career** Broadway début as Blade Stanhope Conway, *The Roof*, 1931; appeared in stage and vaudeville, 1931–35; film début, *Sons of the Desert*, 1933; (as Brice Hutchens) appeared in *The Virginia Judge*, 1935; reverted to own name of Robert Cummings, 1935; contract player, Universal, 1940, released after winning lawsuit, 1945; produced first film, *Let's Live a Little*, 1948; television début, *My Hero*, CBS, 1952; star, *The Bob Cummings Show* (also under name *Love That Bob)*, 1955–59. **Other activities** Aviator. **Awards and honours** Honorary colonel, Air National Guard, 1948; Emmy Award, best actor in a drama, *Studio One* production of *Twelve Angry Men*, 1955. **Stage** *The Roof*, 1931; *Ziegfeld Follies*, 1932; *Faithfully Yours*, 1951. **Films** (As Blade Stanhope Conway) *Sons of the Desert*, 1933; (as Brice Hutchens) *The Virginia Judge*, 1935; *So Red the Rose*, 1935; *Millions in the Air*, 1935; *Desert Gold*, 1936; *Arizona Mahoney*, 1936; *Border Flight*, 1936; *Forgotten Faces*, 1936; *Three Cheers for Love*, 1936; *Hollywood Boulevard*, 1936; *The Accusing Finger*, 1937; *Hideaway Girl*, 1937; *The Last Train from Madrid*, 1937; *Souls at Sea*, 1937; *Sophie Lang Goes West*, 1937; *Wells Fargo*, 1937; *College Swing*, 1938; *You and Me*, 1938; *The Texans*, 1938; *Touchdown Army*, 1938; *I Stand Accused*, 1938; *Three Smart Girls Grow Up*, 1939; *The Under-Pup*, 1939; *Rio*, 1939; *Everything Happens at Night*, 1939; *Charlie McCarthy, Detective*, 1939; *And One Was Beautiful*, 1940; *Private Affairs*, 1940; *Spring Parade*, 1940; *One Night in the Tropics*, 1940; *Free and Easy*, 1941; *The Devil and Miss Jones*, 1941; *Moon Over Miami*, 1941; *It Started With Eve*, 1941; *King's Row*, 1941; *Saboteur*, 1942; *Between Us Girls*, 1942; *Forever and a Day*, 1942; *Princess O'Rourke*, 1943; *Flesh and Fantasy*, 1943; *You Came Along*, 1945; *The Bride Wore Boots*, 1946; *The Chase*, 1946; *Heaven Only Knows*, 1947; *The Lost Moment*, 1947; *Sleep, My Love*, 1948; *Let's Live a Little* (and co-produced), 1948; *The Accused*, 1949; *Free for All*, 1949; *Tell It to the Judge*, 1949; *The Black Book*,

1949; *Paid in Full*, 1950; *The Petty Girl*, 1950; *For Heaven's Sake*, 1950; *The Barefoot Mailman*, 1951; *The First Time*, 1952; *Marry Me Again*, 1953; *Lucky Me*, 1954; *Dial M for Murder*, 1954; *How to Be Very Very Popular*, 1955; *My Geisha*, 1962; *Beach Party*, 1962; *The Carpetbaggers*, 1964; *What a Way to Go!*, 1964; *Promise Her Anything*, 1966; *Stagecoach*, 1966; *Five Golden Dragons*, 1967. **Television** *My Hero*, 1952–53; *Best Foot Forward*, 1954; *Twelve Angry Men*, 1954; *The Bob Cummings Show*, 1955–59; *The New Bob Cummings Show*, 1961–62; *My Living Doll*, 1964–65; *Gidget Grows Up* (film); *The Great American Beauty Contest* (film), 1973; *Partners in Crime* (film), 1973. **Publication** *Stay Young and Vital*, 1960. **Cause of death** Parkinson's disease, kidney failure and complications from pneumonia, at age 80. **Further reading** *International Dictionary of Films and Filmmakers*, volume three, 1986.

LUCY DAWIDOWICZ

American Historian

***Born* New York, 16 June 1915**

***Died* Manhattan, New York, 5 December 1990**

Lucy Dawidowicz wrote about the Holocaust with a passion and commitment which few historians ever attain. Unlike most scholars, she had personal experience of the situation in Europe both before and after World War II. As a young Jewish American studying in Europe in 1938 to 1939, she witnessed the growing fears of the European Jews on the eve of the war, and as an education officer for the American Joint Jewish Distribution Committee in Germany in 1946 she dealt with many of the Holocaust's immediate victims.

Born Lucy Schildkret, she was the daughter of working-class Jewish immigrants from eastern Europe. She received an excellent education in the thriving Jewish community in New York, and graduated from Hunter College with a BA in English in 1937. In another time she might have been content to remain in the United States, but the growing menace of Nazi Germany made her look back towards the land of her ancestors with a mixture of fascination and confusion. To devote herself to English literature at a time when Jews were being persecuted in their millions simply did not make sense. She abandoned her MA studies in English at Columbia University and took up a post-graduate fellowship in Jewish history at the Yivo Institute for Jewish Research in Vilna, Poland. Her parents were alarmed at the thought of their daughter rushing into the heart of a crisis which so many were trying to escape, but she was convinced that it was the right thing to do: "I found that in a world of brutal history whose victims were too often Jews, Wordsworth had become wearisome and even alien."

She was able to spend only a year in Poland before the course of events forced her to join the exodus from eastern Europe back to the United States. "In the year I lived there every day dawned with anxiety for the future and darkened with the terror of history." In August 1939, as war threatened to break out at any moment, she had to find her way across Europe and back home, leaving behind many friends and teachers whom she would not see again, but taking with her a social and scholarly tradition which was soon to be almost completely extinguished. "For now I embodied a specific Jewish continuity, bridging the Yivo's European past and its present American possibilities. I stood between two worlds and was part of both."

She turned to the study and writing of history in order to give expression to her new sense of purpose. During the war years the Yivo branch in New York published many scholarly works on the plight of the Jews in eastern Europe. In 1946, as part of a Jewish American relief team, she toured the camps for displaced persons, discovering for herself what the Holocaust had done. It was at this time that she conceived the idea of writing a history of the Holocaust.

Her career as an academic began with a lectureship at Yeshiva University in New York, and culminated in her appointment to the Eli and Diana Zborowski Chair in Interdisciplinary Holocaust Studies at the same university in 1976. During this time she carried out exhaustive research into the history of the European Jews in the 1930s and 1940s, making use of her knowledge of European languages and Yiddish to consult a wide variety of private and communal sources to build up a comprehensive picture of the lives of the Jews before, during and immediately after World War II. Her major work, *The War Against the Jews 1933–1945*, put forward a radical thesis that the extermination of the Jews and the drive towards "Aryan racial purity" determined Hitler's military and political policies. It was not a theory which won universal assent or approval, particularly as she was inclined to be aggressive in her arguments against other scholars, but it did help to discredit those who tried to fix the blame upon the Jews themselves, or to argue that there was no connection between the long history of anti-Semitism in Europe and the Nazi (and Stalinist) policies towards the Jews. A further work, *The Holocaust and the Historians*, was a shrewd and perceptive analysis of the treatment of the Holocaust by American and European historians, showing how there was a marked tendency to play down its significance, particularly in the New Germany.

Lucy Dawidowicz was a Jew writing about the Jews. She did not shy away from difficult questions, but confronted them and tried to explain them. Her sense of purpose and her close identity with the subject might occasionally have caused her to be too polemical and too forthright in her treatment of contrary views and opinions, but her fellow historians recognized her ability and the high standard of her scholarship. Her achievement as a historian was a fitting tribute to the people whose sufferings she chose to chronicle. As one reviewer of *The War Against the Jews* put it: "Austere and disciplined, this book comes to seem an exemplar of that Jewish belief — or human delusion — that somehow there may still be a moral use in telling what it meant to live and die in the twentieth century."

Born Lucy Schildkret. **Parents** Max and Dora (Ofnaem) Shildkret. **Marriage** Szymon M. Dawidowicz, 1948 (died 1979). **Education** Hunter College, New York, BA, 1936; post-graduate research fellow, Yivo Institute for Jewish Research, Vilna, Poland, 1938–39; Columbia University, MA, 1961. **Career** Assistant to research director, Yivo Institute of Jewish Research, New York City, 1940–46; education officer, displaced persons camps, American Jewish Joint Distribution Committee, Germany, 1946–47; research analyst, American Jewish Committee, 1948–68, research director, 1968–69; faculty, Yeshiva University, New York City, 1969–78, professor of social history, 1974–78, Paul and Leah Lewis Professor of Holocaust Studies, 1970–75, Eli and Diana Zborowski Professor of Interdisciplinary Holocaust Studies, 1976–78. **Related activities** Member, President's Commission on the Holocaust, 1978–79; visiting professor in Jewish civilization, Stanford University, 1981; visiting professor, State University of New York, Albany, 1982; board of directors: Leo Baeck Institute, Library Corporation, Jewish Theological Seminary, Conference on Jewish Social Studies; president, Fund for Translation of Jewish Literature; contributor: *Commentary*, *The New York Times Book Review*, *The Times Literary Supplement*. **Offices and memberships** Member: American Historical Association, American Jewish Historical Society, Conference of Jewish Social Studies, Association for Jewish Studies. **Awards and honours** National Foundation for Jewish Culture Award, 1965; Memorial Foundation for Jewish Culture Award, 1968, 1973, 1974; Atran Foundation Award, 1971; John Slawson Fund for Research Teaching and Education Award, 1972; Gustave Wurzweiler Foundation Award, 1974; Guggenheim Foundation fellowship, 1976; Anisfield-Wolf Prize for *The War Against the Jews, 1933–*

1945, 1976; honorary LHD: Kenyon College, 1978, Hebrew Union College and Jewish Institute of Religion, 1978, Monmouth College, 1982, Yeshiva University, 1983; honorary DHL, Spertus College, 1983. **Publications** (With Leon J. Goldstein) *Politics in a Pluralist Democracy*, 1963; (editor with others) *For Max Weinreich on His Seventieth Birthday: Studies in Jewish Languages, Literature and Society*, 1964; (editor and author of historical introduction) *The Golden Tradition: Jewish Life and Thought in Eastern Europe*, 1967; *The War Against the Jews, 1933–1945*, 1975; *A Holocaust Reader*, 1976; *The Jewish Presence: Essays on Identity and History*, 1977; *The Holocaust and the Historians*, 1981; *On Equal Terms: Jews in America, 1881–1981*, 1982; *From That Place and Time: A Memoir 1938 to 1947*, 1989. **Cause of death** Undisclosed, at age 75.

FRIEDRICH DÜRRENMATT

Swiss Playwright, Novelist, Critic, Essayist and Artist

***Born* Konolfingen, Switzerland, 5 January 1921**

***Died* Neuchâtel, Switzerland, 14 December 1990**

Go to a German-speaking theatre anywhere in the world and, statistically, the chances are that you will see a play by one of three dramatists. Of these, only the first, Bertolt Brecht, is German. The other two are William Shakespeare, and the Swiss writer Friedrich Dürrenmatt. And where many English speakers might have difficulty in grasping how a relatively "lightweight" writer such as Dürrenmatt could ever share the same popularity ratings as Brecht, or even the Bard himself, the fact is that Dürrenmatt's plays and stories have had a gargantuan impact on European literary tastes over the last 20 to 30 years. Dürrenmatt's place in the canon of European contemporary literature is assured; his works have been translated into more than 50 languages and they provide staple food for students of literature all over the world. Just how long he stays a part of that canon remains to be seen.

Taken as a whole, Dürrenmatt's work presents a study in the art of the grotesque, a foray into the world of paradox. Accused of nihilistic self-indulgence, Dürrenmatt constantly proclaimed himself an optimist: "If the world is to be rejected", he once wrote, "then it must first be accepted". Paradoxically, to accept the world as Dürrenmatt portrays it in his plays and stories, is to come to terms with a world full of uncertainty, irony and, above all, absurdity. Our age, he said, was too serious for tragedy; comedy was the only viable form today: "Comedy", he goes on, "supposes an unformed world, a world being made and turned upside down, a world about to fold, like ours." His characters are semi-ridiculous individuals — mad scientists, murderers, dreamers — and his situations border on the fringes of reality.

Dürrenmatt never conformed to any of the mainstream literary traditions and, as a Swiss, he was able to stand apart from the ideological, artistic and economic influences exerted by the much larger German-speaking neighbour to the north. He inherited his independent spirit from his grandfather, a well-known satirist and political poet, and quickly learned to exercise it, giving up his study of theology against the wishes of his parson-father, and opting instead for philosophy, literature and the history of art. Non-conformist he most certainly was, eschewing literary labels and attacking both sides of the political spectrum. For someone who was as well-known in Switzerland for his paintings as he was for his plays, who worked as a graphic artist and theatre critic, and who also wrote cabaret songs, the terms usually used to describe Dürrenmatt, "author and dramatist", are clearly inadequate.

As a young man, Dürrenmatt was at the forefront of the Swiss avant-garde. In addition to German Expressionist drama, writers as diverse as George Bernard Shaw, Pirandello, E.T.A. Hoffmann and Kafka, all exerted an influence on Dürrenmatt as he began to formulate his literary ideas. Essentially, though, he remained an individualist, creating his own blend of sardonic tragi-comedy. Certain major concerns constantly recur in his works: individual and corporate responsibility, the price of justice, the meaning of law and order, the question of shifting morality. In his often grotesque and absurd visions, he shows man failing to cope with his intellectual development, and sets out what critic, Kenneth S. Whitton, describes as "the human condition, the changing moral values in government and politics, the loosening of familial and societal bonds, the despair of 'the little man', suffering at the hands of the well-organised tyrannical bureaucracies."

In his most famous play, *The Visit*, we get what one critic called a "lacerating exposé of human vindictiveness and human greed". A millionairess returns to the town of her childhood with the promise that she will pay the townsfolk as much money as they want. Her only condition: to kill the man responsible for her seduction as a teenager. (It was as a result of this act that she had been forced to enter the world of prostitution.) The fact that he is now a highly respected figure in society serves only to heighten the dramatic tension. With consummate skill, Dürrenmatt depicts the gradual erosion of the townspeople's moral values as they share in the anonymity of corporate responsibility to suppress individual guilt. It is no coincidence that the town where the action takes place is called Gullen, Swiss-German for "liquid cattle dung". The play is a chilling black comedy, a powerful vehicle for Dürrenmatt's abiding themes of greed, hypocrisy and moral degradation.

The question of individual and social responsibility occurs most powerfully in another of his best-known plays, *The Physicists*. Here we are provided with a brief glimpse into the disturbing world of the lunatic asylum, where the dividing line between sanity and insanity, refuge and danger, good and evil, are never quite clear. A physicist has feigned madness to avoid having to divulge knowledge about an invention capable of massive destruction. Unbeknown to him, his inmate friends, Newton and Einstein, are charged with the task of somehow obtaining that knowledge. Who has the right, asks Dürrenmatt, to withhold new wisdom and technology? Can it be withheld at all? With typical irony the final twist comes with the revelation of the hospital psychiatrist's insanity. His megalomaniac designs have clear parallels with any number of the world's tyrannical despots.

Comedy and farce pervade many of his other works, reflecting Dürrenmatt's own interest in the logic of absurdity. In one of his earliest plays, *Romulus*, the founder of the Roman Empire is presented not as a warrior, not as a statesman, but as a chicken-farmer. He is ultimately ousted by no less a fear-inspiring figure than a German trouser-maker. In *The Marriage of Mr Mississippi*, murder and farce become one, while in *The Meteor*, the Lazarus theme is turned on its head when a painter struggles to return to the threat of death from which he has narrowly escaped. *The Executioner and his Henchman*, probably Dürrenmatt's most famous novella, achieved notoriety for its original treatment of the "detective" genre. It remains a favourite "set-book" in schools. For all the common themes of many of his works, however, selecting a representative sample poses a near-impossible challenge. In 1981 a new edition of Dürrenmatt's complete works was published, to commemorate the author's sixtieth birthday. It ran to 30 volumes.

Politically, Dürrenmatt was an interesting and complex character. As a national of neutral Switzerland, he was in the perfect position to attack both East and West. But his attitude to his own nationhood was ambiguous and provocative. "I am glad that I am Swiss", he once exclaimed, "because Switzerland has something grotesque about it. This attempt to remain forever neutral recalls a virgin who wants to make money in a whorehouse while keeping her chastity." Needless to say, such a statement did not endear him to the country's elder statesmen, any more than did his parody of the National Anthem in praise of Swiss banking laws. True, his works dwell constantly on the theme of human greed and on the link between morality and money, and critics on the political left were quick to claim these as attacks on western bourgeois values. But equally, there are as many attacks on eastern-style bureaucracy, on totalitarianism, on the breakdown of social responsibility. In later life, he turned increasingly towards politics, perhaps to divert attention away from the lack of success of his later works. Typical of his individualist stance was his expression of support for Israel in the Yom Kippur war. His *Zusammenhänge: Essay Über Israel* was just one of several treatises which he wrote in the last decade or so of his life. Dealing with the sombre reality of politics, they superseded the absurdist visions of his earlier fiction. From 1970 onwards his dramatic work declined both in quality and quantity. Having declared an interest in the art of stagecraft, and transferring his allegiance from the fictional characters to the purveyors of character, the actors, Dürrenmatt announced that he was abandoning literature for the theatre.

Dürrenmatt was once asked who he thought was the better writer: himself or his compatriot, Max Frisch? After some thought, he answered: "It's like asking 'who is greater: Schiller or Goethe?', to which Goethe replied, 'the Germans should be happy to have us both'." Most people would argue that to compare Dürrenmatt with either Schiller or Goethe, or indeed with Shakespeare and Brecht, is stretching the limits of imagination, even in spite of his immense popularity in Europe. Nevertheless, few would deny he is a writer of great stature.

Born Friedrich Dürrenmatt. **Parents** Reinhold, clergyman, and Hulda (Zimmermann) Dürrenmatt. **Marriages** 1) Lotti Geissler, actress, 1946 (died 1983); 2) Charlotte Kerr, television director, 1984. **Children** Peter, Barbara and Ruth. **Education** Grosshöchstetten School; Freies Gymnasium, Bern; Humboldtianum, Bern; University of Zürich; University of Bern. **Career** First play performed, *Es steht geschrieben*, 1947; drama critic, *Die Weltwoche*, 1951; first international success, *Die Ehe des Herrn Mississippi*, performed as *Fools are Passing Through*, New York, 1958; *Der Besuch der Alten Dame* filmed as *The Visit*, 1958, translated into opera by Gottfried von Einem; *The Physicists*, 1962; co-director, Basel Theaters, 1968–69; co-owner, *Zürcher Sonntags-Journal*, 1969–71. **Awards and honours** Radio Play prize, Berlin, 1957; Italia Prize for radio play, 1958; Scholler Prize, Mannheim, 1959; New York Drama Critics Circle Award, 1959; Schiller Prize, Switzerland, 1960; Grillparzer Prize, 1968; Kanton of Bern prize, 1969; honorary doctorate: Temple University, 1969, Hebrew University, Jerusalem, 1977, University of Nice, 1977, University of Neuchâtel, 1981; Welsh Arts Council International Writers Prize, 1976; Buber-Rosenzweig Medal, 1977; Austrian State Award, 1983; honorary fellow, Modern Language Association, USA. **Plays** *Es steht geschrieben*, 1947, revised as *Die Wiedertäufer*, 1967; *Der Blinde*, 1948; *Romulus der Grosse*, 1949, as *Romulus*, 1962; *Die Ehe des Herrn Mississippi*, 1952, as *The Marriage of Mr Mississippi*, 1966; *Ein Engel kommt nach Babylon*, 1954, as *An Angel Comes to Babylon*, 1964; *Der Besuch der alten Dame*, 1956, as *The Visit*, 1958; *Nächtliches Gespräch mit einem verachteten Menschen (Conversation at Night with a Despised Character)* (radio play), 1957; *Komödien I-III*, 1957–70; *Das Unternehmen der Wega* (radio play), 1958; *Frank V*, 1959; *Der Prozess um des Esels Schatten* (radio play), 1959; *Stranitzky und der Nationalheld* (radio play), 1959; *Abendstunde im Spätherbst* (radio play), 1959, as *Incident at Twilight*, 1968; *Es geschah am hellichten Tag (It Happened in Broad Daylight) (screenplay), 1960; Der Doppelgänger* (radio play), 1960; *Herkules und der Stall des Augias (Hercules and the Augean Stables)* (radio play), 1960; *Die Panne* (radio play), 1961, *as The Deadly Game*, 1966; *Gesammelte Hörspiele*, 1961; *Die Physiker*, 1962, as *The Physicists*, 1963; *Der Meteor*, 1966; as *The Meteor*, 1973; *König Johann* (translation of *King John* by Shakespeare), 1968; *Play Strindberg: Totentanz nach August Strindberg*, 1969, as *Play Strindberg: The Dance of Death*, 1972; *Titus Andronicus* (translation of Shakespeare), 1970; *Porträt eines Planeten*, 1970; *Urfaust* (translation of Goethe), 1970; *Der Mitmacher*, 1973; *Die Frist*, 1977; *Achterloo*, 1983; also: *Rollenspiele, Protokoll, Einer Fiktiven Inszenierung; Achterloo IV*. **Fiction** *Pilatus*, 1949; *Der Nihilist*, 1950; *Der Richter und sein Henker*, 1952, as *The Judge and His Hangman*, 1954; *Die Stadt*, 1952; *Der Verdacht*, 1953, as

The Quarry, 1961; *Grieche sucht Griechin*, 1955, as *Once a Greek ...*, 1965; *Das Versprechen; Requiem auf den Kriminalroman*, 1958, as *The Pledge*, 1959; *Die Panne: Eine noch mögliche Geschichte*, 1960, as *Traps*, 1960, as *A Dangerous Game*, 1960; *Der Sturz*, 1971; *The Assignment*, 1983; *The Execution of Justice*, 1985; *Durcheinandertal*, as *The Valley of Confusion*, 1989. **Other publications** *Theatrerprobleme*, 1955, as *Problems on the Theatre*, 1966; (with Werner Weber) *Der Rest ist Dank* (addresses), 1961; *Die Heimat im Plakat: Ein Buch für Schweizer Kinder*, 1963; *Theater-Schriften und Reden* (edited by Elisabeth Brock-Sulzer, two volumes), 1966–72; *Monstervortrag über Gerechtigkeit und Recht*, 1968; *Sätze aus Amerika*, 1970; *Zusammenhänge: Essay über Israel*, 1976; *Gespräch mit Heinz Ludwig Arnold*, 1976; *Der Mitmacher: Ein Komplex*, 1976; *Frankfurter Rede*, 1977; *Lesebuch*, 1978; *Bilder und Zeichnungen* (edited by Christian Strich), 1978; *Albert Einstein: Ein Vortrag*, 1979; *Werkausgabe* (30 volumes), 1980; *Stoffe 1–3: Winterkrieg in Tibet, Mondfinsternis, Der Rebell*, 1981; *Plays and Essays (edited by Volkmar Sander), 1982*. **Cause of death** Heart failure, at age 69. **Further reading** Murray B. Peppard, *Dürrenmatt*, 1969; Armin Arnold, *Dürrenmatt*, 1972; Timo Tiusanen, *Dürrenmatt: A Study in Plays, Prose and Theory*, 1977; Urs Jenny, *Dürrenmatt: A Study of His Plays*, 1978; Kenneth S. Whitton, *The Theatre of Dürrenmatt: A Study in the Possibility of Freedom*, 1980; *Contemporary Foreign Language Writers*, 1984.

ARMAND HAMMER

American Industrialist and Philanthropist

***Born* Manhattan, New York, 21 May 1898**

***Died* Los Angeles, California, 10 December 1990**

"I love my work. I can't wait to start a new day. I never wake up without being full of ideas. Everything is a challenge", so Armand Hammer lived his life. The Jewish industrialist of Russian ancestry who spent more than one month every year airborne, flying round the world in his private jet, fixing important deals one minute and meeting world leaders the next, has been variously described as egotistical, capricious, a self-publicist. The one thing for which he was never criticized was his prodigious ability for hard work. Even at the age of 89 he was found travelling half way round the world in an attempt to pave the way for the signing of the Geneva Accords. A shirker was he never.

For his admirers, and there were many, the dapper little doctor was a visionary of energy, talent and generosity who built business fortunes several times over. To his detractors he was tough and aggressive. To some he was a guru, a saintly philanthropist and *éminence grise* of world politics. To others he was a sinister figure whose actions were motivated by something very far from altruism.

Hammer, the man and the myth, there was so little separating them. The man who kept the channels of communication between the USA and the USSR open during the height of the cold war, who had personal relationships with most of the world's greatest leaders and was on first-name terms with the British Royal Family, added colour and panache to the grey world of industry and the even greyer world of international diplomacy. A "self-made" man has never courted and been courted as much by the world's leaders and played such an active role on the stage of world politics. Not even his most fervent detractors can dispute this. Hammer was a product of the twentieth century — his life more a Hollywood story than reality; and yet it was in the very real arena of international politics that he made himself known world-wide.

"I am first and foremost a catalyst — I bring people and situations together", he said of himself. He was a twentieth-century "fixer", who knew intuitively when, where and with whom to deal. Some, undoubtedly envious about his supposed "luck", provoked him to say, "People ask how much luck is involved, I tell them that when I work 14 hours a day, seven days a week, I get lucky." His business acumen can certainly be ascribed to more than luck and intuition; he was a man of vision who was willing to take a chance where others were limited by their lack of imagination and their personal ideologies.

Hammer's secret was his ideal of world harmony. Believing that such an ideal could only be achieved through personal contacts, he forged them wherever he could. Be it with Lenin, Brezhnev, Colonel Gadaffi or Deng Xiaoping. With his ideal firmly implanted he felt that he was working for the higher good. It was not only his legacy to the world but his duty, as he saw it, for being in the position to help.

Typical of his altruism was his support for cancer research. His generosity caused publisher Malcolm Forbes (q.v.) to note "Armand is so generous that he is in danger of falling off the list of the 400 richest men." After the magnitude of the Chernobyl nuclear disaster was known he responded immediately, even before official help was sent, by sending the finest specialist in radiation sickness to the USSR. And likewise after the Armenian disaster, his private jet was sent with medical supplies to assist the rescue effort.

The young Hammer was not so inclined to acts of altruism, being perhaps more the hard-headed business man, always looking for another way of augmenting his wealth. His business acumen first came to light when, still at medical school, he saved his father's pharmaceutical business from ruin, when Hammer *père*, a doctor, was in prison for performing an illegal abortion. Going through the books he noticed one item which seemed to be selling well — tincture of ginger. Puzzled, he approached one of his best customers only to discover that this particular customer was mixing the product with soda. When mixed it produced a palatable ginger beer. As the Volstead Act took effect, and prohibition ruled, Armand Hammer's business took off, and within a year he had made his first million. He proudly recounted that not even Gloria Swanson could match that at that time.

Having made his first million before he was 21, what was there left to do? He decided to go to Russia, where there was a typhus epidemic, with the idea of putting his medical qualifications to some use and at the same time collecting the debts owed to his father's business by the Soviet government. (His father had speculated in medicines during the war and his had been the only company to get through the blockade.) It was with a spirit of adventure that Hammer approached the trip which would ultimately result in his spending ten years in the Soviet Union, marrying the daughter of a Russian nobleman and amassing a considerable fortune.

Turning aside from his father's socialism — Julius Hammer had been a founder member of the American Communist Party — but not afraid to use his connections, a vista of opportunities stretched out before him on his arrival. It was never very clear if he ever did treat any of the typhoid patients he had originally gone out to help, or whether he ever recovered his father's debts. What is clear is that this trip started a lifelong partnership with the Soviet Union, in more ways than one. Ten years in the Soviet Union saw him established as one of the few businessmen prepared to negotiate with the new Soviet government, a speculator and art-trader.

Never one to miss an opportunity, he suggested that as a start he could trade American wheat for Soviet minerals. This deal was approved by Lenin personally. The telegram sent to Hammer expressed sympathy for his father's plight and a willingness that he should "exchange American grain for the Urals valuables". These "Urals valuables" ranged from asbestos to furs and, some argue, the rich pickings from the Romanov dynasty.

There is no doubt that during his time in the USSR Hammer managed to accumulate a veritable treasure trove of Romanov heirlooms. At one time he was said to possess, like Malcolm Forbes, more Fabergé eggs than the British Royal Family. His fortune from his Soviet dealings was sealed by a pencil. He negotiated a concession to make pencils, having realized that they were all imported. In the 1960s it was said that most of the Praesidium (inner cabinet) of the USSR Supreme Soviet had learnt to write with a Hammer pencil. It was not so much the manufacturing of pencils that brought him wealth, as a deal with one of Stalin's trade officials, this was the so-called "pencils for art" exchange — a term coined by Hammer and his art fanatic brother. Just when he knew that the pencil factory would be confiscated under Stalin's own economic policies, he negotiated to swap, in effect, the pencils for his "household effects". These were not ordinary domestic items, they were jewels, paintings, wall hangings, ornaments, all relics of the past era.

This was Hammer's last deal with what he often regarded as his second home, for over 20 years. He had no wish to do business with Stalin, and Stalin, although aware of his usefulness and his friendship with Lenin, had no wish for foreign influences in his economy. "I never met Stalin — I never had any desire to do so — and I never had any dealings with him", Hammer was later to explain.

Hammer — the latter-day Midas — returned to the US and for a short while engaged himself in what he regarded as his second love, his art. Even before his return Hammer Galleries, a Manhattan outlet opened with the help of his brother, Victor, had made a name for themselves, but now under his stewardship they proved to be even more profitable.

Just to prove he still was not above "dirty work", Hammer started a cooperage which led to a distillery producing, in his opinion, the best bourbon in Kentucky, which he brazenly called "The Crown Jewel of Kentucky Bourbon". This in turn spawned a cattle-rearing business. It was not until the time of his third marriage in the 1950s and his subsequent retirement to Southern California at the age of 58, when most men are relishing time to themselves, that the international businessman in him was rejuvenated.

Nothing inspired Hammer more than the prospect of a completely new challenge so, when a small oil deal came up, he was excited by something he had never speculated in before — black gold. His Midas touch worked and, five years after Occidental's first significant oil discovery, his turnover was 549 million dollars. His usual perseverance and intuition for a good deal had paid off. Typical of his courage and daring he moved into Libya, having negotiated a deal with King Idris involving the development of Libyan agriculture. Even in 1969 when Colonel Gadaffi came to power, he did not leave. However, his tenacity did not pay off in this case, and when Gadaffi tried to exert pressure on him for more taxes he pulled out. The oil crisis had begun.

His contacts with the Soviet Union, re-established three years after Stalin's death, now came back into their own. He concluded major deals with Brezhnev, and was often a visitor at the Kremlin, where guides still point out the monkey's head Hammer gave Lenin. Having established himself at the forefront of the oil industry, he turned his sights and his interests to something more esoteric — geopolitics.

One of his lawyers once remarked, "Dr Hammer has a great sense of geopolitical relations, almost like Henry Kissinger. He looks at the long term and uses his personal touch." With his access to history and his connection with Lenin, in particular, his kudos was, in the Soviet mind, great. Here was an American with all the correct credentials. When he told Brezhnev that he reminded him of Lenin, Brezhnev's eyes misted over and Hammer succeeded in acquiring a "key" to the Kremlin once more.

He opened the door of the Kremlin at a time when it was closed to the American government and was allowed to play the role of unofficial arbitrator between the superpowers, a role which he relished. In 1980 after the invasion of Afghanistan, Brezhnev told him that the Soviet Union was willing to withdraw if Afghanistan's neighbours were to guarantee its borders and agree to non-interference in Afghan affairs. Hammer travelled to a dozen countries trying to secure international recognition for his offer, but his efforts came to nothing.

He was to see his dream of a possible *rapprochement* between the US and the USSR become reality when Gorbachev became general secretary of the Supreme Soviet. According to Hammer's description, he was "very like Lenin in his pragmatism, resourcefulness, sense of humour and ability". He was partly responsible for dispelling US doubts about the new Soviet leader, Hammer having met him already.

The new spirit of *rapprochement* brought about Hammer's final and most splendid coup — though his role went largely unrecognized — the signing of the Geneva Accords. He spent nine months jetting round the world negotiating with all the leading players. His feelings about Gorbachev were vindicated when the Geneva Accords were signed. Someone who met him at the Geneva meeting noted that he was as excited as a schoolboy, beaming his impish grin, pumping everyone's hand, but modestly refusing publicly to acknowledge his own role. He whispered to one journalist, "We outwitted them all, boy. Now there's going to be peace."

Hammer was always a controversial figure, rarely out of the limelight be it shining on his business deals, his art gallery and museums, his philanthropic work, or personal scandal (he was convicted of making illegal contributions to Nixon's 1972 campaign, but later pardoned). In whatever way he is remembered, no one can dispute the place he had in the hearts and minds of the Soviet nation. In a telegram of condolence sent to his family, the Soviet news agency, Tass, said President Gorbachev described Hammer as "an old and sincere friend of the Soviet Union who did much for Soviet-American relations and for mutual understanding between the two nations." A fitting epitaph for a man whose most sincere wish was to see a reconciliaton between his two "homelands". The stage of international politics is indeed a greyer place without him.

Born Armand Hammer. **Parents** Julius, doctor and pharmaceutical entrepreneur, and Rose (Robinson) Hammer. **Marriages** 1) Baroness Olga von Root, cabaret singer, 1927 (dissolved); 2) Angela Zevely, 1943 (dissolved); 3) Frances (Barrett) Toleman, painter, 1956 (died 1989). **Children** One son, Julian, from first marriage. **Education** Columbia University, New York, MD, 1921. **Military service** US Army Medical Corps, 1918–19. **Career** President, Allied American Corporation, New York, 1923–25; president, Armand Hammer Pencil Company, USSR, 1925–30; president, Hammer Galleries, Incorporated, from 1930; president, J.W. Dant Distilling Company, 1943–54; president/chairman, Mutual Broadcasting System, New York, 1957–58; board chairman, Occidental Petroleum Corporation, 1957–90, chief operating officer, 1957–90; convicted of making illegal campaign contributions, 1976, pardoned 1989. **Related activities** On board of directors: City National Bank, Beverly Hills, 1962–71, Canadian Occidental Petroleum Limited, 1964–90, Raffinerie Belge de Pétroles, 1968–79; member, public advisory committee on US Trade Policy, 1968–69; on National Petroleum Council, 1968–90; on executive committee, Economic Development Board, Los Angeles, 1968–73; chairman, Knoedlers and Company, Incorporated, 1972; on board of governors: US-USSR Trade and Economic Council, Incorporated, 1973, American Petroleum Institute, 1975–90; director, Cities Service, 1982–90; director, Southland Corporation, 1983. **Other activities** Advisory board member, Institute of Peace, 1950–54; on board of governors, Eleanor Roosevelt Cancer Foundation, 1960–90; on board of trustees, Eleanor Roosevelt Memorial Foundation, 1963–74; honorary board member, Florida National Bank, Jacksonville, 1966–72; on executive board of directors, United Nations Association of Los Angeles, 1969–90; on board of governors, Salk Institute for Biological Studies, 1969–90, member, board of trustees, chairman; founder member, Los Angeles Music Center, 1969; on board of directors, United Nations Association of USA, 1970, on board of governors, 1976–90; on board of governors, Association of Harvard Business School, 1975; president, Foundation of International Institute of Human Rights, 1977–90; board member, Pepperdine University, 1979; member, National Support Council, US committee for UNICEF, 1980–90; founder and chairman, Armand Hammer College of American West, New Mexico, 1981; chairman, President's Cancer Panel; advisory board member, Center for Strategic and International Studies, Georgetown University, 1981–90. **Awards and honours** Humanitarian Award, Eleanor Roosevelt Cancer Foundation,

1962; Commander, Order of the Crown, Belgium, 1969; Commander, Order of Andres Bellos, Venezuela, 1975; honorary corresponding member, Royal Academy of Arts, 1975–90; Order of the Aztec Eagle, Mexico, 1977; Commandeur de la Légion d'honneur, France, 1978, Croix de Commandeur, 1983; Order of Friendship between Peoples, USSR, 1978; Royal Order of Polar Star, Sweden, 1978; honorary LLD: Pepperdine University, 1978, South Eastern University, 1978, Columbia University, 1978, Université d'Aix-en-Provence, 1981; honorary DHL: University of Colorado, 1979; honorary doctorate of public service, Salem College, 1979; grand officer, Order of Merit, Italy, 1981; honorary member, Royal Scottish Academy, 1981–90; Gold Medal of Italy, 1983; Commandeur, Ordre des Arts et des Lettres, 1988. **Publications** *Quest of the Romanoff Treasure*, 1932; *Hammer: Witness to History* (autobiography), 1987. **Cause of death** Cerebral arteriosclerosis, at age 92.

KELLY JOHNSON

American Aircraft Designer

***Born* Ishpeming, Michigan, 27 February 1910**

***Died* Burbank, California, 21 December 1990**

The Lockheed Corporation, one of the world's top aircraft producers, has known its hard times. Formed in 1916, by 1932 it was in deep financial trouble, and it was saved from bankruptcy by a businessman called Bob Gross. At the time the judge questioned Gross's wisdom in making the attempt. "Are you sure you know what you are doing?" he asked. Gross was. He assembled a small team to build advanced planes, starting with a streamlined, all-metal airliner to be called the Electra.

Lockheed had no windtunnel, so they sent a model to the University of Michigan for testing. The reply came: "Your design needs further work. The tail does not provide adequate directional control with one engine out." Enclosed was a suggested improvement with a twin-finned tail.

Gross was impressed. He told the young writer to change the model accordingly, and when it succeeded, persuaded him to join the company. In that way Lockheed secured the services of "Kelly" Johnson, certainly one of the world's finest aircraft designers, for the next 42 years.

Born Clarence Johnson, he is said to have acquired the nickname "Kelly" because Clarence sounded too prim for a lad who spent most of his time in fights with other boys. At the age of 12 he decided he wanted to work with aircraft, and from school he went to the University of Michigan where he obtained his BS (Aero) in 1932 and his MS (Aero) in 1933, the year he joined Lockheed.

At Lockheed Johnson, as chief research engineer, was first involved in designing a series of all-metal monoplane airliners. The year 1938 saw a lucky break in the company's fortunes. Shortly after Hitler annexed Austria in March, a delegation from the British Ministry of Aviation visited the US in the search for suitable planes for the Royal Air Force. The Lockheed engineers were given only five days to design a reconnaissance bomber. They produced the "Hudson", a development of the Electra which was the company's most successful commercial air liner. Johnson went to London. He worked away in his hotel room, regularly doing what others would regard as a week's work between one day's meeting and the next. As a result, in June, the British bought 200 Hudsons, "plus as many more as can be delivered by December 1939 up to a maximum of 250". Worth 25 million dollars, it was the biggest order won by any American plane-maker up to that time.

When the US entered World War II, it brought non-stop development work to Johnson and his team, and among other planes Lockheed produced under his direction were the P-38 Lightning, the Constellation and the Neptune. During the war the company produced almost 20,000 aircraft, nine per cent of the American total.

The introduction of jet engines brought about what is perhaps Kelly Johnson's most remarkable legacy to Lockheed. The Army Air Force gave the company 180 days to produce the P-80 Shooting Star from scratch, with the tightest possible security. Johnson gathered his team of top designers into a tent-like structure, completely isolated from everyone else, near the main windtunnel at the Burbank plant. There they worked apparently non-stop, and the first plane was produced in 143 days. That plane, the first American operational jet fighter, later served as the prototype for 1700 variations.

The Advanced Development Projects team formed to create the Shooting Star was not dismantled, but remained as a "factory within a factory" for further secret developments. Known as the "Skunk Works" after the strange factory in the "Li'l Abner" cartoon strip, these included the U-2 spy plane, a plane with long wings and a powerful jet engine which flew at 70,000 feet on missions over the USSR, and the Blackbird, still in service, which cruises at 2100 mph at a height of over 85,000 feet. The problems encountered in designing these planes were immense, and included breaking through what is known as the "thermal thicket", the high heat generated by supersonic flight. This was achieved by using titanium, an especially sleek shape and the black colour of its surface to help radiate the heat. The Blackbird remains one of the fastest and highest flying planes in the world. The Stealth fighter is the latest plane developed in this way.

Johnson disliked the term the "Skunk Works", but it has stuck and is likely to remain. He introduced into it a conceptual management system in addition to the essential technical and design methods. In 1969 he himself moved up to be senior vice-president of Lockheed, but by then he had trained Ben Rich to take over the Skunk Works in his place. After 1975, when Johnson officially retired, he remained as a senior adviser until his death.

In recent years plane designers have not been well known among people in general, but those who study planes and their designs rate Kelly Johnson among the greatest. He played a major part in the design of more than 40 Lockheed aircraft and spacecraft. Nationally and internationally he received some of the most prestigious awards in aviation, as well as three presidential citations and the Medal of Freedom, the top civil award in the US, presented by his namesake President Lyndon Johnson in 1964.

Born Clarence Leonard Johnson. **Marriages** 1) Althea Louise Young (died 1970); 2) Mary Ellen Meade (died 1980); 3) Nancy Powers Horrigan. **Education** Flint Junior College, Michigan; University of Michigan, BS, 1932, MS, 1933. **Career** Consultant, Studebaker Corporation, 1932–33; chief research engineer, Lockheed Aircraft Corporation, 1933–52, chief engineer, 1952–56, vice-president in charge of research and advanced development, 1956–58, vice-president of Advanced Development Projects, 1958–69, senior vice-president, 1969–75, consultant adviser, 1975–80, board of directors. **Offices and memberships** Member: National Academy of Science, National Academy of Engineers; fellow, American Institute of Aeronautics and Astronautics, vice-president, 1948; fellow: American Academy of Arts and Science, Royal Aeronautical Society. **Awards and honours** (include) Sperry Award, American Institute of Aeronautics and Astronautics, 1937, Wright Brothers Medal, Society of Automotive Engineers, 1941; Sylvanus Albert Reed Award, 1956, 1966; Collier Trophy, 1959, 1964; Medal of Freedom, 1964; honorary DE, University of Michigan, 1964; honorary DSc, University of Southern California, 1964; honorary LLD, University of California, Los Angeles, 1965; National Medal of Science, 1966; Thomas D. White National Defense Award, 1966; William Mitchell Memorial Award, 1969; Spirit of St Louis Medal, 1970; Engineering Achievement Award, American Society of Metallurgists;

Theodore Von Karman Award; Founders Medal, National Academy of Engineers, 1971, (with design team, SR-71) National Air and Space Museum trophy, 1990. **Cause of death** Undisclosed, at age 80.

TADEUSZ KANTOR

Polish Director, Actor and Artist

***Born* Wielopole, Poland, 6 April 1915**

***Died* Kraków, Poland, 8 December 1990**

Tadeusz Kantor had been rehearsing his new — and what was to be his final — play the day he died. Ironically the play was called *Today It Is My Birthday*, and the work was to be premièred in Paris in January 1991. Some personal dissatisfaction had thrown Kantor into one of his characteristic rages and he had stormed out of the rehearsal. Later that night he was taken to hospital and one of Poland's most innovative and original artistic figures died in the early hours of the following morning.

His work has been widely praised across Europe and will undoubtedly continue to be viewed as highly original and challenging many years after his death. Michael Billington, chief theatre critic of the *Guardian* newspaper in London, recalls Kantor's first production at the Edinburgh Festival in the following terms, "It was a piece of controlled anarchy that ... made our own avant-garde theatre look arid and inbred." Assessments of his work all focus on Kantor's anarchic use of artistic form — a use which placed him at the heart of the Polish abstract expressionist movement in the 1950s and later among proponents of the Theatre of the Absurd.

By far the strongest overall impression of his work is that of a man who could transform private experience into public art through haunting images. Jack Lang, French minister of culture and one of Kantor's early patrons, said that his great "chamber of the imagination" also turned out to be our own, and as such Kantor is attributed with achieving what Jan Sawka has called "the dream of every theatrically orientated artist".

In the small village of Wielopole, near Kraków, Tadeusz Kantor was born into a war-tormented Poland. His father was fighting at the Front at the time of his birth so his mother moved in with her uncle, the local priest whose house was next door to the Rabbi's. The village was a curious mixture of Jews and Catholics with the only constant element being the army marching through under ever-changing flags. It led to a childhood of confusion and fear — suffering which was to permeate the images in Kantor's later work.

In 1939 Kantor graduated from the Academy of Fine Arts in Kraków. He was trained as a painter but, unable to practise his art, he began to experiment with the theatre — "closet theatre" as he called it, literally underground in cellars and bunkers. When the war came to an end Kantor created avant-garde stage designs for the Teatr Stary in Kraków. Audiences were amazed by the non-conformity of his designs, but it was not until 1956 that he was able to work entirely independently. It was in that year that Kantor established his troupe, Cricot 2 — a troupe which, eventually, was to tour the world.

The key influence on Kantor's work throughout his life was the inter-war Polish visionary, Stanislaw Ignacy Witkiewicz, surrealist painter, writer, philosopher and playwright, who committed suicide in 1939 when the Germans invaded Poland. Kantor can be seen to have revealed Witkiewicz's work to the world — although the compliment can work both ways, so inspired and impressed had Kantor been by the Polish avant-garde during his student days.

Though the critical focus is on his work in the theatre, Kantor the painter is also an important figure. Despite the Stalinist social-realism governing Polish art during the 1950s, Kantor refused to compromise his ideas. His reward came in 1959 when, under the regime of Wladyslaw Gomulka, Polish artists were granted greater freedom of expression, and Kantor, as the leader of the Polish abstract expressionists, exhibited his paintings in a Paris Left Bank gallery. At the time the exhibition was seen by one critic as, "An adventure, a frenzy of living which recalls Jackson Pollock, but goes beyond him." This comparison with the work of Pollock conveys the spontaneity and improvisation of Kantor's work where, as Ryszard Stanislawski, director of the Museum Sztuki in Lodz, and a good friend of Kantor, observed, "his technique consists of mixing fragments of objects fixed to the canvas (for example an umbrella) with traces of themes belonging to the former abstract Informal method".

The shapeless structure of Kantor's paintings was to become the characterizing feature of his theatrical work also, and so it was that, with Cricot 2, Kantor came to be viewed as a theatrical reformer. His own assessment was more that Cricot 2 was "an attempt to create a sphere of free and disinterested artistic behaviour". What this meant in performance was a highly visual production in which the normal linear continuity of the text was broken down, events took place simultaneously, characters spoke at the same time, often with more than one actor playing the same role. The result was a multifocal production which was as much a painting as a play.

In view of his work it seems surprising that it was not until the 1970s that Kantor really became known in western Europe. Jack Lang, then director of the Nancy Festival, introduced Kantor to this wider audience in 1971 with a production of Witkiewicz's *The Water Hen*. Michael Billington saw the same production a year later when Richard Demarco (manager of one of the key fringe venues) brought Kantor over to the Edinburgh Festival. "The result was a revelation. The hawk-profiled Kantor sat in the midst of the actors quietly conducting a series of images depicting our immersion in obsessive, self-appointed tasks: a woman clattered away frantically at a typewriter, a bald-pated chap in drag constantly hauled a heavy trunk, another man danced with a female manikin from whose loins music uncannily issued."

But perhaps the best remembered production was *The Dead Class*. Set in a depressing schoolroom, aged pupils carried the corpses of their childhoods on their backs, forever doomed to repeat in death the mistakes they made whilst alive. Two days after Kantor's death and 15 years after its original performance in the UK, director Peter Brook described the production with all the emotion of his original reaction, recalling the terror, anguish and sadness of the play which he had found when he first visited Poland — "it concentrated the experience of a people in a single image".

This achievement was the key to Kantor's genius. Kantor himself said that his desire to "create" "automatically brought about an essential shift in my attitude towards the past, with its relics and claims, as well as towards the object. For the aim was not to repeat it, but to recapture!" Rsyzard Stanislawski describes the artist's idea of creativity as that of a constantly regenerating phenomenon: "that is, an inner pressure to consider one new problem after another".

So it is that we can understand Kantor's image of "Eternal Wanderers" which first appeared in the "happenings" he staged in the late 1950s and 1960s. It was after 1963 that Kantor defined his work as *emballages*, conveying his attitude to the object as an extension of the human figure portrayed as a carrier of packages, forever in transit. So forceful was this image that suitcases, bags and rucksacks soon appeared in all his productions, and the audience were frequently brought in as part of the image, as in *A Letter* in 1967 when audience members destroyed a huge writing case.

This ability to focus ideas, emotions and events into single images means that Tadeusz Kantor's work cannot rightly be described as "anarchic". His undermining of the traditions of linear text and characterization show him to have been at the forefront of Beckett's Theatre of the Absurd and abstract expressionism. Though isolated from the rest of Europe behind the Iron Curtain, Kantor was in tune with his freer European counterparts and indeed, even by today's standards, must be recognized for his role in leading the theatre into new realms of innovative expression. As Kantor himself wrote,

> In artistic development there are frequent moments when the vital creative act degenerates into a pursuit of a convention, when a work of art no longer involves any risk, adventure, revolt or uncertainty and becomes respectable and well established in its seriousness, dignity and prestige. When this happens, the wisest thing to do is to leave the recognized stage and shift to disinterested activities, on the verge of the ridiculous and shameful, deserving scorn and doomed to neglect.

Such a judgement will never be the fate of Tadeusz Kantor.

Born Tadeusz Kantor. **Parents** Marian and Helena Kantor. **Marriage** Margaret Stangret, painter and actress, 1962. **Education** Academy of Fine Arts, Kraków, 1936–39. **Career** Polish Resistance, directing underground theatre, Kraków, 1942–44; stage designer, Poland, 1944–55; organized first post-war art exhibition, Kraków, 1948; founder-director, Cricot 2 theatre group, Kraków, 1956; first major production outside Poland, *The Water Hen*, France, 1971. **Related activities** Visiting professor, Academy of Fine Arts, Kraków, 1949, 1968; visiting professor, Akademie der Schönen Künste, Hamburg, 1961. **Offices and memberships** Association of Polish Plastic Artists. **Awards and honours** Painting prize, São Paulo, 1967; Premio Marzotto, Rome, 1968; Painting Prize, *Bienal*, São Paulo, 1969; Premio Roma Medal, Galleria Nazionale d'Arte Moderna, Rome, 1969; Tadeusz Boy-Zelenski Theatre Critics' Prize, Warsaw, 1977; Mayor's Medal, Rome, 1978; Cyprian Norwid Art Critics' Prize, Warsaw, 1978; Rembrandt Prize, Goethe-Foundation, 1978; Grand prize, *Le Théâtre des Nations*, Caracas, 1978; Obie prize, New York, 1979, 1982; Mayor's Medal, Milan, 1979; Mayor's Gold Medal, Florence, Italy, 1980; Gold Medal, City of Gdansk, 1980; first prize, Minister of Culture and Art, 1981; commander's cross, Order of Polonia Restituta, 1982; Diploma of Minister of Foreign Affairs, 1982; Chevalier de la Légion d'honneur, 1986. **Productions directed** (include, all Kraków unless otherwise indicated) *Sepia*, 1956; *The Cuttlefish*, 1956; *In a Small House*, 1961; *The Madman and the Nun*, 1963; *Cricotage*, Warsaw, 1965; *Line of Division*, 1966; *The Water Hen*, 1967; *Panoramic Sea-Shore Happening*, Baltic Seashore, 1967; *The Anatomy Lesson — After Rembrandt*, Nuremberg, 1968; *Conference with Rhinocerous*, Nuremberg, 1968; *The Cobblers*, Paris, 1972; *Lovelies and Dowdies*, 1973; *The Dead Class*, 1975; *Où sont les neiges d'antan*, Rome, 1978; *Wielopole, Wielopole*, Florence, 1980; *I Will Never Come Back*, 1988; *Oh Gentle Night*, Avignon, 1990; *Today It Is My Birthday*, 1991. **Exhibitions** Galeria Po Prostu, Warsaw, 1956; Galeria Krzystofory, Kraków, 1957, 1963, 1967, 1968; Muzeum Miejskie, Lublin, 1958; Galleri Samklaren, Stockholm, 1958; Galerie Legendre, Paris, 1959, 1961; Kunsthalle, Düsseldorf, 1959; Sandberg Gallery, New York, 1960; Galerie 54, Gothenberg, Sweden, 1960; Galerie Alice Pauli, Lausanne, Switzerland, 1964; Galeria Foksal, Warsaw, 1965, 1967, 1968, 1970, 1971, 1973; Galerie S.H.S., Kraków, 1966; Galerie Handschin, Basle, 1966; Galerie de l'Université, Paris, 1966; Galleri Pierre, Stockholm, 1966; Kunsthalle, Baden-Baden, 1966; Kunsthalle, Nuremberg, 1968; Musée des Arts Décoratifs, Lausanne, 1971; Henie-Onstand Kunstsenter, Hovikodden, Oslo, 1971, 1976; Atelier des Recherches Théatrales, Dourdan, France, 1971; Galeria Desa, Kraków, 1972; *Emballages*, Muzeum Sztuki, Lodz, 1975; Kulturhuset, Stockholm, 1975; Galeria Zapiecek, Warsaw, 1976; *Emballages* 1960–1976, Whitechapel Art Gallery, London, 1976; Riverside Studios, London, 1976, 1982; Galerie Ricard, Nuremberg, 1977; Galerie de France, 1982; Galerie Eva Poll, West Berlin, 1986. **Group exhibitions** (include) *Modern Art in Poland Since World War II,* Kraków, 1948; *Grupa Krakowska*, Kraków, 1957; *Documenta II*, Museum Fridericianum, Kassel, West Germany, 1958; *30th Biennale*, Venice, 1960; *Polish Painting*, Museum Folkwang, Essen, West

Germany, 1963; *Kunst und Theater*, Kunsthalle, Baden-Baden, 1965; *Bienal de São Paulo*, 1967; *Happening und Fluxus*, Kunstverein, Cologne, 1970; *Painters from the Cricot 2 Theatre*, Rome, 1978. **Collection** Muzeum Sztuki, Lodz. **Publications** *Emballages*, 1976; *Le Théâtre de la mort*, 1978; *La classa morta*, 1981; *Wielopole, Wielopole*, 1981; *Le Théâtre Cricot 2*, 1983. **Cause of death** Heart attack, at age 75. **Further reading** Hanns Sohm, compiler, *Happening and Fluxus*, 1970; Wieslaw Borowski and Ryszard Stanislawski, *Tadeusz Kantor: Emballages*, 1975; Ryszard Stanislawski, *Tadeusz Kantor: Emballages, 1960–1976,* 1976; Witold Filler, *Contemporary Polish Theatre*, 1977; Wieslaw Borowski, *Tadeusz Kantor*, 1982; *Contemporary Artists*, 1989; *Contemporary Designers*, 1990.

FOY KOHLER

American Diplomat

***Born* Oakwood, Ohio, 15 February 1908**

***Died* Jupiter, Florida, 23 December 1990**

Less than a month after his arrival in Moscow as American ambassador Foy Kohler was involved in the gravest conflict between the two superpowers to date — the Cuban missile crisis of October 1962.

Scarcely had Kohler unpacked his bags than he found himself shuttling messages back and forth between John F. Kennedy and Nikita Khrushchev. It was the high point of a diplomatic career which spanned more than three decades. It was also a testing time for Kohler's ability as trouble-shooter. President Kennedy demanded the immediate withdrawal of the Soviet missiles from Cuba — missiles that were believed to be armed with nuclear warheads. Khrushchev in turn demanded that the US lift its naval blockade of Cuba or risk war.

The climax came on 26 October when a Soviet SAM missile brought down an American U2 spy plane over Cuba, and when President Kennedy warned that if another plane were downed the US would invade. The defusing of this conflict was regarded at the time as a model of its kind. It enabled Khrushchev to climb down from his publicly-stated position and to recall the missiles. Kennedy in turn gave assurance that Cuba would be safe from American attack.

If Kohler's nerves were frayed he gave no sign, but then he had been hand-picked by President Kennedy for just such a difficult job. Not only did he have wide experience of eastern Europe, but he spoke Russian fluently, and was well known to Khrushchev, whom he had accompanied on his tour of the United States in 1959.

In contrast to diplomatic careers founded on wealth or political patronage, Kohler earned his spurs by virtue of merit. Born in a small town in Ohio, he worked as a bank teller to finance his studies, graduating from Ohio State University, where he had majored in geography and economics.

Entering the Foreign Service in 1931, his first postings included Bucharest, Belgrade, Athens and Cairo. In April 1946 he began his first tour of duty in Moscow, serving successively as first secretary, counsellor, and minister to the US embassy there before being recalled in 1949 to head Voice of America overseas broadcasting.

This initial contact with the Russians taught Kohler to value the "healthy scepticism" of the average Soviet citizen in the face of official paranoia. "It's up to us to keep their scepticism alive", he told *The New York Times*, "to keep persuading them that the United States doesn't want to attack them, doesn't covet their land, and extends a genuine welcome to them into the family of nations."

Patience likewise was called for in dealing with the Russians. Kohler accompanied Richard Nixon, then US vice-president, on his visit to the Soviet Union in 1959, and was present at the famous "kitchen debate", when an angry Khrushchev took off his shoe and banged it on a table, boasting to Nixon that Russian communism would bury American capitalism alive. On that occasion Kohler saw to it that Nixon's speeches were broadcast in full to the Russian people, and that an American interpreter, rather than a Russian, was used to translate Nixon's informal talks with Soviet officials.

Kohler retired from the Foreign Service soon after completing his tour of duty as US ambassador to Moscow in 1966. From 1968 to 1982 he taught at the University of Miami's graduate Center for Advanced Foreign Studies. He also published a number of books on the Soviet Union.

Dean Rusk, secretary of state under Presidents Kennedy and Johnson, once described Kohler as "one of our greatest professional diplomats". The word "professional" would have pleased him.

Born Foy David Kohler. **Parents** Leander David and Myrtle (McClure) Kohler. **Marriage** Phyllis Penn, 1935. **Education** Scott High School, Toledo, Ohio; University of Toledo, 1924–27; Ohio State University, BS, 1931; Cornell University, New York; National War College, 1946. **Career** Bank teller, Toledo, Ohio, 1924–27; foreign service officer, US Department of State, 1931–67, vice-consul, Windsor, Ontario, 1932–33, Bucharest 1933–35, Belgrade, 1935, legation secretary and vice-consul, Bucharest, 1935–36, Athens, 1936–41, Cairo, 1941, country specialist, Washington, 1941–44, assistant chief of Division of Near Eastern Affairs, 1944–45, first secretary, US embassy, Moscow, 1947–48, counsellor, 1947–48, minister plenipotentiary, 1948–49, director, Voice of America, 1949–52, policy planning staff, 1952–53, counsellor, US embassy, Ankara, 1953–56, detailed to International Cooperation Administration, 1956–58, deputy assistant secretary of state for European affairs, 1958–59, assistant secretary of state for European affairs, 1959–62, US ambassador to Soviet Union, 1962–66, deputy undersecretary of state for political affairs, 1966–67, retired with rank of career ambassador, 1967, consultant 1968–82; professor of international studies, Center for Advanced International Studies, University of Miami, Florida, 1968–78, adjunct professor, 1978–82; senior associate, Advanced International Studies Institute, Washington, 1978–85. **Related activities** Member, Board for International Broadcasting, from 1974; advisory council member, National Convocation of the Challenge for Building Peace; contributor: *Orbis*, *Science*, *Interplay*; co-editor, *Soviet World Outlook*, 1976–85. **Offices and memberships** Member: American Foreign Service Association, American Academy of Political and Social Science, Council on Foreign Relations; board member, American Institute for Free Labor Development. **Awards and honours** Honorary DHL, Ohio State University, 1962; honorary LLD: Toledo University, 1964, University of Akron, 1967, Findlay College, 1967. **Publications** *Understanding the Russians: A Citizen's Primer*, 1970; (author of foreword) *Science and Technology as an Instrument of Soviet Policy*, 1972; (co-author) *Soviet Strategy for the Seventies: From Cold War to Peaceful Coexistence*, 1973; (co-author) *Convergence of Communism and Capitalism: The Soviet View*, 1973; (co-author) *The Role of Nuclear Forces in Current Soviet Strategy*, 1974; (co-author) *The Soviet Union and the October 1973 Middle East War: Implications for Detente*, 1974; (author of foreword) *US-Soviet Cooperation in Space*, 1974; (co-editor) *The Soviet Union: Yesterday, Today, Tomorrow; A Colloquy of American Long-Timers in Moscow*, 1975; (author of introduction) *Custine's Eternal Russia*, 1976; (author of foreword) *War Survival in Soviet Strategy: USSR Civil Defense*, 1976; *Salt II: How Not to Negotiate with the Russians*, 1979. **Cause of death** Undisclosed, at age 82.

ALICE MARBLE

American Tennis Player

***Born* Plumas County, California, 28 September 1913**

***Died* Palm Springs, California, 13 December 1990**

"The founding Amazon of international tennis, with a service to match the most macho." That's what the British national newspaper, the *Guardian*, proclaimed Alice Marble in its headline to her obituary. The British never fail to honour a Wimbledon Triple Champion with verbal superlatives. Americans are more direct. At the height of her fame, Alice Marble received an average of 500 letters a week. Many of them were declarations of undying love. Though she was often criticized for being too "masculine" on the tennis court, off-court she was a glamour girl, a real blonde bombshell who ran with the movie crowd and sang on the radio and in night-clubs. A frequent weekend guest at William Randolph Hearst's castle, San Simeon, her best friends were Carole Lombard and Clark Gable. She taught Marlene Dietrich to play tennis. Charlie Chaplin was another of her pupils. In 1940, she became a radio announcer, predicting the outcome of college football games on station WNEW in New York, and cheerfully telling people, "You know football isn't as difficult a game to play as tennis." She wrote children's stories. She designed sportswear. Her first tour as a professional tennis player earned her 100,000 dollars, enabling her to say, "I have a lovely trust fund and don't have to work." It was too good to be true, no one could have a life that perfect — a life where nothing ever went wrong.

Alice Marble's life was far from perfect — there were things that went very wrong, but she overcame them. In 1934, it seemed her career was over before it even started. She travelled to Paris to play in some international team matches. At the beginning of her first match, she swayed, turned slightly, and fell to the ground. She was diagnosed as having secondary anaemia, and worse, she had tuberculosis. This wasn't the first time she'd collapsed. A year earlier, in Long Island, New York, she'd fainted after playing 108 games in one day. She had a temperature of 104, and that time she was diagnosed as having pleurisy.

Alice Marble returned to America on a stretcher. She was told she needed complete rest. She was also told she would never play tennis again. Friends such as Carole Lombard and Marble's coach, Eleanor "Teach" Tennant rallied around her, helping her fight her way back to health.

In 1936, only two years after being told she'd never play again, Alice Marble won the US National Women's Singles Championship. She won it again in 1938, 1939 and 1940. Meanwhile, she won the US National Doubles Championships four consecutive years, beginning in 1937, and went on to conquer Wimbledon, winning three consecutive mixed doubles titles (1937, 1938, 1939), two ladies' doubles titles (1938, 1939), and the single's championship in 1939, defeating Kay Stammers, Britain's number one, and becoming the first Women's Triple Champion at Wimbledon since Suzanne Lenglen in 1925.

Women's tennis had undergone some changes since Suzanne Lenglen's day. It used to be rather genteel; it was definitely a "ladylike" pursuit. Alice Marble changed all that. According to William F. Long, executive director of the Tennis Hall of Fame, "Alice marked a turning point in the women's game because of her approach to it. She brought the same kind of aggressive, serve-and-volley game that only men did up to that time." Martina Navratilova agrees, saying, "She was one of the first women to serve and volley well and play an aggressive game."

Marble changed the look of women's tennis as well. No flouncey dresses on the court for her, she wore shorts and a white peaked jockey cap. She was a natural crowd-pleaser; she put on a show. She loved playing to the gallery. Following a rare bad shot, she'd boot the offending ball soccer-style or use her racquet like a golf club. Once Hazel Wightman (the donor of the Wightman Cup) scolded her after a match because she'd been more concerned with showmanship than winning the game. Marble fell down, and as Wightman told her later, "instead of getting up and brushing your shorts and getting on with the match, you patted your bottom, and because the crowd enjoyed this you kept on patting as an encore and missed two simple shots which cost you the set."

It was only natural that a tall blonde with a flair for the theatrical (and so many show-business friends) should take a stab at performing. Alice Marble had a good enough voice, and was enough of a celebrity, to make her singing début at New York's Waldorf Hotel in 1938. Singing never became a career, though. Her first love was sport, and smoke-filled night-clubs weren't the best place for an athlete to spend her time, especially one with a history of tuberculosis.

She became a professional tennis player in 1941, embarking on the tour that would ensure her future financial security. The war, however, brought tragedy to her life once more. Her husband, Captain Joe Crowley, was shot down over Germany, leaving her a widow after only three years of marriage. She'd lost their unborn child a few months earlier, as the result of a car accident. An incredibly courageous woman, she agreed to spy for the Allies while touring Switzerland as a tennis pro. She was responsible for obtaining some of the information which would later be used as evidence in the Nuremburg trials. Her work as a spy didn't go smoothly, though. She was shot in the back by a Nazi agent. She made a full recovery and returned to sport as if nothing had happened, rarely even speaking about the incident.

In 1950, she became another kind of champion: a champion of equal rights. A black tennis player, Althea Gibson, had been denied the right to play in the US National on the basis of her colour. Marble publicly condemned the decision, calling the US Lawn Tennis Association's officials "sanctimonious hypocrites". She wrote an impassioned essay for *American Lawn Tennis* magazine, in which she stated that if Gibson were prevented from playing because of her race, she would be "bitterly ashamed". Gibson was allowed to play, and later became a women's singles champion, both in the US and at Wimbledon. Althea Gibson never forgot what Alice Marble had done for her, "She was my idol. She will always be unforgettable to me and to all tennis players."

Alice Marble kept active playing golf, lecturing and coaching until she was well into her seventies. She lived through a time of amazing transformation in people's attitudes towards a woman's place in sport. It was a transformation *she* caused. Thanks to her, women could be respected as athletes. Today's women tennis players owe her a lot, and they know it. Martina Navratilova has called her "a pioneer for women's tennis", while Billie Jean King remembers her as "one of the greatest to play the game". According to Althea Gibson, "She was the greatest ever, definitely."

But tennis wasn't Alice Marble's first love. What she really wanted was to play baseball. As a young girl, she was good enough to be allowed to join the San Francisco Seals' pre-match warm-up. The only reason she took up tennis was to please her family, who were terribly upset that she was interested in anything so unsuitable for a girl as baseball.

Women who play tennis as well as men, and often better than men, are almost commonplace today. They certainly weren't when Alice Marble began her career. One can't help wondering what might have happened if she'd stuck to her original goal of playing baseball.

Born Alice Marble. **Parents** Harry Briggs, cattle rancher, and Jessie (Wood) Marble. **Marriage** Joe Crowley, army intelligence officer (died 1944). **Education** Polytechnic High School, San Francisco, 1931; coached by Eleanor Tennant. **Career** Secretary to Eleanor Tennant; won California junior tennis championship at age of 17; amateur tennis player, 1931–33, 1936–40; member, United States Wightman Cup team, 1933, 1937–39; turned professional, 1941; tennis coach, Palm Desert Country Club until 1987. **Related activities** Tennis clothes designer; lecturer; radio sports announcer. **Other activities** Night-club singer, 1938; intelligence agent, World War

II; author, children's books. **Awards and honours** Member, Tennis Hall of Fame, International Sportsmen's Hall of Fame; Alice Marble Tennis Courts, Greenwich and Hyde streets, San Francisco dedicated to her, 1966. **Major titles** United States singles champion: against Miss Jacobs, 4–6, 6–3, 6–2, 1936, against Miss Wynne, 6–0, 6–3, 1938, against Miss Jacobs, 6–0, 8–10, 6–4, 1939, against Miss Jacobs, 6–2, 6–3, 1940; United States doubles champion with Mrs S.P Fabyan: 1937, 1938, 1939, 1940; United States mixed doubles champion with G. Mako, 1936, with D. Budge, 1938, with H. Hopman, 1939, with R. Riggs, 1940; Wimbledon singles champion, against Miss Stammers, 6–2, 6–0, 1939; Wimbledon doubles champion with Mrs S.P. Fabyan, 1938, 1939; Wimbledon mixed doubles champion with D. Budge, 1937, 1938, with R. Riggs, 1939. **Publications** (include) *The Road to Wimbledon*, 1946; (with Dale Weatherman) *Courting Danger* (autobiography), 1991. **Cause of death** Undisclosed, at age 77.

GIOVANNI MICHELUCCI

Italian Architect

***Born* Pistoia, Italy, 2 January 1891**

***Died* Florence, Italy, 31 December 1990**

When Giovanni Michelucci, arguably the greatest Italian architect of the twentieth century, spoke of "the human scale", he meant the human personality in all its dimensions: its psychology, daily habits, spirituality, and capacity for being good and bad. "Man, nature and architecture are inseparable", he said in one of the last interviews he gave before his death. "Architecture must spring forth from life itself." These convictions grew and sustained him throughout a varied architectural, teaching and academic career spanning most of the century, and they were above all expressed in the continuity which he created between his buildings and the flow of cultural and commercial life around them.

Michelucci leapt to national and international fame in the mid-1930s, under Mussolini's dictatorship, with his Santa Maria Novella Railway Terminus in Florence. When it was built it was the most stylistically advanced station in the world. It represented the triumph, albeit temporary, of modernist or "rationalist" architecture in Italy. This was at a time when the official, neo-classical style favoured by the Fascist state was being wholeheartedly adopted both in Nazi Germany and the Soviet Union, and the persecution of modernist or "decadent" artists in these countries was well underway. Michelucci's design is based on the logical ordering of the building's components, all of which have a clear function and are sharply articulated within a largely rectilinear framework. At the same time the station is open to the through-movement of pedestrians, and further integrated with the city and locality in its use of materials: its marble facade matches the fourteenth-century church of Santa Maria Novella nearby. Michelucci's lifelong concern with materials was the legacy of his artisanal background; he was also strongly imbued with a sense of the characteristic human scale of his native Tuscany, its landscape and building. These two factors contribute to the warmth of his architecture and its appeal to its users, even when, as is the case with Florence Station, it is at its most aesthetically restrained.

Unlike other European countries, Italy had not spawned a strong modern movement in art and design in the earlier part of the century. Its major contribution had been Futurism, which stood for a radical celebration of the machine and violent rejection of the past. Filippo Marinetti, Futurism's founder, was for a time during the 1920s and 1930s able to persuade the dictator to share his particular vision of a "renewal of culture"; Marinetti was a member of the panel which awarded Michelucci and his partners the Florence Station commission. Michelucci's architecture owes little else to Futurism; obliged to join the Fascist party, he recalled that he "held his nose", throwing his party card away on the completion of the project. He did however occupy a number of important academic positions during the late 1930s and the 1940s; he had worked with the team that planned Mussolini's showpiece University City in Rome in 1933, and was responsible for two science institutes. During this period he also published a monograph on the early Renaissance Florentine architect Brunelleschi.

By the late 1940s he was rethinking his rationalist ideals, and was increasingly involved in large-scale plans for integrated, urban rebuilding; his visions had a special urgency for him, given the widespread damage done to Florence towards the end of World War II. He was working towards a far greater freedom in his response to the physical and human environment and in his use of materials; this process culminated in the late 1950s and early 1960s in a series of churches (of which he built a large number during his career; his first building had been a chapel, designed while he was serving with the army during World War I). San Giovanni Battista, at Campi Bisenzio, near Florence, was completed in 1964, and commemorates workers who died constructing the motorway which runs alongside. The strict right angles of *architettura razionale* have gone; a concrete roof sweeps over an exterior of slanting walls roughly faced in stone, while inside branching columns evoke woodland glades or the inside of a tent. The atmosphere of mystery and repose is heightened by multiple, sometimes hidden, sources of light. Michelucci's sense of the "sympathy" welding matter and spirit together is well demonstrated here; it can also be seen in his prolific output of pen-and-ink drawings, in which the curvaceous outlines and structures of buildings fuse in dynamic harmony with the forms of mountains and clouds, and the light they reflect.

Michelucci's post-war work is hard to categorize. It is indebted to the angularity of German Expressionist architecture of the years around World War I, and to the "organicism", the reference to natural forms and structures, of the Catalan Antoni Gaudí; its dramatic curving shapes owe something to Frank Lloyd Wright, particularly to his Guggenheim Museum in New York (completed 1959), and to Le Corbusier's Ronchamp Chapel (completed in 1955). Although Michelucci professed to hate the "enforced functionality" implied in Corbusier's definition of the house as "a machine for living in", he remained a rationalist as well as an organicist; his Florence Post Office, for example, completed in 1965, shares the geometrical order and austerity of his work of the 1930s.

Other projects of the 1960s and 1970s included an "organicist" church at Longarone with an amphitheatre on its roof, and a highly industrialized telecommunications centre at Pisa, flanked by two towers to rival the famous Leaning Tower a few miles away. A branch of the Monte dei Paschi di Siena bank at Colle Val d'Elsa, between Florence and Siena, presents itself as a neighbourhood market, vantage point and local meeting place, rather than as a fortress for the protection of money. A project for a large hospital at Sarzano (La Spezia), which incorporated a restaurant, shops and day-lounges alongside normal medical and support services, was an attempt to transform the image of the hospital: instead of being a ghetto for the ill, it was to be part of the natural course of life in the city. Visitors to Italy will perhaps be most familiar with his reorganization of the Uffizi Gallery in Florence, started in 1957.

Michelucci's practice and his teaching were intimately related. The Fondazione Michelucci, of which he was director, is both an architectural practice and a centre for publication and research. He was known to his students in the Faculty of Architecture in Florence as *Conta Favole* (the teller of fables): his professorial addresses would be stories about man and nature, in which his own moments of discovery and enlightenment were central and technical matters played little part. He required both the stimulus of his contact with the city and ordinary people, and the solitude of his house at Fiesole, outside Florence, to generate the imaginative and empathetic receptiveness out of which architectural ideas and images would emerge. Among his final projects was a plan for a theatre, café and garden inside the Scandicci Prison in Florence, based on proposals made by the prisoners themselves. Such projects, like the New City which he longed to build, he considered less in terms of architectural than of social problems. "The secret of architecture lies in its relationship to people", he said.

Michelucci never worked outside Italy. Without understanding the spirit of an English or Chinese man, he asked, how could he create the corresponding space in which an English or a Chinese person lives? He became known as Italy's "Architect of Hope", responding, in his love of life, hatred of pomp and corruption, and belief in constant change and renewal, to his country's own struggles to create a humane and democratic society.

Born Giovanni Michelucci. **Father** Proprietor, bronze foundry. **Marriage** Aloisia Pacini, 1928. **Education** School of Architecture, Florence, 1908–11, DipArch, 1911; Academy of Fine Arts, Florence, 1911–14. **Military service** Italian Army, 1915–16. **Career** In private practice, Fiesole, 1916 onwards; teacher, Institute of Art, Pisa, 1916–20, Rome, 1920–28; School of Architecture, Florence, professor of interior design, 1928–39, professor, 1939–44, professor of urban planning, 1944–45, professor of architectural design, 1944–45, dean, 1944–45, 1947–48; professor of architectural composition, University of Bologna, faculty of engineering, 1948–66, emeritus professor, 1966 onwards. **Related activities** Founder, Esperienza Artigiana, 1949; director, *La Nuova Città, 1950–52.* **Awards and honours** First Prize, *Italian Gardens Exhibition*, Florence, 1931; First Prize, with others, S. Maria Novella Station Competition, Florence, 1933; First Prize, with others, Master Plan of Pistoia Competition, 1936; highest university degree in interior design, 1939; First Prize, with others, Grazie Bridge Competition, Florence, 1954; Feltrinelli Prize, 1958; San Luca International Prize for Architecture, 1958. **Exhibitions** *Esposizione di Architettura Razionale*, Galleria di Palazzo Ferroni, Florence, 1932; *Ten Italian Architects*, Los Angeles, 1967; *La Città di Michelucci*, Palazzo del Comune, Fiesole, Italy, 1976; *Giovanni Michelucci*, Heinz Gallery, Royal Institute of British Architects, London, 1978. **Works** Chapel, Caporetto, 1916; House, Via Bellini, Pistoia, 1920; War Memorial, Ancona (competition project), 1921; House, Via Rosselli, Montecatini, 1924; Valdissena House, Pescia, 1924; (with Raffaello Fagnoni) Balilla Headquarters, Piazza S. Francesco, Pistoia, 1929; Valiani House, Via Mangili, Rome, 1930; Dining Room Pavilion, *riennale*, Monza, 1930; Valiani Villa, Via Prenestina, Rome, 1931; Alfredo Casella Villa, Rome (project), 1931; (with Pier Niccolo Bernardi, Gherardo Bosio and Sarre Guarnieri) Exhibition Halls, *Fiera Nazionale dell'-Artigianato*, Florence, 1932; (with others) Master plan for University City, Rome, 1933; (with others) S. Maria Novella Station, Florence, 1935; Institute of General Physiology, Psychology and Anthropology, University City, Rome, 1935; Institute of Mineralogy, Geology and Paleontology, University City, Rome, 1935; Covered Market, Piazza de Guidici, Florence (project), 1935; Master plan of Pistoia, Italy (competition project with A. Susini and L. Fuselli), 1936; Façade for *VI Mostra Mercato dell' Artigianato*, Florence, 1936; Government Building, Savona (competition project), 1938; Government Building, Arezzo, 1939; Open-Air Theatre, E.42 District, Rome (project), 1939; Palace of Light and Water, E.42 District, Rome (project), 1939; Government Building, Savona (2nd project), 1939; Villa Contini-Bonacossi extensions, Viale Morin, Forte dei Marmi, 1939; Tower conversion to house and gallery, Via Guicciardini, Florence, 1939; Reconstruction of area around the Ponte Vecchio, Florence, 1946; Tower conversion, Vicolo dei Ramaglianti, Florence, 1947; Funeral Chapel, S. Miniato al Monte, 1948; House, Lido d'Albaro, Genoa, 1948; Cassa di Risparmio Building, Viareggio, 1948; Cassa di Risparmio Building, Volterra, 1948; Stock Exchange, Pistoia, 1950; Bathing Resort, Sori, Genoa (project), 1950; House, Via Montebello, Florence, 1950; Baldassare House, Francavilla al Mare, Chieti (project),

1950; Skyscraper, Marsaglia Park, San Remo, 1950; Caffe Connini, Piazza della Repubblica, Florence, 1953; Master plan for Ferrara (consultant), 1954; Collina di Pentolungo Church, Pistoia, 1954; Grazie Bridge, Florence (competition project with E. Detti and D. Santi), 1954; Carrais Bridge, Florence (competition project with E. Detti and D. Santi), 1954; Vespucci Bridge, Florence (competition project with L. Cestelli-Guidi), 1954; Church of the Virgin, Via Bassa della Vergine, Pistoia, 1956; Residential Zone and Church, Sasso Pisano, 1957; Lardarello Workers Village, Pisa, 1957; Ventura House, Via Guicciardini 24, Florence, 1957; INA Apartment Building, Via Guicciardini, Florence, 1957; House, Via Monte Pania 1, Lido di Camaiore, Lucca, 1957; Cassa di Risparmio Building, Via Bufalini, Florence, 1957; Skyscraper, Livorno (project), 1957; (with L. Lugli) Cabin, Torre S. Lorenzo, 1957; Societa Larderello Building, Pisa, 1957; Uffizi Gallery re-organization, Florence, 1957; Master Plan for Sorgane Quarter of Florence (also co-ordinator), 1958; Citadel Gardens, Pisa, 1958; Galileo Centre, Pisa (project), 1958; Institute of Geology, University of Bologna, 1959; Faculty of Letters and Philosophy, University of Bologna, 1959; Larderello Church, Pisa, 1959; Cemetery Church, Pistoia, Italy, 1959; Institute of Mathematics, University of Bologna, 1959; Belvedere Church, Pistoia, 1961; Apartment buildings and shops, Lungarno del Tempio, Florence, 1961; Giunti House, Viareggio, 1962; Osteria del Gambero Rosso, Collodi, Pistoia, 1963; Memorial to the Victims of Kindu, Pisa Airport, 1963; Apartment/office building, Piazza Brunelleschi, Florence, 1963; Church of St. John the Baptist, Autostrade del Sole, Campi Bisenzio, Florence, 1964; Concert Hall, Montecatini Terme (project), 1964; Concert Hall and Art School, Ravenna (project), 1964; Quadrio House, Milan (project), 1964; Tomb of Dante (project), 1964; Rosetti House, Ravenna (project), 1965; Monument to the Carabiniere, Fiesole, Florence, 1965; School and Village Garden, Arzignano, Vicenza, 1965; Institute of Chemistry, University of Florence (project), 1965; Skyscraper, Livorno, 1966; Borgo Maggiore Church, San Marino, 1966; Arzignano Church, Vicenza, 1967; SIP Headquarters, Via Masaccio, Florence, 1967; Stock Exchange extension, Pistoia, 1967; Cassa de Risparmio Headquarters, Pistoia, 1967; Post Office, Via Verdi, Florence, 1967; Sampiva House, Arzignano, Vicenza, 1969; Bracco Chapel, Trespiano, Florence, 1969; Master plan for Camaiore, Lucca, 1971; Cangioli House, Pistoia, 1972; Scaglietti Chapel, Collodi Cemetary, Pistoia (project), 1972; Orangery reconstruction, Villa Strozzi, Florence (project), 1973; Tozzelli House, Pistoia, 1974; Plan for centre of Sesto Fiorentino, 1974; Bastione Thyrion Secondary School, Pistoia, 1975; Post office, Viareggio, Lucca, with A. Pasquinucci, 1975; Marble Experimental Centre, Foce di Pianza, Carrara, with B. Sacchi, 1975; Monte dei Paschi di Siena Headquarters, Colle Val d'Elsa, Siena (project with B. Sacchi), 1975; Contrada del Palio Valdimontone Headquarters, Siena (project with B. Sacchi), 1975; Bini House, Pescia, Pistoia, with B. Sacchi, 1975; Plan for centre of Arzignano, Vicenza (project with B. Sacchi), 1975; (with M. Innocenti), Telecommunications Centre, Pisa, 1976; (with B. Sacchi) Cassa di Risparmio Headquarters, Via Montalbano, Pistoia, 1976; Church, Livorno (project with B. Sacchi), 1976; Lacani House, Montemarcello, La Spezia (project with B. Sacchi), 1976; Friendship Monument, Church of St. John the Baptist, Autostrade del Sole, Campi Bisenzio, Florence, 1976; (with M. Innocenti) San Bartolomeo Hospital, Sarzana, 1978; Novello Church, Cutigliano, Pistoia (project with B. Sacchi), 1978; Oratorio di San Leonardo conversion, Siena (project with B. Sacchi), 1978; Thermal Centre, Carrara (project with B. Sacchi), 1980–83; Sports Centre, Prato, Florence (project with M. Innocenti), 1980–84; (with B Sacchi) Monte dei Paschi di Siena Bank, Colle Val d'Elsa, Siena, 1982. **Publications** *Filippo Brunelleschi*, 1936; (with A. Ardigo and Franco Borsi) *Il Quartiere di Santa Croce nel Futuro di Firenze*, 1968; *Brunelleschi Mago*, 1972; *La Nuova Città*, edited by R. Risaliti, 1975; *Non sono un Maestro*, 1976; (with Franco Borsi) *Michelucci, il linguaggio dell'architettura*, edited by Maria Cristina Buscioni, 1979; *La felicita dell'architettura*, 1981. **Cause of death** Undisclosed, at age 99. **Further reading** E. Berti and M. Gobbo, *Cassa di Risparmio di Firenze*, 1958; *La Chiesa dell'Autostrada del Sole*, 1964; Franco Borsi, editor, *Giovanni Michelucci*, 1966; F. Clemente and

L. Lugli, *Giovanni Michelucci: Il Pensiero e le Opera*, 1966; M. Cerasi, *Michelucci*, 1968; A. Ottani Cavina, *Firenze Chiesa dell'Autostrada*, 1968; B. Zevi, author of introduction, *Grafica di Giovanni Michelucci* (exhibition catalogue), 1974; Franco Borsi and others, *La Città di Michelucci* (exhibition catalogue), 1976; Fabio Naldi, *Giovanni Michelucci*, 1978; Bruno Sacchi, editor, *Giovanni Michelucci* (exhibition catalogue), 1978; Franco Borsi and others, *La Chiesa di Longarone dell'architetto Giovanni Michelucci*, 1978; Ludovic Quaroni, Salvatore di Pasquale and Giovanni Landucci, *Giovanni Michelucci: la pazienza delle stagioni*, 1980; *Contemporary Architects*, 1987.

MICHAEL OAKESHOTT

British Political Philosopher

Born **Chelmsfield, Kent, 11 December 1901**

Died **Acton, Dorset, 18 December 1990**

Michael Oakeshott was one of the most outstanding in a long line of British political philosophers, and certainly among the most influential liberal thinkers of the twentieth century. Born into a prominent Fabian Socialist family (his father was one of the founders of the London School of Economics (LSE) where Oakeshott was to become a professor) and educated at a progressive co-educational school (in the days when such establishments were a rarity), it was almost inevitable that Michael Oakeshott should have reacted against this background into a philosophy of conservatism. But it was always conservatism without a capital "C". Oakeshott never joined a political party or took up a formal party-political stance. In fact, he always insisted that he had no message, that his teaching of political theory had no connection with political practice and that any lessons to be learned from his lectures and writings were purely those of scholarship with no pragmatic connotations.

Oakeshott went up to Cambridge to read history and stayed on as a history lecturer at Gonville and Caius College for 20 years, and then as a fellow for the rest of his life. The only interruption in his long academic career came with his service in World War II. He enlisted early on in the ranks as a gunner and rose to be an officer in intelligence. In some ways this was one of the happiest periods of his life, for he was a gregarious convivial man, and he appreciated the company of a mixed assortment of characters in his intelligence unit, Phantom — a novel experience outside the somewhat sheltered world of academia. He never let on that he was a Cambridge don in civilian life, and was remembered by his Phantom comrades as an outgoing audacious type ready for any adventure.

Indeed, life was always an adventure for Oakeshott, not in the sense of deeds of derring-do but as an adventure in ideas. In one of his essays he described philosophical reflection as "an intellectual adventure which has a course to follow but no destination". This was in a way an apt description of Oakeshott's own academic achievements. His heroes in the world of political thought were the intellectually and spiritually adventurous — men as different as Benvenuto Cellini and the mystic Saint John of the Cross, and above all, the great human sage and sceptic, Montaigne. Not for nothing did he spend his leisure time during his war service editing a new edition of Hobbes's *Leviathan.* Oakeshott was always a realist. Not for him the didactic ideology of the philosophical system. "His great achievement", he wrote of John Locke, "is to have thought systematically and to have escaped making a system" — a judgement which Oakeshott would have welcomed of his own contribution to political thought.

In a sense it was this aspect of his work which earned him the reputation of being a Conservative, even a Thatcherite, philosopher. Not only did he see clearly the limitations of philosophical systems, he was also well aware of the limitations of government, of ideological politics and of state planning. Most recently his ideas were linked with the extreme theorists of minimal government such as Robert Nozick. But, in what was probably his finest book, written after his retirement, *On Human Conduct,* Oakeshott made it abundantly clear that his overwhelming passion for freedom, both intellectual and practical, was in no sense to be interpreted as a defence of capitalism. Limited politics did not mean for him a free-for-all enterprise culture but rather minimal government in the sense of the classical ideal of civil association, a harking back to the ideas of Hobbes. He saw society as "a multitude of interests, activities and organisations" operating together under the rule of law and common traditions within a freely agreed civil association. He was particularly opposed to "overwhelming concentrations of power such as the trade unions", as he was to the overall imbalance of an over-emphasis on society's economic functions.

Oakeshott's appointment in 1951 to succeed Harold Laski as professor of political science at the London School of Economics came as something of a shock to the academic world. His long-time mentor, Sir Ernest Barker, had campaigned hard for Oakeshott to succeed him at Cambridge. When that failed to come off, Laski's chair was the obvious place, but Oakeshott was not the obvious candidate. As he said in his inaugural lecture, "It seems perhaps a little ungrateful that Professor Graham Wallas and Professor Laski should be followed by a sceptic". But Oakeshott made it clear from the outset that at the LSE he was going to promote academic achievement, not political creeds as his predecessors had done. His weekly lectures on the history of political thought became famous throughout the School; they were attended by students from all disciplines and one had to get to the Old Theatre well in advance to be sure of a seat. His manner was relaxed and informal, even Bohemian — reminiscent of one of his earlier academic escapades, the publication in the 1930s of *A Guide to the Classics,* which turned out to be concerned not with the ancient world but with one of his other passions in life, horse-racing. Among his more notable innovations while at the LSE was his inauguration of a one-year post-graduate course on historiography, largely inspired by his admiration for the work of Benedetto Croce and of Robin Collingwood at Oxford. This attracted students from all over the world, and he continued running the course after he had retired in 1969.

Oakeshott published little during his years at the LSE. Immediately prior to going there he had been preoccupied with his editorship of *The Cambridge Journal* but, apart from contributions to that journal, he had written little since his *Social and Political Doctrines of Contemporary Europe,* written at Barker's suggestion and published in 1939. His great flowering came thick and fast after his retirement with his return to his beloved Hobbes and civil association, his major work *On Human Conduct,* and his preoccupation with historical experience as the basis of all political and social science with *On History.* Always clearly and elegantly written, all his books focused on his central theme of human freedom as the essential characteristic distinguishing mankind from the rest of creation.

Oakeshott was an eminently civilized man. He loved company and good conversation, particularly with the young. Above all, he was a great teacher. He was generous of his time with his students, many of whom remember with affection his accessibility and his never-failing patience and courtesy, and with his colleagues, who enjoyed many an evening discussion ranging far into the night. He was also a man of simple tastes, apart from his love of good wine. He refused all public honours and most honorary doctorates, and passed his long retirement in a tiny cottage in the depths of the country. But his gift for friendship remained as strong as ever, and he welcomed to the end the stimulation of lively company, particularly on his occasional visits to his old college at Cambridge, and the sparkle of new ideas.

Born Michael Joseph Oakeshott. **Parents** Joseph Francis and Frances Maude (Hellicar) Oakeshott. **Marriages** Two; 2) Christel. **Children** One son from first marriage. **Education** St

George's Harpenden; Gonville and Caius College, Cambridge, BA, 1923, MA, 1927. **Military service** Royal Artillery, 1940–45, became captain. **Career** Fellow of Gonville and Caius College, Cambridge from 1925–90, university lecturer in history, 1932–49; professorial fellow, Nuffield College, Oxford, 1949–50; professor of political science, London School of Economics and Political Science, University of London, 1951–69, professor emeritus, 1969 onwards; Muirhead Lecturer, University of Birmingham, 1953; visiting professor, Harvard University, 1958; Ludwig Mond Lecturer, University of Manchester, 1959. **Related activities** Editor, *Cambridge Journal,* 1947–53. **Offices and memberships** Fellow of the British Academy, 1966. **Awards and honours** Honorary doctorate: Colorado University, Durham University, Hull University. **Publications** *Experience and Its Modes,* 1933; (with G. T. Griffiths) *A Guide to the Classics; or, How to Pick the Derby Winner*, 1936, revised edition published as *New Guide to the Derby: How to Pick the Winner,* 1947; *The Social Political Doctrines of Contemporary Europe,* foreword by Ernest Barker, 1939; Thomas Hobbes, *Leviathan; or, The Matter, Forme, and Power of a Commonwealth, Ecclesiasticall and Civil* (editor and author of introduction), 1946; *The Voice of Poetry in the Conversation of Mankind,* 1959; *Rationalism in Politics, and Other Essays,* 1962; *Hobbes on Civil Association,* 1975; *On Human Conduct,* 1975; *On History and Other Essays,* 1983; *Essays on Learning and Teaching,* 1989; *The Voice of Liberal Learning,* 1989. **Cause of death** Undisclosed, at age 89.

VIJAYA PANDIT

Indian Diplomat and Politician

Born **Allahabad, India, 18 August 1900**

Died **Dehra Dun, India, 1 December 1990**

The name Vijaya Lakshmi means "victory and prosperity" and it was given to Mrs Pandit — in accordance with Indian tradition — when she became Mrs Pandit at her marriage in 1921 to advocate Ranjit. It is a fitting name. She spent her life in pursuit of the victory of freedom for India; and prosperity was something she never lacked — indeed, her lavish life-style was to become a bone of contention within her family.

Vijaya Pandit's family was a great one whose members, generation after generation, distinguished themselves in Indian politics. Her father, Motilal Nehru, was a political associate of Mahatma Gandhi and wrote the Nehru Report detailing plans for dominion status for India. She was sister to Jawaharal Nehru, aunt to his daughter Indira and grand-aunt to Indira's son Rajiv — all prime ministers of India for a total of almost 40 years of independent India's 43-year old history. And she was a politician and statesperson of great distinction in her own right.

Born in the northern Indian state of Uttar Pradesh, she was originally named Swarup Kumari after her mother; but amongst family members she was known as Nanhi or "little darling". She grew up under the tutelage of an English governess in an atmosphere of affluence. The Nehrus had their own swimming pool, a large garden, horses, dogs, carriages and automobiles. Nanhi did not attend university; but through association with leaders like Gandhi and her brother, when he returned from Harrow School and Cambridge University in England, she absorbed a mixture of eastern and western cultures as well as political philosophy.

By the time of her marriage in 1921, Gandhi's Civil Disobedience movement to obtain India's freedom by non-violent means was already gaining ground. One by one the Nehru family joined the movement. Both Vijaya Pandit's father and her husband gave up their lucrative law practices to devote their energies to the nationalist struggle. And Pandit herself campaigned selflessly for the cause.

Like her father, husband and brother she was imprisoned for her pains by the British colonial government. Her first spell in jail — a year's sentence for refusing to "refrain from taking part in meetings and processions" — separated her from her three daughters, the youngest of whom was only three. But neither she nor her family ever resisted arrest; they were peaceful prisoners willing to sacrifice their comfort and pleasure to the prospect of independence.

In prison, she found the public washing a problem for a woman of her upbringing; but she did a great deal of reading. "If you meet an Indian who has read Gibbon's *Decline and Fall* right through", she said later, "you can be fairly sure he was a political prisoner."

Repeated jailings focused national and international attention on the Nehru family which together with Gandhi became the symbol for India's struggle for freedom. "There was a certain etiquette about getting oneself locked up", wrote Vijaya Pandit.

> The procedure was to notify the authorities that you intended to break a law, so that they had to arrest you. Mr Gandhi insisted that this should not be done on Sundays — it might prevent the British magistrate from attending church. In our case we knew the magistrate quite well — we'd played tennis with him at one time — and felt sure whatever else he did on Sunday he didn't go to church. But we obeyed the Mahatma's ruling.

In 1936 Vijaya Pandit became the first woman to be elected to India's legislative assembly and was appointed minister for local government and public health. Under previous ministers a subordinate was always sent to observe disaster areas. Pandit personally toured epidemic-plagued villages to see the problems at first hand and to encourage local doctors and the families of victims.

After her last release from prison in 1943 Pandit plunged into the work of helping the famine-stricken inhabitants of Bengal. And in January 1945, a year after the death of her husband, she began her diplomatic career when she was nominated to head an Indian delegation to the Pacific Relations Conference in Virginia in the United States. Soon after that she attended the United Nations Charter Conference in San Francisco as an observer. Here she informed a crowded press conference that the official Indian delegates had not "the slightest representative capacity, no sanction or mandate from any responsible groups in India, and are merely the nominees of the British Government." She successfully stole their limelight by arguing forcefully for India's independence.

Her efforts and those of her family were at last rewarded. At the stroke of midnight on 15 August 1947 India gained its freedom. It was one of Vijaya Pandit's greatest regrets that she was not at home for the historic occasion. Instead she was in Moscow, organizing independent India's embassy, which she then headed. After Moscow she was ambassador in Washington, then Ireland, high commissioner in London, and ambassador in Madrid. She knew Churchill, Stalin and Tito well.

In September 1953 Mrs Pandit was elected president of the United Nations General Assembly — the first woman to hold the office. She was quick to dispel any doubts about her ability to handle the job. At her first press conference as president a reporter asked about the colour of her sari. She shot back: "Did you ask my predecessor the colour of his tie?"

At the UN she vigorously opposed apartheid — India was one of the first countries to sever diplomatic relations with South Africa, a break which continues to this day — and in 1978 she was India's representative to the Human Rights Commission.

In short, for 15 years Vijaya Pandit was a public relations officer for India; she was also living proof that a woman could achieve the highest office and the highest accolades as a diplomat and a politician. For the international career of the diminutive Pandit — sophisticated, silvery and swathed in silks — was unmatched by any woman in her time. She was much in the eye of the public and much interviewed. Wrote one reporter: "What a delight she is proving to be. Small, she has the vivacity of a daring robin that dashes in and steals the tidbit right from under the beak of some bigger, more ferocious bird. It is a joy to listen to her". She was entirely at home in the company of the rich and titled; a few years ago she startled a reporter with a casual reference to her old friend, Queen Elizabeth II as, "not a great intellect, of course, but a warm person of many interests."

But within her family she was not always so popular. Her late husband had left his estate to his daughters which meant that Pandit Nehru had to foot the bill for his sister's extravagant life-style. No light burden, for, as one commentator puts it, Mrs Pandit "spoke — and spent — as a westerner".

There were more serious, more far-reaching sources of family tension. Returning to India in 1961, she became governor of Bombay and then a vociferous critic of her niece Indira Gandhi's government. When, in 1976, Indira Gandhi suspended all civil liberties and declared an internal emergency Vijaya Pandit's opposition was fierce and effective. For her outspokenness, her movements were forcibly curtailed by her prime minister niece. Pandit successfully campaigned against Indira Gandhi's party in the 1977 elections, but declined to accept any office afterwards. Her criticism of government policies extended to Indira Gandhi's son and successor, Rajiv, with whom her relations were frosty to the end.

In public, at any rate. In private, Mrs Pandit was very much the fond matriarch of her distinguished dynasty. Wrote Honor Balfour who first met Mrs Pandit when she was high commissioner in London, "Even when there was considerable tension between her and Indira and some of us even feared for her safety ('No, no,' she'd say, 'Indira wouldn't dare. We in India have too much respect for age.') — when Indira had had a particularly bad Cabinet meeting, she would turn to her aunt, who enfolded her in her arms and let her weep on her bosom as she used to do as a child."

Finally, Vijaya Pandit retired to her house in Dehra Dun, a small town in the foothills of the Himalayas, to write books; and to live in the style to which she was accustomed — the house was designed by Le Corbusier and encircled by rose gardens. Throughout her life she had been a gourmet as well as a woman of sophistication and expensive taste. In her last years she remained a generous hostess, holding dinner parties at Dehra Dun for writers, teachers and politicians.

A small woman physically, Vijaya Pandit achieved the greatest stature as a statesperson and — in no less measure — as the last grand lady of a great family.

Born Swarup Kumari Nehru. **Parents** Motilal, lawyer and joint leader of the Congress Party, and Sarup (Rani) Nehru. **Marriage** Ranjit Sitaram Pandit, lawyer, 1921 (died 1944). **Children** Three daughters, Chandralekha Mehta, Nayantara Sahgal and Rita Dar. **Education** Educated privately at home. **Career** Member, non co-operative movement, 1930; member of board and chairman of education committee, Allahabad Municipal Board, Allahabad, India, 1934–36; minister in charge of portfolios of local self-government and public health, Uttar Pradesh Congress Cabinet, 1936–39, 1946–47; ambassador to the Soviet Union, 1947–49; ambassador to the United States and Mexico, 1949–52; member of congress, Lok Sabha, 1952–54, 1964–68; member of parliament of independent India, 1953–54, 1964–68; high commissioner to Court of St James, London, England; ambassador: to Ireland, 1954–61, to Spain, 1958–61; governor of Maharashtra, India, 1962–64; left Congress Party, joined Congress for Democracy Party, 1977. **Related activities** Delegate, Pacific Relations Conference, Virginia, 1945; observer/delegate, United Nations Charter Conference, San Francisco; leader, Indian delegation to United Nations, 1946–51, 1963; president, General Assembly of United Nations, 1953–54; leader, Indian delegation to Human Rights Commission, 1978–79; lecturer, United States. **Other activities** Imprisoned for one year, 1931; sentenced to three terms of imprisonment, 1932, 1941, 1942; detained, 1942–33. **Offices and memberships** Trustee, Mountbatten Memorial Trust, 1980–90; member: International Women's League for Peace and Freedom, All India Women's Conference. **Awards and honours** Honorary doctorate: University of Allahabad, 1947, Wellesley College, 1950, New York University, 1950, Howards University, 1950, West Virginia State College, 1950, St Louis University, 1950, Lafayette University, 1950, Oklahoma City University, 1951, University of Hawaii, 1951, Nagpur University, 1954, University of London, 1955, University of Wales, 1956, University of Leeds, 1956, McMaster University, 1957, University of Edinburgh, 1960; Doctor of Civil Law, Oxford University, 1964; award from Beta Mu Lambda chapter of Alpha Phi Alpha, 1950, Robert S. Abbot Memorial Award, 1950; award from Bethune-Cookna College, 1951; One World Award, 1952; named Key Woman of the Year, 1954; Woman of Achievement Award, American Federation of Soroptimist Clubs, 1956; Appreciation Award, city of Dayton, Ohio, 1957; Dorothes Schlozer Gold Medal, University of Goettingen, 1958; Padna Vibushan, 1962. **Publications** *So I Became a Minister,* 1939; *Prison Diary,* 1945; *The Evolution of India,* 1958; *The Scope of Happiness: a Personal Memoir,* 1979. **Cause of death** Undisclosed, at age 90. **Further reading** Anne Guthrie, *Madame Ambassador: The Life of Vijaya Lakshmi Pandit,* 1962; Robert Hardy Andrews, *A Lamp for India: The Story of Madame Pandit,* 1967.

SIR DAVID PIPER

British Museum Director and Writer

Born **London, England, 21 July 1918**

Died **Wytham, Oxfordshire, 29 December 1990**

Sir David Piper can best be described, despite his strong anti-Establishment leanings, as an intellectual aristocrat. He was a man who, throughout his life, observed his surroundings with honesty, and often joy, and then discussed them both sensitively and analytically. His many resulting books not only inform but also can be read as literature.

He was educated at Clifton College, Bristol and then read French at Cambridge University. He was just old enough to have completed his education prior to World War II during which he served in the Indian Army. He spent three years as a Japanese prisoner-of-war, an experience which affected him deeply and about which he wrote movingly. In later years he based his novel *Trial by Battle* on his own observations of jungle warfare.

On his return to England in 1945 he was reunited with his future wife, Anne, also a novelist, whom he married soon afterwards. Perhaps because of the horrors he had undergone, his marriage and family were the most important aspects of his personal life and which he valued above all.

His first museum post was as assistant keeper at the National Portrait Gallery on the fringe of London's Trafalgar Square. The gallery in those immediate post-war days was extremely staid and, apart from the pictures, dull. But Piper, besides carrying out the everyday business of administering the gallery, produced a pioneering catalogue in the gallery's series on seventeenth-century portraits, staged an Oliver Cromwell exhibition, and set in train many projects which were to bear fruit in later years. It is as a result of his work that the gallery has developed from being a somewhat minor offshoot of its neighbour, The National Gallery, to having a clear and sought-out identity in its own right. And it was during those years as well that he also wrote his books on *The English Face,* and the delightful *Companion Guide to London* which records the areas of London he explored while walking from his Hammersmith home to the museum each morning. He was made director of the museum in 1964.

In 1967 he was appointed director of the Fitzwilliam Museum in Cambridge where he remained for six years. Although he made a notable contribution to this highly prestigious establishment his time there was spent primarily in wrestling with its financial problems. It did not bring him the joy he was subsequently to find at Oxford's Ashmolean Museum where he took over in 1973 and where he remained until he retired 12 years later.

The Ashmolean had not previously had a director and many viewed the appointment with trepidation but Piper's policy of non-interference with his departmental heads rapidly won him respect and ensured his views were sought and, usually, followed. He was knighted in 1983.

His artistic interests were wide and he continued his parallel career as a writer throughout his life, bringing the work of artists and poets before the British public and demonstrating the connection between creative production and social factors. Each period brings its own particular stimuli and constraints. He always looked for the interface of art and society and, in doing so, produced memorable books, including *Artists' London* and *The Image of the Poet.* Because of his own reticent and self-effacing nature his own personality never detracted from his message. His legacy lies in that fact.

Born David Towry Piper. **Parents** Professor S.H. and Mary Piper. **Marriage** Anne Richmond, novelist, 1945. **Children** One son, Thomas, and three daughters. **Education** Clifton College, Bristol; St Catherine's College, Cambridge, MA. **Military service** Indian Army, 1940–45, Japanese prisoner-of-war, 1942–45. **Career** Assistant keeper, National Portrait Gallery, London, 1946–64, director, 1964–67; Slade Professor of Fine Art, Oxford University, 1966–67; director and Marlay curator, Fitzwilliam Museum, Cambridge, 1967–73; fellow, Christ's College, Cambridge; director, Ashmolean Museum, Oxford, 1973–85; fellow, Worcester College, Oxford, 1973–85, fellow emeritus, 1985; Clark Lecturer, Cambridge University, 1977–78, Rede Lecturer, 1983. **Related activities** Member, Royal Fine Art Commission, 1970–86. **Offices and memberships** Fellow, Society of Antiquaries. **Awards and honours** Commander of the Order of the British Empire, 1969; knighted, 1983; honorary DLitt, Bristol University, 1984. **Publications** *It's Warm Inside* (novel), 1953; *The English Face,* 1957; *Trial By Battle* (novel), 1959; *Catalogue of 17th Century Portraits in the National Portrait Gallery,* 1963; *Companion Guide to London,* 1964; (editor) *Enjoying Paintings*, 1964; *Painting in England, 1500–1880*, 1965; *Shades 1970* (World Cultural Guide series), 1971; (editor) *The Genius of British Painting,* 1975; *The Treasures of Oxford,* 1977; *Kings and Queens of England and Scotland,* 1980; *Artists' London,* 1982; *The Image of the Poet,* 1983; (editor) *The Treasures of the Ashmolean Museum,* 1985. **Cause of death** Undisclosed, at age 72.

TUNKU ABDUL RAHMAN

Malaysian Former Prime Minister

***Born* Alor Star, Malaya, 8 February 1903**

***Died* Kuala Lumpur, Malaysia, 6 December 1990**

"The Tunku" was how Malaya's first prime minister was known affectionately by his fellow countrymen, and even more widely throughout south-east Asia and the Commonwealth. The title denoted that he was of royal descent, and indeed his background was impeccable — the seventh son of the twenty-fourth Sultan of Kedah, a jungle principality which his family had ruled for centuries, a Malay chieftain in a predominantly feudal country. But at the same time he was also thoroughly pro-British in education and outlook, a convivial man far removed from the spartan Muslim tradition, whose fondness for "the good life" almost jeopardized his studies at Cambridge and whose racial tolerance in the end cost him his hold on power. Nevertheless that same breadth of vision in the racially fraught atmosphere of post-World War II Malaya brought his country political stability and economic prosperity which has continued almost unchecked ever since.

Abdul Rahman entered his country's politics almost by accident when the main Malay political party, the United Malays National Organization (UMNO), elected him as their president in 1952, after its founder had walked out following his failure to make the party multi-racial. These were the days of the anti-British "Emergency" spearheaded by the predominantly Chinese Communist guerrillas. The Tunku immediately recognized the importance of forging a communal alliance with the Chinese and Indian communities; some saw this as a result of his own background, with a non-Malay mother from a Burmese Shan dynasty. The Alliance swept to power in the first national elections of 1955 and thereafter the Tunku was the obvious leader to bring the country to independence in 1957.

"Bapa Kanerdekaan" ("Father of Independence") became his sobriquet, but others were to follow. Neighbouring Singapore was sliding into a disintegration which the Tunku saw as threatening the stability of the new independent Malaya. Again his sense of communal balance came to the rescue. Singapore could be safely accommodated within a Malayan federation if its predominantly Chinese population were balanced by an equal Malay insertion by the incorporation of the British colonies of northern Borneo whose populations were akin to the Malays. "Bapa Malaysia" pulled it off, but only at the cost of "confrontation" with Sukarno's Indonesia and three years of bitter guerrilla warfare. The establishment of the Federation was the high spot of the Tunku's career, with his credit high not only among his own Malay community but also throughout the Commonwealth. But it was not to last. Lee Kuan Yew of Singapore proved an uneasy partner. His leadership of a predominantly Chinese opposition threatened the special rights of the Malays under the constitution. At least that was how the Malays interpreted the growing friction between Kuala Lumpur and Singapore, and the Tunku, as the leader of the Malays, was regretfully forced to act. Without demonstrations in any of the territories, Singapore was evicted from the Federation.

This amputation stemmed the fears of the Malay extremists for a time, but by 1969, with electoral defeats for the Alliance, the underlying racial conflict boiled over. The bloody communal riots of May 1969 forced the Tunku to suspend the constitution and delare a state of emergency, and within a year to leave office. His official political career was at an end, but not his political interest and activity. In retirement he wrote a weekly column in a local Penang newspaper, and in his eighties, almost blind and confined to a wheelchair, he was threatening to return to lead his old UMNO party against what he saw as a slide towards dictatorship under the current prime minister, Dr Mahathir Mohamed, whom he had once expelled from the party.

In a multi-racial country like Malaysia, the Tunku's great contribution was his recognition of the need to weld the various immigrant races into one nation, and then into a federation. A man of great personal charm and with all the relaxed easy-going style of the Malays, he yet showed a remarkable strength of political will and a foresight which for a time enabled him to win the allegiance of almost all the strands of the newly independent nation. But in the end his support depended on unquestioning belief in Malay superiority, which he attempted to use as a counterbalance to Chinese economic dominance. When that political superiority was threatened, he had no further weights to throw into the scales. The long retirement ended in struggle and sadness for a man who had claimed at the peak of his career that he was the world's happiest prime minister.

Born Tunku Abdul Rahman Putra al-Haj. **Parents** Sultan Abdul Hamid of Kedah and Makche Menjelara. **Marriages** 1) Name unknown, died 1935; 2) Tun Sharifah Roadziah, 1939. **Children** One son and one daughter by first marriage, one adopted son and three adopted daughters. **Education** Sultan Abdul Hamid College, Alor Star, Bangkok; Penang Free School, Penang; on state scholarship, St Catherine's College, Cambridge, 1922–25, BA; legal studies, 1947–49 (called to the Bar, Inner Temple, London, 1950). **Career** District officer, Kedah State Civil Service, 1931–38; deputy director, civil defence, south Kedah, 1940; Malayan legal service, 1949–51; unofficial member, executive and legislative councils, Malaya, 1952; leader, federal and legislative council; chief minister and minister for home affairs, 1955; first prime minister and minister of external affairs, Malaya, 1957–63, Malaysia, 1963–70, also minister of information and broadcasting, 1963–64, minister of culture, youth and sport at various times. **Related activities** Leader, United Malay National Organization, 1952–70; founder, 1960, and chairman, Muslim Welfare Organization, PERKIM; secretary-general, Islamic Conference, 1963–71. **Other activities** Chancellor, University of Malaya, 1962; chairman, Star Publications and weekly columnist on retirement, *Star,* Penang. **Offices and memberships** President: Malaysian Football Association, Asian Football Confederation; vice-president, for life, Commonwealth Society. **Awards and honours** Order of National Crown of Malaysia; Kedah Order of Merit; Darjah Utama Seri Mahkota Negara; Companion of Honour, United Kingdom; Freedom of the City of London; Distinguished Service Award, United States Sports Academy, 1981; Companion of the Order of Australia, 1988; honorary degree, Oxford University; other honorary degrees and foreign decorations. **Publications** *Mahsuri* (play), 1941, filmed 1966; *Raja Bersiong,* filmed, 1966; *Looking Back,* 1977; *Viewpoints,* 1978; *Lest We Forget, Political Awakening,* 1986. **Cause of death** Heart and kidney problems, at age 87. **Further reading** Harry Miller, *Prince and Premier,* 1959; Roland Mckie, *Malaysia in Focus,* 1963; S. Durai Raja Singam, editor, *Tribute to Tengku Abdul Rahman,* 1963.

ANNE REVERE

American Actress

***Born* Manhattan, New York, 25 June 1903**

***Died* Locust Valley, New York, 17 December 1990**

"Oh, *she's* in this? I forget her name, but she's wonderful!" There is a handful of actors whose presence immediately confers a soothing reassurance that the film you're about to see is going to be pretty worthwhile. Anne Revere belonged to that small group of character actors whose restricted typing hid great breadth of style and professional competence, but who nevertheless could lift the most mundane line, the briefest of parts into something shiny. Revere, with her gaunt, honest face (both attractive and always attracting), often portraying stoic practicality, always kept the kindliness in her eyes and a warmth in her smile. Director Elia Kazan said of her in his 1967 film *Gentleman's Agreement,* where Revere portrayed one of her screen mothers: "She had bite and was at the same time caustic and affectionate." She was also an outstanding actress, bringing assurance and a clear-eyed intelligence to every role, and making maximum effect of screen time which was always far too limited, in over 40 films.

Revere was born into a comfortable New England family—one with a grounded pedigree, as her father was a descendent of Paul Revere. After graduating from Wellesley College, she studied at the respected American Laboratory School in New York (which produced some of the best actors in the 1940s and 1950s). Her drama foundation was further strengthened via repertory companies. Her Broadway début was in *The Great Barrington* in 1931, but she made her greatest impact as one of the teachers accused of lesbianism in Lillian Hellman's riveting (and infamous) play, *The Children's Hour.* The drama polarized audiences because of the subject. Characteristically, Revere was at the forefront of legal action to keep it on stage. She also played to critical acclaim in *As You Like It* and as Masha in *Three Sisters.*

She repeated a stage role in the 1934 film, *Double Door,* a "dark house" thriller, in Hollywood, but didn't move there until 1940. She seemed to be typed from the beginning (Tinseltown producers could not always take chances with imagination), portraying an unmarried teacher in *Remember the Day,* with Claudette Colbert and John Payne. Her next role of note was as a secretary in *Star-Spangled Rhythm,* a Paramount World War II extravaganza full of songs and sketches and no plot. Revere was not shown at her best. But in *The Song of Bernadette,* as Jennifer Jones's mother, she was nominated for Best Supporting Actress. The Oscar-studded film was heavy on celestial chorus and inspiration; Revere was the needed personification of sturdy conviction and earthy wisdom.

After portraying a booming military wife in *Standing Room Only,* and a journalist in *Old Acquaintance,* Revere won, in 1945, her Best Supporting Oscar over formidable competition (Eve Arden (q.v.) in *Mildred Pierce* and Angela Lansbury in *The Picture of Dorian Gray*) for her role as Elizabeth Taylor's mother in *National Velvet.* To many critics, Revere was the best reason to see the emotion-encumbered equine tale. Revere was cast as Gene Tierney's mother in *Dragonwyck* — once more, given her limitations of typecasting, she helped salvage a nonde-script. But in the 1947 *Gentleman's Agreement,* Revere glowed. An earnest indictment of anti-Semitism, with Gregory Peck and John Garfield (all three actors took a severe salary paycut willingly in order to ensure Elia Kazan's film was made), it was the first of a series of anti-racist films. Once again she was able to avoid every cliché-ridden trap; her presence was regal, her portrayal of unsentimental faith in the possibility of turning a bigoted world around impressive.

Again, a period of pleasant but unremarkable films followed; she was a sensible unmarried sister warning Alice Faye that the man she fell for was a beast in *Fallen Angel*, ran a brothel in *Forever Amber,* and was a mother to John Garfield (the two actors respected each other enormously and the chemistry made them a fine filmic team) in the boxing epic *Body and Soul...*

But *A Place in the Sun,* in 1951, was one of her best roles — and one that the movie-going public would hardly recognize. The film was based on Theodore Dreiser's epic novel of American life. But before it was released, the McCarthy plague had begun to take its sickening toll. Revere was blacklisted by the House Un-American Activities Committee, for refusing to testify on Capitol Hill regarding Communist Party Links. Despite being asked by "Ronnie" Reagan to "just name a couple of names", she would not denounce anyone. Revere had also joined the Screen Actors Guild in 1944, and held important offices within it. As a result of her refusal to cast any aspersions on the Guild before the HUAC, she resigned from the board. Later in life, she commented, "I got to know Communists and Communism, but I knew it wasn't for me. I'm a free-thinking Yankee rebel, and nobody's going to tell me what to do." As a result, the subtle nastiness of the Hollywood power system which had bowed to the witch-hunt, did its job. Her roles were cut — most notably in *Place,* which was released a few months after her resignation. Despite the good billing in the credits, much of her work was scissored onto the floor.

According to Revere, several other films (including *Deep Waters* and *The Great Missouri Raid*), were also "irreparably damaged by cutting". But *A Place in the Sun* "was the most tragic. I'd wanted to get away from playing mothers. But she ran a soup kitchen, was a strong influence in the life of the ambitious protagonist...she was actually a villainess. She had to carry a great deal of weight in relatively little footage. I took the part at a reduction in salary. But the film had criticized the American way of life. Before the cutting, my part was the best work I'd ever done in Hollywood." The film won seven Academy awards. Revere didn't work again until 1958.

A highlight of her "bits and pieces" after that period was her year's run in the Broadway smash *Toys in the Attic,* for which she won a Tony Award. In the Lillian Hellman story, she portrayed an inflexible unmarried woman opposite Maureen Stapleton and Jason Robards — the trio were superb together. She appeared several more times on off-Broadway and on television but, as she said, "The blacklist was important to me not only financially but it was my life, the top of my career. My profession. I'm sorry it was cut short as it was, because outside of *Toys,* I never made it."

One more distinguished talent had been ruined by the McCarthy witch-hunt. But if never "making it" meant that millions of film and theatre-goers were never impressed by her performances, or that her reputation as a superb actress was ever dented, then for once Revere could be said to be mistaken.

Born Anne Revere. **Parents** Clinton Revere, stockbroker, and Harriette (Winn) Revere. **Marriage** Samuel Rose, stage director, 1935 (died 1984). **Education** Wellesley College, Massachusetts; American Laboratory School, New York. **Career** Actress, 1930s onwards; Broadway début, *The Great Barrington,* 1931; film début, *Double Door,* 1934. **Other activities** Blacklisted by House Un-American Activities Committee, 1951–58. **Offices and memberships** On board of directors, Screen Actors Guild, 1944–1951, vice-president, 1945, treasurer, 1946–47. **Awards and honours** Academy Award as best supporting actress, 1945; Tony Award for *Toys in the Attic,* 1960. **Stage** (includes) *The Great Barrington,* 1931; *The Children's Hour,* 1934; *Toys in the Attic,* 1960; also: *As You Like It, Three Sisters.* **Films** (include) *Double Door,* 1934; *H.M. Pulham,* 1940; *The Howards of Virginia,* 1940; *Remember the Day,* 1941; *Men of Boy's Town,* 1941; *The Devil Commands,* 1941; *The Flame of New Orleans,* 1941; *Star-Spangled Rhythm,* 1942; *Old Acquaintance,* 1943; *Standing Room Only,* 1943; *The Song of Bernadette,* 1943; *The Keys of the Kingdom,* 1944; *Sunday Dinner for a Soldier,* 1944; *National Velvet,* 1945; *Dragonwyck,* 1946; *Body and Soul,* 1947; *Forever Amber,* 1947; *Scuddo Hoo! Scudda Hay!,* 1948; *The Secret Beyond the Door,* 1948; *Deep Waters,* 1948; *The Great Missouri Raid,* 1950; *A Place in the Sun,* 1951. **Television** (includes) *Six Million Dollar Man*; *The Trojan Women*; *A Time for Us.* **Cause of death** Pneumonia, at age 87.

MARTIN RITT

American Film and Television Director

***Born* Manhattan, New York, 2 March 1914**

***Died* Santa Monica, California, 8 December 1990**

Only a few directors are able to combine an unshakeable sense of social responsibility with an entertaining and thoroughly professional skill. To achieve this without the taint of egotism souring the effect is rare enough. But to do so with perspective, after being betrayed by two industries one has served and enriched, makes Martin Ritt one of the most respected of directors. His reputation has survived the patchy quality of much of his filmic output. Whether flawed or excellent, his films are remembered for their performances, not for any *auteur* affectations.

Following a childhood spent in a tough Lower East Side neighbourhood of Manhattan, Ritt set out to be an actor, and joined the famous Group Theater, which was dedicated to the production of social dramas. His athletic, stocky build helped him win his first job: as a boxing teacher for Luther Adler who needed to prepare for his lead in Clifford Odet's *Golden Boy*. Ritt made his acting début in the same production. After serving in the Army during the war, he appeared in George Cukor's *Winged Victory,* a patriotic film about fighter pilots, but decided he preferred direction and production to performing. His stage productions include *Set My People Free*, *The Man*, *The Front Page* and Arthur Miller's *A View from the Bridge,* which won much praise.

After considerable stage and television experience — Ritt acted in over 150 teleplays and directed over a hundred others in TV's "golden age" of live, superb quality programming — he turned to film. His début film was *Edge of the City* (released in Britain as *A Man is Ten Feet Tall*) in 1957. It dealt with what were then two fashionable themes: waterfront thuggery and social misfits. Starring John Cassavetes, Sidney Poitier and Jack Warden, all unknowns, it was the first American film about an inter-racial friendship. As all of Ritt's films would be, it was bare and clean in direction and execution, with great sympathy for the protagonists (without sticky sentiment) and outstanding, unpretentious location work. From that moment on, Ritt was hooked on film-making. He was also prepared to do battle, to make pictures his way by creating a succession of box-office hits — the only method, Ritt realized, that would eventually buy him creative control. The result would be years of compromise, with a large handful of flawed films.

From the beginning he saw the art of film-making as a collaborative process; he was one of the few directors actors wanted to work with, regardless of the material. Egotism was never to interfere with the act of telling a story or carving out a character. As he was to explain later, "During a shot I concentrate totally upon the actor's face, much more than the text." He was able consistently to extract superb performances from his actors, partly because of his respect for them, and partly because his liberalist sympathy for the underdog remained steadfast. All this was seen in his television work.

But after a stream of productions for CBS TV, Ritt found himself, in 1951, blacklisted, initially because he had been a member of the Communist Party briefly in his youth (until the Soviet-German Pact of 1939). A Syracuse grocer charged him with donating money to Communist China. The McCarthy paranoia was at its most feverish, and Ritt was hauled up before the House Un-American Activities Committee. Like the best people, he never denounced anyone. But his career lay in tatters. He lost the title role of *Marty,* which Paddy Chayefsky had written just for him. He also lost the chance to work in television again. Ritt was reduced to teaching acting classes at the respected Actors Studio; his students included several of his later stars, such as Paul Newman, Lee Remick, Joanne Woodward, Rod Steiger, Maureen Stapleton and Susan Strasberg (daughter of Lee).

But Ritt stayed true to his political views which were consistently to the left of the audiences, and of the film establishment, and continued to devote time and money to liberal causes. Gradually, as the stench of the witch-hunt began to fade, Ritt turned again to the stage as director, and landed the occasional Broadway part. Eventually, Hollywood took him back.

Ritt's 1957 film, *No Down Payment,* took on the subject of promiscuity among the suburban classes. Although the fastened-on ending was considered contrived and moralistic, the film introduced Joanne Woodward, whose performance impressed critics and the public alike. In *The Long Hot Summer,* the same year, with both Woodward and Newman, the studio demanded another happy ending, this time to the story of an unprincipled maverick who disrupts the lives of a "first family" in Mississippi. There was more overheated southern passion in Ritt's production from William Faulkner's novel, *The Sound and the Fury*. Woodward portrayed an illegitimate girl who rebels against her family and its binding traditions.

The Hollywood establishment had not learned its lesson, and insisted upon another soapy ending, this time in *Black Orchid,* with Anthony Quinn and Sophia Loren, widower and widow in a frustrated relationship against the backdrop of a poor Italian neighbourhood. But *Paris Blues* at last redeemed the director. A study of expatriate jazz musicians, with glorious music by Duke Ellington, it was described by one critic as "an exquisite film all about nothing". Ritt had not tempted the powers-that-be with a story-line to sanitize.

Another faltering film, *Adventures of a Young Man,* proved to be a rambling adaptation of Hemingway's "Nick Adam" stories. But artistic and public triumph came with *Hud*, Ritt's at-last uncompromising film about life on a small Texas holding in Nowheresville, USA. Events were seen through the eyes of a young man (Brandon de Wilde) who experiences the conflict between moralistic patriarch Homer (played by Melvyn Douglas), defender of the American Set of Values, and hard-drinking, tough-loving, opportunistic Hud, who was played by Paul Newman in one of his best early performances. While the boy decides upon Homer's standards and values, the ending escaped any jingoism or sugar; the amoral Hud wins what *he* sets after: the ranch away from the older man. Both Douglas and Patricia Neal won Best Supporting Actor awards.

In Ritt's 1965 film, *The Spy Who Came in from the Cold,* Richard Burton gave a brilliant performance as the shabby and disenchanted Leamas, who discovers he's as much a victim of a corrupt society as those whom he defends. Burton abandoned his customary winking nostril and florid stare to act with great concentration and discretion. In *Hombre* Newman played a white man who, brought up by Indians, later avenged himself on his white tormentors. It was not one of Ritt's best. Neither was *The Brotherhood,* an understated study of the Mafia, with an ageing mobster of the Old School in conflict with his younger brother.

Ritt's characters were often underdogs, victims of racism, sexism or capitalism who live lives of quiet dignity, or who disrupt society in the quest for rights of the "common" human being. In *The Molly Maguires,* Ritt matched Sean Connery and Richard Harris in a feud which guaranteed a kind of combustion between the two actors each rarely had with any other co-star. The film was about a rebel miner who leads the Molly Maguires, a terrorist sect which sought to better appalling conditions in the Pennsylvania coalmines during the 1870s...and a Pinkerton detective who infiltrates the sect, only to betray it. Written by Ritt's fellow blacklistee, Walter Bernstein, it was Ritt's favourite film. But it did not do well at the box office. Labour rights seemed not to be a draw, despite leading names.

In 1970 Ritt made *The Great White Hope,* based on the Broadway hit about the first black man to win the World Heavyweight boxing title, who would later be harassed by a racist public due to his involvement with a white woman. The story was true, the actor was a powerful James Earl Jones, and the film did reasonably well. Ritt continued the theme with *Sounder,* co-starring Cicely Tyson and Paul Winfield. The story was about a family struggling to overcome bigotry in Depression-hit Louisiana. Throughout his career, Ritt had made strenuous efforts to combat racism through the kind of stories that put such prejudices to rest. Although the film was powerful, it was also the beginning of a new tone in his work; there was a new warmth and optimism.

Pete 'n Tillie starred Walter Matthau and Carol Burnett as a middle-aged couple torn apart by the death of their son. The reviews were good, the performances unusually good, but unlike the smash-hit *Sounder* it didn't do well. Neither did *Conrack* with Jon Voight as a white teacher living and working among poor Blacks. The story was true, but to Ritt's dismay the film angered many Blacks: "They asked me why I'd made a film about a white Jesus". Ritt was hurt over the snub, and did not return to the subject of racism in that way again.

But he struck gold with the *The Front* with Woody Allen. Ritt was able to handle his own painful memories of the blacklist with humour. In a tale about hypocrisy and hysteria, Allen was paid to pass off the work of a group of blacklisted friends as his own — until forced one day to take a stand at the HUAC himself. At the end credits, the film lists all the people who worked on it, people who had been denied the right to work back then. Even more powerful than the plot was the sight in black and white of the shameful waste of a host of talent. Ironically, the film project was turned down by most of the Hollywood studios; the man who gave it the go-ahead was David Begelman, who was later disgraced in a Hollywoodgate scandal of his own.

Three years later Ritt directed another of his most popular films, again using labour rights as the subject. *Norma Rae* won an Oscar for Sally Field, who portrayed a backwoods factory girl who tries to unionize her fellow workers, and has her consciousness raised at the same time.

In 1987 he directed a flamboyant vehicle for Barbra Streisand, *Nuts,* about a call-girl on trial for manslaughter. Co-starring Richard Dreyfuss and a cast of players from Ritt's earlier days (Maureen Stapleton, Eli Wallach, James Whitmore and Karl Malden), they gave substance to the disturbing exploration of the hooker's supposed "insanity". Ritt's only other film of slight note, after this period until his death, was a pleasant romantic comedy with Field and James Garner called *Murphy's Romance* in 1985. He adds his own two-finger salute in one scene, where both protagonists walk out of a splatter film — an acid Ritt comment on Hollywood's incessant and insulting vomiting of slash-and-smash-and-trash films. In a career spanning over 30 years, he never had to resort to multiple car-crashes, blood-soaked close-ups, or suffocating jingoism to film the subjects he believed in, about people for whom, unmistakably, he cared deeply and about issues that ignited his passion.

John le Carré, author of *The Spy Who Came in from the Cold,* explained Ritt as "a man apart not because he's a power man or vain but because in a painful and ambitious life, he has learned that his own judgement is the only one he can trust."

Born Martin Ritt. **Parents** Morris and Rose Ritt. **Marriage** Adele. **Children** Martina and Michael. **Education** DeWitt Clinton High School, Manhattan, New York; Eton College, North Carolina; St John's University, Brooklyn, New York. **Military Service** United States Army Air Force, 1942–46. **Career** Member, Group Theater, 1937; acting début, *Golden Boy,* 1937; film début, *Winged Victory,* 1944; director, live productions for CBS television, 1948–51; teacher, Actors Studio, 1951–56; début as film director, *Edge of the City,* 1956. **Other activities** Blacklisted by television industry, 1951. **Offices and memberships** Member: Communist Party, until 1939, Screen Directors Guild, American Federation of Television and Radio Artists, Screen Actors Guild. **Stage** (includes, as director unless otherwise indicated) *Golden Boy* (actor), 1937; *Planet of the Sun* (actor), 1938; *The Gentle People* (actor), 1939; *Two on an Island* (actor), 1939; *Mr Peebles and Mr Hooker,* 1946; *The Big People,* 1947; *Set My People Free,* 1948; *The Man,* 1950; *Cry of the Peacock,* 1950; *Golden Boy,* 1954; *Boy Meets Girl,* 1954; *The Front Page,* 1954; *The Flowering Peach* (actor), 1954; *A View from the Bridge,* 1955; *A Memory of Two Mondays,* 1955; *A Very Special Baby,* 1956. **Films** (include, as director unless otherwise indicated) *Winged Victory* (actor), 1944; *Edge of the City* (*A Man is Ten Feet Tall*), 1957; *No Down Payment,* 1957; *The Long Hot Summer,* 1958; *The Sound and the Fury,* 1959; *The Black Orchid,* 1959; *Five Branded Women* (*Jovanka el altri*), 1960; *Paris Blues,* 1961; *Adventures of a Young Man* (*Hemingway's Adventures of a Young Man*), 1962; *Hud* (also co-producer), 1963; *The Outrage,* 1964; *The Spy Who Came in from the Cold* (also co-producer), 1965; *Hombre* (also co-producer), 1967; *The Brotherhood,* 1969; *The Molly Maguires* (also co-producer), 1970; *The Great White Hope,* 1970; *Sounder,* 1972; *Pete'n Tillie,* 1972; *Conrack* (also co-producer), 1974; *The Front* (also producer), 1976; *End of the Game* (*Der Richter und sein Henker*) (actor), 1976; *Hollywood on Trial* (actor), 1977; *Casey's Shadow,* 1977; *Norma Rae,* 1979; *Black Roads,* 1981; *City Heat,* 1984; *Murphy's Romance,* 1985; *Nuts,* 1987; *Stanley and Iris,* 1989. **Cause of death** Complications from heart disease, at age 76. **Further reading** Sheila Whitaker, *The Films of Martin Ritt,* 1972; *International Dictionary of Films and Filmmakers,* volume two, 1991.

LORD SEEBOHM

British Banker and Philanthropist

***Born* Hitchin, Hertfordshire, 18 January 1909**

***Died* 15 December 1990**

The name of Seebohm is one to conjure with in banking and philanthropic circles in Britain. The family originally came from North Germany at the end of the Napoleonic wars, and from its almost 200 years in England Frederic (later Lord) Seebohm inherited traditions of banking (Sharples, Tuke, Lucas & Seebohm in Hertfordshire, ultimately to become part of Barclays Bank), scholarship (his grandfather and namesake was a well-known historian) and social service (Joseph Rowntree of York married two Seebohms, Lord Seebohm's great-aunt and then one of her cousins). This heritage encouraged Frederic Seebohm to lead a life of many facets, in all of which his notable intellectual and personal gifts were invariably to bring him to the top. And his Quaker traditions meant that these many activities were almost always to be directed towards public service.

The young Frederic (Freddie to his many friends) was inevitably destined to take up a banking career and he moved straight into Barclays when he came down from Cambridge in 1929. Ten years later, with the outbreak of World War II, he broke with his family's Quaker traditions to serve with distinction in the Royal Artillery, and this connection was to continue a generation later when he undertook an investigation into the housing and welfare of service families. On his return to civilian life Seebohm rapidly made his way up the banking ladder, becoming a director of Barclays' main board in 1947.

Soon afterwards he joined the board of Barclays DCO, the overseas branch of the business, and from then on his life took a new turn. This was a tricky period in Commonwealth politics and Seebohm developed a remarkable understanding of the problems of the emerging independent countries, especially in Africa where DCO's business was mainly concentrated. He travelled widely, particularly after his appointment in 1955 as vice-chairman and ten years later as chairman of Barclays Bank International (BBI) as it had by then been renamed. He was the chief architect of the transformation of the old paternalistic DCO, with its links primarily with the former British colonies, into a dynamic international bank competing keenly with the major US banks throughout Latin America, Europe and the Far East as well as its former territories. It was in Africa that Seebohm made his outstanding contribution. The new African leaders recognized in him a business acumen with a difference — a wider vision which could see beyond the traditional financing of trade from headquarters in London. After the nationalization of the banks in Egypt, Tanzania and Sudan, Seebohm reorganized Barclays' branches into local subsidiaries with local boards of directors better able to respond to national needs. The one big disappointment of his chairmanship was the criticism of the Bank's activities in South Africa. He abhorred apartheid but at the same time he saw the shortcomings of economic sanctions against the country and stoutly maintained that the Barclays connection was making every effort to ensure the economic prosperity of the entire population. He personally did all he could to promote black Africans on the Banks' staff.

Barclays, where he remained as deputy chairman after his retirement from BBI, was not Seebohm's only connection with the City of London. He was chairman of Friends Provident Life Office and of the Export Guarantees Advisory Council, and on his retirement from active work at Barclays in 1974 (though he remained on the board) he moved on to become Chairman of ICFC and Finance for Industry which ultimately fused to become Investors in Industry (or 3i). Again, this was a job that was slightly out of the ordinary and which appealed to his breadth of vision. Set up jointly by the Bank of England and the clearing banks as a source of venture capital for new enterprises, the organizations weathered the 1970s recession under Seebohm's strong leadership to develop as a major source of equity and loan finance. Seebohm's sharp analytical mind, combined with his remarkable originality of approach, enabled him to see things clearly, and at the same time from a single angle. Above all, he believed in what he was doing, he gave the job his undivided attention, and his practical common sense made all the difference. No wonder one of his business colleagues recounted that he had "the unerring knack of hitting the nail on the head".

Like many Quakers, however, Seebohm had a strong sense of public duty and a particular interest in social work, fostered no doubt by his happy chance posting in his early days to the Barclays branch at York. There, through the family connection with the great Quaker firm of Rowntree, he was instrumental in forming the York Council of Voluntary Service which set him off on his other major life work. To the general public Seebohm's name is undoubtedly best known for his chairmanship of the Joseph Rowntree Memorial Trust and even more for the Seebohm Report of 1968, which led to the wholesale reform of the country's social services into one comprehensive and co-ordinated service — in short, the foundation of the Department of Health and Social Services. That this mammoth creation was ultimately to founder under the weight of bureaucracy is not necessarily a criticism of Seebohm's recognition of the need to tidy up the well-nigh incomprehensible hotch-potch of offices and authorities which preceded it. The main concept of his report was the accessibility and effectiveness of social welfare for all as of right. The present-day Social Services Department owes its genesis to the foresight of Seebohm's recommendations.

This social concern led to many other appointments, the presidency of the National Institute for Social Work, Age Concern, Project Fullemploy, among others. Seebohm's overseas interests also engaged him as chairman of the Overseas Development Institute and of London House, the overseas students' hall of residence at London University, and as president of the Royal African Society. In his later years after his retirement from his business contacts, he was again enlisted by the government to carry out an investigation into the British Council. Seebohm's wise report published in 1981 was vital in rescuing the Council from the penny-pinching attacks of governments of all persuasions and ensuring that its important contribution to Britain's standing in the world should be more firmly established.

Seebohm was knighted in 1970 for his contribution to banking. On his retirement from Barclays International in 1972 the government was not slow to recognize the contribution he could make to debates on social services from a seat in the House of Lords. As a crossbencher, he was a diligent attender and a splendid chairman of many a committee. Politicians in both Houses were glad to listen to what a man of his breadth of experience had to say, not least from what he had learned in almost 20 years as chairman of the Joseph Rowntree Memorial Trust. But he was never dogmatic or opinionated in his contributions. In fact, he always maintained that he was a generalist, and no kind of specialist. Perhaps this was the source of his strength, that he brought an open mind to all questions, that he was prepared to listen and consult and then, when he had assessed the situation, to take decisive action.

"Freddie" Seebohm was a man of great charm, a staunch and generous friend and a reliable and understanding employer. A man of great energy and enthusiasm, he drove himself hard, but at the same time had a remarkable calm and serenity of disposition, shown not least in his hobbies — he was an able water-colour artist and embroiderer, and a keen gardener. Above all, he was blessed with a happy family life. Indeed, he was a true "English gentleman".

Born Frederic Seebohm. **Father** Hugh E. Seebohm. **Marriage** Evangeline Hurst, 1932. **Children** Richard, Victoria and Caroline. **Education** Leighton Park School, Reading; Trinity College, Cambridge. **Military service** Royal Artillery, 1939–45, mentioned in despatches, became lieutenant-colonel. **Career** Joined staff, Barclays Bank Limited, 1929, director, 1947–79, deputy-chairman, 1968–74; vice-chairman Barclays Bank DCO (renamed Barclays Bank International (1965), 1951–79, vice-chairman, 1955–59, deputy-chairman, 1959–65, chairman, 1965–72; vice-chairman, Barclays Bank South Africa, 1968–73. **Related activities** Friends' Provident Life Office, 1952–79, chairman, 1962–68; Industrial and Commercial Finance Corporation (ICFC), 1969–80, chairman, 1974–79; Finance for Industry Limited, 1974–80, chairman, 1974–79; Finance Corporation for Industry Limited, 1974–80, chairman 1974–79. **Other activities** Chairman: Seebohm Committee on Local Authority and Allied Personal Social Services, 1965–68 (*Seebohm Report* published 1968), Joseph Rowntree Memorial Trust, 1966–81, Export Guarantees Advisory Council, 1967–72, London House, 1970–83; president: Age Concern, 1970–89, National Institute for Social Work, Project Fullemploy, 1982 onwards; author, Seebohm Report, British Council, 1981; York Council of Voluntary Service; vice-chairman, Volunteer Centre, 1983 onwards. **Offices and memberships** Governor: London School of Economics, 1965–87, Haileybury Service College, 1970–87; fellow, Chartered Institute of Bankers, president, 1966–68; chairman, Overseas Development Institute, 1972–77; honorary vice-president, Royal African Society, 1978–84, 1984 onwards; trustee and chairman, Bankside Gallery charitable trust, finance committee. **Awards and honours** Territorial Efficiency Decoration; Bronze Star of America, 1945; knighted, 1970; High Sheriff of Hertfordshire, 1970–71; honorary LLD, Nottingham, 1970; created life peer, Baron Seebohm, 1972; honorary DSc, Aston, 1976; honorary member, Royal Watercolour Society. **Cause of death** Road accident, at age 81.

PAUL TORTELIER

French Cellist and Composer

***Born* Paris, France, 21 March 1914**

***Died* Villarçeaux, France, 18 December 1990**

To hear Tortelier play was to experience a rare treat; to see him play was to behold a man in love with music and in love with life. His crop of wavy white hair, his earnest, sparkling eyes, his long, bony fingers — these were the impressive features of a man who emanated warmth, *joie de vivre* and generosity of spirit. This century has seen many fine cellists, and Tortelier rightly ranks among them. But, whether through his performances on the concert platform or through his teaching in the classroom, he will best be remembered as an incomparable communicator, captivating his audience by sheer dint of personality. To hear his concerts or his many masterclasses was to experience at close hand the warmth of this loving and lovable man.

The young Tortelier was no Mozart, however, and had it not been for the frequent admonitions of his single-minded mother to practise, young Paul might just have laid down his child-size bow when others of his age were beginning to take theirs up. Even as a teenager, whilst attending the Paris Conservatoire under the tutelage of the composer Gérard Hekking, Tortelier was often to be found busking in *brasseries* and silent-movie cinemas to help out with the family finances. But by this time Tortelier was beginning to develop his own musical personality and to impress his teachers with his own special brand of rhythmic vitality, intelligence and romanticism. Indicative of that individuality was the occasion of his being awarded first prize in a Conservatoire competition for his performance of the Elgar Cello Concerto, a piece rarely performed at that time outside Elgar's native England. Tortelier was 16, and the concerto won a lasting place in his life-long repertory.

Having once decided on a musical career, no end of playing with the cellos of the Radio Paris Orchestra (which he joined at the age of 18 and to which he returned in 1940), the Monte Carlo

Orchestra, and the Boston Symphony Orchestra, could compensate him for the lack of opportunities for soloists. Only after the war, in 1947, did he get his first major break, marking the start of his international career. As the guest of the English conductor Sir Thomas Beecham, Tortelier played Richard Strauss's *Don Quixote* for the Strauss Festival in London. Suited to his own "quixotic" personality, it was a piece that Tortelier often played and all but made his own. Guest appearances followed with ever greater regularity and the now familiar, totally engaging Tortelier performance was received with ever increasing affection all over the world.

In 1946 he married his second wife, Maud Martin, and found the gift of "reciprocated love" with which he counted himself blessed. With Maud, also a cellist, and their three children, Yan Pascal (now an international conductor in his own right), Maria de la Pau (named after the wife of his great friend, the Spanish cellist Pablo Casals), and Pomona, the Torteliers enjoyed making music as a family. Tortelier himself derived enormous comfort simply from being with his wife and children and it was that sense of togetherness that did so much to inspire his obvious zest for life. As testimony to his love for his wife he dedicated his Double Concerto to Maud and often played it with her in concerts, specifying explicitly that it was a "love affair and must be played by a man and a woman". Of the Torteliers, a family friend once said that "the children had inherited their father's temperament — mad as hatters...Their home pulsated with the exuberance and musicality of this utterly lovable man."

From his pupils he earned great respect and affection; they were, in the words of one commentator, "his extended family", beneficiaries of his untiring enthusiasm, vitality and intelligence. He reached a wider audience through the medium of the televised masterclass. Modest and approachable, he treated his pupils as equals and engaged those listening with down-to-earth anecdotes, emotional outbursts and moments of musical brilliance. At times he could also be mischievous: "Are you a virgin?" he once asked a young "volunteer" as she blushed in front of the cameras, "because you cannot play Brahms if you have not known passion." But though his remarks were often made for effect, they were never dishonest.

If acting technique played a part in his approach to teaching, it had no less a part in his playing. People who saw him perform often spoke of how Tortelier would "live" the piece through his body, a picture of total concentration and absorption. The acrobatics of his left hand never interfered with the clarity and beauty of his tone, the elegance of his phrasing. He was in the business of communication and for a man of such sensitivity as Tortelier, communication came easily. Bach was the composer he most revered, for the discipline of Bach's music appealed to his rhythmic and intellectual bent. But the Elgar, Dvorak and Schumann Cello Concertos and, of course, the *Rococo Variations* by Tchaikovsky were among his favourite and most frequently played works. Given these clearly romantic leanings, it is perhaps not so surprising that Schoenberg inspired only disappointment and antipathy. "Only God, not the avant garde, can start an entirely new school of music", he once exclaimed. A distinguished performer, he also turned his hand to composition, writing a small handful of works which closely reflected his interests and concerns. Among these were the *Symphonie Israélienne (Israel Symphony)*, written shortly after he and his family spent a year on a kibbutz, and *Le Grand Drapeau,* a choral work dedicated to the United Nations. This last work bore witness to Tortelier's firmly held belief in the power of music to foster peace and international understanding. Often, encore pieces like *May Music Save Peace,* some played, others even sung (somewhat eccentrically), by the master cellist, served the same idealistic purpose. As a commentator once wrote: "Everything he did was stamped with his impassioned personality."

An idealist he may have been; he was also a man of high principles. A disagreement over the inclusion of a particular work in the syllabus led to Tortelier's resignation from his professional post at the Paris Conservatoire and to the loss of an assured income and pension. His disapproval of musical competitions was well known; at the second International Cello Competition, for example, Tortelier went against accepted practice by urging that the Gold Medal be shared by two of the competitors. Competitions were a sign of the lack of taste which he saw as a growing trend in musical affairs. Recordings were also part of that trend, and although Tortelier was a familiar face in the recording studio, increasingly he came to question the value of recording.

To see Tortelier perform was to experience some of the enthusiasm and joy by which he himself always lived. It is fitting that his great friend and colleague, Mstislav Rostropovich should have the last word: "He is a great musician. But whatever he does, he is first and foremost a musical philosopher and thinker, totally fused with the artist of temperament and brilliance."

Born Paul Tortelier. **Parents** Joseph, a cabinet-maker, and Marguerite (Boura) Tortelier. **Marriages** Two; 2) Maud Martin, cellist, 1946. **Children** Yan Pascal, Maria de la Pau and Pomona. **Education** Studied with Béatrice Bluhm and Louis Feuillard as a child; studied cello with Gérard Hekking, Conservatoire National de Musique de Paris, winner, premier prix, 1930, studied harmony with Gallon. **Career** Orchestral début, Lamoreux Orchestra, 1931; freelance orchestral player, Orchestre de Radio-Paris and others; first cellist, Monte Carlo Orchestra, 1935–37; solo début, *Don Quixote,* 1937; third cellist, Boston Symphony Orchestra, 1937–40; cellist, radio orchestra, France, 1940; first cellist, Societé des Concerts du Conservatoire de Paris, 1946–47; British début, *Don Quixote,* Festival of Richard Strauss, London, 1947; solo cellist with leading international orchestras, 1947 onwards; American solo début, with Boston Symphony Orchestra, Carnegie Hall, New York, 1955; professor: Conservatoire National Supérieur de Musique de Paris, 1956–69, Folkwang Musikhochschule, Essen, Conservatoire National de Région, Nice, 1978–80; gramophone début as conductor, 1971. **Related activities** Inventor, Tortelier spike. **Offices and memberships** Societé des Auteurs compositeurs et éditeurs de musique; fellow, Royal College of Music, London, 1979. **Awards and honours** Honorary member, Royal Academy of Music, London; honorary DMus: Leicester University, 1972, Oxford University, 1975; Doctor honoris causa, University of Aston, Birmingham, 1979; honorary professor, Central Conservatory, Beijing, 1980. **Compositions** (include) Concerto for Two Cellos; *Symphonie Israélienne;* Cello Sonata Suite for Unaccompanied Cello; *Trois Petits Tours* (cello and piano); *Spirales* (cello and piano); *Elegie; Toccata* (cello and piano); Duos for Two Cellos; *Cadenzas* for Haydn, Schumann, Bocherini and C.P.E. Bach concertos; *Sammartini Sonata;* Concerto for Violin and Orchestra; Concerto for Piano and Orchestra; *Offrande; Le Grand Drapeau; Sonata Breve; Variations on "May Music save Peace"; Mon Cirque* (for unaccompanied cello); Romance and Dance Variations (for flute and piano). **Television** Masterclass series: BBC television, 1964, 1987. **Publications** *How I Play, How I Teach,* 1973; *Self Portrait: in conversation with David Blum,* 1984. **Cause of death** Heart attack, at age 76.

SIR IAN TRETHOWAN

British Journalist, Broadcaster and Administrator

***Born* High Wycombe, Buckinghamshire, 20 October 1922**

***Died* London, England, 12 December 1990**

The central importance of broadcasting, both television and radio, in the life of the second half of the twentieth century can bring great opportunities for those at the helm. But, particularly for the non-commercial side where more subtle influences than the purely commercial dominate the scene, a position such as that of director-general of the British Broadcasting Corporation can prove a bed of nails or at best a constant challenge from an unrelenting watchdog government and a not always sympathetic public. In a life which spanned all sides of the media, as a political journalist in Fleet Street and at Westminster, as a newscaster and diplomatic correspondent for Independent Television News, as head of BBC radio and then television and ultimately director-general, and finally as chairman of a leading commercial television company, Sir Ian Trethowan knew all the tribulations and satisfactions that a career in journalism could bring and faced up to them all fairly and squarely and with remarkable equanimity.

Trethowan's family background was unremarkable. A child of the Depression, his education was cut short at the age of 16 when his father, a retired army officer and part-time sporting journalist, judged that there was little prospect of his winning any further scholarships and that he might as well start earning his living. As the young Ian's only academic attainments had been the publication of a few articles, he was launched into a journalistic career as the personal office boy of the editor of the *Daily Sketch* at the princely salary of one pound a week. With the outbreak of World War II his family moved first to Norwich, where the budding sports reporter (he had by now acquired his lifelong interest in horse-racing) managed to get a job on the *Eastern Daily Press,* and then to York and the *Yorkshire Post* where he obtained a more permanent post to which he returned after war service in the Fleet Air Arm.

By this time Trethowan's interests had taken a more political turn; he joined the parliamentary lobby to become a respected political correspondent of the *Post* and then from 1955 of the *News Chronicle,* at the same time contributing on a regular basis to *The Economist.* Throughout this period he had resisted the new-fangled wiles of television and might well have continued a straightforward press career had not Geoffrey Cox, a former colleague on the *News Chronicle,* managed to persuade him to join him on Independent Television News. Trethowan was later to admit in his autobiography that "a political journalist in his mid-thirties could not turn his back on television", but at the time it was to prove a momentous decision. His skill at handling interviews with leading politicians, and his pleasant television manner, quickly gained him a popular following and he was heralded in the press as Independent Television's answer to Richard Dimbleby.

Not that the BBC was lacking in attempts to win the personable young interviewer over to its side. Ultimately in 1963 it succeeded and over the next six years he became the Corporation's main political commentator, particularly on its newly established second channel. Indeed, it showed every sign of training him up to become Dimbleby's successor; he covered a number of important occasions at home and abroad — including the first televising of the House of Commons in 1966 — at the same time contributing a regular column to *The Times.* Though of a moderate Conservative persuasion, Trethowan was thoroughly objective in his reporting; in fact, all three political parties offered him seats at one time or another, but he preferred to remain the observer rather than becoming active in politics. Indeed, his cool and measured stance in some ways prevented him from achieving the theatrical acclaim of some of his rivals. He was never quite the star performer. His talents lay elsewhere.

By a shrewd turn of fate an old political friend spotted this. Shortly after he became chairman of the BBC, Lord (Charles) Hill persuaded Trethowan to change course and become managing director of BBC Radio. This was probably Trethowan's happiest period at the Corporation. Not that the circumstances were propitious; the radio network was in urgent need of reform which was bitterly opposed by a sizeable section of the staff. Nor did Trethowan have any administrative experience. But his diplomatic talents — a former colleague, Lord Rees-Mogg, was to say what a good ambassador he might have made — enabled him to win over the opposition. "Lack of consultation" was one of the main complaints and Trethowan exercised his political skills to manipulate the various factions, moving around Broadcasting House, inviting producers to dinner, listening to all points of view. His success won him further promotion as Managing Director of Television in succession to Huw Weldon. But this was to be a short-lived posting. Within a year the director-general's position was to be vacant. The new chairman broke with precedent by advertising the job, but, following the BBC tradition of promoting to the top office only from within the Corporation, Trethowan's appointment was more or less a foregone conclusion.

Again the times were difficult. To preside over the BBC at a time of high inflation and increasingly bitter party politics was no easy task. Some have criticized Trethowan for being too easy-going at a time when tough discipline and financial retrenchment were needed, and of failing to face up to the need for reform of an increasingly complacent bureaucracy. But at the same time he negotiated a far more generous licence fee settlement than had been hoped for and a renewal of the charter that left almost all the powers of the Corporation intact. A heart attack at mid-term in 1979 undoubtedly slowed any reforming zeal he might have had; in many ways he was thereafter a somewhat passive director-general, but he was lucky in that by this time he had the never-failing support of a strong chairman in Professor Sir Michael (later Lord) Swann (q.v.).

Retirement from the BBC at the statutory age of 60 in no way meant the end of Trethowan's working career. He became an independent director of *The Times,* a trustee of the British Museum and of Glyndebourne Opera, a consultant and later a director of Thorn EMI, and was on the boards of Barclays Bank and the British Council. He also followed up his interest in the turf by becoming chairman of the Horserace Betting Levy Board. Here again his negotiating skills enabled him to repair the board's financial situation, doubling the levy and prize money and increasing the investment in racecourses.

He was to say that he was happier, and also better paid, after his retirement than during his professional career. He could not keep away from broadcasting, however, and in 1987 became chairman of Thames Television. This soon launched him into controversy with the documentary programme *Death on the Rock* about the shooting of three Irish Republican Army terrorists in Gibraltar. As with earlier controversies at the BBC, Trethowan stoutly stood his ground and defended his right to publish. Despite increasing ill-health and disability, he continued his active chairmanship until a few days before his death.

Ian Trethowan was a man of great personal charm and with a large circle of friends. As a political journalist he was outstanding. As an administrator he had great diplomatic skills but perhaps not the iron in the soul which makes a first-class executive. Perhaps he was too open-minded for the hatchet job he sometimes neglected to carry out.

Born James Ian Raley Trethowan. **Father** Major J. J. R. Trethowan, retired army officer and sporting journalist. **Marriages** 1) Patricia Nelson, 1951 (dissolved); 2) Carolyn Reynolds, 1963. **Children** Three daughters. **Education** Christ's Hospital, Horsham, Sussex, scholar. **Military service** Observer, Fleet Air Arm, 1941–45. **Career** Office boy, later sports writer, the *Daily Sketch;* reporter: *Eastern Daily Press,* Norwich, 1939, *Yorkshire Post,* 1940–41; political correspondent: *Yorkshire Post,* 1947, *News Chronicle,* 1955; newscaster and diplomatic correspondent, then deputy editor, Independent Television News, 1958, later political editor; commentator on politics and current affairs, British Broadcasting Corporation, 1963–70, managing director, BBC Radio, 1970–75, managing director, BBC Television, 1976–77, director-general, 1977–82; director, Thames Television, 1986, chairman, 1987 onwards; also, political contributor: *The Economist,* 1950–58, 1965–67, *The Times,* 1967–69. **Related activities** Member, Committee on Official Secrets Acts, 1971–72; board member, British Council, 1980–87; chairman, Horserace Betting Levy Board, 1982 onwards; independent director, *The Times,* 1982 onwards; director, Barclays Bank, 1982–87; consultant, Thorn EMI, 1982, director, 1986 onwards; president, Cinema and Television Group of the European Commission, 1988 onwards. **Offices and memberships** Fellow, British Institute of Management; trustee: Glyndebourne Arts Trust 1982 onwards, British Museum, 1984 onwards; chairman, British Museum Society, 1982 onwards; governor, Ditchley Foundation. **Awards and honours** University of California Award for *Main Street USA,* 1961;

honorary Doctor of Civil Law, University of East Anglia, 1979; knighted, 1980. **Publication** *Split Screen* (autobiography), 1984. **Cause of death** Motor Neurone disease, at age 68.

Cumulative Alphabetical Index

Cumulative Index of Entrants by Profession

The index is divided into the following categories:

Actors, Actresses and Entertainers

Advertising and Public Relations Executives

Anthropologists and Archaeologists

Architects, Planners and Preservationists

Arms Control Experts

Art Historians, Collectors, Critics and Dealers

Artists and Craftsmen

Arts Administrators

Astronomers and Astrophysicists

Aviators, Aviation Experts, Aerodynamicists and Astronauts

Biographers and Memoirists

Biologists, Botanists, Naturalists, Zoologists and Environmentalists

Business Executives and Industrialists

Chefs, Food Writers and Restaurateurs

Chemists, Biochemists and Nutritionists

Children's Writers and Anthologists

Clairvoyants and Psychics

Clergy and Religious Scholars and Theorists

Composers, Arrangers, Songwriters and Librettists

Criminals

Dancers, Choreographers and Dance Critics

Designers, Design Writers and Fashion Writers

Diplomats

Directors

Earth Scientists (including Geographers, Geologists, Meteorologists, Seismologists, Oceanographers and Demographers)

Economists, Financial Specialists and Bankers

Educators, Educationists and Educational and Foundation/Association Administrators

Engineers and Technologists

Essayists

Explorers and Travellers

Farmers, Horticulturists and Agriculturists

Heads of State, Presidents, Premiers and Governors General

Historians, Classicists, Genealogists and Folklorists

Illustrators, Cartoonists and Animators

Intelligence Officers and Agents

International Affairs Officials

Inventors

Journalists and Editors (including Travel Writers)

Judges, Lawyers and Criminologists

Labour Leaders

Librarians, Museum Curators, Archivists, Antiquarians and Booksellers

Linguistics Experts

Literary Scholars and Critics

Management and Industrial Relations Specialists

Mathematicians, Statisticians and Cryptographers

Medical Practitioners and Researchers

Military Officers and Strategists

Musical Performers and Conductors

Novelists and Short Story Writers (including Humorists)

Performing Arts Critics and Scholars

Philanthropists

Philosophers

Photographers and Cinematographers

Physicists

Playwrights and Scriptwriters

Poets

Political Scientists

Politicians

Pollsters

Producers and Administrators (Film, Stage, Radio, TV and Music)

Psychiatrists, Psychologists and Psychotherapists

Public and Government Officials

Publishers, Newspaper Proprietors and Literary Agents

Radio and Television Personalities

Royalty and Socialites (including notable spouses of famous people)

Social, Political and Human Rights Activists

Social Workers

Sociologists

Sovietologists

Sports and Games Figures

Theatrical/Music Impresarios, Managers, Agents and Club Owners

Translators

CONTENTS

INTRODUCTION

Goddesses hold an important place in history. The myths and legends that surround them, tell us a lot about the societies they originated from. What were our ancestors' values? How did they think life on Earth began? What mattered to them?

Many of humanity's earliest sculptures hold striking similarities to each other. These small figurines, such as the Venus of Willendorf (found in Austria and thought to be around 25,000 years old), are the embodiment of bountiful fertility: all curves – large breasts, stomach, hips and buttocks. Archaeologists and historians have attempted to discern the significance of these figures, with many drawing the conclusion that these are early depictions of goddesses.

Goddess or mortal, these figures demonstrate how divine feminine energy flows throughout history, through our myths and legends, through our artwork, into the fabric of today's storytelling.

THE LITTLE BOOK OF
GODDESSES

ASTRID CARVEL

summersdale

THE LITTLE BOOK OF GODDESSES

Text by Abi McMahon

An Hachette UK Company
www.hachette.co.uk

Summersdale Publishers Ltd
Part of Octopus Publishing Group Limited
Carmelite House
50 Victoria Embankment
LONDON
EC4Y 0DZ
UK

www.summersdale.com

Printed and bound in Poland

ISBN: 978-1-80007-198-8

Creation, fertility, birth and rebirth are prevalent themes among the goddesses of old. But they aren't the only story being told: our feminine pantheon displays the complexity and diversity of sacred feminine energy.

Ishtar, possibly the first deity for whom we have written evidence, was goddess of love. But she was also a tempestuous goddess of war. For every goddess of healing, such as Isis, or fertility, such as Freyja, there is also an embodiment of war, such as Athena or the Morrígan. Some goddesses are of the earth (White Buffalo Calf Woman), some of water (Mami Wata), some of the moon (Mayari) and some of the sun (Amaterasu).

They are kind and ruthless; capricious and steadfast; tricksters and lovers. Through their stories they show us not who we *should* be but who we *can* be, if we choose to tap into our divine femininity.

AMATERASU

OTHER NAMES

Ōhirume-no-Muchi-no-Kami

ORIGIN

Shinto

KEY ATTRIBUTES

Radiant, gentle, originator of power

POWERS AND ABILITIES

Amaterasu is the Shinto goddess of the sun.

MYTHS AND LEGENDS

Amaterasu was one of the three great gods created when Iznagi, one of the Shinto religion's two creator gods, washed his face. Droplets touched his eyes and nose, forming Amaterasu, Tsukuyomi and Susanoo. A personification of the radiance of the sun, she wore a beautiful star necklace and jewel-studded garments.

Amaterasu loved to spin and weave thread - she created her own garments and introduced the skills of spinning and weaving to humans. She preferred to live in peace, although she was often harassed by her storm-god brother, Susanoo. She won one battle of magic, destroying Susanoo's sword by chewing it up and spitting it out. He eventually went too far, killing her dawn-goddess sister Wakahirume, and Amaterasu retreated into exile.

Amaterasu's exile had terrible consequences for the universe, which was plunged into darkness, devoid of new growth. Her fellow gods tried to lure Amaterasu out of her cave, resorting to rambunctious trickery and lascivious dancing by fellow goddess Ame-no-Uzume (p.10). When she rolled aside the boulder blocking the cave entrance, her light shone through the gap, creating the first dawn light.

POPULAR DEPICTIONS

Amaterasu was the godly ancestor of imperial Japan's royal family. She charged her grandson Ninigi with ruling the mortal realm, and he accepted, becoming the first member of the imperial dynasty. As a result of this, and her role as one of the great goddesses of the Shinto religion, she is one of the most worshipped and depicted Shinto gods.

The Ise Grand Shrine is dedicated to Amaterasu and is one of the Shinto religion's holiest sites of worship. It houses the Sacred Mirror, one of the relics gifted to Amaterasu to coax her out of her cave refuge. She later passed it to Ninigi, and when he departed, it became part of the regalia of imperial Japan. The shrine buildings are destroyed and rebuilt every 20 years to represent the Shinto belief of death and the renewal of life.

Amaterasu is often portrayed with rays of light shining out from around her figure, illuminating the beautiful manuscripts and woodprints she adorns. She is one of the few goddesses in any pantheon to represent the sun.

LIFE LESSONS FROM AMATERASU

Sometimes life can wear on you. Remember that, like Amaterasu, you fill your loved ones' lives with light; that, although life may sometimes tempt you to retreat to a cool and mossy cave, you would be missed terribly if you were to move there permanently; and that your return would light up your loved ones' lives like the rays of the first dawn.

Amaterasu was undoubtedly powerful - one of the greatest gods of the Shinto religion. However, she chose to only exercise her power when absolutely necessary, preferring to devote her life to the activities she loved. Power imbalances occur every day - customer and server, employer and employee, teacher and student. You can always choose to withhold your power and exercise kindness and consideration when you have the upper hand. Don't be like Susanoo and bluster around, uncaring of whom you hurt. Be like Amaterasu and be kind to those less powerful than you.

AME-NO-UZUME

OTHER NAMES

The Great Persuader, the Heavenly Alarming Female

ORIGIN

Shinto

KEY ATTRIBUTES

Mirthful, graceful, artistic

POWERS AND ABILITIES

Ame-no-Uzume is the Shinto goddess of happiness.

MYTHS AND LEGENDS

It was Ame-no-Uzume's lascivious dancing that helped lure Amaterasu out from her cave of exile. Ame-no-Uzume – whose name translates as "twirling" – danced outside the cave. As she spun faster and faster, her clothes began to fly off her body. This inspired catcalls from her fellow deities, and this was part of the raucous noise that drew Amaterasu out to become the dawn. Ame-no-Uzume was rewarded for her service by being made a guardian of a precious treasure. Some legends say that she protected a spring of pure water; others, the Milky Way; others, a rainbow.

This precious treasure would grant a mortal immortality, although this state would only be temporary without drinking regularly. Ame-no-Uzume was generous with her gifts and would allow her favoured mortals the chance to drink from her waters.

Ame-no-Uzume fell in love with the powerful earth-bound god Sarutahiko and married him. Together they created a clan consisting of a female court and religious dancers.

POPULAR DEPICTIONS

One of the oldest shrines in Japan, Tsubaki Grand Shrine, is dedicated to Sarutahiko and Ame-no-Uzume. The shrine was established in 3 BCE and is still in use today.

Ame-no-Uzume is the patron of music and dance. *Kagura*, the sacred Shinto music and the dances that accompany it, was said to originate with Ame-no-Uzume. It was inspired by the wild dance she performed to lure Amaterasu from her cave. The original dancers of *Kagura* were shrine maidens, said to be descended from Ame-no-Uzume and Sarutahiko. They would wear masks and carry spears when they danced, channelling the gods through their movement. *Kagura* was originally only performed in shrines, but it gradually spread as an art form and then as worship. Now there are multiple forms of *Satokagura* – non religious *Kagura*. These include *Shishi Kagura*, a lion dance featuring performers in the role of a lion, and *Hayachine Kagura*, a highly energetic dance form performed by artists who embrace an ascetic way of life.

LIFE LESSONS FROM AME-NO-UZUME

Ame-no-Uzume is a delightful goddess who herself delights in life. Let her be a reminder of the power of having fun. Not every great and good deed is one performed with total seriousness. For example, one way to offer support to a struggling loved one is to simply spend time with them. Arrange a date full of activities that you know they'll enjoy, and throw yourselves into them. Providing someone with a safe space to step away from their troubles and experience joy can be as powerful as workshopping solutions.

You deserve to have a good time, too. Sometimes we become consumed with achieving our goals, whether we are thriving or struggling. Scheduling in time to simply be, instead of problem solving or strategizing, opens the door to finding joy in the place you are now.

APHRODITE

OTHER NAMES

Venus (her Roman name)

ORIGIN

Greek

KEY ATTRIBUTES

Powerful, beautiful, desirable and desirous

POWERS AND ABILITIES

Aphrodite blessed or cursed gods and humans with love and lust - and sometimes revulsion.

MYTHS AND LEGENDS

Aphrodite has one of the most memorable "births" across all the world's mythologies. She formed, beauty incarnate, from the sea foam created when the Titan Cronus severed his father Ouranos' penis and threw it into the sea.

The goddess embodies the complexities of love, and her myths show her dividing lovers as often as she unites them. In one tale, she answered lovesick Hippomenes' prayers by gifting him with three golden apples. He used these apples to win the object of his desire, Atalanta, who had sworn to only marry the man who could beat her in a foot race.

Golden apples make another, unhappier, appearance in the tale known as "The Judgement of Paris". Unfortunate prince of Troy, Paris was enlisted to judge who deserved a golden apple inscribed with "for the fairest". Aphrodite, one of the candidates, offered him the most beautiful woman in the world, Helen, little caring that she was married to Menelaus, king of Sparta. Paris granted Aphrodite the apple, she granted him Helen, and the Trojan War was begun.

POPULAR DEPICTIONS

Aphrodite is one of the most popularly portrayed goddesses in Western culture. "The Judgement of Paris" alone is a frequently painted subject, depicted by artists including Botticelli, Renoir, Rubens, Angelica Kauffman and Salvador Dalí.

Botticelli portrayed Aphrodite several times, including in one of the most iconic paintings of the Western canon, *The Birth of Venus*. In this depiction, Aphrodite stands on a giant scallop shell, red-gold hair blown about her naked body by the wind god Zephyr. Aphrodite also appears in another of Botticelli's famous artworks, the pastoral *Primavera*.

The Western literary canon has hardly ignored Aphrodite. The Latin poet Ovid explores tales of Aphrodite throughout his *Metamorphoses*. His Aphrodite feels deeply: in "Venus and Adonis", she "even forgoes the heavens: preferring Adonis to heaven". Shakespeare later wrote his own *Venus and Adonis* and it's saucy stuff: although the lovers only ever exchange a kiss, Shakespeare stuffs his language with plenty of thrusting, riding and sheathing.

LIFE LESSONS FROM APHRODITE

Cynics may note that those who come into contact with Aphrodite, the embodiment of love, are more likely to end up heartbroken, dead or embroiled in a ten-year war than they are to live happily ever after. However, it isn't love itself that causes unhappiness, but how Aphrodite chooses to use it. Remember that it's the choices lovers make, not love itself, which causes their relationship to falter or thrive. You have the power to choose how to act toward those you love, and those that love you have the power to choose how they act toward you. Aphrodite inspires your feelings, but she doesn't dictate your actions.

ASTARTE

OTHER NAMES

Ashtart, Athtart, Queen of Heaven

ORIGIN

Semitic

KEY ATTRIBUTES

Huntress, warrior, associated with royalty, sexuality and fertility

POWERS AND ABILITIES

A fighter, whose divine essence was thought to be a life-giving force.

MYTHS AND LEGENDS

Astarte featured in many pantheons, including ancient Egyptian, Syrian and Greek, under different names. Each religion emphasized different facets of Astarte's powers and strength. In ancient Semitic texts she was portrayed as hunting with fellow goddess Anat, while in Syrian myth she defeated a sea monster with her lover Baal. In a Greek translation of a Phoenician text, Astarte was a daughter of Ouranos and became one of his wives. They had nine children together, including two male children who became known as Love and Desire. The same text tells of how Astarte discovered a fallen star and consecrated it in the holy city of Tyre, which she ruled over.

One Mesopotamian myth describes how her breasts gave forth fertility as if it were milk. Astarte's liquid fertility was found on Earth, too, as the sap in plants. Some myths say that when Astarte's liquid fertility sprayed across the sky, it created the Milky Way – this is a myth she has in common with fellow great goddesses such as Hera.

POPULAR DEPICTIONS

Temples dedicated to the worship of Astarte were said to host sacred servants, known as *hierodoulai*. Sex was one ritual performed by the *hierodoulai*. It was believed to honour the mysterious life force contained in the essences of men and women. The *hierodouleia* was a form of worship practised across many pantheons, most commonly in honour of goddesses or mother goddesses who represented fertility and creation. *Hierodoulai* in Astarte's temples would undergo these sacred rituals on festival days.

Astarte was possibly the origin of fellow love goddess Aphrodite. A dedication to Astarte was found at the site of an ancient temple dedicated to Aphrodite in Erice, Sicily. Astarte is also involved in one of the world's earliest crossover events, as she is namechecked several times in the Old Testament. In 1 Kings 11:5, King Solomon attempts to introduce the cult of Astarte to his kingdom.

LIFE LESSONS FROM ASTARTE

As one of the earliest goddesses of love, Astarte represents some of humanity's first attempts at exploring what love means to us. Celebrate and honour the importance of love in your life. Let your loved ones know how important they are to you. This can be done in small ways, such as remembering to tell them how much you enjoyed the time you spent together the other day, or how you admire a certain positive quality of theirs. Sometimes, familiarity means that we leave certain things unsaid because we assume that the other person knows how we feel. However, even if your loved one knows how you feel deep down, it can only bring joy to hear the words said out loud.

How about dedicating a day to love, in the name of Astarte? It's rare that we give ourselves over to purely pleasurable activities. Mark a day in your calendar and establish the ground rules: no chores, no errands, no saying yes to things you don't want to do. That day is now one day of fun, spent with the people you love.

ATHENA

OTHER NAMES

Athene, Pallas, Minerva (her Roman name)

ORIGIN

Greek

KEY ATTRIBUTES

Wise, honourable, warlike, artistic

POWERS AND ABILITIES

Athena was powerfully intelligent, a master of crafts such as weaving, and a mighty warrior.

MYTHS AND LEGENDS

After Zeus, Athena was the most celebrated and written about of the Greek gods, featuring in hundreds of myths as counsellor, patron and punisher.

Athena's gifts to heroes litter Greek stories and legends. She presented Perseus with the polished shield that helped him kill Medusa the gorgon, gave a horse's bit to Bellerophon so he could tame Pegasus, and helped Odysseus navigate his way home after the Trojan War.

However, like most Greek gods, she was cruel to those who displeased her. When Arachne bested Athena at weaving, Athena turned her into a spider for her troubles. And when Tiresias accidentally saw Athena bathing naked in a spring, Athena cursed him with blindness.

The wise Athena was credited with many inventions, including the art of weaving, a wind instrument known as the *aulos*, and the bit, bridle and saddle. She was the patron of the city-state Athens and in later years became connected with the growing discipline of philosophy.

POPULAR DEPICTIONS

The lost statue *Athena Parthenos* is one of the most famous depictions of Athena. Contemporary accounts report it as being around 11 metres tall and coated in sheets of gold. She held Nike, the goddess of victory, in one outstretched hand and the other clasped the mythical shield aegis, in which the head of Medusa was embedded. *Athena Parthenos* stood in the Parthenon. Her sculptor was the famed Phidias, whose statue of Zeus was one of the Seven Wonders of the World.

The Panathenaea was one of Athens' most important festivals, held in honour of Athena yearly as the Lesser Panathenaea and every four years as the Greater Panathenaea. Yearly festivities included animal sacrifice while the Greater Panathenaea featured a musical contest and the Panathenaic Games. Contests in sports such as wrestling, boxing, chariot racing and javelin took place and the prizes included amphorae containing olive oil. The olive tree was Athena's gift to Athens and was a symbol of the prosperity she granted the city.

LIFE LESSONS FROM ATHENA

Athena was cool-headed, the strategic counterpart to the impulsiveness and violence of fellow Greek god of war Ares. To act when tempers are high is not the Athena way. Instead, take a step back from heated confrontations. If you can, extract yourself from the situation. Sometimes, you may be the hothead, and it is useful in those situations to learn what actions can calm you down. Perhaps just removing yourself from the situation and engaging in a different, simple activity, such as walking, might help. Or perhaps you could learn a short meditative ritual that calms your breath and helps you send away angry emotion. Then, when you are ready, return to the problem. If the issue involves another person, think of it as a challenge for you to overcome as a team. How can you work together to remove this obstacle? Think collaboratively and make the issue the enemy, not the person.

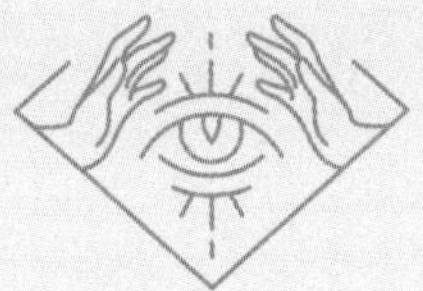

BASTET

OTHER NAMES

Bast, B'sst, Baast, Ubaste, Baset

ORIGIN

Egyptian

KEY ATTRIBUTES

Tender, protective, sometimes fierce

POWERS AND ABILITIES

Bastet is the goddess of the home, domesticity, women's secrets, cats, fertility and childbirth.

MYTHS AND LEGENDS

Early myths tell of Bastet fighting the chaos snake Apep. Apep was locked in battle with Bastet's father, the great sun god, Ra. Sometimes, Apep would get the upper hand over Ra, swallowing him and bringing on an eclipse. In her cat form, Bastet took over the battle one night, in the darkness of Apep's lair, and slew the terrible snake.

Late portrayals of Bastet show her with a cat's head or as a cat. However, early depictions show Bastet with the head of a lioness or as the goddess Sekhmet. One myth explains Bastet's transformation from Sekhmet to her later form. Ra charged Sekhmet to enact a terrible vengeance on his mortal Egyptian subjects. She slaughtered them in great numbers, drinking their blood. Eventually, Ra wished to halt Sekhmet's rampage and attempted to trick her by serving her red beer. Sekhmet drank the beer, believing it to be blood, and fell into a stupor. Pacified, she awoke as the gentler, cat-headed Bastet (perhaps the first person to drink too much and feel better afterwards).

POPULAR DEPICTIONS

Bastet was often depicted holding a *sistrum*, which was an ancient and sacred percussive instrument similar to a rattle.

Bubastis, meaning "Bastet's Place", was a town in the Nile delta. It housed Bastet's temple and, when excavated, over 300,000 mummified cats were found on the temple grounds - some appear to have been sacrifices, although Egyptians were known to mummify beloved pets too. Bubastis was the location of a large festival - some 70,000 people were said to travel yearly to Bubastis to take part. Ancient Greek writer Herodotus compellingly describes the festivities:

> ***Some of the women make a noise with rattles, others play flutes all the way, while the rest of the women, and the men, sing and clap their hands... some shout mockery of the women of the town; others dance, and others stand up and expose their persons... But when they have reached Bubastis, they make a festival with great sacrifices, and more wine is drunk at this feast than in the whole year beside.***

LIFE LESSONS FROM BASTET

Bastet is the perfect goddess inspiration for any aspiring cat mama. Bastet was often depicted with several kittens at her feet. Wouldn't life be better with several cats sat at your feet - or on your lap or about your home? Although in the legends of Bastet the cats were her servants, sadly, as a mortal, you are more likely to be your cats' servant.

There are several ways to throw a party like the festival honouring Bastet. Wine is a must, although perhaps "more wine... than in the whole year" is an inadvisable quantity. Music and dancing are also key elements, and the more live instruments the better. Celebrants of Bastet knew that, sometimes, there is nothing more enjoyable than making a good-natured ruckus. One aspect of these celebrations may be a matter of personal taste - the "day of chewing onions for Bastet". Little is known about the rituals involved in this day, although the name gives a big hint.

COATLICUE

OTHER NAMES

Ilamatecuhtli, Tlaltecuhtli, Tonantzin

ORIGIN

Central American

KEY ATTRIBUTES

Incredibly fertile, a shape-shifter

POWERS AND ABILITIES

A great mother goddess who birthed many gods.

MYTHS AND LEGENDS

Coatlicue's other names are evocative of her qualities: Ilamatecuhtli (Old Goddess), Tlaltecuhtli (Earth-Toad-Knife) and Tonantzin (Our Mother). She was a shape-shifter, once taking the form of a crocodile to do battle. Her commonly depicted form was one of a woman with two facing snakes for a head and a skirt made of snakes and talons, who wore the hearts of her sacrificial victims round her neck. She once had breasts full of the milk of life, but after nursing hundreds of god-sons and countless goddess-daughters, they hung empty.

The father of all but one of her children was Mixcoatl, god of hunting. Her final pregnancy came when, while sweeping at the top of Snake Mountain, a ball of feathers fell into her lap and impregnated her. Outraged at this unusual pregnancy, Coatlicue's sons and daughters decided to murder her. Her son, war god Huitzilopochtli, sprang fully formed and armed from her body and defended her. He overcame his brothers and sisters, beheading Coyolxauhqui and tossing her head into the sky, where it became the moon.

POPULAR DEPICTIONS

One of the most famous depictions of Coatlicue is the Templo Mayor statue sculpted from the volcanic rock andesite. Standing over two metres tall, the statue was first buried in the 1500s after the Spanish colonized the Aztec Empire. It was dug up and then reinterred several times in the centuries since, finally being excavated in the early 1800s. The two snake heads of the statue are thought to represent the decapitation of Coatlicue, as Aztecs used depictions of snakes to represent spurting blood. Little is known about why Coatlicue was portrayed this way; one myth points to an age before humanity when several goddesses sacrificed themselves to allow a new sun to rise. Her feet are jaguar paws, representing Coatlicue's shape-shifting nature. A nearly identical statue was found in the 1900s in the same location, suggesting that this *Coatlicue* was one of a series. As Coatlicue means "Snakes for a Skirt", the new statue was named *Yolotlicue* or "Hearts for a Skirt" as this was the only difference between the statues.

LIFE LESSONS FROM COATLICUE

The biggest lesson to be learned from the myths and legends of Coatlicue is don't clean your home. It will only lead to trouble. Or perhaps Coatlicue wouldn't have become pregnant if she had had access to modern cleaning technology. That ball of feathers was clearly powerful, but could it have withstood the strength of a well-engineered vacuum cleaner?

Coatlicue had a complicated relationship with her family, as did many gods and goddesses. Sometimes those we love don't treat us the way we deserve to be treated. The myths and legends of the world's pantheons show us that while love can be found in unexpected places, loving feelings don't always equate to loving actions. You may be afraid to assert your boundaries with someone because you think your relationship shouldn't need any. Focus not on what "should" be but what is. Don't be afraid to tell someone that their behaviour toward you isn't loving you in the way you deserve to be loved.

CYBELE

OTHER NAMES

Kybele, Great Idaean Mother of the Gods, Mountain Mother

ORIGIN

Phrygian

KEY ATTRIBUTES

Mother goddess, associated with nature and orgiastic rituals

POWERS AND ABILITIES

The protector of nature and the goddess of unrequited lust.

MYTHS AND LEGENDS

The Phrygians were an ancient people originating from the area now known as Turkey. The cult of Cybele spread, and she was adopted into Greek and Roman mythologies.

Early Phrygian depictions of Cybele showed her as a seated, curvaceous woman, often accompanied by wild animals such as hawks and lions - her Mountain Mother form. She was the mother and protector of nature in its pure, uncontrolled form, the antithesis of civilization.

Later myths introduced Attis, her lover. Dozens of myths surround their relationship and love, often laced with death, resurrection and lust. In one myth Cybele and Attis began life as the hermaphrodite deity Agditis. The gods mutilated Agditis and cut their penis in half, the two halves transforming into Cybele and Attis. Cybele lusted for Attis, as either a lover or as the lost other half of herself. In other myths Attis was a handsome youth. When he didn't requite Cybele's love, she drove him mad, until he castrated himself and died. The first violets sprang from his blood.

POPULAR DEPICTIONS

Although Cybele was absorbed into Greek and Roman religions, she was often represented as a wild outsider. Depictions portrayed her driving a chariot pulled by lions, or riding a lion, to the sound of music.

The Corybantes, or Korybantes, were Cybele's half-demonic priests. They wore crested helmets and bore arms, played instruments and danced a frenzied dance that sometimes led to them castrating themselves. This aspect of Cybele's myths intrigued the Roman youth, who formed secret societies to take part in ecstatic dancing rituals. As the centuries passed, Cybele became more ingrained in Roman culture and mythology. The Romans would celebrate Cybele during a long festival, involving a procession, a sacrifice, a week of fasting and a felled pine tree representing Attis. Lucretius described one ritual as involving "yellow-robed, long-haired, perfumed *Galli* [Cybele's mortal priests] waving their knives, wild music of thrumming tympanons and shrill flutes. Along the route, rose petals are scattered, and clouds of incense arise."

LIFE LESSONS FROM CYBELE

Cybele in her earliest Phrygian form was primal, connected with wild and untamed nature. Learn from Cybele by getting back in touch with nature. Spending time in a natural environment is proven to have a positive impact on your mental health. Even time spent in small green spaces, such as your own garden, a park or a wooded area near your home, can reduce stress. However, there is something to be said for the untamed beauty of a truly wild space. In honour of Cybele, plan a trip to a remote place of natural beauty. This could be a mountain, or a lake, or a clifftop. This may take some organizing, especially if you live in a built-up or urban area, but the trip will be worth it - a chance to get back in touch with your sensual, wild divine energy.

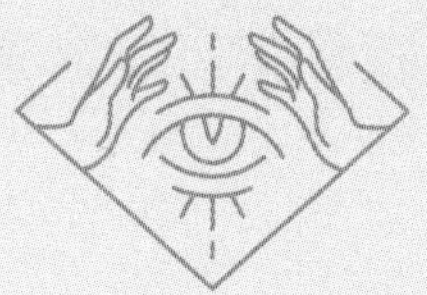

DEVI

OTHER NAMES

Adi Parashakti, Mahadevi, Shakti, Lakshmi

ORIGIN

Hindu

KEY ATTRIBUTES

Great goddess, divine feminine

POWERS AND ABILITIES

Devi is the essence of goddess. In some Hindu myths every goddess is a facet of her essence, from the peaceful mother goddess Uma to warrior goddess Durga.

MYTHS AND LEGENDS

Devi is the Sanskrit word for "goddess". In Hindu myth she is the "divine feminine", although the different traditions of Hinduism conceive her in different ways.

In Shaivism, Devi is the wife and one half of Shiva, her divine femininity creating balance and order with his divine masculinity. In Shaktism, Devi is the supreme divinity, preceding the triad of Brahma, Shiva and Vishnu, who are personifications of her divine essence. She is known as the Supreme Truth or the Eternal One. In the *Markandeya Purana*, the god Brahma addresses Devi and lists her names, counting among them the Great Knowledge, the Great Illusion, the Great Vigour, the Great Memory, the Great Delusion, the Great Goddess, the Great Demon, Good Fortune, Queen, Modesty and Intelligence. This address is part of an exhortation to Devi - in this myth Mahadevi - to defeat two demonic entities, Madhu and Kaitabha. She does, calling forth Vishnu to defeat the demonic entities, which he does by splitting them asunder, "head and buttock".

POPULAR DEPICTIONS

The beautiful hymn "Devi Sukta" is chanted in worship of Devi as part of the goddess-centric tradition of Hinduism, Ṣhaktism. It was composed by Vak Ambhrni, a female *rishi* (sage), and is told from the perspective of Devi as the universal goddess. In one translation the "Devi Sukta" ends:

On the world's summit I bring forth sky the Father:
my home is in the waters, in the ocean as Mother.

Thence I pervade all existing creatures, as their Inner
Supreme Self, and manifest them with my body.

I created all worlds at my will, without any higher
being, and permeate and dwell within them.

The eternal and infinite consciousness is I,
it is my greatness dwelling in everything.

In the Hindu tradition Vaishnavism, Devi is the goddess Lakshmi. Art throughout the centuries portrays her in this form, with 18 hands, sometimes carrying prayer beads, an axe, mace, arrow, thunderbolt, lotus, pitcher, rod, sword, shield, conch, bell, wine cup, trident, noose and discus.

LIFE LESSONS FROM DEVI

Shaktism asserts that every human action is an act of worship of Devi, whether knowingly or unknowingly performed. Think of Devi as the divine feminine, a force that runs through every human, including through you. Consider this connection when contemplating the choices you make. Ask yourself, does this action serve, support or worship the divine femininity within me? Will making this decision support me, further my aims and help me be my best self? Maybe the answers to these questions will help guide your path.

As the divine feminine, the other half of Shiva, Devi brings essential balance to the universe. Sometimes, femininity is seen as a negative. Some people see it as a weakness, wherever they find it. However, femininity is an essential aspect of the universe: it lives within everyone and provides balance. It, like Devi, is multifaceted, containing strength and softness, creation and destruction. Whenever you feel that your femininity is a weakness, remember that it is actually an asset.

FREYJA

OTHER NAMES

Horn (the Flaxen), Valfreyja

ORIGIN

Norse

KEY ATTRIBUTES

Goddess of sexuality, fertility

POWERS AND ABILITIES

Freyja bestowed fertility, protected women in childbirth and governed over half of the fallen Nordic heroes.

MYTHS AND LEGENDS

The Old Norse book the *Prose Edda* describes Freyja's fabulous living arrangements: her dwelling in heaven was a beautiful field known as Folkvang. Here, she lived in a hall called Sessrúmnir and travelled by chariot, pulled by two cats. While half of the valiant slain resided in the great god Odin's Valhalla, the other half were chosen by Freyja to live and celebrate with her in Folkvang.

The *Prose Edda* also tells a screwball tale of how Freyja came into possession of her dazzling necklace, Brísingamen. Freyja saw the gold necklace being made by the dwarves Alfrig, Dvalin, Berling and Grer, and requested it. They agreed, on the condition that Freyja would sleep with them, a price she was willing to pay. Odin, Freyja's lover at the time, sent Loki to secure the necklace, unaware of Freyja's deal with the dwarves. Loki, customarily ready to make trouble, stole it from Freyja, who raised hell with Odin when she discovered what had happened.

POPULAR DEPICTIONS

Friday is derived from Freyja's name. Freyja was one of the last non-Christian deities to be worshipped in Scandinavia during the Christian conversion. Records show that in Iceland around 1000 CE, Hjalti Skeggjason was outlawed for insulting the name of Freyja at the Althing Parliament. Staves – magic sigils – invoking the protection of Freyja have dated to as recently as the eighteenth century in Iceland and she was often invoked in rural Scandinavia in superstitions and folklore.

Freyja features in one of Denmark's two national anthems. "Der er et yndigt land" is Denmark's civil national anthem and was written by poet Adam Oehlenschläger in the early nineteenth century. The last lines of the first stanza read that the name of this lovely country is "old Denmark, and it is Freyja's hall".

Freyja also appears as Freia in Wagner's epic opera series, the *Ring Cycle*. Wotan (the High Germanic name for Odin) has promised the giants Freia as payment for building him a great hall. She is understandably not keen on being payment, and as Wotan tries to find a way to wriggle out of his problems, the saga begins.

LIFE LESSONS FROM FREYJA

Freyja once got into a harsh exchange of words with trickster god Loki, who admonished her for sleeping with many of the Norse gods. She was unmoved and pushed back, the argument only halting when a fellow god defended her, saying that her behaviour was harmless. Although Freyja generally acts with kindness, that doesn't mean she isn't courageous or self-assured. Take strength from Freyja, and know that you can centre values such as kindness and empathy and still assert your boundaries and have the courage of your convictions. Perhaps it would be helpful to reframe disagreement as a conversation instead of conflict. Telling someone "no" is simply giving them the information they need in that moment. You could prepare a couple of scripts to help you while you are getting used to your new perspective. These don't have to be Oscar-worthy! Just simple phrases to have on hand, such as "I can't make that date" or "that's not possible for me", so you feel prepared.

GAIA

OTHER NAMES

Ge, Mother Earth, Terra (her Roman name)

ORIGIN

Greek, Roman

KEY ATTRIBUTES

Mother goddess, creator force

POWERS AND ABILITIES

Gaia was one of the primordial Greek deities, Mother Earth, mother to the Titans and all life.

MYTHS AND LEGENDS

Gaia was the first primordial being to emerge from Chaos. The second was her partner Ouranos (Father Sky). They clung together in a vivid, rather psychedelic creation myth. At first Gaia was formed of rippling hills and crevices. Life, from rivers and oceans to plants and creatures, sprang forth as rain fell from Ouranos into Gaia. The two tore apart, Gaia now a smooth disc floating in the universe, Ouranos suspended above her in cloud and light.

Gaia and Ouranos had many powerful children together, including the 50-headed and 100-handed giants, Cottus, Briareus and Gyges. They also produced three one-eyed Cyclopes.

Myths differ as to Gaia's role in the titanomachy, the epic war between the Titans and Cronus' children, the gods. Some myths have her protecting Zeus after his mother, Gaia's daughter Rhea, hid him from his father, Gaia's son Cronus. Others say that, in defence of the Titans, Gaia created the earth-born giants (perhaps with Tartarus, the primordial underworld) to battle the gods.

POPULAR DEPICTIONS

Gaia was a pivotal figure in Greek and Roman myth and was commonly depicted across the centuries in different art forms.

The titanomachy and gigantomachy were particularly popular mythological subjects, and Gaia featured heavily across most art portraying these epic battles. The frieze on the large Pergamon Altar, created around the second century BCE, shows the gigantomachy. Gaia, her shoulder adorned with fruit, rises from the ground while a winged giant battles Athena. Gaia was often portrayed rising from the ground, as a way to demonstrate her connection to and personification of the earth.

One third-century Roman mosaic portrays Gaia – as the Roman Terra – reclining on the ground with four of her children. The children possibly represent the four seasons, and Gaia herself wears fruit and greenery threaded through her hair.

Gaia has also given her name to a New Age philosophy, Gaianism. Gaianism focuses on the earth as the central meaning of life. Its devotees believe that everyone should honour the earth, attempt to reduce their impact on it and be respectful of all its life forms.

LIFE LESSONS FROM GAIA

Whether you choose to follow Gaianism or not, now is the perfect time to consider your impact on the earth. Almost every scientist agrees that we have reached a crisis point with global warming and that immediate action is required in order to minimize the deadly effects for life on earth. The first form of action you can take is making positive personal choices. Avoid industries with high carbon footprints, such as fast fashion, and instead shop second-hand or with ethical brands. Reduce waste by buying responsibly - avoiding large quantities of plastic packaging - and recycling responsibly. It is also important to recognize that no one person can reverse global warming single-handed. Put pressure on large companies and your local political system by making your voice heard. Write to your local governmental representative with your opinion as their constituent, especially when they are about to vote on environmental policy.

GANGA

OTHER NAMES

Jahanvi

ORIGIN

Hindu

KEY ATTRIBUTES

Purification, forgiveness

POWERS AND ABILITIES

Ganga is the personification of the river Ganges and the Milky Way.

MYTHS AND LEGENDS

The goddess Ganga resided in heaven, flowing around Brahma's home on Mount Meru. The legendary King Bhagiratha learned that 60,000 of his forefathers had been cursed and would not reach heaven. He prayed to Brahma to send Ganga to earth to purify their ashes. Brahma agreed, but Ganga, offended, threatened to drop to earth so heavily that she would drown everything and everyone there. Shiva caught her in his hair on her descent and walked the earth with her, safely releasing her in streams for several years. There, she purified the ashes of Bhagiratha's forefathers, allowing them to reach heaven.

In some myths, Ganga took the form of a beautiful woman, meeting King Shantanu on her banks. She bore him seven children and drowned each of them, as they were reincarnations of Vasyas - elemental gods - cursed to live miserable lives as humans. Shantanu prevented her from drowning their eighth child, who became the wise King Bishma.

POPULAR DEPICTIONS

Ganga Dussehra is a ten-day festival celebrating Ganga's descent to earth. Devotees float lit *diyas* (oil lamps) on the Ganges and dip themselves in her waters. Any person who plunges into the water during this festival is purified – and it is said that their ailments will wash away.

The Ellora caves, a UNESCO World Heritage Site featuring the largest complex of Hindu temple caves in the world, are home to a carving of the goddess Ganga. She is portrayed standing on her mount, a mythological scaled water creature called the makara. Many other religious artworks portray her standing on the makara, often holding a lotus in each hand.

The monument *Descent of the Ganges* is a large relief carved into a pair of boulders. It portrays more than a hundred figures, from gods to mortals to animals, watching Ganga descend through Shiva's hair. A water tank was originally situated between the two boulders and would release water through the *nagas* (serpent deities) carved into the cleft of the rock.

LIFE LESSONS FROM GANGA

Ganga is the goddess of forgiveness. A dip in her waters can wash away the sins of a lifetime. At Kumbh Mela, a festival taking place at the intersection of the rivers Ganges, Yamuna and the mystical (or long-dried) Saraswati every 12 years, roughly 100 million people gather to cleanse their sins. Bring the attitude of Ganga into your life by releasing the petty grudges that take up unnecessary space in your mind. Sometimes, this can be achieved by thinking of the grudge and asking yourself, "How does this serve me?" Although you may feel that you were wronged by another's actions, now is the time to question how hanging on to the bad feeling surrounding them benefits you. Does it make you feel good? Does it give you peace? If the answer is no, release the feelings, letting them flow away like the waters of a river.

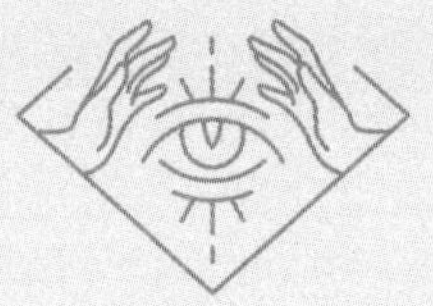

HEL

OTHER NAMES

None in common use

ORIGIN

Norse

KEY ATTRIBUTES

Cold, monstrous, loyal

POWERS AND ABILITIES

Hel was the unfeeling queen of the Norse underworld.

Hel was one of three children born to the Norse trickster god, Loki, and the giantess Angerboda. She was charged with ruling over the part of the underworld where those who died unworthy deaths, such as of sickness, would enter in the afterlife. She offered a cold welcome: her threshold was said to be a stumbling block and her table was called famine.

When her father, Loki, killed the much-loved god Baldur, the war god Hermod rode to Hel to request she return Baldur to life. He appealed to her sensibilities, telling her that all wept for the loss of Baldur. With some of her father's spirit, she retorted that if Hermod could prove that his words were true, she would return Baldur. Hermod sent the message throughout the realms, and all things, even beasts and metals, wept for Baldur. However, Thökk the giantess (thought to be Loki in disguise) refused to weep. So, Hel refused to return Baldur to life.

POPULAR DEPICTIONS

The *Poetic Edda* is a collection of Norse poems by an anonymous author or authors. It was written in the late thirteenth century, although it wasn't discovered until the late seventeenth century. It contains many Norse myths and legends, including tales found in the *Prose Edda*. J. R. R. Tolkien, who studied Old Norse, was greatly inspired by the *Poetic Edda*, lifting several of the concepts within its pages for his own seminal fantasy novel *The Lord of the Rings.* Within the *Poetic Edda* is a vivid description of Hel's realm, Náströnd. It reads:

Venom drops through the smoke-vent down,
For around the walls do serpents wind.

I saw there wading through rivers wild
Treacherous men and murderers too.

It's the kind of description that sends shivers down your spine. In Norse mythology, traitors and murderers were the worst kind of criminal and they would suffer in the miserable halls of Hel.

If you think Hel's name sounds familiar, you'd be right. Hel gave her name to the modern English word "hell".

LIFE LESSONS FROM HEL

Hel is one of the original badasses. There's nothing soft or gentle about her. She ruled over a portion of the dead, in a realm of mist and venom. She is the perfect reminder that divine feminine energy can have hard edges, too. If you feel pressure to present yourself in a limited way then perhaps you can take inspiration from Hel. For example, if society categorizes you as feminine, you may be expected not to be as bold, forthcoming or direct as you'd like. You may even receive comments on your choice of hobbies or dress. However, as you can tell from the goddesses contained in these pages, femininity can take many forms, and has taken many forms throughout history. It's OK to speak up, speak loudly and be yourself.

HOUTU

OTHER NAMES

Di Mu, Di

ORIGIN

Chinese

KEY ATTRIBUTES

Mother goddess, kindly, a problem-solver

POWERS AND ABILITIES

The nourisher of life.

MYTHS AND LEGENDS

Houtu was one of the earliest goddesses in Chinese folklore. Originally, she was known as Mother Earth and, together with Tian, the god of the sky, she was the source of all life. In later myths she is merged with Tian to become Shang Di, the masculine great god.

In one myth, she assisted the great King Yu. Yu wished to channel the flood, which covered his land, to the sea, creating the Yellow River. However, he had channelled westward, where the land was filled with rock, impeding his progress. Houtu mulled on his problem and, using her great wisdom, came up with her solution. She sent one of her divine birds to tell Yu to channel eastward, which he did, succeeding in his goal. Houtu continued to help Yu, at one time using her power to create a large cave for him and his followers to live in.

POPULAR DEPICTIONS

The Houtu Temple in the city of Jiexiu is the oldest temple in the Shanxi Province, and the oldest temple dedicated to Houtu in China. Rebuilt many times throughout history, it is located near the bank of the Yellow River. Han Dynasty emperors would travel to this temple to offer sacrifices and throw ritual feasts in worship of her. The temple was the site of many significant cultural moments in China's history, including the creation of songs and poems. The sixth emperor of the Han Dynasty, Wu-ti, wrote "The Autumn Wind" while on a trip to Houtu Temple. The evocative opening lines possibly describe what he saw at the Houtu Temple:

Autumn wind rises: white clouds fly.
Grass and trees wither: geese go south.
Orchids all in bloom: chrysanthemums smell sweet.

The temple still celebrates Houtu each year on 18 March, the day she was supposedly born. Within the temple she is known as Houtu the Sacred Mother, portrayed as wearing a coronet, a cape and a silk skirt embroidered with phoenixes.

LIFE LESSONS FROM HOUTU

Early worship of Houtu included the act of burying prayers written on scrolls. As Houtu was an earth goddess, it was thought that doing this would help the prayers reach her ears.

There is something rather lovely about the idea of burying a wish or prayer. In a way, it is the opposite of writing a painful letter and then burning it, with the aim of destroying the feelings it contains. Instead, you are planting a seed of hope into fertile ground. Consider creating a ritual based on the worship of Houtu. The next time you want to make a change in your life, buy some seed paper and write your desired outcome in pencil on the paper. Then, following the instructions on the seed paper's packaging, bury the prayer in soil. Care for the plant that grows, and while you tend to it, take steps to make the changes necessary to achieve your dreams.

ISHTAR

OTHER NAMES

Inanna, Ashtart (Ishtar is possibly Astarte's predecessor, see p.18)

ORIGIN

Mesopotamian

KEY ATTRIBUTES

Multifaceted, promiscuous, warlike

POWERS AND ABILITIES

Ishtar was the goddess of love, lust, music and war.

MYTHS AND LEGENDS

Ishtar is one of the earliest recorded goddesses. She was worshipped across the ancient world, and different cultures focused on different facets of her personality.

In the hymn "Inanna and Utu" Ishtar (Inanna) became the goddess of sex. She sought to learn about sex, so she ate the fruit of a tree growing in the underworld. By eating the fruit she learned everything there was to know about sex in one convenient action.

One Sumerian myth describes how Ishtar followed her deceased mortal love Tammuz to the underworld. While she was in the underworld, all reproduction on earth stopped, only resuming once Ishtar persuaded the gods to let her return with Tammuz. Other versions of this story are less romantic. In these, Ishtar offered up Tammuz in her own place, allowing him to be imprisoned in the underworld so she could escape.

Assyrian myth depicted the violent alternative to Ishtar's lustful side. Assyrians worshipped her as a war goddess. Her fearsome war cries would freeze her enemies' blood and her priests would offer up flayed skin in her honour.

POPULAR DEPICTIONS

Ishtar features in the earliest surviving work of fiction, the poem *The Epic of Gilgamesh*, which dates from around 2100 BCE. She is an antagonist of the hero Gilgamesh. First, she desires him to be her lover. However, he rejects her, citing her infamously shoddy treatment of past partners. She is enraged and sends the Bull of Heaven to destroy him. Although the bull is no joke - one breath from him blows a hole in the ground, trapping 100 people - Gilgamesh defeats him. The earliest recorded mention of Ishtar dates from even earlier, around 2300 BCE by the priestess Enheduanna.

As the deity for whom there is potentially the earliest surviving written record, Ishtar and the myths and legends surrounding her echo across the world. You may recognize the themes of Ishtar's descent into the underworld in the later Greek myth of Persephone and Hades. Sharp-eyed readers will also spot the similarities between Ishtar eating sacred fruit to gain sexual knowledge and the biblical tale of Eve in the Garden of Eden.

LIFE LESSONS FROM ISHTAR

Many gods simply possess the attributes that they are known for. For example, there is no myth where Athena learns how to become an expert weaver; she simply is one. Ishtar is interesting because she often wishes to improve her knowledge or power and then takes steps to do so. Learning something new can be engaging and rewarding. It can start you on new roads as you discover a passion for a hobby, subject or even culture. It can be a route to new friends, as you join groups and make connections.

Free yourself from the idea that learning must always be serious. Challenging yourself to learn a new language or pick up a new qualification is a worthy endeavour, but learning something on a small scale can be just as rewarding. Whether it's a physical challenge, such as training yourself to do a really good handstand, or a creative one, such as mastering the art of baking a soufflé, learning can enrich your life.

ISIS

OTHER NAMES

Aset, Eset

ORIGIN

Egyptian

KEY ATTRIBUTES

Loyal wife, dedicated, sometimes great goddess

POWERS AND ABILITIES

Isis was one of the great gods of Egypt, responsible for love, marriage and medicine.

MYTHS AND LEGENDS

Isis was a central player in one of Egypt's key myths, which shows her tenacity and devotion as a mother and wife. Set, jealous of Osiris, his brother and Isis' brother-husband, conspired to kill and dismember him, scattering his body parts around the earth. Isis painstakingly gathered Osiris' body parts and reassembled them, invoking magic spells to return breath to his body. At some point (the stories differ) Isis impregnated herself using the last drop of Osiris' essence. Her son, Horus, would go on to battle and defeat Set.

In the Nile delta Isis was worshipped as the great goddess, having tricked Ra into handing over his powers. Isis used sand and some of Ra's spit to create a snake, which bit Ra. He begged Isis to use her healing powers on his wound but she refused unless he told her his true name, the key to his power. He capitulated and she cured him, gaining his powers and becoming the great goddess.

POPULAR DEPICTIONS

Isis was connected with union and fertility - during the rite to mark her birthday, celebrants would carry a statue of Isis through a field, perhaps hoping the ground would become fertile. However, she was also connected with death and funerary rites. Legends told of her sometimes greeting the dead alongside her husband, Osiris. People would place *tyet* amulets - made with red jasper to represent Isis' blood - on mummies to ensure they had the protection of Isis in the afterlife.

Isis, unlike many other Egyptian gods, including her own son Horus, was portrayed in iconography with a human head. In the tomb of Queen Nefertiti, in the Valley of the Queens, Isis is shown leading Nefertiti by the hand. She carries in her other hand her customary papyrus staff. On her head is a crown made from the horns of a cow and a sun disc.

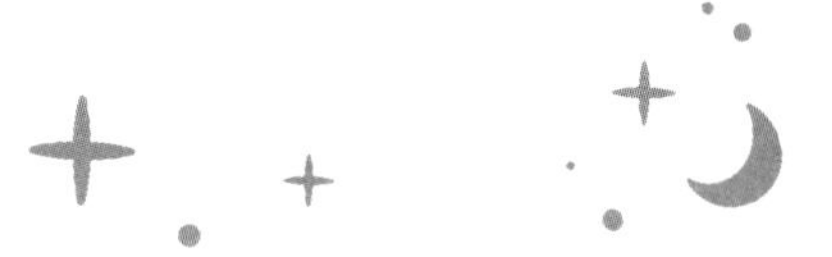

LIFE LESSONS FROM ISIS

When Isis applied herself to a task, she completed it. Sometimes her trials were long and arduous, sometimes she was up against a power much greater than herself. However, her spirits didn't flag. She went to extreme lengths to overcome the obstacles in her way, whether through cunning or kindness. If you feel disheartened by a task that is taking longer than you had hoped, whether it is mastering a skill or simply completing paperwork, bring some of Isis' energy to your life.

Isis was also very good at breaking a task that seemed overwhelming into small parts. For example, reassembling and resurrecting your deceased husband may seem like an insurmountable undertaking. However, by reducing this large project into its component parts - find each body part, reassemble, cast a magic spell - you'll find each element feels more achievable.

IXCHEL

OTHER NAMES

Ix Chel, Chak Chel

ORIGIN

Mayan

KEY ATTRIBUTES

Water-aligned, changeable, hot-tempered

POWERS AND ABILITIES

The Mayan goddess of the moon, fertility and storms.

MYTHS AND LEGENDS

Ixchel was one of the jaguar deities of the Mayan pantheon. These were gods and goddesses who possessed some of the features of the jaguar. Ixchel, in her form as an old woman, was portrayed as having jaguar ears and, in some cases, claws instead of hands. She was variously depicted as a young woman and an old woman, thought to represent the waxing and waning of the moon.

In some legends, Ixchel was the goddess of storms. Jugs of water lined her palace. The Mayan people sacrificed to Ixchel to keep her happy – if they didn't, she would upend the jugs, pouring out the water and flooding the mortal realms below. In some interpretations, she was thought to cause the start of the rainy season.

Her spouse, Itzamna, was a bird deity and the god of the sky. Together they had 13 sons. It was two of these sons who created earth and the humans who inhabit it.

POPULAR DEPICTIONS

Isla Mujeres is the name of an island dedicated to Ixchel, bestowed by a Spanish sailor who stumbled upon it in the early sixteenth century. He chose this name, meaning "the Isle of Women", as it was only inhabited by women. He reported that the priestesses of Ixchel lived on the island in a temple filled with gold, silver and clay statues of the goddess.

Isla Mujeres isn't the only island to be dedicated to Ixchel. The island of Cozumel is filled with temples honouring her, and women would make pilgrimages to these sites to pray for fertility. Some pottery shows Ixchel watching women in childbirth, most likely protecting the mother and child, perhaps in the role of midwife.

Mayans celebrated Ixchel during the festival Ihcil Ixchel. Celebrations would include a feast, where shamans would bring forth small medicine bundles containing idols in the form of Ixchel.

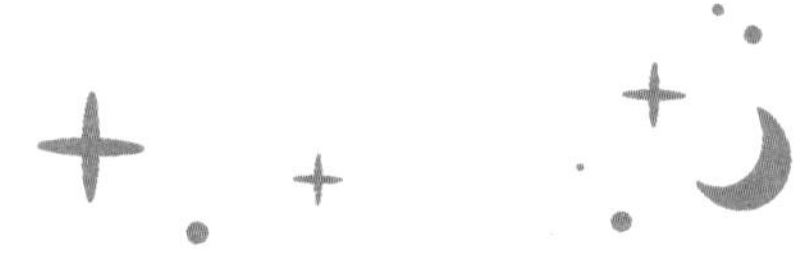

LIFE LESSONS FROM IXCHEL

It's no wonder that Ixchel, a goddess of storms, was also a fertility goddess. The rains are essential to bring forth the harvest and replenish the waters for humans and animals alike. But for most of us, a storm is no longer weather to be celebrated. We connect storms with bad times or challenges - we even refer colloquially to discomforting times as stormy weather. And yet, these are the same storms that are nourishing our crops and refreshing our water supplies. Think like Ixchel when it comes to your own proverbial stormy weather. Some challenges, such as having to navigate conflict or taking on stretch tasks at work, are also opportunities. Their very nature means that you're pushed outside your comfort zone and forced to learn new things about yourself. You may not enjoy the experience while it's happening - and you don't need to try to! - but, on reflection, you may find you've learned a new skill or something new about yourself.

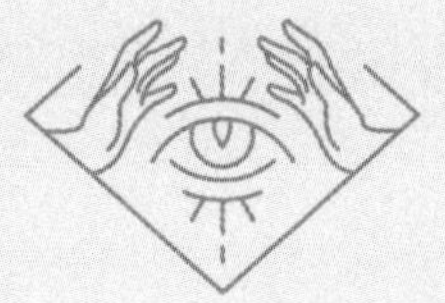

MAMAN BRIGITTE

OTHER NAMES

Gran Brigitte

ORIGIN

Haitian Vodou

KEY ATTRIBUTES

Healing, kindly, sensual and bawdy

POWERS AND ABILITIES

Maman Brigitte is the *lwa* (powerful spirit) of death.

MYTHS AND LEGENDS

Lwa are divine intermediaries between the great god Bondye and the mortal realm. They have certain responsibilities and grant favours to mortals who meet their conditions. Maman Brigitte belongs to the Guede family of *lwa*, who are responsible for death. The Guede family colours are purple and black.

Maman Brigitte uses her healing powers to cure the sick. When a human is fatally ill or wounded, and she cannot cure them, she will guide them to the afterlife. She talks to them while they walk, keeping their spirits up with laughter and kind words. Like the rest of her family, she is foul-mouthed and bawdy, although she respects the dead and teaches others to respect death.

Maman Brigitte is often represented by a black rooster. She enjoys drinking rum laced with chilli peppers, or eating chilli peppers raw. In exchange for an offering of candles or chilli-laced rum, she will stand guard over a grave and keep it safe.

POPULAR DEPICTIONS

Fèt Gede is a festival that takes place over the first two days of November and celebrates the Guede family of *lwa*. Celebrants wear the family colours of black and purple and make offerings of beeswax candles and chilli-laced rum. People gather in jubilant celebration, processing together to graveyards where they offer their ancestors gifts of food. Although this is a festival of death, there is much laughter, music and dancing. The Banda is a special dance honouring the Guede family, performed as part of the Fèt Gede. The dance represents sexuality and death, the characteristics of the Guede family. Maman Brigitte is sometimes thought to rub herself with chilli peppers, pressing them against her genitals – a test sometimes given to women suspected of faking possession during Fèt Gede.

The Vodou *veve* (symbol), for Maman Brigitte features a heart and crossing lines. Maman Brigitte's *veve* is sometimes inscribed on the gravestone of the first woman to be buried in a cemetery.

LIFE LESSONS FROM MAMAN BRIGITTE

Maman Brigitte and the Guede family stand out from many of the world's pantheons for approaching their duties with a sense of fun. Maman Brigitte has the grave responsibility of escorting mortals to the afterlife but she dispatches it with kindness and a bawdy, mischievous sense of humour. There are many serious and sad emotions that accompany an ending of any sort, but there is also an opportunity for celebration. When faced with an ending, or parting, look for the memories that can bring joy. Sometimes, you may feel that it is inappropriate to find joy in a serious situation. However, remember that laughter is a release of emotion. It can be as useful a tool in commemorating the end of an era, or a relationship, as tears can.

MAMA QUILLA

OTHER NAMES

Mama Killa, Mother Moon

ORIGIN

Incan

KEY ATTRIBUTES

Beautiful, maternal, strong

POWERS AND ABILITIES

Mama Quilla was known as the Moon Mother, goddess of marriage and the menstrual cycle. She defended and uplifted women.

MYTHS AND LEGENDS

Mama Quilla was known as the Moon Mother. She married Inti, the sun god, and together they ruled the skies as two of the principal Incan deities.

Incas believed that lunar eclipses were the result of an animal attacking Mama Quilla. They feared that the animal - thought to be a jaguar or serpent - could kill or consume Mama Quilla and the world would be left in darkness. During lunar eclipses people would shout, throw things and make noise in an attempt to scare off the attacking animal and save Mama Quilla.

Such was Mama Quilla's beauty that a fox once fell in love with her. When he ascended into the sky, Mama Quilla pressed him against her, creating the dark spots that can be seen on the moon.

Mama Quilla was often portrayed in art as a large silver disc with human features. She was said to cry silver tears; it was these tears that gave the Incas their rich stores of silver.

POPULAR DEPICTIONS

Quillarumiyoc is a unique archaeological site on a mountain range flanking a fertile valley in the province of Anta, Peru. Its name means "the place of the rock of the moon" for reasons that are quickly understandable. There is a large rock in the centre of the site engraved with a throne, dedicated to Mama Quilla.

Koya Raymi Quilla was the tenth month of the Incan calendar. During this month the Incas held a festival, known as Coya Raymi, celebrating the spring equinox and Mama Quilla. Mama Quilla was a protector of women and a symbol of the divine feminine, and it was women who were the hosts of Coya Raymi. Women of all rank and birth celebrated Coya Raymi and men attended at their invitation. The festival marked the start of the rains and the agricultural season, so was closely linked with fertility.

LIFE LESSONS FROM MAMA QUILLA

Mama Quilla was known as a defender of women. You can embody the same warrior spirit in a non-violent way. There are many small ways to hold space for, uplift and protect your sisters.

One way is to be aware of the dynamics of power in conversation, especially within institutional structures such as workplaces. Who is taking up the most space in the conversation and whose ideas are getting credited? If you notice a woman is often interrupted, can you direct conversation back to her? Can you affirm her in other positive ways, such as being sure to credit her good ideas?

Another way to bring Mama Quilla's values into your life is to support the efforts of others in defending women. Donate money or time, should your own resources allow.

You could even carry forth the spirit of Coya Raymi! Throw festivities with the women in your life; a big feast with all your sisters sounds divine.

MAMI WATA

OTHER NAMES

La Sirene, Watramama

ORIGIN

West, central and southern African

KEY ATTRIBUTES

A healer, sometimes generous, sometimes vengeful

POWERS AND ABILITIES

Mami Wata is a water goddess associated with luck and fortune.

MYTHS AND LEGENDS

Many myths tell of Mami Wata testing mortals in a variety of ways. Should they pass, they would be blessed with wealth and/or good looks. Failure leads to Mami Wata cursing them with bad luck.

Mami Wata is often found in a body of water. One legend has her abducting sailors who traversed the ocean and carrying them to her realm. Should she allow the sailor to return, they would emerge from the water with miraculously dry clothes, improved spiritual enlightenment and wealth. Other myths tell of mortals finding her combing her hair in a river. She would escape the scene, leaving her luxurious possessions behind. If the mortal stole the items, she would appear to them in a dream, asking for their return – plus an additional caveat: if the mortal was a man, he must be sexually faithful to her. Mortals who granted her request would be blessed, those who refused were cursed.

Sometimes Mami Wata can be a harbinger of bad luck. In Cameroon Mami Wata is thought to cause a strong, deadly undertow, while in Nigeria she is blamed for all manner of illnesses.

POPULAR DEPICTIONS

The defining modern image of Mami Wata is that of a beautiful woman, bare-chested, with a snake winding up between her breasts. This is a relatively late depiction of Mami Wata and can possibly be traced back to a lithograph of a real person, a Samoan snake charmer, produced in 1887.

Worship of Mami Wata and her sister water spirits spread across the world, to the Caribbean and North and South America, via the forced displacement of enslaved African people. Contemporary accounts of European slavers talk of their attempts to suppress worship. For example, in Suriname in 1770, colonial authorities passed a law forbidding the "watermamma" and other worship dances. However, these efforts were ultimately futile. In fact, Mami Wata grew in strength through this forced diaspora, her name and characteristics replacing diverse cultures' water spirits and goddesses.

LIFE LESSONS FROM MAMI WATA

Mami Wata is one of the most fluid modern-day goddesses - and not just because she is a water spirit. The forces that attempted to oppress her worship instead inadvertently created the perfect circumstances for her power to rise. Can Mami Wata's resilience inspire you? Her tradition adapted and developed in the face of unspeakable circumstances. How can you tap into Mami Wata's adaptability? Perhaps you could remember that the version of you that you are today isn't the same version of you that has always been - you are made up of every action you've ever taken and every lesson you've ever learned. The future you will be built from the actions that you are taking and the lessons that you are learning today.

MAYARI

OTHER NAMES

Buan, the Maiden in the Moon (her Laguna name)

ORIGIN

Kapampangan, Tagalog

KEY ATTRIBUTES

Beautiful, strong, one-eyed

POWERS AND ABILITIES

Mayari was the goddess of the moon, who ruled over the world at night.

MYTHS AND LEGENDS

Mayari was one of the two children of the great god Bathala. Bathala ruled over everything, but when he died he left behind no will. His son, sun god Apolaki, and his daughter, Mayari, both believed they should rule the world. The two fought, and Mayari lost an eye in the battle. Although he fiercely believed in his right to rule, Apolaki felt sympathy for his sister and offered her a split. When the sun was in the sky, he ruled the earth, and when the moon was risen, she was queen.

Other legends say that Mayari was one of three sisters, fathered by Bathala and born to a mortal woman. Her celestial sisters were Hanan, the goddess of the morning, and Tala, the goddess of the stars. Yet more myths say that Tala was the daughter of Mayari, in her iteration as Buan. Mayari hid Tala, the morning star, in the clouds, to protect her from her jealous brother, the sun.

POPULAR DEPICTIONS

Like Incan myth, Tagalog legend held that eclipses were a result of the moon being attacked by a fearsome beast. The story describes how Laho - a shadow entity in the form of a serpent or dragon - would swallow the moon. People would gather outside and strike bells and other instruments in an effort to scare away the celestial monster and save the moon.

Tagalog and Kapampangan religions are oral traditions and much historical practice has been obliterated by the laws and records of Christian colonizers. Some records show that people would celebrate the coming of the new moon and ask Mayari, in her Buan form, for boons. One prayer was recorded as, "Moon, my Lady, make me rich." In contrast, the lunar eclipse was considered grave luck. It was best to drop everything you were doing during the lunar eclipse, otherwise you were sure not to succeed.

Ceremonies for the Maiden in the Moon included driving a gaggle of roosters to fly in her direction as an offering.

LIFE LESSONS FROM MAYARI

During the new moon, Mayari's devotees would pray for her blessing and ask for abundance. Take Mayari's blessing of abundance and apply it to your own perspective. An abundance mindset isn't about desiring material wealth but about realizing the plenty that is already available to us. For example, a scarcity mindset focuses on the idea that if one person has an opportunity, knowledge or a prized possession, that leaves less out there for everyone else. An abundance mindset focuses on the idea that there is plenty for everyone. The first step to having an abundance mindset is switching your focus from what you don't have to being mindful of what you do have. Notice the little pleasures in each day, practise gratitude and praise yourself for your achievements as much as, if not more than, you chastise yourself for your mistakes.

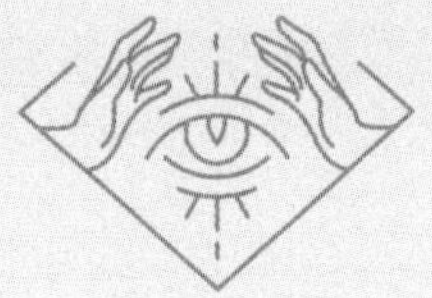

MAZU

OTHER NAMES

Tin Hau, Tian Shang Sheng Mu, Línghuì Fūrén, Ā-mā

ORIGIN

Chinese

KEY ATTRIBUTES

Protector, brave, devout

POWERS AND ABILITIES

Mazu is the goddess of the sea and patron saint of fishermen.

MYTHS AND LEGENDS

Mazu is known by many names. One of her oldest formal titles is Línghuì Fūrén - Lady of Light and Kindness - while in southern China she is known informally as Ā-mā. It's useful to know several different names for Mazu, because using the wrong name at the wrong time can have unforeseen consequences. If you need a quick response from Mazu, use her informal name. Using one of her titles means she will dress in imperial regalia before appearing in front of the plaintiff, which may mean she comes too late!

Some legends say that Mazu was born mortal to a fisherman. She saw in a vision that her father and sons were caught in a great typhoon and used her spiritual powers to save them. Other legends describe how the prophet Laozi brought a star, the Jade Woman of Marvellous Deeds, to earth to serve as a protector for those lost at sea. She was incarnated as Mazu.

POPULAR DEPICTIONS

Mazu watches over those who sail treacherous oceans. She has a particularly good vantage point in Tianjin, where the world's largest statue of her was erected in 2016. Standing over 42 metres tall, she is among the top 60 tallest statues in the world and is the tallest statue of Mazu.

Sailors claim to see Mazu's distinctive red robes on the sea before a storm hits. In the early twelfth century, the Supervising Secretary of China, Lu Yundi, was travelling in a small fleet of eight ships when they were caught in a storm. He claimed to see a goddess dressed in red above the mast of his ship, and his ship was the only one of the eight not to capsize.

Mazu has received official credit from the Chinese government since this adventure. In the late eighteenth century, the government of the last ruling dynasty, the Qing Dynasty, officially credited Mazu with helping their forces defeat the French in battle.

LIFE LESSONS FROM MAZU

Mazu is a protector who extends her hand to those in need. Can you also provide protection for those in need? This could be via an act of giving. Perhaps you could pick a cause that is close to your heart, whether that's supporting animal rights, providing food aid or giving assistance to marginalized groups. Charitable organizations are often most in need of reliable assistance. Could you arrange a monthly donation of money or dedicate your time on a regular basis to this cause?

Perhaps you could make small changes in your life to protect the world around you. For example, you could put out shallow trays of water in summer to help insects - including the endangered bee population - cool and refuel. Or maybe you could avoid purchasing goods that include microplastics, as these pollute the ocean and cause irreversible damage to its flora and fauna. Being a protector isn't about fighting or defending, but sharing your resources and compassion where possible.

THE MORRÍGAN

OTHER NAMES

Mórrigna, Badb, Macha, Nemain, Anand

ORIGIN

Celtic

KEY ATTRIBUTES

Ferocious, foreboding, insatiable and tricksy

POWERS AND ABILITIES

Shape-shifting, inciting battle frenzy, seduction and foresight.

MYTHS AND LEGENDS

The Morrígan is either one of three fearsome warrior sisters or perhaps the collective name for all of them. The three war goddesses are known individually as the Morrígan, Badb and Macha (although names and personas can vary from myth to myth).

The three sisters were masters of transformation and they favoured the form of enormous crows (*badb* is Old Irish for "crow"); those who saw them in crow-form recognized this as an omen of a coming battle.

Although the sisters were known to incite war and drive soldiers to battle frenzy, their favour could secure victory for warriors. One legend has the Morrígan advising the Dagda (the god of life and death) how to secure victory against his foe. She would later turn the tide in that battle by reciting a poem so horrifying that the Dagda's foe fled. The pair would couple in a ceremonial meeting each New Year's Day.

The Morrígan had a complex relationship with hero Cú Chulainn, whom she would alternately attempt to seduce and kill. She would eventually (correctly) predict his death.

POPULAR DEPICTIONS

One of the most enduring depictions of the Morrígan has been through her possible development into the Arthurian faery Morgan le Fay. Historians have found no definitive link between the two but point to the similarity in their names and their complex relationships with great heroes.

The earliest depiction of the Morrígan is in the *Ulster Cycle* - a collection of myths and legends about great Irish heroes. She appears as the foe of Cú Chulainn, successively attempting to seduce him, exchanging sharp words, battling him, tricking him into healing her and finally predicting his death. The first written samples of the Ulster Cycle are found in manuscripts dating back to the twelfth century, although the language can be traced back to around the seventh century and the tales are thought to be set as far back as the first century.

LIFE LESSONS FROM THE MORRÍGAN

In truth, many of the Morrígan's exploits don't translate well to modern life skills. Her methods are only likely to be successful if you can shape-shift into an eel, a red heifer, a beautiful young lady or a wolf. And, although dressing all in black and forecasting doom is a bit of a vibe, it isn't always productive.

However, should there be a time when you need to borrow a little bit of strength and fearlessness, when you are scared to enter a conflict but know it is the right thing to do... perhaps you can imagine that you have the Morrígan's favour. Visualize three warrior goddesses behind you, lending you their strength and spirit. Their fearlessness will become yours and, with that divine energy, you can achieve whatever you need to do.

OMETEOTL

OTHER NAMES

Tōnacātēcuhtli, Tōnacācihuātl, Ōmetēuctli, Ōmecihuātl

ORIGIN

Aztec

KEY ATTRIBUTES

Duality, fertility, great goddess

POWERS AND ABILITIES

Ometeotl is the dual god responsible for all creation.

MYTHS AND LEGENDS

First there was nothing, and then Ometeotl created themself. Ometeotl was a god made up of two halves, the masculine Ōmetēuctli (Two Lord) - and the feminine Ōmecihuātl (Two Lady). They were the first divine being and they resided in the highest of the 13 heavens, Ilhuicatl-Omeyocan (the Place of Duality).

Ometeotl is the source of all life and sustenance in the universe. Ōmecihuātl bore four sons, who became four of the most powerful gods in the Aztec pantheon. Xipe Totec was the god of agriculture; Tezcatlipoca, god of the night; Quetzalcoatl, god of the wind; Huitzilopochtli, god of warfare. These gods became the creator gods for nearly all subsequent life.

One legend says that Ometeotl created the Tzitzimimeh, giant female skeletal deities who lived in the heavens. They were thought to protect humanity. But, should the sun fall, the Tzitzimimeh were poised to descend to earth and devour mortal life.

POPULAR DEPICTIONS

Ometeotl was too lofty for the daily lives of mortals, and was not worshipped in temples or through sacrifice. However, they would be invoked in certain prayers. The *Florentine Codex,* a book written in the sixteenth century by Franciscan monk and Spanish colonizer Bernardino de Sahagún, records the prayers offered at different times in Aztec life. One prayer, spoken by midwives to newborns, talks of Ometeotl. The midwives would bathe the newborn and say, "You were created in the place of duality, the place above the nine heavens. Your mother and father - Ōmetēuctli and Ōmecihuātl, the heavenly lady - formed you, created you."

Some myths say that Ōmecihuātl gave birth to a flint, Tecpatl, which one of her children threw to earth. The Tecpatl was a sacred knife with a double-edged blade. It was used to open the chest of a human sacrifice to enable the removal of their heart.

LIFE LESSONS FROM OMETEOTL

Ometeotl contains both the divine masculine and the divine feminine. Their power originates from their dual nature. While the divine feminine is multifaceted, including kindness and strength, fertility and destruction, and much more, there may be times when you feel that it's not the only source of energy that runs through you. It can be a powerful action to identify with the divine masculine within you and recognize that, like the gods, you contain multitudes. Getting in touch with an unfamiliar divine energy within can be a pretty big task! But, it can be achieved by taking simple steps. For example, be mindful of your thought patterns. If you censor yourself for behaving in a way that you feel is not appropriate for your gender, pause. Notice the negative thought and consciously reject it. Say to yourself that you will not impose limits on yourself and your behaviour. You have the power of the masculine divine and the feminine divine within you, and you will use that power.

OSUN

OTHER NAMES

Oshun

ORIGIN

Yoruba

KEY ATTRIBUTES

The divine feminine, creator, sensual

POWERS AND ABILITIES

Osun was a river goddess who gave life to earth and was patron of the river Osun.

MYTHS AND LEGENDS

Olodumare, the creator god, sent 17 of his children down to earth to complete his work and populate the earth. Despite their great power, the 16 male children were not able to create meaningful life. Finally, they turned to Osun, the youngest and the only goddess. She shared her wisdom and gifted the world with love, beauty and fertility. These gifts made life sweet and gave it meaning - and the work of creation was complete.

The water and mother goddess Yemaya (possibly connected to Mami Wata) saw Osun being chased by Ogun, god of metallurgy. In her desperation to get away, Osun slipped into the flowing river. Yemaya rescued her and gifted her with the realm of fresh water and rivers, and the river was named for her. Since that day Osun has presided over fresh water and the river Osun. Although her primary role was to bring the rains and bless humanity with fertility, she would lash out when angered, causing drought or floods.

POPULAR DEPICTIONS

The city Osogbo in Nigeria was thought to have been built after migrants went to Osun and asked for her blessing to build a home. She gave it, and since then the citizens of Osogbo give their thanks during the festival of Osun. Having run for around 700 years, the festival begins with a lamp-lighting ceremony in the city. Celebrants process to the Osun-Osogbo Sacred Grove, accompanied by drumming and dancing. The festival of Osun culminates in a sacrifice offered to Osun.

The Osun-Osogbo Sacred Grove is a UNESCO World Heritage Site. Osun is thought to live within the densely planted forest, which contains shrines, palaces, temples and other places of worship dedicated to her. It also contains over 400 types of plant life, over 200 of which contain medicinal properties. The New Sacred Art project was launched in the mid-twentieth century and instigated the installation of sculptures in the grove, which continues to this day.

LIFE LESSONS FROM OSUN

The art installed in the Osun-Osogbo Sacred Grove is a beautiful and meaningful way to celebrate the goddess Osun. Creating art, whatever the format, provides an opportunity to engage with a place or event in new ways - and can reveal unexpected perspectives. Art can often fall by the wayside in our daily lives, especially after early schooling ends. However, you don't have to be an artist to create art - and it is always worth the time you invest in it. The reward doesn't necessarily come from art you create, but the process you engage in. For example, you could draw your favourite moment from a day out with friends. Thinking about the time you spent together, reflecting on what you especially enjoyed and considering how to condense these moments into one image may help you recall details you had forgotten. You may be surprised at what you remember, or how the "big" moments weren't necessarily the ones you most enjoyed. By creating art you are giving yourself the chance to relive, reassess and enjoy the occasion all over again.

PAPATŪĀNUKU

OTHER NAMES

Papa

ORIGIN

Māori

KEY ATTRIBUTES

Mother goddess, primordial earth mother

POWERS AND ABILITIES

Papatūānuku is the mother of all life on earth.

MYTHS AND LEGENDS

Papatūānuku, the primordial earth goddess, married Ranginui, the primordial sky god. The two loved each other and were locked in a deep embrace. However, this did not delight their 70 children, who were forced to lie in cramped darkness, stuck between the pair. These children, including the brothers Tāne, god of the forests, Tangaroa, god of the seas, lakes and rivers, and Haumia-tiketike, god of wild food, conspired to push their embarrassing parents apart. Eventually Tāne succeeded and the two were torn asunder.

Not all of Papatūānuku's children agreed that this was the right move: Tāwhirimātea, the god of storms and winds, was infuriated. He relentlessly attacked his siblings until Papatūānuku hid some of them in order to keep them safe. The god of volcanoes and earthquakes, Rūaumoko, was never born and still lives inside Papatūānuku.

To this day, Papatūānuku and Ranginui still long to be reunited. Papatūānuku strains to embrace her love again, while Ranginui rains tears down on to Papatūānuku.

POPULAR DEPICTIONS

Karakia are traditional Māori blessings. They are often used to start a ceremony and invoke the goodwill of the gods and spirits. "Karakia mō te Kai" is a traditional food blessing, used to acknowledge the sources of the food you are about to eat, the land and the gods who provided it, and to express gratitude. It ends: *"Ko Ranginui e tū iho nei/ Ko Papatūānuku e takoto nei/ Tūturu o whiti ka whakamaua kia tina! TINA!/ Hāumi e! Hui e! TĀIKI E!"*

This, translated, means: "I acknowledge the sky father who is above me,/ the earth mother who lies beneath me/ Let this be my commitment to all!/ Draw together! Affirm!"

There are protections in modern New Zealand law which prevent the commercialization of depictions of Papatūānuku. Māori culture prevents the connection of things that are *tapu* (sacred or untouchable) to things that are *noa* (commonplace). The New Zealand Intellectual Property Office specifically namechecks Papatūānuku as a figure who could not be used to brand commonplace items, such as cheese, because she is *tapu*.

LIFE LESSONS FROM PAPATŪĀNUKU

Māori culture contains a deep connection to the land. Papatūānuku birthed all life on earth, meaning that humanity can trace their beginnings back to the earth mother. This powerful connection to the earth has informed the Māori concept *tūrangawaewae*. *Tūrangawaewae* translates literally as "a place to stand", and is a place that we feel a particular connection to, perhaps through ancestral connection, spiritual affinity or comfort with the area. *Tūrangawaewae* is where the external world reflects our inner life. Think about the places that you feel a special connection to. This could be your home town, where you draw confidence from a deep knowledge and ancestral connection to the area, or it could be a place you feel spiritually at home - perhaps a particular landscape such as the ocean or a mountain. If you recognize that a specific location is a source of strength and peace for you, you then have the ability to tap into that strength and peace by visiting it.

PELE

OTHER NAMES

Pele-honua-mea, Madame Pele, Tūtū Pele

ORIGIN

Polynesian

KEY ATTRIBUTES

Hot-tempered, explorer, passionate

POWERS AND ABILITIES

Pele is the goddess of fire and volcanoes and the creator of the Hawaiian islands.

MYTHS AND LEGENDS

Like the Polynesian people, whose ancestors travelled the vast Pacific Ocean and populated the tiny islands, Pele was an explorer. She left her home - some legends say her father cast her out for seducing her sister's husband, others that her brother, Kamohoali'i, king of sharks, gifted her a canoe - and discovered the Hawaiian islands. Pele was soon attacked by her wronged sister, Namakaokahai. Some legends say she was left for dead, others that she died and became a goddess. Most agree that she now lives in the active volcano Kīlauea, on the Big Island.

Pele also often battled her rival, Poli'ahu, the goddess of snow. Poli'ahu was *holua* (lava) sledging with friends when they were joined by a beautiful woman. She joined the race, but when she realized that Poli'ahu was the better sledger, the ground started to shake. Poli'ahu realized that the mysterious beauty was Pele. Pele rained down fire and lava, destroying the lava slide, while Poli'ahu battled her with ice, causing a glacier to form.

POPULAR DEPICTIONS

Polynesian culture has an oral tradition, which means myths, legends and ancestral history are passed down from generation to generation via spoken tales, chants and dances. *Hula Pele* is one of three types of *hula* (sacred dance) and is dedicated to Pele and her family. The movement reflects her energetic, forceful nature and many of the chants tell of her exploits. The chant "E Pele, E Pele" ("O Pele, O Pele") describes the movement of Pele and reflects her connection to fire and lava. It includes the lyrics:

O Pele, O Pele, moving along
O Pele, O Pele, bursting forth
O Pele, O Pele, moving upward
O Pele, O Pele, moving downward.

Chants that are unaccompanied by dance are called *oli*. There are several *oli* in honour of Pele. "Pu'uonioni" was one such chant, performed in a sitting position. The performer recalls watching Pele "burn her way" down to Puna, a district of Hawaii. They implore the goddess, "Take care of your people, they are your choicest possessions."

LIFE LESSONS FROM PELE

Pele was a woman of action and adventure. She was master of the canoe and the sled and a patron of *hula*. Honour Pele by challenging your body and your mind. It doesn't matter if you are not a great mover and shaker – you don't have to run a marathon to enjoy the benefits of exercise.

For example, if you like to be social, what about finding a group activity for you and your loved ones? There may be a local climbing course that is suitable for beginners and includes plenty of fun options such as zip wires, or perhaps a high-octane dance class. For those with a taste for adventure, what about trying something new? You could truly channel the spirit of Pele by starting a course in kayaking or canoeing. Or perhaps you could do something for charity, such as abseiling or even a sky dive. Take Pele's hand and see where her drive for adventure takes you.

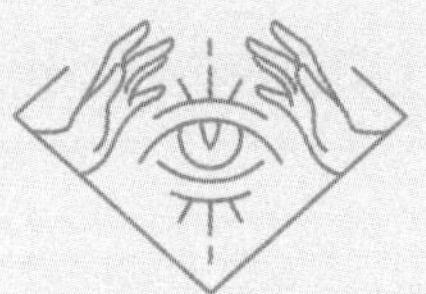

SEDNA

OTHER NAMES

Arnakuagsak, Nuliajuq, Mother of the Deep

ORIGIN

Inuit

KEY ATTRIBUTES

Huntress, creator, vengeful

POWERS AND ABILITIES

Sedna is the goddess of the sea and marine animals.

MYTHS AND LEGENDS

Sedna was known as Mother of the Deep. There are many legends that tell how she came to rule over her kingdom of the sea, many of which see her at odds with her parents. One legend describes Sedna as a giant. Driven by hunger, she attacked her father, who chopped off her fingers. These fingers transformed into seals, whales and walruses. In other stories Sedna was mortal. Her father gave her as a bride to a strange hunter, who revealed himself to be a great bird spirit. Her groom was angered when her father attempted to rescue her, and in the ensuing fight Sedna was thrown into the chilling seas. Her fingers froze and broke off as she tried to hold on to a kayak, and again they became sea creatures. Sedna sank to the bottom of the ocean, where she grew a fish tail and ruled over the monsters of the deep.

POPULAR DEPICTIONS

Inuit hunters would pray to Sedna. They relied on her goodwill, as mother and mistress of all sea creatures, to chase the animals of the deep into their waiting harpoons and nets. However, cursed with unhappy origins, Sedna was a vengeful goddess. If not properly worshipped, Sedna would not release the creatures and so the hunters would have an unsuccessful hunt and their people would go hungry. Inuit people would throw offerings into the sea to appease Sedna, including broken harpoon heads and chunks of meat. However, care of Sedna didn't just take place in the mortal realm. Sometimes the scarcity of creatures would be attributed to Sedna ordering sea shepherd Unga to round them all up. She would do this when mortals had broken taboos, which manifested as dirt and tangles in Sedna's hair. On these occasions shamans were required to astral project to the underworld, where Sedna lived, and comb her hair until the broken taboos were atoned for and she was satisfied.

LIFE LESSONS FROM SEDNA

One thing that the Sedna myths have in common is that they appear to be very extreme examples of "when life gives you lemons, make lemonade." In Sedna's version, it's "when life cuts off your fingers, turn them into sea creatures." Her mythology is a transformative tale, where the events that seem destined to break her instead provide her with the means to grow in strength. Can you think of a time in your own life when you utilized resilience similarly to Sedna? Consider times that you found testing - what did you learn about yourself? How did these experiences arm you with the ability to navigate future strife with deeper knowledge? You have Sedna's strength inside you - all you have to do is tap into it.

SPIDER GRANDMOTHER

OTHER NAMES

Spider Woman, Kokyangwuti, Na'ashjé'ii Asdzáá, Good Spirit

ORIGIN

Native American

KEY ATTRIBUTES

Wise, mentor, creator

POWERS AND ABILITIES

Spider Grandmother is a kind-hearted leader and wise woman.

MYTHS AND LEGENDS

Spider Grandmother exists in many Native American cultures, including the Hopi and Navajo people.

For the Hopi, Spider Grandmother is a creator. She shaped humans from clay and gave them life. In her form Good Spirit, Spider Grandmother guided the mortals through different forms until they settled into their human form in the Fourth World, also known as earth.

In Navajo telling, Spider Grandmother (known as Spider Woman) is a benefactor. When two women petitioned Spider Grandmother for help, she taught them the art of weaving. They, in turn, taught this art to their people, which enabled them all to create rugs to keep them warm during the cold winters. Spider Grandmother also helped the heroic twins Monster Slayer and Born for Water find their father, the sun. She told them where to find him and gave them a protective talisman. Finally, she instructed them in a powerful chant and sent them on their way, blessing their journey by saying, "The trail ahead is now a beautiful trail. Long life is ahead. Happiness is ahead."

POPULAR DEPICTIONS

Spider Grandmother taught the Navajo how to weave. Weavers continue to honour Spider Grandmother and attempt to absorb her skill by rubbing their hands in spiderwebs before starting their work. Some folk tales instruct young weavers to find spiderwebs beaded with the morning dew and rub their hands in them. This is how they will absorb Spider Grandmother's knowledge and skill into their spirits.

Spider Rock is a towering sandstone spire in Arizona's Canyon de Chelly. It is 700 feet of rust-coloured sandstone, bleached white on the top by the sun. Navajo legend says that Spider Grandmother makes her home on top of Spider Rock. She lets down her ladder made of webs to capture misbehaving children, whom she drags back to the top of her rock and eats. The white of the top of Spider Rock is thought to be the bare bones of the children she has captured.

LIFE LESSONS FROM SPIDER GRANDMOTHER

The words that Spider Grandmother says to Monster Slayer and Born for Water are peaceful and hopeful. She finishes with words often found in Navajo chants and prayers, instructing the twins to "walk in beauty". Welcome the wisdom of Spider Grandmother into your life by opening your heart to her words. Perhaps you could repeat them to yourself in the morning, as part of an affirmation that prepares you for the day ahead. You could say the (abridged and adapted) phrase: "The trail ahead is now a beautiful trail. Long life is ahead. Happiness is ahead. I walk in beauty."

The twins used this chant to pass safely and peacefully through many dangers on the road. Be responsible with the words of Spider Grandmother. When you repeat the affirmation, picture yourself walking forward, with strength but also with peace. Imagine yourself meeting challenges with acceptance and self-belief but also with a peaceful heart and actions.

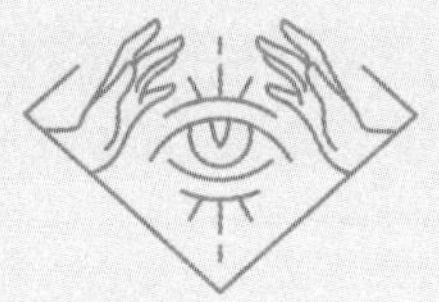

WHITE BUFFALO CALF WOMAN

OTHER NAMES

White She-Buffalo, White Buffalo Maiden

ORIGIN

Lakota

KEY ATTRIBUTES

Mentor, teacher

POWERS AND ABILITIES

White Buffalo Calf Woman was a powerful prophet and teacher for the Lakota Native American people.

MYTHS AND LEGENDS

White Buffalo Calf Woman taught the Lakota people many of their skills and secrets. She appeared one day to Lakota hunters on the plain as a beautiful woman. Although they propositioned her, she refused their advances and told them to build her a lodge fit for her power. They did as she bade, and she gifted them a ceremonial tobacco pipe containing four drops of her breast milk. She told them that if they planted these drops they would grow into corn - which is why corn grains have a milky sheen.

Farming and the ceremonial tobacco pipe weren't White Buffalo Calf Woman's only gifts to the Lakota. She also taught them mysteries, such as the secrets of the wind, and seven rituals to prolong life. These seven rituals include *Inipi*, a purification ritual taking place in a sweat lodge, the Sun Dance and *Huŋkalowaŋpi* (adopted kinship).

When White Buffalo Calf Woman had taught the Lakota everything they needed to know, she turned into a buffalo and disappeared.

POPULAR DEPICTIONS

The White Buffalo Cow Society is an all-woman Mandan society dedicated to White Buffalo Calf Woman. Modern versions of the White Buffalo Cow Society often work to protect women from rape and domestic abuse. According to historic descriptions written by European men, members of the society had tattooed lips and chins, painted one eye in the colour of their choice and wore large headdresses made of buffalo hide and adorned with eagle feathers.

The Sun Dance, given to the Lakota by White Buffalo Calf Woman, is one of the most significant rituals of the year. It is often an arduous ceremony, including fasting beforehand. In some instances, dancers are pierced through the chest and fastened to the pole which they dance around. The Sun Dance ritual often includes a ceremonial drum, a sacred fire and a pipe. The community gathers and prays for the dancers as they complete their ritual performance.

LIFE LESSONS FROM WHITE BUFFALO CALF WOMAN

White Buffalo Calf Woman was a teacher. She was glad to share her wisdom for the benefit of many. Is there a subject that you have expertise in? Perhaps you could help others by sharing your wisdom.

There are many ways to take on a teaching role without joining the profession. If it is your professional skills that you'd like to share, investigate your workplace's mentorship or skill-sharing programmes. Or perhaps you'd like to help people in your profession outside your workplace – are there groups that share knowledge and support across the industry? If you are a passionate hobbyist, you could host hobby-swapping sessions with friends or support new learners by answering queries in forums and online hobbyist groups.

Wanting to share your knowledge is a kind impulse, but make sure that your mentorship is agreed upon and welcomed. Not everyone enjoys receiving top tips and notes for improvement that they didn't expect and certainly didn't ask for.

CONCLUSION

The powerful goddesses in this book have shaped the world. They have left their mark on art and on culture. Even those goddesses that the world has forgotten still influence the way we think and act - we can find them in the etymology of our language, and their stories echo in modern legends and myths. There is no containing the goddesses of old - or of today. They race across the heavens, shift earthly landscapes and forge civilizations in the fire. They loved and created life, they shepherd us through death. They are the sun and the moon, the night sky and the dawn. They are beautiful, monstrous, sage and impulsive.

If these goddesses have one collective lesson to teach, it is that there really is no single way of living. If the whole of human history couldn't decide on one feminine way of being, why should we try to limit ourselves now? There is too much glory in simply

becoming the best version of yourself - whatever form that takes, and however multifaceted that may be! Draw your energy from the sun, the moon or the water. Find her - your divine feminine self - in the fire, in the calm of reflection and in the boldness of action. She is unique, she is glorious and she is wholly you.

Have you enjoyed this book? If so, find us on Facebook at **Summersdale Publishers**, on Twitter at **@Summersdale** and on Instagram at **@summersdalebooks** and get in touch. We'd love to hear from you!

WWW.SUMMERSDALE.COM

Image credits

Goddess icons throughout © Vasya Kobelev/Shutterstock.com
Moon and star icons throughout © maybealice/Shutterstock.com